THE RKO GALS

BY JAMES ROBERT PARISH

As author

THE FOX GIRLS*
THE PARAMOUNT PRETTIES*
THE SLAPSTICK QUEENS
GOOD DAMES

As co-author

THE EMMY AWARDS: A PICTORIAL HISTORY
THE CINEMA OF EDWARD G. ROBINSON
THE MGM STOCK COMPANY: THE GOLDEN ERA*
THE GREAT SPY PICTURES
THE GEORGE RAFT FILE

As editor

THE GREAT MOVIE SERIES
ACTORS' TELEVISION CREDITS: 1950-1972

As associate editor

THE AMERICAN MOVIES REFERENCE BOOK
TV MOVIES

*Published by Arlington House

THE
RKO GALS

JAMES ROBERT PARISH

Editor
T. Allan Taylor

Research Associates
John Robert Cocchi   Florence Solomon

ARLINGTON HOUSE·PUBLISHERS
NEW ROCHELLE, N. Y.

Manufactured in the United States of America

Library of Congress Cataloging in Publication Data

Parish, James Robert.
  The RKO Gals.

  Includes bibliographical references.
  1. Moving-picture actors and actresses—United States—
Biography. 2. RKO Radio Pictures, inc.
I. Title.
PN1998.A2P398   791.43′028′0922 [B]   74-8346
ISBN 0-87000-246-5

Dedicated with Love

To My Parents
Dr. Fred A. Parish
And the late
Ann Lois Parish

Contents

KEY TO THE FILM STUDIOS

AA	Allied Artists Picture Corporation
COL	Columbia Pictures Industries, Inc.
FN	First National Pictures, Inc. (later part of Warner Bros.)
FOX	Fox Film Corporation
MGM	Metro-Goldwyn-Mayer, Inc.
MON	Monogram Pictures Corporation
PAR	Paramount Pictures Corporation
RKO	RKO Radio Pictures, Inc.
REP	Republic Pictures Corporation
20th	Twentieth Century-Fox Film Corporation
UA	United Artists Corporation
UNIV	Universal Pictures, Inc.
WB	Warner Bros. Inc.

Acknowledgments

RESEARCH MATERIAL CONSULTANT
  Doug McClelland
RESEARCH VERIFIER
  Earl Anderson
Elliott Adams
Emily Andersen
Gene Andrewski
Rudy Behlmer
DeWitt Bodeen
Ronald L. Bowers
Richard Braff
Alan Brock
Bruco Enterprises
James Buchanan
Mrs. Loraine Burdick
Cinemabilia Book Shop
  (Ernest Burns)
Classic Film Collector
  (Samuel Rubin)
Olivier Eyquem
Film Collectors Registry
Filmfacts (Ernest Parmentier)
Film Fan Monthly (Leonard Maltin)
Films and Filming
Films in Review
Felix Ganz, Dean—Chicago Music
  College
Stanley Green

Pierre Guinle
Ray Hagen
Mrs. R. F. Hasting
Charles Hoyt
Richard M. Hudson
Ken D. Jones
Lois Kibbee
Jane and Steve Klain
Miles Kreuger
Albert Leonard
Albert B. Manski
David McGillivray
Jim Meyer
Mrs. Earl Meisinger
Peter Miglierini
Norman Miller
Movie Poster Service (Bob Smith)
Jeanne Passalacqua
Michael R. Pitts
Mike Schau
Screen Facts (Alan G. Barbour)
Richard Sisson
Charles Smith
Mrs. Peter Smith
John Springer
Don Stanke
Charles K. Stumpf
Views and Reviews (Jon Tuska)

And special thanks to Paul Myers, curator of the Theatre Collection at the Lincoln Center Library for the Performing Arts (New York City), and his staff: Monty Arnold, Rod Bladel, Donald Fowle, Steve Ross, Maxwell Silverman, Dorothy Swerdlove, Betty Wharton, page Juan Hodelin, and Don Madison of Photo Services.

A publicity pose, c. 1926

5'2"
106 pounds
Ash-blonde hair
Blue-gray eyes
Leo

Ann Harding

One of the biggest of the big movie stars in the early 1930s was RKO's Ann Harding. She was the acme of cool blonde pulchritude, with her long, fair tresses pulled back into a trademark bun and her low, throbbing voice purring those lines of dialog. She was far from being a typical Hollywood glamour girl-flapper. She eschewed the fads of drawn-on eyebrows, overpainted lips, and beaded eyelashes. She was a real lady in the days before "lady" became a dirty word.

Ann once confided to an interviewer, "Perhaps I am that unfortunate creature known as a high-brow." She was! It was this very quality that by the mid-1930s knocked her off the prestigious stardom pedestal. Her staunch determination to bring class to motion pictures, caused her to be frozen into a tiresome screen stereotype as the martyred lady fair whose oversized nobility is only matched by the callousness of the males with whom she is matched so unfortunately in film after film.

Ann learned, to her eventual dismay, that a movie career built upon exaggerated valiancy, and accompanied by highly mannered stage theatrics, becomes very wearing on moviegoers. A little democratic immorality and signs of human flaws are far more engaging traits with which film-viewers can empathize.

11

She was born Dorothy Walton Gatley on August 7, 1901, at Fort Sam Houston, Texas, an Army post near San Antonio, where her West Point-graduate father, Captain George G. Gatley, was stationed. Ann's mother, the former Elizabeth Crabbe, and Captain Gatley were both of old New England stock. Edith, the Gatley's first-born, would later recall that right from the start her younger sister, Ann, had been a strikingly beautiful child, with a pink complexion, penetrating dark blue eyes, and white blonde hair falling to her shoulders in luxuriant curls. Edith remembers that almost from the time Ann could talk, she would diligently repeat the memorized reply their mother taught her to stem the flow of solicitous elders who persistently requested a lock of her hair. "God gave 'em to me," baby Ann would say, "but I'd love to give 'em to you if I could."

Before Ann was two years old, Captain Gatley, a field artillery expert, was transferred to Fort Sheridan on Lake Michigan in Illinois. During one of Mrs. Gatley's shopping expeditions to Chicago with her two girls, the head of the photography department at Marshall Field Department Store spotted Ann. He told her mother that she was undoubtedly the loveliest child he had ever seen and offered complimentary photographs of the entire Gatley family if Mrs. Gatley permitted him to feature Ann's photograph in a store-window display. When Captain Gatley was informed of this "outrageous" incident, he was horrified at the possibility of his child's likeness being displayed in public for commercial gain. His strict code of ethics and his high standards never fluctuated over the years.

Captain Gatley was next stationed at Camp Columbia, a U.S. Army installation near Havana, where he and his corps of instructors were to train the recently formed Cuban Army in the utilization of modern weapons. Mrs. Gatley and the children joined him at the base, and it was there that Ann began her formal schooling, in the camp's one-room schoolhouse.

After two years in Cuba, Captain Gatley was re-assigned to Fort Dix, New Jersey. Mrs. Gatley and the girls first lived with her mother in New York City. Later the family was reunited in a reasonably priced home in nearby Montclair, New Jersey. After completing her primary education in the local public school, Ann was sent to the Baldwin School at Bryn Mawr, Pennsylvania. There she made her stage "debut" in *Macbeth,* the school's Christmas production. Originally Ann had been assigned the part of Ross, but at the last minute the girl who was to portray MacDuff came down with the measles, and Ann went on in her stead. The Shakespearian production was directed by Maude Durbin, the wife of actor Otis Skinner, whose daughter Cornelia was playing Lady Macbeth. Later in the school year Ann was cast as Shylock in the school's edition of *The Merchant of Venice.* Although she contracted a bad case of laryngitis, Ann insisted upon performing, swallowing large doses of a medicated ointment to ease her throat pain. As a result of her ailment Ann found herself projecting her lines in a deep, resonant timbre, which proved not only expedient but quite effective. Recalling this childhood incident, Ann believes it was from this point onward that she utilized the vibrant speaking quality which became her distinctive professional trademark.

Captain Gatley was spared learning of Ann's theatrical forays because he had been sent overseas to serve with the Rainbow Division during World War I, and, in fact, he would remain on the Continent for a year after the Armistice, working with the Army of Occupation. Meanwhile, because of tightened finances, Ann was forced to leave the Baldwin School after one year and complete her education at East Orange High School. In the senior-class play, written by student Garrett Fort, who later became a playwright and scenarist, Ann was (mis)cast as a vamp. For the first time in her lengthy professional career, she wore her hair marcelled.

After graduating high school Ann matriculated at fashionable Bryn Mawr College, planning on a liberal arts degree. She had thoughts of becoming a professional writer, but after one semester she had to withdraw due to financial considerations. Her father, now a colonel, had returned from overseas, and the family was reunited with him at Fort Knox, Kentucky, thirty miles outside of Louisville. There Ann was the typical daughter of the regiment, and her life was a romp of horseback riding, gallant soldier courtships, and so forth. Colonel Gatley was eventually ordered to report to Washington, D.C., to await reassignment; since he could not afford to maintain his family there, Mrs. Gatley and the girls settled in New York City, where they rented a flat in uptown Manhattan in the Nineties. Both of the younger Gatleys found employment, Edith in a stock-brokerage firm, and Ann in a $12.50-a-week post in the welfare division of the Metropolitan Life Insurance Company. Because of her strikingly good looks and her previous stage "experience," Ann was soon being called upon to demonstrate for company executives the correct method of utilizing a new Dictaphone machine.

Ann regarded her pedestrian daytime work as creatively stifling and avidly, but uncertainly, sought an outlet to foster her artistic instinces. She answered an advertisement for freelance assistants with the New York office of the Famous Players-Lasky Company and was hired as an outside reader by Harry Durant, the studio's East Coast scenario consultant. Ann spent her evenings writing synopsis evaluations for Durant of potentially filmable new novels, passing in her assignments each day before heading downtown to Metropolitan Life Insurance. "I had the grand notion," says Ann, "that my work on them would uplift the movies. You know. I was young once."

On one occasion Durant offered her a theatre pass, suggesting she take an evening off and see the show. The divertissement was being presented by the distinguished Provincetown Players at their Macdougal Street showcase theatre in Greenwich Village. Ann was quite impressed with the quality of the show. When she later learned the company was casting a new production, she gathered her courage and auditioned for a small part. Ann gave an expectedly untrained and nervous first reading, but director Jasper Deeter was so impressed by her arresting good looks and her voice that he asked her to

13

report back the following evening. When he inquired her name, she was caught offguard—after all, she was an amateur and this was a lark. Supposedly on the spur of the moment she shot back "Ann Harding," a *nom de plume* she had once thought of using when she was still dreaming of becoming an author.*

Ann arrived the next evening along with the other candidates and listened to Deeter and playwright Susan Glaspell outline the import of their new production, Glaspell's *Inheritors*. Ann was duly requested to read one of the ingenue's longer speeches and was taken aback when later that evening Deeter and Glaspell offered her the part. Ann eventually asked Deeter why he had chosen her. The director replied, "Because you were the only girl present who knew how to listen, and actually carried out what we asked for."

When Ann informed her mother and sister that she was leaving her jobs for a nonpaying fling at acting, it was decided to withhold the "shocking" news from Colonel Gatley. *Inheritors* opened March 21, 1921, to critical approval, with many reviewers acclaiming Ann's performance as Madeline Morton for its earnestness and charm. In the flush of her acting success, forthright Ann wrote her father, advising him of her career plans and expressing the hope that he would come to see her perform.

Colonel Gatley, still of a mind that "one does not receive an actress in one's home," regarded Ann's news as a dictum of heresy. He replied to his younger daughter in writing. "It would hardly be a source of gratification to see my daughter's painted face in public and realize she is displaying herself to the gaping public for money. Such a step is the straight and inevitable road to Hell."

Ann was more successful on the professional front. As a result of her outstanding *Inheritors* performance, which had a run of seventeen performances spread over a four-week-end period, she was courted with tempting offers by such Broadway producers as David Burton, John Cromwell, Adolph Klauber, and Brock Pemberton. When she asked Jasper Deeter's advice in selecting the right part, he stated, "It's time for you to start making your own decisions—and mistakes."

Ann accepted Klauber's bid for her to appear opposite James Gleason in *Like a King* at $100 weekly salary. As this morality play was not to go into production until the fall, Ann joined Jessie Bonstelle's stock company in Buffalo for the summer. The pay there was only $35 a week, but the stage experience was invaluable. When she returned to New York City in the fall she lived in a theatrical boarding house on West 88th Street, and was soon seen being escorted about town by fellow tenant, Monroe Owsley. *Like a King* (39th Street Theatre, October 3, 1921) was set in New England and dealt with the bad repercussions of an American businessman who used too

---

*Cinema historian Gene Ringgold suggests, in his career study of Ann Harding (*Films in Review,* March, 1972), "the fact that it was a Presidential election year (1920) and the successful candidate was Warren G. Harding may have been an unconscious factor." Ann later observed, "I don't suppose a well-thought-out name could have been more suitable, or brought me more good fortune."

much cheek and push in trying to get ahead. The show itself was panned by the New York critics and would close after only sixteen performances. However, Ann fared well with the reviewers in her Broadway debut as Phyllis Weston. The *New York World* described her as a "wholly charming sweetheart" with "golden hair banded like sibyl about her head." The *New York Times* noted she "had indisputable credentials for the play," and the *New York Herald-Tribune,* after adding parenthetically that Ann was "on the stage against parental wishes," went on to laud the newcomer who plays "with a grace, lack of affectations that is as refreshing as is her dainty blond prettiness."

Ann was not long out of work for she accepted a subordinate role in *The Lonely Heart.* But after a bad week in Baltimore, the show folded. Ann returned to stock, this time for the winter season with a Providence, Rhode Island, company. The summer of 1922 was spent with Bonstelle's Buffalo troupe, for whom she appeared in *Peter Pan* (title role), *The Bird of Paradise,* and *The Man Who Came Back.*

Any thoughts Ann may have entertained at this juncture of her career of maneuvering for a promising Broadway venture to establish herself were pushed aside when Jasper Deeter invited her to join his permanent company at the Hedgerow Theatre in Moylan, Pennsylvania, near Philadelphia. She reasoned that the variety of roles offered and the steady salary were plus factors not to be ignored. While with Deeter's group, Ann played Hilda in *The Master Builder,* the title role in *Candida,* Lina in *Misalliance,* and Lady Cecily in *Captain Brassbound's Conversion,* as well as participating in the experimental theatre workshop so much a part of Hedgerow Theatre. Ann has always regarded her Deeter-tutelage period with professional reverence. "Nothing will ever dull my gratitude to him for the things he taught me."

Ann had gotten word that the role of Lelitia Tavis in Gilbert Emery's Broadway-bound *Tarnish* was perfectly suited to her capabilities, and she was overjoyed when she was hired for the upcoming production. However, after two weeks of tryouts, the producer fired Ann. The distraught actress sought out Deeter for consolation. To restore her sapped confidence, he specially mounted a new production of *Inheritors* for the Hedgerow Players to perform, and, during its limited run, Ann found herself being rehired for *Tarnish. Tarnish* (Belmont Theatre, October 1, 1923) co-starred Ann with Albert Gran and Tom Powers in a drama of human frailty. Its plot revolved about a thoughtless father who has lavished his family's funds on his manicurist girlfriend. As the determined daughter of the prodigal, Ann's big theatrical moment in the play occurred when she confronted the mistress and demanded, on behalf of her family, restitution of her father's affections and money. *Tarnish* enjoyed a healthy 255-performance run. Typical of Ann's glowing reviews was the *New York Times's* evaluation: "a rare combination of winsome girlishness, unforced sincerity and poignantly emotional power."

Ann was already established as one of Broadway's most talented newcomers and a fitting adornment for any production of the prolific theatrical season. She was in the privileged position of being able to select among top offers, demanding terms that were the envy of many far more seasoned stage luminaries. But like most players, Ann's talents did not extend to an objective good judgment as to which vehicle would be the best showcase to advance her career. (This same artistic shortsightedness would eventually destroy her film career in the mid 1930s.) She made a bad judgment when she selected *The Horse Thieves* as her next project. The show underwent extensive out-of-town rewrites and reached Broadway retitled *Thoroughbreds* (Vanderbilt Theatre, September 9, 1924). In this folksy play that only a Will Rogers could have saved, George Marion was cast as a Kentuckian who steals his neighbors' horses (because he likes them) and finds himself on trial, with none other than his long-departed daughter, Ann, his court-appointed attorney. As a contemporary Portia, Ann was labled a "human thoroughbred" by the *New York Times* but chided by other critics for her on-again, off-again southern drawl and for allowing herself to be garbed in inappropriate Parisian-designed frocks.

Ann disliked being at liberty for even a few weeks and was quick to accept producer Henry W. Savage's offer to star in the fall of 1925 in *Stolen Fruit,* a loose-fitting translation of a popular Italian play by Dario Micodemi. Ann's joyous expectation was shortlived, for suddenly Savage decided he wanted a dark-complexioned brunette in the lead assignment. Ann was fired. At this disheartening juncture, Ann decided to follow the example of another popular Broadway ingenue, Claudette Colbert, and accept a long-term contract from Al H. Woods, a prolific producer whose Broadway manipulations make David Merrick's later theatre venturing seem like retarded child's play.

One day Woods summoned Ann into his inner office and shoved five scripts in front of her, saying, "Kid, I'll star you in the one you like. Take your pick!" Ann politely but firmly announced that she was not interested in any of these properties, because she had her heart set on playing in *The Green Hat,* which was to be produced in Chicago as of April 25.* Woods understood from Ann's genteel but tenacious stand that she was determined to have either what she wanted or nothing at all. So he acquiesced, and she played Venice Pollen to Katherine Cornell's Iris March and Leslie Howard's Napier. When Henry Savage got word of Ann's success in the part, he had a change of heart re *Stolen Fruit.* Now, however, he had to dicker with Woods, with the result that *Stolen Fruit* became a joint venture for Savage and Woods with Ann playing Marie Millais. (When *The Green Hat* came to Broadway, Margalo Gillmore replaced Ann.) Since Ann's agreement with Woods stated that he received half her salary, Woods found himself in the unique position of paying out money from one pocket which soon thereafter went safely back into another.

Stolen Fruit (Ettinge Theatre, October 7, 1925) presented Ann as a French

---

*She had played Chicago in 1923 in *The Horse Thief* and found the cultural environs stimulating.

peasant girl(!) who is married and deserted by blackguard Rollo Peters. Later she becomes a schoolteacher and learns that her child, who she thought, had died not long after birth, is one of her classroom pupils. The dramatic recognition scene, as Ann tries to guess which child is her own, was the sole highlight of this overly sentimental melodrama. But Ann was cited for realizing her emotional promise and for being "resourceful, honest and economical in her work." More than one toughened aisle-sitter commented that it was no little feat that Ann managed to wring tears from the stubborn first-night audience. Despite a resounding critical roasting, *Stolen Fruit* endured for ninety-six performances—a surprise for all concerned. As an unfortunate side-effect, this professional adventure fully convinced Ann that her forte was in strongly wrought tearjerkers and that she had better not stray too far from the mark. This restricting notion would shape all too narrowly her forthcoming film career.

While emoting in *Stolen Fruit,* energetic Ann made time to appear in a special nine-matinee edition of *The Taming of the Shrew* (Klaw Theatre, December 18, 1925). Ann was Bianca in a cast that included Estelle Winwood (Katherine), Rollo Peters (Petrucio), and Walter Abel, Jessie Ralph, and Allyn Joslyn. The *New York Sun* reported, "For looks and honeyed ways, of course, there was none like Ann Harding." Would that the actress had ventured more often outside her self-imposed acting limitations. Her rationale for deigning to appear in robust comedy was that an opportunity to appear in the Bard's works demanded an exception.

Broadway theatregoers next saw Ann in *Schweiger* (Mansfield Theatre, March 23, 1926), a drama of spiritual remoralization written by Franz Werfel, the author of *Goat Song.* Directed by Jacob Ben-Ami, who starred as the cobbler caught up on a charge of child molestation and homicide, the production had Ann appear as his doleful wife. Audiences were rightly annoyed by the oblique symbolic nonsense, and the show collapsed after thirty-one performances. Ann received her share of critical umbrage. "[She is] ideally fair to look upon, painfully vacant to listen to" *(New York Sun).*

During the summer of 1926, twenty-four-year-old Ann returned to stock, this time with a Detroit repertory group in which she repeated her starring role from *Tarnish* and appeared in such other productions as *Bluebeard's Eighth Wife, The Eskimo,* and *In a Garden.* Besides her acting chores, Ann assumed the additional burdens of producer-business manager-casting director for the stock troupe. In this latter capacity she found herself having to replace the leading man when he suddenly departed for brighter prospects. She sent for Harry Bannister,* an established Broadway performer, to substitute. During their week's work in Detroit and thereafter in New York, they saw a great deal of one another socially.

*Born in 1889 in Holland, Michigan, Bannister made his Broadway debut in *The Passing Show of 1921* (Winter Garden Theatre, December 29, 1920) and earned a fair degree of popularity with his roles in *Czarina, The Rivalry, White Cargo,* and *The Bat.* Hollywood reporter-observer Adela Rogers St. John once described the dapper Bannister as "a handsome, vain actor of the old-fashioned scenery-chewing school."

For her new Al Woods production, Ann agreed to Denison Clift's *A Woman Disputed* (Forrest Theatre, September 28, 1926), a fossilized drama set during World War I with Ann playing a patriotic whore involved with both German villain Lowell Sherman and American officer Louis Calhern. Ann shone as the Alsatian *demimonde*. "There was passion and fire in her, a tartness and tautness that were worthy of better, infinitely better things" (*New York Post*). The show would survive a relatively brief eighty-seven performances. Ann, who could do no wrong as far as the public was concerned, was a favorite interviewee among Broadway-beat reporters. Constantly she was asked if her emotional torrents, a persistent facet of her stage playing, were for real, Ann's flowery reply was typical of her high-toned, lofty public image. "I am encompassed by sorrows as the Walls of Jericho by the hosts of Israel. Am I to suffer them all, eight times a week, with special stress on holiday matinees? . . . A role must be acted, not felt, as a poem must be written and not suffered."

During the run of *A Woman Disputed,* Ann and Bannister were wed on October 22, 1926 at the Little Church Around the Corner.* Dr. Randolph Ray officiated, with Louis Calhern as best man and Ann's sister Edith, Mrs. Robert Nash, as matron of honor. Mrs. Gatley attended her daughter's joyous occasion but General Gatley of Fort McDowell, Angel Island, California, did not reply to Ann's wedding invitation.† During the marriage ceremony a distinguished figure leaned over and whispered to Ann, "I consider it my duty to represent the Army on this occasion." The gentleman was Colonel George Vidmer.

Not until Ann was forced to withdraw from the Chicago company of *A Woman Disputed,* in January, 1927, did she find the time to take a delayed, if brief, honeymoon trip with Bannister. Refreshed from the bout of nervous exhaustion that had caused her to leave *A Woman Disputed,* Ann returned to New York in sufficient time to prepare for Al Wood's latest stage venture, Bayard Veiller's *The Trial of Mary Dugan.*

In its day, *The Trial of Mary Dugan* (National Theatre, September 19, 1927) was considered a fresh, highly effective slant on a courtroom trial, with Ann cast as the heady chorine charged with the murder of her banker sugar daddy. To create the proper atmosphere, Woods had the National Theatre decked out as a courtroom, with the audience as the "jury," "policemen" lounging in the lobby, and "scrubwomen" dusting the onstage furniture during intermission. The sensational melodrama immediately clicked with critics and public alike, who reveled in the hysterical histrionics provided by a radiant Ann. "[She] sniffled and sobbed in a mellow voice with complete verisimilitude" (*New York Times*). Ann objected to one item in the stage business that closed Act I of the show. A seven-foot blowup of a nude Ann was supposed to be brought onstage. Although Woods had superimposed Ann's face on the body of a Follies girl for the photograph, Ann demanded that this

---

*He was then appearing on Broadway in *Yellow.*

†Ann and her father, who had remarried and was now retiring as a brigadier general, would remain estranged until shortly before his death in the mid-1930s.

18

tasteless gimmick be deleted. Woods refused, and she took her righteous cause to Actors' Equity Association. A compromise was reached, and a new, modestly draped figure photograph was utilized instead.

During her five-week summer vacation in 1928 from *The Trial of Mary Dugan*, which would run for 437 performances, Ann gave birth, on July 24, to a daughter, who was christened Jane. One week later Ann returned to the show, but she had lost her enthusiasm for *The Trial of Mary Dugan* because of her increasing disagreements with Woods. The strained relationship with Woods reached an apex when the Theatre Guild offered her the prestigious lead in Eugene O'Neill's *Strange Interlude* and Woods refused to release Ann from her run-of-the-play contract. Ann was keenly disappointed when Lynn Fontanne was substituted in the marathon drama, but with typical ladylike ambiguity, she merely informed the press, "I had no idea Mr. O'Neill was particularly aware of my existence."

After concluding some brief post-Broadway engagements in *The Trial of Mary Dugan*, Ann and Woods canceled their contract. By this time, Bannister had been cast in the national company of *Strange Interlude*. Ann accompanied her husband on tour, which brought them to California. They rented a house in Pasadena for the nine-week Los Angeles run, planning to vacation there for an additional two months before going to Chicago, where Ann was scheduled to assume the lead in *Strange Interlude*.

Ann has always insisted that when she came to Los Angeles in late 1928, planning a long rest and the opportunity to properly care for little Jane, she had no thought whatsoever of a film career. At any rate, with the newfound popularity of talkies, stage stars were being wooed to Hollywood in great droves, and it was not long before the studio executives were apprised that the famous theatre celebrity was vacationing in their own backyard. Soon Ann was besieged with screen offers, which she promptly rejected. It was only when the Bannisters' good friend Frank Reicher, who had recently joined Pathé as a dialog director, suggested Ann submit to a screentest that she agreed to, on condition that Bannister would appear in the test opposite her. It was no surprise that Ann's throaty voice registered extremely well on the still primitive recording equipment.* Studio president J. J. Murdock and executive vice-president E. B. Derr quickly offered Ann an impressively termed contract. Ann still remained firm; she preferred being with her husband and child to becoming a devoted film actress. Eager to acquire Ann's professional services, Pathé took the broad hint and offered Bannister a film contract based on his wife's acceptance of the studio's offer.

Pathé Exchange, Inc., formed in 1914 as a continuation of the original Pathé business organized in the United States in 1904, had long since dropped out of the serial field. Now that both Hal Roach's comedy unit and Cecil B. De Mille's feature-making enterprise had moved over to MGM, the studio was in tough straits to develop a new image for itself as a producer of sound

*Pathé was then utilizing the Photophone process.

feature films. It chose to de-emphasize its string of William Boyd-Robert Armstrong-Eddie Quillan action features in favor of more intimate and sophisticated dramas. In one fell swoop, Pathé grabbed a monopoly of the cosmopolitan leading-lady types, inducing Constance Bennett to return to the cinema, and tempting both Ina Claire and Ann to forsake the Broadway stage for film careers. To direct these ritzy vehicles, Pathé called upon its coterie of contract megaphoners, including Paul Stein, Edward H. Griffith, Gregory La Cava, and Howard Higgin.

For her screen debut, Pathé and Ann selected Philip Barry's scintillating stage hit, *Paris Bound* (1927), which had starred Madge Kennedy on Broadway. Theatre-trained Fredric March was borrowed from Paramount to co-star with Ann in this sophisticated approach to love, in which a young married couple (Ann and March) insist that two persons can remain spiritually true to each other while cavorting with others. When Ann, who has been seeing a great deal of composer Leslie Fenton, discovers that March, while away on a European business trip, has been coupling with ex-flame Carmelita Geraghty at her Antibes villa, she suddenly becomes very properly conventional and considers divorcing March. Director Edward H. Griffith utilized a well-plotted variety of cinema tricks to alleviate the screenplay's staginess, including double exposures to reveal the characters' stream of consciousness. Audiences of the time found *Paris Bound* sufficiently titillating in its peek into worldly domestic life. The screen teaming of Ann and March sparkled sufficiently to insure a full-bodied success for the Pathé release. Critical reaction to Ann's maiden screen performance verified the studio's faith in her film potential. "Miss Harding has a most interesting personality on the screen," announced Mordaunt Hall in the *New York Times.* "She is never twice exactly the same. Her acting is obviously the result of careful thought, which is especially noticeable when she talks over a telephone. Her actions and the cutting off of parts of words are very natural . . . . It is in fact a joyous relief to study the work of an actress in a motion picture who is so modulated in her talking and whose performance throughout is so different from other players."

Her Private Affair, released less than a month later in September, 1929, teamed Ann onscreen with Bannister. Its routine story was sufficiently spiced with élan to fool the public into believing the rehashed beef stew it was being served was cinematic caviar, rich in its reflection of uppercrust living. Within the plot, Ann and her husband (Bannister), a Viennese judge, briefly separate after a quarrel. On a holiday she becomes attracted to Lawford Davidson and later writes some incriminating letters to the gigolo. Thereafter he proceeds to blackmail her, and when she comes to his apartment to retrieve the love notes, the scene is set for high drama.

Ann: "Well. Do I get the letters or must I pay cash on delivery."

Davidson replies by making unwanted advances toward her. In the scuffle, she picks up a revolver, which accidentally discharges and kills him. Although Davidson's butler, charged with the crime, is eventually court-acquitted, she is so weighed down by guilt that she has to confess her sin to the distraught butler. Bannister overhears her recitation, and, as the film concludes, he and Ann are reconciled in a fade-out embrace. *Her Private Affair,* like *Paris Bound,* was released in both silent and sound versions. It did reasonably good box-office business, sustaining Pathé's faith that Ann's essence of hauteur could be commercially disseminated to a movie-hungry public.

Ann's film services were now so much in demand that Pathé took advantage of the opportunity to loan her to Samuel Goldwyn for *Condemned* (1929). Although Ann was now receiving $3,500-a-week from Pathé, she received no extra dividend from the $5,000-a-week tab Goldwyn was paying Pathé for the privilege of her oncamera presence. Suggested by Blair Niles's book *Condemned to Devil's Island, Condemned* dealt with bank-robber Ronald Colman, who is sentenced to the hellish prison island, where he becomes the trusted houseman to brutal penal-colony warden Dudley Digges. As anticipated, it is not long before genteel crook Colman has aroused a spate of passion in Digges's young wife (Ann), and the couple must battle their senses of morality, practicality, and fantasy before they arrive at a happy end. Ann was not particularly at ease in this jungle-set melodrama, and its backlot swamp setting was more effective than the stars.

After one year in the cinema, Ann was now a full-fledged movie star. Her silver-blonde likeness continually graced the covers of fan magazines, which termed her the one "with the sex appeal voice." She now could confess—in rather uncharacteristic jargon—that she got more of a kick out of the appreciation of soundstage crews than she ever had experienced from Broadway audiences: "Those birds are hard-boiled, for a fact. When you do a scene as they like it, you're good." Nevertheless, Ann was extremely self-critical of her screen work and continually carped at what she considered to be low-quality scripts submitted to her by Pathé. Studio officials assumed Ann's "artistic discontentment" was merely a dignified means of demanding more money, so her contract was renegotiated with a two-year extension and escalation clauses to $5,000 weekly. "I earn more in a week than my father, General Gatley, earns in a year," admitted Ann. She was still not happy with the course of her film career, but at least she now could afford to "suffer" in style, even in the bleak months following the Wall Street market crash. She and Bannister built a $125,000 mansion on their newly acquired acreage atop a hill overlooking the Sunset Strip, affording them a view of Los Angeles and the San Fernando Valley from their "dream home."

The Bannisters' home was staffed with a full complement of servants and included special bodyguards hired after the couple received notes threatening the safety of their daughter. In a manner almost as grandiloquent as that of 1920s cinema queen Gloria Swanson, Ann would hold court at tea-time for the ever-curious press, spilling forth the latest "confidences" of the true lady of elegance. "I love it out here. Harry Bannister, my husband, and I have the same kind of contract with Pathé. We can have a house with a front yard with grass in it. The baby plays out there in the mornings. It's hell to go to the studio. I'll never worry about leaving the stage or screen. I'll be just a wife and mother. Harry says I'm a very good one. Isn't that sweet? But he's a sweet person. Can I bum a cigarette from someone?"

Pathé had acquired the screen rights to Philip Barry's *Holiday* as a potential vehicle for Ina Claire, who had signed a nine-month, $175,000 contract with the studio. However, the lengthy production of *The Awful Truth* (1929) left insufficient time for Claire to star in *Holiday* and Ann was handed the plum assignment. Director Edward H. Griffith mounted a stylish production showcasing Ann as wealthy but romantic Linda Seton, who, unlike her materialistic sister, Mary Astor,* sees life as a glorious, uncharted adventure. Ann is matched in her idealistic viewpoint by struggling young lawyer Robert Ames, who prefers Ann's positive do-it-today philosophy to the tradition-bound concepts of his former fiancée (Astor). At the fade-out, Ann and Ames go off on their European jaunt while they are both young enough to enjoy the holiday to its fullest. *Holiday,* released in July, 1930, was a solid hit, comparing most favorably—taking its still primitive sound techniques into consideration—with George Cukor's elegant 1938 remake starring Katharine Hepburn. Ann received her first and only Academy Award nomination for *Holiday,* losing out in the best-actress category to Marie Dressler, who won for *Min and Bill.*

With *Holiday*, Ann solidified her screen image as a partician beauty. Her well-structured face capped in a bun of phosphorescent silver blonde hair was not composed to radiate girlishness, but at twenty-eight years of age, she epitomized the well-bred young matron who had acquired her own distinctive standards of life and love. Her aristocratic standoffishness and her at times icy deep voice often seemed more foreboding than Garbo's aloof screen presence. But, like the Swedish movie star, once Ann's oncamera character was satisfied of her admirer's ardent sincerity, her onscreen reserve melted into refined passion.

Ann's lofty star status provided Pathé with a lucrative bargaining point when other studios bid for her screen services. As part of the package deal for First National's *The Girl of the Golden West* (1930), she insisted that Harry Bannister be offered the second male lead as Sheriff Jack Rance. Not content with his back-door entry into this production, Bannister was soon "instructing" director John Francis Dillon on the proper art of film direction. Despite the growing on-set friction the picture emerged far better than anyone antici-

---

*Years later Mary Astor would recall: "Ann was an actress rather than a star—and there is a difference. Her name ahead of the title, which technically made her a star of the picture, did not affect or enlarge her status on the set. She was one of the first who disregarded the old star-system behavior of special treatment, special chairs, *Miss* Harding, etc. . . . In the picture she went easy on makeup: no beaded eyelashes, no heavily rouged mouth. She had beautiful skin and used practically no greasepaint and she had gorgeous, natural silver-blonde hair. She was thoroughly a member of the company, hard-working, no nonsense. These very qualities made me like her because I felt so uncomfortable with so much of the phony nonsense that seemed to go with being an actress. With me it was a passive irritation; I felt it but didn't scratch. She did. She said, 'I don't want to look like an actress, I want to look like a person.' And she did, and she was—a person."

pated. David Belasco's hoary costume drama had long been considered old hat and no one expected ever-so-genteel Ann to infuse the outing with a respectably convincing performance as swaggering Minnie, the gun-toting girl who wears rough-and-ready garb, owns the Polka Saloon, and falls in love with outlaw Jamie Rennie, the scourge of the gold camp citizenry. All the old familiar scenes were kept intact, including the allegedly suspenseful poker-game finale between Ann and sheriff Harry Bannister with Rennie's freedom as the stakes.

Ann next moved over to Fox for *East Lynne* (1931), the perennial stage antiquity of ultimate misunderstanding and martyred suffering. The picture had first been picturized in 1916 with Theda Bara,* and it should have remained that way, for there was nothing new to say within the mechanics of this hardpressed tearjerker. Ann's Lady Isabel Servern, who is unjustly divorced by her husband (O. P. Heggie) and ostracized from their social circle, has further miseries heaped upon her later when she loses both her beloved Clive Brook and her eyesight. Thanks to Ann's regal manner, Frank Lloyd's astute direction, and the solidly splendid sets of Joseph Urban, *East Lynne* had a modestly successful engagement at the Roxy Theatre (February 20, 1931) and thereafter.

During the production of *East Lynne*, Harry Bannister had proven a source of difficulty to director Frank Lloyd by his constant visits to his wife's sound-stage sets and by offering unwarranted suggestions on how the picture and Miss Harding should really be supervised. It reached the boiling point when Lloyd had the obstreperous Bannister banned from the *East Lynne* sound-stage, and Ann was asked by studio officials to insure that her husband would not reappear on the Fox lot. Bannister was obviously fighting back at the indignities of his enforced role as "Mr. Ann Harding" and his poor luck in establishing his own film career.

At this juncture RCA's president, David Sarnoff, merged Pathé and RKO Radio Pictures into the new RKO Radio-Pathé complex, retaining both studio lots.† In the intricacies of intercorporate double-dealing and consolidation, E. B. Derr, president of Pathé and Ann's staunch protector, was forced to resign, with Lee Marcus substituting as president of RKO-Pathé and Charles R. Rogers installed as production head until October, 1931, when David O. Selznick was brought in to head production for both RKO Radio and RKO-Pathé. If Ann had been number two in box-office power at Pathé, her pres-

---

*Fox had produced a 1925 version of *East Lynne* starring Alma Rubens. Some months after the 1931 Fox edition premiered, there appeared Tiffany's *Ex-Flame* with Neil Hamilton, which was reckoned to be a modernization of *East Lynne*.

†Stockholders of Pathé were disgruntled that a legitimate $1.4 million higher offer for the studio facilities had been ignored in favor of the Sarnoff-RCA absorption proposal, and a minority stockholders' suit was planned but it was never consummated. Largely because of the row over the merger terms, the two studio lots were kept "separate" entities in policy, if not in name or executive personnel.

tigious position was somewhat more diminished at the restructured RKO-Pathé,* but no one would attest to that fact. She, not Constance Bennett, Pola Negri, or Helen Twelvetrees, was given the plushest dressing room on the RKO-Pathé lot. But deferential politeness does not a film star sustain, as would soon become evident under the overall David O. Selznick regime. Of the RKO-Pathé female stars, Selznick was personally most in favor of Constance Bennett, whom he fondly recalled from her past professional association with his producer father in 1920s silent pictures. Besides, her present string of confessional tearjerkers were all making good box-office money. Of the RKO Radio contingent, Selznick had to consider the star power of Oscar-nominated Irene Dunne, who might easily replace both the already departed Bebe Daniels as a musical-comedy-movie star and either Ann or Helen Twelvetrees should they prove to rebel at their new positions in the total RKO Radio-Pathé situation. Moreover, there were several other intriguing contractees to weave into the production schedule, including Mary Astor, Myrna Loy, and Shirley Grey (not to mention the box-office durability of such RKO Radio male magnets as Richard Dix and the comedy team of Wheeler and Woolsey).

Selznick did announce that Donald Ogden Stewart's comedy *Rebound* had been acquired as a vehicle for Ann, to be followed by her top-casting *Jane Eyre,* speculated to be the plushest film on the RKO Radio-Pathé agenda. However, Ann's extended shooting schedule on *East Lynne* precluded her starring in *Rebound* and Ina Claire was substituted. *Jane Eyre* would eventually be shelved, and Ann's suggestion that RKO showcase her in Robert Sherwood's *The Road to Rome,* which the studio had purchased for $35,000, was ignored. Instead, Ann found herself co-starring with Leslie Howard† in *Devotion* (1931), which offered her a change of pace from the stifling histrionics of outmoded melodrama but led her to the incorrigible triteness of contemporary drawing-room heave-and-sigh drama. Ann was Shirley Mortimer, who, having fallen in love with barrister Howard at first sight, soon dons a brown wig, spectacles, old-fashioned frocks, and a Cockney accent to

---

*Extensive trade advertisements for RKO-Pathé in 1931 set forth the executive policy on star status: "The Old Fighting Cock [Pathé's trademark] has the stars! . . . Glamorous Constance Bennett in four pictures. Beautiful Ann Harding in four. Dramatic Helen Twelvetrees in four. Smart Ina Claire in one. Virile Bill Boyd in four. Charming Eddie Quillan in four. And Robert Armstrong to add star-flavor to many of these productions!" Other trade ads found a still different prestige order to the RKO-Pathé stable: Twelvetrees, Claire, Negri, Bennett, Boyd, Quillan, Harding, Armstrong, and (Tom) Keene.

†In a 1933 interview with the British *Film Pictorial,* Howard recalled how, contrary to most film players, Ann seemed decidedly unhappy with Hollywood life. "She has suffered so much and so deeply that she feels that not people, but Fate itself is against her. She has had some hard 'breaks' that make her feel that way.

"She is a most charming person and very artistic. She would rather act in a play she thought was good, in a tiny theatre that holds about twenty people, than play in a show that she felt was less artistic but more popular in appeal. Ann is like that. She is terribly sensitive, too.

"In Hollywood everything is a business—even being artistic. Ann can't see it like that. In consequence her pictures never please her; she is never satisfied with her own work."

win a post as governess to Howard's son. Ann obviously found the challenge of essaying a "dual" role, with one part being decidedly offbeat casting for her, extremely challenging; but there the excitement and gimmick ended, and it was only through the grace and wit of the two genteel stars that *Devotion* did adequately at the box-office. Its limp Cinderella tale set in London had been told too often before.

RKO and Selznick may have become slightly disenchanted with Ann's box-office performance as measured against her astringent contractual demands, but they were not about to allow her to escape back to Broadway. They refused to permit Ann to accept the Theatre Guild's offer for her to play the role of Lavinia Mannon in its production of Eugene O'Neill's *Mourning Becomes Electra*. RKO reasoned that her worth might diminish if she absented herself from the screen for too long a spell. Alice Brady was given the coveted part instead. A still resentful Ann recalls: "I did everything but blow up the entire lot to convince the obtuse gentlemen in command of my fate that it would greatly enhance my value to them to release me for *Electra*. Unable to make them see the light, I tried to break my contract but that proved hopeless as well. It is a major tragedy of my professional life that I was deprived of that great opportunity."

Her next film, *Prestige* (1932), was a dismal entertainment packet filled with hopelessly illogical incident and crudely constructed dialog. Braving assorted dangers to reach the Malayan outpost where her husband (Melvyn Douglas) is commander of the penal colony, Ann finds him a confirmed alcoholic. She is so distraught and vulnerable that she is easily wooed by Douglas's superior officer, Adolphe Menjou. However, fate and Ann's inner sense of decency lead her to remain with Douglas, who again promises to reform. Ann was so distressed by the film ("*Prestige* almost killed mine") that she offered to purchase it from her studio employer. No such luck.

In the midst of her professional problems Ann had to confront the inevitable on the home front. RKO had already settled its $1,250-a-week salary with Bannister for a reported $35,000, and he was itching to find some new avenue to revive his acting career. Obviously Hollywood was not the answer, and Ann could not, or would not, walk out on her film obligations to return to Manhattan with him. Thus, when the couple announced divorce plans, only the movie fan magazines feigned surprise. Bannister told the press:

"During the five and a half years I have been married to Ann Harding, I have had the love and respect and devotion of the very great and lovely person who is my wife.

"Therefore, in order to preserve this in its entirety, we find the apparently drastic course of divorce, the quickest and best solution to our eventual complete happiness."

Ann's public statement added, "We have decided to cut the Gordian knot so he can set forth on his own." Ann complied with Nevada's residency requirement and obtained her Reno divorce on May 7, 1932. She received custody of daughter Jane for ten months out of each year. That evening Bannister gallantly took Ann to dinner in Reno, and when she flew back alone to Hollywood, she advised the press that she intended "no more romance."

Having adjusted to her new status as a divorcee, Ann tried to reconcile herself to being an overpriced ($6,000 a week) commodity at a film factory. "I thought they were paying me for something more than just a face to photograph and a voice to register. But if that's all they will take, that's all I can give them. That's being temperamental, I guess, isn't it?"

Westward Passage (1932) bore many similarities to *Up Pops the Devil* and *Private Lives,* as it traced the marriage of wealthy Ann to novelist Laurence Olivier, he totally scorning money for art. Ann is sympathetic to his tenet until they have a child (Bonita Granville) and she wants the better things of life for their offspring. They divorce and she weds a former suitor (Irving Pichel). She then goes on a European holiday, where, six years later in Lucerne, she encounters Olivier and regains his love.

Judging *Westward Passage* in retrospect, one may lean too heavily in favor of today's artistic standards, but one factor is too obvious—Ann was allowing herself to stagnate in the conventionalities of 1920s stage techniques à la Lynn Fontanne. Ann's silver-screen posing may have been no more subtle than that provided by Norma Shearer, Ruth Chatterton, or Kay Francis. However, unlike these (self) acknowledged chic interpreters of sophisticated drama, Ann allowed her tableau posturing to exclude both sufficient character motivation and enough enchantment in her ebullient masquerade of onscreen personality.* Shortsighted as Ann may have been in revising her frozen screen mold, she did possess the intelligence and graciousness to be generous to her fellow cinema performers. During *Westward Passage* she repeatedly insisted that Laurence Olivier's part be built up and that he be afforded equally sympathetic lighting and close-ups. Ann's enunciated rationale: "You're only as good as your co-star."

RKO had long been seeking a follow-up vehicle to its tremendously successful *Cimarron* as another action showcase for its enduring male star, Richard Dix. David O. Selznick was convinced that *The Conquerors* (1932)†

Westward Passage abounds in Ann's stylized performance, reeking of the grand theatrical manners: continual arms-akimbo posing, handkerchief-in-hand mopping of the brow, swaggering of the head, leaning against pillars, and an obvious concentration on effect rather than motivation. Three scenes in particular demonstrate this point: when she and Olivier quarrel and part seemingly forever, she is left alone in their dismal flat and plays for sympathy with the furniture and woodwork, sitting dejectedly on a sofa arm, leaning wearily against a door, etc. Later, when Ann and her newly found Olivier dock in New York, the couple proceed down the gangplank with their child (Granville) in tow, and the girl in turn dragging along a toy giraffe, which soon becomes the concern of Ann as she and Olivier continue their marital-viewpoint discussion. Ann makes no effort to conceal the cutesiness of this scene, and in the next sequence, in the taxi cab, she proceeds to toy with the giraffe to everyone's distraction. Later she and Olivier revive courtship memories by returning to the Catskill resort home of ZaSu Pitts. During this reconciliation scene, much time is spent at a living room piano, with the couple dabbling at a keyboard duet while charting out their new future. In short, Olivier made his part in *Westward Passage* seem natural, Ann made hers merely another posing outing to display her silver-blonde beauty and for highlighting her stunning wardrobe of white outfits.

†Television title, *Pioneer Builders.*

26

was it. This saga, contrived as a romantic chronicle of America's growing pains during the period 1873-1933, followed the adventures of Dix and his new wife, Ann, the daughter of one of old New York's richest bankers. Together, they travel westward to settle in Fort Allen, Nebraska. As the decades pass Dix and his son die, but their daughter, Julie Haydon, who has wed Donald Cook, has a son (also played by Dix) who eventually carries on the family banking tradition. He is counseled by the elderly Ann who has never forgotten the havoc done to her family by the great depression of 1873, and who has lived to see a complete cycle with the stock market panics of the early twentieth century. Although dynamic, square-jawed Dix with his two major roles had the lion's share of screentime in *The Conquerors,* Ann had what was considered to be an enviable opportunity to display an emotional range as she ages from a young lady of twenty to a decrepit matriarch who lives long enough to see her grandson marching in the World War I armistice parade. The *New York Times* commended Ann for her "charmingly restrained impersonation," but Ann's efforts did not stack up against the robust performance of Irene Dunne in the previous year's *Cimarron.*

David O. Selznick personally supervised Ann's next picture, *The Animal Kingdom* (1932), which utilized both Leslie Howard and William Gargan from the original Broadway cast of Philip Barry's play. Edward H. Griffith directed Ann for a third time and again brought to the fore her finest screen qualities in her role as the mistress of an intellectual publisher (Howard) who is wed to Myrna Loy. Nonconformist Howard refuses to concede that he cannot have two marriages of sorts and sets out to prove his point. The total production emerged both professionally slick and true to Barry's witty original. *The Animal Kingdom* inaugurated the new 3,700-seat RKO Roxy Theatre, situated in the Radio City complex in midtown Manhattan. This picture proved to be the best liked and most successful of Ann's film career.*

As 1932 progressed, Ann's dissatisfaction with Hollywood's tinsel life became even stronger. She visualized a stage return as her creative salvation. "No ermine! No foils, no Paris gowns. No movie spotlight. No X-ray publicity. Dignity, harmony—the pleasure of doing a job you like quietly and the best you can. That's what I hope to do." By the new year she had left Hollywood and was "discovered" that January to be performing with Jasper Deeter's Hedgerow Theatre group in Pennsylvania in Shaw's *Misalliance* and Susan Glaspell's *Inheritors.*

A few months thereafter she was persuaded to return to Hollywood only to find that the new RKO regime was even less enthusiastic about her position and career than the old guard.† If Irene Dunne had been a threat to Ann's dominance as the forerunner of RKO's weepers genre, the presence of iconoclastic and younger Katharine Hepburn proved even more of a stumbling

*RKO ballyhooed the picture and Ann with the caption: "Peerless star in a down to earth drama of Human love." Evidently even the studio publicity department had decided it was time to bring Ann down off her pedestal of idealized upper-class emotionalizing.

†On February 2, 1933, David O. Selznick resigned as production head of RKO Radio Studios, with Merian C. Cooper taking over.

block to Ann's future with the company. Once Hepburn won her Oscar for *Morning Glory,* Ann's fate at the lot was sealed. Thus properties acquired originally as potential vehicles for Ann were being parceled out to others, and not always because Ann had a change of heart about the worthiness of the scenarios. (For example, *Ann Vickers* [1933] went to Irene Dunne and *Christopher Strong* [1933] to Katharine Hepburn.)

Under Ann's modified RKO contract—the studio was still gentlemanly enough to attempt to mollify her major demands—she was allowed to make outside films during her vacation period at whatever salary she herself negotiated. MGM's Louis B. Mayer, long attracted by Ann's well-bred-lady screen image, concluded a three-picture deal with her. The first of these films rematched Ann with her *Animal Kingdom* oncamera adversary, Myrna Loy, in *When Ladies Meet* (1933). Rachel Crothers' dissertation on sophisticated bitchiness found Loy playing a successful novelist with very modern notions on love and marriage. She is convinced that she is enamored of her publisher (Frank Morgan) despite the fact that he is presently wed to urbane Ann. At a weekend party, hostessed by Alice Brady, Ann and Loy are brought together for what proves to be a sparkling scene as the two Morgan-boosters engage in intellectual and emotional sparring. In the acceptable Hollywoodian manner, Ann woos Morgan back to the marriage fold and Loy returns to her long-standing beau, flip newspaperman Robert Montgomery. Despite the essential staginess of the glossy picture, audiences thrived on the fashionable sparring between modish Ann and Loy.* Ironically, Alice Brady, Ann's Broadway substitute for *Mourning Becomes Electra,* nearly upstaged everyone in her role as the overly loquacious, scatterbrained matron.

RKO followed MGM's suit by casting Ann in a would-be elite comedy, *Double Harness,* which had a Radio City Music Hall opening on July 20, 1933. As the young, worldly Joan Colby, Ann is convinced marriage is a woman's business. "I want to marry a man with a future, and make his future mine." She sets her sights on the catch of the San Francisco social season, none other than playboy William Powell, and soon tricks him into marriage. Naturally he learns he has been duped, and Ann is hard-pressed to convince her disillusioned spouse ("Her husband was Like a Cake of Ice," the ads claimed) that she truly does love him and that he should offer her another opportunity. Director John Cromwell effectively established a decorously modulated atmosphere, but the endless stream of glib talk, but little action, about love, marriage, infidelity, and sex, was eventually self-defeating. Ann's performance was marred by what the *New York Herald-Tribune* chose to allude to as a "slightly spinsterish" look and a pose "too determinedly noble for comfort."

Ann's RKO option concluded on May 1, 1933, but instead of returning to Broadway as she had so often mentioned, she renegotiated a new studio agreement. It required her to make six films for RKO at a weekly salary that

---

*MGM would remake *When Ladies Meet* in 1941 with Joan Crawford, Greer Garson, Herbert Marshall, and Robert Taylor, to a far less notable end.

28

would escalate to $9,000 for each of forty weeks of actual work (which brought down her average price per film to about $60,000). Although Ann was now granted the right to select *and* approve her own scripts, the concession was so worded that her approval only extended to properties submitted to her *by* RKO.

Partly by design, partly because of pressure, and partly out of resignation, Ann gave up all pretense of being a potentially versatile grand luminary of the screen to become the queen of modish Hollywood weepers (as Paramount's Sylvia Sidney would be the reigning progenitor of proletarian-oriented soap operas). Each new tearjerker would find Ann suffering nobly from one or all of the following: rationalized infidelity, unrequited love, illegitimate mother-hood, stifled mother love. There is no denying that grand bathos was a pop-ular movie gambit that would last through the 1940s, but, unlike Irene Dunne, Ruth Chatterton, and Margaret Sullavan, who managed to rise above, around, and beyond the maudlin cycle, Ann became engulfed by her rash of weepers. And to make matters worse, she did not possess a necessary tart élan which could be found in Constance Bennett, who rose and fell in 1933 as the highest-paid screen emoter before going into a new phase of screwball screen comedy. The human quality was missing from Ann's self-consciously noble ladies of the screen: She was never frivolous, never spontaneous. *Variety* analyzed, "She needs authentic character and probably for that reason is less successful with literary figures than many actresses of much less intrinsic talent."

The Right to Romance (1933) asked the stultifying question: Can one of New York's foremost plastic surgeons (Ann) find sudden happiness in mar-riage to a playboy flier (Robert Young)? The foreordained answer was—no! Ann belongs with moonstruck admirer-researcher Dr. Nils Asther. Like too many of Ann's screen ventures, *The Right to Romance* was too much chatter and too little picturized action. This film marked the turning point of Ann's general popularity with movie critics. Now, Richard Watts, Jr. of the *New York Herald-Tribune* could unabashedly carp: "In that rather smug style of hers, which I fear is growing characteristic, this most ardently noble of the screen heroines goes in with considerable lugubriousness for the priestly—or, in this case, nunlike—profession of medicine."

In the period before Ann renegotiated her RKO contract in mid-1933, there was trade talk that she would align herself with Darryl F. Zanuck's new Twentieth Century Productions, as had ex-RKO star Constance Bennett and First National's Loretta Young. Ann selected *Gallant Lady* as a test vehicle.*
The picture was a definite contrast for Zanuck, who till then had been consid-ered a specialist in hard-boiled melodramas but now wanted his new produc-tion firm to have a classier image. Ann endured a great deal of emotional turmoil in this turgid tale: her fiancé dies in a plane crash, she allows her illegitimate child (Dickie Moore) to be adopted by Otto Kruger and his wife.

*Remade as *Always Goodbye* (Twentieth Century-Fox, 1938) with Barbara Stanwyck and Herbert Marshall.

Years later, after she has become a successful interior decorator, she encounters now-widowed Kruger, who is about to wed grasping Betty Lawford. Without ever revealing her dark past to Kruger, Ann eventually gains his love and his name, content to be Moore's stepmother. To promote *Gallant Lady*'s opening at the Rivoli Theatre (January 21, 1934), Zanuck and the distributor, United Artists, commissioned the leading commercial artists of the day (James Montgomery Flagg, Diego Rivera, Howard Chandler Christy, McClelland Barclay, Bradshaw Crandall, and Hayden Haydon) to prepare likenesses of Ann to grace the theatre's lobby. The display did nothing to noticeably enhance the box-office receipts.

More melodramatic than any of Ann's films was her adventure when vacationing in Cuba in May, 1933, with Mexican-born stage and screen performer Alexander Kirkland. Ann, Kirkland, and her secretary, Marie Lombard, set out from Havana one bright day in a twenty-foot sailboat. During a subsequent storm the boat capsized. When the Cuban skipper attempted to swim to shore for help, he was killed by sharks. The surviving trio clung to the overturned boat for more than three hours before they were rescued by an English yachtsman, one Captain J. L. Waggill. Before the group reached port, the press erroneously sent out reports that Ann had been lost at sea. The follow-up story was more sensational. According to one of Waggill's crewmen, when the three had been picked up, they were in a state of almost complete undress. Kirkland insisted their clothing had washed away when they stripped off their outer garments to use them to signal a passing airplane. The press was not convinced by this explanation and the reportage reached proper yellow-journalistic levels. Before departing from Cuba to return to Hollywood, Ann settled a $25-a-month pension on the dead skipper's widow.

RKO's *The Life of Vergie Winters* (1934) incorporated every essential ingredient requisite for a top-notch tearjerker, but it still passed out of the studio lab as a carbon copy of the superior *Back Street* and a string of similar efforts. *The Life of Vergie Winters* opens with the funeral of John Boles and a cross-cut to an imprisoned Ann, and then flashes back two decades to the 1910s, when Parksville was just like any other small midwestern town. Ann's romance with genteel Boles suddenly terminates when he is tricked into wedding well-to-do Helen Vinson. Later a repentant Boles adopts his and Ann's illegitimate child (who is played as a grown-up by Betty Furness). Self-sacrificing Ann thereafter establishes herself as a local milliner, settling for a very occasional sidestreet rendezvous with Boles, who is now a U.S. senator. On the day of Furness's wedding, Boles informs Vinson he wants a divorce so he can wed Ann. The enraged legal spouse follows Boles to Ann's apartment and shoots him dead. Rather than reveal the sordid truth to the police, Ann prefers being charged with the homicide. Flipping back to the present, the tale traces Ann's martyred prison existence. It all concludes when Vinson on her deathbed confesses guilt and Ann is freed to be reunited with her daughter in a haloed, tearful meeting. "You keep wishing," moaned one reviewer, "that something solid, something real, would happen."

The Fountain (1934) was "nothing more than a very apt vehicle for Miss Harding," wrote Otis Ferguson in the *New Republic*, "being as it is long and solemn and wonderfully empty." When RKO purchased the screen rights to this popular novel in 1932, literary critics insisted that its mystical sex values could not be properly translated to the screen. RKO's picturization proved them absolutely correct. Even consistently indulgent *Variety* agreed. *The Fountain* was one of the "talkiest talkers yet." Set during World War I, Britisher Ann is residing in Holland at the home of her stern Dutch stepfather, Jean Hersholt. Just as she re-encounters English flier Brian Aherne, her childhood sweetheart, her German husband (Paul Lukas) is sent back from the front lines in a badly mangled state. For much of the eighty-four minutes, the handsome trio brood and brood: Aherne is too self-effacing to admit he ardently loves a married woman, Ann is wracked by guilt for daring to love another while her husband lies in an adjoining room suffering, and Lukas is at once perplexed and pleased, for never before had Ann shown such concern and tenderness for him. Finally, on his deathbed, Lukas eases her from all obligations past and present to him, leaving her free to peacefully (and hopefully ardently) unite with astounded Aherne. Through this vale of tears, Ann did have the chance to provide an offshoot to her screen stereotype: The portrait of a sleek and troubled woman who is rather ruthless in pursuing her heart's desire. RKO promoted *The Fountain* as its contribution to the industry's "back-to-theatre month," insisting that herewith, "RKO delivers another production not a prediction." Audiences, on the other hand, who paid to see the feature at Radio City Music Hall (August 30, 1934), were far more captivated by the companion item on the bill, Pioneer Pictures' Technicolor musical short subject *La Cucaracha,* starring Steffi Duna and Paul Porcasi.

Under her newly revised RKO pact, Ann had signed with Walter Wanger in September, 1934, to appear in *Peacock Feathers,* which was geared to be the pathfinding feature in the new three-color Technicolor process. Unfortunately the production was shelved,* and Pioneer later used Miriam Hopkins to star in its first multihued feature, *Becky Sharp* (1935). But unconsummated film projects and reassignments were becoming a constant way of life for Ann. In 1933 Fox had considered Ann for its lavish *Cavalcade,* but eventually Diana Wynyard was used. Ann's favorite director, Edward H. Griffith, was to showcase her in *The World Outside* (opposite Charles Farrell) as well as in Ernest Hemingway's *The Sun Also Rises* of which RKO owned the screen rights. Likewise, *Alien Corn,* which had spotlighted Katharine Cornell on stage, was purchased by RKO for Ann, first given to European import Dorothea Wieck, then mentioned as a new Katharine Hepburn-John Barrymore vehicle, and finally shelved. Warner Bros. wanted Ann to join Kay Francis and Jean Muir in a biopic of the Bronte sisters. Director John Stahl offered

*It was made in 1946 as *A Night in Paradise* (1946) with Merle Oberon. When Ann tested for this feature to be made post-*Enchanted April* (1935), she gleefully announced, "I haven't known of anything that has stirred my enthusiasm so much since I left the Hedgerow Theatre in Pennsylvania."

to pay Ann $7,300 a week to headline Universal's *Only Yesterday* (1934), but Margaret Sullavan eventually inherited the part.

Ann's excessive inability to carry through on a project she favored stemmed from the growing friction between her and the studio. She accused RKO of stymieing her. Her employers counterclaimed she was just being unsympathetic to Hollywood. Since the RKO stable of actress stars boasted Hepburn, Irene Dunne, and Ginger Rogers, as well as the professional services of Miriam Hopkins, the studio would have been less inclined than ever to kowtow to Ann, even if it had wanted to take the time to properly showcase the distinguished star.

Ann returned to MGM to star in *Biography of a Bachelor Girl* (1934), a project claimed to have been originally intended for Metro star Marion Davies. Unforturnately, Ann was badly miscast in this scrubbed version of S. N. Behrman's Broadway play *Biography* (1932), which had glowed with Ina Claire as its star. "What Miss Harding does to the picture," explained Thornton Delehanty in the *New York Post,* "is to make the central and all-important character as artificial and unbelievable as are compatible with her trite and meaningless gestures." Ann unadroitly essayed the celebrity portrait painter whose forthcoming biography reveals details of her several love affairs, including one with an important politician. There were many striking scenes of silver-blonde Ann elegantly garbed in white floor-length ensembles against off-white decor, but she simply was unbelievable as a sophisticated bohemian who has a frivolous past.

There was not much meat to RKO's *Enchanted April* (1935), her next film, based on the novel by "Elizabeth," and it did nothing to restore Ann's faltering box-office position. As the neglected wife of lionized author Frank Morgan she agrees to share a rented castle on the Italian Riviera with Katharine Alexander, hoping her month-long absence will restore her middle-aged husband to his domestic senses.

Metro recalled Ann for a third and final try, *The Flame Within* (1935). Edmund Goulding, who produced, directed, and wrote the picture, instilled the production with his usual technical skill, sympathetic handling of the performers, and the easy sentiment that was his trademark. But the plotline had little to commend it. British psychiatrist Ann has a lapse of professional ethics when she is overly attracted to her alcoholic and paranoid patient Louis Hayward. He, in turn, has driven his fiancée (Maureen O'Sullivan) to attempted suicide. Ann almost abandons all for Hayward, but regains her perspective and accepts the gentler, more mature love of surgeon Herbert Marshall. This lofty piece of hokum certainly was no companion piece to *Private Worlds* (Paramount, 1935), a much superior study of psychiatrists at work and at love. "Despite her rather studied performance," the *New York Times* admitted . . . Ann "can be brightly charming until the script calls for her to be heroically brave and tragic." The fact that onscreen Hayward seemed so very much younger than Ann did not make this maelstrom of concocted emotions appear too plausible. For its part, MGM had made a valiant try to restore Ann's cinema prestige with a trio of superior women's pictures, but Ann's magnetism was too firmly rooted in the 1920s to appeal to the restless mid-1930s audiences, which craved new personalities, attitudes, and styles.

Although Ann's professional career was being eclipsed by newcomers, her private life was again headline news. In the spring of 1935, Harry Bannister* petitioned the California courts to appoint a suitable guardian for daughter Jane, claiming he had "startling information" to reveal about Ann's moral conduct. A seemingly aghast Ann told the press: "I don't know what to say about it. I've always lived a very quiet and secluded existence, finding my pleasures in the normal, wholesome things that don't seem to interest my Hollywood neighbors. I've tried to live as a lady would, unpretentiously, quietly. That's why all this horrible thing comes as such a shock to me. My only supposition is that Hollywood resents a lady." Bannister and his attorney attempted to link Ann with movie director and playboy Dudley Murphy. Ann retaliated by refusing to answer the court charges, which almost resulted in a contempt-of-court charge. Eventually the matter, for the time being at least, was settled behind closed courtroom doors. Ann received full custody of Jane, with Bannister to have supervision of the girl for two weekends every three months. A further stipulation required that Jane could only leave California with the court's permission.

Hardly had this matter cooled down, when Ann departed for a vacation in Honolulu. Reporters rushed to the airport to inquire whether this trip meant she was planning to see her post-Harry Bannister divorce beau, Major Ben Sawbridge, then stationed at Schofield Barracks in Honolulu. Ann had already announced, in May, 1935, that she would not give up her acting career to wed Sawbridge, and this time around she irately snapped to the newsmen: "I'll announce my own engagement and marriage if I'm ever engaged or married." Among those seeing Ann off at the airport was actor Brian Aherne.

Ann's third and final 1935 release was Paramount's *Peter Ibbetson.*† She had long wanted to make the picture and agreed to accept second billing to Gary Cooper in order to finalize the deal. Under Henry Hathaway's direction *Peter Ibbetson* was a sumptuously mounted film. Ann never appeared to better physical advantage on screen, her beauty accentuated by the period costumes and her ringlet hair-style. Nevertheless audiences were justifiably baffled by the story's "lavender mysticism," which made the venerable stage vehicle seem both old fashioned and too much ahead of its time. Ann's placid, aristocratic existence as the wife of the Duke of Towers (John Halliday) is shattered when architect Cooper arrives at their Yorkshire estate to design new stables. She discovers the interloper is none other than "Gogo," her childhood sweetheart of long-ago Paris days. Ann and Cooper's joyful reunion is misinterpreted by jealous Halliday and in a later confrontation scene, Cooper

---

*He had returned to New York, where in 1933 he produced *Late One Evening* on Broadway with Ursula Jeans starred. The following year he managed the American Music Hall theatre group, whose revival of *The Drunkard* ran for a year.

†Previously filmed by Paramount as *Forever* (1922) with Wallace Reid and Elsie Ferguson.

accidentally kills the Duke. Cooper is sentenced to life imprisonment, but to the amazement of all he survives the grimness of Dartmoor Prison in blissful tranquility. Cooper's secret is that in his "dreams" he and Ann escape the harsh realities of life by meeting in their garden idyll of years past. More time passes and one day the elderly Cooper can no longer envision Ann, for, unknown to him, she has died that very day. He soon thereafter passes away, secure in his knowledge that he and Ann will be reunited for eternity in their beloved garden paradise. It was almost unanimously agreed that Cooper was miscast and out of his element in the strange fantasy world of *Peter Ibbetson*. Ann, on the other hand, thrived in the film's ethereal atmosphere, leading the *New York Herald-Tribune*—no ally to the actress—to admit that her performance was "surprisingly lacking in affection." There was an appealing contrast between Ann's sedate, spiritual character and the more basic flavor supplied by Ida Lupino as Agnes, the woman who loses Cooper to his childhood love. Despite its Radio City Music Hall showcasing (November 7, 1935), *Peter Ibbetson* emerged a substantial box-office casualty, proving to Ann's detractors that she was now thoroughly washed up in movies.

The new Samuel J. Briskin regime, which took over at RKO Radio in October, 1935, inherited Ann with a lot of other commodities it considered overpriced "assets." Nevertheless it was forced to carry through with Ann's contract and obtain what mileage it could from her diminished marquee name. In her more opulent studio days, Ann had urged studio executives to acquire P. J. Wolfson's story, "The Indestructible Mrs. Talbot," but Paramount purchased the property for more than RKO would pay. When Ann went to Paramount to appear in *Peter Ibbetson,* part of the deal included the selling of "The Indestructible Mrs. Talbot" to RKO, along with an agreement that RKO would consider loaning Ann and Irene to Paramount for a picturization of *The Old Maid.* The latter project would eventually be filmed in 1939 by Warner Bros, with Bette Davis and Miriam Hopkins; the other saw release in 1936 as *The Lady Consents.* The picture struggled to present Ann's overplayed screen nobility in a new guise as the eternal wife who hides her tears behind a tight smile.

The premise of *The Lady Consents* offers Ann as a wife of seven years who notices that her physician husband (Herbert Marshall) is far more interested in outdoorsy-type Margaret Lindsay. Without offering any fight she gallantly insists that Marshall divorce her and wed Lindsay, with good sport Ann even attending the ceremony. Largely through the intervention of her sprightly father-in-law (Edward Ellis), Ann wins back Marshall after he discovers the grievous error of his second marriage. The fact that *The Lady Consents* opened at the pedestrian Center Theatre (February 7, 1936) revealed just how little faith RKO had in the property or in Ann's present screen chemistry.

Ann's studio option had not been renewed by the time RKO's *The Witness Chair* went into production in February, 1936. Because her courtroom struggles with Bannister had been so newsworthy, many, including Ann, assumed that *The Witness Chair* was an appropriate project to restore her standing with filmgoers. "I hope," Ann told reporters, "*The Witness Chair* will help me regain my former place in the public eye. Then I'm off to London to make several films. I'm looking forward so much to the trip. It'll be fun working there—and taking my daughter Jane with me. I've taken a new lease on movie life and feel like making pictures forever."

Although *The Witness Chair* (1937) was considered an upswing from some of her recent screen offerings, Ann's RKO swan song was greeted as a "lugubrious and mediocre" film. It did not help matters that the plot structure required Ann to project her character on a single sustained low-key until just before the climax. Then, to save Walter Abel from being convicted on a homicide charge, secretary Ann admits in full court that she accidentally killed her dastardly employer (Douglass Dumbrille), who was conniving to make a false embezzlement charge against business associate Abel. She then explains her gallant gesture to Abel: "Women in love are such fools they can't bear to see their men hurt and would do anything to save them from danger." Their mutual admiration established, it is assumed Ann will be given a verdict of justifiable homicide by the court and will be free to live happily ever after with husband Abel.

In trying her professional luck abroad, Ann clearly hoped to break her repressive movie stereotype as the "premiere sufferer and protectress of young womanhood."* Ann found herself venturing to England, like other American cinema stars, such as Sylvia Sidney and Miriam Hopkins, thinking to re-establish a faltering box-office name through a change of locale. Another fact which induced film celebrities like Ann, Constance Bennett, and William Powell to jaunt to Britain for filmmaking was the beneficial tax break the overseas work provided.

Thus, after completing *The Witness Chair* in March, 1936, Ann applied to the California courts for permission to take Jane to Europe for six months. When Harry Bannister sought to stall her petition, Ann countered by revealing that at the time of their divorce she had settled $100,000 on Bannister and that now he was pressuring her for ownership of half of her property.† It also came out that when Ann had sent Jane to New York in 1934 to stay with Bannister, he had had a bootlegger as a houseguest and there had been several nights of carousing, all a most unfitting atmosphere for an impressionable little girl. The court granted Ann's petition on the condition that she post a $5,000 bond.

The Perils of Pauline could hardly match the real-life drama that followed. Ann and Jane vacationed in Canada before departing for England in June, 1936. When Bannister, busy obtaining a new court order to prevent Jane from

---

*In reviewing *The Lady Consents*, Richard Watts, Jr. (*New York Herald-Tribune*) analyzed: "Always you see Miss Harding as a victim triumphing over the powers of evil by the sheer force of her nobility. In fact, it is my fear that she is so filled with spiritual sweetness that she ends by making you just a trifle resentful of so much greatness of soul."

†Bannister explained that the $100,000 was just part of their joint earnings, a mere 20 percent of their total joint holdings at the time of their divorce.

going abroad, learned that they were about to embark on *The Empress of Australia* from Montreal, he chartered a plane at Roosevelt Field in New York and flew directly to Montreal. At the train station in Montreal, Ann told the eager press: "I'm not afraid of Harry Bannister or of anything he can do." But she altered her plans, detrained at Quebec, and hired a motorboat to take her and Jane aboard the *Duchess of Atholl,* which had just sailed. By the time Bannister arrived in Quebec, Ann and Jane were already at sea. "I think the mother should have the child," Bannister scowled, "but if she establishes a foreign residence I may never see my daughter again."*

Ann and Jane disembarked at Belfast, Northern Ireland, instead of at Liverpool, England, as scheduled. It was mistakenly reported in one Dublin tabloid that Jane had been kidnapped, but really Ann had had her daughter taken ashore by other passengers, rather than subject the child to the turmoil of a sensational press conference.

Hollywood observer Adela Rogers St. John, always a steadfast Ann Harding supporter, could now write of the movie-star expatriate: "No screen story in which she has ever appeared is quite so tragic and quite so pitiful as Ann Harding's own story, and with her going away from us I find my heart aching rather desperately and my mind hammering with questions and my thoughts deeply disturbed. I wonder if people understand exactly what has happened to Ann Harding and what we are losing? Whether any of us realize the great modern problem that lies behind the Bannister-Harding front page scandal or the many strange and devastating torments that face this lovely woman?"

Ann had been scheduled to make several expensively mounted films in London, including a version of *Camille,* but MGM beat the British production company to the punch by preparing its own *Camille* (1936) with Greta Garbo. Instead Ann made *Love from a Stranger* (1937), based on the Agatha Christie story and the Frank Vosper play.† This well-known plot has British national-lottery winner Ann finally able to take a Parisian vacation trip, during which she is wooed by dashing chemical engineer Basil Rathbone, whom she hastily agrees to wed. Belatedly she discovers he has murdered his three previous wives and intends her to become victim number four. This modern Bluebeard tale did not have the requisite zing to make it an outstanding commercial success. Only the climactic cat-and-mouse game between Ann and Rathbone in their cottage in Kent had the needed punch of a first-class screen thriller, but by that time in the film the audience had been lost. When the movie played the United States in 1937 the audience reaction was the same, so it little mattered to Ann's waning screen career that now newspapers like the *New York Daily Mirror* could report, "She is gratifyingly more human in this than in any other picture."

---

*Harry Bannister would marry Leah Moskowitz Welt in 1936, remain a frequent Broadway performer in the 1940s and 1950s and die on February 16, 1961, in Manhattan at the age of seventy-two.

†In 1947 Sylvia Sidney and John Hodiak co-starred in a more pedestrian remake of the chiller.

Vastly disappointed by her bout with British filmmaking,* Ann had high optimism for her London stage bow in George Bernard Shaw's *Candida*. A few weeks before this theatrical event was to occur, Ann surprised her friends and public by marrying symphony conductor Werner Janssen† on January 17, 1937 at London's Caxton Hall Registrar's Office. Among the attendees at the wedding were composer Sir Granville Bantock, Mr. and Mrs. Clive Brook, Paul Dean Thompson of the American Embassy, and, of course, Ann's daughter Jane. As Ann left the Registrar's Office, she blew kisses to the press, saying, "God bless you." It was one of her last moments of nonprofessional prominence.

Ann's connubial tidings had already created a great deal of public interest, which was inflamed further when it was learned that the great George Bernard Shaw had personally attended rehearsals of Ann's *Candida* and thoroughly endorsed her performance. When *Candida* opened at the Globe Theatre (February 10, 1937), Ann received unanimous critical approval, a tribute rarely accorded to any American performer. But Ann only remained with the successful venture until the end of March, when she left for a Scandinavian honeymoon with Janssen. Diana Wynyard, who had replaced Ann in Fox's *Cavalcade* movie years before, became her West End stage replacement in *Candida*.

When the Janssens returned to the United States in 1938, Ann toured with *Candida* and played a season of summer stock with a West Coast troupe. Thereafter she devoted her time to accompanying Janssen on concert tours throughout the United States and South America. Seemingly content with her new role as the wife of one of the brightest young conductors of the 1930s, Ann could tell the press: "It would take an earthquake to lure me back to the films. Of course, if a wonderful plum should be dropped in my lap—that would be something different. But such plums fall only to those who reach for them and I'm tired of reaching for them." Scarcely a year later it was rumored that Ann might star in a movie entitled *Destiny*, based on *The Monster* by Charles MacArthur and Ben Hecht, and would have as co-stars John Howard and Barbara Joe Allen (later known as Vera Vague). But nothing developed.

When Janssen left his post as conductor of the Baltimore Symphony Or-

---

*Said a disgruntled Ann: "Fantastic sums [are] spent inadvisedly—expenditures that don't show on the screen. Production is hand-to-mouth, due to lack of organization and preparation, and the British producers are not prepared to live up to their contracts."

†Born on June 1, 1899 in Manhattan, Janssen was the son of a German expatriate who had made a reputation as the restaurateur-owner of the Hofbrau in New York City. He studied at Dartmouth College where he received his Bachelor of Music degree in 1922 (and an honorary degree as a Doctor of Music in 1935). He held fellowships from the Juilliard Foundation and the American Academy in Rome (1930) and the following years conducted at the latter institution, directing the Royal Symphony Orchestra. Next he embarked on a well-received Continental tour, performing as guest conductor of the Philharmonic Orchestras in Budapest, Berlin, Vienna, Helsinki, Copenhagen, Turin, Milan, and Riga. Janssen made his American debut with the New York Philharmonic Orchestra in 1934, the first native New Yorker to conduct that orchestra. Previously wed to Elsa Schmidt of Indianapolis, whom he divorced in December, 1936, he was the father of two children, Alice, age thirteen, and Werner, Jr., age twelve.

chestra to assume command of his own Hollywood-based orchestra, Ann accompanied him to the West Coast. Louis B. Mayer, who had never forgiven himself for not putting Ann under MGM contract when he had purchased the screen rights to *The Trial of Mary Dugan* back in 1928, now induced her to make her movie return. Mayer had special plans for thirty-nine-year-old Ann. At one point after Norma Shearer rejected *Mrs. Miniver* and before Greer Garson expressed interest in the part, Mayer considered starring Ann in the film. He also had her test in early 1940 for the role of Ma Baxter in the abortive Spencer Tracy version of *The Yearling*. Instead, Ann, who had once been one of the highest-paid stars in Hollywood and its first lady of elegance, found herself making a "comeback" in a minor but offbeat programmer, *Eyes in the Night* (MGM, 1942). In this picture, one of Fred Zimmermann's early directorial efforts, Ann was cast as the stepmother of willful Donna Reed. She appeals to blind detective Edward Arnold to discover whether John Emery, involved with Reed, is really a Nazi agent out to grab a secret formula from her inventor husband (Reginald Denny). The camera was not particularly kind to Ann, and some long-memoried critics noted she was still enacting a version of "those whiny, consciously noble women she used to play."

Having leaped into the fray as a cinema character actress,* she received a good many film offers. Warner Brothers hired Ann to play Mrs. Davies to Walter Huston's Joseph E. Davies, American ambassador to Russia, in the pro-Soviet *Mission to Moscow* (1943). At the time, the elaborately constructed feature received tremendous attention, with the *New York Times's* Bosley Crowther labeling it "clearly the most outspoken picture on a political subject that an American studio has ever made." Ann's opportunities for dramaturgy in this political travelog were minimal, but it was still a prestigious film credit for her in the changed Hollywood of the 1940s.

Later in 1943 Ann was fifth-billed in Samuel Goldwyn's *North Star,* which starred Farley Granger and Anne Baxter. Ann's stock nobility pose was well utilized in her portrayal of the matron of a Russian village overrun by the Nazis during the 1941 invasion. She had her greatest moments of oncamera suffering in this unabashed bit of propaganda when her youngest daughter is killed in a bombing raid and, later, when she herself is tortured by the Nazis.

Ann then turned to screen comedy, playing the vexed mother of Joyce Reynolds in Warner Bros. *Janie* (1944), which, like the Broadway original, was devoted to the premise that American family life is almost completely controlled by brash and precocious youth. In her subordinate role, Ann received even less screen time than Edward Arnold, who essayed her harassed newspaper-editor husband. After being the teacher-chaperone of nine Gamma Theta sorority girls in Columbia's cheapie whodunit *Nine Girls* (1944), Ann

*Ann later admitted that she had greatly rushed the transition from romantic lead to featured player.

returned to RKO to support Robert Young and Laraine Day in an unsubstantial romantic yarn, *Those Endearing Young Charms* (1945). She was cast as the captain in the Women's Uptown (Manhattan) 84th Street Auxiliary, who attempts to steer her impulsive daughter (Day) through a difficult love interlude with gadabout Air Force pilot Young. By now Ann had slipped so completely into her matronly screen-player category, that it was difficult to separate her from lookalike Selena Royle, another practitioner of settled, rather dowdy, mother types. *Janie Gets Married,* Warners' sequel to the fairly popular *Janie,* had been completed in June, 1945, but was not released until a year later. This time Janie (now played by Joan Leslie) has wed Robert Hutton and is undergoing the initial months of domestic confusion. The only bright note to this feeble follow-up was the performance of the late Robert Benchley.

Directly after World War II, Werner Janssen, who had been engaged in wartime volunteer work, resumed his concert-conducting career and Ann accompanied him on the tours. They established their permanent residence in Westport, Connecticut, but Ann returned to Hollywood in 1946 to make two more films. *It Happened on Fifth Avenue* (1947) was the first upper-bracket entry by economy studio Allied Artists, and it proved to be the sleeper of the year.* The whimsical tale found lovable bum Victor Moore utilizing the Manhattan mansion of Charles Ruggles, who has gone South for the season. Ann underplayed her assignment as Ruggles's estranged wife, who joins Moore's menagerie, disguised as a cook. United Artists' *Christmas Eve* (1947)** is one of Ann's most frequently televised features, making it easy for too many of the newer generation of filmgoers to believe that she was always and only an aging character player who had a strong penchant for hamming. Cast as an elderly eccentric matron, Ann eagerly anticipates the arrival of her three adopted sons (George Brent, Randolph Scott, George Raft) to save her from being committed to a mental institution by her stuffed-shirt nephew, Reginald Denny. What resulted were three disjointed tales involving each of the wayward men as they beat a hasty path back to Ann's rescue.

Two years passed before Ann resumed her professional career with a ten-week summer-stock tour of the comedy *Yes, My Darling Daughter.* Henry Jones was cast as her conventional husband. When the star package show played the Cape Playhouse in Dennis, Massachusetts, that theatre's producer, Richard Aldrich, was so charmed by Ann's performance that he induced her to return to Broadway in 1949 in the long-running *Goodbye, My Fancy.*†
Ann explained her Broadway reappearance: "You always have to come back,

---

*On the initial day of shooting on the RKO lot, Ann was greeted at the studio by flowers and a party. with her old canvas chair bearing her name put out for her use. At the time she exclaimed: "I must admit this is one of my life's pleasantest surprises. Hollywood usually ignores actresses at this in-between age, which makes coming back here a double celebration."

**A.k.a. *Sinners Holiday.*

†Ann replaced Ruth Hussey, age thirty-five, who had replaced Madeleine Carroll, age forty-three. Ann was Aldrich's choice after Irene Dunne rejected the bid for a Broadway return.

torture though it may be—you just have to see if you can." Her portrayal of Congresswoman Agatha Reed was well received and she accompanied the road company when it later played Chicago.

MGM and Hollywood again beckoned when her old friend and Broadway co-star, Louis Calhern, wanted her to play his wife in the filmization of his stage success, *The Magnificent Yankee* (1950). Before the two veteran performers emoted in this production, MGM placed them in a Technicolor musical, *Two Weeks with Love* (1950), in which they were reduced to playing comedy foils for the caperings of their brash onscreen daughters, Jane Powell and Debbie Reynolds. Much more impressive but far less of a box-office success was *The Magnificent Yankee,* in which Ann played Fanny Bowditch Holmes to Calhern's Justice Holmes. The film traced their years in Washington, D.C., from 1912 to 1933. Unfortunately, Metro chose to gloss over Holmes's liberal Supreme Court decisions and overaccentuated Mrs. Holmes's influence on her husband, leading to what many termed a "rather humorless *Life with Father.*" A splashy Radio City Music Hall opening did not aid the essentially art-house picture, and *The Magnificent Yankee* fared badly with the public. Ann and Calhern (he being Oscar-nominated for his performance) re-created their roles from *The Magnificent Yankee* on "Lux Radio Theatre" on May 19, 1951.

Her next film, *The Unknown Man* (MGM, 1951), was a promising crime story that faltered along the way with high-sounding principles. Attorney Walter Pidgeon succeeds in winning the freedom of his client Keefe Brasselle, who is charged with murder, only to learn later that Brasselle was probably guilty. Ann was wasted in a side-seat-observer's role as Pidgeon's overly restrained wife. Also in 1951, Ann was featured in an episode of Metro's *It's A Big Country,* but her segment was shorn from the film due to an already inordinately long running time.

It was not until 1956 that Ann appeared in another movie, Twentieth Century-Fox's color expansion of Sloan Wilson's best-selling novel, *The Man in the Gray Flannel Suit.* Reteamed with her *Paris Bound* co-star, Fredric March, Ann had the fleeting assignment of playing the embittered estranged wife of broadcasting tycoon March and the mother of spoiled Gigi Perreau. The mature and quiet authority Ann brought to her very few screen scenes was an excellent contrast to the mercurial emotionalism suppled by Jennifer Jones as the suburban wife of crisis-ridden advertising executive Gregory Peck.

Ann was also in two other 1956 releases, both forgettable programmers. Unlike the more concrete book and film excursion into *The Search for Bridie Murphy, I've Lived Before* was an unconvincing entry in the reincarnation-film cycle, filled with unintended comedy. The plot concerns commerical pilot Jock Mahoney, who believes that through personality transference he has become Ann's long dead fiancé, an Army pilot shot down in 1918 France. *Strange Intruder,* which had scant release, dealt with battle-fatigued GI Edmund Purdom, who has promised his now-dead Korean War buddy to kill the latter's two children so that the unfaithful wife (Ida Lupino) and her lover (Jacques Bergerac) cannot have them. In this slow thriller, Ann and Carl Benton Reid briefly functioned as the parents of the dead neurotic soldier. Plans never materialized for Ann to play a society dowager in Universal's *Tammy and the Bachelor* (1957) and a cafe owner in the same studio's *A Time to Love and a Time To Die* (1958).

From late 1951 through 1965 Ann was a frequent television performer, but unlike the heyday of her movie popularity, there was little fanfare about her many craftsmanlike video outings, all of which were taken for granted by a public that had forgotten, or never knew, that she was once a leading lady of the silver screen. Almost invariably television producers cast the mature Ann in unglamorous assignments as a spinsterish matron, or occasionally as a rather vicious, determined, elder citizen. But whether she was starring on "Lux Video Theatre," "Pulitzer Prize Playhouse," "Play of the Week" (*The Potting Shed, Mornings at Seven*), "Alfred Hitchcock Presents," "Burke's Law," "The Defenders," "Eleventh Hour," or "Ben Casey,"* she consistently turned in well-etched performances. On the March 20, 1960 edition of ABC's "Our American Heritage," in the episode entitled *Autocrat and Son,* she recreated her role as Fanny Bowditch Holmes, with Sir Cedric Hardwicke as her husband.

In 1958, the same year Ann and Janssen sold their California home, Ann made a summer-stock tour with *September Tide,* which had been done on the London stage with Gertrude Lawrence, and then enjoyed a brief foray on Off-Broadway in Tennessee Williams's *Garden District.* She said:

"I read scripts that were dreary, disillusioned, dirty and often loaded with preachment, and then suddenly along came the wonderful opportunity in Mr. Williams' two short plays. I have a marvelous chance to prove myself.

"I couldn't find a better chance to get away from those noble women parts. I've been tired of them for years, and I know everyone else is too."

Critics were enthusiastic over Ann's nuance-filled performance in the two one-acters (*Something Unspoken; Suddenly, Last Summer*) and wondered why Ann had not been considered when the production was first mounted, instead of being a replacement for Margaret Bannerman, who replaced Hortense Allen. When the movie version of *Suddenly, Last Summer* was made the following year, Ann's old RKO rival, Katharine Hepburn, was handed her meaty role of Mrs. Venable.

Four years passed before Ann returned to the theatre, this time as the wife of the commanding officer (William Bendix) at an Army post in Ira Levin's *General Seeger,* directed by George C. Scott. During the Detroit tryout Ann suffered from an inflammation of the intestines, and she fainted onstage during the opening-night performance (February 15, 1962) at the Shubert Theatre. But the game actress recovered in time to appear in the New York

*Her last television performance to date was the "Ben Casey" episode *Because of the Needle, the Haystack Was Lost,* televised October 11, 1965, on ABC-TV.

41

debut (Lyceum Theatre, February 28, 1962), only to have the show close after two performances. She returned to a noble type at the persuasion of playwright-producer Dore Schary, who had been her benefactor at MGM during the 1949-51 period. In *Banderol* Ann was the crippled and neglected wife of movie tycoon Ed Begley. The random production closed in Philadelphia in September, 1962. Ann did not have much better luck with John Sherry's *Abraham Cochrane,* starring Bill Travers, which folded on Broadway after one performance (Belasco Theatre, February 17, 1964).

Ann's domestic situation was even less fruitful. In October, 1961, in a Bridgeport, Connecticut, court, she sued Werner Janssen for divorce, charging him with "intolerable cruelty," and asking alimony and damages of $500,000 and the right to return to her maiden name. She tearfully added that Janssen had persistently sought to control her every minute in order to separate her from her friends. She added that when she decided against returning with him to Germany, where he intended to reside permanently, he had departed without her, and she had not seen him since. The following year Ann dropped her damage suit but was granted her divorce.

After serving a two-month term as guest acting instructor at the School of Speech and Drama at Eastern New Mexico University in June and July of 1964, Ann unofficially retired to her Connecticut home, content, according to her statements, to garden, read, and listen to her collection of classical music. She frequently visits with her daughter, Jane, who, after graduating from the University of California, wed stockbroker Alfred Otto, Jr., in San Francisco in November, 1955, and now lives in a suburb of that city. The Ottos have a daughter, Diana, born in 1958.

At each stage of her well-defined career, Ann was adamant about what she wanted and how she would go about getting it. She is no different about her present retirement. After recovering from an operation for a perforated ulcer during the summer of 1972, she resided with friends in the Los Angeles area, planning to later go and live in Austria. When New York press agent John Springer telephoned Ann not too long ago, requesting her participation in an upcoming film retrospective program, she replied in her still cool, crisp voice: "I beg to be excused. Thank you but no thank you. I am retired. I am no longer involved."

Preoccupied with her simple daily life, Ann is apparently satisfied to abide by her firm philosophy, "If I leave the future alone, I find that it takes care of me so much better than 'the best laid plans of mice and men' could possibly dream up!"

Feature Film Appearances
ANN HARDING

PARIS BOUND   (Pathé, 1929) 73 M.

Supervisor, Maurice Revnes; producer, Arthur Hopkins; director, Edward H. Griffith; based on the play by Philip Barry; adaptation, Horace Jackson; dialog director-dialog, Frank Reicher; music, Josiah Zuro; costumes, Gwen Wakeling; assistant director, William Scully; production manager, George Webster; sound, George Ellis, Charles O'Loughlin; camera, Norbert Brodine, Norbert Scully; editor, Helen Warne.

Ann Harding (Mary Hutton); Fredric March (Jim Hutton); George Irving (James Hutton, Sr.); Leslie Fenton (Richard Parrish); Hallam Cooley (Peter); Juliette Crosby (Nora Cope); Charlotte Walker (Helen White); Carmelita Geraghty (Noel Farley); Ilka Chase (Fanny Shipman).

HER PRIVATE AFFAIR   (Pathé, 1929) 71 M.

Director, Paul Stein, (director for silent version, Rollo Lloyd); based on the play *The Right to Kill* by Leo Urvantzov; adaptation, Francis E. Faragoh, Herman Bernstein; screenplay-dialog, Faragoh; assistant director, E. J. Babille; sound, W. C. Brown, D. A. Cutler; camera, David Abel, Norbert Brodine.

Ann Harding (Vera Kessler); Harry Bannister (Judge Kessler); John Loder (Carl Weild); Kay Hammond (Julia Sturm); Arthur Hoyt (Michael Sturm); William Orlamond (Dr. Zeigler); Lawford Davidson (Arnold Hartmann); Elmer Ballard (Grimm); Frank Reicher (State's Attorney).

CONDEMNED   (UA, 1929) 91 M.

Producer, Samuel Goldwyn; director, Wesley Ruggles; suggested by the book *Condemned to Devil's Island* by Blair Niles; screenplay, Sidney Howard; dialog director, Dudley Digges; settings, William Cameron Menzies; song, Jack Meskill and Pete Wendling; camera, George Barnes, Gregg Toland; editor, Stuart Heisler.

Ronald Colman (Michel Oban); Ann Harding (Madame Vidal); Dudley Digges (Warden Jean Vidal); Louis Wolheim (Jacques Duval); William Elmer (Pierre); William Vaughn (Vidal's Orderly); Albert Kingsley (Felix); Constantine Romanoff (Brute Convict); Harry Ginsberg, Bud Somers, Stephen Selznick, Baldy Biddle, John George, Arturo Kobe, Emile and John Schwartz (Inmates).

HOLIDAY   (Pathé, 1930) 99 M.

Producer, E. B. Derr; director, Edward H. Griffith; based on the play by Philip Barry; screenplay-dialog, Horace Jackson; assistant director, Paul Jones; costumes, Gwen Wakeling; art director, Carroll Clark; music, Josiah Zuro; sound, D. A. Cutler, Harold Stine; camera, Norbert Brodine; editor, Daniel Mandell.

Ann Harding (Linda Seton); Mary Astor (Julia Seton); Edward Everett Horton (Nick Potter); Robert Ames (Johnny Case); Hedda Hopper (Susan Potter); Monroe

Owsley (Ned); William Holden (Edward Seton); Elizabeth Forrester (Laura); Mabel Forrest (Mary Jessup); Creighton Hale (Pete Hedges); Hallam Cooley (Seton Cram); Mary Forbes (Mrs. Pritchard Ames).

THE GIRL OF THE GOLDEN WEST   (FN, 1930) 81 M.

Associate producer, Robert North; director, John Francis Dillon; based on the play by David Belasco; screenplay-dialog, Waldemar Young; camera, Sol Polito.

Ann Harding (Minnie); James Rennie (Dick Johnson); Harry Bannister (Jack Rance); Ben Hendricks, Jr. (Handsome Charlie); J. Farrell MacDonald (Sonora Slim); George Cooper (Trinidad Joe); Johnny Walker (Nick); Richard Carlyle (Jim Larkins); Arthur Stone (Joe Castro); Arthur Housman (Sidney Dick); Norman McNeil (Happy Holiday); Fred Warren (Jack Wallace); Joe Girard (Ashby); Newton House (Pony Express Rider); Princess Noola (Wowkle); Chief Yowlachie (Billy Jackrabbit).

EAST LYNNE   (Fox, 1931) 102 M.

Director, Frank Lloyd; based on the play by Mrs. Henry Wood; adaptation, Bradley King, Tom Barry; settings, Joseph Urban; music, Richard Fall; sound, C. Clayton Ward; dialog director, Claude King; camera, John Seitz.

Clive Brook (Captain William Levison); Ann Harding (Lady Isabel Severn); Conrad Nagel (Robert Carlyle); Cecilia Loftus (Cornelia Carlyle); Beryl Mercer (Joyce); O. P. Heggie (Lord Mount Severn); Flora Sheffield (Barbara Hare); David Torrence (Sir Richard Hare); J. Gunnis Davis (Dodson); Ronald Cosbey (William—as a Baby); Wally Albright (William—as a Boy); Eric Mayne (Doctor).

DEVOTION   (RKO-Pathé, 1931) 84 M.

Producer, Charles R. Rogers; director, Robert Milton; based on the novel *A Little Flat in the Temple* by Pamela Wynne; screenplay, Graham John, Horace Jackson; sound, D. Cutler, H. Stine; camera, Hal Mohr; editor, Dan Mandell.

Ann Harding (Shirley Mortimer); Leslie Howard (David Trent); Robert Williams (Harrington); O. P. Heggie (Mr. Mortimer); Louise Closser Hale (Mrs. Mortimer); Dudley Digges (Sergeant Coggins); Alison Skipworth (Mrs. Coggins); Doris Lloyd (Pansie); Ruth Weston (Margaret); Joan Carr (Marjorie); Joyce Coad (Elsie); Douglas Scott (Derek); Tempe Pigott (Bridget); Forrester Harvey (Gas Inspector); Pat Somerset (Young Man); Margaret Daily (Maid); Olive Tell (Mrs. Trent); Claude King (Junior Partner); Don Stewart (Telegraph Boy); Cyril Delevanti (Reporter).

PRESTIGE   (RKO-Pathé, 1932) 71 M.

Producer, Charles R. Rogers; director, Tay Garnett; based on the novel *Lips of Steel* by Harry Hervey; adaptation, Garnett, Rollo Lloyd; screenplay, Francis Edwards Faragoh; music director, Arthur Lange; sound, Earl Walcott; camera, Lucien Andriot; editor, Joe Kane.

Ann Harding (Therese Du Flos); Adolphe Menjou (Captain Remy Baudoin); Melvyn Douglas (Colonel Du Flos); Guy Bates Post (Major); Carmelita Geraghty (Felice); Rollo Lloyd (Emil de Fontenac); Clarence Muse (Nham).

WESTWARD PASSAGE   (RKO-Pathé, 1932) 73 M.

Executive producer, David O. Selznick; associate producer, Harry Joe Brown; director, Robert Milton; based on the novel by Margaret Ayer Barnes; adaptation, Bradley King; dialog, Humphrey King; costumes, Margaret Pemberton; art director, Carroll Clark; music director, Max Steiner; sound, E. A. Wolcott; camera, Lucien Andriot; editor, Charles Craft.

Ann Harding (Olivia Van Tyne); Laurence Olivier (Nick Allen); Za su Pitts (Mrs. Truesdale); Irving Pichel (Harry Lanman); Juliette Compton (Henrietta); Irene Purcell (Diane Van Tyne); Emmett King (Mr. Ottendorf); Florence Roberts (Mrs. Ottendorf); Ethel Griffies (Lady Caverly); Bonita Granville (Little Olivia); Don Alvarado (The Count); Florence Lake (Elmer's Wife); Edgar Kennedy (Elmer); Herman Bing (The Dutchman); Julie Haydon (Bridesmaid); Joyce Compton (Girl); Nance O'Neil (Mrs. Van Tyne).

THE CONQUERORS   (RKO, 1932) 88 M.

Executive producer, David O. Selznick; director, William A. Wellman; based on the story by Howard Estabrook; screenplay, Robert Lord; music director, Max Steiner; makeup, Ern Westmore; assistant directors, D. M. Zimmer, James Anderson; art director, Carroll Clark; sound, John Tribby; camera, Edward Cronjager; editor, William Hamilton.

Richard Dix (Roger Standish/Roger Lennox); Ann Harding (Caroline Ogden Standish); Edna May Oliver (Matilda Blake); Guy Kibbee (Dr. Daniel Blake); Donald Cook (Warren Lennox); Walter Walker (Mr. Ogden); Wally Albright, Jr., Marilyn Knowlden (Twins); Julie Haydon (Frances Standish); Harry Holman (Stubby); Jason Robards (Lane); Jed Prouty (Auctioneer); Robert Greig (Bit); E. H. Calvert (Doctor).

THE ANIMAL KINGDOM   (RKO, 1932) 95 M.

Director, Edward H. Griffith; based on the play by Philip Barry; screenplay, Horace Jackson; sound, Daniel Cutter; camera, Lucien Andriot; editor, Daniel Mandell.

Ann Harding (Daisy Sage); Leslie Howard (Tom Collier); Myrna Loy (Cecelia Henry); Neil Hamilton (Owen); William Gargan (Regan); Henry Stephenson (Rufus Collier); Ilka Chase (Grace); Leni Stengel (Franc); Donald Dillaway (Joe).

WHEN LADIES MEET   (MGM, 1933) 73 M.

Director, Harry Beaumont; based on the play by Rachel Crothers; adaptation, John Meehan, Leon Gordon; camera, Ray June; editor, Basil Wrangell.

Ann Harding (Clare Woodruf); Robert Montgomery (Jimmie Lee); Myrna Loy (Mary Howard); Alice Brady (Bridget Drake); Frank Morgan (Roger Woodruf); Martin Burton (Walter); Luis Alberni (Pierre).

DOUBLE HARNESS   (RKO, 1933) 69½ M.

Executive producer, Merian C. Cooper; associate producer, Kenneth Macgowan; director, John Cromwell; based on the play by Edward P. Montgomery; adaptation, Jane Murfin; art director, Van Nest Polglase; Charles Kerk; music director, Max Steiner; sound, George D. Ellis; camera, J. Roy Hunt; editor, George Nicholls, Jr.

Ann Harding (Joan Colby); William Powell (John Fletcher); Henry Stephenson (Colonel Colby); Lilian Bond (Monica Page); George Meeker (Dennis); Lucile Brown (Valerie Colby); Reginald Owen (Butler); Kay Hammond (Eleanor Weston); Leigh Allen (Leonard Weston); Hugh Huntley (Farley Drake); Wallis Clark (Postmaster-General); Fredric Santley (Shop Owner).

THE RIGHT TO ROMANCE   (RKO, 1933) 70 M.

Producer, Merian C. Cooper; associate producer, Myles Connolly; director, Alfred Santell; story, Myles Connolly; adaptation, Sidney Buchman, Henry McCarty; sound, W. C. Moore; camera, Lucien Andriot; editor, Ralph Dieterle.

Ann Harding (Dr. Margaret Simmons); Robert Young (Bob Preble); Irving Pichel (Dr. Beck); Alden "Stephen" Chase (Bunny); Nils Asther (Dr. Heppling); Sari Maritza (Lee Joyce); Helen Freeman (Mrs. Preble); Delmar Watson (Bill).

GALLANT LADY   (UA, 1933) 81 M.

Producer, Darryl F. Zanuck; associate producer, William Goetz, Raymond Griffith; director, Gregory La Cava; story, Gilbert Emery, Doug Doty; screenplay, Sam Mintz; camera, Peverell Marley; editor, Richard Day.

Ann Harding (Sally Wyndham); Clive Brook (Dan Pritchard); Otto Kruger (Phillip Lawrence); Tullio Carminati (Cynario); Dickie Moore (Deedy); Janet Beecher (Maria Sherwood); Betty Lawford (Cynthia).

THE LIFE OF VERGIE WINTERS   (RKO, 1934) 82 M.

Producer, Pandro S. Berman; director, Alfred Santell; based on the story by Louis Bromfield; adaptation, Jane Murfin; camera, Lucien Andriot; editor, George Hively.

Ann Harding (Vergie Winters); John Boles (John Shadwell); Helen Vinson (Laura Shadwell); Betty Furness (Joan—at age 19); Frank Albertson (Ranny Truesdale); Lon Chaney, Jr. (Hugo McQueen); Sara Haden (Winnie Belle); Molly O'Day (Sadie); Ben Alexander (Barry Preston); Donald Crisp (Mike Davey); Maidel Turner (Ella Heenan); Cecil Cunningham (Pearl Turner); Josephine Whittell (Madame Claire); Wesley Barry (Herbert Sowerby); Edward Van Sloan (Jim Winters); Wallis Clark (Mr. Preston); Edwin Stanley (Mr. Truesdale); Bonita Granville (Joan—as a Girl); Walter Brennan (Roscoe, a Gossiper); Jed Prouty (Reverend); Mary McLaren (Nurse); Betty Mack (Della, the Maid).

THE FOUNTAIN   (RKO, 1934) 84 M.

Producer, Pandro S. Berman; director, John Cromwell; based on the novel by Charles Morgan; screenplay, Jane Murfin; additional dialog, Samuel Hoffenstein; camera, Henry W. Gerrard; editor, William Morgan.

Ann Harding (Julie von Narwitz); Brian Aherne (Lewis Alison); Paul Lukas (Rupert von Narwitz); Jean Hersholt (Baron Van Leyden); Ralph Forbes (Ballater); Violet Kemble-Cooper (Baroness Van Leyden); Sara Haden (Sophie); Richard Abbott (Allard Van Leyden); Rudolph Anders (Geof Van Leyden); Barbara Barondess (Geof's Wife); Betty Alden (Allard's Wife); Ian Wolfe (Van Arkel); Douglas Wood (de Greve); Frank Reicher (Doctor); Ferike Boros (Nurse); William Stack (Commandant).

BIOGRAPHY OF A BACHELOR GIRL   (MGM, 1934) 84 M.

Director, Edward H. Griffith; based on the play *Biography* by S. N. Behrman; screenplay, Anita Loos; camera, James Wong Howe; editor, William S. Gray.

Ann Harding (Marion); Robert Montgomery (Kurt); Edward Everett Horton (Nolan); Edward Arnold (Feydak); Una Merkel (Slade); Charles Richman (Kinnicot); Greta Meyer (Minnie); Willard Robertson (Process Server); Donald Meek (Mr. Irish).

ENCHANTED APRIL   (RKO, 1935) 66 M.

Producer, Kenneth Macgowan; director, Harry Beaumont; based on the novel by "Elizabeth" and the dramatization by Kane Campbell; screenplay, Samuel Hoffenstein, Ray Harris; set decorator, Van Nest Polglase, Carroll Clark; music director, Roy Webb; camera, Edward Cronjager; editor, George Hively.

Ann Harding (Lotty Wilkins); Frank Morgan (Mellersh Wilkins); Reginald Owen (Henry Arbuthnot); Katharine Alexander (Rose Arbuthnot); Ralph Forbes (Briggs); Jane Baxter (Lady Caroline); Jessie Ralph (Mrs. Fisher); Charles Judels (Domenico); Rafaela Ottiano (Francesca).

THE FLAME WITHIN   (MGM, 1935) 72 M.

Producer-director-screenplay, Edmund Goulding; camera, James Wong Howe; editor, Blanche Sewell.

Ann Harding (Dr. Mary White); Herbert Marshall (Dr. Gordon Phillips); Maureen O'Sullivan (Lillian Belton); Louis Hayward (Jack Kerry); Henry Stephenson (Jock Frazier); Margaret Seddon (Mrs. Grenfell); George Hassell (Rigby); Eily Malyon (Murdock); Claudelle Kaye (Nurse Carter).

PETER IBBETSON   (PAR, 1935) 88 M.

Producer, Louis D. Lighton; director, Henry Hathaway; based on the novel by George du Maurier and the play by John Nathaniel Raphael; adaptation, Constance Collier; screenplay, Vincent Lawrence, Waldemar Young; additional scenes, John Meehan, Edwin Justus Mayer; music, Ernst Toch; sound, Harry D. Mills; art director, Hans Dreier, Robert Usher, Nat W. Finston; special effects, Gordon Jennings; camera, Charles Lang; editor, Stuart Heisler.

Gary Cooper (Peter Ibbetson); Ann Harding (Mary, Duchess of Towers); John Halliday (Duke of Towers); Ida Lupino (Agnes); Douglass Dumbrille (Colonel Forsythe); Virginia Weidler (Mimsey); Dickie Moore (Gogo); Doris Lloyd (Mrs. Dorian); Elsa Buchanan (Madame Pasquier); Christian Rub (Major Duquesnoit); Donald Meek (Mr. Slade); Gilbert Emery (Wilkins); Marguerite Namara (Madame Ginghi); Elsa Prescott (Katherine); Marcelle Corday (Maid); Adrienne D'Ambricourt (Nun); Theresa Maxwell Conover (Sister of Mercy); Colin Tapley, Clive Morgan, Ambrose Barker, Thomas Monk (Clerks); Blanche Craig (Countess); Stanley Andrews (Judge).

THE LADY CONSENTS   (RKO, 1936) 76½ M.

Producer, Edward Kaufman; director, Stephen Roberts; based on the story "The Indestructible Mrs. Talbot" by P. J. Wolfson; screenplay, Wolfson, Anthony Veiller; camera, J. Roy Hunt.

Ann Harding (Anne Talbot); Herbert Marshall (Dr. Michael Talbot); Margaret Lindsay (Jerry Mannerly); Walter Abel (Stanley Ashton); Edward Ellis (Jim Talbot); Hobart Cavanaugh (Yardley); Ilka Chase (Susan).

THE WITNESS CHAIR   (RKO, 1936) 64 M.

Producer, Cliff Reid; director, George Nicholls, Jr.; based on the novella by Rita Weiman; screenplay, Rian James, Gertrude Purcell; camera, Robert De Grasse; editor, William Morgan.

Ann Harding (Paula Young); Walter Abel (Jim Trent); Douglass Dumbrille (Stanley Whittaker); Frances Sage (Connie Trent); Moroni Olsen (Lt. Poole); Margaret Hamilton (Grace Franklin); Maxine Jennings (Tillie Jones); William Benedict (Benny Ryan); Paul Harvey (Martin); Murray Kinnell (Conrick); Charles Arnt (Henshaw); Frank Jenks (Levino); Edward LeSaint (Judge McKenzie); Hilda Vaughn (Anna Yifnick); Barlowe Borland (O'Neil).

LOVE FROM A STRANGER   (UA, 1937) 87 M.

Producer, Max Schack; director, Rowland V. Lee; based on the story by Agatha Christie and the play by Frank Vosper; screenplay, Francis Marion; camera, Philip Tannura; editor, Howard O'Neill.

Ann Harding (Carol Howard); Basil Rathbone (Gerald Lovell); Binnie Hale (Kate Meadows); Bruce Seton (Ronald Bruce); Jean Cadell (Aunt Lou); Bryan Powley (Dr. Gribble); Joan Hickson (Emmy); Donald Calthrop (Holson); Eugene Leahy (Mr. Tuttle).

EYES IN THE NIGHT   (MGM, 1942) 79 M.

Producer, Jack Chertok; director, Fred Zinnemann; based on the novel *Odor of Violets* by Bayard Kendrick; screenplay, Guy Trosper, Howard Emmett Rogers; art director, Cedric Gibbons; camera, Robert Planck, Charles Lawton; editor, Ralph Winters.

Edward Arnold (Capt. Duncan Maclain); Ann Harding (Norma Lawry); Donna Reed (Barbara Lawry); Allen Jenkins (Marty); John Emery (Paul Gerente); Stephen McNally (Gabriel Hoffman); Katherine Emery (Cheli Scott); Reginald Denny (Stephen Lawry); Rosemary de Camp (Vera Hoffman); Stanley Ridges (Hansen); Barry Nelson (Busch); Steve Geray (Anderson); Erik Rolf (Boyd); Reginald Sheffield (Victor); Ivan Miller (Herman); Milburn Stone (Pete); Mantan Moreland (Alistair); Cliff Danielson (Boy); Frances Rafferty (Girl); Edward Kilroy (Pilot); John Butler (Driver); William Nye (Hugo); Fred Walburn, Robert Winkler, Walter Tetley (Boys); Frank Thomas (Police Lieutenant); Marie Windsor (Bit).

MISSION TO MOSCOW   (WB, 1943) 112 M.

Producer, Robert Buckner; director, Michael Curtiz; based on the book by Joseph E. Davies; screenplay, Howard Koch; art director, Carl Jules Heyl; choreography, LeRoy Prinz; technical advisor, Jay Leyda; montages, Don Siegel; camera, Bert Glennon; editor, Owen Marks.

Walter Huston (Joseph E. Davies); Ann Harding (Mrs. Davies); Oscar Homolka (Litvinov); George Tobias (Freddie); Gene Lockhart (Molotov); Eleanor Parker (Emlen Davies); Richard Travis (Paul); Helmut Dantine (Major Kamenev); Victor Francen (Vyshinsky); Henry Daniell (Minister Von Ribbentrop); Barbara Everest (Mrs. Litvinov); Dudley Field Malone (Prime Minister Churchill); Roman Bohnen (Krestinsky); Maria Palmer (Tanya Litvinov); Moroni Olsen (Colonel Faymonville); Minor Watson (Loy Henderson); Maurice Schwartz (Dr. Potkin); Jerome Cowan (Spendler); Konstantin Shayne (Bukharin); Manart Kippen (Stalin); Kathleen Lockhart (Lady Chilston); Kurt Katch (Timoshenko); Felix Basch (Dr. Hjalmar Schact); Frank Puglia (Judge Ulrich); John Abbott (Grinko); Olaf Hytten (Parliament Member); Art Gilmore (Commentator); Leigh Whipper (Haile Selassie); Georges Renavent (Pres. Paul Van Zeeland); Don Clayton (Vincent Massey); Clive Morgan (Anthony Eden); Duncan Renaldo, Nino Bellini (Italian Reporters); Ferd Schumann-Heink, Rolf Liniau, Peter Michael (German Reporters); George Davis, Jean Del Val (French Reporters); Alex Chirva (Pierre Laval); Emory Parnell (Speaker of House); Pat O'Malley (Irish-American); Mark Strong (Englishman); Albert d'Arno (Frenchman); Rudolf Steinbeck (German); Gino Corrado (Italian); Glenn Strange (Southerner); Frank Faylen, Joseph Crehan (Reporters); Isabel Withers (Woman); Edward Van Sloan (German Diplomat); Tanya Somova (Flower Girl); Pierre Watkin (Naval Attaché); Elizabeth Archer (Elderly Woman); Lumsden Hare (Lord Chilston); Robert C. Fischer (Von Schulenberg); Alex Caze (Coulendre); Leonid Snegoff (Kommodov); Edgar Licho (Bookseller); Victor Wong, Luke Chan, Allen Jung (Japanese Diplomats); Frank Ferguson, Bill Kennedy, Louis Jean Heydt, John Hamilton, William Forrest (American Newsmen); Tamara Shayne (Russian Nurse); Alexander Granach (Russian Air Force Officer); Doris Lloyd (Mrs. Churchill); Charles Trowbridge (Secretary of State Cordell Hull); Francis Pierlot (Doctor); Forbes Murray, Edward Keane, William Gould (Isolationists); Harry Cording (Blacksmith); Mike Mazurki (Workman); Lionel Royce (Dr. Schmitt); Tom Tully (Engineer); Hooper Atchley (Father); Betty Roadman (Mother); Eugene Eberly (Son); Arthur Loft (Man with Microphone); Eugene Borden (French Minister); Oliver Blake, Monte Blue, Edmund Cobb, Ernie Adams, Eddie Kane, Howard Mitchell, Frank Wayne, Jack Kenny, Ben Erway, Mauritz Hugo (Hecklers); Al Kunde (Father); Evelynne Smith (Daughter); Frank Hemphill (Grandfather); Cyd Charisse, Michel Panaiess (Specialty Dancers); Gene Gary (Russian Foreman).

THE NORTH STAR   (RKO, 1943) 106 M.

Producer, Samuel Goldwyn; associate producer, William Cameron Menzies; director, Lewis Milestone; screenplay, Lillian Hellman; art director, Perry Ferguson; music,

Aaron Copland; song, Copland and Ira Gershwin; choreography, David Lichine; special effects, R. O. Ginger, Clarence Slifter; camera, James Wong Howe; editor, Daniel Mandell.

Anne Baxter (Marina); Farley Granger (Damian); Jane Withers (Claudia); Eric Roberts (Grisha); Dana Andrews (Kolya); Walter Brennan (Karp); Dean Jagger (Rodion); Ann Harding (Sophia); Carl Benton Reid (Boris); Ann Carter (Olga); Walter Huston (Dr. Kurin); Erich Von Stroheim (Dr. Otto Von Harden); Esther Dale (Anna); Ruth Nelson (Nadya); Paul Guilfoyle (Iakin); Martin Kosleck (Dr. Max Richter); Tonio Selwart (German Captain); Peter Pohlenz (German Lieutenant); Gene O'Donnell (Russian Gunner); Robert Lowery (Russian Pilot); Frank Wilcox (Petrov); Charles Bates (Petya); George Lynn (German Pilot); Minna Phillips (Old Lady in Wagon); Edmund Cobb (Farmer); Bill Walker, Clarence Straight (Young Men in Wagon); Jerry Mickelson (Farmer's Son); Grace Cunard (Farmer's Wife); Martin Faust, Jack Perrin, Bill Nestell, Al Ferguson, Henry Hall, John Judd (Farmers); Bill Borzage (Accordion Player in Wagon); Emma Dunn, Sarah Padden (Old Ladies); Teddy Infuhr (Little Stinker); Grace Leonard (Woman on Bridge); Loudie Claar (Woman on Hospital Cot); Lynne Winthrop (Guerrilla Girl); Joyce Tucker (Little Girl in Hospital); John Bagni (Guard at Desk); John Beverly (Orderly); Ferdinand Schumann-Heink (Doctor's Assistant); Patricia Parks (Sonya); Frederick Brunn (German Motorcycle Officer); Ray Teal (German Motorcycle Officer); Crane Whitney (German Soldier); Lane Chandler, Harry Strang (Guerrillas); Serge Protzenko, Ilia Khmara (Accordion Players); Constant Franke (Boris's Aide); Florence Auer (Woman Farmer); Tommy Hall, Ronn Harvin, George Kole, Jack Vlaskin, William Sabbot, Clair Freeman, Eric Braunsteiner, Tamara Laub, Marie Vlaskin, Inna Gest (Specialty Dancers).

JANIE   (WB, 1944) 106 M.

Producer, Brock Pemberton; director, Michael Curtiz; based on the play by Josephine Bentham, Herschel V. Williams, Jr.; screenplay, Agnes Christine Johnston, Charles Hoffman; songs, Lee David, Sammy Cahn, and Jule Styne; art director, Robert Haas; special effects, Lawrence Butler, William Lynch; camera, Carl Guthrie; editor, Owen Marks.

Joyce Reynolds (Janie Conway); Robert Hutton (Pvt. Dick Lawrence); Edward Arnold (Charles Conway); Ann Harding (Lucille Conway); Robert Benchley (John Van Brunt); Clare Foley (Elsbeth Conway); Barbara Brown (Mrs. Lawrence); Hattie McDaniel (April); Dick Erdman (Scooper Nolan); Jackie Moran (Mickey); Ann Gillis (Paula); Russell Hicks (Col. Lucas); Ruth Tobey (Bernadine Dodd); Virginia Patton (Carrie Lou); Colleen Townsend (Hortense Bennett); William Frambes (Dead Pan); Sunset Carson (Sergeant Carl); Georgia Lee Settle (Susan Wiley); Peter Stackpole, John Alvin (Photographers); Virginia Noe, Ladell Buchanan, Karole Lee, Tanis Chandler (High School Girls); Jim Menzies, Sandy Shaw, Johnny Fleming, Terry Grafton, Roger McGee, Douglas Cooper, Norman Salling, Frank Wierick, Truman Van Dyke, Corky Geil (High School Boys); William Benedict, Joe Gilbert (Soda Jerks); George-Ellen Ferguson (Reardon's Secretary); Jimmy Dodd (Pvt. Frank Parker); Eddie Bruce (Bus Driver); Williams Brothers (Quartette); John Nelson, Danny Jackson, John Forrest, Warren Burr, Keefe Brasselle, Arnold Stanford, Dick Balkney, Michael Carter, Milton Douglas, Martin Lord (Soldiers); Lane Chandler, Monte Blue (Policemen); Virginia Sale (Neighbor); Bill Hunter (M.P. Sergeant); Kirk Barron (M.P.); Harry Leavitt, Bob McGurk, Ricki Tanzi, Jordan Shelly, Jack Robbins, Douglas Pierce, Charles Schrader, Brent Gaylor, Clay Martin (Bits).

NINE GIRLS   (Col., 1944) 75 M.

Producer, Burt Kelly; director, Leigh Jason; based on the play by Wilfred H. Pettitt; screenplay, Karen DeWolf, Connie Lee; art director, Lionel Banks, Ross Bellah; music director, Morris Stoloff; music, John Leopold; camera, James Van Trees; editor, Otto Meyer.

Ann Harding (Grace Thornton); Evelyn Keyes (Mary O'Ryan); Jinx Falkenburg (Jane Peters); Anita Louise (Paula Canfield); Leslie Brooks (Roberta Halloway); Lynn Merrick (Eve Sharon); Jeff Donnell ("Butch" Hendricks); Nina Foch (Alice Blake); Shirley Mills ("Tennessee" Collingwood); Marcia Mae Jones (Shirley Berke); Willard Robertson (Captain Brooks); William Demarest (Walter Cummings); Lester Mathews (Horace Canfield); Grady Sutton (Photographer).

THOSE ENDEARING YOUNG CHARMS   (RKO, 1945) 81 M.

Executive producer, Sid Rogell; producer, Bert Granet; director, Lewis Allen; based on the play by Edward Chodorov; screenplay, Jerome Chodorov; music, Roy Webb; music director, C. Bakaleinikoff; assistant director, William Dorfman; sound, Richard Van Hessen; art director, Albert S. D'Agostino, Walter E. Keller; set decorator, Darrell Silvera, John Sturtevant; special effects, Vernon L. Walker; camera, Ted Tetzlaff; editor, Roland Gross.

Robert Young (Hank); Laraine Day (Helen); Ann Harding (Mrs. Brandt); Marc Cramer (Captain Larry Stowe); Anne Jeffreys (Suzanne); Bill Williams (Jerry); Glenn Vernon (Young Sailor); Norma Varden (Haughty Floor Lady); Lawrence Tierney (Ted); Vera Marshe (Dot); Larry Burke (Singer); Edmund Glover, Robert Clarke (Operations Officers); Johnny Strong, Paul Brinkman, George Holmes (Pilots); Jimmy Jordan (Bellhops); Tommy Dugan (Waiter); Barbara Slater (Girl); John Vosper (Drunk); Georges Renavent (Maitre D'Hotel); Eddy Hart (Bus Conductor); Larry McGrath (Cabby); Tom Dillon (Traffic Cop); Dorothy Vaughn (Matron); George Anderson (Doorman); Aina Constant (Miss Glamour); Dewey Robinson (Doorman); Florence Wix (Customer); Catherine Wallace, Elizabeth Williams, Margaret Farrell, Helen Dickson (Women).

JANIE GETS MARRIED   (WB, 1946) 89 M.

Producer, Alex Gottlieb; director, Vincent Sherman; based on characters created by Josephine Bentham, Herschel V. Williams, Jr.; screenplay, Agnes Christine Johnston; music, Frederick Hollander; music director, Leo F. Forbstein; song, Ted Koehler and M. K. Jerome; art director, Robert M. Haas; montages, James Leicester; camera, Carl Guthrie; editor, Christian Nyby.

Joan Leslie (Janie Conway); Robert Hutton (Dick Lawrence); Edward Arnold (Charles Conway); Ann Harding (Lucille Conway); Robert Benchley (John Van Brunt); Dorothy Malone (Sgt. Spud Lee); Dick Erdman (Lt. Scooper Nolan); Clare Foley (Elsbeth Conway); Donald Meek (Harley P. Stowers); Hattie McDaniel (April); Barbara Brown (Thelma Van Brunt); Margaret Hamilton (Mrs. Angles); Ann Gillis (Paula); Ruth Tobey (Bernadine); William Frambes (Dead Pan); Theo Washington (Rose); Rudy Wissler (Copy Boy); Geraldine Wall, Philo McCullough (Reporters); Jack Mower (Benson); John O'Connor, Monte Blue (Drapery Men); Charles Jordan (Clarke, the City Editor); Rudy Wissler (Copy Boy); Mel Torme, John Sheridan, John Miles, Art Kassel (Dick's Buddies); Lynne Baggett (Hostess); Forbes Murray (Businessman).

IT HAPPENED ON FIFTH AVENUE   (AA, 1947) 116 M.

Producer, Roy Del Ruth; associate producer, Joe Kaufman; director, Del Ruth; story, Herbert Clyde Lewis, Frederick Stephan; screenplay, Everett Freeman; additional dialog, Vick Knight; art director, Lewis Creber; set decorator, Ray Baltz, Jr.; music, Edward Ward; assistant director, Frank Fox; sound, Corson Jowett; songs, Harry Revel and Paul Webster; camera, Henry Sharp; editor, Richard Heermance.

Victor Moore (Aloysius T. McKeever); Charlie Ruggles (Michael O'Connor); Don DeFore (Jim Bullock); Gale Storm (Trudy O'Connor); Ann Harding (Mary O'Connor); Alan Hale, Jr. (Whitey); Dorothea Kent (Margie); Cathy Carter (Alice); Ed Brophy (Felton); Arthur Hohl (Brady); Anthony Sydes (Jackie Temple); Edward Ryan, Jr. (Hank); Grant Mitchell (Farrow); Garry Owen (Detective); George Lloyd (Foreman); George Meader (Music Store Manager); John Hamilton (Harper, the Superintendent); John Arthur (Apartment Manager); Chester Clute (Phillips); Howard Mitchell, Rowland McCracken, William Kline, Al Fenney, Al Winters, Bert Howard, Jack George, Major Kieffer, Lt. George Blagoi, Carl Leviness, Adolph Faylauer, William O'Brien, Vic Travers, David Martell (Executives); Florence Auer (Miss Parker); Charles Lane (Landlord); James Cardwell (Young Man in Barracks); James Flavin, Ed Gargan (Cops); Max Willenz, Leon Belasco (Musicians); Pat Goldin (Waiter); Eddie Marr (Spieler); Dudley Dickerson (Chauffeur); Abe Reynolds (Finklehoffe); Joan Andren (Secretary).

CHRISTMAS EVE   (UA, 1947) 90 M.

Producer, Benedict Bogeaus; director, Edwin Marin; based on stories by Lawrence Stallings, Richard H. Landau; screenplay, Stallings; music director, Heinz Roemheld; music director, David Chudnow; sound, William Lynch; assistant director, Joseph Depew; art director, Ernst Fegte; set decorator, Eugene Redd; camera, Gordon Avil; editor, James Smith.

George Raft (Mario Torio); George Brent (Michael Brooks); Randolph Scott (Jonathan); Joan Blondell (Ann Nelson); Virginia Field (Claire); Dolores Moran (Jean); Ann Harding (Matilda Reid); Reginald Denny (Phillip Hastings); Carl Harbord (Dr. Doremus); Clarence Kolb (Judge Alston); John Litel (FBI Agent); Joe Sawyer (Gimlet); Douglass Dumbrille (Dr. Bunyan); Dennis Hoey (Williams); Molly Lamont (Harriett); Walter Sande (Hood); Konstantin Shayne (Reichman); Claire Whitney (Dr. Bunyan's Wife); Andrew Tombes (Auctioneer); Soledad Jimenez (Rosita); Marie Blake (Girl Reporter); Ernest Hilliard (Assistant Bartender); Al Hill (Bartender); John Indrisano (Gateman); Edward Parks (Beer Drinker); Holly Bane (Page Boy).

TWO WEEKS WITH LOVE   (MGM, 1950) C—92 M.

Producer, Jack Cummings; director, Roy Rowland; musical numbers stager, Busby Berkeley; story, John Larkin; screenplay, Larkin, Dorothy Kingsley; music director, Georgie Stoll; art director, Cedric Gibbons, Preston Ames; song, Arthur Fields and Walter Donovan; set decorator, Edwin B. Willis, Richard A. Pefferle; makeup, William Tuttle; costumes, Helen Rose, Walter Plunkett; special effects, Warren Newcombe; camera, Alfred Gilks; editor, Irvine Washburton.

Jane Powell (Patti Robinson); Ricardo Montalban (Demi Armendez); Louis Calhern (Horatio Robinson); Ann Harding (Katherine Robinson); Phyllis Kirk (Valerie Stressemann); Carleton Carpenter (Billy Finlay); Debbie Reynolds (Melba Robinson); Clinton Sundberg (Mr. Finlay); Gary Gray (McCormick Robinson); Tommy Rettig (Ricky Robinson); Charles Smith (Eddie Gavin).

THE MAGNIFICENT YANKEE   (MGM, 1950) 90 M.

Producer, Armand Deutsch; director, John Sturges; based on the book *Mr. Justice Holmes* by Francis Biddle and the play by Emmett Lavery; screenplay, Lavery; art director, Cedric Gibbons, Arthur Lonergan; music, David Raksin; camera, Joseph Ruttenberg; editor, Ferris Webster.

Louis Calhern (Oliver Wendell Holmes, Jr.); Ann Harding (Fanny Holmes); Eduard Franz (Judge Brandeis); Philip Ober (Mr. Wister); Ian Wolfe (Mr. Adams); Edith Evanson (Annie Gough); Richard Anderson (Reynolds); Guy Anderson (Baxter);

James Lydon (Clinton); Robert Sherwood (Drake); Hugh Sanders (Parker); Harlan Warde (Norton); Charles Evans (Chief Justice Fuller); John R. Hamilton (Justice White); Dan Tobin (Dixon); Robert E. Griffin (Court Crier); Stapleton Kent (Court Clerk); Robert Malcolm (Marshall); Everett Glass (Justice Peckham); Hayden Rorke (Graham); Marshall Bradford (Head Waiter); Holmes Herbert (Justice McKenna); Selmer Jackson (Lawyer); George Spaulding (Justice Hughes); Todd Karns (Secretary); Freeman Lusk (Announcer); David McMahon (Workman); Sherry Hall, Jack Gargan, Dick Cogan, Tony Merrill (Reporters); Robert Board, Wilson Wood, James Horne, Gerald Pierce, Lyle Clark, David Alpert, Tommy Kelly, Bret Hamilton, Jim Drum (Secretaries); Wheaton Chambers, Gayne Whitman (Senators); William Johnstone (Lawyer).

THE UNKNOWN MAN   (MGM, 1951) 86 M.

Producer, Robert Thomsen; director, Richard Thorpe; story-screenplay, Ronald Milar, George Froeschel; art director, Cedric Gibbons, Randall Duell; music, Conrad Salinger; camera, William Mellor; editor, Ben Lewis.

Walter Pidgeon (Dwight Bradley Masen); Ann Harding (Stella Masen); Barry Sullivan (Joe Bucknor); Keefe Brasselle (Rudi Wallchek); Lewis Stone (Judge Hulbrook); Eduard Franz (Andrew Jason Layford); Richard Anderson (Bob Masen); Dawn Addams (Ellie Fansworth); Phil Ober (Wayne Kellwin); Mari Blanchard (Sally Tever); Konstantin Shayne (Peter Hulderman); Don Beddoe (Fingerprint Man); Holmes Herbert (Reverend Michael); Jean Andren (Secretary); Richard Hale (Eddie Caraway); Jeff York (Guard); John Maxwell (Dr. Palmer); John Butler, Harry Hines, Robert Scott, Ronald Brogan, Robert Griffin, Frank Gerstle, Jimmy Dodd, Larry Carr, Eric Sinclair (Reporters); Dabbs Greer (Driver); Mira McKinney (Maid); Richard Karlan (Lieutenant); Wheaton Chambers (Bailiff); Emmett Vogan (Court Clerk); Jack Gargan (Secretary); Moyna Andre, Anna Q. Nilsson, Bess Flowers (Guests); Mae Clarke (Stella's Friend); Harry Cody (Detective); Jack Shea (Sash); Frank Pershing (Jury Foreman).

THE MAN IN THE GRAY FLANNEL SUIT   (20th, 1956) C—152½ M.

Producer, Darryl F. Zanuck; director, Nunnally Johnson; based on the novel by Sloan Wilson; screenplay, Johnson; art director, Lyle R. Wheeler, Jack Martin Smith; music, Bernard Herrmann; sound, Alfred Bruzlin, Harry M. Leonard; set decorator, Walter M. Scott, Stuart A. Reiss; makeup, Ben Nye; costumes, Charles Le Maire; assistant director, Hal Herman; camera, Charles G. Clarke; editor, Dorothy Spencer.

Gregory Peck (Tom Rath); Jennifer Jones (Betsy Rath); Fredric March (Hopkins); Marisa Pavan (Maria); Lee J. Cobb (Judge Bernstein); Ann Harding (Mrs. Hopkins); Keenan Wynn (Caesar Gardella); Gene Lockhart (Hawthorne); Gigi Perreau (Susan Hopkins); Portland Mason (Janie); Arthur O'Connell (Walker); Henry Daniell (Bill Ogden); Connie Gilchrist (Mrs. Manter); Joseph Sweeney (Edward Schultz); Sandy Descher (Barbara); Mickey Maga (Pete); Kenneth Tobey (Mahoney); Geraldine Wall (Miriam); Jack Mather (Police Sergeant); Frank Wilcox (Dr. Pearce); Nan Martin (Miss Lawrence); Phyllis Graffeo (Gina); Dorothy Adams (Mrs. Hopkins's Maid); John Breen (Waiter); Dorothy Phillips (Maid); Otto Reichow, Jim Brandt, Robert Boon (German Soldiers); Harry Lauter, Paul Glass, William Phipps (Soldiers); De-Forrest Kelley (Medic); Roy Glenn (Master Sergeant Mathews); Mario Siletti (Carriage Driver); Lee Graham (Crew Chief); Michael Jeffries (Mr. Sims); King Lockwood (Business Executive); William Philips (Bugala).

I'VE LIVED BEFORE   (Univ., 1956) 82 M.

Producer, Howard Christie; director, Richard Bartlett; screenplay, Norman Jolley, William Talman; art director, Alexander Golitzen, Richard H. Riedel, Alfred Sweeney;

gowns, Bill Thomas; music, Herman Stein; music director, Joseph Gershenson; camera, Maury Gertsman; editor, Milton Carruth, Fred MacDowall.

Jock Mahoney (John Bolan); Leigh Snowden (Lois Gordon); Ann Harding (Jane Stone); John McIntire (Dr. Thomas Bryant); Raymond Bailey (Mr. Hackett); Jerry Paris (Russell Smith); Simon Scott (Robert Allen); April Kent (Stewardess); Vernon Rich (Mr. Anderson); Teri Robin (Stenotypist); Phil Harvey (Dr. Miller); Jane Howard (Secretary); Lorna Thayer (Mrs. Fred Bolan); James Seay (Fred Bolan); Madelon Mitchel (Maid); Brad Morrow (John Bolan—as a Boy); Mike Dale (Pilot); Ray Quinn (Interne); Bill Anders (Air Control Officer); Marjorie Stapp, Mike Portanova, Charles Conrad, Beatrice Gray, Earl Hansen (Spectators); Palmer Wray Sherrill, Jimmy Casino, Blanche Taylor (Bits).

STRANGE INTRUDER   (AA, 1956) 82 M.

Producer, Lindsley Parsons; associate producer, John H. Burrows; director, Irving Rapper; based on the novel *The Intruder* by Helen Fowler; screenplay, David Evans, Warren Douglas; assistant director, Kenneth Walters; music, Paul Dunlap; song, Carroll Coates; camera, Ernest Haller; editor, Maurice Wright.

Edmund Purdom (Paul Quentin); Ida Lupino (Alice); Ann Harding (Mary Carmichael); Jacques Bergerac (Howard); Gloria Talbot (Meg); Carl Benton Reid (James Carmichael); Douglas Kennedy (Parry); Donald Murphy (Adrian); Ruby Goodwin (Violet); Mimi Gibson (Libby); Eric Anderson (Johnny); Marjorie Bennett (Joady).

With Fredric March in PARIS BOUND (Pathé '29)

Center right: Ann Harding as a young girl

Center left: with Harry Bannister in HER PRIVATE AFFAIR (Pathé '29)

With Mary Astor, Robert Ames, and William Holden in HOLIDAY (Pathé '30)

th Leslie Howard in THE
IIMAL KINGDOM (RKO '32)

Obtaining her divorce from
Harry Bannister in 1933

th Melvyn Douglas in PRESTIGE (RKO-Pathé '32)

In EAST LYNNE (Fox '31)

In GALLANT LADY (UA '3

With Josephine Whittell and Molly O'Day in THE LIFE OF VERGIE
WINTERS (RKO '34)

th Gary Cooper in PETER
BETSON (Par '35)

With Werner Janssen in 1937

h Walter Abel in THE LADY CONSENTS (RKO '36)

With Joan Hickson and Jean Cadell in LOVE FROM A STRANGER (UA '37)

With George Tobias, Walter Huston, and Eleanor Parker in MISSION TO MOSCOW (WB '43)

With Edward Arnold and Joyce Reynolds in JANIE (WB '44)

With Gale Storm and Charles Ruggles in IT HAPPENED ON FIFTH AVENUE (AA '47)

With George Brent, Joan Blondell, Dolores Moran, Randolph Scott, and George in CHRISTMAS EVE (UA '47)

With Louis Calhern and Herbert (Guy) Anderson in THE MAGNIFICENT YANKEE (MGM '50)

Above: At the marriage of daughter Jane to Albert Paul Otto in 1955

Left: With Conrad Nagel and Donald Curtis in GOODBYE MY FANCY in 1949

Below: with Jock Mahoney in I'VE LIVED BEFORE (Univ '56)

In GARDEN DISTRICT in 1958

With Maureen O'Sullivan, *second from left*, in THE FLAME
WITHIN (RKO '35)

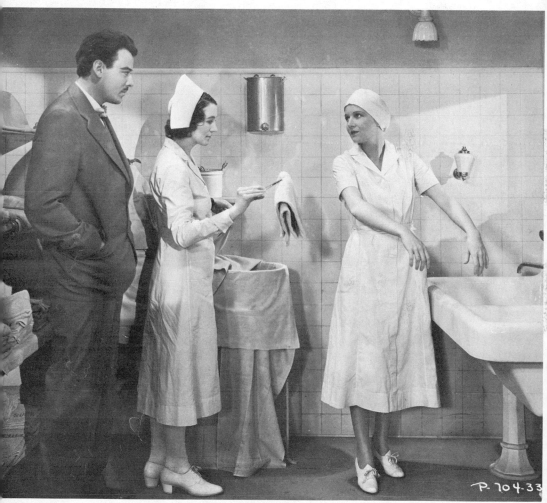

Nils Asther in THE RIGHT TO ROMANCE (RKO '33)

In WHAT PRICE HOLLYWOOD (RKO-Pathé '32)

5'4"
110 pounds
Blonde hair
Blue eyes
Libra

Constance
Bennett

Any survey conducted in the early 1930s to determine which Hollywood stars would be best remembered by the public four decades hence, would certainly have included Constance Bennett's name near the top of the list. In those early Depression years she was considered the epitome of screen chic, not aristocratic like Norma Shearer or Ina Claire, but sanguine and crisp, a woman to pique the imagination with her long-limbed, fluid figure and those luminous wide eyes accenting a pert face. Early in her film talkies career, Constance developed her own rewarding cinema type: the shopgirl forced into immorality who eventually finds the gumption to rise above her degrading situation to a dramatic new respectability. It was a good gimmick and it worked well.

The crest of Constance's popularity could not last indefinitely, but by the mid-1930s she had so quickly plowed her way down from potential super-stardom that the wake of her past fame had its own burning quality, allowing her to coast along for another two decades in minor film roles, onstage, and on radio. Why the tumultuous descent? It goes above and beyond changing times or box-office saturation. Peeling away the superficial factors, there remains the obvious: Constance as a person was not an easy commodity for the motion picture industry or the public to like and respect. She was quixotic, turbulent, stubborn, aggressive, theatrical and full of positive guiles, dynamic and dog-

matic enough (like her famous actor father, Richard Bennett) to force her will on others without thought of the consequences. She was a girl who did not have any sense of diplomacy, and as extravagantly as she dressed or entertained, so she dashingly called a spade a spade with little concern for the inevitable repercussions.

Constance the maverick lived one hell of a life, whether courting a husband-to-be, gambling in the casinos, outmaneuvering a film producer on a sharp-termed deal, or hostessing divertissements in ultralavish style. Eventually it all caught up with Constance and there was the devil to pay: the loss of her following and an increasing unwillingness of film producers to star her in high-priced productions. But Constance, ever the game girl, carried on undaunted, her own little world revolving about her high-powered self. If she missed the mighty accouterments of public idolatry, she hardly ever mentioned it—for like the stage character she eventually played, Auntie Mame, Constance found too many facets of life fascinating and energizing to allow any setback to uptilt her self-made golden apple cart.

She was born in New York City on October 22, 1904, the first of three daughters* of reigning matinee idol Richard Bennett† and his second wife, Adrienne (Mabel) Morrison. Mrs. Bennett was herself a familiar theatre player; in fact she and Bennett had first met when they performed together in *The Royal Family* in 1900. Three years later (November 8, 1903) they wed in Jersey City, New Jersey. After the birth of their three daughters, she made only infrequent stage appearances.

Constance, who inherited her father's excessively independent ways and her mother's beauty, did not utter a word until after she was two years old, and then suddenly popped out with a perfect recitation of the nursery rhyme, "Twinkle, Twinkle, Little Star."‡ Constance's rambunctious nature never endeared her to school authorities, and she frequently was requested to remove her high spirits to another institution of learning. She attended Miss Chandor's

---

*Barbara Jane was born on August 13, 1906; Joan on February 27, 1910.

†Bennett, a very talented and popular stage personality, had made considerable money plying his craft. His first wife, Grena Bennett, whom he wed in 1901 and divorced a year later, had also been one of his leading ladies. Still another of his stage vis-à-vis was the legendary Maude Adams, with whom he successfully co-starred for two seasons in *What Every Woman Knows.* When Miss Adams refused to do a third season of the James B. Barrie show because she wanted to play the title role in *Peter Pan,* Bennett sent her one of the theatre's most famous telegrams: "Congratulations on achieving your long held ambition to be your own leading man."

‡Stage and movie actress Louise Closser Hale, who frequently babysat for the Bennetts, once recalled, "If I told the girls a story Connie remembered every word of it and corrected me if I changed so much as one syllable." Constance was also renowned as a fearless tomboy. Sister Barbara once recollected that on one particular Christmas day the three children were scrambling down the stairs and rushing to the tree. A glimpse of Santa Claus was evident, causing Barbara and Joan to hang back, but Constance marched up and demanded of the stranger, "Why have you stayed here all night? You should be on your way taking care of the other children, mister!" Joan would write in *The Bennett Playbill* (1970), "I loved her, but as a child I was scared to death of her."

Day School on Park Avenue where her sisters would later study, and then transferred to Miss Merrill's Boarding School on Long Island. During this period Richard Bennett was achieving his own notoriety on Broadway, appearing in Eugene Brieux's play *Damaged Goods,* a sex drama dealing with the problem of syphilis. Various civic groups pressured the law to close the show. Bennett countered these moves by climaxing each performance of the drama with an impassioned curtain speech imploring the audience not to allow Art to be censored. These curtain speeches became such an expected part of Bennett's performance that thereafter playwrights and managers often engineered controversies to provide the stepping stone for more platform haranguing by the publicity-hungry Bennett. This bit of showmanship was not lost on the Bennett children, Constance in particular.

Mr. Bennett may have been very outspoken in the theatre, but at home he was a conventional puritanical figure who held to the firm opinion that the woman's place in life was to stay quietly at home; that is, unless she chose to pursue the noble calling of the theatre. Mrs. Bennett, on the other hand, had grown to dislike her prior occupation and frankly did not want any of her three children to "ever set foot on a stage." (This was merely one of the contretemps that led to the several marital separations between the Bennetts.) Thus at the age of ten Constance was already pleading with her parents to allow her to embark on a stage career and to be the fifth generation of Bennett to stand before the footlights.* One gambit she tried was to write herself a letter on Hotel Ansonia stationery (the residence hotel where the Bennetts were then staying). The note stated:

Dear Miss Bennett.

Won't you come over to the Liberty Theatre and try a new leading part, and I wouldn't get any Body else. We have a Starr part for you called the Kidnapped Child it is a great part and just your tipe. Please come if your Mother will let you—

Yours very truly,
Douglas FairBanks

Needless to say, the ingenious gambit did not work on the astute Mrs. Bennett. It was not until 1918 that Constance made her official stage debut at the Neighborhood Players in a production of *Everyman* as the "White Angel," her mother playing "Knowledge."

During Constance's teenage years, as her parents separated and reunited, the family moved from residence to residence. When their Palisades, New Jersey, home burned to the ground in 1914, the Bennetts transferred to Park Hill, near Yonkers, N.Y.; in the spring of 1918 they moved to 22 West 8th Street in a four-storied home near the Washington Square area of Greenwich Village; and in 1920 the family residence changed to Park Avenue. When Bennett was on tour across the country or established in temporary digs during

---

*Ironically, Constance always regarded performing in front of a live audience with trepidation. She would at one point exclaim, "The very thought of that great seething monster out there in the dark, breathing fire, terrifies me!"

one of his frequent "mads," the girls remained with their mother. During one of her separations from Mr. Bennett, Mrs. Bennett took Constance, who had graduated from Miss Merrill's Boarding School on Long Island, to Europe to be enrolled in a Swiss boarding school. But Constance found the atmosphere too confining and sought the friendlier asylum of Madame Balsam's Finishing Academy in Paris, where she remained for a restless year.

When Mrs. Bennett brought Constance home from Europe at the opening of the Roaring Twenties, it was to arrange her society debut in Washington, D.C., and then to set about the traditional task of making a proper marriage. But impulsive, devil-may-care Constance had her own scheme of things. During Easter Week of 1921 at the University of Virginia, she met eighteen-year-old Chester Hirst Moorhead, a pre-law student and the son of a prominent Chicago surgeon. Two months later (June 6, 1921) she eloped with him to Greenwich, Connecticut. Mr. Bennett, then on tour in Los Angeles, was enraged by Constance's inconstant behavior, blaming his wife for the nonsense. His rationale was that if Constance had been gainfully employed with him in the theatre, she would never have had time for such a folly. Meanwhile the more practical and less mercurial Mrs. Bennett brought Constance home from Greenwich without allowing the honeymoon to take place. The "unkissed bride" was packed off to Europe as a diversion from "the recent unpleasantness." Two years later, when the notoriety of the affair had diminished, Constance obtained an annulment from Moorhead, he having resumed his law studies.

In the interim, Richard Bennett, no great admirer of the motion picture medium but a man to take ready cash where he found it, had continued working sporadically in the cinema, sometimes as an actor, and on other occasions as a technical director when the film dealt, for example, with the life of a barnstorming actor. Constance is claimed by cinema historian Gene Ringgold to have made her motion picture debut in 1920 when Mr. Bennett obtained extra roles for her and some girlfriends in one-reel comedies being lensed in New York, for which she received no salary.* Among the many unbilled roles Constance *may* have appeared in at the time were *Adam and Eve* (one reel, 1920), *Men of the Force* (c. 1920), *Has The World Gone Mad?* (seven reels, 1923), *The Daring Years* (seven reels, 1923), and *Clothes* (four reels, 1924). While Constance's participation in these and other early 1920s pictures is still unverified, it is known that in 1922 director Ralph Ince offered her a bit

---

*The May 9, 1914, issue of *Motion Picture News* contains a review of a four-reel action drama, *Fighting Death* (Box Office Attractions), directed by Herbert Blache and starring Rodman Law and Claire Whitney. It was shot largely on location at a Fort Lee, New Jersey, studio. The reviewer notes *a* Constance Bennett in the cast, observing, "Miss Bennett doubles for Claire Whitney in the thrilling part, since Miss Whitney evidently did not care to take such chances. Mr. Law has found in Miss Bennett a partner worthy of his daring. From all reports she is as willing as he to do anything suggested [which included jumping from the Brooklyn Bridge, and leaping from horseback into a frozen lake at some fifty-eight feet distance]." Could the stunt girl in *Fighting Death* have been *the* Constance Bennett? Doubtful, but possible. She, Barbara and Joan Bennett had bits in the feature *The Valley of Decision* (American Mutual, 1916), which starred the girls' parents.

role as a chorus girl in the society drama *Reckless Youth* (Select, 1922), starring Elaine Hammerstein. This six-reel feature film was produced in New York by Lewis J. Selznick. (A decade later, Selznick's two sons, Myron and David O., would be bidding for Constance's professional services.) Miss Hammerstein, long an admirer of Richard Bennett, kindly suggested that Constance should continue her film "career" and found her a larger screen part in Lewis J. Selznick's *Evidence* (1922), in which Constance was the friend of actress Hammerstein. Within the story, Constance wooes away Hammerstein's beau and thereafter conspires to vamp Hammerstein's aristocratic new suitor (Niles Welsh). It was the type of screen part that Constance could play with ease and great flair. The director of *Evidence* recommended Constance to Roy William Neill, then guiding an independent low-budget feature, *What's Wrong with the Women* (Equity, 1922), towards completion. Constance was hired to play a flamboyant flapper who nearly leads Barbara Castleton astray with the jazz way of life, before the latter sensibly returns to her husband (Rod La Rocque). Among the cast of this domestic drama was actress Hedda Hopper, who years later would be chronicling Constance's madcap adventures for public consumption.

Late in 1923 Constance attended the annual Actors Equity Ball escorted by her father. Motion picture producer Samuel Goldwyn was among those attending the elite affair who thought Constance the most startlingly attractive young woman in attendance at the gala. He took Richard Bennett aside and suggested that his vivacious blonde daughter should make a screentest for him (not knowing that Constance had already dabbled in the cinema). Goldwyn was pleased with Constance's subsequent test, and he offered her a role in one of his features, which was to be shot in Hollywood. With the counsel of Richard Bennett, who was well noted for his shrewd contractual bargaining, Constance demanded that all terms of the agreement be put into writing, including a provision that Goldwyn pay her round-trip cross-country expense money in advance.

When Mrs. Bennett learned that her husband had abetted Constance in her Hollywood-bound foolishness, it proved the final straw to their disintegrating marriage. She and Bennett had been officially separated since the fall of 1923, and now she sued him for divorce, charging him with desertion and adultery. On April 24, 1925, she received her final divorce decree, being given custody of their daughters, and alloted suitable alimony.* Ironically, at the

---

*Mrs. Bennett would return to the stage in the modern-dress version of *Hamlet* (1926), would wed literary agent Eric Pinker on June 19, 1927, and thereafter would run a literary agency, which had to be dissolved in the late 1930s largely due to the embezzlements of Pinker (who would serve a two-and-one-half-year term in Sing Sing Prison). Mrs. Bennett made another stage foray in 1940 in *Grey Farm,* which closed within three weeks. She died on November 20, 1940.

Richard Bennett remarried less than a month (July 11, 1927) after his wife, this time to Aimee Raisch Hastings, an actress formerly wed to polo-player Harry Hastings. At the time the couple were performing in the Chicago company of *The Barker,* and the ceremony took place between the matinee and evening performances, with cast member Owen Davis, Jr. as best man. This third marriage for Bennett would end in divorce in 1937. He would continue with infrequent motion-picture roles throughout the early 1940s, dying of a heart attack in Los Angeles on October 22, 1944.

time Mrs. Bennett stated that her one consolation in this turgid domestic situation was that her youngest girl, Joan, had shown no show business aspirations whatsoever.*

Just before Constance was to leave for Hollywood, Paramount tested her and wanted her to sign a player's contract. Mr. Bennett thought the terms offered were favorable, but Constance said, "Oh no." She reasoned: "They wouldn't want me at that figure unless they were satisfied I was going to be good. If I'm good they'll make a lot of money on me. Well, I say if I'm good, I'll make the money myself. I'll take my chance freelancing."

Constance embarked on the Hollywood-bound train with one purpose in mind. To outdo sister Barbara's recent stage success, *The Dancers,* which had temporarily won daughter number two the top spot in Mr. Bennett's affection.

Upon arrival in the cinema capital, Constance was assigned by Goldwyn to *Cytherea* (Strand Theatre, May 25, 1924), which starred Irene Rich as the wronged wife of Lewis Stone. He is a businessman tired of his conventional existence and driven to an intense love affair with married Alma Rubens. Constance's role of Annette Sherwin, an exquisite movie star who loves the brother-in-law (Norman Kerry) of philandering Stone, is said to have been patterned after Lillian Gish. Despite the shortcomings of Frances Marion's conservative script of Joseph Hergesheimer's novel, reviewers and audiences alike were impressed with *Cytherea's* two color sequences. Despite her relatively brief role Constance received flattering critical mention as the calculating, attractive flapper.

Too impatient to await Goldwyn's decision whether to offer her a term contract or not, Constance returned to New York and blithely accepted the first screen work she could find, which was a part in Pathé's ten-reel serial *Into the Net* (1924). Action-hungry audiences may have loved the annual output of cliffhangers so hastily churned out in the 1920s, but to most film people, participating in such "inferior" product clearly indicated that they were either professionally hard up or else extremely "indiscriminating." Trend-setter Constance could hardly have cared less, as she had a lark portraying a hoity-toity Long Island society girl kidnapped by a global crime ring. Edna Murphy and Jack Mulhall starred in this George B. Seitz chapterplay, which was also released in a seven-reel feature version.

While filming *Into the Net* Constance met, and began dating, Philip Morgan Plant, the son of Seldon Manwaring and Mrs. William Hayward, and the adopted child of stepfather Morton F. Plant. As such, young Plant was the heir to huge steamship and railroad fortune. He was attractive, fun-loving, and, despite being a hearty drinker, still a notable catch for any debutante. Plant was almost immediately infatuated with Constance and soon proposed that they get married, an offer which she would accept one day and reject the next. Just because he was so opposed to her continuing in movies, when-

*After wedding Jack Fox on September 15, 1926, Joan would drift into her own stage and motion picture career, which, some five decades later, is still in progress.

ever they fought, she would deliberately go searching for the nearest film offer. Which is probably why she accepted the role of a gin-loving flapper in the shoestring production *Married?*, filmed in New York in 1925 but not released there until February, 1926.

Constance tested Plant's romantic devotion still further by returning to Hollywood, where she obtained a role in Paramount's *The Goose Hangs High* (Rivoli Theatre, March 9, 1925). In this James Cruze-directed comedy, she was the college-bred flapper who, along with her two brothers, puts aside her profligate ways to help her financially and emotionally strapped parents readjust their scheme of life. *Photoplay* magazine rated Constance "splendid."*

If Constance personified the modish flapper onscreen, she was more so offcamera, particularly now that Plant had followed her to Hollywood and was urging her to wed him. Whether flirting or feuding with Plant, Constance insisted upon making more movies—that is, when it did not interfere with her hectic-paced social life, which found her zipping off on a trip to Catalina or down to Mexico on a moment's notice (shooting schedules be damned).

Among Constance's 1925 releases was the ersatz western *Code of the West,* in which she played the well-frocked hellion on wheels who is tamed by cowboy Owen Moore (the audience of the day was more entertained by the film's forest-fire finale). In *My Son* Constance was the city flirt (for a change she was a vamp, not a flapper) who lures Nazimova's adored child (Jack Pickford) into evil ways. The young screen-player won better notices for her appearance than her histrionics.† In *The Goose Woman,*‡ inspired by the Hall-Mills murder case in New Jersey, Constance was a stock-company actress in love with Jack Pickford, who, in turn, was the illegitimate son of a once-famous opera diva (Louise Dresser). The film offered a strong contrast between the embittered Dresser, now an elderly recluse tending geese, and Constance, who shone as the sympathetic heroine.

Constance's most important release of 1925 was MGM's well-appointed *Sally, Irene and Mary,* directed by Edmund Goulding, and teaming Constance with such already established players as Joan Crawford and Sally O'Neill. The feature's trite storyline followed the various romantic entanglements of the chorus-girl trio as they struggled to cope with life while working in a Broadway revue. Constance appeared as an all-knowing woman-of-the-world type who is being kept in rare style by older Henry Kolker. Although Crawford had the most sympathetic part (as Mary, a girl from the Lower East Side who eventually dies in an automobile accident), Constance was so pertly fashionable in her performance that Louis B. Mayer promptly offered her a seven-year player's contract. Only when Mayer agreed to include a clause in the pact allowing Constance to undertake outside film assignments (whenever the

The Goose Hangs High was remade as *This Reckless Age* (Paramount, 1932) with Frances Dee in Constance's old role.

†The *New York Times* reported: "She looks very attractive, as she makes the most of her big eyes, which are set off by exquisitely marcelled hair. She wears alluring frocks that suit her dainty, slender figure."

‡Remade in 1933 as *The Past of Mary Holmes* with Jean Arthur in the Constance Bennett role.

studio had no screen work for her) did she sign with the Culver City lot. A few days after becoming a Metro player, Constance took advantage of this proviso in the agreement to appear in a low-budget quickie, *The Pinch Hitter.* This cheapie film featured Glenn Hunter as a shy baseball-playing collegian who wins the heart of beanery waitress Constance. The production was so tacky in every department—including Constance's (un)intentional imitation of the Gloria Swanson screen persona—that Mayer soon wondered if he had misjudged the potential of this chameleonlike ingenue.

Mayer need not have worried, for soon Plant returned to New York City and events transpired in rapid order to bring about the halt of Constance's film career. Plant announced his engagement and pending marriage (scheduled for June 8, 1925 at St. Bartholomew's Church) to Judith Smith of New York City. Constance is said to have wired her words of congratulation to the future groom, inquiring what he might wish as a wedding present. Plant provided his reply in person. Not long thereafter, Constance asked Mayer to abrogate her MGM contract, saying that as the soon-to-be Mrs. Plant she would never make another picture. Howard Hughes, one of her several frequent escorts at the time, tried to talk her out of wedding Plant, but Constance was firm. Mayer obligingly destroyed her studio contract, promising her that should everything (heaven forbid) not work out as expected, she could certainly return to MGM, but *this time* it would have to be under an exclusive contract.

Constance and Plant returned to New York and on November 3, 1925, they eloped to Greenwich, Connecticut, where Justice of the Peace W. S. M. Fiske (who had married her four years before) performed the ceremony in the lobby of the Pickwick Arms Hotel.* After honeymooning in Florida and Cuba, the couple removed to Europe where they became the darlings of the chi-chi Continental set, roaming about Europe when not stationed at Plant's Biarritz villa, his Swiss Alps lodge, or their leased apartment on Paris' Champs Élysées. Among the stream of movie and international luminaries who were a constant part of Constance and Plant's everwidening stream of acquaintances were Gloria Swanson and her husband, the Marquis, Charles Chaplin, Pola Negri and her Prince escort, and Constance's sister Barbara (who was then professionally dancing as the partner of Maurice Mouvet, the famed ballroom dancer).†

*On the night of the wedding, Mr. Bennett informed a Minneapolis theatre audience: "I'm a little sad tonight. I've just lost a daughter. I don't believe the bridegroom's parents like Constance any better than I like Philip Plant, but they're both twenty-one and it's none of my business. I hope they're happy." Later he told a friend: "Now she can surely go to hell."

†Shortly after Barbara and Mouvet (who had taken a great professional and romantic interest in Constance) returned to New York for an engagement at the Clover Club, Barbara walked out of the show date. Soon thereafter (in March, 1926) she was admitted to a Los Angeles hospital for burns of the face and mouth caused by drinking a bottle of Lysol. She claimed the "accident" was not a suicide attempt. In early 1929 she wed entertainer Morton Downey; they would have five children. Later on Barbara would divorce Downey, subsequently wedding actor Addison Randall. They too divorced, and thereafter she married writer Laurent Suprenant. Barbara and Constance would remain on cool terms right to the time of Barbara's death in 1958.

By the fall of 1928 Constance's marriage to Plant had faltered so badly and so obviously that there was no longer any question of a reconciliation. Early the next year she filed suit for divorce, which was granted that December in Paris. As the ex-Mrs. Plant, she received over $500,000 in a cash settlement. When she suffered from an acute appendicitis attack during this period, it was Plant who was on constant vigil at her bedside, certainly proving he was a gallant man. But the recuperating Constance soon replaced him with Gloria Swanson's estranged husband, Henri de la Falaise, the Marquis de la Coudraye. The latter had been made a titular executive of Pathé Exchange by Joseph P. Kennedy, the business associate and good friend of Swanson.* The Marquis was not totally devoid of good business and artistic sense when he engineered a Pathé contract for Constance, for it was obvious that she photographed well on screen and had merely to reproduce her zesty real-life personality for the camera in order to gain filmgoers' interest.

Constance, who had been on furlough from the movies for over three and one-half years, returned to a Hollywood revolutionized by sound. Pathé Exchange had made the transition to talkie with the same amount of trepidation and toe-stubbing as other companies. Under J. J. Murdock's directorship, the studio had a small lineup of star personalities to carry its rather mediocre product at the box office. William Boyd, Robert Armstrong, and Tom Keene were all carryovers from the company's silent days, while its two leading female players had both been yanked from Broadway stardom at great salary expense to Pathé, but Ann Harding and Ina Claire were considered worth the cost. It was only hoped that Constance would prove a marquee attraction.

Constance's screen reintroduction was *This Thing Called Love* (December, 1929).† Above and beyond its startling color sequence which showed her to good advantage, the feature demonstrated that her husky voice recorded well in the medium. As the *New York Times* reported, she had "an agreeable, easy manner of talking." Constance even managed to outshine such pros as Edmund Lowe and ZaSu Pitts and Roscoe Karns, the latter two of whom played Constance's sister and brother-in-law.

What brought the customers to the box office was not so much Constance's oncamera magnetism (which was considerable at times), but the wide and sensational variety of her personal life as duly recorded in detail by the world press. For example, when she had recently returned to the United States accompanied by the Marquis, the entourage included a five-month-old boy named Peter, who, she claimed, she and Plant had adopted not long before their marital split. The press, however, was not buying their story, and constantly referred to the baby as the Plants' natural son.

After she emoted as a millionaire's daughter in *Rich People* (Pathé, 1929),‡

*After selling his FBO Studios to RCA, Kennedy would finance and release Gloria Swanson's pictures through United Artists, while maintaining a strong financial-executive interest in Pathé until 1931, when that studio was sold and merged with RKO Pictures.

†Remade in 1940 with Rosalind Russell and Melvyn Douglas.

‡In the film she rejects wealthy, dull suitor Robert Ames for salt-of-the-earth insurance salesman Regis Toomey.

the studio loaned her to First National Pictures for Richard Barthelmess's *Son of the Gods* (1930). This revamping of the *Broken Blossoms* theme cast Barthelmess (a veteran of that D. W. Griffith silent picture) as a San Francisco Chinese desperately in love with a beautiful white girl (Constance). This time he is a wealthy college graduate from America who meets sophisticated Constance on the Riviera, only to almost lose her when she discovers his Oriental parentage. Still later a repentant Constance and Barthelmess are able to happily reunite—within 1930s conventions—for lo and behold it is revealed that Barthelmess is not a racial foreigner, but actually the son of a Britisher. Better actresses than Constance also would have faltered in such uninspired surroundings. Constance only came alive in one sequence, in which she was called upon to mercilessly lash Barthelmess with her riding crop. The *New York Times* was so unimpressed by *Son of the Gods* and by Constance's performance that its critic carelessly referred to her as Constance Talmadge throughout the entire review.

The film that established Constance's particular screen forte in talkies was not made at Pathé, but on loan to Fox. *Common Clay* (Roxy Theatre, August 1, 1930) had served Jane Cowl well on Broadway and had been a Pathé feature in 1919 with Fannie Ward. Victor Fleming was assigned to direct this remake film, which immediately became the prototype for all of Constance's most successful vehicles of the 1930-31 period. Its plot, soon to become more hackneyed with overuse, was as follows: The love of music and good times leads working-girl Constance into accepting a job as a speakeasy hostess. After a police raid Constance is given a stern talking to by a thoughtful judge. The sermon sets her right and pushes her in a new direction, leading her to accept a post as maid at the wealthy Fullerton household. Not long thereafter, she finds herself subjected to the unwelcome attentions of both the family butler and the scion to the Fullerton fortune. The latter (Lew Ayres) is most persuasive in his courtship, particularly when his pal informs him that Constance must be a loose girl because he remembers spotting her as a speakeasy girl some time before. For her part, Constance falls in love with Ayres, not wisely but too well . . . A year later she and her mom (Beryl Mercer) call upon the Fullerton lawyer. She now has a baby and wants justice; not money and a quick brush-off, but the respectability of marriage and a legal surname for her child. This embarrassing situation (for alternating playboy-aesthete Ayres cannot decide what to do) leads to a courtroom hearing, and as any initiated devotee of 1930s cinema knows, this is always where the truth comes out in the full dramatic presence of a horde of outraged observers. On the witness stand Constance's mama reveals the sordid truth. Constance is not her daughter! No, she is really the illegitimate product of a union between her girlfriend and an unnamed man. The unmarried mother had thereafter committed suicide rather than bring shame on her paramour. (At this strategic point, to help along less discerning viewers, the camera focuses on the squirming judge, Hale Hamilton.) Less than a reel later, Constance, having coped beautifully with the shock of learning she too is illegitimate, is informed by the recalcitrant Hamilton that he is none other than her father. This immediately triggers an impassioned speech by Constance in which she mounts the proverbial soap box to tell the remorseful elder just what she really thinks of so-called society and the "best people" (a plot ingredient that insured audience empathy in Depression-ridden America). Having concluded her dramatic harangue, Constance turns on her high heels and stamps defiantly out of his chambers, only to have penitent Ayres traipse after her, begging her to forgive his callous ways and now accept the strong love he wishes to offer her. She just cannot refuse her heart's yearnings. Fade-out.

With its sly incorporation of all the essential ingredients guaranteed to snare any distaff audience, *Common Clay* proved a sensation on the distribution circuit in 1930, garnering for Constance a sturdy legion of fans who championed her as the chic new interpreter of cinema soap opera, a youthful demimondaine in the tradition of Gloria Swanson and Ruth Chatterton. Fox certainly did not have to push very much the fact that Constance had a distinguished acting pedigree, for most filmgoers were well aware of her background, given the years of headlined publicity afforded each and every Bennett domestic tiff. What intrigued movie fans even more about Constance was that in her guise as the mother-love princess of the movies, she always fought for her man intelligently and honorably, intent on winning that respectable wedding ring. While Constance was too articulately shrewd and resourceful by nature to be very credible onscreen as the typical stenographer, maid, or artist's model, she compensated for this histrionic shortcoming by providing a surplus of modishness and superiority to her working-girl roles. Her personality plus screen image quickly established a new norm for the accepted movie confessional formula. With one picture, Constance had defined and consolidated her screen reputation.*

Before *Common Clay* had established an acting pattern for Constance, she was thrust into *Three Faces East* (1930) on loan to Warner Brothers. This spy picture provided Constance with her first opportunity to work with that future movie mogul, Darryl F. Zanuck. They quickly established an enduring professional rapport that would several times over the decades rescue Constance's see-sawing film career. *Three Faces East* was nothing more than a hastily assembled remake of a 1926 Jetta Goudal spy thriller. Constance was now the German nurse who is really an Allied secret agent bent on unmasking German spy Erich von Stroheim. The dedicated Prussian is lodged in the home of British War Office head William Holden,† and it is Constance who must stop him at all costs from transmitting vital information back to Germany via a portable wireless. Von Stroheim was obviously indulging in a little oncamera sabotage of his own, attempting to divert the Roy Del Ruth-directed feature into a vehicle more in keeping with his own cinematic pen-

---

*By the time *Common Clay* was remade yet again as *Private Number* (1936) with Loretta Young and Robert Taylor, the subject matter was considered very passé.

†The well-established character actor, not the Holden of today's Hollywood.

chants, but Constance was not guiltless either, for she allowed her thriving sense of the melodramatic to grab hold of her and went overboard in her histrionics on more than one occasion in the slow-paced picture.

After three films away from the home lot, Constance returned to Pathé to star in *Sin Takes a Holiday* (1930), a comedy directed by Paul L. Stein, the studio's prime megaphoner, who had handled Constance's prior *This Thing Called Love.* The ads for the new picture made it quite clear where the emphasis lay in this property: "Ole miss of sophistication, Constance Bennett" and "Oh lady—what clothes!" As a working-girl, Constance, this time a secretary, enters into a marriage of convenience. Her employer (Kenneth MacKenna), a well-known divorce lawyer, needs to marry someone in name only in order to divert the advances of married adventuress Rita La Roy. After dallying with a smoothie (Basil Rathbone) on the Continent, Constance—and the audience, and MacKenna—realizes she truly loves her actual husband.

Pathé, ever anxious to loan out Constance's increasingly valuable services for high fees, shipped her to MGM for *The Easiest Way* (1931),* a project rejected by Metro queen Norma Shearer, but considered desirable by Constance's old *Sally, Irene and Mary* teammate, Joan Crawford. Constance was now at the peak of her box-office power and received a royal welcome from Louis B. Mayer and his chief associate, Irving Thalberg. Her portable dressing room became the site of regal splendor, second only to the trappings and royal protocol of MGM's Marion Davies.

Ironically, *The Easiest Way* is chiefly remembered today as Clark Gable's first MGM feature; but in 1931 it was another of the very popular Constance Bennett pictures then being rushed into distribution. Again she played a brittle, hard-working slum girl who loses her virtue as quickly as she accustoms herself to the lap of luxury. J. Farrell MacDonald transforms her from a department-store clerk into a Brockton Agency model; advertising executive Adolphe Menjou offers her the swank life for a price she believes she can afford; and, finally, young Argentine rancher Robert Montgomery, whom she meets on a trip to Colorado, dangles respectability and love if she will wait for him. Net result? Montgomery is stunned when he is confronted by her easy virtue; Menjou detects an aroma of ennui in his relationship with Constance and walks out, leaving her to her own limited devices. She chooses to become a streetwalker. Needless to say, even in pre-Code Hollywood this sidewalk yarn was gamier than allowable, and it had to be heavily doctored before it could be released (audiences at the time wondered what sections had been deleted in the resultant jerkily told story). In *The Easiest Way,* Constance bore her moral dilemmas almost as well as she wore her Rene Hubert gowns, attempting, as one critic of the day neatly phrased it, to get higher than the subject matter. As for Gable, he was strictly a supporting player in the film. Constance shared a few scenes with the future King of the Movies, as he

---

*The David Belasco stage production had opened on Broadway in 1909 with Frances Starr as Laura Murdock and ran for a total of 282 performances.

enacted her laundry-truck-driver brother-in-law, who does not cotton to having a high-priced tart visiting his modest abode.

By the time Constance returned to Pathé in late 1930 to make *Born to Love* (Mayfair Theatre, April 24, 1931), the studio had been sold to RKO, with David O. Selznick placed in charge of production for the newly combined facilities of the two studios. He not only fondly recalled Constance's previous film work for his father, Lewis J. Selznick, but astutely agreed that her lucrative box-office record had many films to go before public satiation set in. Under director Paul L. Stein, Constance was teamed for the first time with Joel McCrea in *Born to Love*.* The structured premise of the film badly strained viewers' credulity, but it fell within the accepted confines of the typical Constance Bennett (frustrated mother-love) feature that audiences expected and demanded. As an American nurse in a British military hospital during World War I, Constance becomes so enamored of U.S. Army pilot McCrea that she consummates their love without benefit of clergy. (Her rationale is that she knows an officer's wife would not be allowed to remain near the front lines where McCrea is stationed.) When he is later reported missing in action—she has already given birth to his child— she accepts a marriage bid from titled Paul Cavanagh, only to find thereafter that McCrea is very much alive. Cavanagh naturally misunderstands her desire to see McCrea, forcing Constance to leave their London home while he retains custody of the child. Later, when the infant dies of a sudden ailment, McCrea is on hand to comfort the distraught Constance, who is no longer able to cope with the burden of supporting herself (honorably) in a seemingly too cruel world.

With the team of Paul L. Stein directing and Joel McCrea again co-starring, Constance made *The Common Law* (Mayfair Theatre, July 19,1931). † This author considers the picture the apogee of Constance's "outcast-lady" films. The film itself was hastily and crudely constructed with but one aim in mind: to quickly exploit the hotly commercial Constance Bennett screen image. The RKO-Pathé advertising department went overboard with *The Common Law,* promoting Constance as the ultrasophisticated symbol of immoral behavior: "Noted for her Beauty . . . Notorious for her Indiscretion. She didn't care what people said as long as one lone man kept saying 'I Love You.' Her beauty made him the world's greatest artist. But in gaining a reputation for him, she lost her own!"

It would have been impossible, given the mores of the 1930s or even of the 1970s—to have *The Common Law* unreel on screen as blatantly seamy as the ads proclaimed, but within its relatively restricted confines the picture managed to be rather explosive and unconventional. If anything, *The Common Law* could be defined as a salute to the "loose" mores of Parisians. McCrea

---

*Their onscreen romancing gave rise to rumors that it was being duplicated offcamera.

†A remake of the 1923 Corinne Griffith film.

‡The usually commercially-oriented and level-headed critic, P. S. Harrison, became morally strait-laced in his industry organ, *Harrison's Report,* when he wrote, "If RKO Pathé cannot make better than this, they just might as well shut down shop, thus saving their investment."

has left Tarrytown, New York, to become a Left Bank painter in the Paris artistic set. Not long after he has set up his studio in the French capital, he meets Constance, who charmingly inquires if she might model for him. (She has just left her "benefactor," Lew Cody, and is in need of a job and diversion.) McCrea readily accepts her proposal, as he has been planning a large oil painting of a nymph at play and is convinced Constance might just be the nude model for his ambitious project.* Their working and romantic relationship develops splendidly until McCrea happens to learn of her sordid past. Obviously, they must separate—what well-bred young man could accept the affections of such a loose lady?—the idea of marrying such a wanton is initially inconceivable to McCrea. Paris is not too big a city for the two ex-lovers to run into one another at the lavish Four Arts Ball (the highlight of the film) and decide, having spent a glorious night together, that they should embark on a common-law marriage! All of which is fine, until McCrea's society sister (Hedda Hopper) gets wind of the illicit ménage and urges him to come back to America on the pretext that their father is seriously ill. McCrea dutifully returns home, but surprises everyone by showing up with Constance at his side. Hopper is not so easily nonplussed, craftily planning a weekend yachting party during which it is scheduled to have a disgraced Constance as the chief entertainment (Lew Cody has been invited on the high-seas trip). Plans go astray, for McCrea suddenly realizes that the only way to save his beloved from repeated social insults in years to come, is to make the conventional but honorable move of wedding her. The story of *The Common Law,* as adapted by John Farrow and Horace Jackson from Robert W. Chambers's novel, was definitely not the factor that pulled the customers into the theatres. Rather it was Constance's orderly sequence of posturing in preordained and well-rehashed situations that satisfied the moviegoers. As the *New York Times* glibly pointed out in its dissection of *The Common Law,* Constance was " . . . of course, very pretty."

From this pinnacle picture, Constance motored over to the Warner Bros. lot, where she was cast opposite Ben Lyon† and her father, Richard Bennett, in *Bought* (1931). Director Archie Mayo had little difficulty in hewing this adaptation of Harriet Henry's novel, *Jackdaw's Strut,* into a typical Constance Bennett vehicle. In the story Constance is an impoverished working-girl who rebels against the slum existence that brought her seamstress mother to an untimely end. (It might be added that most of mama's efforts were devoted to giving daughter Constance anything her heart desired.) Constance reasons that material luxuries are far more important than high moral standards, and she embarks on a free-living modeling career. Neither elderly Dave Meyer

---

*The sequence in which Constance seemingly poses in the nude is rather badly handled, in the same coy, unsatisfactory manner as a similar situation in Marlene Dietrich's *The Song of Songs* (1933).

†He had wed ex-RKO star Bebe Daniels on June 14, 1930.

(Richard Bennett),* nor struggling writer Lyon can convince the headstrong girl to rethink her new method of social climbing. In fact, it's through Bennett's assistance that she obtains a post in a doctor's office where she meets a swank set of folks, including playboy Raymond Milland. After he seduces her, at his Newport home, she foolishly informs him of the unspeakable truth (her parents were never wed). He promptly rejects her, and storm though she does, the romance is conclusively over. She now realizes who her true friends are, as Bennett brings Constance and Lyon together for a happy finale. Interpolated into this highly synthetic film were fashion shows, house parties, and other glimpses of how the supposed upper crust allegedly lived. One might think it would have alienated less fortunate Americans, but instead moviegoers were agog at this vicarious brush with ritzy living, and in equal measure viewers were compassionately inclined to overlook Constance's onscreen misplaced values, for Constance had the amazing knack (in front of the camera and in real life) to stimulate simultaneous feelings of sympathy and envy.

Before embarking on a European trek during her ten-week vacation in 1931, Constance underwent minor abdominal surgery, officially stated to be removal of adhesions caused by her recent appendectomy. Newsmen, quick to follow up the authenticity of any story involving Constance, met her train when it arrived in Berlin and pointedly reported that also disembarking from the same train as Constance was the Marquis (who later checked into the same hotel as Constance). Not until Constance and the Marquis returned to Hollywood was their relationship legalized. On November 22, 1931, a few weeks after de la Coudraye obtained his final divorce from Gloria Swanson, he and Constance were wed in the Beverly Hills home of director George Fitzmaurice. Constance was given in marriage by her father, with her sister Joan as a matron of honor. Claiming that marriage was the most important career a woman could have, Constance reputedly said she would gladly give up her film career any day for marital bliss, but that her new husband—unlike Philip Plant—encouraged her career and with that her ambition was growing larger.

While Constance was busily pontificating on the rights and privileges of marriage, she was (sub)consciously doing her best to antagonize the press. As a seed of the egotistical Richard Bennett, Constance handled her heirship to fame in an entirely different manner than her sisters: Barbara clashed with the burden of fame throughout her troubled life, and Joan coasted along underplaying her regal heritage. But Constance was very much in the tradition of her father, and, when engulfed by a momentary whim, neither thought nor cared a whit how others about her might interpret her actions. The day of her third wedding was one such occasion, creating the final breach between her and the coterie of reporters assigned to cover the Hollywood scene. They never forgot or forgave Constance's behavior that day. They made darn sure

*Bennett's Dave Meyer takes a fatherly interest in Constance, not realizing she is really his illegitimate daughter.

in the future that the public was always reminded how ungraciously Constance wore the mantle of popularity, suggesting that her indifference to others' feelings and needs was calculated despotism on her part.

It seems that Constance had carefully instructed the RKO-Pathé publicity department that only one press photographer was to cover the ceremony. However, as can be imagined, the social event was too big an occasion not to attract a large turnout of media reporters, each wanting to present his own personal interpretation of the much-anticipated nuptial ceremony. When the slew of cameramen and reporters convened on the spot, they received a very icy welcome from the bride-to-be. "That conceited, ungracious, high-hat, snooty, independent, hateful Constance Bennett!" began one journalist's blast at Constance, while recounting the events of the lavish wedding ceremony. This incensed reporter went on to recount how Constance had cussed at the groom when the Marquis fumbled for the wedding ring, how the movie star had told off some of the guests (in addition to the reporters).* Nor did Constance's intemperate behavior end at the ceremony. Later, when the bride and groom entrained to New York, Constance was accused of snubbing the horde of fans who had waited many hours for a glimpse of their favorite. Thereafter, the slightest breach of etiquette on Constance's part led the press to jump into the fray and lambaste her in any way possible. For example, one irate fan-magazine columnist claimed "Miss Constance Bennett had cavalierly spent over $250,000 for a new wardrobe while the country, as all you dear readers know, was facing disastrous poverty."†

When the newlyweds returned to Hollywood they took up residence in a twenty-room Holmsly Hills mansion where, according to many on-the-scene observers, the lavish social activity ran a close second to the frequent shindigs at Marion Davies's San Simeon. Always noted as a shrewd businesswoman, Constance banked a good third of her $100,000 picture salary, but just as characteristically she threw about a goodly portion of her income for luxurious living and being a tremendous good sport to anyone within reach who presented a tale of woe. She loved good food but could not cook. She was often named one of the country's and the world's best-dressed women but abhorred

*This same journalist went on to recount how Constance, when at MGM for *The Easiest Way,* had refused to be cooperative with the still photography department, declining to pose in her teddy bear. Constance's response at the time made good sense—to everyone but the reporter. Said Constance: "Five years from now when I am married and have a family, I don't want pictures of me in underwear staring at me from the *Police Gazette.*"
This exposé on Constance concluded: "A clever woman. Too clever for Hollywood! Too beautiful; too rich; too attractive to men; too highly paid; too gold-bespooned; too outspoken; too intolerant of stupidity . . . too indifferent to what is said about her; too dominant; too sincerely afraid of other people; too much talked about. Hollywood could not be expected to like her." One wonders whether the author of this piece detested, admired, or just plain stood in awe of Constance.
†In her defense, Constance explained, "I couldn't spend that kind of money in ten years if I used ermine for toilet paper." This statement was reportedly made to Marion Davies. For public hearing she protested: "I have never cut my fans short or discouraged them from seeking autographs. After all, I make pictures for them, not for the critics, if I depended upon critics for popularity I would have been professionally dead a long time ago. Even Walter Winchell compares me to a Swedish servant girl on her day off. Since I have no doubt that Winchell is an authority on such matters, I'll let it go at that. I can imagine much worse things to be."

the title foisted on her. Her favorite hobby was playing poker, and, as one of the sharpest players in Hollywood, she was admitted to gaming tables that ordinarily excluded women. One of Constance's few women friends—for she disliked wasting time at hen sessions—was Marion Davies, whose own genuineness, generosity, and social status were standards to which Constance could relate concretely.

Most agree that RKO's *Lady with a Past* (Mayfair Theatre, February 21, 1932)* was Constance's best picture since *Common Clay,* for it allowed her ample opportunity to emote in high comedy, which was obviously her real screen forte. Ben Lyon, borrowed from Warner Bros, was her leading man as the Paris-based gigolo who, for 2,500 francs a week, imaginatively promises to turn bashful wallflower Constance (yes, Constance as a social dud!) into the most popular woman in Paris and New York. He achieves this miraculous transformation simply by providing her with an intriguing past. This occurs when an elderly viscount commits suicide allegedly because she has rejected his latest marriage bid. Thus in her new guise Constance is able to snub aristocratic David Manners† and all the others who had cast social indignities on her in the past.

The motion picture that insured Constance's reputation with contemporary audiences,‡ and later with more serious-minded cinema historians, was *What Price Hollywood?* (RKO, 1932). It was a project very dear to David O. Selznick, who would later revamp the biting story for his 1937 *A Star Is Born,* produced for his own Selznick-International Pictures.§ *What Price Hollywood?* was the initial RKO directing assignment for George Cukor, who had been recently hired away from Paramount. Perhaps because the director was striving too hard to win a high status on the new lot with his first effort, his penchant for subtle onscreen sophistication was less evident than usual, an unnecessary deficit to this intricately plotted behind-the-scenes account of the movie industry.

The simplified plotline for *What Price Hollywood?* does not do the Adela Rogers St. John story justice.$^{\phi}$ For despite its episodic and seemingly glib glimpses into the milieu of filmdom, the picture is a far more trenchant study

*The same week on Broadway, Richard Bennett was appearing in the play *Arrowsmith* and Joan's movie *She Wanted a Millionaire* debuted.

†He had proposed to her one night while he was drunk, subsequently forgetting the episode altogether.

‡Cukor later reflected, "In those days she was on the crest of the wave and supplied something an audience found glamorous."

§The project, originally entitled *The Truth about Hollywood,* was planned by Selznick as a "sensational comeback" vehicle for Clara Bow.

ϕ In *What Price Hollywood?* Constance played the brittle Brown Derby Restaurant waitress who maneuvers skillfully to wait on important, but constantly drunk, director Lowell Sherman. He in turn paves the way for her to make a screentest, which leads to her eventual movie success as "America's Pal." Along the way she weds carefree, polo-playing Neil Hamilton, who refuses to take second place to her career and divorces his movie-celebrity wife before their son is born. When has-been Sherman commits suicide at Constance's home the scandal rocks the industry and jeopardizes her cinema career. She departs for France with her son, planning on a life of obscurity. However, Hamilton follows her and they are happily reunited, with the promise of a rosy, normal future ahead.

of the Hollywood situation than the acerbic *Once in a Lifetime* filmed the same year. The critics were far more enthused with the overall production of *What Price Hollywood?* than with Constance's performance. "[She] yells quite a bit in the more hysterical of the scenes," reported the *New York Times,* "but performs creditably elsewhere." That she did. The film abounds with memorable sequences, such as the scene in which, late at night at home, Constance rehearses over and over again a bit of dialog for her film debut (hoping that director Sherman will give her another chance to make good), or likewise, the bittersweet, daffy moment when Constance, having stood up Hamilton for dinner, is carried into the hotel dining room by her determined date. She is dressed only in her negligee, and is kicking wildly into the air. "What shall the orchestra play?" Hamilton cheekily inquires.

"A funeral march," says Constance. And the orchestra does!

Whatever the histrionic virtues of Constance's performance in *What Price Hollywood?,* the public was far more curious about what new outrageous real-life prank Constance would pull next. They didn't have long to wait. Because of Constance's enviable box-office track record,* outside studios were constantly vying for her professional services in their latest offering. Jack L. Warner, egged on by his chief studio aide, Darryl F. Zanuck, was one of these big league bidders. According to Hollywood legend, the bargaining proceeded as follows: Warner and Zanuck sent for Constance's agent, Myron Selznick, who, in turn, advised Constance that Warner had stated, "We'll give her $100,000 to make one picture."

"Not enough," was Constance's swift reply to Selznick. "I'll have to have $125,000. I've already been offered that much by another company."

Three weeks later Selznick phoned Constance to say the Warner Bros. contract was ready.

"What contract?" Constance demanded to know.

"Why for that $125,000 you agreed on."

"That was three weeks ago," Constance shot back. "My price is now $300,000." Thereafter Constance personally haggled with Jack L. Warner and came out with a verbal agreement to do two pictures within a ten-week period for $300,000. Later Myron Selznick came to Constance with the written contract, asking, "Where do I come in?"

"You don't. You stay out."

So no contract, and Zanuck warned her that she was risking $270,000 just to save $30,000. "I'll take that gamble," Constance answered. As the situation eventually worked out, Warner agreed to pay Selznick's commission and the income tax on Constance's salary.

With such a fabulous contract at hand, one would certainly expect the picture(s) involved to be equally big-scaled—at least in conception if not in

*Although her movies were considered too sophisticated for some of the rural film markets and thus did not finish in the top-ten film attractions of the year, Constance was among the top moneymakers because of the quantity of her releases, and, while they landed only in the top-twenty-five yearly lists, this still added up to big business.

execution. The film turned out to be the little-remembered *Two against the World* (1932), shot in four and a half weeks by Archie Mayo. Constance, as the scenario pointed out, was the type of thoughtless rich girl who parked in front of fire hydrants and smoked in no-smoking areas. But she has a touch of humanity in moments of crisis (a must for any Constance Bennett vehicle worth its salt), for she comes to admire, and then to love, the young lawyer (Neil Hamilton) who has eloquently pleaded the cause of the widow of a laborer on the Bennett family estate. In fact the milk of human kindness runs so deep within headstrong Constance that when her errant married sister (Helen Vinson) indiscreetly leaves evidence (a vanity casc) at the site of a rendezvous with her lover, Constance shoulders the blame for it so that their brother (Allen Vincent) will not think badly of sis. When enraged Vincent later murders the lover to avenge what he thinks is Constance's besmirched honor, Constance immediately assumes the responsibility for the homicide. No bar association would have approved of Hamilton's subsequent courtroom ethics at the hearing, where he is quite willing to throw the trial to save Constance. (She does fib on the witness stand, and public prosecutor Hamilton is able to save her brother.)

In actuality, *Two against the World* was filled with the type of incredibly outdated cliches that, in their present-day resurrections on television, have given vintage Hollywood features a bad name. What saved the picture at the 1932 box office was, in the elegant description of the *New York American,* Constance's "indefinable glamour."

Constance never made the second picture specified in her Warner deal. Instead she returned to RKO where she appeared in two undistinguished weepers directed by George Cukor. *Rockabye* (1932)* had Constance not as a lady to the manor born, but as a stagestruck young woman who is discovered and molded by theatrical agent Paul Lukas into a Broadway sensation. But Constance's Judy Carroll is, after all, just like any other normal female. She craves the satisfaction of mother love. Her short-lived joy at adopting an infant girl is abruptly ended when the orphanage retakes custody of the child because Constance has become involved in Walter Pidgeon's unsavory trial. She is no longer considered a fit "mother." An abjectly depressed Constance travels abroad and finds consolation in whipping into shape a Broadway-bound production (entitled *Rockabye)* written by fledgling Joel McCrea, which will star her as a streetwalker who becomes a self-sacrificing mother. With requisite Hollywood speed Constance becomes enamored of McCrea, he being estranged from his wife (Virginia Hammond). But on learning that Hammond has just given birth to a baby, Constance nobly sends McCrea back to his forgiving wife. After all, Constance reasons, mother love must be preserved. Before magnanimous Constance walks off into the night, she agrees to wed Lukas, who has been lurking on the sidelines nursing his frustrated love for

*After production was well underway, David O. Selznick had Constance's footage with Phillips. Holmes and Laura Hope Crews scrapped, and their scenes were reshot with Joel McCrea and Jobyna Howland.

her. There were tears enough in *Rockabye* to drown any plot, and the extended silver-screen vision of Constance cooing and prattling with the cute little orphanage girl failed to provide sufficient allure to salvage the weak film at the ticket windows. Jobyna Howland, as Constance's alcoholic stage mother, came off best in this fairy-tale film.

Although Katharine Hepburn was already on the RKO scene and Ann Harding was still majestically portraying the life-suffering sophisticate, studio head David O. Selznick did his best—or so he thought—by Constance. He provided a very handsome mounting for the picturization of Somerset Maugham's play *Our Betters* (1933). The role of Lady Pearl Grayston, the American hardware heiress who discovers the philandering nature of her titled husband (Alan Mowbray) on their wedding night and thereafter sets about twicking London society by its nose, was made to order for regal Constance. Unfortunately, the filmization was lifeless. American audiences, which had once reveled in the satire of Maugham's stage comedy, no longer found the poisonous study of American expatriates amuck in London to be titillating entertainment. Nevertheless, the picture and Constance had their moments, as when duchess Violet Kemble-Cooper inquires how Constance manages to get along in London. Constance tartly replies, "Through strength of character, wit, unscrupulousness." But all in all, neo-Restoration comedy was not entertainment dynamite for middle-class America.*

After the minor fiasco of *Our Betters* RKO wisely reteamed Constance yet again with Joel McCrea for *Bed of Roses* (Radio City Music Hall, June 29,1933.)† There was very little that was edifying about this Gregory La Cava tearjerker, which presented Constance "as the girl who took a short-cut down the primrose path to make herself a . . . BED OF ROSES." For a good many ardent Constance Bennett fans, it was a relief to have her relinquish her lacquered society-matron roles to portray the more picturesque gold digger, for in the latter guise she had more scope within which to display her gusto and humor as a tough broad with a heart of fourteen-karat "good Joe" gold.

In *Bed of Roses* Constance found herself cast as a reform school graduate who, along with her cohort (Pert Kelton), decides that an easy life as a scarlet woman is far more appealing than virtue and honest hard work. Meeting naive Mississippi riverboat captain McCrea changes Constance's slant on life, and eventually she finds herself rejecting New Orleans hymn-book publisher John Halliday to return to saintly McCrea. After all, as McCrea diligently instructs the teary-eyed Constance—now a dime-store clerk, of all things—her unsavory past does not really matter. It is their future together that counts. Constance's interpretation of the redeemed riverboat hooker was virtually a parody of her past screen assignments, and by now the public was fast tiring

---

*Critic Cecilia Agar judged: "Constance Bennett flings herself into the hoity-toity snobsy-wobsy elegance of *Our Betters* like the prodigal hot-footing it home . . . . Every detail is so painstakingly indisputable it sets up a positive nostalgia for the other side of the railroad tracks."

†Not too long before her death, Constance would write Gene Ringgold, then preparing a screen-career article on her for *Films in Review,* "Did I really make a film called *Bed of Roses?*"

of the stereotyped plot and character reactions dogging her every motion picture.

After Tonight (Radio City Music Hall, November 2, 1933), based on Jane Murfin's original screenplay, was more a primer of the do's and don'ts of World War I-period spying than hearty screenfare. RKO director George Archainbaud labored in vain to hoist this creaky melodrama into the stylish, if equally empty, league of Marlene Dietrich's *Dishonored* or Greta Garbo's *Mata Hari*. But he failed. The scenario of *After Tonight* asked the viewer to accept Constance as agent K-14 in the service of the Russian czar, an accomplished lady of the profession who dons several disguises in the course of the proceedings. At one point she poses as a cabaret singer, providing the setting for her to chant "Buy a Kiss." Later she is seen as a humble seamstress sewing coded messages into colleagues' coats, and still later as a Red Cross nurse behind the Austrian lines. Naturally Constance's nemesis proves to be her attractive onscreen leading man, Gilbert Roland, he being an officer of the Austrian intelligence division. (Roland has as much difficulty as the audience in accepting Constance as a spy.) There are extended romantic interludes between husky-toned Constance* and narrow-waisted Roland. The film does have a happy finale, for after the Armistice, they are reunited at a Swiss railway depot. At the time audiences were particularly unenthused about the screen teaming of Constance and Roland, finding their oncamera meanderings unrealistic and undynamic. Which only went to prove the point that screen fantasy is sometimes less exciting than real life. For by the time of *After Tonight,* Constance and Roland, who had met during the making of *Our Betters,* were already engaged in a torrid after-hours romance that would eventually culminate in marriage.

After Tonight completed Constance's RKO contract, and neither party actively sought to renew negotiations. David O. Selznick had left the RKO lot to become an executive producer at MGM, and was replaced by Merian C. Cooper as the RKO production head. Cooper, a strong advocate of Oscar-winning Katharine Hepburn, correctly sized up the situation, concluding that Constance's cinema heyday was over,† and that it simply was not worth the expense or trouble to retain her on the company payroll.‡ Presto. She was gone and quickly forgotten by the RKO factory complex, which was too busy coping with bankruptcy fears and exhibitor demands to worry about one more Hollywood star gone stale.

Constance's pal Darryl F. Zanuck and his business partner Joseph M. Schenck came to her professional rescue, offering her the female leads in two productions for their new Twentieth Century Productions, which released

*Her American twang was a far cry from Romanoff-accented Russian.

†Richard Watts, Jr. (*New York Herald-Tribune*) was not alone in his evaluation of Constance's screen work when he wrote at this time, "Miss Bennett, a striking and attractive young woman who once had ideas about being an actress, has apparently given up the project and is too busy being sophisticated and alluring to bother about a characterization."

‡Because of her frequent tantrums and whimsical demands, many performers simply refused to work in a Constance Bennett picture.

its product through United Artists. Unlike some of the other artists on the Twentieth Century payroll,* Constance's handshake agreement provided that she receive a salary plus percentage on each of her pictures for Zanuck.

She was far from her best in *Moulin Rouge* (Rivoli Theatre, February 7, 1934), a reworking of Constance Talmadge's *Her Sister from Paris* (1925). The gimmick of *Moulin Rouge* was that Constance played a dual role. As the wife of songwriter Franchot Tone, she dons a brunette wig to impersonate her sister in order to reactivate her stage career and revitalize her marriage. Far more appealing than her modest singing of "Coffee in the Morning, Kisses in the Night" and "Boulevard of Broken Dreams," was Constance's onscreen demonstration of a delightful wry quality, never before so fully captured for audience inspection. Obviously she had decided to troup it in this mediocre carbon-copy of *The Guardsman.* Her well-placed tongue-in-cheek pose was a felicitous cinema approach that would stand her in good stead in subsequent years.

The Affairs of Cellini (1934), also for Twentieth Century Productions, demonstrated conclusively that Constance did not photograph well in period trappings, and that she was not adept at providing the grand manner requisite for playing historical romance effectively. Bearded Fredric March, however, was sufficiently braggartly as the Florentine boulevardier and balcony Romeo who took brief respites to produce his works of art,† and Frank Morgan, re-creating his stage role, gave an Oscar-nominated performance as the half-witted duke, who prefers cavorting with March's dumb model, Fay Wray, to mollifying his uppity wife, duchess Constance. Poor Constance seemed lost in this Renaissance period comedy.

Since Constance had last been at MGM in 1931, both Irving Thalberg and studio head Louis B. Mayer had been following her seesawing career with professional interest, wondering if she might be added to the MGM star stable while her marquee luster still had viable commercial value. When it became clear that Constance and Twentieth Century were parting company, Metro offered her a berth at Culver City to make a feature, with the clear understanding that if both parties were satisfied, a long-term contract would ensue. It was first thought to have her star in a version of Somerset Maugham's *The Painted Veil,* but that muddied project went to Greta Garbo. Instead, Constance was ticketed to replace Norma Shearer in a remake of Michael Arlen's drama *The Green Hat.‡* The new edition, called *Outcast Lady* (Capitol Theatre, November 2, 1934), was musty with the fragrance of a bygone era. Madcap Iris March (Constance), prevented from wedding her true love (Herbert Marshall), instead weds her brother's best friend (Ralph Forbes). On their Parisian honeymoon he commits suicide, knowing that a past "unspeakable" crime is about to catch up with him. This is only the beginning of tragedy

---

*Twentieth Century had contracts with, among other players, George Arliss, Wallace Beery, and Loretta Young.

†The audience only once sees him at work in his studio.

‡Made as a Greta Garbo silent picture entitled *A Woman of Affairs* (1928).

for the quixotic March family. Constance's brother (Hugh Williams) becomes a fatal alcoholic. Constance, who has never stopped loving Marshall even though he has reluctantly wed Elizabeth Allan, is dismayed to learn that Marshall had been just about ready to return to her when he recoiled upon discovering her unseemly past. In abject depression Constance kills herself.

By the time *Outcast Lady* premiered, there was little doubt it would be a box-office turkey. Michael Arlen's original story had been so eviscerated that only a bare, unserviceable shell remained.* Besides, it was already fashionable in the mid-1930s to chauvinistically poke fun at the "grand" sophistication of Arlen's polished writing. Ironically, Constance bore a great many similarities to the character of Iris March in *Outcast Lady* and strove to bolster the disjointed characterization with substance borrowed from her own personality. But as Andrew Sennwald (*New York Times*) noticed, "[She] is contributing a very competent, suave and showy emulation of Miss Bennett, and it is simply an unfortunate fact that her irradiations have the tendency to obscure from sad, futile Iris."

During the making of *Outcast Lady,* Constance had been riding high at MGM, her least whim becoming an official command. When she suddenly decided she preferred the services of an MGM cameraman already working on Helen Hayes's *What Every Woman Knows* (1934), Thalberg was forced to yank the cinematographer off that half-finished feature and assign him to *Outcast Lady*. It must have been an amusing victory for Constance to have Herbert Marshall as her leading man in *Outcast Lady,* for it provided her with another coup against her social and professional rival, Gloria Swanson. La Swanson, also combating box-office fatigue, had signed with MGM too, but as yet she and MGM had not been able to settle on a mutually suitable project. To have Constance suddenly arrive on the lot and be given a class production was bad enough, but it was intolerable to have that woman, who had previously acquired her Marquis, demand and receive her current beau (Herbert Marshall) for her leading man. But there was little Swanson could do, for her career doldrums had sapped a great deal of her industry power.

Despite the relative fiasco of *Outcast Lady,* MGM continued its negotiations with Constance when she returned from a European trek to visit the ailing Marquis, and in December, 1934, signed her to a long-term studio pact. The terms were not the same lucrative ones she had enjoyed at RKO-Pathé or Warner Bros., but they kept her in the professional limelight.† At age thirty, one could not hope for much more consideration from an industry where fresh looks were nearly everything.

Metro next cast Clark Gable opposite Constance. The studio heads were certain that the Oscar-winning male lead could provide the proper charisma to make the comedy *After Office Hours* (Capitol Theatre, March 8, 1935) a publicly endorsed winner. Robert Z. Leonard, who had handled *Outcast Lady,*

---

*Variety reported: " . . . if the story hadn't been such a patch-quilt it might have been one of her memorable performances."

†She was still being billed as "the highest paid actress in the world."

directed the new entry. The Herman J. Mankiewicz screenplay provided Constance with sufficient opportunity to shine as the socialite who accepts a reporter's job on Gable's newspaper in order to observe how the other half really lives. She and managing editor Gable clash, make up, fight, and finally accept their mutual love while simultaneously bringing to justice wealthy young Harvey Stephens, who has murdered his mistress (Katharine Alexander). *After Office Hours* proved a popular entry all right, not because of Constance, who had a rather listless part as the purring Miss Hoity-Toity, but due to indomitable Gable, who effortlessly diverted the spotlight from her with his carelessly dynamic performance.

Now that Constance was conclusively no longer top box-office, MGM rather encouraged her to abrogate her studio contract, which had more than a year to go. With a shrug of her pretty shoulders, she packed up her extensive dressing-room gear and left the lot, thereafter departing for Europe to wander around the Continental playground with the Marquis. While abroad Constance made the serviceable Gaumont-British entry, *Everything Is Thunder* (1936). It was another World War I spy melodrama, about a young British officer (Douglass Montgomery) who escapes from a German prisoner-of-war camp and is befriended by a girl (Constance) of the Berlin streets. Oscar Homolka, as the German police detective who hounds Montgomery but allows him to escape in order that Constance not be punished as a collaborator, offered the best performance in this B-picture. Of Constance's emoting, the British *Kine Weekly* noted, "Constance Bennett's American voice jars at first, but the sincerity of her acting as Anna and her quiet control of her histrionics during emotional situations soon insulates the shocks."

When Constance returned to Hollywood in mid-1936, she was alone; the Marquis had remained in France. Darryl F. Zanuck then offered her a part in Twentieth Century-Fox's *Ladies in Love* (1936), more interesting for its on-the-set politics than its romantic-comedy froth.* The premise of *Ladies in Love* is familiar to moviegoers of the last five decades because Fox has reworked it so often. Here three Budapest femmes pool their resources to rent a fancy flat. Constance, the wisest of the trio, is a modiste shopclerk whose affair with affluent manufacturer Paul Lukas abruptly ends when a sixteen-year-old schoolgirl (Simone Simon) steals him from her. More screen time was devoted to Janet Gaynor's romance with doctor Don Ameche, who pulls Loretta Young through when she attempts suicide after losing count Tyrone Power.

As a result of *Ladies in Love*, Hal Roach, then releasing his product through MGM, came to terms with Constance to appear in *Topper* (Capitol Theatre, August 29, 1937), the film for which she is best remembered by post-Roaring

---

*When Zanuck became head of the newly merged Twentieth Century-Fox, he inherited studio star Janet Gaynor, whom he publicly derided, for he much preferred his new contract star, Loretta Young, and his French import, Simone Simon. Constance was hired not only to supply glamour but to add another wedge in his dethroning of Gaynor by making *Ladies in Love* anything but a starring vehicle for her.

Twenties audiences. Constance and Cary Grant were more than adept at personifying Thorne Smith's vivacious ghosts in this Hal Roach production. Much credit goes to Roy Seawright's special camera effects, which allowed the droll ghosts to materialize at will in the presence of harassed bank president Roland Young, whom the madcap duo decide to assist in combatting his shrewish, addlebrained wife (Billie Burke). If Constance and Grant perpetrate this one good deed, they have a fighting chance to gain admittance to Heaven. The public cottoned to the harum-scarum adventures of the ectoplasmic couple. Constance found herself again box office. To perpetuate her new screen image she began posing for gag publicity shots, a bit of business she would never had deigned to undertake in her royal years.

MGM's Norman Z. McLeod, who had helmed *Topper,* was assigned to supervise Constance's next film, *Merrily We Live* (1938), which sought to continue her newly won screen niche in a derivative *My Man Godfrey* story. *Merrily We Live* revolves around the zany Kilbourne family, a conglomerate of each and every standard screwball-comedy type. There were the butterfly-brained mother (Billie Burke), the badgered businessman father (Clarence Kolb), three skittish adult children ranging from eldest child Constance to the youngster of the clan, Bonita Granville, and a full complement of outspoken domestics (Patsy Kelly, Alan Mowbray, Marjorie Kane). *Merrily We Live,* which was well received at the time, does not hold up well, revealing that both Constance and Brian Aherne (as a noted writer posing as a tramp turned chauffeur-confidant) were straining far too hard to be offbeat in their idiosyncratic characterizations.

Nor was Constance's essential hauteur well served by Universal's *Service De Luxe* (1938), vaguely remembered as introducing Vincent Price to screen audiences. As the owner of a swank Manhattan super-secretarial service, Constance was continually being outshone in the picture by such persons as Helen Broderick, who played her brittle business partner; by Mischa Auer, playing a Russian nobleman; and by Charles Ruggles, as an eccentric millionaire who loves to cook. Constance coasted through the film, garnering more acclaim for her succession of interesting costumes than for her performance. Although the fourth estate had reluctantly admitted Constance's talents in *Topper,* they refused to yield a gracious inch regarding her on- and off-screen personality. As the *New York Times* sized up the situation (adding its own backhanded slap in the face), "There is no particular point in continuing to be snobbish toward Miss Constance Bennett just because she was the nation's favorite example of the way Hollywood overpays screen actresses back in the darkest days of the depression."

Constance's unhappy relationship with the press was not helped one whit by her determination in 1938 to spend more time in the courtroom than on the soundstage. In January, 1938, she brought a $250,000 suit against radio commentator James Fidler for alleged defamatory remarks. He said she had snubbed Patsy Kelly, her co-worker on *Merrily We Live.* That case was settled out of court, but not so her next suit, against artist Willi Pogany. He had painted her portrait, which she found extremely unflattering (she said it made her waist and legs look far too heavy), and she refused to pay his fee. Constance gave a great courtroom performance, determined to show the judge and jury that she was far more attractive than the portrait painter had allowed in the "ghastly" canvas she had commissioned. "That woman is an Amazon!" Constance insisted, as she pointed to Exhibit A in the courtroom. "I look like a sack of Portland cement with a rope tied in the middle!" The foreman of the jury, which gave Constance a judicial victory on a technicality, saw fit to state in full court, "I never signed anything so unwillingly in my life."

There was also Constance's suit against Gaumont-British, with which she had contracted in 1935 to make two pictures, the released *Everything Is Thunder,* and the unproduced *The Hawk.* She won that suit but lost a similar action against the producing company of Ben Hecht-Charles MacArthur, which had negotiated for Constance to headline one or more of its projected features. To round out the year, maverick Constance was herself hauled into court by a Hollywood taxi company, which claimed she had refused to pay a $4 fare. Constance's defense was, "He took the long way around . . . It's a point of honor." The court expenses were a costly "point of honor."

By the time Hal Roach and Constance had agreed upon a sequel to *Topper,* Roach had moved his production offices to United Artists, and Cary Grant's salary demands had become so high that Roach could not afford to have him repeat his ghostly assignment in *Topper Takes a Trip* (1939).* Therefore Constance was required to solo the latest adventure of the chic ghost, still out to aid Roland Young in his perennial battles against domineering spouse Billie Burke. This time Burke has gone to the Riviera, where she fast becomes embroiled with a phony baron (Alexander D'Arcy). But with the aid of wispy Constance, Young breaks the bank at Monte Carlo and is eventually reconciled with flibbertigibbet Burke. As a substitute for the sorely missed Grant, the script provided Constance with a new companion, a ghostly wire-haired terrier named Mr. Atlas. Despite the even greater reliance on special effects to carry the show, which was filled with a *déjà vu* quality, audiences were amused by the proceedings. *Topper Takes a Trip* did nicely at the box office, and Constance even earned some nice reviews. "Of all possible ghosts with which one possibly could be affected, Miss Bennett certainly is the most decorative, amusing, and companionable" *(New York Mirror).*

Unfortunately, *Topper Takes a Trip* proved to be yet another watershed mark in the continued career downswing for Constance, for thereafter on-screen she would either be the second female lead in A-productions or the nominal star of programmers. Characteristically she retained the same attitude of indifference to her professional downfall as she had to her sudden ascent, and her screen performances changed not a whit; casual, mocking, at times competent, but always very strong on the nonchalant, high-bred Constance Bennett allure.

*Film clips of Grant from *Topper* were interpolated into the follow-up.

When Loretta Young smartly refused to play second fiddle to Alice Faye in Twentieth Century-Fox's *Tail Spin* (Roxy Theatre, February 10, 1939), Darryl F. Zanuck hired Constance for the role of wealthy Gerry Lester, a society aviatrix who competes in the annual air meet at Cleveland. Her chief rival in the air and on land is Alice Faye, who also thinks she loves wealthy Kane Richmond. *Tail Spin* was as anachronistic a programmer as Warner Bros.' similar *Women in the Air* (1939), which starred Kay Francis. Each picture attempted to take advantage of the publicity garnered by Amelia Earhart, and, in their haste to reach theatrical release, became just concocted trivia. As far as *Tail Spin* went—and down the drain is where it properly headed— neither the inclusion of actual footage from the Cleveland Air Meet of 1938 nor the novelty of four such disparate femmes as Alice Faye, Constance, Nancy Kelly, and Joan Davis could save this ludicrous jumble of phony situations. One brief highlight of the picture was the hair-pulling, slapping brawl between Constance and Faye. Little wonder that in her subordinate screen role Constance merely provided a succession of exceedingly languid poses and quizzical facial expressions.

With her cinema career at a very low ebb, Constance decided to try live theatre. In November, 1939, she played the vaudeville circuit in a skit that incorporated a fashion show interview. After considering, and then discarding, the possibility of playing in *Young Man with a Horn,* Constance made her "official" adult stage bow in Noel Coward's 1925 comedy, *Easy Virtue.* Although her mother especially rewrote the story of an American girl who upsets English customs, Constance frankly admitted, "It's a bomb, but people keep coming to see it and I'll play it as long as they insist on buying tickets." The financially successful, but artistically undistinguished, tour ended in Detroit in late February, 1940, and Constance hastily returned to Hollywood. There was talk of Constance playing the female lead in Columbia's *Adam Had Four Sons,* but the role eventually went to Ingrid Bergman. Instead Constance took second billing to Pat O'Brien in the cliché-ridden programmer *Submarine Zone* (1941). Admittedly, director John Brahm did wonders with the hackneyed *Grand Hotel*-at-sea tale in which Constance was the secretary-mistress of rotten John Halliday. She alternates her shipboard attentions between freewheeling Pat O'Brien and killer-gangster Alan Baxter. All the while the soap opera is progressing aboard the tramp steamer, the vessel is being stalked by a Nazi submarine, giving the tattered tale some topicality. Even a novice filmgoer could see how very easy it was for Constance to project the guise of the shopworn love object who retains her optimism about the future. It was a stereotype she would play over and over again in her remaining Hollywood years.

After finishing *Submarine Zone,* Constance established residence in Nevada and on November 14, 1940, obtained a Reno divorce from the Marquis, whom she charged with having deserted her in January, 1937. While Constance was in Reno she was repeatedly photographed knitting sox for the British War Relief Fund. The Marquis added his own light touch to the divorce suit. He had been stuck in war-torn Europe. In fact, he was among those evacuated from Dunkirk in late March, 1940. He later told bewildered reporters that he endured his ordeals by thinking about how ravishing Constance would appear to other men in widow's weeds.

Largely because of her self-perpetuated and self-gratifying dilettante image, not enough credit was ever given to Constance for her sincere war work. She was one of the first Hollywood celebrities to devote herself to patriotic duties. In August, 1940, she had appeared for three weeks with Douglas Fairbanks, Jr. in the "We Were Dancing" segment of *Tonight at 8:30* at the El Capital Theatre. Others in the stellar cast were Brian Aherne, Gladys Cooper, Dame May Whitty, Reginald Gardiner, Greer Garson, Judith Anderson, Joan Fontaine, C. Aubrey Smith, Roland Young, Basil Rathbone, and Elsa Lanchester. The proceeds went to the British War Relief Fund, a charity that had become a passion with Anglophile Constance. She was also chairman of the International Committee for Refugees of England, and was an ardent fund-raiser, organizer, and speech-maker. She still found time to participate in entertainment shows at various military installations for the servicemen, and she persisted in an effort to create an industry-wide studio tour system for servicemen to see how pictures were made and to meet the stars.

When Miriam Hopkins rejected Warner Bros.' *Law of the Tropics,**
on the grounds that she was too old to play opposite leading man Jeffrey Lynn, Constance, then age thirty-seven, agreed to do the picture for the comparatively paltry salary of $10,000 in toto. She breezed through the role of the cafe singer on the lam from a Jersey City murder rap who finds herself wed to moustachioed South American rubber-plantation-owner Lynn. Her singing of "A Tropical Kiss" was the highlight of a picture geared strictly for action audiences, the majority of whom only vaguely recalled what Constance had meant to early 1930s cinemagoers and the American public at large. When not carping at the hackneyed plot of *Law of the Tropics,* the critics threw bromides at Constance, deciding her maturity was as vulnerable a quality as her persistent overacting.†

At least Constance's basic brittle qualities were well served in the much maligned *Two-Faced Woman* (MGM, 1941), in which she played support to Greta Garbo, the latter in a dual part. Now that multidissection of this George Cukor-directed feature has become part of cinema history, one can review the film and appreciatively watch acerbic Constance parody her own image as a temperamental, catty sophisticate. In the film she plays the bespectacled playwright who loses publisher Melvyn Douglas to ski-instructress Garbo. Constance was paid a token $15,000 for her below-the-title emoting in *Two-Faced Woman.*

In April, 1941, two months before *Two-Faced Woman* went before the

---

*A remake of *Oil for the Lamps of China* with a dash of *Tropic Zone* tossed in.
†*Variety* observed that Constance "isn't exactly the season's first daisy," while the *New York Herald-Tribune* complained, "Does little to help out in refurbishing a broken-down screen script."

MGM cameras, Constance wed for the fourth time. Her groom was Mexican-bred movie actor Gilbert Roland, then age thirty-six, who was a second lieutenant in the U.S. Air Force. The couple eloped to Yuma, Arizona, for the brief ceremony. Not long enough thereafter, to stop gossips' tongues from wagging, they "adopted" a child named Linda (later called Lorinda). In December, 1942, their daughter, Gyl Christina, was born.*

Meanwhile, Constance appeared in a trio of undistinguished B-pictures. *Wild Bill Hickok Rides* (Warner Bros., 1941), which top-cast Bruce Cabot as the whitewashed historical figure, emerged from the production-line mill as just another horse opera, lacking all the rootin'-tootin' verve and spectacle that characterized the same studio's Errol Flynn sagebrush epics. As the gambling lady involved with Cabot, Constance won no plaudits. "Of all the fine screen ladies who have frequented Western dance halls in their times, Miss Bennett, the erstwhile orchid of salons and lightly scented bowers, is the one you could least have expected to find in such a place. She, too, seems to sense the incongruity of it." Constance, who always claimed "My voice is right here in my feet" sang "The Lady Got a Shady Deal" in *Wild Bill Hickok Rides*. That she certainly did in this film.!

Mae West and Marlene Dietrich had perceptively rejected *Sin Town* (Universal, 1942), Constance's third 1941-42 feature under Ray Enright's craftsmanlike, but uninspired, direction. She and fellow con artist Broderick Crawford (in his less beefy days) arrive in the oil-boom hamlet of Carsin, Oklahoma, a backlot manufactured town filled to the budget brim with gamblers, brawlers, and boomers. More noteworthy than Constance's grappling with the trite part of the blonde accomplice who maneuvers to hold onto her man (Crawford) were the occasional bouts of bone-crushing fisticuffs among the male leads and extras.

It did not require much perception to realize that Constance, who weds war correspondent Don Porter in *Madame Spy* (Universal, 1942) and then cavorts with Axis agents in New York, is not a Nazi sympathizer, but really an undercover FBI agent. The production values here were as flimsy as the obvious plotline and her lacklustre leading man.

Offscreen, when not following husband Roland from Air Force base to Air Force base, Constance found time to participate in a national tour of Philip Barry's *Without Love,* which had starred her RKO star successor Katharine Hepburn on Broadway. The economy edition of *Without Love* featured Steve Cochran, a cinema newcomer whom Constance had screentested with at Warner Bros. The critics described the Constance of *Without Love* as "patrician" and a "cool, delightful comedienne." Constance was less laudatory in her self-appraisal. "I'm a lot more sartorial than thespian. They come to see me and go out humming costumes." It was also in 1943 that Constance engaged in another well-publicized court battle, this time contesting the will of

---

*Gyl, who studied acting at the American Academy of Dramatic Arts, most recently appeared onscreen as an airline stewardess in *Black Gunn,* lensed in June, 1972, by Champion Productions.

her late second husband, Philip Plant. She was bent on winning son Peter a share of the tremendous Plant fortune. The Connecticut Supreme Court reached a strange verdict. They agreed with the executors of the will that the facts showed Peter was adopted and "really" the illegitimate child of Constance's cousin, Sabina Armstrong, who was residing in England at the time of the infant's birth on January 21, 1939. But the court did allow Peter $150,000 for "attorney expenses." Constance offered a typically forthright reaction to this bizarre settlement. "It's obvious nonsense—obviously. Either Peter is the son of myself and Philip, and should legally share in his grandfather's estate, or he isn't our son and shouldn't get a cent. The court awarded him $150,000. That should be proof enough that the court is certain Philip did not 'die without issue' as the executors of the estate tried to show."*

Perhaps noting the mild success her former onscreen rival, Gloria Swanson, was enjoying with her various business enterprises, Constance set aside time during the World War II years to open a cosmetic firm (which she later sold in the nick of time, before it became insolvent), and to endorse Fashion Frocks, Inc., which sold modestly priced garments door to door, each bearing the label "Designed by Constance Bennett."

Constance had been an infrequent radio performer in the late 1930s,† but in 1945 she not only became an occasional panelist member, along with Binnie Barnes, Dorothy Kilgallen, Lucille Ball, Eloise McElhone, *et al.*, on Mutual Network's "Leave It to the Girls," a program devoted to topical problems, but in May of that year she began her own daily fifteen-minute radio show, during which she dispensed fashion hints and women's news, and interviewed Hollywood celebrities.

During production of *Paris—Underground,* Constance had not been above seeking the professional advice of her long-time friend Darryl F. Zanuck, who in turn offered her several film roles in the ensuing years. She rejected the part of Suzanne in *The Razor's Edge* (1946), a part subsequently considered by Gloria Swanson but played by no one as it was deleted from the final shooting script. Constance also declined the part in *Gentleman's Agreement* (1947) that won Celeste Holm a best-supporting-actress Oscar. But she did accept a part in the Otto Preminger-directed *Centennial Summer* (Roxy Theatre, August 17, 1946). Just before this Twentieth Century-Fox period comedy went into production, studio head Zanuck, spurred on by the success of his' company's musicalized remake of *State Fair* (1945), added a Jerome Kern-Oscar Hammerstein II, Leo Robin-E. Y. Harburg score to the picture. As fifth-billed Zenia Lascalles, Constance played to the hilt the gay Parisienne

---

*Years later, after Constance and Roland had divorced in May, 1945, Constance aired her decision that she did not ever desire to see Peter again because he had remained loyal to ex-spouse Roland.

†She was heard on "Lux Radio Theatre" in the episode *I Found Stella Parrish* (CBS, July 4, 1938). While touring in Philip Barry's *Without Love* in 1943-44, she dickered with Decca Records about the possibility of recording an album of love scenes from the play with linking musical background.

widowed sister of Dorothy Gish, arriving in Philadelphia in May, 1876, to visit her family and view the forthcoming Philadelphia Centennial. This was Constance's first full-length Technicolor picture and only the second time in her cinema career that she wore period costumes. She photographed maturely (enough to make her devotees wince at the passage of time), but radiated a delightful coquettishness that unfortunately was buried in the background of the story. She joined in the group singing of "Up with the Lark."

A month before the mildly received *Centennial Summer* debuted, Constance wed for a fifth time on June 22, 1946. Led up the aisle by son Peter at the St. Francis Chapel at the Mission Inn, Riverside, California, she married U.S. Army Colonel John Theron Coulter.* Mrs. Darryl F. Zanuck was her matron of honor, with sister Joan and her current husband, Walter Wanger, in attendance, along with Constance's two daughters, Lorinda and Gyl. Constance's painstaking efforts to placate the press this time around produced another of the many Constance Bennett statements that have become Hollywood legend. Reportedly she told the press: "Hurry and get the pictures, boys. I've been doing this for twenty years and I'm a little tired. I'd like to go lie down."

Although the newlyweds resided at Hamilton Field near San Francisco for some time, Constance jaunted to Hollywood on occasion to appear in a batch of increasingly less worthwhile film ventures. In *The Unsuspected* (Warner Bros., 1947), a complex murder mystery directed by Michael Curtiz but salvaged by the bravura performance of Claude Rains as a producer-writer of radio crime shows who makes his vocation his way of life, Constance had a small assignment as Rains's wisecracking secretary. She put plenty of pep into her few onscreen moments. *The Unsuspected* was touted as a successor to *Laura*—promoted with the catchline, "You can't foresee it. You can't forget it!"—but more than one critic tagged the new thriller as "seedy."

Further along on the downhill swing was *Smart Woman,* let loose by Monogram Pictures in 1948, with Constance as a crafty lady lawyer who locks professional horns with crusading special prosecutor Brian Aherne. Constance's Adrian gowns were the best feature of this dull programmer. Aherne also joined Constance in the abysmal *Angel on the Amazon* (Republic, 1948). This bizarrely charted picture found pilot George Brent wedding Vera Ralston only to later learn, via Dr. Constance Bennett's layman's explanation, that his spouse's pristine beauty is due to a severe shock having retarded her natural aging processes. When another trauma pushes Ralston over the brink of Geritol-induced rescue, Brent blithely turns to romancing a most eager Constance. Some time after making this film, Constance admitted she did not know what possessed her to become involved in such a rancid turkey.

Her last motion picture for the duration was Twentieth Century-Fox's *As Young as You Feel* (1951), a thinly-premised comedy which relied on the already overexposed talents of Monty Woolley and Thelma Ritter to carry it

---

*Joan Bennett later said, "At last, she'd met her match in a perfect husband who adored her but would not suffer temperamental nonsense."

over with audiences. Constance was briefly seen in the fifth-billed role as the neglected wife of business executive Albert Dekker. He is too busy making advances to his curvaceous secretary (Marilyn Monroe).*

After spending three years abroad, where her husband was Wing Commander of the Air Lift Base at Fassberg, Germany,† Constance embarked on a pre-Broadway venture entitled *I Found April (*a. k. a., *A Date With April)*. It was a flimsy comedy by George Barson, which dragged onto Broadway (Royale Theatre, April 15, 1953) and closed within thirteen performances. In this triangle love tale, Constance was cited as a "handsome woman with a nice taste for clothes." That summer she staged twelve weeks of shows at the 4,000-seat Carter Barron Amphitheatre in Rock Creek Park, near Washington, D.C., where her husband was then stationed.

As a favor to George Cukor she appeared as herself as a panelist in the Judy Holliday comedy *It Should Happen To You* (Columbia, 1954). She continued her infrequent video guest shots,‡ toured in *Sabrina Fair* in 1955, had a five-day-a-week radio show in 1956, and during that same year did a one-woman show from Oklahoma to Louisiana. When plans to appear in *The Best of Steinbeck* on Broadway in the fall of 1956 fell through, Constance reached out to a new medium by making her club debut in Miami, Florida, in early 1956, followed by a well-covered New York City opening on April 24, 1956, at the Cotillion Room of the Hotel Pierre. Her act, staged by Herb Ross, included her rendition of "Boulevard of Broken Dreams" along with other Marlene Dietrich-type songs, which she sang in her "throaty but nice" voice. The climax to her routine found Constance offbeatly costumed in blue jeans, denim shirt, a custom-made outfit gussied up with patch pockets with rhinestone and diamond sequins. She parodied the current rash of rhythm 'n blues songs by performing "A Teen-Age Prayer," "Lipstick, Candy, and Rubber Soled Shoes," and "Dungaree Doll." She even danced a jitterbug.

After a summer tour of *Silk Stockings* in 1957, Constance played the lead in the national company of *Auntie Mamie* (Travis Banton did her outfits). After a six-week holiday in July, 1958, she was back on this tour, which concluded later that year after a twenty-city outing and a gross of $1.5 million,

*Constance is supposed to have said of Marilyn Monroe, "There's a broad who's got a future behind her!"

†During her Germany years Constance flew back and forth to the United States to organize professional companies of *Over 21, Dear Ruth,* and *John Loves Mary* to play Fassberg and other military bases in Europe. She also did a brief stateside tour of *Skylark* in 1951.

‡Constance's video appearances include a scene from *Love Letters* on the "Faith Baldwin Show" (ABC, July 14, 1951); a scene from *Eastward in Eden* on the "Betty Crocker Star Matinee" (ABC, December 1, 1951); guest shots on the "Ken Murray Show" (CBS, 1951) and "Martha Raye Show" (NBC, 1952); a brief reunion with *Topper* co-star Roland Young on the panel show "It's New to Me" (CBS, 1952); a televersion of *Twentieth Century* with Fred Clark on "Broadway TV Theatre" (Channel 9, New York City, 1953); the *Sinora Isabel* (NBC, 1956) and *Onions in the Stew* (NBC, September 17, 1956) episodes of "Robert Montgomery Presents"; and an episode of the "Ann Sothern Show" (CBS, February 23, 1961) in which she and John Emery, the ex-Mr. Tallulah Bankhead, did a parody of Tallulah and John Barrymore. Constance's last video appearance was on "The Reporter" series in the episode *The Man behind the Badge* (CBS, November 6, 1964).

a good deal of the take due to Constance's chic trouping in the marathon role. Therefore she engaged in some more citronella-circuit outings: *Call Me Madam* (1959) and *The Marriage-Go-Round* (1960), followed by what proved to be her last stage production, the national touring company of Lillian Hellman's *Toys in the Attic*. From the start, Constance was ill at ease in the role of the ingenue's mama who has a black lover. After a few weeks of touring in the part in 1961, she quit the production. While in Chicago, she told Irv Kupcinet, on his television show, the reasons for her withdrawal. "There's too much sickness and unhappiness in the world for anyone to want to see *Toys in the Attic*. This is a very unpleasant play. It's merely an acting exercise for me. My forte is really comedy. My agent, Geoffrey Barr, thought this might change my image. Wait until I get back to New York. I'll change his image!"*

In 1962, while on holiday in Switzerland with her husband (now a brigadier general and commander of the New York Air Defense Sector), she suffered a triple leg fracture in a skiing mishap. After several weeks of hospitalization there she returned to the United States, but she was forced to be bedridden for months thereafter, this being one of the few times in her entire life when Constance stayed put for more than a day at a time.

There was a great deal of surprise in the Hollywood community when it was announced, in late January, 1965, that Constance would be returning to the movies, after a twelve-year layoff, to play—of all things—Lana Turner's mother-in-law (!) in the remake of *Madame X* (Universal, 1966). It was a role that did not exist in the original play. Producer Ross Hunter had reportedly first offered the role to Kay Francis, who rejected it, and then to Myrna Loy, who was unavailable because of her commitment to the national company of *Barefoot in the Park*. Hunter threw a big, splashy soundstage party at Universal welcoming Constance back to Hollywood. She radiated in the rash of attention like a bee nosediving to honey. As in the old days, she found time to pontificate in the best Richard Bennett manner on a wide variety of subjects, but all having one common denominator: herself.

On youth: "If there's a secret it's working like a beaver to be happy. What I mean is I've always been interested in everything I did, or else I wouldn't do it. When you're that interested in anything, you're happy."

On beauty: "The worst enemy of a female is having a resentful personality. Any woman who habitually has shown meanness and envy will find in time they'll show in her face and make her unattractive."

On luxury: "Listen, there are worlds to enjoy that aren't made of mink and sables. And the world of mink and sable isn't free of drudgery and heartache. It's all what you make it."

On her children: "At their ages, I don't know whether I find it harder to keep up with them, or they find it tougher to keep up with me."

On the scope of her life: "I've done practically everything except magic and

*Toys in the Attic producer Kermit Bloomgarden counter-attacked in *Variety:* "Miss Bennett's sharp words were obviously made with an eye to her own future. Frankness in ladies is now considered both daring and amusing, and television interviewers enjoy leading them on."

mine coal." Any regrets? "No. Only I tell my kids I'll beat their brains out if they ever try to do what Mama has done."

On Hollywood: "Back in the thirties, there were more pictures about women. The roles were glamorous and the clothes divine. They weren't dramatic roles, they were synthetic. But they were exciting and the actresses acted like movie queens. Pictures have certainly changed today!"

Of her more than fifty-five pictures over a five-decade period,* Constance would admit partiality to only five titles: *Common Clay, The Common Law, What Price Hollywood?, Our Betters,* and *Topper.*

Almost immediately after completing her co-starring assignment in *Madame X,* Constance entered Walter Reed Hospital in Bethesda, Maryland, for surgery on a severe middle-ear ailment. She was released on May 28, 1965. On July 24 of the same year, a few days after she conferred with agent Geoffrey Barr about a possible Broadway play and another motion picture assignment, Constance collapsed in her McGuire Air Force Base home in New Jersey,† and she died that evening of a cerebral hemorrhage in the nearby Fort Dix Hospital. General Coulter was at her bedside.

The funeral was held the following Tuesday afternoon at Frank E. Campbell's Upper East Side Manhattan funeral home. Over two hundred people attended the twelve-minute Episcopal ceremony,‡ including movie executives Walter Wanger and Spyros P. Skouras, actor Lee Bowman, and sister Joan, who had flown into New York from a summer-stock engagement in Franconia, New Hampshire.§ Constance's closed coffin was draped in a blanket of white chrysanthemums, with a centerpiece of small red roses. The large white floral cross from Joan was stationed nearby. In constant attendance with General Coulter were Constance's son, Peter, his wife, Audrey, and the late star's two daughters, California sculptress Lorinda and New York actress Gyl. Constance was buried the following morning at eleven o'clock at Arlington National Cemetery. The grave marker lists only her name and the date of her death.ϕ

Constance's last motion picture, *Madame X,* was not released until April, 1966, when it was distributed on a saturation showcase basis, in the hope of wangling as many playoff engagements as possible before bad word-of-mouth

---

*A favorite story of Constance's was that in the 1950s and 1960s, when she toured in plays, elderly ladies would come up to her and say, "Oh Miss Bennett, you were my favorite actress when I was a child." To which Constance added (at a later date), "Dear God, I guess no adults ever saw my films!"

†The Coulters at the time were planning to move into Manhattan on a permanent basis, with their new residence at 171 West 57th Street.

‡Canon Timothy Case of St. James Episcopal Church officiated, commencing the ceremony by reading "I am the Resurrection" and then quoting from "The Order for Burial of the Apostle" from the thirteenth chapter of the First Epistle of St. Paul to the Corinthians.

§Joan returned to New Hampshire that same evening to give a performance of *Never Too Late,* reasoning, "When you are a show business family for one hundred years as we are, the cliché about 'The show must go on' is not really a cliché but a fact of life." Moreover, said Joan, "Connie would want it that way."

ϕConstance remained vain about her age right to the end. When she was brought to the Fort Dix Hospital she insisted to the admitting authorities that she had been born in 1914. As she once said, "It's never been properly recorded and it's never going to be!"

destroyed its curiosity potential. This fourth adaptation of the venerable stage play had been brought up to date in costuming and appointments, but at heart it was still a mildewed tearjerker, reverently coasting along from "ache to pain and worse." What drew most critical (and gossip-column) notice was the fact that sixty-one-year-old Constance, with her chic darker-blonde-colored hair styled in an attractive neck-length pageboy, looked far younger than forty-four-year-old Lana Turner. Constance even had a few scenes that smacked of her best dialog moments in 1930 movies. For example, after the death of Lana Turner's lover, modish Constance glides onto the scene, coolly appraises the situation, and says to distraught Turner: "So you've killed your lover, my girl. You're still only a shop girl and you should've stayed on the other side of the counter." The critics, for once—and now it was too late for Constance to read their words of praise—gave Constance her proper due. "Excellent" said the *New York Times,* and ". . . endows [her] role with quiet dignity and strength" asserted *Variety.*

While Constance was in Hollywood emoting in *Madame X,* cinema historian Gene Ringgold contacted her about an article on her career he was planning to write for *Films in Review.** In thanking him for his interest in her professional work to date, she cautioned: "I'm flattered that you would want to write about me. But, if you do, keep it light. And be truthful about my film work. After all, I was no Sarah Bernhardt. Good luck."

*It appeared in the issue of October, 1965.

Feature Film Appearances
CONSTANCE BENNETT

FIGHTING DEATH (Box Office Attractions, 1914) 4 reels.

Director, Herbert Blache.

With: Rodman Law, Claire Whitney, Constance Bennett.*

*It is doubtful whether this is *the* Constance Bennett of *The RKO Gals*.

THE VALLEY OF DECISION (American Mutual, 1916) 5 reels.

Director, Ren Berger.

With: Richard Bennett (Arnold Gray); Adrienne Morrison (Jane Morton); Blanche Hanson (Rhoda Lewis); George Periolat (Dr. Brainard); Constance Bennett, Barbara Bennett, Joan Bennett (Unborn Souls); Blanche Bennett (Woman).

RECKLESS YOUTH (Select, 1922) 5,700'

Presenter, Lewis J. Selznick; director, Ralph Ince; based on the story by Cosmo Hamilton; screenplay, Edward J. Montagne; camera, Jules Cronjager, Jack Brown.

Elaine Hammerstein (Alice Schuyler); Niles Welch (John Carmen); Myrtle Stedman (Mrs. Schuyler-Foster); Robert Lee Keeling (Mr. Schuyler-Foster); Huntley Gordon (Harrison Thomby); Louise Prussing (Mrs. Dahlgren); Frank Currier (Cumberland Whipple); Kate Cherry (Martha Whipple); Constance Bennett (Chorus Girl).

EVIDENCE (Select, 1922) 4,642'

Presenter, Lewis J. Selznick; director, George Archainbaud; story-screenplay, Edward J. Montagne; camera, Jack Brown, Jules Cronjager.

Elaine Hammerstein (Florette); Niles Welch (Phillip Rowland); Holmes Herbert (Judge Rowland); Constance Bennett (Edith); Marie Burke (Mrs. Bascom); Matilda Metevier (Louise); Ernest Hilliard (Walter Stanley).

WHAT'S WRONG WITH THE WOMEN? (Equity, 1922) 7,254'

Presenter, Daniel Carson Goodman; director, Roy William Neill; story-adaptation, Goodman; sets, Tilford Cinema Studios; camera, George Folsey.

Wilton Lackaye (James Bascom); Montagu Love (Arthur Belden); Rod La Rocque (Jack Lee); Huntley Gordon (Lloyd Watson); Paul McAllister (John Mathews); Julia Swayne Gordon (Mrs. Bascom); Constance Bennett (Elise Bascom); Barbara Castleton (Janet Lee); Helen Rowland (Baby Helen Lee); Hedda Hopper (Mrs. Neer); Mrs. Oscar Hammerstein (A Friend).

CYTHEREA (Associated FN, 1924) 7,400'

Presenter, Samuel Goldwyn; director, George Fitzmaurice; based on the novel *Cytherea, Goddess of Love* by Joseph Hergesheimer; adaptation, Frances Marion; technical director, Ben Carré; camera, Arthur Miller; editor, Stuart Heisler.

Irene Rich (Fanny Randon); Lewis Stone (Lee Randon); Norman Kerry (Peyton Morris); Betty Bouton (Claire Morris); Alma Rubens (Savina Grove); Charles Wellesley (William Grove); Constance Bennett (Annette Sherwin); Peaches Jackson, Mickey Moore (Randon Children); Hugh Saxon (Randons' Butler); Lee Hill (Groves' Butler); Lydia Yeamans Titus (Laundress); Brandon Hurst (Daniel Randon).

INTO THE NET (Pathé, 1924) Serial—10 chapters (also released in a feature version)

Director, George B. Seitz; based on the story by Richard E. Enright; screenplay, Frank Leon Smith.

With: Edna Murphy, Jack Mulhall, Constance Bennett, Harry Semels, Bradley Barker, Frank Lacteen, Frances Landau, Tom Goodwin, Paul Porter.

Chapter titles: (1) "The Shadow of the Web"; (2) "The Clue"; (3) "Kidnapped"; (4) "Hidden Talons"; (5) "The Raid"; (6) "The House of the Missing"; (7) "Ambushed"; (8) "The Escape"; (9) "To the Rescue"; (10) "In the Tolls."

THE GOOSE HANGS HIGH (Par., 1925) 6,186′

Presenter, Adolph Zukor, Jesse L. Lasky; director, James Cruze; based on the play by Lewis Beach; screenplay, Walter Woods, Anthony Coldeway; camera, Karl Brown.

Constance Bennett (Lois Ingals); Myrtle Stedman (Eunice Ingals); George Irving (Bernard Ingals); Esther Ralston (Dagmar Carroll); William R. Otis, Jr. (Hugh Ingals); Edward Peil, Jr. (Bradley Ingals); Gertrude Claire (Granny); James A. Marcus (Elliott Kimberly); Anne Schaefer (Rhoda); Z. Wall Covington (Noel Derby); Cecille Evans (Mazie).

MARRIED? (Herman Jans, 1925) 55 M.

Director, George Terwilliger; story, Marjorie Benton Cooke; camera, Walter Blakely, Louis Dunmyre.

Owen Moore (Dennis Shawn); Constance Bennett (Marcia Livingston); Evangeline Russell (Kate Pinto); Julia Hurley (Madame Du Pont); Nick Thompson (Joe Pinto); Antrim Short (Chuck English); Frank Walsh (Harvey Williams); Betty Hillburn (Mary Jane Paul); Helen Burch (7-11 Sadie); Gordon Standing (Clark Jessup); John Costello (Judge Tracey); Rafaela Ottiano (Maid).

CODE OF THE WEST (Par., 1925) 6,777′

Presenter, Adolph Zukor, Jesse L. Lasky; director, William K. Howard; based on the novel by Zane Grey; screenplay, Lucien Hubbard; camera, Lucien Andriot.

Owen Moore (Cal Thurman); Constance Bennett (Georgia May Stockwell); Mabel Ballin (Mary Stockwell); Charles Ogle (Henry Thurman); David Butler (Bid Hatfield); George Bancroft (Enoch Thurman); Gertrude Short (Mollie Thurman); Lillian Leighton (Ma Thurman); Edward Gribbon (Tuck Merry); Pat Hartigan (Cal Bloom); Frankie Lee (Bud).

WANDERING FIRES (Arrow, 1925) 5,866′

Producer-director, Maurice Campbell; story, Warner Fabian; camera, Harry Stradling.

Constance Bennett (Guerda Anthony); George Hackathorne (Raymond Carroll); Wallace MacDonald (Norman Yuell); Effie Shannon (Mrs. Satorius); Henrietta Crosman (Mrs. Carroll).

MY SON   (FN, 1925) 6,552′

Presenter-director, Edwin Carewe; based on the play by Martha M. Stanley; screenplay, Finis Fox; assistant director, Wallace Fox; art director, John D. Schulze; camera, L. W. O'Connell; editor, Laurence Croutz.

Nazimova (Ana Silva); Jack Pickford (Tony, Her Son); Hobart Bosworth (Sheriff Ellery Parker); Ian Keith (Felipe Vargas, a Fisherman); Mary Akin (Rosa Pina); Charles Murray (Captain Joe Bamby); Constance Bennett (Betty Smith); Dot Farley (Hattie Smith).

THE GOOSE WOMAN   (Univ., 1925) 7,500′

Presenter, Carl Laemmle; director, Clarence Brown; based on the story by Rex Beach; screenplay, Melville Brown; titles, Dwinelle Benthall; art director, E. E. Sheeley, William R. Schmidt; assistant director, Charles Dorian; camera, Milton Moore; editor, Ray Curtiss.

Louise Dresser (Mary Holmes/Marie de Nardi); Jack Pickford (Gerald Holmes); Constance Bennett (Hazel Woods); James O. Barrows (Jacob Riggs); George Copper (Reporter); Gustav von Seyffertitz (Mr. Vogel); George Nichols (Detective Lopez); Marc MacDermott (Amos Ethridge).

SALLY, IRENE AND MARY   (MGM, 1925) 5,564′

Director, Edmund Goulding; based on the play by Edward Dowling, Cyrus Wood; screenplay, Goulding; art director, Cedric Gibbons, Merrill Pye; camera, John Arnold; editor, Harold Young, Arthur Johns.

Constance Bennett (Sally); Joan Crawford (Irene); Sally O'Neil (Mary); William Haines (Jimmy Dugan); Henry Kolker (Marcus Morton); Douglas Gilmore (Nester); Ray Howard (College Kid); Kate Price (Mrs. Dugan); Aggie Herring (Mrs. O'Brien); Sam De Grasse (Officer O'Dare); Lillian Elliott (Mrs. O'Dare); Edna Mae Cooper (Maggie).

THE PINCH HITTER   (Associated Exhibitors, 1925) 6,259′

Director, Joseph Henabery; story, C. Gardner Sullivan; camera, Jules Cronjager.

Glenn Hunter (Joel Martin); Constance Bennett (Abby Nettleton); Jack Drumier (Obadiah Parker); Reginald Sheffield (Alexis Thompson); Antrim Short (Jimmy Slater); George Cline (Coach Nolan); Mary Foy (Aunt Martha); James E. Sullivan (College Dean); Joseph Burke (Charlie).

THIS THING CALLED LOVE   (Pathé, 1929) 6,697′

Associate producer, Ralph Block; director, Paul L. Stein; based on the play by Edwin Burke; screenplay, Horace Jackson; art director, Edward Jewell; assistant director, E. J. Babille; sound, Charles O'Laughlin, Ben Winkler; camera, Norbert Brodin; editor, Duane Harrison.

Edmund Lowe (Robert Collings); Constance Bennett (Ann Marvin); Roscoe Karns (Harry Bertrand); ZaSu Pitts (Clara Bertrand); Carmelita Geraghty (Alvarez Guerra); John Roche (de Witt); Stuart Erwin (Fred); Ruth Taylor (Dolly); Wilson Benge (Dumary); Adele Watson (Secretary); Jean Harlow (Bit).

RICH PEOPLE   (Pathé, 1929) 75 M.

Associate producer, Ralph Block; director, Edward H. Griffith; stager, Anthony Brown; based on the story by Jay Gelzer; screenplay, A. A. Kline; art director, Edward Jewell; set decorator, Ted Dickson; costumes, Gwen Wakeling; assistant director, E. J. Babille; sound, George Ellis, Cliff Stein; camera, Norbert Brodine; editor, Charles Craft.

Constance Bennett (Connie Hayden); Regis Toomey (Jeff MacLean); Robert Ames (Noel Nevins); Mahlon Hamilton (Beverly Hayden); Ilka Chase (Margery Mears); John Loder (Captain Danforth); Polly Ann Young (Sally Vanderwater).

SON OF THE GODS   (FN, 1930) 93 M.

Director, Frank Lloyd; based on the story by Rex Beach; screenplay, Bradley King; song, Ben Ryan and Sol Violinsky; camera, Ernest Haller.

Richard Barthelmess (Sam Lee); Constance Bennett (Allana); Dorothy Mathews (Alice Hart); Barbara Leonard (Mabel); James Eagles (Spud); Frank Albertson (Kicker); Mildred Van Dorn (Eileen); King Hoo Chang (Moy); Geneva Mitchell (Connie); E. Alyn Warren (Lee Ying); Ivan Christie (Cafe Manager); Anders Randolf (Wagner); George Irving (Attorney); Claude King (Bathurst); Dickie Moore (Boy); Robert Homans (Dugan).

COMMON CLAY   (Fox, 1930) 68 M.

Presenter, William Fox; director, Victor Fleming; based on the novel by Cleves Kincaid; screenplay, Jules Furthman; assistant director, William Tummel; set decorator, William Darling; costumes, Sophie Wachner; sound, B. J. Kroger, Eugene Grossman; camera, Glen MacWilliams; editor, Irene Morra.

Constance Bennett (Ellen Neal); Lew Ayres (Hugh Fullerton); Tully Marshall (W. H. Yates); Matty Kemp (Arthur Coakley); Purnell B. Pratt (Richard Fullerton); Beryl Mercer (Mrs. Neal); Charles McNaughton (Edwards); Hale Hamilton (Judge Samuel Filson); Genevieve Blinn (Mrs. Fullerton); Ada Williams (Hugh's Sister).

THREE FACES EAST   (WB, 1930) 71 M.

Producer, Darryl F. Zanuck; director, Roy Del Ruth; based on the play by Anthony Paul Kelly; screenplay, Oliver H. P. Garrett, Arthur Caesar; sound, Harry D. Mills; camera, Chick McGill; editor, William Holmes.

Constance Bennett (Frances Hawtree/Z-1); Erich Von Stroheim (Valdar [Schiller: Blecher]); Anthony Bushell (Captain Arthur Chamberlain); William Holden (Sir Winston Chamberlain); William Courtenay (Yates); Charlotte Walker (Lady Catherine Chamberlain); Craufurd Kent (General Hewlett); Ulrich Haupt (Colonel); William Von Brincken (Kruger, an Aide); Paul Panzer ("Kirsch," the Decoy).

SIN TAKES A HOLIDAY   (Pathé, 1930) 86 M.

Producer, E. B. Derr; director, Paul L. Stein; story, Robert Milton, Dorothy Cairns; screenplay, Horace Jackson; art director, Carroll Clark; assistant director, E. J. Babille; costumes, Gwen Wakeling; sound, Charles O'Loughlin, L. A. Carmen; camera, John Mescall; editor, Daniel Mandell.

Constance Bennett (Sylvia); Kenneth MacKenna (Gaylord Stanton); Basil Rathbone (Durant); Rita La Roy (Grace); Louis John Bartels (Richards); John Roche (Sheridan); ZaSu Pitts (Anna); Kendall Lee (Miss Munson); Murrell Finley (Ruth); Judith Wood (Miss Graham); Fred Walton (Butler).

THE EASIEST WAY   (MGM, 1931) 86 M.

Director, Jack Conway; based on the play by Eugene Walter; screenplay, Edith Ellis; sound, J. Russell Franks; gowns, Rene Hubert; art director, Cedric Gibbons; camera, John Mescall; editor, Frank Sullivan.

Constance Bennett (Laura Murdock); Adolphe Menjou (Willard Brockton); Robert Montgomery (Johnny Madison); Anita Page (Peg Murdock); Marjorie Rambeau (Elfie St. Clair); J. Farrell MacDonald (Ben Murdock); Clara Blandick (Agnes Murdock); Clark Gable (Nick Felici); Francis Palmer Tilton (Artist); Charles Judels (Genster); Johnny Harron (Chris Swobeda); Bill O'Brien (Wales—Butler); Hedda Hopper (Clara Williams); Dell Henderson (Bud Williams); Lynton Brent (Associate).

BORN TO LOVE   (RKO-Pathé, 1931) 84 M.

Director, Paul L. Stein; story-screenplay, Ernest Pascal; sound, Charles O'Laughlin, Ben Winkler; camera, John Mescall; editor, Claude Berkeley.

Constance Bennett (Doris Kendall); Joel McCrea (Barry Craig); Paul Cavanagh (Sir Wilfred Drake); Frederick Kerr (Lord Ponsonby); Anthony Bushell (Leslie Darrow); Louise Closser Hale (Lady Agatha Ponsonby); Mary Forbes (Duchess); Elizabeth Forrester (Evelyn Kent); Edmund Breon (Tom Kent); Reginald Sharland (Foppish Gentleman); Daisy Belmore (Tibbetts); Martha Mattox (Head Nurse); Fred Esmelton (Butler); Eddy Chandler (Captain Peters); Robert Greig (Hansom Cabby); Eily Malyon (Nurse); Olaf Hytten (Aide to Major General); Billy Bevan (Departing British Soldier); Bill Elliott (Extra at Hotel Desk).

THE COMMON LAW   (RKO-Pathé, 1931) 77 M.

Producer, Charles R. Rogers; associate producer, Harry Joe Brown; director, Paul L. Stein; based on the novel by Robert W. Chambers; screenplay, John Farrow; dialog, Horace Jackson; art director, Carroll Clark; costumes, Gwen Wakeling; music director, Arthur Lange; sound, Earl Wolcott, J. Grubb; camera, Hal Mohr; editor, Charles Craft.

Constance Bennett (Valerie West); Joel McCrea (John Neville, Jr.); Lew Cody (Cardemon); Robert Williams (Sam); Hedda Hopper (Mrs. Clare Collis); Marion Shilling (Stephanie Brown); Paul Ellis (Querido); Walter Walker (John Neville, Sr.); Emile Chautard (Doorman); George Irving (Doctor); Nella Walker (Yacht Guest); Dolores Murray (Queen at the Ball).

BOUGHT   (WB, 1931) 70 M.

Director, Archie Mayo; based on the novel *Jackdaw's Strut* by Harriet Henry; screenplay, Charles Kenyon, Raymond Griffith; camera, Ray June; editor, George Marks.

Constance Bennett (Stephany Dale); Ben Lyon (Nicky Amory); Richard Bennett (Dave Meyer); Dorothy Peterson (Mrs. Dale); Ray Milland (Charles Carter); Doris Lloyd (Mrs. Barry); Maude Eburne (Mrs. Chauncy); Mae Madison (Natalie Ransome); Clara Blandick (Miss Sprigg); Arthur Stuart Hull (Carter, Sr.); Edward J. Nugent (Jimmy Graham); Paul Porcasi (Rapello).

LADY WITH A PAST   (RKO-Pathé, 1932) 80 M.

Producer, Charles R. Rogers; associate producer, Harry Joe Brown; director, Edward H. Griffith.

Constance Bennett (Venice Muir); Ben Lyon (Guy Bryson); David Manners (Donnie Wainwright); Don Alvarado (The Argentine); Albert Conti (Rene); Merna Kennedy (Ann Duryea); Blanche Frederici (Nora); Astrid Allwyn (Lola); Nella Walker (Aunt Emma); Helene Millard (Mrs. Bryson); John Roche (Karl); Donald Dillaway (Jerry); Freeman Wood (Patterson); Cornelius Keefe (Spaulding); George Irving (Mr. Patridge); Arnold Lucy (Butler); Bruce Cabot (Dance Extra); Don Terry (Friend); Bill Elliott (Brown).

WHAT PRICE HOLLYWOOD?   (RKO-Pathé, 1932) 87 M.

Executive producer, David O. Selznick; associate producer, Pandro S. Berman; director, George Cukor; based on the story by Adela Rogers St. John; adaptation, Gene Fowler, Rowland Brown; screenplay, Jane Murfin, Ben Markson; art director,

Carroll Clark; music director, Max Steiner; montages, Slavko Vorkapich; costumes, Margaret Pemberton; camera, Charles Rosher; editor, Jack Kitchin.

Constance Bennett (Mary Evans); Lowell Sherman (Maximilian Carey); Neil Hamilton (Lonny Borden); Gregory Ratoff (Julius Saxe); Brooks Benedict (Muto); Louise Beavers (Bonita, the Maid); Eddie Anderson (James); Bryant Washburn (Washed-up Star); Florence Roberts (Diner); Gordon DeMain (Yes Man); Heinie Conklin (Car Owner); Eddie Dunn (Doorman at Grauman's Chinese Theatre); Phil Teal (Jimmy, Assistant Director).

TWO AGAINST THE WORLD   (WB, 1932) 71 M.

Director, Archie Mayo; based on the novel *A Dangerous Set* by Marion Dix, Jerry Horwin; screenplay, Sheridan Bigney; camera, Charles Rosher; editor, Bert Levy.

Constance Bennett (Dell Hamilton); Neil Hamilton (Dave Norton); Helen Vinson (Corinne); Allen Vincent (Bob); Gavin Gordon (Victor Linley); Maude Truax (Dowager); Clara Blandick (Aunt Agatha); Alan Mowbray (George); Leila Bennett (Bootlegger); Oscar Apfel (District Attorney); Dennis O'Keefe (Dance Extra).

ROCKABYE   (RKO-Pathé, 1932) 75 M.

Executive producer, David O. Selznick; director, George Cukor; based on the play by Lucia Bronder; screenplay, Jane Murfin; art director, Carroll Clark; music director, Max Steiner; songs, Nacio Herb Brown and Harry Akst; Jeanne Borlini and Edward Eliscu; sound, George D. Ellis; camera, Charles Rosher; editor, George Hively.

Constance Bennett (Judy Carroll); Joel McCrea (Jacobs Van Riker Pell); Paul Lukas (Anthony de Sola); Jobyna Howland ("Snooks" Carroll); Walter Pidgeon (Comm. Al Howard); Clara Blandick (Brida); Walter Catlett (Jimmy Dunn); Virginia Hammond (Mrs. Van Riker Pell); J. M. Kerrigan (Fagin); June Filmer (Lilybet); Charles Middleton (D.A.); Lita Chevret (Party Guest); Edgar Kennedy (Driver); Sterling Holloway (Speakeasy Customer); Edwin Stanley (Defense Attorney); Richard Carle (Doc).

OUR BETTERS   (RKO, 1933) 82 M.

Executive producer, David O. Selznick; director, George Cukor; based on the play by W. Somerset Maugham; screenplay, Jane Murfin, Harry Wagstaff Gribble; technical advisor, Elsa Maxwell; costumes, Hattie Carnegie; art director, Van Nest Polglase; interiors, Hobe Erwin; music director, Max Steiner; sound, George D. Ellis; camera, Charles Rosher; editor, Jack Kitchin.

Constance Bennett (Lady Pearl Grayston); Violet Kemble-Cooper (The Duchess); Phoebe Foster (Princess); Charles Starrett (Fleming Harvey); Grant Mitchell (Thornton Clay); Anita Louise (Bessie); Gilbert Roland (Pepi D'Costa); Minor Watson (Arthur Fenwick); Hugh Sinclair (Lord Henry Blayne); Alan Mowbray (Lord George Grayston); Harold Entwistle (Poole); Tyrell Davis (Ernest); Virginia Howell (Mrs. Saunders); Walter Walker (Mr. Saunders).

BED OF ROSES   (RKO, 1933) 67 M.

Producer, Merian C. Cooper; associate producer, Pandro Berman; director, Gregory La Cava; story-adaptation, Wanda Tuchok; screenplay, Tuchok, Eugene Thackrey; art director, Van Nest Polglase, Charles Kirk; music director, Max Steiner; assistant director, Edward Kelly; sound, George Ellis; camera, Charles Rosher; editor, Basil Wrangel.

Constance Bennett (Lorry Evans); Joel McCrea (Dan); Pert Kelton (Minnie); Samuel S. Hinds (Father Doran); John Halliday (Steve Paige).

AFTER TONIGHT   (RKO, 1933) 71 M.

Executive producer, Merian C. Cooper; associate producer, H. N. Swanson; director, George Archainbaud; story, Jane Murfin; screenplay, Murfin, Albert Shelby LeVino, Worthington Miner; art director, Van Nest Polglase, Al Herman; music director, Max Steiner; sound, John L. Cass; song, Steiner; camera, Charles Rosher; editor, William Hamilton.

Constance Bennett (Carla [K-14]); Gilbert Roland (Captain Rudi Riber); Edward Ellis (Major Lieber); Sam Godfrey (Franz); Lucien Prival (Erlich); Mischa Auer (Adjutant Lehar); Ben Hendricks, Jr. (Sergeant Probert); Leonid Snegoff (Private Muller); Evelyn Carter Carrington (Frau Stengel); John Wray (Major Mitika); Vera Lewis (Anna Huber, a Cleaner); William Wagner (Overcoat Spy); Edward Keane (Intelligence Officer); William von Brincken (Captain—Officer of the Day); Hans Furberg (Man); Adrienne d'Ambricourt (Woman); Herman Bing (Railroad Ticket Clerk); George Davis (Frenchman); Frank O'Connor (Officer on Train); Selmer Jackson (Spy); Julie Haydon (Hysterical Nurse); Frank Reicher (Major—Medical Officer); Hooper Atchley (Contact Who Is Captured); Landers Stevens (Major); Major Sam Harris (German Officer); Virginia Weidler (Olga, Carla's Niece).

MOULIN ROUGE   (UA, 1934) 69 M.

Producer, Darryl F. Zanuck; associate producer, William Goetz, Raymond Griffith; director, Sidney Lanfield; based on the play by Lyon de Bri; adaptation, Nunnally Johnson, Henry Lehrman; music director, Alfred Newman; songs, Al Dubin and Harry Warren; choreography, Russell Markert; camera, Charles Rocher; editor, Lloyd Nibley.

Constance Bennett (Helen Hunt/Raquel); Franchot Tone (Douglas Hall); Tullio Carminati (Victor Le Maire); Helen Westley (Mrs. Morris); Andrew Tombes (McBride); Russ Brown (Joe); Hobart Cavanagh (Drunk); Georges Renevant (Frenchman); Fuzzy Knight (Eddie); Russ Columbo, The Boswell Sisters (Themselves); Ivan Lebedeff (Ramon).

THE AFFAIRS OF CELLINI   (UA, 1934) 90 M.

Producer, Darryl F. Zanuck; associate producer, William Goetz, Raymond Griffith; director, Gregory La Cava; based on the play *The Firebrand* by Edwin Justus Mayer; screenplay, Bess Meredyth; music, Alfred Newman; assistant director, Fred Fox; ballet master, Adolph Bolm; camera, Charles Rosher; editor, Barbara McLean.

Fredric March (Benvenuto Cellini); Constance Bennett (Duchess of Florence); Frank Morgan (Alessandro, Duke of Florence); Fay Wray (Angela); Vince Barnett (Ascanio); Jessie Ralph (Beatrice); Louis Calhern (Ottaviano); Jay Eaton (Polverino); Paul Harvey (Emissary); John Rutherford (Captain of Guards); Irene Ware (Girl); Lucille Ball (Lady-in-Waiting); Lionel Belmore (Court Member); Harry Wilson (Henchman); Ward Bond, James Flavin (Guards); Constantine Romanoff, Theodore Lorch (Executioners); Lane Chandler (Jailer); Russ Powell (Servant); Dewey Robinson (Steward).

OUTCAST LADY   (MGM, 1934) 79 M.

Director, Robert Z. Leonard; story, Michael Arlen; screenplay, Zoe Akins; camera, Charles Rosher, William Le Vanway.

Constance Bennett (Iris March); Herbert Marshall (Napier Harpenden); Mrs. Patrick Campbell (Lady Eve); Hugh Williams (Gerald March); Elizabeth Allan (Venice); Henry Stephenson (Sir Maurice Harpenden); Robert Loraine (Hilary); Lumsden Hare (Guy); Leo Carroll (Dr. Masters); Ralph Forbes (Boy Fenwick); Alec B. Francis (Truble).

AFTER OFFICE HOURS   (MGM, 1935) 73 M.

Producer, Bernard F. Hyman; director, Robert Z. Leonard; story, Laurence Stallings, Dale Van Every; screenplay, Herman J. Mankiewicz; camera, Charles Rosher; editor, Tom Held.

Clark Gable (Jim Branch); Constance Bennett (Sharon Norwood); Stuart Erwin (Hank Parr); Billie Burke (Mrs. Norwood); Harvey Stephens (Tommy Bannister); Katharine Alexander (Mrs. Patterson); Hale Hamilton (Mr. Patterson); Henry Travers (Cop); Henry Armetta (Italian); Charles Richman (Jordan); Herbert Bunston (Barlow); Margaret Dumont (Mrs. Murchison); Mary McLaren (Maid); William Demarest, Pat O'Malley (Detectives); Tom Dugan (Motor Cop); Bud Jamison (Cop); Dale Van Sickel (Dancing Extra).

EVERYTHING IS THUNDER   (Gaumont-British, 1936) 76 M.

Director, Milton Rosmer; based on the novel by J. B. Hardy; screenplay, Marion Dix, John Orton; camera, G. Krampf.

Constance Bennett (Anna); Douglass Montgomery (Hugh McGrath); Oscar Homolka (Detective Gretz); Roy Emerton (Kostner); Frederick Lloyd (Muller); George Merrit (Webber).

LADIES IN LOVE   (20th, 1936) 97 M.

Producer, B. G. DeSylva; director, Edward H. Griffith; based on the play by Ladislaus Bus-Fekete; screenplay, Melville Baker; music director, Louis Silvers; camera, Hal Mohr; editor, Ralph Dietrich.

Janet Gaynor (Martha Kerenye); Loretta Young (Susie Schmidt); Constance Bennett (Yoli Haydn); Simone Simon (Marie Armand); Don Ameche (Dr. Rudi Imre); Paul Lukas (John Barta); Tyrone Power (Karl Lanyi); Alan Mowbray (Paul Sandor); Wilfrid Lawson (Ben Horvath); J. Edward Bromberg (Brenner); Virginia Field (Countess Helena); Frank Dawson (Johann); Egon Brecher (Concierge); Vesey O'Davoren (Fritz); Hayne Regan (Mrs. Dreker); John Bleifer (Porter); Eleanor Weselhoeft (Charwoman); William Brisbane (Chauffeur); Monty Woolley (Man in Box Seat); Lynn Bari (Clerk).

TOPPER   (MGM, 1937) 97 M.

Producer, Hal Roach; associate producer, Milton H. Bren; director, Norman Z. McLeod; based on the novel by Thorne Smith; screenplay, Jack Jevne, Eric Hatch, Eddie Moran; art director, Arthur Rouce; music arranger, Arthur Morton; music conductor, Marvin Haltey; song, Hoagy Carmichael; camera effects, Roy Seawright; camera, Norbert Brodine; editor, William Terhune.

Constance Bennett (Marion Kerby); Cary Grant (George Kerby); Roland Young (Cosmo Topper); Billie Burke (Henrietta Topper); Alan Mowbray (Wilkins); Eugene Pallette (Casey); Arthur Lake (Elevator Boy); Hedda Hopper (Mrs. Stuyvesant); Virginia Sale (Miss Johnson); Theodore Von Eltz (Hotel Manager); J. Farrell MacDonald (Policeman); Elaine Shepard (Secretary); Doodles Weaver, Si Jenks (Rustics); Three Hits and a Miss (Themselves); Donna Dax (Hat-Check Girl at Rainbow Nightclub); Hoagy Carmichael (Bill, the Piano Player); Claire Windsor, Betty Blythe (Ladies).

MERRILY WE LIVE   (MGM, 1938) 90 M.

Executive producer, Milton H. Bren; producer, Hal Roach; director, Norman Z. McLeod; screenplay, Eddie Moran, Jack Jevne; art director, Charles D. Hall; song, Paul Charig and Arthur Quenzer; music director, Marvin Hatley; special effects, Roy Seawright; camera, Norbert Brodine; editor, William Terhune.

Constance Bennett (Jerry Kilbourne); Brian Aherne (Wade Rawlins); Billie Burke (Mrs. Emily Kilbourne); Alan Mowbray (Grosvenor); Patsy Kelly (Rosa, the Cook); Ann Dvorak (Minerva Harlan); Tom Brown (Kane Kilbourne); Bonita Granville (Marion Kilbourne); Marjorie Rambeau (Senator's Wife); Phillip Reed (Herbert Wheeler); Clarence Kolb (Mr. Kilbourne); Marjorie Kane (Rosa, the Maid); Paul Everton (Senator); Willie Best (G. W. Jones).

SERVICE DE LUXE   (Univ., 1938) 85 M.

Associate producer, Edmund Grainger; director, Rowland V. Lee; story, Bruce Manning, Vera Caspary; screenplay, Gertrude Purcell, Leonard Spigelgass; camera, George Robinson; editor, Ted J. Kent.

Constance Bennett (Helen Murphy); Vincent Price (Robert Wade); Charles Ruggles (Robinson); Helen Broderick (Pearl); Mischa Auer (Bibenko); Joy Hughes (Audrey); Frances Robinson (Secretary); Halliwell Hobbes (Butler); Raymond Parker, Frank Coghlan, Jr. (Bellhops); Nina Gilbert (Mrs. Devereaux).

TOPPER TAKES A TRIP   (UA, 1939) 85 M.

Producer, Hal Roach; associate producer, Milton H. Bren; director, Norman Z. McLeod; based on the novel by Thorne Smith; screenplay, Eddie Moran, Jack Jevne, Corey Ford; special effects, Roy Seawright; art director, Charles D. Hall; camera, Norbert Brodine; editor, William Terhune.

Constance Bennett (Marion Kerby); Roland Young (Cosmo Topper); Billie Burke (Clara Topper); Alan Mowbray (Wilkins); Verree Teasdale (Nancy Parkhurst); Franklin Pangborn (Louis); Alexander D'Arcy (Baron de Rossi); Skippy (Mr. Atlas); Paul Hurst (Bartender); Eddy Conrad (Jailer); Spencer Charters (Judge Wilson); Irving Pichel (Prosecutor); Paul Everton (Defender); Duke York (Gorgan); Leon Belasco (Bellboy); Georges Renavent (Magistrate); George Humbert, Alphonse Martell (Waiters); James Morton (Bailiff); Torben Meyer (Doorman); George Davis (Porter); Armand Kaliz (Clerk); Cary Grant (George Kerby—in scenes from *Topper*).

TAIL SPIN   (20th, 1939) 84 M.

Producer, Darryl F. Zanuck; associate producer, Harry Joe Brown; director, Roy Del Ruth; screenplay, Frank Wead; art director, Bernard Herzbrun, Rudolph Sternad; set decorator, Thomas Little; costumes, Gwen Wakeling; technical director, Paul Mantz, Clifford W. Henderson; music director, Louis Silvers; song, Mack Gordon and Harry Revel; sound, Eugene Grossman, Roger Heman; camera, Karl Freund; editor, Allen McNeil.

Alice Faye (Trixie Lee); Constance Bennett (Gerry Lester); Nancy Kelly (Lois Allen); Joan Davis (Babe Dugan); Charles Farrell (Bud); Jane Wyman (Alabama); Kane Richmond (Dick "Tex" Price); Wally Vernon (Chick); Joan Valerie (Sunny); Edward Norris (Speed Allen); J. Anthony Hughes (Al Moore); Harry Davenport (T. P. Lester); Mary Gordon (Mrs. Lee); Harry Rosenthal (Cafe Manager); Irving Bacon (Storekeeper); Sam Hayes (Announcer).

SUBMARINE ZONE   (Col., 1941) 74 M.

Producer, Sam Bischoff; director, John Brahm; story, Sidney Biddell, Frederic Frank; screenplay, P. J. Wolfson; camera, Franz Planer; editor, Al Clark.

Pat O'Brien (Mike Farrough); Constance Bennett (Christine Blaine); John Halliday (John Morgan); Melville Cooper (Penney); Alan Baxter (Larry Perrin); Edgar Buchanan (Charles Atterbee); Marjorie Gateson (Mrs. Winslow); Francis Pierlot (Professor Mudge); Jessie Busley (Mrs. Mudge); Stanley Logan (Captain Hollister); Frank Sully (Tommy Malone); Erwin Kalser (Dr. Behrens); Don Beddoe (Chief

Engineer); Leslie Denison, Rex Post (First Mates); Bruce Bennett (Lieutenant); Dick Rich (Harry); Wyndham Standing (Man); Frank Baker, Arthur Mulliner (Detectives); Olaf Hytten (Agent); Frank Benson, Dave Dunbar, Bobby Hale, Jimmie Kilgannon (Sailors); Jean Prescott (Mrs. Hollister); Hans Schumann (Submarine Commander); Norbert Schiller (Submarine First Officer); Franz Von Altenberger (Submarine Radio Operator); Fred Wolff, Hans Von Morhart, Paul Michael (German Sailors); Arno Frey (Submarine Gunner); Douglas Gordon (Lookout).

LAW OF THE TROPICS (WB, 1941) 76 M.

Associate producer, Ben Stoloff; director, Ray Enright; based on the novel *Oil for the Lamps of China* by Alice Tisdale Hobart; screenplay, Charles Grayson; music, Howard Jackson; dialog director, Jo Graham; camera, Sid Hickox; editor, Frederick Richards.

Constance Bennett (Joan Madison); Jeffrey Lynn (Jim Conway); Regis Toomey (Tom Marshall); Mona Maris (Rita Marshall); Frank Puglia (Tito); Thomas Jackson (Lieutenant Maguire); Paul Harvey (Alfred King); Craig Stevens (Alfred King, Jr.); Hobart Bosworth (Boss Frank Davis); Charles Judels (Captain); Cliff Clark (Bartender); Roland Drew (Desk Clerk); Luis Alberni (Native); Martin Garralaga (Pedro, the Bookkeeper); Creighton Hale (Wilson, the Clerk); Rolfe Sedan (Julio Andre, the Tailor); Demetrius Emanuel (Waiter); Paco Moreno (Vendor); Anna Demetrio (Maria, the Vendor); Don Orlando (Messenger); John Eberts, Juan Duval (Natives); Mayta Palmera (Dancer); Dale Van Sickel (Double for Craig Stevens).

TWO-FACED WOMAN (MGM, 1941) 94 M.

Producer, Gottfried Reinhardt; director, George Cukor; based on a play by Ludwig Fulda; screenplay, Sidney H. Behrman, Salka Viertel, George Oppenheimer; art director, Cedric Gibbons, Daniel B. Cathcart; set decorators, Edwin B. Willis, Cathcart; choreography, Bob Alton; sound, Douglas Shearer; costumes, Adrian; music, Bronislau Kaper; orchestrator, Leo Arnold; camera, Joseph Ruttenberg; editor, George Boemler.

Greta Garbo (Karin); Melvyn Douglas (Larry Blake); Constance Bennett (Griselda Vaughn); Roland Young (O. O. Miller); Robert Sterling (Dick Williams); Ruth Gordon (Miss Ellis); George Cleveland (Sheriff); George P. Huntley, Jr. (Mr. Wilson); James Spencer (Carl); William Tannen (Ski Guide); Frances Carson (Miss Dunbar); John Marston (Graham); Olive Blakeney (Phyllis); Douglas Newland, Roy Gordon (Men); Hilda Plowright, Eula Guy (Women); Mary Young (Wife); Mark Daniels (Bellboy); Vinton Haworth (Guide); Connie Gilchrist, Bess Flowers (Receptionists); Paul Leyssac, Cliff Danielson (Clerks); Walter Anthony Merrill (Stage Manager); Arno Frey (Waiter); Andre Cheron (Headwaiter); Lorin Raker, Tom Herbert, Grace Hayle, Emily Fitzroy (Rhumba Dancers); George Calliga (Hotel Clerk); Gloria De Haven, Michaele Fallon (Debutantes); Robert Alton (Cecil).

WILD BILL HICKOK RIDES (WB, 1941) 81 M.

Associate producer, Edmund Grainger; director, Ray Enright; screenplay, Charles Grayson, Paul Gerard Smith, Raymond Schrock; camera, Ted McCord; editor, Clarence Kolster.

Bruce Cabot (Bill Hickok); Constance Bennett (Belle Andrews); Warren William (Jim Farrel); Betty Brewer (Janey); Walter Catlett (Sylvester Edmunds); Howard da Silva (Ringo); Frank Wilcox (Martin); Faye Emerson (Peg); Julie Bishop (Violet); Lucia Carroll (Flora); Russell Simpson (Nolan); J. Farrell MacDonald (Judge Hathaway); Lillian Yarbo (Daisy); Cliff Clark (Kersey); Trevor Bardette (Sam Bass); Elliott Sullivan (Bart Hanna); Dick Botiller (Sager); Ray Teal (Beadle).

SIN TOWN (Univ., 1942) 73 M.

Producer, George Waggner; director, Ray Enright; screenplay, W. Scott Darling, Gerald Geraghty; additional dialog, Richard Brooks; assistant director, Gil Valle; art director, Jack Otterson; music director, H. J. Salter; camera, George Robinson; editor, Edward Curtiss.

Constance Bennett (Kye Allen); Broderick Crawford (Dude McNair); Anne Gwynne (Laura Kirby); Patric Knowles (Wade Crowell); Andy Devine (Judge Eustace Vale); Leo Carrillo (Angelo Colins); Ward Bond (Rock Delaney); Arthur Aylsworth (Sheriff Bagby); Ralf Harolde (Kentucky Jones); Charles Wagenheim (Dry Hole); Billy Wayne (Hollister); Hobart Bosworth (Humiston); Bryant Washburn (Anderson); Jack Mulhall (Hanson); Paul Bryar (Grady); Oscar O'Shea (Conductor); Eddy Waller (Forager); Clarence Muse (Porter); Ben Erway (Dr. Pendergrast); Ed Peil, Sr. (Hedges); Harry Strang (Jessup); Guy Usher (Man on Train); Rebel Randall, Jean Trent (Dance Hall Girls); Victor Zimmerman, George Lewis, Ed Peil, Sr. (Oil Men); Larry McGrath (Stick Men); Murray Parker (Juggler); Frank Hagney (Bartender); Neely Edwards, Jack C. Smith (Gamblers); Kernan Cripps, Art Miles, Charles Marsh, Frank Coleman (Men).

MADAME SPY (Univ., 1942) 63 M.

Associate producer, Marshall Grant; director, Roy Neill; story, Clarence Upton Young; screenplay, Lynn Riggs, Young; camera, George Robinson; editor, Ted J. Kent.

Constance Bennett (Joan Bannister); Don Porter (David Bannister); John Litel (Peter); Edward S. Brophy (Mike Reese); John Eldredge (Carl Gordon); Nana Bryant (Alicia Rolf); Selmer Jackson (Harrison Woods); Edmund MacDonald (Drake); Jimmy Conlin (Winston); Nino Pipitone (Miro); Cliff Clark (Inspector Varden); Johnny Berkes (Hotel Clerk); Grace Hayle, Norma Drury, Mira McKinney (Red Cross Women); Billy Wayne (Driver's Helper); Pat West (Driver); Reid Kilpatrick (Announcer); William Gould (Minister); Phil Warren (Reporter); Anne O'Neal (Woman); John Dilson (Proprietor); Thornton Edwards (Foreign Cab Driver); Irving Mitchell (Man); Sidney Miller (Newsboy); Alexander Lockwood, Charles Sherlock, Pat Costello, Frank Marlowe (Cab Drivers); Eddie Coke (Attendant); Rico de Montez (Filipino Servant); Gerald Pierce (Page Boy).

PARIS—UNDERGROUND (UA, 1945) 97 M.

Executive producer, Constance Bennett; executive assistant producer, Carley Harriman; director, Gregory Ratoff; based on the novel by Etta Shiber; screenplay, Boris Ingster, Gertrude Purcell; production designer, Nicolai Remisoff; art director, Victor Greene; set decorator, Sydney Moore; music, Alexander Tansman; music supervisor, David Chudnow; assistant director, Ad Schaumer; sound, John Carter; camera, Lee Garmes; editor, James Newcom.

Constance Bennett (Kitty de Mornay); Gracie Fields (Emmyline Quayle); George Rigaud (Andre de Mornay); Kurt Kreuger (Captain Kurt von Weber); Leslie Vincent (Lieutenant Gray); Charles Andre (Father Dominique); Eily Malyon (Madame Martin); Vladimir Sokoloff (Undertaker); Richard Ryan (Mr. Renard).

CENTENNIAL SUMMER (20th, 1946) C—102 M.

Producer-director, Otto Preminger; based on the novel by Albert E. Idell; screenplay, Michael Kanin; art director, Lyle Wheeler, Lee Fuller; set decorator, Thomas Little; songs, Jerome Kern and Oscar Hammerstein II; Leo Robin and E. Y. Harburg; music director, Alfred Newman; orchestrator, Maurice de Packh, Herbert Spencer, Conrad Salinger; assistant director, Arthur Jacobson; choreography, Dorothy Fox; sound,

W. D. Flick, Roger Heman; special camera effects, Fred Sersen; camera, Ernest Palmer; editor, Harry Reynolds.

Jeanne Crain (Julia); Cornel Wilde (Philippe Lascalles); Linda Darnell (Edith); William Eythe (Benjamin Franklin Phelps); Walter Brennan (Jesse Rogers); Constance Bennett (Zenia Lascalles); Dorothy Gish (Harriet); Barbara Whiting (Susanna Rogers); Larry Stevens (Richard Lewis, Esq.); Kathleen Howard (Deborah); Buddy Swan (Dudley Rogers); Charles Dingle (Snodgrass); Avon Long (Specialty); Florida Sanders (Dance Specialty); Gavin Gordon (Trowbridge); Eddie Dunn (Mr. Phelps); Lois Austin (Mrs. Phelps); Harry Strang (Mr. Dorgan); Frances Morris (Mrs. Dorgan); Reginald Sheffield (President Grant); William Frambes (Messenger Boy); Paul Everton (Senator); John Farrell (Drunk); Billy Wayne (Attendant); Robert Malcolm (Kelly, the Engineer); Edna Holland (Nurse); Ferris Taylor (Governor); Winifred Harris (Governor's Wife); Clancy Cooper, Budd Fine (Carpenters); Roger Neury, Perc Launders (Waiters); Alexander Sacha, Peter Conrad (Frenchmen); William Forrest, Jr. (Man); Sam McDaniel, Nicodemus Stewart, Fred "Snowflake" Toones, Napoleon Whiting (Redcaps); Hans Moebus (Used in Still Pictures); Rodney Bell (Emcee); Joe Whitehead (Railroad Clerk); Alex Melesh, Max Willenz ("Napoleons").

THE UNSUSPECTED (WB, 1947) 103 M.

Producer, Charles Hoffman; associate producer, George Amy; director, Michael Curtiz; story, Charlotte Armstrong; adaptation, Bess Meredyth; screenplay, Ranald MacDougall; art director, Anton Grot; set decorator, Howard Winterbottom; music, Fran Waxman; music director, Leo F. Forbstein; assistant director, Robert Vreeland; sound, Everett A. Brown; special effects, David C. Kertesz; camera, Woody Bredell; editor, Frederick Richards.

Joan Caulfield (Matilda Frazier); Claude Rains (Victor Grandison); Audrey Totter (Althea Keane); Constance Bennett (Jane Maynihan); Hurd Hatfield (Oliver Keane); Michael North (Steven Francis Howard); Fred Clark (Richard Donovan); Harry Lewis (Max); Jack Lambert (Mr. Press); Ray Walker (Donovan's Assistant); Nana Bryant (Mrs. White); Walter Baldwin (Justice of the Peace).

SMART WOMAN (Mon., 1948) 93 M.

Producer, Hal E. Chester; associate producer, Bernard W. Burton; director, Edward A. Blatt; story, Leo Gutterman, Edwin V. Westrate; adaptation, Adela Rogers St. John; screenplay, Alvah Bessie, Louise Morheim, Herbert Margolis; art director, F. Paul Sylos; set decorator, Ray Boltz, Jr; music, Louis Gruneberg; music director, Constantine Bakaleinikoff; assistant director, Melville Shyer; makeup, Dave Grayson; costumes for Constance Bennett, Adrian; dialog director, G. Joseph Dell; sound, Tom Lambert; camera, Stanley Cortez; editor, Frank Gross; editing supervisor, Otho Lovering.

Brian Aherne (Robert Larrimore); Constance Bennett (Paula Rogers); Barry Sullivan (Frank McCoy); Michael O'Shea (Johnny Simons); James Gleason (Sam); Otto Kruger (District Attorney Bradley Wayne); Isobel Elsom (Mrs. Rogers); Richard Lyon (Rusty); Selena Royle (Mrs. Wayne); Taylor Holmes (Dr. Jasper); John Litel (Clark); Nita Hunter (Patty Wayne); Lee Bonnell (Joe, the Secretary); Benny Baker (Fat Photographer); Al Bridge (Hotel Clerk); Larry Haze (Bellboy); Robert Riordan (Burkette); Phyllis Kennedy (Telephone Operator); Netta Packer (Woman); Wally Walker (Man); John Phillips (Fred Johnson); Willie Best (Porter); Jimmy Ames (Bellhop); George Carleton (Elderly Judge); Paul Bryar (Bartender); Phil Arnold (Elevator Operator); Jack Mower (Bailiff); Ralph Sanford (Petitioner/Man's Voice); Doris Kemper (Woman Driver); Milton Parsons (Conrad, the Witness); Margaret Tracy (Anna, the Maid); Eddie Gribbon (Man in Bar); Iris Adrian (Sob-Sister Newspaper Columnist); Houseley

Stevenson (Joe Smith); Joseph Fields (Paula's Assistant); Gladys Blake (Elsie); John Eldredge (Lester Flynn, the Reporter); Lesley Farley (Woman in Bar); Charles Lane, Wallace Scott, Peter Virgo (Reporters); Douglas Aylesworth (Court Clerk); Lois Austin (Woman Juror); Frank Mayo (Uniformed Guard); Paul Maxey (Wise); Jimmy Conlin (Miller, the Printer); John H. Elliott (Harker); Horace MacMahon (Lefty); Edward Gargan (Interrogator); Harry Strang, Michael Gaddis, Stanley Blystone (Cops); Cliff Clark (Police Captain).

ANGEL ON THE AMAZON   (Rep., 1948) 86 M.

Associate producer-director, John H. Auer; story, Earl Felton; screenplay, Lawrence Kimble; art director, James Sullivan; set decorator, John McCarthy, Jr., George Milo; music, Nathan Scott; music director, Morton Scott; assistant director, Lee Lukather; makeup, Bob Mark; sound, Victor B. Appel, Howard Wilson; special effects, Howard and Theodore Lydecker; camera, Reggie Lanning; editor, Richard L. Van Enger.

George Brent (Jim Warburton); Vera Ralston (Christine Ridgeway); Brian Aherne (Anthony Ridgeway); Constance Bennett (Dr. Karen Lawrence); Fortunio Bonanova (Sebastian Ortega); Alfonso Bedoya (Paulo); Gus Schilling (Dean Hartley); Richard Crane (Johnny MacMahon); Walter Reed (Jerry Adams); Ross Elliott (Frank Lane); Konstantin Shayne (Dr. Jungmeyer); Charles LaTorre, John Trebach (Waiters); Elizabeth Dunne (Housekeeper); Alberto Morin (Radio Operator); Dick Jones (George); Alfredo DeSa (Brazilian Reporter); Tony Martinez (Bellhop); Gerardo Sei Groves (Native); Manuel Paris (Night Desk Clerk).

AS YOUNG AS YOU FEEL   (20th, 1951) 77 M.

Producer, Lamar Trotti; director, Harmon Jones; story, Paddy Chayevsky; screenplay, Trotti; art director, Lyle Wheeler, Maurice Ransford; music director, Lionel Newman; camera, Joe MacDonald; editor, Robert Simpson.

Monty Woolley (John Hodges); Thelma Ritter (Della Hodges); David Wayne (Joe); Jean Peters (Alice Hodges); Constance Bennett (Lucille McKinley); Marilyn Monroe (Harriet); Allyn Joslyn (George Hodges); Albert Dekker (Louis McKinley); Clinton Sundberg (Frank Erickson); Minor Watson (Cleveland); Wally Brown (Gallagher); Rusty Tamblyn (Willie); Ludwig Stossel (Conductor); Renie Riano (Harpist); Roger Moore (Saltonstall); Dick Cogan (Benson); Charles Conrad (Information Clerk); James Griffith (Cashier); Harry Shannon (Kleinbaum); Charles Cane (Rogell); Billy Lechner (Mailboy); Harry Cheshire (President of Chamber of Commerce); Anne Tyrrell (Secretary); Gerald Oliver Smith (Butler); Paul Burns (Printer); Robert Dudley, Houseley Stevenson (Old Men); David Clarke (Chauffeur); Carol Savage (Librarian); Helen Brown (Clancy); Don Beddoe (Head of Sales); Raymond Greenleaf (Vice President); Emerson Treacy (Director of Public Relations); Harry McKim (Page Boy); Frank Wilcox (Lawyer).

IT SHOULD HAPPEN TO YOU   (Col., 1953) 81 M.

Producer, Fred Kohlmar; director, George Cukor; story-screenplay, Garson Kanin; art director, John Meehan; music, Frederick Hollander; assistant director, Earl Bellamy; camera, Charles Lang; editor, Charles Nelson.

Judy Holliday (Gladys Glover); Peter Lawford (Evan Adams III); Jack Lemmon (Pete Sheppard); Michael O'Shea (Brod Clinton); Vaughn Taylor (Entrikin); Connie Gilchrist (Mrs. Riker); Walter Klavun (Bert Piazza); Whit Bissell (Robert Grau); Arthur Gilmore (Don Toddman); Rex Evans (Con Cooley); Heywood Hale Broun (Sour Man); Constance Bennett, Ilka Chase, Wendy Barrie, Melville Cooper (Panelists); Ralph Dumke (Beckhard); Lennie Bremen (Allie); Chick Chandler (Engineer); Frank

Nelson (Salesman); Mary Young (Old Lady Customer); Cora Witherspoon (Saleslady); James Nusser, Edwin Chandler, Stan Malotte, Robert Berger, Earl Keen, George Becwar, Tom Hennesy, Leo Curley (Board Members); Ted Thorpe, Tom Cound (Assistant Photographers); Sandra Lee, Stephany Hampson (Teenagers); Harold J. Kennedy (Photographer); James Hyland (Bartender); Margaret McWade (Elderly Lady); George Kitchel (Lieutenant); Don Richards (Photographer); Jack Kruschen (Joe); Stanley Orr (Makeup Man); Herbert Lytton (Sound Man); John Saxon (Boy Watching Argument in Park).

MADAME X   (Univ., 1966) C—100 M.

Producer, Ross Hunter; director, David Lowell Rich; based on the play by Alexandre Bisson; screenplay, Jean Holloway; assistant director, Doug Green; art director, Alexander Golitzen, George Webb; set decorator, John McCarthy, Howard Bristol; music, Frank Skinner; music supervisor, Joseph Gershenson; gowns, Jean Louis; sound, Waldon O. Watson, Clarence Self; camera, Russell Metty; editor, Milton Carruth.

Lana Turner (Holly Parker); John Forsythe (Clay Anderson); Ricardo Montalban (Phil Benton); Burgess Meredith (Dan Sullivan); Constance Bennett (Estelle Anderson); Keir Dullea (Clay Anderson, Jr.); Warren Stevens (Michael Spalding); John Van Dreelen (Christian Torben); Virginia Grey (Mimsy); Frank Marth (Combs, the Detective); Frank Maxwell (Dr. Evans); Teno Pollick (Manuel Lopez); Teddy Quinn (Clay, Jr.—as a Boy); Joe DeSantis (Carter); Jill Jackson (Police Matron); Neil Hamilton (Scott Lewis); Bing Russell (Sergeant Riley); Matilda Calhan (Miss Monteaux); Karen Verne (Nurse Riborg); Rudolfo Hoyos (Patronc); Jeff Burton (Bromley); Duncan McCleod (Official); Ruben Moreno, George Dega (Men); Mark Miranda (Mexican Boy); Byrd Holland (Cronyn, the Butler); Kris Tel (Danish Woman); Brad Logan, Richard Tretter (Merchant Marines); Paul Bradley (Dancing Extra).

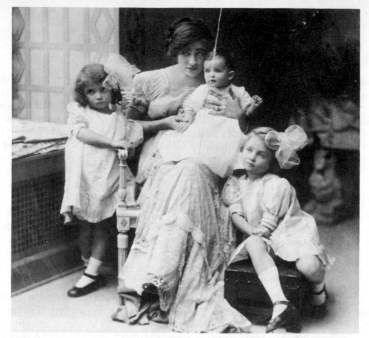

The Bennetts in 1914: Barbara, Mrs. Bennett, Joan and Constance

With Lewis Stone in CYTHEREA (Associated FN '24)

th Edward Peil, Jr., and Myrtle Stedman in THE GOOSE HANGS HIGH
ar '25)

With Joan Crawford and Sally O'Neil in SALLY, IRENE AND MARY (MGM '25)

With Richard Barthelmess i
SON OF THE GODS (FN '30

In mid-1931

With Ben Lyon in LADY WIT
A PAST (RKO-Pathé '3:

With Gene Markey, Joan Bennett, and the Marquis de la Falaise in 1931

th her father, Richard Bennett, in 1931

With Clara Blandick (*second from the left*), Dennis O'Keefe (*rear*), and Neil Hamilton in TWO AGAINST THE WORLD (WB '32)

With June Filmer in ROCKABYE (RKO-Pathé '32)

With Herbert Marshall in OUTCAST LADY (MGM '34)

With Joel McCrea in BED OF ROSES (RKO '33)

With Gloria Swanson, Marion Davies, and Jean Harlow at Davies's 1934 costume party in Hollywood

With Loretta Young and Janet Gaynor in LADIES IN LOVE (20th '36)

Constance Bennett of the fan
magazines (1934)

With Billie Burke, Tom Brown, and Bonita Granville in MERRILY WE LIVE
(MGM '38)

With Helen Broderick in
SERVICE DE LUXE (Univ '38)

With Alice Faye in TAIL SPIN
(20th '39)

With Jeffrey Lynn in LAW OF
THE TROPICS (WB '41)

With John Litel in MADAME
SPY (Univ '42)

With Kurt Kreuger in PARIS
UNDERGROUND (UA '45)

With Dorothy Gish in
CENTENNIAL SUMMER (20th
'46)

With husband Gilbert Roland
and daughter Christina in
April, 1942

With husband-to-be Col. John
Theron Coulter in May, 1948

With Walter Reed in ANGEL
ON THE AMAZON (Rep '48)

In her New York City
nightclub-act debut (April,
1956)

At home, c.

MADAME X (Univ '66)

With Spencer Tracy in A GUY NAMED JOE (MGM '43)

5'5"
115 pounds
Brown hair
Hazel eyes
Sagittarius

Irene Dunne

In the annals of the cinema there have been few more versatile or gracious screen luminaries than Irene Dunne. No one more rightfully deserved the title, "First Lady of Hollywood." Throughout the 1930s and 1940s Irene shone in a wide variety of film genres, bringing forth new aspects of her multiple talents to enhance each fresh film venture: chronicle drama (Cimarron), *soap opera* (Back Street), *musical comedy* (Show Boat), *romantic drama* (Love Affair), *madcap comedy* (The Awful Truth), *or period piece* (I Remember Mama).

On camera Irene was the epitome of regal beauty, her trim figure topped by a classic, delicately dimpled face, with a patrician nose, cool dark eyes, a flow of dark brown hair, and capped by her well-modulated voice, which could imply so much with just the slightest inflection. Offscreen Irene was a devoted wife and mother, who found gadfly socializing on the Hollywood scene as repellent as sitting down to an afternoon of bridge with the girls. Just as Irene was too much the complete woman to repeat the dirt about her co-workers or neighbors, so she always found it strange that interviewers could really be interested in her opinions on life. In fact, to protect herself from revealing what she considered extraneous data on her life and thoughts, she developed a "charming vagueness" with which she could politely deter even the most ardent of reporters from ferreting too deeply into the private thoughts of private citizen Irene Dunne.

Away from the active swirl of show business for nearly two decades, Irene remains a perennial screen favorite with fans who fondly recall her wide range of superior screen work. This tribute to her enduring popularity is all the more potent when one considers that the bulk of her prime cinema work (Cimarron, Back Street, Roberta, Show Boat—*and until very, very recently,* Theodora Goes Wild, Love Affair, Anna and the King of Siam, *and* Life with Father) *was out of television circulation due to copyright problems involving remakes and (re) telecasts.*

Irene Marie Dunn,* of German-Irish descent, was born December 20, 1898,† in Louisville, Kentucky, the older of two children‡ born to Joseph John Dunn and Adelaide Antoinette (Henry) Dunn. Her father followed in the family profession of Mississippi riverboat building and operating, later becoming a ship inspector for the federal government. Irene was sent to Saint Benedict's Academy in downtown Louisville to receive a Catholic education from the Sisters of Loretto.

Irene was not yet twelve when her father, several years older than her mother, died. Mrs. Dunn took her two children to live with her parents in Madison, Indiana. Mrs. Dunn, an accomplished pianist, had for several years nurtured the conviction that Irene's voice was capable of sophisticated training and that if properly handled, it could lead to a full-fledged operatic career. Once in Madison, Irene was embarked on a series of voice, dance, and language courses at nearby Indianapolis' Fine Arts Academy. In September, 1918, Irene enrolled in the Conservatory Division of the Chicago Musical College,§ from which she was awarded a senior diploma in voice on June 19, 1919; she was also the gold medal winner for that year. Irene returned to the college in the fall for the 1919-20 school year, following the same curriculum, except that she studied French instead of Italian and doubled up on voice lessons. She retained her free scholarship in music history, and her voice lessons were still paid for by Mr. Syndacker.

By 1920 Mrs. Dunn felt her daughter was ready for the long-planned Metropolitan Opera House audition and Irene made her first trip to Manhattan. She promptly failed the Met's test, but while in New York, she accompanied the daughter of one of her mother's friends to an audition for the proposed road company of the musical comedy *Irene.* "What are you here for? Do you sing?" Irene was asked by an imperious assistant stage man-

---

*Irene added a final *e* to her surname after she entered show business.
†Some sources insist the year of her birth was 1901, 1904, or 1907.
‡There was a younger brother, Charles.
§Her course of study included: voice, sight reading, harmony, Italian, and music history (taught by the president of the College, who granted Irene a free scholarship in music history). Her voice lessons were paid for by one H. M. Syndacker.

ager. She explained, but then as a lark—so the story goes—she offered a rendition of "Kiss Me Again." She was immediately hired for the lead role in *Irene** and made her stage debut when the show tour opened in Chicago. (Jeanette MacDonald played Eleanor in the Chicago Company.)

When no further roles developed as a result of her four-month tour in *Irene,* she considered the possibility of teaching music in the Chicago public-school system, but was spurred on by her mother's enthusiasm to return to New York and pursue additional musical studies while waiting for her next professional break. Her opportunity came via an agent when she was hired to play in the Henry W. Savage production of *The Clinging Vine* (Knickerbocker Theatre, December 25, 1922). Peggy Wood starred as an efficient businesswoman in that musical comedy by Zelda Sears and Harold Levey. Irene's small part as Tessie the secretary was over less than four minutes after the curtain went up on Act I. But Irene already possessed a knowledgeable flair for attracting attention, even in this apprentice period of her career. She wrote Miss Sears a thank-you note—which was well circulated—complimenting the playwright for her foresight in making the role of Tessie so short and within the play's initial first four minutes, leaving Irene plenty of free time to complete her daily studies.

After *The Clinging Vine,* which lasted for 188 performances, Irene eased into a new career niche as a musical-comedy replacement. Peggy Wood came down with laryngitis while touring with *The Clinging Vine* in Cleveland and producer Savage rushed Irene from New York to replace the star until the latter recovered. Later in 1924 Irene succeeded Gloria Dawn as Virginia in the musical *Lollipops* (Knickerbocker Theatre, January 21, 1924), another divertissement written by Zelda Sears. In this production, Irene, still wearing her Mary Pickford-style curls, sang the duet "Love in a Cottage" with Leonard Culey.

The following season Irene won a small role in the musicalization of *The Fortune Hunter,* entitled *The City Chap* (Liberty Theatre, October 26, 1925). Skeets Gallagher and Phyllis Cleveland were the stars. It was the first of several occasions on which Irene would perform in a Jerome Kern-scored production. The *New York Evening World* noted, "Irene Dunne stands out in the beauty section." Among the other featured players of *The City Chap* was George Raft.

Irene was not originally in the cast of *Sweetheart Time* (Imperial Theatre, January 19, 1926) when it debuted, but two months thereafter she was hired to succeed Genevieve Tobin in the second female lead role of Violet Stevenson. She thus had the opportunity to solo the title tune and to duet "Girl in Your Arms" with star Eddie Buzzell.† Next came *Yours Truly* (Shubert Theatre, January 25, 1927). Irene opened in this musical playing Diana, but

---

*Played by Edith Day on Broadway the previous year.

†He later became a motion picture director in Hollywood, but he and Irene never worked on a film together.

two months later she succeeded Marion Harris as Leon Errol's vis-à-vis. This show had a fair run of 129 performances, which surprisingly outdistanced *She's My Baby* (Globe Theatre, January 3, 1928), which boasted a Richard Rodgers-Lorenz Hart score and a cast that included Beatrice Lillie, Clifton Webb, Irene, and Jack Whiting. The show was directed by Edward Royce and found Irene dueting "You're What I Need" and "If I Were You," both with Whiting.

The Shubert Brothers were the producing outfit that finally allowed Irene to originate her first full-fledged musical comedy lead in their *Luckee Girl* (Casino Theatre, September 15, 1928). In this adaptation of the French musical *Un Bon Garçon,* Irene played Arlette Armidnette, a pert French miss who duets "A Flat in Montmartre" with Irving Fisher and soloes "I Love You So." Although shapely Doris Vinton and funnyman Billy House received more than their share of critical praise, the reviewers and the public at last took an appreciative evaluation of Irene's virtues as a musical comedy prima donna. The *New York Post* extolled, "[She has a] charming voice, unusually lovely face and a bright, guileless clarity which was not without dignity too." The *New York Herald-Tribune* analyzed that Irene was "a cool, pleasantly detached young lady." As Irene's luck would have it, the show only ran eighty-one performances.

At this point, twenty-nine-year-old Irene was not certain whether she would continue with her show business career, for on July 16, 1928 she had wed New York City-based Dr. Francis J. Griffin, then age forty-two. The couple had met at a Manhattan party a few years earlier. Being of a conservative New England background, Griffin was not attracted to the theatre and theatre people, but he refused to stand in his wife's way should she decide to continue her career.* The couple honeymooned in Europe and then returned to New York, where Irene played the title role of *Luckee Girl.*

It was at this professional impasse that fate, so Irene insists, took a firm hand. One day early in 1929, she entered a midtown Manhattan office building on the way to see a theatrical agent. She stepped into a crowded elevator. One of the passengers happened to be producer Florenz Ziegfeld. With his sharp eye for beauty he quickly spotted Irene, who was wearing a most attractive blue hat. She exited the elevator on her appointed floor, Ziegfeld on the next, where he promptly ordered an associate to go downstairs and find the pretty girl with the blue hat. As a result of their initial meeting

---

*Several years later Dr. Griffin would publicly recall: "After we decided to get married I was kind of opposed to Miss Dunne continuing her stage career. Also I didn't like the moral tone of show business.

"Although she was a star, I was never that impressed with her talent. After she got to Hollywood and *Cimarron*—she went to the top.

"Then I didn't feel I could ask her to drop her career. If she didn't have talent, I would have. I really didn't think marriage and the stage were compatible but we loved each other and we were both determined to make our marriage work."

Irene was offered the role of Magnolia in Ziegfeld's road company of *Show Boat*.* During her very successful Chicago engagement, she won plaudits for her singing of the Jerome Kern score and for the quality of her stage presence. It was not long before she came to the attention of RKO studio officials who, over a kippered-herring lunch, offered Irene a studio contract.

The relatively new RKO Radio studios were anxious to continue doing films in the screen genres in which they had already achieved marketable success—namely, musical comedy. Ex-Paramount comedienne Bebe Daniels had made a great personal hit with *Rio Rita* (1929) and had already been assigned to *Dixiana* (1930), paired again with the commercially hot comedy team of Wheeler and Woolsey. Studio president J. J. Murdock and executive vice-president E. B. Derr reasoned that another musical-comedy ingenue on the roster would be sound business, albeit Irene was already thirty years of age.

In view of Irene's later imperial screen career, the cheeky *Leathernecking* (Globe Theatre, September 12, 1930) appears in retrospect a very strange production in which to have introduced her to screen audiences. Yet probably nothing at the time seemed more logical. Irene was an unproven screen commodity, and casting her in a role that either contractee Dorothy Lee or Dorothy Jordan could have played equally as well, was a safe way of publicly screen-testing her for her future box-office potential. RKO had acquired the Richard Rodgers-Lorenz Hart-Herbert Fields stage musical *Present Arms*† as a logical property for the musical screen, but when the vogue for song-and-dance features died in 1930, the project was quickly converted into a straightforward service comedy. "The film's chief virtue," decided the *New York Times,* "is its failure to take itself seriously," and, with its prefabricated plot, that was a blessing.

The rambling story of *Leathernecking* has upper-crust socialite Irene tossing a swank party at her Honolulu abode, inviting Eddie Foy, Jr., whom she has been led to believe is a captain in the Marine Corps stationed there. In reality he is a lowly buck private, gauche and chipper as they come. When his true rank is exposed, she denounces him, but her good pal Lilyan Tashman maneuvers the two of them together on her yacht, leading to their being marooned on a desert island during a storm. When they return home, Foy is tossed into the brig, and Irene refuses to relent until a fortuneteller (Rita La Roy) advises her that Foy is bound for disaster. She rushes to his rescue, only to learn that he has been retroactively elevated to a captaincy for his bravery during the recent Nicaraguan campaign. So everyone is happy! With the scene-stealing mugging of Foy, Louise Fazenda, and Ken Murray, the

*Ziegfeld's father, Dr. Florenz Ziegfeld, had founded the Chicago Musical College in 1867, so it would seem likely that Irene would have had an introduction to the Broadway impresario long before this happenstance situation.

†Mansfield Theatre, April 26, 1928; 155 performances.

arch comedy of Ned Sparks, and the effortless performance of tony Lilyan Tashman, little wonder that Irene was overlooked by reviewers and audiences alike.*

Originally Irene had been scheduled to follow *Leathernecking* with a role in RKO's proposed rendition of Victor Herbert's *Babes in Toyland*.† But with the further cutback in Hollywood screen musicals, it was decided to postpone the costly production. Meanwhile Richard Dix‡ had been handed the lead role in the studio's upcoming epic production of Edna Ferber's *Cimarron* (1930), the best-selling novel about the 1889 Oklahoma Territory land rush and the subsequent molding of the territory into a state. Stage star Fay Bainter was the leading contender for the role of Sabra Cravat, who ages in the film from seventeen to sixty. But Dix, who had a sterling reputation for aiding unknown and featured players with an almost unheard-of generosity, had seen Irene perform on the stage back in New York and was convinced she would be ideal for the role. According to "fact" it was Dix who prevailed upon his good friend, RKO producer William Le Baron, to persuade director Wesley Ruggles and the other studio executives that Irene should have the key part. Irene had already grasped the movie-business maxim that he who does, gets; and she persuaded makeup expert Ernest Westmore and cameraman Ernest Bracken to devote a Saturday afternoon to recording on film the proof that she was right for the role.

Ruggles soon learned he had made a wise choice§ in allowing Irene to portray the gentle Kansas girl Sabra who weds poet, gunslinger, and lawyer Dix, and then moves with him to the Oklahoma Territory, participating in the great land rush of April 22, 1889,ϕ and settling the new town of Osage. She affirmatively takes charge of the liberal *Oklahoma Wigwam* when wanderlust causes robust Dix to seek out new frontiers, only to be reunited with him in 1930 when he is an elderly, dying oil worker and she is a senior Congresswoman.

There was no doubt when the 131-minute *Cimarron* premiered at the Globe Theatre (January 26, 1931) that it was an inspired piece of Americana owing as much to Ruggles's direction as to Ferber's original sprawling novel. "Magnificent in scope, powerful in treatment, admirable in action . . . . It is one of the few talking picture productions which inspires rather than awes," decreed the *New York Daily News* in its four-star review. The picture went

---

Leathernecking is currently unavailable for television screenings.

†Two-page color trade ads in June, 1930, announced that *Babes in Toyland* would be directed by Luther Reed, with sets and costumes by Max Ree, choreography by Pearl Eaton, and that under the musical direction of Victor Baravelle, it would star: Wheeler and Woolsey. Joseph Cawthorne, Irene, Dorothy Lee, Ned Sparks, Marguerite Padula, Edna May Oliver, the Tiller Sunshine Girls, and "2,000 others."

‡Ex-Paramount leading man Dix had re-established his waning screen career as a talking-picture star at RKO with the popular *Seven Keys to Baldpate* (1929).

§Ruggles would later say of Irene: "She can sing, play comedy or drama. She's bound to have one of the most enviable careers in Hollywood—if she signs with a top agent."

ϕA spectacularly photographed sequence whose excitement has rarely been duplicated on screen.

on to gross two million dollars, win three Oscars, and claim a permanent niche in screen history as one of the best westerns ever made.*

It was no surprise when Richard Dix turned in a fine, Academy Award-nominated performance in *Cimarron,* but nearly everyone was caught off-guard when Irene provided a spunky portrayal in the picture, which earned her an Oscar bid.† Perhaps the keynote to Irene's adept portrayal was her ability to essay convincingly a wide range of moods, from the innocent young bride who trustingly leaves civilization behind to follow her rugged husband to the new territory, to the aging matriarch who cradles her dying husband in her arms. One scene which is always cited as a mark of Irene's innate acting excellence is the moment early in the film when she and Dix are strolling down the street of a western town. Along comes Stanley Fields, the prime scoundrel, who jeeringly points a gun at the unflinching Dix. Instinctively and without such oncamera business being written into the script, Irene lurches forward at Fields with her parasol outstretched like a weapon, which she uses to hit the opponent. Despite the screenplay's strong focus on Dix's characterization and the wealth of spicy supporting players (ranging from Edna May Oliver's town busybody, to loyal Jewish merchant George E. Stone, to Estelle Taylor's shady lady), Irene more than held her own in her *Cimarron* assignment, which demanded strong oncamera perseverance and strength of character. She provided just that with her realistic portrayal of continued faith in Dix as he wanders in and out of her life, by her unshakable conviction in the growth of Oklahoma into statehood, and by her belief that she must represent the area in Congress. If there was any weakness to Irene's characterization of Sabra Cravat, it was her flittery maneuvering as an onscreen mother who sees her beloved son killed in a railroad accident, and as a steadfast grandmother who wavers too much between authoritarianism and gooeyness. More than a decade later Irene would repeat her *Cimarron* characterization on radio's "The Cavalcade of America" (December 1, 1941).

Although advance word on *Cimarron* and Irene's performance was excellent, an actress could not make a full-fledged movie career of appearing only in epics—there were too few produced by the Hollywood film factories—so William Le Baron § next cast Irene in a conventional role as a virtuous working-girl in *Bachelor Apartment* (1931), one of the typical early 1930s urbane comedies, directed by and starring an underrated debonair film figure, Lowell Sherman. The sophisticated story was on surer ground with its

*Because of the much inferior 1960 MGM remake of *Cimarron,* the original RKO version is unavailable for video use.

†The other nominees were Marie Dressler, Norma Shearer, Ann Harding, and Marlene Dietrich, with Miss Dressler winning for *Min and Bill.*

Regarding her congressional acceptance speech in *Cimarron,* Will Rogers is reported to have said, "If women like Irene Dunne would run for Congress, I'd vote for them."

§Executive producer in charge of production at RKO Radio, he would assume similar duties over the combined RKO Radio-Pathé facilities in early 1931, assuring that his favorite Irene had a good choice of leading roles in the new studio's lineup of product.

elaborately modernistic setting than its tattered account of womanchasing bachelor Sherman, who decides his fickle predilection for married women (Mae Murray in particular) is becoming too dangerous an occupation (Murray's enraged husband Purnell Pratt had threatened to kill him), so he wisely chooses to wed Irene, a girl only recently arrived in the big city with her flighty sister (Claudia Dell). Perhaps Irene seemed a bit too aristocratic to play a working girl as in *Bachelor Apartment,* but audiences were sufficiently intrigued by her intrinsic chic and her directness of manner in handling boudoir champs like mustachioed Sherman, to overlook such inconsistencies in casting.

Ironically it was not RKO but MGM that first made practical use of Irene's singing talents, for Metro borrowed her to play an opera singer in *The Great Lover* (1931). MGM had already learned that its contracted Metropolitan Opera stars, Lawrence Tibbett and Grace Moore, were not fitting cinema material at this point in each of their careers. Thus Metro cast Adolphe Menjou to play the tempermental Continental baritone in *The Great Lover,* a suave philanderer who experiences true love with his protegee Irene, only to sacrifice his desires in order that she can find happiness with Neil Hamilton. The latter was seen as Carlo Joneus, really Carlo Jones of Buffalo. His handling of the role was his typically unsubtle best. He proved no asset to the film, nor, surprisingly, did Irene, as the sentimental budding prima donna who realizes a sensational debut on the stage, but cannot appreciate her achievement because she is emotionally torn between telling mentor Menjou that she respects but does not love him, and stifling her palpitating yearning for Hamilton in order to properly repay all of Menjou's kindness by wedding him. (After all, did not Menjou's Jean Paurel lose his stage voice training Irene for her debut and did not he have to endure the shame of seeing his understudy [Hamilton] go on in his place and achieve great success?) Within the context of *The Great Lover,* Menjou postured through the approved degrees of unctuousness and was occasionally touching, while Olga Baclanova offered yet another of her satisfying toughlady screen interpretations. One could have done very nicely indeed without the low comedy routines of Cliff Edward, Roscoe Ates, and Herman Bing, but their presence was a necessary evil, considered essential by MGM's Irving Thalberg in order to pacify the lower intellectual denominations of filmgoers.

Back at RKO Irene was top-billed in a gentle little romance, *Consolation Marriage* (1931). Irene and news reporter Pat O'Brien meet in a speakeasy and are amused to discover that they have a good deal in common since both have been jilted by their sweethearts (Lester Vail, Myrna Loy). Feeling sorry for one another, they quickly decide to marry, but very carefully state that whenever one or the other should become bored with the domestic arrangement, they can get a fast divorce. Time passes, and then one bright day Loy gets back in touch with O'Brien, but he has just learned that Irene is pregnant and does not follow through on the appointed rendezvous with his former flame. However, when, a year later, he encounters fetching Loy, he just cannot resist re-establishing contact. Irene is aware of the dangerous situation and, bound to hurt before she is wounded, she agrees to return to Vail, who has just informed her he is divorcing his wife. However, the contrived finish has O'Brien realizing he loves his wife, daughter, and Fuzzy, their St. Bernard dog, a lot more than blonde menace Loy.

Consolation Marriage was not much of a film, but it proved a point that would not be lost on the RKO Radio-Pathé regimes. Whereas silver-blonde Ann Harding had been considered the queen of screen tearjerkers since her film debut in Pathé's 1929 product lineup, she had clearly demonstrated that her airy, regal bearing was only appropriately utilized when she was cast as an aristocratic young grand dame, maneuvering on a high plateau of social interaction and refined emotional turmoil. On the other hand, Irene, who was older than Ann Harding, had the capacity to appear equally at ease as a manor-born sophisticate or as a level-headed shopgirl whose pedestrian heart knows no practical reason where romance is involved. To boot, Irene could sing, was far more pliable in accepting roles handed to her, and was then earning a great deal less than the patrician Miss Harding.

Thus, when RKO Radio and Pathé merged their operations,* Irene and the slightly younger Ann Harding were vying for the same roles, with the increasingly more frequent result that Irene or two short-term RKO Radio contractees (Myrna Loy and Mary Astor) drew parts that would have automatically gone to Miss Harding in days gone by. (When Katharine Hepburn entered the scene in 1932 the star-stable balance of power would change its complexion all over again.)

Irene was next seen in *Symphony of Six Million* (1932).† This Fannie Hurst tearjerker was the type of project usually handled with precision by Warner Bros., which possessed the expanded facilities and adroitness of staff to whittle down such a maudlin tale of Lower East Side New York Jewish family life into a social commentary that would be both fast moving and entertaining. But giving credit where it is due, RKO did not do badly with Gregory La Cava at the megaphone, for he directed the production with sincerity. In *Symphony of Six Million,* Meyer and Hannah Klauber (Gregory Ratoff, Anna Appel) wish for nothing more in life than that their elder son (Ricardo Cortez) should grow up to become a fine doctor—a surgeon, no less. Cortez readily complies with their dream and after completing his medical studies devotes himself to caring for the neighborhood poor. But his very Americanized brother (Noel Madison) urges him and goads his parents to persuade the "doctor" to move his practice to a better neighborhood so he

*In the merger takeover, William Le Baron departed the lot and David O. Selznick took over as head of studio production. Pandro S. Berman, former RKO Radio chief editor, who had been a production assistant to Le Baron, was now made an associate producer under the Selznick regime. He was very favorably inclined to the casting of the increasingly popular Irene in as many vehicles as possible.

†Along with such disparate Hollywood personalities as Buster Keaton, Joe E. Brown, Norma Shearer, Laurel and Hardy, Edward G. Robinson, and Maurice Chevalier, Irene appeared in the Masquers Club two-reel short, *The Slippery Pearls* (1932).

can amass worthy returns on his years of arduous study. Cortez transfers his practice from the ghetto to West End Avenue and then to the acme of success, a Park Avenue suite. He is now a famous specialist, but inwardly he feels guilty, dissatisfied with catering to the whims of his rich clientele. When Cortez's father becomes desperately ill, mama Klauber urges—demands—that Cortez use his "million-dollar hands" to help papa. The surgery fails to save Mr. Klauber's life, and Cortez is so demoralized that his entire medical future is in jeopardy. But Fannie Hurst did not create the character of Jessica (Irene) for nothing. She is the practical middle-class schoolteacher, a cripple who has unstintingly devoted most of her time to helping blind children. One of Irene's most touching moments in *Symphony of Six Millions* occurs when she drags herself to Cortez's Park Avenue office to gently berate him for not attending one of her dying "boys," but nothing seems to bring the benumbed Cortez to his senses. Only when he learns that Irene must have corrective surgery on her spine and that she insists he perform the life-or-death operation, does he regain his lease on his career and sense of values. With Irene safely on the path to recovery, Cortez announces that he is returning to work amont the poor, who really require his ministrations. Devotees of the sob-story genre were quick to point out that *Symphony of Six Million* had more tears per reel than even MGM's prime weeper, *Emma,* which starred Marie Dressler.

For all the multifaceted judgmental errors attributable to the Universal Studio regime of the early 1930s, Carl Laemmle, Jr. must be credited with an astuteness for pushing into production both a series of classic horror films (*Dracula, Frankenstein, The Old Dark House,* etc.) and a collection of showy soap operas that was kicked off when he had the studio purchase Fannie Hurst's literary gold mine, *Back Street.* Since Irene had already graced one Fannie Hurst-derived picture, it was logical for Laemmle to negotiate to borrow her from RKO to star in what proved to be the most popular of picturizations of Fannie Hurst material.

Even in 1932, much of the storyline of *Back Street* was considered outmoded lavender and old lace, with its contrived teary formula to propagate the evil of the double standard used by selfish males to manipulate sweet and innocent females. The heartrending chronicle opens in Cincinnati near the turn of the century, where Irene, the daughter of middle-class German parents, meets well-born banker John Boles. Through a medley of errors, an appointed park meeting between Irene and Boles's mother does not take place, and six years pass before Irene and her admirer encounter again. This time it is in New York, and Boles has long since wed wealthy Doris Lloyd and is the father of two children. Irene has never forgotten her high-toned love, and now she rejects the matrimonial offer of George Meeker in order to remain even a small part of Boles's busy life, wherever and however she can. Which means she must become his discreet mistress, estalished in an apartment on one of the city's less-traveled streets. When Boles jaunts off to Europe on business he blithely forgets to continue his monthly subsidy of Irene, but she has her love to keep her strong and she takes to painting designs on china to earn the requisite income. When he returns their great love (at least on her part) builds to a new height. Throughout the years, Boles's wife has remained discreetly silent about Boles's obvious extramarital activities, but their two grown children, particularly William Bakewell, make no bones about their disgust at this immoral relationship. Irene refuses to be cowed, continuing firm in her devotion to the seemingly unworthy Boles. The end comes nearly thirty years after the lovers first met. Boles is attending the Reparation Commission meetings in Paris. This time he has paid for Irene's Continental trip and she is residing in a flat not far from his suite. One day the gray-haired mistress receives a phone call from Bakewell, who was urged by his father to call her, for the banker has suffered a stroke and is dying. Irene tearily bids her loved one goodbye, knowing full well that even with his death, convention demands that she remain on the sidelines while his legal wife and children participate in the funeral farewells.

Universal gave *Back Street* (Mayfair Theatre, August 28, 1932) a hard sell and reaped a tidy box-office return, bringing the studio more money than its previous record holder, *All Quiet on the Western Front* (1930).* The publicity campaign for *Back Street* raged: "Waiting—always waiting—in the shadows of the back street . . . longing for the man she loves . . . asking nothing, receiving nothing—yet content to sacrifice all for him. WHY?" Irene, billed over the title, managed to overcome much that was lachrymose in this account of the trials and tribulations of a kept woman, not the least problem being immobile John Boles's artificial characterization as the genteel man who enjoyed sipping hot chocolate and eating gingerbread at Irene's back-street flat, and rather patronizingly subsidized her with a $200 monthly allowance. Instead of being the lovable cad as intended, Boles emerged more of a dreary effete, but this was within the framework of typical 1930s soap-opera male leads, and no one complained too severely. Irene was required to convey credibility to a character who, while being naive and self-sacrificing, is perceptive enough to know "There's not one woman in a million who's found happiness in the back streets of a man's life." As Boles's auxiliary wife she willingly becomes a social outcast for his small portions of love, and for over ninety-three minutes she is obliged to overreact to the alleged exigencies of her character's besmirched situation. Adding to the acting challenge of *Back Street* were the handicaps of coping with excessively mushy dialog and director John Stahl's decision to end each "dramatic" episode of the film with a jerking strain to the camera's and the movie's flow of continuity.

The lofty *New York Times* condescended that Irene in *Back Street* "does well enough considering the wobbly character she plays." But other critics,

Back Street was nationally reissued in 1935; there were two subsequent remakes (in 1941 with Margaret Sullavan, in 1961 with Susan Hayward), as a result of which the Irene Dunne version was taken out of possible television circulation.

particularly distaff members of the reviewing profession, like Regina Crewe *(New York American)*, heralded, "She stands almost alone as the last remaining graceful, gracious gentle lady in-the-cinema." The *London Times* amplified, "[Irene Dunne] always has her part perfectly in hand, . . . she is consistently natural and unforced, both as the young girl radiantly and idealistically in love and as the mature, experienced woman."

Irene enjoyed working with director John Stahl but regarded the message-laden *Back Street* as "trash." Nevertheless, it was *Back Street* which consolidated Irene's star status in Hollywood and to the public, typecasting her as the beautiful first lady of soap opera, more viable at the box office than either of her silver-screen competitors, Ann Harding and Ruth Chatterton. It was now agreed by nearly all that Irene's screen charisma could stabilize the shakiest of four-handkerchief film vehicles. She might not be as chic as RKO's fashionable Constance Bennett, but Irene was more dependable in her performance, and more adept at portraying all facets of womanhood in chronicle tearjerkers in which she could effortlessly develop the exigencies of aging, sainted, back-street women.

Until the overwhelming success of *Back Street,* Irene had merely considered herself a temporary Hollywood resident; in fact her RKO contract specifically provided that after the completion of each film she could return to New York to be with her husband, and that the studio had to provide her with ten days notice before the opening shooting day of any future cinema commitment. Irene's unique marital setup* was a constant source of speculation in Hollywood, but she remained the imperturbable lady as onscreen. Occasionally Irene would venture some statement on the subject to the press: "Our geographical separation is an unfortunate circumstance, but we manage to see each other often. . . . I believe, aside from the fact that we are in love with each other, the secret of our happiness is that we are in different vocations."

RKO may have pampered Irene's domestic-life whims, but they were ever anxious to make full use of her screen services. The hastily assembled potboiler *Thirteen Women* had its release delayed (Roxy Theatre, October 14, 1932) to take full advantage of Irene's mushrooming marquee lure from *Back Street.*† Director George Archainbaud converted Tiffany Thayer's melodrama into such a straight-laced, stark horror outing that it quickly collapsed into laughable hokum. In casting *Thirteen Women,* RKO utilized nearly all of its roster of distaff players, ranging from gracious Jill Esmond to neurotic ingenue-type Julie Haydon. Myrna Loy, who had yet to escape her Oriental stereotype onscreen, was required to play a half-Javanese, half-Hindu lunatic, a girl slighted at finishing school by her uppity classmates. For years she has harbored resentment and now determines to dispose of

---

*Conventional in comparison to Shirley MacLaine's global separations from her husband in the show business world of the 1960s and 1970s.

†Although Irene was second-billed to studio contract lead Ricardo Cortez.

her alleged persecutors, one by one. With the aid of a fake swami (C. Henry Gordon), she instills a growing fear into the boarding school graduates, who now realize their unknown assailant intends to have each of them meet the fate of Peg Entwhistle, one of their number who is hysterically seduced into committing suicide. Irene and Esmond are the two most stable members of the group, refusing to give in to the fears that are destroying their number. With good reason Irene conveyed little credulity in her sketchy part, forced to be kittenish with police sergeant Ricardo Cortez (who appears too late in the story and too briefly to instill any masculine luster to the proceedings), maternal to her toddler child (Wally Albright), and resolutely firm in combating her mystical adversary (Loy).

It was no secret that after David O. Selznick became production head of RKO and newcomer Katharine Hepburn emerged as an Oscar-winning top star, a sharp re-evaluation of the star stable had occurred at the studio. Constance Bennett, Mary Astor, Helen Twelvetrees, and Myrna Loy had departed the lot, or soon would, and Ann Harding was yanked down from her imperial top-lady-of-the-lot throne to a lesser post more on a par with ever-rising Irene. But both these ladies were considered—more so by the RKO executives than the public—a shade below the eccentric screen novice Hepburn. Given the seesawing balance of star status, Ann Harding and Katharine Hepburn continued to make strong demands on the studios as to the type of picture they would grace or how a particular new role should and would be handled. Irene, on the other hand, remained quite pliable to studio dictates, which continued to cast her in a rash of weepers.

Irene was so entrenched in the public's mind as the screen's new queen of martyrdom figures that when *No Other Woman* opened (Roxy Theatre, January 29, 1933), Richard Watts, Jr. of the *New York Herald-Tribune* could safely enunciate; "The lady Gandhi of the cinema stars is Hollywood's most determined representative of the mobility of passive resistance. Ever gentle and long suffering, whether in the role of wife or mistress, she has never been more completely sacrificial. In fact, I am sure that she should be an inspiration to all of us and a fine example to American Womanhood."

The plot of *No Other Woman* was the old pap of how money corrupts. Industrious Irene, who keeps a boarding house for mine workers in an ugly Pennsylvania steel town, weds steel-mill employee Charles Bickford. She encourages her rough husband to work with "pencil-pusher" Eric Linden from the mill office, who has been experimenting with new refining processes. The men's research efforts lead to sudden wealth. The once humble, happy couple (Irene and Bickford) move to a posh Pittsburgh abode and things predictably deteriorate in their domestic life. On one of Bickford's periodic trips to New York he meets designing Gwili Andre, who properly tags him as an easy mark. Fast playing, quick drinking Bickford decides he wants to shed Irene and their son to wed fun-loving, mercenary blonde Andre. What about Irene? She is ever the Christian martyr, refusing to be shaken by the unfortunate change of circumstances. Even when she is playing a round of golf at the country club and she hears malicious gossip about Bickford's extramarital activities, she calmly plays out her round before marching off to New York to get Bickford back. But egged on by Andre, Bickford pushes Irene into divorcing him, leading to a very messy courtroom trial in which Bickford behaves most reprehensibly. Under oath he testifies to deliberate falsehoods about Irene, stating that he is not the father of their child. Does Irene crumble under such unfair abuse? No! As she dramatically envisions her home life slipping away, she stoically rises in court and acknowledges the lies, all of which so affects Bickford that he now must shout out his perjury (for which he is sent to jail for a short period). A year later the couple are reunited.

Movie fans of the day heartily approved of the morality and predetermined plot manipulations of *No Other Woman,* with distaff members of the film-going audience vicariously thrilled to watch Irene act out a story in which "not one woman in a million would have done the desperate things she did to hold her own!" Without a doubt Irene seemed to be the sterling onscreen example of ladylike behavior, radiating "America's idea of the perfect woman, wife, mother, and sweetheart." Under the then-existing movie-star system, reviewers and public alike gave little attention to the supporting players, but in *No Other Woman* J. Carroll Naish offered a particularly effective performance as Bickford's devious shyster lawyer, far outshining the much-touted emoting of Gwili Andre, who came across oncamera as just another smart-mouth, bankbook-minded gal.

RKO next lent Irene's services (at a tidy profit to the company) to MGM for *The Secret of Madame Blanche* (1933), a thin remake of First National's *The Lady* (1925), which had starred Norma Talmadge. *The Secret of Madame Blanche* was firmly in the conventional mold established at MGM with the Oscar-winning *The Sin of Madelon Claudet* (1931), but without any of that film's essential felicity, a factor which surely had deterred any of the MGM female-star stable from accepting the role in the first place. The premise establishes Irene as a pure American chorus girl of 1890s London who is picked up by insipid British aristocrat Phillips Holmes, whom she foolishly weds. He cannot support them and his heartless father (Lionel Atwill) denies any monetary assistance; Holmes commits suicide, leaving Irene to face a bleak future. Later in Paris she gives birth to a son, and thereafter she obtains a job at a notorious cafe. Claiming Irene is certainly an unfit mother, Atwill gains custody of the child. Years pass—it is now 1918, and as "Madame Blanche," proprietress of a rowdy French cafe, Irene is suddenly given the opportunity to protect her soldier son, who has accidentally killed another in a drunken scuffle in her establishment. When Irene discovers the youth's identity she attempts to assume the blame for the shooting, but the French court demands to know her real identity and why she claims to have killed the victim for no apparent reason. In true *Madame X* style, mother and son are then reunited, he to endure a light prison sentence, followed by a bright future for them both in America. The critics were tolerant to Irene's soft-keyed interpretation. "[She] does a good deal to mitigate the anguished banalities of this theme" *(New York Evening Post)*. "[Irene Dunne] plays the familiar and sometimes slightly embarrassing part with reticence and feeling" *(New York Herald-Tribune)*.

Although Irene was handed *The Silver Cord* (Radio City Music Hall, May 4, 1933) as a reward for her consistently fine box-office achievements, the picture itself was not really such a career blessing.* For no matter how scenarist Jane Murfin tried to rearrange the emphasis of Sidney Howard's stage play, *The Silver Cord* remained a strong indictment of twisted mother love with the memorable role belonging to the dictatorial mama, played on stage and oncamera by Laura Hope Crews. It was also ironic that on the first cinema occasion that Irene had a young, virile, and quite popular leading man, Joel McCrea, he was forced to play a mother-plagued man almost as hamstrung by his filial devotion as his weak-spined brother (Eric Linden). Within the story's framework, young scientist Irene weds promising architect McCrea on the Continent and returns with him to his small American hometown only to find that what seemed at first to be a happy mother-son relationship is not so. In reality, mother Crews, who suffered from a faulty marriage and now has a subconscious desire for revenge against males, dishes out frightening overdoses of possessiveness guised in the traditional "mother knows best" sweetness. Her tactics have already emotionally crippled her younger son (Linden), causing him to break off his engagement to Frances Dee, and Irene is convinced the same fate awaits McCrea. Pregnant Irene sternly informs McCrea that he must choose between his mother and her, for she is packing her bags and returning to New York. At the last dramatic moment, McCrea emancipates himself and joins Irene.

Like the stage original, *The Silver Cord* is a very talky exercise with little action, relying on the shock value of Crews's excessive selfishness to give the tale its entertaining bite. Director John Cromwell was more successful with Frances Dee (as the sweet, lovesick girl who attempts suicide when Linden rejects her) than with Irene in breaking up the oversized speeches for effective cinematic theatrics. Irene's role in this emotional tug-of-war demanded a new facet to her screen persona, for she had to eschew the passive and take an active stance to retain her man's love.†

Merian C. Cooper, who replaced David O. Selznick as production head of RKO in February, 1932, continued with his predecessor's penchant for acquiring literary projects for filming. Sinclair Lewis's novel *Ann Vickers* was purchased early in 1933 and produced as a movie for release that same year. The studio's hopes to make *Ann Vickers* as commercially successful as *Arrowsmith* (United Artists, 1931) fell far short of the mark, as there was such an inherent overslickness to *Ann Vickers* (as both a novel and a film) that its

---

*Both Katharine Hepburn and Ann Harding had previously been announced to play the lead female role.

†Because of complicated changes of copyright ownership to *The Silver Cord*, this feature is presently unavailable for TV viewing.

very episodic drama refused to coagulate into a coherent piece of entertainment.

As Lewis's tract of the feminist social worker opens, dedicated charity worker Ann Vickers (Irene) is assisting at an institution social. There she encounters World War I Army captain Bruce Cabot, who greatly appeals to her romantic nature. But the viewer shortly learns from Irene's own lips, "I'm not ready for love yet." Nevertheless, she soon falls prey to Cabot's glib ways; in their on-again off-again romance, she becomes pregnant by him, but loses the baby in childbirth. Yet Irene's Ann Vickers is able to bounce back from this traumatic episode very quickly, for she is enveloped by her do-gooder ambitions. "Ann" proclaims her autocratic doctor friend, Edna May Oliver, "has a passion for helping. She's going to make the world over if it takes her all winter." Which is a fair appraisal of Irene's drive. She zings out West to work at the Copper Gap State Prison. Her revealing experiences there of human cruelty are all captured in her book *Ninety Days and Nights in Prison,* which becomes a best seller, going through twenty printings. With her newfound prominence in the social work-reform movement, Irene quickly becomes head of the Stuyvesant Industrial Home, receiving honorary degrees, and making the acquaintance of salty judge Walter Huston. The two seemingly disparate types fall in love so strongly that when he is sent to prison on a corruption charge Irene stands firm in her loyalty to him, even though her allegiance costs her job and social standing. While he is in jail, she gives birth to their child, supporting herself and the baby by writing syndicated articles on prison reforms. After three years, Huston is released on probation. He returns to industrious Irene, who now admits that career is not everything, for she has been freed too—from the "prison of ambition and desire."

The studio's promotion of *Ann Vickers,* which found Irene coiffed and garbed rather unattractively and possessed of an unbecoming Katharine Hepburn-like nasality, would have been far more effective in the liberal 1970s, but they made a game try to convince 1930s audiences that this movie was something different from the usual presentation of an idealized woman, for here was a heroine who has modern ideas about love and the courage to do something with them. "These are the times of overturning. RKO Radio does not believe that the truth should be suppressed. The screen dares to produce what Lewis dared to write. The picture now pleads guilty to destroying human faith in certain pleasant lies. It will inflame the nation like a purifying fire. But *Ann Vickers* is not a sermon!!"

Even by 1934, when Irene was a major star, she was required, like other studio movie queens, to turn out a minimum of three to four pictures a year. But Irene was still not wont to fight too hard with studio executives over choice of projects at this stage of her career. Her set-tos were usually confined to disagreements with the directors of her projects over the shape of her characterization and its relationship to the picture as a whole.

On the surface, *If I Were Free* (Radio City Music Hall, January 4, 1934) seemed promising subject matter. Under the title *Behold We Live,* The John Van Druten play had been performed to respectable results on the London stage with Gertrude Lawrence and Gerald du Maurier starred. In that format it seemed less mundane, what with the glittery distraction of the two theatre luminaries. Oncamera, however, *If I Were Free* emerged just another tastefully mounted but conventional triangular love drama, much in the vein of *Only Yesterday* (Universal, 1933), which starred Margaret Sullavan. In *If I Were Free,* British barrister Clive Brook, ever so proper and distinguished, is floundering in Paris, a much misunderstood husband. Also in Paris is Irene, so unhappily wed to the dissolute Nils Asther that she almost prefers the notion of death to her current unhappiness. But fortuitously for the plot and the characters, the two distraught figures chance upon one another and together feel there is a way to contentment on earth, particularly after Brook gently pushes Asther out of Irene's life for the time being. The happy couple cross the Channel to London, where Brook rises again in the legal profession and Irene establishes a rather successful interior decorating-antique business. The viewer is treated to a prim, idealistic, romantic excursion between Irene and Brook as they sneak happy moments together, punting on the Thames, listening to church music on the quiet, etc. But their earthly paradise is shortlived; Irene is frankly told by Brook's friend (Henry Stephenson) that her relationship with Brook is hurting his career. After all, she has attained her divorce from Asther, but Brook has had no such luck with his obstinate wife (Lorraine MacLean). At this strategic point, gross melodrama grabs hold of the film. A totally distraught Brook, feeling life once again is too burdensome to continue onward, risks a dangerous operation to have a bullet from a World War I injury removed from his lung. While he is fighting for his life on the surgeon's table, Irene and MacLean engage in a battle of wills to determine who will have Brook should he survive the operation.

As the basic plotline fully indicates, there was very limited potential to Irene's role, particularly in view of her having fairly well exhausted all variations of the genre.* As the *New York Sun* reviewed the situation, "[She] plays simply, sincerely, and well and remains that likeable Miss Wholesomeness that she always is."

This Man Is Mine (1934) was no better constructed a vehicle ("mediocre, verbose," *New York Times*), with some contemporary critics suggesting the problem drama should have been a farce, not a drama. The movie did benefit from John Cromwell's graceful direction, which geared the deluxe production qualities to the taste of married women filmgoers. The premise found Irene wed to rather bovine playboy Ralph Bellamy, spending most of her days dabbling in painting and playing classical selections on the piano. Irene's contentment with this simple, homey existence is not shared by Bellamy, and within a few years he is obviously weary of life in Westchester,

---

*Irene did sing snatches of a German lullaby.

New York, sweet Irene, and their fine tyke of a son. So with scarcely a wink of the eye, he resumes a romance with snippy, feline Constance Cummings, who had ditched him at the altar some three years back, but is now back from a Reno divorce and eager for fresh prey. To round out the domestic crisis there is soft-spoken blueblood Sidney Blackmer, who offers to take Irene away on his yacht. Before the seventy-sixth-minute finale, Irene has daringly smashed a picture over Bellamy's fat head and Bellamy has socked Cummings in the eye, To round out matters, Bellamy contritely returns to Irene, while bubbly Cummings decide to wed affluent Blackmer, a decision which knocks out Irene's potential for revenge.

There was no doubt that *This Man Is Mine* was an Irene Dunne picture, but the plot was so peculiarly structured that her role was actually no more important than that of Cummings (as the rather awkward femme fatale) or Kay Johnson (as Cummings's sardonic, sagacious sister-in-law). (There was also Vivian Tobin for standard, but expertly handled, comic side-relief.) All of which demonstrated that Irene was not always master of her oncamera productions. Almost unknowingly—and thanks largely to director John Cromwell's sensibilities—Irene began a professional transition of genre specialty in *This Man Is Mine,* which would gravitate her from turgid drawing-room drama to lighthearted comedy. The almost imperceptible changes in her screen image were leading Irene further and further away from the anonymous hoity-toity nobility pose that, for example, was ruining Ann Harding's box-office draw.* But at this stage in the transformation, Irene was neither here nor there, wavering between essaying the lofty martyred wife a la Ann Harding and the practical, level-headed miss so adroitly essayed by Carole Lombard.†

When Irene had signed an exclusive new two-year RKO Radio contract in September, 1933, she was slated to make *My Gal Sal,* a Gay Nineties musical, but that did not come to pass. *Stingaree* (1934), which reunited Irene with Richard Dix did.‡ It provided Irene with an opportunity to utilize her vocal talents for the first time in four years at her home studio. In this William Wellman-directed costumer set in 1874 Australia, Irene was cast as Hilda Bouverie, the dependent of rancher Henry Stephenson. When her jealous foster mother (Mary Boland) tosses a grand bash, uninvited Dix, the Robin Hood of Down Under, shows up at the party intending to relieve the

---

*Critics were fast to disparage Ann Harding's commanding film status, as did the *New York Herald-Tribune* review of *This Man Is Mine.* "If you can close your eyes and imagine Miss Ann Harding in the role, you will realize how fine Miss Dunne is."

†Tough New York film critic Cecilia Ager wryly pointed out; "She's still noble Irene Dunne in *This Man Is Mine,* but she's loosening up. She says 'jake' once, and saying it, makes it sound like a swear word; she smashes a glass in temper, but smashes it against the fireplace where its destruction will cause the least untidyness; and most revolutionary of all, she confesses to an ardent dislike for—what is this world coming to?—her mother!"

‡It had been touted that Irene and Dix would co-star in *The Ace,* but instead he made the picture (retitled *The Ace of Aces* [1933] with Elizabeth Allan). Leslie Banks was the original choice for Irene's co-star in *Stingaree;* when Dix was substituted, Irene remained top-billed.

assembled guests of their riches. But the music-loving bandit is so entranced with comely Irene that he forgets his original mission and instead forces the gathering to listen to the girl sing operatic arias. Irene at first tolerates the outspoken stranger because she assumes he is compser Conway Tearle, but by the time she learns her admirer's true occupation, she has become terribly infatuated with him. But their romance (he has kidnapped her to his out-of-the-way abode) is short-lived, for he insists that she travel to Italy to study opera under the best teachers. A series of montage shots reveal that she attains prima donna status as easily and successfully as Dix continues to plunder the Australian upper classes. Eventually Irene returns to Australia, even though her mentor (Tearle) has begged her to become his wife and go to England. She is to make her local debut at a Melbourne gala to be attended by the governor-general (Reginald Owen). When Dix learns of Irene's forthcoming appearance, he holds up Owen's party and substitutes himself in the dignitary's box at the concert. Upon spotting Dix in the audience Irene turns in an inspired performance, but she does not stay to bask in her long-awaited success for she quickly agrees to ride off with Dix to future bliss in the bush country.

Certainly the plot of *Stingaree* was as fantastic and improbable as one could imagine. It was no coincidence that Dix's roguish outlaw bore a striking resemblance to that flippant gentleman thief Raffles, for both characters were created by E. W. Hornung. If Dix was larger than life with his over-cosmeticized countenance and his theatrical variation of the chivalrous cowboy, Irene was equally out of proportion as the budding prima donna. She and the film were most at ease in the early sequence when she and Dix share their intimate tête-á-têtes. But when it came to the actual operatic sequences (here from *Faust* and *Martha*), Irene seemed unusually tense and stiff; she did much better with the two contemporary tunes composed for the picture, handling them in a carefree, unsteamy style.

Katharine Hepburn was having her own problems on the RKO lot finding a proper vehicle and decided that *The Age of Innocence* (1934) was not her cinematic cup of tea. Therefore Edith Wharton's delicate satire of 1870s New York society was reassigned to Irene. As a starting handicap, the screenplay dealing with stifling mid-Victorian conventions was no improvement upon the stodgy rendition of the novel that had stumbled onto Broadway in 1928 with Katharine Cornell. As the film was assembled, art director Van Nest Polglase and costumer Walter Plunkett created the proper waxed-flower atmosphere, but nothing could bolster the overly restrained storyline and emoting. The "painstaking but emotionally flaccid photoplay" *(New York Times)* was hardly geared to win the approval of Depression-oppressed moviegoers, who wanted escapism of a less aesthetic nature.

The too-delicately-woven yarn found John Boles, a young lawyer and a member of New York's high society, engaged to wed Julie Haydon, a typical Manhattan socialite with all the restrictions and forms adopted by that privileged class. Into their serene surroundings comes Countess Ellen Olenska

(Irene), a New York girl of irreproachable pedigree who has married a Polish nobleman on the Continent but wishes a divorce from him. Just the rumors of a pending divorce are sufficient to cast a taint of impropriety about Irene, causing her to be ostracized from New York's finer social circles. Only her flighty but good-natured grandmother (Helen Westley) takes pity on Irene, forcing her beloved granddaughter down the throats of local society. It develops that as a child Irene had greatly admired Boles, but he had foolishly snubbed her. Now, of course, he is captivated by her, as is Lionel Atwill, an unscrupulous married businessman whose persistent attentions to Irene add nothing to her tenuous reputation. Boles succeeds in winning Irene's daring divorce and although he loves her, he feels bound to wed her conventional cousin, Haydon. After his honeymoon, he and Irene meet again and their girdled passions flare, coming within inches (but this was post-Code Hollywood and discretion was the necessary part of commercial valor) of surrendering. Instead noble Irene exiles herself to Europe, leaving Boles to carry on dignifiedly with his wife.

Obviously the new Merian Cooper regime at RKO hoped that within the more dignified approach of *The Age of Innocence,* Irene and Boles could recreate the box-office magic of their prior *Back Street.* No way. The interaction and romancing of the new drama was as constricted as the tight-laced moral code that separated the two lovers from eventual happiness. Irene may have worn sixteen coiffures and an equal number of becoming period outfits, but only Helen Westley as the social arbiter came alive with her brief apearance as the mellow dowager. (*The Age of Innocence* would turn up on radio on "Theatre Guild of the Air" on April 20, 1947, with Gene Tierney, and on November 11, 1951, with Claudette Colbert.)

Irene was more than agreeable when Warner Bros. coaxed her, in August, 1934, to accept an attractive loan-out offer to star in *Sweet Adeline* (1935), based on the stage musical.* It had all the ingredients that augured for a quite popular screen success: a genteel nostalgic, turn-of-the-century story, music by Jerome Kern and Oscar Hammerstein II, screen direction by Mervyn LeRoy, and the efficient Warner Bros. production and stock company. Oncamera, bustle-skirted Irene was extremely winsome in the Mae West-era story with its atmosphere of beer gardens, bicycles built for two, and straw-hatted, handlebar-mustachioed men. But somehow Irene lacked the charisma that reviewers attributed to Helen Morgan's magic presence in the stage rendition. Particularly in this role, Irene was too much the assured metropolitan to play the innocent maid. Her cool, high soprano singing of "Don't Ever Leave Me" and "Why Was I Born?" and her dueting of "We Were So Young" (with Irish tenor Phil Regan) were pleasant but unmemorable, more than can be said for the loosely reworked screen story: Irene,

---

*Written by Jerome Kern and Oscar Hammerstein II for Helen Morgan as a follow-up vehicle for their star of *Show Boat.* It opened September 3, 1929, at the Hammerstein Theatre, running for 234 performances.

the saner daughter (there is flighty Nydia Westman) of Hoboken-German beer-garden-owner Joseph Cawthorn, attracts the attention of composer Donald Woods and Spanish-American War Army major Louis Calhern (dastardly down to his waxed mustache), both vying for Irene's approval, with Calhern promising to help back Wood's latest operetta if Irene is given the lead. Midst the silly plot and the perambulations of sulky hero Woods, there were the dependable joys of Ned Sparks (the dour stage-manager), Hugh Herbert (the simpleminded millionaire backer and secret service agent), Winifred Shaw (Irene's vengeful stage rival), and the host of veteran players peppering the minor bits. And, yes, Irene does become the toast of Broadway and make a splashy opening in Woods's operetta, but she returns to the emotional safety of her father's quaint beer garden before she and Woods reconcile.

Back at RKO, executive producer Pandro S. Berman was having phenomenal success with the screen teaming of Fred Astaire and Ginger Rogers, who had initially clicked as a subordinate love team in *Flying Down to Rio* (1933) and then confirmed their audience popularity with their starring project, *The Gay Divorcee* (1934). But he felt the screen adaptation of the Jerome Kern-Otto Harbach stage hit *Roberta** required additional box-office insurance, and thus cast Irene in the top-billed role of this distinguished screen outing, which premiered at Radio City Music Hall on March 7, 1935. Irene, cast as the unobtrusive Russian princess serving as assistant to Helen Westley, owner of Roberta's elite Paris dressmaking shop, finds herself sparring in and out of love with husky young American football player Randolph Scott (heir to the establishment when his Aunt Westley dies). Mingled into their mundane romance is the overshadowing auxiliary story of Astaire, an American band player stranded in Paris who discovers that Countess Scharwenka (Rogers) is none other than his old childhood sweetheart, Lizzie Gatz. The latter duo perform four inspired dance routines, with Rogers singing "I'd Be Hard to Handle" with a mock heavy French-Slavic accent, and duet-dancing "I Won't Dance," making tough competition for Irene, who had a rather confining part as the priggish noblewoman, who in the course of the movie sings those two still popular standards, "Smoke Gets in Your Eyes" and "Lovely to Look At," and also "Yesterdays." *Roberta* may have top-cast Irene, but it is remembered best for the Astaire-Rogers interludes.†

By the time *Roberta* went into release, Irene had left RKO, wisely deciding she could obtain better deals on a less restrictive basis. She turned down such offers as *Enter Madame* and *Peter Ibbetson* (both in 1935 at Paramount) and did not proceed with negotiations for her and Ann Harding to co-star in *The Old Maid* at the same studio. Instead she accepted a lucra-

*Opened November 18, 1933 at the New Amsterdam Theatre for a 295-performance run.
†When MGM acquired the screen rights to *Roberta* for its remake, *Lovely to Look At* (1952), the RKO version disappeared from circulation, only to reappear in the 1970s on a limited art-house theatrical-release basis.

tive short-term contract with Universal, a studio attempting to bolster its roster of female stars, which included Margaret Sullavan and, on a part-time basis, Claudette Colbert and Carole Lombard. It was announced that Irene's premier Universal attraction would be *Magnificent Obsession* (1935). "Heavy dramatic roles are essential for an actress of my type," Irene reasoned. "I know definitely that the status I have achieved has been achieved through tears. So for my career I cry."

Like most screen translations of weepy chronicles, *Magnificent Obsession* emerged choppy and at times unconvincing, but it was—and still is—on a par with the three other top soap operas of the 1930s: *Back Street, Imitation of Life,* and *Stella Dallas.* The familiar plot of *Magnificent Obsession* finds Irene the wife of an eminent surgeon who dies of a heart attack at the opening of the picture. His demise is attributed in part to the fact that the only available pulmotor resuscitator equipment in the vicinity was then being used in pumping lake water from bachelor Robert Taylor,* who had smashed his speedboat during a drunken bout. Only as a widow does Irene begin to fathom what a wonderful man her husband, Dr. Hudson, had been, discovering his many acts of quiet philanthropy and unobtrusive Christian charity. Thus, when she finally encounters arrogant Taylor, her anger is unbounded, particularly when he has the audacity to make romantic overtures. In fact, during one of their tug-and-pull arguments, he so distracts her that she rushes across the street without noting an oncoming automobile, and is desperately injured, being blinded. Now with Irene's eye impairment on his conscience, the once morally reprehensible Taylor vows to God (and the audience) that he will return to his dropped medical studies. Within a few brief years he becomes a Nobel Prize-winning surgeon, so skilled, in fact, that he operates on Irene and restores her shattered vision. Once able to see, she is amazed to discover that her recent medical benefactor is none other than a transformed Taylor, totally changed in morality by having adopted Dr. Hudson's philosophy on righteousness and the rewards of brotherly love.

Thus, hovering throughout *Magnificent Obsession* was author Lloyd Douglas's continual metaphysical propaganda (incarnated in the movie in the semispiritual influence of Ralph Morgan). Audiences were not only to have a good cry at the well-calculated emotional tugs in this weeper, but to feel salubriously purified by its pseudoreligious ambience. Extravagantly silly, yes, but the film was enormously popular, proving once again the power of Irene's box-office draw.†

In his tribute to the golden age of film musicals, *Gotta Sing, Gotta Dance* (1970), cinema writer John Kobal observes, "[Jeanette] MacDonald's only rival as the thirties' first lady of film song, was Irene Dunne, similar in style

---

*It was Irene who gently suggested to John M. Stahl, the director of *Magnificent Obsession,* that newcomer Robert Taylor might be ideal for the male lead. Her suggestion was heeded by Stahl.

†Because of Universal's lucrative remake of *Magnificent Obsession* (1954, with Jane Wyman and Rock Hudson), the original screen version has been withdrawn from television circulation.

and appearance." A good deal of Irene's reputation in the song-and-dance genre stems from her performance in Universal's second version of *Show Boat* (Radio City Music Hall, May 14, 1936). The bulk of the Jerome Kern-Oscar Hammerstein II score, removed from the 1929 version to make way for now-forgotten other numbers, was restored to the expansive new edition, lavishly helmed by James Whale, who demonstrated here that his cinematic expertise did not rest only in the horror film genre.

A five-acre tract along the Los Angeles River was utilized for the site of Boonville on the Mississippi River, one of the docking spots for the show-boat *Cotton Blossom,* captained by Charles Winninger and his shrewish wife, Helen Westley. Helen Morgan re-created her stage role as Julie, the mulatto torch singer who hastily departs the riverboat troupe with her lover, Donald Cook, when her racial background is discovered. Morgan's best friend on the *Cotton Blossom* was Winninger's daughter, Irene, who now finds herself performing in the boat show as Morgan's replacement. It is not long before lovely Irene becomes appealing to river gambler Gaylord Ravenal (Allan Jones) and he begins a hasty courtship. Despite her mother's sound warnings, Irene weds this romantic luck-pusher. Before their subsequent child, Kim, is more than a few years old, Irene has cause to regret her marriage, for Jones has suffered a losing streak at the gaming tables and has decided that Irene and their child would be better off without him. She returns to the world of show business, obtaining a post at the Trocadaro Club (replacing a drunken Morgan, who deliberately walks out on her club contract to give Irene a break). At her club opening the sudden appearance of Winninger turns Irene's likely disastrous debut into a quick success, for he eggs her into transforming her ladylike performance into something more popular for the audience to appreciate. More years pass, and Irene's daughter, Kim, has followed in her mother's footsteps by becoming an actress. At Kim's debut performance a gray-haired Irene and Jones (now an elderly stage-doorman) have a teary reunion, able to jointly rejoice in their daughter's professional success.

For a rare change the elastic screen medium was used to nearly full advantage in this *Show Boat,* recapturing the grandeur of the showboat era with the lachrymose flavor and lilting score that made the stage show such a perennial crowd-pleaser. Irene, albeit a mature Magnolia, was accomplished, beautiful, and versatile. Her shuffling and trucking during the "Can't Help Lovin' Dat Man" number remains a joyous scene with Irene at her liberated screen best. With her leading man Jones, Irene sang "You Are Love," "Why Do I Love You?," "I Have the Room Above," and the best-remembered "Make Believe." The number "Why Do I Love You?" ended up on the cutting-room floor. Irene, Jones, and Winninger re-created their *Show Boat* roles on "Lux Radio Theatre" on June 24, 1940.*

*In 1938, MGM acquired the screen rights to *Show Boat* from Universal, planning a new screen version to star Jeanette MacDonald and Nelson Eddy, but it was not until 1951 that a new rendition finally appeared, causing the 1936 version to be withdrawn from circulation.

Nineteen hundred and thirty-six was a full-course watershed mark for thirty-seven-year-old Irene. With a changeover in regimes at Universal, Irene decided to parcel out her screen commitments on a wider scale, resulting in a picture-a-year pact with Columbia, then with Paramount, and later with her old home lot, RKO. This multiallegiance system had been inaugurated on a successful basis by Claudette Colbert earlier in the decade and was adopted later by Carole Lombard, as well as by Irene and others. Irene, who had received $100,000 from Universal in 1936 for *Show Boat,* rose to a $150,000 ceiling on her forthcoming pictures, although her initial Columbia ventures were pacted at a $40,000-salary-plus-percentage pay scale.

When Irene signed with Harry Cohn's Columbia in June, 1935, it had been agreed that her first venture there would be a comedy, a nice change of pace after her years of weepers, But as the time for production grew nearer, Irene suddenly became skeptical of her planned laugh debut in *Theodora Goes Wild* (Columbia, 1936) and hastily embarked on a six-week vacation trip to Europe with Dr. Griffin. Ostensibly the purpose of the Continental jaunt was to meet with the daughter of Madame Curie in preparation for Universal's projected screen biography of the great woman scientist, which was to star Irene.*

Irene finally returned to Hollywood, where Cohn had placed her on salary suspension, and she saw that she had little option but to appear in the screen comedy. When she was advised that former Moscow Art Theatre director Richard Boleslawski was to handle the project, she was even more skeptical. Harry Cohn graciously allowed Irene the option of replacing Boleslawski after one week of shooting if she were not fully satisfied with his abilities by that point. For some strange, happy reason, Boleslawski proved amazingly adept at conveying small-town Americana, so the film proceeded to everyone's satisfaction.

The screwball plot of *Theodora Goes Wild* has Thomas Mitchell, editor of the *Lynnfield* (New England) *Bugle,* stirring up a hornet's nest when he publishes the first installment of the "racy novel," *The Sinner,* by one Caroline Adams. The townsfolk are shocked, especially maiden aunts Elisabeth Risdon and Margaret McWade, who urge their seemingly proper niece Irene (who teaches Sunday school and plays the church organ) to protest the publication, not fathoming that this twenty-five-year-old miss is really *the* Caroline Adams. The sudden publicity of her book prompts Irene to visit her New York publisher to urge him to keep her identity a secret.

However, sophisticated Melvyn Douglas, who illustrated her book turns up at the publisher's office. Douglas is immediately attracted to prim Irene and when she returns home she—but not the audience—is surprised to find him at her front gate (having hoodwinked her aunts into hiring him as an

*Universal had selected *Madame Curie* as a substitute vehicle for Irene after rescheduling *Road to Reno* (1938) for Hope Hampton. Eventually *Madame Curlie* was sold to MGM as a possible Greta Garbo vehicle, with F. Scott Fitzgerald working on one version of the screenplay, before the biopicture finally emerged as a Greer Garson—Walter Pidgeon picture of 1943.

itinerant gardener.) Under the influence of Douglas's courtship, Irene puts aside her prim facade and jaunts back to New York, where she takes up residence at Douglas's residence and finally meets his wife, from whom he has been separated for the past five years.

Perky Irene is now determined to free Douglas from his matrimonial burden, deliberately giving wild interviews and allowing herself to be named the "other woman" in a divorce action between her publisher and his wife. Irene wins her point when Douglas's unwanted spouse finds "tainted" Miss Authoress dancing with the governor at the state ball. Irene further implicates Douglas in her wild melees, and Douglas at last wins his wife's agreement to a legal end to their marriage. Along the way Irene even finds herself custodian of an unwanted baby, which is how she manages to become the shocking Theodora Lynn, the girl named in two divorce suits, and the "mother" of a fatherless baby. But by the finale she has had enough of liberating, capricious behavior and informs Douglas that Theodora is not wild anymore.

The joy of *Theodora Goes Wild* is obviously not in the plot, but in the effervescent manner in which the former queen of soap opera (now displaying a new, longer, hair style) glided through the onscreen shenanigans. A good many critics were unprepared for Irene's successful maiden voyage into the arena of screen comedy. "She surprises with a spirited gift for clowning . . . the role is the most exacting which she has played, and none of Hollywood's dizzier comediennes could have invoked the small town moral of it," *(New York Daily News)*. Although Irene received her second Oscar nomination,* there were some detractors on the scene who carped that "farce does not set too well upon the lovely shoulders of Irene Dunne" and that, as the *New York Herald-Tribune* pointed out, "she strains a bit too hard for laughter on occasion and some of her mannerisms and her drawling chuckles are likely to remind you of Lynn Fontanne."

There was also a "great divide" in Irene's personal life in 1936. Dr. Griffin gave up his New York City practice entirely, and he and Irene made their well-appointed (French Provincial) Holmsby Hill home, which she had been sharing with her mother, their permanent residence.† On March 17, 1936, the couple adopted four-year-old Anna Mary Bush from the New York Founding Hospital. On December 17 of that year, Irene's mother (and constant companion) died in Hollywood of a cerebral hemorrhage; she was survived by Irene and her brother.

---

*Luise Rainer won for *The Great Ziegfeld* (MGM).

†Dr. Griffin reasoned, "I either stayed out there [Hollywood] to be with my wife or we wouldn't have much of a marriage." He first busied himself on the Coast by being Irene's manager, but found the task too complicated for his inexpertise and turned to real-estate management to fill his semiretirement days, as well as accompanying Irene on location trips for her pictures. "I think a man married to a career woman in show business has to be convinced that his wife's talent is too strong to be denied or put out. Then, he can be just as proud of her success as she is and inside, he can take a bow himself for whatever help he's been. That's gratification enough."

While Irene was readjusting to her changed life-style, film offers continued to pour in from the major studios. Paramount wanted her to star in the tear-jerker *Valiant Is the Word for Carrie* (1936), but she decided the venture could not be properly filmed because of the movie industry's revised censorial code, so the project went to Gladys George. Irene also rejected *Swing High, Swing Low* (Paramount, 1937), which went to Carole Lombard, but she did agree to appear in Paramount's *High, Wide and Handsome* (1937). ˜

The production history of *High, Wide and Handsome* is more interesting—at least to this author—than the resulting picture. Rouben Mamoulian, who had just finished directing *The Gay Desperado* (United Artists, 1936), was not eager to attack another screen musical, but he owed Paramount a picture, and studio executives, including Irene's prior RKO mentor, William Le Baron, were convinced he was the proper talent to shepherd Irene through *High, Wide and Handsome,* as he had done so expertly with her screen rival, Jeanette MacDonald, in *Love Me Tonight* (1932). For the music, Paramount hired Jerome Kern and Oscar Hammerstein II, who were determined to create a new *Show Boat* for Irene. They chose for their source material the founding of the Tidewater Oil Company in the western Pennsylvania of the 1850s. What resulted was a shaky mixture of part-musical, part-romance, and part-specious melodrama, not at all the overflowing brimful of picturesque Americana originally intended.

The tricky plot of *High, Wide and Handsome* concerns Irene, who is stranded with her medicine-sideshow father (Raymond Walburn) in a small western Pennsylvania town of 1859. While their damaged wagon is being repaired, Irene meets and becomes enraptured with Randolph Scott and his farming life ("It's like a picture book"). They wed and he promises her that wonderful dwelling just like "The Folk Who Live on the Hill." But his marital promises go down the cinematic drain when the neighboring farmers decide to band together to commercialize the untapped local oil supply. While Scott is organizing the men and combating the transportation syndicate headed by Alan Hale, crony Charles Bickford, and Greek honky-tonk keeper Akim Tamiroff, Irene becomes perturbed at Scott's neglect of her, and she joins a traveling circus. As a warbling soprano (putting forth such ballads as "Can I Forget You?") she soon becomes the prime attraction of the show. But when she learns that Scott and his helpers are in dire need of help, she returns to him and prompts her circus friends to fight off Hale's men and aid Scott in completing his oil pipelines.

The faults within *High, Wide and Handsome* are not difficult to trace. Mamoulian had insisted on having Hammerstein's original script rewritten to no good effect. The Kern-Hammerstein songs as a whole were disappointing, and there was nothing else of sufficient interest to offset the plethora of unessential plotline. Randolph Scott, never much on heavy acting, was certainly unable to provide Irene with the proper springboard for an adequate give-and-take performance (Gary Cooper had been the original choice for the role of Peter Cortlandt.) Not that Paramount's own sarong-girl, Dorothy Lamour, came off much better in the film as the saloon singing Jezebel who is befriended by Irene and later, as Tamiroff's mistress, has an opportunity to repay her debt to Irene.

As for Irene in *High, Wide and Handsome,* there was something amiss with her musical performance. Her numbers, ranging from the rousing opening moment when she launches into the title tune, to her ballad "Can I Forget you?" (sung in a moonlit orchard and reprised at the circus) to the lilting "The Folk Who Live on the Hill" and the somewhat catchy "Allegheny Lil" (sung on a saloon table-top with Lamour), had variety of tempo and style. Nevertheless, no matter how hard Mamoulian tried, Irene was no Jeanette MacDonald,* nor was Irene's presence being bolstered by a storyline as bubbly and sophisticated as the film needed. As *Variety* tactfully noted, Irene was "perhaps a shade too mature." Irene herself, perhaps sensing the widening gap between reality and her screen ingenue roles, lapsed into her old bad habit of gallumphing along in long shots, a telltale trait whenever she became overconscious in her attempt to be young and feminine.

High, Wide and Handsome, which cost a reputed $1.9 million to produce, opened at the Astor Theatre on July 21, 1937, at a $2.20 ticket top on a two-shows-a-day basis. Audience reaction was less than enthusiastic, and for its less than enthusiastic general release thereafter, Paramount pared down the running time from an originally unruly 110 minutes to an easier under-100-minute version.

Irene's other 1937 release, Columbia's *The Awful Truth,†* was far more successful in all ways. Irene no longer had any doubts about her abilities as a screen comedienne and gladly agreed to play with Cary Grant in *The Awful Truth.* The script was directed by Leo McCarey, who also became the film's producer. Irene was not prepared, however, for McCarey's iconoclastic methods of soundstage operation, in which he would often devise the day's shooting takes on the set that very morning, while playing impromptu tunes on a piano. During these inspiration sessions, Irene, Grant, and the others would sit around, waiting for genius to strike the former gag-master. But the results were eminently worthwhile. McCarey won an Oscar as best director of the year, and *The Awful Truth* ranked as one of the year's most successful films. It was a slapstick picture in the best screwball tradition, elevating Irene to equality with the genre's leading practitioner, Carole Lombard, which was no mean feat for a middle-aged screen actress firmly entrenched in both her own mind and that of the public as a great lady of

---

*Irene's gown and garb in the circus number amazingly resembled Jeanette MacDonald's cinematic stock-in-trade image.

†After the fairly popular Broadway stage-play original (Henry Miller Theatre, September 12, 1922—144 performances) there was the Producers Distributing Corp. filmization with Agnes Ayres in 1925, and in 1929 Ina Claire recreated her stage role for the Pathé picturization. In 1953 Columbia would churn out an indifferent musical remake of the story, entitled *Let's Do It Again,* with Jane Wyman and Ray Milland starred.

the four-handkerchief weepers.* Irene's achievement in her new forte was corroborated by members of the Academy of Motion Pictures Arts and Sciences, who nominated her for an Oscar. (She again lost out to Luise Rainer, the latter winning this time for *The Good Earth.*)

When she was passed over by Columbia in favor of her old RKO rival, Katharine Hepburn, for the studio's remake of *Holiday* (1938),† Irene returned to her alma mater RKO for her first picture there in over three years. The studio's new corporate president, George Schaefer, packaged a Jerome Kern-Dorothy and Herbert Fields musical in which Irene costarred opposite Douglas Fairbanks, Jr. Unfortunately there is a good deal of overt straining on everyone's part in *Joy of Living,* so much so, that at times the serviceable comedy almost comes to a halt as the humor dissipates before one's eyes.

The structured comedy plot of *Joy of Living* presents Irene as a $10,000-a week Broadway musical-comedy star, too busy catering to the multitudinous whims of her parasitic family to enjoy the fruits of her fame or her fast dwindling fortune. And then along comes madcap Fairbanks, the black sheep of his Back Bay Boston clan (he has refused to follow in the traditional family business of banking), who insists that life has something to offer a freewheeling individual and that his personal Shangri-La is sailing his yacht to a particular South Sea Island retreat. Obviously, when Irene and Fairbanks meet, they clash, for his persistent *joie de vivre* is an anathema to her practical nature. After escapade upon escapade of trying to shake this Ronald Colman-like figure, she succumbs to his infectious philosophy, tells off her money-grubbing relatives (sister Lucille Ball in particular), walks out of her Sutton Place home, and jaunts off with him.

In the final analysis, one either liked *Joy of Living* immensely or detested it greatly. If one accepts the picture, one also must accept Fairbanks's annoying habit of imitating Donald Duck's quacking and Irene's arch mannerisms, and one must agree to follow willingly along with the couple on their wild (yes, improbable) two-dollar evening in Manhattan's Yorkville German section. This nocturnal escapade ranges from a beer garden stopover, where Irene becomes soused, to their lark at a roller-skating rink, to the ultimate end where the iconoclastic duo walk down New York's streets in their bare feet.

One of the more intriguing factors in *Joy of Living* is the imaginative fashion in which director Tay Garnett set the scene for Irene to sing her several songs: "Just Let Me Look at You" (performed as her play-within-the-movie finale, and repeated in a chauffeur-driven car, and in court), "You Couldn't Be Cuter" (sung to Lucille Ball's twin daughters, while Irene is

---

*It was McCarey's perception to capitalize on the visual incongruity of having such an obviously genteel lady as Irene involved in nutty happenings. Certainly *The Awful Truth* had more than its share of screwball situations what with Irene and Cary Grant playing a couple who get divorced only to discover belatedly that they are still in love, even if neither will admit it.

†Losing out on *Holiday* came as a great disappointment to Irene.

playing their nursery toy piano), "What's Good About Good Night?" (vocalized at the radio station broadcast), and "A Heavenly Party" (sung into a twenty-five-cent recording device at the carnival). Ironically—and particularly sad for those of her fans who liked her, disliked the picture—*Joy of Living* was Irene's swan song in screen musicals!*

It was at this strategic point in her career that Irene publicly theorized: "Comedy is more difficult than drama. Good comedy techniques are harder to acquire. The shadings of meaning and character are subtler, the timing is everything. A flick of a finger can be important—if it's flicked in the right way, and the whole gesture is small. Once learned, comedy techniques can be used for drama merely by slowing them down. An actress who can do comedy can do drama, but the vice versa isn't necessarily true. Big emotional scenes are much easier to play than comedy. An onion can bring tears to your eyes, but what vegetable can make you laugh?"

Columbia proposed that Irene star in the *Elizabeth Blackwell Story,*† but that project was dropped and, being at the peak of her multigenre screen success, she chose RKO's *Love Affair* (1939) as the first of three releases that year, each for a different studio. Under the producing-directing aegis of Leo McCarey, *Love Affair* became an obvious sentimental drama with only a surface glitter of bittersweet sophisticated comedy in the opening sequences. "Soiled" club singer Irene and down-and-out playboy-artist Charles Boyer, each devoted to pink champagne and good repartee, meet on a New York-bound transatlantic liner. Although each is scheduled to wed another upon arrival in the United States—more for financial security than love—they allow themselves the temporary luxury of a shipboard romance, which ultimately develops into such a serious relationship that Boyer insists on having Irene meet his elderly grandmother (Maria Ouspenskaya) on a Madeira stopover. When they reach New York, the love birds agree to give their love a six-month test, deciding to meet on July 1 at five in the afternoon at the top of the Empire State Building ("the nearest thing to heaven in New York"). Half a year later, as Irene joyfully rushes to meet Boyer, she hastily crosses a street and is struck by a car, and is left an apparent cripple. When Irene does not keep the date, Boyer initially loses faith in her, but his deeper feelings push him to search for her. At Christmas time he locates the wheelchair-bound Irene at a Washington Heights orphanage where she is a music instructor and general morale booster, teaching the children to sing such cheery songs as "Just Keeping on Wishing." When Irene realizes Boyer has

---

*Gallant Douglas Fairbanks, Jr. offered an astute appraisal of his *Joy for Living* co-star; "One of the most civilized women. She's a dream, an absolute dream, one of the most professional women I've ever known. Nothing is instinctive, everything she does is carefully thought out, she knows every movement, every intonation, every nuance. She's a first-class craftswoman. Her hours are like office hours, she's never late, she never slips, but instead of being dull and perfect, she's absolutely enchanting and perfect."

†The plotline would have had Irene cast as an English girl who defies convention by coming to the United States to attend and graduate from the New York Medical School at Geneva.

155

discarded his dissolute ways and is now concentrating again on becoming a serious painter, she exclaims, "Miracles do happen. If you can paint, then I can walk." Finis.

Under Rudolph Mate's delicate camerawork, Irene never looked lovelier

high-minded working girl who realizes that love is more important than material betterment. In combination with Continental Charles Boyer, Irene radiated more than ever before oncamera. Only a few critics, such as Archer Winsten *(New York Post),* were able to carp about the fairytale romance and Irene: "Your enjoyment of it will depend on your tolerance of her peculiarly breathlessness. She also sings two songs in the fashion that always makes me fear she is going to miss the note by an infinitesimal margin."

Not long ago Irene reminisced about *Love Affair.* "*Love Affair* is my favorite of all of my films not only because it was so well done, but also because we had such a good time making it. I always worked well with Boyer, and Leo McCarey was a marvelous director and a very dear friend. We shot in continuity and we had such a good time doing the shipboard sequences (much of which was improvised) that when the story had us dock in New York, we felt a real letdown, just as if we had returned from a real trip. Nobody could think of anything to do to pep up the script and they had to bring in teams of extra writers."*

It was eight years since Irene had worked under Wesley Ruggles's direction in *Cimarron;* now they were reunited in Universal's *Invitation to Happiness* (1939). Her screen partner in this boxing film was Fred MacMurray, whose broad comedy technique was far more effective when combined with the quick-tongued vivacity of the likes of Claudette Colbert than with Irene's cooler style of comedy. *Invitation to Happiness* sought to rise above its basic prizefight premise, but its side excursions into class discrimination and realization of success through failure only bogged the story further into a morass of stodginess.

Irene remained at Universal for *When Tomorrow Comes* (1939)† produced and directed by John M. Stahl. Top-billed Irene was again matched with Charles Boyer in this often persuasive love story. Irene was presented in *When Tomorrow Comes* as a union-flag-waving waitress who falls in love with concert pianist Boyer, only to later learn that he is wed to a woman (Barbara O'Neil) of his own class who suffers from periodic bouts of insan-

---

*Irene would recreate her *Love Affair* role opposite William Powell on "Lux Radio Theatre" on April 1, 1940. Because of the 1957 Twentieth Century-Fox remake of the picture as *An Affair to Remember* (with Deborah Kerr and Cary Grant), Irene's version is no longer available for television showings.

†The genesis of *When Tomorrow Comes* is rather fascinating. It derives from the same James M. Cain story which was the basis of *Serenade* (1956), and *When Tomorrow Comes* itself was remade as *Interlude* (1956 and 1968 versions). The *Daily Worker* had an interesting in-slant on Irene's performance as the union-loving waitress: "She is by no means the youngest of the stars, but her performance is distinctly youthful and tremendously sincere."

ity. Whether spouting food orders in hashhouse lingo ("Ferdinand without flour"), rapturously listening to Boyer's piano playing, or cozily snuggling with the pianist in a church-attic retreat during a hurricane, Irene (and Boyer) overcame the patchwork plot and mundane dialog. Many a lesser talent would have fallen by the wayside with such clichéd dialog as:

Irene: "Why didn't you tell me who you really are?"

Boyer: "Would it have made any difference?"

When Tomorrow Comes concludes with Boyer leaving on his scheduled Paris trip, promising Irene that "I shall return," but each knows (as does the audience) that joint happiness is never to be theirs.

Moving into the 1940s, Irene almost went over to Warner Bros. to assume the lead opposite Charles Boyer in *All This and Heaven Too* (1940), but the thought of losing such a prize role was more than Warner's *femme terrible,* Bette Davis, could bear, and she returned to the lot from a suspension walkout to make the picture. Since Irene was grossing about $100,000 a year, she felt safe in continuing to refuse vehicles that just were not up to her standards. Along with Jean Arthur, Claudette Colbert, and Ginger Rogers, Irene rejected Columbia's remake of *The Front Page,* to be called *His Girl Friday* (1940). Rosalind Russell was borrowed from MGM for that Cary Grant comedy.

Irene also rejected the opportunity to return to Broadway in *Lady in the Dark* (Alvin Theatre, January 23, 1941—462 performances). She refused the role, which went to Gertrude Lawrence; because Dr. Griffin had already made the transition to Hollywood, she was perfectly content with her screen career, and moreover, she did not want to give it up for a chancy Broadway fling.

But Irene did accept the female lead in RKO's *My Favorite Wife* (1940) opposite Cary Grant.* The film's scenario is sweetly to the point. Legally presumed dead after being lost at sea for seven years, Irene suddenly returns home in time to prevent "husband" Grant from loving Gail Patrick. The situation leads to a four-handed game of romance and jealousy, for it develops that Irene's deserted-isle mate was not a mealy-mouthed weakling (as she had told Grant) but lanky Randolph Scott. Irene was enthused enough about the prospects of the picture and her percentage deal to attend the special premiere of the film held in her hometown of Louisville, Kentucky, before the movie's official debut at Radio City Music Hall (May 4, 1940).

*Originally director Leo McCarey planned this feature as a Jean Arthur vehicle entitled *Woman Overboard.* Instead Arthur made the very similar *Too Many Husbands,* and Irene was hired on at $100,000 salary plus a percentage of the profits. McCarey had slated himself to both produce and direct this variation of the Enoch Arden theme, but due to illness he was forced to hand over the helming chores to newcomer Garson Kanin, although the latter insists that McCarey controlled the day-by-day course of direction. *My Favorite Wife* was remade by Twentieth Century-Fox in the 1960s, first as the abortive *Something's Gotta Give* (1963) with Marilyn Monroe, and then as Doris Day's *Move Over, Darling* (1963). Consequently, Irene's *My Favorite Wife* is unavailable for video showings.

Irene made yet another film with her expert teammate Cary Grant, *Penny Serenade* (Columbia, 1941), a rather maudlin romantic drama produced and directed by George Stevens in his typical overextended fashion. The plot has Irene determined to leave her husband (Grant). Just at the point of departure she happens to replay some of the recordings which they had purchased over the years. Each record triggers memories (via flashbacks) of specific episodes in their joint lives: from courtship to marriage, to her miscarriage suffered during an earthquake while with her newspaper-reporter hubby in Tokyo, to their ownership of a small-town newspaper, to the joy of adopting a little girl and the abject sorrow they endure when she dies. But a boost from the scripters and good sense bring Irene and Grant together again before the fade-out. As an added bit of optimism, they are encouraged by the knowledge that the orphanage has another child waiting for their tender, loving care. Otis Ferguson *(New Republic)* confided to his readers, "[Irene is] one of the very few gals who could sustain a part like this." Irene herself explained one especial reason for her success with this turgid assignment: "I don't think I've ever felt as close to any picture. It's very much the scheme of my personal life." Irene and Edgar Buchanan, joined by Joseph Cotten, performed *Penny Serenade* over "Lux Radio Theatre" on May 8, 1944.

Irene had always felt most comfortable performing with directors with whom she had had previous professional experience. Therefore she readily accepted Universal's comedy-package offer for her to star in *Unfinished Business* (1941), produced and directed by Gregory La Cava, who had last directed Irene in *Symphony of Six Million* (1932). Irene had faith that megaphoner La Cava would turn out another screwball-comedy masterpiece à la *My Man Godfrey,* but she was sadly mistaken. *Unfinished Business* was slick and smooth, but neither Irene nor Robert Montgomery could bolster the slight, trite tale to major entertainment heights. The film itself posed the question, How can there be a new love when the old love is unfinished? A choir singer (Irene) from the small town of Messine, Ohio, has spent most of her life to date bringing up her younger sister and dreaming of romance. After her sister marries, Irene jaunts to New York on a fling. On the train she meets charming Preston Foster, who easily wins her heart (so she thinks), but he has only been indulging in a mild flirtation. Later she meets his brother (Robert Montgomery), whom she thereafter weds. Nevertheless Irene still has lingering thoughts about Foster, which persist in hovering in her (sub)conscious till fate (the script) brings Irene and Foster together face to face. Irene now realizes her attraction to Foster was only a fancy.

Irene had ample opportunity to demonstrate her flawless sense of timing in *Unfinished Business,* whether as the game nightclub switchboard operator ("This is the cafe Col-ti-noor, Sterling 3-6924") exchanging barbs with restaurateur Walter Catlett, performing as a forlorn milkmaid in the chorus of the opera *Martha,* or drifting into inebriation and flying off with Montgomery for an overnight elopement in South Carolina. Irene's performance was blemished in *Unfinished Business*—even if there are those who will deny it—by her old nemesis: once again she emerged too poised and cultured a person to be the ingenuous *Way Down East* type of girl Nancy Andrews is structured to be in the film's opening scenes. When Irene was heard in the "Lux Radio Theatre" rendition of *Unfinished Business* on October 6, 1941, Don Ameche was her male lead, and her role interpretation remained much the same as on film.

Still at the height of her professional popularity, forty-three-year-old Irene could afford moments of candor in her increasingly rare interviews with the press. She had a long discussion on the subject of temperament with Irene Thirer of the *New York Post* in 1941. "Anyone will tell you," claimed the movie star, neither boastfully nor overly modest, "that I'm the easiest person to get along with on the set. What my fellow players and members of the unit don't know is that I've thrashed it all out before hand. Mine is the calm after the storm. Two weeks before I'm scheduled to begin a picture I go into conference with my producer and director—and a terrific battle invariably ensues. However, by the time shooting commences, it's all over. Everything is nice and peaceful. . . . Why I fought constantly with my husband for nearly two years before we were married."

Gregory La Cava's recurring illnesses during the shooting of *Lady in a Jam* (Universal, 1942) have always been cited as the cause for that film being a bomb in which the tediousness of a prefabricated "comedy" plot and synthetic characterizations reached new heights. Scatterbrained socialite Irene suddenly learns in *Lady in a Jam* that her fortune (left to her by her grandfather) is almost gone, and through a series of misadventures she ends up on her grandmother's Arizona ranch, flirting with her childhood flame (Ralph Bellamy) to raise the jealousy factor within psychiatrist Patric Knowles, who is posing as her chauffeur. Complicated? Not really! Enjoyable filmfare? Not really! Irene, in fact, offered a very jittery performance in this fallen souffle.

It was very logical that Irene would eventually return to MGM, where her refined screen manner could be appreciated at closer hand by studio head Louis B. Mayer. It was indeed unfortunate that Irene and Mayer did not come to terms before she had passed beyond her fortieth birthday into the "dangerous" decade of a screen actress's career, and ahead of Mayer's discovery of Greer Garson, whom he soon came to regard as the epitome of the idealized well-bred woman. Irene might have been very effective in *Mrs. Miniver* (1942) or in her once-designated vehicle, *Madame Curie* (1943), two roles that did much to make Garson the queen of the Metro lot.

At any rate, after performing as guest artist with the Chicago Symphony Orchestra in the 1941-42 season, Irene concluded an MGM pact, which put her on the Culver City lot with two other RKO alumnae, Katharine Hepburn (who had found a new lease on her cinema career as Spencer Tracy's leading lady) and Ann Harding (who had foolishly resigned herself to film character parts). As a matter of fact, it was rather ironic that Irene's first

1940s Metro role should be with Hepburn's latest screen partner, Spencer Tracy, in the film entitled *A Guy Named Joe* (1943).

Borrowing heavily from the philosophy of *Outward Bound,* the spriteness of *Blithe Spirit,* and the commercial drollery of *Here Comes Mr. Jordan, A Guy Named Joe** was irretrievably a syrupy patriotic tale, pandering to the current mystical view of plane pilots and crews. The England-set plot centers on American flyer Tracy, who, on his last flight before returning to the United States as a pilot instructor, embarks on a suicide mission, crashing his plane into a German aircraft carrier. In the flyers' valhalla he is assigned by celestial general Lionel Barrymore to return to earth to counsel Air Force cadets. The presence of Tracy's returned "spirit" is constantly felt by his past girlfriend, Irene of the Ferry Command Squadron, and particularly by millionaire novice serviceman Van Johnson. Johnson is impudent and young (both of which qualities annoy Tracy), but more importantly to Tracy's consternation, he falls deeply in love with Irene and they wed while he is based in New Guinea. In a particularly foolhardy *Perils of Pauline*-style climax, Johnson is assigned a dangerous flight task, but Irene impetuously goes up in the readied plane to perform the mission instead. With Tracy's unseen help she succeeds. Now Tracy can return to heaven, leaving the couple to their earthly happiness.

From the start there was no doubt but that *A Guy Named Joe*† would be exceedingly commercial film fare for entertainment-hungry World War II filmgoers, which it was. It was the first movie in several years that did not have Irene topcast, a status position that Tracy insisted upon, particularly when the rambunctious Oscar-winner took an immediate dislike to Irene's natural high-bred manner. He made no bones about grumbling over his dissatisfaction at having to work with her on this film. Only when movie newcomer Van Johnson was severely injured during filming and Louis B. Mayer threatened to replace him, did Johnson's mentor (Tracy) agree to adopt a far more civil attitude to Irene in exchange for an assurance that production would be held up until Johnson recovered sufficiently to resume his role in the film.

While Johnson recuperated from the head injury which had almost put him out of total commission, MGM put into production *The White Cliffs of Dover* (Radio City Music Hall, May 10, 1944), which meant that in the course of the latter picture's long film schedule and the resumption of *A Guy Named Joe,* Irene had to work on two big-budgeted movies at once. "I always lived the characters I played," says Irene, "and to have to be those two entirely different women at the same time was unbearable. And yet I think *A Guy Named Joe* is one of the finest pictures I ever made." Certainly *The White Cliffs of Dover* does not stand up as well today, largely because it was such a blatant hands-across-the-sea World War II propaganda gesture with all its emotional stops pulled out. What *Mrs. Miniver* had done for

*The film's title derived from a remark made by General Claire Chennault, who said about flying, during the early part of World War II, "When I'm behind the stick, I'm just a guy named Joe."

†Everett Riskin produced both *Here Comes Mr. Jordan* and *A Guy Named Joe.*

Greer Garson and America's impression of Britishers on the home front, *The White Cliffs of Dover* was to do for Irene and Anglo-American relationships. Thus it was no accident that Sidney Franklin produced both of these MGM pictures.

For a woman of age forty-five, Irene still photographed as an amazingly youthful person as she played an innocent American who comes on a visit to England in 1914 and weds Devon landowner Alan Marshall only to have him die in World War I in the autumn of 1918, leaving her to raise their child in her husband's homeland. The decades pass, and when England becomes embroiled in a new global conflict, Irene immediately volunteers as a Red Cross nurse supervisor. By happenstance, she passes by the bed where her wounded soldier son (Peter Lawford) lies dying. The wistful tearjerker ends on a sobbing, patriotic note as Irene repeats the words of a fatally wounded American boy as just quoted to her by Lawford: "We must not break faith with the dead again; this time we must fight for a peace that will stick . . . "*

Irene was commended for offering "a nice glow of American charm" *(New York Times)* in *The White Cliffs of Dover,* but had the picture not been so speciously intent upon showing Americans only their own preconceived notions of Britain and Britishers, Alice Duer Miller's famous poem might have been properly picturized to convey the actual message "There will always be an England," and Irene would have had the full-bodied showcase she deserved but did not receive.

While Louis B. Mayer was pondering Irene's fate on his lot, she arranged to make *Together Again* (Columbia, 1944), her third and final screen outing with Charles Boyer. It was a sticky confection in which the two co-stars worked busily to no effect and with little sparkling of romance and fun. Irene played the widow of the mayor of a small New England town (Brookhaven). Under the prompting of her father (Charles Coburn), she treks off to New York City to commission a sculptor to chisel a statue in honor of her late husband. She meets artist Boyer and falls in love with him, much to the consternation of her junior miss daughter (Mona Freeman). Producer and co-scripter Virginia Van Upp too often relied in *Together Again* on Coburn's stock elderly Cupid image and stylization, along with overly fortuitous heavenly interventions—rainstorms and thunderstorms—to solve sticky plot manipulations. The *New York Herald Tribune* properly labeled the picture a turkey.

Irene then settled into a professional routine of making only one picture a year, while keeping her star status amazingly intact. Columbia had paid an exorbitant $350,000 for the screen rights to Ruth Gordon's Broadway success, *Over 21* (1945).† Harry Cohn shoved the property at versatile, if uninspired, director Charles Vidor, to prepare as an Irene Dunne picture.

*Irene had her own evaluation of the message in *The White Cliffs of Dover:* "I don't think it smacks of propaganda, but if it does, then I'm glad. I feel everything possible should be done to cement friendship between the two nations that are most alike and speak the same language."

†Opened at the Music Box Theatre on January 3. 1944, and ran for 221 performances.

Unfortunately Gordon had conceived the lead role (based on Dorothy Parker) as a juicy part for herself on the stage; it was almost impossible to re-tailor it to Irene's very different personality. This being the case, Cohn and Vidor decided to have Irene remake her screen presence herein as closely as possible to that of Miss Gordon. Irene's copying of Gordon's peculiar public guise might have been a good private acting exercise, but it hardly created any stimulating screen fare.

The story, much in the vein of *Pillar to Post,* had a famous woman screen writer (Irene) forced to cope with the mundane problems of the wartime housing shortage and the makeshift accommodations of bungalow-court life while her thirty-nine-year-old newspaper editor husband (Alexander Knox) attends officers' training camp. Charles Coburn was typecast as the grumpy newspaper publisher who intends to have Knox back where he belongs—at his newspaper desk—and enlists Irene's cooperation to insure the fact.

After completing *Over 21* in March, 1945, Irene traveled to Chicago to accept an honorary degree of doctor of music from the Chicago Musical College, positive that when she returned to Hollywood in mid-June that year she would again be at work at MGM on a new project. But such was not to be the case, for in the post-World War II cutback, Louis B. Mayer and the Metro hierarchy decided that younger Greer Garson was more than adequate to handle any major role on the studio's production schedule that required a high-toned lady. Irene had finally become a victim of the occupational disease from which there is no cure: over-age.

But Irene was an industrious strategist; if MGM did not require her professional services, Twentieth Century-Fox was more than pleased to have her sign a contract to star in *Anna and the King of Siam* (Radio City Music Hall, June 20, 1946). The superbly mounted feature was in production for eighty-eight days under John Cromwell's direction.* Irene applied a restrained touch to her focal role, which could easily have degenerated into pompous histrionics.† The now-familiar story has Irene as Anna Owens, the British widow who arrives with her young son in the Siam of 1862 to be the teacher to the king's harem of wives and children and, as she later discovers, to advise the monarch on all facets of the English way of life. Just as the wily king (Rex Harrison) learns much from the noble and triumphant Anna, so she acquires a better understanding of life from the ruler, a man who desperately wishes to leap in one bound from semibarbarism to civilized life. As she fervently exclaims near the end of this 128-minute black-and-white feature, "He tried so hard, no one will ever know. He was like a little boy sometimes . . . . nobody understood, not really." When the king dies and the prince (Tito Renaldo) becomes ruler, the new monarch's first proclamation is

---

*The set decorations and Arthur Miller's camera work earned Academy Awards.

†According to the advertisements for *Anna and the King of Siam*, the thrust of the film concerned "the incredible . . . . but true . . . . story of a woman who braved and won a world, more glorious than any dream."

to abolish the age-old custom of groveling, a practice over which Anna had staunchly fought the late king. Through her veil of tears, Anna realizes that in her small way she has wrought great changes in the Siamese culture; her once unimportant life now has a grand, unselfish meaning. She is fulfilled, almost enough to make up for the loss of her son, who has died in a riding accident.

In her first screen epic since *Cimarron*, Irene emerged with flying colors (performing, according to *Newsweek*, "with charm, good sense, and a nice appreciation of Occidental independence in an Oriental oligarchy"). She re-created her memorable role in *Anna and the King of Siam* on "Lux Radio Theatre" on May 30, 1949, with James Mason as the king.*

Riding a new crest of cinematic popularity after *Anna and the King of Siam,* Irene had many offers from which to choose. When Warner Bros. packaged *Life with Father* (1947)† and studio director Michael Curtiz vetoed the original choice of Mary Pickford (in what would have been her film come-back) to play Vinnie Day, Irene accepted the part. In her first color feature, Irene had her hair dyed red‡ to match the shade used by the other members of the oncamera Day family. Clarence Day's play was translated almost in toto to the screen with William Powell admirably suited to his portrayal of the irascible New Yorker of the 1890s whose favorite word is "gad!" and who is aghast at the thought that his wife and flock of children are maneu-vering to overcome an omission on the part of his parents, i.e., to have him baptized. It requires Vinnie's illness for her bluff and independent husband to agree to being christened on the promise, of course, that she return an atro-cious china dog which she had the audacity to charge to him. Finally, and to everyone's relief, the family is seated in the carriage heading off to Audubon Park and the church baptism. As the carriage is about to depart from their 420 Madison Avenue home, the cop on the beat inquires where Powell is off to in such a dither. Powell's answer is, "To be christened, damn it!"

There was almost universal approval for the Warner Bros. rendition of *Life with Father*, with praise being heaped on each and every talent depart-ment connected with the film. Perhaps the biggest controversy involving this

---

*In the subsequent multimedia offerings of *Anna and the King of Siam*, Gertrude Lawrence played Anna in the Broadway musical version entitled *The King and I*, a role re-created by Deborah Kerr in the 1956 movie musical version; in the embarrassingly puerile television situ-ation comedy adaptation of *The King and I* (1972), an inept Samantha Eggar portrayed the American teacher at Yul Brynner's Siam-set court. Because of these various remakes of Margaret Landon's original best-selling book, Irene's 1946 film version of *Anna and the King of Siam* did not have its television premiere until December 26, 1969, at which time Irene earned plaudits from a new generation unfamiliar with her modulated interpretation of the de-manding yet potentially cloying role.

†Opened January 8, 1939 at the Empire Theatre and ran for 3,224 performances.

‡Years later, Irene recalled; "They sent us all down to [Perc] Westmore's one Sunday morning to get our hair dyed red. When they went to rinse the dye off they discovered that there was no water—the plumbing for the whole block had been turned off because they were repairing the street. We called up the Mayor and everybody we could think of, but to no avail. Fortunately, somebody hit upon the idea of diluting the dye with gallons of cold cream; otherwise we would have been bald, hair dyes were so crude in those days."

film concerned the billing. How was the studio to acknowledge the equal popularity of both Irene and William Powell? Warner Bros.' ingenious solution is still remembered today in Hollywood circles. Onscreen, during the credit unrolling, flashing lights first have Irene's name in the top spot, then William Powell's name in that position. In printed media advertisements, Irene's name would appear first one day, Powell's would be top-spotted the next.

For those who adored the screen version of *Life with Father*, and fondly recalled Irene's jaunty performance as the matronly but vivacious mother of the Day brood and wife to the temperamental William Powell, it was a long wait until the feature finally appeared on television. When copyright and contractual negotiations were finally solved for a CBS-TV premiere on December 25, 1970, audiences were somewhat disappointed to note that the 118-minute feature had been chopped down by several scenes to fit into its allotted video screening time. But at least there was Irene once again proudly perambulating down the streets of 1890s New York, an effervescent bounce to her stride which could not be hampered in any way by the harassing from her delightful tyrant of a husband (Powell).

It was a new RKO to which Irene returned in 1947 to star in *I Remember Mama* (1948). Dore Schary was now in charge of the truncated studio facilities, whose player roster now boasted the likes of Barbara Hale, Jane Greer, Robert Mitchum, Kirk Douglas, and Martha Hyer, a distinct change of box-office pace from the studio's heyday in the early 1930s, when Irene, Ann Harding, Constance Bennett, and Katharine Hepburn ruled the company's marquee roost.

Initially, when producer Harriet Parsons considered turning Kathryn Forbes's novel, *Mama's Bank Account*, into a film, she had Katina Paxinou in mind for the lead role. But then RKO and Parsons were financially persuaded to hold up the forthcoming screen adaption while a John Van Druten Broadway production (1944) was mounted. When that New York venture, starring Mady Christians, proved so popular (lasting 714 performances), Harriet Parsons approached Greta Garbo about the lead assignment in the delayed movie version.* Garbo said no, but Irene gave an affirmative nod. Production got underway in late 1947 under the aegis of executive producer-director George Stevens. Irene, in a braided wig and with a thick Norwegian accent, played the 1910s San Francisco (Larker Street) housewife and mother, performing so realistically that it seemed as if "the fjords were only recently behind her." As she had been the tower of strength behind the monarch in *Anna and the King of Siam* and her upper-class family in *Life with Father*, so she was the backbone of her Scandinavian-extract household in *I Remember Mama*, displaying a sense of strength and sympathy that made her symbolize

---

*Garbo, who had been offered the lead in *The Paradine Case* at this time, rejected both roles, saying, "No mamas, no murderesses."

mothers everywhere. * Whether proceeding through the solemn ceremony of counting out the household money on Saturday nights, offering maturing daughter Barbara Bel Geddes her first cup of coffee, keeping a promise to daughter June Hedin that she will visit her in the hospital after her tonsillectomy (Irene has to don the outfit of a scrubwoman to sneak by the institution's authorities), or comforting cantankerous Uncle Chris (Oscar Homolka) on his deathbed, Irene thoughtfully performed her assignment in this idyllic series of nostalgic vignettes. She received her fifth Oscar nomination (her fourth being a decade earlier for *Love Affair*) for *I Remember Mama, but* lost out to Jane Wyman, who won the Best Actress Award for *Johnny Belinda*. Irene, Barbara Bel Geddes, and Oscar Homolka would recreate their *I Remember Mama* roles on "Lux Radio Theatre" on August 30, 1948.

Nineteen hundred and forty-nine was a year of award receiving for Irene. The University of Notre Dame selected her for its annual tribute as the outstanding member of the American Catholic laity, and in June of that year she received an honorary degree from Mount St. Mary. She was offered the replacement lead in the Broadway hit *Goodbye, My Fancy*, but rejected the chance to make a stage return. Instead Irene agreed to star in *Never a Dull Moment* (RKO, 1950), a very mild comedy which reteamed her with aging male lead Fred MacMurray. Producer Harriet Parsons and director George Marshall tried to carbon-copy Universal's box-office bonanza *The Egg and I* (which had co-starred Claudette Colbert and MacMurray), but the formula did not jell in this insipid spinoff. As the sophisticated New York music writer who weds a rodeo performer, Irene did her best to instill lightness into the city-dude-comes-to-a-Wyoming-ranch tale, but television-attuned audiences would not buy this modest domestic-comedy package. Irene's singing of "Once You Find Your Guy," "Sagebrush Lullaby," and "A Man with a Big Felt Hat" was pleasant but modest.

In retrospect it is easy enough to perceive why Irene thought *The Mudlark* (Twentieth Century-Fox, 1950) would be a challenge. The film offered her an opportunity to hark back to her 1930s roles, in which makeup altered her youthful, chic screen image to that of a dowdy old matron. However, in *The Mudlark* she went one better, for throughout the entire film Irene was garbed, contorted, and facially remolded as the small, dumpy, elderly Queen Victoria. Unfortunately the sight of Irene in this guise was the British-lensed feature's only gimmick, and that was shot in the first twenty minutes, when the camera zooms in for a close-up, and a much-corseted Irene sits in her regal chair awaiting the audience's appreciative appraisal of her transformation into the famed monarch. Once the viewer has gasped, "That can't be Irene Dunne! How did they do it?" there is very little of entertainment value left to the pic-

*Not even Peggy Wood, in the well-remembered, Emmy Award-winning television series "[I Remember] Mama," could outdo Irene's portrayal of the wise, kind, generous, and thrifty turn-of-the-century Mama.

ture, particularly if one is not impressed by Alec Guinness's effete portrayal of politician Disraeli or the *Oliver Twist*-like cuteness of Cockney Andrew Rey, who sneaks into Windsor Castle to get a peek at the still-mourning Queen. (She is forced out of retirement back into the political humdrum, no matter how much she grieves for her late, beloved Prince Albert). At the time it was made, there was much consternation among the British that an American should be cast to play the Queen. One London M.P. exclaimed it was the greatest insult to Britain since Hollywood cast Erroll Flynn in *Objective Burma* (1945) and allowed him to capture the enemy outpost singlehandedly.

Not only did *The Mudlark* fail to find public favor, but Irene was criticized for giving more a measured impersonation than a performance since her characterization lacked both humanity and depth. Compared to other performances—by Helen Hayes, Anna Neagle, and Julie Harris, among others—of Queen Victoria, Irene's interpretation falls far short of the mark. Irene, nevertheless, did see fit to recreate her *The Mudlark* role on "Lux Radio Theatre" on August 27, 1951 with Sir Cedric Hardwicke as her co-star.

It is a pity that *It Grows on Trees* (Universal, 1952) should be Irene's last feature film to date. The inexpensively mounted comedy would have made a fine half-hour television episode, but its thin, fanciful plot (of a lady who discovers five-dollar and ten-dollar bills growing on trees in her backyard) could not bear the extended screen treatment. Critics kindly referred to Irene as "that inexhaustible lady" in *It Grows on Trees*, but little could be said of the giddy little comedy fantasy, or for that matter of the scope of Irene's role as the nice middle-class housewife who alters her harried suburban Connecticut existence by her marvelous backyard discovery.

Seemingly, the finale of Irene's three-decade film career would be the end of her professional work, but she surprised not a few in the film industry by accepting a hostess post on television's "Schlitz Playhouse of Stars" (May-November, 1952), leaving the job when, she said, too many of her fans wrote to her protesting her appearance on a video show sponsored by a brewery. Thereafter she was an infrequent performer on the small-screen medium.*

*On television, she was seen to advantage in the lead role in *Sister Veronica* on "Ford Theatre" (NBC, April 15, 1954); in *A Touch of Spring* on "Ford Theatre" (NBC, February 3, 1955), with Gene Barry as the younger man in her life; and portraying Dr. Gina Kersten, the real-life physician who treated mentally retarded children, in *The Opening Door* segment of "The June Allyson Show" (CBS, October 5, 1959). She was among the nearsighted hostesses (she refused to wear glasses and squinted instead) who emceed the special Academy Awards nomination special on NBC (February 12, 1955); sang selections from *Show Boat* on the "Perry Como Show" (NBC, September 15, 1956); and guested on the October 7, 1960 Eleanor Roosevelt *Diamond Jubilee Plus One* NBC special. She appeared on an episode of NBC's "Saints and Sinners" series (October 15, 1962). When Irene guested on the *Go Fight City Hall* segment of "G.E. Theatre" (CBS, January 28, 1962), playing a widow who is drawn into political action, she insisted this would not lead to a series about the lady politico. "When I was at the Revue Studios filming this show," Irene said, "I felt so sorry for all those people who were there doing series and knowing they were unable to do their best. It just can't be done every week, can it?

"I think of the lonely lives they must lead. They are so busy with the series that they have no time to do anything else.

"And those commercials! I don't want to downgrade television, but having to do commercials doesn't really do anything for a star, do you think?"

Much more important to Irene in the 1950s were her political involvements. Early in the decade she let it be known that she held staunch Republican views. "It wasn't very bright of me, I suppose," said Irene, recalling the years when she was branded a right-wing Republican. (Long an endorser of General Eisenhower, she later added: "I'm a Nixon Republican, not a Goldwater one. I don't like extremism in any case. The extreme rights do as much harm as the extreme lefts.") In 1957, as a result of her supporting him, President Eisenhower appointed her an alternative delegate to the Twelfth General Assembly of the United Nations in New York.* After giving her maiden speech to the Assembly on October 2, 1957 (speaking on the state of trusteeships), Irene told the press, "I've played many parts, but this offers the greatest challenge of all." She remained with her U.N. post for a year, and then returned to Hollywood.

Not so much because she was a post-middle-aged star who had difficulty finding proper roles, but more because she wanted to devote her full concentration to being a mother and a wife, Irene eased out of show business completely by the 1960s. Her name continued to appear in the news: turning down a leading part in MGM's *The Swan* (1956), receiving an honorary law degree at Notre Dame University in 1958 and one at Loyola of Los Angeles in the same year, entering into a rhubarb with Mrs. Eleanor Roosevelt over Irene's participation in the right-to-work campaign in 1958 in California. Irene's fans knew time was marching on, but never so clearly as when, in August, 1959, she became a grandmother for the second time. (Her daughter had married Richard Lee Skinnick in the mid-1950s, giving birth to her first child in 1958.)

Throughout her thirty-seven-year marriage to Dr. Griffin, Irene had led such a placid domestic life—always politely deferring to Dr. Griffin's wishes in her daily professional existence—that there was never the slightest taint to their wedded years, a remarkable record in fast-paced Hollywood.† On Oc-

---

*Regarding Irene's United Nations post, good friend Loretta Young said, "She will do a magnificent job. She never did any other as a wife, a mother, or an actress."

From the Lower Park Avenue address where the United States delegation to the U.N. maintained its headquarters, Irene told the press re speechmaking; "I'm Miss Stagefright herself. I never could overcome it; really, cameras scare me half to death. But I'm not the least bit nervous making a U.N. speech. Maybe that's because, as an actress, I am impersonating someone else, while here I'm saying the things I feel."

One of the several entertaining anecdotes to come out of Irene's new U.N. post was the time she completed a speech at the Assembly, pledging twenty-one million on behalf of the Congress. As she left the rostrum, a man tapped her elbow, saying "Your autograph, madam."

Irene thought it an odd place to ask for such a fan request, till she looked at the paper handed her—it was the official agreement binding the U.S. to give aid to refugees.

†Dr. Griffin rarely assumed any personality in public. On only one occasion in later years did he speak on his subordinate role. In 1958 he told reporter Joe Hyams that Irene's career "paled him into insignificance" and "I've been insignificant ever since." He rarely boasted of his sharp business acumen, whether as a real-estate investor, bank trustee, or partnered with his own family in the Griffin Equipment Company (of New York), which distributed diesel engines for heavy construction work, and the Griffin Wellpoint Company, which manufactured special equipment for soil dewatering processing. Dr. Griffin's chief hobbies were his memberships in Catholic groups, as a Knight of the Holy Sepulchre and a Knight of Malta.

tober 15, 1965, Dr. Griffin died of a heart ailment at the age of seventy-nine. Irene stated that it required a good deal of time (five years) and the benevolent assistance of the Almighty for her to recuperate from the shock of losing her beloved husband.

Thereafter Irene appeared even less frequently in the news. She was occasionally mentioned for receiving yet another honorary degree or award for her philanthropic work, or when she was elected to the Board of Directors of Technicolor, Inc., in 1965 (noteworthy for her being the first woman so selected). She did make an appearance, so to speak, on Broadway in the 1965 season when she was among the celebrities shown larking in candid home movies taken by Ken Murray and used in his stage show *Ken Murray's Hollywood* (John Golden Theatre, May 11, 1965). In 1967, Irene was among those present at the televised Oscarcast, she being assigned to present the Jean Hersholt Humanitarian Award.

Today, Irene's life is very full but very private. She tends the extensive real-estate holdings that she and Dr. Griffin acquired, as well as the various corporate offices she filled in his place upon his demise. There are visits with her daughter and two grandchildren, and various charitable works (particularly fund raising for St. John's Hospital and serving on the California Arts Commission). Usually she has afternoon tea at three o'clock in her well-appointed library in the Holmsby Hills home she still maintains. Thereafter, towards dusk, she usually goes alone to a little Westwood chapel for late afternoon Mass. "A Mass takes twenty-five minutes and it's no sacrifice for me to give that much time to say, 'Praise you, my Lord.' I'm just grateful that I'm well enough to go."

In the fall of 1970 Irene did agree to take cognizance of her lengthy and very successful film career by appearing at a special tribute program sponsored by the Los Angeles County Museum and the California Palace of the Legion of Honor. In the course of the retrospective, Irene graciously answered questions posed by the public, many of whom had never seen the bulk of her film work in theatrical release or on television (due largely to copyright problems involving remakes).

Irene looks back fondly on the studio system of the 1930s and 1940s "where there was a great simpatico feeling between a person under contract and the studio to whom you belonged. You had a great feeling of security."

But Irene claims she does not miss stardom. "I knew all along acting was not everything there was." Of her peak fame years: "I never really had time to enjoy my success. Time! All my mother wanted was me and my time. I could buy her a new car, but I couldn't go around to the shops with her. I didn't have time. I had good governesses for my daughter and yet with these grandchildren I see how much time they demand, how much of you they demand. [When my mother died] I was devastated. I couldn't go on. When I go, my daughter will be able to carry on."

Feature Film Appearances

IRENE DUNNE

LEATHERNECKING (RKO, 1930) 80½ M.

Associate producer, Louis Sarecky; director, Edward Cline; based on the play *Present Arms* by Herbert Fields, Richard Rodgers, Lorenz Hart; adaptation, Alfred Jackson; continuity, Jane Murfin; titles, John Krafft; art director, Max Ree; music director, Victor Baravalle; choreography, Pearl Eaton; assistant director, Frederick Fleck; song, Benny Davis and Harr Akst; music, Oscar Levant; camera, J. Roy Hunt.

Irene Dunne (Delphine Witherspoon); Ken Murray (Frank); Louise Fazenda (Hortense); Ned Sparks (Sparks); Lilyan Tashman (Edna); Eddie Foy, Jr. (Chick Evans); Benny Rubin (Stein); Rita La Roy (Fortune teller); Fred Santley (Douglas); William von Brinken (Richter); Carl Gerrard (Colonel); Werther Weidler, Wolfgang Weidler (Richter's Sons).

CIMARRON (RKO, 1931) 131 M.

Producer, William Le Baron; associate producer, Louis Sarecky; director, Wesley Ruggles; based on the novel by Edna Ferber; screenplay, Howard Estabrook; assistant director, Doran Cox, Dewey Starkey; art director-costumes, Max Ree; sound, Clem Portman; camera, Edward Cronjager; editor, William Hamilton.

Richard Dix (Yancey Cravat); Irene Dunne (Sabra Cravat); Estelle Taylor (Dixie Lee); Nance O'Neil (Felice Venable); William Collier, Jr. (The Kid); Rosco Ates (Jess Rickey); George E. Stone (Sol Levy); Stanley Fields (Lon Yountis); Robert McWade (Louie Heffner); Edna May Oliver (Mrs. Tracy Wyatt); Frank Darien (Mr. Bixley); Eugene Jackson (Isaiah); Dolores Brown (Ruby Big Elk—elder); Gloria Vonic (Ruby Big Elk—younger); Otto Hoffman (Murch Rankin); William Orlamond (Grat Gotch); Frank Beal (Louis Venable); Nancy Dover (Donna Cravat—elder); Helen Parrih (Donna Cravat—younger); Donald Dillaway (Cim—elder); Junior Johnson (Cim—younger); Douglas Scott (Cim—youngest); Reginald Streeter (Yancey, Jr.); Lois Jane Campbell (Felice, Jr.); Ann Lee (Aunt Cassandra); Tyrone Brereton (Sabney Venable); Lillian Lane (Cousin Bella); Henry Roquemore (Jouett Goforth); Nell Craig (Arminta Greenwood); Robert McKenzie (Pat Leary); Clara Hunt (Indian Girl); Bob Kortman (Killer); Dennis O'Keefe (Extra); William Janney (Worker).

BACHELOR APARTMENT (RKO, 1931) 77 M.

Producer, William Le Baron; associate producer, Henry Hobart; director, Lowell Sherman; story, John Howard Lawson; screenplay, J. Walter Ruben; costumes-scenery, Max Ree; sound, Clem Portman; camera, Leo Tover; editor, Marie Halvey.

Lowell Sherman (Wayne Carter); Irene Dunne (Helene Andrews); Mae Murray (Agatha Carraway); Norman Kerry (Lee Carlton); Claudia Dell (Lita Andrews); Ivan Lebedeff (Henri de Moneau); Noel Francis (Janet); Roberta Gale, Arline

Judge (Whoopee Girls); Purnell Pratt (Henry Carraway); Charles Coleman (Rollins); Kitty Kelly (Miss Clark); Bess Flowers (Charlotte); Arthur Housman (Tippler); Florence Roberts (Mrs. Halloran); Boston Winston (Brown); Lee Phelps (Traffic Cop).

GREAT LOVER   (MGM, 1931) 79 M.

Director, Harry Beaumont; story, Leo Dietrichstein, Frederic and Fanny Hatton; screenplay, Gene Markey, Edgar Allan Woolf; camera, Merritt B. Gerstad; editor, Helen Warne.

Adolphe Menjou (Jean Paurel); Irene Dunne (Diana Page); Ernest Torrence (Potter); Neil Hamilton (Carlo); Baclanova (Mme. Savarova); Cliff Edwards (Finny); Hale Hamilton (Stapleton); Rosco Ates (Rosco); Herman Bing (Losseck); Else Janssen (Mme. Neumann Baumbach).

CONSOLATION MARRIAGE   (RKO, 1931) 82 M.

Producer, William Le Baron; associate producer, Myles Connolly; director, Paul Sloane; story, Bill Cunningham; screenplay, Humphrey Pearson; scenery-costumes, Max Ree; sound, John E. Tribby; music director, Max Steiner; song, Connolly and Steiner; camera, J. Roy Hunt; editor, Archie Marshek.

Irene Dunne (Mary); Pat O'Brien (Steve Rollo Porter); Myrna Loy (Elaine); John Halliday (Jeff); Matt Moore (The Colonel); Lester Vail (Aubrey); Wilson Benge (Butler).

SYMPHONY OF SIX MILLION   (RKO, 1932) 94 M.

Executive producer, David O. Selznick; associate producer, Pandro S. Berman; director, Gregory La Cava; based on the novel by Fannie Hurst; screenplay, Bernard Schubert, J. Walter Ruben; additional dialog, James Seymour; music, Max Steiner; art director, Carroll Clark; sound, George Ellis; camera, Leo Tover; editor, Archie Marshek.

Irene Dunne (Jessica); Ricardo Cortez (Felix Klauber); Gregory Ratoff (Meyer Klauber); Anna Appel (Hannah Klauber); Lita Chevret (Birdie Klauber); Noel Madison (Magnus); Helen Freeman (Miss Spencer); Julie Haydon (Nurse-Receptionist); Josephine Whittell (Mrs. Gifford); Oscar Apfel (Doctor); Harold Goodwin (Intern); John St. Polis (Dr. Schifflen); Eddie Phillips (Birdie's Husband); Lester Lee (Felix, as a boy).

BACK STREET   (Univ., 1932) 93 M.
Producer, Carl Laemmle, Jr.; associate producer, E. M. Asher; director, John M. Stahl; based on the novel by Fannie Hurst; screenplay, Gladys Lehman; dialog, Lynn Starling; art director, Charles D. Hall; assistant director, Scott R. Beal; costumes, Vera; sound, C. Roy Hunter; camera, Karl Freund; editor, Milton Carruth.

Irene Dunne (Ray Schmidt); John Boles (Walter Saxel); June Clyde (Freda Schmidt); George Meeker (Kurt Shendler); ZaSu Pitts (Mrs. Dole); Shirley Grey (Francine); Doris Lloyd (Mrs. Saxel); William Bakewell (Richard Saxel); Arletta Duncan (Beth Saxel); Maude Turner Gordon (Mrs. Saxel, Sr.); Walter Catlett (Bakeless); James Donlan (Profhero); Paul Weigel (Mr. Schmidt); Jane Darwell (Mrs. Schmidt); Robert McWade (Uncle Felix). Paul Fix (Hugo Hack); Russell Hopton, Gene Morgan, James Flavin (Reporters); James Farley (Conductor); Bob Burns (Streetcar Conductor); Rolfe Sedan (Croupier); Grace Hayle (Lady in Street); Jack Chefe (Onlooker); Mahlon Hamilton, Virginia Pearson, Caryl Lincoln, Beulah Hutton, Rosalie Roy, Tom Karrigan, Rose Dione.

THIRTEEN WOMEN (RKO, 1932) 73 M.

Executive producer, David O. Selznick; director, George Archainbaud; based on the novel by Tiffany Thayer; screenplay, Bartlett Cormack; sound, Hugh McDowell; camera, Leo Tover; editor, Buddy Kimball.

Ricardo Cortez (Sergeant Barry Clive); Irene Dunne (Laura Stanhope); Myrna Loy (Ursula Georgi); Jill Esmond (Jo Turner); Florence Eldridge (Grace Coombs); Kay Johnson (Helen Dawson); Julie Haydon (Mary); Harriet Hagman (May Raskob); Mary Duncan (June Raskob); Peg Entwistle (Hazel); Marjorie Gateson (Martha); Elsie Prescott (Nan); Wally Albright (Bobby Stanhope); C. Henry Gordon (Swami Yogadachi); Ed Pawley (Burns); Blanche Frederici (Miss Kirsten); Phyllis Fraser (Twelfth Woman); Betty Furness (Thirteenth Woman); Audrey Scott, Aloha Porter (Equestriennes); Clayton Behee, Eddie Viera, Eddie DeComa, Buster Bartell (Trapeze Acts); Teddy Mangean (Wire Walker); Cliff Herbert (Circus Act); Lee Phelps (Conductor); Edward LeSaint (Police Chief); Lloyd Ingraham (Inspector); Mitchell Harris (Detective); and: Leon Ames, Kenneth Thomson, Clarence Geldert, Violet Seaton, Louis Natheaux, Oscar Smith, Allan Pomeroy.

NO OTHER WOMAN (RKO, 1933) 58 M.

Executive producer, David O. Selznick; director, J. Walter Ruben; based on the play *Just a Woman* by Owen Francis; adaptation, Wanda Tuchock; music, Max Steiner; assistant director, James Anderson; sound, Clem Portman; camera, Edward Cronjager; editor, William Hamilton.

Irene Dunne (Anna Stanley); Charles Bickford (Big Jim Stanley); J. Carroll Naish (Bonelli); Eric Linden (Joe Lacovia); Gwili Andre (Margot Von Dearing); Buster Miles (Bobbie Stanley); Lelia Bennett (Susie); Christian Rub (Eli); Hilda Vaughn (Governess); Brooks Benedict (Chauffeur); Joseph E. Bernard (Butler); Frederick Burton (Anderson); Theodore Von Eltz (Sutherland); Edwin Stanley (Judge).

THE SECRET OF MADAME BLANCHE (MGM, 1933) 85 M.

Director, Charles Brabin; based on the play *The Lady* by Martin Brown; screenplay, Frances Goodrich, Albert Hackett; music, Dr. William Axt; camera, Merritt B. Gerstad; editor, Blanche Sewell.

Irene Dunne (Sally); Lionel Atwill (Aubrey St. John); Phillips Holmes (Leonard St. John); Una Merkel (Ella); Douglas Watson (Leonard, Jr.); C. Henry Gordon (State's Attorney); Jean Parker (Eloise); Mitchell Lewis (Duval).

THE SILVER CORD (RKO, 1933) 74 M.

Producer, Pandro S. Berman; director, John Cromwell; based on the play by Sidney Howard; screenplay, Jane Murfin; sound, Clem Portman; camera, Charles Rosher; editor, George Nicholls, Jr.

Irene Dunne (Christina Phelps); Joel McCrea (David Phelps); Frances Dee (Hester); Eric Linden (Robert Phelps); Laura Hope Crews (Mrs. Phelps); Helen Cromwell (Delia).

ANN VICKERS (RKO, 1933) 72 M.

Executive producer, Merian C. Cooper; producer, Pandro S. Berman; director, John Cromwell; based on the novel by Sinclair Lewis; screenplay, Jane Murfin; art director, Van Nest Polglase, Charles Kirk; music director, Max Steiner; sound, Paul F. Wiser; camera, David Abel, Edward Cronjager; editor, George Nicholls, Jr.

Irene Dunne (Ann Vickers); Walter Huston (Barney Dolphin); Conrad Nagel (Lindsey Atwell); Bruce Cabot (Captain Resnick); Edna May Oliver (Malvina Wormser);

Mitchell Lewis (Captain Walde); Murray Kinnell (Dr. Slenk); Helen Eby-Rock (Kitty Cognac); Gertrude Michael (Mona Dolphin); J. Carroll Naish (Dr. Sorell); Sarah Padden (Lil); Reginald Barlow (Chaplain); Rafaela Ottiano (Feldermus); Irving Bacon (Waiter); Geneva Mitchell (Leah Burbaum); Mary Foy (Matron); Frederic Santley (Sam, Reform Assistant); Wally Albright (Mischau); Edwin Maxwell (Defense Attorney); Larry Steers (Prosecutor); Arthur Hoyt (Mr. Penny); Jane Darwell (Mrs. Gates); Sam Hardy (Ignati).

IF I WERE FREE (RKO, 1933) 66 M.

Producer, Merian C. Cooper; director, Elliott Nugent; based on the play *Behold, We Live* by John Van Druten; adaptation, Dwight Taylor; sound, George D. Ellis; camera, Edward Cronjager; editor, Arthur Roberts.

Irene Dunne (Sarah Cazenove); Clive Brook (Gordon Evers); Nils Asther (Tono Cazenove); Henry Stephenson (Hector Stribling); Vivian Tobin (Jewel Stribling); Laura Hope Crews (Dame Evers); Tempe Pigott (Mrs. Gill); Lorraine MacLean (Mrs. Evers).

THIS MAN IS MINE (RKO, 1934) 76 M.

Producer, Pandro S. Berman; director, John Cromwell; based on the play *Love Flies in the Window* by Anne Morrison Chapin; screenplay, Jane Murfin; music director, Max Steiner; camera, David Abel; editor, William Morgan.

Irene Dunne (Tony Dunlap); Constance Cummings (Francesca Harper); Ralph Bellamy (Jim Dunlap); Kay Johnson (Bee McCrea); Charles Starrett (Jud McCrea); Sidney Blackmer (Mort Holmes); Vivian Tobin (Rita); Louis Mason (Slim).

STINGAREE (RKO, 1934) 76 M.

Producer, Pandro S. Berman; director, William A. Wellman; based on the stories of E. W. Hornung; screenplay, Becky Gardiner; songs, Gus Kahn and W. Franke Harling; Edward Eliscu and Max Steiner; music director, Steiner; Camera, James Van Trees; editor, James B. Borley.

Irene Dunne (Hilda Bouverie); Richard Dix (Stingaree); Mary Boland (Mrs. Clarkson); Conway Tearle (Sir Julian Kent); Andy Devine (Howie); Henry Stephenson (Mr. Clarkson); Una O'Connor (Annie); George Barraud (Inspector Radford); Reginald Owen (Governor-General); Snub Pollard (Victor).

THE AGE OF INNOCENCE (RKO, 1934) 81 M.

Executive producer, Pandro S. Berman; director, Philip Moeller; based on the novel by Edith Wharton and the play by Margaret A. Barnes; screenplay, Sarah Y. Mason, Victor Heerman; music, Max Steiner; associate director, James Loring; costumes, Walter Plunkett; art director, Van Nest Polglase, Al Herman; sound, John L. Case; camera, James Van Tree; editor, George Hively.

Irene Dunne (Countess Ellen Olenska); John Boles (Newland Archer); Lionel Atwill (Julius Beaufort); Laura Hope Crews (Mrs. Welland); Helen Westley (Granny Mingott); Julie Haydon (May Welland); Herbert Yost (Mr. Welland); Theresa Maxwell Conover (Mrs. Archer); Edith Van Clive (Janey Archer); Leonard Carey (Butler).

SWEET ADELINE (WB, 1935) 85 M.

Producer, Edward Chodorov; director, Mervyn LeRoy; based on the play by Jerome Kern, Oscar Hammerstein II, Harry Armstrong, Dick Gerard; screenplay, Erwin S. Gelsey; songs, Kern and Hammerstein; ensemble director, Bobby Connolly; costumes, Orry-Kelly; art director, Robert Haas; camera, Sol Polito; editor, Harold McLernon.

172

Irene Dunne (Adeline Schmidt); Donald Woods (Sid Barnett); Ned Sparks (Dan Herzig); Hugh Herbert (Rupert Rockingham); Winifred Shaw (Elysie); Louis Calhern (Major Jim Day); Nydia Westman (Nellie Schmidt); Joseph Cawthorn (Oscar Schmidt); Dorothy Dare (Dot, the Band Leader); Phil Regan (Juvenile); Noah Beery, Sr. (Sultan); Don Alvarado (Renaldo); Martin Garralaga (Dark Young Man); Emmett Vogan (Captain); Howard Dickinson (Civilian); Eddie Shubert (Eddie); Nick Copeland (Prop Man); Ferdinand Munier (General Hawks); William V. Mong (Cobbler, a Spy); Johnny Eppelite (Young Jolson); Mary Treen (Girl); Milton Kibbee (Stage Hand); Joseph Bernard (Waiter); Charles Hickman (Manx); Howard H. Mitchell (Bartender); Landers Stevens, William Arnold (Men); David Newell (Young Man); Evelyn Wynans (Woman); Harry Tyler (Louise); Jack Mulhall (Bob).

ROBERTA (RKO, 1935) 105 M.

Producer, Pandro S. Berman; director, William A. Seiter; based on the novel *Gowns by Roberta* by Alice Duer Miller, and the musical play *Roberta* by Jerome Kern and Otto Harback; screenplay, Jane Murfin, Sam Mintz; additional dialog, Glenn Tryon, Allan Scott; choreography, Fred Astaire; ensemble director, Hermes Pan; music director, Max Steiner; art director, Van Nest Polglase, Carroll Clark; set decorator, Thomas K. Little; songs, Kern and Harback; Kern and Bernard Dougall; Kern, Oscar Hammerstein II, Dorothy Fields, and Jimmy McHugh; Kern, Fields, and McHugh; gowns, Bernard Newman; sound, John Tribby; camera, Edward Cronjager; editor, William Hamilton.

Irene Dunne (Stephanie); Fred Astaire (Huck); Ginger Rogers (Countess Scharwenka [Lizzie Gatz]); Randolph Scott (John Kent); Helen Westley (Roberta [Aunt Minnie]); Victor Varconi (Ladislaw); Claire Dodd (Sophie); Luis Alberni (Voyda); Ferdinand Munier (Lord Delves); Torben Meyer (Albert); Adrian Rosley (Professor); Bodil Rosing (Fernando); Lucille Ball, Jane Hamilton, Margaret McChrystal, Kay Sutton, Maxine Jennings, Virginia Reid, Lorna Low, Lorraine DeSart, Wanda Perry, Diane Cook, Virginia Carroll, Betty Dumbries, Donna Roberts (Mannequins); Mike Tellegen, Sam Savitsky (Cossacks); Zena Savine (Woman); Johnny "Candy" Candido, Muzzi Marcellino, Gene Sheldon, Howard Lally, William Carey, Paul McLarind, Hal Bown, Charles Sharpe, Ivan Dow, Phil Cuthbert, Delmon Davis, William Dunn (Orchestra); Judith Vosselli, Rita Gould (Bits): Mary Forbes (Mrs. Teal); William B. Davidson (Purser); Grace Hayle (Reporter); Dale Van Sickel (Dance Extra).

MAGNIFICENT OBSESSION (Univ., 1935) 112 M.

Producer, John M. Stahl; associate producer, E. M. Asher; director, Stahl; based on the novel by Lloyd C. Douglas; screenplay, George O'Neil, Sarah Y. Mason, Victor Heerman; camera, John Mescall; editor, Milton Carruth.

Irene Dunne (Helen Hudson); Robert Taylor (Bobbie Merrick); Sara Haden (Nancy Ashford); Charles Butterworth (Tommy); Betty Furness (Joyce); Arthur Hoyt (Perry); Gilbert Emery (Dr. Ramsey); Marion Clayton (Amy); Arthur Treacher (Horace); Ralph Morgan (Randolph); Inez Courtney, Georgette Rhodes, Helen Brown, Joyce Compton, Norma Drew (Nurses); Alan Davis (Dr. Justin); Craufurd Kent (Dr. Thomas); Edward Earle (Dr. Miller); Sumner Getchell (Jimmy); William Arnold (Chief Inspector); Leah Winslow, Ethel Sykes (Women on Boat); Sherry Hall, Allen Connor, William Worthington, Louis LaVoie (Men on Boat); Oscar Rudolph (Western Union Boy); Eddy Chandler (Mechanic); Mickey Daniels (Boy in Ford); Beryl Mercer (Little Woman); Sidney Bracy (Butler); Alice Ardell (Maid); Cora Sue Collins (Girl in Park); Roy Brown, Gretta Gould, Frank Mayo, John M. Saint Polis, George Hackathorne, Beth Hazelton (Ex-Patients); Sid Marion (Sword Swallower); Arnold Korff, William Stack, Frank Reicher, Leonard Mudie, Frederic Roland, Fredrik Vogeding, Theodor Von Eltz (Doctors); Rollo Lloyd (Tramp); Charles Coleman (Butler); Purnell Pratt

(Attorney); Walter Miller (Chauffeur); Walter Walker (Grandfather); Vance Carroll, Henry Hale, Ray Johnson, Louis Natheau, Jack Hatfield, Gladden James, Donald Kerr (Reporters).

SHOW BOAT   (Univ., 1936) 110 M.

Producer, Carl Laemmle, Jr.; director, James Whale; based on the novel by Edna Ferber and the play by Oscar Hammerstein II, Jerome Kern; screenplay-songs, Hammerstein, Kern; music director, Victor Baravelle; choreography, LeRoy J. Prinz; costumes, Doris Zinkeison; special effects, John P. Fulton; assistant director, Joseph A. McDonough; camera, John Mescall; editor, Ted Kent, Bernard W. Burton.

Irene Dunne (Magnolia Hawks); Allan Jones (Gaylord Ravenal); Charles Winninger (Captain Andy Hawks); Helen Westley (Parthy Hawks); Paul Robeson (Joe); Helen Morgan (Julie); Donald Cook (Steve); Sammy White (Frank); Queenie Smith (Ellie); J. Farrell MacDonald (Windy); Arthur Hohl (Pete); Charles Middleton (Vallon); Hattie McDaniel (Queenie); Francis X. Mahoney (Rubberface); Sunnie O'Dea (Kim— elder); Marilyn Knowlden (Kim—younger); Patricia Barry (Kim—as a baby); Dorothy Granger, Barbara Pepper, Renee Whitney (Chorus Girls); Harry Barris (Jake); Charles Wilson (Jim Green); Clarence Muse (Sam); Stanley Fields (Jeb); "Tiny" Stanley J. Sandford (Backwoodsman); May Beatty (Landlady); Bob Watson (Lost Child); Jane Keckley (Mrs. Ewing); E. E. Clive (Englishman); Helen Jerome Eddy (Reporter); Donald Briggs (Press Agent); LeRoy Prinz (Dance Director); Eddie Anderson (Young Black Man); Patti Patterson (Banjo Player); Helen Hayward (Mrs. Brecenbridge); Flora Finch (Woman); Theodore Lorch (Simon Legree); Arthur Housman (Drunk); Elspeth Dudgeon (Mother Superior); Monte Montague (Old Man); Lois Verner (Small Girl); Grace Cunard (Mother); Maralyn Harris (Little Girl); Jimmy Jackson (Young Man); Harry Barris (Jake); Eddy Chandler, Lee Phelps, Frank Mayo, Ed Peil, Sr., Edmund Cobb, Al Ferguson (Gamblers); Maude Allen (Fat Woman); Artye Folz, Barbara Bletcher (Fat Girls); Forrest Stanley (Theatre Manager); Jack Latham (Juvenile); George H. Reed (Old Black Man); Georgia O'Dell (School Teacher); Selmer Jackson (Hotel Clerk); George Hackathorne (YMCA Worker); Ernest Hilliard, Jack Mulhall, Brooks Benedict (Race Fans).

THEODORA GOES WILD   (Col., 1936) 94 M.

Associate producer, Everett Riskin; director, Richard Boleslawski; based on the story by Mary McCarthy; screenplay, Sidney Buchman; sound, George Cooper; assistant director, William E. Muel; music director, Morris Stoloff; costumes, Bernard Newman; art director, Stephen Goosson; camera, Joseph Walker; editor, Otto Meyer.

Irene Dunne (Theodora Lynn); Melvyn Douglas (Michael Grant); Thomas Mitchell (Jed Waterbury); Thurston Hall (Arthur Stevenson); Rosalind Keith (Adelaide Perry); Spring Byington (Rebecca Perry); Elizabeth Risdon (Aunt Mary); Margaret McWade (Aunt Elsie); Nana Bryant (Ethel Stevenson); Henry Kolker (Jonathan Grant); Leona Maricle (Agnes Grant); Robert Greig (Uncle John); Frederick Burton (Governor Wyatt); Mary Forbes (Mrs. Wyatt); Grace Hayle (Mrs. Cobb); Sarah Edwards (Mrs. Moffat); Mary MacLaren (Mrs. Wilson); Wilfred Hari (Toki); Laura Treadwell (Mrs. Grant); Corbet Morris (Artist); Ben F. Hendricks (Taxi Driver); Frank Sully (Clarence); James T. Mack (Minister); William Benedict (Henry); Carolyn Lee Bourland (Baby); Paul Barrett (Adelaide's Husband); Leora Thatcher (Miss Baldwin); Billy Wayne, Harold Goodwin, Jack Hatfield (Photographers); Harry Harvey, Don Brodie, Eddie Fetherstone, Ed Hart, Lee Phelps, Sherry Hall, Ralph Malone, Beatrice Curtis (Reporters); Maurice Brierre (Waiter); Sven Borg (Bartender); Dennis O'Keefe (Man); Rex Moore (Newsboy); Georgia Cooper, Jane Keckley, Jessie Perry, Noel Bates, Betty Farrington, Stella Adams, Isabelle LaMal, Georgia O'Dell, Dorothy Vernon (Women).

HIGH, WIDE AND HANDSOME   (Par., 1937) 110 M.

Producer, Arthur Hornblow, Jr.; director, Rouben Mamoulian; screenplay, Oscar Hammerstein II; additional dialog, George O'Neill; songs, Jerome Kern and Hammerstein; assistant director, Joe Youngerman; art director, Hans Dreier, John Goodman; set decorator, A. E. Freudeman; music director, Boris Morros, orchestrator, Robert Russell Bennett; choreography, LeRoy Prinz; sound, Charles Hisserich, Don Johnson; technical adviser, William Gilmore Beymer; special effects, Gordon Jennings; camera, Victor Milner, Theodor Sparkuhl; editor, Archie Marshek.

Irene Dunne (Sally Watterson); Randolph Scott (Peter Cortlandt); Dorothy Lamour (Molly Fuller); Raymond Walburn (Doc Watterson); Alan Hale (Walter Glennan); Elizabeth Patterson (Grandma Cortlandt); Charles Bickford (Red Scanlon); William Frawley (Mac); Akim Tamiroff (Joe Varese); Ben Blue (Samuel); Irving Pichel (Stark); Lucien Littlefield (Dr. Lippincott); Helen Lowell (Mrs. Lippincott); Roger Imhof (Pop Bowers); Purnell Pratt (Colonel Blake); Edward Gargan (Foreman); Tommy Bupp (Boy); Russell Hopton (John Thompson); Billy Bletcher (Shorty); Stanley Andrews (Lem Moulton); Frank Sully (Gabby Jonson); Jack Clifford (Walsh Miller); James Burke (Stackpole); Claire MacDowell (Seamstress); and: Connie Bergen.

THE AWFUL TRUTH   (Col., 1937) 90 M.

Producer, Leo McCarey; associate producer, Everett Riskin; director, McCarey; based on the play by Arthur Richman; screenplay, Vina Delmar; art director, Stephen Goosson, Lionel Banks; assistant director, William Mull; music director, Morris Stoloff; interior decorator, Babs Johnstone; gowns, Kalloch; songs, Ben Oakland and Milton Drake; sound, Edward Bernds; camera, Joseph Walker; editor, Al Clark.

Irene Dunne (Lucy Warriner); Cary Grant (Jerry Warriner); Ralph Bellamy (Daniel Leeson); Alexander D'Arcy (Armand Duvalle); Cecil Cunningham (Aunt Patsy); Molly Lamont (Barbara Vance); Esther Dale (Mrs. Leeson); Joyce Compton (Dixie Belle Lee [Toots Binswanger]); Robert Allen (Frank Randall); Robert Warwick (Mr. Vance); Mary Forbes (Mrs. Vance); Claud Allister (Lord Fabian); Zita Moulton (Lady Fabian); Scott Colton (Mr. Barnsley); Wyn Cahoon (Mrs. Barnsley); Paul Stanton (Judge); Mitchell Harris (Jerry's Attorney); Alan Bridge, Edgar Dearing (Motor Cops); Leonard Carey (Butler); Miki Morita (Japanese Servant); Frank Wilson (Emcee); Vernon Dent (Police Sergeant); George C. Pearce (Caretaker); Bobby Watson (Hotel Clerk); Byron Foulger (Secretary); Kathryn Curry (Celeste); Edward Peil, Sr. (Bailiff); Bess Flowers (Viola Heath); John Tyrrell (Hank); Edward Mortimer (Lucy's Attorney).

JOY OF LIVING   (RKO, 1938) 90 M.

Producer, Felix Young; director, Tay Garnett; story, Dorothy Fields, Herbert Fields; screenplay, Gene Towne, Graham Baker, Allan Scott; music, Jerome Kern and Dorothy Fields; music director, Frank Tours; special effects, Vernon L. Walker; camera, Joseph Walker; editor, Jack Hively.

Irene Dunne (Maggie); Douglas Fairbanks, Jr. (Dan); Alice Brady (Minerva); Guy Kibbee (Dennis); Jean Dixon (Harrison); Eric Blore (Potter); Lucille Ball (Salina); Warren Hymer (Mike); Billy Gilbert (Cafe Owner); Frank Milan (Bert Pine); Dorothy Steiner (Dotsy Pine); Estelle Steiner (Betsy Pine); Phyllis Kennedy (Marie); Franklin Pangborn (Radio Broadcast Orchestra Leader); James Burke (Mac); John Qualen (Oswego); Spencer Charters (Magistrate); George Chandler (Taxi Driver); Grady Sutton (Florist).

LOVE AFFAIR   (RKO, 1939) 87 M.

Producer-director, Leo McCarey; story, Mildred Cram, McCarey; screenplay, Delmer Daves, Donald Ogden Stewart; assistant director, James Anderson; montage, Douglas Travers; songs, B. G. DeSylva; Harold Arlen and Ted Koehler; special effects, Vernon L. Walker; camera, Rudolph Mate; editor, Edward Dmytryk, George Hively.

Irene Dunne (Terry McKay); Charles Boyer (Michel Marnet); Maria Ouspenskaya (Grandmother); Lee Bowman (Ken Bradley); Astrid Allwyn (Lois Clarke); Maurice Moscovich (Maurice Cobert); Scotty Beckett (Boy on Ship); Bess Flowers, Harold Miller (Couple on Deck); Joan Leslie (Autograph Seeker); Dell Henderson (Cafe Manager); Carol Hughes (Nightclub Patron); Ferike Boros (Boarding-House Keeper); Frank McGlynn, Sr. (Orphanage Superintendent ["Picklepuss"]); Oscar O'Shea (Priest); Tom Dugan (Drunk with Christmas Tree); Lloyd Ingraham, Leyland Hodgson (Doctors); Phyllis Kennedy (Maid); Gerald Mohr (Extra).

INVITATION TO HAPPINESS   (Par., 1939) 95 M.

Producer-director, Wesley Ruggles; screenplay, Claude Binyon; art director, Hans Dreier, Ernst Fegte; music, Frederick Hollander; song, Frank Loesser and Hollander; process camera, Farciot Edouart; camera, Leo Tover; editor, Alma Macrorie.

Irene Dunne (Eleanor Wayne); Fred MacMurray (Albert "King" Cole); Charles Ruggles (Pop Hardy); Billy Cook (Albert Cole, Jr.); William Collier, Sr. (Mr. Wayne); Marion Martin (Lola); Oscar O'Shea (Divorce Judge); Burr Caruth (Butler); Eddie Hogan (The Champ); Gordon Jones (Dutch Arnold); Allen Wood, Don Laterre (Youths); Mack Gray (Usher); Bob Evans (Galliette); Jack Roper (Scat); Billy Newell (Waiter); Heinie Conklin (Cook); Franklin Parker, Wheaton Chambers, Joseph Franz, Jack Gargan, Jack Knoche, Robert Stevenson, Jerry Fletcher, Harry Hayden (Reporters); Lee Moore (Headwaiter); Doodles Weaver (Band Leader); Myra Marsh (Maternity Nurse); Virginia Brissac (Eleanor's Nurse); William Orr (Bellboy); Bill Knudsen (Attendant); Emerson Treacy (Photographer); Hank Hankison (Fighter); Joe Cunningham (Announcer); Guy Usher (Spectator); Joe Caits (Man in Office); Russ Clark, Charles Randolph (Referees).

WHEN TOMORROW COMES   (Univ., 1939) 90 M.

Producer-director, John M. Stahl; based on the story by James Cain; screenplay, Dwight Taylor; assistant director, Joseph A. McDonough; camera, John J. Mescall; editor, Milton Carruth.

Irene Dunne (Helen); Charles Boyer (Charles); Nydia Westman (Lulu); Onslow Stevens (Holden); Fritz Feld (Butler); Barbara O'Neil (Madeleine); Nella Walker (Mrs. Dumont); Constance Moore (Bride); Jerry Marlowe (Groom); Doris Weston, Frances Robinson, Bobbe Trefts, Helen Lynd, Myrtis Crinley, Kitty McHugh, Florence Lake, Dorothy Granger, Mary Treen, Inez Courtney, Helen MacKellar, Helen Brown, Ruth Warren, Dorothy Appleby, Virginia Sale, Mira McKinney, Claire Du Brey, Greta Granstedt, Diana Gibson, Jane Barnes, Sally Payne, Jennifer Gray, Claire Whitney, Mary Field (Waitresses); Harry C. Bradley (Minister); Milton Parsons (Organist); William Davidson (Army Captain); Addison Richards (Refugee Leader); Tom Dugan (Bum); Greta Meyer (Nurse); Howard Hickman (Wealthy Man); Natalie Moorhead, Margaret McWade, Gladys Blake (Women); Frank Darien (Boat-House Caretaker); George Humbert (Vendor); Wade Boteler (Policeman); Milburn Stone (Bus Boy Head); Emmett Vogan (Head Waiter); Gaylor Steve Pendleton (Bus Boy); Edward Keane Alden, Stephen Chase, Landers Stevens, John Dilson (Men); Vinton Haworth, Gordon Jones, Stanley Taylor (Radio Technicians); Eddie Acuff (Bus driver); Edward Earle (Assistant Manager); Philip Trent (Service Man); James Flavin (Coast

Guard Man); Otto Hoffman (Farmer); Mickey Kuhn, Tommy Bupp, Ray Nichols, Payne Johnson, Sonny Bupp, Delmar Watson (Boys); Hally Chester (Newsboy); Lilian Elliott (Character Woman); James Morton (Chef); Ed Peil, Sr. (Janitor); George Offerman, Jr. (Farmer's Son); Dick Winslow (Accordian Player).

MY FAVORITE WIFE   (RKO, 1940) 88 M.

Producer, Leo McCarey; director, Garson Kanin; story, Sam and Bella Spewack, McCarey; screenplay, the Spewacks; camera, Rudolph Mate; editor, Robert Wise.

Irene Dunne (Ellen Arden); Cary Grant (Nick Arden); Randolph Scott (Stephen Burkett); Gail Patrick (Bianca); Ann Shoemaker (Ma); Scotty Beckett (Tim Arden); Mary Lou Harrington (Chinch Arden); Donald MacBride (Hotel Clerk); Hugh O'Connell (Johnson); Granville Bates (Judge); Pedro de Cordoba (Dr. Kohlmar); Brandon Tynan (Dr. Manning); Leon Belasco (Henri); Harold Gerald (Assistant Clerk); Murray Alper (Bartender); Earle Hodgins (Court Clerk); Cyril Ring (Contestant); Clive Morgan, Bert Moorhouse (Lawyers); Florence Dudley, Jean Acker (Witnesses); Joe Cabrillas (Phillip); Frank Marlowe (Photographer); Thelma Joel (Miss Rosenthal); Horace MacMahon (Truck Driver); Chester Clute (Little Man); Eli Schmudkler (Janitor); Franco Corsaro (Waiter); Cy Kendall (Detective); Pat West (Caretaker).

PENNY SERENADE   (Col., 1941) 125 M.

Producer, George Stevens; associate producer, Fred Guiol; director, Stevens; based on the story by Martha Cheavens; screenplay, Morrie Ryskind; music director, Morris Stoloff; music, W. Franke Harling; camera, Joseph Walker; editor, Otto Meyer.

Irene Dunne (Julie Gardiner); Cary Grant (Roger Adams); Beulah Bondi (Miss Oliver); Edgar Buchanan (Applejack); Ann Doran (Dotty); Eva Lee Kuney (Trina—at age 6); Leonard Willey (Dr. Hartley); Wallis Clark (Judge); Walter Soderling (Billings); Baby Biffle (Trina—at age 1); Edmund Elton (Minister); Billy Bevan (McDougal); Nee Wong, Jr. (Sung Chong); Michael Morris (Bill Collector); Grady Sutton, Stanley Brown (Men); Beryl Vaughn (Flower Girl); John Tyrrell (Press Operator); Iris Han (O-Hanna-San); Otto Han (Cook Sam); Ben Taggart (Policeman); Frank Moran (Cab Driver); Lynton Brent (Reporter); Al Seymour (Bootlegger); Dick Wessel (Joe); Charles Flynn (Bob); Arline Jackson, Mary Bovard, Georgia Hawkins (Girls); Snowflake (Train Porter); Ed Peil, Sr. (Train Conductor); Eddie Laughton (Cab Driver); Doris Herbert (Minister's Wife); Bess Flowers (Mother); John Ferguson (Father); Lani Lee (Chinese Waitress); Rollin Moriyama, Ben Kumagai (Rickshaw Boys); Lillian West (Nurse); Henry Dixon (Old Printer); Dorothy Adams (Mother); Albert Butterfield (Boy).

UNFINISHED BUSINESS   (Univ., 1941) 95 M.

Producer-director, Gregory La Cava; screenplay, Eugene Thackery; art director, Jack Otterson; music director, Franz Waxman; camera, Joseph Valentine

Irene Dunne (Nancy Andrews); Robert Montgomery (Tom Duncan); Eugene Pallette (Elmer); Preston Foster (Steve Duncan); June Clyde (Clarisse); Phyllis Barry (Steve's Wife); Thomas W. Ross (Lawyer); Richard Davies (Jimmy); Esther Dale (Aunt Mathilda); Walter Catlett (Billy Ross); Samuel S. Hinds (Uncle); Dick Foran (Best Man); Kathryn Adams (Bride); Chester Clute, Paul Everton, John Sheehan, Matt McHugh, Larry Kent, Fred Santley, Reed Hadley, Boyd Irwin, Quen Ramsey (Men); Pierre Watkin (Lawyer); Helen Lynd, Phyllis Kennedy, Margaret Armstrong, Grace Hayle, Dorothy Vaughan, Grace Stafford, Dorothy Granger, Dora Clemant, Hillary Brooke, Sheila Darcy, Flo Wix, Virginia Engels, Gwen Seager, Isabelle LaMal, Dorothy Hass, Ruth Dwyer (Women); Paul Fix, Jack Voglin, Eddie Fetherstone (Reporters); Virginia Brissac (Aunt); Josephine Whittell (Wardrobe Woman); Mary Gordon (Charwoman); Harry Rosenthal (Pianist); George Davis, Bob Perry (Waiters); Helen Millard (Helen); Fortunio Bonanova (Impresario); Reverend Neal Dodd (Minister); Hope Landin (Groom's Mother); Frank Coghlan, Jr. (Page Boy); Jacques Vanaire (Head Waiter); Yolande Mellot (Manicurist); Frank Shannon (Groom's Father); Hugh Beaumont (Groom); Eugene Jackson (Bootblack); Lester Dorr (Yes Man); Mary Jo Ellis (Bridesmaid); Amanda McFarland (Baby).

LADY IN A JAM   (Univ., 1942) 78 M.

Producer-director, Gregory La Cava; screenplay, Eugene Thackey, Frank Cockrell, Otho Lovering; music director, Charles Previn; music, Frank Skinner; art director, Jack Otterson; assistant director, Joseph A. McDonough; camera, Hal Mohr; editor, Russell Schoengath.

Irene Dunne (Jane Palmer); Patric Knowles (Dr. Enright); Ralph Bellamy (Stanley); Eugene Pallette (Billingsley); Queenie Vassar (Cactus Kate); Jane Garland (Strawberry); Robert Homans (Faro Bill); Samuel S. Hinds (Dr. Brewster); Hobart Cavanaugh (Reporter); Mira McKinney (Lady of the Evening); Sarah Padden (Miner's Wife); Clara Blandick (Tourist); Sam H. Underwood (Desert Rat); Kathleen Howard, Josephine Whittell, Kitty O'Neil, Claire Whitney, Isabelle LaMal, Mona Barrie (Women); Russell Hicks (Manager); Irving Bacon (Motel Proprietor); Hardie Albright (Chauffeur); Charles Lane (Government Man); Fuzzy Knight, Eddie Fetherstone (Cab Drivers); Robert Emmett Keane (Coupe Driver); Charles Cane (Cop); Holmes Herbert, Garry Owen, Reed Hadley, Charles Coleman (Men); Phyllis Kennedy (Drunk Tourist); Rex Lease, Syd Saylor, Ruth Warren (Drunks); Eddie Dunn (Bartender); Thomas Kilshaw (Auctioneer); Chief Thundercloud (Himself); Eddy Chandler (Waiter); Lester Dorr (Assistant Manager); Al Bridge (Furniture Mover); Fred Stanley (Tourist); Dick Alexander (Fighter); Billy Benedict (Barker); Bess Flowers (Nurse); Casey MacGregor (Case Keeper); Jack Gardner (Auctioneer's Clerk).

A GUY NAMED JOE   (MGM, 1943) 118 M.

Producer, Everett Riskin; director, Victor Fleming; story, Charles Sprague, David Boehm, Frederick H. Brennan; screenplay, Dalton Trumbo; music, Herbert Stothart; art director, Cedric Gibbons; song, Roy Turk and Fred Ahlert; special effects, Arnold Gillespie, Donald Jahraus, Warren Newcombe; camera, George Folsey, Karl Freund; editor, Frank Sullivan.

Spencer Tracy (Pete Sandidge); Irene Dunne (Dorinda Durston); Van Johnson (Ted Randall); Ward Bond (Al Yackey); James Gleason ("Nails" Kilpatrick); Lionel Barrymore (The General); Barry Nelson (Dick Rumney); Don DeFore ("Powerhouse" O'Rourke); Henry O'Neill (Colonel Hendricks); Addison Richards (Major Corbett); Charles Smith (Sanderson); Mary Elliott (Dance-Hall Girl); Earl Schenck (Colonel Schenck); Maurice Murphy (Captain Robertson); Gertrude Hoffmann (Old Woman); Mark Daniels (Lieutenant); William Bishop (Ray); Esther Williams (Ellen Bright); Eve Whitney (Powerhouse Girl); Kay Williams (Girl at Bar); Walter Sande (Mess Sergeant); Gibson Gowland (Bartender); John Whitney, Kirk Alyn (Officers in Heaven); James Millican (Orderly); Ernest Severn (Davy); Edward Hardwicke (George); Raymond Severn (Cyril); Yvonne Severn (Elizabeth); Christopher Severn (Peter); John Frederick (Lieutenant); Frank Faylen, Phil Van Zandt (Majors); Marshall Reed, Blake Edwards (Fliers); Matt Willis (Lieutenant Hunter); Peter Cookson (Sergeant Hanson); Jacqueline White (Helen); Bill Arthur, John Bogden, Herbert Gunn, Bob Sully, Johnny Dunn, James Martin, Richard Woodruff, Ken Scott, Louis Hart, Fred Beckner (Cadets); Craig Flannagan, Melvin Nix, Earl Kent, Michael Owen (U.S. Lieutenants); Joan Thorsen, Leatrice Gilbert, Mary Ganley (Girls in Chinese Restaurant); Charles King II (Lieutenant Collins); Eddie Borden (Taxi Driver); Arthur Space (S. F. Airport Captain); Alan Wilson (Sergeant in Jeep); Leslie Vincent (Sentry).

THE WHITE CLIFFS OF DOVER (MGM, 1944) 126 M.

Producer, Sidney Franklin; director, Clarence Brown; based on the poem "The White Cliffs" by Alice Duer Miller; additional poetry, Robert Nathan; screenplay, Claudine West, Jan Lustig, George Froeschel; art director, Cedric Gibbons; Randall Duell; set decorator, Edwin B. Willis, Jacques Mersereau; costume supervisor, Irene; makeup, Jack Dawn; technical advisor, Major Cyril Seys Ramsey-Hill; sound, Douglas Shearer; special effects Arnold Gillespie, Warren Newcombe; camera, George Folsey; editor, Robert J. Kern.

Irene Dunne (Susan Ashwood); Alan Marshal (Sir John Ashwood); Frank Morgan (Hiram Porter Dunn); Roddy McDowall (John Ashwood II—as a boy); Peter Lawford (John Ashwood II—age 24); Dame May Whitty (Nanny); C. Aubrey Smith (Colonel); Gladys Cooper (Lady Jean Ashwood); Van Johnson (Sam Bennett); John Warburton (Reggie); Jill Esmond (Rosamund); Brenda Forbes (Gwennie); Norma Varden (Mrs. Bland); Elizabeth Taylor (Betsy—age 10); June Lockhart (Betsy—age 18); Charles Irwin (Farmer Kenney); Jean Prescott (Mrs. Kenney); Tom Drake (American Soldier); Isobel Elsom (Mrs. Bancroft); Edmond Breon (Major Bancroft); Miles Mander (Major Loring); Ann Curzon (Miss Lambert); Steven Muller (Gerhard); Norbert Muller (Dietrich); Molly Lamont (Helen); Lumsden Hare (The Vicar), Arthur Shields (Benson); Doris Lloyd (Plump Lady at the Boarding House); Matthew Boulton (Immigration Officer); Ethel Griffies (Woman on Train); Herbert Evans (Footman); Keith Hitchcock (Duke of Waverly); Vera Graaff (Duchess); Anita Bolster (Miller); Ian Wolfe (Skipper); Alec Craig (Billings); Clyde Cook (Jennings); Bunny Gordon (John—at six months); George Kirby (Old Man); Wilson Benge (Chauffeur); Harry Allen (English Cabby); Nelson Leigh (British Naval Officer); Mabel Row (Housemaid); James Menzies (Telegraph Boy); Kay Deslys (Blonde Woman); Leo Mostovoy (Bandmaster); George Davis (Boots).

TOGETHER AGAIN (Col., 1944) 93 M.

Producer, Virginia Van Upp; director, Charles Vidor; story, Stanley Russell, Herbert Biberman; screenplay, Van Upp, F. Hugh Herbert; art director, Stephen Goosson, Van Nest Polglase; music, Werner R. Heymann; music director, Morris W. Stoloff; camera, Joseph Walker; editor, Otto Meyer.

Irene Dunne (Anne Crandall); Charles Boyer (George Corday); Charles Coburn (Jonathan Crandall, Sr.); Mona Freeman (Diana Crandall); Jerome Courtland (Gilbert Parker); Elizabeth Patterson (Jessie); Charles Dingle (Morton Buchanan); Walter Baldwin (Witherspoon); Fern Emmett (Lillian); Frank Puglia (Leonardo); Janis Carter (Miss Thorn); Adele Jergens (Gloria LaVerne); Edwin Mills (Potter Kid); Virginia Sale (Secretary); Jessie Arnold, Isabel Withers, Virginia Brissac (Women); Sam Flint, Ferris Taylor, Fred Howard, Charles Marsh (Men); Carole Mathews, Shelley Winters, Adelle Roberts, Ann Loos (Girls); Carl Alfalfa Switzer (Elevator Boy); Jimmy Lloyd (Master of Ceremonies); Rafael Storm (Artist); Nina Mae McKinney (Maid); Ralph Dunn, James Flavin (Policemen); Constance Purdy, Jody Gilbert (Fat Women); Wally Rose (News Cameraman); Charles Arnt (Clerk); Paul Burns, Milton Kibbee (Workmen); Nora Cecil (Woman at Recital); Dudley Dickerson (Porter); Hobart Cavanaugh (Perc Mather); Jimmy Carpenter, Billy Lord, Bobby Alden (Newsboys); Billy Newell (Cab Driver).

OVER 21 (Col., 1945) 102 M.

Producer, Sidney Buchman; director, Charles Vidor; based on the play by Ruth Gordon; screenplay, Buchman; art director, Stephen Goosson, Rudolph Sternad; set decorator, Louis Diage; music, Marlin Skiles; music director, Morris W. Stoloff; assistant director, Ray Nazarro; sound, Howard Fogetti; camera, Rudolph Mate; editor, Otto Meyer.

Irene Dunne (Paula Wharton); Alexander Knox (Max Wharton); Charles Coburn (Robert Gow); Jeff Donnell (Jan Lupton); Loren Tindall (Roy Lupton); Lee Patrick (Mrs. Foley); Phil Brown (Frank MacDougal); Cora Witherspoon (Mrs. Gates); Charles Evans (Colonel Foley); Pierre Watkin (Joel I. Nixon); Anne Loos (Mrs. Dumbrowski); Nanette Parks (Mrs. Clark); Adelle Roberts (Mrs. Collins); Jean Stevens (Mrs. Greenberg); Billy Lechner (Little Boy); Robert Williams (Taxi Driver); Abigail Adams, Francine Ames, Pat Jackson, Marilyn Johnson, Carole Mathews, Jo Gilbert, (Officer-Candidates' Wives); Charles Marsh (Howell); Dan Stowell (Male Secretary); Robert Emmett Keane (Kennedy); Forbes Murray (Meredith); Cosmo Sardo (Barber); Alfred Allegro, Lillian Bronson (Secretaries); George Carleton (Hinkle); Doug Henderson, Michael Owen, George Peters, John James, Bob Meredith, William Hudson (Officer-Candidates); James Flavin (Captain); Rube Schaefer (Athletic Instructor); George Bruggeman, Chuck Hamilton, LeRoy Taylor (Lieutenants); Gladys Blake (Girl); Wallace Pindell (Publicity Man).

ANNA AND THE KING OF SIAM   (20th, 1946) 128 M.

Producer, Louis D. Lighton; director, John Cromwell; based upon the book by Margaret Landon and the books by Anna H. Leonowens; screenplay, Talbot Jennings, Sally Benson; art director, Lyle Wheeler, William Darling; set decorator, Thomas Little, Frank E. Hughes; music, Bernard Herman; assistant director, Saul Wertzel; sound, Bernard Fredericks, Roger Heman; special camera effects, Fred Sersen; camera, Arthur Miller; editor, Harmon Jones.

Irene Dunne (Anna Owens); Rex Harrison (King Mongkut); Linda Darnell (Tuptim); Lee J. Cobb (Kralahome); Gale Sondergaard (Lady Thiang); Mikhail Rasumny (Alak); Dennis Hoey (Sir Edward); Tito Renaldo (Prince—grown up); William Edmunds (Moonshee); Richard Lyon (Louise Owens); John Abbott (Phya Phrom); Leonard Strong (Interpreter); Mickey Roth (Prince); Connie Leon (Beebe); Diana Van Den Ecker (Princess Fa-Ying); Si-lan Chen (Dancer); Marjorie Eaton (Miss MacFarlane); Helena Grant (Mrs. Cortwright); Stanley Mann (Mr. Cortwright); Addison Richards (Captain Orton); Neyle Morrow (Phra Palat); Yvonne Rob (Lady Sno Kim); Julian Rivero (Government Clerk); Lorette Lucz, Chabing, Marianne Quon, Lillian Molieri, Buff Cobb, Sydney Logan (Wives of King); Oie Chan (Old Woman); Ted Hecht, Ben Welden (Judges); Aram Katcher, Rico DeMontes (Guards); Pedro Regas (Guide); Hazel Shon (Slave).

LIFE WITH FATHER   (WB, 1947) C—118 M.

Producer, Robert Buckner; director, Michael Curtiz; based on the play by Howard Lindsay, Russell Crouse; screenplay, Donald Ogden Stewart; art director, Robert Hass; sets, George James Hopkins; wardrobe, Milo Anderson; music, Max Steiner; music director, Leo F. Forbstein; assistant director, Robert Vreeland; dialog director, Herschel Daugherty; technical advisor, Mrs. Clarence Day; makeup, Perc Westmore; sound, C. A. Riggs; montages, James Leicester; special effects, William McGann; special effects director, Ray Foster; camera, Peverell Marley, William V. Skall; editor, George Amy.

William Powell (Clarence Day); Irene Dunne (Vinnie Day); Elizabeth Taylor (Mary); Edmund Gwenn (Rev. Dr. Lloyd); ZaSu Pitts (Cora); Jimmy Lydon (Clarence); Emma Dunn (Margaret); Moroni Olsen (Dr. Humphries); Elisabeth Risdon (Mrs. Whitehead); Derek Scott (Harlan); Johnny Calkins (Whitney); Martin Milner (John); Heather Wilde (Annie); Monte Blue (Policeman); Nancy Duff (Delia); Mary Field (Nora); Queenie Leonard (Maggie); Clara Blandick (Miss Wiggins); Frank Elliott (Dr. Somers); Clara Reid (Scrub Woman); Philo McCullough (Milk Man); Lois Bridge (Corsetierre); George Meader (Salesman); Douglas Kennedy (Mr. Morley); Phil Van Zandt

(Clerk); Russell Arms (Stock Quotation Operator); Faith Kruger (Hilda); Jean Del Val (Francois); Michael and Ralph Mineo (Twins); Creighton Hale (Father of Twins); Jean Andren (Mother of Twins); Elaine Lange (Ellen); Jack Martin (Chef); Arlene Dahl (Girl in Delmonico's); Gertrude Valerie, David Cavendish, Henry Sylvester, Hallene Hill, Laura Treadwell (Churchgoers); John Beck (Perkins, the Clerk); James Metcalf (Customer); Joe Bernard (Cashier); Lucille Shamberger (Nurse Maid).

I REMEMBER MAMA   (RKO, 1948) 134 M.

Executive producer, George Stevens; producer, Harriet Parsons; director, George Stevens; based on the novel *Mama's Bank Account* by Kathryn Forbes and the play by John Van Druten; screenplay, DeWitt Bodeen; art director, Albert S. D'Agostino, Carroll Clark; set decorator, Darrell Silvera, Emil Kuri; music, Roy Webb; music director, C. Bakaleinikoff; sound, Richard Van Hessen, Clem Portman; assistant director, John H. Morse; makeup, Gordon Bau; costumes, Edward Stevenson, Gile Steele; special effects, Russell A. Cully, Kenneth Peach; camera, Nicholas Musuraca; editor, Robert Swink, Tholen Gladden.

Irene Dunne (Mama); Barbara Bel Geddes (Katrin); Oscar Homolka (Uncle Chris); Philip Dorn (Papa); Sir Cedric Hardwicke (Mr. Hyde); Edgar Bergen (Peter Thorkelsen); Rudy Vallee (Dr. Johnson); Barbara O'Neil (Jessie Brown); Florence Bates (Florence Dana Moorehead); Peggy McIntyre (Christine); June Hedin (Dagmar); Steve Brown (Nels); Ellen Corby (Aunt Trina); Hope Landin (Aunt Jenny); Edith Evanson (Aunt Sigrid); Tommy Ivo (Cousin Arne); Lela Bliss, Constance Purdy (Nurses); Stanley Andrews (Minister); Franklyn Farnum (Man); Cleo Ridgley (School-teacher); George Atkinson (Postman); Howard Keiser (Bellboy); Ruth Tobey, Alice Kerbert, Peggy McKim, Peggy Kerbert (Girls).

NEVER A DULL MOMENT   (RKO, 1950) 89 M.

Producer, Harriet Parsons; director, George Marshall; based on the novel *Who Could Ask for Anything More* by Kay Swift; screenplay, Lou Breslow, Doris Anderson; songs, Swift; music director, C. Bakaleinikoff; art director, Albert S. D'Agostino, Walter E. Keller; camera, Joseph Walker; editor, Robert Swink.

Irene Dunne (Kay); Fred MacMurray (Chris); William Demarest (Mears); Andy Devine (Orvie); Gigi Perreau (Tina); Natalie Wood (Nan); Philip Ober (Jed); Jack Kirkwood (Papa Dude); Ann Doran (Jean); Margaret Gibson (Pokey); Lela Bliss (Mama Dude); Irving Bacon (Tunk Johnson); Victoria Horne, Connie Van, Virginia Mullen, Edna Holland (Women); Gene Evan, Olin Howlin, Paul Newman (Hunters); Ann O'Neal (Julia Craddock); Chester Jim Hawkins (Chalmers); Alan Dinehart III (Sonny Boy); Jo Ann Marlowe (Sister); Jacqueline De Witt (Myra Van Elson); Bob Thom, Carl Sklover, Art Dupuis (Vendors).

THE MUDLARK   (20th, 1950) 99 M.

Producer, Nunnally Johnson; director, Jean Negulesco; based on the novel by Theodore Bonnett; screenplay, Johnson; art director, C. P. Norman; music, William Alwyn; sound, Buster Ambler; camera, Georges Perinal; editor, Thelma Myers.

Irene Dunne (Queen Victoria); Alec Guinness (Disraeli); Andrew Ray (Wheeler); Beatrice Campbell (Lady Emily Prior); Finlay Currie (John Brown); Anthony Steel (Lieutenant Charles McHatten); Raymond Lovell (Seargeant Footman Naseby); Marjorie Fielding (Lady Margaret Prior); Constance Smith (Kate Noonan); Ronan O'Casey (Slattery); Edward Rigby (Watchman); Robin Stevens (Herbert); William Strange (Sparrow); Kynaston Reeves (General Sir Henry Ponsonby); Wilfred Hyde-White (Tucker); Ernest Clark (Hammond); Eric Messiter (Ash, Lieutenant of Police);

Pamela Arliss (Princess Christian); Ian Selby (Prince Christian); Maurice Warren (Christian); Michael Brooke (Albert); Jane Short (Victoria); Howard Douglas (Broom); Richmond Nairne (Didbit); George Dillon (Jailer); Leonard Sharp (Ben Fox); V. Kaley (Mrs. Feeney); Freddie Watts (Iron George); Y. Yanai (Al Hook); Paul Garrard (Petey); Leonard Morris (Hooker Morgan); Marjorie Gresley (Meg Bownes); Bob Head (Dandy Fitch); Vi Stevens (Mrs. Dawkins); Alan Gordon (Disraeli's Valet); Grace Denbeigh Russell (Queen's Maid).

IT GROWS ON TREES   (Univ., 1952) 84 M.

Producer, Leonard Goldstein; director, Arthur Lubin; story-screenplay, Leonard Praskins, Barney Slater; assistant director, John Sherwood; music, Frank Skinner; art director, Bernard Herzbrun, Alexander Golitzen; set decorator, Russell A. Gausman, Julia Heron; sound, Leslie I. Carey, Richard DeWeese; camera, Maury Gertsman; editor, Milton Carruth.

Irene Dunne (Polly Baxter); Dean Jagger (Phil Baxter); Joan Evans (Diane Baxter); Richard Crenna (Ralph Brown); Edith Meiser (Mrs. Pryor); Sandy Descher (Midge Baxter); Dee Pollock (Flip Baxter); Les Tremayne (Finlay Murchison); Malcolm Lee Beggs (Henry Carrollman); Forrest Lewis (Dr. Harold Burrows); Frank Ferguson (John Letherby); Bob Sweeney (McGuire); Dee Pollack (Flip Baxter); Emile Avery (TV Man); John Damler (Cleanshave); Clark Howat (Mustache); Elmer Peterson (Commentator); Dee J. Thompson (Miss Reid); Thurston Hall (Sleamish); Cliff Clark (Sergeant); Madge Blake (Woman); Hal K. Dawson (Tutt); Jimmy Dodd (Treeburger Proprietor); Anthony Radecki, Perc Launders, Charles Gibb, Charles McAvoy (Policemen); Mary Benoit, Vera Burnett (Assitants); William O'Leary (Gonnigle); Bob Carney (Bus Driver); Burman Bodel (Badge Vendor); Ralph Montgomery (Umbrella Vendor); Jack Reynolds (Reporter); Bob Edgecomb (Interviewer); Jeanne Blackford (Lady); Frank Howard, Robert Strong (Ad Lib Cameramen); Walter Clinton (Delivery Man); Chuck Courtney (Paper Man).

th Eddie Foy, Jr. in
ATHERNECKING (RKO '30)

In CIMARRON (RKO '31)

the RKO lot, c. 1932

With Wally Albright in
THIRTEEN WOMEN (RKO '32)

With Ricardo Cortez, Lita Chevret, Anna Appel, Gregory Ratoff, and Noel Madison in SYMPHONY OF SIX MILLION (RKO '32)

With John Boles in BACK STREET (Univ '32)

On the set of IF I WERE FREE (RKO '33) with Clive Brook and director Elliott Nugent

h Phillips Holmes in THE
CRET OF MADAME
ANCHE (MGM '33)

With Ralph Bellamy in THIS
MAN IS MINE (RKO '34)

Louis Calhern and Joseph Cawthorn in SWEET ADELINE (WB '35)

In ROBERTA (RKO '35)

In MAGNIFICENT OBSESSI
(Univ

With Helen Westley in THE AGE
OF INNOCENCE (RKO '34)

h Charles Winninger in
OW BOAT (Univ '36)

In THE AWFUL TRUTH
(Col '37)

Margaret McWade and Elisabeth Risdon in THEODORA GOES WILD
'36)

With Marion Martin and Fred MacMurray in INVITATION TO HAPPINESS (Par '39)

With Philip Trent in WHEN TOMORROW COMES (Univ '39)

With Robert Montgomery in UNFINISHED BUSINESS (Univ '41)

With Charles Boyer in
TOGETHER AGAIN (Col '44)

With Alexander Knox and
Charles Coburn in OVER 21
(Col '45)

With Rex Harrison in ANNA
AND THE KING OF SIAM
(20th '46)

With William Powell in LIFE
WITH FATHER (WB '47)

With Baldy Cooke and Barbara
Bel Geddes in I REMEMBER
MAMA (RKO '48)

With Gigi Perreau, Natalie
Wood, Fred MacMurrary, and
Andy Devine in NEVER A DULL
MOMENT (RKO '50)

h her husband, Dr. Griffin,
nid-1950s

At the United Nations in 1957

n Finlay Currie and Alec Guinness in THE MUDLARK (20th '50)

In KITTY FOYLE (RKO '40)

Ginger Rogers

5'5"
115 pounds
Gold-blonde hair
Green eyes
Cancer

In analyzing the superstardom qualities of living legend Ginger Rogers, writer-director Garson Kanin once stated, "She retains the nerve of a newcomer, and the courage of a champion." This may well explain why Ginger has endured for over four decades as a radiant exponent of wholesome glamour. Above and beyond her magical screen teaming with Fred Astaire in ten tasteful musical films (between 1933 and 1949)—a solid chunk of nostalgia which Ginger milks to the commercial limit—Ginger has been most resourceful in reshaping her established show business image to fit the new molds demanded by changing times and her advancing age.

Like lesser RKO co-worker Anne Shirley, Ginger was initially very much a product of her own backstage mama. Mrs. Lela Rogers guided Ginger's career with a firm hand and a blindness to any obstacle in her daughter's professional path: despite Ginger's husbands, the girl's limited dramatic-acting range, and long-standing film-executive indifference to Ginger's true screen potential. Ginger acknowledges her mother's very helping hand, demurely saying, "Pushing is necessary in achieving stardom. Someone should."

Once Ginger matured into cinema stardom, she became the exponent of the chic, worldly, witty, slick, brittle girl, always ready with a tart word, but basically having that proverbial heart of gold. It is a state of being that remains with Ginger today, when, well past her movie-star years, she continues to be active in a variety of guises: stage performer, television guest artist, fashion-design pitchwoman. One might wish that Ginger would pursue intellectual avenues as savagely as she does wholesome morality, but that would not be the athletic, well-wishing Ginger who has remained a public favorite for more years than even Joan Crawford would care to admit. Ginger's creed still remains: "Life is activity, or activity is life. I'm not sure which. Anyway, I keep active."

She was born Virginia* Katherine McMath on July 16, 1911, in Independence, Missouri, the daughter of Eddins and Lela Emogene (Owens) McMath.†
When Ginger was scarcely more than a year old, the McMaths moved to Ennis, Texas, where the father had accepted employment. The stagnant atmosphere of their new hometown did nothing to smooth over the disintegrating domestic relationship between Mr. and Mrs. McMath, and it was not long before the couple decided to separate. Mrs. McMath and Ginger moved into a nearby hotel for the time being. Suddenly, Mr. McMath, deciding he wanted Ginger at his own fireside, "kidnapped" the girl. The Texas courts branded this action "reckless behavior." Not only was McMath required to return his daughter to the custody of his wife, but his visitation rights were sharply curtailed. Incensed by this unjust state of being, he "kidnapped" little Ginger again and left the state.

A most determined Mrs. McMath and her parents employed private detectives, who ultimately tracked Mr. McMath and Ginger to St. Louis. The girl was promptly taken from her father again.‡ Mrs. McMath bundled herself and Ginger off to Kansas City to live with her parents, where she intended to map out a new life for herself and her daughter.

Years later, in a mother-of-a-star-talks-about-her-daughter booklet, Mrs. McMath would recall, with appropriate aplomb: "Ginger Rogers was the most beautiful baby anyone could have wished for, and began dancing before she could even walk. At the age of three she was singing the popular numbers of the day. The words pronounced in her own baby way, but right on the nose with the time and the beat." When gangling Ginger was not even five years old, her ambitious mother maneuvered the girl a job appearing in a few (obscure) advertising films produced in Kansas City. For some of these screen outings, the versatile if not so talented or experienced Mrs. McMath directed the oncamera proceedings. It developed a taste for moviemaking that neither McMath was to ever lose.

*It is always said that it was Ginger's cousin and lifelong friend Phyllis Fraser (later Mrs. Bennett Cerf), unable to pronounce "Virginia," who developed the habit as a child of calling her relative "Ginger."

†Mr. McMath, an electrical engineer, had met his wife-to-be in a Kansas City dancing school. When her father, a building contractor, was about to move his business and his family to Utah, McMath rose to the occasion and wed Lela on her eighteenth birthday (Christmas Day). The McMath's first child died in infancy, and another, conceived after Ginger's birth, was stillborn.

‡She would only see him a few times thereafter, for he died when she was eleven years old.

Thereafter a success-craving Mrs. McMath charged her parents with caring for the freckled-faced Ginger while she went to Hollywood to try her luck in the cinema capital. Her announced goal was to become a scriptwriter. Eventually Fox Studios purchased one of her efforts—more for its title (*Honor System* [1917]) than for its content—and soon she was able to secure scenarist jobs, writing for the likes of Gladys Brockwell, Theda Bara, and Baby Marie Osborn.* As a staff writer for the Baby Marie vehicles, Mrs. McMath was later sent to New York City. Once there, and finding herself with sufficient income, she sent for Ginger to join her in residence at Manhattan's Hotel Bristol.

Not too long after Ginger arrived in New York and began appearing on the movie sets with mama, Burton George, a Fox film director, brought Ginger to the company's Fort Lee, New Jersey, studio and gave her a tiny part in a then-shooting George Walsh picture. When Mrs. McMath learned of this adventure, she unexpectedly took a conservative stand on the matter, and declined to allow Ginger to return to the studio for the two additional days required to finishing shooting the part. Another girl was substituted. Referring to this incident years later, Ginger would wistfully say, "No one knows this, but I could have been a child star at six. I was offered a contract but Mom said I was too young."

While Ginger's potential film career was being snafued, the global political situation of 1917 exploded into America's entry into World War I. Ginger was hastily sent back to Kansas City to her grandparents, while the ubiquitous Mrs. McMath moved on to Washington, D.C., to write publicity copy for the Marine Corps magazine, *The Leatherneck*. For this journalistic venture, she used the pen name of Lela Leibrand.

When the Armistice came two years later, Mrs. McMath reappeared in Kansas City to re-establish herself both as Ginger's mother and in a decent paying job. She found employment as a reporter on the *Kansas City Post*. By the time she was officially widowed in 1922 (with the death of Mr. McMath) she had re-established a social relationship with John Logan Rogers, whom she had dated years before. They wed that year and in the course of their seven-year marriage Mr. Rogers legally adopted Ginger. When business required the Rogerses to transplant themselves to Fort Worth, Texas, adaptable Lela was quick to find a post on the *Fort Worth Record* as reporter and theatre critic. Just to keep her days full, she served as manager of a local symphonic orchestra; for the pure recreation of it all, she composed short plays concerned with Texas history. When one of these divertissements, entitled *The Death of St. Dennis*, was performed at the Fort Worth Central High School in 1924, it was only natural that thirteen-year-old Ginger should have a role in it.†

---

*She would be Ginger's movie stand-in during the 1930s, and Betty Hutton's in the 1940s.

†In Kansas City, Ginger had attended the Benton Boulevard Elementary School; in Fort Worth she matriculated at the Elementary School. At the age of eleven she fulfilled an earlier childhood ambition by appearing publicly as a pianist. Her rendition of MacDowall's "To a Wild Rose" met with enthusiastic response from the auditorium audience, but Ginger did not seriously pursue her music studies, preferring to concentrate on acting and dancing.

Mrs. Rogers was convinced that Ginger's future lay in the show business world, and she did everything possible to pave the path for her daughter's blossoming in the predetermined field. According to mama Rogers, "Actors, musicians and opera singers were guests in my house for after-theatre snacks of southern fried chicken, biscuits and honey. By the age of fifteen Ginger had met them all, plus the local theatre managers, who were my friends." She did not really have to push Ginger very hard, for early in life Ginger had decided, like her mother, that there was nothing quite so glamorous as a life upon the "wicked" stage. Ginger's first big opportunity was not long in coming in this conducive grease-paint-oriented atmosphere. Vaudeville star Eddie Foy was playing the Fort Worth circuit one week in 1925 and required a fill-in dancer, posthaste. Mrs. Rogers learned about the opening through her grapevine and Ginger found herself on the scene auditioning for the stage assignment. She won the part and proved more than adequate in actual performance.

In defense of Lela Rogers, who over the years has received more than her share of rebuke for her dedication to becoming the prize stage mother of all time, she did try at this time to induce Ginger to attend college, savvy enough to the vicissitudes of show business to realize that further education would be a tremendous asset to Ginger should she later have to find another occupation. But the theatre was already Ginger's first love, and she was scarcely able to contain herself to completing her high school requirement. So grudgingly (or so the story goes) Mrs. Rogers assisted her daughter in creating the white-rhinestone-encrusted gown that Ginger would wear in a Charleston contest, leading to her entry in the state finals held in Dallas on January 12, 1926. Ginger, who had inherited her mother's competitive spirit, enjoyed the challenge, and, more so, the victory. Her prize was a month-long booking on the Texas-Oklahoma theatre circuit. At Lela Roger's instigation, the two runner-ups in the Charleston events were hired to join her in the act, which went under the tag, "Ginger and her Redheads."*

After this professional outing, it took all of Mrs. Rogers's cunning to woo Ginger into returning to high school for another year. But the following summer, Ginger was back on the show business tack, dancing and singing in a cafe in Galveston, Texas, a club spot which led to a road tour which concluded its run in St. Louis, where Ginger was enjoying billing as "The Original John Held, Jr. Girl."†

For the next three years Ginger toured on the vaudeville circuit—largely in the Midwest and South—with Mrs. Rogers, the latter accepting 20 percent of

---

*"My mother decided that my solo Charleston act needed pepping up for the tough theatres ahead. She remembered that in the finals at the Dallas hotel there had been a couple of runners-up from Houston. One was a strapping seventeen-year-old boy named Earl Leach and his partner was a peppy girl named Josephine Butler. The fact that they both had red hair gave mother an idea."

†John Held, Jr., a Utah Mormon, was famed for his drawings and paintings of college-age youngsters in the 1920s. The "Held girl," who appeared in the original *Life, Vanity Fair,* and *Harper's Bazaar,* characteristically had well-structured, long, racy legs, slender hands, and a lovely neck. She was the Cosmetic Ideal of the fun girl who smelled wonderful.

Ginger's salary for serving as agent, costumiere, confidante, and supplier of most of the material for the act. Eventually Ginger found steady employment on the Paramount-Publix vaudeville circuit in short musical revues at $350-a-week salary. Her standard routine consisted of singing and dancing, and most memorably offering bits of baby talk "recalations about the anumals, including Mama Nyceroserous and Papa Hippopapumis." (These diverting—when performed, not when discussed—ga-ga-cooing toddler-lingo sessions would become standard fare in Ginger's later film work, and offcamera they remain to this day a fixed part of her repertoire to amuse her friends.)

In 1928, during a three-week layoff, Ginger decided to marry Jack Edward Culpepper, whom she had known when they were both children in Texas. He was now a hoofer on the vaudeville circuit, known as Jack Pepper. After a very brief honeymoon the couple embarked on a road tour billed as "Ginger and Pepper." The act was no more successful than the marriage. After ten months, much to Mrs. Rogers's relief, the couple called it quits (a divorce would be obtained in 1931).

After her marital failure Ginger reverted to a solo act, headlining a show with Eddie Lowry and his band, which played St. Louis for thirty-two weeks and later Chicago's Oriental Theatre for an additional eighteen weeks. In the latter engagement she was co-featured with comedian Willie Howard, whom she has always thanked for teaching her a great deal about milking an audience for applause. Next she was a featured singer with Paul Ash and his orchestra, which led to an engagement at the Paramount Theatre in Brooklyn. An overzealous Mrs. Rogers, thrilled that her daughter had finally broken out of the provincial grind into the "big time," tried to induce Eddie Cantor, who caught one of the Brooklyn shows, to include Ginger in his new Broadway musical, *Whoopee*. Cantor declined the proffered suggestion.

But Charlie Morrison, owner of the Mocambo Nightclub in Hollywood, had spotted Ginger in her vaudeville act and mentioned her favorably to songsmiths Bert Kalmar and Harry Ruby, who were seeking a snappy young soubrette for their new musical comedy, *Top Speed* (46th Street Theatre, December 25, 1929). Ginger was hired as the second female lead, in support of Lester Allen, Paul Frawley, and Irene Delroy. She was cast as Babs Green, a wealthy miss who falls for a stockbroker's clerk. Shame! Shame! She and Lester Allen performed "Keep Your Undershirt On" and she led the ensemble in the lively number "Hot and Bothered," a tune which aroused a good deal of favorable critical and audience reaction.* John Boyle and LeRoy Prinz staged the choreography for *Top Speed* while Hermes Pan, who would later

---

*The reviewers had a field day poking jovial barbs at Miss Rogers's nickname. "The surprise performance of the show is given by the aforementioned Miss Rogers (we prefer to remember only her surname)," wrote Howard Barnes (*New York Herald-Tribune*). "Ginger may not disturb the terpsichorean hall of fame, but she has it with Ginger flavor" (*New York American*). Brooks Atkinson (*New York Times*) was more catholic in his appraisal of Ginger's stage abilities, calling reader attention to "an impudent young thing, Ginger Rogers, who carries youth and humor to the point where they are completely charming."

be dance director on the Fred Astaire-Ginger Rogers RKO pictures, was just a member of the *Top Speed* chorus.

Although Ginger and Mrs. Rogers were pleased by the warm reception of the *Top Speed* performance, they were concerned with eradicating the growing word-of-mouth among less enthusiastic Broadway observers that Ginger was merely another hoofer in the Zelma O'Neal musical comedy tradition, and that she was destined to be nothing more than a carbon-copy of the then very popular Helen "Betty Boop" Kane. Then too, the Rogerses had to ponder the advisability of pursuing Ginger's film career. Paramount producer Walter Wanger had been among the attendees of the opening-night performance of *Top Speed,* and he had been immediately convinced of Ginger's ripe screen potential.* He persuaded her to make a movie test to prove that his snap judgment was correct.

Supercharged Ginger decided to give feature films a proper fling and signed a contract with Paramount, who were informed by East Coast executive Wanger that the new player might well be the stand-by for Helen Kane that the studio was seeking. But, in typical moviemaking tradition, Ginger was not utilized in the real capacity she had been signed for (musical comedy) but was instead thrust into the wisecracking mold already becoming closely associated with Warner Brothers' Joan Blondell. On her free mornings and nonmatinee afternoons, Ginger would trek out to Paramount's studio in Astoria, Long Island, to emote oncamera, her first feature being *Young Man of Manhattan* (Paramount Theatre, April 18, 1930). In this newspaper story, which boasted Broadway's own Claudette Colbert, Ginger was seen chasing after Charles Ruggles and then diverting her amorous advances to Norman Foster. When she finally captures her prey, smart-mouthed flapper Puff (Ginger) snaps out the now classic line, "Cigarette me, Big Boy." The film gave her the opportunity to sing "I've Got It But It Don't Do Me No Good," leading the *New York Times* to evaluate: "[She] is attractive and bright and sings well." But Ginger's reaction was more critical. "My stomach did a flip-flop. I so wanted to do it all over again."

But the studio was not about to reshoot the comedy-relief scenes of the supporting female player. Instead she was thrust into another churned-out feature, *The Sap from Syracuse* (1930), paired with a smart-alecky Jack Oakie. He was a crane driver in this tongue-in-cheek comedy that had more than its share of funny moments, something that could not be said for *Queen High* (1930), which featured Charles Ruggles and Frank Morgan as partners in the garter business, and Ginger as background set-dressing.

At this point, Paramount offered to send Ginger of the spit curls and bee-stung lips to its Hollywood filmmaking plant, complete with a new contract.

---

*During Ginger's Paramount-Publix vaudeville touring days, she had made several one- and two-reel short subjects, part of the Checker Comedy series, with Ginger utilizing a great deal of her stage material for her oncamera scenes. Her three-reel short, *Campus Sweethearts,* which starred Rudy Vallee, was filmed in a third-dimensional process (Natural Vision). It was made during her Brooklyn Paramount Theatre stint. Later there would be such short subjects as *A Night in the Dormitory,* and that delight of home-movie devotees, *Office Blues.*

However, at the end of the Broadway run of *Top Speed,* the opportunity presented itself for her to appear in George Gershwin's *Girl Crazy* (Alvin Theatre, October 14, 1930) and she could not resist the formidable chance to shine in this Broadway show. Besides, *Girl Crazy* would pay her more than $1,000 a week, while Paramount was only offering her $350 weekly at the time. Ginger also rejected the opportunity to appear in Douglas Fairbanks's filmed musical comedy *Reaching for the Moon* (United Artists, 1931), which was to be shot in California.

In *Girl Crazy* Ginger was cast as Molly Gray, postmistress of Custerville, a rural locale upon which a Broadway Romeo and his coterie of beauties descend to open a dude ranch. Willie Howard had the comedy lead as the Manhattan taxi driver who took his Lochinvar passenger to Custerville, and stayed himself to become the local sheriff. Ginger, with her soft but sweet voice, was assigned some of Gershwin's best numbers, including "But Not for Me" and "Embraceable You" as well as the comic ditty "Cactus Time in Arizona."* But the surprise hit of opening night and the show was not Ginger, or established Willie Howard, or the DeMarcos, or Red Nichols and his Orchestra, but gutsy Ethel Merman, who belted out "I Got Rhythm" and "Boy! What Love Has Done for Me." Overnight Merman became a Broadway sensation, while the less bombastic Ginger would have to wait for Hollywood to properly capitalize on her much gentler entertaining talents.†

During the 272-performance run of *Girl Crazy,* Ginger had little opportunity to relax at her new 55 Central Park West digs, for she had to complete her standing Paramount contract. There was *Follow the Leader* (1930), Ed Wynn's debut in full-length talking films, in which Ginger was the saucy understudy who replaces Ethel Merman in the big show (within the movie) when the latter is suddenly kidnapped. More entertaining in all cinematic departments was *Honor among Lovers* (1931), yet another newspaper story, in which Ginger was the lively girlfriend of reporter Charles Ruggles.

Exhausted by the strenuous pace of filming at the Astoria lot by day and performing on the Broadway stage at night, Ginger negotiated a release from her Paramount contract.‡ This sudden consideration for her health was more a ploy on the part of Ginger and Mrs. Rogers than a fact, for the young actress seriously doubted that there was any substantial future for her with Paramount Pictures. The musical comedy competition was too keen at that company. No, she reasoned, she might do much better to accept the lucrative

---

*During rehearsals of *Girl Crazy,* Broadway dancing star Fred Astaire was called in to assist co-producer Alex Aarons in staging the "But Not for Me" number, which, due to lack of better facilities, was being rehearsed in the Alvin Theatre lobby. Although Ginger and Astaire occasionally dated in this period, neither one had any inkling that they soon would be dancing together as a screen team.

†In her autobiography Ethel Merman recalled: "Ginger was pretty, she could act, she could dance, but no one called her The Voice. Ginger's voice was a pleasing one, but small. The way she sang 'Embraceable You' was charming, but the songs she sang didn't require power."

‡Supposedly Paramount studio producer Jesse Lasky sighed upon granting Ginger's release, "I'm afraid a day will come when I'll regret this."

199

contract offered by Charles R. Rogers,* the newly appointed production head of RKO Pathé. Mrs. Rogers was particularly certain this was Ginger's big silver-screen break, so the mother-daughter team said a quick goodbye to Broadway and embarked on the cross-country train to Hollywood.

Arriving back on the Hollywood scene was a pleasant experience for Mrs. Rogers, but Ginger had second thoughts about her future on the Pathé lot, where there were such established luminaries as Helen Twelvetrees, Ina Claire, Pola Negri, Ann Harding, and one of Ginger's screen idols, Constance Bennett. Ginger's intuition about Pathé proved correct, for she found herself being cast to the winds in *The Tip Off* (1931), a rather depressing tale involving the prizefight game and the underworld. Her male leads were studio (and, believe it or not, public) favorites Eddie Quillan and Robert Armstrong, both of the "ah shucks" school of acting. To this day Ginger has unkind words about this debut Hollywood feature. At the time *The Tip Off* opened at the Broadway Theatre (October 21, 1931) the companion entertainment bill, which contained a practical demonstration of television, received more enthusiastic notices.

Suicide Fleet (1931) was not much better. William "Hopalong Cassidy" Boyd, Robert Armstrong, and James Gleason all join the World War I Navy, each insisting he is madly in love with candy-hawker Ginger. Ginger's preference runs to Boyd—which makes sense since he was the picture's star—who used to work as a Coney Island shooting-gallery shill. She spent most of *Suicide Fleet* proving to the jealous gobs that one boyfriend was quite sufficient. As "dramatic" relief from this romantic setup there were naval engagements in which the Allied forces attempted to cope with the German U-boat squadrons. *Carnival Boat* (RKO-Pathé, 1932) was on the same par. Ginger was the sexy young showboat entertainer whose snazzy presence distracts William Boyd from devoted duty to the timber business operated by his father (Hobart Bosworth). This picture did provide her with the screen chance to sing "How I Could Go for You."

At this indecisive juncture in her meandering film career, Ginger was quite willing to spout forth on any subject for the fan magazines. "I don't know which I like best," she told one reporter, "I love the applause on the stage. But pictures are so fascinating. You reach so many millions through them. And you make more money, too." Pathé was as little impressed with Ginger's range of oratory as it was with her box-office lustre to date; her studio option was dropped.

Ginger was not about to be ruled off the Hollywood scene by this setback. With characteristic abandon she plunged herself into filmmaking activity, accepting each and every offer that turned up, whether the film seemed promising or not. By the law of averages, so she and mama Rogers figured, one of the projects might turn out to be a showcase part for her that would pave the way for a better studio berth. Thus Ginger's remaining four 1932 releases saw

*No relation to Ginger.

200

her jumping from studio to studio and genre to genre, seeking a "comeback" in whatever proved to be her proper screen niche. At First National, a lighter-haired Ginger performed as straight woman for cavernous-mouthed Joe E. Brown in *The Tenderfoot.* As the secretary who Texas-rich Brown is sure can take over for leading lady Vivienne Oakland in *Her Golden Sin,* the play-within-the-movie, Ginger spent most of the picture registering oversized reactions to cowboy Brown's outrageous onscreen behavior. Next Ginger hotfooted it over to Monogram Pictures on poverty row for *The Thirteenth Guest.** The modest thriller owed more to *The Cat and the Canary* than to its director Albert Ray, what with the stock setting of a haunted house (at 122 Old Mill Road), a frightened heiress (Ginger), her detective Lochinvar (Lyle Talbot), and the standard dense law-enforcer (Brandon Hurst). Ginger was certainly not in Fay Wray's league as a screaming movie heroine, but she was growing more comely picture after picture, having learned by experiment to soften her once-stereotyped tough-red-head screen image. Over at Fox, Ginger found herself playing third fiddle to hat check girl Sally Eilers (cast as a good girl from Brooklyn) and Ben Lyon (seen as a playboy falsely accused of murdering crook Monroe Owsley). There was less entertainment value than met the eye in *Hat Check Girl,* but it did provide a venue for Ginger to test her refined screen posture as Eilers' wisecracking pal who does not mind making a few *dishonest* dollars here and there; in this instance, in the bootlegging racket.

Joe E. Brown had found Ginger an amiable leading lady and requested her for *You Said a Mouthful* (First National, 1932), which was far more of a slap-stick venture than their previous *The Tenderfoot.*† As a dense inventor of an unsinkable bathing suit, Brown lands in California to collect his late aunt's estate, only to find instead that she left a bundle of debts. That is bad enough for the star of *You Said a Mouthful,* but he also must cope with Ginger, who mistakes him for a champion swimmer and enthusiastically enlists him in a pending aqua race. Yes. This is the vintage film in which beachside-clad Ginger finds herself drenched in mud.

If Hollywood had yet to cotton to Ginger, she had enthusiastic opinions of the movie industry and its colony of celebrities. Being pert, fun-loving, and single she was a popular girl on the social scene, but she chose to devote her attention to one gentleman in particular, Warner Bros. director Mervyn LeRoy. So serious was their dating, that many Hollywood bystanders were convinced the couple would soon wed. While Ginger never did say yes to that important question, she did heed LeRoy's advice to accept a replacement job for Joan Blondell in Warners' *42nd Street* (Strand Theatre, March 9, 1933).

---

*Remade as *The Mystery of the 13th Guest* (1943). The earlier version became a television staple in late 1940s and early 1950s video programming.

† Since Brown had a persistent reputation of being difficult to deal with on the set, unless everything on- and offcamera revolved about him, it must have required a good deal of diplomacy on Ginger's part to ingratiate herself with the limelight-loving comedian.

That trend-setting screen musical,* directed in crisp, smooth, flowing style by Lloyd Bacon, did much to consolidate the future film career of kaleidoscopic-prone dance stager Busby Berkeley, and it established the viable box-office teaming of Dick Powell and Ruby Keeler. Ginger had hoped for a bigger part in the ninety-eight-minute feature, but while she only had the opportunity to sing a few choruses of "Shuffle off to Buffalo" with Una Merkel, and to make occasional flip talk as the society-aspiring, monocled, cane-carrying chorine known as Anytime Annie,† she did make an indelible impression with audiences for her glib ability to dish out wise talk in the best Joan Blondell-Glenda Farrell tradition. For this author, a far more telling indication of Ginger's seasoning screen talents could be found in the film's scene in which, as the new mistress of show-backer Guy Kibbee, she admits to not being talented enough to take over for ailing Bebe Daniels, but says she knows a girl in the chorus who is just right for the part. (Ruby Keeler, of course!).

By the time *42nd Street* was released, Ginger had appeared in the short subject *Hollywood on Parade* (1933) and more importantly been selected as a WAMPAS Baby Star of 1932, along with Lillian Bond, Mary Carlisle, Eleanor Holm, Evalyn Knapp, Patricia Ellis, Gloria Stuart, and others. But she had no time to bask in any industry puffery for she was to make eight other films that would see release in 1933. She hopped from Warner Bros. to Fox for *Broadway Bad.*‡ This movie was hogwash that made dull work of the Great White Way, had a badly photographed Joan Blondell in the lead, and found Ginger cast as a chorus girl with a predictable sentimental streak. Fortunately Mervyn LeRoy came to Ginger's rescue again, having her cast in *Gold Diggers of 1933* (Warner Bros., 1933). § Not that she had one of the lead roles, for there was established-cinema-name Warren William as the snooty Bostonian brother of would-be songwriter Dick Powell, with Ginger very much the fourth-hand member of the gold-digging quartet of chorines, headed by Joan Blondell, Ruby Keeler, and Aline MacMahon. As Fay Fortune, Ginger literally opened the picture as the prime interpreter of that Depression-born song "We're in the Money," sung to the accompaniment of swaying oversized coins, which made an interesting contrast to Ginger's shimmering gown of sparkling shekels. To this day Ginger insists that the utilization of her singing stanzas of the soon-to-become famous Money song in pig Latin ("e'rewa ina the oneyma; e'rewa ina the oneyma") came about from her joking on the set one day, and studio producer Darryl F. Zanuck deciding the lark should be

---

*The *New York Times* called *42nd Street* the "liveliest and one of the most tuneful screen musicals to come out of Hollywood."

†"The only time Anytime Annie said no, she didn't hear the question."

‡Directed by Sidney Lanfield, who had helmed *Hat Check Girl.*

§ *The Gold Diggers,* starring Ina Claire, opened on Broadway on September 30, 1919, and ran for 720 performances. In 1923 it was picturized by Warner Bros. with Hope Hampton, Louise Fazenda, Gertrude Short, and Arita Gillman. In 1929, the studio remade it as *Gold Diggers of Broadway* with Nacy Welford, Winnie Lightner, Ann Pennington, and Lilyan Tashman in the top femme roles.

integrated into the overall production number.* As cinema writer Homer Dickens has already pointed out,† fledgling star Ginger was also featured in another production number subsequently deleted from the release print of *Gold Diggers of 1933,* in which she was garbed in a black decollete' outfit, singing in front of a white piano.

Ginger's industrious agent ‡ thereafter landed her a leading role, no less, at RKO in *Professional Sweetheart* (Radio City Music Hall, July 13, 1933),§ another one of those tattered musicals deriving its sputtering energy from taking to task the sacred cow of radio. Director William Seiter guided Ginger through her undemanding paces as the "Purity Girl of the Air," the star of the "Ippie Wipsie Radio Hour," sponsored by Gregory Ratoff, the iconoclastic head of the Ipswitch Washcloth Company. Because Ginger has tired of her professional post as the pedestaled virgin of the airwaves and wants a little human romance (with hickish Kentuckian Norman Foster), she upsets Ratoff's cloth cart by joining the employ of dishrag-industry rival Edgar Kennedy. However, timely mergers, both commercial (Ratoff and Kennedy) and matrimonial (Ginger and Foster), bring the picture to a happy conclusion. The *New York Times* could not compliment the listless story, but it reported that "Ginger Rogers has rarely been more entertaining." What the newspaper failed to grasp—and the public as well—was that, according to musicologist Miles Kreuger, for the first and only time onscreen Ginger's small but melodic voice was dubbed. RKO hired black songstress Etta Moten to function as her vocal ghost.ᵠ

Before RKO had the opportunity to tabulate Ginger's impact on audiences in *Professional Sweetheart,* she was off and running on yet another of her marathon filmmaking chores. (Ginger has often enunciated her workaday philosophy as, "I like to use every minute of every day purposefully; even when I lounge it is because I believe it helps me to get the best out of my next spell of activity.") *A Shriek in the Night* (Allied Pictures, 1933) reteamed Ginger with poverty-row leading man Lyle Talbot and director Albert Ray (both from *The Thirteenth Guest*) in a penny-dreadful thriller. Ginger and Talbot functioned as rival reporters who are determined to crack a murder case, while finding romance along the way. As the game heroine (unfortunately she only has one shrieking scene), Ginger is not astute enough to de-

---

* For those filmgoers who missed Ginger's flippant rendition of "We're in the Money" in the initial or subsequent theatrical releases of the feature or on innumerable video showings, the sequence was included in *Bonnie and Clyde* when Warren Beatty takes a few hours off from bank robbing to lounge in a movie theatre playing the picture.

† *Films in Review* career study (March, 1966).

‡ By 1935 her professional ten-percenter would be powerful Myron Selznick.

§ By this point RKO Radio and Pathé had for all intents and purposes combined their facilities, with a changeover of executive command, paving the way for Ginger's reappearance on the lot.

ᵠShe had functioned so powerfully, if briefly, in the "Forgotten Man" number of *Gold Diggers of 1933.*

cipher janitor Harvey Clark's peculiar behavior and is only rescued in the nick of time from ending up as ash in an incinerator.

Universal's *Don't Bet on Love* (1933) was more memorable for pairing Ginger with her future real-life husband number two (Lew Ayres) than for its *Guys and Dolls*-like yarn, which found manicurist Ginger agog over racetrack devotee Ayres, he a plumber by trade. She was next rematched with Jack Oakie in *Sitting Pretty* (Paramount, 1933) a filmusical set in Hollywood. Ginger was perfectly at ease as the lunch-counter proprietress who bolsters songwriters Oakie and Jack Haley on their way to cinematic fortune, although she almost loses roly-poly Oakie to Acme Studio's own prima donna, Thelma Todd. The picture's prime melody, "Did You Ever See a Dream Walking," became one of the top-ten pop songs of the year. Ginger got her own round of praise for *Sitting Pretty* when Richard Watts, Jr. (*New York Herald-Tribune*) referred to her as "a girl who combines looks, grace, and an unaffected wit."

In mid-1933 Mrs. Rogers was still angling for a proper studio home for Ginger. She had her daughter test anew at Columbia Pictures because that company's mogul, Harry Cohn, had seen several of Ginger's films and thought she had definite potential beyond her limited showcasing to date. But parsimonious Cohn could not make up his mind whether or not to sign her to a term contract. While he was debating the advisability of this maneuver, Ginger's Columbia screentest came to the attention of Merian C. Cooper.* Cooper's RKO production unit had utilized Ginger in *Professional Sweetheart,* but it was the inverse catalyst of screening Ginger's embarrassingly stilted (and downright bad) Columbia movie test† that decided Cooper to have a long talk with Lela Rogers. The net result of this conference was that Ginger signed a seven-year pact with RKO,‡ forcing her to drop out of Paramount's *Take a Chance* (1934) with James Dunn and Cliff Edwards. June Knight took her place.

Within a limited overall budget Cooper had been doing wonders at RKO, ranging from *King Kong* to *Little Women* (both 1933) and now he was preparing a fairly lush screen musical, *Flying Down to Rio* (1933). Exotic Dolores Del Rio and bland Gene Raymond had been cast as the picture's leads, with Hollywood newcomer Fred Astaire as the dancing second lead.§ According to Cooper, "I selected Ginger Rogers—at that time not a big name—as Astaire's partner. Originally I was going to use my wife [Dorothy Jordan] to play opposite him, but our marriage made me revise that plan. While the numbers were in rehearsal I brought in Robert Benchley to write some additional dialogue for Astaire, and in other ways we built up the parts of Astaire and Rogers."

*He had replaced Dore Schary (reberthed at MGM) as production head of the combined RKO Radio and Pathé facilities.

†According to the privileged group who have seen this screen test, Ginger played-hammed is closer to the mark-a mature woman lawyer.

‡Ginger's cousin, Phyllis Fraser, had been at RKO since 1932.

§Long a proven Broadway name, Astaire was considered a nervous movie bet, despite his brief but effective outing in Joan Crawford's *Dancing Lady* (MGM, 1933).

When *Flying Down to Rio* opened at the Radio City Music Hall on December 22, 1933, no one was surprised by the innocuous screen billing-and-cooing by Del Rio and Raymond. However, the novel onscreen combination of Ginger and Astaire grabbed everyone's interest. When the tasteful twosome launched into the "Carioca" dance, audiences suddenly realized they were witnessing a vibrant, delectable slice of cinema magic. This extended segment of ballroom virtuosity goosed *Flying Down to Rio* from the level of simply pleasant screen musical fare into the ranks of distinctiveness. Ginger and Astaire, as has so often since been analyzed, were not merely performing for the cinematographer to capture as best he could. They were working in combination with the camera's lens, which followed their terpsichorean flirtation, tracing the couple's every graceful elegant gesture. Despite the instantaneous success of *Flying Down to Rio* and Ginger and Astaire (the team became the strong selling point for the film), it would be many months before the players were reunited for another cinema outing.

While everyone was praising the new onscreen Ginger, with her fresh, sleek screen look (especially her restyled long-hair coiffure), *Chance at Heaven** crept into the Rialto Theatre on Christmas Day, 1933. "She acts the part better than it deserves" claimed the *New York Times,* referring to Ginger's effort to breathe life into the paltry account of a rural miss (Ginger) who loses her gas-station-owner sweetheart (Joel McCrea) to urban socialite Marian Nixon, only to rewin him after he discovers it is no picnic being wed to spoiled Miss Nixon.

With the spiffy box-office drive of *Flying Down to Rio,* exhibitors were in a tizzy for a new Fred Astaire-Ginger Rogers (as the couple was always billed) vehicle, but Merian C. Cooper refused to be rushed into launching the singing-dancing duo into just any picture encore. Instead; Astaire went to London to play *Gay Divorce* there, and Ginger was employed by RKO on the home lot and in loan-out for five additional pictures before returning to the on-camera arms of Astaire.

RKO made a big fuss about seeking a new surname for Ginger, in keeping with her growing movie prominence; they would have been well advised to hunt out better film projects for her instead. William Seiter, who had mauled *Chance at Heaven,* performed similar chores on *Rafter Romance* (1934). The novelty of the film's premise was hardly explored in the allotted seventy-minute presentation. Struggling Greenwich Village artist Ginger shares her attic room with impoverished young artist Norman Foster. Since she works in the daytime and he as a night watchman is occupied in the evenings, they never meet, although each has a firm conviction that the other must be a bad number. When they do encounter at a Sunday picnic they are, naturally, mutually attracted. Even *Variety,* usually generous with its accolades, termed *Rafter Romance* as fit only for the "rear rank of a double feature bill."

Finishing School (RKO, 1934) was of a much higher calibre but still rather slim film fare. For her role in this Frances Dee starrer, Ginger reverted from

*Made at RKO before *Flying Down to Rio.*

205

sweet heroine back to her *Gold Digger* type of worldly-wise dame, albeit here on a more subdued level as the Swiss-boarding-school roommate of Dee. It was lovely Miss Dee who had the catchall part of a debutante miss who enters hesitantly on a romance with impetuous intern Bruce Cabot, fearful of the consequences, which do all come true. On the other hand, Ginger ambled through the film delighting in her defiance of headmistress Beulah Bondi and flaunting her violations of the hypocritical rules governing the exclusive educational emporium.

Warner Bros.' *20 Million Sweethearts* (1934)* offered Ginger as song-stress Peggy Cornell, the "Cinderella Girl" on Consolidated Broadcasting's "Carlotta Soap Hour." In the film Ginger takes an immediate shine to beer garden singing-waiter Dick Powell and manages to provide him with his big audio break, risking her job in the gesture. Dynamic Consolidated talent scout Pat O'Brien is ordered by the big brass to break up the youngsters' budding romance for the sake of each's radio image. But, thank heavens, love does win out. The songs in *20 Million Sweethearts* may have been plugged a bit too hard and the lack of lavish production numbers was all too evident, but director Ray Enright conveyed a pleasant, spoofy flavor to the works. The *London Times* rated zingy Ginger and her new screen partner Powell as "intelligent and charming."

Next on the agenda it was back to Fox and the mild soap opera *Change of Heart* (1934), in which she, Janet Gaynor, Charles Farrell, and James Dunn were miscast as college graduates who seek happiness in that big old wicked New York City. Gaynor hopes to become a writer, Farrell a lawyer, and Dunn has ambitions to crash the success barriers as a crooner. As for brash Ginger, she wants luxury the easy way, and does not much care how she attains her goal. Needless to say, since the film was made in post-Production Code Hollywood, the script carefully details that Ginger has her own change of heart before the finale.

Ginger returned yet again to Warner Bros. for *Upperworld* (1934), a triangular love drama involving railroad magnate Warren William, his social-climbing wife (Mary Astor), and chorus girl Ginger, to whom William turns in lieu of his thoughtless spouse. This Ben Hecht story culminates with Ginger's valiant sacrifice of her own life. Why? Well, her sinister blackmailing boss (J. Carrol Naish) pulls a gun on discreet William and is about to plug the gent, when noble Ginger steps into the path of the speeding bullet. It was the only time in Ginger's long cinema career in which she would die oncamera. The death scene was far from memorable, for it naturally allowed no chance for Ginger to demonstrate her cinematic stock-in-trade, her gay spontaneity.

At long last Fred Astaire wound up his London fling and returned to Hollywood and RKO to participate in the filmization of his Broadway and West End success, *Gay Divorce,*† retitled for the decorous cinema as *The Gay Divorcee*

---

*Remade as *My Dream Is Yours* (1949) with Doris Day.
†Opened at the Ethel Barrymore Theatre on November 29, 1932, for a 248-performance run.

(1934). As would become *de rigeur* with Astaire-Rogers vehicles, the storyline was fragile, with only slight variation from film to film. Astaire was nearly always the American dancer who simply must convince high-hatting Ginger that he is morally and socially good enough to fit into her life's plan of a very suitable marriage. They flirt ever so decorously in song and dance, battle off the dance-room floor, and eventually decide—with nary a screen kiss—that they are meant for one another. In *The Gay Divorcee* only one song, "Night and Day," was carried over from Cole Porter's original Broadway score. It provided a nice duet for Ginger and Astaire, but it was the inventive "Continental" dance sequence (lasting nearly twenty minutes) which convinced industry figures and moviegoers alike that Ginger and Astaire were an established box-office wow. Thanks to Astaire's painstaking rehearsal procedures and the smoothing subtlety of dancing director Hermes Pan, the "Continental" routine elevated the film into the ranks of a minor screen classic.

RKO, intent, like any other commercial-minded studio, on gaining full value from its players, immediately tossed Ginger from the cultivated ambience of *The Gay Divorcee* into the bathos-drenched setting of *Romance in Manhattan* (1934), in which she assisted Czech immigrant Francis Lederer in finding work and love in the metropolis.

Just about the time *Romance in Manhattan* was receiving its resounding pans in theatres throughout the country, Ginger ventured into matrimony for the second time. On November 14, 1934, at the Little Church of the Flowers, she married twenty-five-year-old Lew Ayres. Cousin Phyllis Fraser and friend Janet Gaynor were her matrons of honor. The ceremony was followed by a reception at the swank Ambassador Hotel with many of Hollywood's notables in attendance. The very guests who were swilling champagne at Ginger's reception were among the movie-colony observers who bet that the marriage between vivacious Ginger and introspective Ayres would not last a year. (They were wrong, not in judgment, but in the length of time it took for disillusionment and irreparable conflict to set in.) Because of the couple's busy film schedule, they had to delay their Hawaiian honeymoon, which, when they finally took it nearly a year later, had to be cut short because of the studio's demand that Ginger return for a new project (*In Person*).

Meantime, producer Pandro S. Berman, who would become production head of RKO in 1936,* urged the studio to purchase the Jerome Kern-Otto Harback Broadway hit *Roberta*† for a Fred Astaire-Ginger Rogers vehicle, but shrewdly decided that a marquee bonus would greatly enhance the film's potential revenue. Thus RKO leading lady Irene Dunne was cast in the top-billed role of the member of Russian royalty serving as an able assistant to Helen Westley in the latter's modish Parisian couturiere establishment. The resulting motion picture, which debuted at Radio City Music Hall on March 7, 1935, was a model of urbanity. Ginger and Astaire danced to "I Won't

---

*Replacing Sam Briskin, who had replaced Merian C. Cooper.
†Opened at the New Amsterdam Theatre on November 18, 1933, for a run of 295 performances.

Dance," "Let's Begin," and "Smoke Gets in Your Eyes," and Ginger soloed "I'll Be Hard to Handle," in her mock Continental accent. As predicted, Ginger and Astaire's screen chemistry outshone the magical presence of both Irene Dunne and the ornate fashion-show finale filmed in color.*

While the RKO brass were preoccupied with selecting the next Astaire-Rogers project, and Astaire was working out new dance routines to weave into the chosen format, Ginger popped up in RKO's *Star of Midnight* (1935). Because suave William Powell had the lead and the picture was a sophisticated whodunit geared to a lighthearted vein, it was a natural situation for critics and viewers alike to compare the RKO effort with the already launched MGM *Thin Man* series, which was flourishing with Powell and teammate Myrna Loy. Ginger looked like a million in *Star of Midnight* and ably bandied smart repartee with Powell, and if audiences refused to accept her as a substitute Loy, she nevertheless deserved credit for making this entry one of the smoothest of the 1930s murder mysteries. The occasions in the film when Ginger and Powell engaged in frivolous banter as they downed another cocktail provided some of Ginger's slickest movie moments to that date.

Top Hat (Radio City Music Hall, August 29, 1935) found Ginger and Astaire "increasingly dexterous" *(New York Times)*. Perhaps of all the team's joint RKO screen outings, *Top Hat* contained the plushest of Van Nest Polglase sets, with the giant art moderne hotel rooms, radiant white furniture, glistening Venetian canals, elegant parks filled with formally attired extras; creating a totally unreal atmosphere in which Ginger and Astaire could banter, romance, dance, sing, argue, and make up. Mark Sandrich, who had directed *The Gay Divorcee* and would helm two subsequent Astaire-Rogers pictures, handled *Top Hat* with resplendent adroitness, allowing the screen team to shine in their major production number "The Piccalino," as well as the adagio "Cheek to Cheek," the duet "Isn't This a Lovely Day (to be Caught in the Rain)," and Astaire's solos "Top Hat, White Tie and Tails" and "No Strings— I'm Fancy Free." Thanks to the success of *Top Hat,* Ginger and Astaire were rated number-four box-office attractions in the country for 1934, right behind Shirley Temple, Will Rogers, and Clark Gable.

After *Top Hat,* Ginger's programmer *In Person* (1935) seemed a bigger disappointment than it really was. (The huff-and-puff overtone to the heavy-handed comedy sequences directed by William A. Seiter did not aid the cause of *In Person* one whit.) Ginger portrayed Carol Corliss, a grand cinema star suffering from agoraphobia as a result of having been mauled by her over-enthusiastic fans at a recent premiere. She seeks refuge at a mountain hunting retreat where her acquaintanceship with George Brent deepens into love. He is the man for high-strung Ginger because he is intuitively smart enough to rebuke the lass for overindulging her myriad of whims. Once again Ginger revealed a growing flair for comedy, rising to the cause when she dons a

---

*Remade as *Lovely to Look At* (MGM, 1952), *Roberta* until recently (1970) was not available even for art-house reissue.

disguise to escape detection from her public. As would prove true throughout Ginger's cinema sojourn, she was always the most sparkling when her screen character was pretending to be something other than what she was.

Nineteen hundred and thirty-six found Ginger dramatically slowing down her filmmaking activities, with only two pictures in release, both with Fred Astaire. Mark Sandrich directed *Follow the Fleet,* based on the Herbert Osborne play *Shore Leave* (1922).* At a lengthy 110 minutes, there was ample opportunity to include a wealth of Irving Berlin tunes; Ginger sang "We Saw the Sea" with the chorus and "Let Yourself Go," and Astaire vocalized "I'm Putting All My Eggs in One Basket." "Let's Face the Music and Dance" was the team's specialty dance number in *Follow the Fleet.* For entertainment variety there were screen newcomer Harriet Hilliard to handle "But Where Are You" and "Get Thee Behind Me Satan," and rising RKO blondine Betty Grable as one of the curvaceous back-up chorus members.

Having sufficiently proven her dexterity as a song-and-dance star, Ginger yearned for the opportunity to prove her dramatic worth onscreen. Studio executives were aghast when Ginger seriously suggested she wished to be tested for the upcoming John Ford-directed *Mary of Scotland* (1936), which was to star Katharine Hepburn in the title role.† Ginger was certainly aware that, as she has often put it, "Great acting's not my line," but she calculated —and so did mama Rogers—that she deserved an opportunity to sink her thespian teeth into a meaty role. She ventured that the part of the Queen of England in this historical epic was just the right cinematic opportunity for her. Abetted by Mrs. Rogers, Ginger perpetrated her own scheme to win the denied screentest. She arrived at the casting office, gussied up in her best *The Gay Divorcee* Mayfair accent, with self-effacing makeup, a new voice, and a fearless approach to bolster her disguise. She eventually won a test. However, the desirable role went to Florence Eldridge, wife of the film's male lead, Fredric March. As one RKO executive reasoned the vetoing of Ginger for *Mary of Scotland,* "Hell! Nobody'll know it's her [i.e., Ginger] and if they do know, they'll keep waiting for Queen Elizabeth to crack wise or get up and do a number!"

While Ginger was having problems with the home-lot big wigs, her marriage was on the proverbial rocks. When she and Ayres were first married, she had earnestly tried to adapt to his intellectual, perpetually meditating

---

Shore Leave had been filmed in 1925 with Richard Barthelmess and Dorothy Mackaill. In 1927 it became the Broadway musical *Hit the Deck,* which in itself was twice filmed, in 1930 and 1955.

†Throughout the overlapping reigns of Ginger and Hepburn on the RKO lot of the 1930s, the former held the latter in professional reverence. However, Ginger also maintained the notion that, given the proper showcasing, she might close the dramatic-prowess gap between herself and Hepburn. There was no such friendly rivalry between Ginger and departing RKO cinema queen Ann Harding, the latter on such a high plateau as a lady of dramatic elegance that Ginger never seriously dreamed of filling her vacated throne. As for Irene Dunne, although Ginger, with the assistance of Astaire, had outshone Dunne in *Roberta,* it was not until the late 1930s that the two actresses would compete for the same daffy comedy-type assignments.

nature. She patiently listened as day after day he explained the intricacies of his favorite pursuit, astronomy, and for a long period she complied with his wish to lead a placid, unpublic existence. She took up drawing and painting, anything that would keep her fruitfully occupied while Ayres was charting the skies and stargazing. But soon Ginger's boundless energies pushed to the fore, and she returned to her usual schedule of bounding from the studio set to the tennis courts and the swimming pools and then for a harmless sally about the nightspots.

If Ginger was not Ayres's ideal of the perfect housewife (as a cook, Ginger admitted, "I even managed to get lumps in gravy"), her rising career status was another sore point. Since his career-opening performance in *All Quiet on the Western Front* (1930), Ayres's movie assignments had been on a downward swing, in direct contrast to Ginger's steadily improving screen image; a situation that added no sweetness to their marriage. Thus in 1936 the couple separated, much to Mrs. Rogers's delight. When Ginger and Ayres first wed, gossipmongers had suggested that Ginger was (sub)consciously seeking a father figure in marrying the sedate actor. To which Ginger scoffingly replied, "I hardly knew my real father. I liked my stepfather a great deal but never saw him after he divorced my mother. So why would I need a father figure?" By the time she separated from Ayres, she would have her own theories for the marriage's failure, politely boosting Ayres's image while revealing the source of their incompatibilities, "He is a brilliant fellow, like so many who are introverted, he doesn't show his true brilliance. He's written books and plays and all kinds of music, including symphonic." But in the last analysis he was not what Ginger craved in a mate, a fun-loving twenty-four-hour-a-day partner who equally enjoyed sparkling in the public eye.

All through these years, Mrs. Rogers was never far from Ginger's side, many insisting she was the primary cause of each of Ginger's marriage failures. Whatever the truth of that may be, there is no doubt she was proving to be the prime stumbling block to Ginger's success at RKO. Studio executives could easily cope with the martyred type of stage mother (e.g., Anne Shirley's mama, Mimi), but coping with the ever-present Lela Rogers was another matter, as even decorous Fred Astaire found out in picture after picture, when Mrs. Rogers attempted to woo the cast and crew to her daughter's "side" so that Ginger would shine above Astaire. Eventually RKO came up with a plausible solution. Mrs. Rogers was officially put in charge of the New Talent Acting School at RKO, a position which not only fed her ego, but soon kept her constantly occupied. It was a happy coincidence that her film-business acumen led her to effectively promote from the ranks such RKO newcomers as Lucille Ball and Jack Carson (another of her protégés was Tyrone Power, who would prove his cinematic worth as a Twentieth Century-Fox leading man).

With both *Mary of Scotland* and Lew Ayres lost causes,* Ginger returned

*Throughout the late 1930s there were repeated rumors that Ginger and Ayres might reconcile, but each reapprochement ended in a battle over the same old conflicts, even after Ayres had attained renewed screen popularity with his MGM *Dr. Kildare* series.

to the bread-and-butter films with Fred Astaire. Ginger had played a honky-tonk singer in *Follow the Fleet* with Astaire as a gum-chewing gob; in *Swing Time* (1936), directed by George Stevens, the couple was far more elegant. Stevens prodded cameraman David Abel to use innovative, flowing photography to properly capture new aspects of Ginger and Astaire's lilting dancing of "Waltz in Swing Time" and the Academy Award-winning "The Way You Look Tonight." Ginger sang "A Fine Romance," while Astaire performed the gymnastic "Bojangles of Harlem."

Despite the excellence of *Swing Time,* there was a noticeable decline in box-office revenue, and it was rumored that *Shall We Dance?* (1937), directed by Nathaniel Shilkret, would be the last screen teaming of the Astaire-Rogers combination. With a score by George and Ira Gershwin, *Shall We Dance?* benefited greatly by the plot conceit, which presented Astaire as a ballet star and Ginger as a swing dancer. It obviously allowed for a logical variety of contrasting dance rhythms. Ginger sang "They All Laughed," Astaire crooned "I've Got Beginner's Luck," and the duo roller-skated to "Let's Call the Whole Thing Off," laid against a Central Park setting.

It was during this period that Ginger purchased property in Coldwater Canyon where she constructed the hilltop home in which she lived until recently. Van Nest Polglase and the RKO set-art design department were recruited to help style the abode in accordance with Ginger's carefree personality. Ginger matched her independence on the real-estate front by demanding a chance to do a non-Fred Astaire picture. Three in a row of such film musicals were more than enough for Ginger (and Mrs. Rogers), who felt the reddish-blonde star should no longer be sharing screen billing—secondary at that—and celluloid footage with Mr. Astaire. While RKO scurried around to find a replacement for Ginger to team with Astaire in *A Damsel in Distress* (1937),* Ginger maneuvered and won a co-starring spot opposite Katharine Hepburn in the picturization of the Edna Ferber-George S. Kaufman play *Stage Door.*†

Stage Door (Radio City Music Hall, October 7, 1937) owed some of its success to the revamping work done by scenarists Morrie Ryskind and Anthony Veiller, who gutted a great deal of the stage original to bring the drama more within the specifications required for the silver screen, and by the assorted unique personalities assigned to work under Gregory La Cava's ad-lib-style direction: ranging from Andrea Lecds as the overly dedicated aspiring actress (who commits suicide), to the contrasting wise-dame portrayals by Lucille Ball and Eve Arden, to the superannuated leading-lady type essayed by Constance Collier ("Can you picture an older woman in the part?"). Ginger's tart performance as Jean Maitland, the salt-of-the-earth roommate of dilettante Hepburn was a fine enunciation of Ginger, the now robust screen comedienne who combined unostentatious beauty with a realistic mixture of flipness and gentleness. It required someone of Ginger's finesse to toss out the line (said to Hepburn), "Some day they're going to cut you open and find a

---

*RKO's Joan Fontaine was given the part.
†Opened at the Music Box Theatre on October 26, 1936, for a 169-performance run.

211

rock where your heart ought to be." Other performers would have said such dialog with the delivery of a gagster's automated mouthpiece, but Ginger had learned to vary her brittle line readings with a touch of warmth. In fact, the essence of Ginger's successful portrayal in *Stage Door* was that she conveyed her character's multilevel nature, a girl with a persistent fear of professional failure who hides her insecurities under the guise of humorous casualness. Ginger would recreate her popular *Stage Door* role on "Lux Radio Theatre" on February 20, 1939, accompanied by Adolphe Menjou and Rosalind Russell.

When Katharine Hepburn refused to gutter her artistic level and play the soppy lead in RKO's *Mother Carey's Chickens* (1938), the role was turned over to Ginger. She dyed her hair brown for the part, determined to shed glamour for a sincere performance. However, RKO suddenly decided that perhaps Ginger was worthy of better ventures and tucked her into *Having Wonderful Time* (1938) instead, in which she was blonde again. Anne Shirley was given another "break" by being called into action to play the hand-me-down lead assignment in *Mother Carey's Chickens*.

Over the years *Having Wonderful Time* has taken a shellacking from critics and moviegoers alike, who bemoan the fact that the screenplay denatured the Jewish flavor of the stage original and lost its viability as a social statement. More to the aesthetic point was the fact that the movie edition of the play sidetracked much of the show's innate charm and romantic tenderness, substituting in its stead unsubtle slapstick.* As *Variety* appraised the transfer from stage to screen, *Having Wonderful Time* was "just another film." Nor was there much rejoicing at Ginger's obvious performance as the Manhattan-weary secretary who escapes city life to a nondescript resort where she falls in love with loafing Douglas Fairbanks, Jr. (he was even more miscast than Ginger).

A step back in the right direction was *Vivacious Lady* (1938), produced and directed by George Stevens, which offered Ginger as a brash nightclub singer who meets and weds shy botany professor James Stewart, only to find herself in domestic conflict when he takes her back home to meet his small-town parents (Charles Coburn and Beulah Bondi) and his old flame (Frances Mercer).

Succumbing to exhibitor demands, RKO paired Ginger and Astaire yet again in *Carefree* (Radio City Music Hall, September 22, 1938). It was Astaire's idea to be cast as something other than a dancer in the by-now-too-standardized formula for the Astaire-Rogers film outings. In *Carefree* he was presented as a psychiatrist who becomes involved with temperamental radio songstress Ginger. At eighty-three minutes, *Carefree,* directed by Mark Sandrich, was the shortest of the team's ten musicals, and perhaps the least popular. There were such Irving Berlin numbers as "Change Partners" and "The Night Is Filled with Music," and the intricately staged "The Yam," as well

---

*That the screenplay to *Having Wonderful Time* should be such a letdown was all the more unexpected because the scenario had been written by the playwright, Arthur Kober.

as the comedy relief provided by Ginger,* who created chaos with the sets whenever she is under hypnosis. The finished product, even with its gadgety dream sequences and slow motion photography, had more than a touch of *ennui* and *déjà vu*. Not only was the premise of *Carefree* the slimmest and draggiest of the Astaire-Rogers canon, but twenty-seven-year-old Ginger photographed poorly. Even pandering to the publicity-induced gimmick which had prevented Ginger and Astaire from kissing properly onscreen, by having the couple finally engage in tasteful osculation (at the end of the slow-motion dream dance, "I used to be Color Blind") did not stir the anticipated public enthusiasm.

Despite the disappointment of *Carefree*, Ginger was approaching the crest of her box-office popularity, earning a sizable $208,767 in 1938. She may have lost out in the Howard Hughes romance sweepstakes,† and suffered momentary disfavor in the screen colony when she refused to appear almost gratis on Louella Parsons's "Hollywood Hotel" radio program, but she was considered, all in all, a perfect example of the American dream girl, saucy but gentle, wholesome, athletic, and fun to be with. She had come a long way from the Charleston contests of 1926; but her struggling days were not so far in her past that she did not realize the necessity of complying with her studio bosses' wishes when her job might be on the line. During her tenure at RKO she had already seen such studio stalwarts as Katharine Hepburn and Ann Harding fall from favor, and both Ginger and her mother decided she was not yet in so lofty a position that she could afford to balk too strongly against company dictates. Thus Ginger agreed to make what was publicly announced—"It's the end of an era, my dear!"—as the final Astaire-Rogers film, *The Story of Vernon and Irene Castle* (1939). It was determined that this last joint effort should be entirely different in two major aspects: first, it would be the couple's initial period-costume affair, and secondly and more important, it was to be a screen biography in which Ginger and Astaire would not be playing variations of themselves, but rather would portray their famed ballroom predecessors, Vernon and Irene Castle.

What emerged under H. C. Potter's lethargic direction was a tasteful if episodic recreation of a bygone period, authentic within the bounds of cinematic storytelling.‡ Within the picture's ninety minutes, Ginger and Astaire participated in fourteen song interludes and bits of some sixty-seven musical numbers as they went through their paces redoing the Castles' most famous

---

*The *New York Times* wagered that Ginger "has become one of the gayest of our comediennes, equally practiced with the verbal foil or the slapstick."

†Ironically, it was Ginger who broke off her fling with millionaire Hughes. Hughes's chief aide, Noah Dietrich, would later report that once he came into his boss's office to find the executive nearly in tears, moaning, "It's Ginger—she's left me. She caught me cheating with another girl, and now she won't even talk to me."

‡The real-life Irene Castle was well acquainted with Fred Astaire and his dancing charisma, but she did not approve of casting Ginger to play the oncamera Mrs. Castle. Nevertheless, Irene Castle served as technical advisor for the picture.

dance steps including the One-Step, the Fox Trot, Maxixe, and the Castle Walk. Most of the tunes were drawn from the 1910s ("When You Wore a Tulip," "Darktown Strutters' Ball," etc.), but one new song, "Only When You're in My Arms," was created for Astaire to sing and for him and Ginger to dance to later in the film. In *The Story of Vernon and Irene Castle,* Ginger had two particularly outstanding scenes, one in which she did a rendition of performer Bessie McCoy's "The Yama Yama Man," and the final sequence, which also provided another innovation for an Astaire-Rogers film—a tragic ending! At the Texas hotel she is dressed for an evening celebration-reunion with Astaire, when she learns from their business manager-confidante, Edna May Oliver, that he has died in a plane crash during military dress-parade maneuvers that afternoon. Although tears are streaming down her face, she gathers together her courage and makes a stand, knowing she must now carry on alone. This screen moment—in what would become the best June Allyson tradition—revealed that within bounds Ginger could certainly handle vital dramatic assignments.

The box-office returns on *The Story of Vernon and Irene Castle* were respectable but a good indication not only that the screen magic of the Astaire-Rogers team had paled, but that the public was somewhat indifferent to seeing the couple in noncontemporary surroundings. The spotty reaction to *The Story of Vernon and Irene Castle* convinced the new RKO regime headed by George Schaefer that Ginger, if she were to remain a viable studio commodity, must go her own separate screen path. She was more than willing. (Although he has never been blunt enough to say so, Astaire had had more than his fill of combating the combined offensives of Ginger and Mrs. Rogers on their movie sets.)

With her once-fashionable screen musicals behind her, Ginger launched full force into her solo star-personality period. *Bachelor Mother* (1939) was the type of slightly screwball comedy that Irene Dunne was handling so well elsewhere at this time.* Under Garson Kanin's direction, Ginger emoted as an out-of-work shopgirl who finds herself in charge of an abandoned baby. The net results are that everyone, including David Niven, the grandson of department store owner Charles Coburn, takes pity on her, leading to a rash of comic results. Although *Bachelor Mother* provided Ginger with an engaging Charleston number, the film relied on her comic prowess for buoyancy. *Variety* aptly summed up the "new" Ginger Rogers: "[She] should not have to depend on her dancing feet for future film assignments. She blossoms forth as a most competent comedienne, trouping through in grand style, displaying sincerity in the lightness with which she plays the role." Ginger re-created her *Bachelor Mother* role on "Lux Radio Theatre" (January 22, 1940) with Fredric March as her new vis-à-vis.†

---

*She was no longer under exclusive RKO contract.

†*Bachelor Mother* would be dusted off and remade as *Bundle of Joy* (1956), a vehicle for the abortive screen team of Debbie Reynolds and Eddie Fisher.

Producer-director Gregory La Cava provided Ginger with her next vehicle, *Fifth Avenue Girl* (1939), which proved to studio executives, if not to more and more demanding Ginger, that she was not yet capable of carrying a picture alone at the box-office. The frayed story was no particular aid, as Ginger was cast as an unemployed girl—seemingly her screen specialty at this time—who is hired by millionaire Walter Connolly to pose as a gold digger in order to make his thoughtless family jump back into humane line. Ginger has her own reward in the story, for she falls in love with Connolly's son, Tim Holt. Ginger repeated her *Fifth Avenue Girl* portrayal on "Lux Radio Theatre" (December 16, 1940), accompanied by Edward Arnold and John Howard.

With the coming of the new decade, it was decided that Ginger, now prize female commodity at RKO, should expand her range of screen emoting. *Primrose Path* (Roxy Theatre, March 22, 1940) was certainly the offbeat vehicle to accomplish this aim. Very loosely based on the novel *February Hill* by Victoria Lincoln and the 1939 play adaptation by Robert Buckner and Walter Hart, the picture told in very veiled terms the story of the shantytown Adams family,* ruled by Marjorie Rambeau,† a stern-on-the-surface tart, who must support her mama (Queenie Vassar),‡ a drunken husband (Miles Mander), and two daughters (Ginger and young Joan Carroll). Tomboyish Ginger (at age twenty-nine she was asked to play an unpretentious seventeen-year-old) encounters hamburger-stand-operator Joel McCrea, with whom she becomes totally infatuated. They soon wed, but when stalwart McCrea discovers her unsavory pedigree his immediate reaction is to split the scene. Confused and penniless, Ginger reasons that now only one course remains open to her, to succumb to her sordid heritage and follow in the family trade. For the sake of the Production Code and of Ginger Rogers fans everywhere, McCrea returns in time to save her from such a horrendous fate. In its genteel way *Primrose Path* was a somewhat graphic presentation of a daring subject. It may have afforded Ginger little opportunity for her expected comedy-relief playing, but she felt more than compensated by the opportunity the film allowed for emoting in a "controversial" dramatic showcase.

Ginger was among the many who rejected the lead in Columbia's remake of *The Front Page*,§ but she did accept a part in RKO's *Lucky Partners* (1940), dying her hair dark brunette for the role. It required a good deal of diplomacy on RKO's part to insure Ginger's presence on the set of *Lucky Partners,* for not only was veteran leading man Ronald Colman top-billed over her, but he had the more splashy role. The Lewis Milestone-directed comedy hinged on a peculiar bit of whimsy, so capricious in nature that it might easily have been

*Years later Ginger would recall: "I did a picture once, *The Primrose Path* about a family of prostitutes, but there wasn't anything indecent on the screen or soundtrack. Audiences had to be pretty sophisticated to get it, I suppose, but we didn't stoop to rub people's noses in dirt. That's what I despise about so much of today's [c. mid-1960s] so-called entertainment."

†She received an Academy Award nomination for her part.

‡Repeating her stage assignment.

§Rosalind Russell accepted the lead opposite Cary Grant in this comedy, called *His Girl Friday* (1940).

rejected by somber World War II audiences if cast with less VIP talent. Greenwich Village painter Colman introduces himself to Ginger in a street flirtation. He soon suggests that they share a sweepstakes ticket for good luck, proposing a honeymoon trip in platonic style if they win the prize. Colman does win, but he has a deuce of a time overcoming the objections of Ginger's dumbbell suitor, Jack Carson. Eventually they have their Niagara Falls trip, with a tag ending in a rural court presided over by Harry Davenport. Yes. Strong-willed Ginger does weaken to Colman's irresistible charm. As *New Republic* critic Otis Ferguson jovially pointed out about *Lucky Partners,* "Ginger Rogers has changed her hair but not whatever it is she's got that gets us."

Back in December, 1939, while Ginger was busily filming *Lucky Partners,* RKO had purchased for $50,000 the screen rights to Christopher Morley's very popular novel, *Kitty Foyle.* At the time, Ginger was exhausted from her nonstop filmmaking schedule and declined to even consider the property. She was eventually persuaded to read the book, and later admitted: "I knew it was a colorful, adult role—the sort of thing for which I was constantly looking to shake off this image of a girl who has danced her way to success—but I didn't think it was for me. I called up the producer [David Hempstead] and said 'I don't want to do it.' " Hempstead remained unflappable and with much gentle prodding finally persuaded Ginger to tackle the assignment.

As *Kitty Foyle* (1940) evolved on the screen, it was not Morley's study of a white-collar girl who is involved in some tawdry situations, but rather a fairly conventional slow-talking account which relied on Ginger to invest it with truth and beauty. The Dalton Trumbo screenplay opens with Ginger trying to choose between Dennis Morgan, the man she madly loves but who can't wed her, and the other suitor, James Craig, who is waiting at the church to marry her. Her mirrored voice-of-conscience refreshes her memory as to the many factors leading up to the present dilemma, allowing *Kitty Foyle* to lapse into flashback. She is a girl from the wrong side of the Philadelphia tracks who falls in a big way for Main Line blueblood Morgan. She follows him to New York and they eventually wed. But his strait-laced family vetoes the union, leading to his divorcing her. Their baby dies, leaving Ginger to make her own way in the big city. Her past hurts make her all the more vulnerable to the kindness of doctor James Craig, a man from her own lower social set. Although Morgan has remarried one of his own class level, he returns to Ginger with an offer of shrouded romance. End of flashback and back to the present. Ginger's Kitty Foyle now knows what decision she must make. Her future is clear.

RKO provided *Kitty Foyle* with an exceptionally hard sell, geared to equating Ginger's working-girl portrayal with the All American Miss. "If there isn't one in your family," proclaimed the studio advertising copy, "there's one across the street, or one facing you across an office desk or in the subway or streetcar." In fact, after completing *Kitty Foyle* Ginger was whisked off to New York by RKO to receive a special "award" from a group of Manhattan stenographers for playing the ever-so-average white-collar worker. Ginger disembarked at Grand Central Station, radiantly white-collared, with a diamond brooch, gold earrings, and a long mink coat. (There was certainly nothing working-girl about this expensive outfit!) This cheery sight led the usually jaded *Time* magazine to editorialize: "Ginger with her shoulder-length tresses, her trim figure, her full lips, her prancing feet and honest-to-goodness manner is the flesh-and-blood symbol of the United States working girl."

The public doted on *Kitty Foyle* in a big way, and the critics were especially considerate of Ginger's slick but dramatically vulnerable performance. (Even in 1940 there was special consideration for the already-nostalgic legend who had graced those wonderful Astaire-Rogers musicals that had enchanted an entire decade of filmgoers.) "[She] plays her with as much forthright and appealing integrity as one can possibly expect" *(New York Times)*. Hollywood observers had predicted that Ginger might well receive an Oscar nomination for the "sensational" *Primrose Path,* but it was for *Kitty Foyle* that she received her first (and only) Oscar bid to date. In a year of very stiff competition* she amazed many by winning the coveted Award.† At the Hollywood-based Oscar ceremonies in the spring of 1941, Ginger rushed to the rostrum to accept the statue from Lynn Fontanne and Alfred Lunt, the stage couple then in town in Los Angeles with *There Shall Be No Night.* Miss Fontanne, who had known Ginger in 1930s Hollywood, confided to the winner, "I told you, you'd make good." Ginger was too excited by her victory to acknowledge the Lunts' presence, but instead immediately launched into her rehearsed speech, thanking her mother (of course) and concluding with the comment, "This is the happiest moment of my life." For those who had missed Ginger's onscreen emoting in *Kitty Foyle,* she, Dennis Morgan, and James Craig would re-create their roles from this picture on "Lux Radio Theatre" on May 5, 1941.

After years of teetering on and off the brink of divorce, Ginger and Lew Ayres finally made it legal in 1940. The final break supposedly came when Ayres allegedly brusquely told Ginger, "I wish you'd go home to your mother and stay there." During the judicial processing of the split, Lew Ayres's only official comment for the press was, "I never had time to see my wife."

Ginger's follow-up to *Kitty Foyle* was an RKO comedy, *Tom, Dick and Harry* (1941), which many consider the epitome of the bubbling full essence of the screen personality known as Ginger Rogers. It offered her an opportunity to effervesce in three contrasting guises, for the story's Janie is an imaginative telephone operator who projects personality changes on herself as she pictures marital life with each of three suitors of differing class, financial, and temperamental backgrounds. There is persuasive George Murphy, the auto salesman; easy-going garage mechanic Burgess Meredith; and wealthy Alan Marshall. Ginger dreams of being married to each of the trio, but naturally has to decide

---

*Bette Davis *(The Letter),* Joan Fontaine *(Rebecca),* Katharine Hepburn *(The Philadelphia Story),* and Martha Scott *(Our Town).*

†Fred Astaire would years later quip about Ginger and his *Damsel in Distress* co-star Joan Fontaine, "They dance with me, then go on to Academy Awards for Acting."

217

upon just one.* If only reality could be as lighthearted as her daydreaming in *Tom, Dick and Harry.†* For this stunning excursion into frivolity, Ginger garnered affirmative nods from a wide range of critical corners.‡ Ginger and the three Ms (Murphy, Meredith, and Marshall) repeated their assignments on "Lux Radio Theatre" on September 1, 1941.

Having enjoyed the relative luxury of making only one picture in 1940, which allowed for plenty of opportunity to enjoy her newly acquired Rogers Rogue Ranch in Oregon (complete with trout stream), Ginger decided it was high time to expand her industry availability. She followed the suit of such past motion-picture-contract trend-setters as Claudette Colbert and Irene Dunne, by arranging a nonexclusive pact with RKO, which allowed her to agent outside film commitments for herself.§ Her first venture under this arrangement was a loan-out to Twentieth Century-Fox for *Roxie Hart* (1942)ϕ directed by William A. Wellman. Ginger was asked in this role to revert to her prior screen type as the brazen flapper whose husband has shot her lover and tagged her as the prime suspect. The film is set in the wild Prohibition era when a comely murderess, especially in Chicago, was just as likely to become the sensation of the vaudeville circuit as be condemned to death, because, says flavorful crime reporter Lynne Overman, "This country wouldn't hang Lucretia Borgia." So red-headed (her hair styled to a bubble cut), gum-chewing Ginger hires Chicago's best criminal lawyer (Adolphe Menjou), a histrionic type whose shortcomings in legal knowledge are outweighed by his way with juries. The burlesque film was divided into three acts á la the play original, with Part I in Roxie's apartment, Part II in Roxie's cellblock in Cook County Jail, and Part III in the pell-mell courtroom. Wisecracking Ginger discovers that the jury considers her shapely gams and her expected motherhood (a lie) her best defense, and that her involvement in the homicide has put her right up in the headlines with all the big wheels. Ginger does win her freedom in *Roxie Hart,* but settles for anonymity and the quiet life as the wife of cub reporter George Montgomery. Everything in the film was painted in the broadest strokes to allow for punchy episodes, causing James Agee (*Time* magazine) to observe, "America's own Ginger Rogers is attractive but unbelievable in her [role]. The star plays second fiddle to the era."

Ginger remained on at Fox for *Tales of Manhattan* (1942), a gimmicky

---

*Director Garson kept the ending secret from the cast too.

†Remade as *The Girl Most Likely* (1957) with Jane Powell.

‡"She plays the girl as no other actress we know could, with a perfect combination of skepticism and daffiness" (Bosley Crowther, *New York Times*). "The good Lord knows where she gets it, but Ginger Rogers has got every range of the working-girl character and a direct projection far ahead of the lines themselves . . . She has learned more of the right things faster than any actress today; and is still at it."

§RKO was feeling an economic pinch and was happy to reduce some of the studio overhead by sharing the contracts of some of its players (Charles Laughton, Ginger, Maureen O'Hara) with other companies.

ϕBased on the 1926 play by Maurice Watkins, which had been a film, *Chicago* (1927), with Phyllis Haver.

multiepisode picture tied together by a narrative thread (i.e., the case history of a dress suit). In the second, and perhaps the weakest, of the five episodes directed by Julien Duvivier, Ginger is convinced that Cesar Romero is two-timing her and shifts her affections to his shy friend, Henry Fonda. Ginger's shoulder-length brunette pageboy haircut was the most startling facet of her performance in this film.

Ginger was on much surer footing in Billy Wilder's *The Major and the Minor* (Paramount, 1942), a wacky comedy that hit the mark with World War II-weary audiences.* Ginger was cast as a disillusioned New York career gal who disguises herself as a little girl in order to obtain half-fare passage on the train trip back home. Aboard the express train she is befriended by Ray Milland, an Army major stationed at a boys' school. Always at her best when she is pretending to be what she is not, Ginger excelled—save for a telltale double-chin profile on occasion—as Sue-Sue the twelve-year-old who accepts Milland's patronizing friendship and later falls in love with him.† Ironically, and as director-co-scenarist Wilder intended, it is a real child (Diana Lynn), the precocious younger sister of Milland's fiancée (Rita Johnson), who sees through Ginger's disguise. Just to keep the film a family affair, Mrs. Rogers played Ginger's mom in the picture, repeating her role along with Ginger and Milland for "Lux Radio Theatre" (May 31, 1943).

After a year away from RKO, Ginger returned to her home lot in full glory. The studio proudly announced that its Oscar-winning star, who had been considering a version of the Somerset Maugham-derived *Rain* or Theodore Dreiser's *Sister Carrie,* would make *Once upon a Honeymoon* (1942) with Cary Grant as her co-star and Leo McCarey as the producer-director.‡ Ginger was offered (wearing a pageboy hair-do with her hair color back to blonde) as a former stripper from Flatbush, whose ritzy diction came and went as she pleased. She is a naive gold digger about to wed influential Nazi Walter Slezak. However, American war correspondent Grant takes a political interest in the planned union. As he follows Ginger and devious Slezak throughout East Europe, Grant finds he has fallen in love with her. When Ginger finally comprehends that weasel Slezak is really Hitler's prime fingerman, she ditches her Axis-loyal husband, and escapes with Grant through Scandi-

---

*This was the film in which Robert Benchley utters to Ginger that snappy line, "Why don't you step out of those wet clothes and into a dry martini?"

†The *New York Herald-Tribune* rated Ginger's work here "nothing short of magnificent."

‡RKO had been in the financial doldrums throughout much of George Schaefer's recent short-term leadership. His successor, Charles Koerner, had determinedly restructured the studio's product lineup to squeeze the most revenue possible out of stringently budgeted features. While the resultant series programmers made a steady profit, this shift from A- to B-films did much to dilute the company's status as a "major" studio. (George Jessel's oft-repeated joke at the time was not as apocryphal as it sounded. He quipped that if the Japs ever bombed California, the safest place for a bomb shelter would be at RKO, because it had been so long since they had a real hit.) Koerner was resolute about making at least one big, splashy picture for 1942 release, and he gave the okay for a $1 million budget to the McCarey project, with Grant receiving a reported $175,000 salary.

navia, eventually landing in France. On the boat to America, Ginger and Grant discover a familiar figure aboard; none other than Slezak, who is on his way to perpetrate skulduggery in America. Later, in one of the more perversely structured sequences of any American-made World War II film, Ginger and Grant good-naturedly banter about the length of time it would take to stop the ship and send out a lifeboat to pick up nonswimmer Slezak, whom Ginger has not so gingerly shoved overboard. They and the ship's captain decide it would hardly be worth the effort—fade-out from the scene. At the time of its release, *Once upon a Honeymoon* (Radio City Music Hall, November 12, 1942) met with audience resistance.* Filmgoers who were zealous patriots—which encompassed the bulk of 1940s moviegoers—could hardly be expected to take the tongue-in-cheek adult comedy-drama as it was intended, and the film suffered accordingly. *Time* magazine offered the majority review when it commented about the film, "Principals Rogers and Grant exude a general impression that they know something has gone very wrong, and that nothing much can be done about it." Nevertheless, taken in the proper light, *Once upon a Honeymoon,* like Ernst Lubitsch's even more maligned *To Be or Not to Be* (United Artists, 1942), holds up very well indeed. For this author, at least, Ginger offers her finest 1940s performance in *Once upon a Honeymoon,* providing a characterization that is part show, but more earnest emoting, with the flip veneer lightly covering a sincere heart that needs the proper direction to induce its owner to become a responsible citizen and a most appealing woman.

Throughout World War II, Ginger was as devoted as the next star to doing her bit for the war effort, and she participated in several patriotic short-subject films whenever time and the occasion permitted. She appeared in the training picture *Safeguarding Military Information,* narrated with Walter Huston; co-narrated with Spencer Tracy the Garson Kanin-directed *Battle Stations* (1944), a one-reeler devoted to the Coast Guard Spars, who performed shore jobs formerly handled by males, and was in the five-minute trailer *Ginger Rogers Finds A Bargain,* promoting the fourth War Loan Drive. On a more personal level, Ginger joined in several USO tours.

During one such outing to San Diego, she met Marine Jack Briggs,† whom she wed a few months later (January 6, 1943) in a quiet Methodist church service in Pasadena. "Jack," said a starry-eyed Ginger, "is all I've ever dreamed of." A few days after the ceremony he returned to military duty and Ginger to her picture-making.

Tender Comrade (1943) was a picture both RKO and Ginger had cause to regret, for, a few years later, when Senator McCarthy turned the nation's eyes to the Communist threat in Hollywood, *Tender Comrade* was one of the

---

*RKO's ad campaign did not help sell tickets either. "She finished the man who started the war! He [Grant] kissed her all over the map . . . of Europe!"

†Prior to being drafted, he was an actor, appearing in small roles in *Ladies' Day* (RKO, 1943) and other films.

prime pictures held up as being Red-tinged throughout.* Which would have surprised no one in early 1943—but Communism was not then a dirty word— for the film's director (Edward Dmytryk) and its scripter (Dalton Trumbo) were quite frankly Red sympathizers.

The plotline of *Tender Comrade* is basically a very cozy affair. Ginger has only one night with her husband (Robert Ryan) before he is shipped overseas with his military unit. He leaves the next day and she returns to her welder's job at the Douglas Aircraft plant. During a lunch break she persuades three of her married co-workers (Ruth Hussey, Patricia Collinge, and Kim Hunter) to pool their resources and rent a large house in which all four can live "just like a democracy." Ginger soon decides they need a housekeeper and they acquire the services of German refugee Mady Christians whose husband is fighting the Nazis. The girls bawl out war wife Ruth Hussey for dating another man and she then learns her husband has been lost in action at sea. Ginger recalls—with pain—her brief moment with Ryan, particularly her arguments because of his overtime hours—overtime he was putting in to leave her financially well off when he was overseas. Returning to the present, time passes, and Ginger has the baby she and Ryan had planned for them to have after the war is over. She later learns that Ryan has been killed in action. In a teary finale Ginger tells her baby that Ryan died to make the world safe for democracy.†

Ginger offered a rather stagey performance in *Tender Comrade,* what with her overly cutesy handling of pet expressions for her husband, her weak approach to the essence of the material, and in counterpoint to the overexaggerated brave playing of Ruth Hussey and the other cast members. Not that the bulk of the blame for the failure of *Tender Comrade* can be thrust at Ginger, for the film was rather hard to take, no matter what one's political persuasions might be. *Time* magazine labeled the film "kind of *Little Women* of World War II" in which the scenario's misguided logic makes one feel as if the players "had been brained with a powder puff." Just for the record, one could hardly expect to find a five-bedroom house in the West Adams section

*In 1947, when Lela Rogers was a staunch member of the Motion Picture Alliance for the Preservation of American Ideals, along with John Wayne, Adolphe Menjou, Charles Coburn, Ward Bond, and Leo McCarey (and boosted by Hedda Hopper), she claimed that at the time of the making of *Tender Comrade* she had begged Ginger not to participate in the project, regarding it as a Communistic-style study of communal living. Ginger, also post the fact, claimed that she had felt strongly about some of the dialog in *Tender Comrade,* which ripped into America's democratic ideals, and that she had refused to voice them oncamera (the lines were subsequently redrafted for other actresses in the picture to say).

†The original ending for *Tender Comrade* was almost shelved as being too much of a squirm-inducer. RKO executives ordered it re-edited, and then had a new ending filmed, with Ginger getting the bad news, biting her lips, and then going off to work—bravely! That finish was dropped and the initial finale restored (in which Ginger wakes up the baby, holds Ryan's uniformed picture in front of the kid, and says: "Little guy . . . you two aren't ever going to meet . . . . He went and died so you could have a better break when you grow up than he ever had . . . .. Don't ever let anybody say he died for nothing. . . . Chris boy." Ginger then comes downstairs into a huge close-up. End.

of Los Angeles for $90 rental, or a free housekeeper of the caliber of Mady Christians.

After the unpleasantness generated by *Tender Comrade,* it seemed a happier day professionally for Ginger when she was cast in the prize role of Liza Elliott in Paramount's picturization of Moss Hart's *Lady in the Dark.** As part of her three-picture studio deal, Ginger was paid $122,500 for her participation in this generously budgeted feature film†—her first in color—which went into production in December, 1942, but did not see release until February, 1944. Paramount executive producer B. G. De Sylva was so intent upon creating a richly frosted entertainment treat that the basic storyline and the complex character of Liza were often submerged for reels at a time.‡ Devotees of the Broadway version and of Gertrude Lawrence's particular interpretation of the Kurt Weill-Ira Gershwin score, were distressed that the outstanding "My Ship" song was only briefly hummed by Ginger in the film, that much of the childhood dream sequence was deleted, and that Ginger, as Bosley Crowther observed in the *New York Times,* "moves through it all in a variety of stunning costumes but in a plain brown study most of the time." On the other hand, in the screen part Garbo had once considered undertaking, *Time* magazine confided, "Ginger Rogers is suitably dramatic and a lovely neurotic." Despite the split critical vote on Ginger's performance § and the quality of the film itself, *Lady in the Dark* went on to gross $4.5 million.

Ginger had considered entering into a $3 million independent-production-company venture with RKO executive Charles Koerner, but that did not materialize, nor did the planned Technicolor *Gibson Girl* slated to go before the RKO color cameras in January, 1944, nor the announced Twentieth Century-Fox musical *Bandwagon* by Howard Dietz and Arthur Schwartz. Despite Ginger being the number-one star attraction on the RKO roster, the studio could not come up with a suitable vehicle for her, so instead she finally agreed to go on loan-out to David O. Selznick as a replacement for the recalcitrant Joan Fontaine. The picture was *I'll Be Seeing You* (1944), in which Ginger

*Opened at the Alvin Theatre on January 23, 1941, with Gertrude Lawrence and Danny Kaye in the top roles, and ran for 467 performances.

†At this time Claudette Colbert was earning $150,000 per film, Betty Grable $124,000, and Bette Davis about $120,500.

‡Frigid, tailored Ginger is the chic editor of a prominent fashion magazine, working overly hard in order to avoid participation in the mainstream of life. When she has a near nervous breakdown, she consults a psychiatrist (Barry Sullivan), relating to him details about the three men in her life. There is her office associate and nemesis, Ray Milland, who calls her Boss Lady. In contrast, she admires Warner Baxter, whose pending divorce suit will set him free to remarry, but there is also muscular movie star Jon Hall. In her four therapeutic visits to Sullivan she relates her bizarre and very Freudian dreams: one finds her being painted as a caricature old maid by Milland, climbing a huge wedding cake while vast choirs sing her praises; in another she is performing in a circus, which melds into a trial with a squabbling jury of clowns and freaks.

§Director Mitchell Leisen and co-star Ray Milland would both later vehemently denounce Ginger's performance in the film, claiming she hadn't the least idea of the story's psychological ramifications, or any capacity to duplicate the charisma of Gertrude Lawrence's stage performance.

played the women's-prison inmate on Christmas furlough who brings happiness to shell-shocked war veteran Joseph Cotten. Each tries to hide his/her embarrassing past from the other, but after they adjust to the trauma of reality, they realize their mutual love has grown stronger, and they can plan for a future together. Under William Dieterle's direction, Ginger played her part a bit too archly, failing to underline the potential sensitivity of her character—a girl who had thought her dream of apple-pie happiness was gone forever, but now has renewed hope.

Rolling into the mid-1940s, Ginger temporarily berthed at MGM for *Weekend at the Waldorf* (Radio City Music Hall, October 4, 1945), a tacky updating of Vicki Baum's *Grand Hotel.* In the revamped rendering, more facile but shallower than the 1932 original, Ginger mingled with members of Metro's star stock-company (Walter Pidgeon, Van Johnson, Lana Turner) as she assumed Greta Garbo's role (transformed to a sure-footed film actress) with Pidgeon playing opposite her in the John Barrymore part (now a celebrated war correspondent). As director Robert Z. Leonard shifted from story fragment to fragment, one wondered if staying at the famed Manhattan hostelry was worth the cost; everyone seemed so preoccupied and bored in their robot-like portrayals. Ginger had a dozen or so Irene costumes and an accompanying change of hair style for each outfit, but she had difficulty remaining in the limelight, whether ousted from the focal point by pipe-smoking Pidgeon, who steals into her room one night (for professional reasons rather than the amorous ones she imagines) or outdistanced by Rosemary DeCamp as her accented maid. Then for stronger distraction there was Lana Turner, certainly a dream stenographer in looks if not office skills, and Van Johnson's wholesome Air Force captain, who mistakenly believes he has a fatal illness. All in all Ginger seemed just a smidgen too recherché as the tired and unhappy movie star who would give up all her luxuries for a real, level-headed fellow.

Few people at the time, and certainly Ginger was not one of them, realized that *Weekend at the Waldorf* marked the downhill slide of the thirty-four-year-old movie star.* She would continue in leading assignments for the next decade, but now it was a visible strain on her to retain her post-ingenue glow and for audiences to accept her in non-junior matron roles.

Ginger's RKO return for *Heartbeat* (Palace Theatre, May 10, 1946) † was hardly the cinematic treat for which everyone hoped.‡ As *Photoplay* magazine punned, "The heartbeat is irregular and sadly ailing." Sam Wood, who had helmed *Kitty Foyle,* was at loggerheads to direct Ginger and *Heartbeat* to a satisfying level. Ginger was tempting the fates by attempting to portray an eighteen-year-old French gamin who, when released from reform school,

*For 1945, she earned a whopping $292,159, making her the highest-paid Hollywood star, and the eighth biggest salary earner in the United States.
†A remake of Danielle Darrieux's *Battement de Coeur* (1939).
‡It would have been far better for Ginger's career if RKO had allowed her to go over to Paramount for *To Each His Own* (1946), a role which netted Olivia de Havilland an Oscar.

takes up professional thievery. She picks the pocket of diplomat Adolphe Menjou, but he in turn uses her to flirt with Jean Pierre Aumont, who in turn has been carrying on with Menjou's wife (Mona Maris). There was little that was either Gallic or gay about *Heartbeat*. At this point in her career, Ginger's insistence upon demonstrating wide-eyed innocence to the nth degree was cloying, not charming. The meager highlight of the picture was the performance of Basil Rathbone, playing a modern-day Fagin who operates a school for pickpockets.

Ginger's succeeding film ventures were not much of an improvement. *Time* magazine neatly summed up *Magnificent Doll* (1946), the first of her pictures on freelance now that her RKO contract had finally expired. Said that journal, Ginger was "forced into a role above her head and a script that is beneath it." Perhaps Ginger was intrigued by the opportunity to wear flouncy period costumes and to play a historical figure in a politically oriented love tale. Whatever, her Dolly Madison was far more interested in correctly displaying her Vera West gowns and her Lilly Dache hats than in bringing out the proper dramatic values of the Irving Stone screenplay. (Granted the script forced her to utter such banal lines as [to jailed traitor Aaron Burr as played by David Niven], "I hope all this will make you think, Aaron."). The fictionalized historical whimsy, as recounted by Ginger the narrator, made mincemeat of the real-life Dolly Madison, who loses her first husband (Stephen McNally) and gives up dashing traitor Niven to wed meek President-in-the-making James Madison (Burgess Meredith). One of the pretentious film's most amusing moments quite unintentionally occurred during the British invasion of Washington, D.C. with Ginger snatching documents and paintings from the White House right under the Englishers' noses.

The post-World War II economy drives had not yet seriously hurt Ginger's financial status, for she was earning $175,000 a picture plus a percentage of the profits. *It Had to Be You* (Columbia, 1947) was a broad farce with psychological and whimsical overtones. Ginger was seen as a predatory sculptress, a would-be bride who has run out on three prospective bridegrooms and is just about to try a fourth's patience when a snappy young Indian (Cornel Wilde) enters her life and pursues the reckless lass with very resolute persistency on his part. Never had Ginger before or since been asked to play such an outlandish saphead onscreen.

Ginger took a moratorium from filmmaking in 1947 and for most of 1948, spending much of her time at her Oregon ranch with her demobilized husband, Jack Briggs. For a spell, while mama Rogers was busy platforming for her right-wing committee, Ginger had a notion of running for Congress on the Republican ticket, but she soon dropped the idea. Not until late 1948, when Judy Garland became so emotionally and physically ill that it was necessary to replace her in *The Barkleys of Broadway* (1949), did Hollywood beckon to Ginger again. She was paged from her Oregon ranch to rush pronto to the Culver City soundstage to join her old dancing partner, Fred Astaire, in a new movie musical. Her publicized reaction to this nostalgic but commercial gesture belied hidden fears she may have possessed about being capable of re-creating her screen dance magic of a decade ago. "I don't want to do musicals," Ginger announced, "and I am satisfied to keep on with the straight ones. But I guess it'll turn out all right! Anyway, we'll have some fun."

On the whole, the color *The Barkleys of Broadway* turned out dandy, belying to a great extent the maturity of the two lead players. As the high-strung husband-and-wife Broadway team, Ginger and Astaire donned kilts to perform "My One and Only Highland Fling." drifted into nostalgia with a recap of Gershwin's "They Can't Take That Away from Me,"* and had the kidding hillbilly routine, "The Courtin' of Elmer and Ella." There was more than a dash of reality to Ginger's screen assignment as Dinah Barkley, the song-and-dance sensation of the Great White Way who craves to be a dramatic star. Ginger's Dinah has her dream fulfilled when she is hired to star in a legitimate play based on the life of *Young Sarah Bernhardt,* which has for its emotional highlight Ginger's emphatic recitation of "La Marseillaise" in front of the judging panel of the Académie Française. This sequence has become the camp favorite among Ginger aficionados. Ginger would re-create her *The Barkleys of Broadway* role on "Lux Radio Theatre" on January 1, 1951 with George Murphy as her co-star.

What Ginger's intimate friends had been predicting for some time, came true on September 7, 1949, when she divorced Jack Briggs. Now at domestic loose ends, Ginger was more than ever anxious to dig into a good film role. But in the television-plagued film business there were few enough parts available for the new crop of younger screen personalities, let alone an over-seasoned pro. Ginger talked of starring in *The Story of Molly X* at Universal, but June Havoc ended up making this tale of a gangster's widow who sets out to find her husband's killer. When Judy Garland was removed from *Annie Get Your Gun* (1950), Ginger immediately telephoned MGM studio chief Louis B. Mayer and told him, "I've found your Annie." But the veteran executive was not convinced. He explained, "Keep your high heels and your silk stockings, you're not raucous enough." So rejected Ginger motored over to Warner Bros. for *Perfect Strangers* (1950),† based on an outmoded play written by Ben Hecht and Charles MacArthur for Helen Hayes in the 1930s. During jury duty, divorcee Ginger cares more about romancing married man Dennis Morgan (who has two children) than dealing with the matter of justice in a murder case. After a good deal of seemingly endless talk, interspersed with comedy relief by Thelma Ritter as a lowbrow, slightly stupid housewife, both Ginger and Morgan go their separate paths at the end of *Perfect Strangers.* A rather bored audience had already yawned its indifferent way out of the theatre long before the end title hit the screen.

---

*Ginger insists to this day it was she and not producer Arthur Freed who thought of dredging up the Gershwin song for appropriate nostalgia.

†Based on the play *Ladies and Gentlemen,* which opened on Broadway, October 17, 1939, with Helen Hayes starred and ran for 105 performances.

Hardly had Ginger completed *Perfect Strangers* when that film's producer, Jerry Wald, requested her to fill in the breach and take over for a balking Lauren Bacall in Warners' *Storm Warning* (1950). Director Stuart Heisler was obviously influenced by the documentary techniques of *Boomerang* and *Lost Boundaries,* but producer Wald was pushing for another *Flamingo Road.* The result was a mishmash, hardly reminiscent of Warners' social-indictment dramas of the 1930s, which carried punch and nifty entertainment values. In this weakling effort, Ginger was the New York model who comes South to visit her sister(!), Doris Day, and witnesses a Ku-Klux Klan execution engineered by white-sheet-member Steve Cochran, her brother-in-law. Before Ginger can leave town, she is sexually assaulted by Cochran, whipped by the Klan, and subpoenaed by district attorney Ronald Reagan; altogether more than enough punishment for any self-respecting screen heroine to endure in one picture.

Ginger thought it time to renew her acquaintance with screen comedy by doing *The Groom Wore Spurs* (1951), made for Fidelity Pictures but released by Universal. The resultant picture, which suffered from exceptionally bad editing, was a fitful comedy presenting Ginger as a woman attorney who maneuvers cowboy star Jack Carson out of one Las Vegas scrape after another, resulting in their marriage. The strained comedy, with Ginger looking plump and quite middle-aged, was a sad sight to behold.

Nineteen hundred and fifty-one marked Ginger's fortieth birthday, and she was quite justified in regarding this chronological turning point as a dangerous age; the film offers were simply not coming in. For a once-luscious movie star who still kept herself in astoundingly good physical shape, she considered the inability to present herself for public display a sad waste. Why not return to Broadway, she reasoned. Louis Verneuil's *Love and Let Love* (Plymouth Theatre, October 19, 1951) was a weak vehicle in which to essay a stage comeback. The show was plagued by problems: author-director-leading man Verneuil suffered a heart attack long before the show opened; Sally Benson was hired to do rewrites, but she became ill, leaving a bemused Ginger and Paul McGrath to cope with the vapid script as best they could. Ironically the show did financially well on the road—Ginger in person still had plenty of drawing power for Middle America—but Ginger wanted to bring it to Broadway ("I'd rather be a sitting duck in a big pond"). Once in New York, it died after fifty-six performances. The reviewers tore into the play but gave Ginger, who essayed a dual role, credit for her vibrant looks and her poise in wearing the Jean Louis outfits.* Said Brooks Atkinson of the *New York Times,* "No one that gorgeous can be entirely overwhelmed by a playwright's dullness." After the death of *Love and Let Love,* Ginger said, "I'm not the type that can be discouraged." The game star had offers to remain on Broadway for up-

*In 1958 Ginger would find cause to comment about this flop: "The only person who liked that was the author. He adored it. He later went back to France and cut his throat with a razor, even though he had no beard and didn't shave. I thought that was odd."

226

coming projects, such as *Jezebel's Husband* with Claude Rains, but she chose to return to the safer ground of Hollywood.

The pickings were not plush in the drastically tightened film economy of the 1950s. Many of Ginger's contemporaries had fallen by the professional wayside, but Ginger's name and enthusiasm still counted for something. She netted a role in another multiepisode picture, *We're Not Dressing* (Twentieth Century-Fox, 1951), playing opposite Fred Allen in the first of five sketches. The duo were rather droll as a veteran husband-and-wife radio team ("wed" for twenty-one years) who ignore each other in the living room, bedroom, and bath, but purr over one another once on the air with their daily breakfast show.

Ginger had much more prominence with her two 1952 releases. *Monkey Business* reunited her with Cary Grant* in a funny comedy about adults seeking the fountain-of-youth elixir and, when accidentally gaining it, acting more childish than any rambunctious kiddie would ever dream of. The screwball plot was reminiscent of director Howard Hawks's earlier outing with Grant in *Bringing up Baby* (1939), in which Katharine Hepburn was the zany female foil. As a result of favorable audience reactions to Ginger in this slapstick fare, Fox producer Sol Siegel cast her in the second-billed assignment opposite prissy Clifton Webb in *Dream Boat.* The film's atypical premise offered Ginger one of her most diverting cinema parts, that of a mature former star of the silent screen who finds herself a celebrity again when a perfume company sponsors television showings of her most famous 1920s flicks, all of which embarrasses her former leading man (Webb), now a prim college professor and the conservative father of a grown daughter (Anne Francis).

After these novelty roles it was a welcome relief for Ginger to appear in a solid, if tritely executed, bit of film fare, Paramount's *Forever Female* (1953). Ginger was plucky enough to essay the role of an aging actress who refuses to admit that the passage of time has disqualified her for starring onstage as the ingenue in William Holden's new play or to be his romantic partner offstage. As depicted in *Forever Female,* the glamour world of Broadway was not in the same league with *All about Eve,* but it had its share of lustrous ambience. Ginger dug into her "silly and somewhat brutal role" with surprising honesty, and proved especially effective in the telling sequence in which she acknowledges that her emotional age must stay in keeping with her chronological maturity.

Even before *Forever Female* was released,[†] Ginger had played her on-camera role in real life by romancing and marrying twenty-six-year-old Jacques Bergerac on February 7, 1953 in Palm Springs.[‡] The newspapers all

*This time Grant was top-cast.

[†] It was the first feature film to have its premiere on American television, being shown as a prime attraction on the innovative Telemeter system at Palm Springs, where for $1.35 viewers could view the first-run film.

[‡] Evelyn Keyes had introduced Ginger to the ex-hotel clerk-drama student-lawyer on the Riviera in 1952.

played up the sixteen-year age difference. Charming Bergerac diplomatically told the media, "In France when a man and his wife love each other nobody asks when they were born." Ginger was too ecstatic over her love to do anything much but gurgle to the press: "When you're happy, you don't count the years—in the same way that you don't count calories when you eat. I'll always be 15 days older than Jacques."

While Bergerac matriculated at MGM (thanks to Ginger's intervention) to study acting and to appear in several supporting film roles, Ginger reported to the Twentieth Century-Fox lot to co-star in the CinemaScope and color whodunit, *Black Widow* (1954). Mid a cast of equal veterans (Gene Tierney, Van Heflin, George Raft, Reginald Gardiner, and Peggy Ann Garner), Ginger was noticeably restrained in her interpretation of a glittering, catty stage star involved in homicide. The Nunnally Johnson-produced-directed-scripted drama was too obviously constructed to contain much in the way of surprise, and the illicit love theme was handled so tactfully that all titillation value was destroyed. Nevertheless, the film coasted by at the box-office due to its clustering of familiar marquee names and its then still novel use of the wide-screen process.

More as a boon to her fledgling-actor husband than as a step in the right direction for her waning movie career, Ginger traveled to England to make the modestly budgeted melodrama *Twist of Fate* (1954). Since Ginger had invested in the film, there was no question about Bergerac receiving a smallish part in the project. As to her act of nepotism, Ginger responded, "I found talent before and it has succeeded, Jacques can do so as well."

The same year Ginger made her long-awaited (at least for some) television debut in an expensively mounted, highly touted "Producers Showcase" special (NBC, October 18, 1954), appearing in three of Noel Coward's nine playlets from *Tonight at 8:30*. Otto Preminger directed her in *Red Peppers, Still Life,* and *Shadow Play,* with a cast that included Trevor Howard, Gig Young, Ilka Chase, Martyn Green, Gloria Vanderbilt, and Margaret Hayes. Ginger's attempt at shouldering a dramatic showcase that had once starred Gertrude Lawrence on stage, was greeted with mild enthusiasm, leading one to wonder whether Ginger had been rather presumptuous when she said, before starting rehearsals for the special, "[Until now] I can honestly say that I have never yet seen a TV dramatic show which has made me say, 'I wish I'd done that.'" It would be four years before Ginger tackled television again, and then she appeared as a subject on Edward R. Murrow's "Person to Person" (CBS, March 7, 1958). Mrs. Lela Rogers emerged with more appealing zest in this interview than her illustrious daughter. As Ginger embarked on production plans for her special, *The Ginger Rogers Show* (CBS, October 15, 1958), which featured Ray Bolger and the Ritz Brothers, she casually told the press, "I think I may have waited too long." The sixty-minute musical-review show did not create the excitement expected (Ginger was more at ease in her spoofing than in her vocalizing), but there was sufficient interest in Ginger as a TV name. She starred in an NBC half-hour variety-show pilot on February

228

28, 1959 that did not garner future sponsors for a series; jaunted over to England to headline *Carissima* for the BBC, playing the forty-five-year-old head of an American cosmetic firm, receiving £2,500 for her performance. Subsequently there was an episode of the "June Allyson Show" entitled *The Tender Shoot* (CBS, October 19, 1959), the *Never Too Late* segment (CBS, February 4, 1960) of the "Zane Grey Theatre," the lead in an unsold situation-comedy pilot, "A Love Affair for Just Three," playing twins (it was eventually aired on "Vacation Playhouse" [CBS, July 22, 1963]). She and Walter Pidgeon were the regal cast members of the CBS musical special *Cinderella* (February 22, 1966). Thereafter Ginger guested on the *Terror Island* segment (NBC, February 26, 1966) of "Bob Hope Chrysler Theatre," and later starred in a chapter of "Here's Lucy" (CBS, November 8, 1971).

Sandwiched in between her meandering forays into television, Ginger plied her art in feature film work, when and as it became available. She finally conceded to the passage of time when she played an unstarched—but still fairly shapely—gangland moll in Columbia's programmer *Tight Spot* (1955). She gave unexpected zest to her role of the former doll, who is released from prison, in the special custody of law-enforcer Edward G. Robinson, in the hope that she will provide the tipoff on racketeering operations. Within the close confines of the hotel-suite set, director Phil Karlson created a fast-paced drama, bolstered by the presence of Brian Keith (that year's hot television find) as a surprise baddie. Ginger was right at home mouthing her tough dialog, making it quite clear that her Sherry Conley was a brassy dame of the Glenda Farrell school. Ginger's finest crack in *Tight Spot* was appropriately saved for the climax, when she is escorted into the courtroom, having endured brutal pressure from gangsters out to eliminate her before she can possibly testify. Sworn in on the witness stand, she is asked her occupation. Without a bat of an eye, she snaps out, "Crime buster!"

A great deal of to-do was raised over Ginger's return to her RKO alma mater for *The First Traveling Saleslady* (1956). "It was good to be home again," Ginger confessed. "They gave me the same dressing room. It was a little dusty, but that was taken care of in a hurry. Many of the same people were still around the studio. To tell you the truth, it really hasn't changed much at all." Ginger must have been befogged with nostalgia, for the RKO of the mid-1950s was in sad straits. What the 1940s antitrust production-distribution suits and television had not wreaked on the Culver City studio, Howard Hughes did within a short eight-year period, leaving the facilities a shell of their former self when he parceled off his shares in the company in 1955-56. William Dozier was production chief in charge of what was left of RKO moviemaking, at the time of *The First Traveling Saleslady*. Having failed to lure Mae West out of movie retirement, he called upon Ginger to provide a Westian characterization as the corset saleslady who is a bug on women's rights. Ginger evidently thought the would-be comedy western had potential. She was sadly mistaken. Dozier supplied Ginger with three familiar video male leads (Barry Nelson, David Brian, James Arness) to goose up the mild comedy, but under the direction of Arthur Lubin* the movie flopped so badly it kept Ginger's iconoclastic co-star, Carol Channing, away from pictures for years to come. Later Ginger would quip that almost singlehandedly she had helped to close down RKO.

Ginger's next two assignments at Fox were merely stopgaps in her asphyxiating film career. *Teenage Rebel* (1956) was based on *Roomful of Roses,* which had failed on Broadway the year before, with Betty Field in the lead. Betty Lou Klein reprised her stage assignment as the fifteen-year-old daughter of divorced parents (Ginger and John Stephenson) who finds it difficult to adjust to living with her mother and stepfather (Michael Rennie). Ginger did rather well with her conventional mother's role in a quiet, hackneyed screen melodrama. *Oh Men! Oh, Women!* (1957), also derived from a Broadway show, was produced-directed in overly broad strokes by Nunnally Johnson, making the film just another one of the many forgettable, allegedly sophisticated fun sessions from the mid-1950s Twentieth Century-Fox production mill. The subject at hand here was the vicissitudes of patients who think they really must rely completely on the judgment of their psychiatrist (David Niven), when in reality they each could have solved their problems rather simply. Ginger played the wife of movie star Dan Dailey, telling Dr. Niven that she is forced to live an Ibsenesque *Doll's House* existence. Tony Randall, as the unstrung fiancé of Barbara Rush, hogged most of the screen time with his blatant temper-tantruming.

During these cinematic off-years, Ginger's marriage to Bergerac fell apart, just as had been predicted by the Hollywood set some four years earlier. In June, 1957, she sued for divorce from the Frenchman, who, it was rumored, had been overly attentive to actress Phyllis Kirk. Ginger told the Santa Monica court judge that she and Bergerac had separated in May, 1956, and that Bergerac had persistently and "wrongfully inflicted grievous mental suffering" upon her, stating as examples that he would hardly speak to her for days at a stretch, that he deliberately drove unreasonably fast, knowing full well it upset her greatly, and that he had the audacity to read French classics aloud in his native tongue in front of their party guests. Ginger realistically asked for no alimony. Bergerac's movie career was stagnating, to put it politely.

At the time of her divorce-getting, Ginger thought of starring in the independently produced feature *Flight to Vienna* by Fred Finklehoffe, which was to be made on location, but instead she ventured into the nightclub field, 1950s style. Unfortunately, Ginger's act was whipped into shape by talented Kay Thompson, who injected more Thompson personality than Ginger, and wrongly chose to ignore the nostalgia value of the movie star's past film work. After completing her break-in engagement in Havana, Ginger decided to turn to the stock circuit as a safer bet, and picked *Bells Are Ringing* for her vehicle. Her rationale for her pursuit of a hectic work schedule went as follows: "I'm

*Best known for directing the *Francis, the Talking Mule* film series at Universal.

not married any longer, so why shouldn't I work as hard as I can? Idleness breeds mischief or depression, so I'm going to keep busy." The following year (1959) Ginger headlined a pre-Broadway comedy (which became musicalized on the road), *The Pink Jungle,* which dealt with the cosmetic industry. "I don't think of myself as a creampuff actress," Ginger ventured before embarking on this expensively mounted Leslie Stevens project. As with *Love and Let Love,* audiences in the hinterland flocked to see Ginger, who, for entirely different reasons than contemporaries Joan Crawford, Bette Davis, Katharine Hepburn, and the older Gloria Swanson, had maintained her allure for legions of former filmgoers, as well as newer generations who had grown up watching her old films on television and listening to their parents sigh for the good old days when movies were movies and Ginger and Fred . . . Despite a $350,000 Broadway advance, *The Pink Jungle* folded in Boston on December 12, 1959, for "rewrites." There were rumors that excessive clashes between Ginger's constant traveling advisor, mama Rogers, and the play's other female lead, Agnes Moorehead, had created irreparable friction. Game Ginger insisted that *The Pink Jungle* interlude was a positive episode in her career: "I don't feel the experience was a loss."

While more and more of Ginger's contemporaries fell into unavoidable semiretirement or snatched at straws by debasing themselves in mock-horror-movie quickies, Ginger plied the stock circuit, a safe but lucrative means of keeping her name before the public and herself professionally busy. In the early 1960s she traveled on the road with *Annie Get Your Gun, Bell, Book and Candle, The Unsinkable Molly Brown,* and *Tovarich,* seemingly revitalized by her marriage to forty-five-year-old actor William Marshall.* They were wed on March 17, 1961, with Marshall's sixteen-year-old son (by his former marriage to Michele Morgan) as the best man. The couple purchased a two-acre tract in Jamaica, West Indies, and soon publicized the fact that they intended to create a movie-studio facility there, under a joint venture with the local government, which saw a $10 million investment over a ten-year period. The only picture that resulted from the enterprise was *The Confession* (made in 1964 and receiving spotty release as *Seven Different Ways* in the early 1970s before being sold to television). In a cast that included Ray Milland, Barbara Eden, and Elliott Gould, Ginger donned a dark wig to play the madam of an Italian bordello. After this unpromising start, the Marshalls soon abandoned their Jamaica filmmaking project.

Ginger made her official screen return in the Electronovision version of *Harlow* (1965), shot in eight days in black and white to beat out the plusher competition edition being turned out by Joseph E. Levine. Ginger Rogers found herself a last-minute substitute for an ailing Judy Garland, who had been scheduled to play the mother of the 1930s blonde bombshell Jean Harlow (Carol Lynley). In this grainy film, characterization was tossed to the

*Ginger and Marshall had met when they both were touring with *Bell, Book and Candle.* He had previously been wed to French actresses Michele Morgan and Micheline Presle.

231

wind, along with any fidelity to facts, ambience, or entertainment values. While the other performers careened through their *Harlow* roles like bulldozers, Ginger gave indications of having been lost along the way as the aggressive mama; certainly no threat whatsoever to the carnivorous performance of Angela Lansbury as Mama Jean in Paramount's *Harlow* (1965).

The failure to resurrect her screen career was wiped out by Ginger's triumph when, on August 9, 1965, she took over for Carol Channing as the new Dolly Levi in Broadway's long-running musical hit, *Hello, Dolly!** Ginger had no qualms about being a replacement attraction. "I have spent my life doing things created by someone else. There is no stigma in doing something someone else has already done . . . But then I'm a kid who has turned down more good things than anybody you know. I tried to talk myself out of *Kitty Foyle* and I turned down *Snake Pit*. Anything I know I'm not right for, that's it. I should do it." While the critics generally refused to be locked into a corner by comparing quieter Ginger with galvanic Carol Channing as far as interpretations of Dolly Levi went, the public thoroughly endorsed Ginger's rendition, loving every bit of the star legend she brought to the show (including her standard, well-rehearsed, teary curtain speech each evening). In fact, it is agreed in theatrical circles that few performers could have punched up the failing momentum of ticket sales to *Hello, Dolly!* as Ginger did for the Jerry Herman musical during the one and a half years she remained with the Broadway production (thereafter taking one of the national touring companies).

In February, 1967, while she was the toast of Broadway with *Dolly!*, the Gallery of Modern Art in New York arranged a special film tribute to Ginger. "Is she ready for the museum?" asked one national magazine. Evidently in this capacity, yes, for Ginger and the movie retrospective (ranging from *Office Blues* to *The Barkleys of Broadway* to *Kitty Foyle* to *Gold Diggers of 1933*) proved a substantial hit. A dewy-eyed Ginger said at the festivities: "It ain't really me up there. Just images, lights and shadows. Me's here. . . Believe me. I don't deserve this tribute. Great women like Jackie Kennedy have earned such honors, some women have risen from the worst predicaments to become successful. All I ever did was make a shambles of my life." The tribute provided a good springboard for the media to interview Ginger anew and capture her opinions on a rash of subjects.

About being the good girl next door: "It's the columnists who built that image and put me on a pedestal. And I'd be happy to get off because I hate that phony facade." She also had another pet peeve: "I hate people who give me their own personal screen test and scream, 'Oh Miss Rogers, how beautiful you are!' What are they trying to find? They make believe the wrinkles do not exist!"

About herself: "I have the body of a beauty, but the soul of Satan. My beauty is strictly on the surface, but inside where a woman should really be

*Opened at the St. James Theatre on January 16, 1964.

beautiful, I'm not. . . . I only wish I had taken as much care of my soul as I did of my face and figure. For true beauty is within a person, not where you can see it. And I'm ugly inside." (For the record, Ginger is an active Christian Scientist.)

On dancing: "The truth is I hate dancing whether for theatrical or social purposes. It's become too much of a chore for me." Fred Astaire: "He was a real professional and only pros turn me on. . . It makes me sick to be around inept performers."

On marriage: "Maybe it was because I married men too young for me. They made me feel younger but perhaps I was too demanding and impatient with them. I never really gave my marriages a chance to work out.

"It's different with Bill [Marshall]. He's the only good thing I've got to show for forty-two years of hard work. He knows all my shortcomings and is helping me to become a more understanding and compassionate person than I've ever been before."

On stardom: "The most important thing for a star's talent is to work it. You must keep it working, not sit back and wait for the plums to come your way, keep it pliable. Does it improve? Yes, I think so because I believe that anything smoother is better."

After touring the West Coast and points east with *Hello, Dolly!* in 1967, Ginger continued to keep her name in front of the public with occasional television variety-show appearances, and by quietly feeding the nostalgic passion for the still comely distaff side of the fabled Astaire-Rogers dance team.* Neither she nor the affable, shy Astaire ever alluded to the personality problems which caused them to split up and end the possibility of further moviemaking together—even had they been able to find a backer in the 1950s —and each in his/her own way fostered the still-a-building glow that even now surrounds the strains of "The Continental," "Cheek to Cheek," "Let's Call the Whole Thing Off," all part of the requisite equipment to recall the Wonderful Thirties, when refined ballroom dancing, chic, idealized romance, gracefulness, all were symbolized by the screen charisma of Astaire and Rogers.

Ginger had refused yet another take-over role for debilitated Judy Garland in Twentieth Century-Fox's *Valley of the Dolls* (1967),† but she did agree to walk in the shoes of Angela Lansbury by starring in the London company of *Mame* (Drury Lane Theatre, March 14, 1969). It was an offer she could hardly refuse: a year's salary of $250,000, plus many other fringe benefits to insure that she and husband William Marshall would enjoy their London stay. When

*On occasion Ginger could be flip about the Astaire-Rogers allure. When asked if the duo might ever reteam, she said (c. 1958), "Why not? Television seems to be bringing everything else out of mothballs."

†Susan Hayward accepted the role of Helen Lawson in the film, which Ginger said was too smutty for her serious consideration. "I simply couldn't say those words. I simply could not stand having my ears hear that kind of language, coming out of my mouth, and I don't think anyone else could either."

Ginger docked at Southhampton there was a flock of press and fans to greet her, and a special *Mame* car for her on the train to London. Her extensive rehearsals paid off, for although *Mame* received qualified reviews as a show per se, Ginger captured the hearts of nearly all attendees. ("Miss Rogers has only to start dancing to provide the same lift of the heart, the quickening of the breath that she could inspire in her younger days" [*London Financial Times*].) Ginger's year with *Mame* in London did much to consolidate her enduring superstar status. She gave the public what they wanted, and everyone was happy.

Plans did not jell for Ginger to take *Mame* to Paris in December, 1970, with a French-language version, so she and Marshall returned to the States. There were more television guest appearances, (ranging from "The Dean Martin Show" to "Hollywood Squares") and then a touring edition of *Coco,* the Broadway musical which had been such a personal success for her former RKO co-worker, Katharine Hepburn. Ginger garnered most publicity in *Coco* when she announced, for any press man in the country to hear, that she would not use the four-letter word employed at the opening of the show's Act II. "When I was asked to play *Coco,*" Ginger explained with sincerity, "I said if that word had to be uttered, include me out. I'm not a prude but cleaning up the stage and movies has to start somewhere." The *Coco* stint garnered no particular laurels for anyone concerned; it was not a part to which the Ginger Rogers personality could add luster.

So what new venture could sixty-one-year-old Ginger tackle? In April, 1972, she announced she had become fashion consultant to the J. C. Penney chain, an organization which claims to dress more American women than any other retail company. "Ginger" panty hose and Penney's fashions (modeled by Ginger) are represented in the company's huge new catalog, and Ginger is zipping about the country to all the store openings. "I'm doing a whole wardrobe layout for Mrs. America for her trip or two-week tour. And I put it all in one suitcase, isn't that great?" explains and exclaims Ginger, who is seemingly as excited about this new career turn as she was about *Flying Down to Rio* or *Kitty Foyle.* Wearing a J. C. Penney wardrobe (a $42 knit suit) may not be the same as sporting the latest Jean Louis movie budget haute couture, but Ginger is still her same snappy self, her almost platinum hair styled just as when she danced with Fred Astaire four decades ago. For Ginger, playing Mrs. Consumer is another way of entertaining the public, and at the same time being serviceable to what she feels is the public good (as when she wrote an editorial on religious freedom in 1957 for the *Los Angeles Examiner* and won the Freedom Foundation Award, or when she campaigned for Richard Nixon's gubernatorial race in 1960s California). Reasons Ginger: "I've always tried to make my name stand for the better things in life—the things which involve goodness and morality and cleanliness. And, most important, consideration for other people. . . That's how I've managed to stay a star. You don't stay on top by compromising your ideals."

Ginger's resurgent wholesomeness campaign leaves little room these days for talk of other facets of her life, present (she spends most of her free time at her Oregon ranch) or past. Blessedly she has not lost any of her zingy ability for a quick comeback on any question. During the still recent Howard Hughes-Clifford Irving rhubarb, the press besieged her with questions on her dating days with mysterious Hughes. Snapped a still dazzling Ginger, "I'm saving my Howard Hughes anecdotes for my own autobiography. I'm not going to hire a ghost writer, especially not Clifford Irving."

Asked what she would like to be remembered for, Ginger will most frequently answer, "I want nothing more than that Ginger Rogers be known as a trailblazer for quality—for all things of the highest levels of goodness, understanding, communication, morality, cleanliness, and consideration." A tall order to fill, but then so has been her entire professional life to date.

Feature Film Appearances

GINGER ROGERS

YOUNG MAN OF MANHATTAN   (Par., 1930) 80 M.

Director, Monta Bell; based on the play by Katherine Brush; adaptation, Robert Presnell; songs, Irving Kahal, Pierre Norman, and Sammy Fain; sound, Ernest F. Zatorsky; camera, Larry Williams; editor, Emma Hill.

Claudette Colbert (Ann Vaughn); Norman Foster (Toby McLean); Ginger Rogers (Puff Randolph); Charles Ruggles (Shorty Ross); Leslie Austin (Dwight Knowles); H. Dudley Hawley (Doctor); Four Aalbu Sisters (Sherman Sisters).

QUEEN HIGH   (Par., 1930) 85 M.

Producer, Frank Mandel, Laurence Schwab; director, Fred Newmeyer; based on the play by Schwab, B. G. De Sylva, and Lewis Gensler and the play *A Pair of Sixes* by Edward Henry Peple; songs, Arthur Schwartz and Ralph Rainger; De Sylva and Gensler; E. Y. Harburg and Henry Souvain; Dick Howard and Rainger; music arranger, John W. Green; sound, C. A. Tuthill; camera, William Steiner; editor, Barney Rogan.

Stanley Smith (Dick Johns); Ginger Rogers (Polly Rockwell); Charles Ruggles (T. Boggs Johns); Frank Morgan (George Nettleton); Helen Carrington (Mrs. Nettleton); Theresa Maxwell Conover (Mrs. Rockwell); Betty Garde (Florence Cole); Nina Olivette (Coddles); Rudy Cameron (Cyrus Vanderhold); Tom Brown (Jimmy).

THE SAP FROM SYRACUSE   (Par., 1930) 75 M.

Director, A. Edward Sutherland; based on the book by John Wray, Jack O'Donnell, John Hayden; screenplay, Gertrude Purcell; songs, E. Y. Harburg, John W. Green, and Vernon Duke; Harburg and Green; sound, Edwin Schabbehar, Gordon New; camera, Larry Williams.

Jack Oakie (Littleton Looney); Ginger Rogers (Ellen Saunders); Granville Bates (Hycross); George Barbier (Senator Powell); Sidney Riggs (Nick Pangolos); Betty Starbuck (Flo Goodrich); Veree Teasdale (Dolly Clark); J. Malcolm Dunn (Captain Barker); Bernard Jukes (Bells); Walter Fenner (Henderson); Jack Daly (Hopkins).

FOLLOW THE LEADER   (Par., 1930) 86 M.

Director, Norman Taurog; based on the play *Manhattan Mary* by William K. Wells, George White, Buddy De Sylva, Lew Brown, Ray Henderson; screenplay, Gertrude Purcell, Sid Silvers; dialog director, Albert Parker; songs, Brown, De Sylva, and Henderson; E. Y. Harburg and Arthur Schwartz; Irving Kahal and Sammy Fain; dialog stager, Al Packer; sound, Ernest F. Zatorsky; camera, Larry Williams; editor, Barney Rogan.

Ed Wynn (Crickets); Ginger Rogers (Mary Brennan); Stanley Smith (Jimmy Moore); Lou Holtz (Sam Platz); Lida Kane (Ma Brennan); Ethel Merman (Helen King); Bobby

Watson (George White); Donald Kirke (R. C. Black); William Halligan (Bob Sterling); Holly Hall (Fritzie Devere); Preston Foster (Two-Gun Terry); James C. Morton (Mickie); Tammany Young (Bull); William Gargan (Chuck); Jack La Rue (Hood).

HONOR AMONG LOVERS   (Par., 1931) 75 M.

Director, Dorothy Arzner; story-screenplay, Austin Parker; dialog, Parker, Gertrude Purcell; camera, George Folsey; editor, Helen Turner.

Claudette Colbert (Julia Traynor); Fredric March (Jerry Stafford); Monroe Owsley (Philip Craig); Charles Ruggles (Monty Dunn); Ginger Rogers (Doris Blake); Avonne Taylor (Maybelle); Pat O'Brien (Conroy); Janet McLeary (Margaret); John Kearney (Inspector); Ralph Morgan (Riggs); Jules Epailly (Louis); Leonard Carey (Butler).

THE TIP OFF   (Pathé, 1931) 70 M.

Producer, Charles R. Rogers; director, Albert Rogell; story, George Kibbe Turner; screenplay, Earl Baldwin; dialog director, Ralph Murphy; sound, Charles O'Loughlin, T. Carman; camera, Edward Snyder; editor, Charles Craft.

Eddie Quillan (Tommy Jordan); Robert Armstrong (Kayo McClure); Ginger Rogers (Baby Face); Joan Peers (Edna Moreno); Ralf Harolde (Nick Vatelli); Charles Sellon (Pop Jackson); Mike Donlin (Swanky Jones); Jack Herrick (Jack); Cupid Ainsworth (Miss Waddums); Frank Darien (Uncle); Dorothy Granger (Hat Check Girl); Ernie Adams (Slug McGee); Harry Wilson (Hood); James Burtis (Men's Room Patron); Luis Alberni (Searno); Charles Sullivan (Chuck—bouncer).

SUICIDE FLEET   (Pathé, 1931) 87 M.

Producer, Charles R. Rogers; director, Albert Rogell; story, Commander Herbert A. Jones; screenplay, Lew Lipton, F. McGrew Wills; sound, D. A. Cutler; camera, Sol Polito; editor, Joe Kane.

Bill Boyd (Baltimore); Robert Armstrong (Dutch); James Gleason (Skeets); Ginger Rogers (Sally); Harry Bannister (Commander); Frank Reicher (Holtzman); Ben Alexander (Kid); Henry Victor (Captain von Stuben); Han Joby (Schwartz).

CARNIVAL BOAT   (RKO-Pathé, 1932) 64 M.

Producer, Charles R. Rogers; associate producer, Harry Joe Brown; director, Albert Rogell; story, Marion Jackson, Don Ryan; screenplay, James Seymour; music director, Max Steiner; songs, Bernie Grossman and Harold Lewis; Steiner and Arthur Lange; art director, Carroll Clark; costumes, Gwen Wakeling; sound, L. John Myers; camera, Ted McCord; editor, John Link.

Bill Boyd (Buck Gannon); Ginger Rogers (Honey); Fred Kohler (Jack Logan); Hobart Bosworth (Jim Gannon); Marie Prevost (Babe); Edgar Kennedy (Baldy); Harry Sweet (Stubby); Charles Sellon (Lane); Eddie Chandler (Jordon); Walter Percival (DeLacey); Jack Carlyle (DeLacey's Assistant); Joe Marba (Windy); Bob Perry (Bartender).

THE TENDERFOOT   (FN, 1932) 70 M.

Director, Alfred Santell; based on the play *The Butter and Egg Man* by Grace Miller White; screenplay, S. N. Behrman, Sonya Levien, Rupert Hughes; sound, W. D. Fink; camera, Hal Mohr.

Joe E. Brown (Peter Jones); Ginger Rogers (Ruth); Lew Cody (Sam Lehman); Vivien Oakland (Miss Martin); Robert Greig (Mack); Wilfred Lucas (Patterson); Spencer Charters (Oscar); Ralph Ince (Dolan); Mae Madison (Cafe Maid); Marion

Byron (Kitty); Lee Kuhlmar (Waiter); Harry Seymour (Newsstand Proprietor); Richard Cramer (Rackstein); Douglas Gerrard (Stage Director); Jill Bennett (Cafe Cashier).

THE THIRTEENTH GUEST   (Mon., 1932) 69 M.

Producer, M. H. Hoffman; director, Albert Ray; based on the novel by Armitage Trail; adaptation, Francis Hyland, Arthur Hoerl; dialog, Trail; assistant director, Gene Anderson; production manager, Sidney Algier; camera, Harry Neumann, Tom Galligan.

Ginger Rogers (Marie Morgan/Lela); Lyle Talbot (Phil Winston); J. Farrell MacDonald (Captain Ryan); James Eagles (Harold "Bud" Morgan); Eddie Phillips (Thor Jensen); Erville Alderson (John Adams); Robert Klein (John Barksdale); Crauford Kent (Dr. Sherwood); Frances Rich (Marjorie Thornton); Ethel Wales (Aunt Joan Thornton); Paul Hurst (Detective Grump); William Davidson (Captain Brown); Phillips Smalley (Uncle Dick Thornton); Harry Tenbrook (Cabby); John Ince (John Morgan); Allan Cavan (Uncle Wayne Seymour); Alan Bridge (Policeman); Tom London (Detective Carter); Henry Hall (Sergeant—jailer); Tiny Sandford (Mike—jailer); Kit Guard (Prisoner).

HAT CHECK GIRL   (Fox, 1932) 65 M.

Director, Sidney Lanfield; story, Rian James; screenplay, Philip Klein, Barry Conners; assistant director, Lesley Felander; costumes, Rita Kaufman; music director, George Lipschultz; settings, Gorton Wiles; camera, Glenn MacWilliams; editor, Paul Weatherwax.

Sally Eilers (Gerry Rand); Ben Lyon (Buster Collins); Ginger Rogers (Jessica King); Monroe Owsley (Tod Reese); Arthur Pierson (Phil Cornwall); Noel Madison (Stoney Stone [Charles Beaton]); Dewey Robinson (Tony Carlucci); Harold Goodwin (Walter Marsh); Eulalie Jensen (Mrs. Marsh); Purnell Pratt (Collins); Henry Arnetta (Water Wagon Driver); Ed Brady (Traffic Cop); Hooper Atchley ("Detective" Monahan); Richard Carle (Professor); Dennis O'Keefe, Bill Elliott (Guests); Bert Roach, Arthur Housman (Drunks); Eddie Anderson (Waiter); Lee Moran (Subway Rider); Harry Schultz (Hotel Waiter); Joyce Compton, Astrid Allwyn (Gossips at Party); Sherry Hall (Bartender); Harvey Clark (Colonel).

YOU SAID A MOUTHFUL   (FN, 1932) 75 M.

Director, Lloyd Bacon; story, William B. Dover; screenplay, Robert Lord, Bolton Mallory; camera, Richard Towers; editor, Owen Marks.

Joe E. Brown (Joe Holt); Ginger Rogers (Alice Brandon); Sheila Terry (Cora); Guinn Williams (Joe Holt, a Swim Champ); Harry Gribbon (Harry Daniels); Oscar Apfel (Armstrong); Edwin Maxwell (Dr. Vorse); Frank Hagney (Holt's Manager); Selmer Jackson (Armstrong's Secretary); Mia Marvin (Jones); Harry Seymour (Announcer); James Eagles (Messenger); Arthur S. Byron (Elliott); Anthony Lord (Bookkeeper); Bert Moorhouse (Office Manager); Farina (Sam); Preston Foster (Dover, a Swimmer); Walter Walker (Mr. Brandon); Don Brodie (Judge's Assistant); Wilfred Lucas (Official).

42nd STREET   (WB, 1933) 98 M.

Director, Lloyd Bacon; based on the novel by Bradford Ropes; screenplay, James Seymour, Rian James; assistant director, Gordon Hollingshead; art director, Jack Okey; songs, Al Dubin and Harry Warren; costumes, Orry-Kelly; choreography, Busby Berkeley; camera, Sol Polito; editor, Thomas Pratt.

Warner Baxter (Julian Marsh); Bebe Daniels (Dorothy Brock); George Brent (Pat Denning); Una Merkel (Lorraine Fleming); Ruby Keeler (Peggy Sawyer); Guy Kibbee

(Abner Dillon); Dick Powell (Bill Lawler); Ginger Rogers (Ann Lowell); George E. Stone (Andy Lee); Robert McWade (Al Jones); Ned Sparks (Thomas Barry); Eddie Nugent (Terry Neil); Allen Jenkins (MacElroy); Harry Akst (Jerry); Clarence Nordstrom (Groom in Production Number); Henry B. Walthall (The Actor); Al Dubin, Harry Warren (Song Writers); Toby Wing ("Young and Healthy" Girl); Jack La Rue (A Mug); Wallis Clark (Dr. Chadwick); Tom Kennedy (Slim Murphy); Louise Beavers (Pansy); Dave O'Brien (Chorus Boy); Patricia Ellis (Secretary); George Irving (House Doctor); Charles Lane (Author); Milton Kibbee (News Spreader); Rolfe Sedan (Stage Aide); Lyle Talbot (Geoffrey Waring); Pat Wing, Gertrude Keeler, Helen Keeler, Joan Barclay, Ann Hovey, Renee Whitney, Dorothy Coonan, Barbara Rogers, June Glory, Jayne Shadduck, Adele Lacy, Loretta Andrews, Margaret La Marr, Mary Janc Halsey, Ruth Eddings, Edna Callaghan, Patsy Farnum, Maxine Cantway, Lynn Browning, Donna Mae Roberts, Lorena Layson, Alice Jans (Chorus Girls).

BROADWAY BAD   (Fox, 1933) 59 M.

Director, Sidney Lanfield; story, William R. Lipman, A. W. Pezet; screenplay, Arthur Kober, Maude Fulton; art director, Gordon Wiles; camera, George Barnes; editor, Paul Weatherwax.

Joan Blondell (Tony Landers); Ricardo Cortez (Craig Cutting); Ginger Rogers (Flip Daly); Adrienne Ames (Aileen); Spencer Charters (Lew Gordon); Ronald Cosbey (Big Fella); Frederick Burton (Robert North, Jr.); Margaret Seddon (Bixby); Donald Crisp (Darrall); Max Wagner, Harold Goodwin (Reporters); Eddie Kane (Jeweler); John Davidson (Prince); Larry Steers (Business Associate); Matty Roubert, Eddie Berger (Newsboys); Henry Hall (Bailiff).

GOLD DIGGERS OF 1933   (WB, 1933) 96 M.

Director, Mervyn LeRoy; based on the play *Gold Diggers* by Avery Hopwood; adaptation, Erwin Gelsey, James Seymour; dialog, David Boehm, Ben Markson; choreography, Busby Berkeley; songs, Harry Warren and Al Dubin; camera, Sol Polito; editor, George Amy; art director, Anton Grot; gowns, Orry-Kelly.

Warren William (J. Lawrence Bradford); Joan Blondell (Carol King); Aline MacMahon (Trixie Lorraine); Ruby Keeler (Polly Parker); Dick Powell (Brad Roberts [Robert Treat Bradford]); Guy Kibbee (Faneuil H. Peabody); Ned Sparks (Barney Hopkins); Ginger Rogers (Fay Fortune); Clarence Nordstrom (Gordon); Robert Agnew (Dance Director); Sterling Holloway (Messenger Boy); Tammany Young (Gigolo Eddie); Ferdinand Gottschalk (Clubman); Lynn Browning (Gold Digger Girl); Charles C. Wilson (Deputy); Billy Barty ("Pettin in the Park" Baby); Fred Toones, Theresa Harris (Black Couple); Joan Barclay (Chorus Girl); Wallace MacDonald (Stage Manager); Charles Lane, Wilbur Mack, Grace Hayle (Society Reporters); Hobart Cavanaugh (Dog Salesman); Bill Elliott (Dance Extra); Dennis O'Keefe (Extra during Intermission); Busby Berkeley (Call Boy); Fred Kelsey (Detective Jones); Frank Mills (First Forgotten Man); Etta Moten ("Forgotten Man" Singer); Billy West (Medal of Honor Winner).

PROFESSIONAL SWEETHEART   (RKO, 1933) 70 M.

Producer, Merian C. Cooper; director, William Seiter; story-screenplay, Maurine Watkins; song, Edward Eliscu and Harry Akst; camera, Edward Cronjager; editor, James Morley.

Ginger Rogers (Glory Eden); Betty Furness (Reporter); Gregory Ratoff (Ispwich); Sterling Holloway (A Scribe); Frank McHugh (Speed); ZaSu Pitts (Elmerada de Leon); Allen Jenkins (O'Connor); Norman Foster (Jim Davey); Edgar Kennedy (Kelsey); Lucien Littlefield (Announcer); Franklin Pangborn (Childress); Frank Darien (Appleby); Theresa Harris (Maid).

239

A SHRIEK IN THE NIGHT (Allied, 1933) 64 M.

Director, Albert Ray; story, Kurt Kempler; story, Frances Hyland; camera, Harry Neumann, Tom Galligan; editor, L. R. Brown.

Ginger Rogers (Patricia Morgan); Lyle Talbot (Ted Rand); Arthur Hoyt (Wilfred); Prunell Pratt (Inspector Russell); Harvey Clark (Janitor); Lillian Harmer (Augusta); Maurice Black (Martini); Louise Beavers (Maid); Clarence Wilson (Editor Perkins).

DON'T BET ON LOVE (Univ., 1933) 62 M.

Director-story, Murray Roth; screenplay, Roth, Howard Emmett Rogers; sound, Gilbert Kurland; camera, Jackson Rose; editor, Robert Carlisle.

Lew Ayres (Bill McCaffery); Ginger Rogers (Molly); Charles Grapewin (Pop McCaffery); Merna Kennedy (Ruby); Thomas Dugan (Scotty); Robert Emmett O'Connor (Sheldon); Lucile Webster Gleason (Mrs. Gilbert).

SITTING PRETTY (Par., 1933) 85 M.

Producer, Charles R. Rogers; director, Harry Joe Brown; story suggested by Nina Wilcox Putnam; screenplay, Jack McGowan, S. J. Perelman, Lou Breslow; choreography, Larry Ceballos; songs, Mack Gordon and Harry Revel; camera, Milton Krasner.

Jack Oakie (Chick Parker); Jack Haley (Pete Pendleton); Ginger Rogers (Dorothy); Thelma Todd (Gloria Duval); Gregory Ratoff (Tannenbaum); Lew Cody (Jules Clark); Harry Revel (Harry, the Pianist); Jerry Tucker (Buzz); Mack Gordon (Meyers, the Song Publisher); Hale Hamilton (Vinton); Walter Walker (George Wilson); Kenneth Thomson (Norman Lubin); William B. Davidson (Director); Lee Moran (Assistant Director); The Pickens Sisters, Arthur Jarrett, Virginia Sale (Guest Stars); Irving Bacon, Stuart Holmes (Dice Players); Fuzzy Knight (Stock Clerk); Harvey Clark (Motorist); Wade Boteler (Jackson, Aide to Wilson); Russ Powell (Counterman); Frank La Rue (Studio Gateman); Charles Williams, George and Olive Brasno (Neighbors); Sidney Bracy (Manager); Rollo Lloyd (Director); Lee Phelps (Studio Aide); Harry C. Bradley (Set Designer); Phil Tead (Aide); Dave O'Brien (Assistant Cameraman); Jack Mower (Clark's Aide, a Bouncer); Henry Hall, Larry Steers (Party Guests); Charles Coleman (Butler); Frank Hagney (Bar Manager); James Burtis (Foreman of Movers).

FLYING DOWN TO RIO (RKO, 1933) 89 M.

Executive producer, Merian C. Cooper; associate producer, Lou Brock; director, Thornton Freeland; based on a play by Anne Caldwell, from an original story by Brock; screenplay, Cyril Hume, H. W. Hanemann, Erwin Gelsey; art director, Van Nest Polglase, Carroll Clark; music director, Max Steiner; choreography, Dave Gould; songs, Vincent Youmans, Edward Eliscu, and Gus Kahn; sound, P. J. Faulkner; costumes, Walter Plunkett; camera effects, Vernon Walker; camera, J. Roy Hunt; editor, Jack Kitchin.

Dolores Del Rio (Belinha de Rezende); Gene Raymond (Roger Bond); Raoul Rouline (Julio Rubeiro); Ginger Rogers (Honey Hale); Fred Astaire (Fred Ayres); Blanche Frederici (Dona Elena); Walter Walker (Senor de Rezende); Etta Moten (Black Singer); Roy D'Arcy, Maurice Black, Armand Kaliz (The Three Greeks); Paul Porcasi (Mayor); Reginald Barlow (Banker); Eric Blore (Butterbass, the Head Waiter); Franklin Pangborn (Hammersmith, the Hotel Manager); Luis Alberni (Carioca Casino Manager); Jack Goode, Jack Rice, Eddie Borden (Yankee Clippers); Alice Gentle (Concert Singer); Martha La Venture (Dancer); Ray Cooke (Banjoist); Harry Bowen (Airport Mechanic); Lucile Browne, Mary Kornman (Belinha's Friends); Sidney Bracy (Rodriquez, the Chauffeur); Clarence Muse (Caddy in "Haiti"); Movita Castaneda (Singer); Harry Semels (Sign Poster); Manuel Paris (Extra at Aviator's Club); Gino Corrado (Messenger); Adrian Rosley (Club Manager); Wallace MacDonald (Pilot who Performs Marriage); The American Clippers Band, The Brazilian Turunas

(Themselves); Howard Wilson, Betty Furness, Francisco Maran, Helen Collins, Carol Tevis, Eddie Tamblyn, Alice Ardell, Rafael Alivir, Barbara Sheldon, Douglas Williams, Alma Travers, Juan Duval, Eddie Boland, Julian Rivero, Pedro Regas (Bits).

CHANCE AT HEAVEN   (RKO, 1933) 70 M.

Producer, Merian C. Cooper; associate producer, H. N. Swanson; director, William Seiter; based on the story by Vina Delmar; screenplay, Julian Josephson, Sarah Y. Mason; art director, Van Nest Polglase, Perry Ferguson; music director, Max Steiner; sound, Forrest Perley; camera, Nick Musuraca; editor, James B. Morley.

Ginger Rogers (Marje Harris); Joel McCrea (Blacky Gorman); Andy Devine (Al); Marion Nixon (Glory Franklyn); Virginia Hammond (Mrs. Franklyn); Lucien Littlefield (Mr. Harris); Ann Shoemaker (Mrs. Harris); George Meeker (Sid Larick); Betty Furness (Betty); Herman Bing (Chauffeur); Harry Bowen (First Reporter).

RAFTER ROMANCE   (RKO, 1934) 72 M.

Director, William Seiter; story, John Wells; screenplay, H. W. Hanneman, Sam Mintz, Glenn Tryon; camera, David Abel; editor, James Morley.

Ginger Rogers (Mary Carroll); Norman Foster (Jack Baron); George Sidney (Max Eckbaum); Robert Benchley (Hubbell); Laura Hope Crews (Elise); Guinn Williams (Fritzie).

FINISHING SCHOOL   (RKO, 1934) 73 M.

Executive Producer, Merian C. Cooper; associate producer, Kenneth MacGowan; director, Wanda Tuchock, George Nicholls, Jr.; story, David Hempstead; screenplay, Tuchock, Laird Doyle; music, Max Steiner; art director, Van Nest Polglase, Al D'Agostino; camera, J. Roy Hunt; editor, Arthur Schmidt.

Frances Dee (Virginia); Billie Burke (Mrs. Radcliff); Ginger Rogers (Pony); Bruce Cabot (MacFarland); John Halliday (Mr. Radcliff); Buelah Bondi (Miss Van Alstyn); Sara Haden (Miss Fisher); Marjorie Lytell (Ruth); Adalyn Doyle (Madeline); Dawn O'Day (Billie); Claire Myers, Susanne Thompson, Edith Vale (Girls); Rose Coghlan (Miss Garland); Irene Franklin (Aunt Jessica); Ann Cameron (Miss Schmidt); Caroline Rankin (Miss Weber).

20 MILLION SWEETHEARTS   (FN, 1934) 89 M.

Director, Ray Enright; story, Paul Finder Moss, Jerry Wald; screenplay, Warren Duff, Harry Sauber; songs, Harry Warren and Al Dubin; camera, Sid Hickox; editor, Clarence Kolster.

Dick Powell (Buddy Clayton); Pat O'Brien (Rush Blake); Ginger Rogers (Peggy Cornell); Four Mills Brothers, Ted Fio Rito and His Band, The Radio Rogues (Themselves); Allen Jenkins (Pete); Grant Mitchell (Chester A. Sharpe); Joseph Cawthorn (Herbert Brockman); Leo Forbstein (Conductor); Bill Ray (Announcer); Marjorie Briggs, Dorothy Hill, Betty Noyes (Debutantes); Grace Hayle (Martha Brockman); Muzzy Marcellino (Himself); Bob Perry (Cafe Manager); Nora Cecil (Lady in Bed); Charles Sullivan (Cabby); Milton Kibbee (Pete's Announcer); Charles Lane (Reporter); Sam MacDaniel (Deacon, the Waiter); William Davidson (Woodcliff Inn Manager); George Humbert (Headwaiter); Eddie Kane, William Elliott (Boys in Perry's); Jean Wheeler (Marge); Henry O'Neill (Lemuel Tappan); Johnny Arthur (Secretary).

CHANGE OF HEART   (Fox, 1934) 74 M.

Director, John G. Blystone; based on the novel *Manhattan Love Song* by Kathleen Norris; screenplay, Sonya Levien, James Gleason, Samuel Hoffenstein; song, Harry Akst; camera, Joseph Aiken; editor, Margaret Clancy.

Janet Gaynor (Catherine Furness); Charles Farrell (Chris Thring); James Dunn (Mac McGowan); Ginger Rogers (Madge Rountree); Beryl Mercer (Harriet Hawkins); Gustav von Seyffertitz (Dr. Kreutzmann); Shirley Temple (Shirley); Irene Franklin (Greta Hailstrom).

UPPERWORLD   (WB, 1934) 75 M.

Director, Roy Del Ruth; based on the sotry by Ben Hecht; screenplay, Ben Markson; art director, Anton Grot; gowns, Orry-Kelly; Vitaphone Orchestra conductor, Leo F. Forbstein; camera, Tony Gaudio; editor, Owen Marks.

Warren William (Alexander Stream); Mary Astor (Hettie Stream); Ginger Rogers (Linda); Andy Devine (Oscar, the Chauffeur); Theodore Newton (Rocklen); Henry O'Neill (Banker); Robert Barrat (Commissioner Clark); Dickie Moore (Tommy Stream); J. Carrol Naish (Lou Colima); Sidney Toler (Officer Moran); Ferdinand Gottschalk (Marcus); Rogert Greig (Caldwell, the Butler); Willard Robertson (Captain Reynolds); John M. Qualen (Chris, the Janitor); Frank Sheridan (Inspector Kellogg); Nora Cecil (Housekeeper); Lester Dorr (Steward); Wilfred Lucas (Captain); Cliff Saum (Sailor); William Jeffrey (Bradley); Edward Le Saint (Henshaw); Armand Kaliz (Maurice); John Elliott (Crandall); Milton Kibbee (Pilot); Marie Astaire, Loyce Owen, Lucille Collins (Chorus Girls); Douglas Cosgrove (Johnson); Guy Usher (Captain Carter); Jay Eaton (Salesman); James P. Burtis, Henry Otho (Cops); Clay Clement (Medical Examiner); James Durkin, Monte Vandergrift; Jack Cheatham (Detectives); William B. Davidson (City Editor); Edwin Stanley (Joe, the Fingerprint Expert); Howard Hickman (Judge); Frank Conroy (Attorney); Tom McGuire (Bailiff); Bert Moorhouse (Court Clerk); Sidney DeGrey (Foreman).

THE GAY DIVORCEE   (RKO, 1934) 107 M.

Producer, Pandro S. Berman; director, Mark Sandrich; based on the novel and play *Gay Divorce* by Dwight Taylor; musical adaptation, Kenneth Webb, Samuel Hoffenstein; screenplay, George Marion, Jr., Dorothy Yost, Edward Kaufman; music director, Max Steiner; choreography, Dave Gould; songs, Cole Porter; Con Conrad and Herb Magidson; Mack Gordon and Harry Revel; art director, Van Nest Polglase, Carroll Clark; costumes, Walter Plunkett; sound, Hugh McDowell, Jr.; camera effects, Vernon Walker; camera, David Abel; editor, William Hamilton.

Fred Astaire (Guy Holden); Ginger Rogers (Mimi Glossop); Alice Brady (Hortense Ditherwell); Edward Everett Horton (Egbert Fitzgerald); Erik Rhodes (Rodolfo Tonetti); Betty Grable (Dancer); Charles Coleman (Guy's Valet); William Austin (Cyril Glossop); Paul Porcasi (French Headwaiter); E. E. Clive (Chief Customs Inspector); Charles Hall (Call Boy at Dock); Lillian Miles (Guest); George Davis, Alphonse Martell (French Waiters).

ROMANCE IN MANHATTAN   (RKO, 1934) 78 M.

Producer, Pandro S. Berman; director, Stephen Roberts; story, Norman Krasna, Don Hartman; adaptation, Jane Murfin, Edward Kaufman; music director, Al Colombo; camera, Nick Musuraca; editor, Jack Hively.

Francis Lederer (Karel Novak); Ginger Rogers (Sylvia Dennis); Arthur Hohl (Attorney Pander); Jimmy Butler (Frank Dennis); J. Farrell MacDonald (Officer Murphy); Helen Ware (Miss Anthrop); Eily Malyon (Miss Evans); Lillian Harmer (Landlady); Donald Meek (The Minister); Sidney Toler (Police Sergeant); Oscar Apfel (Judge); Reginald Barlow (Chief Customs Inspector); Christian Rub (Immigrant); Frank Sheridan (Customs Inspector); Irving Bacon (Counterman); Andy Clyde (Scotch Liquor Store Owner).

ROBERTA   (RKO, 1935) 105 M.

Producer, Pandro S. Berman; director, William A. Seiter; based on the novel *Gowns by Roberta* by Alice Duer Miller, and the musical play *Roberta* by Jerome Kern and Otto Harbach; screenplay, Jane Murfin, Sam Mintz; additional dialog, Glenn Tryon, Allan Scott; choreography, Fred Astaire; ensemble director, Hermes Pan; music director, Max Steiner; art director, Van Nest Polglase, Carroll Clark; set decorator, Thomas K. Little; songs, Kern and Harbach; Kern and Bernard Dougall; Kern, Oscar Hammerstein II, Dorothy Fields, and Jimmy McHugh; Kern, Fields, and McHugh; gowns, Bernard Newman; sound John Tribby; camera, Edward Cronjager; editor, William Hamilton.

Irene Dunne (Stephanie); Fred Astaire (Huck); Ginger Rogers (Countess Scharwenka [Lizzie Gatz]); Randolph Scott (John Kent); Helen Westley (Roberta [Aunt Minnie]); Victor Varconi (Ladislaw); Claire Dodd (Sophie); Luis Alberni (Voyda); Ferdinand Munier (Lord Delves); Torben Meyer (Albert); Adrian Rosley (Professor); Bodil Rosing (Fernando); Lucille Ball, Jane Hamilton, Margaret McChrystal, Kay Sutton, Maxine Jennings, Virginia Reid, Lorna Low, Lorraine DeSart, Wanda Perry, Diane Cook, Virginia Carroll, Betty Dumbries, Donna Roberts (Mannequins); Mike Tellegen, Sam Savitsky (Cossacks); Zena Savine (Woman); Johnny "Candy" Candido, Muzzi Marcellino, Gene Sheldon, Howard Lally, William Carey, Paul McLarind, Hal Bown, Charles Sharpe, Ivan Dow, Phil Cuthbert, Delmon Davis, William Dunn (Orchestra); Judith Vosselli, Rita Gould (Bits); Mary Forbes (Mrs. Teal); William B. Davidson (Purser); Grace Hayle (Reporter); Dale Van Sickel (Dance Extra).

STAR OF MIDNIGHT   (RKO, 1935) 90 M.

Producer, Pandro S. Berman; director, Stephen Roberts; based on the novel by Arthur Somers Roche; screenplay, Howard J. Green, Anthony Veiller, Edward Kaufman; music director, Max Steiner; camera, J. Roy Hunt; editor, Arthur Roberts.

William Powell (Clay Dalzell); Ginger Rogers (Donna Mantin); Paul Kelly (Kinland); Gene Lockhart (Swayne); Ralph Morgan (Mr. Classon); Leslie Fenton (Tim Winthrop); J. Farrell MacDonald (Doremus); Russell Hopton (Tommy Tennant); Vivien Oakland (Mrs. Classon); Frank Reicher (Abe Ohlman); Sidney Toler (Cleary); Francis McDonald (Kinland Gangster); Paul Hurst (Corbett); Spencer Charters (Doorman); George Chandler (Witness); Charles McMurphy (Officer Lewis); Hooper Atchley (Hotel Manager); John Ince (Doctor).

TOP HAT   (RKO, 1935) 101 M.

Producer, Pandro S. Berman; director, Mark Sandrich; based on the play *Gay Divorce* by Dwight Taylor and a play by Alexander Farago and Aladar Laszlo; screenplay, Taylor Allan Scott; choreography, Fred Astaire; ensemble director, Hermes Pan; art director, Van Nest Polglase, Carroll Clark; set decorator, Thomas K. Little; costumes, Bernard Newman; songs, Irving Berlin; music director, Max Steiner; sound, Hugh McDowell, Jr.; special effects, Vernon L. Walker; camera, David Abel; editor, William Hamilton.

Fred Astaire (Jerry Travers); Ginger Rogers (Dale Tremont); Edward Everett Horton (Horace Hardwick); Helen Broderick (Madge Hardwick); Erik Rhodes (Alberto Beddini); Eric Blore (Bates); Lucille Ball (Flower Girl); Leonard Mudie (Flower Salesman); Donald Meek (Curate); Florence Roberts (Curate's Wife); Edgar Norton (London Hotel Manager); Gino Corrado (Toledo Hotel Manager); Peter Hobbes (Call Boy); Ben Holmes, Nick Thompson, Tom Costello, John Impolite, Genaro Spagnoli, Rita Rozelle, Phyllis Coghlan, Charles Hall (Bits); Dennis O'Keefe (Elevator Extra).

IN PERSON   (RKO, 1935) 85 M.

Producer, Pandro S. Berman; director, William A. Seiter; based on the novel by Samuel Hopkins Adams; screenplay, Allan Scott; camera, Edward Cronjager; editor, Arthur Schmidt.

Ginger Rogers (Carol Corliss); George Brent (Emory Muir); Alan Mowbray (Jay Holmes); Grant Mitchell (Judge Thaddeus Parks); Samuel S. Hinds (Dr. Aaron Sylvester); Joan Breslau (Minna); Louis Mason (Sheriff Twing); Spencer Charters ("Parson" Lunk); Bob McKenzie (Theatre Manager); Lee Shumway (Studio Representative); Lew Kelly (Man Giving Directions); William B. Davidson (Bill Sumner, the Director).

FOLLOW THE FLEET   (RKO, 1936) 110 M.

Producer, Pandro S. Berman; director, Mark Sandrich; based on the play *Shore Leave* by Hubert Osborne; screenplay, Dwight Taylor, Allan Scott; songs, Irving Berlin; music director, Max Steiner; choreography, Hermes Pan; art director, Van Nest Polglase, Carroll Clark; set decorator, Darrell Silvera; gowns, Bernard Newman; technical advisor, Lt. Commander Harvey Haislip; sound, Hugh McDowell; special effects, Vernon Walker; camera, David Abel; editor, Henry Berman.

Fred Astaire (Bake Baker); Ginger Rogers (Sherry Martin); Randolph Scott (Bilge Smith); Harriet Hilliard (Connie Martin); Ray Mayer (Dopey); Astrid Allwyn (Iris Manning); Harry Beresford (Captain Hickey); Jack Randall (Lieutenant Williams); Russell Hicks (Jim Nolan); Brooks Benedict (Sullivan); Lucille Ball (Kitty Collins); Betty Grable, Joy Hodges, Jennie Gray (Trio); Tony Martin, Edward Burns, Frank Jenks, Frank Mills (Sailors); Jane Hamilton (Waitress); Maxine Jennings (Hostess); Herbert Rawlinson (Webber).

SWING TIME   (RKO, 1936) 103 M.

Producer, Pandro S. Berman; director, George Stevens; story, Erwin Gelsey; screenplay, Howard Lindsay, Allan Scott; songs, Jerome Kern and Dorothy Fields; music director, Nathaniel Shilkret; ensemble director, Hermes Pan; choreography, Fred Astaire; art director, Van Nest Polglase, Carroll Clark; special settings-costumes, John Harkrider; set decorator, Darrell Silvera; gowns, Bernard Newman; sound, Hugh McDowell; special effects, Vernon Walker; camera, David Abel; editor, Henry Berman.

Fred Astaire (John "Lucky" Garnett); Ginger Rogers (Penelope "Penny" Carrol); Victor Moore (Dr. Cardetti [Pop]); Helen Broderick (Mabel Anderson); Eric Blore (Mr. Gordon); Betty Furness (Margaret Watson); George Metaxa (Ricardo Romero); Landers Stevens (Judge Watson); John Harrington (Dice Raymond); Pierre Watkin (Al Simpson); Abe Reynolds (Schmidt); Gerald Hamer (Eric); Edgar Dearing (Policeman); Harry Bowen, Harry Bernard (Stagehands); Donald Kerr, Jack Good, Ted O'Shea, Frank Edmunds, Bill Brand (Dancers); Frank Jenks (Red); Ralph Byrd (Hotel Clerk); Charles Hall (Taxi Driver); Jean Perry (Dealer); Olin Francis (Muggsy); Floyd Schackleford (Romero's Butler); Ferdinand Munier (Minister); Joey Ray (Announcer); Jack Rice (Wedding Guest).

SHALL WE DANCE   (RKO, 1937) 116 M.

Producer, Pandro S. Berman; director, Mark Sandrich; suggested by the story "Watch Your Step" by Lee Loeb, Harold Buchman; screenplay, Allan Scott, Ernest Pagano, P. J. Wolfson; music director, Nathaniel Shilkret; songs, George and Ira Gershwin; ensemble director, Hermes Pan; ballet director, Larry Losee; art director, Van Nest Polglase, Carroll Clark; set decorator, Darrell Silvera; gowns for Miss Rogers, Irene; sound, Hugh McDowell; special effects, Vernon L. Walker; camera, David Abel; editor, William Hamilton.

Fred Astaire (Petrov [Pete Peters]); Ginger Rogers (Linda Keene); Edward Everett Horton (Jeffrey Baird); Eric Blore (Cecil Flintridge); Jerome Cowan (Arthur Miller); Ketti Gallian (Lady Tarrington); William Brisbane (Jim Montgomery); Harriet Hoctor (Herself); Ann Shoemaker (Mrs. Fitzgerald); Ben Alexander (Bandleader); Emma Young (Tai); Sherwood Bailey (Newsboy); Pete Theodore (Dancing Partner); Marek Windheim, Rolfe Sedan (Ballet Masters); Charles Coleman (Cop in Park); Frank Moran (Charlie, the Big Man).

STAGE DOOR   (RKO, 1937) 92 M.

Associate producer, Pandro S. Berman; director, Gregory La Cava; based on the play by Edna Ferber, George S. Kaufman; screenplay, Morrie Ryskind, Anthony Veiller; art director, Van Nest Polglase, Carroll Clark; set decorator, Darrell Silvera; assistant director, James Anderson; makeup, Mel Burns; costumes, Muriel King; music, Roy Webb; sound, John L. Cass; camera, Robert De Grasse; editor, William Hamilton.

Katharine Hepburn (Terry Randall); Ginger Rogers (Jean Maitland); Adolphe Menjou (Anthony Powell); Gail Patrick (Linda Shaw); Constance Collier (Catherine Luther); Andrea Leeds (Kaye Hamilton); Samuel S. Hinds (Henry Sims); Lucille Ball (Judy Canfield); Pierre Watkin (Richard Carmichael); Franklin Pangborn (Harcourt); Elizabeth Dunne (Mrs. Orcutt); Phyllis Kennedy (Hattie); Grady Sutton (Butcher); Jack Carson (Milbank); Fred Santley (Dukenfield); William Corson (Billy); Frank Reicher (Stage Director); Eve Arden (Eve); Ann Miller (Annie); Jane Rhodes (Ann Braddock); Margaret Early (Mary); Norma Drury (Olga Brent); Jean Rouverol (Dizzy); Harriet Brandon (Madeline); Peggy O'Donnell (Susan); Katharine Alexander, Ralph Forbes, Mary Forbes, Huntley Gordon (Cast of Play); Lynton Brent (Aide); Theodor Von Eltz (Elsworth); Jack Rice (Playwright); Harry Strang (Chauffeur); Bob Perry (Baggageman); Larry Steers (Theatre Patron); Mary Board, Frances Gifford (Actresses); Whitey the Cat (Eve's Cat).

HAVING WONDERFUL TIME   (RKO, 1938) 70 M.

Producer, Pandro S. Berman; director, Alfred Santell; based on the play by Arthur Kober; screenplay, Kober; music director, Roy Webb; songs, Sam Stept and Charles Tobias; camera, Robert de Grasse; editor, William Hamilton.

Ginger Rogers (Teddy); Douglas Fairbanks, Jr. (Chick); Peggy Conklin (Fay); Lucille Ball (Miriam); Lee Bowman (Buzzy); Eve Arden (Henrietta); Dorothea Kent (Maxine); Richard "Red" Skelton (Itchy); Donald Meek (P. U. Rogers); Jack Carson (Emil Beatty); Clarence H. Wilson (Mac); Grady Sutton (Gus); Shimen Ruskin (Shrimpo); Dorothy Tree (Frances); Leona Roberts (Mrs. Shaw); Harlan Briggs (Mr. Shaw); Inez Courtney (Emma); Juanita Quigley (Mabel); Ann Miller (Vivian); Kirk Windsor (Henry); Hooper Atchley, Ronnie Rondell (Subway Riders); Dean Jagger (Charlie); George Meeker (Fresh Subway Rider).

VIVACIOUS LADY   (RKO, 1938) 90 M.

Executive producer, Pandro S. Berman; producer-director, George Stevens; story, I. A. R. Wylie; screenplay, P. J. Wolfson, Ernest Pagano; art director, Van Nest Polglase; music, Roy Webb; song, George Jessel, Jack Meskill, and Ted Shapiro; camera, Robert de Grasse; editor, Henry Berman.

Ginger Rogers (Francey); James Stewart (Peter); James Ellison (Keith); Beulah Bondi (Mrs. Morgan); Charles Coburn (Mr. Morgan); Frances Mercer (Helen); Phyllis Kennedy (Jenny); Franklin Pangborn (Apartment Manager); Grady Sutton (Culpepper); Jack Carson (Waiter Captain); Alec Craig (Joseph); Lee Bennett (Student);

Willie Best (Porter); June Johnson (Miss Barton); Tom Quinn (Maitre d'); Vinton Haworth (Druggist); Frank M. Thomas (Conductor); Spencer Charters, Maude Eburne (Couple in Pullman); Lee Bennett (Dance Extra); Hattie McDaniel (Hattie); Lloyd Ingraham (Professor Noble); Ed Mortimer (Professor).

CAREFREE (RKO, 1938) 83 M.

Producer, Pandro S. Berman; director, Mark Sandrich; story, Marian Ainslee, Guy Endore; adaptation, Dudley Nichols, Hagar Wilde; screenplay, Ernest Pagano, Allan Scott; ensemble stager, Hermes Pan; assistant director, Argyle Nelson; songs, Irving Berlin; music director, Victor Baravalle; art director, Van Nest Polglase, Carroll Clark; set decorator, Darrell Silvera; gowns for Miss Rogers, Howard Greer; costumes, Edward Stevenson; sound, Hugh McDowell; special effects, Vernon L. Walker; camera, Robert de Grasse; editor, William Hamilton.

Fred Astaire (Dr. Tony Flagg); Ginger Rogers (Amanda Cooper); Ralph Bellamy (Stephen Arden); Luella Gear (Aunt Cora); Jack Carson (Connors); Clarence Kolb (Judge Travers); Franklin Pangborn (Roland Hunter); Walter Kingsford (Dr. Powers); Kay Sutton (Miss Adams); Tom Tully (Policeman); Hattie McDaniel (Maid); Robert B. Mitchell and St. Brendan's Boys Choir (Themselves).

THE STORY OF VERNON AND IRENE CASTLE (RKO, 1939) 90 M.

Executive producer, Pandro S. Berman; producer, George Haight; director, H. C. Potter; based on stories by Irene Castle; adaptation, Oscar Hammerstein, Dorothy Yost; screenplay, Richard Sherman; songs, Bert Kalmar and Harry Ruby; Harold Atteridge and Harry Carroll; Colin Davis and Karl Hoschna; Albert Bryan and Fred Fisher; A. Seymour Brown and Nat D. Ayer; Otto Harbach and Karl Hoschna; Joseph McCarthy and Jimmy Monaco; L. Wolfe Gilbert and Lewis E. Muir; Shelton Brooks; Cecil Macklin; Fisher; Worton David and Bert Lee; Con Conrad, Herman Ruby, and Bert Kalmar; choreography, Hermes Pan; music, Victor Baravelle; assistant director, Argyle Nelson; technical advisor, Irene Castle; special effects, Vernon Walker, Douglas Travers; camera, Robert de Grasse; editor, William Hamilton.

Fred Astaire (Vernon Castle); Ginger Rogers (Irene Castle); Edna May Oliver (Maggie Sutton); Walter Brennan (Walter); Lew Fields (Himself); Etienne Girardot (Papa Aubel); Janet Beecher (Mrs. Foote); Rolfe Sedan (Emile Aubel); Leonid Kinskey (Artist); Robert Strange (Dr. Foote); Douglas Walton (Student Pilot); Clarence Derwent (Papa Louis); Sonny Lamont (Charlie); Frances Mercer (Claire Ford); Victor Varconi (Grand Duke); Donald MacBride (Hotel Manager); Marge Champion (Girl Friend).

BACHELOR MOTHER (RKO, 1939) 81 M.

Executive producer, Pandro S. Berman; producer, B. G. De Sylva; director, Garson Kanin; story, Felix Jackson; screenplay, Norman Krasna; assistant director, Edward Killy; special effects, Vernon Walker; camera, Robert de Grasse; editor, Henry Berman, Robert Wise.

Ginger Rogers (Polly Parrish); David Niven (David Merlin); Charles Coburn (J. B. Merlin); Frank Albertson (Freddie Miller); E. E. Clive (Butler); Elbert Coplen, Jr. (Johnnie); Ferike Boros (Mrs. Weiss); Ernest Truex (Investigator); Leonard Penn (Jerome Weiss); Paul Stanton (Hargraves); Frank M. Thomas (Doctor); Edna Holland (Matron); Dennie Moore (Mary); June Wilkins (Louise King); Donald Duck (Himself).

FIFTH AVENUE GIRL (RKO, 1939) 82 M.

Producer-director, Gregory La Cava; story, Allan Scott; assistant director, Edward Killy; camera, Robert de Grasse; editor, William Hamilton, Robert Wise.

Ginger Rogers (Mary Grey); Walter Connolly (Mr. Borden); Verree Teasdale (Mrs. Borden); James Ellison (Mike); Tim Holt (Tim Borden); Kathryn Adams (Katherine Borden); Franklin Pangborn (Higgins); Ferike Boros (Olga); Louis Calhern (Dr. Kessler); Jack Carson (Sailor in Park); Theodor Von Eltz (Terwilliger); Alexander D'Arcy (Maitre d'Hotel).

PRIMROSE PATH   (RKO, 1940) 92 M.

Producer-director, Gregory La Cava; based on the play by Robert L. Buckner, Walter Hart and the novel *February Hill* by Victoria Lincoln; screenplay, Allan Scott, La Cava; assistant director, Edward Killy; special effects, Vernon L. Walker; camera, Joseph H. August; editor, William Hamilton.

Ginger Rogers (Ellie May Adams); Joel McCrea (Ed Wallace); Marjorie Rambeau (Mamie Adams); Henry Travers (Gramp); Miles Mander (Homer); Queenie Vassar (Grandma); Joan Carroll (Honeybell); Vivienne Osborne (Thelma); Carmen Morales (Carmelita).

LUCKY PARTNERS   (RKO, 1940) 98 M.

Producer, Harry E. Edington; director, Lewis Milestone; based on the story "Bonne Chance" by Sacha Guitry; screenplay, Allan Scott, John Van Druten; art director, Van Nest Polglase; music, Dimitri Tiomkin; assistant director, Argyle Nelson; special effects, Vernon L. Walker; camera, Robert de Grasse; editor, Henry Berman.

Ronald Colman (David); Ginger Rogers (Jean); Jack Carson (Freddie); Spring Byington (Aunt); Cecilia Loftus (Mrs. Sylvester); Harry Davenport (Judge); Hugh O'Connell (Niagara Clerk); Brandon Tynan (Mr. Sylvester); Leon Belasco (Nick#1); Edward Conrad (Nick#2); Lucile Gleason (Ethel's Mother); Helen Lynd (Ethel); Walter Kingsford (Wendell); Otto Hoffman (Clerk); Alex Melesh (Art Salesman); Dorothy Adams (Maid in Apartment); Frank Mills (Bus Driver); Murray Alper, Billy Benedict (Bellboys); Al Hill (Motor Cop); Robert Dudley (Bailiff); Grady Sutton (Reporter); Nora Cecil (Club Woman); Harlan Briggs (Mayor).

KITTY FOYLE   (RKO, 1940) 105 M.

Producer, David Hempstead; director, Sam Wood; based on the novel by Christopher Morley; screenplay, Dalton Trumbo; additional dialog, Donald Ogden Stewart; assistant director, Argyle Nelson; art director, Van Nest Polglase; music, Roy Webb; special effects, Vernon L. Walker; camera, Robert de Grasse; editor, Henry Berman.

Ginger Rogers (Kitty Foyle); Dennis Morgan (Wyn Strafford); James Craig (Mark); Eduardo Ciannelli (Giono); Ernest Cossart (Pop); Gladys Cooper (Mrs. Strafford); Odette Myrtil (Delphine Detaille); Mary Treen (Pat); Katharine Stevens (Molly); Walter Kingsford (Mr. Kennett); Cecil Cunningham (Grandmother); Nella Walker (Aunt Jessica); Edward Fielding (Uncle Edgar); Kay Linaker (Wyn's Wife); Richard Nichols (Wyn's Boy); Florence Bates (Customer); Heather Angel (Girl in Prologue); Tyler Brooke (Boy in Prologue); Frank Milan (Parry); Charles Quigley (Bill); Ray Teal (Saxophonist); Joey Ray (Drummer); Joe Bernard, Tom Herbert (Waiters); Hilda Plowright (Nurse); Helen Lynd (Girl in Elevator); Spencer Charters (Father); Frank Mills (Taxi Driver).

TOM, DICK AND HARRY   (RKO, 1941) 86 M.

Producer, Robert Sisk; director, Garson Kanin; story-screenplay, Paul Jarrico; special effects, Vernon L. Walker; camera, Merrit Gerstad; editor, John Sturges.

Ginger Rogers (Janie); George Murphy (Tom); Alan Marshal (Dick Hamilton); Burgess Meredith (Harry); Joe Cunningham (Pop); Jane Seymour (Ma); Lenore Lonergan (Babs); Vicki Lester (Paula); Betty Breckenridge (Gertrude); Phil Silvers

(Ice Cream Man); Sid Skolsky (Announcer); Edna Holland (Miss Schlom); Jack Briggs (Boy); Jane Patten (Girl); Jane Woodworth (Bit); Gus Glassmire (Music Store Proprietor); Netta Packer (Sales Clerk); Tommy Seidel, Jane Woodworth (Bits); Ellen Lowe (Matron); Sarah Edwards (Mrs. Burton); Gertrude Short (Bridge Matron); Edward Colebrook (Stalled Car Driver); Gayle Mellott (Brenda); Dorothy Lloyd (Gypsy Oracle); Maurice Brierre (French Waiter); Lurene Tuttle (Girl Lead).

ROXIE HART   (20th, 1942) 72 M.

Producer, Nunnally Johnson; director, William A. Wellman; based on the play *Chicago* by Maurine Watkins; screenplay, Johnson; choreography, Hermes Pan; art director, Richard Day, Wiard B. Ihrien; set decorator, Thomas Little; costumes, Gwen Wakeling; makeup, Guy Pearce; sound, Alfred Bruzler, Roger Heman; camera, Leon Shamroy; editor, James B. Clark.

Ginger Rogers (Roxie Hart); Adolphe Menjou (Billy Flynn); George Montgomery (Homer Howard); Lynne Overman (Jake Callahan); Nigel Bruce (E. Clay Benham); Phil Silvers (Babe); Sara Allgood (Mrs. Morton); William Frawley (O'Malley); Michael "Ted" North (Stuart Chapman); Helene Reynolds (Velma Wall); George Chandler (Amos Hart); Charles D. Brown (Charles E. Murdock); Morris Ankrum (Martin S. Harrison); George Lessey (Judge); Iris Adrian (Gertie); Milton Parsons (Announcer); Billy Wayne (Court Clerk); Charles Williams (Photographer); Leon Belasco (Waiter); Lee Shumway, Jim Pierce, Phillip Morris, Pat O'Malley, Stanley Blystone (Policemen); Frank Orth, Alec Craig, Edward Clark (Idlers); Larry Lawson, Harry Carter (Reporters); Jack Norton (Producer); Arthur Aylesworth (Mr. Wadsworth); Margaret Seddon (Mrs. Wadsworth).

TALES OF MANHATTAN   (20th, 1942) 118 M.

Producer, Boris Morros, S. P. Eagle; director, Julien Duvivier; original stories-screenplay, Ben Hecht, Ferenc Molnar, Donald Ogden Stewart, Samuel Hoffenstein, Alan Campbell, Ladislas Fodor, Laslo Vadnay, Laszlo Gorog, Lamar Trotti, Henry Blankfort; assistant director, Robert Stillman; original music, Sol Kaplan; art director, Richard Day, Boris Leven; sound, W. D. Fleck, Roger Heman; camera, Joseph Walker; editor, Robert Bischoff.

Sequence A: Charles Boyer (Orman); Rita Hayworth (Ethel); Thomas Mitchell (Halloway); Eugene Pallette (Luther); Helene Reynolds (Actress); Robert Greig (Lazar); William Halligan (Webb); Charles Williams (Agent); Jack Chefe (Tailor); Eric Wilton (Holloway Butler).

Sequence B: Ginger Rogers (Diane); Henry Fonda (George); Cesar Romero (Harry); Gail Patrick (Ellen); Roland Young (Edgar, the Butler); Marian Martin (Squirrel); Frank Orth (Second-Hand Dealer); Connie Leon (Mary).

Sequence C: Charles Laughton (Charles Smith); Elsa Lanchester (Mrs. Smith); Victor Francen (Arturo); Christian Rub (Wilson); Adeline deWalt Reynolds (Grandmother); Sig Arno (Piccolo Player); Forbes Murray (Dignified Man); Buster Brodie (Call Boy); Frank Jaquet (Musician); Will Wright (Skeptic); Dewey Robinson (Proprietor); Frank Darien (Grandpa); Rene Austin (Susan).

Sequence D: Edward G. Robinson (Browne); George Sanders (William); James Gleason (Father Joe); Harry Davenport (Professor); James Rennie (Hank Bronson); Harry Hayden (Davis); Morris Ankrum (Judge); Don Douglas (Henderson); Mae Marsh (Molly); Barbara Lynn (Mary); Alex Pollard (Waiter); Don Brodie (Whistler); Ted Stanhope (Chauffeur); Joseph Bernard (Postman).

Sequence E: Paul Robeson (Luke); Ethel Waters (Esther); Eddie Anderson (Lazarus); J. Carrol Naish (Costello); Hall Johnson Choir (Themselves); Clarence Muse (Grandpa); George Reed (Christopher); Cordell Hickman (Nicodemus); Alberta Gary (Girl); Charles Tannen (Pilot); Phillip Hurlic (Jeff); Charles Gray (Rod); Lonnie Nichols (Brad); John Kelly (Monk).

THE MAJOR AND THE MINOR   (Par., 1942) 100 M.

Producer, Arthur Hornblow, Jr.; director, Billy Wilder; suggested by the play *Connie Goes Home* by Edward Childs Carpenter and the story "Sunny Goes Home" by Fannie Kilbourne; screenplay, Charles Brackett, Wilder; art director, Hans Dreier, Roland Anderson; music, Robert Emmett Dolan; assistant director, C. C. Coleman, Jr.; costumes, Edith Head; sound, Harold Lewis, Don Johnson; camera, Leo Tover; editor, Doane Harrison.

Ginger Rogers (Susan Applegate); Ray Milland (Major Kirby); Rita Johnson (Pamela Hill); Robert Benchley (Mr. Osborne); Diana Lynn (Lucy Hill); Edward Fielding (Colonel Hill); Frankie Thomas (Cadet Osborne); Raymond Roe (Cadet Wigton); Charles Smith (Cadet Korner); Larry Nunn (Cadet Babcock); Billy Dawson (Cadet Miller); Lela Rogers (Mrs. Applegate); Aldrich Bowker (Rev. Doyle); Boyd Irwin (Major Griscom); Byron Shores (Captain Durand); Richard Fiske (Will Duffy); Norma Varden (Mrs. Osborne); Getl Dupont (Mrs. Shackleford); Stanley Desmond (Shumaker); Dell Henderson (Doorman); Ed Peil, Sr. (Station Master); Ken Lundy (Elevator Boy); Ethel Clayton, Gloria Williams (Women); Marie Blake (Bertha); Mary Field (Mother in Railway Station); Will Wright, William Howell (Ticket Agents); Tom Dugan (Dead Beat); Carlotta Jelm (Little Girl in Train Station); George Anderson (Man with Esquire); Stanley Andrews, Emory Parnell (Conductors); Guy Wilkerson (Farmer, Truck Driver); Milton Kibbee (Station Agent); Archie Twitchell (Sergeant); Alice Keating (Nurse); Billy Ray (Cadet Summerville); Don Wilmot, Jack Lindquist, Billy Glauson, John Borgden, Bradley Hail (Cadets).

ONCE UPON A HONEYMOON   (RKO, 1942) 116 M.

Producer-director, Leo McCarey; story, McCarey, Sheridan Gibney; screenplay, Gibney; assistant director, Harry Scott; music, Robert Emmett Dolan; camera, George Barnes; editor, Theron Warth.

Ginger Rogers (Katie); Cary Grant (Pat); Walter Slezak (Baron Von Luber); Albert Dekker (LaBlanc); Albert Basserman (Borelski); Ferike Boros (Elsa); Harry Shannon (Cumberland); John Banner (Kleinoch); Natasha Lytess (Anna); Peter Seal (Polish Orderly); Alex Melesh (Hotel Clerk—Warsaw); Major Nichols, Dina Smirnova, Alex Davidoff, Leda Nicova (Travelers—Warsaw); Ace Bragunier (Plane Pilot); Emil Ostlin (German Captain); Otto Reichow (German Private); Henry Guttman, Johnny Dime (Storm Troopers); Dell Henderson (American Attaché); Carl Ekberg (Hitler); Fred Niblo (Ship Captain); Oscar Lorraine (Ship Steward); Claudine De Luc (Hotel Proprietor); Brandon Beach (Civilian); Eddie Licho (French Waiter); Joseph Kamaryt (Czech Official); Walter Stahl (Baron's Guest); Joe Diskay (Warsaw Desk Clerk); Eugene Marum (Anna's Son); Gordon Clark, Jack Martin, Manart Kippen, George Sorel, Walter Bonn, Bill Martin (German Officers); Lionel Royce (Marshall Mocha); Jacques Vanaire (French Radio Announcer); Frank Alten (Spontaneity); Boyd Davis (Chamberlin); Emory Parnell (Quisling).

TENDER COMRADE   (RKO, 1943) 101 M.

Producer, David Hempstead; associate producer, Sherman Todd; director, Edward Dmytryk; story-screenplay, Dalton Trumbo; art director, Albert S. D'Agostino, Carroll Clark; music, Leigh Harline; music director, C. Bakaleinikoff; camera, Russell Metty; editor, Roland Gross.

Ginger Rogers (Jo); Robert Ryan (Chris); Ruth Hussey (Barbara); Patricia Collinge (Helen Stacey); Mady Christians (Manya); Kim Hunter (Doris); Jane Darwell (Mrs. Henderson); Mary Forbes (Jo's Mother); Richard Martin (Mike); Richard Gaines (Waldo Pierson); Patti Brill (Western Union Girl); Euline Martin (Baby); Edward Fielding (Doctor); Claire Whitney (Nurse); Donald Davis, Robert Anderson (Boys).

LADY IN THE DARK   (Par., 1944) C—100 M.

Executive producer, B. G. De Sylva; producer, Dick Blumenthal; director, Mitchell Leisen; based on the play by Moss Hart, Kurt Weill, and Ira Gershwin; screenplay, Frances Goodrich, Albert Hackett; set decorator-costumes, Raoul Pene du Bois; art director, Hans Dreier; songs, Gershwin and Weill; Johnny Burke and Jimmy Van Heusen; Robert E. Dolan; Clifford Grey and Victor Schertzinger; special effects, Gordon Jennings; camera, Ray Rennahan; editor, Alma Macrorie.

Ginger Rogers (Liza Elliott); Ray Milland (Charley Johnson); Jon Hall (Randy Curtis); Warner Baxter (Kendall Nesbitt); Barry Sullivan (Dr. Brooks); Mischa Auer (Russell Paxton); Mary Philips (Maggy Grant); Phyllis Brooks (Allison DuBois); Edward Fielding (Dr. Carlton); Don Loper (Adams); Mary Parker (Miss Parker); Catherine Craig (Miss Foster); Marietta Canty (Martha); Virginia Farmer (Miss Edwards); Fay Helm (Miss Bowers); Gail Russell (Barbara—age 17); Kay Linaker (Liza's Mother); Harvey Stephens (Liza's Father); Rand Brooks (Ben); Pepito Perez (Clown); Charles Smith (Barbara's Boyfriend); Audrey Young, Eleanor DeVan, Jeanne Straser, Arlyne Varden, Angela Wilson, Dorothy O'Kelly, Betty Hall, Fran Shore, Lynda Grey, Christopher King, Maxine Ardell, Alice Kirby, Louise LaPlanche (Office Girls); Paul Pierce, George Mayon, James Notaro, Jacques Karre, Byron Poindexter, Kit Carson (Specialty Dancers); Bunny Waters, Susan Paley, Dorothy Ford, Mary MacLaren (Models); Paul McVey (Librarian); Marten Lamont, Tristram Coffin, Dennis Moore (Men); Jack Mulhall (Photographer); Murray Alper (Taxicab Driver); Dorothy Granger (Autograph Hunter); Emmett Vogan, Lester Dorr, Grandon Rhodes (Reporters); Johnnie Johnson, John O'Connor, Buster Brodie (Clowns); Herbert Corthell (Senator); Herb Holcomb (Aquatic Clown); Charles Bates (David); Theodore Marc (Daniel Boone Clown); Armand Tanny (Strong-Man Clown); Stuart Barlow (Accordion Clown); Leonora Johnson (Bird's Nest Clown); Harry Bayfield (Snow Clown); Larry Rio (Farmer Clown); Buz Buckley (Freckle-faced Boy); Priscilla Lyon (Little Girl at Circus); Marjean Neville (Liza—Ages 5 and 7); Phyllis Brooks (Barbara—age 7); Billy Dawson (Boy at Circus).

I'LL BE SEEING YOU   (UA, 1944) 83 M.

Producer, Dore Schary; director, William Dieterle; based on the radio play by Charles Martin; screenplay, Marion Parsonnet; song, Sammy Fain and Irving Kahal; music, Daniele Amfitheatrof; art director, Mark-Lee Kirk; camera, Tony Gaudio; editor, William H. Ziegler.

Ginger Rogers (Mary Marshall); Joseph Cotten (Zachary Morgan); Shirley Temple (Barbara Marshall); Spring Byington (Mrs. Marshall); Tom Tully (Mr. Marshall); Chill Wills (Swanson); Dare Harris (Lieutenant Bruce); Kenny Bowers, John Derek (Sailors on Train); John James (Soldier on Train).

WEEKEND AT THE WALDORF   (MGM, 1945) 130 M.

Producer, Arthur Hornblow, Jr.; director, Robert Z. Leonard; suggested by the play *Grand Hotel* by Vicki Baum; adaptation, Guy Bolton; screenplay, Sam and Bella Spewack; art director, Cedric Gibbons, Daniel B. Cathcart; set decorator, Edwin B. Willis, Jack Bonar; choreography, Charles Walters; music, Johnny Green; songs, Sammy Fain and Ted Koehler; Pepe Guizar; assistant director, William Lewis; sound, Douglas Shearer; special effects, Warren Newcombe; camera, Robert Planck; editor, Robert J. Kern.

Ginger Rogers (Irene Malvern); Walter Pidgeon (Chip Coolyer); Van Johnson (Capt. James Hollis); Lana Turner (Bunny Smith); Robert Benchley (Randy Morton); Edward Arnold (Martin X. Edley); Constance Collier (Mme. Jaleska); Leon Ames (Henry Burton); Warner Anderson (Dr. Campbell); Phyllis Thaxter (Cynthia Drew);

Keenan Wynn (Oliver Webson); Porter Hall (Stevens); Samuel S. Hinds (Mr. Jessup); George Zucco (Bey of Aribajan); Xavier Cugat (Himself); Lina Romay (Juanita); Bob Graham (Singer); Michael Kirby (Lt. John Rand); Cora Sue Collins (Jane Rand); Rosemary DeCamp (Anna); Jacqueline DeWit (Kate Douglas); Frank Puglia (Emile); Charles Wilson (Hi Johns); Irving Bacon (Sam Skelly); Miles Mander (British Secretary); Nana Bryant (Mrs. H. Davenport Drew); Russell Hicks (McPherson); Ludmilla Pitoeff (Irma); Naomi Childers (Night Maid); Moroni Olsen (House Detective Blake); William Halligan (Chief Jennings); John Wengraff (Alix); Ruth Lee (Woman); Jack Luden (Clerk); Ruth Warren, Hope Landin, Karen Lind, Gertrude Short, Jean Carpenter, Ethel King (Telephone Operators); Rex Evans (Pianist); Harry Barris (Anna's Boyfriend); Byron Foulger (Barber); Arno Frey (Maitre D'Hotel); Gordon Richards (Headwaiter); Dorothy Christy (Cashier); Dick Hirbe (Newsboy); Shirley Lew, Billie Louie (Chinese Girls); Bess Flowers, Sandra Morgan, Dick Gordon, Oliver Dross, Ella Ethridge (Guests); Charles Madrin (Assistant Hotel Manager); Kenneth Cutler (Desk Clerk); Frank McClure (Florist); Estelle Etterre (Assistant Florist); Barbara Powers (Cigarette Girl).

HEARTBEAT   (RKO, 1946) 102 M.

Producer, Robert Hakim, Raymond Hakim; director, Sam Wood; screenplay, Hans Wilhelm, Max Kolpe, Michel Duran; adaptation, Morrie Ryskind; additional dialog, Roland Leigh; production designer, Lionel Banks; set decorator, George Sawley; assistant director, John Sherwood; music, Paul Misraki; music director, C. Bakaleinikoff; songs, Misraki and Erwin Drake; sound, John Tribby; camera, Joseph Valentine; editor, Roland Gross.

Ginger Rogers (Arlette); Jean Pierre Aumont (Pierre); Adolphe Menjou (Ambassador); Basil Rathbone (Professor Gristide); Mikhail Rasumny (Yves Cadubert); Melville Cooper (Roland Medeville); Mona Maris (Ambassador's Wife); Henry Stephenson (Minister).

MAGNIFICENT DOLL   (Univ., 1946) 93 M.

Producer, Jack H. Skirball, Bruce Manning; director, Frank Borzage; story-screenplay, Irving Stone; assistant director, John F. Sherwood; art director, Alexander Golitzen; set decorator, Russell A. Gausman, Ted Offenbecker; music, Harry J. Salter; sound, Charles Felstead; camera, Joseph Valentine; editor, Ted J. Kent.

Ginger Rogers (Dolly Payne); David Niven (Aaron Burr); Burgess Meredith (James Madison); Stephen McNally (John Todd); Peggy Wood (Mrs. Payne); Frances Williams (Amy); Robert H. Barrat (Mr. Payne); Grandon Rhodes (Thomas Jefferson); Henri Letondal (Count D'Arignon); Joe Forte (Senator Ainsworth); Erville Alderson (Darcy); George Barrows (Jedson); Francis McDonald (Barber Jenks); Emmett Vogan (Mr. Gallentine); Arthur Space (Alexander Hamilton); Byron Foulger (Servant); Joseph Crehan (Williams); Larry Blake (Charles); Pierre Watkin (Harper); John Sheehan (Janitor); Ruth Lee (Mrs. Gallentine); George Carleton (Howard); Jack Ingram (Lane, the Courier); Olaf Hytten (Blennerhassett); Sam Flint (Waters); Boyd Irwin (Hathaway); Lee Phelps (Hatch, a Bettor); Lois Austin (Grace Phillips); Harlan Briggs (Quinn); John Hines (Dr. Ellis); Ferris Taylor (Mr. Phillips); Eddy Waller (Arthur, the Coachman); Stanley Blystone (Bailiff); Stanley Price (Man at Platform); Victor Zimmerman (Martin); Ja George (Governor Stanley); Ethaln Laidlaw (Sanders, a Soldier); Mary Emery (Woman); Carey Hamilton (Senator Mason); Dick Dickinson (Man Who Falls); Larry Steers (Lafayette); Frank Erickson (Captain White); Grace Cunard (Woman with Baby); Tom Coleman (Mr. Carroll); Pietro Sosso (Mr. Anthony); Jack Curtis (Edmund); Harry Denny (Mr. Calot); Garnett Marks (Justice Drake); Jerry Jerome (Thomas); John Michael (Ned).

251

IT HAD TO BE YOU   (Col., 1947) 98 M.

Producer, Don Hartman; assistant producer, Norman Deming; director, Hartman, Rudolph Mate; story, Hartman, Allen Boretz; screenplay, Norman Panama, Melvin Frank; assistant director, Sam Nelson; art director, Stephen Goosson, Rudolph Sternad; set decorator, Wilbur Menefee, William Kierman; music director, Morris W. Stoloff; sound, Jack Haynes; camera, Rudolph Mate; editor, Gene Havlick.

Ginger Rogers (Victoria Stafford); Cornel Wilde (George/Johnny Blaine); Percy Waram (Mr. Stafford); Spring Byington (Mrs. Stafford); Thurston Hall (Mr. Harrington); Ron Randell (Oliver H. P. Harrington); Charles Evans (Dr. Parkinson); William Bevan (Evans); Frank Orth (Conductor Brown); Harry Hays Morgan (George Benson); Douglas Wood (Mr. Kimberly); Mary Forbes (Mrs. Kimberly); Nancy Saunders (Model); Douglas D. Coppin (Boyfriend); Michael Towne, Fred Sears (Firemen); Paul Campbell (Radio Announcer); Carol Nugent (Victoria—age 6); Judy Nugent (Victoria—age 5); Mary Patterson (Victoria—age 3); Myron Healey (Standish); Harlan Warde (Atherton); Anna Q. Nillson (Saleslady); George Chandler (Man); Edward Harvey (Dr. Thompson); Allen Wood (Cab Driver); Vera Lewis (Mrs. Brown); Cliff Clark (Fire Chief); Victor Travers (Drug Store Manager).

THE BARKLEYS OF BROADWAY   (MGM, 1949) C—109 M.

Producer, Arthur Freed; director, Charles Walters; screenplay, Betty Comden, Adolph Green; songs, Harry Warren and Ira Gershwin; choreography, Robert Alton; Astaire's choreography, Hermes Pan; music, Lennie Hayton; art director, Cedric Gibbons, Edward Carfagno; camera, Harry Stradling; editor, Albert Akst.

Fred Astaire (Josh Barkley); Ginger Rogers (Dinah Barkley); Oscar Levant (Ezra Millar); Billie Burke (Mrs. Livingston Belney); Gale Robbins (Shirlene May); Jacques Francois (Jacques Pierre Barredout); George Zucco (Judge); Clinton Sundberg (Bert Fisher); Inez Cooper (Pamela Driscoll); Carol Brewster (Gloria Amboy); Wilson Wood (Larry); Jean Andren, Laura Treadwell (Women); Allen Wood (Taxi Driver); Margaret Bert (Mary, the Maid); Alphonse Martell, Howard Mitchell, Marcel de la Brosse, Wilbur Mack (Ad Lib Judges); Larry Steers, Lillian West (Ad Lib Guests); Forbes Murray, Bess Flowers, Lois Austin, Betty Blythe, Bill Tannen (Guests in Theatre Lobby); Betty O'Kelly, Pat Miller, Bobbie Brooks, Charles Van, Richard Winters, Mickey Martin, Dick Barron (Bobby-Soxers); Lorraine Crawford (Cleo Fernby); Mahlon Hamilton (Apartment Doorman); Dee Turnell (Blonde); Reginald Simpson (Husband); Hans Conreid (Ladislaus Ladi); Sherry Hall (Chauffeur); Frank Ferguson (Mr. Perkins); George Boyce, John Albright, Butch Terrell (*Look* Photographers); Edward Kilroy (Standees); Nolan Leary (Stage Doorman); Joe Granby (Duke de Morny); Esther Somers (Sarah's Mother); Helen Eby-Rock (Sarah's Aunt); Joyce Mathews (Genevieve); Bob Purcell (Voice); Max Willenz (Clerk); Jack Rice (Ticket Man); Roger Moore, Wheaton Chambers (Men); Roberta Jackson (Clementine).

PERFECT STRANGERS   (WB, 1950) 87 M.

Producer, Jerry Wald; director, Bretaigne Windust; based on the play *Ladies and Gentlemen* by Charles MacArthur, Ben Hecht; adaptation, George Oppenheimer; screenplay, Edith Sommer; music, Leigh Harline; art director, Stanley Fleischer; camera, Peverell Marley; editor, David Weisbart.

Ginger Rogers (Terry Scott); Dennis Morgan (David Campbell); Thelma Ritter (Lena Fassler); Margalo Gillmore (Isobel Bradford); Anthony Ross (Robert Fisher); Howard Freeman (Timkin); Alan Reed (Harry Patulle); Paul Ford (Judge Byron); George Chandler (Lester Hubley); Frank Conlan (John Brokaw); Charles Meredith (Lyle Pettijohn); Harry Bellaver (Bailiff); Frances Charles (Eileen Marcher); Marjorie Bennett (Mrs. Moore); Paul McVey (District Attorney); Edith Evanson (Mary Travers); Whit Bissell (Defense Attorney); Summer Getchell (John Simon); Ford

Rainey (Ernest Crag); Sarah Selby (Mrs. Wilson); Alan Wilson (Court Clerk); Ronnie Tyler (Newsboy); Isabelle Withers (Woman); Max Mellenger (Official); Boyd Davis (Judge); Ezelle Poule (Secretary); Creighton Hale, John Albright, Frank Marlowe, Ed Coke (Reporters); Dick Kipling (Autopsy Surgeon).

STORM WARNING (WB, 1950) 93 M.

Producer, Jerry Wald; director, Stuart Heisler; story-screenplay, Daniel Fuchs, Richard Brooks; music, Daniele Amfitheatrof; art director, Leo K. Kuter; camera, Carl Guthrie; editor, Clarence Kolster.

Ginger Rogers (Marsha Mitchell); Ronald Reagan (Burt Rainey); Doris Day (Lucy Rice); Steve Cochran (Hank Rice); Hugh Sanders (Charlie Barr); Raymond Greenleaf (Faulkner); Lloyd Gough (Rummel); Ned Glass (George Athens); Paul E. Burns (Hauser); Walter Baldwin (Bledsoe); Lynn Whitney (Cora Athens); Stuart Randall (Walters); Sean McClory (Shore); Dave McMahon (Hollis); Robert Williams (Jaeger); Charles Watts (Wally); Charles Phillips (Bus Driver); Dale Van Sickel (Walter Adams); Anthony Warde (Jukebox Collector); Paul Brinegar (Cameraman); Len Hendry, Ned Davenport (Cops); Frank Marlowe (Al, a Bus Driver); Leo Cleary (Barnet); Alex Gerry (Basset); Charles Conrad (Jordan); Lillian Albertson (Mrs. Rainey); Eddie Hearn (Mr. Rainey); Harry Harvey (Mr. Louden); Janet Barrett (Mrs. Adams); Lloyd Jenkins (Interne); King Donovan (Ambulance Driver); Tommy Walker (Bob); Dewey Robinson, Gene Evans (Klansmen).

THE GROOM WORE SPURS (Univ., 1951) 80 M.

Producer, Howard Welsch; director, Richard Whorf; based on the story "Legal Bride" by Robert Carson; screenplay, Carson, Robert Libbott, Frank Burt; art director, Perry Ferguson; music, Emily Newman, Arthur Lance; song, Newman and Leon Pober; camera, Peverell Marley; editor, Otto Ludwig.·

Ginger Rogers (Abigail Furnival); Jack Carson (Ben Castle); Joan Davis (Alice Dean); Stanley Ridges (Harry Kallen); James Brown (Steve Hall); John Litel (District Attorney); Victor Sen Yung (Ignacio); Mira McKinney (Mrs. Forbes); Gordon Nelson (Ricky); George Meader (Bellboy); Kemp Niver (Killer); Robert B. Williams (Jake Harris); Richard Whorf (Man).

WE'RE NOT MARRIED (20th, 1952) 85 M.

Producer, Nunnally Johnson; director, Edmund Goulding; story, Gina Kaus, Jay Dratler; adaptation, Dwight Taylor; screenplay, Johnson; music, Cyril Mockridge; art director, Lyle Wheeler, Leland Fuller; music director, Lionel Newman; camera, Leo Tover; editor, Louis Loeffler.

Ginger Rogers (Ramona); Fred Allen (Steve Gladwyn); Victor Moore (Justice of the Peace); Marilyn Monroe (Annabel Norris); David Wayne (Jeff Norris); Eve Arden (Katie Woodruff); Paul Douglas (Hector Woodruff); Eddie Bracken (Willie Fisher); Mitzi Gaynor (Patsy Fisher); Louis Calhern (Freddie Melrose); Zsa Zsa Gabor (Eve Melrose); James Gleason (Duffy); Paul Stewart (Attorney Stone); Jane Darwell (Mrs. Bush); Tom Powers (Attorney General); Victor Sutherland (Governor Bush); Alan Bridge (Detective Magnus); Harry Golder (Radio Announcer); Kay English (Wife); Lee Marvin (Pinky); O. Z. Whitehead (Postman); Marjorie Weaver (Ruthie); Dabbs Greer (Man); Forbes Murray (Mississippi Governor); Maurice Cass (Organist); Margie Liszt (Daughter on Radio); Maude Wallace (Autograph Hound); Richard Buckley (Mr. Graves); Alvin Greenman, Eddie Firestone, (Men in Radio Station); Phyllis Brunner (Wife); Steve Pritko, Robert Dane (MPs at Railroad Station); James Burke (Master Sergeant Nuckols); Robert Forrest, Bill Hale (MPs); Ed Max (Counterman); Richard Reeves (Brigadier General); Ralph Dumke (Twitchell); Harry Antrim (Justice of the Peace); Byron Foulger (License Bureau Clerk); Harry Harvey (Postman); Selmer Jackson (Dr. Ned); Harry Carter (Chaplain Hall); Dabbs Greer (Man at Miss Mississippi Contest); Emile Meyer (Beauty Contest Announcer); Henry Faber, Larry Stamps (State Troopers).

MONKEY BUSINESS   (20th, 1952) 97 M.

Producer, Sol C. Siegel; director, Howard Hawks; story, Harry Segall; screenplay, Ben Hecht, Charles Lederer, I. A. L. Diamond; music, Leigh Harline; art director, Lyle Wheeler, George Patrick; set decorator, Thomas Little, Walter M. Scott; music director, Lionel Newman; camera, Milton Krasner; editor, William P. Murphy.

Cary Grant (Barnaby Fulton); Ginger Rogers (Edwina); Charles Coburn (Mr. Oxley); Marilyn Monroe (Lois Laurel); Hugh Marlowe (Harvey Entwhistle); Henri Letondal (Siegfried Kitzel); Robert Cornthwaite (Dr. Zoldeck); Larry Keating (Mr. Culverly); Douglas Spencer (Dr. Brunner); Esther Dale (Mrs. Rhinelander); George "Foghorn" Winslow (Little Indian); Emmett Lynn (Jimmy); Gil Stratton, Jr. (Yale Man); Faire Binney (Dowager); Harry Carey, Jr. (Reporter).

DREAM BOAT   (20th, 1952) 83 M.

Producer, Sol C. Siegel; director, Claude Binyon; based on the story by John D. Weaver; screenplay, Binyon; music, Cyril Mockridge; art director, Lyle Wheeler, Maurice Ransford; set decorator, Thomas Little, Fred J. Rode; orchestrator, Bernard Mayers; camera, Milton Krasner; editor, James B. Clark.

Clifton Webb (Thornton Sayre); Ginger Rogers (Gloria); Anne Francis (Carol Sayre); Jeffrey Hunter (Bill Ainslee); Elsa Lanchester (Dr. Coffey); Fred Clark (Sam Levitt); Paul Harvey (Harrington); Ray Collins (Timothy Stone); Helene Stanley (Mimi); Richard Garrick (Judge Bowles); George Barrows (Commandant); Jay Adler (Desk Clerk); Marietta Canty (Lavinia); Emory Parnell (Used-Car Salesman); Laura Brooks (Mrs. Gunther); Gwen Verdon, Matt Mattox, Frank Radcliffe (Performers in Commercial); May Wynn (Cigarette Girl); Vici Raaf, Barbara Wooddell (Receptionists); Robert B. Williams, Tony De Mario (Photographers); Steve Carruthers (Busboy); Joe Recht (Waiter); Victoria Horne (Waitress); Bob Nichols (Student); Alphonse Martel (Maitre D'); Mary Treen (Wife); Fred Graham (Bartender); Richard Karlan (Husband); Jean Corbett (Girl).

FOREVER FEMALE   (Par., 1953) 93 M.

Producer, Pat Duggan; director, Irving Rapper; suggested by the play *Rosalind* by J. M. Barrie; screenplay, Julius J. and Philip G. Epstein; music, Victor Young; art director, Hal Pereira, Joseph MacMillan Johnson; camera, Harry Stradling; editor, Archie Marshek.

Ginger Rogers (Beatrice Page); William Holden (Stanley Krown); Paul Douglas (E. Harry Philips); Pat Crowley (Sally Carver); James Gleason (Eddie Woods); Jesse White (Willie Wolfe); Marjorie Rambeau (Herself); George Reeves (George Courtland); King Donovan (Playwright); Vic Perrin (Scenic Designer); Russell Gaige (Theatrical Producer); Marian Ross (Patty); Richard Shannon (Stage Manager); Kathryn Grant, Sally Mansfield, Rand Harper (Young Hopefuls); Henry Dar (Boggia Felix); Victor Romito (Maitre D'); Hyacinthe Railla, Alfred Paix (Waiters); Joel Marston (Photographer); Almira Sessions (Mother); Michael Darrin (Jack).

BLACK WIDOW   (20th, 1954) C—95 M.

Producer-director, Nunnally Johnson; based on a story by Patrick Quentin; screenplay, Johnson; music, Leigh Harline; art director, Lyle Wheeler, Maurice Ransford; camera, Charles G. Clarke; editor, Dorothy Spencer.

Ginger Rogers (Lottie); Van Heflin (Peter); Gene Tierney (Iris); George Raft (Detective Bruce); Peggy Ann Garner (Nancy Ordway); Reginald Gardiner (Brian); Virginia Leith (Claire Amberly); Otto Kruger (Ling); Cathleen Nesbitt (Lucia); Skip Homeier (John); Hilda Simms (Anne); Harry Carter (Welch); Geraldine Wall (Miss Mills); Richard Cutting (Sergeant Owens); Mabel Albertson (Sylvia); Aaron Spelling (Mr. Oliver); Wilson Wood (Costume Designer); Tony De Mario (Bartender); Virginia Maples (Model); Frances Driver (Maid); Michael Vallon (Coal Dealer); James F. Stone (Stage Doorman).

TWIST OF FATE   (UA, 1954) 89 M.

Producer, Maxwell Setton, John R. Sloan; director, David Miller; story, Rip Van Ronkel, Miller; screenplay, Robert Westerby, Carl Nystrom; art director, Geoff Drake; assistant director, James Ware; music, Malcolm Arnold; camera, Robert Day, Ted Schaife; editor, Alan Osbiston.

Ginger Rogers ("Johnny" Victor); Herbert Lom (Emil Landosh); Jacques Bergerac (Pierre Clement); Stanley Baker (Louis Galt); Margaret Rawlings (Marie Galt); Eddie Byrne (Luigi); Lily Kann (Nicole); Coral Browne (Helen); Lisa Gastoni (Yvette); John Chandos (Nino); Ferdy Mayne (Chief of Police); Rudolph Offenbach (Yacht Captain).

TIGHT SPOT   (Col., 1955) 95 M.

Producer, Lewis J. Rachmil; director, Phil Karlson; based on the play *Dead Pigeon* by Lenard Kantor; screenplay, William Bowers; art director, Carl Anderson; music director, Morris Stoloff; music, George Duning; sound, John Livadary, Lambert Day; gowns, Jean Louis; assistant director, Milton Feldman; camera, Burnett Guffey; editor, Viola Lawrence.

Ginger Rogers (Sherry Conley); Edward G. Robinson (Lloyd Hallett); Brian Keith (Vince Striker); Lucy Marlow (Prison Girl); Lorne Greene (Benjamin Costain); Katherine Anderson (Mrs. Willoughby); Allen Nourse (Marvin Rickles); Peter Leeds (Fred Packer); Doye O'Dell (Mississippi Mac); Eve McVeagh (Clara Morgan); Helen Wallace (Warden); Frank Gentle (Jim Hornsby); Gloria Ann Simpson (Miss Masters); Robert Shield (Carlyle); Norman Keats (Arny); Kathryn Grant (Girl Honeymooner); Will J. White, Patrick Miller (Plainclothesmen); Bob Hopkins (TV Salesman); Kenneth N. Mayer, Dean Cromer (Policemen); Tom de Graffenried (Doctor); Joseph Hamilton (Judge); Alan Reynolds (Bailiff); Robert Nichols (Boy Honeymooner); Alfred Linder (Tonelli); Ed Hinton, John Larch (Detectives).

THE FIRST TRAVELING SALESLADY   (RKO, 1956) C—92 M.

Producer-director, Arthur Lubin; screenplay, Devery Freeman, Stephen Longstreet; music, Irving Gertz; art director, Albert S. D'Agostino; set decorator, Darrell Silvera; sound, S. G. Haughton, Terry Kellum; songs, Gertz and Hal Levy; assistant director, Richard Mayberry; costumes, Edward Stevenson; camera, William Snyder; editor, Otto Ludwig.

Ginger Rogers (Rose Gillray); Barry Nelson (Charles Masters); Carol Channing (Molly Wade); David Brian (James Carter); James Arness (Joel Kingdom); Clint Eastwood (Jack Rice); Frank Wilcox (Marshal Duncan); Robert Simon (Cal); Daniel M. White (Sheriff); Harry Cheshire (Judge Benson); John Eldredge (Creavy); Robert Hinkle (Pete); Jack Rice (Dowling); Kate Drain Lawson (Annie Peachpit); Edward Cassidy (Theodore Roosevelt); Fred Essler (Schlessinger); Bill Hale (Sheriff's Deputy); Lovyss Bradley (Mrs. Bronson); Nora Bush (Mrs. Pruett); Ann Kunde (Mrs. Cobb); Hans Herbert (Night Clerk); Lynn Noe, Joan Tyler, Janette Miler, Kathy Marlowe (Models); Roy Darmour, Peter Croyden, Al Cavens, Paul Bradley, Hal Taggart (Men); Ian Murray (Prince of Wales); Robert Easton (Young Cowboy); Lester Dorr, Frank Soannel, Paul Keast (Salesmen); Mauritz Hugo, Julius Eyans, Stanley Farrer (Buyers); Lane Chandler (Rancher).

TEENAGE REBEL   (20th, 1956) 94 M.

Producer, Charles Brackett; director, Edmund Goulding; based on the play *Roomful of Roses* by Edith Sommer; screenplay, Walter Reisch, Brackett; music, Leigh Harline; costumes, Mary Wills; assistant director, Eli Dunn; song, Lionel Newman and Carroll Coates; Ralph Freed and Goulding; art director, Lyle R. Wheeler, Jack Martin Smith; camera, Joe MacDonald; editor, William Mace.

Ginger Rogers (Nancy Fallon); Michael Rennie (Jay Fallon); Mildred Natwick (Grace Hewitt); Rusty Swope (Larry Fallon); Lili Gentle (Teenager at Races); Louise Beavers (Willamay); Irene Hervey (Helen McGowan); John Stephenson (Eric McGowan); Betty Lou Keim (Dodie); Warren Berlinger (Dick Dewitt); Diane Jergens (Jane Hewitt); Susan Luckey (Madeleine Johnson); James O'Rear (Mr. Heffernan); Gary Gray (Freddie); Pattee Chapman (Erna); Richard Collier (Cab Driver); Wade Dumas (Porter); James Stone (Pappy Smith); Sheila James (Teenager); Joan Freeman (Teenager in Malt Shop); Gene Foley (Soda Fountain Girl).

OH, MEN! OH, WOMEN!   (20th, 1957) C—90 M.

Producer-director, Nunnally Johnson; based on the play by Edward Chodorov; screenplay, Johnson; assistant director, Hal Herman; wardrobe, Charles LeMaire; music, Cyril J. Mockridge; art director, Lyle R. Wheeler, Maurice Ransford; special camera effects, Ray Kellogg; camera, Charles G. Clarke; editor, Marjorie Fowler.

Dan Dailey (Arthur Turner); Ginger Rogers (Mildred Turner); David Niven (Dr. Alan Coles); Barbara Rush (Myra Hagerman); Tony Randall (Cobbler); Natalie Schafer (Mrs. Day); Rachel Stephens (Miss Tacher); John Wengraf (Dr. Kraus); Cheryll Clarke (Melba); Charles Davis (Steward); Clancy Cooper (Mounted Policeman); Joel Fluellen (Cab Driver); Franklin Pangborn (Bartender); Franklin Farnum (Steamship Clerk); Hal Taggart (Passenger).

THE CONFESSION   (Golden Eagle Films, 1964) C—100 M.

Producer, William Marshall; director, William Dieterle; screenplay, Allen Scott; art director, Jim Sullivan, Willis Connor; music, Michael Colicchio; title designs, Sal Maimovie; production supervisor, Lee Lukather; camera, Robert Brenner; editor, Carl Lerner.

Ginger Rogers (Mme. Renaldi); Ray Milland (Mano Forni); Barbara Eden (Pia Pacelli); Carl Schell (Beppo); Michael Ansara (Mayer Pablo); Elliott Gould (The Mute); Walter Abel (The Thief); Vinton Hayworth (Augesta); David Hurst (Gustave); Pilla Scott (Gina); Cecil Kellaway (The Bishop); and: Michael Youngman, Julian Upton, Mara Lynn, Carol Ann Daniels, Leonard Cimino.

HARLOW   (Magna, 1965) 107 M.

Executive producer, Brandon Chase; producer, Lee Savin; director, Alex Segal; screenplay, Karl Tunberg; music, Al Ham, Nelson Riddle; assistant director, Greg Peters, Johnny Wilson, Dick Bennett; art director, Duncan Cramer; set decorator, Harry Gordon; camera, Jim Kilgore.

Carol Lynley (Jean Harlow); Efrem Zimbalist, Jr. (William Mansfield); Ginger Rogers (Mama Jean); Barry Sullivan (Marino Bello); Hurd Hatfield (Paul Bern); Lloyd Bochner (Marc Peters); Hermione Baddeley (Marie Dressler); Audrey Totter (Marilyn); John Williams (Jonathan Martin); Audrey Christie (Thelma); Michael Dante (Ed); Jack Kruschen (Louis B. Mayer); Celia Lovsky (Maria Ouspenskaya); Robert Strauss (Hank); James Dobson (Counterman); Sonny Liston, Nick Demitri (Fighters); Cliff Norton (Billy); Paulle Clark (Waitress); Jim Plunkett (Stan Laurel);

John "Red" Fox (Oliver Hardy); Joel Marston (Press Agent); Christopher West (Bern's Secretary); Fred Conte (Photographer); Catherine Ross (Wardrobe Woman); Buddy Lewis (Al Jolson); Danny Francis (Casino Manager); Frank Scannell (Doctor); Maureene Gaffney (Miss Larsen); Ron Kennedy (Assistant Director); Harry Holcombe (Minister); Lola Fisher (Nurse); Fred Klein (Himself).

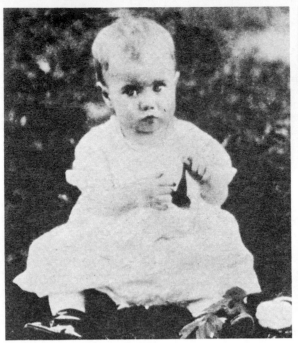

The infant Ginger Rogers

With Eddie Quilla
THE TIP OFF (Pathe

With Sally Eilers and Monroe Owsley in HAT CHECK GIRL (Fox '32)

With Ruby Keeler and Una Merkel in FORTY-SECOND STREET (WB '33)

With Lew Ayres in DON'T BET ON LOVE (Univ '33)

With Jerry Tucker, Jack Oakie, and Jack Haley in SITTING PRETTY (Par '33)

With Betty Furness and Lela Rogers at the opening of the Hollytown Theatre, Los Angeles, in December, 1933

With Howard Hughes (c. 1934)

With Fred Astaire in ROBERT (RKO '35)

With Edward Everett Horton, Helen Broderick, Eric Blore, Fred Astaire, and Erik Rhodes in TOP HAT (RKO '35)

With Katharine Hepburn on the set of STAGE DOOR (RKO '37)

With Walter Connolly and Franklin Pangborn in FIFTH AVENUE GIRL (RKO '39)

With Fred Astaire in
CAREFREE (RKO '38)

With Lynn Fontanne accept
the Oscar for KITTY FO
in 1

With Queenie Vassar, Joan Carroll, and Miles Mander in PRIMROSE PATH
(RKO '40)

With Adolphe Menjou in
ROXIE HART (20th '42)

With Tom Dugan in THE
MAJOR AND THE MINOR
(Par '42)

With her husband, John Calvin
Briggs, in January, 1943

With Robert Ryan in TENDER
COMRADE (RKO '43)

With Ray Milland, Phyllis
Brooks, and Jon Hall in LADY
IN THE DARK (Par '44)

With Joseph Cotten in I'LL BE
SEEING YOU (UA '44)

With Clifton Webb in DREAM
BOAT (20th '52)

With Jacques Bergerac in
TWIST OF FATE (UA '54)

With Helen Wallace and Brian
Keith in TIGHT SPOT (Col '55)

...th Stephen McNally in
...GNIFICENT DOLL (Univ. '46)

With Steve Cochran in STORM
WARNING (WB '50)

...n Fred Astaire in THE BARKLEYS OF BROADWAY (MGM '49)

With Barry Nelson in THE
FIRST TRAVELING SALESLADY
(RKO '56)

With Barbara Eden in THE
CONFESSION (Golden Eagle
'64)

With David Burns in HELLO,
DOLLY! in 1965

Carol Lynley in HARLOW (Magna '65)

A publicity pose of 1938

5' 7"
110 pounds
Brown hair
Blue eyes
Scorpio

Katharine

Hepburn

Now in her late-sixties, Katharine Hepburn remains the most active of the enduring cinema-bred superstars. As blunt and candid today as she was back in the 1920s, Kate, nevertheless, is still a deliberate enigma made up of iconoclastic contradictions. She is a hearty mixture of toughened but still striking beauty, stark individualism in all matters, fierce loyalty and partiality, and she possesses a razor-sharp mind that brooks no double-talk from others and no pandering to anyone's self-delusions.

Kate has never made it easy on her fans. Admirers of the actress are so baffled by her determined, self-sufficient course of life that empathy for her must remain outside the scope of their admiration. "I strike people as peculiar in some way," Kate once said, "although I don't quite understand why. Of course, I have an angular face, an angular body, and I suppose, an angular personality which jabs into people."

When Kate was Queen of the RKO lot in the 1930s, she was most often termed Katharine of Arrogance. Onscreen and off—during that decade—she created a deliberate image of the spoiled little rich girl, what with her rampant willfulness, her tomboyishness, her piquant face, her strident little nasal-twanged voice, all wrapped up in fascinating but most annoying mannerisms. With the coming of the 1940s and her professional-personal relationship with

Spencer Tracy, a new, softer Kate emerged, just as self-possessed, but far more full-bodied in all ways. As the years slipped by, the ramrod matriarch slipped into, as Garson Kanin observed, "a world of her own, and she lives in it happily ever after. She is its Empress, its leading citizen, and the most common of its commoners."

Kate is one of the few great stars from whom the public derives sustenance, and not the reverse. She admits of no nostalgia for her past, and is definitely not the type to watch her old movies on television or in revival theatres. ("There's a certain melancholy in watching yourself rot. It's a long trip to the grave, and mine is longer than some. I don't want to sit and study the process.") Kate is the first to admit that her life has been a combination of hard work and lucky breaks. "And the curious thing is—when I started out, I didn't have any great desire to be an actress or to learn how to act. I just wanted to be famous."

Katharine Houghton Hepburn was born on November 9, 1907, in Hartford, Connecticut, the second of the six children of Dr. Thomas Norval Hepburn and Katharine Houghton Hepburn.* By the time of Katharine's birth the couple were about to move from their shared rented house to 133 Hawthorne Street in Hartford, and less than a decade later, they would be able to afford a tasteful brick residence on Bloomfield Avenue in aristocratic West Hartford.

All six of the Hepburn children (Thomas, Katharine, Richard, Robert, Marion, and Peggy) were reared according to their parents' iconoclastic child-development plan, with each youth having a great deal of unheard-of freedom, and an equal amount of physical culture, a combination which stood the youths in good stead during the years when their parents were the subject of tempered ostracism by the Hartford social set.

Katharine was encouraged to become an all-around tomboy, able to wrestle,† swim, and skate with the best of her male competition. Her mother had

---

*Virginia-born Dr. Hepburn, a graduate of Randolph-Macon College in Virginia, had met his wife-to-be while he was a student at Johns Hopkins Medical School, and they were wed in his final year there. Dr. Hepburn became a prominent surgeon and urologist, but was more noted for his rather advanced medical concepts, which included publicizing the facts concerning venereal disease. He and Harvard's Dr. Charles Eliot founded the Connecticut Social Hygiene Association, and it was Dr. Hepburn who actively participated in the distribution of the English translation of Eugene Brieux's play *Damaged Goods,* a graphic drama dealing with the problems engendered by society's habit of smothering the causes and treatment of syphilis. Despite his publicity-engendering crusade, Dr. Hepburn was and always remained an essentially private person, opposed to any form of publicity, which he thought vulgar and demeaning.

Mrs. Hepburn was born with a very respected Boston pedigree, including a relative who served as American ambassador to Great Britain. So proud was she of her heritage, that Mrs. Hepburn would have each of her children bear her maiden surname as a middle name. She graduated from Bryn Mawr College in 1898, later earning a M.A. in art at Radcliffe College. Like her husband, Mrs. Hepburn was a spirited liberal, her *causes célèbres* being the suffragette movement and birth control. She was among the prominent suffragette leaders who picketed the White House in the hope of persuading an undecided President Woodrow Wilson to see the light.

† To remove any possible disadvantage from her distaff status, each summer Kate would have her head shaven, so her tussling opponents could not yank at her hair.

special plans for Katharine to follow in her crusading footsteps. At an early age Katharine found herself assisting mater with the suffragettes' Votes for Women crusade; she was assigned to passing out leaflets on street corners, a task she thoroughly enjoyed. Katharine made her public debut at the age of eight, when, dressed as a Dutch girl, she graced a float furnished by a kitchen-cleanser manufacturer, for the women's big liberation-day parade. As Katharine would later enunciate, "I learned early what it is to be snubbed for a good cause. Snobbery has never worried me since." When not busily campaigning for mama, Katharine could be found engrossed in her home-based puppet theatres, or rushing out to the Saturday movie matinee to see her beloved William S. Hart in his latest horse opera.

Tragedy struck Kate* when she was just twelve years old. Her family was spending the Easter holiday in New York; Kate and fifteen-year-old Thomas were taken to see a matinee performance of *A Connecticut Yankee in King Arthur's Court*. The youngsters were particularly fascinated by one portion of the play, in which a character performed a rope trick with a noose. On Easter Eve, the children attended a party during which Thomas was the subject of a juvenile taunt. The next morning, when he failed to appear for breakfast, it was a much-concerned Kate who discovered him in the attic, hanging from a noose. She cut him down and rushed pell-mell out of the house to find the nearest doctor. It was far too late, for the youth had been dead for some several hours. This unexplainable event, which most think was an accident, justifiably left Kate morose, and the Hepburns considered it a great relief when that summer, at their Long Island Sound vacation home in Fenwick, Connecticut, Kate took to amusing herself in dramatics, forming a local stock company to present children's plays. It seemed that Kate, now the eldest living child of the Hepburn brood, found her theatrical preoccupation a diverting release from her post as assistant mother to her younger brothers and sisters.

In her earliest years, headstrong Kate had endured private tutors—and the instructors had endured her. Thereafter her family sent her to the West Middle School and then to the Oxford School for Girls, both situated at Hartford. At each institution, she was categorized as a moody and difficult child, apparently hell-bent to be the center of attention. In 1924, sixteen-year-old Kate entered Bryn Mawr College in suburban Philadelphia, where she soon discovered that her willful ways made not a bit of difference to her instructors, who were well used to coping with girls of varying degrees of uniqueness. In fact, during her freshman year, Kate almost flunked out for academic reasons, but realizing that she could not participate in college plays unless she attained far higher grades, she set her mind to studying and won the needed marks. That same first year at Bryn Mawr she was briefly suspended when

*Dr. Hepburn called her Redtop, later Reddy. As an adult her nieces and nephews called her Aunt Kath; her screen co-player Spencer Tracy frequently called her Kathy, but mostly Miss Hepburn.

the college authorities found her smoking forbidden cigarettes.* However, during the remainder of her college years, Kate passed muster within the rules, her grades continuing to swing upward, particularly in her history major. (One of her weakest courses was a Shakespearian survey class, which left her bored and restless.) In her final two years at Bryn Mawr, Kate, regarded by her classmates as a "self-conscious beauty," became a firm part of the school's drama group, playing a male youth in A. A. Milne's *The Truth about Blayds* and then Teresa in *The Cradle Song.* When respected Shakespearian scholar Horace Howard Furness bestowed on her the honor of playing Pandora in the school pastoral, *The Woman in the Moone,* Kate became convinced, once and for all, that a theatrical career was her life's destiny.

The Kate of these pre-adult years was a rather lanky girl, with a long, bony face, whose angularity was accentuated by her abundance of freckles, and crowned by her tightly bunned crop of red hair. Her loose-limbed stance and gangling posture gave her a gawky individuality which less considerate observers termed masculine ease. Like her parents, Kate was exceedingly opinionated, and, her thoughts, expressed in her piercing, brittle voice, had a very authoritarian ring, made all the more intriguing (to admirers, at least) by its strong New England nasal twang. Improbable as it may have seemed, Kate did have her gaggle of admirers. Among her swains were Robert McKnight, a graduate of the Yale Art School, who sculpted a bust of her and later proposed marriage. She rejected his offer as she did that of four other suitors during her Bryn Mawr years.

In the spring of her last year at Bryn Mawr, Kate trundled off to Baltimore where she had an entree to meeting Edwin H. Knopf.† Despite her letter of introduction from a mutual acquaintance, John S. Clarke, Knopf was far from impressed with Kate, either in her unsettling physical appearance or her obvious lack of stage presence. "She was tremendously sincere, but awkward, green, freaky-looking, I wanted no part of her. But," added Knopf, "it wasn't so easy to get rid of Hepburn."

Although her initial foray into the Knopf camp had not netted Kate any assurance of forthcoming theatre work, immediately upon graduation from Bryn Mawr in June, 1928, she reported back to Baltimore and nagged her way into a supernumerary part as a lady-in-waiting in *The Czarina,* starring Mary Boland. The next week in this stock troupe she was cast as a flapper in *The Cradle Snatchers.* Then she suddenly departed the Knopf players, to no one's great regret, although some of the company had begun to comprehend that beneath the standoffish veneer, Kate was not a snobbish dilettante but a sincere apprentice actress. Her leave-taking from the Baltimore theatre was

---

*Kate had indulged in other pranks which seemingly did not offend the school's code of ethics; for example, the time she decided to bathe in the library fountain and then roll herself dry in the grass.

†Brother of the famed book publisher, and later an MGM producer.

not a case of quickly-admitted defeat; rather, she had received some sound words of advice from the company's stage manager, Kenneth McKenna,* who convinced her that if she really wished to pursue a theatrical career she must obtain proper training. So Kate scurried off to New York, determined to bring herself up to professional snuff. For her voice coach, she elected Frances Robinson-Duff and for movement and dance, Michael Mordkin. The combination of disciplined teaching from these two renowned coaches did much to shape the stage presence of the Kate of later years. Almost needless to say, while Kate was studying with these two expert but expensive tutors, it required a great deal of diplomacy on her part to win her father's confidence in her show business venturing, so that he would agree to assist in subsidizing her extended training period. The Hepburn of these years soon became a familiar sight in theatrical circles, as she proudly made her ways on casting rounds, refusing to bend one iota from her individualist manner of bearing, costuming, or thinking; convinced that her unique qualities would be recognized for their proper worth by the right creative force.

But Kate was not above inducing this meeting of theatre employer and employee. When she heard that Edwin H. Knopf had closed his Baltimore showcase and was bringing a new play to Broadway with Kenneth McKenna in the lead role, she quickly got in touch with her former boss. Eventually she was offered the tiny role of the secretary in *The Big Pond*† and given the opportunity to understudy the leading lady. A short time into rehearsal, Knopf fired his original stage ingenue and offered Kate the choice part. Kate promptly accepted and ordered Miss Robinson-Duff to work overtime with her to smooth out the rough corners of her histrionic technique. The tryout engagement for *The Big Pond* was held in Great Neck, Long Island. There are many versions of the causes leading up to Kate's opening-night fiasco. One account has it that her unintended imitation of co-star McKenna's adopted French stage accent created a burst of audience laughter which threw Kate offguard. Another explanation was that she and director Knopf fought and she was too flustered to proceed on an even keel; yet another version was that she grew overconfident at her big chance and barged ahead at full steam, losing the audience in her barrage of unintelligible dialog.

Among the audience on that traumatic opening night (and, for Kate, closing night) were the show's producers, Arthur Hopkins and A. H. Woods, who promptly hired Kate for Katharine Clugston's *These Days* (Cort Theatre, November 12, 1928). That show lasted a mere eight performances. Hopkins next assigned Kate to understudy blue-blood-dabbling actress Hope Williams in Philip Barry's *Holiday,* then in try-out in New Haven.‡ After only two

---

*An actor, he later became a story editor at MGM and one of actress Kay Francis's several husbands.

†The George Middleton and A. E. Thomas play would be filmed by Paramount in 1930 with Claudette Colbert and Maurice Chevalier starring in both the English- and French-language editions.

‡Opened at the Plymouth Theatre on November 26, 1928, for a 229-performance run.

weeks in this post, Kate quit the show to marry Ludlow Ogden Smith. The groom-to-be, a Philadelphia aristocrat, was a graduate of the University of Grenoble in southeastern France. He had met Kate while she was a Bryn Mawr junior. The couple were married on December 12, 1928, at her parents' home in West Hartford, with her grandfather, the Reverend S. S. Hepburn, the oldest Episcopal clergyman in Virginia, officiating at the ceremony. The newlyweds honeymooned in Bermuda and by the time they returned, Kate had convinced her husband to change his surname; she just could not picture herself as Kate Smith. So he altered his name to Ogden Ludlow and agreed to move from Philadelphia to New York, where they obtained an East 39th Street walk-up apartment, and he maneuvered a post as an insurance broker. But three weeks of being a housewife were enough for Kate and she sought out Arthur Hopkins to beg for reinstatement as Hope Williams's *Holiday* understudy. Unfortunately for Kate, Miss Williams never missed a performance of the play. After *Holiday* closed in June, 1929, Kate and Ogden Ludlow (whom she called Luddy) went to Europe for a brief vacation. When they returned from abroad, the Ludlows decided to separate, although Luddy remained friendly with the Hepburn clan.

The Theatre Guild hired Kate for the ingenue's part in S. N. Behrman's *Meteor* (1929).* Kate was quite naturally pleased by the opportunity and the respectable $225 weekly stipend; she was at least making a bit of a success in her chosen career, a situation not paralleled in her domestic situation. Particularly at this stage of her life, Kate was an overly ambitious lass, and she was not above resigning from her Guild pact to accept a bigger role in the dramatic fantasy, *Death Takes a Holiday.* She was cast as Grazia to Philip Merivale's Prince Sirki; but not for long. After five weeks of pre-New York tryouts, in which Kate received only qualified notices, producer Lee Shubert ordered her to resign from the show. "Resign hell!" was Kate's reaction. "If he wants me out of the cast, he can kick me out!" And so Rose Hobart inherited the role of Grazia when *Death Takes a Holiday* opened at the Ethel Barrymore Theatre on December 26, 1929, for a 180-performance run.

Undaunted, Kate returned to the theatrical arena very quickly, for the forgiving Theatre Guild offered her $35 a week to understudy Nazimova in Turgenev's *A Month in the Country* (Guild Theatre, March 17, 1930); later Kate played the maid in this well-mounted offering. Through professional associates of Frances Robinson-Duff Kate was next offered a summer stock season at the Berkshire Playhouse in Stockbridge, Massachusetts. According to the Shubert Alley grapevine, at Stockbridge Kate's inherent arrogance overrode her professional humility and after performing in a few of the season's productions, she quit. That fall, through the auspices of Kenneth Macgowan,† who was co-producing a repertory season at the Maxine Elliott

---

*Opened at the Guild Theatre on December 23, 1929, for a ninety-two-performance run.

†Macgowan would gravitate to Hollywood in early 1932, first as story editor under David O. Selznick's regime at RKO, then as an associate producer at the studio, with *Little Women* (1933), starring Kate, as one of his first big hits.

Theatre with Jane Cowl as principal player, Kate obtained the role of Cowl's daughter in *Art and Mrs. Bottle* (November 18, 1930). Benn W. Levy, the British author of that comedy, had severe reservations regarding Kate: "She looks a fright, her manner is objectionable, and she has no talent." Because of Levy's unfavorable reaction to Kate, she was fired from the cast, but when a string of other actresses proved even more unlikely in the part, Cowl persuaded Levy to rehire Kate—at a higher salary. *Art and Mrs. Bottle* provided Kate with her first round of critical praise, leading Howard Barnes *(New York Herald-Tribune)* to write, "She is agreeable to look at, assured and altogether a proficient actress." Miss Cowl would later tell the press that in her lengthy theatrical experience she had never seen a young actress so totally absorbed in her work or so thrilled by working in the theatre.

After a subsequent summer season at the Ivoryton Playhouse in Connecticut, Kate won the juicy role of Daisy Sage in Philip Barry's new comedy, *The Animal Kingdom.* Author Barry was all for extending Kate's role in this sophisticated outing, but star and co-producer Leslie Howard objected to the shift of dramatic emphasis, and before the play opened in Boston, Kate was replaced by Frances Fuller. *The Animal Kingdom* opened on Broadway on January 12, 1932, and became a very popular White Way entry.

Kate was not without work for long, for she landed the lead role in Julien Thompson's farce, *The Warrior's Husband.* Before the play, dealing with an Amazon queen who becomes a love slave to a Greek, opened at the Morosco Theatre (March 11, 1932), Kate had been fired from the production and rehired. In the course of the show, as Antiope the Amazon queen, she hurdled down a ramp lugging a prop deer, wrestled with co-star Colin Keith-Johnston, made prodigious leaps across the stage, and most importantly (for some audience members) wore a short tunic outfit which showed to advantage her long, lovely legs. The critics enthused more about Kate's captivating stage abandon than the quality of the play itself. Said Richard Garland *(New York World-Telegram):* "Miss Katharine Hepburn comes into her own as Antiope. . . . [she] makes the most of it, bringing out its tenderness, its humor, its bite. It's been many a night since so glowing a performance has brightened the Broadway scene." Kate was now finally a Broadway star, even if the play only lasted a mere eighty-three performances.

During the run of *The Warrior's Husband,* Paramount was quick to offer her a picture deal, but she rejected it. On the other hand, when David O. Selznick, then production head of RKO Radio Pictures, was informed of the unique being known as Katharine Hepburn,* he offered her a studio contract. Instead of being overawed at the sudden beckoning of the cinema, arty Kate spit out the following comment about crass moviemakers: "They didn't like me until I got into a leg show." Although Kate was only making $79.50 a week from *The Warrior's Husband,* she was so sure Hollywood was a ridiculous place for her, that she demanded an absurd salary, $1,500 weekly. RKO did not say no, but politely requested that she screentest for

*Some say it was Kenneth Macgowan who suggested Kate to Selznick.

277

them in New York. At that time the studio was planning a screen rendition of *A Bill of Divorcement* and was requiring all newcomers to do a filmed reading from that play.* Kate was aware of the situation, and stated categorically that it was "impossible" for her to do the scene requested, asking instead to substitute a bit from *Holiday*. She made the test with actor Alan Campbell.† Years later Kate recalled this life-changing screentest. "I could imagine what it was like sitting in a projection room watching one girl after another play the same scene—over and over again. Finally, they get so immune to the scene, it doesn't have any meaning—so when I came on, looking sort of strange and mysterious—and may I say, photogenic?—they heard a new scene—and a damn good one too, by the way—and it worked. I'm not going to deny that luck has a lot to do with everything good that happens to us, but there's a little brainwork mixed up in it, too—don't forget that."

Kate was as surprised as anyone when her agent, Leland Hayward, advised that RKO had accepted her overpriced demands. After completing a previously arranged stock-company engagement in Ossining, New York, Kate embarked for Hollywood. Perhaps no one before or since has ever headed West with so determined a notion to set the movie industry on its collective heels, not so much to feather her own nest (indeed an important ingredient of her psyche) but to prove to the allegedly base film colony that artistic integrity was far more important than mere cinematic presence. To this day, no one has yet properly evaluated just how much of Kate's nonconformist stand in the early 1930s was inherited self-sufficiency, and how much was an offshoot of her extroverted pose of snobbishness to conceal her widespread insecurities. What is uncontroverted is that Kate's rebellious attitudes (offbeat acting style, bizarre manner of dressing, and cavalier handling of the supposedly all-important press) were considered heresy at the time; today these values would be regarded as commonplace (but then the Kate Hepburn of today has developed into a new extension of her avant-garde self).

At any rate, Kate, accompanied by her long-standing actress friend Laura Harding,‡ disembarked at the Pasadena, California, railway station on July 4, 1932. Myron Selznick, who had accompanied his partner, Leland Hayward, to greet their client, was reported as having uttered, "My God! Are we sticking them $1,500 a week for this!" Such was Kate's initial impact on the film colony.

From the start, Kate made it quite clear to RKO executives in all departments that she was not to be treated like any standard silver-screen apprentice ingenue, and more importantly that she would have none of the usual nonsense dished out by studio publicists, nor would she pander to the corps of news reporters covering the Hollywood scene. Most shocking of all was her staunch belief that autograph hounds should *not* be indulged under any circumstances.

---

*Opened at the George M. Cohan Theatre on October 10, 1921, for a 173-performance run, with Katharine Cornell in the lead.

†He later gained more recognition as the husband of writing wit Dorothy Parker.

‡A fellow student of Frances Robinson-Duff, she had worked with Kate at the Berkshire Playhouse in the summer of 1930.

RKO quite naturally wondered what it had let itself in for with this demanding stage actress, who was being needlessly insulting to everyone (from top to bottom), giving inane interviews, and being abusive to the press in general. Kate had yet to prove herself in the film medium, and the studio had its own stable of star ladies and promising newcomers to meet its casting needs, without having to contend with this unmanageable easterner. Then George Cukor* suddenly announced that he wanted Kate, not MGM's Norma Shearer or RKO's Irene Dunne, Jill Esmond or Anita Louise, for the plum role in *A Bill of Divorcement* (1932). Cukor would later explain his seemingly rash casting choice. "I saw a test that she'd done in New York. She was quite unlike anybody I'd ever seen. Though she'd never made a movie, she had this very definite knowledge and feeling right from the start . . . a quality of cutting through 'correctness.' " Not that genteel Cukor was agog over the emerging Hepburn mystique, for he often described her attitude in those early Hollywood years as "subcollegiate idiotic."

Once on the set, Kate settled down to business and under Cukor's patient tutelage†, her raw talent was reshaped into a fine, deliberately edged performance. Dealing with the picture's star, John Barrymore, was another matter for Kate. Oncamera she was to emote as his understanding daughter, the one constant force who remains loyal to him when, after escaping from an insane asylum, he returns to the family home to find that his wife (Billie Burke) is about to remarry. Newsmen, already out to shoot Kate down, were quick to report that on the first day of shooting, womanizing Barrymore attempted to seduce Kate in his luxurious soundstage dressing room. Another version had a distraught Kate yelling at the Great Profile, "I'll never play another scene with you." To which Barrymore is said to have calmly replied, "But my dear, you never have."‡

When *A Bill of Divorcement* opened in September, 1932, it proved a commercial hits,§ with the limelight shared by Barrymore, in his most sensitively shaded screen performance, and by Kate. Richard Watts, Jr. *(New York Herald-Tribune)* went so far as to pen, "The most effective portrayal of the film, however, is provided by Miss Katharine Hepburn, who is both beautiful and distinguished as the daughter, and seems definitely established for an important cinema career."

Directly after the completion of *A Bill of Divorcement,* Kate and her infrequently seen husband went to Europe. By the time they returned, word of

---

*Cukor had moved over to RKO from Paramount. He quickly impressed his new employer by helming the well-received *What Price Hollywood?* (1932), starring Constance Bennett.

†"In the pictures in which I have directed her," Cukor would later explain, "she has never at any time been unreasonable. She has had good ideas which she will fight for at the drop of a hat, at the same time admitting being in the wrong, if such happens to be the case."

‡Sometime later Kate would admit: "I learned a tremendous lot from Barrymore. One thing in particular has been invaluable to me—when you're in the same cast with people who know nothing about acting, you can't criticize them, because they go to pieces. He never criticized me. He just shoved me into what I ought to do before the camera. He taught me all that he could to one greenhorn in that short time."

§The 1940 remake with Maureen O'Hara starred would be a pale imitation in all departments.

her screen success was in the air, and the press was even more eager to learn details of her background, particularly concerning the rumor that she was married. For whatever reason—and there are many versions—Kate handled the matter quite flippantly, telling reporters she couldn't really recall if she were married, but she did know for a fact that she had five kids, "three of them colored." This eccentric behavior did nothing to endear her to the fourth estate, the studio officials, the public, or, for that matter, the shadowy Ogden Ludlow. He would remain in the East while Kate returned to Hollywood, where she shared hideaway bachelor digs with Laura Harding. Seldom was Kate on the Hollywood social scene, preferring to remain the rarely seen loner in public, the type of person who wore baggy sweaters and patched dungaree pants, and read her mail sitting on the curb outside the swank RKO studio. Kate did make one exception to her nonfraternization rule with the movie colony, and that was George Cukor, with whom she shared a growing camaraderie. She often participated in his Sundays-at-home where such celebrities as Tallulah Bankhead, Mary Garden, and Greta Garbo were frequent guests.

After the public's endorsement of Kate's work in *A Bill of Divorcement*, Kate's stock with David O. Selznick soared. He immediately saw her as the promising new leading lady of the RKO Radio-Pathé complex. *Christopher Strong* (1933), which had been scheduled for Ann Harding and Leslie Howard as a follow-up to their popular *The Animal Kingdom*, was reticketed with Kate and Colin Clive now in the leads.* To say the most, *Christopher Strong* was a strange tale, and it certainly fell within the precepts of Thornton Delehanty's *New York Post* warning, issued in his *A Bill of Divorcement* review: "All she [Kate] needs is a little more familiarity with the microphone, . . . and a firm determination not to let her producers exploit her as a second Garbo, a second Joan Crawford, or a second anything."

Christopher Strong attempted to make Kate into a leading lady of drawing-room tearjerkers. Granted the role of Lady Cynthia Darrington allowed Kate ample opportunity to exude that burgeoning screen quality of hers, as a strong-willed, independent individual, but Dorothy Arzner, the film's director, tended to stress the conventional aspects of this potentially unique if stately tragedy.† What emerged in the final print of *Christopher Strong* was not at all what the public had been led to expect as Kate's follow-up picture,

---

*At the time of Selznick's change of mind, Kate had already begun pre-production work on *Three Came Unarmed,* which was to co-star her with Joel McCrea and to be directed by Gregory La Cava.

†The unusual plot of *Christopher Strong* concerns pell-mell aviatrix Lady Cynthia Darrington (Kate), who meets conservative married man Clive. She is as absorbed in her flying avocation as he is with politics, but neither can deny their strong mutual attraction. They wisely decide to separate, she to undertake a global flight, he to fulfill a government mission to New York. They happen to meet in Manhattan, and once again their passion for each other is aroused. Later, after she has promised to abandon her dangerous hobby, Kate discovers she is pregnant, and in her distress she accepts a dare to break the world's aviation altitude record. As her craft noses above the 30,000-foot mark, she dramatically removes her oxygen mask, losing control of the plane and crashing to her death.

and it failed to arouse much box-office business.* Even the critics, while still enthusiastic about Kate's potential, carped that she was losing her special screen qualities by being shoved into the silver-screen mode of RKO's tear-jerker queens, Ann Harding and Irene Dunne. There are a few curiosity consolations to *Christopher Strong;* mostly visual, such as the sight of Kate garbed in her John Wayne leathernecking outfit complete with tight-fitting cap and goggles, and the arresting vision of Kate in her mothlike party costume, with its gossamer cape, lamé evening dress, and matching-antennae skullcap.

Kate and audiences had much better luck identifying with her character in *Morning Glory* (Radio City Music Hall, August 17, 1933), in which she was top-billed as Eva Lovelace. The story, based on Zoe Akins's play,† was old hat, but its energetic presentation was noteworthy. Kate was cast as a stage-struck miss from a small town in Vermont who is up against it, trying to win a professional niche in New York City. Elderly actor C. Aubrey Smith takes pity on her and offers her acting tips and an entree to a splashy Broadway party where she promptly becomes tipsy on a few glasses of champagne. In her inebriated state Kate's Eva launches into a recital of *Hamlet's* "To Be or Not to Be" soliloquy and the balcony scene from *Romeo and Juliet.* Most of the guests are offended or embarrassed by this display, but not play manager Adolphe Menjou, who soon maneuvers her into a love affair. However, it is not middle-aged, suave Menjou who captures her lifelong affections, but young playwright Douglas Fairbanks, Jr. When temperamental leading lady Mary Duncan walks out of Fairbanks's latest Broadway effort, Kate, who knows the part by heart, is substituted and is acclaimed an "overnight" star.

Contemporary audiences were well aware of the artistic deficiencies in *Morning Glory,* particularly in Lowell Sherman's unsubtle direction and Howard J. Green's trite screenplay; nevertheless, nearly everyone was convinced by the intense sincerity of Kate's performance, a characterization drawn no doubt from her own Broadway experiences. For the first time on-screen, Kate had occasion to portray an ingenuous, youthful soul who is both trusting and innately wise. Kate offered such a winning portrayal that she was Oscar-nominated and beat out May Robson *(Lady for a Day)* and Diana Wynyard *(Cavalcade)* for the Academy Award.

Louisa May Alcott's children's classic, *Little Women,* had been one of the prime projects on David O. Selznick's production lineup during his RKO tenure; he had been planning to cast Helen Mack as Beth and Dorothy Wilson as Jo. Before he departed RKO for a similar berth at MGM, Selznick

---

*RKO's advertising department offered a strong, but unsuccessful, pitch: "The personal story of a million daughters. Higher and higher! Faster and faster! She gave herself to the great god Speed, and tried to run away from the fires within her! Three hundred miles an hour, then the crash!"

†Miss Akins's play would not be produced until 1938, when it had a Pasadena Playhouse tryout preparatory to a Broadway spin which never occurred. *Morning Glory* would be indifferently remade as the movie *Stage Struck* (1958) with Susan Strasberg in Kate's old role.

assigned George Cukor to direct the major project. It was Cukor who decided that Kate should be the tomboy Jo, who in the course of the story is transformed from a headstrong lass into a courageous, loyal young lady.*

Little Women premiered at Radio City Music Hall on November 16, 1933 where it proceeded to break box-office records, foreshadowing its tremendous welcome in all parts of the country. Unlike the later MGM remake, the Cukor-directed rendition of *Little Women* hewed closely to the original book, retaining a balance of sincere sentiment and poignancy. Cukor had the cooperation of art director Van Nest Polglase and especially set decorator Hobe Erwin in avoiding the "chi-chi," clearing the way for the Civil War-period atmosphere to emerge in tasteful re-creation. With the support of her screen sisters (Frances Dee as Meg, Jean Parker as Beth, and Joan Bennett as Amy), Kate offered a splendidly hoydenish performance.† "Miss Hepburn steps up the ladder, if anything, by her interpretation of Jo," Mordaunt Hall *(New York Times)* decided. "She talks rather fast at times, but one feels that Jo did, and after all one does not wish to listen to dialogue in which every word is weighed when the part is acted by a Katharine Hepburn." At the Venice Film Festival of 1934, Kate was voted the best actress of the year.

As has been typical throughout Kate's professional career, a success was followed by a failure. Merian C. Cooper, the new production head of RKO, refused to loan Kate, the studio's prize property, to Jesse Lasky for the film version of *The Warrior's Husband* (Fox, 1933), which eventually starred Elissa Landi, nor would he allow her to be considered for Lasky's projected picturization of the life of ballerina Anna Pavlova, to be entitled *The Flight of the Swan.* Instead Cooper assigned Kate to *Spitfire* (1934).‡

"Completely and daringly different from anything she has ever done," read the posters advertising Kate in *Spitfire.* That it was, with Kate portraying an illiterate tomboy, an Ozark Mountain girl who believes herself a faith healer. Because of her strange "powers" her neighbors grow to fear her, and drive her from the community. The brave girl announces she will return sometime within the year to reoccupy her mountain cabin and to rekindle her romance with her protector, Ralph Bellamy. Unfortunately director John Cromwell had little success in conveying much reality to Kate's mystic healer from the far hills. Her inherent urbanity and her nasal voice conflicted with the essential simplicity of the characterization. As so often was her wont in these RKO years, Kate substituted vim and vigor for the subtly shaded portrayal she might have given.

Kate had performed in *Spitfire* as a concession§ to RKO executive Cooper

---

*†Kate would re-create her role of Jo on radio's "Theatre Guild of the Air," on December 30, 1945, with a repeat on December 21, 1947.

‡The film derived from the Broadway play *Trigger* by Lula Vollmer, which had opened on December 5, 1927 for a fifty-performance run at the Little Theatre, with Claiborne Foster in the lead.

§Kate's RKO contract had accidentally been allowed to expire during the protracted filming of *Spitfire,* and with the finale of the film yet to be lensed, Kate was able to charge the studio some $10,000 in overtime work.

so that he would finally okay her return to the Broadway stage to star in the New York edition of the London stage success, *The Lake* (Martin Beck Theatre, December 26, 1933).* The play opened with a sizable advance sale due to Kate's growing screen reputation. Despite Kate's insistence upon extensive coaching sessions from Frances Robinson-Duff (which would last throughout the run of the play), she was not prepared for the mantle of stage stardom. "There is no point pursuing Miss Hepburn with her limitations as a dramatic actress," wrote Brooks Atkinson *(New York Times).* "The simple fact is that as a result of her sensational achievement on the screen she has been projected into a stage part that requires more versatility than she has had time to develop. She still needs considerable training, especially for a voice that has unpleasant timbre." Dorothy Parker, one of the opening night audience at *The Lake,* was more caustically to the point, telling friends in the theatre lobby that Kate "runs the gamut of emotions all the way from A to B!" Kate was so disturbed by her unwieldy performance in *The Lake* that she bought her way out of the run-of-the-play contract with the producer for $15,500, even though the show was still doing above-par business.

Having freed herself from *The Lake,* Kate recuperated with a short European trek, and then journeyed to Merida, Yucatan, where on May 9, 1934 she obtained a divorce from Ogden Ludlow.† Years later Kate would admit of her Ludlow domestic partnership, "because I behaved very badly, I vowed I would never marry again."

Before Kate left RKO and Hollywood, there had been talk of starring her in either Edith Wharton's *Age of Innocence* (which Irene Dunne did for RKO in 1934), a biopicture about Queen Elizabeth, the life of Nell Gwynn, or Melville Baker and Jack Kirkland's original screenplay, *Without Sin.* Now RKO was seeking to lure Kate back to the picture-making fold with such variously touted projects as a rendition of *The Forsyte Saga,* the life of George Sand, and a filmed tribute to Joan of Arc. On her part, Kate was seriously considering remaining on the Broadway scene with a version of *Pride and Prejudice* to be produced under Arthur Hopkin's auspices. Then there was an offer to star in the Ivoryton Playhouse summer-season premiere of *Dark Victory,* but the play was temporarily shelved when co-star Stanley Ridges became ill.

Kate did succumb to RKO's importuning, and signed a lucrative $300,000 contract for six films to be made within a two-year period. Because she had both a film and a stage failure to her recent mark *(Spitfire, The Lake),* Kate

---

*Producer Jed Harris had wanted Kate to take the only female lead in the controversial *The Green Bay Tree* with Laurence Olivier and James Dale, but she and agent Leland Hayward said no; instead choosing Harris's British import, *The Lake.*

†Thirty-two-year-old Ludlow was apparently as shocked as his mother by Kate's precipitous action; and eight years later, uncertain as to the validity of the Yucatan divorce, he sued for divorce in Hartford, Connecticut, charging desertion. Five days after the decree was granted (September 18, 1942) he applied for a marriage license to wed twenty-four-year-old Bostonian Elisabeth K. Albers.

was more than anxious to make professional amends, and she tore into her new picture role with dedicated abandon. The screen version of James M. Barrie's *The Little Minister* (1934),* it was hoped, would be a popular follow-up to *Little Women*†; it was not, being too chock-full of obstructive pseudocharm.‡ Moreover, Kate's attempts at reaching a new histrionic maturity fell by the wayside, leaving a very mannered, cloying performance, full of synthetic whimsy. As Eileen Creelman *(New York Sun)* aptly analyzed, Kate was "just Miss Hepburn, arch, vivid, varying little, adored by a vast public. Wistful is not a Hepburn characteristic."

Kate was next thrust into the directorial care of Philip Moeller for *Break of Hearts* (1935). This contemporary soap opera left a great deal to be desired, both in story and in direction.§ Boyer was merely matinee idol Boyer,φ and Kate, well—while a good many critics bestowed praise on her still fresh and glowing vitality and her ability to rise above the maudlin story, there was a small but determined clique of critics who warned, "Still performing as the heroine of *Little Women,* Miss Hepburn makes it clear that unless her employers see fit to restore her to roles in keeping with her mannerisms, these will presently annoy cinemaddicts into forgetting that she is really an actress of great promise and considerable style." (*Time* magazine).

From the trivia of *Break of Hearts,* Kate launched into *Alice Adams* (Radio City Music Hall, August 15, 1935).** When production on the picture was to begin, Kate was furious to learn that novice director George Stevens had

*Barrie's work was first a novel (1891), then a play (1897), which was later transferred to the American stage with Maude Adams (in 1907 and a very successful 1915 revival). There were two silent-feature versions of *The Little Minister*—both in 1921: Vitagraph's edition starred Alice Calhoun and Jimmy Morrison, while Paramount's more elaborate rendition headlined Betty Compson and George Hackathorne.

†Kate would later confess: "I didn't really want to play it until I heard another actress [Margaret Sullavan] was desperate for the role. Then of course it became the most important thing in the world for me that I should get it. Several of my parts in those days I fought for just to take them from someone who needed them."

‡Within the plot of *The Little Minister,* seemingly demure Lady Babbie (Kate) delights in posing as a rambunctious gypsy wench, cavorting with the impoverished weavers of the Auld Licht Kirk in 1840s Thrums. She is an arch adherent of their social welfare causes, and takes every opportunity to warn them whenever her titled guardian (Frank Conroy) dispatches troops to put down their rebellious outbursts. Equally iconoclastic is her dalliance with the Kirk's new minister (John Beal). The two promptly fall in love, he knowing her only as the gypsy lass, which leads to a parish scandal. At the critical moment her noble lineage is revealed and all ends well.

§In *Break of Hearts,* unknown composer Kate trips into blissful romance with well-established musical conductor Charles Boyer, not knowing that he is seeing another woman. The appearance of sincere John Beal seems to be the answer to her dilemma for he offers her marriage. However, she rejects Beal, for her beloved Boyer has now sunk into alcoholism, and she is convinced that only her constant attention will restore his self-confidence and resurrect him from the depths of dipsomania.

φThe role of Franz Roberti was originally scheduled for John Barrymore; when he was dropped from the production lineup, Francis Lederer was given the part, but he could not work with Kate, and Boyer was thus substituted.

**Kate had suggested a screen rendition of Booth Tarkington's *Seventeen,* with William Wyler to direct. But Wyler was contracted elsewhere, so RKO whipped up a version of Tarkington's Pulitzer Prize-winning novel, *Alice Adams.*

been foisted on her, but after the star and megaphoner recuperated from their initial battles of will, they developed a fine personal rapport. More importantly, he squeezed from "Miss Rebel" one of her best performances, shrewdly manipulating her acting vices into character-portrayal virtues.

Perhaps of all Kate's 1930s films, *Alice Adams** best reveals her potential richness of variety in acting technique, demonstrating that subtlety was not beyond her professional reach. In *Alice Adams*, Mr. Adams (Fred Stone) is contentedly employed at Lamb's Wholesale Drugs in the little town of South Ranford. But his wife (Ann Shoemaker) wants their daughter (Kate) to marry well, so she cajoles him into leaving his job by using a glue formula he has invented to branch out into business for himself. Later it is learned that their son (Frank Albertson) has misappropriated funds from Mr. Lamb (Charles Grapewin), and it requires a good deal of humbling on Stone's part before Grapewin not only forgives the son's misdeed but agrees to join in partnership with Stone in his faltering but promising glue business. In the midst of these tumultuous events, Kate experiences the tribulations of growing womanhood; anxious for social recognition by her more aristocratic girlgriends, she is persistently oblivious to their continual snubs. At a big party, she fortuitously meets engineer Fred MacMurray, who takes an interest in her and eventually, after many false starts, asks her to wed him.

Alice Adams contains two enormously effective sequences. The first occurs at the elegant party given by Mildred Palmer (Evelyn Venable), which finds Kate being invited only as a not-so-polite afterthought. Kate cannot afford a new dress for the occasion and must remodel a two-year-old white ensemble. To give her restitched costume the proper finishing touch, she illegally scoops up a bunch of violets from the park to make the corsage which she cannot afford to purchase and which she knows no would-be swain will provide for her. In fact, she and her mother have had to nag her uncouth brother into escorting the dewy-eyed Kate to the big function. Kate is nearly heedless that due to a rainstorm she must drape her father's unbecoming old raincoat around her shoulders, although she does express distinct misgivings at having to be conveyed to the Palmers' (Hedda Hopper, Jonathan Hale) in the wobbly old car her brother has borrowed for the occasion. Once at the crowded dance, Kate experiences (and fully reacts to) the total range of agonies endured by anyone who has ever been forced into the position of wallflower-for-the-night. She toys neurotically with her corsage, stares abstractly into space, fidgets in her chair, pretends to be engaged in conversation with the snooty hosts, who are oblivious to her presence, makes extended pleasant chitchat with the seated group of elders, and experiences momentary overjoyment when bloated dunce Grady Sutton asks her to dance with him. (She makes a valiant effort to ignore the looks of derision from the assembled smartaleck guests, as she and cloddish Sutton whirl about the

---

*The story had been filmed before in 1923 by Associated Exhibitors with Florence Vidor in the lead; it was a far more faithful rendition of Tarkington's story.

dance floor.) Then, as if by a miracle, charming, handsome Fred MacMurray pops into sight and Kate manages to win his attention and interest. Despite losing him to his distant cousin (Evelyn Venable) for the time being, the evening has had its brief moments of reward, sufficient upon which to weave a whole fantasy of social acceptance. The emotional horrors she endured that night have had their compensations.

The other sequence in *Alice Adams* is even more vital to the canon of great screen moments in Kate's film career. Many at the time—and even today—freely read into the scene (and Kate's performance through the picture) that her acting approach herein was very indicative of Kate the real-life person. For in the famous dinner scene* all the pretentious foibles and maddeningly artificial poses of socially ambitious Alice Adams come to the embarrassing foreground. They are made all the more dramatically effective because of the persistent acts of misfate which all but reduce the evening and Kate to shambles, counterbalanced by MacMurray's slick portrayal of the polite guest who tries very hard to ignore the sting of the *faux pas*. To begin with, the maid hired for the evening turns out to be gum-chewing Hattie McDaniel, whose lack of parlor etiquette is all too evident. The domestic is more concerned with retaining her constantly slipping starched servant's cap on her head than in dishing out the dinner in the approved Emily Post manner. No matter. The increasingly nervous, and twitching, Kate guides the family (from squirming Stone, who cannot adjust to his formal dinner outfit, to oversolicitous Shoemaker; Albertson has refused to participate in the charade) through a dinner that is a paragon of bad planning. It is one of the hottest nights of the summer and the Adams' dining room suffers from lack of proper ventilation, causing everyone but Kate to skip the soup course. As for the main dish of sweetbreads, Kate digs into her helping, but even MacMurray can only make a feeble attempt at toying with his serving. The dinner is capped by a dessert of melted vanilla ice cream.

Granted, there are many gawky moments in *Alice Adams,*† and several critics, including Otis Ferguson *(New Republic),* carped that "she shouldn't have made her performance in it simply a smudged copy of something that in time leaves open to easy jeers qualities that are essentially enough to take an ordinary person's breath away." Other more fervent detractors of the Hepburn screen image, insisted that her performance in *Alice Adams* was merely an unintentional mocking of all the idiosyncrasies of mannerism that had plagued her since she first trod the acting footboards.

On the other hand, a sufficient number of respected aesthetic judges sided with Kate's performance in this acknowledged bit of screen hokum, that she

---

*In the context of the story, Kate's heroine has been nagged by her mother into inviting MacMurray to dinner. Until now, Kate has always managed to hold her courtship meetings with MacMurray on the neutral front porch, thus avoiding having to explain away her middle-class home and family.

† As when MacMurray finally proposes to the moon-struck Kate. In the resultant big close-up of her, all she can say is a ludicrous "Gee Whiz!"

was nominated for her second Academy Award, but she lost out to Bette Davis, who won the best-actress Oscar for *Dangerous*. (In her autobiography, *The Lonely Life* [1962], Davis says she thinks Kate should have won the prize.)

RKO's *Sylvia Scarlett* (1936) reunited Kate with director George Cukor, the latter borrowed from MGM where he was already entrenched in directing that studio's bevy of women stars to considerable advantage. The controversial nature of the story to *Sylvia Scarlett*—in which Kate masquerades as a boy in order to escape to France with her larceny-bent father (Edmund Gwenn)—far outshone the picture itself, which was very poorly received. Despite the prestige presence of Kate and Cary Grant (in his new screen persona as a drawing-room comedian), the Pandro S. Berman production lost well over $200,000.*

After the dismal failure of the avant-garde *Sylvia Scarlett*,† Kate was rather eager to divert her creative talents to stage work, in particular by accepting Max Reinhardt's offer for her to star in a summertime production of *Twelfth Night* at the Hollywood Bowl. But Pandro S. Berman and RKO remained firm that her film schedule was too crowded to permit such frivolities. To prove their point, it was announced that the studio had Anthony Veiller at work adapting the Hungarian play *Marie Bashkirtseff*, in which Kate was to star. (She never did make that film.) Then there was the publicized discussion between RKO and MGM about the former lending Metro the services of Kate for its upcoming historical romancer, *The Gorgeous Hussy*. (It was made in 1936 with Joan Crawford.)

While these projects did not materialize for Kate, a screen adaptation of Maxwell Anderson's *Mary of Scotland* (1936)‡ did. It is readily fathomable why director John Ford selected the patriotic project and equally understandable why Kate was enamored of her role as the doomed Queen of Scots. But noble intentions do not make a good film. Scenarist Dudley Nichols removed much of Anderson's blank verse, hoping to enliven the historical drama, while director Ford concentrated on the epic pageantry so much a part of sixteenth-century Britain. But there were too many strikes against the film for it to be viable entertainment. (On the strength of its marquee names and production values it did garner respectable revenues.) Fredric March, admittedly one of this author's least favorite screen performers, went to unsubtle lengths to exert a manly Scottish aura as the Earl of Bothwell, who becomes not only Mary Stuart's (Kate) protector but also her lover. An even larger casting de-

---

*George Cukor enjoys recounting the disastrous preview evening of *Sylvia Scarlett*. "A nightmare. People rushing out up the aisles! Then Kate went to the ladies' john, and there was a woman lying down there. Kate asked, 'Was the picture so bad?' and the woman just raised her eyes up to heaven. . . . Then we got into my car, and Kate hit her head. . . . [Back at his house, they met Berman] And Kate and I said, 'Pandro, scrap the picture, we'll do another picture for you for nothing! and he said, not kidding, 'I never want to see either of you again!'

† In recent years the picture has gained its own underground reputation.

‡Opened November 23, 1933, at the Alvin Theatre for a run of 248 performances, with Helen Hayes as Mary and Helen Menken as Elizabeth.

ficiency resulted from acceding to March's wish that his real-life wife, actress Florence Eldridge, be utilized as Queen Elizabeth.* I believe that it would have been more astute casting to have Kate and Eldridge (once she was locked into the production) switch roles. The fierce resoluteness which the heavily costumed Kate radiated in the film was more in keeping with the realities of the nature of the Queen of England, while the flittery, namby-pamby strutting of the pompous Eldridge might have sufficed for the more feminine Mary Stuart.

Be that as it may, *Mary of Scotland* emerged a resplendent historical panorama, visually somewhere between *Queen Christina* and *The Private Lives of Elizabeth and Essex*. The RKO epic was short on expansive sets, but long on mood-evoking kilts, bagpipes, native ditties, and thick burrs.† With its wealth of historically twisted facts, including a fictional encounter between the two Queens, *Mary of Scotland* plodded its way through to its tragic end.‡ On the whole, this picture did more to bolster the studio's artistic standing within the industry than to fill its corporate coffers.

Kate's role as the steadfast Queen who prefers death as a "traitor" to signing away all claims to the English throne, had a surefire finale. After a lengthy internment at Fotheringay, Kate's Mary Stuart mounts the long stairway to the chopping block. As she undertakes the long, final climb, the camera pans upward from her prayer-bent eyes past the castle and to heaven. There are repeated peals of thunder as she and the audience hear, wafting in the great above, refrains from the piping of her dead lover (March).

There were many, especially critics abroad, who complained that Kate's accent in *Mary of Scotland* was pure Hepburnian and not a whit resembling the famed Mary Stuart, but even her detractors had to admit that Kate had dramatic gumption,§ and that she was straining in earnest to offer a sincere characterization above and beyond her accustomed bag of histrionic tricks.

Kate moved from this costume picture to two more such RKO entries. *A Woman Rebels* (1936) presented her as Pamela Thistlewaite, a young woman of Victorian England who fights to win emancipation in the face of the strict conventions of the 1870s. The well-appointed picture, hampered by the pres-

*RKO's Ginger Rogers and Warner Brothers' Bette Davis were among the actresses who craved this meaty part.

†Has anyone ever counted the number of "laddies" uttered by Donald Crisp in the course of this film?

‡While the plethora of talky sequences leaves one a bit anesthetized long before the emotion-evoking finale comes into view, this version created far more empathy for the characters than the 1971 *Mary, Queen of Scots* starring Glenda Jackson (Elizabeth) and Vanessa Redgrave (Mary Stuart).

§Otis Ferguson *(New Republic)* essayed: "For when the spotlight and scenic effects have faded, there still remains the fact that for all her digressions into mannerism and poor type parts as of the past, for all her naive reliance on her own resources and befuddled trying, this girl, with the curious wide mouth and lips and flesh tight over her facial bones, is an artist in our theatre by virtue of combining personal strength and fire with the grace of giving out to people. Her work is not in mimicry or in a ridiculous building of many parts, but it is creative in itself, a sort of bright emanation."

ence of genteel but dull Herbert Marshall as her patient suitor, may have appealed to the women's liberation spirit of Kate and her campaigning mother, but it left the majority of filmgoers entertainment-hungry. But RKO and Kate remained undaunted. Searching for yet another vehicle in the mold of *Little Women,* they turned to *Quality Street* (1937).* Like *The Little Minister,* this archaic bit of flim-flam was from the whimsical pen of James M. Barrie and had also starred Maude Adams onstage. George Stevens directed this airy drawing-room romance of Napoleonic England, and for those who bothered to witness this ornamented production, Fay Bainter as the level-headed sister (of Kate) seemed far more appealing than bantering wistful Kate, who had a dual role as the drab schoolteacher Phoebe Throssel and as the flirtatious Livvy out to win back the dashing soldier, Franchot Tone.

Having completed her six-picture RKO pact, Kate was determined to return to her first professional love, the stage. She gladly accepted the Theatre Guild's offer to star in Helen Jerome's adaptation of Charlotte Brontë's *Jane Eyre,* at $1,500-a-week salary. The play opened its tryout tour in New Haven on December 26, 1936, to less than enthusiastic notices, but in its four months on the road it did booming box-office business. For by this time, Kate, who had dated her agent, Leland Hayward, before he wed Margaret Sullavan, had become the constant companion of Howard Hughes, a seemingly unfathomable man whose romances would include a wide range of actresses, including Billie Dove, June Lang, Ginger Rogers, Gina Lollobrigida, and Jean Peters. The much heralded romance between Kate and Hughes was headlined during the entire course of her fourteen-week play tour, with news photographers eagerly snapping shots of Kate dashing down a runway for a rendezvous with Hughes. Those in the know say that what intrigued the mercurial Hughes most about Kate was the combination of her wit, and their mutual enjoyment of flying and golfing. Like *Jane Eyre,* the Hepburn-Hughes romance never reached an official finish, for she and Hughes drifted apart, and *Jane Eyre,* after earning a terrific $340,000 gross on the road, shuttered without reaching New York. Many speculated that Kate did not have the internal fortitude to face bad stage reviews still one more time.

Regimes came and went at RKO—Pandro S. Berman was now head of production—but thirty-year-old Kate was still considered a commodity of value to the studio's welfare, particularly now that its string of prestigious leading ladies had left the lot,† leaving a big gap to fill in its A-picture programming. Thus RKO still needed Kate and reached a new four-picture contract with her, the terms of which remained peculiarly secret even in gossip-bent

---

*It had better served Marion Davies a decade before in a silent-picture version.

†Ann Harding, Constance Bennett, and Irene Dunne were no longer under (exclusive) RKO contract. Ginger Rogers, largely via her co-starring musicals with Fred Astaire, had risen to a top studio berth, but had yet to show her capabilities in dramatic or whimsical comedy entries— the established fortes of Kate. Of the studio's newcomers, Joan Fontaine was being given the big RKO push.

Hollywood. Tied to a new studio agreement, Kate gave up notions of starring in Max Gordon's planned revival of *Peter Pan*. She closed up the East 49th Street brownstone in Manhattan where she had lived since 1934, but had only finished buying in 1937. (In contrast, to this day she has never owned a Hollywood home, reasoning, "I never expected to stay.")

RKO announced that Kate would star in *The Mad Miss Manton*, a comedy originally planned for the departed Irene Dunne. But the 1937 screwball entry went to Barbara Stanwyck, for the studio decided to showcase Kate in a contemporary picture backed by the best talent available on the lot. The studio acquired the screen rights to the Edna Ferber-George S. Kaufman broadway success *Stage Door*.* Scenarists Morrie Ryskind and Anthony Veiller revamped the stage original to emphasize Kate's role of Terry Randall as the lead part.† Kate's Terry is the smug debutante who sashays into Manhattan's Footlights Club to harvest theatrical flavor from the earnest group of impoverished would-be actresses residing there. Soon highfalutin Kate has attracted the attention of dapper Broadway producer Adolphe Menjou, who hires her for the ingenue part in the upcoming production of *Enchanted April*. Only when Andrea Leeds, yet another of the Footlights girls, becomes distraught about losing the *Enchanted April* role—a part she was born to play—and commits suicide on opening night, does the unfeeling Kate experience a catharsis of humanity. As superannuated Constance Collier informs the near-hysterical Kate, "You've got to give the performance she wanted you to give. Then maybe you can bring her peace wherever she is." Kate then glides onto stage, offers an inspired performance, and is acclaimed a stage find.‡ More important to the girls of the Footlights Club, her humble curtain speech reveals she has awakened to reality, shaken loose from the tinsel arrogance.

The success of *Stage Door* (Radio City Music Hall, October 7, 1937), which grossed over $2 million at a production cost of $900,000, was not entirely due to Kate. Inspired director Gregory La Cava, famed for working off the cuff, instilled a spontaneity among his troupe of contrasting femme types at the Footlights Club, ranging from tart Lucille Ball and Eve Arden, to the zingy presence of Ginger Rogers, who, as Kate's basic roomie, proved her screen talents were not limited to the ballroom floor. Most noteworthy was the well-etched performance of Andrea Leeds, who received an Oscar nomination (best supporting actress) for her emoting in *Stage Door*. As to Kate's generally well received performance, Mordaunt Hall *(New York Times)* expressed it all, when he wrote: "It is the type of role in which Miss Hepburn excels. Where most actresses in dealing with the part of a stagestruck girl

---

*The drama opened October 21, 1936, at the Music Box Theatre for a run of 169 performances. Kate's longstanding professional rival, Margaret Sullavan, had the lead on Broadway.

†George S. Kaufman quipped of the movie version, "It should be called *Screen Door*."

‡Yes, this is the play-within-the-movie in which Kate says, "The calla lilies are in bloom again," and the movie in which her character's pet expression was "really" (pronounced by Kate as "raer-leh").

might be tempted to over-act, Miss Hepburn realizes the need for restraint, evidenced by her brilliant work several years ago in *Morning Glory,* and in this current picture she is equally effective. Her Terry is a vivacious, honest, intelligent girl."

Inspired by Kate's reception in *Stage Door* in which she demonstrated a flair for comedy, RKO concocted *Bringing Up Baby* (Radio City Music Hall, March 3, 1938), which reteamed her with Cary Grant under the direction of Howard Hawks. Even a mere year before this madcap comedy was made, no one would have suspected that mannered, whimsical Kate could have excelled in screwball comedy, a genre formerly regarded as the exclusive province of Carole Lombard and more recently of Irene Dunne and even melodramatic Miriam Hopkins. But as the devil-may-care heiress who appears on the scene to cause zoology professor Grant to lose his fiancée (Virginia Walker), a rare dinosaur bone, the promised $1 million museum endowment from her aunt (May Robson), and nearly his sanity, Kate is as sleek and lightning-paced in her timing here as "Baby," the pet Brazilian leopard she leaves in Grant's care in *Bringing Up Baby.* The picture's situations were downright improbable and the slapstick fantastic, but it was a revelatory joy to see the once prissy, self-contained Kate letting loose in a comedy in which she trips over logs, falls flat on her face, and has a knock-out encounter with Grant. To this day, *Bringing Up Baby* remains one of Kate's best remembered performances; in fact her zany interpretation of the headstrong miss with "bounding, brassy nerve" and the picture itself served as the prototype for Peter Bogdanovich's *What's Up Doc* (1971), starring Ryan O'Neal and Barbra Streisand.

Almost perversely, as good as Kate had been in *Bringing Up Baby,* her professional status took a sudden nosedive. Exhibitor Harry Brandt, spokesman of the Independent Theatre Owners of America, came out with his now legendary listing of luminaries whom his membership considered box-office poison. Among the stars attacked were Edward Arnold, Fred Astaire, Joan Crawford, Marlene Dietrich, Kay Francis, Greta Garbo, Mae West—and Katharine Hepburn. Rather than express dismay—at least publicly—Kate insisted: "They say I'm a has-been. If I weren't laughing so hard, I might cry." But RKO was not so cavalier about the situation. Suddenly Kate was "requested" to star in what at best could be classified a high-grade programmer, in a role that was quite alien to the personality of the thirty-one-year-old star. Kate realized that accepting the lead in RKO's *Mother Carey's Chickens* was professionally untenable. Therefore, she bought herself out of her RKO contract for $200,000.*

After her RKO pact was dissolved, Kate beat out Irene Dunne for the lead in Columbia's remake of *Holiday* (1938), directed by George Cukor and again teaming her with Cary Grant. At last Kate had the opportunity to tear

*Ginger Rogers next inherited *Mother Carey's Chickens,* before it was finally, and far more appropriately, ticketed to Anne Shirley.

into the role of Linda Seton, which she had understudied on Broadway a decade before. Because the essence of *Holiday* is the study of a nonconformist social dropout (Grant) who looks askance at the misplaced values of unthinking rich folk, the film remains topical today. So does Kate's performance as the life-loving tomboy sister of conventional Doris Nolan, who agrees with Grant that adventures should be undertaken when one is young enough to enjoy and benefit from the experiences. The "new Hepburn" (as the Columbia press copy labeled her) gave "her liveliest performance since appearing in his [Cukor's] *Little Women*" (*Time* magazine). Gone were most of Kate's previous telltale hysterical overtones and jittery mannerisms, replaced by a slick, new deep-voiced smoothness, precise and to the contemporary point. Co-star Grant would later evaluate Kate: "As an actress she's a joy to work with. She's in there trying every minute. There isn't anything passive about her; she 'gives.' And as a person, she's real. There's no pretense about her. She's the most completely honest woman I've ever met."

When Kate bought out of her RKO pact, refusing to play in *Mother Carey's Chickens* was not her sole reason. Like most every other actress in Hollywood—or woman in the world, for that matter—she had her heart set on winning the dearly held role of Scarlett O'Hara in *Gone with the Wind*. She employed all her ingenuity to convince that epic's producer, David O. Selznick, that gone were her *Little Women* days, that she was now correct for the part. "The part was practically written for me. I am Scarlett O'Hara." But she had several odds in her disfavor. Selznick wrote in a memo on November 18, 1938: "I think Hepburn has two strikes against her—first, the unquestionable and very widespread intense public dislike of her at the moment, and second, the fact that she is yet to demonstrate that she posesses the sex qualities which are probably the most important of all the many requisites of Scarlett." Equally important was the fact that, unlike such other strong contenders as Jean Arthur, Joan Bennett, Loretta Young, and Paulette Goddard, Kate refused to test for the part, claiming "If you don't know whether I can act by now, you never will." In the final analysis, Selznick stuck with his original impression, "I just can't imagine Rhett Butler [Clark Gable] chasing you for ten years."

Shattered by her loss of *Gone with the Wind* and the public apathy to her career, Kate remained secluded in Connecticut for much of the summer and fall of 1938, refusing play offers and such film pacts as that extended by MGM at $5,000 weekly (but with no script approval clause). However, when playwright Philip Barry approached Kate with a new play, that was a different story. The comedy *(The Philadelphia Story)*, and particularly the part of Tracy Lord, appealed to her greatly; Kate not only consented to star in the stage venture but to provide one-fourth of the backing.* In lieu of salary Kate agreed to accept 10 percent of the gross profits from the New York engagement and 12½ percent from any road-company editions. Even wiser was her decision to acquire the screen rights to *The Philadelphia Story*.

*Barry, the Theatre Guild, and Howard Hughes were the other partners in the production.

292

As the play went through its arduous rehearsals, the part of Tracy Lord was remolded to suit Kate, and Kate adapted her acting approach to fit the role. By the time *The Philadelphia Story* opened on March 29, 1939, at the Shubert Theatre, Kate and the cast (which included Joseph Cotten, Shirley Booth, Van Heflin, and Nicholas Joy) were prepared to greet Broadway with a perfectly modulated evening of theatre. Both *The Philadelphia Story* and Kate were registered immediate hits. "She acts it like a woman who has at last found the joy she has always been seeking in the theatre . . . There are no ambiguous corners in this character portrayal. Dainty in style, it is free and alive in its darting expression of feeling" (Brooks Atkinson, *New York Times*).

Kate remained with *The Philadelphia Story* throughout its 415-performance-Broadway run, and headlined the touring company for 254 performances. When the road version closed on February 15, 1941, in Philadelphia (the same city where the show had first tried out some two years before), Kate provided a most touching curtain call. She brought the electricians and stagehands to stage center. "When I started this play," she informed the hushed audience, "these people knew I was on the spot. They could have treated me as a climber and a phony. Instead they treated me as an actress and a friend." Everyone then joined in the singing of "Auld Lang Syne." This was a far cry from the Kate of even a few years prior.

Several studios had competitively bid for the screen rights to *The Philadelphia Story,* but it was Louis B. Mayer at MGM who offered Kate the package she wanted: she to star as Tracy Lord, George Cukor to direct, Cary Grant* and James Stewart as her co-stars, and—an essential point for her—reasonable consultation on the screenplay. With Cukor directing and a slick screenplay by Donald Ogden Stewart, which smoothly incorporated new scenes into the storyline while modifying the original to fit the film medium, the movie emerged a tremendous box-office hit, breaking attendance records at Radio City Music Hall (opened December 26, 1940), where in its six-week engagement it grossed almost $600,000. Those who had seen both the stage and film versions, insisted that Kate had improved her performance in the movie translation. As the spoiled, vacillating Tracy Lord on the eve of her second marriage, the *Christian Science Monitor* found, "There is a sheen now to her vividness, and her abrupt, electric style of motion has taken on flow and grace. There is no doubt of her validity in the role of Tracy Lord." The New York Film Critics bestowed their coveted best-actress award on Kate, but Hollywood was not so forgiving to its prima donna. While *The Philadelphia Story* received six Oscar nominations—including best picture, best actress (Kate), best actor (James Stewart), best supporting actress (Ruth Hussey), best director (Cukor), and best screenplay (Donald Ogden Stewart)—only the two Stewarts won actual Oscars. Kate lost to her old RKO teammate Ginger Rogers, who earned her Academy Award for *Kitty Foyle.*

*Grant received top-billing in the film, the first time Kate was subordinated in screen credit since *A Bill of Divorcement.*

Kate and the cast members of the film would re-create their *The Philadelphia Story* roles on "Lux Radio Theatre" on July 20, 1942.

Oncamera Kate of the 1940s could be as mannered and overblown as the role of Tracy Lord, by the very nature of its creation in her image, but away from the set she displayed a new vulnerability. It was no secret she greatly desired a new studio berth and had her hopes set on joining the MGM celebrity stable. But Louis B. Mayer, with "more stars than there are in heaven," had his chubby hands full balancing the company's production schedule and did not immediately come up with a suitable vehicle for Kate. After Kate supplied the narration for the Office of War Information documentary short subject *Women in Defense* (1941),* she turned packaging agent for the second time in her film career, and proved to be a shrewd businesswoman.

Admittedly fate played an important role in the subsequent events, which were to irrevocably alter the course of her screen career and her private life. Ring Lardner, Jr. brought an outline draft of a proposed screenplay to Garson Kanin, with the hope that the latter could develop it into a viable film project. However, Garson Kanin had just been drafted into the Army, so he suggested that Lardner work with his younger brother, Michael Kanin, on a complete version of the project, which would incorporate any suggestions the elder Kanin found time to offer. Furthermore, Kanin advised the fledgling screenwriters to bring their finished work to the attention of Kate. They did; she was tremendously impressed with the project and in turn sent it on to Louis B. Mayer, who bought the "anonymous" package for $211,000. Kate gave each of the young scenarists $50,000, taking $100,000 for herself in addition to $11,000 in commissions and agent's fees. Climaxing her coup, she wrung from Mayer the star contract she sought, with the concession that she not only would star in *Woman of the Year* but would have her choice of director and leading man.

Kate wanted and got George Stevens as director, but obtaining Spencer Tracy, whom she had never met but admired as a performer, was another story. Tracy was then on location in Florida for what proved to be the abortive first attempt at filming *The Yearling*. When the project was abandoned for the time being, Tracy returned to Hollywood and found himself free to meet the challenge of dealing with the headstrong, authoritarian Miss Hepburn.

Kate had not encountered anyone quite like the forty-one-year-old Tracy on the MGM lot. After meeting her co-star to be, she told producer Joseph L. Mankiewicz, "I'm afraid I'm a little tall for Mr. Tracy."† It was Mankiewicz, not Tracy, who uttered that immortal retort, "Don't worry, Miss Hepburn. He'll cut you down to size."

*Kate did the narration because "it's the first time in my life anyone wanted me for my voice."

†A strange remark on Kate's part, considering she had gotten into the habit at MGM of wearing three-inch platform shoes to make her tower over such short Metro executives as Louis B. Mayer, Ben Thau, Eddie Mannix, and Sidney Franklin.

As many critics of the day and thereafter have analyzed to the nth degree, the teaming of two such disparate types as Spencer Tracy and Katharine Hepburn worked exceedingly well,* each complementing the other's contrasting acting style, adding new dimensions of humaneness to both players' already rich screen presence. *Woman of the Year* (Radio City Music Hall, February 5, 1942) established the brand of cinema chemistry between Tracy and Kate that would endure for eight additional pictures over the next twenty years. She is aggressive, maneuvering, challenging, and forever coy; he is the solidly affirmative, but innately shy, personality who in the long run proves to be the more resilient, imaginative, and, at heart, a true romantic.

In *Woman of the Year,* Kate plays global-affairs columnist Tess Hardings, who comes to loggerheads with craggy sports writer Sam Craig (Tracy) over the estimable subject of baseball. The two opponents not only come to terms regarding the sport, but soon marry, much to the surprise of their acquaintances. Yet Kate's Tess is not about to sacrifice her booming career for a heavy dose of domesticity, causing Tracy to eventually quit the homefront. Belatedly—but still in the nick of time—she learns that being a good wife means more than being named Woman of the Year. With new resolve, she exerts total effort (if not success, in the hilarious breakfast-making scene) into becoming a model spouse for homebody Tracy.

Critics and public alike cottoned to the new, liberated Kate,† no longer an icy figure on a self-made pedestal, but a feeling woman who acknowledges her responsibilities to the man in her life. She was nominated for her fourth Academy Award, but lost out to Greer Garson, who won for MGM's *Mrs. Miniver.* Although she missed out on the Oscar accolade, she had convinced MGM that she could successfully work together with contract star Spencer Tracy, and it was decided that this latest screen team should join the gallery of Metro star pairs (including William Powell-Myrna Loy, Greer Garson-Walter Pidgeon, Mickey Rooney-Judy Garland) for many more go-rounds at the box office.‡

After completing *Woman of the Year* in late 1941, Kate came East to co-star with Elliott Nugent in Philip Barry's *Without Love,* which the playwright had created with her in mind. The show opened at the McCarter Theatre in Princeton, New Jersey, on March 5, 1942, for a tryout engagement, and then toured for three months, including a stand at the Bushnell Memorial Hall in Hartford, Connecticut. While Barry proceeded to rewrite portions of the show, Kate returned to Hollywood, not to do Cecil B. De

* Tracy insisted upon and always received top-billing in his joint assignments with Kate.

†"Katharine Hepburn wouldn't win a screen-test for pretties, yet she has that rare quality of composing all the lines of her face and figure, sense and feeling into a pattern that is seen and felt as a thing of beauty. And she has never before seemed able to condense into one performance so much of this almost outrageous challenge and appeal, deliberate affectation, and genuine, delightful ease" (Otis Ferguson, *New Republic*).

‡ The Tracy-Hepburn combination would repeat their *Woman of the Year* roles on a "Screen Guild of the Air" radio broadcast.

Mille's *Reap the Wild Wind* at Paramount as had been rumored, but to co-star with Tracy in *Keeper of the Flame* (1942), based on I. A. R. Wylie's chilling novel. The quiet Gothic thriller, with overtones of *Citizen Kane* and reminiscent of Alfred Hitchcock's pervading moods of terror, was entrusted to George Cukor, who sought to prove that the oncamera combination of Tracy and Hepburn could push far and above the screen comedy of *Woman of the Year*. As the widow with a secret about her late husband,* she comes into conflict with Tracy, a renowned correspondent assigned to delve into the legend surrounding her deceased "national hero" husband. Tracy discovers in time that Kate's peculiar silence is not a result of evil complicity in the man's murder, but rather derives from love of country and a refusal to shatter the myth at such a critical time in America's history. *Keeper of the Flame* was a slickly turned out psychological thriller, but it was quite unsatisfactory as a whole, unresolved in its ideological and romantic implications. For all of Tracy's admirable restraint in his detached role as the investigator, Kate retained the limelight as the grieving widow whose life is clouded with an impenetrable mysteriousness. *Keeper of the Flame* proved to be a watershed mark for the film career of thirty-five-year-old Kate, being the last time she would essay a romantic glamour-girl part oncamera.

With the second Tracy-Hepburn film in the can, Kate returned to New York to open *Without Love* (St. James Theatre, November 10, 1942). The critics snapped testily about Philip Barry's fuzzy characterizations and the playwright's insistence upon lumping together an unhomogeneous blend of politics and romance. Kate came in for her share of critical raps for being as mechanical as the script. But on the strength of star and playwright, *Without Love* strung out for 113 performances. During the show's run Kate volunteered her services to the American Theatre Wing by appearing as herself in the all-star tribute picture *Stage Door Canteen* (United Artists, 1943), filmed in New York.

There was talk of Kate heading a filmization of George Bernard Shaw's *The Millionairess,* but, like plans for Paramount borrowing her for Daphne du Maurier's *Frenchman's Creek* (1944), it came to naught. Instead she reported back to MGM in Culver City for what she considered a most challenging assignment, the role of Jade in Pearl Buck's best-selling novel of World War II China, *Dragon Seed* (1944). Metro assembled a stellar cast, the only fault being—and no one let the studio forget it once the picture was released—most of the players were Occidentals playacting at being Orientals. When accepting this difficult *Dragon Seed* part, which was fraught with obvious pitfalls, Kate was comforted by the thought that a similar role in *The Good Earth* netted Luise Rainer an Academy award. Moreover, the character of Jade would allow her to play a zealous patriot, determined as a Chinese to fight for her homeland, and equally resolved as a woman to fight for

---

*He was far from being the superphilanthropist he pretended to be but was really the sinister force behind a fascist movement.

the dignity and safety of her family. As *Dragon Seed* turned out, Walter Huston and Aline MacMahon, as Kate's honorable parents, garnered the best notices, while Kate, once the critics grew accustomed to her nasal twang and sharply Anglo-Saxon features juxtaposed in a Chinese setting, was accorded accolades for generating a portrayal so glowing in benevolent grandeur.

Harold S. Bucquet, who had co-directed *Dragon Seed,* helmed the film edition of *Without Love* (1945), which united Tracy and Hepburn onscreen for the third time. Once again Donald Ogden Stewart was on hand to update, polish, depoliticalize, and refine a Philip Barry stage original for the cinema. The premise remained essentially the same, though; a comely widow (Kate), in wartime-crowded Washington, proposes to share her spacious home with house-hunting experimental scientist Tracy, strictly on a platonic marriage basis. Gradually, and to no one's surprise, as she assists him perfecting a new aeronautical oxygen helmet, the couple shed their romantic off-limits policy, becoming man and wife in the true sense of the relationship. As Fay Bainter had bolstered the pacing of *Woman of the Year,* so did wisecracking Lucille Ball and noisy Keenan Wynn benefit the unwinding of *Without Love.*

Neither Kate nor Robert Taylor* seemed at ease in the psychological chiller, *Undercurrent* (1946). It certainly did not help matters that the well-mounted feature was directed in lugubrious style by Vincente Minnelli, a talent far more accustomed to helming musical comedy than to guiding leery players through their uncertain paces in a wobbly murder tale. Only Robert Mitchum on loan-out from RKO provided a sure characterization, he playing Taylor's much-talked-about younger brother. All the subtlety that had earmarked the similar but superior *Suspicion* was lacking in this broadly etched tale of a professor's matronly daughter (Kate), who weds an aggressive industrialist (Taylor) only to discover that marriage to a chameleonlike aristocrat can be near fatal. At best Kate was judged competent in this melodrama. Much more sound was her participation in 1946 in *The American Creed,* an American Brotherhood Week trailer, produced by David O. Selznick, and containing appearances by such celebrities as Ingrid Bergman, Van Johnson, Edward G. Robinson, and Walter Pidgeon.

The Sea of Grass (1947), filmed before *Undercurrent,* was sprawling in every sense but entertainment value. Soap opera strung out on the plains of the nineteenth-century New Mexico Territory made for passable reading in Conrad Richter's novel, but as abysmally attenuated for the screen it set up obstacles that neither director Elia Kazan nor the star trio of Kate, Spencer Tracy, and Melvyn Douglas could possibly overcome. In the course of its seemingly endless 131 minutes, cattle baron Tracy loses his wife Kate, who runs off to Denver where she has an affair with his stern adversary (Douglas). Later, at the urging of grown daughter Phyllis Thaxter, Kate returns

---

*In his first picture after three years of World War II naval service.

to console the bereft Tracy, who is mourning the death of their other child, son Robert Walker. In *The Sea of Grass,* Kate resorted to a bad display of oversized mannerisms, Tracy shrunk into dramatic reticence, and Douglas remained his crisply speaking, resolute self. One of the few assets of this lame costume drama was the magnificent photography of Harry Stradling, which captured the beauty of the on-location Nebraska lensing.

Kate fared even worse in her other period-drama release of 1947, *Song of Love.* Metro producer-director Clarence Brown, inspired by the success of Columbia's *A Song to Remember* (1945), assembled a plush film play to showcase the combined musical talents of pianist Clara Wieck (Kate) and her composer husband, Robert Schumann (Paul Henreid). Interspersed among the plentiful classical-music interludes was a hackneyed account of Kate's endless devotion to her husband and their seven children. Kate's Clara is so steadfastly loyal to hubby that she nobly rejects the love offer of infatuated young Johannes Brahms (Robert Walker), who has come to study with the Schumanns. But for tormented Henreid a loyal wife and devoted family are not enough—he craves recognition for his compositions. He has a nervous collapse and later dies in an asylum, and resolute Kate careens back to the concert stage to forcefeed her husband's neglected music to a previously indifferent public.

Although 1947 filmgoers were vaguely aware of musical dubbing being involved when movie stars impersonated pianists onscreen (e.g., Mary Astor in *The Great Lie,* Cornel Wilde in *A Song to Remember*), a good many of the audience who witnessed *Song of Love* being unreeled assumed that Kate was actually offering a lusty and impressive accounting at the keyboard. Why not? In her almost two decades before the public eye, she had demonstrated that she was capable of most anything she put her mind to. In actuality, Kate's imitation of Clara Schumann's piano virtuosity was the result of Kate having arduously studied for weeks with pianist Laura Dubman, so that the actress could mock play for the cameras while offscreen Artur Rubinstein's keyboard renditions were blended onto the actual soundtrack. Despite all this preparation for *Song of Love,* post-World War II audiences just would not buy the sudsy story.

With two more box-office turkeys on her scorecard, one can only wish that Kate had had the opportunity to star in, as announced, *Green Dolphin Street* (Lana Turner did in 1947), or the picturization of John Van Druten's play *The Damask Cheek* or even John B. Marquand's *B. F.'s Daughter* (which went to Barbara Stanwyck).

While Kate's star status was slipping at the box office, her personal popularity dipped due to an outburst of unorthodox political belief. In May, 1947, she made an impassioned protest speech to a crowd of some 30,000 spurred on by her anger at the groups which barred former Vice President Henry Wallace from using the Hollywood Bowl to present his defense against the charge, made at House Committee on Un-American Activities hearings, that he had been a Communist Party dupe. Kate was equally adamant against that committee's chairman, J. Parnell Thomas, for pushing his nose into the "state" of the motion picture industry. "Today J. Parnell Thomas is engaged in a personally conducted smear campaign of the motion picture industry. He is aided and abetted in his efforts by a group of super patriots who call themselves the Motion Picture Alliance for the Preservation of American Ideals. For myself, I want no part of their ideals or those of Mr. Thomas. The artist since the beginning of time has always expressed the aspirations and dreams of his people. Silence the artist and you have silenced the most articulate voice the people have."

Thus it was with some trepidation that producer-director Frank Capra and MGM (which was releasing this Liberty Films production) agreed to substitute Kate for an overdemanding Claudette Colbert in *State of the Union.** Cast in a contemporary story into which they could sink their collective teeth, both Tracy and Kate excelled in this searing rendition of the political campaign of a staunch Republican who discovers that expediency and gullibility have made him unfit to serve the people, while at the same time realizing that he prefers his forthright, fiery wife (Kate) to the overbearing love of Machiavellian Angela Lansbury. In a very large way the firm directorial hand of Capra and the strong screen presence of Lansbury and Adolphe Menjou (as a conniving politician) forced Kate into rising above her usual dramatic reach, delivering a performance that was, in the words of Howard Barnes *(New York Herald-Tribune),* "restrained, persuasive, and altogether delightful."

Screen-star teams require a genre change of pace if they are to retain their marquee allure for long (e.g., witness the declining popularity of Greer Garson and Walter Pidgeon in the late 1940s). Garson Kanin and his actress-writer wife, Ruth Gordon, came to the fore in 1949 with MGM's *Adam's Rib,* which served Kate and Tracy as well as they served their comedy vehicle. Cast as an upper-middle-class Mr. and Mrs. lawyer couple, they become involved on opposite sides of the legal fence when Kate, a dynamic supporter of women's rights, defends dumb blonde Judy Holliday, accused of shooting her husband, whom she found in the arms of another woman. The courtroom arena allows barrister Kate to parade her favorite theory that women deserve equality right down the line, a proposition which infuriates Tracy, the prosecuting law-enforcer and put-upon husband. In battling the point who should wear the pants in the family at home and on the job, Kate and Tracy created a smash box-office hit. A good deal of credit for the film's success rightly went to director George Cukor and to newcomer Holliday, the latter

---

*The Pulitzer Prize-winning Howard Lindsay-Russell Crouse play opened at the Hudson Theatre on November 14, 1945, and ran for 765 performances. It had been written for Helen Hayes, who rejected it, and was subsequently refused by Margaret Sullavan and Kate. Ex-MGM player Ruth Hussey was eventually given the female lead.

heading a superior supporting cast. It was typical of Kate, long considered a meddler on the set by detractors, that she should take such an enthusiastic interest in bolstering the career of Holliday, insuring that the comedienne dominated each of the scenes in which they jointly appeared.

Always reaching for new channels of artistic fulfillment and new avenues in which to ply her histrionic trade now that she had reached and passed the dangerous age of forty, Kate brushed up on her Shakespeare under the tutelage of Constance Collier to prepare for the role of Rosalind in the Theatre Guild's revival of *As You Like It*. Before the comedy opened at the Cort Theatre (January 26, 1950) Kate was repeatedly asked why she had chosen the Bard's work for her Broadway return. "The part of Rosalind is really a test of how good an actress you are, and I want to find out." (With 749 lines, it is one of Shakespeare's longest roles.) To another newsman, Kate confided that she was encouraged in her choice of playwrights here by the knowledge that her mother greatly respected the Bard. "I suppose that's why I did it, really—for her."

As You Like It proved a sturdy commercial success, achieving recognition as much for Kate's still shapely legs (encased in tights) as for her recreation of the Elizabethan drama about a girl masquerading as a boy. The fourth estate was sharply divided on the virtues of Kate's interpretation of the Shakespearian lines, with Brooks Atkinson *(New York Times)* arguing that she is "too sharply defined a personality for such romantic make-believe . . . she has to design the character too meticulously." Richard Watts, Jr. *(New York Post)* represented the opposing camp. "She plays with spirit, tenderness, humor, grace, and vitality, and looks so beautiful, that her Rosalind becomes a characterization of sheer loveliness. No actress I have ever seen in this celebrated role has approached . . . [Kate] in bringing it to poetic life." Argue the critics might and did; audiences were rather enchanted with the magnetic personality who made Shakespeare's comedy so palatable theatre fare. The production established a new record for *As You Like It,* with 145 consecutive performances, followed by a twenty-two-week tour starting in Hershey, Pennsylvania, and onward to Michigan, Illinois, Missouri, Oklahoma, Kansas, Colorado, California, Oregon, and Wisconsin, before concluding in October, 1950.

Kate was considering—and it was remarkable at even this mid-stage of her long career that offers were still pouring in for her consideration, a situation not enjoyed by many of her professional contemporaries forced into semiretirement or face-saving minor efforts—starring in a play production of *The Taming of the Shrew* when director John Huston approached her about starring in a movie rendition of C. S. Forester's 1935 novel, *The African Queen,**

---

*In the late 1940s the book was considered as a possible vehicle for Bette Davis and John Mills; a few years later MGMer Deborah Kerr urged her Metro employers to buy it as a showcase for her latent screen talents.

being scripted by James Agee and already cast with Humphrey Bogart.*
Kate agreed to the atypical venture and offbeat screen teaming, bought a financial interest in the film, and packed her bags to join the cast and production crew for the arduous on-location filming in the African Congo along the Ruki River. After two months of difficult jungle lensing, the unit became so debilitated and depleted by illness that it was necessary to return to London to complete filming there. The resultant film proved a box-office powerhouse with a $4.3 million domestic gross, and single-handedly insured Kate's screen reputation for decades to come.

Set in German East Africa at the outbreak of World War I in 1914, *The African Queen*—Kate's first color movie—finds the actress playing Rose Sayer, who, with her bulbous Methodist missionary brother (Robert Morley), supervises a pathetic outpost at Kungdo, ministering to the converted heathen. The opening shot of Kate pounding away at the foot organ during the hymn-singing service, makes one fully aware of her overzealous nature. Despite her suffocating outfit (long dress with wrist cuffs and high-neck collar, smooth leather boots, and wide-brim brown hat) she is oblivious to the heat, caught up in her desire to ease Morley in this humiliating church assignment.† "God has not forsaken this place as my brother's presence bears witness," Kate insists to Bogart, a Canadian machinist who originally came to Africa to help construct a bridge. Although Kate and Morley have been exiled for nearly a decade from their fondly remembered home in the English Midlands, they still maintain as much decorum as possible in their crude African surroundings, causing Kate to twitch with discomfort at the vulgarity so much a part of unkempt, stomach-gurgling Bogart.

The story shifts into full force when German soldiers destroy the native village, leading to Morley's death. Gin-swilling Bogart returns in the nick of time to offer Kate sanctuary on his thirty-foot boat, *The African Queen,* proposing that in these dangerous times, the best course of action would be to

---

*Bogart would say of his co-star, "She talks a blue streak. We listened for the first couple of days when she hit Africa and then began asking ourselves 'How affected can you be in the middle of Africa?' She used to say that everything was 'divine.' 'Oh, what a *divine* native!' she'd say. 'Oh, what a *divine* pile of manure!' You had to ask yourself, "Is this really the dame or is this something left over from *Woman of the Year?'*

"She does pretty much as she goddam pleases. She came in lugging a full-length mirror and a flock of toothbrushes. She brushed her teeth all the time and she habitually takes four or five baths a day. She talks at you as though you were a microphone. I guess she was nervous, though, and scared of John and me. She lectured the hell out of us on temperance and the evils of drinking.

"She's actually kind of sweet and loveable, though, and she's absolutely honest and absolutely fair about her work. None of this late on the set or demanding close-ups or any of that kind of thing. She doesn't give a damn how she looks. She doesn't have to be waited on, either. You never pull up a chair for Kate. You tell her 'Kate, pull up a chair willya and while you're at it get one for yourself.' I don't think she tries to be a character. I think she is one."

Kate kept her own diary of the adventures on *The African Queen* set, which might well have been publishable, but it was lost en route back to California.

†Morley had been a dunce at the seminary and received this no-man's-land ministry as a last resort on his superiors' part.

301

travel the lesser-used byways and somehow drift out of harm's way. Kate is not convinced of the rightness of this plan. Nevertheless they embark on Bogart's planned trek, only to have Kate become inspired by a new mission, to maneuver their craft down-river and somehow blow up the one-hundred-foot German gunboat *Louisa,* which patrols a vital lake expanse against possible British occupation. It is a constant pull-and-tug for Kate to stir the lazy, drunken—even cowardly—Bogart into action, while combating assorted obstacles (ranging from malaria, to leeches, to gunfire from a German fort and the dangerous swamp stillwaters). When Bogart is really stewed he calls his partner "You crazy psalm-singing skinny old maid." His prime argument against Kate's preposterous scheme is that it just cannot be done, for they cannot successfully fight nature. Undaunted Kate replies, "Nature is what we are put into the world to rise above."

From this author's point of view, Kate has enjoyed no finer onscreen moment than the one in which, as they proceed down the Ulanga River which turns into the Bora, they shoot their first rapids. Exhilarated beyond belief by this challenging episode, Kate rhapsodizes to Bogart, shouting in her sing-song voice to be heard over the rushing waters, "I never dreamed such a mere physical experience could be so exciting!" As they pilot onward, warming up to each other as they grow more vitalized by their mission, they experience their first joint sexual encounter. A few moments thereafter, Kate says to her newly found and first-loved one—and this always brings appropriate titters from audiences—"Dear. What is your first name?" This bit of seemingly incongruous sidetalk is capped thereafter when they disagree as to procedures for carrying out their plan. "Oh, Charlie," sighs Kate in the most feminine voice her mannish character can summon up, "We're having our first quarrel."

The African Queen reaches her destination, but during a storm both passengers are swept overboard and picked up by the crew of the *Louisa,* whose captain (Peter Bull) sentences the couple to death. As a parting gesture, Bogart asks the captain to marry them, leading to an amusing moment as Kate primps herself to her respectable best for a ceremony in which she never thought she would personally participate. Just as the wedding service is completed, the torpedo-staffed wreckage of *The African Queen* rams into the *Louisa* and blows it up. A spared Kate and Bogart are thrown into the water and soon are paddling to shore on a piece of debris.

Kate and Bogart were both nominated for Oscars for their *The African Queen* performances; she lost to her *Gone with the Wind* rival, Vivien Leigh;* but Bogart won. As he accepted his award on the stage of the Hollywood Pantages Theatre, he said, "I want to pay tribute to John Huston and Katharine Hepburn, who helped me to be where I am now."

From the primitive setting of *The African Queen,* Kate jumped into the robust locale of MGM's *Pat and Mike* (1952), her final film under her MGM

*Leigh won her second Oscar for *A Streetcar Named Desire.*

contract. She was reunited with director George Cukor, the writing team of Garson Kanin-Ruth Gordon, and, of course, her longstanding screen team-mate, Spencer Tracy. Situated in what was a new film atmosphere for her—the world of active sports—Kate, as, a lively college physical-education in-structor, had ample chance to demonstrate her real golfing and tennis prow-ess, while matching quips with shady sports promoter Tracy* and debating the wisdom of her romance with staid William Ching. Perhaps the key in-gredient for the film's commercial popularity was summed up nearly twenty years after the fact by director Cukor. "The whole thing has a *dégagé* air. It's not played from point to point, but lets the chips fall where they may. When it gets a laugh it's not playing for laughs. It's an unusually discreet kind of love story." (Kate and Tracy only touch one another once in the course of the film, and that occurs when he massages her leg after she has strained a muscle. The embarrassed look on Tracy's face during this bit of screen business is memorable.)

After completing *Pat and Mike* Kate was at liberty, but the forty-five-year-old star was not about to slow down her pace; energetic work was too much a necessary part of her everyday life. She crossed the Atlantic to make her London stage debut at the New Theatre in the first full-scale production of George Bernard Shaw's *The Millionairess,* directed by Michael Benthall, who had handled *As You Like It.* The British critics did not change their opinion of this lesser Shavian work, but they were forced to admit that Kate was a captivating success, "dominating, forceful, bossy, talkative, energetic and bursting with electric vitality."

Kate insisted that *The Millionairess* was not geared for American tastes ("Vitality is not such a novelty in America"), but the producers deter-minedly shut down the London production on September 20 in time for the show to be reassembled for a ten-week limited Broadway engagement opening October 10, 1952, at the Shubert Theatre.

Kate then did an about-face and shied away from both stage and screen for over a year and a half.† Not until the summer of 1954, when David Lean offered her the leading role in *Summertime* (premiere, Venice Film Festival, May 29, 1955), did she return to her chosen craft, arriving in Italy for the on-the-spot lensing of Broadway's wistful tearjerker, *The Time of the Cuckoo.*‡ The film deleted the more sordid aspects of Arthur Laurents's theatre origi-nal, glamorizing the study of the aging-spinster American schoolteacher who finds momentary love with married antique-dealer Rossano Brazzi. Jack Hildyard's picture-postcard photography took a close second to Kate in creating a credible romantic flavor in which a middle-aged woman sheds life-long practicality for a fleeting episode of idyllic love. The sequence in *Sum-*

---

*Tracy says of Kate, "There ain't much meat on her, but what there is, is choice."

†She was supposed to appear in a screen version of *Miss Hargreaves* for John Huston, play-ing a seventy-year-old woman who scandalizes a cathedral town.

‡Opened at the Empire Theatre on October 15, 1952, for a run of 263 performances, with Shirley Booth in the lead part.

mertime in which vigorous tourist Kate falls into a Venetian canal made global headlines long before the picture was generally released in June, 1955. Kate's performance in *Summertime* was hailed a revelation, with *The Hollywood Reporter* insisting: "She is the closest thing on the screen today to a Greta Garbo and it is a public misfortune that she is not seen more often." Kate was nominated for her sixth Oscar, but lost to Anna Magnani, who won for *The Rose Tattoo.*

While *Summertime* was enjoying a healthy release, Kate was in Australia with Robert Helpmann and the Old Vic Company, touring in three Shakespearian works (as Isabella in *Measure for Measure,* as Portia in *The Merchant of Venice,* and as Katharina in *The Taming of the Shrew*). The next year Kate returned as another screen spinster, this time as the Kansas farmwoman in Paramount's *The Rainmaker* (1956).* In this Joseph Anthony-directed study one could not always believe that Kate was "just a homely little primitive" wilting on a drought-plagued farm, but she was more than persuasive at conveying the frustration of a woman hell-bent on having herself a man without the least notion of how to attract him.† That box-office-oriented casting saddled her with stylized Burt Lancaster as her fast-talking faker, was a deficit that Kate almost overcame. She was again Oscar nominated, but lost to Ingrid Bergman, who won for *Anastasia.* Before Kate returned to Hollywood from abroad to film *The Rainmaker,* she had stopped over in England to co-star with Bob Hope—of all people—in a loosely fitting screen comedy entitled *The Iron Petticoat* (released abroad in mid-1956, not until nearly a year later in the United States). The black-and-white VistaVision "comedy" was plagued with production problems from the start. It was bad enough that scripter Ben Hecht became so infuriated that he walked off the project, because of constant script tampering by Hope and his crew of gag writers, but Hope and Kate clashed on the set as to scene interpretation and character importance. Worst of all, *The Iron Petticoat* was a comedy with a very slim ration of laughs. In fact, the applause meter reached such a low on *The Iron Petticoat* that the film was declared an international disaster. The offbeat teaming of Kate and Hope proved not unique but grotesque, and the notion of this strange duo falling in love onscreen was an embarrassing travesty. All the blame could not be settled at Hope's feet, for Kate was not very convincing as the Russian Air Force captain who in a fit of anger flies her MIG to an American base in Germany and agrees to tour London with American flier Hope. The novelty of square-jawed Kate in stark military

---

*The movie derived from N. Richard Naish's television drama (NBC, August 16, 1953) starring Joan Potter and Darren McGavin, and the Broadway version, which opened on October 28, 1954, at the Cort Theatre for a 124-performance run with Geraldine Page in the starring role. Naish would rehash the essence of *The Rainmaker* for Lucille Ball's musical, *Wildcat* (1960), before utilizing the drama yet again for the basis of the stage musical, *110 in the Shade* (1964).

†One can still hear Kate telling her oncamera rancher father (Cameron Prud'homme), "I'll get myself some bright lip rouge—and paint my mouth so it looks like I'm always whistling."

outfit, mouthing such pseudo-Slavic-accented lines as "I am villink to go to the Vastern Vorld" soon wore off, leaving the viewer with too much free time to wonder why he had not elected instead to see a revival of the similar Greta Garbo *Ninotchka* or even the latter's stage (or movie) musical version, *Silk Stockings.*

Kate was on much surer ground in Twentieth Century-Fox's *The Desk Set* (1957),* which teamed her for the eighth and next-to-last time with Spencer Tracy. (It was their first joint venture in CinemaScope and color.) As the very knowledgeable head of a sizable television-network reference library, Kate was indeed chic, something her last three screen parts had denied her. Tracy appears on the cinema scene as the surefooted methods engineer who has concocted a computer brain cell (the Emmarac Electro-Magnetic Memory Research Arithmetical Calculator), which, he proudly announces, can answer any and all questions. Naturally Kate and her staff fear the possible loss of their jobs, which establishes the necessary plotline rivalry between Kate and Tracy. The latter soon learns that Miss Know-It-All has more quick answers than he has sly, difficult questions; she in turn realizing that it is not slow-to-propose executive Gig Young whom she wants as a husband, but unassuming, portly, white-haired Tracy, particularly after she finds that his electronic memory bank is not about to do her and the girls out of their livelihoods. Adult filmgoing audiences were pleased at having a fresh Tracy-Hepburn vehicle to enjoy, easily accepted the second-rate movie as entertaining filmfare, enlivened by the slick work of the perennial screen team.

Like the rough Connecticut Yankee she was, Kate turned a deaf ear to past criticism of her Shakespearian role playing and accepted a guest-star post at the American Shakespeare Festival at Stratford, Connecticut, in the summer of 1957 for the salary of $350 weekly. Teamed with Alfred Drake in *The Merchant of Venice* and *Much Ado about Nothing,* Kate was judged more noteworthy for her game try than for her enthusiastic but incomplete attack on the particularly difficult role of Portia in *The Merchant of Venice.*

Kate was then professionally inactive until 1959 when she returned to England to co-star with Elizabeth Taylor and Montgomery Clift in an expansion of Tennessee Williams's somewhat controversial one-act play, *Suddenly, Last Summer.*† She was paid a salary of $175,444 for emoting in this Sam Spiegel production directed by Joseph L. Mankiewicz, portraying the first of her several full-bodied screen character roles to date. Here she was the eccentric(!), wealthy New Orleans widow who sternly requests brain surgeon Clift to perform a lobotomy on her beauteous cousin (Taylor), the latter now incarcerated at a private sanitarium. Kate's Mrs. Venable offers $1 million to the hospital where the no-questions-asked operation will be performed,

---

*The stage play with Shirley Booth starring, opened at the Broadhurst Theatre on October 24, 1955, for a 296-performance run.

†Part of a double-bill show, *Garden District,* which opened at the York Playhouse on January 9, 1958, for a 216-performance run. Ann Harding was among the several actresses to play the middle-aged female lead.

but neurosurgeon Clift is suspicious of this heinous creature. Instead he administers a truth serum to incoherent Taylor, who has been babbling about "the dreadful things" that occurred to Mrs. Venable's poet son, who died suddenly last summer in North Africa of what has been alleged to be a heart attack surrounded by strange circumstances. Under the influence of the drug, Taylor reveals that the dead Sebastian had been a doting homosexual, for whom Mrs. Venable had procured his prey until her beauty faded, when Taylor had taken over the chore. Sebastian's death—more symbolic than real—at the hands of cannibalistic beach urchins, was deemed a fitting end to his cruel debasing of the corrupted young ones.

For Kate's deft handling of the witchlike Mrs. Venable,* she was nominated (as was Taylor) for an Oscar, but she lost out to Simone Signoret, who won for *Room at the Top.*

In the summer of 1960 Kate was invited back as guest star at the American Shakespeare Festival in Connecticut, having far better success with her performance as Cleopatra to Robert Ryan's Marc Antony in *Antony and Cleopatra,* than as Viola in *Twelfth Night.* Because of her Stratford commitment, Kate was unavailable to star in the tryout of *The Night of the Iguana,* which Tennessee Williams adapted from his own short story, with Kate in mind for the lead.

Two years passed—it was not easy for a fifty-five-year-old superstar to find any, let alone proper, roles in the diminished film market—before Kate made another screen appearance. So intrigued was she by the idea of portraying Mary Tyrone in the New York-based filmization of Eugene O'Neill's *Long Day's Journey into Night* (Embassy, 1962)† that she accepted a mere $25,000 salary plus a percentage of whatever profits there might be. Her co-stars in this somber study were Ralph Richardson, Jason Robards, Jr., and Dean Stockwell, each of whom had his full minutes in front of the spotlight as the marathon drama of interfamily anguish wound its way to the conclusion, demonstrating that one day (in 1912) of the Tyrones' family life at their seaside Connecticut home was almost more than audiences could bear to watch. Director Sidney Lumet allowed little compromising of the original in this arty 108-minute picture‡ in which Kate was on occasion either excellent or manner-prone as the guilt-ridden mother who transmitted tuberculosis to son Stockwell and who became dope-addicted as the result of an illness suffered during his birth. She was nominated for her ninth Academy Award but lost the Oscar to Anne Bancroft, who won on the strength of her performance in *The Miracle Worker.*

---

*Can one forget the bizarre sight of her descending in her French elevator into the tropical hothouse garden (filled with monstrous plants) and launching into an edgy monolog about the poetic character of her dead son?

† The O'Neill drama was finally presented in full stage version at the Helen Hayes Theatre on November 7, 1956, for a run of 390 performances. Fredric March and his wife Florence Eldridge had the leads originally.

‡ The original film version ran 174 minutes!

Not long after the release of *Long Day's Journey into Night,* Kate's eighty-two-year-old father died on November 20, 1962, and the following summer her constant companion, Spencer Tracy, suffered a "congested lung condition" and was hospitalized. For the next five years Kate ignored her career (dropping out of the proposed film version of Ruth Gordon's *A Very Rich Woman,* which was made as *Rosie!* with Rosalind Russell, and from the Shirley MacLaine film musical of *Bloomer Girl,* which was never done) to devote her entire energies to caring for the periodically ailing Tracy.* Her friendship with the already married Catholic Tracy, carefully nurtured by studio hands as Hollywood's best-kept secret love affair,† was in reality closer to the camaraderie of two good pals who each approved of the other's professional expertise and simultaneously admired yet cajoled at his/her established life-style. There is no doubt of the couple's total admiration for one another, with Kate extolling Tracy's virtues right up to his untimely end. "Spencer Tracy is one of the few actors capable of total concentration. All based on truth. He and Laurette Taylor are the two best actors I've ever seen."

Finally, at the prompting of Tracy's very good friend, producer-director Stanley Kramer, Kate agreed to return to the screen with Tracy in an original screenplay, *Guess Who's Coming to Dinner?* (Columbia, 1967). The making of this "social comedy" (a euphemistic term to say the least) was considered big news everywhere, for it was well established that Tracy was a very ill man, that Kate had been inactive for several years, and (at least so it was touted) that the William Rose story dealt in pathfinding terms with the touchy problem of interracial marriage. With Sidney Poitier cast in the second-billed spot and Kate's niece Katharine Houghton signed to play her daughter, the film could not miss being a well-documented venture.

Shortly after completing this film, Spencer Tracy died on June 10, 1967, which made his posthumously-released performance all the more box-office-worthy. The film took in a domestic gross of $25.5 million, proving that Kramer's naive conception of social significance was at least well attuned to the public's threshold of acceptance. Sidney Poitier's stereotyped performance as the saintly black man is less compelling upon each viewing, particularly taken in the context of the even-then-emerging black liberation movement. On the other hand, Kate's side-seat portrayal as the chic San Francisco art gallery owner has a resiliency that rises to the fore in many unexpected spots throughout the picture, giving her presence added dimension. In the film she is a liberal in deed as well as talk, unlike her "crusading" newspaper publisher husband (Tracy). When their daughter (Houghton) breezes home from

*Kate did find time to contribute an article on "The Right of Privacy, the Predicament of the Public Figure," which appeared in a 1965 issue of the *Virginia Law Quarterly.* Among her statements in this piece was, "Everything has to be considered in relation to the world we are living in—I do not know how you can relate privacy to this world—they would seem to contradict each other."

†In his book *Tracy and Hepburn* (1971), Garson Kanin panders to this misconception of the relationship between the two performers.

a Hawaiian vacation with her husband-to-be (Poitier) in tow, the parents have a quick decision to make; either accept Poitier as their girl's chosen spouse or deny their blessings and witness Poitier's departure from the scene. After adjusting to the initial shock of the dilemma, Kate gallantly endorses whatever will make Houghton happy, but stubborn Irish Tracy is not so tractable, particularly when confronted with Poitier's Los Angeles parents, who parallel his and Kate's positions on the pending marriage. The film cops out to a happy finale, with Tracy—in view of his very subsequent real-life death—offering a heart-breaking curtain speech; but it was effervescent Kate who buoyed the production into the tidy gossamer package of palatable entertainment for Middle America.

Kate confounded her acquaintances by launching into an immediate barrage of work following Tracy's death,* co-starring with Peter O'Toole in the movie edition of *Lion in Winter* (Avco-Embassy, 1968),† and then moving on to Nice to join the name cast of *The Madwoman of Chaillot* (Warner Bros.-7 Arts, 1969). While in the south of France lensing *The Lion in Winter,* Kate, garbed in her Eleanor of Aquitaine wardrobe, filmed a brief segment of the April, 1967, Academy Awards telecasts discussing the first decade of the Oscar's history.‡ Kate was already in Nice on the sets of *The Madwoman of Chaillot* when her housekeeper phoned from Hollywood to tell her "*YOU* won the Oscar [for *Guess Who's Coming to Dinner?*]."

Kate calmly inquired, "Did Mr. T win it too?

"No, Madame."

Kate: "Well, that's okay. I'm sure mine is for the two of us."

To the gathered Nice press, Kate said, "I am enormously touched." She later cabled the Academy of Motion Picture Arts and Sciences. "It was delightful, a total surprise. I feel I have received a big, affectionate hug from fellow workers. They don't usually give these things to old girls, you know."

All of which left her unprepared for the following year's Academy Award announcement that she (for *The Lion in Winter*) and Barbra Streisand (for *Funny Girl*) had "tied" for the best actress Oscar. As the exiled, embittered, and imprisoned wife of middle-aged Henry II (Peter O'Toole), Kate joins her husband and their three sons (John Castle, Anthony Hopkins, Nigel Terry) to decide upon the succession to the throne of England, joined in their Yuletide squabbling by the young King of France (Timothy Dalton) and his sister Alais (Jane Merrow). The *London Observer* termed the drama "a medieval variant on *The Little Foxes*," while Judith Crist (*New York* magazine) summed up the majority opinion when she judged Kate's performance as "simply stunning." It was indeed regal, rich, and full of nuance, but filled with dis-

---

*She tactfully refrained from attending the funeral services.

†The Broadway version opened at the Ambassador Theatre on March 3, 1966, closing after a brief ninety-two-performance run. Robert Preston was Henry II and Rosemary Harris was Eleanor, his wife.

‡Prior to this first television appearance, Kate had narrated (unbilled) a telefilm documentary on the Connecticut River, produced by her brother-in-law, Ellsworth Grant.

tracting, annoying, gallant overtones ("She's about as tough as Helen Hayes," said Pauline Kael of *The New Yorker*) and an unfortunate nervous tic to her head that made the more skittish viewer shy away from watching her too carefully in the close-ups.

Eleven times nominated and three times an Oscar winner, Kate suffered a professional reversal with *The Madwoman of Chaillot*,* which belatedly limped into the Plaza Theatre on October 12, 1969. John Huston had originally signed Kate for the lead role in Jean Giraudoux's long acclaimed stage fantasy (1945), but Huston bowed out of the project due to a conflict over the script. Bryan Forbes replaced him. At the time Kate exclaimed: "I think *The Madwoman of Chaillot* has more relevance today than it did twenty years ago. The world has gone cuckoo. We're still dominated by greed, and that's what Giraudoux was talking about. The Madwoman represents the possibilities of man, she represents a hope." The international cast gathered for the costly movie venture was as much at sea as Kate in translating Giraudoux's proselytizing drama to the screen. It was one of the bigger artistic fiascos of the 1960s cinema. It emerged lifeless and at times ludicrous, nearly always tedious viewing. Not the least fault of the production was Kate's too timid and sentimental interpretation of the dotty Parisian countess who determines to do away with a claque of war-minded capitalists out to transform her beloved Paris into an oversized oil field.

At this juncture in the career of sixty-one-year-old Kate, there hardly seemed any new histrionic avenue for her to realistically accept,† but she proved characteristically unique when she agreed to star in the Alan Jay Lerner-Andre Previn musical *Coco*.‡ Kate was to be paid the astronomical— by Broadway standards—sum of $15,000 a week plus a percentage of the net profits in this $900,000-to-mount musical. After extensive vocal lessons with coach Sue Seaton (so Kate could talk-sing-growl such "tunes" as "Mademoiselle Cliché de Paris," "On the Corner of the Rue Cambon," and "Always Mademoiselle"), Kate debuted in this extravaganza at the Mark Hellinger Theatre on December 18, 1969. The Cecil Beaton sets and costumes, re-

*After the original Paris stage version starring Margeurite Moreno and Louis Jouvet, it was thought that Laurette Taylor would play it on Broadway, but she died before this could take place. The drama opened at the Belasco Theatre on December 27, 1948, with Martita Hunt as the Madwoman and John Carradine as the Ragpicker. It ran for 368 performances. The release of the film version was delayed for well over a year due to the competing and equally disastrous stage-musical version of Giraudoux's work, entitled *Dear World*, which starred Angela Lansbury.

†Kate was heard but not seen discussing David O. Selznick on the television special *Hollywood: The Selznick Years* (NBC, March 21, 1969). Clips from *A Bill of Divorcement* were shown.

‡Producer Frederick Brisson at one time intended the show as a vehicle for his wife, Rosalind Russell, but the Parisian couturiere vetoed that casting notion. After meeting Kate, the eighty-five-year-old Coco approved of her. Kate on her part said, "She's the real article. She's not stupid. And she has fundamentally a good sense of humor." (Coco Chanel would die in Paris on January 10, 1971).

creating the 1953 fashion world of Coco Chanel as she attempts a designer's comeback, were well appointed but hardly startling—and this creative aspect was the sturdiest part of the weakly structured musical with its potpourri of forgettable tunes. Clives Barnes *(New York Times)* reported his opening-night reaction to Kate: "Miss Hepburn is a blithe spirit, a vital flame. Her voice is like vinegar on sandpaper, her presence is a blessing. She growls out the most ordinary lines as if they were pearls of great price, gems of wit, nuggets of wisdom. She grins and she is enchanting. She prowls, gloweringly down to the footlights, mutters a word for ordure in an idiomatically terse fashion, and remains devastatingly charming."

He further stated: "This is not acting in any of the accustomed fashions of acting. Her singing voice is unique—a neat mixture of faith, love and laryngitis, unforgettable, unbelievable and delightful. Dear Miss Hepburn—perhaps they should have made a musical of your life rather than the dress designer. They say some beauty is ageless—yours is timeless."

Being on Broadway in *Coco* led Kate to two unusual (for her) media ventures. She participated in the Paramount original-cast-album recording of *Coco* (a horrid listening experience, but a collector's item),* and because she was nominated for a Tony Award (she lost to pal Lauren Bacall, who won the best musical actress award for *Applause!*), Kate appeared in a taped clip of the number "Always Mademoiselle" on the nationally televised Tony ceremonies in April, 1970.

When Kate left the Broadway cast of *Coco,*† she departed immediately for Spain to participate in Michael Cacoyannis's screen rendition of Aristophanes' *The Trojan Women.* Lensed on a sensible budget with a sturdy cast, the resulting road-show film (Fine Arts Theatre, September 27, 1971) nevertheless was a stodgy mess, which died on the vine. "As Hecuba she almost holds the film together; challenged, she responds with fire, but sometimes there's a too querulous tone to her grief and it is then that Hecuba's impassioned dignity eludes her" *(British Monthly Film Bulletin).*

After lensing the unsucessful *The Trojan Women,* Kate returned to the United States to head the national touring company of *Coco,* which opened at the Public Music Hall in Cleveland on January 11, 1971, and closed on June 26, 1971, at the Chandler Pavilion in Los Angeles. Once again, the public flocked in ticket-party droves to witness the living legend, Katharine Hepburn, "sing" her way through a flat musical, and like Broadway audiences they were shocked when, at the opening of Act II, at which time Coco has suffered a professional setback, she utters the unexpected expletive, "Shit!"‡

*The studio reportedly paid $2.7 million for the right to film the play (eventually) with Kate in the lead.

†Danielle Darrieux took over for Kate in *Coco* on August 3, 1970, and although she offered a sensitive performance, the show soon had to fold, suffering from the lack of a strong enough marquee name.

‡ Kate is said to have contributed this bit of dialog to the show.

Kate received her share of unwanted publicity in the course of 1971. In February, 1971, while playing *Coco* in Hartford, her former maid-chauffeur, Louella G. West, age fifty-four, broke into the home of Kate's stepmother, Madeline Hepburn, and in a fight with Kate, bit the actress hard on a finger of her right hand. Kate was treated at the Hartford Hospital, while the distraught attacker was put into custody for a later hearing and trial, which were handled very quietly. In August of that year, Kate sued the Vita Herring Company and its advertising agency for $4 million, regarding a commercial which featured "Harriet Hubert Herring, one of the great herring experts of our times." Kate charged that the voice used was patterned to sound like her, stating in her complaint that her well-known voice was "distinctive, with a unique characteristic quality of sound, style, pitch, inflection and accent." The verdict in this suit has not yet been reached.

In 1972, Kate attended to some family business (she purchased the Hepburn family home from the estate, and gave it to Hartford University), dickered with the idea of going to Australia to do *Daisy Bates* with a screenplay by Chester Erskine (which did not come to be), and was almost on the starting line for Grahame Greene's *Travels with My Aunt,* to be directed by George Cukor. However, there were disagreements over the script, as well as the producer's refusal to utilize Kate's latest protégée (Joy Bang) in a key role in the film. Kate withdrew from the project and Maggie Smith was substituted. After some months of quiet, Kate quietly signed to play a lead part in the film of Edward Albee's drama *A Delicate Balance,** which was to costar Paul Scofield, Lee Remick, Kate Reid, Joseph Cotten, and Betsy Blair, and would be directed by Tony Richardson in London in late 1972.

Ten, five, or even one year ago, Kate would have said "Ne-e-v'r," if anyone had suggested that she would become the surprise delight of American television. Yet with three distinctly different video appearances, she has made it incontestably clear that she is just as vivid, vivacious, and determined in the 1970s as she was four decades ago on the RKO lot. On October 2nd and 3rd, 1973, Kate was the solo guest on ABC-TV's "Dick Cavett" show, during which, to quote the *New York Times*, she " . . . discusses herself and her career with enough wit, intelligence, humor and typical Hepburn vitality to leave the average talk-show personality speechless." While there was much to carp with concerning Anthony Harvey's direction of ABC-TV's version of *The Glass Menagerie* (December 16, 1973) as produced by David Susskind, there was little fault to find with Kate's interpretation of Tennessee Williams' pathetic but sterling character, Amanda Wingfield. One might have wished Hepburn had submerged her strong, highly mannered personality a little more deeply into her portrait or that her nervous head shaking had not led her to so much compensating posturing. However, in her evocation of the sadness of an existence that verges on tragedy, she gave humanity and sensibility to a role

*Opened at the Martin Beck Theatre on September 22, 1966, for a run of 132 performances; starring Jessica Tandy, Hume Cronyn, Rosemary Murphy, and Carmen Mathews.

that others often have made merely an exercise in feminine foolishness. In this production, unfortunately ignored by home viewers, she was amply aided by Sam Waterston (the Tony Perkins act-a-like) as son Tom, the narrator, and by Michael Moriarty, as the embarrassed gentleman caller.

Most astounding of all was Hepburn's decision to appear on the Academy Award telecast (April 9, 1974) in order to present the Irving Thalberg Award to her friend and co-worker producer Lawrence Weingarten. Striding out onto the stage in a becoming pants suit, she begged the industry's forgiveness for her selfishness in not attending any of the past forty-one Oscar ceremonies, and then suggested, in her tribute speech to Weingarten, just how grateful she is for being part of such a noble profession. Some attributed the standing ovation she received as a paeon to nostalgia; others thought it was a testament to her fortitude in continuing in her craft, unbowed by age, infirmities, or personal sorrows. Post-show reports of Kate's preparation for her special appearance, indicated that she is ever regal, demanding, precise, and responsive. A growing affection for humility has not mellowed her professional standards or her iconoclastic life style. Having taken three new steps in the video medium, Kate is presently preparing to film a tv dramatic special with Lord Laurence Olivier in London.

Of all the professional avenues still open to Kate, directing a film is the most challenging. Both Louis B. Mayer and John Ford seriously offered her the chance some twenty-three years ago, but she never took the opportunity to do so. In recent years she has frequently mentioned her interst in Irene Mayer Selznick's production of *Martha,* based on two Margery Sharp novels, dealing with a British gal who hikes off to Paris to become an artist. *"Martha,"* Kate has said, " . . . is my first real chance, and I think I can do a damn good job of it."

Today Kate nonchalantly admits: "I'm a legend because I've survived over a long period of time. I'm revered rather like an old building. And I still seem to be the master of my fate. I'm still paddling the boat myself, you know. I'm not sitting being paddled by anybody. Now, it may just be a canoe, but nevertheless, I'm paddling it."

Having established the modus operandi of her life and career, Kate enunciates few regrets: "With my ruthless ambition I don't think that I would have been fit to bring up children. I think I was too interested in myself. I think I have become nicer through the years, I've improved with time, but I don't deceive myself that I can have everything."

Will the elusive, publicity-shy, iconoclast retire from her craft? Hardly likely. "I've always had a strange and strong dream that if I stopped acting and went back to Hartford, Connecticut, I wouldn't remember a thing about my acting career. Not one damn thing." Overriding this theory is her stronger belief: "I like hard work. To get anywhere in the world today, you have to work hard."

Feature Film Appearances
KATHARINE HEPBURN

A BILL OF DIVORCEMENT (RKO, 1932) 75 M.

Executive producer, David O. Selznick; director, George Cukor; based on the play by Clemence Dane; screenplay, Howard Estabrook, Harry Wagstaff Gribble; art director, Carroll Clark; assistant director, Dewey Starkey; music director, Max Steiner; costumes, Josette De Lima; technical director, Marion Balderstone; sound, George Ellis; camera, Sid Hickox; editor, Arthur Roberts.

John Barrymore (Hilary Fairfield); Billie Burke (Margaret Fairfield); Katharine Hepburn (Sidney Fairfield); David Manners (Kit Humphrey); Henry Stephenson (Dr. Alliot); Paul Cavanagh (Gray Meredith); Elizabeth Patterson (Aunt Hester); Gayle Evers (Bassett); Julie Haydon (Party Guest); Dennis O'Keefe (Dance Extra).

CHRISTOPHER STRONG (RKO, 1933) 77 M.

Producer, David O. Selznick; associate producer, Pandro S. Berman; director, Dorothy Arzner; based on the novel by Gilbert Frankau; screenplay, Zöe Akins; art director, Van Nest Polglase, Charles Kirk; music, Max Steiner; costumes, Howard Greer; makeup, Mel Burns; assistant directors, Edward Killy, Tommy Atkins; sound, Hugh McDowell; special effects, Vernon L. Walker; camera, Bert Glennon; editor, Arthur Roberts.

Katharine Hepburn (Lady Cynthia Darrington); Colin Clive (Sir Christopher Strong); Billie Burke (Lady Elaine Strong); Helen Chandler (Monica Strong); Ralph Forbes (Harry Rawlinson); Irene Browne (Carrie Valentin); Jack La Rue (Carlo); Desmond Roberts (Bryce Mercer); Gwendolyn Logan (Bradford, the Maid); Agostino Borgato (Fortuneteller); Margaret Lindsay (Girl at Party); Donald Stewart (Mechanic); Zena Savina (Maid); Pat Somerset (Bobby); Miki Morita (Japanese Announcer).

MORNING GLORY (RKO, 1933) 74 M.

Executive producer, Merian C. Cooper; producer, Pandro S. Berman; director, Lowell Sherman; based on the play by Zoe Akins; screenplay, Howard J. Green; art director, Van Nest Polglase, Charles Kirk; makeup, Mel Burns; costumes, Walter Plunkett; music, Max Steiner; assistant director, Tommy Atkins; sound, Hugh McDowell; camera, Bert Glennon; editor, George Nicholls, Jr.

Katharine Hepburn (Eva Lovelace); Douglas Fairbanks, Jr. (Joseph Sheridan); Adolphe Menjou (Louis Easton); Mary Duncan (Rita Vernon); C. Aubrey Smith (Robert Harley Hedges); Don Alvarado (Pepe Velez); Fred Santley (Will Seymour); Richard Carle (Henry Lawrence); Tyler Brooke (Charles Van Dusen); Geneva Mitchell (Gwendolyn Hall); Helen Ware (Nellie Navarre); Theresa Harris (Maid).

LITTLE WOMEN (RKO, 1933) 115 M.

Executive producer, Merian C. Cooper; associate producer, Kenneth Macgowan; director, George Cukor; based on the novel by Louisa May Alcott; screenplay, Sarah

Y. Mason, Victor Heerman; art director, Van Nest Polglase; set decorator, Hobe Erwin; music, Max Steiner; assistant director, Edward Killy; makeup; Mel Burns; costumes, Walter Plunkett; sound, Frank H. Harris; special effects, Harry Redmond; camera, Henry Gerrard; editor, Jack Kitchin.

Katharine Hepburn (Jo); Joan Bennett (Amy); Paul Lukas (Professor Bhaer); Edna May Oliver (Aunt March); Jean Parker (Beth); Frances Dee (Meg); Henry Stephenson (Mr. Laurence); Douglass Montgomery (Laurie); John Davis Lodge (Brooke); Spring Byington (Marmee); Samuel S. Hinds (Mr. March); Mabel Colcord (Hannah); Marion Ballou (Mrs. Kirke); Nydia Westman (Mamie); Harry Beresford (Dr. Bangs); Marina Schubert (Flo King); Dorothy Gray, June Filmer (Girls at Boarding House); Olin Howland (Mr. Davis).

SPITFIRE   (RKO, 1934) 88 M.

Executive producer, Merian C. Cooper; associate producer, Pandro S. Berman; director, John Cromwell; based on the play *Trigger* by Lula Vollmer; screenplay, Jane Murfin, Vollmer; art director, Van Nest Polglase, Carroll Clark; music, Max Steiner; assistant director, Dewey Starkey; makeup, Mel Burns; costumes, Walter Plunkett; sound, Clem Portman; camera, Edward Cronjager; editor, William H. Morgan.

Katharine Hepburn (Trigger Hicks); Robert Young (J. Stafford); Ralph Bellamy (G. Fleetwood); Martha Sleeper (Eleanor Stafford); Louis Mason (Bill Grayson); Sara Haden (Etta Dawson); Virginia Howell (Granny Raines); Sidney Toler (Mr. Sawyer); Bob Burns (West Fry); Therese Wittler (Mrs. Sawyer); John Beck (Jake Hawkins).

THE LITTLE MINISTER   (RKO, 1934) 110 M.

Producer, Pandro S. Berman; director, Richard Wallace; based on the novel and play by Sir James M. Barrie; screenplay, Jane Murfin, Sarah Y. Mason, Victor Heerman; additional scenes, Mortimer Offner, Jack Wagner; art director, Van Nest Polglase, Carroll Clark; set decorator, Hobe Erwin; assistant director, Edward Killy; music, Max Steiner; costumes, Walter Plunkett; makeup, Mel Burns; technical adviser, Robert Watson; special camera effects, Vernon L. Walker; sound, Clem Portman; camera, Henry Gerrard; editor, William Hamilton.

Katharine Hepburn (Babbie); John Beal (Gavin); Alan Hale (Rob Dow); Donald Crisp (Dr. McQueen); Lumsden Hare (Thammas); Andy Clyde (Wearyworld); Beryl Mercer (Margaret); Billy Watson (Micah Dow); Dorothy Stickney (Jean); Mary Gordon (Nanny); Frank Conroy (Lord Rintoul); Eily Malyon (Evalina); Reginald Denny (Captain Halliwell); Leonard Carey (Munn); Harry Beresford (John Spens); Barlowe Borland (Snecky); May Beatty (Maid).

BREAK OF HEARTS   (RKO, 1935) 80 M.

Producer, Pandro S. Berman; director, Philip Moeller; based on a story by Lester Cohen; screenplay, Sarah Y. Mason, Victor Heerman, Anthony Veiller; art director, Van Nest Polglase, Carroll Clark; music, Max Steiner; makeup, Mel Burns; assistant director, Edward Killy; sound, John Tribby; costumes, Bernard Newman; camera, Robert De Grasse; editor, William Hamilton.

Katharine Hepburn (Constance Dane); Charles Boyer (Franz Roberti); John Beal (Johnny Lawrence); Jean Hersholt (Professor Talma); Sam Hardy (Marx); Inez Courtney (Miss Wilson); Helene Millard (Sylvia); Ferdinand Gottschalk (Pazzini); Susan Fleming (Elise); Lee Kohlmar (Schubert); Jean Howard (Didi Smith-Lennox); Anne Grey (Phyllis); and: Inez Palange, Jason Robards, Sr., Egon Brecher, Dick Elliott.

ALICE ADAMS   (RKO, 1935) 99 M.

Producer, Pandro S. Berman; director, George Stevens; based on the novel by Booth Tarkington; adaptation, Jane Murfin; screenplay; Dorothy Yost, Mortimer Offner; art director, Van Nest Polglase; music, Max Steiner; costumes, Walter Plunkett; makeup, Mel Burns; song, Steiner and Dorothy Fields; assistant director, Edward Killy; sound, Denzil A. Cutler; camera, Robert De Grasse; editor, Jane Loring.

Katharine Hepburn (Alice Adams); Fred MacMurray (Arthur Russell); Fred Stone (Mr. Adams); Evelyn Venable (Mildred Palmer); Frank Albertson (Walter Adams); Ann Shoemaker (Mrs. Adams); Charles Grapewin (Mr. Lamb); Grady Sutton (Frank Dowling); Hedda Hopper (Mrs. Palmer); Jonathan Hale (Mr. Palmer); Janet McLeod (Henrietta Lamb); Virginia Howell (Mrs. Dowling); Zeffie Tilbury (Mrs. Dresser); Ella McKenzie (Ella Dowling); Hattie McDaniel (Malena); Harry Bowen (Laborer).

SYLVIA SCARLETT   (RKO, 1936) 97 M.

Producer, Pandro S. Berman; director, George Cukor; based on the novel *The Early Life and Adventures of Sylvia Scarlett* by Compton MacKenzie; screenplay, Gladys Unger, John Collier, Mortimer Offner; art director, Van Nest Polglase, Sturges Carne; music, Roy Webb; music director, P. J. Faulkner, Jr.; makeup, Mel Burns; assistant director, Argyle Nelson; costumes for Miss Hepburn, Muriel King; sound, George D. Ellis; camera, Joseph August; editor, Jane Loring.

Katharine Hepburn (Sylvia Scarlett); Cary Grant (Jimmy Monkley); Brian Aherne (Michael Fane); Edmund Gwenn (Henry Scarlett); Natalie Paley (Lily); Dennie Moore (Maudie Tilt); Lennox Pawle (Drunk); Harold Cheevers (Bobby); Robert Adair (Turnkey); Lionel Pape (Sergeant Major); Peter Hobbes, Leonard Mudie, Jack Vanair (Stewards); Harold Entwistle (Conductor); Adrienne D'Ambricourt (Stewardess); Gaston Glass, Michael S. Visaroff (Pursers); Bunny Beatty (Maid); E. E. Clive, Edward Cooper, Olaf Hytten (Customs Inspectors); Dina Smirnova (Russian); George Nardelli (Frenchman); and: Daisy Belmore, Elspeth Dudgeon, May Beatty, Connie Lamont, Gwendolyn Logan, Carmen Beretta.

MARY OF SCOTLAND   (RKO, 1936) 123 M.

Producer, Pandro S. Berman; director, John Ford; based on the play by Maxwell Anderson; screenplay, Dudley Nichols; art director, Van Nest Polglase, Carroll Clark; set decorator, Darrell Silvera; music, Nathaniel Shilkret; orchestrator, Maurice De Packh; costumes, Walter Plunkett; assistant director, Edward Donahue; makeup, Mel Burns; sound, Hugh McDowell, Jr.; special camera effects, Vernon L. Walker; camera, Joseph H. August; editor, Jane Loring; assistant editor, Robert Parrish.

Katharine Hepburn (Mary Stuart); Fredric March (Earl of Bothwell); Florence Eldridge (Elizabeth Tudor); Douglas Walton (Darnley); John Carradine (David Rizzio); Robert Barrat (Morton); Monte Blue (Messenger); Jean Fenwick (Mary Seton); Gavin Muir (Leicester); Ian Keith (James Stuart Moray); Moroni Olsen (John Knox); Donald Crisp (Huntley); William Stack (Ruthven); Molly Lamont (Mary Livingston); Walter Byron (Sir Francis Walsingham); Ralph Forbes (Randolph); Alan Mowbray (Throckmorton); Frieda Inescort (Mary Beaton); David Torrence (Lindsay); Anita Colby (Mary Fleming); Lionel Belmore (English Fisherman); Doris Lloyd (His Wife); Bob Watson (His Son); Lionel Pape (Burghley); Ivan Simpson, Murray Kinnell, Lawrence Grant, Nigel De Brulier, Barlowe Borland (Judges); Mary Gordon (Nurse); D'Arcy Corrigan (Kirkcaldy); Brandon Hurst (Arian); Leonard Mudie (Maitland); Wilfred Lucas (Lexington); Cyril McLaglen (Faudoncide); Robert Warwick (Sir Francis Knellys); Earle Foxe (Duke of Kent); Wyndham Standing (Sergeant); Gaston Glass (Chatelard); Neil Fitzgerald (Nobleman); Paul McAllister (Du Croche); Jean Kirchner and Judith Kirchner (Prince James).

A WOMAN REBELS   (RKO, 1936) 88 M.

Producer, Pandro S. Berman; director, Mark Sandrich; based on the novel *Portrait of a Rebel* by Netta Syrett; screenplay, Anthony Veiller, Ernest Vajda; art director, Van Nest Polglase, Perry Ferguson; set decorator, Darrell Silvera; assistant director, Dewey Starkey; makeup, Mel Burns; choreography, Hermes Pan; costumes, Walter Plunkett; music, Roy Webb; orchestrator, Maurice De Packh; music director, Nathaniel Shilkret; sound, George D. Ellis; camera, Robert de Grasse; editor, Jane Loring.

Katharine Hepburn (Pamela Thistlewaite); Herbert Marshall (Thomas Lane); Elizabeth Allan (Flora Thistlewaite); Donald Crisp (Judge Thistlewaite); Doris Dudley (Young Flora); David Manners (Alan); Lucile Watson (Betty Bumble); Van Heflin (Gerald); Eily Malyon (Piper); Margaret Seddon (Aunt Serena); Molly Lamont (Young Girl); Lionel Pape (Mr. White); Constance Lupino (Lady Gaythorne); Lillian Kemble-Cooper (Lady Rinlake); Nick Thompson (Signor Grassi); Inez Palange (Signora Grassi); Tony Romero (Italian Boy); Joe Mack (Italian Bit); Marilyn French (Flora—as an infant); Bonnie June McNamara (Flora—age 5); Marilyn Knowlden (Flora—age 10).

QUALITY STREET   (RKO, 1937) 84 M.

Producer, Pandro S. Berman; director, George Stevens; based on the play by Sir James M. Barrie; screenplay, Mortimer Offner, Allan Scott; art director, Van Nest Polglase; set decorator, Darrell Silvera; assistant director, Argyle Nelson; makeup, Mel Burns; costumes, Walter Plunkett; music, Roy Webb; orchestrator, Maurice De Packh; sound, Clem Portman; camera, Robert de Grasse; editor, Henry Berman.

Katharine Hepburn (Phoebe Throssel); Franchot Tone (Dr. Valentine Brown); Fay Bainter (Susan Throssel); Eric Blore (Sergeant); Cora Witherspoon (Patty); Estelle Winwood (Mary Willoughby); Florence Lake (Henrietta Turnbull); Helena Grant (Fanny Willoughby); Bonita Granville (Isabella); Clifford Severn (Arthur); Sherwood Bailey (William Smith); Roland Varno (Ensign Blades); Joan Fontaine (Charlotte Parratt); William Bakewell (Lieutenant Spicer); Yorke Sherwood (Postman); Carmencita Johnson (Student).

STAGE DOOR   (RKO, 1937) 92 M.

Associate producer, Pandro S. Berman; director, Gregory La Cava; based on the play by Edna Ferber, George S. Kaufman; screenplay, Morrie Ryskind, Anthony Veiller; art director, Van Nest Polglase, Carroll Clark; set decorator, Darrell Silvera; assistant director, James Anderson; makeup, Mel Burns; costumes, Muriel King; music, Roy Webb; sound, John L. Cass; camera, Robert de Grasse; editor, William Hamilton.

Katharine Hepburn (Terry Randall); Ginger Rogers (Jean Maitland); Adolphe Menjou (Anthony Powell); Gail Patrick (Linda Shaw); Constance Collier (Catherine Luther); Andrea Leeds (Kaye Hamilton); Samuel S. Hinds (Henry Sims); Lucille Ball (Judy Canfield); Pierre Watkin (Richard Carmichael); Franklin Pangborn (Harcourt); Elizabeth Dunne (Mrs. Orcutt); Phyllis Kennedy (Hattie); Grady Sutton (Butcher); Jack Carson (Milbank); Fred Santley (Dunkenfield); William Corson (Billy); Frank Reicher (Stage Director); Eve Arden (Eve); Ann Miller (Annie); Jane Rhodes (Ann Braddock); Margaret Early (Mary); Jean Rouverol (Dizzy); Norma Drury (Olga Brent); Harriett Brandon (Madeline); Peggy O'Donnell (Susan); Katharine Alexander, Ralph Forbes, Mary Forbes, Huntley Gordon (Cast of Play); Lynton Brent (Aide); Theodor Von Eltz (Elsworth); Jack Rice (Playwright); Harry Strang (Chauffeur); Bob Perry (Baggageman); Larry Steers (Theatre Patron); Mary Bovard, Frances Gifford (Actresses); Whitey the Cat (Eve's Cat).

BRINGING UP BABY   (RKO, 1938) 102 M.

Producer, Howard Hawks; associate producer, Cliff Reid; director, Hawks; based on a story by Hagar Wilde; screenplay, Dudley Nichols, Wilde; art director, Van Nest Polglase, Perry Ferguson; set decorator, Darrell Silvera; assistant director, Edward Donahue; makeup, Mel Burns; costumes, Howard Greer; music, Roy Webb; sound, John L. Cass; special camera effects, Vernon L. Walker; camera, Russell Metty; editor, George Hively.

Katharine Hepburn (Susan Vance); Cary Grant (David Huxley); Charles Ruggles (Major Horace Applegate); May Robson (Aunt Elizabeth); Walter Catlett (Constable Slocum); Barry Fitzgerald (Gogarty); Fritz Feld (Dr. Fritz Lehmann); Leona Roberts (Mrs. Hannah Gogarty); George Irving (Alexander Peabody); Tala Birell (Mrs. Lehmann); Virginia Walker (Alice Swallow); John Kelly (Elmer); Asta (George, The Dog); George Humbert (Louis, the Headwaiter); Ernest Cossart (Joe, the Bartender); Brooks Benedict (David's Caddy); Richard Lane (Circus Manager); Jack Carson (Roustabout); Ward Bond (Motor Cop).

HOLIDAY   (Col., 1938) 93 M.

Associate producer, Everett Riskin; director, George Cukor; based on the play by Philip Barry; screenplay, Donald Ogden Stewart; art director, Stephen Goosson, Lionel Banks; set decorator, Babs Johnstone; music, Sidney Cutner; music director, Morris Stoloff; assistant director, Clifford Broughton; costumes, Kalloch; sound, Lodge Cunningham; camera, Franz Planer; editor, Otto Meyer, Al Clark.

Katharine Hepburn (Linda Seton); Cary Grant (Johnny Case); Doris Nolan (Julia Seton); Lew Ayres (Ned Seton); Edward Everett Horton (Nick Potter); Henry Kolker (Edward Seton); Binnie Barnes (Laura Cram); Jean Dixon (Susan Potter); Henry Daniell (Seton Cram); Charles Trowbridge (Banker); George Pauncefort (Henry); Charles Richman (Thayer); Mitchell Harris (Jennings); Neil Fitzgerald (Edgar); Marion Ballou (Grandmother); Howard Hickman (Man in Church); Hilda Plowright (Woman in Church); Harry Allen, Edward Cooper (Scotchmen); Margaret McWade (Farmer's Wife); Frank Shannon (Farmer); Aileen Carlyle (Farm Girl); Matt McHugh (Taxi Driver); Maurice Brierre (Steward); Esther Peck (Mrs. Jennings); Lillian West (Mrs. Thayer); Luke Cosgrave (Grandfather); Bess Flowers (Countess); George Hickman (Telegraph Boy); Maude Hume (Maid).

THE PHILADELPHIA STORY   (MGM, 1940) 112 M.

Producer, Joseph L. Mankiewicz; director, George Cukor; based on the play by Philip Barry; screenplay, Donald Ogden Stewart; art director, Cedric Gibbons, Wade B. Rubottom; set decorator, Edwin B. Willis; music, Franz Waxman; costumes, Adrian; makeup, Jack Dawn; assistant director, Edward Woehler; sound, Douglas Shearer; camera, Joseph Ruttenberg; editor, Frank Sullivan.

Cary Grant (C. K. Dexter Haven); Katharine Hepburn (Tracy Lord); James Stewart (Mike Connor); Ruth Hussey (Liz Imbrie); John Howard (George Kittredge); Roland Young (Uncle Willie); John Halliday (Seth Lord); Virginia Weidler (Dinah Lord); Mary Nash (Margaret Lord); Henry Daniell (Sidney Kidd); Lionel Pape (Edward); Rex Evans (Thomas); Russ Clark (John); Hilda Plowright (Librarian); Lita Chevret (Manicurist); Lee Phelps (Bartender); David Clyde (Mac); Claude King (Willie's Butler); Robert De Bruce (Dr. Parsons); Veda Buckland (Elsie); Dorothy Fay, Florine McKihney, Helene Whitney, Hillary Brooke (Main Liners).

WOMAN OF THE YEAR   (MGM, 1942) 112 M.

Producer, Joseph L. Mankiewicz; director, George Stevens; screenplay, Ring Lardner, Jr., Michael Kanin; art director, Cedric Gibbons, Randall Duell; set decorator,

Edwin B. Willis; music, Franz Waxman; costumes, Adrian; makeup, Jack Dawn; assistant director, Robert Golden; sound, Douglas Shearer; camera, Joseph Ruttenberg; editor, Frank Sullivan.

Spencer Tracy (Sam Craig); Katharine Hepburn (Tess Harding); Fay Bainter (Ellen Whitcomb); Reginald Owen (Clayton); Minor Watson (William Harding); William Bendix (Pinkie Peters); Gladys Blake (Flo Peters); Dan Tobin (Gerald); Roscoe Karns (Phil Whittaker); William Tannen (Ellis); Ludwig Stossel (Dr. Martin Lubbeck); Sara Haden (Matron at Refugee Home); Edith Evanson (Alma); George Kezas (Chris); Henry Roquemore (Justice of the Peace); Cyril Ring (Harding's Chauffeur); Ben Lessy (Punchy); Johnny Berkes (Pal); Duke York (Football Player); Winifred Harris (Chairlady); Joe Yule (Building Superintendent); Edward McWade (Adolph); William Holmes (Man at Banquet); Jimmy Conlin, Ray Teal (Reporters).

KEEPER OF THE FLAME (MGM, 1942) 100 M.

Producer, Victor Saville; associate producer, Leon Gordon; director, George Cukor; based on the novel by I. A. R. Wylie; screenplay, Donald Ogden Stewart; art director, Cedric Gibbons, Lyle Wheeler; set decorator, Edwin B. Willis, Jack Moore; sound, Douglas Shearer; costumes, Adrian; music, Bronislau Kaper; makeup, Jack Dawn; assistant director, Edward Woehler; special effects, Warren Newcombe; camera, William Daniels; editor, James E. Newcom.

Spencer Tracy (Steven O'Malley); Katharine Hepburn (Christine Forrest); Richard Whorf (Clive Kerndon); Margaret Wycherly (Mrs. Forrest); Donald Meek (Mr. Arbuthnot); Stephen McNally (Freddie Ridges); Audrey Christie (Jane Harding); Frank Craven (Dr. Fielding); Forrest Tucker (Geoffrey Midford); Percy Kilbride (Orion); Howard da Silva (Jason Richards); Darryl Hickman (Jeb Richards); William Newell (Piggot); Rex Evans (John); Blanche Yurka (Anna); Mary McLeod (Janet); Clifford Brooke (William); Crauford Kent (Ambassador); Mickey Martin (Messenger Boy); Manart Kippen, Donald Gallaher, Cliff Danielson (Reporters); Jay Ward (Pete); Rita Quigley (Susan); Major Sam Harris, Art Howard, Harold Miller (Men); Dick Elliott (Auctioneer); Edward McWade (Lawyer); Irvin Lee (Boy Reporter); Diana Douglas, Gloria Tucker (Girls); Robert Pittard (Tim); Louis Mason (Gardener); Dr. Charles Frederick Lindsley (Minister's Voice).

STAGE DOOR CANTEEN (UA, 1943) 132 M.

Producer, Sol Lesser; associate producer, Barnett Briskin; director, Frank Borzage; screenplay, Delmer Daves; art director, Hans Peters; set decorator, Victor Gangelin; music, Freddie Rich; music director, C. Bakaleinikoff; songs, Lesser, Al Dubin, and Jimmy Monaco; Lorenz Hart and Richard Rodgers; Dubin and Monaco; Joe McCoy; Elmer Schoebel, Billy Meyers, and Jack Pitts; Franz Schubert; Rimsky-Korsakov; assistant director, Lew Borzage, Virgil Hart; costumes, Albert Deano; production designer, Harry Horner; sound, Hugh McDowell; camera, Harry Wild; editor, Hal Kern.

Cheryl Walker (Eileen); William Terry (Ed "Dakota" Smith); Marjorie Riordan (Jean Rule); Lon McCallister ("California"); Margaret Early (Ella Sue); Sunset Carson ("Texas"); Dorothea Kent (Mamie); Fred Brady ("Jersey" Wallace); Marion Shockley (Lillian); Patrick O'Moore (Australian); Ruth Roman (Girl); Judith Anderson, Henry Armetta, Benny Baker, Kenny Baker, Tallulah Bankhead, Ralph Bellamy, Edgar Bergen & Charlie McCarthy, Ray Bolger, Helen Broderick, Ina Claire, Katharine Cornell, Lloyd Corrigan, Jane Cowl, Jane Darwell, William Demarest, Virginia Field, Dorothy Fields, Gracie Fields, Lynn Fontanne, Arlene Francis, Vinton Freedley, Billy Gilbert, Lucile Gleason, Vera Gordon, Virginia Grey, Helen Hayes, Katharine Hepburn, Hugh Herbert, Jean Hersholt, Sam Jaffe, Allen Jenkins, George Jessel,

Roscoe Karns, Virginia Kaye, Tom Kennedy, Otto Kruger, June Lang, Betty Lawford, Gertrude Lawrence, Gypsy Rose Lee, Alfred Lunt, Bert Lytel, Harpo Marx, Aline MacMahon, Elsa Maxwell, Helen Menken, Yehudi Menuhin, Ethel Merman, Ralph Morgan, Alan Mowbray, Paul Muni, Elliott Nugent, Merle Oberon, Franklin Pangborn, Helen Parrish, Brock Pemberton, George Raft, Lanny Ross, Selena Royle, Martha Scott, Cornelia Otis Skinner, Ned Sparks, Bill Stern, Ethel Waters, Johnny Weissmuller, Arleen Whelan, Dame May Whitty, Ed Wynn (Stage Door Canteen Stars); Count Basie & His Band, Xavier Cugat & His Orchestra, with Lina Romay; Bennie Goodman & His Orchestra, with Peggy Lee; Kay Kyser & His Band, Freddy Martin & His Orchestra, Guy Lombardo & His Orchestra (Themselves).

DRAGON SEED   (MGM, 1944) 145 M.

Producer, Pandro S. Berman; director, Jack Conway, Harold S. Bucquet; based on the novel by Pearl S. Buck; screenplay, Marguerite Roberts, Jane Murfin; art director, Cedric Gibbons, Lyle R. Wheeler; set decorator, Edwin B. Willis, Hugh Hunt; music, Herbert Stothart; makeup, Jack Dawn; sound, Douglas Shearer; costumes, Valles; assistant director, Al Shenberg; technical director, Wei F. Hsueh; special effects, Warren Newcombe, camera, Sidney Wagner; editor, Harold F. Kress.

Katharine Hepburn (Jade); Walter Huston (Ling Tan); Aline MacMahon (Mrs. Ling Tan); Akim Tamiroff (Wu Lien); Turhan Bey (Lao Er); Hurd Hatfield (Lao San); Frances Rafferty (Orchid); Agnes Moorehead (Third Cousin's Wife); Henry Travers (Third Cousin); Robert Lewis (Captain Sato); J. Carrol Naish (Japanese Kitchen Overseer); Robert Bice (Lao Ta); Jacqueline De Wit (Mrs. Wu Lien); Clarence Lung (Fourth Cousin); Paul E. Burns (Neighbor Shen); Anna Demetrio (Wu Sao); Ted Hecht (Major Yohagi); Abner Biberman (Captain Yasuda); Leonard Mudie (Old Peddler); Charles Lung (Japanese Diplomat); Al Hill (Japanese Officer); J. Alex Havier, Jay Novello (Japanese Soldiers); Philip Van Zandt (Japanese Guard); Roland Got (Speaker with Movies); Robert Lee (Young Farmer); Frank Puglia (Old Clerk); Claire Du Brey (Hysterical Woman); Lee Tung Foo (Innkeeper); Leonard Strong (Japanese Official); Lionel Barrymore (Narrator); Benson Fong (Student); Spencer Chan, Beal Wong (Farmers).

WITHOUT LOVE   (MGM, 1945) 111 M.

Producer, Lawrence A. Weingarten; director, Harold S. Bucquet; based on the play by Philip Barry; screenplay, Donald Ogden Stewart; art director, Cedric Gibbons, Harry McAfee; set decorator, Edwin B. Willis, McLean Nisbet; music, Bronislau Kaper; assistant director, Earl McEvoy; makeup, Jack Dawn; montage, Peter Ballbusch; costumes, Irene, Marion Herwood Keyes; sound, Douglas Shearer; special effects, A. Arnold Gillespie, Danny Hall; camera, Karl Freund; editor, Frank Sullivan.

Spencer Tracy (Pat Jamieson); Katharine Hepburn (Jamie Rowan); Lucille Ball (Kitty Trimble); Keenan Wynn (Quentin Ladd); Carl Esmond (Paul Carrell); Patricia Morison (Edwina Collins); Felix Bressart (Professor Grinza); Emily Massey (Anna); Gloria Grahame (Flower Girl); George Davis (Caretaker); George Chandler (Elevator Boy); Clancy Cooper (Sergeant); Wallis Clark (Professor Thompson); Donald Curtis (Professor Ellis); Charles Arnt (Colonel Braden); Eddie Acuff (Driver); Clarence Muse (Porter); Franco Corsaro (Headwaiter); Ralph Brooks (Pageboy); William Forrest (Doctor); Garry Owen, Joe Devlin, William Newell (Soldiers); James Flavin (Sergeant); Hazel Brooks (Girl on Elevator).

UNDERCURRENT   (MGM, 1946) 116 M.

Producer, Pandro S. Berman; director, Vincente Minnelli; based on a story by Thelma Strabel; screenplay, Edward Chodorov; art director, Cedric Gibbons, Randall

Duell; set decorator, Edwin B. Willis, Jack D. Moore; music, Herbert Stothart; costumes, Irene; makeup, Jack Dawn; assistant director, Norman Elzer; sound, Douglas Shearer; camera, Karl Freund; editor, Ferris Webster.

Katharine Hepburn (Ann Hamilton); Robert Taylor (Alan Garroway); Robert Mitchum (Michael Garroway); Edmund Gwenn (Professor "Dink" Hamilton); Marjorie Main (Lucy); Jayne Meadows (Sylvia Lea Burton); Clinton Sundberg (Mr. Warmsley); Dan Tobin (Professor Joseph Bangs); Kathryn Cord (Mrs. Foster); Leigh Whipper (George); Charles Trowbridge (Justice Putnam); James Westerfield (Henry Gilson); Billy McLain (Uncle Ben); Bess Flowers (Julia Donnegan); Sarah Edwards (Cora); Betty Blythe (Saleslady); Eula Guy (Housekeeper); Wheaton Chambers (Proprietor); Gordon Richards (Headwaiter); Helen Eby-Rock (Fitter); Ellen Ross (Gwen); Hank Worden (Attendant); William Eddritt (Butler); Phil Dunham (Elevator Man); Jack Murphy, William Cartledge (Messengers); Sydney Logan (Model); Robert Emmett O'Connor (Stationmaster); Rudy Rama (Headwaiter); Nina Ross, Dorothy Christy, Jane Green (Women).

THE SEA OF GRASS (MGM, 1947) 131 M.

Producer, Pandro S. Berman; director, Elia Kazan; based on the novel by Conrad Richter; screenplay, Marguerite Roberts, Vincent Lawrence; art director, Cedric Gibbons, Paul Groesse; set decorator, Edwin B. Willis; sound, Douglas Shearer; music, Herbert Stothart; costumes, Walter Plunkett; makeup, Jack Dawn; assistant director, Sid Sidman; camera, Harry Stradling; editor, Robert J. Kern.

Katharine Hepburn (Lutie Cameron); Spencer Tracy (Colonel James Brewton); Melvyn Douglas (Brice Chamberlain); Phyllis Thaxter (Sarah Beth Brewton); Robert Walker (Brock Brewton); Edgar Buchanan (Jeff); Harry Carey (Doc Reid); Ruth Nelson (Selena Hall); William "Bill" Phillips (Banty); James Bell (Sam Hall); Robert Barrat (Judge White); Charles Trowbridge (George Cameron); Russell Hicks (Major Harney); Robert Armstrong (Floyd McCurtin); Trevor Bardette (Andy Boggs); Morris Ankrum (Crane); Nora Cecil (Nurse); Glen Strange (Bill Roach); Douglas Fowley (Joe Horton); Buddy Roosevelt, Earle Hodgins, Robert Bice (Cowboys); Vernon Dent (Conductor); John Vosper (Hotel Clerk); John Hamilton (Forrest Cochran); Joseph Crehan (Senator Graw); Whit Bissell (Ted, the Clerk); Gertrude Chorre (Indian Nurse); Patty Smith (Sarah Beth—at age 4½); Ray Teal, Eddie Acuff (Cattlemen); Lee Phelps, Jack Baxley, George Magrill, Charles McAvoy, Nolan Leary (Homesteaders); Carol Nugent (Sarah Beth—at age 7); Jimmie Hawkins (Brock—at age 5½); Dick Baron (Newsboy); William Challee (Deputy Sheriff); Stanley Andrews (Sheriff).

SONG OF LOVE (MGM, 1947) 119 M.

Producer-director, Clarence Brown; based on the play by Bernard Schubert, Mario Silva; screenplay, Ivan Tors, Irmgard Von Cube, Allen Vincent, Robert Ardrey; art director, Cedric Gibbons, Hans Peters; set decorator, Edwin B. Willis; sound, Douglas Shearer; music director, Bronislau Kaper; piano recordings, Artur Rubinstein; costume supervisor, Irene; women's costumes, Walter Plunkett; men's costumes, Valles; makeup, Jack Dawn; music advisor, Laura Dubman; assistant director, Al Raboch; special effects, Warren Newcombe; camera, Harry Stradling; editor, Robert J. Kern.

Katharine Hepburn (Clara Wieck Schumann); Paul Henreid (Robert Schumann); Robert Walker (Johannes Brahms); Henry Daniell (Franz Liszt); Leo G. Carroll (Professor Wieck); Else Janssen (Bertha); Gigi Perreau (Julie); "Tinker" Furlong (Felix); Ann Carter (Marie); Janine Perreau (Eugenie); Jimmie Hunt (Ludwig); Anthony Sydes (Ferdinand); Eilene Janssen (Elsie); Roman Bohnen (Dr. Hoffman); Ludwig Stossel (Haslinger); Tala Birell (Princess Valerie Hohenfels); Kurt Katch (Judge);

Henry Stephenson (King Albert); Konstantin Shayne (Reinecke); Byron Foulger (Court Officer); Josephine Whittell (Lady in Box); Betty Blythe (Lady with Opera Glasses); Clinton Sundberg (Dr. Richarz); Andre Charlot (Pompous Gent); Mary Forbes, Winifred Harris (Women at Party); Lela Bliss (Mrs. Heller).

STATE OF THE UNION   (MGM, 1948) 124 M.

Producer, Frank Capra; associate producer, Anthony Veiller; director, Capra; based on the play by Howard Lindsay, Russell Crouse; screenplay, Veiller, Myles Connolly; art director, Cedric Gibbons, Urie McCleary; set decorator, Emile Kuri; sound, Douglas Shearer; music, Victor Young; assistant director, Arthur S. Black, Jr.; costumes, Irene; special effects, A. Arnold Gillespie; camera, George J. Folsey; editor, William Hornbeck.

Spencer Tracy (Grant Matthews); Katharine Hepburn (Mary Matthews); Van Johnson (Spike McManus); Angela Lansbury (Kay Thorndyke); Adolphe Menjou (Jim Conover); Lewis Stone (Sam Thorndyke); Howard Smith (Sam Parrish); Maidel Turner (Lulubelle Alexander); Raymond Walburn (Judge Alexander); Charles Dingle (Bill Hardy); Florence Auer (Grace Orval Draper); Pierre Watkin (Senator Lauterback); Margaret Hamilton (Norah); Irving Bacon (Buck); Patti Brady (Joyce); George Nokes (Grant, Jr.); Carl Switzer (Bellboy); Tom Pedi (Barber); Tom Fadden (Waiter); Charles Lane (Blink Moran); Art Baker (Leith); Rhea Mitchell (Jenny); Arthur O'Connell (Reporter); Marion Martin (Blonde Girl); Tor Johnson (Wrestler); Stanley Andrews (Senator); Dave Willock (Pilot); Russell Meeker (Politician); Frank I. Clarke (Joe Crandall); David Clarke (Rusty Miller); Dell Henderson (Broder); Edwin Cooper (Bradbury); Davison Clark (Crump); Francis Pierlot (Josephs); Brandon Beach (Editor); Eddie Phillips (Television Man); Roger Moore, Lew Smith, Gene Coogan, Douglas Carter, Charles Sherlock, Wilson Wood, George Barton, Harry Anderson, Charles Coleman, Stanley Price, Fred Zendar, Jack Boyle (Photographers); Maurice Cass (Little Man); Eve Whitney (Secretary); Bert Moorhouse, Thornton Edwards, Marshall Ruth (Men).

ADAM'S RIB   (MGM, 1949) 101 M.

Producer, Lawrence Weingarten; director, George Cukor; story-screenplay, Garson Kanin, Ruth Gordon; art director, Cedric Gibbons, William Ferrari; set decorator, Edwin B. Willis, Henry Grace; sound, Douglas Shearer; music, Miklos Rozsa; songs, Cole Porter; assistant director, Jack Greenwood; costumes, Walter Plunkett; camera, George J. Folsey; editor, George Boemler.

Spencer Tracy (Adam Bonner); Katharine Hepburn (Amanda Bonner); Judy Holliday (Doris Attinger); Tom Ewell (Warren Attinger); David Wayne (Kip Lurie); Jean Hagen (Beryl Caighn); Hope Emerson (Olympia La Pere); Eve March (Grace); Clarence Kolb (Judge Reiser); Emerson Treacy (Jules Frikke); Polly Moran (Mrs. McGrath); Will Wright (Judge Marcasson); Elizabeth Flournoy (Dr. Margaret Brodeigh); Janna Da Loos (Mary, the Maid); James Nolan (Dave); David Clarke (Roy); John Maxwell Sholes (Court Clerk); Marvin Kaplan (Court Stenographer); William Self (Benjamin Klausner); Gracille La Vinder (Police Matron); Ray Walker (Photographer); Tommy Noonan (Reporter); De Forrest Lawrence, John Fell (Adam's Assistants); Sid Dubin (Amanda's Assistant); Joe Bernard (Mr. Bonner); Madge Blake (Mrs. Bonner); Marjorie Wood (Mrs. Marcasson); Lester Luther (Judge Poynter); Anna Q. Nilsson (Mrs. Poynter); Roger David (Hurlock); Louis Mason (Elderly Elevator Operator); Rex Evans (Fat Man); Charles Bastin (Young District Attorney); E. Bradley Coleman (Subway Rider); Paula Raymond (Emerald); Glenn Gallagher, Gil Patric, Harry Cody (Criminal Attorneys); George Magrill, Bert Davidson (Subway Guards); Tom Noonan (Reporter).

THE AFRICAN QUEEN (UA, 1951) C—105 M.

Producer, S. P. Eagle; director, John Huston; based on the novel by C. S. Forester; screenplay, James Agee, Huston; music, Alan Gray; sound, Eric Wood; costumes for Miss Hepburn, Doris Langley Moore; costumes, Connie De Pinna; makeup, George Frost; assistant director, Guy Hamilton; camera, Jack Cardiff; editor, Ralph Kemplen.

Humphrey Bogart (Charlie Allnut); Katharine Hepburn (Rose Sayer); Robert Morley (Rev. Samuel Sayer); Peter Bull (Captain of *Louisa*); Theodore Bikel (First Officer); Walter Gotell (Second Officer); Gerald Onn (Petty Officer); Peter Swanwick (First Officer of Shona); Richard Marner (Second Officer of Shona).

PAT AND MIKE (MGM, 1952) 95 M.

Producer, Lawrence Weingarten; director, George Cukor; story-screenplay, Ruth Gordon, Garson Kanin; art director, Cedric Gibbons, Urie McCleary; set decorator, Edwin B. Willis, Hugh Hunt; sound, Douglas Shearer; music, David Raskin; wardrobe for Miss Hepburn, Orry-Kelly; makeup, William Tuttle; assistant director, Jack Greenwood; montage, Peter Ballbusch; special effects, Warren Newcombe; camera, William Daniels; editor, George Boemler.

Spencer Tracy (Mike Conovan); Katharine Hepburn (Pat Pemberton); Aldo Ray (Davie Hucko); William Ching (Collier Weld); Sammy White (Barney Grau); George Mathews (Spec Cauley); Loring Smith (Mr. Beminger); Phyllis Povah (Mrs. Beminger); Charles Bronson (Hank Tasling); Frank Richards (Sam Garsell); Jim Backus (Charles Barry); Chuck Connors (Police Captain); Owen McGiveney (Harry MacWade); Lou Lubin (Waiter); Carl Switzer (Bus Boy); William Self (Pat's Caddy); Billy McLean, Frankie Darro, Paul Brinegar, "Tiny" Jimmie Kelly (Caddies); Mae Clarke, Elizabeth Holmes, Helen Eby-Rock (Woman Golfers); Hank Weaver (Commentator); Tom Harmon (Sportscaster); Charlie Murray (Line Judge); Don Budge, Helen Dettweiler, Betty Hicks, Beverly Hanson, Babe Didrikson Zaharias, Gussie Moran, Alice Marble, Frank Parker (Themselves); Kay English, Jerry Schumacher, Sam Pierce, Bill Lewin, A. Cameron Grant (Reporters); John Close, Fred Coby, Russ Clark (Troopers); Tom Gibson, Kay Deslys (Shooting Gallery Proprietors); Barbara Kimbrell, Elinor Cushingham, Jane Stanton (Tennis Players); Louis Mason (Railway Conductor); King Mohave (Linesman); Frank Sucack (Chairman); Crauford Kent (Tennis Umpire); Sam Hearn (Lawyer).

SUMMERTIME (UA, 1955) C—99 M.

Producer, Ilya Lopert; associate producer, Norman Spencer; director, David Lean; based on the play *The Time of the Cuckoo* by Arthur Laurents; screenplay Lean, H. E. Bates; art director, Vincent Korda, W. Hutchinson, Ferdinand Bellan; sound editor, Winston Ryder; music, Alessandro Cicognini; makeup, Cesare Gamberelli; assistant director, Adrian Pryce-Jones, Alberto Cardone; continuity, Margaret Shipway; camera, Jack Hildyard; editor, Peter Taylor.

Katharine Hepburn (Jane Hudson); Rossano Brazzi (Renato Di Rossi); Isa Miranda (Signora Fiorini); Darren McGavin (Eddie Yaeger); Mari Aldon (Phyl Yaeger); Jane Rose (Mrs. McIlhenny); MacDonald Parke (Mr. McIlhenny); Gaitano Audiero (Mauro); Andre Morell (Englishman); Jeremy Spencer (Vito Di Rossi); Virginia Simeon (Giovanna).

THE RAINMAKER (Para., 1956) C—121 M.

Producer, Hal B. Wallis; associate producer, Paul Nathan; director, Joseph Anthony; based on the play by N. Richard Nash; screenplay, Nash; art director, Hal Pereira, Walter Tyler; set decorator, Sam Comer, Arthur Krams; sound, Harold

Lewis, Winston Leverett; music, Alex North; costumes, Edith Head; makeup, Wally Westmore; assistant director, C. C. Coleman, Jr.; special camera effects, John P. Fulton; camera, Charles Lang, Jr.; editor, Warren Low.

Burt Lancaster (Starbuck); Katharine Hepburn (Lizzie Curry); Wendell Corey (File); Lloyd Bridges (Noah Curry); Earl Holliman (Jim Curry); Cameron Prud'-homme (H. C. Curry); Wallace Ford (Sheriff Thomas); Yvonne Lime (Snookie); Dottie Bee Baker (Belinda); Dan White (Deputy); Ken Becker (Phil Mackey); Stan Jones, John Benson, James Stone, Tony Merrill, Joe Brown (Townsmen).

THE IRON PETTICOAT (MGM, 1956) C—87 M.

Producer, Betty E. Box; director, Ralph Thomas; story Harry Saltzman; screenplay, Ben Hecht; art director, Carmen Dillon; set decorator, Vernon Dixon; sound editor, Roger Cherrill; costumes, Yvonne Caffin; assistant director, James H. Ware; makeup, W. T. Partleton, camera, Ernest Steward; editor, Frederick Wilson.

Bob Hope (Chuck Lockwood); Katharine Hepburn (Vinka Kovelenko); James Robertson Justice (Colonel Sklarnoff); Robert Helpmann (Ivan Kropotkin); David Kossoff (Dubratz); Alan Gifford (Colonel Tarbell); Paul Carpenter (Lewis); Noelle Middleton (Connie); Nicholas Phipps (Tony Mallard); Sidney James (Paul); Alexander Gauge (Senator); Doris Goddard (Maria); Tutte Lemkow (Sutsiyawa); Sandra Dorne (Tityana); Richard Wattis (Lingerie Clerk); Maria Antippas (Sklarnoff's Secretary); Martin Boddey (Grisha).

DESK SET (20th, 1957) C—103 M.

Producer, Henry Ephron; director, Walter Lang; based on the play *The Desk Set* by William Marchant; screenplay, Phoebe and Henry Ephron; art director, Lyle Wheeler, Maurice Ransford; set decorator, Walter M. Scott, Paul S. Fox; sound, E. Clayton Ward, Harry M. Leonard; music, Cyril J. Mockridge; music director, Lionel Newman; orchestrator, Edward B. Powell; costumes, Charles Le Maire; makeup, Ben Nye; assistant director, Hal Herman; special camera effects, Ray Kellogg; camera, Leon Shamroy; editor, Robert Simpson.

Spencer Tracy (Richard Sumner); Katharine Hepburn (Bunny Watson); Gig Young (Mike Cutler); Joan Blondell (Peg Costello); Dina Merrill (Sylvia); Sue Randall (Ruthie); Neva Patterson (Miss Warringer); Harry Ellerbe (Smithers); Nicholas Joy (Azae); Diane Jergens (Alice); Merry Anders (Cathy); Ida Moore (Old Lady); Rachel Stephens (Receptionist); Sammy Ogg (Kenny); King Mojave, Charles Heard, Harry Evans, Hal Taggart, Jack M. Lee, Bill Duray (Board Members); Dick Gardner (Fred); Renny McEvoy (Man); Jesslyn Fax (Mrs. Hewitt); Shirley Mitchell (Myra Smithers).

SUDDENLY, LAST SUMMER (Col., 1959) 114 M.

Producer, Sam Speigel; director, Joseph L. Mankiewicz; based on the play by Tennessee Williams; screenplay, Gore Vidal, Williams; art director, William Kellner; set decorator, Scott Slimon; sound editor, Peter Thornton; costumes for Miss Hepburn, Norman Hartnell; makeup, David Aylou; assistant director, Bluey Hill; music, Buxton Orr, Malcolm Arnold; special camera effects, Tom Howard; camera, Jack Hildyard; editor, Thomas G. Stanford.

Elizabeth Taylor (Catherine Holly); Katharine Hepburn (Mrs. Venable); Montgomery Clift (Dr. Cukrowicz); Albert Dekker (Dr. Hockstader); Mercedes McCambridge (Mrs. Holly); Gary Raymond (George Holly); Mavis Villiers (Miss Foxhill); Patricia Marmont (Nurse Benson); Joan Young (Sister Felicity); Maria Britneva (Lucy); Sheila Robbins (Dr. Hockstader's Secretary); David Cameron (Young Intern); Roberta Woolley (Patient).

323

LONG DAY'S JOURNEY INTO NIGHT (Embassy, 1962) 108 M.

Producer, Ely Landau, Jack J. Dreyfus, Jr.; director, Sidney Lumet; based on the play by Eugene O'Neill; screenplay, O'Neill; production designer, Richard Sylbert; music, Andre Previn; costumes, Motley; camera, Boris Kaufman; editor, Ralph Rosenblum.

Katharine Hepburn (Mary Tyrone); Ralph Richardson (James Tyrone, Sr.); Jason Robards, Jr. (James Tyrone, Jr.); Dean Stockwell (Edmund Tyrone); Jeanne Barr (Cathleen).

GUESS WHO'S COMING TO DINNER (Col., 1967) C—108 M.

Producer, Stanley Kramer; associate producer, George Glass; director, Kramer; screenplay, William Rose; production designer, Robert Clatworthy; set decorator, Frank Tuttle; assistant director, Ray Gosnell; song, Billy Hill; costumes, Joe King; music, Frank De Vol; special effects, Geza Gasper; process camera, Larry Butler; camera, Sam Leavitt; editor, Robert C. Jones.

Spencer Tracy (Matt Drayton); Sidney Poitier (John Prentice); Katharine Hepburn (Christina Drayton); Katharine Houghton (Joey Drayton); Cecil Kellaway (Monsignor Ryan); Roy E. Glenn, Sr. (Mr. Prentice); Beah Richards (Mrs. Prentice); Isabel Sanford (Tillie); Virginia Christine (Hilary St. George); Alexandra Hay (Car Hop); Barbara Randolph (Dorothy); Tom Heaton (Peter); D'Urville Martin (Frankie); Grace Gaynor (Judith); Skip Martin (Delivery Boy); John Hudkins (Cab Driver).

THE LION IN WINTER (Avco-Embassy, 1968) C—134 M.

Executive producer, Joseph E. Levine; producer, Martin Poll; associate producer, Jane C. Nusbaum; director, Anthony Harvey; based on the play by James Goldman; screenplay, Goldman; art director, Peter Murton; set decorator, Peter James; sound, Simon Kaye; assistant director, Kip Gowans; costumes, Margaret Furse; music, John Barry; makeup, William Lodge; camera, Douglas Slocombe; editor, John Bloom.

Peter O'Toole (Henry II); Katharine Hepburn (Eleanor of Aquitaine); Jane Morrow (Princess Alais); John Castle (Prince Geoffrey); Timothy Dalton (King Phillip); Anthony Hopkins (Prince Richard the Lion-hearted); Nigel Stock (William Marshall); Nigel Terry (Prince John).

THE MADWOMAN OF CHAILLOT (WB-7 Arts, 1969) C—142 M.

Executive producer, Henry T. Weinstein; producer, Ely Landau; associate producer, Anthony B. Ungar; based on the play by Jean Giraudoux as translated into English by Maurice Valency; director, Bryan Forbes; screenplay, Edward Anhalt; production designer, Ray Simm; art director, Georges Petitot; set decorator, Dario Simoni; music, Michael J. Lewis; assistant director, Louis-Alain Pitzeie; makeup, Monique Archambault; song, Lewis and Gil King; camera, Claude Renoir, Burnett Guffey; editor, Roger Dwyre.

Katharine Hepburn (Aurelia, the Madwoman of Chaillot); Charles Boyer (Broker); Claude Dauphin (Dr. Jadin); Edith Evans (Josephine, the Madwoman of La Concorde); John Gavin (Reverend); Paul Henreid (General); Oscar Homolka (Commissar); Margaret Leighton (Constance, the Madwoman of Passy); Giulietta Masina (Gabrielle, the Madwoman of Sulpice); Nanette Newman (Irma); Richard Chamberlain (Roderick); Yul Brynner (Chairman); Donald Pleasence (Prospector); Danny Kaye (Ragpicker); Fernand Gravey (Police Sergeant); Gordon Heath (Folksinger); Gerald Sim (Julius).

THE TROJAN WOMEN (Cinerama, 1971) C—111 M.

Executive producer, Josef Shaftel; producer, Michael Cacoyannis, Anis Nohra; director, Cacoyannis; based on the translation by Edith Hamilton of the play by

Euripides; screenplay, Cacoyannis; assistant director, Stavros Konstantarakos, Joe Maria Ochoa, Robert Cirla; art director, Nicholas Georgiadis; music, Mikis Theodorakis; costumes, Annalisa Rocca; special effects, Basilio Corti; sound editor, Alfred Cox; camera, Alfio Contini; editor, Cacoyannis.

Katharine Hepburn (Hecuba); Vanessa Redgrave (Andromache); Genevieve Bujold (Cassandra); Irene Papas (Helen); Patrick Magee (Menelaus); Brian Blessed (Talthybius); Aoberto Santz (Astyanaz); Maria Farantouri (Singer); and: Pauline Letts, Rosaline Shanks, Pat Becket, Anna Bentinck, Esermalda Adam, Maria Garcia Alonso, Nilda Alvarez, Victoria Ayllon, Elizabeth Billencourt, Margarita Calahora, Elena Castillo, Anna Maria Espojo, Maria Jesus Hoyos, Conchita Leza, Margarita Matta, Mirta Miller, Conchita Morales, Virginia Quintana, Yvette Rees, Carmen Segarra, Esperanza Alonso, Consolation Alvarez, Adela Armengol, Gloria Berrogal, Maria Borge, Carmen Cano, Renee Eber, Katie Ellyson, Gwendoline Kocsis, Maureen Mallall, Ivi Mavridi, Livia Mitchell, Ersie Pittas, Catherine Rabone, Clara Sanchiz, Laura Zarrabeitia.

A DELICATE BALANCE   (American Film Theatre, 1973) C—132 M.

Executive producer, Mort Abrahams; producer, Neil Hartley; director, Tony Richardson; based on the play by Edward Albee; screenplay, Albee; art director, David Brockhurst; set dresser, Harry Cordwell; costume designer, Maggie Purse; wardrobe, Norman Dickens, Gloria Barnes; makeup, Bill Lodge; assistant director, Andrew Grieve; camera, David Watkin; editor, John Victor Smith.

Katharine Hepburn (Agnes); Paul Scofield (Tobias); Lee Remick (Julia); Kate Reid (Claire); Joseph Cotten (Harry); Betsy Blair (Edna).

With Henry Stephenson and John Barrymore in A BILL OF DIVORCEMENT (RKO '32)

With Douglas Fairbanks, Jr. in MORNING GLORY (RKO '33)

With Henry Stephenson and Douglass Montgomery in LITT WOMEN (RKO '33)

Fred MacMurray in ALICE ADAMS (RKO '35)

With Robert Young in SPITFIRE (RKO '34)

With Brian Aherne in SYLVIA SCARLETT (RKO '36)

In MARY OF SCOTLAND (RKO '37)

With Eric Blore on the set of
QUALITY STREET (RKO '37)

With Andrea Leeds in STAGE
DOOR (RKO '37)

With Jean Dixon and Edward
Everett Horton in HOLIDAY
(Col '38)

In PHILADELPHIA STORY on Broadway in 1939

With John Howard in THE PHILADELPHIA STORY (MGM '40)

With Eddie Phillips, *third from left*, in WOMAN OF THE YEAR (MGM '42)

In KEEPER OF THE FLAME (MGM '42)

With Turhan Bey in DRAGON
SEED (MGM '44)

With Spencer Tracy in
WITHOUT LOVE (MGM '45)

With Robert Walker and Paul
Henreid in SONG OF LOVE
(MGM '47)

n Spencer Tracy in STATE
THE UNION (MGM '48)

With Humphrey Bogart in THE
AFRICAN QUEEN (UA '51)

Katharine Hepburn of 1951

Onstage in 1952 with THE
MILLIONAIRESS

With Gaitano Audiero in
SUMMERTIME (UA '55)

With Bob Hope in THE IRON
PETTICOAT (MGM '56)

With Joan Blondell and Spence
Tracy in DESK SET (20th '57)

n Montgomery Clift, director
eph L. Mankiewicz, and
abeth Taylor on the set of
DDENLY, LAST SUMMER (Col '59)

With Dean Stockwell in LONG
DAY'S JOURNEY INTO NIGHT
(Embassy '62)

Katharine Houghton,
ey Poitier, Roy E. Glenn, Sr.,
Beah Richards in GUESS
'S COMING TO DINNER (Col '67)

Post-performance of *Coco* on
Broadway (December, 1969)

In THE LION IN WINTER (Avco-Embassy '68)

h Paul Scofield in
DELICATE BALANCE (American
n Theatre, 1973)

In BOY SLAVES (RKO '39)

5'2"
100 pounds
Red-blondish hair
Amber eyes
Aries

Anne Shirley

One need only mention the name Anne Shirley to earn a quick smile from most any seasoned filmgoer. Anne may have been perfect as the gooey heroine of Anne of Green Gables *or as the put-upon daughter in* Stella Dallas, *but more often than not, in her string of 1930s RKO programmers she was an unintentional mockery of her true-blue screen type, thus preventing anyone from taking her performance or the picture very seriously. Anne was earnest enough playing the unsophisticated country lass who suffers all kinds of abuse at the hands of snobbish city society folk. But unfortunately every picture she did seemed to end à la Shirley Temple, with Anne's screen character overcoming her despair with a tear and sigh, and then pushing on to a just reward with a benevolent guardian or helpmate.*

Even more deleterious to the oversized image of Anne as America's own dear oncamera child were the published legends detailing the drudgery and anguish endured by Anne and her dear, devoted (determined, dogged) mother. According to the stories, these two embattled females hung on to hope while earning mere pennies for several years, until fate rewarded Anne with an escape from the perilous ranks of being an anonymous child extra and promoted her to the status of studio contract player. It seemed to be Mrs. Shirley's theory that by making both studio executives and the public feel sorry and guilty about Anne's tawdry apprentice years, fame would be immediately thrust into her daughter's lap.

Ironically, once Anne dropped the mantle of screen player and retired in the mid-1940s, she allowed herself to blossom as a full person. Her previously well-concealed wit and general intelligence made her the surprise and the joy of the Hollywood scene.

Less than eight months before the World War I armistice was signed, Anne was born in Manhattan on April 17, 1918. She was christened Dawn Evelyeen Paris, the only child of New Yorkers Mr. and Mrs. Paris. Anne was hardly a year old when her father died.* The "widowed" Mrs. Mimi Paris—and she never allowed Anne, the movie industry, or the public to forget her marital status—was left with the dual burden of caring for an infant daughter and earning a living to support them both. Having neither college nor business-school training, the best position Mrs. Paris could find was as a saleswoman. Six dollars of her weekly $16 salary was paid to a charwoman to look after baby Anne. Mrs. Paris soon gave up that job, for she discovered that the untrained babysitter was so completely careless with her charge that Anne suffered an almost complete mutilation of her right hand. Resolutely, Mrs. Paris next found a position as a housekeeper for a widower and his three children. She was paid $4 a week plus room and board. More important, she was allowed to have Anne live on the premises. But one night, just like a page yanked from a penny-dreadful novel, her employer attempted to enter her room long after she had retired. The uncooperative Mrs. Paris and little Anne were promptly sent packing.

In the fall of 1919 Mrs. Paris embarked on a new money-earning gambit, one that slowly had been formulating in her mind for some time. She set about transforming sixteen-month-old Anne into a professional model. The venture did not immediately pay dividends, but Mrs. Paris was convinced that her cute and exceedingly well disciplined child could, and would, become as famous and as well paid as, say, Baby Madge (Evans) of a few years before. With a persistence that would grow stronger over the ensuing years, Mrs. Paris took Anne on the rounds of commercial photographic studios. In good weeks the income amounted to $8. Not a monumental beginning, but it was a start.

Two years later Mrs. Paris decided Anne was now old and experienced enough to embark on the next phase of her career, the much more lucrative area of motion pictures—then still flourishing in Manhattan. In the days of silent pictures, well-tempered cooperation was the most vital prerequisite for a toddler screen thespian. And Anne had diligently learned from mama early in the game that the fashion photographer and/or film director was the complete boss, to be treated with the same unquestioning respect and obedience

*Over the years Anne and her mother would both deliberately skirt any public mention of the mysterious Mr. Paris, which suggests that his convenient "death" may well have been a useful way of explaining his disappearance from the home scene.

one would bestow on a beloved father. From that time forward, whenever Mrs. Paris heard rumors that an upcoming production-call for a motion picture might require a little child, tiny Anne with her curly hair was dragged from film studio to studio. To commemorate the launching of Anne's career, Mrs. Paris created a new surname for the future breadwinner, who was henceforth known as Dawn O'Day.*

There was still competition for the few worthwhile juvenile roles in the flicks, and it was some time before Anne got to make her motion picture debut in Allan Dwan's *The Hidden Woman*,† released in April, 1922. A few months later Mrs. Paris's daily rounds earned Anne a role in Herbert Brenon's western *The Miracle Child: He Giveth and Taketh*, released by Fox under the title *Moonshine Valley* in August, 1922. This time Anne had a real part, as little Nancy, the catalyst in restoring the broken marriage of drunkard William Farnum and his ex-wife, Sadie Mullen.

On the casual but considered advice of both Allan Dwan and Herbert Brenon, Mrs. Paris decided to move to California and have her daughter compete at the center of the film industry. As Mrs. Paris would recall in a *Photoplay* magazine interview in August, 1935: "I had come from New York to put my baby into pictures, and I wept because I could find no other way of surviving in a world that has no work to offer a mother who insists upon keeping her child with her."‡ Director Herbert Brenon was kind enough to take pity on Mrs. Paris and particularly Anne, and he maneuvered a bit role for the novice actress in Paramount's *The Rustle of Silk* (1923), a romantic British-set drama starring Betty Compson and Conway Tearle. Anne received a modest salary of $17 a week for this picture, just about sufficient for Mrs. Paris to rent a small four-room cottage in Los Angeles and to somehow find enough surplus funds to have professional photographs made of Anne to circulate at the casting offices of the various studios.

Brenon and his actress wife became very fond of little Anne and urged Mrs. Paris to allow them to adopt her in exchange for a substantial monetary settlement. Mrs. Paris firmly refused, but did persuade the director to hunt up a role for the girl in his upcoming Paramount production, *The Spanish Dancer* (1923). Since it was then still customary for actresses to play male children,§ no one much noticed when Anne found herself decked out as the aristocratic Don Balthazar Carlos, particularly since the $2 million historical romance, set during the reign of King Philip IV of Spain, had been hastily adapted to allow Pola Negri to portray the lead in a film role originally intended for

---

*Reportedly it was movie casting director Jimmy Ryan who suggested the new surname of O'Day.

†Unconfirmed but likely as her screen debut.

‡Later in the article, Mrs. Paris phrased it more dramatically: "I had in my handbag two letters to two prominent directors and those bits of paper represented my final hope of keeping a single roof over both our heads, and the certainty of a quart of milk a day for Anne. And I let those tired and bitter tears fall because I had to trade my baby's beauty for such necessities."

§E.g., Mary Pickford in *Little Lord Fauntleroy*; Betty Bronson in *Peter Pan*.

Rudolph Valentino. (Ironically, at this very time Negri's former director-friend, Ernst Lubtisch, was busy directing Mary Pickford's *Rosita* [1923], which like *The Spanish Dancer,* was a picturization of the play *Don César de Bazan.*)

Through the auspices of Anne's personal and most devoted agent—her mother—Anne was kept on at Paramount for *The Man Who Fights Alone* (1924). Mrs. Paris convinced the Marathon Street Studio that it was only logical to give Anne the part of Dorothy, since the girl had already played William Farnum's daughter in *Moonshine Valley.* Likewise a similar plea to Paramount's casting office earned Anne the role of Betty Compson's daughter in the jazz age domestic drama *The Fast Set* (1924).

But then Anne and Mrs. Paris's luck ran out. From late 1924 to mid-1925, Anne found no screen work whatsoever. She was at the junior gawky stage (four to six), too old to pose as a precocious, adorable toddler, yet too immature for a more substantial juvenile role. However, Mrs. Paris was not about to give up the quest for success. She rented out three rooms of their four-room home, and when no roomers were to be had she sold the furniture piece by piece. When the situation became even more desperate she took a job as a combination switchboard operator and janitress for a ramshackle social clubhouse in exchange for a small room with cold running water, where she and Anne resided. They had to walk a mile to a friend's home to bathe. On many occasions during this bleak period they relied on the kindness of Mrs. Searle (mother of actor Jackie) and Mrs. Wynenah Johnson (mother of seven young performers) to keep at a bare subsistence level.

Mrs. Paris's perseverance paid off, for Anne eventually found employment in Walt Disney's series of *Alice* one-reelers, released by Winkler and Pathé, in which she was the only noncartoon, live performer. Then Anne was hired for *The Callahans and the Murphys* (1927), one of the several MGM features to star the team of Marie Dressler and Polly Moran. Anne was barely visible among Dressler's tenement-bred brood, but she fondly recalls the great kindness Miss Dressler showered on her on the set. Hopscotching back and forth across Hollywood to the various studios, Mrs. Paris was able to find Anne enough film work so that their income averaged out to $17 a week, better than many other families were earning, even in the inflationary days before the Wall Street market crash.

Anne had her best casting-office luck at the Fox studios, where she made five of her eight feature film appearances between 1928 and the beginning of 1929. Usually Anne was featured briefly in the prologue sequence, playing the picture's female lead as a child.* In Fox's *City Girl*, released in 1930 and directed by F. W. Murnau, Anne appeared in both the silent and "full sound" versions, portraying the daughter of Charles Farrell and Mary Duncan. This rural drama was filmed on location in Pendleton, Oregon. In *Liliom* (1930),

*E.g., Madge Bellamy as a youngster in *Mother Knows Best* (1928), Jean Arthur as a child in Paramount's *Sins of the Fathers* (1928), and the young Janet Gaynor in *Four Devils* (1929), the latter being one of Anne's larger film assignments during this period.

also starring Charles Farrell, Anne had the subordinate role of Louise, the daughter of Budapest carnival-man Farrell and his wife, Rose Hobart.

Despite Anne's craftsmanlike work and disciplined behavior on the set, during these years she was never able to leap out of the semi-extra league into the ranks of moppet stardom. Not that Mrs. Paris realistically expected Anne to be a latter-day Baby Peggy, but still . . . To make sure that no possible avenue of talent went untapped, Anne was enrolled in the Lawlor Professional School for acting, dance, and voice lessons. Among her classmates were Anita Louise, Mitzi Green, Mickey Rooney, Judy Garland, and Virginia Weidler.

Anne was passing through another awkward stage of physical transition in 1930, and that year she landed only one feature-film assignment—in Paramount's *Rich Man's Folly,* playing Frances Dee as an *eight*-year-old. In these hard times Mrs. Paris was forced to accept a $15-a-week grocery-clerk job in Long Beach to make ends meet. Anne did obtain a few bit parts in Vitaphone short subjects, and by 1932 she was back in the cinema running, albeit on a very minor scale, with appearances in six films. These assignments were obtained by politely pressuring former co-workers and past employers for special consideration: e.g., Marie Dressler's *Emma* (MGM, 1932), Frank Borzage's *Young America* (Fox, 1932). Mrs. Paris and Anne had become well-known faces at all the Hollywood casting offices, but it was at Warner Bros.' Burbank studio that Anne was most frequently hired during 1932-33. In William Wellman's *So Big* (1932) Anne was seen as Selina Peake, whose grown-up incarnation in the filmization of the Edna Ferber weeper was played by Barbara Stanwyck; in Wellman's *The Purchase Price* (1932), also starring Stanwyck, Anne was cast as a farmer's daughter. Mervyn LeRoy's tidy entertainment package *Three on a Match* (1932) had Anne as the child version of the adult character played by Ann Dvorak (the preadult Joan Blondell role was played by Virginia Davis, the Bette Davis role by Betty Carse). Anne then returned to MGM to portray Princess Anastasia, the youngest daughter of the Russian Czar, in *Rasputin and the Empress* (1932), her most prestigious role to that date, though still a tiny one.

After playing along with Mickey Rooney as one of the youngsters in Archie Mayo's *The Life of Jimmy Dolan* (Warner Bros., 1933), Anne experienced another stretch of no work. To her dismay Mrs. Paris discovered that her years of maneuvering to impress casting directors with Anne's name and face had horribly backfired. Whenever Anne was considered for a possible part, she was being ignored in favor of newcomers, usually because everyone concerned still thought of her as Baby Dawn O'Day, not as a maturing young lady of fifteen. Anne had not even matched the track record of her younger competitor of a decade before, Cora Sue Collins. It was only because of the graciousness of Mrs. Paris's landlady, who was willing to wait a year and a half for the rent, that Anne and her mother were able to pass through this very lean period.

Finally, in late 1933, Anne was back in the money. Vitaphone utilized her in a few additional short subjects (*Picture Palace* [1934], *Private Lessons* [1934]), and she was paid to decorate *This Side of Heaven* (MGM, 1934) and *The Key* (Warner Bros., 1934) as a flower girl.

But the role that would prove the turning point for Anne was in *Finishing School* (1934), produced at RKO during Merian C. Cooper's regime. For some reason, Mrs. Paris sensed that even a small part in this feature would launch Anne onto a new screen career as a teenage player. She cajoled, pleaded, and maneuvered. Finally she convinced the RKO casting department to consider Anne. Eventually it was decided that the role of Billie, one of the boarding-school girls, was to be Anne's. Two weeks later Mrs. Paris and Anne learned via the trade papers that RKO had changed its corporate mind. Fourteen-year-old Mitzi Green, a semi-film and stage name, was being imported back from vaudeville for the role. Mrs. Paris, who knew no pride where Anne's career was concerned, begged the RKO casting director to give her poor daughter the consolation of at least a bit—an extra's job even—in the production. That was agreeable, and Anne, a ten-year-plus cinema veteran, found herself once more thrust on the sidelines, while being coached by her mother that no matter how badly she might feel she was not to show her disappointment in any way whatsoever on the soundstages. Throughout this depressing episode Mrs. Paris remained convinced that *Finishing School* still could be Anne's big break, and she proved to be correct. Suddenly, a week later, Mitzi Green withdrew from the picture and wended her way back to New York. Papa Green had decided the role of Billie was not big enough for his daughter. Anne was immediately reinstated in the role.

Finishing School (Casino Theatre, April 29, 1934) was merely one of the several features churned out by Hollywood in vague imitation of the arty German picture *Mädchen in Uniform* (1933), which had realerted film producers to the dramatic potential of movies with girls'-school settings. Under the co-direction of Wanda Tuchock and George Nicholls, Jr., *Finishing School* focused on the hypocritical snobbery at the exclusive Crockett Hall School in Switzerland. Established ingenue Frances Dee and up-and-fast-coming Ginger Rogers, both RKO contractees, may have had the major roles, but unlike tenth-billed Anne, they were beyond the proper predebutante age to properly convey their characterizations. At the time it seemed that Anne's very minimal screen footage went virtually unnoticed by the industry or the public.

Right after completing *Finishing School* Anne was hired by the independent producing company, Liberty, for its shoestring production of *School for Girls* (1934). The institution depicted was a far cry from the Crockett Hall Finishing School, for it was a reform home supervised by sadistic Lucille La Verne. The rather implausibly structured tale, filmed in very black-and-white terms, cast twenty-five-year-old Sidney Fox* as a teenaged delinquent girl who eventually arouses the romantic interest of Paul Kelly. As a member

*In her thirteenth and final movie role.

of the outside visiting committee, he has her paroled in his custody and later weds her. Anne was buried way down in the cast, along with such former silent-screen stars as William Farnum and Charles Ray.

And then came *Anne of Green Gables* (1934).* RKO had had very good sales luck with the Kenneth Macgowan-produced *Little Women* (1933) and readily agreed that another quaint children's classic would be ideal screen fare. What could be more appropriate than the perennial girls' favorite, *Anne of Green Gables*, written by Canadian Lucy Maud Montgomery in 1908, a book whose lead character had often been described as fiction's dearest child since *Alice in Wonderland*. George Nicholls, Jr., former RKO film editor, assistant director, and co-director of *Finishing School*, was assigned to the economically budgeted *Anne of Green Gables*. He remembered Anne's work in *Finishing School* and had her tested and signed for the film. By the time of the picture's debut at the Roxy Theatre (December 21, 1934) Anne had been placed under a $75-a-week studio contract, and she acquired a new professional name when she legally adopted the name of her character from her first starring feature, Anne Shirley.

The Arcadian idyll followed closely Montgomery's plot of the braided red-haired orphan girl who arrives one day at the train station in Bright River, where she is to become the child of middle-age farmer O. P. Heggie and his acerbic, but essentially sweet, sister, Helen Westley. Heggie appears at the train station, expecting to find a little boy, having requested one to help with the farm chores, but Anne has been sent instead. "My name is Anne Shirley— Anne spelled with an *e*," she informs the bemused man. "I was afraid you weren't coming for me, and I was imagining all the things that could happen to prevent you." Heggie takes the waif back to the little village of Avonlea on Prince Edward Island where she becomes a firm part of the Cuthbert home life, growing into young womanhood, attending boarding school, and at the finale about to wed Gilbert Blythe (Tom Brown).†

With the premiere of *Anne of Green Gables*, Anne enjoyed a successful transition from a nonentity to becoming a recognized name both within the film industry and to the public. The critics enthused: "The outstanding find of the season" (*Liberty* magazine); "Her performance is as warm, as honest

---

*More so than other major studios, RKO had a penchant for extreme duality in its production program. On one hand, it had a strong reputation for its grade-A line of sophisticated women's pictures, starring Ann Harding, Helen Twelvetrees, Constance Bennett, Irene Dunne, and Katharine Hepburn. Yet each season the company was equally inclined to turn out a heavy string of programmers consciously dealing with rural Americana. Not only were these homespun country yarns easy to manufacture at a relatively low cost—having modest production values and no real star names—but they were satisfying a very precise film-audience need for familiar, folksy accounts of American country life, past or present. RKO's cinematic excursions into pastoral-land were generally devoid of the Warner Bros. style of hard-hitting political polemics, which tended to show how the Depression and corruption had filtered down from the city to hurt the countryfolk. Rather RKO followed in the path of Fox with its glossy Will Rogers and Janet Gaynor pictures, which gently chided the so-called better life enjoyed by city-slickers.

†Who had received equally obnoxious publicity two years prior when he adopted his new professional name after winning the lead role in *Tom Brown of Culver*.

and as beguiling a piece of acting as Hollywood has offered us all year" (*New York Times*).

After she made a token appearance in RKO's short subject *A Night at the Biltmore Bowl* (June, 1935),* RKO was quite agreeable to loaning Anne's services to Fox for *Steamboat 'Round the Bend* (Radio City Music Hall, September 19, 1935),† which proved to be the last made, but not the last released, starring vehicle for Will Rogers, who was killed in a plane crash on August 15, 1935, in Point Barrow, Alaska. Rogers's Fox features, especially those directed by John Ford, who was helming *Steamboat 'Round the Bend*, were always given class-A mounting and exhibition. RKO knew it would be an excellent showcase for their Anne at no expense to themselves. Blending in well with the folksy Mississippi River atmosphere, Anne was cast as Fleety Belle, the little mudlark from the swamp area who becomes the heart's desire of John McGuire, nephew of patent medicine hawker-riverboat pilot Rogers. When McGuire commits manslaughter in self-defense to protect Anne's honor and is thrust into jail waiting to be hung, he makes a last request: to wed his beloved Anne. The townsfolk comply and in a rather comic sequence the two young'uns are legally hitched. Thereafter Rogers, who has acquired the steamboat *Claremore Queen*, devotes all his energies to navigating up and down the river to locate the one eyewitness who can prove McGuire's innocence. At the same time Rogers becomes enmeshed with Irvin S. Cobb, captain of the rival *Pride of Paducah,* and the two engage in a climactic riverboat race, the outcome of which finds Rogers the champion of the contest and the savior of his nephew's life.

In the tradition set by such past heroines of Will Rogers pictures (Marian Nixon, Anita Louise, Rochelle Hudson, Evelyn Venable), Anne was more than adequate in her subordinate role, being complimented for her "delightfully whimsical innocence" (*New York Times*) and for being "so natural, sincere and so winning" (*New York Mirror*). In retrospect Anne's performance in *Steamboat 'Round the Bend* does not measure up to these accolades, for both the limited scope of her screen role and her own unprepossessing personality combined to submerge her Fleety Belle (at times mostly sullen, frightened, and homely) in the face of Rogers's scene-grabbing crackerbarrel philosopher, or such other ersatz folk as half-crazed evangelist Berton Churchill, lazy jailor Eugene Pallette, and drunken stoker Francis Ford.

Back at RKO, Anne was reunited with *Anne of Green Gables* director George Nicholls, Jr. and performers Helen Westley and O. P. Heggie in *Chasing Yesterday* (1935). It seemed a strange choice to select Anatole France's Gallic-set *The Crime of Sylvestre Bonnard* as the next project for the studio's new Mary Pickford gamin, particularly when she had originally

---

*Which also includes glimpses of such other Hollywood night lifers as RKO contract personalities Bert Wheeler, Edgar Kennedy, Preston Foster, Betty Grable, Lucille Ball, Joy Hodges, and Edgar Kennedy.

†During filming Fox merged with Darryl F. Zanuck's Twentieth Century Productions to become Twentieth Century-Fox Pictures.

been scheduled to play opposite Tom Brown in the more suitable *Freckles* (1935)* or, as an alternative, in the touted RKO version of Charles Dickens's *Little Dorrit*. Despite a $200,000 budget, Nicholls all too carefully recreated the methodically slow pace of Anatole France's original, but without the integral atmosphere or substance. The seventy-seven-minute film emerged as both heavy-handed and artificial. In this lachrymose tale, elderly archaeologist Heggie tries to renew his lost youth by making Anne, the daughter of the woman he once loved, his ward. He and his housekeeper (Westley) are prepared to sacrifice everything, including his prized library, to have the lovable girl properly educated and made to feel a part of a real household. *Variety* hit the mark when its reviewer cited that straw-brim-hatted Anne "is merely playing a part, seldom living it."

By late 1935, when Sam Briskin, the newly-appointed head of RKO production, had settled into office, it was executively decided that Anne's potential as the screen princess of rural Americana† was so close to realization that her contract should be renegotiated accordingly. Her salary jumped to $400 weekly, permitting her and her mother—now officially known as Mimi Shirley—to move out of their three-room flat over a hardware store, to a better apartment only five blocks from the studio. Although Anne was no longer being publicized as a cute adolescent,‡ the studio carefully maintained an elasticity to her public image so that she could continue to play adolescents of any age demands.

One of Anne's sharpest performances in this period was in *Chatterbox* (1936). Director George Nicholls, Jr. laced the unpretentious production with a gentle tongue-in-cheek quality, utilizing to full advantage Anne's growing reputation as Miss Innocence of the silver screen. In fact *Liberty* magazine commended Anne's performance herein for having "the appeal of a younger [Katharine] Hepburn or a less cloying Janet Gaynor." In *Chatterbox*, naive Jenny Yates (Anne), a comely Vermont miss, yearns to follow in her late mother's footsteps as a stage actress. Her fondest desire is to re-create one of mama's biggest stock-company triumphs, as the heroine of *Virtue's Reward*. A chance meeting with artist Phillips Holmes leads her to New York, and as luck (and the script) would have it, she is propelled to the auditions for a production of *Virtue's Reward*. Everyone involved in the play within the film is aware that the hoary old melodrama is to be played strictly for laughs— except abnormally sensitive Anne, who takes everything seriously, partic-

*Eighteen-year-old Carol Stone was utilized instead to play the young lead in this Gene Stratton Porter story.

†Anne was certainly less cloying than such other contenders as Dorothy Jordan or the too beautiful Jean Parker. By this point the twenty-seven-year-old RKO star and the twenty-nine-year-old Fox luminary, Janet Gaynor, had drifted away from their tomboy and/or gamin country-girl roles.

‡For a long spell, fan-magazine readers were deluged with stories of Anne's large doll collection (gifts from stars she had worked with years before) and reports that her best little pal was her Scotty dog, Angel Cake. RKO now even deigned to allow photos to be taken of *seventeen-year-old* Anne behind the wheel of her black coupe, a gift from her studio.

ularly her assignment as the pure stage heroine. On opening night her gawky, overly earnest portrayal is greeted with gales of audience laughter. Suddenly she realizes what a fool she has been and beats a hasty retreat back to grandpa's (Edward Ellis) farm. Holmes follows to console the lost lamb. With its gently-spiced plot twist, *Chatterbox* was able to grab dual levels of audience empathy. There were filmgoers—a tremendous number of them in the mid-1930s—who could sympathize with the plight of Anne's Jenny Yates, an overly articulate, bucolic lass whose bible of etiquette was *Smith's Compendium of Learning*. Then there were the slightly more sophisticated movie viewers who could patronizingly observe the homey miss as a less fortunate creature than themselves.

A good deal of Anne's success in portraying such a character convincingly stemmed from her repressed upbringing, in which she was never allowed to express her own ambitions or sentiments. Mother Shirley's close supervision of Anne's professional and private life had made the actress a seemingly tractable young lady, as apparently unknowledgeable of the more stimulating and harsher aspects of life as any character she portrayed onscreen. Time would dispel this theory, but for the present only a rare review even suggested that Anne's oncamera work was not a total reflection of her offcamera personality.*

The fact that Anne was regarded as the perfect Louisa May Alcott heroine had provided her with the needed entree to screen success, but such constant typecasting was also her professional undoing. During the two decades that RKO was at its prime, the 1930s and 1940s, no contract actress, with the possible exception of Lucille Ball, slaved so diligently and continuously in one-toned programmers as did Anne. Each time her career would reach a possible momentum upward, the studio would bypass "good old Anne" in favor of some newcomer who received the prize assignment that might have led Anne to a far more distinguished cinema-industry footing. The first such example was in February, 1936, when the studio announced that Anne would co-star in Maxwell Anderson's *Winterset*. But by the time the property went before the cameras, Margo had been imported from Broadway to re-create her stage role along with the play's lead, Burgess Meredith. The filmization of *Winterset* (1936) did wash out as a proverbial artistic failure, but the heroine's role might well have led RKO or other studios to consider Anne for assignments that would soon become the specialty of Warner Bros.' Priscilla Lane and Jane Bryan: the socially conscious Depression heroine. Instead Anne was assigned to her fifth George Nicholls, Jr.-directed feature, *M'liss* (Roxy Theatre, August 7, 1936), a picture *Variety* characterized as "heavy doses of mush . . . mixed with a sprinkling of sarsaparilla."

Anne was as miscast in *M'liss* as Ann Harding had been in *The Girl of the Golden West* (First National, 1930). The two actresses were at opposite poles of the screen-image continuum in looks, breeding, and sophistication; yet

*The *New York Times* bandied re *Chatterbox*: "[She] performs with her customary coyness."

neither could successfully adopt the midway guise of a rambunctious, self-sufficient, western-town saloon girl. Admittedly in *M'liss*, Anne had the easier task, for Bret Harte's story of M'liss, the spitfire shanty-house daughter of a drunkard (Guy Kibbee) who washes dishes at the local saloon, was so laundered that the rustic film was as innocent as a Sunday School picnic. John Beal, once a promising RKO lead player and now demoted to B-films, was inappropriately cast as the new teacher come to town who takes a shine to ungrammatic Anne and eventually weds her. Anne's best sequence here was a carryover from *Chatterbox*, a scene in which she offers a heart-felt rendition of "I'll Hang My Heart on the Weepy Willow," performed with full primitive dramatics in front of the saloon patrons to earn sufficient money so she can attend school. Throughout the film, and despite the allegedly seamy events at the saloon, with its contingent of rowdy gamblers, miners, and farmers, Anne remains a naïve lass respected by the entire village, save by mayor Arthur Hoyt, his wife (Margaret Armstrong), and their pesky daughter (Barbara Pepper). Anne's obvious uneasiness with the role of M'liss filtered through her performance, emphasizing the still unpolished aspects of her acting talents. The critics, who were usually kind to Anne's winning screen emoting, were particularly sharp in their opinions of her in *M'liss*. "Not our idea of an actress" *(New York Herald-Tribune)*; "determinedly ingenuous" (*New York Sun*); "Anne Shirley in the title role can hardly be said to be much of an actress" (*Brooklyn Daily Eagle*).

Anne's third and final 1936 release was *Make Way for a Lady*, which provided her with a new director (David Burton) and an attempted change of image to being a Miss-Fix-It. The role of a precocious busybody adolescent was suitable for the likes of Shirley Temple, Deanna Durbin, Judy Garland, or Jane Withers, but Anne was then eighteen years old* and not a cute youngster who could dispel the essential stickiness of her moon-struck character with a mere dimpled smile or a quick song and dance. RKO surrounded Anne with a superior cast, including top-billed Herbert Marshall as her widowed father, who Anne believes loves novelist Margot Grahame (he really craves schoolteacher Gertrude Michael); nevertheless, the *New York American* reviewer sighed, "In all my movie-going days I have seldom seen a passable young player in so impossible a situation."

While RKO's new executive vice-president in charge of production, Pandro S. Berman, was fumbling with Anne's oncamera image, the private Anne was undergoing her own personal milestones and enunciated personality changes. In January, 1936, Anne and her mother negotiated a new five-year RKO contract,† which provided for further salary escalations, as well as a standard

---

*A mature Shirley Temple would fare equally poorly in MGM's *Kathleen* (1941), a similar story, which also featured Herbert Marshall as the dad.

†In May, 1936, it was revealed that Anne legally had two "mothers," Mrs. Mimi Shirley and Mrs. Lena Sage, the latter a family friend since Anne first came to Hollywood and appeared in *The Spanish Dancer* along with her son. The dual guardianship was devised to "protect" Anne in case anything happened to Mrs. Shirley.

cancellation clause should she wed. A well-coached Anne told the press: "I want to spend the next five years in serious picture work, without anything to distract me. By the end of that time, if all goes well, I will be in a position to provide for mother and myself for life [her goal was to present her mother with a $50,000 life annuity policy]—and then, if I wish, I can start thinking about romance. But right now I'm too young for that sort of thing, and a special clause seemed the best way to insure my present independence. . . . This way I automatically cease being an actress when I marry." On June 10, 1936, Anne graduated from her private-tutor high school, and that September she made her first trip back East for a public appearance tour in New York. Her first presentation was at the Brooklyn RKO Albee Theatre on September 30, 1936.

That fall eighteen-year-old Anne gave some slight intimations that there was a well-developed individual personality buried behind the smokescreen of her mother's and RKO's publicity mill. "All through the years," Anne confided to one reporter, "it seemed to me there was nothing else to do but act in pictures, because I had been in them from the time I was hardly more than a baby. Now that I have grown older, I am going to do the best I can to make more of myself—perhaps to be a great star." Anne and her mother were still sharing a six-room bungalow on the wrong side of the Hollywood tracks, but now the actress had a confederate in arms. For more than a year Phyllis Fraser, Ginger Rogers's cousin, had been a permanent guest at the Shirley home. What had begun as an engineered-goodwill favor by Mrs. Shirley to court the pleasure of Rogers's mother, Mrs. Lela Rogers, then heading a talent-coaching department at RKO, ended in bringing about Anne's emancipation. For soon Anne and Phyllis Fraser began breaking away from the studio-designed dating with the likes of Tom Brown, and Owen Davis, Jr., and started attending social functions of their choice.

That Anne was professionally stagnating at RKO was clearly indicated by her first two 1937 releases. *Too Many Wives* was a tepid attempt at screwball comedy with proletarian Anne, cast as an heiress no less, flirting with John Morley, who for want of better diversion has made himself a society dog-watcher. Anne, billed over the title, was badly photographed and radiated tackiness rather than glamour. Contrary to RKO's mild promotional campaign, Morley was not a find, but a detriment to the film. Rather it was Barbara Pepper, wasted in a brief assignment in *Too Many Wives*, who proved the most capable in this skittish comedy dud. *Meet the Missus* had Anne taking third billing to contract comedians Victor Moore and Helen Broderick, who for a change had a picture to themselves instead of playing second-bananas to Fred Astaire and Ginger Rogers. Small-town barber Moore is so henpecked he inevitably finds himself the one stuck doing the housewife while his dominating wife (Broderick), being too preoccupied with her contest-entering, issues instructions. Through a fluke, Broderick, undoubtedly Fosterboro's least experienced and most untalented housewife, finds herself entered in the Happy Noodle Company's "Mrs. Mid-Western

Housewife" contest, with the finals taking place in Atlantic City. Daughter Anne, in a very subordinate role, tags along and while at the oceanside resort strikes up a romance with noodle salesman Alan Bruce. *Meet the Missus* would have been much better as a two-reeler, but with two pros heading the cast, director Joseph Santley was able to stretch it out to sixty minutes. On two times at bat, Anne had clearly demonstrated that screwball screen comedy was not her forte.

The picture for which Anne is best remembered is Samuel Goldwyn's *Stella Dallas* (Radio City Music Hall, August 5, 1937). When Goldwyn announced he would redo his 1925 feature, which had starred Belle Bennett, Ronald Colman, and Lois Moran, film-industryites chuckled that the veteran producer had lost his touch, and that the old-warhorse tale could not possibly hold up under the scrutiny of 1930s audiences. They proved wrong and Goldwyn right, for the famous sob-promoter picture clicked with the public and was a rousing financial success. It had been an easy decision to cast handsome, immobile John Boles (of *Back Street* and *The Life of Vergie Winters*) in the typecast cardboard role of Stephen Dallas, and after some debate whether the queen of mother-love screenfare, Ruth Chatterton, might be more appropriate, it was decided to offer the title role to the younger, and more popular, Barbara Stanwyck. As for the role of the daughter, Laurel, it was a fluke of perception that Anne was even considered for the important assignment, after her recent rash of RKO mini-fiascoes. The more attractive, equally talented Andrea Leeds, who would perform in several Goldwyn pictures, would have been an equally good choice for the part, but it was eighteen-year-old Anne, who had worked briefly twice before with Stanwyck, who was given the casting go-ahead. Despite her on-the-set problems with director King Vidor, Anne rose to the occasion magnificently.*

Barbara Stanwyck's Stella Dallas is a blatant caricature of a coarse, common woman with atrocious taste in clothes, friends, and life-style. Her one redeeming quality is a misguided sense of overwhelming mother love. On the other hand, Anne's Laurel provides the threads of credibility upon which the film hangs. In the context of the film, Anne's character matures from a gawky,

---

*Not so long ago Anne reminisced about *Stella Dallas*. "Oh, it's hopelessly old-fashioned. It was hopelessly old-fashioned when we did it. No girl in real life, even back then, would have carried on the way I did in that picture. If she'd been unhappy with or embarrassed by her mother, she would have simply gone off to another town and changed her name.

"You know, I did a dreadful thing while we were making that one. Our director was King Vidor, and though he's a dear man socially, on the set he gives you absolutely no direction—just lets you shift for yourself—and never says whether you're doing well or terribly. Well, I wasn't used to that kind of treatment and it bugged me terribly. So I finally made an appointment to see Sam Goldwyn and when I was ushered into his office, I promptly burst into tears and told that poor man. 'Mr. Goldwyn, you've got to replace me. I can't finish this picture. I can't work like this.'

"I was too young to realize that one just doesn't tell someone like Sam Goldwyn anything like that; certainly not for the reasons I finally gave him. But Sam was very dear about it. He told me to dry my eyes, go back to the set and that he felt certain I'd have no more problems. I was later told that he immediately called Vidor and told him, 'I don't care *what* you tell the kid . . . tell her she's lousy if she's great or great if she's lousy. Tell her any damn thing you please. I just can't cope with hysterical females and I don't want to be bothered again!"

shy girl of thirteen to a graceful young debutante who marries aristocratic Tim Holt. Anne's Laurel is a polite young girl torn between a strong love for the crude mother with whom she lives and an equal, but unchanneled, attachment to her blueblood father, who resides in New York and associates with such magnificent ladies as widow Barbara O'Neil (whom he later marries). Continual holiday visits to New York prompt Anne to compare her small-town common home surroundings—which generally included Stanwyck's loud-mouthed drunken salesman beau, Alan Hale—with the luxurious appointments of O'Neil's residence and the stellar deportment of her three gentlemanly sons. Fate and human nature lead Anne to eventually reside with her father and his new wife. In the climactic wedding scene she has no knowledge that her devoted low-class mother is watching the ceremony from the dank street outside.

In *Stella Dallas* Anne performs three particularly moving sequences. On the day of her junior-miss birthday party, dressed in the new outfit sewn by Stanwyck, beribboned Anne runs the gamut from bubbling enthusiasm to resigned disappointment, as one by one her classmates' parents phone to say their child will not be attending the festivities.* Finally, late in the afternoon, dejected Anne realizes that not one of the guests will have the decency to make an appearance, so she bravely says to baffled, hurt Stanwyck,† "We'll go in together," determined to celebrate the occasion properly—no matter what, no matter how.

Later on, when Stanwyck comes to the conclusion that she should make wealthy Boles pay for Anne so that her daughter can enjoy all the luxuries of life that are a normal part of O'Neil's existence, mother and daughter traipse off to the fancy Mirador Resort. There Anne meets eligible, collegiate Tim Holt and an instant romance develops. In the lengthy feature's one idyllic sequence, with Anne very attractively photographed by Rudolph Mate, she and Holt partake of a countryside bicycle jaunt and stop by a pond to talk. As they sit on the hillside rocks with the sun reflecting in the water, they engage in easily comprehensible pantomine as Holt presents her with his fraternity pin. Anne suddenly realizes the pathway to an elite future lies open to her. The mimed expressions on Anne's changing countenance are a mere indication of the acting potential she possessed even at this time.

Still later in *Stella Dallas*, after Anne demands that she and her mother immediately pack up and leave the resort,‡ Anne lies sleepless in the Pullman-car upper berth. Suddenly she (and Stanwyck in the berth beneath) hear passengers giddily gossiping about the gaudily dressed, painted dame (Stanwyck) who was running loose at the resort that day. Stanwyck finally comprehends Anne's sudden decision to leave the vacation spa, but she pretends

*Nasty rumors have spread about town concerning Stanwyck's close relationship with Hale.

†The mother has put tremendous energy and great expense into dressing herself and fixing up the flat for the occasion.

‡The vision of Stanwyck stalking across the resort patio dressed outlandishly in a loud print dress, excess of bows, jewelry, makeup, adorned shoes, and a hideous white-fox boa, is unforgettable.

to be asleep when the daughter, overwhelmed with remorse, jumps down from her berth to snuggle next to her rejected mother. For the first time, and circumstances in the plot prove it to be the final time, Anne is in a position to comfort her mother on a mature basis, reversing their usual roles.

Anne's reviews for *Stella Dallas* were like a press agent's dream: "sensitive and expressive" (*London Times*); "Little short of magnificent" (*New York World-Telegram*); "flawless" (*New York Times*); "The outstanding performance in the photoplay is that of Anne Shirley, as the daughter Laurel. Eager and unaffected, she carries the character from the hair-ribboned innocence of the birthday party through the heart-breaks of adolescence to maturity with steady and brilliant assurance. This is acting of distinction and great promise" (Howard Barnes, *New York Herald-Tribune*). With these critical raves confirmed by audience reactions, Anne was nominated for her first and only Academy Award.* But it was veteran performer Alice Brady who won the best supporting actress award for her performance in *In Old Chicago*. Anne, Stanwyck, and Boles would re-create their *Stella Dallas* roles on "Lux Radio Theatre" on October 11, 1937.†

Ironically, at the very time when Anne's career star should have been shooting skywards, it was dangerously close to crashing to a complete halt. Goldwyn's prime production of *Stella Dallas* took longer to complete than expected, leaving only a few weeks between the finish of that feature and the time in late 1937 when Anne's RKO option was due. It was too late to sandwich Anne into a studio programmer, and RKO executives, ever alert to paring down the contract roster by removing "deadwood," were unsure whether Anne's important role in the unpreviewed *Stella Dallas* would pay dividends for RKO, making her viable box office again. As former RKO studio executive Sam Briskin recalled after the fact: "One of our most difficult problems has been to cast Miss Shirley properly. . . . She is not old enough to play leads, and so stories must be found adaptable to her special talent. We tried to follow the success of *Anne of Green Gables* with *M'liss,* which was exactly the same type, but unfortunately, the picture did not come through quite so well. I convinced Samuel Goldwyn of the girl's desirability as Laurel in *Stella Dallas* and although he did not agree at first, tests proved that we were right in our appraisal of her. We had hoped that *Stella* would be completed before Miss Shirley's option came up, but when we saw that it would not, we debated and discussed among ourselves the advisability of retaining an actress who presented so many problems. We were convinced of her value, and although we were unable to view any of her work in *Stella,* we exercised the option anyway because of the confidence we have in her."

All of which was not exactly factual. For suddenly Anne had become eman-

---

*Ironically, Andrea Leeds was also nominated that year, for her role in RKO's *Stage Door,* a part studio-contractee Anne could have handled well.

†Anne was heard in such other "Lux Radio Theatre" adaptations as *The Voice of Bugle Ann* (July 6, 1936) with Lionel Barrymore, *Come and Get It* (November 15, 1937) with Edward Arnold, and *Poppy* (March 7, 1938) with W. C. Fields and John Payne.

cipated. On August 22, 1937, in Santa Barbara, she wed twenty-five-year-old actor John Payne.* Anne had met Payne two months before, during the production of *Stella Dallas,* when she and Phyllis Fraser happened to attend one of Lee Bowman's cocktail parties. After the marriage, Anne and Payne rented a modest Hollywood apartment, with Phyllis moving to an apartment across the hall from them. From this time forward, Mimi Shirley—both in public and private—played a continually decreasing role in Anne's life.

The RKO decision-makers were unsure whether once pliable, tractable Anne would become independent and difficult to manage now that she was married. She seemed so different since her *Stella Dallas* loan-out. She had totally abandoned her modest little country-girl guise. Her reddish-gold hair was worn in a mature, down style, and she now favored shorter skirts and even wore eye makeup. RKO decided to gamble and renewed Anne's option at a yearly cost of under $30,000. Immediately it was announced that Anne would be rematched on film with Barbara Stanwyck, the latter still having additional picture commitments to RKO. The vehicle selected was *Condemned Women,* a distaff-oriented entry in the current prison-film cycle. By the time it went into production in December, 1937, Stanwyck was instead starring in the comedy *The Mad Miss Manton* (RKO, 1938), but Anne was thrust into the inferior *Condemned Women* (1938) in support of Sally Eilers and Louis Hayward. The final screen results were as unrewarding as Paramount's *Prison Farm* (1938) starring Shirley Ross. Neither movie was a *Caged*—or even a *Women's Prison.* Director Lew Landers created a humdrum account that was neither starkly realistic nor fancifully entertaining. The plot finds naive young Anne jailed for a crime she did not commit, all in the name of love to protect her boyfriend so he can become an attorney. Among her prison associates are sweet shoplifter Eilers (also displaying a marcelled hairdo) and tough babe Lee Patrick. Most of the yarn focuses on Eiler's romance with prison psychiatrist Hayward, and the attempts of visionary warden George Irving to regenerate Eilers while steering her away from Hayward so the latter's career will not be tainted. Yes, there is the *de rigeur* prison break in which a matron is killed, and, yes, Eilers is placed on trial for her participation. But both Hayward and Irving come to her rescue and see that her sentence is reduced because of mitigating circumstances. Almost forgotten Anne straggles through to her own satisfactory rewards.

Less than a week after *Condemned Women* opened, *Law of the Underworld* followed it into the Rialto Theatre on April 27, 1938. It was still another cut-rate affair dispensed by Robert Sisk's RKO programmer division and directed in mediocre style by Lew Landers. Square-jawed Chester Morris, who

*Born May 23, 1912, in Roanoke, Virginia, Payne attended Mercersburg Academy in Pennsylvania, where he was a star swimmer. While at Roanoke College he was a water-sports champ and a noted singer. Later he was employed as a pulp-magazine writer while working his way through Columbia University and the Juilliard School of Music. For a spell he played the Shubert Brothers summer-stock circuit and was a solo vocalist on many radio programs. In the Broadway revue *At Home Abroad* he was both a soloist and a quartet member. Later that year he went to Hollywood, making his film debut in the role of Harry in Samuel Goldwyn's *Dodsworth* (1936).

had appeared in the story's Broadway original (*Crime* [1927])* now starred as the society gangster who becomes the benefactor of Anne and her true love, Richard Bond. The young couple become the innocent dupes of Morris's chief henchman, sneering Eduardo Ciannelli, who uses them to carry out a shop robbery, leading to their arrest, but big-hearted Morris bumps off rebellious Ciannelli and turns himself over to the cops to clear the ingenuous young couple.

By the time *Stella Dallas* was in release and garnering fine notices for Anne, she was cast in *Mother Carey's Chickens* (Radio City Music Hall, August 4, 1938),† her first prime RKO vehicle in over two years. Even now Anne did not rate as the first choice for the picturization of the Kate Douglas Wiggin novel. Studio star Ginger Rogers had been the original selection, but she wisely rejected the lavender-scented project to continue onward with her Fred Astaire musicals and alternating grade-A-produced comedy-drama assignments. Rowland V. Lee, once scheduled to guide Anne in *Condemned Women*, whipped some robustness into the fragile period account of Mother Carey (Fay Bainter), who brooks every obstacle to keep her family of four children (Anne, Ruby Keeler, Donnie Dunagan, Jackie Moran) together after Captain Carey (Ralph Morgan) is killed in the Spanish-American War. Bainter hits upon the idea of solving the family's economic problem by renting a beautiful, rickety old house and turning it into a boarding house for schoolteachers. A romantic crisis arises when the two oldest girls fall for Latin teacher James Ellison, but since Anne was top-billed over ex-Warner Bros. tippy-tap star Keeler, it was obvious who would win this contest. (Keeler is relegated to finding "happiness" with Dr. Frank Albertson, a young doctor she meets when her youngest brother becomes ill.) The final calamity occurs when the homestead is up for sale because of unpaid back taxes. The resourceful Carey brood frighten away prospective purchasers by leading them to believe the abode is haunted, and eventually they are able to keep the house. Certainly this quaint film lacked the sentimental chemistry of *Anne of Green Gables,* and in the new production Anne was no more than competent in her role, running "through her part in an acceptable manner" (*New York Herald-Tribune*). It was three-year-old Dunagan and ten-year-old veteran Virginia Weidler (as the neighborhood girl with the wrong shoes on each foot) who provided the touchstone to this folksy picture and who earned the bulk of critical and viewer attention.

Far more impressive was RKO's unheralded remake of its *One Man's Journey* (1933), entitled *A Man to Remember* (1938) and given to Broadway-recruit Garson Kanin as his premier directorial assignment. Kanin capitalized on the picture's low budget by turning out a sensible film that amazed contemporary critics, who were aghast with delight that so workmanlike a product could be created on the proverbial shoestring. The film opens at the funeral of elderly Dr. Edward Ellis, longtime physician of Westport, a small mid-

---

*First filmed by RKO in 1930 as *The Pay-Off* with Lowell Sherman, Marian Nixon, and Hugh Trevor.

†A project rejected by both Katharine Hepburn and Ginger Rogers.

western town. Banker Granville Bates, merchant Harlan Briggs, and newspaper editor Frank M. Thomas gather in the local lawyer's office to press their combined $360 claim against the late doctor's estate. In going through his papers they recall events in the citizen's laudatory life. There is a flashback to twenty years prior when humble country doctor Ellis arrives in Westport to conduct his practice, convinced that big-city ways are not his style. In the course of his ministrations to the townfolk, he rescues little Jean (played as a child by Carole Leete, as an adult by Anne) from her father, who cannot forgive or forget that she was indirectly responsible for her mother's death in childbirth. Ellis's ward grows up to love and cherish the doctor's own son (Lee Bowman), who later rejects a big-city neurology practice to return to his hometown to become a country doctor like his esteemed father, and, of course, to renew his romance with Anne. Anne was commended as "one of the most ringingly true little actresses in films" (*New York Daily Mirror*), but it was Ellis who made this film memorable, and a far cry above other examples of the then-current physician-film cycle.*

By mid-1938 Anne reached yet another plateau in her film career. Although having lost out in the 1937 Academy Award sweepstakes, RKO proved its continued interest in Anne by announcing that she would star in a remake of *A Bill of Divorcement* with the clear intention that she was to be groomed into an adult dramatic star. Topping this announcement was the fact that Anne was among the many seriously tested by David O. Selznick for his forthcoming MGM release, *Gone with the Wind*. She, Andrea Leeds, and Elizabeth Allen were among those in the top running for the part of Melanie, but they all lost out to Olivia de Havilland. As 1938 wore on, RKO went through another of its constant executive shake-ups, and under the new George Schaefer regime, Anne found herself again being passed over, much like the poor relative who can always be counted on as a last-minute substitute for lesser offerings.

Anne was loaned to Columbia for their catchpenny *Girls' School* (1938), in which she was the forlorn central victim of boarding-school snobbery. This uninvigorating study of class distinction, incipient romance and threatened expulsion at Magnolia Hall, gave Anne a liberal opportunity to exercise her abilities as a prime silver-screen martyr. She was the poverty-stricken scholarship member of the senior class who must earn her keep at the exclusive institution by working after class in the library and serving in the undesirable post of class monitor. In fact, she earns her classmates' total scorn when she informs the school officials that spoiled Nan Grey actually spent an entire night away from the dormitory. At the senior prom events come to a crisis for snubbed, ostracized Anne. Plumber's assistant Noah Beery, Jr. not only arrives to escort Anne to the dance in a shabby delivery truck, but at the prom she is accused of stealing Grey's corsage. However, before the evening is over, the students learn what four years of association with Anne has failed to

*Which included MGM's *The Citadel* and *Young Dr. Kildare* and RKO's own *Dr. Christian* series, featuring studio contractee Dorothy Lovett in an Anne Shirley-type of recurring role.

demonstrate, that she is a regular chum to be admired, not despised. *Girls'
School* came and went generally unnoticed on the programmer film circuit,
its workmanlike direction by German import John Brahm taken for granted,
and Anne's impersonation of the blacklisted, frightened, and humiliated
Natalie Freeman overlooked by an indifferent public.* It was just this sort of
performance that demonstrated Anne's rightness for the ingenue part in Warner Bros.' *Old Maid* (1938) for which she was tested, but bypassed in favor
of Bette Davis's protégée, Jane Bryan.

And so it was back to RKO programmers. Anne was the nominal lead in
Boy Slaves (1939) a sturdy indictment of forced-labor camps for juvenile
delinquents. Eleanor Roosevelt may have endorsed the picture as "almost as
exciting as *Jesse James*," but the movie was less a general-audience entertainment entry than a sidetracked preachment (complete with a melodramatic
foreword) aimed at welfare and social workers.† This time the setting was at
Charles Lane's turpentine camp where the free youthful labor is treated
sadistically. The picture follows the particular plight of waif Roger Daniel,
considered a stool pigeon by his tramp comrades until the climax where, by
his brave death during an escape plot, he proves his courageous spirit. In this
top-heavy study of brute horror, Anne provided the one sympathetic feminine
touch as the orphaned girl who is forever cooking and cleaning. Near the
finale she has an extended speech imploring the boys not to run away from
the camp but to await the arrival of the police and explain to them the horrendous situation as it actually was. It was this scene of camera-holding dramatics
that led the *New York Herald-Tribune* to wager that Anne's "star is ascend-
ing."

In *Sorority House* (RKO, 1939) Anne was back at her familiar post as the
ingenuous daughter of a small-town grocer (J. M. Kerrigan), who does not at
first appreciate the sacrifice made by her father when he sells his store to a
big chain so that she can attend Talbot University. Once at college wide-eyed
Anne falls prey to the social-climbing mania in which any coed who is not a
sorority girl is immediately classified a "dreep" (combination of dreary and
weep). Countrified Anne would never have had a bid to the Gamma House,
but she had the good fortune of quickly becoming acquainted with the campus
hero (James Ellison), who pities Anne's bewilderment and helps her adjust
to the big-league social system. Ellison's squiring and the sorority-girls' sudden
interest in her go to Anne's head and she becomes—ever so temporarily—one
of those 1930s villainesses, *a social snob!* Who should show up on the most
important night of her entire life—the Gamma Sorority pledge party—but her
bucolic father, and Anne is beside herself with unjustified embarrassment.
She cold-shoulders dad only to later realize the meaning of her dreadful
behavior, rediscovering that she has nothing to be ashamed of, least of all in

*Howard Barnes *(New York Herald-Tribune)* did note of Anne: "Catches up all the moving
quality of the piece in an eloquent performance."
†William Wellman's *Wild Boys of the Road* (First National, 1933) was not only more to the
sociological point but had far more drive and entertainment value.

the honest, self-sacrificing person of her father. As a dramatic gesture she tears up her Gamma Sorority bid. Among the bit players enacting coeds in *Sorority House* were future celebrities Veronica Lake and Marge Champion, but Anne's heartrending performance led Regina Crewe of the *New York American* to observe that Anne "proves again she is one of the ablest actresses on Hollywood's long roster."

As her third and final release of 1939 RKO tucked Anne into *Career,* another grade-B picture enhanced by the earnest portrayal of Edward Ellis. Playing the owner of a hardware store in the small midwestern town of Pilville, Iowa, he proves to be the salvation of his fellow citizens. Not that he is a completely flawless person. Years before banker Samuel S. Hinds wed the woman Ellis loved and now, because of that long-ago incident, Ellis is unfavorably inclined toward Hinds's daughter, Anne, the devoted love of Ellis's son (John Archer), just now starting a career as a medical researcher. When Ellis suspects Hinds's bank may close, he engineers a near panic by withdrawing his own funds, and in retaliation Hinds convinces the aroused townsfolk to go after the storekeeper. But everyone regains a modicum of sense, and the bank is saved, Ellis and Hinds reach a truce, and the town realizes how fortunate it is to have such men as Ellis and Hinds. *Career* could be called a poor man's offshoot of *Ah, Wilderness!*, with all the action transpiring between July 4th and Christmas and the emphasis likewise on contrived local color. In this picture Anne was stuck with a secondary role, playing Hinds's considerate daughter, willing to sacrifice her future happiness by wedding wealthy Charles Drake in order to obtain needed funds to restore the bank's solvency. But the fates and the scriptwriters provided a happy ending for her. Bosley Crowther *(New York Times)*, never much of an Anne Shirley fan, labeled her here as "little more than a face with a voice."

With the end of another decade in the cinema, Anne could not resist the opportunity to spell out her own reflections as a lifelong show-business veteran. "I don't think I missed any of the 'natural' life that comes to the average child, and if I did there have been compensatory factors. I don't regret a single day I've spent here in Hollywood. I love the town and my work in pictures, and I only hope I'll be here—and working—for many years to come."

Evidently RKO did not share Anne's optimistic outlook on her career, for they dealt her possible career another blow: the promised role in *A Bill of Divorcement* went to the studio's new favorite contract player, young Maureen O'Hara. It was little consolation to Anne to have the opportunity to work with a top-rate director, George Stevens, in a first-class production but his film, *Vigil in the Night* (1940),* proved to be a box-office clinker and reflected no

---

*Anne frankly admitted a few years ago about this film: "Oh, it had its moments and of course it was directed by George Stevens, who was a genius even then. It's for directors like him and Bill Dieterle that actors and actresses are willing to turn themselves inside out . . . they're just so great that you sometimes think you are, too, just working with them. But the picture was something else. It was all so ghastly stark and tragic. . . . Everyone is in tears at one time or another. It's the wettest movie I ever did. And then there was Carole Lombard. I thought she did a magnificent job in the film, but the public, used to her as a light comedienne, felt differently. They just wouldn't accept Carole as a tragic heroine."

glory on third-billed Anne. The slickly produced rendition of A. J. Cronin's novel proved much too severe for 1940s audiences, even if Carole Lombard was starred.*

Vigil in the Night cast Anne against type, as the willful younger sister of nurse Lombard. Anne is forever rebelling against the monotony and drabness of a profession she entered only to please Lombard, and as a result she treats her nursing career too cavalierly. Dedicated Lombard assumes the guilt for the death of a child resulting from Anne's negligence during her training period in a hospital in Manchester, England. Lombard is forced to take a post at another hospital where she falls in love with doctor Brian Aherne, but later she is pushed into leaving that institution for failing to fraternize with a hospital benefactor. Meanwhile Anne is in London, having wed her hometown sweetheart. She is again in difficulty, in danger of being tried for criminal negligence in the suicide death of a patient. Both Lombard and Aherne come to her timely rescue. Thereafter both sisters volunteer to return to the Manchester hospital to work in the isolation ward during a diphtheria epidemic. Anne dies during the travail, while Lombard is rewarded for her devotion to duty by being reinstated to her former position and reuniting with Aherne.

RKO attempted to spark audience interest in *Vigil in the Night* by utilizing sensational advertising for the film, but word of mouth killed this misleading approach to what was an essentially somber drama, crowded with significant but disjointed action and too few saving romantic touches. If comedienne Lombard was criticized for being too subdued and severe in the picture, and Aherne's performance was passed off as too pat, Anne was lauded as being "splendid" *(New York Daily News).* Attractively garbed in her nurse's outfit, Anne was "as superb," insisted the *New York Herald-Tribune*'s Howard Barnes, "as many of us have always thought she would be when given a role worthy of her talents." One poignant sequence in *Vigil in the Night* occurs near the film's conclusion, when Anne is desperately fighting to save the life of a child, determined to make amends for the one who died during her training days. Her successful efforts are reflected in the intent little faces of the other ward patients, children who silently acknowledge her life-saving efforts.

It was little more than a happy accident that Anne was even cast in Warner Bros.' *Saturday's Children* (1940). That studio's Jane Bryan had been assigned the part, but she suddenly decided to retire from the screen to wed. Warner's contract star Olivia de Havilland went on suspension rather than accept the role. Thus Anne was a hasty third choice to play opposite John Garfield in this remake of Maxwell Anderson's Pulitzer Prize-winning play.† Garfield portrayed an uncharacteristic assignment as a slow-thinking, bespectacled young man who constantly devises impractical inventions. He is about to embark on a new career in the Philippines when Anne, on the advice of her married older sister (Lee Patrick), tricks him into wedding her. "We

*She was then freelancing under a special RKO pact and was Hollywood's highest-salaried nonstudio star.

†Gregory La Cava had directed the original 1929 screen version, which starred Corinne Griffith, Grant Withers, and Charles Lane, as more of a romantic comedy.

married on $20 a week and we're sitting on top of the world" ran the film's ad copy, but soon within the plot the tenement-living newlyweds discover that in a still financially depressed America a small salary leads to tumultuous marital discord, particularly when the husband is unhappily trapped in a minor clerical post. It is only the near successful sacrifice of her father (Claude Rains), who attempts to commit suicide so his family can collect the insurance money, that awakens Garfield and Anne to the life opportunities available to the young and willing. However, by 1940, such Depression-drab tales had become too commonplace, and with the approach of World War II prosperity the story was excessively quaint and archaic. Thus *Saturday's Children* received short shrift at the box office. In a typically sensitive portrayal, Rains claimed the best of the review notices, with Anne scarcely mentioned in passing.

During the production of *Saturday's Children* Anne told the press that she was pregnant. (On August 10, 1940, her daughter, Julie Anne, was born.) Despite the fact of her approaching motherhood, RKO cast Anne in *Anne of Windy Poplars* (Palace Theatre, August 22, 1940), an unnecessary sequel to *Anne of Green Gables.* "I guess they must think I don't have much here," Anne said about her unwanted assignment as she pointed to her brain area. "I'm really not that kind of a person at all. I'm grown up now. I'm not the sweet girl they make me out to be. I'm not terribly sophisticated but I do know more than that. I don't know exactly what to do about it. I just have to play the parts they give me. It's such a nice studio and I don't like to make any trouble.

"I'd like to make a complete change. Even have another name. Anne Shirley. It just doesn't end. It just sort of dies out. I'd like a strong name."

Anne proved absolutely correct in her prediction. *Anne of Windy Poplars* was a dull and uninteresting entry, an escapee from a pre-gaslight era. The story's lead character (played by Anne) is now a mature young woman who arrives at Pringleton, on Canada's Prince Edward Island, where she is to be the new vice-principal and teach high school classes. Because elderly Ethel Griffies had wanted that very post, Anne earns the emnity of Griffies's influential family. But not for long, because she manages to overcome the hostility and brings happiness (just like Pollyanna) into the lives of some of her new friends. At the wholesome conclusion of *Anne of Green Gables,* Anne was set to wed Gilbert Blythe (Tom Brown), but in the sequel Blythe (now played by Patric Knowles) is away studying to become a doctor. She temporarily became enamored of local townsman James Ellison but realizes he truly loves fellow schoolteacher Louise Campbell. This observation paves the way for Anne's reunion with Knowles and their adoption of orphan Joan Carroll. The picture was charitably regarded as the "closest thing to a Sunday school picnic that's come to Broadway in a long, hot summer" *(New York Times).* But filmgoers were not buying this brand of sweetness at this point in the twentieth century.

More than a year after the birth of Anne's daughter, Anne was back on the screen via loan-out to Paramount for their *West Point Widow* (Loew's Criterion, September 10, 1941). It was a picture that certainly did not live up to its dramatic title and so enraged the critics that even the usually placid Kate Cameron of the *New York Daily News* wrote that the movie gives West Point an undeserved "black eye" and "deserves nothing but our contempt." The speciously plotted junk found Academy plebe Richard Denning breaking the institution's strict rule by wedding Anne. But later, through the influence of his snobbish Park Avenue mother, the couple split and Anne agrees to an annulment. Naive Anne does not inform her ex-groom that she is pregnant, for in her simple way she is certain he will later live up to his promise to rewed her. Anne has her child, joins a hospital's nursing staff, and eventually, after recovering from Denning's calculated marriage to socialite Frances Gifford, herself marries Dr. Richard Carlson. As the film winds up, Anne sails off into the sunset toward Panama and a new future, hand in hand with Carlson and her infant child. One of the big-newspaper reviewers, William Boehnel *(New York World-Telegram)*, took space and time away from blasting the banally scripted feature to editorialize: "But Miss Shirley never seems to be able to get out of the B class. Why? I don't know, because she is a good-looking young lady, has charm and lots of acting ability. A darn sight more than most of the cuties who have been pushed toward stardom."

Undaunted, RKO saw fit to pitch Anne into the flimsy *Unexpected Uncle* (1941), more a minor showcasing for Charles Coburn than a vehicle for her. He played a steel tycoon who has walked out of his $40,000-a-year post to find the bluebird of happiness as an itinerant horseshoe pitcher lodged at a Florida trailer camp. Anne was presented as a sappy lingerie salesgirl whose romance with discontented shoe millionaire James Craig is engineered by aging Coburn. The film's slender proposition (one should never be a slave to one's money— particularly if you have lots of it!) was not aided by the lax performances, colorless direction by Peter Godfrey, and sloppy production values. Anne breezed through her assignment looking innocent and smiley when required and crying ever so prettily on cue when things in the plot go wrong.

Ironically, Anne's favorite picture is one of the programmers in which RKO (and evidently she) threw discretion to the wind and allowed her to camp it up outrageously. *Four Jacks and a Jill* (1941), a shoddy remake of *That Girl from Paris* (1936),* cast Anne in the role originated by Lily Pons. This time around Anne was the hungry out-of-work girl adopted by four struggling musicians (including hoofer-drummer Ray Bolger). Their gambit is to have Anne pose as a European singer who has been very intimate with a newsworthy Balkan king, the latter on occasion impersonated by the bongo-playing taxi-driver member of the crew, Desi Arnaz. To make the untidy package complete (and pad out the running time to sixty-eight minutes), the group is

*In itself a remake of *Street Girl* (1930), starring Betty Compson.

involved with gangsters and gem pilfery. Naturally the climax finds Anne and Bolger "that way" about one another. If a moviegoer could forgive the grammar-school scripting, he or she could scream still at the abundance of worn-out sight gags and tedious joking. Finally, to make matters worse, Anne, who definitely had a most untrained singing voice, was given the go-ahead to burst forth into several songs, none of which she could handle with finesse. (It is rumored that ace dubber Martha Mears provided some of the onscreen singing for Anne.) Anne's partiality for this humdrum filler film is purely personal. She liked it "not because it was a good film. It wasn't. But I loved Ray Bolger and everyone else in it and we had more fun working on that than any other picture I'd ever done." Simple enough logic, but too bad RKO and Anne could not have gotten together for a Sunday-school-picnic session on a more noteworthy project—say even one of the studio's *Saint* or *Falcon* detective series entries where equivalent breeziness was required but was not always given by the inexperienced leading lady at hand.

Anne wrapped up 1941 with a token appearance in *All That Money Can Buy* (Radio City Music Hall, October 16, 1941), part of RKO's program to bring "art" to the American public. Most every industryite save the RKO executives involved with the picturization of Stephen Vincent Benet's short story "The Devil and Daniel Webster"* were quick to predict that the unorthodox metaphysical melodrama would be a commercial failure—and it certainly was! By the time the RKO authorities came to the same awesome conclusion the picture was past the stopping point in production and all that could be economically changed at that stage was the title, which switched from the original tag to *Here Is a Man* to *All That Money Can Buy*. The yarn's premise was based on Daniel Webster's statement that "if two New Hampshire men aren't a match for the Devil, we might as well give the country back to the Indians."

The story is set into motion in 1840s New Hampshire when young farmer James Craig meets a stranger named Mr. Scratch (Walter Huston) who promises him a ripe future for the price of his soul. Craig agrees, and sure enough he becomes a prosperous country farmer. At the end of the seven years, on the night of the birth of Craig's son, Huston's comely assistant Simone Simon, who claims to be from a neighboring valley, appears on the scene to insure that Craig lives up to his bargain. All this proves too much for Craig's honest, patient wife (Anne), who soon leaves home seeking refuge at the nearby farm of Daniel Webster (Edward Arnold). Arnold later engages in a dialectical match with Huston, staking Craig's soul as the prize. The illustrious orator Arnold wins the debate. Turnip-munching Huston, having stolen a piece of Ma Jane Darwell's fresh peach pie, departs for new conquests. As he ambles along he turns to the camera's eye to warn the filmgoer that he might well be the next victim—so watch out.

---

*It had been presented on radio previously and in May, 1939, had been seen as a one-act opera, which was quickly withdrawn as a novelty without sufficient merit.

Despite Huston's sly performance and Arnold's bravura oratory, producer-director William Dieterle could not turn a cinematic turkey into a profit-making film venture like the fantasy *Here Comes Mr. Jordan* (Columbia, 1941). *Variety* astutely categorized the picture: "It's a twist on the Faust theme, but Benet isn't Goethe." Ann in her special "and" billing had to cope with a slight, one-dimensional characterization which added nothing to the progression of the plot or the pseudo-New England atmosphere.

In November, 1941, twenty-one-year-old Anne signed a new seven-year contract with RKO, which scarcely was recorded by the trade press even though officially Anne was one of the studio's five top leading ladies (Lucille Ball, Phyllis Brooks, Maureen O'Hara, and Ginger Rogers were the others). Anne received more news space after voicing her opinions on the industry per se: "Do you know what makes a movie actress feel ancient?" the screen veteran asked the press. "I'll tell you. It's seeing remakes of your old films, with yourself being supplanted by a newer comer who now more closely suits the role." Anne, now herself a mother, supplanted Mrs. Mimi Shirley as the purveyor of advice for would-be professional children: "If that's what they really want, either for ambition or because they need the money, okay. I could tell them a lot of things more important to a child's career than learning a time-step before it's a year old. First, I'd teach it to mind—not just me, but anybody I told it to. My mother never let me forget for a minute that the director was the man in charge. I'd teach a child to be quiet and to go to anybody who held out arms to it."

Anne's rather sterile stand on professional children may have been a reaction to her increasing domestic problems. She took her responsibilities as a mother very seriously, while John Payne, now a rising Twentieth Century-Fox contract lead player, thoroughly enjoyed the Hollywood nightlife. On January 30, 1942, Anne filed for divorce, which was granted more than a year later on March 1, 1943, at which time she confessed: "I had never been on my own before John and I parted, and I have found it a lot of fun being entirely free and independent. . . . because I married when I was quite young it is a real novelty for me to do exactly as I please for the first time in my life." All of which reveals a great deal about Ann's relationships with her mother and with Payne.* Anne became a film colony nightlife figure, frequently seen in the company of another Twentieth Century-Fox playboy star, Victor Mature.

*Payne would enter military service after completing *Hello, Frisco, Hello* (1943), and the following year would wed MGM starlet Gloria de Haven, by whom he had two children before they divorced in 1950. Subsequently he married Alexandra Curtis (1953). After completing his Twentieth Century-Fox contract in 1947, Payne spent several years making Paramount actioners, and then in the 1950s top-lined modest programmers. He starred in the western teleseries "Restless Gun" (1958) but thereafter was plagued by bad professional luck. He was replaced by Craig Stevens in the Broadway-bound musical *Here's Love,* a tuner version of his last Fox feature, *Miracle on 34th Street* (1947). He did play in the subsequent West Coast production of *Here's Love.* Later, in the mid-1960s, he was the victim of an automobile accident while crossing a Manhattan street. Since then he has been in poor health, making only occasional film or television appearances. In late 1973 he and Alice Faye began production on the pre-Broadway tour of *Good News,* another nostalgia-craze revival.

At this time he was between his on-again, off-again engagement to Rita Hayworth. Although there was serious speculation that Anne and Mature would wed, they did not (Mature accepted active duty in the Coast Guard during World War II). Instead Anne and former Warner Bros. stock-company sidekick Eddie Albert became a serious twosome on the social circuit and, on more than one occasion before he joined the Navy in late 1942, he and Anne were rumored to have married. They did not, for two days before his military discharge in 1945 he wed Margo, the actress who had replaced Anne in *Winterset* nearly a decade before. For a time in early 1943 Anne dated Sergeant Joe Johnson, but her continual comment, "We're just good friends," proved correct, for they soon drifted apart.

Meanwhile Anne continued sporadically with an undemanding film schedule at the RKO lot. Her only 1942 release was the inexpensively produced *Mayor of 44th Street,* which relied on the drawing power of second-string MGM hoofer George Murphy for whatever box-office lure the picture had. (*P.M.'s* on-the-spot verdict judged the film a "real, unrelieved stinker.") As director Alfred Green put his cast through their mechanical paces, Murphy enacted the head of a dance-band agency who runs afoul of a group of young kids who organize their jitterbugging pals into a gang of hooligans who break up dance sessions in order to receive a hefty payoff from the band at hand. William Gargan was a friendly cop, Anne wandered in and out as Murphy's former dance partner, and silent-screen star Richard Barthelmess appeared as a recently paroled hood who intends to organize the juvenile gang on a more streamlined basis. The only "redeeming" features of this sad little entry were Murphy's breezy performance, the music of Freddy Martin's band, and the vocalizing of Joan Merrill.

The Powers Girl, completed in late 1942 but not released until March, 1943, again starred George Murphy and featured Carole Landis more prominently than second-billed Anne. The movie failed to live up to its exploitable element, with the bevy of starlets used as the long-stemmed American beauty models played down for minimal exposure. Anne was a schoolmarm come to New York, Murphy a candid cameraman, and Landis was Anne's younger sister, who craved to be a John Robert Powers (Alan Mowbray) model. Get the setup? Both sisters fall for lively Murphy, à la his *Two Girls on Broadway* (MGM, 1940), but it is mousey Anne from the sticks who lands him while Landis becomes the top Powers girl of 1943. Benny Goodman and his Orchestra provided the swing music interludes, and Dennis Day, in his standard unisex guise, offered a medley of forgettable tunes. That Anne, the ex-gingham girl, had her own sense of physical pride was revealed during completion of this double-bill item. She sued producer Charles R. Rogers for utilizing a double's legs in a hosiery scene close-up. Said a disgruntled Anne regarding the gams in question: "Besides they were of an unflattering dimension, less shapely and half again as large as mine." The case was settled out of court.

Paramount thought some publicity mileage would accrue from casting Anne with Eddie Albert in its budgeter *Lady Bodyguard* (1943), in which the emphasis was on presenting Anne as a madcap, glamorous type, an image that failed to catch any more public interest in 1943 than it had in 1937 with RKO's *Too Many Wives*. In *Lady Bodyguard* a malicious secretary alters an insurance policy for $1,000 to $1,000,000, and company public-relations gal Anne unknowingly hands the doctored policy to test pilot Albert as a promotional gimmick. Three of Albert's barroom cronies, named as policy beneficiaries, attempt to rub out Albert while Anne is avidly pursuing the pilot to retrieve the troublesome document. She and daffy Albert fall in love and marry. As a wedding present he agrees to cancel the policy. But now Anne's insurance company says no—it would not look right—so the newlyweds must beat a hasty retreat from the pursuing trio of crooks. This leads to a forced and hardly amusing plane chase before the conspirators are jailed. The contrived horseplay on the road to romance might have been more palatable if Anne and vis-à-vis Albert did not create such a bland couple, he even milder than usual and she being her restrained oncamera sweet self.

Anne did her share of war charity work during World War II, including her participation in the short subject *Show Business at War* (1943), shot by Twentieth Century-Fox for *The March of Time* series. Among the personalities participating in this report were: Louis Armstrong and his Band, Ethel Barrymore, Jack Benny, Linda Darnell, Marlene Dietrich, Irene Dunne, Kay Francis, Rita Hayworth, Hedy Lamarr, George Murphy, Lily Pons, Ginger Rogers, Frank Sinatra, Lana Turner, Orson Wells, and Darryl F. Zanuck.

Bombardier (1943) was a rah-rah formula World War II service account, whose only distinction—and a mild one at that—was being the first feature film dealing with the training of bombardier cadets. The picture was made at the suggestion of the U.S. Air Force and earned the studio needed concessions regarding restricted building supplies. RKO's newly pacted contract lead, middle-aged Pat O'Brien, headed the cast as the prototype of Colonel Paddy Ryan, noted for perfecting the modern bombsight. O'Brien was abetted on-screen by officer Randolph Scott, who congenially argues with his superior about whether the pilot or bombardier is more essential in combat duty. The test of their argument occurs when O'Brien leads a bombing raid over Japan, during which time Scott is forced down. Scott later sets a truck on fire (killing himself) to light the target for an oncoming Allied air assault. That neither O'Brien nor Scott (who dies clutching a letter from Anne) win Anne was a slight novelty, for the script had ordained that she become the sweetheart of service novice Walter Reed. Eddie Albert had a rather straight assignment as Anne's brother, an air cadet killed saving the life of a comrade. *Bombardier* was panned as a "cheap, fictitious film" *(New York Times)*.

Once again when RKO produced one of its increasingly rarer major productions, *Government Girl* (1943), the studio relied on the services of an outside star to add glitter to the box-office package. This time Warner Bros.' Olivia de Havilland was borrowed to star in the comedy, directed and produced by Dudley Nichols, while contract-lead Anne was relegated to an inconsequential role in the slapdash affair. *Government Girl* was several cuts below Columbia's *The More the Merrier* (1943) and Warner Bros.' rendition of Broadway's *The Doughgirls* (1944), which also dealt with a "hilarious" look at the problems engendered by overcrowded living conditions in wartime Washington. Compounding the other disabling factors of *Government Girl* was the bizarre casting. De Havilland, on much surer ground in heavy drama and costumers, was obviously out of her depth as a pretty but daffy secretary in the War Department who takes a shine to dollar-a-year man Sonny Tufts in the nation's capital. Tufts, who had made such a noteworthy showing that year in *So Proudly We Hail* (Paramount, 1943), was heavyhanded (downright oafish) as the go-getting bomber-production chief who strives to untie the morass of War Department red tape to push his pet project into being. Anne's role as de Havilland's ever-hungry roommate was no more than a living running gag. She has wed Sergeant James Dunn, and accommodating de Havilland insists she will somehow, some way, vacate their hotel suite, which is commandeered at the last minute by Tufts. Anne and Dunn appear periodically throughout the proceedings to reinforce and overwork the gag, being two too-weary souls anxious for their hotel accommodations before Dunn has to return to duty. By the predictable climax, at which point no one could care too much either way, Anne and Dunn finally get their long-awaited room.

Anne, who just refused to complain about the shabby treatment RKO was affording her, was then loaned to Republic for *Man from Frisco* (1944) directed by Robert Florey. The picture was as automated as its plot about the Henry Kaiser-like Irish engineer (Michael O'Shea) who develops a new method for prefabricating wartime ships. According to formula, Anne, the secretary daughter of shipbuilding supervisor Gene Lockhart, looks unfavorably on wiseacre O'Shea when he hits their California coastal community. Not only does his arrival with new methods bring about her father's dismissal, but the timesaving production system accidentally leads to the death of her young brother (Tommy Bond). But O'Shea's methods prove dramatically successful in the overall wartime situation and Anne, realizing that the rough and tough man has a heart after all, politely gives in to his romantic advances. The resulting feature was definitely not the sweepingly magnificent picture the subject suggested, nor did Anne contribute much more than animate set decoration.* *Man from Frisco* did not have even the grace to be timely, for by its June, 1944, release the United States was already undergoing cutbacks in its defensing shipbuilding program.

The story thread of *Music in Manhattan* (1944) was enough to tax anyone's patience, except for programmer-driven RKO. As the star of the Broadway-bound "Gay Forties" musical, Anne must get to Washington, D.C., to persuade a prospective backer to loan the show additional funds. She obtains a priority plane reservation by claiming to be the wife of service hero Phillip Terry, which leads to expected complications when she is shown to his hotel

*Stephanie Bachelor, as the war worker whose hubby is in the Navy, did far better with her small part.

suite in the nation's capital and the expected consequences ensue. Her song-and-dance partner (Dennis Day) is jealous, Terry joshingly insists on his marital rights, and the arrival of his mother (Jane Darwell) adds additional threads to the circumstantial spider's web, with Anne caught in one compromising situation after another. Throughout the modest picture, Anne quietly engaged in song duets and undemanding softshoeing with Day, but neither partner looked particularly pleased with the low-keyed production numbers. It was rather late in the cinema game for twenty-six-year-old Anne to suddenly aspire to pinup status as a musical-comedy lead and not many viewers bought the gambit.

Murder, My Sweet (1944) is one of the rare movie remakes to be better than the original.* Here RKO dusted off Raymond Chandler's novel *Farewell, My Lovely*—which had earlier been transformed into George Sanders' *The Falcon Takes Over* (1942)—as a new starring vehicle for Dick Powell, who was anxious to reshape his crooner screen image. Powell played hard-boiled detective Philip Marlowe, who is hired by a stir-happy ex-convict (Mike Mazurki) to find his girlfriend, who has disappeared. At the same time unscrupulous Powell is hired by Claire Trevor, the tough wife of wealthy Miles Mander, to locate a jade necklace that has been stolen. The trail leads to blackmail, murder, mental sanitariums, and quacks, with Powell absorbing more than his share of brutal beatings in his search for the missing girl and the jade necklace. Slowly he pieces together the puzzle and finds that the cases have merged since the missing jewelry and the disappearing girl of the ex-convict have become involved in the same plot. Third-billed Anne was cast as Trevor's innocent daughter, who knows too much for her own safety and that of her apparently helpless dad. But as Anne rightly appraised, it was Trevor, in the role of the scheming blonde *femme fatale,* who stole the limelight next to Powell, who made quite an impact in his offbeat casting.

A month before *Murder, My Sweet* opened a successful engagement at the Palace Theatre (March 8, 1945) Anne and thirty-three-year-old Adrian Scott,† producer of the taut corpse opera, were wed on February 9, in Las Vegas. It was the second marriage for each.

*"Now, there was a really good film," Anne enthusiastically recalled. "I loved it. Not for myself, actually, but because it pulled wonderful Dick Powell out of those insipid 'singing hero' roles and gave him a whole new and better image. You know, I read the script and even though it wasn't a large role, I fell in love with the Claire Trevor part. I was dying to play a heavy. Then Claire told me she was sick of doing heavies and would love to do the role assigned to me. Claire and I put our heads together and conspired to reverse the femme casting. We even ganged up on the producer and director, probably giving better performances for their benefit than we did in the film. But it all did us no good. Claire went back to being bad and fascinating and I went back to being good and dull. But I decided that I was going to wear a mink coat since the girl I played was very wealthy. Well, I did. But as luck would have it, that scene was shot so much in shadows that I almost could have been nude, for all anyone in the audience would have known."

†Born February 6, 1912, in Arlington, New Jersey, Scott graduated from Amherst College, was involved with Broadway stage productions, and then came to Hollywood where he collaborated on the screenplays of *Keeping Company* (MGM, 1941), *The Parson of Panamint* (Paramount, 1941), and *We Go Fast* (Twentieth Century-Fox, 1941). He then joined RKO, where he scripted *Mr. Lucky* (1943) and produced *My Pal Wolf* (1944) and *Murder, My Sweet.*

After more than two decades in front of the camera, Anne was more than content to retire, and she decided that *Murder, My Sweet* was an appropriate swan song. Since her husband was connected with RKO, a satisfactory settlement was made to Anne's existing contract. She finally became a private citizen, maintaining her professional ties only through her husband and by socializing on the Hollywood scene. Scott, who went on to produce *So Well Remembered* and *Crossfire,* both in 1947 under Dore Schary's RKO regime, was among the Unfriendly Ten involved in the House Committee on Un-American Activities hearings and was promptly fired by Schary as having breached the morality terms of his studio contract. On August 23, 1948, Anne announced that she and Scott, who had already separated, would divorce. She refused to comment on whether his political plight had any part in her decision.*

On October 19, 1949, Anne, in a very posh ceremony, wed writer-producer-director Charles D. Lederer† at the East 62nd Street, Manhattan, home of Bennett Cerf. His former wife happened to be Anne's good friend, Phyllis Fraser. In August, 1950, Anne gave birth to a son, who was named Daniel Davies Lederer. Throughout the 1950s the Lederers were very big Hollywood party-givers and solid participants in the local social life. In the 1960s, by which time Anne had become estranged (on and off) from Lederer, she continued to participate in the nightlife scene, seen in such diverse company as that of Jennings Lang and Dean Martin. Anne occasionally appeared in the news, as when her daughter Julie (from whom she was frequently estranged) made her show business debut.

Whenever someone inquires of Anne whether she will ever consider the possibility of returning to motion pictures, she has a very definite reply: "No, I don't want to go back to it. I was never really dedicated. I like to think I was competent but I know I was never better than that. I don't care to write my memoirs either, but I am trying to work up a treatment about a young girl who is forced to go into the profession and denied a normal childhood by a

---

* Scott, who had been very ill throughout the late 1940s, finally served a year's prison term in 1950 and paid a $1,000 fine for contempt of Congress in refusing to answer the Committee's question whether or not he was ever a Communist. In 1951-52, Scott sued RKO for back salary due under his contract, but lost his case. Later he returned to film production, and in the late 1960s he was associated with Universal Pictures. On December 26, 1972, Scott died in Los Angeles of cancer at the age of sixty-one.

†Born around 1906, Lederer, the son of theatrical producer George W. Lederer and actress Reine Davies, sister of Marion, had been a Broadway figure before coming to Hollywood in 1931 to collaborate on the screenplay of *The Front Page.* Thereafter he was frequently employed to co-script films, such as *Topaze* (RKO, 1933), *Within the Law* (MGM, 1939), *His Girl Friday* (Columbia, 1940), and *Love Crazy* (MGM, 1941). Occasionally he directed features, such as *Fingers at the Window* (MGM, 1942), *On the Loose* (RKO, 1951), and *Never Steal Anything Small* (Universal, 1959), which he also scripted. Besides his screenplays in the 1950s, which included *The Thing* (RKO, 1952), *Gentlemen Prefer Blondes* (Twentieth Century-Fox, 1953), and *It Started with a Kiss* (MGM, 1958), he co-wrote the Broadway show *Three Wishes for Jamie* (1951), the stage musical *Kismet* (1953), and the theatre flop *Festival* (1956). In the 1960s his career trailed off with scenario credits for *Ocean's Eleven* (Warner Bros., 1961), *Follow That Dream* (United Artists, 1962), and *Mutiny on the Bounty* (MGM, 1964). In 1948 he was divorced from Virginia Nicholson, the ex-Mrs. Orson Welles.

too-ambitious mother; how she married too young and too soon to escape, only to find herself in a worse bind. (John and I were much too young when we got married, much too young and much, much too foolish—and how, but why go on?) Obviously it will be autobiographical, but that's the closest to an autobiography I ever plan to get."

Today Anne, known simply as Anne Lederer, is content to lead a relatively quiet life at her beachfront Malibu home. Her neighbors, Johnny Mathis and Beau Bridges, perhaps know as little of Anne's intriguing past as the public of today.

Feature Film Appearances
ANNE SHIRLEY

As Dawn O'Day:

THE HIDDEN WOMAN (Nanuet Amusement-American Releasing, 1922) 4,626′
Producer-director, Allan Dwan.

Evelyn Nesbit (Ann Wesley); Crauford Kent (Bart Andrews); Murdock MacQuarrie (Iron MacLoid); Ruth Darling (Vera MacLoid); Albert Hart (Bill Donovan); Russell Thaw (Johnny Randolph); Mary Alden (Mrs. Randolph); Jack Evans (Derelict); Dawn O'Day* (Girl).

*Unconfirmed but likely as her screen debut.

MOONSHINE VALLEY (Fox, 1922) 5,679′

Presenter, William Fox; director, Herbert Brenon; story, Mary Murillo, Lenora Asereth; screenplay, Murillo, Brenon; camera, Tom Malloy.

William Farnum (Ned Connors); Sadie Mullen (His Wife); Holmes Herbert (Dr. Martin); Dawn O'Day (Nancy, a Child); Jean Bronte (Jeane, the Dog).

THE RUSTLE OF SILK (Par., 1923) 6,947′

Presenter, Adolph Zukor; director, Herbert Brenon; based on the novel by Cosmo Hamilton; screenplay, Sada Cowan, Ouida Bergère; camera, George R. Meyer, James Van Trees.

Betty Compson (Lola De Breze); Conway Tearle (Arthur Fallaray); Cyril Chadwick (Paul Chalfon); Anna Q. Nilsson (Lady Feo); Leo White (Emil); Charles Stevenson (Henry De Breze); Tempe Piggot (Mrs. De Breze); Frederick Esmelton (Blythe); Dawn O'Day (Girl).

THE SPANISH DANCER (Par., 1923) 8,434′

Presenter, Adolph Zukor; producer-director, Herbert Brenon; based on the novel *Don César de Bazan* by Adolphe Philippe Dennery, Philippe Francois Pinel; adaptation, June Mathis, Beulah Marie Dix; camera, James Howe.

Pola Negri (Maritana); Antonio Moreno (Don César de Bazan); Wallace Beery (King Philip IV); Kathlyn Williams (Queen Isabel of Bourbon); Gareth Hughes (Lazarillo); Adolphe Menjou (Don Salluste); Edward Kipling (Marquis de Rotundo); Dawn O'Day (Don Balthazar Carlos); Charles A. Stevenson (Cardinal's Ambassador); Robert Agnew (Juan).

THE MAN WHO FIGHTS ALONE (Par., 1924) 6,337′

Presenter, Adolph Zukor, Jesse L. Lasky; director, Wallace Worsley; based on the novel *The Miracle of Hate* by William Blacke, James Shelley Hamilton; screenplay, Jack Cunningham; camera, L. Guy Wilky.

William Farnum (John Marble); Lois Wilson (Marion); Edward Everett Horton (Bob Alten); Lionel Belmore (Meggs); Barlowe Borland (Mike O'Hara); George Irving (Dr. Raymond); Dawn O'Day (Dorothy); Rose Tapley (Aunt Louise); Frank Farrington (Struthers).

THE FAST SET   (Par., 1924) 6,754'

Presenter, Adolph Zukor, Jesse L. Lasky; director, William De Mille; based on the play *Spring Cleaning* by Frederick Lonsdale; screenplay, Clara Beranger; camera, L. Guy Wilky.

Betty Compson (Margaret Sones); Adolphe Menjou (Ernest Steele); Elliott Dexter (Richard Sones); ZaSu Pitts (Mona); Dawn O'Day (Little Margaret Sones); Grace Carlyle (Jane Walton); Claire Adams (Fay Colleen); Rosalind Byrne (Connie Gallies); Edgar Norton (Archie Wells); Louis Natheaux (Billy Sommers); Eugenio De Liguoro (Walters); Fred Walton (Simpson).

RIDERS OF THE PURPLE SAGE   (Fox, 1925) 5,578'

Director, Lynn Reynolds; based on the novel by Zane Grey; screenplay, Edfrid Bingham; camera, Dan Clark.

Tom Mix (Jim Lassiter); Beatrice Burnham (Millie Erne); Arthur Morrison (Frank Erne); Seesel Ann Johnson (Bess Erne—as a Child); Warner Oland (Lew Walters/Judge Dyer); Fred Kohler (Metzger); Charles Newton (Herd); Joe Rickson (Slack); Mabel Ballin (Jane Withersteen); Charles Le Moyne (Richard Tull); Harold Goodwin (Bern Venters); Marion Nixon (Bess Erne); Dawn O'Day (Fay Larkin); Wilfred Lucas (Oldring).

THE CALLAHANS AND THE MURPHYS   (MGM, 1927) 6,126'

Director, George Hill; based on the novel by Kathleen Norris; screenplay, Frances Marion; titles, Ralph Spence; sets, Cedric Gibbons, David Townsend; wardrobe, René Hubert; camera, Ira Morgan; editor, Hugh Wynn.

Marie Dressler (Mrs. Callahan); Polly Moran (Mrs. Murphy); Sally O'Neil (Ellen Callahan); Lawrence Gray (Dan Murphy); Eddie Gribbon (Jim Callahan); Frank Currier (Grandpa Callahan); Gertrude Olmsted (Monica Murphy); Turner Savage (Timmy Callahan); Jackie Coombs (Terrance Callahan); Dawn O'Day (Mary Callahan); Monty O'Grady (Michael Callahan); Tom Lewis (Mr. Murphy).

NIGHT LIFE   (Tiffany, 1927) 6,235'

Director, George Archainbaud; story, Albert S. Le Vino; continuity, Gertrude Orr; titles, Viola Brothers Shore, Harry Braxton; sets, Burgess Beall; camera, Chester Lyons; editor, Desmond O'Brien.

Alice Day (Anna); Johnny Harron (Max); Eddie Gribbon (Nick); Walter Hiers (Manager); Lionel Braham (War Profiteer); Kitty Barlow (His Wife); Dawn O'Day, Mary Jane Irving, Audrey Sewell (His Daughters); Earl Metcalf (An Amorous Swain); Patricia Avery (Maid); Leopold, Archduke of Austria (Chief of Detectives); Snitz Edwards (Merry-Go-Round Manager); Violet Palmer (Beer Garden Waitress); Lydia Yeamans Titus (Landlady).

MOTHER KNOWS BEST   (Fox, 1928) 10,116'

Presenter, William Fox; director, John Blystone; dialog supervisor, Charles Judels, Dave Stamper; based on the story by Edna Ferber; screenplay, Marion Orth; dialog, Eugene Walter; titles, William Kernell, Edith Bristol; music, Erno Rapee, S. L. Rothafel; song, William Kernell; assistant director, Jasper Blystone; sound, Joseph Aiken; camera, Gilbert Warrington; editor, Margaret V. Clancey.

Madge Bellamy (Sally Quail); Louise Dresser (Ma Quail); Barry Norton (The Boy); Albert Gran (Sam Kingston); Joy Auburn (Bessie); Annette De Kirby (Bessie—as a child); Stuart Erwin (Ben); Ivor De Kirby (Ben—as a child); Lucien Littlefield (Pa Quail); Dawn O'Day (Sally—as a child).

SINS OF THE FATHER   (Par., 1928) 7,845′

Director, Ludwig Berger; story, Norman Burnstine; adaptation-continuity, E. Lloyd Sheldon; titles, Julian Johnson; music, Hugo Riesenfeld; camera, Victor Milner; editor, Frances Marsh.

Emil Jannings (Wilhelm Spengler); Ruth Chatterton (Gretta); Barry Norton (Tom Spengler); Jean Arthur (Mary Spengler); Jack Luden (Otto); ZaSu Pitts (Mother Spengler); Matthew Betz (Gus); Harry Cording (The Hijacker); Arthur Housman (The Count); Frank Reicher (The Eye Specialist); Douglas Haig (Tom—as a boy); Dawn O'Day (Mary—as a girl).

FOUR DEVILS   (Fox, 1929) 9,496′

Presenter, William Fox; director, F. W. Murnau; stager, A. H. Van Buren, A. F. Erickson; based on the novel *De Fire Djaevle* by Herman Joachim Bang; adaptation, Berthold Viertel, Marion Orth; screenplay, Carl Mayer; dialog, John Hunter Booth; music, S. L. Rothafel; song, Erno Rapee and Lew Pollack; assistant director, Erickson; sound, Harold Hobson; camera, Ernest Palmer, L. W. O'Connell; editor, Harold Schuster.

First Sequence: Farrell MacDonald (The Clown); Anders Randolf (Cecchi); Claire McDowell (Woman); Jack Parker (Charles—as a boy); Philippe De Lacy (Adolf—as a boy); Dawn O'Day (Marion—as a girl); Anita Fremault (Louise—as a girl); Wesley Lake (Old Clown).

Second Sequence: Janet Gaynor (Marion); Charles Morton (Charles); Nancy Drexel (Louise); Barry Norton (Adolf); Mary Duncan (The Lady); Michael Visaroff (Circus Director); George Davis (Mean Clown); André Cheron (Old Roué).

CITY GIRL   (Fox, 1930) 77M.

Presenter, William Fox; director, F. W. Murnau; stage director, A. H. Van Buren, A. F. Erickson; based on the play *The Mud Turtle* by Elliott Lester; adaptation-screenplay, Berthold Viertel, Marion Orth; dialog, Elliott Lester; titles, Katherine Hilliker, H. H. Caldwell; music, Arthur Kay; assistant director, William Tummel; costumes, Sophie Wachner; sound, Harold Hobson; sets, Harry Oliver; camera, Ernest Palmer; editor, Katherine Hilliker, H. H. Caldwell.

Charles Farrell (Lem Tustine); Mary Duncan (Marie); David Torrence (Tustine); Edith Yorke (Mrs. Tustine); Dawn O'Day (Mary Tustine); Tom Maguire (Matey); Dick Alexander (Mac); Pat Rooney (Butch); Ed Brady, Roscoe Ates, Jack Pennick, Guinn Williams (Reapers); Ivan Linow (Taxi Driver); Helen Lynch (Girl on Train); Mark Hamilton (Hungry Reaper); Arnold Lucy (Cafe Patron).

LILIOM   (Fox, 1930) 8,472′

Presenter, William Fox; director, Frank Borzage; based on the play by Ferenc Molnár; screenplay, S. N. Behrman; continuity, Sonya Levien; assistant director, Lew Borzage; costumes, Sophie Wachner; music, Richard Fall; songs, Fall and Marcella Gardner; art director, Harry Oliver; sound, George P. Costello; camera, Chester Lyons; editor, Margaret V. Clancey.

Charles Farrell (Liliom); Rose Hobart (Julie); Estelle Taylor (Madame Muskat); Lee Tracy (Buzzard); James Marcus (Linzman); Walter Abel (Carpenter); Mildred Van Dorn (Marie); Guinn Williams (Hollinger); Lillian Elliott (Aunt Hulda); Bert Roach (Wolf); H. B. Warner (Chief Magistrate); Dawn O'Day (Louise).

RICH MAN'S FOLLY   (Par., 1931) 80 M.

Director, John Cromwell; based on the novel *Dombey and Son* by Charles Dickens; screenplay, Grover Jones, Edward Paramore, Jr.; camera, David Abel.

George Bancroft (Brock Trumbull); Frances Dee (Anne Trumbull); Robert Ames (Joe Warren); Juliette Compton (Paula Norcross); David Durand (Brock Junior); Dorothy Peterson (Katherine Trumbull); Harry Allen (McWylie); Gilbert Emery (Kincaid); Guy Oliver (Dayton); Dawn O'Day (Anne—as a child); George McFarlane (Marston).

EMMA   (MGM, 1932) 73 M.

Director, Clarence Brown; story, Frances Marion; screenplay, Leonard Praskins, Zelda Sears; sound, A. MacDonald; camera, Oliver T. Marsh; editor, William Levanway.

Marie Dressler (Emma Thatcher); Richard Cromwell (Ronnie Smith); Jean Hersholt (Frederick Smith); Myrna Loy (Isabelle); John Miljan (District Attorney); Purnell E. Pratt (Haskins); Leila Bennett (Matilda); Barbara Kent (Gypsy); Kathryn Crawford (Sue); George Meeker (Bill); Dale Fuller (Maid); Wilfred Noy (Drake); Andre Cheron (Count Pierre); Dawn O'Day (Girl); Dorothy Peterson (Woman).

YOUNG AMERICA   (Fox, 1932) 70 M.

Director, Frank Borzage; based on the play by John Frederick Ballard; screenplay, William Conselman; assistant director, Lew Borzage; music director, George Lipschultz; sound, Eugene Grossman; camera, George Schneiderman.

Spencer Tracy (Jack Doray); Doris Kenyon (Edith Doray); Tommy Conlon (Arthur Simpson); Ralph Bellamy (Judge Blake); Beryl Mercer (Grandma Beamish); Sarah Padden (Mrs. Taylor); Robert Homans (Patrolman Weems); Raymond Borzage (Nutty); Dawn O'Day (Girl); and: Betty Jane Graham, Louise Beavers, Spec O'Donnell, William Pawley, Eddie Sturgis.

SO BIG   (WB, 1932) 82 M.

Producer, Jack L. Warner; director, William A. Wellman; based on the novel by Edna Ferber; screenplay, J. Grubb Alexander, Robert Lord; music, W. Franke Harling; costumes, Orry-Kelly; camera, Sid Hickox; editor, William Holmes.

Barbara Stanwyck (Selina Peake); George Brent (Roelf); Dickie Moore (Dirk—as a Boy); Guy Kibbee (August Hemple); Mae Madison (Dallas O'Mara); Hardie Albright (Julie Hemple); Robert Warwick (Simeon Peake); Arthur Stone (Jan Steen); Earle Foxe (Pervus Dejong); Alan Hale (Klaas Pool); Dorothy Peterson (Maartje); Dawn O'Day (Selina—as a little girl); Dick Winslow (Roelf—as a boy); Harry Beresford (Adams Ooms); Eulalie Jensen (Mrs. Hemple); Elizabeth Patterson (Mrs. Tibbits); Rita LeRoy (Paula); Blanche Frederici (Widow Parrlenbing); Willard Robertson (The Doc); Harry Hollman (Country Doctor); Lionel Belmore (Reverend Dekker).

THE PURCHASE PRICE   (WB, 1932) 68 M.

Director, William A. Wellman; based on the story "Mud Lark" by Arthur Stringer; screenplay, Robert Lord; camera, Sid Hickox; editor, Bill Holmes.

Barbara Stanwyck (Joan Gordan); George Brent (Jim Gilson); Lyle Talbot (Ed Fields); Hardie Albright (Don Leslie); David Landau (Bull McDowell); Murray Kinnell (Spike Forcon); Leila Bennett (Emily); Matt McHugh (Waco); Clarence Wilson (Justice of the Peace); Lucille Ward (His Wife); Crauford Kent (Peters); Dawn O'Day (Farmer's Daughter); Victor Potel (Clyde); Adele Watson (Mrs. Tipton); Snub Pollard (Joe).

THREE ON A MATCH   (WB, 1932) 64 M.

Associate producer, Samuel Bischoff; director, Mervyn LeRoy; story, Kubec Glasmon, John Bright; screenplay, Lucien Hubbard; art director, Robert Haas; camera, Sol Polito; editor, Ray Curtis.

Joan Blondell (Mary Keaton); Warren William (Robert Kirkwood); Ann Dvorak (Vivian Revere); Bette Davis (Ruth Westcott); Lyle Talbot (Mike); Humphrey Bogart (Harve); Patricia Ellis (Linda); Sheila Terry (Naomi); Grant Mitchell (Principal Gilmore); Glenda Farrell (Reformatory Girl); Frankie Darro (Bobby); Clara Blandick (Mrs. Keaton); Hale Hamilton (Defense Attorney); Dick Brandon (Horace); Junior Johnson (Max); Dawn O'Day (Vivian—as a child); Virginia Davis (Mary—as a child); Betty Carse (Ruth—as a child); Buster Phelps (Junior); John Marston (Randall); Edward Arnold (Ace); Allen Jenkins (Dick); Sidney Miller (Willie Goldberg); Herman Bing (Prof. Irving Finklestein); Jack LaRue, Stanley Price (Mugs); Spencer Charters (Street Cleaner); Hardie Albright (Lawyer); Ann Brody (Mrs. Goldberg); Mary Doran (Prisoner); Blanche Frederici (Miss Blazer, a Teacher); Selmer Jackson (Voice of Radio Announcer); Harry Seymour (Jerry Carter).

RASPUTIN AND THE EMPRESS   (MGM, 1932) 133 M.

Director, Richard Boleslavsky; story-screenplay, Charles MacArthur; art director, Cedric Gibbons, Alexander Toluboff; costumes, Adrian; assistant director, Cullen Tate; music, Herbert Stothart; sound, Douglas Shearer; camera, William Daniels; editor, Tom Held.

John Barrymore (Prince Paul Chegodieff); Ethel Barrymore (Empress Alexandra); Lionel Barrymore (Rasputin); Ralph Morgan (Emperor Nikolai); Diana Wynyard (Natasha); Tad Alexander (Alexis); C. Henry Gordon (Grand Duke Igor); Edward Arnold (Doctor); Gustav von Seyffertitz (Dr. Wolfe); Dawn O'Day (Anastasia); Jean Parker (Maria); Sarah Padden (Landlady); Henry Kolker (Chief of Secret Police); Frank Shannon (Professor Propotkin); Frank Reicher (German Language Teacher); Hooper Atchley (Policeman); Leo White, Lucien Littlefield (Revelers); Maurice Black, Dave O'Brien (Soldiers); Mischa Auer (Butler); Charlotte Henry (Girl).

THE LIFE OF JIMMY DOLAN   (WB, 1933) 85 M.

Director, Archie Mayo; based on the play by Bertram Milhauser, Beulah Marie Dix; camera, Arthur Edeson; editor, Bert Levy.

Douglas Fairbanks, Jr. (Jimmy); Loretta Young (Peggy); Aline MacMahon (The Aunt); Guy Kibbee (Phlaxer); Lyle Talbot (Doc Woods); Fifi D'Orsay (Budgie); Harold Huber (Reggie Newman); Shirley Grey (Goldie); George Meeker (Magee); David Durand (George); Farina (Sam); Mickey Rooney (Freckles); Dawn O'Day (Mary Lou); Arthur Hohl (Marvin).

FINISHING SCHOOL   (RKO, 1934) 73 M.

Producer, Merian C. Cooper; director, Wanda Tuchock, George Nicholls, Jr.; story, David Hempstead; screenplay, Tuchock, Laird Doyle; sound, John L. Cass; camera, J. Roy Hunt; editor, Arthur Schmidt.

Frances Dee (Virginia); Billie Burke (Mrs. Radcliff); Ginger Rogers (Pony); Bruce Cabot (MacFarland); John Halliday (Mr. Radcliff); Beulah Bondi (Miss Van Alstyn); Sara Haden (Miss Fisher); Marjorie Lytell (Ruth); Adalyn Doyle (Madeline); Dawn O'Day (Billie); Claire Myers, Rose Coghlan, Susanne Thompson, Edith Vale (Girls); Irene Franklin, Ann Cameron (Bits).

THIS SIDE OF HEAVEN   (MGM, 1934) 78 M.

Director, William K. Howard; based on the novel *It Happened One Day* by Marjorie Bartholomew Paradise; screenplay, Zelda Sears, Eve Green, Edgar Allan Wolf, Florence Ryerson; camera, Hal Rosson; editor, Frank Hull.

Lionel Barrymore (Martin Turner); Fay Bainter (Francene Turner); Mae Clarke (Jane Turner); Una Merkel (Dirdie); Mary Carlisle (Peggy Turner); Tom Brown (Seth Turner); Onslow Stevens (Walter); C. Henry Gordon (Mr. Barnes); Edward Nugent (Vance); Henry Wadsworth (Hal); Edwin Maxwell (Sawyer); Richard Tucker (Producer); Claire Du Brey (Miss Blair); Sumner Getchell (Gus); Nell O'Day (Secretary); Herbert Prior (Grouch); Edward LeSaint (Minister); Phil Tead (Radio Announcer); Lee Phelps (Policeman); Paddy O'Flynn (Taxi Driver); Geneva Mitchell, Ailene Carlyle (Nurses); Paul Stanton, Theodor Von Eltz (Doctors); Nell Craig (Nurse Attendant); Bobby Watson (Interior Decorator); Dawn O'Day (Flower Girl); Dickie Moore (Boy); Charles Williams (Reporter); James Durkin (Raymond); Charles Giblyn (Harvey); Mickey Daniels (Stinky Bliss); Ed Norris (Upper Classman); Billy Taft (School Boy); Niles Welch (Druggist); Stanley Taylor (Intern).

THE KEY   (WB, 1934) 70 M.

Director, Michael Curtiz; story, R. Gore-Browne, J. L. Hardy; screenplay, Laird Doyle; camera, Ernest Haller; editor, William Clemens.

William Powell (Captain Tennant); Edna Best (Norah Kerr); Colin Clive (Andre Kerr); Halliwell Hobbes (General); Hobart Cavanaugh (Homer); Henry O'Neill (Dan); J. M. Kerrigan (O'Duffy); Donald Crisp (Conlan); Arthur Treacher (Lt. Merriman); Maxine Doyle (Pauline O'Connor); Arthur Aylesworth (Kirby); Lew Kelly (Angular Man); Dixie Loftin (Irish Man); Olaf Hytten, David Thursby, Desmond Roberts (Regulars); Robert Homans, Ralph Remley (Bartenders); Gertrude Short (Barmaid); Luke Cosgrave (Man); John Elliott (Padre); James May (Driver); Douglas Gordon (Operator); Wyndham Standing (Officer); Pat Somerset (Laramour); Mary McLaren (Street Walker); Aggie Herring, Kathrin Clare Ward (Flower Women); Dawn O'Day (Flower Girl); Charles Irwin (Master of Ceremonies); Lowin Cross (Dispatch Rider); Edward Cooper (Lloyd).

SCHOOL FOR GIRLS   (Liberty, 1934) 73 M.

Associate producer, M. H. Hoffman, Jr.; director, William Nigh; suggested by the story "Our Undisciplined Daughters" by Reginald Wright Kauffman; story-screenplay, Albert De Mond; production manager, Rudolph Flothow; camera, Harry Neumann; editor, Mildred Johnston.

Sidney Fox (Annette Eldridge); Paul Kelly (Garry Waltham); Lois Wilson (Miss Cartwright); Lucille La Verne (Miss Keeble); Dorothy Lee (Dorothy Bosworth); Toby Wing (Hazel Jones); Dorothy Appleby (Florence Burns); Lona Andre (Peggy); Russell Hopton (Elliott Robbins); Barbara Weeks (Nell Davis); Kathleen Burke (Gladys Deacon); Anna Q. Nilsson (Dr. Anne Galvin); Purnell Pratt (Inspector Jameson); Robert Warwick (Governor); William Farnum (Charles Waltham); Charles Ray (Duke); Mary Foy (Miss Gage); Dawn O'Day (Catherine Fogarty); Myrtle Stedman (Mrs. Winters); Edward Kane (Ted); Gretta Gould (Mrs. Smoot); George Cleveland (Reeves); Helene Chadwick (Larson); Helen Foster (Eleanor); Fred Kelsey, Harry Woods (Detectives); Edward LeSaint (Judge); Jack Kennedy (Hansen).

As Anne Shirley:

ANNE OF GREEN GABLES   (RKO, 1934) 79 M.

Producer, Kenneth Macgowan; director, George Nicholls, Jr.; based on the novel by L. M. Montgomery; screenplay, Sam Mintz; camera, Lucien Andriot; editor, Arthur Schmidt.

Anne Shirley (Anne Shirley); Tom Brown (Gilbert Blythe); O. P. Heggie (Matthew Cuthbert); Helen Westley (Marilla Cuthbert); Sara Haden (Mrs. Barry); Murray Kinnell (Mr. Phillips); Gertrude Messinger (Diana); June Preston (Mrs. Blewett's Daughter); Charley Grapewin (Dr. Tatum); Hilda Vaugh (Mrs. Blewett).

STEAMBOAT 'ROUND THE BEND   (20th, 1935) 80 M.

Producer, Sol M. Wurtzel; director, John Ford; based on the novel by Ben Lucien Burman; screenplay, Dudley Nichols, Lamar Trotti; music, Samuel Kaylin; art director, William Darling; set decorator, Albert Hogsett; assistant director, Edward O'Fearna; camera, George Schneiderman; editor, Alfred De Gaetano.

Will Rogers (Dr. John Pearly); Anne Shirley (Fleety Belle); Eugene Pallette (Sheriff Rufe Jeffers); John McGuire (Duke); Berton Churchill (The New Moses); Stepin' Fetchit (George Lincoln Washington); Francie Ford (Efe); Irvin S. Cobb (Capt. Eli); Roger Imhof (Pappy); Raymond Hatton (Matt Abel); Hobart Bosworth (Chaplain); Louis Mason (Boat Race Organizer); Charles B. Middleton (Fleety Belle's Father); Si Jenks (A Drunk); Jack Pennick (Ringleader of Boat Attack); William Benedict (Breck); Hobart Cavanaugh (A Listener); Fred Kohler, Jr. (Fleety Belle's Suitor); John Lester Johnson (Uncle Jeff); Ben Hall (Fleety Belle's Brother); Dell Henderson (Salesman); Grace Goodall (Sheriff's Wife); Ferdinand Munier (Governor); D'Arcy Corrigan (Hangman); James Marcus (Warden); Heinie Conklin (Jailbird); Luke Cosgrave (Labor Boss); Captain Anderson (Jailer); Otto Richards (Prisoner).

CHASING YESTERDAY   (RKO, 1935) 77 M.

Producer, Cliff Reid; director, George Nicholls, Jr.; based on the novel *The Crime of Sylvestre Bonnard* by Anatole France; screenplay, Francis E. Faragoh; camera, Lucien Andriot; editor, Arthur Schmidt.

Anne Shirley (Jeanne); Helen Westley (Therese); John Qualen (Coccoz); O. P. Heggie (Sylvestre Bonnard); Elizabeth Patterson (Prefere); Trent Durkin (Henri); Etienne Girardot (Mouche); Doris Lloyd (Mme. De Gabry); Hilda Vaughn (Slavey).

CHATTERBOX   (RKO, 1936) 68 M.

Producer, Robert Sisk; director, George Nicholls, Jr.; story, David Carb; screenplay, Sam Mintz; camera, Robert De Grasse; editor, Arthur Schmidt.

Anne Shirley (Jenny Yates); Phillips Holmes (Philip Greene, Jr.); Edward Ellis (Uriah Lowell); Erik Rhodes (Archie Fisher); Margaret Hamilton (Emily Tipton); Granville Bates (Philip Greene, Sr.); Allen Vincent (Harrison); Lucille Ball (Lillian Temple); George Offerman, Jr. (Michael Arbuckle); Maxine Jennings (Actress); Richard Abbott (Blythe); Wilfred Lucas, Margaret Armstrong (Character People).

M'LISS   (RKO, 1936) 66 M.

Producer, Robert Sisk; director, George Nicholls, Jr.; based on the story by Bret Harte; screenplay, Dorothy Yost; music director, Alberti Colombo; art director, Van Nest Polglase, Perry Ferguson; sound, George D. Ellis; camera, Robert De Grasse; editor, William Morgan.

Anne Shirley (M'liss Smith); John Beal (Stephen Thorne); Guy Kibbee (Washoe Smith); Douglass Dumbrille (Lon Ellis); Moroni Olsen (Jake); Frank M. Thomas

(Alf Edwards); Arthur Hoyt (Mayor Morpher); Barbara Pepper (Clytie Morpher); Margaret Armstrong (Mrs. Morpher); Esther Howard (Rose); James Bush (Jack Farlan).

MAKE WAY FOR A LADY   (RKO, 1936) 65 M.

Producer, Zion Myers; director, David Burton; based on the novel *Daddy and I* by Elizabeth Jordan; screenplay, Gertrude Purcell; camera, David Abel; editor, George Crone.

Herbert Marshall (Christopher Drew); Anne Shirley (June Drew); Gertrude Michael (Miss Emerson); Margot Grahame (Valerie); Clara Blandick (Miss Dell); Frank Coghlan, Jr. (Billy Hopkins); Mary Jo Ellis (Mildred Jackson); Maxine Jennings (Miss Moore); Taylor Holmes (George Terry); Helen Parrish (Genevieve); Willie Best (Townley); Maidel Turner (Mrs. Jackson); Murray Kinnell (Dr. Barnes); Grace Goodall (Mrs. Hopkins); Johnny Butler (Briggs); Alan Edwards (Gregory).

TOO MANY WIVES   (RKO, 1937) 61 M.

Producer, William Sistrom; director, Ben Holmes; story, Richard English; screenplay, Dorothy Yost, Lois Eby, John Grey; art director, Van Nest Polglase; camera, Nick Musuraca; editor, Desmond Marquette.

Anne Shirley (Betty Jackson); John Morley (Barry Trent); Gene Lockhart (Mr. Jackson); Dudley Clements (Mr. Mansfield); Barbara Pepper (Angela Brown); Frank Melton (Clabby Holden); Charles Coleman (Rogers); Dot Farley (Mrs. Potts); Jack Carson (Hodges); George Irving (Mr. Otto).

MEET THE MISSUS   (RKO, 1937) 60 M.

Producer, Albert Lewis; director, Joseph Santley; based on the novel *Lady Average* by Jack Goodman, Albert Rice; screenplay, Jack Townley, Bert Granet, Joel Sayre; art director, Van Nest Polglase; music director, Roy Webb; camera, Jack Mackenzie; editor, Frederick Knudtson.

Victor Moore (Otis Foster); Helen Broderick (Emma Foster); Anne Shirley (Louise Foster); Alan Bruce (Steve Walton); Edward H. Robins (Gordon Cutting); William Brisbane (Prentiss); Frank M. Thomas (Barney Lott); Ray Mayer (Mr. White); Ada Leonard (Princess Zarina); George Irving (Magistrate); Alec Craig (College President); Willie Best (Mose); Virginia Sale (Mrs Moseby); Jack Norton (Mr. Norton).

STELLA DALLAS   (UA, 1937) 104 M.

Producer, Samuel Goldwyn; associate producer, Merritt Hubbind; director, King Vidor; based on the novel by Olive Higgins Prouty; screenplay Victor Heerman, Sara Y. Mason; dramatization, Harry Wagstaff Gribble; art director, Richard Day; music director, Alfred Newman; costumes, Omar Kayan; sound, Frank Maher; camera, Rudolph Mate; editor, Sherman Todd.

Barbara Stanwyck (Stella Martin Dallas); John Boles (Stephen Dallas); Anne Shirley (Laurel Dallas); Barbara O'Neil (Helen); Alan Hale (Ed Munn); Marjorie Main (Mrs. Martin); Edmund Elton (Mr. Martin); George Walcott (Charlie Martin); Gertrude Short (Carrie Jenkins); Tim Holt (Richard); Nella Walker (Mrs. Grosvenor); Bruce Satterlee (Con); Jimmy Butler (Con —as an adult); Jack Egger (Lee); Dickie Jones (John); Ann Shoemaker (Miss Phillibrown).

CONDEMNED WOMEN   (RKO, 1938) 77 M.

Producer, Robert Sisk; director, Lew Landers; story-screenplay, Lionel Houser; music director, Roy Webb; camera, Nick Musuraca; editor, Desmond Marquette.

Sally Eilers (Linda Wilson); Louis Hayward (Phillip Duncan); Anne Shirley (Millie Anson); Esther Dale (Matron Glover); Lee Patrick (Big Annie); Leona Roberts (Kate); George Irving (Warden Miller); Richard Bond (David); Netta Packer (Sarah); Rita LaRoy (Cora); Florence Lake (Prisoner); Jack Carson, Edmund Cobb (Detectives); Dorothy Adams (Nurse); Edythe Elliott (Dr. Barnes); John Marston (Defense Attorney); Hooper Atchley (Prosecutor); Paul Stanton (Judge); Vivien Oakland (Mrs. Hempstead); Kathryn Sheldon (Matron).

LAW OF THE UNDERWORLD   (RKO, 1938) 58 M.

Producer, Robert Sisk; director, Lew Landers; based on the play *Crime* by Samuel Shipman; screenplay, Bert Granet, Edmund L. Hartmann; camera, Nicholas Musuraca; editor, Ted Cheesman.

Chester Morris (Gene Fillmore); Anne Shirley (Annabelle); Eduardo Ciannelli (Rocky); Walter Abel (Rogers); Richard Bond (Tommy); Lee Patrick (Dorothy); Paul Guilfoyle (Batsy); Frank M. Thomas (Captain Gargan); Eddie Acuff (Bill); Jack Arnold (Eddie); Jack Carson (Johnny); Paul Stanton (Barton); George Shelley (Frank); Anthony Warde (Larry).

MOTHER CAREY'S CHICKENS   (RKO, 1938) 82 M.

Producer, Pandro S. Berman; director, Rowland V. Lee; based on the novel by Kate Douglas Wiggin; screenplay, S. K. Lauren, Gertrude Purcell; camera, J. Roy Hunt; editor, George Hively.

Anne Shirley (Nancy Carey); Ruby Keeler (Kitty Carey); James Ellison (Ralph Thurston); Fay Bainter (Mrs. Carey); Walter Brennan (Mr. Popham); Donnie Dunagan (Peter Carey); Frank Albertson (Tom Hamilton); Alma Kruger (Aunt Bertha); Jackie Moran (Gilbert Carey); Margaret Hamilton (Mrs. Fuller); Virginia Weidler (Lally Joy); Ralph Morgan (Captain Carey); Phyllis Kennedy (Annabelle); Harvey Clark (Mr. Fuller); Lucille Ward (Mrs. Popham); George Irving (Mr. Hamilton).

A MAN TO REMEMBER   (RKO, 1938) 80 M.

Producer, Robert Sisk; director, Garson Kanin; based on the novel *Failure* by Katharine Haviland-Taylor; screenplay, Dalton Trumbo; art director, Van Nest Polglase; montage, Douglas Travers; music, Roy Webb; camera, J. Roy Hunt; editor, Jack Hively.

Edward Ellis (John Abbott); Anne Shirley (Jean); Lee Bowman (Dick Abbott); William Henry (Howard Sykes); Granville Bates (George Sykes); Harlan Briggs (Homer Ramsey); Frank M. Thomas (Jode Harkness); Charles Halton (Perkins); John Wray (Johnson); Gilbert Emery (Dr. Robinson); Dickie Jones (Dick Abbott—as a child); Carole Leete (Jean—as a child).

GIRLS' SCHOOL   (Col., 1938) 71 M.

Associate producer, Samuel Marx; director, John Brahm; story, Tess Slesinger; screenplay, Slesinger, Richard Sherman; art director, Stephen Goosson; music director, Morris Stoloff; music, Gregory Stone; camera, Franz Planer; editor, Otto Meyer.

Anne Shirley (Natalie Freeman); Nan Grey (Linda Simpson); Ralph Bellamy (Michael Hendragin); Dorothy Moore (Betty Fleet); Gloria Holden (Miss Laurel); Marjorie Main (Miss Armstrong); Margaret Tallichet (Gwennie); Peggy Moran (Myra); Kenneth Howell (Edgar); Noah Beery, Jr. (George); Cecil Cunningham (Miss Brewster); Pierre Watkin (Mr. Simpson); Doris Kenyon (Mrs. Simpson); Heather Thatcher (Miss Bracket); Virginia Howell (Miss MacBeth); Joanne Tree (Sudie).

BOY SLAVES (RKO, 1939) 72 M.

Producer, Pandro S. Berman; associate producer-director, P. J. Wolfson; story, Albert Bein; screenplay, Bein, Ben Orkow; camera, J. Roy Hunt; editor, Desmond Marquette.

Anne Shirley (Annie); Roger Daniel (Jesse); James McCallion (Tim); Alan Baxter (Graff); Johnny Fitzgerald (Knuckles); Walter Ward (Miser); Charles Powers (Lollie); Walter Tetley (Pee Wee); Frank Malo (Tommy); Paul White (Atlas); Arthur Hohl (Sheriff); Charles Lane (Albee); Norman Willis (Drift Boss); Roy Gordon (Judge); Helen Mackellar (Mother).

SORORITY HOUSE (RKO, 1939) 64 M.

Producer, Robert Sisk; director, John Farrow; based on the story "Chi House" by Mary Coyle Chase; screenplay, Dalton Trumbo; camera, Nick Musuraca; editor, Harry Marker.

Anne Shirley (Alice); James Ellison (Bill); Barbara Reed (Dotty); Pamela Blake (Merle); J. M. Kerrigan (Lew Fisher); Helen Wood (Mme. President); Doris Jordan (Neva Simpson); June Storey (Norma Hancock); Elisabeth Risdon (Mrs. Scott); Margaret Armstrong (Mrs. Dawson); Selmer Jackson (Mr. Grant); Chill Wills (Mr. Johnson); Veronica Lake, Marge Champion (Coeds).

CAREER (RKO, 1939) 80 M.

Producer, Robert Sisk; director, Leigh Jason; based on the novel by Phil Stong; screenplay, Dalton Trumbo, Bert Granet; camera, Frank Redman; editor, Arthur E. Roberts.

Anne Shirley (Sylvia Bartholomew); Edward Ellis (Stephen Cruthers); Samuel S. Hinds (Clem Bartholomew); Janet Beecher (Amy Cruthers); Leon Errol (Mudcat); Alice Eden (Merta Katz); John Archer (Ray Cruthers); Raymond Hatton (Deac); Maurice Murphy (Mel Bartholomew); Harrison Greene (Ben Burnett); Charles Drake (Rex Chaney); Hobart Cavanaugh (Jim Bronson).

VIGIL IN THE NIGHT (RKO, 1940) 96 M.

Executive producer, Pandro S. Berman; producer-director, George Stevens; based on the novel by A. J. Cronin; screenplay, Fred Guiol, P. J. Wolfson, Rowland Leigh; assistant director, Syd Fogel; art director, Van Nest Polglase, L. P. Williams; set decorator, Darrell Silvera; costumes Walter Plunkett; music, Alfred Newman; camera, Robert de Grasse; editor, Henry Berman.

Carole Lombard (Anne Lee); Brian Aherne (Dr. Prescott); Anne Shirley (Lucy Lee); Julien Mitchell (Matthew Bowley); Robert Coote (Dr. Caley); Brenda Forbes (Nora); Rita Page (Glennie); Peter Cushing (Joe Shand); Ethel Griffies (Matron East); Doris Lloyd (Mrs. Bowley); Emily Fitzroy (Sister Gilson).

SATURDAY'S CHILDREN (WB, 1940) 101 M.

Producer, Jack L. Warner, Hal B. Wallis; associate producer, Henry Blanke; director, Vincent Sherman; based on the play by Maxwell Anderson; screenplay, Julius J. and Philip G. Epstein; camera, James Wong Howe; editor, Owen Marks.

John Garfield (Rims Rosson); Anne Shirley (Bobby Halevy); Claude Rains (Mr. Halevy); Lee Patrick (Florrie Sands); George Tobias (Herbie Smith); Roscoe Karns (Willie Sands); Dennie Moore (Gertrude Mills); Elizabeth Risdon (Mrs. Halevy); Berton Churchill (Mr. Norman).

ANNE OF WINDY POPLARS (RKO, 1940) 86 M.

Executive producer, Lee Marcus; producer, Cliff Reid; director, Jack Hively; story, L. M. Montgomery; screenplay, Michael Kanin, Jerry Cady; costumes, Edward Stephenson; sound, John L. Cass; camera, Fred Redman; editor, George Hively.

Anne Shirley (Anne Shirley); James Ellison (Tony Pringle); Henry Travers (Matey); Patric Knowles (Gilbert Blythe); Slim Summerville (Jabez Monkman); Elizabeth Patterson (Rebecca); Louise Campbell (Catherine Pringle); Joan Carroll (Betty Grayson); Katharine Alexander (Ernestine Pringle); Minnie Dupree (Kate); Alma Kruger (Mrs. Stephen Pringle); Marcia Mae Jones (Jen Pringle); Ethel Griffies (Hester Pringle); Clara Blandick (Mrs. Morton Pringle); Gilbert Emery (Stephen Pringle); Wright Kramer (Morton Pringle); Jackie Moran (Boy).

WEST POINT WIDOW (Par., 1941) 63 M.

Producer, Sol C. Siegel; associate producer, Colbert Clark; director, Robert Siodmak; based on the story "The Baby's Had a Hard Day" by Anne Wormser; screenplay, F. Hugh Herbert, Hans Kraly; art director, Hans Dreier, Haldane Douglas; camera, Theodor Sparkuhl; editor, Archie Marshek.

Anne Shirley (Nancy Hull); Richard Carlson (Jimmy Krueger); Richard Denning (Rhody Graves); Frances Gifford (Daphne); Maude Eburne (Mrs. Willits); Janet Beecher (Mrs. Graves); Cecil Kellaway (Dr. Spencer); Archie Twitchell (Joe Martin); Lillian Randolph (Sophie); Patricia Farr (Miss Hinkle); Sharon Lynne and Deanna Jean Hall (Jennifer); Eddy Conrad (Mr. Metapoulos); Jack Chapin (Bill); Charles Coleman (Mr. Appleton); Jean Phillips (Betty); Eleanor Stewart (Pearl); Catherine Craig (Hilda); Keith Richards, Richard Webb, Jack Luden (Internes); Nina Guilbert (Supervisor of Nurses); Kate Drain Lawson (Elderly Nurse); Ethel Clayton, Gloria Williams (Nurses); Ray Cooke (Father in Hospital); Nell Craig (Switchboard Operator); Grace Hayle (Dowager); Rita Owin (Beauty Operator); Harry McKim, Robert Winkler (Fresh Kids); Lee Shumway (Cop); Sam Ash (Pedestrian); Mike Frankovich (Announcer at Football Game); Lillian West (Manageress); Gladys Blake (Salesgirl); Marjorie Deanne (Young Girl at Bar); Catherine Wallace (Woman in Bar); Gilbert Wilson, Louis Natheaux (Men at Bar); Leonard Carey (Simpson); Frances Raymond (Old Lady at Beach); Herbert Holcombe (George); Matt McHugh (Drunk at Football Game); Harry Barris (Hot Dog Vendor); Audra Siddons (Girl at Football Game).

UNEXPECTED UNCLE (RKO, 1941) 67 M.

Producer, Tay Garnett; director, Peter Godfrey; based on the novel by Eric Hatch; screenplay, Delmer Daves, Noel Langley; music, Anthony Collins; art director, Albert S. D'Agostino; camera, Robert de Grasse; editor, William Hamilton.

Anne Shirley (Kathleen); James Craig (Johnny); Charles Coburn (Seton); Ernest Truex (Wilkins); Renee Godfrey (Carol West); Russell Gleason (Tommy); Astrid Allwyn (Sara Cochran); Jed Prouty (Sanderson); Thurston Hall (Jerry Carter); Virginia Engels (Mrs. Carter); Hans Conried (Clayton); Arthur Aylesworth (Quenton); Matt Moore (Detective); Jack Mulhall (Policeman); Russell Hicks (Cafe Manager); Eleanor Counts (Cigarette Girl); Pat Flaherty (Mounted Cop); George Dolenz (Headwaiter); Joey Ray (Club Singer); Mary Gordon (Landlady); Edith Conrad (Flower Woman).

FOUR JACKS AND A JILL (RKO, 1941) 68 M.

Producer, John Twist; director, Jack Hively; story-screenplay, Twist; songs, Mort Greene and Harry Revel; camera, Russell Metty; editor, George Hively.

Ray Bolger (Nifty); Anne Shirley (Nina); Desi Arnaz (Steve); June Havoc (Opal); Jack Durant (Noodle); Eddie Foy, Jr. (Happy); Henry Daniels, Jr. (Bobo); Fritz Feld

(Maurice Hoople); Jack Briggs (Nat); William Blees (Eddie); Robert Smith (Joe); Fortunio Bonanova (Mike); Norman Mayes (Bootblack); Mary Gordon (Landlady); Amarilla Morris (Girl—Door Gag); Leo White (Perfumer); Frank Martinelli (Ditchdigger); Rosemary Coleman (Salesgirl); Jane Woodworth (Bit); Armand "Curley" Wright (Hot Dog Vendor); Florence Lake (Counter Girl); Mantan Moreland (Attendant); Charles Arnt, Ted O'Shea, Grady Sutton (Drunks); Eddie Dunn, Frank Mills (Cops); Raphael Storm (Headwaiter); Eddie Hart (Taxi Driver); Constantine Romanoff, Bob Perry (Gorillas); Nina Waynler (Katherine); Max Luckey (Otto); Roy Crane (Keva); Jack Carr (Big Guy); Jack Gardner (Usher); Joe Bernard (Jailer); Patti Lacey (Jitterbug Specialty).

ALL THAT MONEY CAN BUY   (RKO, 1941) 106 M.

Producer, William Dieterle; associate producer, Charles L. Glett; director, Dieterle; based on the short story "The Devil and Daniel Webster" by Stephen Vincent Benet; screenplay, Dan Totheroh; assistant director, Argyle Nelson; art director, Van Nest Polglase; music, Bernard Hermann; special effects, Vernon L. Walker; camera, Joseph August; editor, Robert Wise.

Edward Arnold (Daniel Webster); Walter Huston (Mr. Scratch); Jane Darwell (Ma Stone); Simone Simon (Belle Dee); Gene Lockhart (Squire Slossum); John Qualen (Miser Stevens); H. B. Warner (Justice Haythorne); Frank Conlan (Sheriff); Lindy Wade (Daniel Stone); George Cleveland (Cy Bibber); Anne Shirley (Mary Simpson); James Craig (Jabez Stone); Jeff Corey (Tom Sharp); Sonny Bupp (Martin Van Buren Alden); Alec Craig (Eli Higgins); Carl Stockdale (Van Brooks); Walter Baldwin (Hank); Sarah Edwards (Lucy Slossum); Virginia Williams (3-Month-Old Baby); Stewart Richards (Doctor); Patsy Doyle (Servant); Harry Hook (Tailor); Anita Lee (Infant Baby); Jim Toney, Eddie Dew (Farmers); Harry Humphrey (Minister); Ferris Taylor (President); Robert Dudley (Lem); Frank Austin (Spectator); Bob Pittard (Clerk); Sunny Boyne (Bit); Charles Herzinger (Old Farmhand); Robert Strange (Court Clerk); Sherman Sanders (Caller); Robert Emmett Keane, Fern Emmett (Married Couple); James Farley (Studio Gateman); William Alland (Guide); Bob Burns (Townsman).

MAYOR OF 44th STREET   (RKO, 1942) 86 M.

Producer, Cliff Reid; director, Alfred Green; suggested by the magazine article by Luther Davis, John Cleveland; screenplay, Lewis R. Foster; choreography, Nick Castle; songs, Mort Greene and Harry Revel; music director, C. Bakaleinikoff; camera, Robert de Grasse; editor, Irene Morra.

George Murphy (Joe Jonathan); Anne Shirley (Jessie Lee); William Gargan (Tommy Fallon); Richard Barthelmess (Ed Kirby); Joan Merrill (Vicki Lane); Freddie Martin & Orchestra (Themselves); Rex Downing (Bitz McCarg); Millard Mitchell (Herman); Mary Wickes (Maisie); Eddie Hart (Gromm); Robert Smith (Eddie, the House Manager); Marten Lamont (Shoemaker, Kirby's Attorney); Walter Reed (Lew Luddy); Roberta Smith (Red); Lee Bonnell (Head Waiter); Kenneth Lundy (Dude); Esther Muir (Hilda, Switchboard Operator); John H. Dilson (Carter, the General Manager); Monty Collins (Piano Player); Pete Theodore (Dancer); Jack Byron (Bandleader); Jane Patten (Girl at Office); Gerald Pierce (Mickey, the Messenger Boy); David Kirkland (Petey); Rosemary Coleman, Wayne McCoy, Richard Martin (Office Clerks); Jane Woodworth, Linda Rivas (Actresses); John McGuire (Curley Sharp); Reginald Barlow (Watchman); Jack Gardner, Clarence Hennecke, Johnny Tryon (Photographers); James Mena (Filipino Servant); Matt Moore (Jerry, the Office worker); Ken Christy (District Attorney); George Ford (Phil, the Dancer); Lola Jensen (Phil's Partner); Norman Mayes (Rathskeller); Barbara Clark (Dancing Girl); Frank O'Connor (Cop); Donald Kerr, Mike Lally (Mugs).

THE POWERS GIRL   (UA, 1942) 93 M.

Producer, Charles R. Rogers; director, Norman Z. McLeod; based on the book by John R. Powers; story, William A. Pierce, Malvin Wald; screenplay, Edwin Moran, Harry Segall; songs, Jule Styne and Kim Gannon; music director, Louis Silvers; camera, Stanley Cortez; editor, George Arthur.

George Murphy (Jerry Hendricks); Anne Shirley (Ellen Evans); Carole Landis (Kay Evans); Dennis Day (Himself); Benny Goodman & Orchestra (Themselves); Alan Mowbray (John Robert Powers); Jean Ames (Googie); Mary Treen (Nancy); Raphael Storm (Vandy Vandegrift); Helen MacKellar (Mrs. Hendricks); Harry Shannon (Mr. Hendricks); Roseanna Murray (Edna Lambert); Jayne Hazard, Lillian Eggers, Linda Stirling, Evelyn Frey, Eloise Hart, Patricia Mace, Barbara Slater, Rosemary Coleman (Models); George Chandler (Harry); Willie Best (Waiter); Minerva Urecal (Maggie); Jack Daley (Bruised Waiter); Peggy Lee (Herself); Jack Baxley (Judge).

LADY BODYGUARD   (Par., 1943) 69 M.

Producer, Sol C. Siegel; associate producer, Burt Kelly; director, William Clemens; based on a story by Edward Haldeman, Vera Caspary; screenplay, Edmund Hartmann, Art Arthur; art director, Hans Dreier, Haldane Douglas; camera, Daniel Fapp; editor, Billy Shea.

Eddie Albert (Terry Moore); Anne Shirley (A. C. Baker); Raymond Walburn (Avery Jamieson); Ed Brophy (Harry Gargan); Donald MacBride (R. L. Barclay); Maude Eburne (Mother Hodges); Clem Bevans (Elmer Frawley); Roger Pryor (George Mac-Alister); Gus Schilling (Bughouse Sweeney); Olin Howlin (Mr. Saunders) Charles Halton (Edwards); Warren Ashe (Fletcher); Jack Norton (Henderson); Mary Treen (Miss Tracy); Greta Granstedt (Gertie); Oscar O'Shea (Justice of the Peace); Emmett Vogan (Stone); John H. Dilson (Doctor); Harlan Briggs (Gaston); George M. Carleton, Gordon DeMain (Directors); Frances Morris (Receptionist); Jack Stoney, Fred Graham, Kernan Cripps, Murray Alper (Attendants); Charles R. Moore (Porter); Sam Ash, Wilbur Mack, Jack Gardner (Salesmen); Al Hill (Mechanic); Matt McHugh (Drunk); Peter Leeds (Intern); Harry Tyler (Weasel-faced Salesman); William Newell (Chef); Stanley Blystone (Police Officer); Gloria Williams, Ethel Clayton (Women).

BOMBARDIER   (RKO, 1943) 99 M.

Producer, Robert Fellows; director, Richard Wallace; story, John Twist, Martin Rackin; screenplay, Twist; song, M. K. Jerome and Jack Scholl; music, Roy Webb; music director, C. Bakaleinikoff; art director, Albert S. D'Agostino, Al Herman; special effects, Vernon L. Walker; camera, Nicholas Musuraca; editor, Robert Wise.

Pat O'Brien (Major Chick Davis); Randolph Scott (Captain Buck Oliver); Anne Shirley (Burt Hughes); Eddie Albert (Tom Hughes); Walter Reed (Jim Carter); Robert Ryan (Joe Connor); Barton MacLane (Sergeant Dixon); Richard Martin (Chito Rafferty); Russell Wade (Paul Harris); James Newill (Captain Rand); Bruce Edwards (Lieutenant Ellis); John Miljan (Chaplain Craig); Harold Landon (Pete Jordan); Margie Stewart (Mamie); Joe King (General Barnes); Leonard Strong (Jap Officer); Abner Biberman (Jap Sergeant); Russell Hoyt (Photographer); Wayne McCoy, Charles Russell (Instructors); Bud Geary (Sergeant); Warren Mace, George Ford, Mike Lally (Co-Pilots); Kirby Grant, Eddie Dew (Pilots); Erford Gage (Mayer); Charles Flynn (Radio Operator); Neil Hamilton, Lloyd Ingraham (Colonels); Stanley Andrews, John Sheehan, Walter Fenner, Bert Moorhouse (Congressmen); Lee Shumway, Ed Peil, Robert Middlemass (Officers); Paul Parry (Captain Driscoll); James Craven (Major Morris); Cy Ring (Captain Randall); Joan Barclay, Marty Faust (Bits); Larry Wheat (Doctor); Joey Ray, Dick Winslow (Navigators); Paul Fix (Big Guy); John Calvert (Illusionist); John James (Lieutenant); Hugh Beaumont (Soldier); Allen Wood (Army Clerk).

GOVERNMENT GIRL   (RKO, 1943) 94 M.

Producer, Dudley Nichols; associate producer, Edward Donahue; director, Nichols; story, Adela Rogers St. John; adaptation, Budd Schulberg; screenplay, Nichols; music, Leigh Harline; music director, C. Bakaleinikoff; special effects, Vernon L. Walker; camera, Frank Redman; editor, Roland Gross.

Olivia de Havilland (Smokey); Sonny Tufts (Browne); Anne Shirley (May); Jess Barker (Dana); James Dunn (Sergeant Joe); Paul Stewart (Branch); Agnes Moorehead (Mrs. Wright); Harry Davenport (Senator MacVickers); Una O'Connor (Mrs. Harris); Sig Rumann (Ambassador); Jane Darwell (Miss Trask); George Givot (Count Bodinsky); Paul Stanton (Mr. Harvester); Art Smith (Macqueenie); Joan Valerie (Miss MacVickers); Harry Shannon (Mr. Gibson); Emory Parnell (The Chief); Ray Walker (Tom Holliday); J. O. Fowler (Man); Russell Huestes, Larry Steers, James Carlisle, Bert Moorhouse, Fred Norton, Demetrius Alexis, Larry Williams, Chester Carlisle, Harry Denny, Tom Costello, Ronnie Rondell, Charles Meakin (Business Men); Norman Mayes, Karl Miller (Janitors); Clive Morgan (Officer); Harold Miller (Naval Officer); Major Sam Harris (American General); Rita Corday, Patti Brill, Margaret Landry, Mary Halsey, Barbara Coleman, Barbara Hale, Marion Murray (Bits); Lawrence Tierney, Bruce Edwards, Ralph Dunn, Al Hill, David Newell, George Ford, Alex Melesh (FBI Men); Fred Fox, Babe Green, Frank McClure, Harry Bailey, Donald Hall, Louis Payne, Wally Dean, James Kirkwood (Senators); Ralph Linn, Josh Milton, Tom Burton, Harry Clay, Steve Winston (Reporters); June Booth (Secretary); Ivan Simpson (Judge Leonard); Charles Halton (Clerk); Ian Wolfe (Hotel Clerk); David Hughes (Guest); J. Louis Johnson (Mr. Wright's Father); Chef Milani (Hotel Waiter); Frank Norman (Tough Sergeant); John Hamilton, Edward Keane, George Melford (Irate Men); Joe Bernard (Workman); George Riley (Cop).

MAN FROM FRISCO   (Rep., 1944) 91 M.

Associate producer, Albert J. Cohn; director, Robert Florey; story-adaptation, George Worthington Yates, George Carlton Brown; screenplay, Ethel Hill, Arnold Manoff; art director, Russell Kimball; music, Marlen Skiles; camera, Jack Marta; editor, Ernest Nims.

Michael O'Shea (Matt Braddock); Anne Shirley (Diana Kennedy); Gene Lockhart (Joel Kennedy); Dan Duryea (Jim Benson); Ray Walker (Johnny Rogers); Robert Warwick (Bruce McRae); Forbes Murray (Maritime Commissioner); Ann Shoemaker (Martha Kennedy); Tommy Bond (Russ Kennedy); Charles Wilson, Ed Peil, Sr., William Nestell, Roy Barcroft (Key Men); Russell Simpson (Dr. Hershey); Erville Alderson (Judge McLain); Olin Howlin (Eben Whelock); Stanley Andrews (Chief Campbell); Martin Garralaga (Mexican); Ira "Buck" Woods (Black Worker); Stephanie Bachelor (Ruth Warnecke); Charles Sullivan (Irishman); William Haade (Brooklyn); Sid Gould (Russian); Tom London (Old Salt); George Cleveland (Mayor Winter); Nolan Leary, Hal Price, Jack Low, Harry Tenbrook, Dick Alexander, Sam Bernard, Lee Shumway, George Lloyd (Workmen); Judy Cook (Worker); Eddy Waller (Older Worker); Tom Chatterton (Doctor); Minerva Urecal (Widow Allison); Jack Gardner, Rex Lease, Roy Darmour (Men); Effie Laird (Mrs. Hanson); Virginia Carroll, Marjorie Kane (Girls); Patricia Knox (Girl Welder); Gino Corrado (Tony D'Agostino); Frank Moran (Mr. Hanson); Norman Nesbitt (Announcer); H. Michael Barnitz (Ruth Warnecke's Baby); Chester Conklin (Baggage Man); Rosina Galli (Mrs. Palaski); George Neise (Narrator); Monte Montana (Montana); Frank Marlowe (Tough Guy); Ben Taggart (Superintendant); Sam Flint (Chief of Police); Grace Lenard, Weldon Heyburn (Couple in Trailer); Jimmy Conlin (Mayor's Secretary); Harrison Greene (Politician); John Hamilton (Governor); Bud Geary (Bit Man); Kenne Duncan, Jack Kirk (Foremen); Larry Williams (Sam); Maxine Doyle (Woman); John Sheehan (Gang Boss).

MUSIC IN MANHATTAN   (RKO, 1944) 81 M.

Producer-director, John H. Auer; story, Maurice Tombragel, Hal Smith, Jack Scholl; screenplay, Lawrence Kimble; music, Leigh Harline; music director, C. Bakaleinikoff; choreography, Charles O'Curran; songs, Herb Magidson and Lew Pollack; art director, Albert S. D'Agostino, Al Herman; camera, Russell Metty; editor, Harry Marker.

Anne Shirley (Frankie); Dennis Day (Stanley); Phillip Terry (Johnny); Raymond Walburn (Professor); Jane Darwell (Mrs. Pearson); Patti Brill (Gladys); Charlie Barnett & Orchestra, Nilo Menedez & Rhumba Band (Themselves); Minerva Urecal (Landlady); Don Dillaway (Major Hargrove); Edmund Glover, Carl Kent, Michael Road, Steve Winston, John Shaw (Officers); Mary Halsey (Operator); Margie Stewart (Airplane Hostess); Sherry Hall (Chauffeur); Chris Drake (Bellboy); John Hamilton (Banker); Gerald Pierce (Elevator Boy); Ralph Peters (Truck Driver); Jason Robards (Desk Clerk); David Thursby (Clancy); Harry Clay, Bert Moorhouse, Tom Bryson (Photographers); Frank Mayo (Doorman); Robert Homans (Justice of Peace); Georgia Cooper (Judge's Wife); Chester Carlisle (Businessman); Bob Mascagno, Italia De-Nubila (Dance Specialty); Byron Foulger (Ticket Agent); Bert Roach (Fat Man); Joan Barclay (Chorus Girl).

MURDER, MY SWEET   (RKO, 1944) 95 M.

Producer, Adrian Scott; director, Edward Dmytryk; based on the novel *Farewell My Lovely* by Raymond Chandler; screenplay, John Paxton; art director, Albert S. D'Agostino, Carroll Clark; music, Roy Webb; music director, C. Bakaleinikoff; special effects, Vernon L. Walker; camera, Harry J. Wild; editor, Joseph Noriega.

Dick Powell (Philip Marlowe); Claire Trevor (Mrs. Grayle); Anne Shirley (Ann); Otto Kruger (Amthor); Mike Mazurki (Moose); Miles Mander (Mr. Grayle); Douglas Walton (Marriott); Don Douglas (Lt. Randall); Ralf Harolde (Dr. Sonderborg); Esther Howard (Mrs. Florian); John Indrisano (Chauffeur); Jack Carr (Short Guy); Shimen Ruskin (Elevator Operator); Ernie Adams (Bartender); Dewey Robinson (The Boss); Larry Wheat (Butler); Sammy Finn (Headwaiter); Bernice Ahi (Dancer); Don Kerr (Cab Driver); Paul Phillips (Detective Nulty); Ralph Dunn, George Anderson (Detectives); Paul Hilton (Boy).

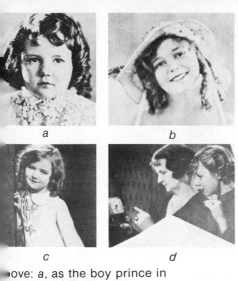

a

b

c

d

ove: *a*, as the boy prince in
IE SPANISH DANCER (Par
); *b*, in THE FAST SET (Par
); *c,* in THE CALLAHANS AND
IE MURPHYS (MGM '27); *d*,
th Mimi Shirley, c.1934

In FINISHING SCHOOL (RKO '34)

John Maguire and Irvin S. Cobb in STEAMBOAT 'ROUND THE BEND (20th '35)

With O. P. Heggie in CHASING YESTERDAY (RKO '35)

With Edward Ellis in CHATTERBOX (RKO '36)

With Barbara Stanwyck and Alan Hale in STELLA DALL (UA '37)

With husband John Payne in
September, 1937

With James Ellison in MOTHER
CAREY'S CHICKENS
(RKO '38)

With Mimi Shirley in 1938

With Dorothy Moore, Margaret Tallichet, and Peggy Moran in GIRLS' SCHOOL (Col '38)

With Carole Lombard in VIGIL IN THE NIGHT (RKO '40)

With John Garfield in SATURDAY'S CHILDREN (W '40)

With Patric Knowles and Joan Carroll in ANNE OF WINDY POPLARS (RKO '40)

In Los Angeles court (February, 1942) obtaining a divorce from John Payne

Jane Darwell in ALL THAT ...NEY CAN BUY (RKO '41)

With Eddie Albert and Walter Reed in BOMBARDIER (RKO '43)

On the Hollywood scene with
Victor Mature in 1942

With her third husband, Cha
D. Lederer (October, 1

With James Dunn, Olivia de Havilland, Rita Corday, and Patti Brill in
GOVERNMENT GIRL (RKO '43)

With daughter Julie in February, 1959

Miles Mander and Dick Powell in MURDER, MY SWEET (RKO '44)

With George Brent in LOVER COME BACK (Univ '46)

5'6"
120 pounds
Red hair
Blue eyes
Leo

Lucille
Ball

From a raw-boned Ziegfeld chorus girl to the matron-queen of global tele-vision comedy is a big transition, and the transformation has not always been easy for Lucille Ball. Before hitting the professional big time with the phenomenally successful "I Love Lucy" video series in the early 1950s, brassy comedienne Lucy suffered through two decades of unfulfilling screen work. She progressed from being a Goldwyn Girl to joining the roster of stock players at Columbia, and then emerged as the Queen of B-pictures at the disintegrating RKO Radio Studios. From there she ambled through five unrewarding years at glittery MGM before hitting the freelance path. Along the way there would be an occasional good smart-aleck role (Stage Door), a solid dramatic role (The Big Street), or a glamorous assignment (The Ziegfeld Follies). By and large, however, Lucy was stuck with run-of-the-mill programmer junk, which did its darnedest to drag her down to rock bottom. Amazingly, she survived the ordeal and went on to prove to enter-tainment executives and public alike that what she did best, seemingly no one could do better: slapstick tomfoolery.

Lucille Desirée Ball was born on August 6, 1911, in Jamestown, New York, a farming and manufacturing community some sixty miles south of Buffalo, on the southern shore of Lake Chautauqua.* Lucy's father, Henry Dunnell Ball, made his living as a telephone lineman, the same work pursued by his father, who had been the black sheep of a financially well-off local family. Lucy's mother, Desirée Hunt, derived from respected Jamestown stock; Desiree's father had been a carpenter much in demand (and a Socialist to boot) and her mother, Florebelle Orcutt Hunt,† was an effervescent, civic-minded person who often functioned as a midwife. There was a time when Lucy's mother earnestly hoped to pursue a concert-pianist career, and when that ambition did not materialize, she bided her time, hoping that one of her children might have the "calling."

In 1915 Lucy's father, then a lineman for the Anaconda Copper Company in Butte, Montana, contracted typhoid fever and died. Mrs. Ball, who had remained in Jamestown with Lucy, was then already pregnant with their second child (Frederick). Mrs. Ball elected to return to her parents' home in a suburb of Jamestown called Celoron. Five years later she wed a salesman named Ed Peterson. "[He was] a handsome-ugly man, very well-read," Lucy recently recalled. "He was good to me and Freddy, but he drank too much. . . . He was the first to point out the magic of the stage." Later, in 1920, Lucy's mother and stepfather moved to Detroit where he had a new territory to cover, leaving her and Frederick with his old-fashioned Swedish parents who, for the brief period that they supervised Lucy's upbringing, maintained a strict, tight control over the child. However, it was not long before Lucy's mother decided that her husband's drinking problem was too much for her to handle, and she returned home and sued for divorce.

Lucy's mother resumed the surname of Ball and found employment in a Jamestown dress shop, earning enough to support her two children and an orphaned niece, Cleo Van Marter. ‡ Musically inclined Mrs. Ball prevailed upon Lucy to study piano at the Chautauqua Institute. But Lucy, who was bumbling her way through school ("I wasn't smart. I had to take algebra five times"), had no affinity for the piano. While at the Chautauqua Institute she witnessed a performance by monologist Julius Tannen and decided

*For a stretch in her early career years Lucy claimed she had been born in Butte, Montana, which is actually where her father died. In fact, for a while she tried to tell everyone her nickname was "Montana."

†Lucy once reminisced: "Grandpa Hunt was a marvelous jack of all trades, a wood turner, eye doctor, mailman, bon vivant, hotel owner (and also a Populist-Socialist). He met my grandmother, Flora Belle, a real pioneer woman and the pillar of our family, when she was a maid in his hotel. She was a nurse and midwife, an orphan who brought up four pairs of twin sisters and brothers all by herself."

‡She is the daughter of Mrs. Ball's sister and has often been referred to by the press as Lucy's sister. She made a momentary appearance with Lucy in *Having Wonderful Time* (RKO, 1938), thereafter marrying press agent Ken Morgan, who would later be employed by Lucy's Desilu Company. After divorcing Morgan, Cleo married Cecil Smith, the television critic of the *Los Angeles Times*. Most recently, Cleo has functioned as a "producer" for Lucy's videoseries.

that show business was the only vocation for her. She was just as apt to perform an overly enthusiastic Apache dance at the Jamestown Masonic Social (with so much gusto she dislocated an arm) as to participate in the local edition of *Charley's Aunt.* *

For several years it was a tradition in the springtime for Lucy to run away from home, walking towards New York until she was found and brought home. Finally, in the summer of 1926, her family faced the inevitable. Lucy wanted to go into show business, and she was determined to make her start in New York. She convinced her mother to allow her to enroll in the John Murray Anderson-Robert Milton drama school in New York City. Says Lucy, "I was a tongue-tied teenager spellbound by the school's star pupil—Bette Davis." Despite Lucy's enthusiasm for her future profession, she was not a born actress. Her instructor wrote Mrs. Ball: "Lucy's wasting her time and mine. She's too shy and reticent to put her best foot forward."

Although she flunked all her courses at the drama school, Lucy was still convinced of her destiny in show business, if not as a lofty "artiste," then possibly as a musical-comedy performer, or even as a lowly chorus girl, if necessary. She accepted any sort of employment available (soda jerk, salesgirl, etc.) to pay for her Manhattan room and board while endeavoring to become a chorus girl.† As a statuesque blonde with a shapely figure she eventually came to the attention of Florenz Ziegfeld's casting agent, then preparing the third road company of the Broadway success *Rio Rita*. But after several weeks of intensive rehearsal for the road-company edition, the distraught stage manager exclaimed to Lucy: "It's no use, Montana. You're not meant for show business. Go home!" Lucy was too full of pride, naïvete, and perseverance to accept the well-meant advice. She made the chorus audition rounds and some months later landed a part in the girlie line of an upcoming musical, *Step Lively*. However, two weeks later the choreographer fired Lucy. Her terpsichorean activity still left a great deal to be desired. Looking back from the safe side of success on these disillusioning show business breaks, Lucy can now say: "But where I was different from the other dumb showgirls is that I learned from every experience and some of them don't. I also had a grab on respectability. My grandparents had raised me to have a conscience. I was very observant. I watched the other girls make their mistakes. I turned down a lot of so-called 'opportunities' because they were only 'maneuvers.' My ambition wasn't high. I just wanted to work."‡

*"I played the lead, directed it, cast it, sold the tickets, printed the posters, and hauled furniture to the school for scenery."

† It was during this financially fraught, but essentially carefree, period that Lucy became acquainted with Manhattan artist Roger Furse, who painted several full-length studies of blonde Lucy. Furst, who died in mid-1972, would gain real prominence as a motion-picture set and constume designer, winning an Academy Award for his creative work on Laurence Olivier's *Hamlet* (1948).

‡ On another occasion Lucy pontificated: "I got thrown in with older Shubert and Ziegfeld dollies and, believe me, they were a mean, closed corporation. I don't understand kids today who get easily discouraged and yap about doing their own things. Don't they know what hard work is. Where are their morals? I always knew when I did wrong, and paid penance."

At this juncture in her very unfulfilled career, Lucy dropped her "Montana" moniker, substituting the more aristocratic professional name of Diane Belmont. Having taken new stock of herself, she decided she had at least two tangible major assets: her striking physical appearance and her ability to wear clothes. Both of these assets pointed in one logical direction. It was not too difficult to become a mannequin, the trick was to retain the job, and this required another feat of physical determination. Lucy took modeling assignments where she found them, usually rushing back and forth between the Seventh Avenue midtown dress center and the 14th Street fur shops. Her usual weekly take-home pay was $25, but soon she acquired sufficient finesse to be hired by the posh Hattie Carnegie establishment at $35 a week. As if her daytime schedule were not busy enough,* Lucy did freelance modeling at night for commercial photographers and such magazine illustrators as McClelland Barclay and John Lagata. In full reaction to her severe upbringing, playful Lucy took complete advantage of the extensive Manhattan late-evening social scene, and was to be seen in the posh club spots with a variety of escorts. The youthful Lucy of this period was a far cry from the conservative matron of today.

There are at least two versions of the ailment which sent Lucy back home to Jamestown for a long recuperative period. Account No. 1 (and until recently Lucy has refused to publicly recall this painful episode in her hectic life) has it that one afternoon, while modeling at the Hattie Carnegie emporium, she was stricken with severe pains "which pierced my insides." The illness was diagnosed as a combination of severe malnutrition combined with excessive fatigue. Account No. 2, the far more dramatic but even less likely rendition, is that, exhausted by the pace of her modeling career, she had "decided to give it all up and go for a holiday." She was driving home from a Carnegie fashion show when her car skidded on a slick, icy street, and turned over. Lucy was thrown clear but lay still. It was an infrequently used byway and there were no on-lookers.† She lay in the roadway several hours before a passerby found her and telephoned for the police and an ambulance. The doctor at first diagnosed her condition only as extensive shock. She was advised to rest, but when, after a day or two, she tried to rise, she found she could not. The physicians re-examined her, discovered she was paralyzed, and said that she would never walk again. Life became a succession of operations and treatments, and after nearly a year confined to the hospital room, she was advised she could go home, as there was no further treatment to be tried. Her mother came with a wheelchair to take her back to Jamestown by train. For more than two years she remained there in her bedroom except for brief outings in the wheelchair. Determined to

---

*It was not uncommon for a Carnegie model to demonstrate several dozen frocks daily, and in those pre-airconditioned-showroom days, coping with the heat was a major task in itself.

†On a recent talk show Lucy said the site was in front of the old Ziegfeld Theatre at 54th Street and Sixth Avenue.

walk—even to dance again—she pursued a strenuous, painful, self-exercise course and surprised everyone by regaining the use of her lower limbs.

Whichever, if either, version is true, it is an undisputed fact that Lucy hurdled a physical barrier that would have defeated most other performers-in-the-making, particularly someone who had been informed on three separate occasions by professionals that she had no talent whatsoever. This phenomenal self-determination and willpower were key factors in bolstering Lucy's spirit through her subsequent unrewarding years as an apprentice in show business.

As Lucy's strength returned she found herself spending more and more time with Gert Kratzert, a Jamestown hairdresser and friend. They often discussed the possibility of venturing to New York; finally one afternoon they decided to stop talking and actually took the bus to Manhattan. They rented a room in the Hotel Kimberley at 72nd Street and Broadway. Lucy was reinstated at Hattie Carnegie's, while her friend obtained employment in the Amsterdam Hotel beauty salon. But Miss Kratzert soon became homesick and decided to return to Jamestown. Not Lucy.

Her break came as a result of her myriad modeling assignments, which brought her to the attention of Liggett and Myers' advertising department, which was seeking a model to be used for its Chesterfield Cigarette posters. The resultant national exposure led to Lucy's Hollywood movie career. She had already made her debut in the New York-filmed *Broadway Thru a Key-hole* (United Artists, 1933), a nightclub backstage story said to be based on the romance and careers of Ruby Keeler and Al Jolson. Along with Ann Sothern, she was a blondine cutie walk-on in a beach scene. Footage of Lucy from this feature was among the tests sent to producer Samuel Goldwyn, then releasing his product through United Artists. He was seeking twelve "Goldwyn Girls" to dress up the background of his latest Eddie Cantor film, *Roman Scandals* (1933), and to later promote the picture to the public. Goldwyn signed Lucy to a short-term contract and she found herself on her way to California.*

While on the Goldwyn lot Lucy had a bit in the gangster thriller *Blood Money* (1933), starring George Bancroft and Frances Dee, which was released before *Roman Scandals*. In the latter picture, Broadway man-about-town Cantor dreams himself back in Italy of old, with Lucy playing one of the slave girls. Even while performing such menial cinema chores, Lucy was convinced that a little industry and imagination could land her at the top of

---

*Busby Berkeley, who was the dance director of *Roman Scandals*, later reminisced: "Goldwyn asked me to join him in the screen room one afternoon in '33 to look at the screentests of some girls from New York he was thinking of placing under contract. Some of the girls he liked and some he didn't, and among those he didn't was Lucille Ball. I liked her and said so and the next day I asked his secretary if he had sent for that girl I liked and she said he had. So that's how Lucille Ball got her first break in films—because Sam respected my judgment. If I hadn't been with him that afternoon he would have let his personal likes and dislikes rule her out."

the heap.* In the next year she maneuvered bits in eight features at United Artists and Fox. She was again a chorus girl (in the nightclub sequence) in *Moulin Rouge* (1934), a near extra in *Nana* (1934), an unbilled girl in Spencer Tracy's *Bottoms Up* and likewise in James Dunn's *Hold That Girl,* both made at Fox in 1934. Back at United Artists, she was a mere walk-on in *Bulldog Drummond Strikes Back* (1934), and a lady-in-waiting in the costume drama *The Affairs of Cellini* (1934). Her final assignment at Goldwyn-United Artists was in Eddie Cantor's *Kid Millions* (1934), which benefited from the presence of Ethel Merman, Ann Sothern, and George Murphy.† A rather somber but striking blonde Lucy was to be seen as a "1934 Goldwyn Girl."

Lucy was perceptive enough to realize that she was existing on borrowed time at Goldwyn-United Artists. When her player's option expired in 1933 she hastily made the rounds of studios, coming up with a $75-a-week offer from Columbia. That company, still struggling to rise above its poverty-row origins, had a healthy short-subject program. Its casting-talent department quickly decided that 5-foot, 6-inch Lucy would be a perfect dumb-blonde type—in the burlesque tradition—for its range of lowbrow comedies. Lucy was immediately thrust into Leon Errol's two-reeler *Perfectly Mismated* (Columbia, November 1, 1934), which featured such short-subject regulars as Vivian Oakland and Dorothy Granger. Lucy had a walk-on as a secretary in that film. Before the end of 1934 Lucy was volleying back and forth between additional short-subject assignments, such as her part in the Three Stooges' *Three Little Pigskins* (Columbia, December 8, 1934), and bits in such 1934 studio features as a blonde telephone operator in Frank Capra's *Broadway Bill,* quickie work in Nancy Carroll's *Jealousy* and Bruce Cabot's *Men of the Night,* and playing a beauty-shop operator in *Fugitive Lady.*

Lucy was sufficiently experienced by now in the here-today-gone-tomorrow world of show business to know that her Columbia contract offered no realistic security. But it was a start! She was also wise enough to realize that having her family on the scene might well prevent her from making any im-

---

*"I came out to Hollywood to do an Eddie Cantor picture with twelve or fourteen showgirls, right? They had more experience, more money, knew their way around. Yet I made it and they didn't. Why? Maybe because they turned down more working jobs or social opportunities and I did just the opposite. As a result, I've never been out of work in this town except for two hours once between contracts."

† Murphy reminisced back over four decades: "I had been puzzled by Lucille's behavior on the set [of *Kid Millions*]. During the shooting of the musical numbers, we would get five-minute breaks for a smoke or other, more urgent, duties. Lucille would invariably be late in returning. The assistant would have to call her name over the loudspeaker, 'Miss Ball—Miss Ball—on the set please.'

"This got to be too much for the assistant director, Benny Silvie. . . . Finally he told her off for holding up shooting.

"I took Lucille aside. 'Honey, I don't understand you' I said. 'One of these days Benny will get so angry he'll fire you.'

"'Oh,' she said, matter-of-factly, 'that may be true. But one thing you can be sure of—they'll know who I am.'"

pulsive personal decisions that could harm her potential professional standing. Lucy later phrased her decision thusly: "I was alone in Hollywood. I didn't belong to anyone. I was unhappy. One night I went on the roof of my house to think over what was the matter with me. I decided that I wasn't doing my part in the world, and, as Columbia had just given me a stock contract to do bits, I decided to share this good fortune. Straight away I went out and wired my mother, my grandfather, my brother, and a cousin to leave Jamestown, my home, and come out to Hollywood." With her family settled in with her at the small house she had rented on Ogden Drive in Hollywood Hills, Lucy now had roots in Hollywood, giving her further incentive to maneuver some way to establish her mark in the film industry.

Just when it seemed that Lucy might be emerging from the bit players' rank (she received her first screen billing as a nurse, in Lee Tracy's *Carnival* [1935], playing along with Geneva Mitchell and Lillian West), Columbia underwent one of its periodic economy waves. The studio discharged a goodly number of its bit players, including Lucy. She immediately made the rounds of studio casting departments.* RKO agreed to hire her, but only at fifty dollars a week. Lucy needed the money and decided to gamble on the offer. She accepted and joined the Culver City studio in the summer of 1934.

RKO had been under the production leadership of Merian C. Cooper for over a year. While the company was still noted for its posh women's pictures starring Katharine Hepburn, Irene Dunne, and Ann Harding, it had become equally well known (and solvent) for its string of Fred Astaire-Ginger Rogers musicals, rural dramas starring Anne Shirley, and Richard Dix action products. RKO received full value from Lucy's contractual presence on the lot, sandwiching her into five 1935 releases plus one short subject. Someone in the casting department must have remembered (or did Lucy remind them?) that she had been a Hattie Carnegie model. It was natural, therefore, for Lucy to be among the mannequins in the extended fashion-show sequence of *Roberta* (1935). Swathed in ostrich feathers, she descended the staircase onto the promenade ramp, making the most of what she has called "halfway between an extra and a bit."†

In Charles "Buddy" Rogers' film return, the college musical *Old Man Rhythm* (1935), Lucy joined with other RKO femme contractees (Kay Sutton, Jane Hamilton, Maxine Jennings, Marian Darling) in adorning the campus background as shapely coeds. But most noticeable in this picture was rising RKO family member Betty Grable, who was not only blonder than Lucy but could tap dance and sing far better. Lucy's second appearance in a Fred Astaire-Ginger Rogers vehicle found her as a flower clerk in *Top Hat* (1935),

*It is possible Lucy was in Paramount's *Murder at the Vanities* (1934), and it has been suggested she was in United Artists' *The Bowery* (1933).

†In very recent years *Roberta* has had limited theatrical reissue in the United States. Invariably there is a cascading flow of surprised audience whispers when Lucy makes her theatrical screen entrance.

most of the time with her back to the camera and less than a scant line of dialog. Lucy is alleged to have had a bit in the studio's rendition of Alexandre Dumas's *The Three Musketeers* (1935), but screenings of that picture fail to reveal her visual presence. But there is no question that Lucy was in *I Dream Too Much* (Radio City Music Hall, November 28, 1935), which offered the unspectacular cinema debut of the "pocket soprano" opera singer Lily Pons. While most of the footage was devoted to petite French girl Pons, who weds composer Henry Fonda (and sings the "Bell Song" from *Lakme,* "Caro Nome" from *Rigoletto,* and some Jerome Kern selections), Lucy was in evidence as the striking daughter of Lucien Littlefield and Esther Dale. Evidently, Lucy's complaining to the front office had done some good at RKO. No longer would she be among the anonymous players of a picture. To wrap up 1935 in the movies, Lucy was among the RKO stable players, including Betty Grable, Anne Shirley, Edgar Kennedy, Preston Foster, Joy Hodges, Bert Wheeler, and Jimmy Greer and Orchestra, who appeared in the studio's two-reeler *A Night at the Biltmore Bowl.*

Lucy now regularly received small featured roles in RKO productions, not only because she was becoming a familiar face to the studio casting department, but because she enthusiastically participated in the lot's dramatic school supervised by Ginger Rogers' mother, Mrs. Lela Rogers. Lucy's rapport with the influential Mrs. Rogers and her industrious study of acting techniques paid dividends. *Chatterbox* (1936), one of the string of B-pictures starring the studio's own Miss Rural, Anne Shirley, found Lucy cast as Lillian Temple, a savvy member of the stock troupe to which Shirley aspires. In the Fred Astaire-Ginger Rogers *Follow the Fleet* (1936), Lucy was Kitty Collins, a sailor-happy pal of Rogers, although once again it was Betty Grable who, next to Rogers and fourth-billed Harriet Hilliard, made far more of an audience impression than fuzzy-haired Lucy. *The Farmer in the Dell* (1936) was an attempt at low-level satirizing of Hollywood by having an Iowa family—parents Fred Stone and Esther Dale, daughter Jean Parker—traipse off to tinsel town where a newly imposed set of values temporarily leads them astray. Lucy's role was Gloria, the wise-mouthed script girl. *Bunker Bean* (1936), the third filming of Lee Wilson Dodd's play based on Harry Leon Wilson's 1913 novel, was a low-keyed rendition of a mousey stenographer (Owen Davis, Jr.) who rises to dizzy heights of power under the influence of a quack savant professor, Berton Churchill. Lucy, as Miss Kelly, was one of Davis's fellow office workers. Lucy was still a sufficiently unproven commodity to be tossed into the breach in the Jean Yarbrough-directed short *So and Sew* (RKO, August 24, 1936), in which she was top-billed as the fiancée of an interior decorator. In Leon Errol's two-reeler *One Live Ghost* (RKO, November 6, 1936), Lucy was featured along with Vivien Oakland. While Lucy and fellow-player Barbara Pepper were merely set-dressing "girls" in the arty production of *Winterset* (1936), Lucy had a much better assignment in *That Girl from Paris* (Radio City Music Hall, December 3, 1936). Since Lily Pons's elegantly mounted *I Dream Too*

Much had failed to create the public interest anticipated, RKO executive producer Pandro S. Berman decreed that her follow-up vehicle should low-pedal the star's operatic techniques and contain more comedy relief. That it did! Jane Murfin's story begins in Paris, where opera luminary Pons walks out on her marriage to stuffy Gregory Gaye and encounters Gene Raymond, whose swing band, which includes Jack Oakie, Frank Jenks, and Mischa Auer, is just about to depart for the U.S.A. Pons stows away on the trans-Atlantic crossing and nearly makes Raymond forget his state-side fiancée, Lucy. But when the ship docks there is blonde dancer Lucy all set to tie the marital knot. When Raymond expresses continued interest in her competitor, Lucy tells the feds about Pons's illegal entry into America, all of which nearly ruins the gang's New Jersey club act. Since Pons was the star of the picture and Lucy was fifth-billed, Pons wins Raymond, but Lucy received her first set of worthwhile critical notices: " . . . an attractive blonde who contributes a diverting dance routine [with Jackie Oakie to the tune "Moon Face"]" *(New York Evening Journal).* The *New York Daily Mirror* was far more enthusiastic. "One Miss Lucille Ball, an able actress and an agile dancer, contributes an exquisite scene as a dancer with soaped shoes . . . [it] is so beautifully done it is worth the whole price of admission. Miss Ball plays it quite straight, intensifying the comedy of each disaster. She rates, thereby, more conspicuous roles and more intense promotion. She is a comedienne, which always means a 'find.'"

Before *That Girl from Paris* reached the public, Lucy had been propelled into *Don't Tell the Wife* (1937), directed by Christy Cabanne. This film, an Americana comedy, found small-town executive Guy Kibbee innocently involved in a fraudulent stock-market scheme engineered by Lynne Overman. Babbitt-like Kibbee, however, turns the tide by discovering a new vein of ore on the Gold Nugget property, making the once worthless paper very valuable currency. Lucy? Well she was along for the ride as local color to flesh out the thin story.

Although Lucy was grateful for the bigger, if not better, assignments RKO was dishing out to her, she still yearned for the big time. When playwright Barlett Comack announced he was seeking talent for a Broadway-bound play, *Hey Diddle Diddle,* Lucy auditioned and was awarded a role. The unhomogeneous cast, which included Martha Sleeper, O. Z. Whitehead, Conway Tearle, Alice White, Keenan Wynn, et al., entrained for New York to begin rehearsals in late December, 1936, under the supervision of producer-director Anne Nichols. The play was written as a sort of *Boy Meets Girl,* only this time told from the point of view of three movie extra girls, (including Lucy as Julie Tucker) who share a Hollywood apartment. *Hey Diddle Diddle* had its premiere at the McCarter Theatre in Princeton, New Jersey, on January 21, 1937, and received mixed notices. *Variety* enthused over Lucy's stage "debut": "[She] fattens a fat part and almost walks off with play. She outlines a consistent character and continuously gives it logical substance. Has a sense of timing and, with a few exceptions, keeps her comedy under control." *Hey Diddle Diddle* wobbled next to Philadelphia, but after a week's engagement in Washington it closed on February 13, 1937, for extensive rewrites. There was talk of later remounting the production—only Lucy from the original cast was asked to be in the new version—but nothing further came of the project.

Lucy returned to California and the RKO lot. Mrs. Lela Rogers told Lucy that the studio was going to put the screen version of George S. Kaufman and Edna Ferber's *Stage Door* (1937) into production, and that a role in this winner was a *must* for her screen career. Mrs. Rogers had a conference with Ginger, who had been awarded the second female lead to Katharine Hepburn's starring role, and Ginger in turn "suggested" to RKO executives that Lucy be given a break in *Stage Door*. She was.

The heavy dramatics and glamour were handled by the triumvirate of Hepburn, Rogers, and Andrea Leeds, with eighth-billed Lucy cast as Judy Canfield, one of the gamier residents at Manhattan's Footlight Club for aspiring actresses. Director Gregory La Cava neatly balanced the production with its diverse range of moods. The main focus in *Stage Door* was on the unofficial competition between dedicated actress Leeds and smug debutante Hepburn for the lead role in Adolphe Menjou's upcoming stage production of *Enchanted April,* paralleling the sandpaper rapport between snooty Hepburn and her down-to-earth roommate Rogers. Nevertheless there were plenty of moments devoted to the other Footlight Club girls: aging character player-coach Constance Collier; bedraggled Phyllis Kennedy, who is dating plump butcher Grady Sutton; and the two wiseacres of the crowd, Lucy and Eve Arden. While Arden slunk about the boarding-house living room with Whitey the Cat draped around her shoulders and tossing out acid remarks,* Lucy postured in and out of the scenes, snapping off her own acerbic remarks, but revealing an inner sense of practicality when it came to selecting the security of a steady beau in preference to gambling on becoming an accepted Broadway stage commodity.

RKO was sufficiently pleased with Lucy's *Stage Door* showing to revise her contract in October, 1937, with an escalated salary-increase clause. *Joy of Living* (1938) may have boasted the presence of Irene Dunne and Douglas Fairbanks, Jr. and a Jerome Kern-Dorothy Fields score, but it struggled with an unjoyous plotline for its mechanical comedy effects. Seventh-billed Lucy was part of Broadway star Dunne's parasitic family, playing the selfish younger sister who is always whining such phrases as, "If I were in your shoes." When Dunne succumbs to the entreaties of renegade Back Bay Boston banking heir Fairbanks to leave town for a simpler life, she literally

*Although emotionally and stylistically different, for a spell Lucy and Eve Arden were categorized as similar screen types. "She and I competed for years," Lucy later recalled. "One of us would be the lady executive and the other would be 'the other woman.' They were the same roles, for we'd walk through a room, drop a smart remark, and exit. I called us 'the drop-gag girls.' I didn't dig it at all, for in such parts you lose your femininity. That was one of the reasons I wasn't too fond of staying in pictures."

tells prima donna Lucy to step into her shoes and carry on with the lead role in her current Broadway musical. As the spoiled wife of loafer Frank Milan and the thoughtless mother of pampered twins, Dorothy and Estelle Steiner, Lucy had a most conventional, subordinate role, an unsympathetic part that she was incapable of instilling with any redeeming qualities.

Nor was being handed the female lead in *Go Chase Yourself* (1938) much of a break. This programmer, featuring Joe "You Wanna Buy a Duck" Penner, was guileless slapstick comedy geared for the family trade. Lucy's role as Penner's nagging spouse was an offshoot of the stereo typed character usually essayed by Vivien Oakland or Dorothy Granger in those domestic-comedy short subjects of the 1930s: the domineering spouse who must follow her weak-willed hubby to set things straight but who usually creates havoc of staggering proportions. In *Go Chase Yourself,* singing teller Penner of the Williamstown First Union National Bank wins a trailer in a raffle, which is fine, except, as wife Lucy points out, that they have no car. That night, after a fight with Lucy, Penner camps out in the trailer parked outside their house, only to become the unwilling passenger of a bank-robbing trio (Richard Lane, Tom Kennedy, Bradley Page) who hitch up their getaway car to his mobile home. Naturally the police and even Lucy are convinced Penner's disappearance proves he is part of the gang, so they charge about in merry pursuit. The *New York Journal American* quickly passed off this cinema trivia, but tagged Lucy as "one gorgeous eyeful."

Lucy returned to more sophisticated surroundings in *Having Wonderful Time* (Radio City Music Hall, July 6, 1938). Arthur Kober distilled his Broadway success of life at a Jewish Catskill resort into a Gentile-oriented screenplay, tailored for the talents of Ginger Rogers and Douglas Fairbanks, Jr. Lucy, in her fifth and final supporting role in a Rogers vehicle, had a larger assignment than fellow Camp Kare-Free guest Eve Arden, but again it was a part not built to endear Lucy with audiences. Lucy was jealous Miriam, who views the arrival of Bronxite Rogers with very jaundiced eye, quickly realizing that this demure lass can (and does) have her pick of the eligible males at the adult resort camp. Lucy shared a few scenes with screen newcomer Red Skelton, playing the camp's social director who has a penchant for dunking donuts.

RKO had taken note of the oncamera rapport of Lucy and Jack Oakie (i.e., *That Girl from Paris)* and cast them together in *The Affairs of Annabel* (1938), which the studio proudly announced would become a screen series. Ex-Paramount star Oakie, whose career had been declining as rapidly as he had gained weight, was back in his best overbearing form as the gimmick-a-second Wonder Pictures press agent assigned to bolster the career of temperamental film star Annabel Allison (Lucy). When Lucy's Annabel made *Behind Prison Bars* (in the movie within the movie), did he not dream up the clever stunt of sending her to jail as a publicity gag? Was it his fault that it took a month to obtain her release? Now that Lucy's Annabel is to headline *A Maid and a Man,* does it not make good sense to hire her out as a domestic? And of course the lucky family in question happens to be the crackpot Fletchers (Elisabeth Risdon, Granville Bates, Thurston Hall, et al.). Before long poor Lucy is involved with kidnappers and wanted by the police for supposed complicity. When the studio learns of this newest dilemma, her upcoming picture is hastily rewritten as *The Diamond Smugglers* to take full advantage of the new real-life situation. *The Affairs of Annabel* concludes with Lucy on her way back to jail, thanks to Oakie's backfiring press agentry, leaving the film with a "here we go again folks" ending and RKO with a moderately successful B-picture to distribute. For her efforts in this comedy the *New York Times's* Frank S. Nugent accorded that Lucy was "rapidly becoming one of our brightest comediennes."

Then came *Room Service,* which RKO was insistent would be a resounding hit, if only because it had paid a record $225,000 for the screen rights to the long-running Broadway hit, and because it had temporarily lured the zany Marx Brothers away from MGM. But the RKO effort proved a paragon of miscasting and misdirecting (William A. Seiter), creeping along at a snail's pace and nearly devoid of the inspirational verbal and physical humor so characteristic of prior Marx Brothers film outings. To complete the cinematic *faux pas,* statuesque Lucy, who was by now a proficient screen mugger, had only a small role, allowing her little or no comedy interplay.* Most of the screen story occurs in Groucho's room at the White Way Hotel, just off Broadway and Times Square. As the producer of an in-rehearsal play, (*Hail and Farewell*), Groucho has conned his brother-in-law (Cliff Dunstan), the hotel manager, into extending $1,200 in credit to him and his cast of twenty-two performers in exchange for a 10 percent interest in the show. As the plot-heavy feature continues, the Marx Brothers find they must devise a way of remaining at the hotel, over the protests of hotel supervisor Donald MacBride, until a new would-be backer (Philip Wood) returns the next morning. Audiences expecting Groucho to wrestle with a femme vis-à-vis, Harpo to play a harp solo, and Chico to tinkle at the keyboard were sadly disappointed by this too tightly controlled picture. As one of the actresses in the play-within-the-movie, Lucy had virtually a walk-on role. She helps the boys con a producer and aids in their other tactical diversions, but her onscreen moments were few and far between. One can only wonder what the results would have been if Lucy could have met Groucho head onward in repartee and antics as Eve Arden did in the later *At the Circus* (MGM, 1939). Ironically, *Room Service* received almost unqualified critical approval at the time.†

Good pictures or bad, Lucy kept churning out roles for RKO. She received top-featured billing for the first time in *The Next Time I Marry* (1938), one

---

*Likewise pert RKO contractee Ann Miller had little chance to display her singing and dancing talents here either.

†Groucho Marx later dissected: "It was the first time we had tried doing a play we hadn't created ourselves. And we were no good. We can't do that. We've got to originate the characters and the situations ourselves. Then we can do them. Then they're us. But we can't do gags or play characters that aren't ours. We tried it, and we'll never do it again."

of those mindless minor screwball comedies that cannot survive close scrutiny. RKO's new *wunderkind* director, Garson Kanin, who had made such a fine showing with his premier effort, *A Man to Remember* (1938), was not so fortunate with this assignment. Kanin followed the tried and true, derivative, *It Happened One Night* formula, but there were many moments of pretentious straining as Kanin fumbled with the delicate genre. In this film Nancy Fleming (Lucy) is one of America's wealthiest heiresses, but to collect her loot she must marry and do so pronto. WPA ditchdigger James Ellison pops into sight and he becomes her prime target. She intends to wed him, acquire her legacy, and then hastily divorce him and marry a fortune-hunting foreigner, count Lee Bowman. Naturally Ellison has integrity and truly loves Lucy, and on the cross-country trailer trip to Reno (one of his prerequisite demands before agreeing to a divorce) she realizes his true values. Despite the banality of the sloppily steered film, the *New York Mirror* could report that Lucy "has individuality and wears smart clothes exceptionally well. She's a very interesting addition to Hollywood's roster of madcap heiresses."

As her seventh—yes, seventh!—1938 release, RKO offered the public a second helping of Jack Oakie and Lucy in *Annabel Takes a Tour*. This series follow-up again was aimed at kidding Hollywood, but it lacked the prefabricated enthusiasm of the original. Lucy's Annabel is now on a personal appearance tour, and again must cope with the engineered publicity stunts of balmy public relations man Oakie. He links her with a "titled" Britisher (Ralph Forbes), which leads to complications when a way must be found to break the headlined engagement. Ruth Donnelly again played wisecracking confidante Josephine, and puffy-cheeked Oakie was still very good for a laugh in the pinch. Twenty-seven-year-old Lucy was at her "attractive colloquial comedienne" best. RKO fully intended to churn out additional *Annabel* segments, but Oakie demanded $50,000 per picture for future installments, which would have brought the budget to over $200,000 per segment, and economy-minded RKO just decided to junk the series.

With this steady diet of RKO programmers, there was good reason for one Hollywood pundit to venture that during this phase of Lucy's studio tenure "she was classified with the scenery." Even Lucy must have wondered where she was heading at RKO where she just could not break out of the B-unit into grade-A features.* Each new regime that came and went was content to leave dynamic Lucy in the programmer division, where her shoestring features were grossing quite respectable box-office returns. Although RKO casting chief Ben Piazza included Lucy among the eight stock girls to test for David O. Selznick's *Gone with the Wind,* Lucy was not fooled for a

---

*RKO's B-unit had such femme stalwarts as Anne Shirley, Joan Fontaine, Wendy Barrie, Betty Grable, Harriet Hilliard, Kay Sutton, Whitney Bourne, Marjorie Lord, Constance Worth, Barbara Pepper, Patricia Wilder, and Margot Grahame, and such veteran stalwarts as Gertrude Michael, Lee Patrick, and Helen Broderick.

moment into believeing that either RKO or Selznick himself would think her capable of playing the demanding Scarlett O'Hara part. Lucy was the first to admit that her ability to drawl out such lines as "I do declare, Ashley Wilkes, I don't for the life of me understand what you see in that skinny little Melanie . . . ," was minimal, and that no amount of at-home rehearsing would improve the situation. But she eventually drove over to the Selznick studio in Culver City for her session with Will Price, a southern scholar hired as an advisor and coach for the would-be candidates. Still later on, she forced herself to appear at Mr. Selznick's office, soaked to the skin from an inconsiderate cloudburst, chattering with cold and fear. While waiting for Selznick to appear, Lucy gave one final practice reading of her test scenes, unaware that Selznick had quietly slipped into the office. She finished reading her lines and looked up at Selznick.

Selznick: "Very good, Miss Ball."

Lucy: "Did you really think so?"

Selznick: "Indeed. We'll let you know our decision. Meanwhile, thanks for coming."

Lucy: "Then I can go now."

Selznick: "Yes. Here. Let me help you."

Only as Selznick hustled around the desk to assist her to her feet did Lucy realize she had performed her entire audition on her knees.

The new year was inaugurated by Lucy participating in additional budget features. *Beauty for the Asking* (1939) may have been just another quickie entry, but it had the distinction of offering Lucy a very sympathetic, if one-dimensional, role. Former actor Glenn Tryon, who had turned first to scriptwriting and now to directing, guided Lucy through her paces as she played an earnest beauty-shop operator who invents a startlingly effective facial cream, which advertising man Donald Woods promotes into a dramatic financial success. Part of Lucy's backing comes from rich plain-duckling Frieda Inescort, whose bank account is sufficient to cause cad Patric Knowles to jilt Lucy for Inescort's richer berth. It takes Lucy most of the picture's sixty-eight minutes to comprehend that Knowles has played her for a sucker and that Woods is really *the* man for her. Reviewer Kate Cameron, the culture leader of *New York Daily News* film-page readers, estimated in her two-and-one-half-star review of *Beauty for the Asking* that Lucy "plays the young career woman with a great deal of zest and competence in handling the dialogue that infuses the mediocre story with an atmosphere of reality usually lacking in films of its type. As a matter of fact, Miss Ball rises high enough above her material to remind us that she is of the stuff that stars are made of." RKO executives, in true Hollywood style, took no heed of Miss Cameron's evaluation. It served the studio's short-term purposes far better to use Lucy's abilities in programmers than to stretch her limits in more demanding fare.

Lucy was next scheduled to make *Glamour Boy #2*, again paired with Joe Penner, but he was instead cast in *The Day the Bookies Wept* (1939) with former Paramount player Betty Grable, and Lucy took second billing to RKO's veteran leading man Richard Dix in *Twelve Crowded Hours*. Obviously assembled for the action market, the picture had director Lew Landers challenge the credibility gap by jamming a plethora of events into the stereotyped proceedings. The plotline had star crime reporter Dix, who is determined to save Allan Lane, the brother of fiancée Lucy, corral the town's policy-game operators, which leads to the expected climactic shootout which nicely eliminates all the bad guys. The picture's most imposing figure was 250-pounder Cyrus W. Kendall as the master crook.

With a total lack of artistic conscience, RKO threw Lucy to the dogs in *Panama Lady* (1939), perhaps the nadir of her B-picture period. Directed by ex-film editor Jack Hively for Cliff Reid's studio economy unit, *Panama Lady* was the type of tropical melodrama that was antiquated when *Sadie Thompson* was still fresh. Lucy portrayed a cabaret entertainer named Lucy, who is stranded in Panama. Her marriage plans with commercial aviator Donald Briggs have fallen apart because she has learned that he is a gunrunner with a price on his head and that he cannot be depended upon to keep his promises. Local cabaret proprietress Evelyn Brent offers Lucy a club post, if she will be cooperative, such as helping to roll Allan Lane, an American geologist on an oil-prospecting trek. Lane does not take the robbery lightly and only drops police charges when Lucy agrees to be his "housekeeper" back at his camp. Like the famed bad penny, Briggs turns up at Lane's camp seeking revenge on Lucy for what he believes was a double-cross. In the ensuing scuffle Briggs is shot and Lucy, convinced she has killed him, allows Lane to help her escape. Time elapses and back in New York City Lucy, existing in poverty, is now very much a redeemed woman. Lane comes to Manhattan to tell Lucy the belated good news: it was really Cheema (Steffi Duna), a native girl who loved Lane and was jealous of Lucy, who fired the fatal shots into Briggs. Lucy and Lane now have a bright future together. It was a tossup which was more ludicrous, the hackneyed situations or the production team's juvenile approach in suggesting an ambience of sin. Once again the *New York Daily News*'s Wanda Hale did battle for Lucy, editorializing in her two-star pan of *Panama Lady*,* "[The film] is another minor triumph for Lucille Ball. But it is high time RKO recognized her potential and put her in something more deserving of her ability than the last things she has appeared in. I don't contend that she is a Duse, but she is one of the most up-and-coming young players around."

With no thanks to RKO top-level policy, Lucy's next picture, *Five Came Back* (1939), emerged a pleasant contrast to its programmer predecessor, *Panama Lady*. Director John Farrow worked wonders with his modest budget and gave the film real distinction. It contained all the *Grand Hotel*-style clichés still used in the genre today (e.g., *Skyjacked* [1972]), but it packed within its seventy-four minutes more tension and credibility than the more

---

*Lucy had the distinction of being billed above the title in this bauble.

heavily mounted *The High and the Mighty* or *Airport.* Relying on the cream of its programmer stock company, Farrow peppered *Five Came Back* with Chester Morris and Kent Taylor as the pilots of the clipper *Silver Queen,* which is on the run from Los Angeles to Panama (that country again!). Aboard the aircraft are Lucy, a girl with a dubious past whom the others snub; professor C. Aubrey Smith and his wife (Elisabeth Risdon); secretary Wendy Barrie, who is eloping with her wealthy employer Patric Knowles; Casey Johnson, a gangster's son being taken to safety by henchman Allen Jenkins; political murderer Joseph Calleia in the custody of law-enforcer John Carradine; and steward Dick Hogan. Part way to their destination, the plane falters off course and crashes to the jungle floor. Hogan is killed and in the following days the passengers have ample occasion to display their essential natures. Carradine and Knowles become drunkards, Calleia demonstrates an inner decency, and aging Smith and his wife renew their love for one another. Hard-boiled Lucy exhibits good instincts, which win her the friendship of Barrie as well as the others, especially Morris. With so many interweaving subplots to focus on, each performer was constantly on and offcamera. Rightly so, the focal point in *Five Came Back* came to be the jungle itself, with the sounds of beating native drums the center of attention, as the Caucasians seek to escape before it is too late. In their few scenes together it was instructive to observe Wendy Barrie floating through her acting business on a personality bubble, while Lucy, as the bad girl gone square, was churning with visible brain waves to put across her hazy characterization. *Five Came Back* would be remade by Farrow in 1956 as *Back From Eternity* with Anita Ekberg in Lucy's old part.

As Lucy's fifth and final 1939 picture assignment, she decorated *That's Right, You're Wrong,* the screen debut of Kay Kyser, who was then riding the crest of his popularity as the bandleader-emcee of the radio show "Kollege of Musical Knowledge." To showcase Kyser and his band group (including Ginny Simms, Harry Babbitt, and Ish Kabibble), there were five song interludes. The thin plotline had Kyser signed to a movie contract at Four Star Pictures. But when he and his band arrive on the Coast, temperamental producer Adolphe Menjou wants no part of this airwave celebrity from Rocky Mount, North Carolina. A test scene from *Romeo and Juliet* is clear evidence that Kyser is no John Barrymore. Even the ace screenwriting team of Edward Everett Horton and Hobart Cavanaugh cannot whip together a picture for Kyser, and Menjou is determined to get rid of Kyser once and for all. Just to keep the story rolling along, the picture sported glamorous movie star Lucy, glib press agent Roscoe Karns, Kyser's perky grandmother, May Robson, and the bandleader's genteel manager, Dennis O'Keefe (who conveniently has a yen for Lucy). It was the type of potpourri concocted musical nonsense that RKO would turn out to an increasing degree in the 1940s.

Meanwhile, in mid-1939 RKO executives had negotiated a contract with the genius of Mercury Theatre, Orson Welles. The agreement provided for

Welles and his troupe to relocate in Hollywood and appear in Mercury film productions for RKO release. Studio president George Schaefer reasoned that this coup would give RKO a new lease on artistic prestige within the industry. Anyway, as has been well documented elsewhere, Welles's initial project, based on Joseph Conrad's *Heart of Darkness,** was shelved due to continuing policy disagreements on the project between Welles and RKO's financial board. The studio then suggested that Welles helm the detective thriller *The Smiler With the Knife* written by English poet Cecil Day Lewis. Welles, who demanded that fresh screen faces be used in pictures he supervised,† was aghast when RKO heads "suggested" that either Carole Lombard (then under a special RKO pact) or Rosalind Russell would be most suitable for the film. Welles did not have to fumble for long with ways to say no to the ladies, for both these stars rejected the idea almost at once. For a while the studio considered using its queen of the B-pictures, Lucy, for the film, but finally *The Smiler with the Knife* was also shelved. Welles went on to *Citizen Kane* and *The Magnificent Ambersons,* and Lucy returned to her old stamping grounds and more programmers.

The Marines Fly High (1940) had originally been conceived as a further continuation of the successful teaming of Victor McLaglen and Edmund Lowe *(What Price Glory, Cockeyed World, Hot Pepper),* particularly now that Mexican spitfire Lupe Velez (the distaff interest of *Hot Pepper)* was currently under RKO contract. But the purchase price for the Quirt-Flagg characters proved so high that RKO dropped the line of attack and converted the nascent property into a formula actioner for Richard Dix, Chester Morris, and third-billed Lucy. Despite the adept proletarian cast, *The Marines Fly High* proved extremely sluggish film fare. The plot had leathernecks Dix and Morris combating, usually via airplanes, a local villain named El Vengador, who is raiding the territory's cacao plantations. One such estate owner (Lucy) soon finds herself relying rather heavily on the presence of Dix and Morris for both protection and spare-time romance. Dix, of course, wins Lucy's fair hand. Steffi Duna was again a tempestuous native girl, and the mysterious El Vengador? Well. Keep your eyes on Lucy's apparently respectable plantation foreman, John Eldredge.

Scarcely two months after *The Marines Fly High* was grinding away at the Rialto Theatre, *You Can't Fool Your Wife* rolled into the Palace Theatre (May 23, 1940). Aimed as a bedroom farce, the picture tumbled out an "inconsequential but occasionally chuckling charade of domestic crisis" *(New York Times).* The picture had Lucy and James Ellison wed fresh out of college, and, five years later, despite the perpetually aggravating presence of Lucy's mom (Emma Dunn), the couple (he an accountant, she a drab housewife) have not unhitched their matrimonial knot. But then one evening hubby arrives home not only very late but quite inebriated. He claims his

*Budgeted at over $1 million.
†Welles's Mercury Company included Joseph Cotten, Ruth Warrick, Ray Collins, Agnes Moorehead, Paul Stewart, and George Coulouris.

condition is merely the result of entertaining British playboy client Robert Coote, but Lucy is suspicious and the episode triggers a separation. The script of *You Can't Fool Your Wife,* in obvious obeisance to the trend-setting *The Guardsman,* has apologetic Coote suggest to Lucy that she pose as an alter ego to make Ellison sufficiently jealous and repentant. So for the last reels of the picture Lucy is bounding in and out of the set as both homebody Clara Hinklin and (by donning a Spanish mantilla) South American coquette Mercedes Vasquas. The picture sank very quickly into the sheer nonsense that one expected from RKO's *Mexican Spitfire* series, all very obvious and trite.

If Lucy personally decried being denied the glamour treatment given to RKO's Ginger Rogers both on and offcamera, she was equally miffed that RKO executives had sidetracked her possible professional elevation by association with the arty Orson Welles in *The Smiler With the Knife.* Lucy was objective enough to realize she lacked the essential intangibles to follow in the Madeleine Carroll tradition as recently departed RKO B-picture leading lady Joan Fontaine had, but the presence of redheaded Irish Maureen O'Hara on the studio lot presented a very real threat. Brought to the studio as a protegee of actor-producer Charles Laughton and producer Erich Pommer, who each had impressive RKO pacts, O'Hara had already co-starred in the expensively mounted *The Hunchback of Notre Dame* and had assumed the lead role, no less, in the remake of Katharine Hepburn's *A Bill of Divorcement.* O'Hara's talents at this point were mostly visual, and Lucille was in no way about to yield her spot on the studio totem pole to this potential usurper. Thus, when producer Pommer, having cast O'Hara and Louis Hayward in the leads of a new musical, *Dance, Girl, Dance* (1940), requested Lucy for the third-star spot of Bubbles, Lucy was determined to show everyone once and for all that she was not a performer to be consistently shortchanged.

In the canon of backstage musicals, *Dance, Girl, Dance* contained all the stock ingredients (except a healthy dose of comedy relief). Director Dorothy Arzner did her best to inject class into the production-line product, and she had fine assistance from her two contrasting leading ladies. The two redheads were showcased as members of Maria Ouspenskaya's nightclub dance troupe. Gold-digging Lucy and culture-conscious O'Hara (she yearns to be a ballet performer) both latch onto playboy Hayward, despite the presence of his ex-wife (Virginia Field) and ballet producer Ralph Bellamy's wish to provide O'Hara with life's finer things. Fireball Lucy soon breaks away from the troupe to become a go-getting burlesque performer. The frivolous miss clicks as a stripper and before long she is regarded as a queen of the circuit. Magnanimously Lucy even finds O'Hara a job as her onstage stooge. Although vocally not up to par (requiring her voice to be dubbed), Lucy demonstrated that in all other departments she was a cinematic tornado. Whether tossing off wisecracks, having a tussle fight with O'Hara, performing a hula and then a jitterbug, or offering her electric interpretation of a strip while "singing" "Oh Mother, What Do I Do Now?" Lucy grabbed the limelight, making *Dance, Girl, Dance* very much her picture. Audiences were wowed anew by their programmer favorite and the critics politely raved. (" . . . gives an amazingly knowing interpretation. . . . It is a hard, unsympathetic role, but it is bound to be a springboard for the new star's rise" [New York *Herald-Tribune*].)

This time RKO heeded the enthusiastic response to Lucy's performance and handed her the lead in *Too Many Girls* (Criterion Theatre, November 20, 1940), derived from the Richard Rodgers-Lorenz Hart-George Marion, Jr. Broadway musical.* Stage director George Abbott, along with original cast members Desi Arnaz, Eddie Bracken, and Hal LeRoy, were imported to Hollywood to translate the show to the screen. Lucy inherited Marcy Wescott's role as the spoiled heiress whose father (Harry Shannon) hires four football players (Arnaz, Bracken, Richard Carlson, LeRoy) to act as her protectors while she attends Pottawatomie College in Stop Gap, New Mexico. Lucy learns she is not the only dangerous coed on campus, for toe-tapping Ann Miller and tune-chirping Frances Langford are also engaged in taunting the male collegians. Before the rah-rah tale comes to its happy conclusion, Lucy has won crew-cut Carlson and the college's football team is on its joyous way to the Rose Bowl competition.

Unfortunately, *Too Many Girls* was not the joyous screen musical anticipated. Abbott, whose last movie directing was in 1930, was too inclined to merely reproduce on film what he had conceived for the live stage, hoping that an occasional production number top-heavy with chorus extras would pass muster. As the wistful heroine, Lucy "sang" two numbers: "I Didn't Know What Time It Was" and "You're Nearer."† The limelight, however, fastened more clearly on bongo-tapping Arnaz with his "Spic and Spanish" number, tap dancing LeRoy, and ever-effervescent terpsichorean Miller. Even bucolic Bracken, here with a southern drawl, was a scene-grabbing diversion. So *Too Many Girls* can hardly be classified as Lucy's picture.

Lucy's initial meeting with her *Too Many Girls'* co-star Desi Arnaz‡ occurred in the RKO studio commissary during the filming of her *Dance, Girl, Dance*. "He had on a dirty green leather jacket," Lucy clearly remembers. "I heard him whisper, 'That girl's not going to play my ingenue, No!'" Rap-

---

*Opened October 18, 1939, at the Imperial Theatre for a run of 249 performances. RKO paid $100,000 for the screen rights.

†Both dubbed by Trudy Erwin.

‡ Born Desiderio Arnaz y de Acha on March 3, 1917, in Santiago, Cuba, where his father was the mayor. During the 1933 Cuban revolution his father was jailed, and Desi and his mother fled to Miami. After a series of odd jobs, he became part of a seven-piece rhumba band, which played Miami's plush Roney Plaza Hotel. Xavier Cugat hired Desi two years later as a band vocalist, and some months later Arnaz formed his own south-of-the-border band. While he was touring with it, producer-director George Abbott spotted Arnaz and offered him the third lead in the stage production of *Too Many Girls* as a Latin lover. (In the early 1940's during the height of the "good neighbor" policy, Arnaz was promoted as a South American, never a Cuban.) After RKO put him under contract for the movie version of *Too Many Girls,* the studio used him in *Father Takes a Wife* (1941), *Four Jacks and a Jill* (1941), and *The Navy Comes Through* (1942).

port between the two players, however, obviously improved, for by the time *Too Many Girls* completed production on August 11, 1940, Lucy and Arnaz were a steady twosome. Thereafter, Arnaz completed a band tour and Lucy made a nationwide personal appearance trek. They remet in New York and on November 11, 1940, eloped to Greenwich, Connecticut, where they were wed in a civil ceremony. (Later they were remarried in a Catholic ceremony in California, and Lucy, who was reared as a Protestant, agreed to raise any children they might have as Catholics.) Hollywood observers gave the marriage six weeks at the most. It was well known that Lucy, ever anxious for respectability and security, had pursued temperamental playboy Arnaz with indiscreet abandon, and the six-year age difference was a sore point to all concerned. Lucy and Arnaz purchased a five-acre San Fernando Valley ranch,* but they were not fated to spend much of the war years together. When he was not on band tour, he was away for what proved to be a three-year hitch in the United States Army.†

Meanwhile Lucy returned to moviemaking. Programmers, what else? The title of *A Girl, A Guy, and a Gob* (1941), starring Lucy, Edmond O'Brien, and George Murphy, tells all there is to be told about this film. Shipping magnate O'Brien is a big career success but has no inkling of how to grab a bit of *joie de vivre*. Employee Lucy, who has a sizable crush on him, and errant, but sympathetic, naval gunner Murphy attempt to remedy this deficiency. To allow for wacky interludes, the script provides daffy Lucy with a screwball family who are forever indulging in monkeyshines. The fact that former cinema-comedy kingpin Harold Lloyd was producing the first picture in which he did not star neither helped the quality of the film (as RKO so persistently claimed) nor hindered the matter of the performances. Even here at the age of thirty Lucy's screen presence elicited critical approval, a tribute to her sustained striking looks. For example, "most luscious little dish to have come this way in many a long moon!" *(New York Morning Telegraph);* "Lucille Ball may not be made of Indian rubber, but she has as much bounce" *(New York Times).*

At this juncture Lucy, along with Ginger Rogers, Maureen O'Hara, Anne Shirley, and Phyllis Brooks, was considered, and listed accordingly in trade advertisements, as one of RKO's "woman contractees," to be differentiated from the roster of distaff featured players, occasional studio performers, or actresses not possessed of current box-office magnetism.‡ With its rather anemic roster, RKO was anxious to retain Lucy's screen services and negotiated a new seven-year pact with her in March, 1941, which provided for

---

* Contrary to popular misconception, Arnaz was earning far more than Lucy in the early 1940s. Between his band engagements and recording sessions, he was grossing $100,000 yearly, while Lucy was earning a relatively paltry $40,000-$50,000.

† Arnaz declined a commission in the Cuban Army and instead joined the U.S. Army in February, 1943.

‡ This mongrel group included Wendy Barrie, Signe Hasso, Anne Hunter, Michele Morgan, Lupe Velez, Jane Wyatt, Joan Carroll, Dorothy Comingore, Frances Neal, Janes Pattern, Virginia Vale, Ruth Warrick, and Jane Woodworth.

a salary that would spiral upward to $1,500 weekly.* There was talk in July, 1941, that producer Erich Pommer would star Lucy with Joseph Cotten in *Passage to Bordeaux* under the direction of Britisher Robert Stevenson. That film did not come to pass, but *Look Who's Laughing* (1941) did.† The whole affair was strictly makeshift filmfare, with vacationing Edgar Bergen experiencing airplane engine trouble and landing his small craft in the rural community of Wistful Vista. There he sets about aiding the determined Fibber McGee and Molly in promoting a new plane factory for the town, with none other than the burg's mayor, Throckmorton P. Gildersleeve (Harold Peary), as their arch opponent. Typical casting found Lucy wasted as Bergen's assistant and playing stooge to Charlie McCarthy's wisecracks. When not engaged in these unchallenging frivolities, Lucy was flirting with Lee Bonnell (Bergen's manager, who really loves Dorothy Lovett) and Bergen. Fortunately, Lucy was spared being the third fiddle in the picture's disastrous follow-up, *Here We Go Again* (1942).

By now RKO was recovering from the debacle of George Schaefer's regime and embarking on a sterner attempt to gear its product to the escapist needs of World War II audiences. The studio followed the lead of Universal and Columbia in being determined to give the customers the least possible in order to earn the most revenue conceivable. *Valley of the Sun* (1942) was such a venture. A totally undistinguished escapee from the studio's programmer division, this western was grandly bandied as RKO's biggest outdoor picture since *Cimarron*. Set in the 1860s when Arizona was still Indian territory, the plot had James Craig assume the guise of an apparently discredited Indian scout who marches into the area, ready to take advantage of any promising skulduggery. All of which is fine with crooked Indian agent Dean Jagger, who needs new aides in bilking the poor savages. Craig not only proves to be a virtuous government agent out to protect the redskins, but he prevents Lucy, who owns the town's only eatery, from making the ghastly error of wedding skunk Jagger. For momentary comic diversion there was Billy Gilbert as the farcical justice of the peace, Tom Tyler as the rebel leader Geronimo, and former silent-screen star Antonio Moreno as the solemn Chief Cochise. Needless to say, Lucy, who was more at home in Lindy's on Broadway, and not in the wild wild West, was sorely out of keeping in this George Marshall-directed sagebrush tale. In fact Lucy had reached such a low ebb in her career that *Variety* classified her and Craig as "low voltage marquee strength."

Although Lucy was still receiving her $1,500 weekly paychecks, her RKO prospects were pretty dim. New studio head Charles Koerner appreciated Lucy's artistic dissatisfaction, but he had bigger problems—keeping the studio

---

* Some sources list the price range as high as $3,500 weekly.
† RKO was in the midst of its grab-a-radio-star-for-movie-appeal methods, and was persuaded by colossal talent packager Music Corporation of America to contract as a package Edgar Bergen (with dummy Charlie McCarthy), Jim and Marian Jordan (better known as radio's "Fibber McGee and Molly"), and director Allan Dwan.

on the solvency map. It was only by a freakish bit of good luck that Lucy found herself playing opposite Henry Fonda in *The Big Street* (Palace Theatre, August 13, 1942). The previous year Carole Lombard had introduced Lucy to Broadway's flavorful raconteur, Damon Runyon, then completing negotiations to make his debut as an RKO motion picture producer. Runyon selected his own story, "Little Pinks," for the initial studio project, and urged RKO to borrow Henry Fonda for the meek busboy lead. Then, to everyone's surprise, Runyon demanded that Lucy be given the meaty second-billed role as the petulant butterfly, Gloria.* Many agree, this author included, that *The Big Street* offered Lucy her finest screen moments.

Within the fairytale setting of the picture, Lucy's Gloria is depicted as one of the Great White Way's most notorious gold diggers. Her philosophy is "a girl's best friend is a dollar," reasoning that all love gives a gal is "a one-room apartment, two chins and three kids." Like all Runyon characters, she comes on strong with the colloquial dialog, prone to telling anyone in sight to "evaporate," "button your lip," or "drop dead," depending on how the conversation is running. After all, the denizens of Runyon's Broadway do not call Lucy's Gloria "Your Highness" or "Princess" for nothing. Then one day, everything changes for the doll. She informs her crooked club-owner paramour (Barton MacLane), "I'm closing my account. I'm thinking of doing business with another bank." His immediate reaction is to slap her face; she falls down a flight of stairs and ends up in the hospital, a permanent cripple. Naturally the most faithful hospital visitors prove to be those very persons she ignored most when she was a high and mighty club singer: Nicely Nicely Johnson (Eugene Pallette), Violette (Agnes Moorehead), and of course Little Pinks (Fonda), the timid Mindy's busboy who has long nurtured a crush on the snobbish redhead. Now at her most vulnerable, Lucy's Gloria slowly realizes who her true friends are, but she must feign toughness when Fonda arrives at the hospital. She says to a friend: "How about that little weasel? Send him in." Later, in one of the film's most fanciful segments, Fonda pushes Lucy all the way to Florida in her wheelchair, for she is determined to have one more crack at landing the rich playboy who previously showed a great deal of interest in her. (And Fonda is equally determined to give the doll anything her heart desires, for the doctor has told him that if she cannot surmount her emotional depression she will surely die.)

Despite Lucy's careful planning, her wealthy friend discovers the ruse and the well-bred beach bum leaves her high and dry, sending the delectable dish into one huge funk. But she has not counted on the imaginative devotion of Fonda, who rises to the situation, aided by all the ex-Broadwayites in the area. He risks aggravating the long arm of the law by arranging a huge dance at a swank Miami club (owned by MacLane), forcing a horde of big-time swells to come and pay homage to ailing Lucy. In total glory she manages to have one dance with Fonda, before climbing a flight of stairs

*At one point in pre-production planning, Mercury Player Dorothy Comingore had the part.

and dying in happiness. For she has become her heart's desire, a true lady.

A few diehards may have labeled *The Big Street* a poor man's *Of Human Bondage* and complained that the dubbing of Lucy's singing voice* was too obvious, but the general consensus was that *The Big Street* was the snappiest product from RKO in a long time, what with its array of quaint but lovable characters and its fanciful sob story of unrequited love. Fonda was praised for his highly sympathetic interpretation, but it was Lucy who rightfully garnered the critical spotlight, leading James Agee to write his famous evaluation: "Pretty Lucille Ball, who was born for the parts Ginger Rogers sweats over, tackles her 'emotional' role as if it were sirloin and she didn't care who was looking."

But fast on the heels of *The Big Street* was the forgettable *Seven Days' Leave* (1942), which had an unredeemable B-picture patina. Victor Mature† was cast as a conceited Army draftee who has been left a legacy of $100,000. But the will has one major hitch: he must wed a society heiress (Lucy) before a certain date, and he only has a week's leave. "Can I make any girl love me in seven days!" smirking Mature ponders. "It'd be different if I had two weeks." To round out the plot complication of this "highly unappetizing cinematic goulash" (*New York Herald-Tribune*), Mature's original fiancée, Mapy Cortes, does her best to retain her beau's affection and eliminate Lucy from the scene. As if to match Mature's posturing, Lucy badly overacted as the haughty socialite, giving an unsatisfying performance compounded by the fact that she was ineffectually photographed as well. The best bits of this "tune-filled" picture were re-creations of sections of two radio programs, "The Court of Missing Heirs" and Ralph Edwards's "Truth or Consequences."

Ironically, just as *The Big Street* leaped into release and Lucy was garnering good reviews, her status at RKO was further deteriorating. She had gone on suspension earlier in 1942 for refusing the second female role in a loan-out to Twentieth Century-Fox for Betty Grable's *Footlight Serenade*.‡ Although studio head Charles Koerner was personally fond of Lucy as a performer, he was under strict orders to pare down the weekly overhead, which meant contractees who were high-priced (by RKO standards anyway) had to go. It no longer seemed feasible to pay Lucy $1,500 for headlining programmer pictures which could coast by with far less expensive help.§ So Lucy's option was allowed to expire.

But fortunately for Lucy, she proved to be the answer to MGM's casting problems. Metro had acquired the screen rights to the Cole Porter-B. G. De Sylva-Herbert Fields Broadway success, *Du Barry Was a Lady*.φ Although

*By Martha Mears
†His last picture assignment for the duration of World War II, as he joined the Coast Guard after it was completed.
‡Jane Wyman was substituted.
§Especially in the new thrift-budget series: *The Falcon, The Saint,* and Val Lewton's chiller unit.
φThe show had opened at the 46th Street Theatre on December 6, 1939, with a run of 406 performances.

415

there was little difficulty in scrubbing the saucy dialog for the screen or in converting Bert Lahr's stage role into a screen part for Red Skelton, there was a very real problem in finding an actress with enough zest to recapture the vibrato of Ethel Merman's title part. The most likely candidate on the MGM lot was neglected Ann Sothern, who had just that year jumped out of her *Maisie*-series rut to grapple with the Merman role in Cole Porter's *Panama Hattie* (1942). However, studio executives figured one such outing as this for Ann was enough for filmgoers to digest. So producer Arthur Freed was at loose ends in selecting a suitable alternative. After viewing Lucy's performance as a golddigging thrush in *The Big Street* he was convinced she could rise to the occasion in *Du Barry Was a Lady* (1943).

So Lucy moved from one Culver City lot to another and finally starred in her first Technicolor feature. Parading a new strawberry-pink hair color, Lucy proved she clearly understood musical comedy in *Du Barry,* giving a biting edge to her performance as club chanteuse May Daly, who would much sooner have Gene Kelly or Douglass Dumbrille pursue her than buffoon Skelton. But when Skelton wins a $150,000 lottery and acquires the club, it is a different story. Lucy now agrees to marry him. At the celebration party Skelton worries that Kelly's unabated pursuit might bear fruit, so he plans to put knockout drops in his competitor's drink. By error Skelton downs the mickeyed drink himself, which leads to an extended dream (nightmare) in which his subconscious casts him as duncish dandy King Louis XV with his love-of-life Lucy as none other than Madame Du Barry. Even in his manipulated dreams Skelton discovers being monarch is not all fun and games, and when he awakens, he is a wiser man, deciding Kelly should wed Lucy and that hat-check girl Virginia O'Brien is a much better match for him. Lucy, who "sang" such numbers as "Friendship" and "Madame, I Love Your Crepes Suzettes,"* made a valiant stab at lassoing the limelight (particularly in her fantasyland minuet with Skelton, during which she was dressed to the nines in period finery, with a stick of celery in her mouth), but mugging Skelton emerged as the film's focal point. Acerbic O'Brien of the stone-faced song delivery and iconoclastic Zero Mostel (as the club soothsayer) were not far behind Skelton in audience favor.

But Lucy soon had a second chance. Metro's own Lana Turner, who had performed a walk-on in *Du Barry Was a Lady,* was forced to bow out of Arthur Freed's next Technicolor musical, *Best Foot Forward* (1943),† because of her all-too-obvious pregnancy. The hand-me-down assignment proved to be only a moderate blessing, since most of the more charming elements of the stage show, which had starred Rosemary Lane, were eventually deleted from the screen reworking. Lucy recapped her *Annabel* portrayals in playing herein a glamorous movie star whose film career is on the skids. To rebolster her sagging screen allure, press agent William Gaxton convinces

---

*Dubbed by Martha Mears
†The stage version had opened at the Ethel Barrymore Theatre on October 1, 1941, with a run of 326 performances.

her to accept an invitation from lovelorn fan Tommy Dix to be his military-school prom date.* Once Lucy arrives at Winsocki, cadet Dix admits his incapability of coping with the impossible situation, which is aggravated by his steady girlfriend Virginia Weidler, who sets out to bring Lucy down to size (they later engage in a drag-out tussle, leaving an embarrassed and tattered Lucy in her slip). Writing in the *New York Post,* Archer Winsten pinpointed the cinematic problems of *Best Foot Forward:* "[Lucy] is really something to conjure with, but it is one of the weaknesses of *Best Foot Forward,* that no one gets much of a chance to conjure with her." Nor did Lucy's dubbed† performance of "You're Lucky" enhance her aura in this production. The two performers who benefited most from *Best Foot Forward* were a pair of recruits from the Broadway edition, Nancy Walker and June Allyson.

For her third 1943 MGM release, Lucy joined with Ann Sothern and Marsha Hunt in a skit for the all-star revue *Thousands Cheer.* The girl trio were seen as prospective WAVES about to receive a medical examination from lascivious Dr. Frank Morgan. It played on screen much neater than the burlesque skit sounds.

Meet the People (1944)‡ had been a cozy little Los Angeles-originated revue, which received a Broadway cold shoulder before being distorted into a message-laden vaudeville movie show. Lucy was top-starred as a Broadway star who has a dual purpose in accepting a job at the Morganville, Delaware, shipyard. Not only will she have a well-publicized opportunity to "meet the people," but there will be a chance to show budding playwright Dick Powell that he was wrong in dismissing her as too snooty for his stage production. Welder-of-the-day Lucy becomes the yard's queen and wins Powell's heart, but it was Virginia O'Brien who was most pleasing on camera, especially with her rendition of "Say That We're Sweethearts Again."§

Nineteen forty-four proved to be very downbeat for Lucy. Despite her effort to mesh career and homelife, professional dictates usually kept Lucy and Arnaz apart. φ Previously he was usually on the road with a band tour while she remained based in Hollywood. By 1944, when he was a corporal in the Army, stationed at Camp Arlington near Riverside, California, he was usually able to return to their ranch home in the San Fernando Valley for weekends. But their domestic harmony had so deteriorated that early in 1944 Lucy filed for a divorce, claiming that Arnaz had frequent and excessive temper tantrums. The couple re-thought their hasty split, for Lucy soon dropped her legal suit.

The situation at MGM was even less stable. Louis B. Mayer and his studio

*Later in 1943 Paramount's programmer-series entry *Henry Aldrich Gets Glamour* used the same premise with less pretentious results.

†By Gloria Grafton.

‡Opened at the Manfield Theatre on December 25, 1940, for a run of 160 performances.

§O'Brien had been signed to an MGM contract as a result of her appearance in the Los Angeles edition of the revue.

φLucy had performed with Arnaz in a stage act at Loew's State Theatre in January, 1942.

regime had promised Lucy a big buildup, initially showing their good intentions by installing her in Norma Shearer's former star dressing room and assigning the lot's most experienced makeup artists to remold her screen image. Everything went smoothly until Lucy was tossed into the mediocre *Meet the People,* which fared poorly. The studio immediately lost interest in Lucy as a major personality. Had Metro not been blessed with the uncomplaining services of Ann Sothern and Angela Lansbury—who each deserved better breaks themselves—Lucy might have been able to make a go at the studio in her old sharp, tart screen types. But that avenue was closed and so were most of the other possible pigeonholed screen types, since MGM was still top-heavy with a huge roster of assorted femmes, who were given preference over floundering Lucy. So for the bulk of her remaining MGM years Lucy sat it out in an office in an obscure section of the lot, passing the time of day with another equally neglected contract player, Buster Keaton, then under a studio pact as a joke consultant for Red Skelton pictures.

Thanks to Lucy's friendly relationship with Katharine Hepburn in their RKO *Stage Door* days, Lucy wangled a third co-starring spot in *Without Love* (1945), based on Hepburn's qualified Broadway success in 1942.* Lucy inherited the wisecracking role of sophisticated real-estate agent Kitty Trimble, a part handled in the Theatre Guild stage production by Audrey Christie. Lucy pitched her witty lines like an expert ballplayer, but the focus was so clearly on the contrived tale of two practical scientists (Hepburn and Spencer Tracy) in overcrowded Washington who wed for convenience, that Lucy and Keenan Wynn (as the amiable souse) were quickly lost in the shuffle.

Later in 1945 Metro dropped drifting Lucy into *Abbott and Costello in Hollywood* as a guest "star" along with such other studio non-celebrities as Preston Foster and Rags Ragland. Lucy and Foster were performers who graciously open a talent agency to promote the budding career of a young singer, Frances Rafferty.

Ziegfeld Follies finally saw release in 1946, having sat in the can for almost two years. It was made in a period when MGM still had faith in Lucy, and she therefore had appropriate billing and showcasing in this star-clustered Technicolor entry. She appeared to stunning advantage in the opening production number, "Bring on the Girls," sung and danced to by Fred Astaire. Lucy is introduced as one of the "beautiful girls" Astaire is crooning about, and she drifts into sight riding one of the live horses on the merry-go-round. High-toned Lucy is clad in a fabulous pink outfit topped by a headdress of huge plumes of feathers. Lucy steps off the horse, whirls her pink cloak at the camera, and then commences to crack her whip at a bevy of chorines (dressed in black cat costumes) encased behind the streamer bars of an abstract cage. Tiger-tamer Lucy dominates the action as the "cats" writhe through their feline dance routine. This brief sequence was a virtual show-

*The stage version opened at the St. James Theatre (November 10, 1942) for a 113-performance run.

stopper of the talent-stuffed film, and the image of pink-clad Lucy at her Ziegfeld best, remains one of the visual highlights of her long career to date.

When Twentieth Century-Fox requested Lucy's screen services to bolster a medium-budgeted murder mystery, *The Dark Corner* (Roxy Theatre, May 8, 1946), she consented to the loan-out. After her semi-ostracism at MGM she had nothing to lose, and perhaps everything to gain, by being in Darryl F. Zanuck's playground. Lucy's part in *The Dark Corner* proved to be much the same type of assignment her long-standing professional rival Eve Arden was handling so deftly at Warner Bros. With no trouble at all, Lucy essayed the acid-tongued secretary of private detective Mark Stevens, he being almost railroaded to jail on a trumped-up manslaughter charge. Clifton Webb was used too sparingly to rephrase the ruthless aesthete he had honed to a fine point in *Laura,* with William Bendix slobbering away as Stevens's disloyal ex-partner.

The Dark Corner was a journeyman credit for Lucy, but Metro's *Easy to Wed* (Capitol Theatre, July 11, 1946) was an entirely different story. MGM had dusted off its *Libeled Lady* (1936) as a vehicle for Van Johnson and Esther Williams, a sure-fire combination in post-World War II America. The plot remained essentially the same as the original, which meant that Jean Harlow's role was up for grabs, and Lucy seized it when neither Ann Sothern nor Angela Lansbury was available. The plotline has managing-editor Keenan Wynn faced with a hefty libel suit by a shy, rich playgirl (Williams). He inveigles his much ignored fiancée (Lucy) to pose as the bride of Johnson in order to make Williams appear to be a husband-stealing vixen. Lucy excelled in her interplay with Wynn, and as the nightclub performer she "sang" a dazzling musical-comedy number, "The Continental Polka." "She snaps her lines over the heads of the other characters," enthused the *New York Herald-Tribune,* "and in pantomime manages to be as scatterbrained and indignant as a wet hen." The Technicolor romp grossed a rosy $4.5 million.

Despite Lucy's overt robbery of the best notices in *Easy to Wed,* Metro and Louis B. Mayer were content to waste her in *Two Smart People* (1946). This B+ picture co-scripted by detective writer Leslie Charteris and directed by Jules Dassin, was a dogeared tale romanticizing crooks to no one's advantage. Con artist John Hodiak is allowed a five-day sidetrip before commencing a jail term in New York. He is determined to have himself a gustatory fling, and, after stopping off in El Paso, Texas, he heads for New Orleans and the Mardi Gras. On his trail are rival cheater Lucy, a benign detective (Lloyd Nolan), and rascal Elisha Cook, Jr., all very interested in discovering where Hodiak has secreted $500,000 in government certificates. MGM palmed off this hodgepodge picture on the dual-bill market.

Two Smart People proved to be Lucy's MGM swan song. The studio persistently refused to cast her in the type of comedy (or even drama) she felt equipped to handle. Decorating musicals, in which half her performance was the offstage dubbed singing of another person, gave her no satisfaction. So she hit the freelance trail. Universal hired her for *Lover Come Back* as a backstop player to male lead George Brent. The feckless comedy presented Lucy as a chic fashion editor (with shoulder-length hair styles and Travis Banton gowns), who discovers that while her husband (Brent) was a war correspondent overseas he had a high old time for himself. In retaliation she dashes off to Nevada determined to win a divorce. Naturally philandering Brent wins her forgiveness. Although Lucy was attractively garbed in *Lover Come Back,* her overbent dramatics were as tiresome as Brent's phlegmatic walk-through performance.

Next Lucy tried United Artists. Perhaps the chief delight of that studio's *Lured* (1947) (a.k.a. *Personal Column)* was its London setting. In the film Scotland Yard inspector Charles Coburn attempts to solve a rash of killings committed by a contemporary Bluebeard. Lucy, an American taxi dancer* stranded in London, confers with Coburn about her missing roommate and ends up working on the case as a lure for the killer. Her adventures lead her into contact with such bizarre types as George Sanders and his business partner, Sir Cedric Hardwicke, artist Boris Karloff, and white-slave dealer Joseph Calleia. Neither Lucy nor the production team for *Lured* won any thanks for their modest contributions to the public's entertainment.

An even less likely piece of claptrap was Columbia's *Her Husband's Affairs* (1947). Despite a Ben Hecht screenplay, the film remained high-paced nonsense going nowhere fast. Franchot Tone and Lucy are a marital team employed at Edward Everett Horton's advertising agency. The duo merchandise a new face cream for waterless, razorless shaving, a by-product of inventor Mikhail Rasumny's embalming fluid. When the cream proves to grow hair instead, they quickly change their ad campaign, pushing the item as a new cure for balding heads. Meanwhile the couple are undergoing severe marital discord, what with Lucy always bailing her less-than-practical husband out of difficulties and displaying too much superiority at the wrong time. A few critics compared Lucy's work here to that of the late Carole Lombard, but the box-office take on *Her Husband's Affairs* was minimal.

Thirty-six-year-old Lucy came to a firm decision in 1947: if she could not achieve top stardom in the movies, perhaps it was finally time to diversify into other show business media on a much larger scale. Thus she embarked on a twenty-two-week West Coast tour of Elmer Rice's *Dream Girl,* and in July, 1947, debuted as a radio series star.† Lucy's choice of a radio vehicle proved sound. "My Favorite Wife," based on characters created by Isabel Scott Rorick in the novel *Mr. and Mrs. Cugat* (which also served as the basis of Paramount's *Are Husbands Necessary?* [1942] featured first Lee Bowman, and then Richard Denning, as Lucy's husband, and Gale Gordon as

---

*Annette Warren dubbed Lucy's vocal interludes.

† She had previously been heard as a regular on Jack Haley's weekly "Wonder Bread Show" for CBS in 1938; been on "Lux Radio Theatre" in *They Drive By Night* (with George Raft and Lana Turner, June 21, 1941) and *Lucky Partners* (with Don Ameche, September 25, 1944); guested on such anthology series as "Suspense" and "Screen Guild Playhouse"; and participated on the panel show "Leave It to the Girls."

Rudolph Atterbury. The program would run until March, 1951, thereafter being transferred to television with Joan Caulfield.

Whatever this rash of activity may have done for Lucy's professional standing, it did nothing to stabilize Lucy's shaky marriage to Arnaz.* It was Lucy who jokingly told the press at this time: "I drive along Ventura Boulevard and pretty soon Desi comes along driving the other way from our ranch to Hollywood. We wave to each other as we pass. Then I have dinner and go to bed early, to be bright and rested for the next day's work, and he'll stay up all night playing (with his band). That's married life?"

After a two-year hiatus from feature films, Lucy returned to the soundstages at the request of Bob Hope, who asked her to team with him in Paramount's *Sorrowful Jones* (1949). Shirley Temple had stolen the spotlight in *Little Miss Marker* (1934), the original picturization of the Damon Runyon story, but Mary Jayne Saunders, her counterpart in the remake, was not up to such a scene-stealing task. This luck proved to be a mixed blessing, for it now allowed wiseacre Hope, as the nimble racetrack tout who unofficially adopts a waif, to hog the camera. Obviously, in this focal shift, the whimsical farce lost its point of view. As in Runyon's *The Big Street*, Lucy was again cast as a club singer,† but this outing was a relatively small part. She did what she could to gussie up her role as the vitriolic doll who grows as fond of Saunders as Hope does, but the buildup of her comedy-foil pranks was nearly all extraneous to the main plot. At best *Sorrowful Jones* was a middling Hope-Lucy Ball showcase. The duo repeated their *Sorrowful Jones* characterizations on "Lux Radio Theatre" on November 21, 1949.

There was even less glory in Lucy's return to RKO for *Easy Living* (1949). That studio was undergoing severe survival pains. Its star roster was so reduced that the Howard Hughes regime considered itself lucky to still have the acting services of Jane Russell, Robert Mitchum, and Jane Greer. But one thing had not altered. Seven years prior Lucy had played second fiddle to Victor Mature in an RKO clinker (*Seven Days Leave*), and now in 1949 she was again doing yeoman's duty in support of Mature in an RKO bomb, *Easy Living*. This empty football story told of an aging bigtime gridiron star (Mature) who, to satisfy his luxury-hungry wife, Elizabeth Scott, is driven to continue playing on the field instead of coaching from the sidelines. Lucy was badly wasted as the understanding team secretary, a hard-shelled babe with a soft heart for all who needed a big sister's shoulder on which to cry.

S. Sylvan Simon, who had directed Lucy in *Abbott and Costello in Hollywood* and *Her Husband's Affairs*, convinced his Columbia boss Harry Cohn that Lucy could be utilized to full advantage by top-casting her in modestly mounted slapstick. Thus Columbia offered Lucy a three-picture, $85,000-per-

---

*After his Army discharge, Arnaz did not return to MGM but trotted over to Universal for *Cuban Pete* (1946) and then to Columbia for *Holiday in Havana* (1948), both slipshod quickies. After several band tours, he became musical director for Bob Hope's radio show.

†Her singing was dubbed by Annette Warren.

film deal, and she readily accepted. Simon, who had now graduated to producer status, assigned Lucy to *Miss Grant Takes Richmond* (1949). Under Lloyd Bacon's smooth direction Lucy had ample occasion to exercise her ever-refining expertise as a dimwitted miss. This time Lucy was a birdbrained secretary (recall the sequence in which her typewriter carriage zooms off its mount?) who discovers that her boss (William Holden) is using his real-estate business as a front for a bookmaking operation. She convinces him to turn honest and boost a new low-cost housing project. The comedy had a very solid gag foundation,* and even the usually wooden Holden demonstrated a flair for flip remarks.

After making a cameo appearance in Rosalind Russell's *A Woman of Distinction* (Columbia, 1950), Lucy returned to Paramount to co-star with Bob Hope again, this time in a color-musical remake of *Ruggles of Red Gap* (1935). This fourth screen edition of Harry Leon Wilson's tale of an English butler who sets an American western town on its heel, was revamped to situate Hope as a ham actor stranded in England and mistakenly hired by Lucy's *nouveau riche* family to serve in the manse back in Red Gap, New Mexico (c. 1912). Bruce Cabot, who had functioned as the villain in *Sorrowful Jones*, was again the baddie in *Fancy Pants*, determined that wealthy Lucy should not fall out of his clutches by wedding bumbling Hope. Much more so than *Sorrowful Jones*, the George Marshall-directed *Fancy Pants* relied on sight gags and illogical slapstick to push the vehicle along to its draggy conclusion. The moviegoing public, however, bought the package. Lucy had gone on a road tour to Chicago with Desi Arnaz to work out the frogs in her "uneasy soprano" voice so she could sing her own numbers in *Fancy Pants*.† The critics politely focused on her looks ("gorgeously brazen" said the *New York Times*) and ignored her vocal gymnastics. Lucy and Hope would recreate their *Fancy Pants* roles on "Lux Radio Theatre" on September 10, 1951.

Lucy had legitimate high hopes of winning the coveted female lead in Columbia's *Born Yesterday* (1950) but eventually lost out in the talent competition to Judy Holliday.‡ As a consolation, S. Sylvan Simon handed her *The Fuller Brush Girl* (1950), which he produced and Lloyd Bacon directed.§ The comedy taught the moviegoing public two essentials: that

---

*Harry Cohn took no chances with the release of *Miss Grant Takes Richmond*. According to reporter-author Bob Thomas in his *King Cohn* (1967), the mogul persuaded pal Frank Sinatra to request the fun-but-mild film comedy as the feature to be booked on the bill at the Capitol Theatre when he played an engagement there in October, 1949. When the packaged bill garnered $122,000 during its first week of showcase there, Cohn was able to promote the picture as a big moneytaker in trade-paper advertisements.

†Including the duet "Home Cooking" sung with Hope.

‡Harry Cohn, initially unenthusiastic about the screen potential of stage performer Judy Holliday, considering using either Lucy or Jean Parker (then heading the national company of the show) for the role.

§Simon had directed Columbia's *The Fuller Brush Man* (1948) with Red Skelton, then on loan-out from MGM.

Fuller Brush girls do not necessarily peddle brushes (cosmetics was Lucy's game), and that Lucy was by now a most adept farceur. In the course of the film, Lucy and her lamebrained boyfriend (Eddie Albert) are involved in homicide, tangle with kidnappers, and take it on the lam from misunderstanding cops. The entire show was heavily laced with broad slapstick antics, but they were entirely in keeping with the film's tone. Red Skelton even provided a walk-on cameo as a goodwill gesture to his onscreen successor in the *Fuller Brush* series. One of the funnier scenes in *The Fuller Brush Girl* occurs when Lucy pursues the murderers to a burlesque theatre, where she is forced to rig herself up as one of the performers (proving her apprentice screen work in *Dance, Girl, Dance* had not been for naught). As a dumb-Dora comedienne Lucy jumped handsprings around Columbia's perennial asinine-housewife heroine, Penny Singleton of *Blondie* fame.

After these partial successes, how did forty-year-old Lucy end up as a scantily clad harem princess in Columbia's *The Magic Carpet* (1951)? There was still one more feature to go under her three-film Columbia pact. S. Sylvan Simon died, and Harry Cohn, already happily reconciled to promoting Judy Holliday as the lot's prime nonsense queen, wished to renege on his deal with Miss Ball. Lucy wanted the $85,000 from Cohn, picture or no picture. During this impasse, Lucy's agent came up with a fine offer for a co-starring part in Cecil B. De Mille's *The Greatest Show on Earth* (Paramount, 1952), in which Lucy would play Angel the elephant girl. She begged Cohn to postpone her Columbia commitment, but he refused and demanded that she fulfill her obligation by appearing in *The Magic Carpet*. One look at the script was enough to confirm that this projected film was a piece of the worst kind of *dreck,* not even fit for the moppet trade. But Lucy surprised Cohn by accepting the lead in the Sam Katzman color quickie (shot in eight days) with a much younger John Agar as her Lochinvar. Only after the programmer was finished did Lucy advise Cohn that the reason for her telltale weight gain was not overeating but pregnancy. She had the last laugh on a usually astute Cohn, but her impending motherhood cost her the part in De Mille's circus epic. She was replaced in that film by Gloria Grahame. Ironically, Lucy would have a miscarriage just as she had suffered one previously during the first year of her marriage to Arnaz.

After Lucy recuperated, she toured the declining vaudeville circuit with Arnaz and his band, performing in a situation-comedy skit very closely akin to her radio series, "My Favorite Husband." In fact Arnaz had designed this sketch as a testing ground for a potential video series, reasoning there was more money to be made on the small-screen medium than his $150,000 yearly gross from strenuous cross-country club touring.* Another pregnancy cut short this tour, and on July 17, 1951, Lucy gave birth, by Caesarean section, to a girl whom she and Arnaz named Lucie Desirée.

---

*Lucy and Desi had already appeared as guest artists on such 1950 video variety shows as those hosted by Ed Wynn and Bob Hope.

Despite all their domestic differences, Lucy has always credited Arnaz with the concept and business execution of the project which became television's "I Love Lucy." With $5,000 in equity capital, Lucy and Arnaz launched Desilu Productions, Inc., and he sold CBS-TV on the situation-comedy series to star Lucy and himself. It was Arnaz who convinced the CBS brass that the half-hour show must be performed in front of a live audience,* and it was Arnaz who refused to give up ownership to the films (later videotapes) that would record the live telecasts. Arnaz also persuaded Philip Morris Cigarettes to sponsor the pilot shot of "I Love Lucy," which cost $30,000.

With scripts written by Jess Oppenheimer, Madalyn Pugh, and Bob Carroll (the team that had scripted Lucy's "My Favorite Husband" radio show) and photography by the expert Karl Kreund, "I Love Lucy" debuted on Monday evening, October 15, 1951. Arnaz had given in to CBS's demand that the show should focus on a still struggling Cuban bandleader and his daffy wife, rather than mirror their real-life selves. And it all worked out for the better. William Frawley and Vivian Vance were cast as their landlord-neighbors, Fred and Ethel Mertz, who provided the straight persons and accomplices necessary to spin out Lucy's wild escapades. From the start the adventures of Ricky and Lucy Ricardo of Manhattan made a vivid impression on American televiewers (and later on watchers all over the world). The program fast climbed into the top-ten viewer favorites and remained there for all six seasons on the air. In the flush of her newfound success, Lucy admitted: "I don't know if I'll ever work again in a theatre movie. It doesn't interest me a bit. . . . TV is like a long, cool relaxing drink." As for her submergence into lowbrow hijinks: "Look. I'm just a slob. I have no desire to play heavy drama. I want to do things with heart in them. Yes. That's as much drama as I care about."

In 1951, when Red Skelton won an Emmy Award as best comedian on the video screen, he told the audience, "Ladies and gentlemen, you've given it to the wrong redhead." The following year Lucy won the first of four Emmy Awards for her television work.†

On "I Love Lucy," middle-class Lucy Ricardo was always up to some wild scheme to foster one of her outrageous pet ambitions: (1) to make Ricky demonstrate his undying love for her; (2) to finally gain a foothold in the elusive world of show business like her bongo-playing husband; (3) to outdo one of her more affluent friends; (4) to squirm out of a horrendous predicament engendered by her bragging, stupidity, or kindheartedness; or (5) to prove a point to Ricky and/or the Mertzes. With one of the above premises quickly established, the program would escalate promptly into the major comedy skit, with Lucy just as likely to appear in the guise of Harpo Marx, as to be found stealing John Wayne's cemented footprints from the lobby area of

* Lucy's perky performance during the recent road tour proved that point.
† Lucy won in 1952, 1955, 1966, 1967, and has a total of eleven Emmy nominations to date.

Grauman's Chinese Theatre. Since the show continually abounded with references to persons and places from Lucy's childhood in Jamestown, New York, it was no wonder that when she became pregnant again, the situation was utilized to full advantage on the show, with an episode planned to coincide with the birth of her real-life child (born by Caesarean section on January 19, 1953, and christened Desi).*

Because Lucy was riding the crest of international popularity she was quickly able to slough off an unfortunate episode from her past, which cropped up in the wake of the House Committee on Un-American Activities hearings. According to Lucy's testimony before the committee, in 1936 she had signed a nomination petition for a Communist candidate to the California State Assembly. She claimed it was done at the insistence of her grandfather, Fred C. Hunt, then living with her in Los Angeles. This reasoning did not impress King Features columnist Westbrook Pegler, who on September 23, 1953, devoted most of his column to "this Ball woman [who] knew what she was doing when she registered with the Communists." But the loyal public would not accept any such contra-remarks about their beloved redhead, and the incident soon dropped from the news. Her network employer, CBS-TV, showed its good faith during this crisis by signing an $8 million long-term pact with Desilu Productions.

The next year was even more successful for Lucy. Taking into consideration her phenomenal television triumph, MGM, now under the aegis of Dore Schary, begged Lucy (and Desi Arnaz) to return there for feature-filmmaking. For a combined $250,000 salary, the husband-wife duo starred in Vincente Minnelli's *The Long, Long Trailer* (Radio City Music Hall, February 18, 1954) a truly hilarious color comedy essentially constructed on one joke (i.e., how an oversized trailer can nearly but not quite bring clumsy Lucy to terms). Lucy demonstrated on the wide screen her masterful flair for becoming a symbol of frustrated humanity coping with a pesky inanimate object. Arnaz was again her straight man, and far more professional in his thankless role than most people have credited him over the years on television or in the 1950s movies. *The Long, Long Trailer* made a fine showing in theatrical release. Later in 1954 Ed Sullivan devoted the entire hour of a "Toast of the Town" program (October 3, 1954) to saluting the phenomenal show business success of Lucy and Arnaz. Thereafter MGM anxiously pursued the couple to make another feature for the studio, *Forever Darling* (Loew's State, February 9, 1956). It was an unsteady mixture of domestic comedy, fantasy, and slapstick that left filmgoers baffled and unsatisfied, what with James Mason as the guardian angel come to earth to patch up the homelife squabbles of a young research chemist (Arnaz) and his spoiled, immature wife (Lucy). The weak box-office returns on this Desi Arnaz-produced feature suggested that perhaps Lucy and Arnaz had passed the peak of their popularity.

*On television, actor Richard Keith would play little Ricky.

Lucy and Arnaz held the same opinion, for after the conclusion of the sixth video season (in May, 1957) of "I Love Lucy," it was duly announced the show was being shelved. With the $5 million earned from selling CBS the rerun rights to the segments, Desilu acquired the then-idle RKO Studios at a reported $6.15 million price tag. In its years of activity Desilu had outgrown its five acres and nine soundstages and obviously needed additional production space. The RKO acquisition gave the teleproduction outfit fifteen acres and sixteen soundstages at the Gower Street lot in Hollywood and fourteen acres and eleven soundstages (plus twenty-eight acres of backlots) in Culver City.

In the fall of 1957, Lucy, Arnaz, Vivian Vance and William Frawley returned to television in a series of one-hour specials, utilizing an expanded "I Love Lucy" format and relying on guest stars (from Ernie Kovacs to Betty Grable to Tallulah Bankhead) to carry the proceedings. This program later merged into the "Westinghouse Desilu Playhouse," a continually less-than-scintillating hour anthology-drama show hosted by Arnaz.*

Meanwhile Lucy's marriage to Arnaz had become so stormy that it could no longer be kept under conventional wraps. She admitted that Desilu and "I Love Lucy" had been initially spawned as a means to restore harmony into their homelife, but that it no longer provided a saving crutch to their relationship. On February 26, 1960, their separation was publicly announced, and on May 4, 1960, Lucy received an interlocutory divorce decree. Each party retained a half-interest in Desilu Productions, Lucy got their Beverly Hills home and $450-a-month child support. Arnaz received their ranch in Riverside, California, with their Palm Springs hotel placed in trust for the children. The headlined divorce prompted newsmen to recurrently pepper Lucy with questions on her marital split. Lucy explained: "It was romance—out of step. It was romantic, and fun, occasionally. It was emotional. But our senses of values were different." She says that once she decided on a divorce action, "I understood I would have to rearrange my life, and find out what it means to be really selfish. Selfishness means to be true to oneself and to what one needs, I decided." And to the repeated query: "Am I happy? No. Not yet. I will be. I've been humiliated. That's not easy for a woman."†

But Lucy had little opportunity to think of her uncertain personal life, for she was soon involved in a $400,000-plus Broadway musical, *Wildcat,* whose too obvious similarity to *The Rainmaker* was largely due to N. Richard Nash having authored both Broadway shows. *Wildcat* was set in the Mexican border town of Centavo City in 1912, with Lucy playing a wildcatter equally determined to strike oil, to provide a good future for her lame sister (Paula

*Lucy made her television "dramatic" debut on the series in the episode *K. O. Kitty* (November 17, 1958).

†After his divorce from Lucy, Arnaz married Edith Mack Hirsch in 1963 and two years later formed his own television production company, which packaged "The Mothers-in-Law," with Eve Arden and Kaye Ballard, among other shows. Arnaz not only produced that comedy series but directed and appeared in several episodes during its two-season run on the air.

Stewart), and to subdue to marital status the burly drill-team boss, Joe Dynamite (Keith Andes). The songs by Cy Coleman and Carolyn Leigh, save for the catchy "Hey, Look Me Over!" (shouted rather than sung by Lucy), were unremarkable, and director Michael Kidd was far better at choreographing the dance ensembles and manipulating the Peter Larkins sets than at manipulating the cast to good advantage. During the out-of-town tryouts, Arnaz was frequently in evidence as a consultant (since Desilu had pushed several hundred-thousands into the show). *Wildcat* dragged into New York on December 15, 1960, at the Alvin Theatre to very mixed notices. For forty-nine-year-old Lucy, performing the arduous one-woman show proved to be too much of a physical chore, and when she collapsed on stage on April 20, 1961, it was decided to close the musical after only 171 performances. Over $165,000 in advance ticket sales had to be refunded, a good deal of it at personal cost to her. "When I left the show I was so tired they almost carried me out in a coffin," Lucy sadly recalls. But she adds with vehemence: "I learned something good, even from a horrible experience like *Wildcat*. I learned the people came to the theatre to see the Lucy they knew and I didn't give it to them."

In the interim Lucy's third co-starring vehicle with Bob Hope, *The Facts of Life* (1960), opened to very respectable notices, if not sensational box-office receipts. Filmed at Desilu Studios under Melvin Frank's direction, the black-and-white feature ably depicted the amusing vicissitudes of two middle-aged marrieds of the Pasadena suburban set who decide that it is just too darn much trouble to have an affair. More than any of the other Lucy-Hope ventures, *The Facts of Life* was grounded in reasonable plausibility, making its spoof of extramarital jaunting all the more delightful. There were the expected sight gags (not as funny as before since both Lucy and Hope were showing distinct signs of aging), but more of the humor derived from the on-target repartee between the two top-notch gagsters. Even the occasional bit of stale dialog sounded fresh with their rapid-fire delivery, as, for example, when Lucy and Hope prepare to check into a motel for a clandestine evening. Lucy advises him to give the registration clerk "a real married-sounding name." Hope retorts, "How about George and Martha Washington?" Likewise, when Lucy informs Hope that she cannot make their rendezvous because her son is ill, and Hope complains, Lucy counters, "If you were flat on your back with a fever of 102, would you like to be left alone with my mother?"

During the strenuous run of *Wildcat* Lucy had been persuaded by co-star Paula Wayne to accept a blind date, who turned out to be stand-up comedian Gary Morton.* The couple soon found themselves steady dating, and thereafter Lucy and Morton, he six years her junior, were wed on November 19,

---

*Born Goldapper, Morton had learned the rudiments of his comedian art while in the Army's special services during World War II and had been performing largely on the Catskill club circuit. By 1960, however, he had graduated to occasional bookings at the Copacabana Club in Manhattan. He had been previously wed to actress Jacqueline Inmoor, but that marriage was annulled.

1961 at Manhattan's Marble Collegiate Church with the Reverend Norman Vincent Peale officiating.* Instead of a honeymoon, Morton completed a pre-arranged nightclub tour and Lucy, after selling her recently acquired $30,000 New York City apartment, returned to California, where she recuperated for a year from her *Wildcat* outing. But life was not all non-business, for she was now madame chairman of Desilu Productions, Inc., and felt a very strong obligation to promote her company's product (which at various times included such video shows as "The Untouchables," "The Ann Sothern Show," "The Greatest Show on Earth," and such space lessees as "The Real McCoys," "Star Trek," "Mission: Impossible," and "The Danny Thomas Show"). Lucy realized the best way to sell CBS on Desilu's shakier video pilot shows was to use her possible appearance in a new teleseries as a bargaining wedge.

Thus on October 1, 1962, she returned to television in the "Here's Lucy" program, which cast her as a widow with two children and Vivian Vance as a divorcee, both living in Westchester. William Frawley, who had gone on to *My Three Sons,* was replaced by Gale Gordon, who functioned as an all-purpose straight man. Lucy was still Lucy—older and deeper of voice, and pressing harder for laughs, but still Lucy. The public loved it and so did CBS-TV. Each spring, as if by preordained plan, Lucy and CBS would under-go the same publicized courtship ritual: the question was *not* whether CBS would renew Lucy's program, but whether Lucy would renew the network. With a step up in deferred bonuses and a green light to other Desilu video products Lucy would sign on the dotted line. The professional coquette had become the number-one female comedy attraction in American television (and the world). "Here's Lucy" moved its locale to California in the 1965 season with Vivian Vance departing the show to freelance and Gale Gordon appearing first as Lucy's employment-agent boss and then as her relative and bank-manager employer.

In 1967, for a reported $7 million, Lucy sold the major part of her Desilu stock† to Gulf and Western (the parent company of Paramount Pictures) and, sighing with audible relief, announced: "Now I've just sold the whole damn thing to a bigger corp. and pretty soon they'll take my name off the door and I'll be free, opening for everything. It's really exciting." Lucy, who had appeared in assorted CBS variety-show specials, including *Lucy in London* (October 24, 1966), and had even replaced Gary Moore for a spell in the fall of 1964 as the moderator of a loosely formated CBS-radio weekly day-time show, continued onward as the matron queen of video comedy. In 1968 she decided that it was time to bring her two children (Desi, Jr. and Lucie) into the "Lucy Show" family, not so much to milk audience curiosity, which

---

*Present at the wedding were Lucy's mother, her two children, and Paula Wayne and her comedian husband, Jack Carter.

†In 1962 Lucy had acquired from Arnaz his stock in Desilu at a price of over two million, giving her 600,650 shares (52 per cent of the outstanding stock). Lucy surprised Hollywood observers by her assumption of Arnaz's post as corporate head and her successful running of the business for the next five years. There were many times when her overeager desire to take part in every facet of corporate business was a detriment to Desilu.

happened, of course, but, as she phrased it, to get them away from the "unhappy misfits" at Los Angeles High School where boys took drugs and girls got pregnant.

Lucy's fourth and final theatrical feature to date with Bob Hope was *Critic's Choice* (Warner Bros., 1963), a none-too-smooth screen adaptation of Ira Levin's satirical stage comedy, which had starred Henry Fonda on Broadway.* There was very little reality to Hope's broad portrayal of a theatre critic for a large New York newspaper who fears the dread effects resulting from his wife's play being presented on the Great White Way. Lucy did her darnedest to be sincere in the color feature, whether dealing with Hope's tired flippancies or the sirenish advances of his ex-wife (Marilyn Maxwell), resisting the flirtations of bohemian stage-director Rip Torn, or trying to toss some motherly advice to their precocious son (Ricky Kelman). The overblown feature fell apart at the seams most spectacularly in the scene in which an inebriated Hope covers the opening night of Lucy's play, weaving and muttering his precarious way in and onto the theatre's crowded balcony. By opting for inexcusably low slapstick at this strategic point, director Don Weis sank the film for good.

Four years later Lucy was induced to return to films with a cameo part in Twentieth Century-Fox's *A Guide for the Married Man* (1967), directed in haphazard fashion by Gene Kelly. In one of the lesser blackout skits, Lucy is seen as the wife of blue-collar worker Art Carney, he demonstrating how a husband can break out of the domestic fold for an evening by simply utilizing aggressive behavior. A combination of an unbecoming upsweep hairdo, excessive pancake makeup, and unflattering photography made Lucy look every one of her fifty-six years.

But the following year Lucy redeemed herself by packaging and starring in *Yours, Mine and Ours* (United Artists, 1968), based on the true story of Navy Warrant Officer Francis L. Beardsley. Lucy had initially selected Fred MacMurray for the male lead, but when he was unavailable she settled for her *The Big Street* co-star, Henry Fonda. In an easygoing characterization reminiscent of his *Mr. Roberts* role, Fonda provided a perfect counterpart to the frantic San Franciscan Lucy, a widowed mother of eight who contemplates marriage to widower Fonda, the father of ten children. Lucy selected her old MGM pal Van Johnson to essay the contrived role of oncamera matchmaker. Surprisingly, director Melville Shavelson whipped the seemingly trite story into fine shape and it emerged one of the box-office winners of the year with a domestic rental gross of $11.5 million. One has only to compare *Yours, Mine and Ours* to the similar but more ridiculous *With Six You Get Egg-roll* (Doris Day, Brian Keith, 1968) to appreciate the virtues of Lucy's version.

Ever since selling Desilu to Gulf and Western Lucy has been content to bathe in the rosy glow of her seemingly unassailable position as the popular veteran star of a top-twenty teleseries, and more particularly as a mother hen

*Opened at the Ethel Barrymore Theatre on December 14, 1960, and ran for 189 performances.

to her two children and to Hollywood in general.* The change from the rip-roaring Lucy of the 1920s and early 1930s to the Lucy of today is a fantastic one, with each year seeing her becoming more conservative in philosophy as she strives harder to outwardly convey a contemporaneousness to her thoughts and actions, which display too well the generation gap.† She registered parental dismay when son Desi became involved with established older actress Patty Duke, the latter claiming that her child (born in 1971) was fathered by young Desi. Lucy is increasingly more prone to—therapeutically?—talk about that disastrous episode in young Desi's life: "I had my doubts if the baby was Desi's at all. I said to him, "You feel responsible? Boy, you're all of 16½, you want to spend the rest of your life with this neurotic person?" On the other hand, when Desi, Jr. later began squiring Liza "Cabaret" Minnelli about the world, Lucy tacitly offered her sanction, even though Liza had yet to divorce singer Peter Allen. (Lucy explained, "I'm glad Desi, Jr. found her. Especially after the ghastly thing with Patty Duke. . . I try to be a mother to her [Liza]." As for daughter Lucie, Lucy is quite proud of the girl, especially because she has never been a real problem like Desi, Jr. Part of Lucy's approval of Lucie is that she remains close at mother's side, continuing to be an active part of the teleseries (to no one's advantage). Lucy admits she was disappointed that her daughter's marriage and divorce from twenty-nine-year-old producer-actor Philip Vandervort had to occur, but remains silent about Lucie's new beau, once-divorced female impressionist Jim Bailey. Said Lucy at one point during her children's many personal crises, "I worked for years for a quiet personal life and to have it personally impinged on, with no recourse, is hard."

Although Lucy never got around to doing a stage rendition of *Hello Dolly!* (she was also considered for the movie version directed by Gene Kelly) or appearing with Jackie Gleason in a telespecial devoted to Lillian Russell and Diamond Jim Brady, she is now finally achieving her 1960s ambition, which may prove the climax to her show business career. In early 1973 she stepped before the Warner Bros. cameras as the lead in the movie rendition of *Mame,* directed by Gene Saks. Seven years before, when the musical had opened on Broadway‡ and Angela Lansbury astounded everyone but herself by becoming the toast of New York as the singing and dancing *Auntie Mame,** it was assumed that Lansbury would play in the eventual filmization. But by the time Warner Bros. completed its $3 million purchase price of the screen

*In 1971 Lucy moved Lucille Ball Productions from Paramount-Desilu to Universal Studios, where in the same year Desi, Jr. made his motion picture debut in *Red Sky at Morning,* receiving better notices than the film itself. Later in 1971 he appeared to personal advantage in the telefeature *Mr. and Mrs. Bo Jo Jones* (ABC) and he is currently starred in the feature film *Marco* in the title role.

†Lucy of today unequivocally says: "Women's Lib? I don't know the meaning of it! Politics? Definitely not on my agenda. I'm tired of the ugly. Fred Astaire and Ginger Rogers dancing, that's my idea of entertainment. As an entertainer, I don't believe in messages."

‡*Mame* opened on Broadway at the Winter Garden Theatre on May 24, 1966, and ran for 1,058 performances.

*Rosalind Russell starred on Broadway and in the movies as Auntie Mame.

rights, Lansbury had gone on to such Broadway failures as *Dear World* and *Prettybelle* and destroyed her magical allure. During the various changeovers in Warners' executive leadership the *Mame* project remained in a hazy background, with no one willing to make an official pronouncement on who would be the new Mame oncamera. Persistent rumors had it that when Lucy broke her ankle in a skiing accident in mid-1972 she relinquished her potential for the choice part in a movie-starved Hollywood. But the game lady pulled more than one string and not only salvaged her "Lucy Show" 1972-73 season by having scripts rewritten to take into account her physical disability, but she parlayed her marquee name against Warners' need to recoup its investment, and got that studio's brass to hold up production till her injury healed.

Clearly Lucy is still one of the major entertainment forces to reckon with on the Hollywood or any other scene. But (sub)consciously she is enough of a realist to know that *Mame* may well be the last high-water mark of her professional career, certainly of her film work. As such, she has been observed as twice the bundle of growing energy she usually is on the job, pushing her present status of queen bee to the ultimate, almost in a frenzy of controlled desperation to make each oncamera moment count to the fullest. As she told reporter Charles Higham: "Up to *Mame* my only exercise had been never sitting down for two seconds, running around constantly. For *Mame* I had to learn not only to walk again [referring to her skiing accident], but to dance again. I hadn't danced in a movie for 30 years or more. Now I'm up at 5 every day. No social life, nothing. Jesus! Making movies! It's like you're running backward!"

Lucy the self-indoctrinator is convinced that making *Mame* has a purpose above and beyond its entertainment value. "I hope that in *Mame*," she told Higham, "we'll glorify a little something called hope and faith and love. The only thing that worries me about it is will anybody want to go see it. The queues are for sex and violence."

Today in her sixties, Lucy has outsurvived and outbested most all of her stage and screen female contemporaries, a fact tacitly admitted by her queenly, sometimes waspish pose on recent television talk-show outings. There was genuine consternation, regret, and wistfulness when Lucy announced in March, 1974 that she was withdrawing from the weekly tv show arena, planning to focus on occasional video specials and additional family-oriented motion pictures. Her exhaustive cross-country tour to promote *Mame* has convinced her, if not the critics or more sophisticated moviegoers, that America is still eager for her brand of entertainment. She remains outwardly insistent that people yet crave the type of wholesome, semi-slapstick comedy that was the mainstay of the 1950s "I Love Lucy" outings. Any suggestions that this thinking or the lady herself is old hat are met by icy glares of denial by Queen Lucy. Obviously having worked so hard to attain her show business throne, she intends to keep it and her subjects intact.

Now that her professional future is taking a somewhat different tact, Lucy can occasionally take some time out of her determinedly busy daily schedule to hold court at her 1000 Roxbury Drive, Beverly Hills, home.† Nowadays she is no longer a practicing Catholic but instead attends services conducted by Norman Vincent Peale. She is vocally anti-President Nixon and the handling of the Vietnam situation, yet arch conservative on most other major issues. Gracious when necessary yet always dogmatic, the enormously wealthy Lucy firmly believes in keeping her fingers in all phases of show business, whether appearing on multistar tele-specials, attending industry functions, or setting up scholarships like the one in dramatic writing at the University of California at Los Angeles. Her continued driving force stems from the same rationale that pushed her to and over so many professional hurdles throughout the decades: "I have to work or I am nothing."

† Lucy's mother lives nearby, and brother Fred manages the Palm Springs hotel complex.

Feature Film Appearances
LUCILLE BALL

BROADWAY THRU A KEYHOLE (UA, 1933) 90 M.

Director, Lowell Sherman; story, Walter Winchell; screenplay, Gene Towne; songs, Mack Gordon and Harry Revel; camera, Barney McGill; editor, Maurice Wright.

Constance Cummings (Joan Whelan); Russ Columbo (Clark Brian); Paul Kelly (Frank Rocci); Blossom Seeley (Sybil Smith); Gregory Ratoff (Max Mefooski); Texas Guinan (Tex Kaley); Hugh O'Connell (Chuck Haskins); Hobart Cavanaugh (Peanuts Dinwiddle); C. Henry Gordon (Tim Crowley); William Burress (Thomas Barnum); Helen Jerome Eddy (Esther); Lucille Ball, Ann Sothern (Girls at Beach).

BLOOD MONEY (UA, 1933) 66 M.

Producer, Joseph M. Schenck, Darryl F. Zanuck; associate producer, William Goetz, Raymond Griffith; director, Rowland Brown; screenplay, Brown, Hal Long; music director, Alfred Newman; camera, James Van Trees; editor, Lloyd Nosler.

George Bancroft (Bill Bailey); Frances Dee (Elaine Talbart); Chick Chandler (Davy); Judith Allen (Ruby Darling); Blossom Seeley (Singer); Etienne Girardot (Bailey's Assistant); George Regas (Charlie); Theresa Harris (Maid); Ann Brody (Client); Sandra Shaw (Job Seeker); Henry Kolker (Managing Editor); Bradley Page (District Attorney); Joe Sawyer (Red); Noel Francis (Red's Girl); Clarence Wilson (Judge); John Webb (Detective); Lucille Ball (Davy's Girl at Race); John Bleifer (Henchman); Theresa Harris (Jessica).

ROMAN SCANDALS (UA, 1933) 93 M.

Producer, Samuel Goldwyn; director, Frank Tuttle; story, George S. Kaufman, Robert E. Sherwood; adaptation, William Anthony McGuire; additional dialog, George Oppenheimer, Arthur Sheekman, Nat Perrin; songs, Al Dubin and Harry Warren, L. Wolfe Gilbert and Warren; choreography, Busby Berkeley; chariot sequence director, Ralph Cedar; sound, Vinton Vernon; camera, Gregg Toland; editor, Stuart Heisler.

Eddie Cantor (Eddie); Ruth Etting (Olga); Gloria Stuart (Princess Sylvia); David Manners (Josephus); Verree Teasdale (Empress Agrippa); Edward Arnold (Emperor Valerius); Alan Mowbray (Major Domo); Jack Rutherford (Manius); Grace Poggi, Aileen Riggin (Slave Dancers); Willard Robertson (Warren F. Cooper); Harry Holm (Mayor of West Rome); Lee Kohlmar (Storekeeper); Stanley Fields (Slave Auctioneer); The Abbottiers (Florence Wilson, Rose Kirsner, Genevieve Irwin, Dolly Bell) (Slave Market Soloists); Charles C. Wilson (Police Chief Charles Pratt); Clarence Wilson (Buggs, the Museum Keeper); Stanley Andrews (Official); Stanley Blystone (Cop/Roman Jailer); William Wagner (Slave Buyer); Louise Carver (Lady Slave Bidder); Francis Ford (Citizen); Charles Arnt (Food Taster); Harry Cording, Lane Chandler, Duke York (Soldiers); Michael Mark (Assistant Cook); Dick Alexander (Guard); Frank

Hagney (Lucius, an Aide); John Ince (Senator); Paul Porcasi (Chief); Jane Darwell (Beauty Salon Manager); Billy Barty (Little Eddie); Iris Shunn (Girl); Katharine Mauk, Rosaline Fromson, Mary Lange, Vivian Keefer, Barbara Pepper, Theo Plane, Lucille Ball (Slave Girls).

MOULIN ROUGE   (UA, 1934) 70 M.

Producer, Darryl F. Zanuck; director, Sidney Lanfield; screenplay, Nunnally Johnson, Henry Lehrman; art director, Richard Day, Joseph Wright; music director, Alfred Newman; choreography, Russell Markert; songs, Al Dubin and Harry Warren; camera, Charles Rosher; editor, Lloyd Nosler.

Constance Bennett (Helen Hall); Franchot Tone (Douglas Hall); Tullio Carminati (Le Maire); Helen Westley (Mrs. Morris); Andrew Tombes (McBride); Russ Brown (Joe); Hobart Cavanaugh (Drunk); Georges Renavent (Frenchman); Fuzzy Knight (Eddie); Russ Columbo, The Boswell Sisters (Themselves); Lucille Ball, Barbara Pepper (Chorus Girls); Ivan Lebedeff (Ramon); Richard Powell (Doorman); Stanley Blystone (Cop); Larry Steers (Extra).

NANA   (UA, 1934) 89 M.

Producer, Samuel Goldwyn; director, Dorothy Arzner; based on the novel by Emile Zola; screenplay, Willard Mack, Harry Wagstaff Gribble; songs, Lorenz Hart and Richard Rodgers; camera, Gregg Toland; editor, Frank Lawrence.

Anna Sten (Nana); Phillips Holmes (Lt. George Muffat); Lionel Atwill (Col. Andre Muffat); Richard Bennett (Gaston Greiner); Mae Clarke (Satin); Muriel Kirkland (Mimi); Reginald Owen (Bordenave); Jessie Ralph (Zoe); Lawrence Grant (Grand Duke Alexis); Lucille Ball (Chorus Girl).

BOTTOMS UP   (Fox, 1934) 85 M.

Producer, B. G. De Sylva; director, David Butler, story-screenplay, De Sylva, Butler, Sid Silvers; songs, Harold Adamson and Burton Lane; Gus Kahn and Richard Whiting; music director, C. Bakaleinikoff; art director, Gordon Wiles; choreography, costumes, Russell Patterson; sound, Joseph Aiken; camera, Arthur Miller; editor, Irene Morra.

Spencer Tracy (Smoothie King); Pat Paterson (Wanda Gale); John Boles (Hal Reede); Harry Green (Louis Baer, the Producer); Herbert Mundin (Limey Brock); Sid Silvers (Spud Mosco); Thelma Todd (Judith Marlowe); Dell Henderson (Director Lane Worthing); Douglas Wood (Baldwin); Robert Emmett O'Connor (Detective Rooney); Suzanne Kaaren (Beer's Secretary); Johnny Boyle (Dance Specialty); Sammy Glasser (Harmonica Player); Walter Hardwick (Waiter); David Field (Reporter); Samuel E. Hines (Bellboy); Mariska Aldrich (Opera Singer); Ernest Wood (Hotel Clerk); Johnny Murray (Radio Announcer); Allen Connor (Ticket Taker); Ned Norton, William R. Arnold, Arthur Loft ("Yes" Men); Loretta Rush, Vera Payton, Opal Ernie, Lucille Ball (Girls); Frank O'Connor (Director); Richard Carle, Cecil Cunningham, Ferdinand Munier (Bits).

HOLD THAT GIRL   (Fox, 1934) 66 M.

Director, Hamilton MacFadden; story-screenplay, Dudley Nichols, Lamar Trotti; sound, Al Protzman; songs, George Marion, Jr. and Richard Whiting; Furman Brown and Frederick Hollander; camera, George Schneiderman.

James Dunn (Barney Sullivan); Claire Trevor (Tony Bellamy); Alan Edwards (Tom Mallory); Gertrude Michael (Dorothy Lamont); John Davidson (Ackroyd); Robert McWade (McCloy); Effie Ellser (Grandmother); Jay Ward (Warren); Lucille Ball (Girl).

BULLDOG DRUMMOND STRIKES BACK   (UA, 1934) 83 M.

Producer, Samuel Goldwyn; director, Roy Del Ruth; based on the novel by H. C. McNeile; adaptation, Henry Lehrman; screenplay, Nunnally Johnson; camera, Peverell Marley; editor, Allen McNeil.

Ronald Colman (Captain Hugh Drummond); Loretta Young (Lola Field); C. Aubrey Smith (Inspector Neilsen); Charles Butterworth (Algy); Una Merkel (Gwen); Warner Oland (Prince Achmed); George Regas (Singh); Mischa Auer (Hassan); Kathleen Burke (Jane Sothern); Arthur Hohl (Dr. Sothern); Ethel Griffies (Mrs. Field); H. N. Clugston (Mr. Field); Douglas Gerrard (Parker); William O'Brien (Banquet Servant); Vernon Steele, Creighton Hale, Pat Somerset (Wedding Guests); Gunnis Davis (Man with Harsh Voice); Charles Irwin (Cockney Drunk on Street); Halliwell Hobbes, E. E. Clive, Yorke Sherwood (Bobbies); Wilson Benge (Neilsen's Valet); Olaf Hytten (Hotel Clerk); Charles McNaughton (Hotel Manager); Lucille Ball (Girl); Bob Kortman (Henchman); Doreen Monroe (Woman in Hotel Room); Billy Bevan (Man in Hotel Room).

THE AFFAIRS OF CELLINI   (UA, 1934) 90 M.

Director, Gregory La Cava; based on the play *The Firebrand* by Edwin Justus Mayer; screenplay, Bess Meredyth; assistant director, Fred Fox; ballet master, Adolph Bolm; music, Alfred Newman; camera, Charles Rosher; editor, Barbara McLean.

Fredric March (Benvenuto Cellini); Constance Bennett (Dutchess of Florence); Frank Morgan (Alessandro, Duke of Florence); Fay Wray (Angela); Vince Barnett (Ascanio); Jessie Ralph (Beatrice); Louis Calhern (Ottaviano); Jay Eaton (Polverino); Paul Harvey (Emissary); John Rutherford (Captain of Guards); Irene Ware (Girl); Lucille Ball (Lady-in-Waiting); Lionel Belmore (Court Member); Harry Wilson (Henchman); Ward Bond, James Flavin (Guards); Constantine Romanoff, Theodore Lorch (Executioners); Lane Chandler (Jailer); Russ Powell (Servant); Dewey Robinson (Steward).

KID MILLIONS   (UA, 1934) 92 M.

Producer, Samuel Goldwyn; director, Roy Del Ruth; story-screenplay, Arthur Sheekman, Nat Perrin, Nunnally Johnson; music director, Alfred Newman; choreography, Seymour Felix; songs, Walter Donaldson and Gus Kahn, Burton Lane and Harold Adamson, Irving Berlin; assistant director, Benjamin Silvie; camera, Ray Rennahan; editor, Stuart Heisler.

Eddie Cantor (Eddie Wilson, Jr.); Ethel Merman (Dot); Ann Sothern (Joan Larrabee); Warren Hymer (Louie the Lug); George Murphy (Gerald Lane); Berton Churchhill (Colonel Larrabee); Paul Harvey (Shiek Mulhulla); Jesse Block (Ben Ali); Eve Sully (Tanya); Otto Hoffman (Khoot); Doris Davenport (Toots); Jack Kennedy (Pop); Edgar Kennedy (Herman); Stanley Fields (Oscar); John Kelly (Adolph); Guy Usher (William Salde); Nicholas Brothers (Specialty Number); Mathew Beard (Stymie); Henry Kolker (Attorney); Tommy Bond (Tommy); Leonard Kibrick (Leonard); William Arnold (Steward); Harry C. Bradley (Bartender); Edward Peil, Sr. (Assistant Bartender); Harry Ernest (Page Boy); Eddie Arden (Busboy); Ed Mortimer (Ship's Officer); Zack Williams, Everett Brown (Slaves); Fred Warren, Harrison Greene (Spielers); George Regas, Noble Johnson (Attendants); Lon Poff (Recorder); Constantine Romanoff, Tor Johnson (Torturers); Ivan Linow, Lalo Encinas, Bud Fine, Leo Willis, Larry Fisher (Warriors); Sam Hayes (Eddie's Announcer); Malcolm Waite, Bob Reeves (Trumpeteers); Clarence Muse (Colonel Witherspoon); Steve Clemento,

Art Mix, Silver Harr, M. Rourie, Bob Kortman, Robert Ellis (Desert Riders); Louise Carver (Native Woman); Theodore Lorch (Native Fakir); Bobbie LaManche (Native Boy); Bobby Jordan (Tourist); J. Macher, John Dowd, Charles Hall (Natives); Mickey Rentschler, Jacqueline Taylor, Carmencita Johnson, Patricia Ann Rambeau, Ada Mae Hender, Billy Seay, John Collum, Wally Albright (Children on Tug); Lucille Ball (A 1934 Goldwyn Girl).

BROADWAY BILL   (Col., 1934) 105 M.

Director, Frank Capra; story, Mark Hellinger; screenplay, Robert Riskin; camera, Joseph Walker; editor, Gene Havlick.

Warner Baxter (Dan Brooks); Myrna Loy (Alice Higgins); Walter Connolly (J. L. Higgins); Helen Vinson (Margaret Brooks); Douglass Dumbrille (Eddie Morgan); Raymond Walburn (Colonel); Lynne Overman (Happy); Clarence Muse (Whitey); Margaret Hamilton (Edna); Paul Harvey (Whitehall); Claude Gillingwater, Sr. (J. P. Chase); Charles C. Wilson (Collins); Frankie Darro (Jockey Williams); Harry Todd (Pop); Ward Bond, Charles Lane (Morgan's Henchmen); George Cooper (Joe); George Meeker (Henry Early); Jason Robards (Arthur Winslow); Helen Flint (Mrs. Early); Helene Millard (Mrs. Winslow); Clara Blandick (Mrs. Peterson, Secretary); Alan Hale (Orchestra Leader); Edmund Breese (Presiding Judge); Ed Tucker (Jimmy Baker); Robert Allen (Reporter); Inez Courtney (Nurse); Forrester Harvey (Horse Trainer); Charles Middleton (Veterinary); Herman Bing (Waiter); Harry Holman (Rube); Irving Bacon (Hot Dog Stand Owner); Tom Ricketts (Johnson, the Butler); Harry C. Bradley (Bookkeeper); A. R. Haysel (Mike); Eddy Chandler (Onlooker); Dick Summer (Policeman); Joan Standing (Secretary); Richard Heming, Arthur Rankin, Pat O'Malley, Jack Mulhall, Dennis O'Keefe, Babe Lawrence, Bert Moorhouse, Reginald Simpson, Harry Keaton, Brooks Benedict, Leigh Williams, Gene McKay, Herman Marks, George Morrell (Men); Kay McCoy, Iris Morman, Janet Harper, Alice Lake, Edith Craig, Anita Pike, Lillian West, Peggy Leon, Janet Eastman, Margaret Morgan, Violet Carlton, Ethel Bryant, Patricia Caron (Women); Ky Robinson, Frank Holliday (Deputy Sheriffs); William H. Strauss (Pawnbroker); Gladys Gale (Head Nurse); Lucille Ball (Blonde Telephone Operator); Harry Semels (Conductor).

JEALOUSY   (Col., 1934) 68 M.

Director, R. William Neill; story, Argyle Campbell; screenplay, Joseph Moncure March, Kubc Glasmon; camera, John Stumar; editor, Roy Snyder.

Nancy Carroll (Jo Douglas); George Murphy (Larry O'Roarke); Donald Cook (Mark Lambert); Raymond Walburn (Phil); Arthur Hohl (Mike Callahan); Inez Courtney (Penny); Josephine Whittell (Laura); Arthur Vinton (Tony); Ray Mayer (Hook); Ray Cooke (Line); Huey White (Sinker); The Nicholas Brothers (Themselves); Lee Ramage (Fighter); James Burtis (Brownie); Niles Welch (Police Doctor); Selmer Jackson (Radio Announcer); James J. Jeffries (Captain Scott); Charles Keppen (Announcer); Edwin Stanley (Editor); Harry Holman (Man with Dog); Edward Keane (District Attorney); Montague Shaw (Judge); Kathrin Clare Ward (Jury Woman); Phil Dunham (Jury Man); Abe Roth (Referee); K. S. Hubley (Ramage's Manager); Freddy Welsh (Russ); Robert Graves (Headwaiter); Broderick O'Farrell (Minister); Gladden James (Court Clerk); James Farley (Bailiff); Pietro Sosso (Chaplain); Emmett Vogan, Sherry Hall, James Bradbury, Jr., Jack Kenney, Jack La Barba, Mike Schwartz, Jack Mack, James Quinn, Billy West, Sammy Blum, Charles Marsh (Reporters); William Irving, Stanley Mack, Ernest Young (Photographers); Tom London, Charles King, Bobbie Dale, Theodore Lorch, Sidney D'Albrook, Billy Engle, John Beck, Dutch Hendrian, Max Asher, William Ryno (Men); Dulcie Day (Nurse); Edward Le Saint (Hospital Doctor); Ethan Laidlaw (Taxicab Driver); Alice Dahl, Jean

Dudley, Patricia Royale, Irene Coleman, Ann Hughes, Jean Eddy, Pat O'Neill, Elinor Fields (Women); Lucille Ball (Girl); Matty Roubert (Newsboy); Jack Cheatham (Guard); Charles McAvoy, Ky Robinson (Detectives); Amelia Batchelor (Stand-in for Nancy Carroll); Chuck Colean (Stand-in for George Murphy).

MEN OF THE NIGHT   (Col., 1934) 58 M.

Director-story-screenplay, Lambert Hillyer; camera, Henry Freulich.

Bruce Cabot (Kelly); Judith Allen (Mary); Ward Bond (Connors); Charles Sabin (Davis); John Kelly (Chuck); Mathew Betz (Schmidt); Walter McGrail (Louie); Maidel Turner (Mrs. Webley); Arthur Rankin (Pat); Charles C. Wilson (Benson); Frank Darien (Mr. Webley); Harry Holman (Fat Man at Pig Stand); James Wang (Chop Suey Parlor Owner); Al Hill, Louis Natheau (Hold-up Men); Eddie Foster (Pedro); Frank Marlowe (Gas Station Attendant); Gladys Gale (Mrs. Everett); Robert Graves (Mr. Everett); Pearl Eaton (Ethel); Frank Meredith (Motorcycle Officer); Jack Mack (Bill); Tom London (Dave Burns); Dick Rush (Conductor); Lucille Ball (Peggy); Frank O'Connor (Boss Painter); Lee Shumway (Detective); Mitchell Ingraham (Telegraph Operator); Jack King, Matty Roubert (Newsboys); Ernie Adams (Sandy); Charles McMurphy (Policeman); Bruce Randall (Police Car Driver); Herman Marks (Crook); Dutch Hendrian (Henchman); Jeanne Lawrence, Isabel Vecki, Peggy Leon, Phyllis Crane, Nell Baldwin, Louise Dean, Lucille De Never (Women).

THE FUGITIVE LADY   (Col., 1934) 66 M.

Director, Al Rogell; story-screenplay, Herbert Asbury, Fred Niblo; camera, Al Siegler; editor, John Rawlins.

Neil Hamilton (Donald Brooks); Florence Rice (Ann Duncan); Donald Cook (Jack Howard); Clara Blandick (Aunt Margaret); Nella Walker (Mrs. Brooks); William Demarest (Steve Rogers); Matt McHugh (Bert Higgins); Wade Boteler (Rudy Davis); Ernest Wood (Joe Nelson); Rita La Roy (Sylvia Brooks); Rita Gould (Mrs. Clifford); Harvey Clark (Mr. Creswell); Maidel Turner (Mrs. Young); Harry Holman (Mr. Young); James Curtis (Motorcycle Officer); Jessie Pringle (Mrs. Carfax); Warner Richmond (Saunders); Howard Hickman (Doctor); Betty Alden (Nurse); Maude Truax (Mrs. Adams); Gladys Gale (Miss Smith); Edward Le Saint (Judge); Billie Seward (Miss Hyland); Phillips Smalley (Mr. Wolsey); Margaret Morgan (Mrs. Wolsey); Sam Flint (Conductor); Billy Dooley (Simmons); Pat O'Malley (Renham); Lucille Ball, Virgina Pine, Bess Flowers (Beauty Operators); Isabelle La Mal (Mrs. Brown); A. R. Haysel (Hallahan); Beulah Hutton (Edna); Wilson Benge (Butler); Buddy Roosevelt (Fight Double); Adalyn Hall (Mrs. Goddard); Wedgwood Nowell (Court Clerk); James Adamson (Black Man); Cy Schindell, Mike Lally, Bert Starkey, Allen Caran (Men); Irene Colman, James Blakeley (Bridal Couple); Evelyn Mackert (Stand-in for Florence Rice).

CARNIVAL   (Col., 1935) 76 M.

Producer, Samuel J. Briskin; director, Walter Lang; story-screenplay, Robert Riskin; camera, Al Siegler; editor, Richard Cahoon.

Lee Tracy (Chick); Sally Eilers (Daisy); Jimmy Durante (Fingers); Florence Rice (Miss Holbrook); Thomas E. Jackson (Mac); John Richard Walters (Poochy); George and Olive Brasno (Midgets); Helen Jerome Eddy (Dr. Hodges); Oscar Apfel (Mr. Lawson); Sheila Bromley (Puppet Assistant); Geneva Mitchell, Lucille Ball, Lillian West, Helen Barclay, Betty Alden (Nurses); Lee Moran, Phil Tead, Frank Mills, Bert Starkey, Ernie Adams, Eddie Featherstone (Barkers); Howard C. Hickman (Doctor); Wade Boteler (Sheriff); T. Roy Barnes (Salesman); Paul Hurst, Ben Taggart (Policemen); Charles Sabin (Intern); Inez Courtney, Billee Van Every, Evelyn Pierce, Doris

McMahan (Girls); Mr. and Mrs. Clemons (Knife-Throwing Act); Wilshire Doll House (Puppets); Edward LeSaint (Hospital Superintendent); Ada Mae Moore (Snake Charmer); Frank Rico (Clown); Stanley Blystone, James Farley (Detectives); Edward Mundin (Technical Advisor); Selmer Jackson, Gladys Gale, Montague Shaw, Brenda Fowler (Baby Judges); A. R. Haysel (Conductor); Kathryn Sheldon, Jessie Arnold, Isabelle La Mal, Helen Dickson, Marie Wells, Mabel Forrest, Cora Beach Shumway, Gladys Joyner, Dorothy Shearer (Women); Mrs. Bob McKenzie (Mother); Bert Wilson (Tattooed Man); Arthur Belasco (Guard); Lillian Worth (Half Man-Half Woman); Cecil Weston, Violet Knights (Small Town Women); Baby Ricardo Lord Cezon (Baby); Bill Irving (Waiter); Arthur Millette (Los Angeles Cop); Burr Caruth (Justice of the Peace); Vester Pegg, J. P. Lockney (Small-Town Men); Budd Fine (Fireman).

ROBERTA (RKO, 1935) 105 M.

Producer, Pandro S. Berman; director, William A. Seiter; based on the novel by Alice Duer Miller and the play *Gowns by Roberta* by Jerome Kern, Otto Harbach; adaptation, Jane Murfin, Sam Mintz; additional dialog, Glenn Tryon, Allan Scott; choreography, Fred Astaire; ensemble director, Hermes Pan; music director, Max Steiner; songs, Kern and Harbach, Dorothy Fields and Jimmy McHugh; art director, Van Nest Polglase, Carroll Clark; costumes, Bernard Newman; sound, John Tribby; camera, Edward Cronjager; editor, William Hamilton.

Irene Dunne (Stephanie); Fred Astaire (Huck); Ginger Rogers (Countess Scharwenka [Lizzie Gatz]); Randolph Scott (John Kent); Helen Westley (Roberta [Aunt Minnie]); Victor Varconi (Ladislaw); Claire Dodd (Sophie); Louis Alberni (Voyda); Ferdinand Munier (Lord Delves); Torben Meyer (Albert); Adrian Rosley (Professor); Bodil Rosing (Fernando); Lucille Ball, Jane Hamilton, Margaret McChrystal, Kay Sutton, Maxine Jennings, Virginia Reid, Lorna Low, Lorraine DeSart, Wanda Perry, Diana Cook, Virginia Carroll, Betty Dumbries, Donna Roberts (Mannequins); Mike Tellegen, Sam Savitsky (Cossacks); Zena Savine (Woman); Johnny "Candy" Candido, Muzzy Marcellino, Gene Sheldon, Howard Lally, William Carey, Paul McLarind, Hal Brown, Charles Sharpe, Ivan Down, Phil Cuthbert, Delmon Davis, William Dunn (Orchestra); Mary Forbes, William B. Davidson, Judith Vosselli, Rita Gould (Bits).

OLD MAN RHYTHM (RKO, 1935) 74 M.

Associate producer, Zion Myers; director, Edward Ludwig; based on the story by Lewis Gensler, Sig Herzig, Don Hartman; screenplay, Herzig, Ernest Pagano; additional dialog, H. W. Hanemann; choreography, Hermes Pan; art director, Van Nest Polglase; songs, Gensler and Johnny Mercer; music director, Roy Webb; camera, Nick Musuraca; editor, George Crone.

Charles "Buddy" Rogers (Johnny Roberts); George Barbier (John Roberts, Sr.); Barbara Kent (Edith Warren); Grace Bradley (Marian Beecher); Betty Grable (Sylvia); Eric Blore (Phillips); Erik Rhodes (Frank Rochet); John Arledge (Pinky Parker); Johnny Mercer (Colonel); Donald Meek (Paul Parker); Dave Chasen (Andy); Joy Hodges (Lois); Douglas Fowley (Oyster); Evelyn Poe (Honey); Margaret Nearing (Margaret); Ronald Graham (Ronald); Sonny Lamont (Blimp); William Carey (Bill); Lucille Ball, Marian Darling, Jane Hamilton, Maxine Jennings, Kay Sutton (College Girls); Jack Thomas, Erich Von Stroheim, Jr., Carlyle Blackwell, Jr., Bryant Washburn, Jr., Claude Gillingwater, Jr. (College Boys).

TOP HAT (RKO, 1935) 101 M.

Producer, Pandro S. Berman; director, Mark Sandrich; based on the play *Gay Divorce* by Dwight Taylor and a play by Alexander Farago and Aladar Laszlo; screenplay, Taylor Allan Scott; choreography, Fred Astaire; ensemble director, Hermes Pan; art director, Van Nest Polglase, Carroll Clark; set decorator, Thomas K. Little; costumes, Bernard Newman; songs, Irving Berlin; music director, Max Steiner; sound, Hugh McDowell, Jr.; special effects, Vernon L. Walker; camera, David Abel; editor, William Hamilton.

Fred Astaire (Jerry Travers); Ginger Rogers (Dale Tremont); Edward Everett Horton (Horace Hardwick); Helen Broderick (Madge Hardwick); Erik Rhodes (Alberto Beddini); Eric Blore (Bates); Lucille Ball (Flower Girl); Leonard Mudie (Flower Salesman); Donald Meek (Curate); Florence Roberts (Curate's Wife); Edgar Norton (London Hotel Manager); Gino Corrado (Toledo Hotel Manager); Peter Hobbes (Call Boy); Ben Holmes, Nick Thompson, Tom Costello, John Impolite, Genaro Spagnoli, Rita Rozelle, Phyllis Coghlan, Charles Hall (Bits); Dennis O'Keefe (Elevator Extra).

I DREAM TOO MUCH (RKO, 1935) 95 M.

Producer, Pandro S. Berman; director, John Cromwell; based on the story by Elsie Finn, David G. Wittels; screenplay; Edmund North, James Gow; songs, Jerome Kern and Dorothy Fields; costumes, Bernard Newman; camera, David Abel.

Lily Pons (Annette); Henry Fonda (Jonathan); Eric Blore (Roger); Osgood Perkins (Darcy); Lucien Littlefield (Mr. Dilley); Esther Dale (Mrs. Dilley); Lucille Ball (Gwendolyn Dilley); Mischa Auer (Pianist); Paul Porcasi (Tito); Scotty Beckett (Boy on Merry-Go-Round).

CHATTERBOX (RKO, 1936) 68 M.

Producer, Robert Sisk; director, George Nicholls, Jr.; from the play by David Carb; screenplay, Sam Mintz; camera, Robert De Grasse; editor, Arthur Scmidt.

Anne Shirley (Jenny Yates); Phillips Holmes (Philip Greene, Jr.); Edward Ellis (Uriah Lowell); Erik Rhodes (Archie Fisher); Margaret Hamilton (Emily Tipton); Granville Bates (Philip Greene, Sr.); Allen Vincent (Harrison); Lucille Ball (Lillian Temple); George Offerman, Jr. (Michael Arbuckle); Maxine Jennings (Actress); Richard Abbott (Blythe); Wilfred Lucas (Character Man); Margaret Armstrong (Character Woman).

FOLLOW THE FLEET (RKO, 1936) 110 M.

Producer, Pandro S. Berman; director, Mark Sandrich; based on the play *Shore Leave* by Hubert Osborne; screenplay, Dwight Taylor, Allan Scott; songs, Irving Berlin; music director, Max Steiner; choreography, Hermes Pan; art director, Van Nest Polglase, Carroll Clark; set decorator, Darrell Silvera; gowns, Bernard Newman; technical advisor, Lt. Comdr. Harvey Haislip; sound, Hugh McDowell; special effects, Vernon Walker; camera, David Abel; editor, Henry Berman.

Fred Astaire (Bake Baker); Ginger Rogers (Sherry Martin); Randolph Scott (Bilge Smith); Harriet Hilliard (Connie Martin); Ray Mayer (Dopey); Astrid Allwyn (Iris Manning); Harry Beresford (Captain Hickey); Jack Randall (Lieutenant Williams); Russell Hicks (Jim Nolan); Brooks Benedict (Sullivan); Lucille Ball (Kitty Collins); Betty Grable, Joy Hodges, Jennie Gray (Trio); Tony Martin, Edward Burns, Frank Jenks, Frank Mills (Sailors); Jane Hamilton (Waitress); Maxine Jennings (Hostess); Herbert Rawlinson (Webber).

BUNKER BEAN (RKO, 1936) 67 M.

Producer, William Sistrom; director, William Hamilton, Edward Killy; based on the novel by Harry Leon Wilson and the play *His Majesty, Bunker Bean* by Lee Wilson

Dodd; screenplay, Edmund North, James Gow, Dorothy Yost; camera, David Abel; editor, Jack Hively.

Owen Davis, Jr. (Bunker Bean); Louise Latimer (Mary Kent); Robert McWade (J. C. Kent); Jessie Ralph (Grandmother); Edward Nugent (Mr. Glab); Lucille Ball (Miss Kelly); Berton Churchill (Professor Balthazer); Hedda Hopper (Mrs. Kent); Pierre Watkin (Mr. Barnes); Charles Arnt (Mr. Metzger); Russell Hicks (A. C. Jones); Leonard Carey (Butler); Ferdinand Gottschalk (Mr. Meyerhauser); Sibyl Harris (Countess); Joan Davis (Telephone Operator); Ed Dearing, Edward LeSaint (Cops).

THAT GIRL FROM PARIS   (RKO, 1936) 105 M.

Producer, Pandro S. Berman; director, Leigh Jason; based on a story by Jane Murfin suggested by a story by J. Carey Wonderly; adaptation, Joseph A. Fields; screenplay, P. J. Wolfson, Dorothy Yost; music director, Nathaniel Shilkret; songs, Arthur Schwartz and Edward Heyman; operas conducted by Andre Kostelanetz; art director, Van Nest Polglase, Carroll Clark; set decorator, Darrell Silvera; gowns, Edward Stevenson; camera, J. Roy Hunt; editor.

Lily Pons (Nikki Martin); Gene Raymond (Windy McLean); Jack Oakie (Whammo); Herman Bing (Hammacher); Lucille Ball (Claire Williams); Mischa Auer (Butch); Frank Jenks (Laughing Boy); Patricia Wilder (Coat Room Girl); Vinton Haworth (Reporter); Willard Robertson (Immigration Officer); Gregory Gaye (Paul De Vry); Ferdinand Gottschalk (Uncle); Rafaela Ottiano (Marie); Harry Jans (Purser); Landers Stevens (Ship's Captain); Edward Price (Photographer); Alec Craig (Justice of the Peace); Michael Mark, Louis Mercier, Richard Carle (Bits); Pat Hartigan (Immigration Officer).

WINTERSET   (RKO, 1936) 78 M.

Producer, Pandro S. Berman; director, Alfred Santell; based on the play by Maxwell Anderson; screenplay, Anthony Veiler; music director, Nathaniel Shilkret; music arranger, Maurice De Packh; camera, Peverell Marley; editor, William Hamilton.

Burgess Meredith (Mio); Margo (Miriamne); Eduardo Ciannelli (Trock); Paul Guilfoyle (Garth); John Carradine (Romagna); Edward Ellis (Judge Gaunt); Stanley Ridges (Shadow); Maurice Moscovich (Esdras); Myron McCormick (Carr); Willard Robertson (Policeman); Mischa Auer (Radical); Barbara Pepper, Lucille Ball (Girls); Alec Craig (a Hobo); Helen Jerome Eddy (Maria Romagna); Fernanda Eliscu (Piny); George Humbert (Lucia); Murray Alper (Louie); Paul Fix (Joe); Alan Curtis (Sailor); Arthur Loft (District Attorney); Otto Hoffman (Elderly Man); Grace Hayle (Woman); Al Hill (Gangster); Bobby Caldwell (Mio as a boy).

DON'T TELL THE WIFE   (RKO, 1937) 62 M.

Producer, Robert Sisk; director, Christy Cabanne; based on the play *Once Over Lightly* by George Holland; screenplay, Nat Perrin; art director, Van Nest Polglase, Feild Gray; sound, John E. Tribby; costumes, Renie; camera, Harry Wilde; editor, Jack Hively.

Guy Kibbee (Malcom Winthrop); Una Merkel (Nancy Dorset); Lynne Overman (Steve Dorset); Thurston Hall (Major Manning); Guinn Williams (Cupid); William Demarest (Larry Tucker); Lucille Ball (Ann Howell); Harry Tyler (Mike Callahan); Frank M. Thomas (Sergeant Mallory); Harry Jans (Martin); George Irving (Warden); Alan Curtis (Customer's Man); Donald Kerr (Smith); Bill Jackie (Rooney); Bradley Page (Hagar); Aggie Herring (Charwoman); Barney Furey (Sign Painter); Hattie McDaniel (Nancy's Maid); Si Jenks (Sam Taylor); Charles West (Joe Hoskins).

STAGE DOOR   (RKO, 1937) 92 M.

Associate producer, Pandro S. Berman; director, Gregory La Cava; based on the play by Edna Ferber, George S. Kaufman; screenplay, Morrie Ryskind, Anthony Veiller; art director, Van Nest Polglase, Carroll Clark; set decorator, Darrell Silvera; assistant director, James Anderson; makeup, Mel Burns; costumes, Muriel King; music, Roy Webb; sound, John L. Cass; camera, Robert De Grasse; editor, William Hamilton.

Katharine Hepburn (Terry Randall); Ginger Rogers (Jean Maitland); Adolphe Menjou (Anthony Powell); Gail Patrick (Linda Shaw); Constance Collier (Catherine Luther); Andrea Leeds (Kaye Hamilton); Samuel S. Hinds (Henry Sims); Lucille Ball (Judy Canfield); Pierre Watkin (Richard Carmichael); Franklin Pangborn (Harcourt); Elizabeth Dunne (Mrs. Orcutt); Phyllis Kennedy (Hattie); Grady Sutton (Butcher); Jack Carson (Milbank); Fred Santley (Dukenfield); William Corson (Billy); Frank Reicher (Stage Director); Eve Arden (Eve); Ann Miller (Annie); Jane Rhodes (Ann Braddock); Margaret Early (Mary); Norma Drury (Olga Brent); Jean Rouverol (Dizzy); Harriet Brandon (Madeline); Peggy O'Donnell (Susan); Katharine Alexander, Ralph Forbes, Mary Forbes, Huntley Gordon (Cast of Play); Lynton Brent (Aide); Theodor Von Eltz (Elsworth); Jack Rice (Playwright); Harry Strang (Chauffeur); Bob Perry (Baggageman); Larry Steers (Theatre Patron); Mary Bovard, Frances Gifford (Actresses); Whitey the Cat (Eve's Cat).

JOY OF LIVING   (RKO, 1938) 90 M.

Producer, Felix Young; director, Tay Garnett; story, Dorothy Fields, Herbert Fields; screenplay, Gene Towne, Graham Baker, Allan Scott; music, Jerome Kern and Dorothy Fields; music director, Frank Tours; special effects, Vernon L. Walker; art director, Van Nest Polglase, Carroll Clark; assistant director, Kenneth Holmes; camera, Joseph Walker; editor, Jack Hively.

Irene Dunne (Maggie); Douglas Fairbanks, Jr. (Dan); Alice Brady (Minerva); Guy Kibbee (Dennis); Jean Dixon (Harrison); Eric Blore (Potter); Lucille Ball (Salina); Warren Hymer (Mike); Billy Gilbert (Cafe Owner); Frank Milan (Bert Pine); Dorothy Steiner (Dotsy Pine); Estelle Steiner (Betsy Pine); Phyllis Kennedy (Marie); Franklin Pangborn (Radio Broadcast Orchestra Leader); James Burke (Mac, the Cop); John Qualen (Oswego); Spencer Charters (Magistrate).

GO CHASE YOURSELF   (RKO, 1938) 70 M.

Producer, Robert Sisk; director, Edward F. Kline; story, Walter O'Keefe; screenplay, Paul Yawitz, Bert Granet; song, Hal Raynor, Burton Lane, and Joe Penner; music director, Roy Webb; art director, Van Nest Polglase; Feild M. Gray; special effects, Vernon L. Walker; gowns, Renie; editor, Desmond Marquette.

Joe Penner (Wilbur P. Meely); Lucille Ball (Carol Meely); Richard Lane (Nails); June Travis (Judith Daniels); Fritz Feld (Count Pierre de Louis-Louis); Tom Kennedy (Ice Box); Granville Bates (Halliday); Bradley Page (Frank); George Irving (Mr. Daniels); Arthur Stone (Warden); Jack Carson (Warren Miles); Frank M. Thomas (Police Chief); Jack Green (Officer); George Shelley (Detective); Ted Oliver (Detective Clark); Margaret Armstrong (Mrs. Daniels); Phillip Morris (Cop); John Ince (John Weatherby); Lynton Brent (Photographer); Clayton Moore, Alan Bruce, William Corson (Reporters); Napoleon Whiting (Porter); Donald Kerr (Gas Station Attendant); Edith Craig (Mother); Bobs Watson (Junior); Diana Gibson, Rita Oehmen (Diners); Billy Dooley (Linesman); Edward Hearn (Raffle Seller); Chester Clute (Excited Man).

HAVING WONDERFUL TIME   (RKO, 1938) 70 M.

Producer, Pandro S. Berman; director, Alfred Santell; based on the play by Arthur Kober; screenplay, Kober; music director, Roy Webb; songs, Sam Stept and Charles Tobias; camera, Robert de Grasse; editor, William Hamilton.

Ginger Rogers (Teddy); Douglas Fairbanks, Jr. (Chick Kirkland); Peggy Conklin (Fay); Lucille Ball (Miriam); Lee Bowman (Buzzy Armbruster); Eve Arden (Henrietta); Dorothea Kent (Maxine); Richard "Red" Skelton (Itchy); Donald Meek (P.U. Rogers); Jack Carson (Emil Beatty); Clarence H. Wilson (Mac); Grady Sutton (Gus); Shimen Ruskin (Shrimpo); Dorothy Tree (Frances); Leona Roberts (Mrs. Shaw); Harlan Briggs (Mr. Shaw); Inez Courtney (Emma); Juanita Quigley (Mabel); Dean Jagger (Charlie).

THE AFFAIRS OF ANNABEL   (RKO, 1938) 69 M.

Producer, Lee Marcus, Lou Lusty; director, Lew Landers; based on the story *Menial Star* by Charles Hoffman; screenplay, Bert Granet, Paul Yawitz; music director, Roy Webb; camera, Russell Metty; editor, Jack Hively.

Jack Oakie (Lanny Morgan); Lucille Ball (Annabel Allison); Ruth Donnelly (Josephine); Bradley Page (Howard Webb); Fritz Feld (Valdimir Dukoff); Thurston Hall (The Major); Elizabeth Risdon (Margaret Fletcher); Granville Bates (Jim Fletcher); James Burke (Officer Pat Muldoon); Lee Van Atta (Robert Fletcher); Edward Marr (Martin); Anthony Warde (Bailey); Leona Roberts (Mrs. Hurley); Maurice Cass (Dr. Rubnick, the Jiu-Jitsu Teacher); John Sutton (Man At Newsstand); Kane Richmond, (Detective); Charles Coleman (Perkins, the Butler); Wade Crosby (Scriptwriter); George Irving (Warden); Stanley Blystone (Cop).

ROOM SERVICE   (RKO, 1938) 78 M.

Producer, Pandro S. Berman; director, William A. Seiter; based on the play by John Murray, Allen Boretz; screenplay, Morrie Ryskind; art director, Van Nest Polglase, Al Herman; set decorator, Darrell Silvera; music director, Roy Webb; camera, J. Roy Hunt; editor, George Crone.

Groucho Marx (Gordon Miller); Harpo Marx (Faker Englund); Chico Marx (Harry Binelli); Lucille Ball (Christine); Ann Miller (Hilda Manney); Frank Albertson (Leo Davis); Donald MacBride (Wagner); Cliff Dunstan (Gribble); Philip Loeb (Timothy Hogarth); Alexander Asro (Sasha); Charles Halton (Dr. Glass); Philip Wood (Simon Jenkins).

THE NEXT TIME I MARRY   (RKO, 1938) 64 M.

Producer, Lee Marcus; director, Garson Kanin; story, Thames Williamson; screenplay, John Twist, Helen Meinardi; camera, Russell Metty; editor, Jack Hively.

Lucille Ball (Nancy Fleming); James Ellison (Tony Anthony); Lee Bowman (Count Georgi); Granville Bates (H. E. Crocker); Mantan Moreland (Tilby); Elliot Sullivan (Red); Murray Alper (Joe).

ANNABEL TAKES A TOUR   (RKO, 1938) 69 M.

Producer, Lee Marcus, Lou Lusty; director, Lew Landers; story, Joe Bigelow, Bert Granet; screenplay, Granet, Olive Cooper; camera, Russell Metty; editor, Harry Marker.

Jack Oakie (Lanny Morgan); Lucille Ball (Annabel Allison); Ruth Donnelly (Josephine); Bradley Page (Howard Webb); Ralph Forbes (Viscount); Frances Mercer (Natalie); Donald MacBride (Thompson); Alice White (Marcella, the Manicurist); Chester Clute (Pitcairn); Pepito (Poochy); Jean Rouverol (Laura); Clare Verdera

(Viscountess); Edward Gargan (Longshoreman); Mary Jo Desmond (Girl); Wesley Barry (Bellhop); Rafael Storm (Count).

BEAUTY FOR THE ASKING   (RKO, 1939) 68 M.

Producer, B. F. Fineman; director, Glenn Tyror; story, Edmund L. Hartmann; screenplay, Doris Anderson, Paul Jarrico; camera, Frank Redman; editor, George Crone.

Lucille Ball (Jean Russell); Patric Knowles (Denny Williams); Donald Woods (Jeffrey Martin); Frieda Inescort (Flora Barton); Inez Courtney (Gwen Morrison); Leona Maricle (Eve Harrington); Frances Mercer (Patricia Wharton); Whitney Bourne (Peggy Ponsby); George Andre Beranger (Cyril); Kay Sutton (Secretary); Ann Evers (Lois Peabody).

TWELVE CROWDED HOURS   (RKO, 1939) 64 M.

Producer, Robert Sisk; director, Lew Landers; story, Garret Fort, Peter Ruric; screenplay, John Twist; camera, Nick Musuraca; editor, Harry Marker.

Richard Dix (Nick Green); Lucille Ball (Paula Sanders); Allan Lane (Dave Sanders); Donald MacBride (Inspector Keller); Cyrus W. Kendall (Costain); Granville Bates (McEwen); John Arledge ("Red"); Dorothy Lee (Thelma); Bradley Page (Tom Miller); Addison Richards (Berquist); Murray Alper (Allen); John Gallaudet (Jimmy); Joseph De Steffani (Rovitch).

PANAMA LADY   (RKO, 1939) 64 M.

Producer, Cliff Reid; director, Jack Hively; story, Garrett Fort; screenplay, Michael Kanin; art director, Van Nest Polglase; music director, Roy Webb; special effects, Vernon L. Walker; camera, J. Roy Hunt; editor, Theron Warth.

Lucille Ball (Lucy); Allan Lane (McTeague); Steffi Duna (Cheema); Evelyn Brent (Lenore); Donald Briggs (Roy); Bernadene Hayes (Pearl); Abner Biberman (Elisha); William Pawley (Bartender); Earle Hodgins (Foreman).

FIVE CAME BACK   (RKO, 1939) 74 M.

Producer, Robert Sisk; director, John Farrow; story, Richard Carroll; screenplay, Jerry Cady, Dalton Trumbo, Nathaniel West; art director, Van Nest Polglase; music, Roy Webb; special effects, Vernon L. Walker; camera, Nicholas Musuraca; editor, Harry Marker.

Chester Morris (Bill); Lucille Ball (Peggy); Wendy Barrie (Alice Melhorne); John Carradine (Crimp); Allen Jenkins (Peter); Joseph Calleia (Vasquez); C. Aubrey Smith (Professor Henry Spengler); Kent Taylor (Joe); Patric Knowles (Judson Ellis); Elisabeth Risdon (Martha Spengler); Casey Johnson (Tommy); Dick Hogan (Larry).

THAT'S RIGHT—YOU'RE WRONG   (RKO, 1939) 91 M.

Producer-director, David Butler; story, Butler, William Conselman; screenplay, Conselman, James V. Kern; art director, Van Nest Polglase; music arranger, George Dunning; songs, Walter Donaldson; Johnny Burke and Frankie Masters; James Kern, Hy Heath, Johnny Lange, and Lew Porter; Charles Newman and Sammy Stept; Jerome Brainin and Allan Roberts; Dave Franklin; special effects, Vernon L. Walker; assistant director, Fred A. Flecke; camera, Russell Metty; editor, Irene Morra.

Lucille Ball (Sandra Sand); Dennis O'Keefe (Chuck Deems); Kay Kyser and His Band (Themselves); Adolphe Menjou (Stacey Delmore); May Robson (Grandma); Edward Everett Horton (Tom Village); Roscoe Karns (Mal Stamp); Moroni Olsen (J. D. Forbes); Hobart Cavanaugh (Dwight Cook); Ginny Simms (Ginny); Harry

Babbitt (Harry); Sully Mason (Sully); Ish Kabibble (Ish); Dorothy Lovett (Miss Cosgrave); Lillian West (Miss Brighton); Denis Tankard (Thomas); Fred Othman, Erskine Johnson, Sheilah Graham, Hedda Hopper, Jimmy Starr, Feg Murray (Themselves); Stephen Chase, Forbes Murray, Vinton Haworth (Producers); Charles Judels (Luigi, the Makeup Man); Horace McMahon, Elliott Sullivan (Hoods); Kathryn Adams (Elizabeth).

THE MARINES FLY HIGH   (RKO, 1940) 68 M.

Producer, Robert Sisk; director, George Nicholls, Jr., Ben Stoloff; story, A. C. Eddington; screenplay, Jerry Cady, A. J. Bolton; music director, Roy Webb; camera, Frank Redman; editor, Frederic Knudtson.

Richard Dix (Lieutenant Darrick); Chester Morris (Lieutenant Malone); Lucille Ball (Helen Grant); Steffi Duna (Teresa); John Eldredge (J. Henderson); Paul Harvey (Colonel Hill); Horace MacMahon (Monk O'Hara); Dick Hogan (Corporal Haines); Robert Stanton (Lieutenant Hobbs); Ann Shoemaker (Mrs. Hill); Nestor Paiva (Fernandez); Ethan Laidlaw (Barnes).

YOU CAN'T FOOL YOUR WIFE   (RKO, 1940) 68 M.

Producer, Cliff Reid; director Ray McCarey; based on the story "The Romantic Mr. Hinklin" by Richard Carroll, McCarey; screenplay, Jerry Cady; art director, Van Nest Polglase; music, Roy Webb; camera, J. Roy Hunt; editor, Theron Warth.

Lucille Ball (Clara Hinklin/Mercedes Vasquez); James Ellison (Andrew Hinklin); Robert Coote (Battincourt); Virginia Vale (Sally); Emma Dunn (Mom Fields); Elaine Shepard (Peggy); William Halligan (J. R. Gillespie); Oscar O'Shea (Chaplain).

DANCE, GIRL, DANCE   (RKO, 1940) 88 M.

Producer, Erich Pommer; director, Dorothy Arzner; story, Vicki Baum; screenplay, Tess Slesinger, Frank Davis; songs, Edward Ward, Chester Forrest, and Robert Wright; choreography, Ernst Matray; camera, Russell Metty; editor, Robert Wise.

Maureen O'Hara (Judy); Louis Hayward (Jimmy Harris); Lucille Ball (Bubbles); Virginia Field (Elinor Harris); Ralph Bellamy (Steve Adams); Maria Ouspenskaya (Madame Basilova); Mary Carlisle (Sally); Katharine Alexander (Miss Olmstead); Edward Brophy (Dwarfie); Walter Abel (Judge); Harold Huber (Hoboken Gent); Ernest Truex, Chester Clute (Baileys); Lorraine Krugger (Dolly); Lola Jensen (Daisy); Emma Dunn (Mrs. Simpson); Sidney Blackmer (Puss in Boots); Vivian Fay (Ballerina); Ludwig Stossel (Caesar); Erno Verebes (Fitch).

TOO MANY GIRLS   (RKO, 1940) 85 M.

Producer, Harry Edington, George Abbott; director, Abbott; based on the play by George Marion, Jr., Richard Rodgers, and Lorenz Hart; screenplay, John Twist; songs, Rodgers and Hart; art director, Van Nest Polglase; special effects, Vernon L. Walker; camera, Frank Redman; editor, William Hamilton.

Lucille Ball (Connie Casey); Richard Carlson (Clint Kelly); Ann Miller (Pepe); Eddie Bracken (Jojo Jordan); Frances Langford (Eileen Eilers); Desi Arnaz (Manuelito); Hal LeRoy (Al Terwilliger); Libby Bennett (Tallulah Lou); Harry Shannon (Mr. Casey); Douglas Walton (Mr. Waverly); Chester Clute (Lister); Tiny Person (Midge Martin); Ivy Scott (Mrs. Tewkbury); Byron Shores (Sheriff Andaluz); Van Johnson (Boy#41); John Benton (Boy); Janet Lavis, Anna Mae Tessle, Amarilla Morris, Vera Fern, Mildred Law, Ellen Johnson (Coeds); Michael Alvarez (Joe); Sethma Williams (Marie); Averell Harris (Detective); Tommy Graham (Hawker); Grady Sutton (Football Coach); Homer Dickinson (Butler); Iron Eyes Cody, Jay Silverheels (Indians); Chief John Big Tree (Chief); Pamela Blake (Student).

A GIRL, A GUY, AND A GOB   (RKO, 1941) 91 M.

Producer, Harold Lloyd; director, Richard Wallace; screenplay, Frank Ryan, Bert Granet; assistant director, James H. Anderson; special effects, Vernon L. Walker; camera, Russell Metty; editor, George Crone.

Lucille Ball (Dot Duncan); Edmond O'Brien (Stephen Herrick); George Murphy (Coffee Cup); George Cleveland (Pokey); Henry Travers (Abel Martin); Franklin Pangborn (Pet Shop Owner); Kathleen Howard (Jawme); Marguerite Chapman (Cecilia Grange); Lloyd Corrigan (Pigeon); Mady Correll (Cora); Frank McGlynn (Pankington); Doodles Weaver (Eddie—Growing Sailor); Frank Sully (Salty, the Sailor); Nella Walker (Mrs. Grange); Richard Lane (Recruiting Officer); Irving Bacon (Mr. Merney); Rube Demarest (Ivory, the Sailor); Charles Smith (Messenger); Nora Cecil (Charwoman); Bob McKenzie (Porter); George Lloyd, George Chandler, Vic Potel (Bits); Vince Barnett (Pedestrian); Jimmy Bush, Jack Lescoulie (Sailors); Joe Bernard (Tattoo Artist); Fern Emmett (Middle-Aged Woman); Wade Boteler (Uniformed Attendant); Charles Irwin (Dance Hall Emcee); Carol Hughes (Dance Hall Girl); Warren Ashe (Opera Ticket Taker); Jimmy Cleary (Program Boy); Ralph Brooks, Cy Ring, Tommy Quinn (Hustlers); Alex Pollard (Butler); Mary Field (Woman on Street); Snub Pollard (Attendant); Geraldine Fissette (Native Dancer); Leon Belasco (Taxi Driver); Hal K. Dawson (Photographer); Dewey Robinson (Bouncer).

LOOK WHO'S LAUGHING   (RKO, 1941) 78 M.

Producer-director, Allan Dwan; screenplay, James V. Kern; art director, Van Nest Polglase; music, Roy Webb; special effects, Vernon L. Walker; camera, Frank Redman; editor, Sherman Todd.

Edgar Bergen (Himself); Jim Jordan (Fibber McGee); Marian Jordan (Molly McGee); Lucille Ball (Julie Patterson); Lee Bonnell (Jerry); Dorothy Lovett (Marge); Harold Peary (The Great Gildersleeve); Isabel Randolph (Mrs. Uppington); Walter Baldwin (Bill); Neil Hamilton (Hilary Horton); Charles Halton (Cudahy); Harlow Wilcox (Mr. Collins); Spencer Charters (Motel Manager); Jed Prouty (Mayor); George Cleveland (Mayor Kelsey); Bill Thompson (Veteran); Sterling Holloway (Rusty, the Soda Jerk); Jed Prouty (Mayor Duncan); Florence Wright (Evelyn); Harlan Briggs, Arthur Q. Bryan (Mayor Duncan's Aides); Charles Lane (Club Secretary); Edna Holland (Mrs. Hargrave); Dell Henderson (Mr. Wentworth); Jack George (Orchestra Leader); Matty Kemp (Harry); Louise Currie (Jane); Louis Payne (Butler); Joe Hickey (Dancing Partner); Donald Kerr (Father); Sally Cairns (Girl); Eleanor Counts, Yvonne Chenal (Bits); Dorothy Lloyd (Maisie/Matilda).

VALLEY OF THE SUN   (RKO, 1942) 79 M.

Producer, Graham Baker; director, George Marshall; based on the story by Clarence Budington Kelland; screenplay, Horace McCoy; music, Paul Sawtell; camera, Harry Wild; editor, Desmond Marquette.

Lucille Ball (Christine); James Craig (Jonathan); Sir Cedric Hardwicke (Warrick); Dean Jagger (Jim Sawyer); Peter Whitney (Willie); Billy Gilbert (Justice of the Peace); Tom Tyler (Geronimo); Antonio Moreno (Chief Cochise); George Cleveland (Bill Yard); Hank Bell (Shotgun); Richard Fiske, Don Terry (Lieutenants); Chris Willow Bird (Apache Indian); Fern Emmett (Spinster); Carleton Young (Nolte); Carl Sepulveda (Pickett); George Melford (Dr. Thomas); Pat Moriarty (Mickey Maguire); Stanley Andrews (Major); Chester Clute (Secretary); Al St. John, Harry Lamont, Al Ferguson, Chester Conklin, Ed Brady; Lloyd Ingraham, Frank Coleman (Men on Street); Ethan Laidlaw (Johnson); Steve Clemento (Knife Thrower); George Lloyd (Sergeant); Bud Osborne (Rose); Tom London (Parker); Francis McDonald (Interpreter); Harry Hayden (Governor).

THE BIG STREET   (RKO, 1942) 87 M.

Producer, Damon Runyon; director, Irving Reis; based on the story "Little Pinks" by Runyon; screenplay, Leonard Spigelgass; music director, C. Bakaleinikoff; art director, Albert S. D'Agostino; choreography, Chester Hale; songs, Mort Greene and Harry Revel; special effects, Vernon L. Walker; camera, Russell Metty; editor, William Hamilton.

Henry Fonda (Little Pinks); Lucille Ball (Gloria); Barton MacLane (Case Ables); Eugene Pallette (Nicely Nicely Johnson); Agnes Moorehead (Violette); Ozzie Nelson And His Orchestra (Themselves); Sam Levene (Horsethief); Ray Collins (Professor B); Marion Martin (Mrs. Venus); William Orr (Decatur Reed); George Cleveland (Col. Venus); Vera Gordon (Mrs. Lefkowitz); Louise Beavers (Ruby); Juan Varro (Lou Adolia); Hans Conried (Louie); Harry Shannon (Doctor); William Halligan (Detective); John Miljan (McWhirter); Don Barclay (Emcee); Julius Tannen (Judge Bamberger); Eddie Dunn (Mulvaney); Bert Hanlon (Philly the Weeper); Bob Perry (Heart of Gold); Anthony Blair (O'Rourke); Art Hamburger (Joel Duffle); Addison Richards (Dr. Mitchell); Sally Wadsworth, Mary Stuart, Mary Halsey, Richard Martin, Russell Wade (Bits); Ann Summers (Cashier); Chester Huntley (Radio Announcer); Sammy Stein, Johnny Indrisano, Warren Jackson, Tony Merlo, George Magrill, Peter Duray, Arnold Virt, Jack Chefe, Joe Niemeyer, Don Kerr (Mugs at Mindy's); Joe Scadato (Spanish Joe); Walter Soderling (Doctor at Mindy's); Frank Moran, James O'Gatty (Mugs); Marie Windsor (Girl); Ralph Peters (Florist); Mimi Doyle (Nurse); Dewey Robinson, Elliott Sullivan (Tramps); Donald Kirke (Surgeon); George Noisom (Newsboy).

SEVEN DAYS' LEAVE   (RKO, 1942) 87 M.

Producer, Tim Whelan; associate producer, George Arthur; director, Whelan; screenplay, William Bowers, Ralph Spence, Curtis Kenyon, Kenneth Earl; music director, C. Bakaleinikoff; choreography; Charles Walters; songs, Frank Loesser and Jimmy McHugh; art director, Albert S. D'Agostino, Carroll Clark; special effects, Vernon L. Walker; camera, Robert de Grasse; editor, Robert Wise.

Victor Mature (Johnny Grey); Lucille Ball (Terry); Harold Peary (The Great Gildersleeve); Mapy Cortes (Mapy); Ginny Simms (Ginny); Freddy Martin & His Orchestra, Les Brown & His Orchestra; Lynn Royce & Vanya; Cast of "The Court of Missing Heirs"; Ralph Edwards & Company of "Truth or Consequences"; Peter Lind Hayes (Jackson); Marcy McGuire (Mickey); Walter Reed (Ralph Bell); Wallace Ford (Sergeant Mead); Arnold Stang (Bitsy); Buddy Clark (Clarky); Charles Victor (Charles); King Kennedy (Gifford); Charles Andre (Andre); Harry Holman (Justice of Peace); Addison Richards (Captain Collins); Sergio Orta (Himself); Jack Gardner (Announcer); Willie Fung (Houseboy); Ronnie Rondell (Miller, the Chauffeur); Richard Martin, Frank Martinelli, Russell Hoyt (Financial Trio); Henry DeSoto (Maitre d' Hotel); Charles Hall, Ed Thomas (Waiters); Max Wagner (Military Police); Ralph Dunn (Cop); Allen Wood (Groom); Charles Flynn (Guard).

DU BARRY WAS A LADY   (MGM, 1943) C—101 M.

Producer, Arthur Freed; director, Roy Del Ruth; based on the play by B. G. De Sylva and Herbert Fields; screenplay, Irving Brecher; songs, Cole Porter; Lew Brown, Ralph Freed, and Roger Edens; Freed, Brown, and Burton Lane; Freed and Lane; E. Y. Harburg, Freed, and Lane; Edens; music adaptator, Roger Edens; choreography, Charles Walters; art director, Cedric Gibbons; camera, Karl Freund; editor, Blanche Sewell.

Lucille Ball (May Daly/Mme. Du Barry); Red Skelton (Louie Blore/King Louis) Gene Kelly (Alec Howe/Black Arrow); Douglass Dumbrille (Willie/Duc De Rigor)

Rags Ragland (Charlie/Dauphin); Donald Meek (Mr. Jones/Duc De Choiseul); George Givot (Cheezy/De Roquefort); Zero Mostel (Rami, The Swami/Cagliostro); Tommy Dorsey & Band (Themselves); Virginia O'Brien (Ginny); Louise Beavers (Niagra); Charles Coleman (Doorman); Dick Haymes (Dorsey singer); Cecil Cunningham, Harry Hayden (Couple); Clara Blandick (Old Lady); Marie Blake (Woman); Andrew Tombes (Escort); Don Wilson (Announcer's Voice); Pierre Watkins (Patron); Sig Arno (Nick); Ernie Alexander (Delivery Man); Hugh Beaumont (Footman); William Forrest (Guard Captain); Charles Judels (Innkeeper); Dick Alexander, Art Miles, Paul Newlan (Men); Chester Clute (Doctor); Michael Visaroff, William Costello, Dell Henderson, Edward Cooper, Thomas Clarke, Emmett Casey (Flunkies); Christian Frank (Lackey); Emory Parnell (Gatekeeper); Mitchell Lewis (Renel); Maurice Costello (Passerby); Ava Gardner, Kay Aldridge, Hazel Brooks, Kay Williams (Girls); Lana Turner (Guest Star).

BEST FOOT FORWARD (MGM, 1943) C—95 M.

Producer, Arthur Freed; director, Edward Buzzell; based on the play by John Cecil Holmes; screenplay, Irving Brecher, Fred Finklehoffe; songs, Hugh Martin and Ralph Blane; music director, Lennie Hayton; choreography, Charles Walters; art director, Cedric Gibbons; camera, Leonard Smith; editor, Blanche Sewell.

Lucille Ball (Lucille); William Gaxton (Jack Haggerty); Virginia Weidler (Helen Schelssenger); Tommy Dix (Bud Hooper); Nancy Walker (Blind Date); June Allyson (Minerva); Kenny Bowers (Dutch); Gloria De Haven (Ethel); Jack Jordan (Hank); Beverly Tyler (Miss Delaware Water Gap); Chill Wills (Chester Shoat); Henry O'Neill (Major Reeber); Sara Haden (Miss Talbert); Darwood Kaye (Killer); Bobby Stebbins (Greenie); Donald MacBride (Capt. Bradd); Morris Ankrum (Colonel Harkrider); Nana Bryant (Mrs. Dalyrimple); Harry James & His Music Makers (Themselves); Jack Wagner, Jack McGee, Hugh Sheridan (Boys); Billy Bletcher (Waxer); Robert Emmet O'Connor (Conductor); Art Thompson, Lulu Mae Bohrman (Elderly Couple); Harry Hayden (Professor); Isabel Randolph (Wife); Bess Flowers (Mrs. Bradd).

THOUSANDS CHEER (MGM, 1943) C—126 M.

Producer, Joseph Pasternak; director, George Sidney; based on the story "Private Miss Jones" by Paul Jarrico, Richard Collins; screenplay, Jarrico, Collins; music director, Herbert Stothart; songs, Ralph Blane and Hugh Martin, Ralph Freed and Burton Lane, Paul Francis Webster and Walter Jurmann, E. Y. Harburg and Earl Brent, Harold Adamson and Ferde Grofe, Andy Razaf and Fats Waller, Harburg, Harold Rome, and Stothart, Blane, Martin, and Roger Edens, George R. Brown and Lew Brown, Walter Ruick; art director, Cedric Gibbons; camera, George Folsey; editor, George Boemler.

Kathryn Grayson (Kathryn Jones); Gene Kelly (Eddie Marsh); Mary Astor (Hyllary Jones); Jose Iturbi (Jose); John Boles (Colonel Jones); Dick Simmons (Captain Avery); Ben Blue (Chuck); Frank Sully (Alan); Wally Cassell (Jack); Ben Lessy (Silent Monk); Frances Rafferty (Marie); Mary Elliott (Helen); Odette Myrtil (Mama Corbino); Will Kaufman (Papa Corbino); Kay Kyser Orchestra (Themselves); Lionel Barrymore (Announcer); Betty Jaynes (Girl at Station); Sig Arno (Uncle Algy); Connie Gilchrist (Taxicab Driver); Bea Nigro (Woman); Daisy Buford (Maid); Pierre Watkin (Alex); Ray Teal (Ringmaster); Paul Speer (Specialty Dancer); Myron Healey, Don Taylor (Soldiers); Carl Saxe (Sergeant Major); Bryant Washburn, Jr. (Colonel Brand); Harry Strang (Captain Haines); Florence Turner (Mother at Station); June Allyson, Margaret O'Brien, Gloria De Haven, Marilyn Maxwell, Donna Reed, Lena Horne, Mickey Rooney, Judy Garland, Red Skelton, Eleanor Powell, Virginia O'Brien, Don Loper, Maxine Barrat (Guests); MGM Orchestra and the United Na-

447

tions Chorus, Bob Crosby and His Orchestra, Benny Carter and His Orchestra (Themselves); *Frank Morgan Sketch:* Frank Morgan (Barber); Ann Sothern, Lucille Ball, Connie Gilchrist, Marsha Hunt (Girls); Sara Haden, Marta Linden (Nurses); John Conte (Doctor).

MEET THE PEOPLE   (MGM, 1944) 100M.

Producer, E. Y. Harburg; director, Charles Reisner; based on the play by Louis Lantz, Sol and Ben Barzman; screenplay, S. M. Herzig, Fred Saidy; art director, Cedric Gibbons; music director, Lennie Hayton; choreography, Sammy Lee, Charles Walters, Jack Donahue; songs, Ralph Freed and Sammy Fain; Lorenz Hart and Richard Rodgers; Harburg and Burton Lane; Earl Brent; camera, Robert Surtees; editor, Alexander Troffey.

Lucille Ball (Julie Hampton); Dick Powell (William "Swanee" Swanson); Virginia O'Brien ("Woodpecker" Peg); Bert Lahr (Commander); Rags Ragland (Mr. Smith); June Allyson (Annie); Steve Geray (Uncle Almost); Paul Regan ("Buck"); Howard Freeman (Mr. Peetwick); Betty Jaynes (Steffi); John Craven (John Swanson); Miriam Lavelle (Miriam); Ziggie Talent (Ziggie); Spike Jones & His City Slickers, Vaughan Monroe & His Orchestra (Themselves); Morris Ankrum (Monte Rowland); Kay Medford (Mrs. Smith); Joey Ray (Dance Director); King Sisters (Themselves); Thelma Joel, Barbara Bedford, Mary Ganley, Katharine Booth, Mary McLeod (Girls); Lucille Casey, Natalie Draper, Alice Eyland, Noreen Nash, Linda Deane, Hazel Brooks, Eve Whitney, Erin O'Kelly, Peggy Maley, Kay Williams, Florence Lundeen (Show Girls); Patsy Moran (Homely Girl); Pat West (Man); Roger Moore (Chauffeur); Celia Travers (Secretary); Robert Emmett O'Connor (Attendant); Fred "Snowflake" Toones (Pullman Porter); Bobby Blake (Jimmy—Age 7); Dickie Hall (Billy—Age 5); Russell Gleason (Bill); Myron Healey (Marine); Creighton Hale (Hotel Clerk); Leon Belasco (Dress Designer).

WITHOUT LOVE   (MGM, 1945) 111 M.

Producer, Lawrence A. Weingarten; director, Harold S. Bucquet; based on the play by Philip Barry; screenplay, Donald Ogden Stewart; art director, Cedric Gibbons, Harry McAfee; set decorator, Edwin B. Willis, McLean Nisbet; music, Bronislau Kaper; assistant director, Earl McEvoy; makeup, Jack Dawn; montage, Peter Ballbusch; costumes, Irene, Marion Herwood Keyes; sound, Douglas Shearer; special effects, A. Arnold Gillespie, Danny Hall; camera, Karl Freund; editor, Frank Sullivan.

Spencer Tracy (Pat Jamieson); Katharine Hepburn (Jamie Rowan); Lucille Ball (Kitty Trimble); Keenan Wynn (Quentin Ladd); Carl Esmond (Paul Carrell); Patricia Morison (Edwina Collins); Felix Bressart (Professor Grinza); Emily Massey (Anna); Gloria Grahame (Flower Girl); George Davis (Caretaker); George Chandler (Elevator Boy); Clancy Cooper (Sergeant); Wallis Clark (Professor Thompson); Donald Curtis (Professor Ellis); Charles Arnt (Colonel Braden); Eddie Acuff (Driver); Clarence Muse (Porter); Franco Corsaro (Headwaiter); Ralph Brooks (Pageboy); William Forrest (Doctor); Garry Owen, Joe Devlin, William Newell (Soldiers); James Flavin (Sergeant); Hazel Brooks (Girl on Elevator).

ABBOTT AND COSTELLO IN HOLLYWOOD   (MGM, 1945) 83 M.

Producer, Martin Gosch; director, S. Sylvan Simon; story, Nat Perrin, Martin Gosch; screenplay, Perrin, Lou Breslow; songs, Ralph Blane and Hugh Martin; choreography, Charles Walters; music director, George Bassman; sound, Douglas Shearer; art director, Cedric Gibbons, Wade B. Rubottom; set decorator, Edwin B. Willis; assistant director, Earl McAvoy; camera, Charles Schoenbaum; editor, Ben Lewis.

Bud Abbott (Buz Kurtis); Lou Costello (Abercrombie); Frances Rafferty (Claire Warren); Robert Stanton (Jeff Parker); Jean Porter (Ruthie); Warner Anderson (Norman Royce); Rags Ragland, Lucille Ball, Preston Foster, Robert Z. Leonard, Jackie "Butch" Jenkins (Themselves); Carleton G. Young (Gregory LeMaise); Mike Mazurki (Klondike Pete); Robert Emmet O'Connor, Edgar Dearing (Studio Cops); Katharine Booth (Louise); Lyttle Sisters (Singers); Marion Martin (Miss Milbane); Arthur Space (Director); Dean Stockwell, Sharon McManus (Child Stars); William "Bill" Phillips (Kavanaugh's Assistant); Chester Clute (Mr. Burvis); Marie Blake (Secretary); Wheaton Chambers (Pedestrian); Harry Tyler (Taxi Driver); William Tannen (Hard-Boiled Assistant); Skeets Noyes (Wardrobe Man); Nolan Leary (Assistant); Forbes Murray (George Washington); Ed O'Neill (Abe Lincoln); Joe Bacon (Nubian Slave); Dick Alexander (Prop Man); Hank Worden (Gangling Guy); Dick Winslow (Orchestra Leader); Jane Hale, Mitzie Uehlien (Cigarette Girls); Frank Scannell, William Hawley, Arno Frey (Waiters); Lee Phelps (House Detective); William Tannen (Dr. Snide's Voice); Milton Kibbee (Counterman); Joe Devlin (Counterman); Beverly Haney, Barbara Combs, Zaz Vorka, Mary Donovan (Manicurists); Peter Miles (Little Boy with Horn); Del Henderson (Benson).

ZIEGFELD FOLLIES   (MGM, 1946) C—110 M.

Producer, Arthur Freed; director, Vincente Minnelli, Robert Lewis, Lemuel Ayers; art director, Cedric Gibbons, Merill Pye, Jack Martin Smith; puppet sequence, William Ferrai; set decorator, Edwin B. Willis, Mac Alper; choreography, Robert Alton, Eugene Loring; music adapter, Roger Edens; orchestrator, Conrad Salinger, Wally Heglin; music director, Lennie Hayton; songs, Douglas Furber and Philip Braham; Kay Thompson and Edens, Arthur Freed and Harry Warren, Arthur Freed and Earl Brent, Ralph Blane and Hugh Martin, Brent and Edens, Ralph Freed and Edens, Ira and George Gershwin; sound, Douglas Shearer; assistant director, Jack Greenwood, Al Shenberg; camera, George Folsey, Charles Rosher; editor, Albert Akst.

William Powell (Florenz Ziegfeld);

Ziegfeld Days: Fred Astaire, Bunin's Puppets; *Meet The Ladies:* Fred Astaire, Lucille Ball, Virginia O'Brien; *A Water Ballet:* Esther Williams; *Traviata:* James Melton, Marion Bell; *Pay the Two Dollars:* Victor Moore, Edward Arnold, Ray Teal (Special Officer); Joseph Crehan (Judge); William B. Davidson (Presiding Judge); Harry Hayden (Warden); Eddie Dunn, Garry Owen (Officers); *This Heart of Mine:* Fred Astaire (The Imposter); Lucille Bremer (The Princess); Count Stefenelli (The Duke); Naomi Childers (The Duchess); Helen Boice (The Countess); Robert Wayne (Retired Dyspeptic); Charles Coleman (The Major); Feodor Chaliapin (The Lieutenant); Sam Flint (The Flunky); *Number Please:* Keenan Wynn; *Love:* Lena Horne; *When Television Comes:* Red Skelton; *The Sweepstakes Ticket:* Fannie Brice (Norma); Hume Cronyn (Monty); William Frawley (Martin); Arthur Walsh (Telegraph Boy); *Limehouse Blues:* Fred Astaire (Tai Long); Lucille Bremer (Moy Ling); Captain George Hill, Jack Deery (Men); *A Great Lady Has an Interview:* Judy Garland, Rex Evans (Butler); *The Babbit and the Bromide:* Fred Astaire, Gene Kelly; *There's Beauty Everywhere:* Kathryn Grayson.

THE DARK CORNER   (20th, 1946) 99 M.

Producer, Fred Kohlmar; director, Henry Hathaway; based on a story by Leo Rosten; screenplay, Jay Dratler, Bernard Schoenfeld; art director, James Basevi, Leland Fuller; set decorator, Thomas Little, Paul S. Fox; music, Cyril Mockridge; music number, Eddie Heywood; music director, Emil Newman; assistant director, Bill Eckhardt; sound, W. D. Flick, Harry M. Leonard; special camera effects, Fred Sersen; camera, Joe MacDonald; editor, J. Watson Webb.

Lucille Ball (Kathleen); Clifton Webb (Cathcart); William Bendix (White Suit); Mark Stevens (Bradford Galt); Kurt Kreuger (Tony Jardine); Cathy Downs (Mari Cathcart); Reed Hadley (Lieutenant Frank Reeves); Constance Collier (Mrs. Kingsley); Eddie Heywood & Orchestra (Themselves); Molly Lamont (Lucy Wilding); Forbes Murray (Mr. Bryson); Regina Wallace (Mrs. Bryson); John Goldsworthy (Butler); Charles Wagenheim (Foss); Minerva Urecal (Mother); Raisa (Daughter); Matt McHugh (Milkman); Hope Landin (Scrub Woman); Gisela Werbisek (Mrs. Schwartz); Donald MacBride, Lee Phelps, Charles Cane, John Russell, Ralph Dunn, John Kelly (Policemen); Eugene Goncz (Practical Sign Painter); Steve Olsen (Barker); Mary Field (Cashier); Ellen Corby (Maid); Charles Tannen (Cabbie); Alice Fleming (Woman in Galt's Apartment); John Elliott, Pietro Sosso, Peter Cusanelli (Men); Frieda Stoll (Frau Keller); Thomas Martin (Major-Domo); Colleen Alpaugh (Little Girl); Lynn Whitney (Stenographer); Eloise Hardt (Saleswoman).

EASY TO WED (MGM, 1946) C—110 M.

Producer, Jack Cummings; director, Edward Buzzell; based on the screenplay *Libeled Lady* by George Oppenheimer, Maurine Watkins, Howard Emmett Rogers; screenplay, Dorothy Kingsley; music, Johnny Green; art director, Hans Peters; set decorator, Edwin B. Willis, Jack Bonar; choreography, Jack Donahue; songs, Ted Duncan and Green; Robert Franklin and Green; Ralph Blane and Green; Osvaldo Farres; sound, Douglas Shearer; assistant director, Herman Webber; camera, Harry Stradling; editor, Blanche Sewell.

Van Johnson (Bill Chandler); Esther Williams (Connie Allenbury); Lucille Ball (Gladys Benton); Keenan Wynn (Warren Haggerty); Cecil Kellaway (J. B. Allenbury); Carlos Ramirez (Carlos); Ben Blue (Spike Dolan); Ethel Smith (Ethel); June Lockhart (Babs Norvell); Grant Mitchell (Homer Henshaw); Josephine Whittell (Mrs. Burns Norvell); Jean Porter (Frances); Paul Harvey (Farwood); Jonathan Hale (Boswell); James Flavin (Joe); Celia Travers (Farwood's Secretary); Robert Emmett O'Connor (Taxi Driver); Charles Sullivan, Frank Hagney (Truck Drivers); Sybil Merritt (Receptionist); Dick Winslow (Orchestra Leader); Joel Friedkin (Justice of the Peace); Milton Kibbee (Private Detective); Tom Dugan (Waiter); Katherine Black (Masseuse); Walter Soderling (Mr. Dibson); Sarah Edwards (Mrs. Dibson); Jack Shea (Lifeguard); Mitzie Uehlein, Mildred Sellers, Phyllis Graffeo, Kanza Omar, Louise Burnett, Patricia Denise (Girls at Pool); Fred Fisher, Alex Pollard (Waiters); Charles Knight, John Valentine, Guy Bates Post (Butlers).

TWO SMART PEOPLE (MGM, 1946) 93 M.

Producer, Ralph Wheelwright; director, Jules Dassin; story, Ralph Wheelwright, Allan Kenward; screenplay, Ethel Hill, Leslie Charteris; art director, Cedric Gibbons, Wade Rubottom; set decorator, Edwin B. Willis, Keough Gleason; music, George Bassman; songs, Ralph Blane and Bassman; assistant director, S. Sidman; sound, Douglas Shearer; camera, Karl Freund; editor, Chester W. Schaeffer.

Lucille Ball (Rickie Woodner); John Hodiak (Ace Connors); Lloyd Nolan (Bob Simms); Hugo Haas (Senor Rodriquez); Lenore Ulric (Senora Maria Ynez); Elisha Cook, Jr. (Fly Feletti); Lloyd Corrigan (Dwight Chadwick); Vladimir Sokoloff (Monsieur Jacques Dufour); David Cota (Jose); Clarence Muse (Porter); George Magrill (Taxi Driver); Mary Emory, Maria Dodd, Helen Dickson (Women); Bobby Johnson (Waiter); Leo Mostovoy (Headwaiter in French Restaurant); Shelley Winters (Princess); Frank Johnson (Fat Man); Lynn Whitney (Swedish Girl); Erwin Kalser (Franz); Connie Weiler (Hat Check Girl); Fred Nurney (Victoire); Marek Windheim (Captain); William Riley (Pete, the Bellboy); William Tannen (Clerk); Fred "Snowflake" Toones (Red Cap); Cleo Morgan (Cleopatra); Peter Virgo (Indian Attendant); Gloria Ander-

450

son (Grecian Girl); Harold De Garro (Stilt Walker); Jimmy Magill (Reveler); John Piffl (Jolly Fat Man); Tom Quinn (Sheik); Gabriel Canzono (Monkey Man); Emil Rameau (Riverboat Waiter); Paul Kruger (Cop); Bess Flowers, Jean Andren (Police-women); Lorenzo Lopez (Gardener); Phil Dunham (Drunk); Harry Depp (Spectator); George Calliga (Stewart); Margaret Jackson (Bystander).

LOVER COME BACK   (Univ., 1946) 90 M.

Producer, Michael Fessier, Ernest Pagano; director, William Seiter; screenplay, Fessier, Pagano; art director, Jack Otterson, Martin Obzina; set decorator, Russell A. Gausman, Ted Offenbecker; music, Hans J. Salter; sound, Bernard B. Brown; costumes, Travis Banton; assistant director, Fred Frank; camera, Joseph Valentine; editor, Ray Snyder.

George Brent (Bill Williams); Lucille Ball (Kay); Vera Zorina (Madeline Laslo); Charles Winninger (Pa); Carl Esmond (Paul); Raymond Walburn (J. P. Winthrop); Elisabeth Risdon (Ma); Louise Beavers (Martha); Wallace Ford (Tubbs); Franklin Pangborn (Hotel Clerk); William Wright (Jimmy Hennessey); George Chandler (Waiter); Joan Shawlee (Janie); Audrey Young (Receptionist); Eddy Waller (Mr. Russel); Dorothy Christy (Receptionist); George Davis (Maitre D'); Dorothy Ford (Brunette); Edward Martendel (Slocum); Anne O'Neal (Mrs. Tubbs); Frank Scannell, Harold Goodwin, Perc Launders (Reporters); Lane Chandler, Jack Shutta, Jerome Root (Bellhops); Lloyd Ingraham (Partner); Geraldine Jarman (Blonde); Louis Wood (Room Steward); Mary Moore, Joan Graham, Gwen Donovan, Shirley O'Hara (Show Girls); Lottie Harrison (Mother); Katherine York (Redhead); Bill Hudson (Young Man).

LURED   (UA, 1947) 102 M

Producer, James Nasser; associate producer, Henry Kesler; director, Douglas Sirk; screenplay, Leo Rosten; production design-art director, Nicholai Remisoff; music, Michel Michelet; assistant director, Clarence Eurist; sound, H. Connors; camera, William Daniels; editor, James E. Newcom, John M. Foley.

George Sanders (Robert Fleming); Lucille Ball (Sandra Carpenter); Charles Coburn (Inspector Temple); Boris Karloff (Artist); Alan Mowbray (Maxwell); Cedric Hard-wicke (Julian Wilde); George Zucco (Officer Barrett); Joseph Calleia (Dr. Moryani); Tanis Chandler (Lucy Barnard); Alan Napier (Inspector Gordon); Robert Coote (Officer); Jimmie Aubrey (Nelson); Dorothy Vaughan (Mrs. Miller).

HER HUSBAND'S AFFAIRS   (Col., 1947) 83 M.

Producer, Raphael Hakim; director, S. Sylvan Simon; screenplay, Ben Hecht; art director, Stephen Goodson, Carl Anderson; camera, Charles Lawton, Jr.; editor, Al Clark.

Lucille Ball (Margaret Weldon); Franchot Tone (William Weldon); Edward Everett Horton (J. B. Cruikshank); Mikhail Rasumny (Professor Glinka); Gene Lockhart (Peter Winterbottom); Nana Bryant (Mrs. Winterbottom); Paul Stanton (Dr. Frazee); Jonathan Hale (Governor Fox); Mabel Paige (Mrs. Josper); Frank Mayo (Vice President Starrett); Pierre Watkin (Vice President Beitler); Carl Leviness (Vice President Brady); Dick Gordon (Vice President Nicholson); Jack Rice (Slocum); Clancy Cooper (Window Washer); Douglas Wood (Tappel); Charles C. Wilson (Police Captain); Charles Trowbridge (Brewster); Selmer Jackson (Judge); Arthur Space (District At-torney); Cliff Clark (Gus); Douglas D. Coppin (Milkman); Virginia Hunter, Doris Colleen (Secretaries); Stanley Blystone (Ike); Fred Miller (Dan); Larry Parks (Him-self); Nancy Saunders, Wanda Cantlon, Edythe Elliott (Nurses); Harry Cheshire (Mayor); Gerald Oliver Smith (Harold); Robert Emmett Keane (Manager); Emmett Vogan (Mr. Miller); Fred Sears (Man at Mayor's Party); Bob Cason (Heckler); Tommy

Lee, James B. Leong, Hom Wing Gim, Owen Song (Acrobats); George Douglas, Stephen Bennett (Vice Presidents); Fred Howard (Bailiff); Bill Wallace, Charles Hamilton, Russell Whitman (Policemen); Charles Bates, Buz Buckley, Teddy Infuhr, Dwayne Hickman, (Boys); Charles Williams (Clerk); William Gould (Jailer); Frank Wilcox (Floorwalker); Susan Simon (Girl); Dan Stowell (Willowcombe); Victor Travers (Jury Foreman); Eric Wilton (Governor's Butler); Buddy Gorman (Youth).

SORROWFUL JONES   (Par., 1949) 88 M.

Producer, Robert L. Welch; director, Sidney Lanfield; based on the story "Little Miss Marker" by Damon Runyon; screenplay adaptation, William R. Lipman, Sam Hellman, Gladys Lehman; screenplay, Melville Shavelson, Edmund Hartmann, Jack Rose; art director, Hans Dreier, Albert Nozaki; set decorator, Sam Comer, Bertram Granger; music, Robert Emmett Dolan; songs, Jay Livingston, Ray Evans; assistant director, Oscar Rudolph; makeup, Wally Westmore; costumes, Mary Kay Dodson; sound, Harold Lewis, John Cope; special effects, Gordon Jennings; process Camera, Farciot Edouart; camera, Daniel L. Fapp; editor, Arthur Schmidt.

Bob Hope (Sorrowful Jones); Lucille Ball (Gladys O'Neill); William Demarest (Regret); Bruce Cabot (Big Steve Holloway); Thomas Gomez (Reardon); Tom Pedi (Once-Over Sam); Paul Lees (Orville Smith); Houseley Stevenson (Doc Chesley); Mary Jayne Saunders (Martha Jane Smith); Claire Carleton (Agnes "Happy Hips" Noonan); Ben Welden (Big Steve's Bodyguard); Harry Tyler (Blinky); John "Skins" Miller (Head Phone Man); Charley Cooley (Shorty); Marc Krah (Barber); Sid Tomack (Waiter at Steve's Place); Patsy O'Byrne (Charwoman); Ralph Peters (Cab Driver); Ed Dearing (Police Lieutenant Mitchell); Arthur Space (Plainclothesman); Emmett Vogan, Maurice Cass (Psychiatrists); John Shay, Selmer Jackson (Doctors); John Mallon, Frank Mills, Tony Cirillo, Allen Ray, Sam Finn, Bob Kortman, James Davies, James Cornell, Jack Roberts, Douglas Carter, Michael A. Cirillo, (Horseplayers); Pat Lane, Billy Snyder, Kid Chissell, Eddie Rio (Bookies); William Yip, George Chan (Chinamen); Sally Rawlinson, Louise Lorimer (Nurses).

EASY LIVING   (RKO, 1949) 77 M.

Producer, Robert Sparks; director, Jacques Tourneur; based on the story "Education of the Heart" by Irwin Shaw; screenplay, Charles Schnee; art director, Albert S. D'Agostino, Alfred Herman; set decorator, Darrell Silvera, Harley Miller; music, Roy Webb; music director, C. Bakaleinikoff; assistant director, James Lane, Joel Freeman, Nate Slott; makeup, Robert M. Cowan, Lee Greenway; costumes, Edward Stevenson; sound, Earl Wolcott; camera, Harry J. Wild; editor, Frederic Knudtson.

Victor Mature (Pete Wilson); Lucille Ball (Anne); Lizabeth Scott (Liza Wilson); Sonny Tufts (Tom McCarr); Lloyd Nolan (Lenahan); Paul Stewart (Argus); Jack Parr (Scoop Spooner); Jeff Donnell (Penny McCarr); Art Baker (Howard Vollmer); Gordon Jones (Bill Holloran); Dick Erdman (Buddy Morgan); William "Bill" Phillips (Ozzie); Charles Lang (Whitey); Kenny Washington (Benny); Julia Dean (Mrs. Belle Ryan); Everett Glass (Virgil Ryan); James Backus (Dr. Franklin); Robert Ellis (Urchin); Steven Flagg (Gilbert Vollmer); Alex Sharp (Don); Russ Thorson (Hunk Edwards); June Bright (Billy Duane); Eddie Kotal (Curley); Audrey Young (Singer); The Los Angeles Rams (Themselves); Robert Graham, Warren Schannon, Jackie Jackson, Alan Dinehart III (Urchins); Dick Ryan (Bartender); Erin Selwyn (Nurse); Albin Robeling (Chef); Steve Crandall (Reporter); W. J. O'Brien, Gene Leslie (Vendors); Ray George (Referee); William Erwin, Carl Saxe (Men).

MISS GRANT TAKES RICHMOND   (Col. 1949) 87 M.

Producer, S. Sylvan Simon; director, Lloyd Bacon; story, Everett Freeman; screenplay, Nat Perrin, Devery Freeman, Frank Tashlin; art director, Walter Holscher; set decorator, James Crowe; music, Heinz Roemheld; music director, Morris Stoloff; assistant director, Carl Hiecke; makeup, Clay Campbell; costumes, Jean Louis; sound, Lambert Day; camera, Charles Lawton, Jr.; editor, Jerome Thoms.

Lucille Ball (Ellen Grant); William Holden (Dick Richmond); Janis Carter (Peggy Donato); James Gleason (J. Hobart Gleason); Gloria Henry (Helen White); Frank McHugh (Kilcoyne); George Cleveland (Judge Ben Grant); Stephen Dunne (Ralph Winton); Arthur Space (Willacombe); Will Wright (Roscoe Johnson); Jimmy Lloyd (Homer White); Loren Tindall (Charles Meyers); Ola Lorraine (Jeanie Meyers); Claire Meade (Aunt Mae); Roy Roberts (Foreman); Charles Lane (Woodruff); Harry Harvey (Councilman Reed); Harry Cheshire (Leo Hopkins); Nita Mathews (Ruth); Glen Thompson (Carpenter Stunt); Peter Brocco, Toni Newman, Marjorie Stapp, Don Hayden, Bradley Johnson, Robert Strong, Bret Hamilton, Tom Kingston (Bits); Syd Saylor (Surveyor); Michael Cisney (Lawyer); Eddie Acuff (Bus Driver); Bill Lechner (Soda Clerk); Charles L. Marsh (Court Clerk); Charles "Chuck" Hamilton (Cop); Wanda Cantlon (Maid); Stanley Waxman (Sig Davis); Cosmo Sardo (Maitre D'); Cliff Clark (Job Boss); Wanda Perry (Ruth); Charles Sullivan (Worker); Ted Jordan, Jerry Jerome, Jack Overman, Paul Newlan, Michael Ross (Hoods).

A WOMAN OF DISTINCTION   (Col., 1950) 85 M.

Producer, Buddy Adler; director, Edward Buzzell; story, Hugh Butler, Ian McClellan Hunter; screenplay, Charles Hoffman; art director, Robert Peterson; music director, Morris Stoloff; camera, Joseph Walker; editor, Charles Nelson.

Ray Milland (Alec Stevenson); Rosalind Russell (Susan Middlecott); Edmund Gwenn (Mark Middlecott); Janis Carter (Teddy Evans); Mary Jane Saunders (Louisa); Francis Lederer (Paul Simone); Jerome Courtland (Jerome); Alex Gerry (Herman Pomeroy); Charles Evans (Dr. McFall); Charlotte Wynters (Miss Withers); Clifton Young (Chet); Gale Gordon (Station Clerk); Jean Willes (Pearl); Wanda McKay (Merle); Elizabeth Flournoy (Laura); Harry Tyler (Charlie); Lucille Ball (Unbilled Cameo); Robert Malcolm, William E. Green (Conductors); Dudley Dickerson (Waiter); Gail Bonney, Napoleon Whiting, Wilda Biber, Kathryn Moore, Patricia Reynolds, Ethel Sway, Elaine Towne (Bits); Billy Newell (Bartender); Charles Trowbridge (Bartender); Richard Bartell, Charles Jordan, Harry Strang, Donald Kerr, Larry Barton, Ted Jordan (Reporters); Mira McKinney, Lelah Tyler (Members); Lois Hall (Stewardess); Myron Healey (Cameraman); Ed Keane (Sergeant); Lucille Browne (Manicurist); Marie Blake (Wax Operator); Walter Sande (Officer); Maxine Gates (Goldie).

FANCY PANTS   (Par., 1950) C—92 M.

Producer, Robert Welch; director, George Marshall; based on the story "Ruggles of Red Gap" by Harry Leon Wilson; screenplay, Edmund Hartman, Robert O'Brien; art director, Hans Dreier, Earl Hedrick; music, Van Cleve; songs, Ray Evans and Jay Livingston; camera, Charles B. Lang, Jr.; editor, Archie Marshek.

Bob Hope (Humphrey); Lucille Ball (Agatha Floud); Bruce Cabot (Cart Belknap); Jack Kirkwood (Mike Floud); Lea Penman (Effie Floud); Hugh French (George Van-Basingwell); Eric Blore (Sir Wimbley); Joseph Vitale (Wampum); John Alexander (Teddy Roosevelt); Norma Varden (Lady Maude); Virginia Kelly (Rosalind); Colin Keith-Johnson (Twombley); Joe Wong (Wong); Robin Hughes (Cyril); Percy Helton (Major Fogarty); Hope Sanberry (Millie); Grace Gillern Albertson (Dolly); Oliver Blake (Mr. Andrews); Chester Conklin (Guest); Edgar Dearing (Mr. Jones); Alva Marie Lacy (Daisy); Ida Moore (Betsy and Bessie); Ethel Wales (Mrs. Wilkins); Jean Ruth (Miss Wilkins); Jimmie Dundee, Bob Kortman (Henchmen); Major Sam Harris (Umpire); Gilchrist Stuart (Wicket Keeper); Charles Cooley (Man); Olaf Hytten (Stage Manager); Alex Frazer (Stagehand); Almira Sessions (Belle); Howard Petrie, Ray Bennett (Secret Service Men); Harry Martin (Englishman); Gilbert Alonzo, David

Alvarado, Robert Dominguez, Vincent Garcia, Henry Mirelez, Alfred Nunez (Indian Boys); Hank Bell (Barfly).

THE FULLER BRUSH GIRL   (Col., 1950) 85 M.

Producer, S. Sylvan Simon; director, Lloyd Bacon; screenplay, Frank Tashlin; art director, Robert Peterson; music director, Morris Stoloff; camera, Charles Lawton; editor, William Lyon.

Lucille Ball (Sally Elliot); Eddie Albert (Humphrey Briggs); Carl Benton Reid (Christy); Gale Robbins (Ruby Rawlings); Jeff Donnell (Jane Bixby); Jerome Cowan (Harvey Simpson); John Litel (Watkins); Fred Graham (Rocky Mitchell); Lee Patrick (Claire Simpson); Arthur Space (Inspector Rodgers); Sid Tomack (Bangs); Billy Vincent (Punchy); Lorin Raker (Deval); Lelah Tyler (Mrs. North); Sarah Edwards (Mrs. East); Lois Austin (Mrs. West); Isabel Randolph (Mrs. South); Isabel Withers (Mrs. Finley); Donna Bosell (Sue/Lou); Gregory Marshall (Alvin/Albert); Gail Bonney (Baby Sitter); Joel Robinson, Shirley Whitney (Dancers); Sumner Getchell (Magazine Salesman); Red Skelton (Fuller Brush Man); Jay Barney (Fingerprint Man); John Doucette, Charles Hamilton, Cy Malis, Joseph Palma (Cops); Jack Little, James L. Kelly (Comics); Myron Healey (Employee); Bud Osborne (Old Sailor); Barbara Pepper, Paul Bryar (Couple); Jean Willes (Mary).

THE MAGIC CARPET   (Col., 1951) C—84 M.

Producer, Sam Katzman; director, Lew Landers; story-screenplay, David Mathews; art director, Paul Palmentola; music director, Mischa Bakaleinikoff; camera, Ellis W. Carter; editor, Edwin Bryant.

Lucille Ball (Narah); John Agar (Ramoth); Patricia Medina (Lida); George Tobias (Gazi); Raymond Burr (Boreg); Gregory Gay (Ali); Rick Vallin (Abdul); Jo Gilbert (Marcus); William Fawcett (Akkmid); Dretta Johnson (Tanya); Linda Williams (Estar); Perry Sheehan (Copah); Eilia Howe (Vernah); Winona Smith (Nedda); Minka Zorka (Ziela).

THE LONG LONG TRAILER   (MGM, 1954) C—96 M.

Producer, Pandro S. Berman; director, Vincente Minnelli; based on the novel by Clinton Twiss; screenplay, Albert Hackett, Frances Goodrich; art director, Cedric Gibbons, Edward Carfagno; set decorator, Edwin B. Willis, Keogh Gleason; assistant director, Jerry Thorpe; makeup, William Tuttle; special effects, A. Arnold Gillespie, Warren Newcombe; music, Adolph Deutsch; songs, Haven Gillespie, Seymour Simmons, and Richard A. Whiting; camera, Robert Surtees; editor, Ferris Webster.

Lucille Ball (Tacy Collini); Desi Arnaz (Nicholas Carlos Collini); Marjorie Main (Mrs. Hittaway); Keenan Wynn (Policeman); Gladys Hurlbut (Mrs. Bolton); Moroni Olsen (Mr. Tewitt); Bert Freed (Foreman); Madge Blake (Aunt Anastasia); Walter Baldwin (Uncle Edgar); Oliver Blake (Mr. Judlow); Perry Sheehan (Bridesmaid); Charles Herbert (Little Boy); Herb Vigran (Trailer Salesman); Emmett Vogan (Mr. Bolton); Edgar Dearing (Manager); Karl Lukas (Inspector); Howard McNear (Mr. Hittaway); Jack Kruschen (Mechanic); Geraldine Carr, Sarah Spencer (Girl Friends); Dallas Boyd (Minister); Ruth Warren (Mrs. Dudley); Edna Skinner (Mrs. Barrett); Alan Lee (Mr. Elliott); Robert Anderson (Carl Barrett); Phil Rich (Mr. Dudley); John Call (Shorty); Wilson Wood (Garage Owner); Dorothy Neumann (Aunt Ellen); Howard Wright (Uncle Bill); Connie Van (Grace); Dennis Ross (Jody); Christopher Olsen (Tom); Ida Moore (Candy Store Clerk); Emory Parnell (Officer); Fay Roope (Judge); Peter Leeds (Garage Manager); Ruth Lee (Mrs. Tewitt); Dick Alexander (Father); Judy Sackett (Bettie); Janet Sackett (Kay); Norman Leavitt (Driver); Juney Ellis (Waitress); Frank Gerstle (Attendant).

FOREVER, DARLING (MGM, 1956) C—96 M.

Producer, Desi Arnaz; associate producer, Jerry Thorpe; director, Alexander Hall; story-screenplay, Helen Deutsch; art director, Ralph Berger, Albert Pyke; music, Bronislau Kaper; song, Sammy Cahn; assistant director, Jack Aldworth, Marvin Stuart; wardrobe, Elois Jenssen; camera, Harold Lipstein; editor, Dann Cahn, Bud Molin.

Lucille Ball (Susan Vega); Desi Arnaz (Lorenzo Xavier Vega); James Mason (Guardian Angel); Louis Calhern (Charles Y. Bewell); John Emery (Dr. Edward R. Winter); John Hoyt (Bill Finlay); Natalie Schafer (Millie Opdyke); Mabel Albertson (Society Reporter); Ralph Dumke (Henry Opdyke); Nancy Kulp (Amy); Willis Bouchey (Mr. Clinton); Ruth Brady (Laura).

THE FACTS OF LIFE (UA, 1960) 103 M.

Producer, Norman Panama; associate producer, Hal C. Kern; director, Melvin Frank; screenplay, Panama, Frank; art director, J. MacMillan Johnson, Kenneth A. Reid; song, Johnny Mercer; music, Leigh Harline; assistant director, Jack Aldworth; wardrobe, Edith Head, Edward Stevenson; camera, Charles Lang; editor, Frank Bracht.

Bob Hope (Larry Gilbert); Lucille Ball (Kitty Weaver); Ruth Hussey (Mary Gilbert); Don DeFore (Jack Weaver); Louis Nye (Charlie Busbee); Philip Ober (Doc Mason); Marianne Stewart (Connie Mason); Peter Leeds (Thompson); Hollis Irving (Myrtle Busbee); William Lanteau (United Airlines Clerk); Robert F. Simon (Hotel Clerk); Louise Beavers (Gilberts' Maid); Mike Mazurki (Husband in Motel Room).

CRITIC'S CHOICE (WB, 1963) C—100 M.

Producer, Frank P. Rosenberg; director, Don Weis; based on the play by Ira Levin; screenplay, Jack Sher; assistant director, Russell Llewellyn; music, George Duning; costumes, Edith Head; sound, Stanley Jones; makeup, Gordon Bau; set decorator, William L. Kuehl; camera, Charles Lang; editor, William Ziegler.

Bob Hope (Parker Ballantine); Lucille Ball (Angela Ballantine); Marilyn Maxwell (Ivy London); Rip Torn (Dion Kapakos); Jessie Royce Landis (Charlotte Orr); John Dehner (S. P. Champlain); Jim Backus (Dr. William Von Hagedorn); Rickey Kelman (John Ballantine); Dorothy Green (Mrs. Champlain); Marie Windsor (Sally Orr); Evan McCord (Phil Yardley); Richard Deacon (Harvey Rittenhouse); Joan Shawlee (Marge Orr); Jerome Cowan (Joe Rosenfield); Donald Losby (Godfrey Von Hagedorn); Lurene Tuttle (Mother); Ernestine Wade (Thelma); Stanley Adams (Bartender); Soupy Sales (Desk Clerk); James Flavin (Security Guard); Rhoda Williams, Stacy King (Telephone Operators); Linda Rand, Marilee Jones (Usherettes); Theona Bryant (Beauty Operator); Stephen Coit (Wait); Allan Ray (Apartment Doorman); Breena Howard (Girlfriend); Kelly Benson, Elizabeth Thompson, Anita Samuels (Members of audience); Hal Smith (Drunk); Jimmy Gaines (Boy); Michael St. Angel, Ray Montgomery (Actors); Lillian Culver (Fat Woman); Joy Monroe (Vicki); Beverly Powers, Nancy Vaughn (Pretty Girls); Desiree Sumarra (Trophy Girl); Patricia Olson (Barbara Yardley); Mimi Dillard (Maid); Tommy Jackson (Doorman); Frank London (Butcher); Sam Flint, Louis Cavalier (Little League Rooters); Arthur Passarella, Art Stewart (Umpires).

A GUIDE FOR THE MARRIED MAN (20th, 1967) C—91 M.

Producer, Frank McCarthy; director, Gene Kelly; based on the book by Frank Tarloff; screenplay, Tarloff; assistant director, Paul Helmick; art director, Jack Martin Smith, William Glasgow; set decorator, Walter M. Scott, Raphael Bretton; music, Johnny Williams; song, Williams and Leslie Bricusse; costumes, Moss Mabry; sound,

Harry M. Lindgren, David Dockendorf; special camera effects, L. B. Abbott, Art Cruickshank, Emil Kosa, Jr.; camera, Joe MacDonald; editor, Dorothy Spencer.

Walter Matthau (Paul Manning); Robert Morse (Ed Stander); Inger Stevens (Ruth Manning); Sue Anne Langdon (Irma Johnson); Claire Kelly (Harriet Stander); Linda Harrison (Miss Stardust); Elaine Devry (Jocelyn Montgomery); Michael Romanoff (Maitre d'Hotel); Jason Wingreen (Mr. Johnson); Fred Holliday, Pat Becker (Party Guests); Lucille Ball, Jack Benny, Polly Bergen, Joey Bishop, Sid Caesar, Art Carney, Wally Cox, Jayne Mansfield, Hal March, Louis Nye, Carl Reiner, Phil Silvers, Terry-Thomas, Ben Blue, Ann Morgan Guilbert, Jeffrey Hunter, Marty Ingels, Sam Jaffe (Guest Stars); Heather Carroll (Mrs. Miller); Robert Patten (Mr. Miller); Eddie Quillan (Cologne Salesman); Dale Van Sickel (Stunt Driver); Mickey Deems (Waiter); Aline Towne (Mrs. Mousey Man); Chanin Hale (Mrs. Crenshaw).

YOURS, MINE AND OURS   (UA, 1968) C—110 M.

Producer, Robert F. Blumofe; director, Melville Shavelson; story, Madelyn Davis, Bob Carroll, Jr.; screenplay, Shavelson, Mort Lachman; assistant director, Dick Bremerkamp, Louis Nocoletti, Jim Benjamin; art director, Arthur Lonegan; music, Fred Karlin; sound, Pete Peterson; camera, Charles Wheeler; editor, Stuart Gilmore.

Lucille Ball (Helen North); Henry Fonda (Frank Beardsley); Van Johnson (Darrel Harrison); Tom Bosley (Doctor); Jennifer Leak (Colleen North); Kevin Burchett (Nicky North); Kimberly Beck (Janette North); Mitchell Vogel (Tommy North); Margot Jane (Jean North); Eric Shea (Phillip North); Gregory Atkins (Gerald North); Lynnell Atkins (Teresa North); Timothy Matthieson (Mike Beardsley); Gilbert Rogers (Rusty Beardsley); Nancy Roth (Rosemary Beardsley); Suzanne Cupito (Louise Beardsley); Gary Goetzman (Greg Beardsley); Holly O'Brien (Susan Beardsley); Michele Tobin (Veronica Beardsley); Maralee Foster (Mary Beardsley); Tracy Nelson (Germaine Beardsley); Stephanie Oliver (Joan Beardsley); Ben Murphy (Larry).

MAME   (WB, 1974) C—132 M.

Producer, Robert Fryer, James Cresson; director, Gene Saks; based on the musical play by Jerome Lawrence, Robert E. Lee, Jerry Herman and the play *Auntie Mame* by Lawrence, Lee; from the novel by Patrick Dennis; screenplay, Paul Zindel; songs, Herman; choreography, Onna White, Martin Allen; costumes, Theadora van Runkle; orchestra, Ralph Burns, Billy Byers; sound, Al Overton; camera, Phil Lathrop; editor, Maury Wintetrobe.

Lucille Ball (Mame); Robert Preston (Beauregard); Beatrice Arthur (Vera); Kirby Furlong (Young Patrick); Bruce Davidson (Older Patrick); Joyce Van Patten (Sally Cato); Don Porter (Mr. Upson); Audrey Christie (Mrs. Upson); Jane Connell (Agnes Gooch); John McGiver (Mr. Babcock); Doris Cook (Gloria Upson); Bobbi Jordan (Pegeen); George Chiang (Ito).

With Betty Grable on the RKO lot in 1935

With Patricia Wilder and Anne Shirley in a 1936 RKO publicity pose

With Fred Astaire and Ginger Rogers in FOLLOW THE FLEET (RKO '36)

With Ginger Rogers in STAGE DOOR (RKO '37)

With Groucho in ROOM SERVICE (RKO '38)

With Ralph Forbes, Jack Oakie and Alice White in ANNABEL TAKES A TOUR (RKO '38)

With Chester Morris in FIVE CAME BACK (RKO '39)

With George Chandler and George Murphy in A GIRL, A GUY, AND A GOB (RKO '41)

With Marian Jordan, Jim Jordan, and Edgar Bergen in LOOK WHO'S LAUGHING (RKO '41)

With Billy Gilbert and Dean Jagger in VALLEY OF THE SUN (RKO '42)

With Henry Fonda in THE BIG STREET (RKO '42)

With Victor Mature in SEVEN DAYS' LEAVE (RKO '42)

Top left: with Gene Kelly, Red Skelton, Virginia O'Brien, and Kay Kyser in DU BARRY WAS A LADY (MGM '43)

Right: Lucille Ball in 1943

Center: with Virginia Weidler, Tommy Dix, William Gaxton, and Chill Wills in BEST FOOT FORWARD (MGM '43)

Bottom: with Keenan Wynn in EASY TO WED (MGM '46)

With Cedric Hardwicke in
LURED (UA '47)

With John Agar, *right, in* THE
MAGIC CARPET (Col '51)

With children Desi, Jr. and
Lucie in 1953

On "I Love Lucy" (CBS-TV, c. 1955) with Vivian Vance, Desi Arnaz, and William Frawley

With husband Desi Arnaz in 1955

With James Mason, Louis Calhern, and Desi Arnaz in FOREVER, DARLING (MGM '56)

With Angelo Didio on "I Love Lucy" (CBS-TV, 1956)

With Bob Hope in THE FACTS OF LIFE (UA '60)

With Mitchell Vogel, Timoth[y] Matthieson, Henry Fonda, a[nd] Gilbert Rogers in YOURS, M[INE] AND OURS (UA '68)

On Broadway in *Wildcat* (1961)

With husband Gary Morton in 1968

In REBECCA (UA '40)

5'3"
108 pounds
Blonde hair
Hazel eyes
Libra

Joan
Fontaine

With her Dresden doll-like delicacy, and her cool, elegant manner, aristo-
cratic Joan Fontaine should have been a ranking international cinema star
for much longer than the World War II period. However, before her rise to
movie fame as the fragile heroine of Gothic filmfare, she was a frightened,
if crisp, B-picture leading lady in the late 1930s at RKO. After Rebecca *and*
the Oscar-winning Suspicion, *she was an imperious star grown too fond of the*
high-society life that she so carefully cultivated, and far too uninterested in
promulgating her potentially rich acting career as a mature player. (She is
more versatile beneath the surface than her more famous sister, Olivia de
Havilland.)

A decade ago one interviewer wrote of her: "Joan Fontaine is the complete
actress. After an hour's conversation, you have no clearer idea who she is, or
what she thinks, or why, than if you'd been talking to a figure on the celluloid
screen." No one, least of all her potential fans, has ever been able to success-
fully fathom what are the essential ingredients of this actress. She seems
physically vulnerable, yet radiates a mixture of being both an emotionally
solid figure and a skittish female in great need of a helping hand. For all her
demonstrated capabilities as a cook, interior decorator, golfer, and eques-
trienne, Joan has never seen fit to become a completely realized human being

in her media work. The clothes of the social arbiter fit too quickly and smoothly for her to visibly care otherwise.

Joan de Beauvoir de Havilland was born on October 22, 1917, in the International Settlement in Tokyo, the second child (Olivia was born on July 1, 1916) of Walter de Havilland and the former Lilian Ruse.* Because of Olivia's and Joan's recurring ailments, the de Havillands came to San Francisco in November, 1919, planning to follow the advice of specialists and take their children to the warmer Italian climate. But Olivia's condition worsened and further traveling was out of the question. Mrs. de Havilland and the two girls settled in at a resort inn in nearby Saratoga, a town of 1,000 people, while her husband returned to his lucrative Tokyo enterprises. It soon became clear to Mrs. de Havilland that it would be best to end her quarrelsome marriage. While preparing the necessary divorce papers, she built a small home in Saratoga proper.

Ironically, while Olivia's health improved in the California climate, Joan remained a sickly child, constantly in need of medical attention. Because of the necessity of restricting Joan's physical activities, "Livvy can, Joan can't" soon became a familiar expression in the de Havilland household. This practical—but irrational to a child—curtailment of Joan's *modus operandi* naturally led to an unresolved rivalry between the sisters.

While Mrs. de Havilland was back in Tokyo to complete her divorce suit,† gregarious Olivia made the acquaintance of neighbor George M. Fontaine, the manager of a San Jose department store, who had a son by a previous marriage. Mrs. de Havilland arrived back in Saratoga and soon decided that Fontaine was the new man in her life. The couple wed in 1925.

Like her older sister, Joan had an extremely high IQ‡ and spent most of her time immersed in books due to her restricted daily physical program. It was a common sight to see her sitting in the graveyard near home, propped up against a tombstone and reading poetry. As one of her mother's acquaintances later recalled: "This melancholy pursuit seemed suitable since she was a wasted looking creature and to all appearances had one foot planted in the area."

---

*Born in Berkshire, England, Lilian Ruse had first come to Japan to visit her brother. At an embassy tea she was introduced to Walter de Havilland ("He spoke like God, but behaved like the devil," she later recalled). He was a descendant of Sir Peter de Havilland, a supporter of Cromwell against Charles I, and of Lord and Lady Nolesworth, patrons of Gilbert and Sullivan. His cousin, Sir Geoffrey de Havilland, founded the famed Aircraft company. Walter de Havilland himself was well to do and with his scholarly bent chose to be an English instructor. Happening to be living in Tokyo he decided to teach at the Imperial University and in his spare time operate a patent law firm. He proposed to Lilian, but she declined in order to return to England to continue her music and voice studies at Sir Beerbohm Tree's Dramatic Academy. In 1914, when he returned to England to enlist, he re-established his acquaintance with her, and when he was rejected for military service, she returned to Japan with him as his wife. Their first child, Olivia, was born in Tokyo.

†Mr. de Havilland would subsequently marry his household maid.

‡At the age of three Joan scored 160 on a scientific intelligence test.

468

Because Mrs. de Havilland had never pursued her own theatrical career, she was convinced that one or both of her daughters might make the grade in the profession she had sacrificed to become Walter de Havilland's wife. During their California years, it became a daily ritual for Mrs. de Havilland to correct their diction and have the children recite aloud from Shakespeare and other playwrights. ("We were nauseating," Joan recalls.) Both girls attended Saratoga primary schools and then went to nearby Los Gatos High School, where, on their mother's advice, they learned typing and shorthand. For a time the girls were enrolled at the Notre Dame Convent in Belmont, California. Living at home eventually became odious to Olivia and Joan, for Mr. Fontaine was a stern disciplinarian who strongly opposed the girls' proposed show-business careers. Thus, when Olivia was sixteen and Joan was fifteen, they "left" home and went to live with a friend of their mother. After school they would work at odd jobs (Joan as a waitress) to contribute to their own support.

Frail and delicate Joan soon became ill again and cabled her father in Tokyo for help. He invited her to visit him in Japan, while advising Olivia that he would provide financial assistance for her budding stage career in California. Once in Japan, Joan shucked all signs of the anemia that had caused her dismal adolescence. She blossomed into a wraithlike beauty, and while enjoying the novelty of having a slew of beaus in panting polite pursuit, she voraciously gobbled up courses at the American School in Tokyo in subjects ranging from Oriental art to ballet and amateur theatrics. By the time she returned to California in early 1934 she had collected five engagement rings, for as a matter of principle she never broke a betrothal!

Finding that Olivia had already made some headway in the acting field, competitive Joan launched her own professional career by joining a San Jose theatre group. Through a family friend, Homer Curran, Joan later made her first professional appearance in San Francisco in Curran's production of *Kind Lady* starring May Robson, Ralph Forbes and Robert Kent. But San Jose was too smalltime for Joan and she moved on to Los Angeles.

To celebrate her move to the big city Joan adopted a new surname, first St. John,* then Burfield, determined that she would in no way trade upon Olivia's emerging success. At this juncture Joan came to the attention of director George Cukor, who tested her at MGM. Thereafter he offered her a bit in *No More Ladies* (1935), to be directed by Edward H. Griffith and himself. It seemed a good beginning: employment at swank MGM in no less than a classy Joan Crawford vehicle. But when *No More Ladies* premiered at the Capitol Theatre on June 21, 1935, ninth-billed Joan (Burfield) was scarcely in evidence. Cast as the *thirty-five-year-old* sophisticate Caroline, she had a minuscule role as one of the several ladies (including Gail Patrick and Vivi-

---

*St. John was concocted for its alliterative rhythm but proved clumsy; Burfield was derived from a Los Angeles street. Fontaine was ultimately selected when, according to Joan, being advised by a local numerologist that she really should have a last name ending in *e*, she dug out this new surname from her family genealogy.

enne Osborne) who lose dissolute philanderer Robert Montgomery to sympathetic socialite Crawford.

Following *No More Ladies* Joan experienced more than a year and a half of professional inactivity* and was very willing to accept a role in Henry Duffy's stage production of *Call It a Day* when it was offered. This rehash edition of Dodie Smith's domestic comedy opened at the El Capitan Theatre in Hollywood in mid-June, 1936, for a two-week run. Undoubtedly, part of Joan's enthusiasm for the show derived from the fact that Olivia, already an established Warner Bros. contract player, had just completed playing the same ingenue role in the picturization of *Call It a Day* (1937).

Among the opening-night audience at Henry Duffy's rendition of *Call It a Day* was veteran film producer Jesse L. Lasky, who was attracted not to the mature stars of the show, Violet Heming and Conway Tearle, but to newcomer Joan. He already was making a habit of contracting new screen talent via his "Gateway to Hollywood" radio program, and he suggested Joan screentest for him. She did and soon thereafter signed a player's contract with Lasky. One of the provisos of the pact stated that Lasky was in no way to exploit the fact that she was Olivia de Havilland's "baby sister."

Because of Lasky's then-current production-distribution agreement with RKO, Joan's personal contract was in turn assumed by that studio. Overnight she found herself an RKO studio gal, on the same lot where Katharine Hepburn, Irene Dunne, and Ginger Rogers had already assumed the top spots held only a few years before by Ann Harding, Constance Bennett, Bebe Daniels, and Helen Twelvetrees. Company production head Pandro S. Berman immediately had the new contractee cast in Hepburn's *Quality Street* (Radio City Music Hall, April 8, 1937), directed by George Stevens. Joan was assigned the tiny role of Charlotte Parratt, the proper fiancée of ensign Roland Varno.

Several generations of theatregoers may have loved the whimsy of *Quality Street,* but Sir James M. Barrie's comedy of manners did not measure up to expectation in this new screening, falling short, in many people's estimation, of the 1927 silent film starring Marion Davies. Thirteenth-billed Joan was only oncamera fleetingly, but she wore the period costumes well. In her one remaining close-up in the final-release print, her well-chiseled features photographed attractively. At the time director Stevens, who was struggling to provide Hepburn with a vehicle as successful as his *Alice Adams* (1935) had been, found time to observe that he was convinced Joan had the makings of a real star.

---

*During this period, Joan often roomed with far more affluent Olivia and frequently borrowed money, wardrobe, and the use of a car from her sister. Joan can now say, "I'll always be grateful to her for that," but at the time it was a crushing blow to her pride to be forced to accept succor from big sister. This period saw the culmination of Joan's rancor at being second-best to Olivia, but she still masked her feelings with such circuitous statements as, "We had to share the same bathroom together too long . . . ," which was her way of saying that Olivia's small Hollywood cottage was too small to contain the competitive de Havilland girls.

RKO, however, was not yet convinced of Joan's box-office potential,* but was reasonably sure that, at the very least, the well-bred girl with the sophisticated British accent could lend class to its increasing string of programmers, previously dominated by studio-stable players Frances Dee, Lucille Ball, and Anne Shirley (and by Wendy Barrie in the future).

The Man Who Found Himself (1937), a contrived double-bill item, featured Joan in the vapid role of a flying field nurse who helps ex-doctor John Beal to regain his past professional standing and to patch up personal differences with his father (George Irving). The picture, which was released at about the same time as *Quality Street,* gave critics their first opportunity to play compare-and-contrast, with Joan as their latest victim. One fan magazine contingent insisted Joan was a lookalike for Kathryn Carver,† who was about to give up her promising screen career again for yet another marriage. *Variety,* while admitting Joan "handles herself quite well" and "photographs lusciously," carped about her "seeming desire to ape the voice mannerisms of Katharine Hepburn." Kate Cameron in the *New York Daily News* assured her many readers that "Miss Fontaine is as blonde as Miss de Havilland is dark, but she has the same charm and poise which makes her sister one of the most promising of the younger actresses in Hollywood." Still others insisted Joan revealed definite traits of being the new Madeleine Carroll. The net result was that twenty-year-old Joan was being dissected and reassembled for public approval as everyone and everything but herself.

You Can't Beat Love (1937) was a fragile lark with a plot which suggested that love will conquer all. Devil-may-care playboy Preston Foster is a game guy who will take any dare, from digging a ditch in full-dress suit to accepting the challenge of the mayor's comely daughter (Joan) that he campaign against her dad. In a plot solution that was illogical and verged on the offensive, Foster pulls out of the political race at the crucial moment to please his lady love (Joan). The *New York Mirror* confirmed what astute filmgoers already knew, that Joan could effortlessly rise above her mediocre material: " . . . the sole distinction [of *You Can't Beat Love*] is that it permits her fans to meet the pretty Joan Fontaine, new RKO Radio starlet who is being pushed vigorously by the studio. She is pretty, has a winning smile, gives an unsensational performance in a role which demands nothing more." Ironically, *You Can't Beat Love* opened on a double-bill program at the RKO Palace along with another programmer, Olivia's *Call It a Day*. As if two pictures were not enough

---

*RKO's female-player roster at the time included: Lucille Ball, Diana Barrington, Helen Broderick, Claudette Colbert and Irene Dunne (both on special multistudio deals), Diana Gibson, Betty Grable, Margot Grahame, Katharine Hepburn, Harriet Hilliard, Harriet Hoctor, Anne Hovey, Maxine Jennings, Lorraine Kreuger, Thelma Leeds, Ada Leonard, Marjorie Lord, Marie Marks, Melissa Mason, Gertrude Michael, Dorothy Moore, Patsy Lee Parsons, Lee Patrick, Barbara Pepper, Lily Pons, Leona Roberts, Ginger Rogers, Anne Shirley, Ann Sothern, Barbara Stanwyck (special multistudio deal), Jane Walsh, Patricia Wilder, and Constance Worth.

†The onetime wife of Ira L. Hill, she had later married Adolphe Menjou and after divorcing him wed a stockbroker. She died in 1947 at the age of thirty-nine.

to lure patrons, the theatre's management offered the added inducement of including a film reportage of the Jim Braddock-Joe Louis boxing match.

Jesse L. Lasky considered utilizing Joan in the lowbrow musical *Radio City Revels* (1937), but newcomer Ann Miller was substituted as being much more suited to cavorting with the likes of Jack Oakie, Kenny Baker, Bob Burns, Helen Broderick and Victor Moore in this bumpkin revue show. Instead Joan was cast in the more prestigious *Music for Madame* (1937). This was the third Lasky screen vehicle for operatic tenor Nino Martini, but it was not the same caliber as his previous pleasant diversion, *The Gay Desperado* (United Artists, 1936, co-starring Ida Lupino with Martini). *Music for Madame* had the good sense not to surfeit the viewer with an overdose of operatic excerpts while spinning out its gossamer plot. Aspiring singer Martini arrives in Hollywood bent on achieving fame and fortune. Unwittingly he becomes the dupe of jewel thieves, who use him as a singing diversion at a wedding reception while they systematically rob the host's gems. Since Martini is dressed in a clown's disguise at the time, the police can only refer to the unknown accomplice as the "mysterious tenor." But because the law has a good description of his vocal style he dares not sing in public, a blessing in disguise for the movie's viewers. Young composer Joan also crashed this same party, determined to play her latest composition for guest Alan Mowbray, he being a distinguished, if outrageously eccentric maestro. Naturally Joan and Martini meet and fall in love while extricating themselves from complicity in the robbery.

Through instinct and an ingrained sense of authoritarian presence, Joan had glided through past screen roles with relative oncamera ease. But *Music for Madame* asked her to function in a genre alien to her basic temperament: lighthearted farce. Her role as the serious-bent composer, Jean Clemens, required her to be the brunt of several gag situations and wisecracks.* Joan attempted to mask her uneasiness behind a solemn onscreen tone, forcing out a smile on cue or timidly joining with Martini in the song "I Want the World to Know." But neither she nor heavily accented Martini blended homogeneously with the dominating screwball performances of Mowbray, detective Alan Hale, Erik Rhodes (as Martini's competitor, Spaghetti Nacio), or hyperfrenetic Billy Gilbert in a recap of his sneezing bit.

RKO was not exhibiting reckless abandon when it chose to overlook Joan's relative awkwardness in *Music for Madame* and handed her the plum assignment of appearing opposite Fred Astaire in *A Damsel in Distress* (1937). Ginger Rogers wanted a break from her steady diet of co-starring musicals with Astaire. Exhibitors were demanding the promised new Astaire picture, production time was drawing near, and no suitable replacement for Rogers had yet been found.† Director George Stevens was convinced that despite

---

*E.g., district attorney Grant Mitchell advises Joan, "If you're a composer you'll have to face the music."

†Astaire rejected ex-Warner Bros. star Ruby Keeler as being inappropriate to portray an English aristocrat.

Joan's unfamiliarity with musical-comedy protocol, she could handle the part, especially if he and Astaire exerted their imagination to skirt around her singing-dancing limitations. And RKO, which had invested some coin and energy in promoting Joan as a versatile high-toned leading lady, decided to put her to the brutal test. Thus George Burns and Gracie Allen were imported from Paramount to handle the bulk of the singing-dancing-comedy collaboration with Astaire, particularly in the already devised and intricate fun-house dance scene.

In this modern cinematic fairy tale Joan was lovely but tense as the gracious British miss trapped in a brooding English castle by her conventional relatives, and finally "rescued" by dapper American dancing star Astaire. But no matter how director Stevens disguised the situation, there was inevitable audience comparison between Joan's performance and the known quantity of a Ginger Rogers enactment. When the plotline of *A Damsel in Distress* finally calls for Joan to join Astaire in a brookside dance (to George and Ira Gershwin's "Things Are Looking Up"), choreographer Hermes Pan and cinematographer Joseph H. August did their utmost to keep mobile Joan in semi-long shots, as Astaire swung her around the soundstage hillside. The same setup held true in the castle hallway finale where Astaire and Joan lightstepped to the Gershwins' "I Can't Be Bothered Now." As a result of everyone overprotecting Joan's oncamera image in *A Damsel in Distress,* she emerged as a passive, forgettable screen heroine, vastly overshadowed by the top-billed star trio and by such superb supporting players as Reginald Gardiner and Constance Collier. *Life* magazine's verdict was among the kinder notices Joan received: "[She] tries hard but lacks Ginger's grace!"

Embarrassed by its own foible of miscasting Joan in *A Damsel in Distress,* RKO officially lost all interest in Joan's screen career and blithely tossed her back to the anomaly of B-pictures. The Joan of this period was too shy and introverted to press her legitimate claims for better opportunities and resignedly set about fulfilling her studio contract.

For her final 1937 release Joan was farmed out to Puritan Pictures for the cheaply assembled *A Million to One.* She and Bruce Bennett were the children of two separate past Olympic contenders. The children romance and eventually reunite their warring dads, with Bennett going on to championship victory. Joan respectfully requested not to be forced into *Maid's Night Out* (1938), but RKO insisted, and Joan was in no professional or financial position to go on suspension. In this film, as yet another lightheaded heiress—here the daughter of arch society matron Hedda Hopper—she is mistaken for a maid by Allan Lane, who she thinks is the milkman. But since the film was a dedicated, if feeble, screwball comedy, the rules required that no one really be what he seems. Lane has a bet with his wealthy dairy-owner father that he can hold down a milkman's delivery job for a month; as a reward, if successful, he can borrow the family yacht to study marine biology in the South Seas. Not only is Joan not a domestic, but also she is not totally the spoiled little debutante she seemed on first meeting. The only remarkable feature of *Maid's Night Out* was that it provided Joan with her first instance of top screen billing.

Although *Blond Cheat* (1938) boasted a strong British cast, it was far from a first-class drawing-room comedy. Cecil Kellaway hires actress Joan to break up his daughter's romance with Derrick de Marney. The conventional results found Joan taking her job too seriously and becoming very attached to the lad.

RKO's *Sky Giants* (Rialto Theatre, July 19, 1938) in no way matched MGM's *Test Pilot* (1938), but its aerial photography of stunting and spinning planes was commendable. Unfortunately, when the story hit the ground it exploded into formula drivel. Harry Carey, retired from the Army to head a new aviation school, has veteran flyer Richard Dix assigned as his chief instructor. Soon Dix and Carey's reckless son (Chester Morris) are vying for Joan's affections, but they remain steadfast, cooperative airmen when involved in the climatic transarctic flight to Moscow. It was traditional for reviewers to label programmer heroines "decorative," but the *New York World-Telegram* tripped over itself when complimenting Joan: "Joan Fontaine is so attractive as Meg that it doesn't matter much whether her performance is good or bad."

Despite its Radio City Music Hall sendoff (December 15, 1938), United Artists' *The Duke of West Point* was an uneven sentimental saga of the U. S. military academy and the unenviable lot of West Point plebes. Louis Hayward provided one of his typical low-keyed interpretations as the British-born American who finds the discipline more than he bargained for, particularly when he is nearly cashiered for performing a noble deed (sneaking off post one night to wire money to Richard Carlson's poor widowed mother so that his roommate can remain at the academy). Just to give the picture a hopefully new twist, football was not the focal sport. Instead the brutal game of hockey, with a "big" game between the Point and Canada's Royal Academy, provided the film's few exciting scenes. Producer Edward Small utilized Joan for the rather colorless heroine: the hockey coach's daughter who perceives the integrity behind Hayward's glib facade.

Back at RKO, director George Stevens again came to Joan's career rescue by casting her in his expansive production of *Gunga Din* (Radio City Music Hall, January 26, 1939). Rudyard Kipling's famed poem was transformed into a thunderous cavalcade of action set in nineteenth-century India where the resolute British armed forces battle the upsurging native Thuggees led by Eduardo Ciannelli. Since Sam Jaffe in the title role of the loyal native waterboy ("You're a better man than I am, Gunga Din") only received fourth billing in the picture, it is no wonder that Joan's sixth-billed role as Douglas Fairbanks, Jr.'s fiancée received short shrift. The picture stuck to its focus on the musketeerlike adventures of British soldiers Cary Grant, Fairbanks, and Victor McLaglen, as they capered through one episode after another. When romance threatened to dominate the storyline, it was quickly thrust aside. In fact, in one of Joan's few scenes at the Army post, Grant and McLaglen scheme to separate refined Joan from Fairbanks so they won't lose their comrade-in-arms to matrimony. The million-dollar-plus eastern-western was in production for 104 days with location lensing at Lone Pine, California, near the slopes of Mt. Whitney. (Joan's inconsequential sequences were shot at the home lot.) When released, *Gunga Din* proved an enormously successful excursion into the adventure-epic genre so clearly dominated by Warner Bros. in the 1930s. It would be reissued several times over the years before being sold to television.* Once again Joan gained no career boost from appearing in a major production. Unlike sister Olivia, who had successfully graced several large-scale Errol Flynn costumers at Warners, Joan had yet to prove herself as more than a tastefully pretty programmer heroine. And Hollywood was overrun with such types at this time.

Before Joan's RKO contract option expired in late 1938, she was loaned to Republic for *Man of Conquest* (1939) as part of a package deal including star Richard Dix and director George Nicholls, Jr. The million-dollar tribute to the eccentric American hero Sam Houston (Dix) traces his action-charged life from the battle of Horseshoe Bend, where he becomes a lifelong friend of Andrew Jackson (Edward Ellis), through Houston's presidency of Texas following the defeat of Mexico. In her initial unsympathetic screen assignment, Joan was presented as Eliza Allen, Houston's demanding first wife, whom he weds on the eve of his re-election as governor of Tennessee. She is a pretty but petulant miss who will not abide Dix's peccadillos, including his carousing, and she leaves him in a permanent huff. Although Joan's Eliza was subordinate to Gail Patrick's slick portrait of Houston's picture-book-staunch-and-true second wife, Joan displayed a previously untapped histrionic resourcefulness, giving her crudely written role some nourishing bite. *Man of Conquest* proved she was very capable at handling her share of non-sweetness-and-cream roles.

After two years at RKO, twenty-two-year-old Joan was now at liberty, a semi-acknowledged Hollywood personality in a town teeming with box-office names. But Joan the adult was no longer the repressed adolescent and she was already showing signs of displaying the tenacity and tarantula quality that would make her capable of dealing with producers and directors alike when she became a 1940s bigtime screen star. Whether Joan cares even now to admit it or not, it was because of her much more famous sister, Olivia, that she found herself ushered again into the august presence of director George Cukor, this time to consider the value of accepting the offered privilege of reading for the secondary-female-lead role of Melanie in David O. Selznick-MGM's *Gone with the Wind* (1939).† Hurt that she had not been considered for the Scarlett O'Hara job, Joan politely but haughtily declined performing more than a brief reading for Melanie, reinforcing both Selznick and Cukor's

Sergeants Three (1962), the Frank Sinatra-Dean Martin-Peter Lawford-Sammy Davis, Jr. western remake of *Gunga Din* had Ruta Lee playing Joan's old role.

†In *Memo From David O. Selznick* (1972), cinema historian Rudy Behlmer offers a November 11, 1938, memo from Selznick to attorney Daniel T. O'Shea: "Certainly I would give anything if we had Olivia de Havilland under contract to us so that we could cast her as Melanie ... It should also be borne in mind that it is a long time since George has seen [her sister Joan] Fontaine. . . . She certainly should have readings."

original belief that sister Olivia was the de Havilland girl they should have tested for the role. In the course of events, Selznick replaced Cukor with Victor Fleming, and Cukor was transferred to helming Metro's *The Women* (1939). Cukor remembered Joan and cast her in the film.

Joan found herself in very heady company in this bitchy rampage translated from Clare Boothe Luce's 666-performance Broadway smash success. Next to Norma Shearer's lead part, Joan's Peggy Day (the lamb of the group) was the only other essentially sympathetic role in the all-female cast. Joan's Peggy is the docile young wife who finds herself spouting forth the vitriolic sentiments instilled in her flibbertigibbet mind by her strong-willed pals. Thus the almost simpering Peggy—flighty of mind and movement, with arms limply drifting about and head moving like a magnet to whomever is dominating her at the moment—is led to admit that "you can trust no man further than you can kick a lemon pie." But once in Reno she has a decided change of heart—and characterization—and is prompted to calling her almost ex-spouse to tell him that she is pregnant and wants to come home. She leaves the scene of battle, a contrite miss. Despite the oddity of her about-face characterization, Joan made her presence felt in the film, displaying at some moments hints of the warmhearted elegance that would be so much a part of her best 1940s screen work.*

Less than a month after *The Women* debuted at the Capitol Theatre, Joan wed dapper, mature screen star Brian Aherne on August 20, 1939, at St. John's Episcopal Church in Del Monte, California. It was the first marriage for each. Joan was attended by her unmarried sister, Olivia, and associate producer Louis D. Lighton served as best man. Olivia's presence at the ceremony was gracious but fraught with tension, since the previous year Aherne, her co-star in *The Great Garrick* (1937), had been among her steadier and more promising beaus. On the other hand, flirtatious, nightclub-hopping Joan had most frequently been escorted about Hollywood by forty-three-year-old veteran actor Conrad Nagel. Columnist Hedda Hopper later reported having cautioned Joan about Nagel. "Take a good look at me," Hopper instructed Joan. "I married a man five years older than my father. We had a wonderful son and I've worked every day since—without a husband." Whatever influence Hedda Hopper's regal advice may have had, Joan soon discarded Nagel and wed thirty-seven-year-old Englisher Aherne, who had made his screen debut in the British silent film *The Eleventh Commandment* (1924). If Joan had been seeking a playmate with excellent deportment she hardly could have picked a better candidate. But she did not reckon that a fast-approaching reversal in their positions in the constellation of silver-screen players, would turn her

---

*Director Cukor recently recalled: "Joan was a very pretty girl. . . . I'd always remembered her. She had a not very successful career as a leading lady at RKO, and she was free at this time. I told the studio [MGM] they ought to take an option on her, but they didn't. Anyway, it was an interesting moment when she played her scene on the telephone. Up to then she'd wanted to be an actress but was never really sure she could act. Now she felt a power, and as a result of this scene, the experience it gave her, she felt, 'Yes, I was right to try, I can act . . . ' I think it had a great deal to do with her getting the part in *Rebecca*."

spouse's debonair manner and facile wit into an icy exterior punctuated with acid observations on her immodest emergence from a stock ingenue's shadowy cocoon into the limelight of a self-impressed, demanding cinema queen.

When Joan and Aherne departed on their honeymoon trip to the North country she left Hollywood as an unemployed, floundering actress. She returned a week later a star-in-the-making. There are three versions of this watershed period. According to Joan, it was all merely a pleasant quirk of fate. As she recollected, some months before her wedding to Aherne she had been included in the select circle invited to dine at Pickfair with Mary Pickford and others. She found herself seated next to David O. Selznick at the dinner table. When the mighty producer smiled at her she thought she had better start a conversation pronto so he would not have the opportunity to inquire on what picture she was then working. For, if the horrible truth be known, she was without any legitimate offers whatsoever.

"I have just finished reading the most interesting book," Joan told Selznick in her best finishing-school-hostess manner.

"What was the name of it?" Selznick politely asked.

"*Rebecca,*" said Joan.

"You finished reading it today? I finished buying it today. How would you like to test for it?"

With proper modesty Joan suggested that Margaret Sullavan, the acknowledged weeper queen of the cinema, would really be a far better candidate for the vulnerable heroine. With equal conviviality, Selznick admitted the notion had crossed his mind but nevertheless asked Joan if she wouldn't care to test for the picture. Matching his decorum to hide her inner glee, she agreed she would like to try her hand at the part, and so she did make one screentest, then another and yet another. But seemingly Selznick could not make up his mind, which was nothing new to Hollywood. By the time her August wedding to Aherne took place, eight other actresses had tested for the lead in Daphne du Maurier's latest best seller and Joan had given up, so she says, on any hope of winning the showcase assignment. Furthermore, according to Joan, while she and Aherne were in the wilds of northern Oregon hunting and fishing, she was called off the lake and her Hollywood agent told her by telephone that she had been victorious in winning *Rebecca.* Joan would insist that right there and then she told her ten-percenter: "But I don't want it." Joan claims it was Aherne who said: "Oh, why don't you do it for hat money?"

Aherne waited some three decades to relate his side of the story, as cavalierly told in his flippant, wispy autobiography, *A Proper Job* (1969): "Almost on impulse I married Joan Fontaine, sister of Olivia de Havilland, young, pretty, gay and utterly charming—and no actress, thank God, or at least so I thought until the fifth day of our honeymoon in the Oregon woods, when my dream was abruptly shattered by a phone call from David Selznick offering her the lead in his picture, *Rebecca.* Over my despairing protests, the honeymoon was instantly abandoned, and we rushed back to Hollywood, where she was launched into orbit as a big new motion picture star. Soon after this disaster—and I had seen too much of the marriages of stars to believe it would be anything else—the Second World War broke out and my life, like those of people all over the world, became filled with new and unsuspected problems."

Only recently, with the publication of a small portion of David O. Selznick's prolific and lengthy file of memos, has the producer's version of what "really happened" come to light.

Selznick considered *Rebecca* almost as exciting a project as *Gone with the Wind,* infusing his participation in the making of the Daphne du Maurier thriller with all the hoopla, decision-pondering, and creative re-evaluations that surrounded the making of the classic Civil War epic movie. Selznick states he had been following Joan's career since her early RKO days and at one point in considering her for *Rebecca* hoped to interest Sam Goldwyn and Hal Roach in a three-way producers' contract to utilize her acting services. As Selznick states: "She was thought by some people in Hollywood to have so little talent that they called her 'the wooden woman.' Nobody at our place could see her for dust in this role, nor could they understand why I kept turning down the great and important stars that were dying to play the part."

Eventually, after considering such disparate types as Loretta Young, Vivien Leigh, and Olivia de Havilland for *Rebecca,* the final choices came down to Margaret Sullavan,* Anne Baxter, and Joan. After much viewing of the assorted screentests, many of the creative talents—including director John Cromwell, who had made Joan's first *Rebecca* test, and Alfred Hitchcock, who was to helm the movie itself—voted in favor of her.

On August 19, 1939, Selznick, in communicating to an associate, revealed the following: "Now, the situation on Fontaine is curiously complicated since her engagement to Brian Aherne, whom she is marrying tomorrow, Saturday." The producer went on to relate that intellectually he was still shadowboxing with his conscience whether Joan could handle such an in-depth role without becoming monotonous, and that the best thing for Joan to do, would be to make additional tests in order "to get the full range of her performance. Unfortunately, her face is swollen with an impacted wisdom tooth (and not so good for a honeymoon) and therefore she couldn't make the tests today or any time before her marriage tomorrow. She said she would be delighted to cut her honeymoon short, coming back after a week if we decide to put her in the part; and further that she would cut her honeymoon short to make further tests . . . "

Regardless of which of the three accounts of that week in August, 1939, one prefers, Joan did cut her honeymoon short—she did return to Hollywood—and she did play *Rebecca.*

Joan signed a long-term personal contract with Selznick in early September, 1939. Her natural British manner was very helpful in her portrayal of the heroine, and director Hitchcock, making his first American-lensed picture,

*Sullavan had played the role of the second Mrs. de Winter with Orson Welles in a radio version of *Rebecca.*

surrounded her with a largely English cast: Laurence Olivier (somewhat angered that his wife, Vivien Leigh, was not given the film's lead), Judith Anderson, George Sanders, Nigel Bruce, C. Aubrey Smith, Gladys Cooper, Melville Cooper, and Leo G. Carroll.

The psychological thriller presented Joan as the pretty but mousy paid companion of a wealthy American, who jumps at the opportunity to escape her onerous position by quickly wedding the gallant but mysterious stranger, Maxim de Winter (Olivier). "The first time I saw Manderley," Joan's Rebecca speaks in the voice-over prologue, "I had just married Maxim de Winter. I had been looking forward to seeing the de Winter mansion but as our car drew nearer, and the rain began, I realized I dreaded Manderley. Max had lived there with Rebecca, the first Mrs. de Winter who died so suddenly, so mysteriously." And so the chiller is launched into motion with Fontaine becoming increasingly intimidated by her austere surroundings. Her fear is intensified by the authoritarian housekeeper, Mrs. Danvers (Anderson), and the unexplainable atmosphere of dread and death that permeates the castle. Slowly she comprehends that Olivier is still deeply possessed by the spirit of his first wife. Not until the finale, when Rebecca's drowning has been (lamely) put into proper perspective, and Anderson has perished along with the Manderley she sets aflame, does the tormented heroine dare hope for any fruitful future with her moody, tempestuous husband.

Throughout the production of *Rebecca* it was a well-known fact in the Hollywood community that it was a touch-and-go affair whether Joan would emerge with flying colors or be dismissed as a flash in the pan who fizzled out in her big acting opportunity.*

But a combination of Hitchcock's pushing,† Selznick's soothing, Joan's sharpened native talents,‡ and a superior supporting cast, caused the actress to exhibit a much wider range to her screen acting than had ever been imagined possible. Particularly in her ability to display all shadings of vulnerability,

---

*In an unsent memo from Selznick to Hitchcock, discovered by Rudy Behlmer for his book *Memo from David O. Selznick,* the producer commiserated with an exasperated Hitchcock, both of whom bemoaned the possibilities of ever getting the necessary performance from Joan. "I am aware that it takes time to get the performance out of Joan Fontaine, but every picture I have ever worked on had some such difficulty. . . . Miss Fontaine . . . requires work—but so has every other girl who has been aimed at stardom and who requires an enormous amount of work in her first big opportunity."

†Years later Hitchcock reflected: "In the early stages of the actual shooting, I felt that Joan Fontaine was a little self-conscious, but I could see her potential for restrained acting and I felt she could play the character in a quiet, shy manner. At the outset she tended to overdo the shyness, but I felt she would work out all right, and once we got going, she did."

‡Joan later told hubby Brian Aherne why she felt such an affinity for *Rebecca:* "When I was a little girl unable to hold my own with those who should have been my friends, I knew the same quality of unhappiness the second Mrs. de Winter knew. I was fearful and timid, and I lived in constant horror of criticism."

Sister Olivia had her own rationale for Joan's success with the screen part: "Joan couldn't have been as wonderfully good as she was in *Rebecca* if she hadn't been married with Brian and her home foremost in her life. She was able to be objective about her work. She didn't get too intense. We try too hard in our family. We get too anxious about things."

Joan gave dimension to this Charlotte Brontë-esque story of suspenseful mood. Her affinity for vulnerableness would become the essential quality of Joan's 1940s star image. Most critics were enraptured by her performance in *Rebecca*. "Miss du Maurier never really convinced me," wrote Frank S. Nugent in the *New York Times,* "any one could behave quite as the second Mrs. de Winter behaved and still be sweet, modest, attractive and alive. But Miss Fontaine does it not simply with her eyes, her mouth, her hands and her words, but with her spine. Possibly it's unethical to criticize performances anatomically. Still we insist Miss Fontaine has the most expressive spine— and shoulders we've bothered to notice this season." The *New York Post* was one of the few sources to carp at Joan's latest cinema effort: "This studied performance will be hailed as a great performance by anyone who is not repelled by the pat familiarity of it." Mr. Archer Winsten's opinion gained few supporters.

Rebecca debuted at the Radio City Music Hall on March 28, 1940, and within its first four days 117,735 patrons had paid to see it. All of which surprised its distributor, United Artists, which still had a grudge to settle with Selznick for having released *Gone with the Wind* through MGM. While both the film and its stars were generally praised, it was not until *Rebecca* won an Oscar as best picture of the year that United Artists really promoted this product.*

Although Oscar-nominated Joan lost the Academy Award to Ginger Rogers's *Kitty Foyle* (RKO, 1940), doubtless it was with satisfaction that Joan returned to her old home lot to co-star with Cary Grant in Alfred Hitchcock's *Suspicion* (RKO, 1941). Joan was now exercising her full options as a major motion-picture star, rejecting projects like Universal's *Back Street* (1941), which did not meet her approval. Despite the high-pressure directives from David O. Selznick, who rightly felt he deserved to make as much capital as possible from his investment in Joan the actress by frequently loaning her acting services to the highest bidder, she stood firm on her own artistic decisions. She was now every bit the tenacious woman that sister Olivia had been at Warner Bros. in her many artistic battles with lot mogul Jack L. Warner.

Suspicion was based on Francis Iles's topnotch thriller novel, *Before the Fact* (1932). Once more the setting was English and again Joan's character, a well-bred sensitive spinster, has rushed into a potentially fatal marriage to a charming man (Grant) of whom she knows very little save that he is an irresponsible, penniless playboy who, her father (Cedric Hardwicke) predicts, will cause her infinite problems. Each day of their marital union brings home new revelations of Grant's shiftless, gambling nature, which comes to a frightening focus when his best pal, bumbling Nigel Bruce, mysteriously dies in Paris and Joan learns Grant had been seen with him that fateful evening.

---

*It grossed $2 million in the United States and $1 million in England during its first release. During the period of September-December, 1945, in its first British reissue, *Rebecca* grossed another $460,000. In 1956 the picture was theatrically revived before being sold to television.

Joan's suspicion mounts to rising hysteria as she becomes convinced Grant is planning to murder her for her trust fund inheritance. But once again Joan's screen counterpart is too much in love with her mate to step away from certain danger, and even daringly drinks the glass of milk she suspects is spiked with poison. Despite the tame happy ending to *Suspicion** and its failure to match up to the fine standards of *Rebecca,* the film remains a taut exercise in credulity versus reality.†

Joan received heady plaudits for her *Suspicion* emoting. Howard Barnes *(New York Herald-Tribune)* commended the "beauty and artistry" of her "memorable performance," and Bosley Crowther *(New York Times)* ranked Joan as unquestionably "one of the finest actresses on the screen." The New York Film Critics voted Joan the best actress of the year, and the Academy of Motion Picture Arts and Sciences bestowed an Oscar on Joan.‡

The much overpublicized feud between Joan and Olivia got its first real airing as a result of the Academy Awards ceremonies held on the night of February 27, 1942. The two highly competitive sisters had been especially skeptical of one another's professional and social successes in recent years.§ At the time of the 1942 Oscar nominations the de Havilland rivalry stood in a dead heat: Olivia had been nominated for best supporting actress for *Gone with the Wind* (1939) but had lost, as did Joan in 1940 for *Rebecca.* The following year Joan was nominated for *Suspicion* and Olivia for her performance in Paramount's *Hold Back the Dawn.* "We were at the same table," Joan remembers of that tense Award ceremony night, "when my name was called. I thought she was going to pull out my hair." In a later reflective moment Joan admitted "it really wasn't cricket" winning the Oscar for *Suspi-*

*Hitchcock had wanted to end *Suspicion* with Joan writing her mother that she now knows Grant is a killer and though she would rather die she believes society should protect itself by punishing Grant. She completes the note just as Grant enters the room. She asks him to post the letter, drinks the milk, and dies. Chipper Grant mails the letter.

†Joan, Brian Aherne, and Nigel Bruce were heard in an audio adaptation of *Suspicion* on "Lux Radio Theatre" on May 4, 1942.

‡Hitchcock, who has long exercised a penchant for grooming icy-cold blonde types for stardom (including Madeleine Carroll, Joan, Grace Kelly, Vera Miles, and Tippi Hedren), has in recent years had a reversal of thoughts about some of his protégées, particularly Joan. During his publicity tour for *Frenzy* (1972) he took deliberate occasion, during several talk-show and newspaper interviews, to lambast her abilities as anything beyond a puppet. He claimed that in *Suspicion* her entire performance was nothing more than a cut-and-paste job, culling snatches of movement which he carefully directed in hopes that some bits could be blended into a modulated whole.

§In playing up the sibling rivalry, the press delighted in pointing out that both actresses were on the outs with their father, Walter de Havilland, who in the rash of anti-Occidental policy in Japan in the 1930s had become impoverished. He and his wife migrated to California in the early 1940s, where he was cold-shouldered by both daughters. When his Japanese wife was forced to move inland to one of the internment camps for Japanese established for "America's protection" during World War II, he accompanied her. It was not until 1950, on his seventy-eighth birthday, that Joan and her father reconciled when she came to visit him at his abode in Victoria, British Columbia.

In late 1972, when Joan was a guest on Merv Griffin's television talk show, she commented about her father, who had died at the age of ninety-six: "My mother, my sister and I took his ashes to Guernsey and sprinkled them on the water. No one wrote about that!"

cion, which most people acknowledged was a rebound victory for having lost the year before. On her part, Olivia later recollected of that traumatic night: "I thought, 'Oh, my God, I've lost prestige with my own sister,' and it was true. She was haughty to me after that." With their increasingly strained relationship, plans to co-star Olivia and Joan in Warner Bros.' story of the literary Brontë sisters were dropped, but Olivia made the picture the following year teamed with Ida Lupino.

With an Oscar and two box-office successes to her credit, Joan's professional services were much in demand in World War II Hollywood. No longer termed the Cinderella sister of Olivia de Havilland, Joan was a major screen name on her own. She could have found more than one suitable vehicle per year to intrigue her, but Selznick believed that her particular marquee appeal was enhanced by a limited amount of screen exposure at a salary which would escalate to $125,000 to $200,000 per picture. But Joan realized very little of the amount Selznick charged for her loan-outs, a situation which increasingly irked her.* That the professional relationship between Joan and Selznick was on a continual downward bent could be measured by the quality of Christmas gifts Selznick gave to his troublesome employee.† An obvious factor in Joan's disenchantment with Selznick was his growing preoccupation with his other contractees, including Ingrid Bergman, Shirley Temple, and Dorothy McGuire, but particularly the future Mrs. Selznick, Jennifer Jones. As late as 1969, Joan would say of her late boss, who was the subject of an NBC-TV special, *Hollywood: The Selznick Years:* "I admired his tremendous ability and good taste, but he became a peddler in horseflesh rather than a creative movie maker. . . . Oh he made our lives absolute hell unless we acceded to his demands."

Joan balked when in October, 1941, Selznick informed her that she was to report to Twentieth Century-Fox to play second fiddle to Tyrone Power in *This Above All,* based on Eric Ambler's patriotic novel. She wanted something different, something more in keeping with her star status. Selznick threatened her with suspension, and so Joan arrived at the Fox lot on schedule in early November, 1941, for the six weeks of filming.

Under Anatole Litvak's cosmopolitan direction, *This Above All* (Astor Theatre, May 12, 1942) emerged far more than just a love story set in the war-torn England of 1940. Joan, as Prudence, the headstrong daughter of a London surgeon, has joined the Women's Auxiliary Air Force. On a blind date she meets conscientious objector Power, who, it develops, is an Army deserter. Joan soon throws discretion to a tasteful wind, rendezvousing with him at a bleak seashore inn in Dover. Slowly Joan pieces together Power's back-

---

*$17,500 for *Rebecca,* well over $30,000 for *Suspicion,* $75,000 for *This Above All* (Joan was paid $1,000 a week for six weeks of filming). Even in her peak 1940s heyday, four-fifths of the salary went directly to Selznick.

†After the first year of Joan's contract with Selznick, he sent her a set of English bone china, plus a bonus check of $30,000. The following year, after many squabbles, he sent her a potted geranium with a $5 price tag.

ground, aided by a chance meeting with his Army buddy Thomas Mitchell. She begins to understand why Power's ideals have been shattered and why he ponders whether England, with its smug, self-satisfied aristocrats, is really worth fighting for. Back in London Power displays his resilient courage by ignoring his own safety in order to rescue a woman and two children during an air raid. While recuperating in the hospital he suddenly regains his former zealous patriotism, convinced anew, "We must win. We must win."*

The well-engineered flag-waving tale was bound to be popular with World War II audiences and met with full rounds of approval in release. Joan's role as the clear-thinking aristocrat may have been secondary to Power's characterization, but it provided her with a rousing climactic monolog delivered soon before she and Powers are to wed in the hospital. Her Prudence has continually urged the disgruntled Power to look into his own heart and reawaken to the global human tragedy. In a cogent address to her beloved (and the camera's eye) she reiterates her heartfelt belief that their beloved England is worth fighting for and saving at any cost. Joan's ability to cloak her performance with a surface restraint that covers an inner emotional intensity, did much to make her Prudence a palatable, lovely creature.

There had been talk during the early 1940s that Joan might "return" to the stage. Selznick, in fact, had announced in June, 1941, the formation of the Hollywood Summer Theatre to be headquartered at the Lobero Theatre in Santa Barbara. John Houseman was to be the managing director, with Joan, Ingrid Bergman, and perhaps Vivien Leigh as resident stars. The project with Joan's participation never did materialize, and Joan's only California stage activity for the duration was a brief appearance with Gladys Cooper and Philip Merivale in the "Family Album" playlet from Noel Coward's *Tonight at 8:30* presented to aid the British War Relief Fund.

During her frequent nonworking weeks, Joan tried to devote herself to being a dutiful wife, hostessing at the plush white Georgian-style Beverly Hills home she shared with her husband. According to Brian Aherne's directives, the couple had daily tea at 4 P.M. and dressed formally for dinner each night, whether there were guests present or not. Joan and Aherne also owned a 160-acre ranch at Indio, California, which they obligingly converted into a stock and vegetable farm during World War II. Fan magazine readers, who pictured Joan as only costumed in the highest of fashions, were constantly amazed to see photographs of the star garbed in blue jeans and work shirt, hoeing farm crops at the Indio spread. Aherne also held title to a tract of land in Phoenix, Arizona, which during the war years was converted into Thunderbird and Falcon Air Fields, serving as the training ground for British, Chinese, and American pilots. The latter real-estate holdings were quite lucrative, but demanded Aherne's constant personal supervision.

Joan may have been publicly stumbling in her relationships with her sister,

---

*Was it cricket of the scriptwriters to pound home their philosophy while a man (Power) was down and out, flat on his back?

father, and husband, but there was no doubt in anyone's mind but that she had come fully to grips with her star status. No longer was she the same outwardly insecure girl who only a few years before had gone along so willingly with David O. Selznick's personality consultant Anita Colby, who condescendingly advised: "Make Fontaine smart, feminine, and refined."* Unlike her hesitant, deferring screen characters, Joan now spoke her mind—and rather bluntly at times—to any business associate or social acquaintance. This frank manner did not endear her to industry figures and at times caused a strain between her and the press.† Because Joan was so successful in her career, few believed that her recurring la-de-da posing was not a bad side-effect of her screen achievements, forgetting the defense mechanisms that had long ago made Joan the precipitous poseur intent on matching her illustrious sister in professional stature. This incessant "grand dame" manner would lead Joan to utter such absurd, snobby remarks as: "Oh, it's a hectic calling, the movies, but there is money in it."

The other side of Joan, the conscientious war worker, often was ignored. She devoted herself assiduously to charity activities, functioning as a Red Cross nurse's aide, and participating in bond-selling tours. On one Canadian War Loan Drive she was joined by her relative, Sir Geoffrey de Havilland, in making a morale tour of the de Havilland aircraft plant in Canada. On April 23, 1943, Joan, a British subject who had never been to England, became an American citizen.

Joan's next screen assignment came about in a curious way, but in a manner that is still typical of the film industry. She and Aherne had returned from a British War Relief tour and went directly out to dinner at Romanoff's Restaurant, even though she was exhausted and looked bedraggled (by her standards). Warner Brothers director Edmund Goulding stopped by their table to say hello to Aherne and happened to comment: "We're having an awful time trying to find a puny, weak looking, freckle-faced, string-haired girl to play Tessa [in *The Constant Nymph*]."

According to Joan she popped up, "How would I do?"

Goulding replied, "Who are you?"

Aherne then introduced Joan to Goulding. The director apologized for his *faux pas* and then beat a hasty retreat to telephone studio boss Jack L. Warner. "I've found Tessa!" he informed the film mogul.

As pat as the account may be, Joan had wanted to play Tessa in the projected new version of Margaret Kennedy's well-received novel, which had already been a play and the source for two British-made features: a 1929 silent with Frances Dibble, and a 1934 remake, which starred Leonora Corbett and Brian Aherne. In fact, so great was Joan's desire to tackle this assign-

*In confiding to one reporter how she had gained confidence and poise, Joan reasoned: "Perhaps I had learned my trade and knew it. I try to live each character I play; this calls, for me at least, much concentration."

†In 1943 the Hollywood Women's Press Club selected Joan as the least cooperative actress of the year, occasioned more by her constant and still painful shyness and distrust of inquiring persons, than any basic feeling of being put upon by the news reporters.

ment that Selznick used it as a wedge to coerce her into making *This Above All*, telling Joan, no Fox picture, no Tessa.

The Constant Nymph (1943) contains Joan's favorite screen role: a fifteen-year-old girl suffering from a heart condition and from unfulfilled love for composer Charles Boyer, who has wed her haughty cousin (Alexis Smith). Under Goulding's direction and backed by a rich Erich Wolfgang Korngold score,* twenty-five-year-old Joan made her taffy-color-pigtailed Tessa and *The Constant Nymph* viable screenfare. Granted her restrained screen personality was at odds with her oncamera sisters (Warner Brothers contractees Brenda Marshall, Joyce Reynolds, and Jean Muir) in the opening sequence at the family chalet in the Alps, but it was appropriate, for her character was a sickly girl existing in her own dream world.† Only a very small percentage of 1943 filmgoers were unwilling to accept the conventions of this tearjerker, which showcased Joan and Boyer (in his best boudoir manner) as they stifle their growing love, only to have the girl pass away one night while listening to her beloved perform a concert for a radio audience. For her "radiant performance" Joan received her third Academy Award nomination, but she lost the Oscar to another Selznick protégé, Jennifer Jones, who won for *The Song of Bernadette.*

Ever since Samuel Goldwyn's screen success with Emily Brontë's *Wuthering Heights* (1939), it had been a foregone conclusion that some Hollywood producer would jump on the bandwagon and engineer a remake of Charlotte Bronte's *Jane Eyre.*‡ David O. Selznick, a gluttonous man where assembling film projects was concerned, began preparations for such a picture while in the midst of finalizing *Gone with the Wind,* but the opportunity and financial backing never became available for Selznick to go ahead with the actual filming. Finally he sold the package to Twentieth Century-Fox in 1943 with Joan contracted to play the title role. Although Miss Fontaine was a star of the first magnitude now, the studio agreed that it would sacrifice top billing to have Orson Welles play the cornerstone role of brooding Edward Rochester.

Despite an articulate script, this new edition of *Jane Eyre* (Radio City Music Hall, February 3, 1944) took too many liberties with the original in making Welles, as the sire of Thornfield Hall, even more a key figure in the tale. The opening segment, featuring Jane Eyre as a sad orphan child (played by Peggy Ann Garner) at Lowood School, seems unnecessarily remote from the remainder of the picture in which Joan, as the forlorn, sternly self-controlled governess, arrives at dank Thornfield Hall to assume her duties and there experiences a sudden, uncontrollable attraction for sardonic Welles. Fox's

---

*Joan's "singing" of "Tomorrow (When You Are Gone)" was provided by Sally Sweetland's offcamera voice.

†The similarities between Joan's childhood and that of the character Tessa are obvious, perhaps providing the key to Joan's ultra-strong affinity to the role. To this day she insists *The Constant Nymph* would make a solid Broadway musical, although she no longer fancies herself for the lead part.

‡The 1921 *Jane Eyre* starred Mabel Ballin and Norman Trevor, while the 1934 Monogram rendition featured Virginia Bruce and Colin Clive.

publicity for *Jane Eyre* boldly proclaimed: "A LOVE STORY EVERY WOMAN WOULD GIVE A THOUSAND DEATHS TO LIVE!" which even in movie industry lingo was hearty exaggeration. There was actually very little oncamera rapport between Welles's ferocious Rochester and Joan's modest and subdued screen figure, who only came alive in moments of tense anxiety. As in *Rebecca,* Joan's closest onscreen relationship was not to other characters in *Jane Eyre* but in her adaptation and reaction to the gloomy manse in which she finds herself an emotional prisoner. One obtained very little sense of the passionate love that supposedly existed between Rochester and Jane Eyre, making the melodramatic finale unconvincing and unsatisfying.* In theatrical release, *Jane Eyre* was far from the popular success that either *Wuthering Heights* or *Rebecca* had been. A much too pretty Joan received what in retrospect seem better-than-deserved notices for her *Jane Eyre* performance: "Only Miss Fontaine could have made the title role so luminous and appealing that her plight is understandable" *(New York Herald-Tribune);* "A sensitive, wholly believable portrait from the early Victorian era" *(New York Journal-American).*

Joan's marriage to Aherne had turned sour, even in public, long before she filed for a divorce in Los Angeles court on June 2, 1944.† In court Joan charged Brian Aherne with the traditional extreme cruelty, citing, "His butler ran the home to such an extent that I felt like sort of a guest." In her complaint she also detailed that he insisted she accompany him to their Indio desert ranch, knowing full well that she was allergic to the dust and hot, dry climate. Moreover, she attested, they had been separated by conflicting work assignments so much during their years of marriage that they might as well divorce. Left unstated in Joan's petition was the fact that Joan's cinema standing was soaring, while Aherne, at age forty-two, had dissipated his potentially superior screen career into second-string-male-lead role types. Later Joan would say of Aherne: "He was too much a gentleman to fight with me. A wife likes a nice fight occasionally."

Meantime Joan starred in her second 1944 release, Paramount's *Frenchman's Creek* (Rivoli Theatre, September 20, 1944). Selznick reportedly collected a fat $250,000 for Joan's services, while under her escalated contract with him she received only $35,000 compensation. She was against doing the film ("That was a film I made because the studio pressured me with lawyers' letters until I broke. If I had been a man, I'd have told the studio to go four-letter-word and gone fishing. But I'm a woman and I broke. I'd never do one like it again."). Joan was rightly convinced that she was unsuited for this reckless romantic depicted in Daphne du Maurier's historical best seller.

*Jane Eyre, sensing that Rochester needs her desperately, returns to Thornfield Hall to find that a fire has destroyed the estate house, killing the insane Mrs. Rochester and leaving the master sightless.

†Aherne recalls that Joan visited their ranch from a film location in Oregon where she was then starring in *Frenchman's Creek* and said to her husband: "How long have we been married?"
Aherne: "Nearly four years."
"What?" Joan cried. "My God! I never meant to stay married to you that long."
Two days later, Aherne says, he read in Louella Parsons's column that she was divorcing him.

Next to MGM's huge outlay for *Ziegfeld Follies,* Paramount's close to $4 million budget for *Frenchman's Creek* made it *the* colossal movie of the year. "She found the love all women dream of knowing," read the studio advertising copy. "We've made it Big. But we've made it Entertaining." This last statement about this oversized Technicolor period piece set in 1668 England was not precisely true. Joan never looked lovelier* onscreen with her long flowing brown-golden hair billowing over her lavish costumes† supervised by producer-director Mitchell Leisen. But when all was said and done, *Frenchman's Creek* was a gorgeously comported picture unsupported by its ludicrous storyline; besides, for an alleged swashbuckling yarn it had an amazing lack of action. Lady Dona St. Columb (Joan) suffers from an overdose of London-bred ennui and, angered by the constant advances of lord Basil Rathbone, scoops together her belongings and two small children, and takes an imperious leave of her bewildered foppish husband (Ralph Forbes). But where to? To the majestic country castle on the Cornish coast. Upon arrival at the estate she finds a new caretaker (Cecil Kellaway) in charge of the house. He is so pleasantly folksy that Joan is unperturbed when she discovers he is really the gentle mate of the notorious Gallic pirate Jean Benoit Aubrey (Arturo de Cordova), who has hidden his ship in the local inlet.‡ Joan is later kidnapped by de Cordova's men, but soon finds life aboard the *Adventurer* romantically conducive. Before long she is just one of the boys and insists upon joining her new paramour in coastal skirmishes, relishing her rambles disguised as a cabin boy. Then along comes Forbes to reclaim his wife, accompanied by Rathbone, who intends to carry through on his initial seduction of tantalizing Joan. Dastardly Rathbone is properly disposed of, but does Joan sail off into the multihued sunset with phlegmatic de Cordova? No! Why? "A woman," says Joan's Dona, "can only escape for a night and a day." She cannot bear the thought of leaving her children behind, so, like any martyred middle-class wife, she remains with her stolid husband. She does take time out to strategically stand on the hillside (with the camera stationed behind her) to artistically watch de Cordova and crew sail over the horizon.

Perhaps the major flaw in Talbot Jennings's screenplay was allowing Joan's thirty-year-old Lady Dona to be nothing more than a well-bred trollop who revels in piratical raids which kill her neighbors. Even taking into consideration the conventions of seventeenth-century British nobility, there is no excuse (and thus no audience empathy) for her irrational behavior in which even love does not conquer all. Thus we have a majestically beautiful Joan sweeping about at her haughty best in floor-length gowns at London balls,

---

*Joan arrived on the Paramount lot preceded by one of Selznick's famous lengthy memos (this one was forty pages) detailing how the studio should treat the visiting star both on the set and in her debut color feature.

†Appropriately padded to fill out her figure.

‡Director Leisen was unhappy from the start with the casting of Joan and Arturo de Cordova, having hoped to instead have Claudette Colbert and Ray Milland star. Leisen blamed much of the picture's extended production schedule and mounting costs on Joan's temperament and de Cordova's ineptness.

and coyly parrying her wit with her dinner guests at country dinner parties (singing the "Nell Gwynne" song and tossing oranges at her tableside audience). Whether she is mooning or embarking on escapades with de Cordova there is a prevalent snide, tongue-in-cheek quality to Joan's performance that alienates the viewer. In fact one almost feels sorry for her cuckolded husband, with the result that "all the audience gets out of her poses and posturing is a snicker" *(New York Daily News)*.

The "new" Joan was billed over the title in *Frenchman's Creek,* but the bewigged and belaced feature did far less for her career than Paramount's more entertaining *Kitty* (1945), starring Paulette Goddard and also directed by Mitchell Leisen. It was not immediately evident, but from this point onward Joan's mighty screen career began a steady descent into mediocrity.

Joan was the first to admit she needed a change of pace in her screen outings, and she agreed to star in Paramount's *The Affairs of Susan* (Rivoli Theatre, March 28, 1945). After completing this William A. Seiter-directed picture, Joan told the press: "I was sick of being the sad-sack of the screen. I've shed gallons of tears and moped all over the place. I wanted to play comedy, and now that I've done it I'm happier than I've ever been in Hollywood."

In *The Affairs of Susan* airplane manufacturer Walter Abel hosts a bachelor party in honor of his forthcoming marriage to actress Joan. From the "if you knew Susie like I know Susie" reminiscences of Abel and the three guests (producer George Brent, wealthy oil man Don DeFore, and poet Dennis O'Keefe) one learns that Joan's Susan Darell has managed to be all things to all men. Interestingly enough, and the factor which instills her heroine with charm, she has been refreshingly honest as to how she felt at the given time with each swain. Joan was amazingly adept at presenting her contrasting poses as she dallies with each of the quartet. Within the structured confines of drawing-room comedy she could comfortably allow her antics to be merely glib tricks rather than attempt to be amusing per se. And Joan well understood the art of Neo-Restoration comedy of manners (she lived it), which allowed her to eschew the bane of so many cinema ingenues, offering a lethal dose of unbounding ebullience. The plot of *The Affairs of Susan* ends on a cute twist as Joan returns from her USO tour and makes a decision as to which of the men present she wants to claim. Given the film's limitations, Joan is more successful in her multifaceted characterization than Ginger Rogers or Betty Hutton were in two other Paramount segmented-personality stories, *Lady in the Dark* and *Dream Girl*.

Joan's stormiest contretemps with David O. Selznick occurred over her adamant refusal to star in *I'll Be Seeing You* (1944), a project which eventually featured Ginger Rogers. As a result of again displeasing her employer she spent the bulk of 1945 on contractual suspension with each party threatening to go to court. Joan's increased professional toughness was matched by her new personal image, allegedly a reaction resulting from her Brian Aherne British-aristocrat years. Now she swung the other way, adopting a shock technique to prove that at heart she was really a regular girl. Now she could and did admit: "I express my feelings by action. I have a frightful temper, and

I can fly into rages about almost anything that gets on my nerves at any time of day or night."

Joan returned to the screen and to the postwar RKO to star in *From This Day Forward* (1946). More so than any of the other major film studios, RKO had undergone a deglamorization process during World War II, when the bulk of its profits derived from undemanding programmers, mostly decorated with humdrum stock players. The few prestigious projects at the RKO lot were generally the result of special pacts with outside acting talent. *From This Day Forward* opens with returning war veteran Mark Stevens job-searching at the U. S. Employment Service, indicating that perhaps director John Berry was going to deal head-on with a vital, contemporary problem. But while enduring the Employment Service's red tape, Stevens thinks back eight years prior to when he and Joan wed just at the time when America was coming out of the Depression. The couple endured the usual travails (i.e., fear of unemployment, overstretched budgets, in-law trouble, etc.), even taking into stride Stevens's draft into the Army and their wartime separation. The picture concludes on an optimistic note with both Stevens and Joan confident of their future.

Ambitious and overblown as this lachrymose soap opera was, it was no *Saturday's Children* and Joan's tattered Bronx tenement housewife was noticeably unconvincing.* *From This Day Forward* demonstrated again that Joan's screen image personality had decided limitations. After essaying variant English misses in four British-set features, Joan had proven she could play a contemporary American heroine in *The Affairs of Susan*. But there was a total aura of cultured aristocracy about Joan that kept her from digging into a role termed in Hollywood casting language the "Joan Crawford working-girl." Joan Fontaine by the stretch of no one's imagination, particularly her own, could ever convincingly be the salt-of-the-earth.

Shortly after completing *From This Day Forward,* Joan eloped with thirty-eight-year-old RKO producer William Dozier to Mexico City, where, on May 2, 1946, they were wed in a civil ceremony. It was the second marriage for each, he having divorced Katherine Foley earlier that year. Upon their return to California they settled into a large Fordyce Road home in the Santa Monica mountain area, a showplace home in which she resided until 1960, when she leased it.†

By now William Dozier had moved over to Universal-International where he became vice-president and associate head of production. A four-picture pact was negotiated for Joan with the studio. There she made the period English shocker *Ivy* (1947), which wrapped up her David O. Selznick deal.‡ Joan's part in *Frenchman's Creek* had been that of a self-willed fatuous

---

*The contrast of Joan "slumming" in her impoverished surroundings was highlighted by the typically fine performance of Rosemary DeCamp as her cynical older sister, wed to shiftless but likable Harry Morgan.

†In 1961 the house and its contents were totally destroyed in the Bel Air-Brentwood blaze.

‡Selznick garnered $225,000 from Universal for Joan's services, and she in turn was doled out $36,000 by Selznick for her *Ivy* chores.

charmer, but *Ivy* took her one step farther as an adulterous Edwardian who juggles her busy amorous schedule (husband Richard Ney, lover Patric Knowles) by an insidious use of poison, hoping to clear the way so she can land Herbert Marshall, the attentive catch of the London season. If director Sam Wood had been allowed to focus more attention on Ivy's multiromantic interludes rather than highlighting the lush tapestry of early twentieth-century England,* the results would have been far more persuasive, notably in view of the Motion Picture Production Code, which demanded an illogical crime-does-not-pay ending. Certainly Joan's scheming Ivy did not emerge the vicious horror intended, nor was Joan's unbridled, artificial performance the hoped-for tour de force that would lead her to another Oscar. In fact, had Universal been able to hire the de Havilland of their first choice (Olivia, who rejected the part), they would have been better off than with the package of a mis-guided Joan in the title role and her mother, Lilian Fontaine, playing Lady Flora.†

For the first time in four years Joan was forced to accept second billing —in Paramount's *The Emperor Waltz* (1948).‡ Motion pictures were under-going a sharp retrenchment. Even for seasoned Oscar winners who at the age of thirty-one still retained a fresh chic glamour, it was not easy to come up with suitable vehicles. So Joan played straight woman to Bing Crosby in *The Emperor Waltz,* which even director Billy Wilder could not inject with much more of a bite than other Crosby-Paramount musical outings. Joan photo-graphed gorgeously in the period trappings as the haughty Hapsburg countess of 1901 Austria-Hungary who succumbs to the yokel charms of yodeling Amer-ican phonograph salesman Crosby. It was a toss-up whether Crosby tried harder in *The Emperor Waltz* to sell Emperor Franz Josef one of his new-fangled musical instruments, or whether Joan was the more industrious soul as she struggled to cope with the picture's farcical tone. The net result was that Joan's cardboard role was totally unmemorable, while Crosby at least had the saving grace of having reintroduced the old standard, "I Kiss Your Hand, Madame."

Joan personally selected Stefan Zweig's romantic novel *Brief Einer Un-bekannten* as the lead off vehicle for Rampart Productions, a company founded by her and Dozier in late 1947, with Universal to release their product. She was convinced the resultant *Letter from an Unknown Woman* (1948) would

---

*The well-appointed sets were supervised by producer William Cameron Menzies.

†She had made her screen debut portraying Jane Wyman's mother in *Lost Weekend* (1945). Also in 1947 she played a dowager in Universal's *Time Out of Mind* and had a tiny role in Para-mount's *Suddenly, It's Spring.* Later she would play Ida Lupino's landlady in *The Bigamist* (1953), which starred Joan. Interestingly, Lilian Fontaine never appeared in any of Olivia's many feature films.

‡There had been much advance publicity about Joan starring with Gregory Peck in *Earth and High Heaven,* based on the popular novel by Gwethalyn Graham concerning the marriage of a Jew and a Gentile. When Joan was signed for the picture in October, 1946, by Samuel Goldwyn, he stated he had been waiting over one and a half years for Joan's schedule to allow the project to be made, and that production would commence in May, 1947. Filming of *Earth and High Heaven* never got under way.

be the type of high-class woman's picture that audiences craved and missed. Despite offering one of her best screen performances ("virtually wrings herself dry," *New York Times*) under Max Ophuls's controlled direction, the John Houseman-produced picture proved unworthy at the box office and died. Disillusioned Universal tossed it away when finally released abroad.

All the proper plot ingredients were present in *Letter from an Unknown Woman* except for the actor cast as the male lead.* Louis Jourdan was too perpetually *dégagé* in manner to lend any credence to his characterization as a heartless rake who has, buried beneath his surface chill, an untapped sensitive streak. It did not take many minutes for an astute filmgoer to wonder why Joan, whether as the fourteen-year-old or as an adult, was going through martyrdom for this yawning, blasé continental type.

If only Universal's *Kiss the Blood off My Hands* (1948) had measured up to its perversely compelling title or to the promising ad copy: "With every footstep a menace . . . every shadow a threat . . . They stole their love!" But instead the picture was a confused account of two lost postwar souls. Neither Joan as the prim London nurse nor Burt Lancaster's merchant-marine-on-the-run is a viable character. Instead, director Norman Foster allowed Robert Newton, as the sinister Cockney who witnessed Lancaster's skull-cracking of a pubkeeper, to become the most intriguing element in the British-set movie. After Newton is stabbed by Joan when he attempts to blackmail her, *Kiss the Blood off My Hands* disintegrates into tedious incredibility, capped by a finale which has the escaping Joan and Lancaster suddenly do a turnabout and decide to give themselves up to the law.

Much more successful was Rampart's second Universal project, *You Gotta Stay Happy* (Radio City Music Hall, November 4, 1948). The wild comedy owes almost as much to Joan's airy playing of multimillionaire heiress Dee Dee Dillwood as to James Stewart's laconic ex-Army pilot struggling with partner Eddie Albert to make a go of their two-plane cargo-shipping outfit.

---

*The ninety-minute feature traces the sad life of Joan from the age of fourteen in 1890 Vienna when she became foolishly enamored of her pianist neighbor, Louis Jourdan, and wants to be the woman in his life. She finds herself more interested in glimpsing his amorous conduct with his parade of women than in listening from the garden below to his daily piano playing. She is heartbroken when her widowed mother remarries and they move to another town. Years later she returns to Vienna as a dress-shop model and is picked up by Jourdan one night. Although she is crushed that he does not recall his former child admirer, she and the roué have their moment of love. When he promptly ditches her, she never returns to tell him that she is pregnant by him ("I wanted to be the one woman who asked him for nothing"). Later she marries middle-aged, Austrian aristocrat Marcel Journet, but her heart is still starved for Jourdan. One night at the opera she and her amour encounter. Thereafter she abandons her husband for Jourdan, but soon discovers that she is nothing but a meaningless new conquest for the aging rake. ("I came to offer you my whole life. And you didn't even remember me," she murmurs to her unworthy love object.) Later Joan and her son contract diphtheria, the boy dies, and while she is lying gravely ill in a hospital, she writes Jourdan the letter of the title which he has received at the picture's opening. After reading her missive (which states "I love you now as I have always loved you") Jourdan tries hard to recall the lovesick girl of years before and finally a vague picture of her holding open the door for him flutters through his mind. Instead of fleeing the city as he had planned, Jourdan decides to fight the probably fatal duel with the enraged Journet. As he leaves his abode he pins to his lapel one of the blossoms Joan gave him on their last meeting.

491

By adopting a breathless style, Joan's Dee Dee, more a product of the 1930s screwball comedies than post-World War II America, was acceptably pleasant. This fickle, romantic woman runs out on her newly acquired stuffed-shirt spouse (Willard Parker) and finds herself on a transcontinental flight with Stewart, Albert, and a bizarre cargo that includes embezzler Porter Hall, a GI and his bride (Arthur Walsh and Marcy McGuire), a cigar-smoking chimpanzee, a corpse, and a shipment of lobsters and whitefish. Midst the episodes of incredible nonsense, Joan and Stewart engage in a predictable romance. Joan's approach to cinema light comedy was still more mechanical than the standards once set by genre experts Carole Lombard and Jean Arthur, but she offered a far better, more effervescent performance than in the prior *The Affairs of Susan.* Joan and Stewart recreated their *You Gotta Stay Happy* roles on "Lux Radio Theatre" on January 17, 1949.

The same month as *You Gotta Stay Happy* was released, Joan gave birth at St. John's Hospital in Santa Monica to Deborah Leslie, her first and only child. She was off the screen in 1949, but not out of moviegoers' minds, for the fan magazines continued to fan the flames of sibling rivalry that had erupted yet again between Joan and Olivia. It was at the Academy Awards celebrating the winners of the 1946 sweepstakes that the de Havilland girls had clashed again so noticeably. Olivia was onstage accepting her award for best actress in *To Each His Own,* and Joan, as a previous winner, was among those present in an officiating capacity. When Olivia left the rostrum, award in hand, Joan put forth a hand and a congratulatory smile. Olivia abruptly brushed by Joan, refusing to acknowledge her sister's greeting. The bombastic but quietly sophisticated confrontation was caught for posterity by photographer Hymie Fink and subsequently appeared in *Photoplay* magazine. For those who knew the actresses, this scene was a logical conclusion to an emotional tug-of-strength that had been in progress throughout the 1940s, especially after Joan's *Suspicion* victory.*

Joan returned to the screen in 1950, not in *Trilby,* which was to have been filmed in England, but in RKO's *Born to Be Bad,* a project once considered

---

*There is an endless wealth of stories available to document this continuing battle for supremacy. Once, when Olivia came home from on-location filming so ill she had to be taken off the train on a stretcher, Joan happened to meet her and soon was noted vying for the limelight with the accompanying press. On another 1940s occasion, Olivia, who was in the process of changing residences, preferred sleeping in her car to calling on Joan when she could find no accommodations so late at night.

Joan's evaluation of the tortuous situation was: "Being the little sister of a movie star *does* hurt. You discover that people are your friends only to reach your sister. People would rave to me that a certain performance of hers could never be matched. I served the cakes at Livvie's parties. I drove her to the studio and waited outside."

For her part, Olivia confided in the 1950s that the major break with Joan had actually occurred when she wed novelist Marcus Goodrich in 1946. "Joan is very bright and sharp and can be cutting. She said some things about Marcus that hurt me deeply. She was aware there was an estrangement between us. . . . I swore that I would never reconcile with Joan until she apologized. But when I returned to Hollywood after my separation from Marcus [in 1950], it seemed silly to demand an apology then."

Not to be left out of the matter, Olivia and her mother were on the outs from 1947 until January 1957, when Joan and Mrs. Fontaine went to France to meet Olivia's new husband (Pierre Paul Galante) and see the couple's new child, Giselle. Mrs. Fontaine died in 1958.

for her while under contract to David O. Selznick. The tired story was set in San Francisco with Joan ineffectually portraying a honey-voiced *femme fatale* whose obvious machinations go unobserved by her supposedly bright male acquaintances (including wealthy gadabout Zachary Scott, novelist Robert Ryan, and artist Mel Ferrer). Her unscrupulous Christabel was physically attractive but not the desired scheming, selfish bitch. The film misfired not only because of its bland distillation of Anne Parrish's novel *All Kneeling* and Nicholas Ray's diffuse direction, but also due to Joan's inability to portray excessive venality as a realistic character trait rather than a pose.

September Affair (world premiere: Venice Film Festival, August 25, 1950; American debut: Radio City Music Hall, February 1, 1951) was the initial entry of Joan's three-picture deal with Paramount and the last financially successful major film in which she was first-billed. Despite the low-grade romantics of the rambling drama, inhibited even further by somnambulistic Joseph Cotten and a lethargic, dumb ending, audiences took to this would-be *Intermezzo* with sizable relish.* The trade rationale for the film's success was the combination of the Naples-Florence location filming and the well-integrated utilization of Walter Huston's singing of "September Song."

Joan was far from her best mouthing with such sticky dialog as: "The concert's a month away and I'm scared of it, and the world's in an awful mess and—oh, let's be unconventional. . . . " She gave in to a distressing habit of swallowing words as she recited her lines, looking straight ahead as if peering at a cue card, only occasionally pausing to glance sideways for dramatic effect. Leonard Pennario dubbed Joan's oncamera piano solos, and Francoise Rosay, as the music teacher who highly disapproves of Joan's wayward life, gave the actress more backing than the film deserves. At least Joan could be complimented, for more often than not she suppressed the coy flirtatiousness indigenous to her character. She and Cotten repeated their *September Affair* roles on "Lux Radio Theatre" on January 26, 1953.

Domestic strife, which had halted the making of Rampart Productions' three remaining Universal Pictures, led to Joan and William Dozier divorcing in January, 1951. Joan declared: "He walked out of the house on August 4, 1949, and never came back. . . . He told me that our marriage did not suit him."† A bitter custody fight ensued over daughter Deborah, which was

---

*Concert pianist Joan and successful middle-aged engineer Cotten, he unhappily married to Jessica Tandy and the father of two children, meet and fall in love in Italy. When they miss their plane back to New York and the flight crashes, with them both being listed among the victims, the couple decide to begin life anew. But eventually they are forced back to reality, each to accept his own responsibilities. All they have left are beautiful memories (which is more than the responsible viewer obtained).

†Tactfully left unrepeated at the courtroom hearing was that when Joan jaunted to Italy in August, 1949, to film *September Affair*, it was publicly understood—even by the fan magazines— that the Doziers were separated and that he would move out of the house before she returned in October of that year. It was later revealed that on her transatlantic flight Joan chatted with columnist Hedda Hopper, who was then heading to Paris. Joan impulsively invited Hopper to accompany her to Rome, to which the flattered gossip arbiter agreed. Then, according to biographer George Eels in *Hedda and Louella* (1972), Joan met photographer "Slim" Aarons and a hectic romance developed in which Hopper was totally ignored. The columnist never forgave Joan for this unwarranted social slight.

settled in 1958 by a court order which ruled the child was to stay with her father in Beverly Hills. Meanwhile, Joan, who had been linked with Prince Ali Khan during the early 1950s when he was separated from his wife, Rita Hayworth, adopted a Peruvian infant, Martita Pareja Caldron, whom she had found while attending a South American film festival in 1952.

Joan fared badly with her other Paramount releases. *Darling, How Could You!* (1951) was a feeble adaptation of Sir James M. Barrie's *Alice-Sit-By-The Fire,* an antiquated drama once considered as a follow-up picture for Gloria Swanson after her *Sunset Boulevard* comeback. "Everybody acts so gol-danged cute," *Cue* Magazine reported, "you get the feeling they're all talking oozy-woozy baby talk." The *New York Times* ruled this unsatisfying peek at Washington Square society a "lustreless flapdoddle" and as if that was not sufficient derision, went on to complain that Joan, "exquisite as usual, flutters, gasps, manipulates her eyebrows like flags." Mona Freeman as the precocious teenaged daughter of Dr. John Lund, who thinks her mother (Joan) is having an affair with dad's best friend, was more vapidly saccharine than she had been in her Paramount *Dear Ruth (Dear Wife, Dear Brat)* days.

Something to Live For, completed July 20, 1951, and released March 7, 1952, was also ground out in black and white, and found Joan taking an undesirable back seat to Ray Milland, he recapping his Oscar-winning *Lost Weekend* alcoholic. Only this time Milland is a reformed drunkard whom AA sends to counsel dipsomaniac Joan, a flamboyantly glamorous stage star unable to cope with pressing professional demands. Will Milland leave his pregnant wife (Teresa Wright) for new love Joan? The unconvincing climax did not deal at all successfully with the picture's moral dilemma. Nor was Joan's overly polite, chic drunk anywhere as interesting a focal point as James Cagney's reformed alcoholic in *Come Fill the Cup* (1951). It had been thirteen years since Joan had last been professionally associated with George Stevens. Then he had been more of a newsworthy item than *Gunga Din* heroine Joan. Now, as the Oscar-winning director of *A Place in the Sun,* he was again more in demand within the industry and a more commercial name to the public than Joan.

Joan was at liberty and traveling abroad when MGM paged her to replace Margaret Leighton as the well-bred Rowena in Metro's *Ivanhoe.* Her pallid role, subordinate to stars Robert Taylor and Elizabeth Taylor (as the Jewess Rebecca) demanded only that she pose quietly in the background and await Robert Taylor to claim her after the final tournaments and castle storming.

While abroad Joan agreed to star with Louis Jourdan in RKO's *Decameron Nights* (1953) filmed on the cheap in Spain. Director Hugo Fregonese wrung very little of the richness of Boccaccio's original tales into his low-grade programmer, which coasted along on its pretentions of classiness. Joan was attracted to the project because it offered a variety of four roles (maid, wife, matron, and widow) in which she could cavort. The multiepisode hodgepodge suffered as much from Jourdan's *déjà vu* ennui as from Joan's leering coquetry and the sparseness of the production values. Binnie Barnes, wife of the film's producer, M. J. Frankovich, turned in the best performance as the Contessa and the old witch.

Following close on the art house failure of *Decameron Nights* was Paramount's *Flight to Tangier* (1953). Neither color nor the novelty of 3-D photography salvaged the low-caliber thriller. It was a toss-up who looked more shifty-eyed and bewildered, Joan (as a trench-coated FBI agent no less), Jack Palance, or Corinne Calvet, all hopelessly enmeshed in a tale of the retrieval of a $3 million letter of credit and other negotiables being smuggled into Tangier from behind the Iron Curtain.

Perhaps the most intriguing aspect of *The Bigamist* (Astor Theatre, December 25, 1953) was the personal relationship of its producer director, and players. On November 25, 1952, at the home of her mother and stepfather in Saratoga, California, Joan had wed forty-five-year-old producer Collier Young, who had previously been married to Ida Lupino and then to sophisticate Valerie Edmonds. *The Bigamist* was a production of Filmakers, an organization created by Young when he was married to Lupino (1948-50). The inexpensively mounted film was directed by Lupino, who co-starred as the waitress second wife of traveling sales executive Edmond O'Brien, already legally bound to swank Joan.* Even in 1953 the subject of adultery was intriguing still-conservative Americans, but the presentation here could not overcome its television-style production values, a weak ending,† and the lethargic performances of its detached leads. The biggest flaw of all was the incongruous casting. Why, for any reason, would O'Brien want to wed his strung-out, pregnant, lower-class mistress (Lupino) when he has back home such a smart, upper class wife who enjoys nothing more than closing business deals for hubby over homespun dinner parties?

Completed before the above two pictures but not released until April 18, 1954, was Paramount's *Casanova's Big Night*. It was a hit-and-miss affair that did nothing to halt Bob Hope's screen decline. Several years earlier Hope had kidded the britches off of romantic costume dramas in *Monsieur Beaucaire* (1946), but that was in a decade when the genre was still fashionable and there was something viable to satirize. Joan was equally at sea in this new Hope spoof, which was strung together by director Norman Z. McLeod. With no one to guide her, her fey qualities ran rampant, which was certainly no antidote to her obvious uneasiness with the fuzzy characterization she had to portray in *Casanova's Big Night*. The telltale sign of her inward rebellion at the part was her stooped-over gait (very prominent here), accompanied by a pained, gracious expression, and an equally insincere tone to her usually cool, crisp voice (as she smirked and giggled her way through the sight-gag trivia). Poor Joan did not belong as Hope's sparring partner in 1700s Venice; he was cast as the apprentice tailor forced to impersonate the great lover,

---

*To make the family circle complete, Joan's mother, Lilian Fontaine, played Lupino's landlady, and Collier Young had his own silent bit as a barfly.

†The judge who hears bewildered O'Brien's tale of woe will not pass sentence until a later date, leaving the picture with a non-ending.

and she was the sophisticated grocer's widow who accompanies the cowardly dunce on his madcap adventures.

Joan had been scheduled to make her Broadway stage debut in 1940 in a revival of *The Beaux' Stratagem* co-starred with her then husband Brian Aherne and Cornelia Otis Skinner. That project never came to be, nor did Chester Erskine's *Curtain Going Up,* which producer Cheryl Crawford intended as a joint project for Joan and Aherne. But on June 1, 1954, Joan replaced Deborah Kerr* in the Broadway edition of Robert Anderson's *Tea and Sympathy,* with Anthony Perkins taking over the part originated by John Kerr. Richard Watts, Jr. *(New York Post)* reported: "If she lacks something of the warmth and romantic glamor that Miss Kerr brought to her interpretation, she has the virtue of being without the slight air of self-conscious nobility that occasionally crept into her predecessor's characterization." Brooks Atkinson *(New York Times)* championed Joan's mainstem presence: "She is personally modest and professionally able, and her performance is a revealing piece of acting. This is one of the better lend-lease deals with Hollywood."

Joan thrived on her Broadway experience, reveling in the critical acclaim, the live public adoration, and a renewal of acquaintanceship with the perky Manhattan social life. "Sometimes you don't get the feel of a success till long after," Joan told reporters. "I remember when they gave me my Oscar for *Suspicion;* there was so much excitement that I felt nothing at all. Here at the theatre, though, I knew a wonderful thing was happening to me. And I was grateful even for the bad times and the frustrations I could look back on." She continued with the show through February 8, 1955, when a sledding accident aggravated a bout of bursitis in one arm and forced her to withdraw.

Unfortunately Joan's run with *Tea and Sympathy* did nothing for her screen career. Her sole 1955 cinema appearance was an unbilled cameo in United Artists' *Othello,* done as a lark for producer-director-star Orson Welles when she was on European location for *Decameron Nights* back in 1952. There was talk of Joan and equally adrift Van Johnson starring in a movie musical based on *Die Fledermaus* with the setting changed from Vienna to Salzburg. This Gottfried Reinhardt production for Warner Bros. collapsed, but Joan did sign for another Warners' release, *Serenade* (1956).

Serenade derived from a James Cain story Warners had owned since 1937 but never before could turn into a Production Code-approved scenario. Even in the more permissive 1950s, *Serenade*'s storyline was considered laundered for viewer suitability.† Those employed on this elaborate Anthony Mann-directed musical (fourteen songs, including two pop tunes) attest that star

---

*Thirty-three years old and a refugee from an unsatisfactory MGM contract, Deborah Kerr was then at the height of her box-office popularity, a far more lustrous box-office name in 1954 than Joan.

†In *Serenade* her deportment in a lush Howard Shoup wardrobe gave the movie some style, even if the *New York Journal American* insisted she overplayed her celebrity-gathering siren with a "cat that swallows the canary expression."

Mario Lanza had not improved his temperament or decorum in the three years since he was last in front of the cameras at MGM. Joan, among others, abhorred the whole filming experience, having to steel herself daily before she could bear the thought of exiting her dressing room to confront the tenor's latest breach of civility. Joan's revulsion with the distasteful situation showed itself clearly onscreen. She was cast as the irresistible Kendall Hale, a wanton storyland-type blueblood who sadistically thrives on cold, calculated romances. Her Kendall picks up young California vineyard worker Lanza (unexplainably paunchy) and soon she is launching the would-be tenor on his operatic career. When she ditches him on the eve of his New York debut, he falls into a colossal (widescreen and color) funk that is only belatedly counteracted by a long sojourn in Mexico and the revitalizing love of a bullfighter's daughter (Sarita Montiel). Also caught in this claptrap was Vincent Price as Lanza's cynical entrepreneur.

Serenade marked the beginning of Joan's glacial, older-woman screen phase. At age thirty-nine she could not and would not attempt to portray the skittish heroines that year-older sister Olivia was still attempting onscreen. Because Joan's natural chic lent such class to any production she graced, she was an asset to any drawing-room drama and found herself in sufficient demand in this limited capacity.

By the mid-1950s Joan was a steady television performer. In 1953, when she made the last of her "Theatre Guild on the Air" radio broadcasts,* she pondered the possibility of headlining a teleseries to be produced by husband Collier and to co-star his ex-wife, Ida Lupino. But she decided against the deal, maintaining: "I'm not the kind of person who relishes getting up at five in the morning five days a week for two to three years. I've had series offers and series offers but until something really strikes my fancy, I'll forgo this. The story's always the thing and nothing's hitting home." Instead, she chose to ply her name, face, and a modicum of her talent on an assortment of anthology series, commencing with the *Girl on the Park Bench* episode of "GE Theatre" (CBS, December 3, 1953). Two years passed before she returned to the medium, this time as a guest performer on the *Trudy* episode of "Four Star Playhouse" (CBS, May 26, 1955), a series which featured Ida Lupino as a recurring guest regular. Thereafter she popped up as a one-shot substitute hostess for Loretta Young on the latter's NBC teleseries (December 18, 1955), and was seen to modest advantage in the Gene Tierney role in the video remake of *The Ghost and Mrs. Muir* on "Twentieth Century-Fox Hour," "Stranger in the Night" (CBS October 17, 1956); guested on an episode of Ida Lupino and Howard Duff's comedy series "Mr. Adams and Eve" (CBS, October 18, 1957); and made several more appearances on "GE Theatre"

*Having already starred on that dramatic anthology series in *Pride and Prejudice* (November 18, 1945), *The Shining Hour* (November 16, 1947), *Camille* (April 3, 1949), *Great Expectations* (April 16, 1950), *A Farewell to Arms* (October 22, 1950), *Main Street* (September 30, 1951), *The Major and the Minor* (October 14, 1951), *The House of Mirth* (December 13, 1952), and *Vanity Fair* (March 8, 1953).

and other series throughout the mid-1960s. She hostessed CBS's *Model of the Year Pageant* (May 30, 1967), and on NBC's *Hollywood: The Selznick Years* (March 21, 1969) was seen in clips from *Rebecca* and in a taped interview regarding her former boss.

Joan again demonstrated that in Hollywood business often takes precedence over personal feelings when she returned to her old studio, RKO, in March, 1956, under a new three-picture deal. The terms were far from the lucrative ones bargained for by David O. Selznick in the old days. The head of the once major RKO complex was her ex-husband William Dozier, vice-president in charge of production since Howard Hughes had bled the facilities dry and sold the shell to General Tire in 1955.

Beyond a Reasonable Doubt (Loew's State Theatre, September 13, 1956) was as drab a picture as director Fritz Lang's earlier effort that year, RKO's *While the City Sleeps*. In a halfhearted manner the RKO publicity staff made much of the fact that the story and screenplay for *Beyond a Reasonable Doubt* was concocted by lawyer Douglas Morrow.* Yet the film displayed a flagrant disregard for the actuality of the law, particularly regarding the subject of pardons in capital-crime cases.† Not only did the plot of *Beyond a Reasonable Doubt* stretch one's credibility to the cracking point, but the gimmick was not the novelty claimed.‡ Joan's noble guise was as shallow and unconvincing as Andrews's great show of innocence. *Beyond a Reasonable Doubt* quickly disappeared from the theatrical-release circuit.

Joan never completed her RKO contract, for the studio soon went out of the production business. Instead she signed to appear in Twentieth Century-Fox's *Island in the Sun* (Roxy Theatre, June 12, 1957), Darryl F. Zanuck's first independent production since technically resigning as production head of Fox. The mogul promoted the picturization of Alex Waugh's potboiler as the film industry's first major step toward maturely dealing with racial integration since Zanuck's previous *Pinky* (Twentieth Century-Fox, 1949). The resultant picture, filmed in Grenada and Barbados, did treat the racial issue in a manner of speaking,§ but the novel's thrust was lost in a diffuse account of assorted life, love, and hate on the mythical island of Santa Marta in the British West

---

*He won an Oscar for his screenplay to *The Stratton Story* (MGM, 1949).

†Newspaper publisher Sidney Blackmer plans a graphic case to demonstrate the fallibility of justice. He and daughter Joan's fiance, writer Dana Andrews, plot a case of circumstantial evidence against Andrews. After Andrews's murder conviction Blackmer is to reveal his cohort's innocence via photographic proof. When a nightclub dancer is murdered, their plan is set into motion, with not even Joan being informed of the facts. Andrews is duly convicted, but his alibi disappears when Blackmer is killed in an auto crash in which all the evidence of innocence is apparently destroyed. At the very last minute a clarifying letter is found in Blackmer's safety deposit box and Andrews is about to be pardoned. But alas—Joan next happens upon conclusive evidence that Andrews really did commit the crime and was merely using her father's scheme to beat a murder rap. She finally telephones the governor's office to report the latest development and Andrews is returned to death row.

‡The plot ploy had been incorporated into Clara Bow's *Capital Punishment* (1925).

§The film was banned in many southern states, or at least had the "offensive" integration sequence heavily censored.

Indies. In a cast bursting with British-clipped accents, second-billed Joan played the neurotic, "mature" sister of aristocratic Patricia Owens. The gimmick of Joan's role was that, within the film's framework, she has the audacity to develop a yen for calypso-singing native labor-organizer Harry Belafonte. Unlike another segment in *Island in the Sun,* which does climax in a logical manner,* Joan's participation ends in frustrated anticipation for both the characters in the film and the people in the audience. After all, the hoopla had implied that something very passionate and graphic would transpire between Joan and Belafonte, but the daring of the film's producers had its limits. Stymied in winning her predatory way with Belafonte (she wants to go off to England with her muscular black would-be lover), the two clash head-on for a potentially violent parting. But the airport scene deteriorates into hackneyed dialog with Belafonte informing Joan: "But a white girl, a girl like you as my wife. . . . that would only mean snubs . . . misery. . . . Besides the girl would one day forget herself and call me a nigger." Joan seemed very ill at ease in this embarrassing rejection sequence, stalking away from an equally perplexed Belafonte.

Despite the inherent faults of *Island in the Sun* and the critical harangues by disgruntled reviewers who tore into the CinemaScope, DeLuxe color feature with a fury,† the Zanuck entertainment package made a nifty bundle in release, garnering over $5 million in United States and Canadian gross rentals.

Joan then went to MGM for *Until They Sail* (1957), Robert Wise's well-manipulated study of New Zealand women coping with the loneliness imposed on them by World War II. Had the black-and-white feature been produced a decade earlier its impact would have been far greater. Scrubbed and starched Joan appeared as the eldest of the four parentless Leslie girls (Joan, Jean Simmons, Piper Laurie, Sandra Dee). She is a frosty spinster who finds the Yankee GI's "indecent" until she experiences the awakening joys and grief of an affair with a gentle Marine captain (Charles Drake) from Oklahoma. Drake is killed in action, leaving the once aloof Joan to cope with pregnancy and her illegitimate son on her own terms. But Joan's role, as finely as it was handled, was clearly subordinate to star Jean Simmons and her relationship with tough, disillusioned Marine captain Paul Newman.

Thereafter Joan returned to Twentieth Century-Fox to complete her Darryl F. Zanuck-Fox agreement. As a joke she made an unbilled appearance as a native-girl extra in Joshua Logan's *South Pacific* (Magna, 1958) and then was utilized in the same year's *A Certain Smile* to provide mature elegance for the loafish adaptation of Francoise Sagan's novelette. The very plushness of the Milton Krasner-lensed Gallic backdrops, accompanied by Alfred New-

*Cast member John Justin and Belafonte's oncamera ex-mistress, Dorothy Dandridge, hurdle the racial barrier, with the British government aide taking his black amour to London and, hopefully, marriage.

† *Time* magazine called the picture the "sexiest West Indian travelogue ever made" and cited Joan's white-cargo appearance as "obviously too old for [Belafonte]."

man's lushly orchestrated soundtrack, made the feeble screenplay all the weaker. Joan was reduced to worldly sideline observation as the patient wife of charming Rossano Brazzi, being ever so decorously understanding when he indulges in a week-long Riviera romance with his teenaged niece, Christine Carere. Joan and Brazzi must indulge in an awkwardly handled forgiveness scene, a blatantly obvious pacifier to viewers who in 1958 might object to Brazzi's seemingly cavalier love affair. Even director Jean Negulesco recognized that his spun-sugar brew sagged badly midway and installed an extraneous lengthy insert within *A Certain Smile* of Johnny Mathis singing the title tune in a swank Parisian club setting. Joan earned her pay for her appearance in this sequence alone. Magnificently costumed in evening garb, she was the epitome of cool elegance as she politely sat viewing Mathis's gyrations, all the time sneaking looks at her table companions, the cooing Brazzi and Carere.

In early 1958 Joan contracted hepatitis and mononucleosis. After hospitalization at UCLA Medical Center in Los Angeles, she recuperated at her Maine home. She was well enough by mid-1959 to tour in Gerald Savory's *Hillary*. Joan was commended for her "bubbling zest" in this Broadway-bound venture, but the show never made it to Manhattan. The following summer she toured in *Susan and God,* and then returned to Hollywood to complete her Twentieth Century-Fox pact. "I'm very self-reliant," Joan admitted to an unastonished press, "that's what being ill taught me. When you find yourself flat on your back, unable to work, to read or do anything, without friends to cheer you up, believe me, you learn self-reliance."

While on the subject of herself, she provided a few new thoughts she had on the problems of marriage. "It's a very difficult situation. You work hard from dawn until evening. Then you go home and your husband expects you to put in full time as a wife. If you don't, he is resentful."

Joan's solution: "I think the ideal situation would be to marry a diplomat. Then he couldn't resent your position; in fact, your fame would help him in entertaining."

One would hardly expect to find Joan portraying a world-renowned psychologist in a science-fiction movie, but there she was along with such diverse personalities as Walter Pidgeon, Peter Lorre, Barbara Eden, and Frankie Avalon in *Voyage to the Bottom of the Sea* (Twentieth Century-Fox, 1961). It was all part of producer-director Irwin Allen's Jules Verne-esque cycle of widescreen entries geared to grab a good piece of the still profitable action-film market. Joan played a scientist who is convinced that Pidgeon, skipper of the nuclear-powered *Seaview* submarine, is insane, and intends to sabotage his mad plan to save the world from the Van Allen radiation belt. Her fate? She is eaten alive in the ship's shark tank. The special effects of this $3 million entry were the only rewarding aspect of the picture, which spawned the later Richard Basehart teleseries.

F. Scott Fitzgerald's *Tender Is the Night* (1932), considered his best, if least popular, novel, defied screen adaptation for decades, but David O.

Selznick was convinced it could be made with his forty-three-year-old wife, Jennifer Jones, as the star. It proved a very costly error. Twentieth-Century-Fox backed the production, utilizing studio contract players to fill out the supporting roles. Thus Joan found herself assigned to work again with her old boss Selznick. (During production there were several reports that Joan and longstanding friend Jones were feuding. "Ridiculous," Joan retorted. "There's no feud. We've known each other for years and we adore each other.") When the topheavy 142-minute production premiered at the Paramount and Plaza Theatres on January 20, 1962, reviewers applauded the recreation of the gay 1920s look ("gorgeous, inviting and remote") but critically slammed all concerned for allowing Miss Jones to pose as the far younger Nicole, a psychotic who regains her wavering mental stability at the emotional expense of her romantic-weakling husband, Jason Robards, Jr. Only Joan, in the brief part of Jones's shallow older sister, Baby Warren, conveyed the proper Fitzgeraldian tone and was roundly complimented for her mature flapper characterization.*

Meanwhile, on January 3, 1961, Joan, draped in a mink coat ("my Christmas present to myself"), appeared in a Los Angeles court to win her divorce from Collier Young, from whom she had been separated since May, 1960. As part of the settlement she received a one-half interest in one of his television production firms and stock in two others. Thereafter her escorts included Adlai Stevenson among others, but it was Alfred Wright, editor of *Sports Illustrated* magazine, whom she wed on January 27, 1964. They would separate in early 1966† and finally agree to a Mexican divorce in 1969. At one point in 1966 during their see-sawing relationship, Joan expounded: "Believe it or not, I take the job of being a wife very seriously. I love to entertain, I cook well, I have my own electric drill, my own soldering iron. I am an excellent handywoman. I took my first watch apart when I was eight, changed my first tire when I was thirteen. So I am not helpless."

Joan merely dabbled with her acting career in the 1960s, tempered by a realization that only younger actors and actresses could be the new decade's top recognized personalities. There were occasional television assignments. She was scheduled to film a Norah Lofts-written project in London in the fall of 1964, but that was postponed (and later shelved) when she joined the out-of-town tryout of Iris Murdock's *A Severed Head*.‡ During the Philadelphia run, Joan left the ill-fated project, later returning to the still lucrative summer-

---

*"Only Joan Fontaine, as Baby, is authentic. She conveys something of the haughty well-groomed American golden girl, glimpsed in Pullmans and hotel lobbies, who is the Fitzgerald dream and devil" (Stanley Kaufman, *New Republic*).

†"Alfred has his homes in golf clubs all over the country," Joan explained. "We've seen each other maybe three months in the last two years. I've tried to go along, but I'm a terrible nuisance —I'm in the way, really. There he is in the press tent writing, and I'm sitting in the club with room service. That's not a marriage."

‡Joan's reason for doing the play: "I was tired of loafing, and it was a boring summer out on the [Long] Island."

theatre circuit with *Dial M for Murder* (1966) and *The Spider's Web* (1967). There was talk of Joan trying out Nord Riley's farce *The Armored Dove* with Tom Ewell, but it remained just that, talk. And so did Alan Eyckborn's *Relatively Speaking,* which was to be imported from the London stage in 1970.

Joan once stated that "producers used to be able to smell a good picture," so she must have had a very persistent head cold when she bought the rights to Peter Curtis's novel *The Devil's Own,* made in England on the cheap and showcase-released by Twentieth Century-Fox in 1967 as a double-bill entry. It was rather late in the game for Joan to embark on the horror-film trail, à la Bette Davis, Joan Crawford, and sister Olivia. Nor was Joan's belated fright-picture entry well plotted or directed, being filled with an abundance of loopholes and unintended laughs.* As too often happens to stars in decline who accept a role under a misconception of its possible screen potential, Joan's characterization emerged without enough substance to allow her any legitimate dramatic scope. The best that could be said of Joan in *The Devil's Own* was that she looked as lovely and gracious as always, and had that same frightened-out-of-her-mind look she had perfected in *Rebecca* and *Suspicion.*

Joan's most recent film venture was the abortive *A Girl Called Jules,* based on a risqué novel by Melina Milani, and being produced by Francisco Mazzei to co-star Anna Moffo. On January 27, 1970, in a well-publicized huff, Joan packed her bags and left the location site in Cortina d'Ampizzo, Italy, claiming there had been a grievous mistake in contractual terms and she was not being paid her weekly salary in advance as the pact had detailed. When Joan reached Rome on her hasty way back to New York, the producer had the legal authorities impound her luggage (she traveled on without them) and later he initiated a $500,000 damage suit against Joan that has yet to be settled.

In early 1972 Joan took another summer-stock fling, again starring in *Dial M for Murder.* She displayed her well-known imperiousness during the ten-week South African tour when she called a press conference in Durban (post her final week's salary having been cabled to New York) to complain that the management had failed, among other essential items, to supply transportation to and from the theatres, meals between performances, a personal maid, and the opportunity to perform before a black audience. When the show played the New England stock circuit in the summer of 1972, Joan looked as fetching as ever, but was allowed to fall back on her immature cutesy performing habits of the 1930s.

---

*While teaching at a mission school in central Africa, Joan is subjected to a traumatic encounter with a voodoo witch doctor. She recovers from the nervous collapse and accepts a headmistress post in a small provincial English school. Her prize pupil there, thirteen-year-old Ingrid Brett, is later suspected by the villagers of being spiritually possessed. When Martin Stephens disappears from the classroom sphere, everyone is sure he is the prey of local voodooists who are planning to offer him as a sacrifice. Joan suffers a new breakdown and goes to a nursing home where she recovers her memory, escaping in time to return to the village. There she finds that writer Kay Walsh is the leader of the local cult.

Today Joan resides in New York in her East 72nd Street apartment, and besides participating in an active nightlife, she is an ardent golfer, licensed pilot, interior decorator, and equestrienne. "I'm enjoying life more now than I ever did," Joan recently exclaimed. "I've been a nurse's aide for years in New York City hospitals and I try to do some hospital work in whatever city I'm appearing.

"I'm having the best time of my life right now. If you take good care of yourself, life after fifty can be the very best time."

Daughter Deborah is completing her college degree at the University of Southern California and Martita is now married and living in Massachusetts. On and off throughout the 1960s Joan was dating New York society figure Dr. Ben Kean. Although marriage never developed from their relationship, quick-witted Joan is the first to note, regarding her value as a spouse: "I certainly made a much more exciting life for the man. Life was never humdrum with me."

As for her present rapport with sister Olivia—the latter was Joan's guest at her Central Park South apartment during the zesty Manhattan Christmas season of 1961, but since then they have remained tactfully apart. "We're getting closer together as we get older, but there would be a slight problem of temperament. In fact," admits Joan, "it would be bigger than Hiroshima."

Suspicion is not one of Joan's favorite films ("That was just a mystery"), but she has a sneaking fondness for *Rebecca, The Constant Nymph,* and *Letter from an Unknown Woman,* because they "were far more sensitive and of a higher quality than any of the others."

Joan's rare video appearances these days are limited to panel-show guest shots because several of the programs are based in New York, the money is good, and it keeps her name in front of the public. As for motion pictures, she now insists: "One of the reasons I stopped making pictures is so nobody could do to me what they did to poor Ray Milland in *Love Story.* He looked half-dead. No toupee and those big closeups. His face looked like the craters of the moon."* Which seems a strange rationale for Joan to pursue, since she still boasts an unblemished complexion and a smooth-featured face.

What of Joan's future plans in general? Besides her occasional lapses into proletarian commercialism (i.e., her Arnold Bread TV commercials), the naturally cultured Joan has a deep-rooted love for her present ritzy social standing and continues to enjoy all the best that money can buy. Since she wants for no "creature comforts," she can look at you with a twinkle in her eyes and a wry smile planted on her lips, as she purrs her "fondest" wish: "Only to grow into an imperious, demanding old woman. I want to be just as rude to young people as old people were to me when I was young."

*On another occasion not so long ago Joan admitted about movie making, "I don't want character roles nor do I want to play mothers, so I don't quite know what to do." In June, 1973, it was announced Joan would portray Czarina Alexandra in Dico Dimitrov's production of *The Escape of Nicholas and Alexandra,* in which Rossano Brazzi, her *A Certain Smile* co-star would be Czar Nicholas II, and Victor Mature would be cast as an American government official. The project apparently never got off the ground.

Feature Film Appearances
JOAN FONTAINE

As Joan Burfield:

NO MORE LADIES   (MGM, 1935) 81 M.

Producer, Irving Thalberg; director, Edward H. Griffith, George Cukor; based on the play by A. E. Thomas; screenplay, Donald Ogden Stewart, Horace Jackson; costumes, Adrian; art director, Cedric Gibbons; sound, Douglas Shearer; camera, Oliver T. Marsh; editor, Frank E. Hull.

Joan Crawford (Marcia); Robert Montgomery (Sherry); Edna May Oliver (Fanny); Franchot Tone (James); Charlie Ruggles (Edgar); Gail Patrick (Theresa); Reginald Denny (Oliver); Vivienne Osborne (Lady Diana Moulton); Joan Burfield (Caroline); Arthur Treacher (Lord Moulton); David Horsley (Duffy); Jean Chatburn (Sally); William Wagner (Butler); Charles Coleman (Stafford); Isabelle La Mal (Jacquette); Frank Dawson (Dickens); Walter Walker (Bit); E. J. Babiel (Desk Clerk); Ed Hart (Taxi Driver); Tommy Tomlinson (Dick); Charles O'Malley (Bellboy); Lew Harvey, David Thursby (Bartenders); Sherry Hall (Captain); Clem Beauchamp (Drunk); Veda Buckland (Maid); Mabel Colcord (Cook).

As Joan Fontaine:

QUALITY STREET   (RKO, 1937) 84 M.

Producer, Pandro S. Berman; director, George Stevens; based on the play by Sir James M. Barrie; screenplay, Mortimer Offner, Allan Scott; art director, Van Nest Polglase; set decorator, Darrell Silvera; assistant director, Argyle Nelson; makeup, Mel Burns; costumes, Walter Plunkett; music, Roy Webb; orchestrator, Maurice De Packh; sound, Clem Portman; camera, Robert de Grasse; editor, Henry Berman.

Katharine Hepburn (Phoebe Throssel); Franchot Tone (Dr. Valentine Brown); Fay Bainter (Susan Throssel); Eric Blore (Sergeant); Cora Witherspoon (Patty); Estelle Winwood (Mary Willoughby); Florence Lake (Henrietta Turnbull); Helena Grant (Fanny Willoughby); Bonita Granville (Isabella); Clifford Severn (Arthur); Sherwood Bailey (William Smith); Roland Varno (Ensign Blades); Joan Fontaine (Charlotte Parratt); William Bakewell (Lt. Spicer); Yorky Sherwood (Postman); Carmencita Johnson (Student).

THE MAN WHO FOUND HIMSELF   (RKO, 1937) 67 M.

Associate producer, Cliff Reid; director, Lew Landers; story, Alice F. Curtis; screenplay, J. Robert Bren, Edmund L. Hartman, G. V. Atwater; special effects, Vernon L. Walker; camera, J. Roy Hunt; editor, Jack Hively.

John Beal (Jim Stanton); Joan Fontaine (Doris King); Philip Huston (Dick Miller); Jane Walsh (Barbara Reed); George Irving (Dr. Stanton); James Conlin (Nosey);

Frank M. Thomas (Roberts); Diana Gibson (Helen); Dwight Frye (Patient); Billy Gilbert (Fat Hobo).

YOU CAN'T BEAT LOVE   (RKO, 1937) 82 M.

Producer, Robert Sisk; director, Christy Cabanne; based on the story by Olga Moore; screenplay, David Silverstein, Maxwell Shane; camera, Russell Metty; editor, Ted Cheesman.

Preston Foster (Jimmy Hughes); Joan Fontaine (Trudy Olson); Herbert Mundin (Jasper); William Brisbane (Clem Bruner); Alan Bruce (Scoop Gallagher); Paul Hurst (Butch Mehaffey); Bradley Page (Dwight Parsons); Berton Churchill (Chief Brennan); Frank M. Thomas (Mayor Olson); Harold Huber (Pretty Boy Jones); Paul Guilfoyle (Louie, the Weasel); Barbara Pepper (May Smith).

MUSIC FOR MADAME   (RKO, 1937) 81 M.

Producer, Jesse L. Lasky; director, John Blystone; story, Robert Harari; screenplay, Gertrude Purcell, Harari; music director, Nathaniel Shilkret; songs; Gus Kahn and Rudolf Friml; Eddie Cherkose and Shilkret; Herb Magidson and Allie Wrubel.

Nino Martini (Nino Maretti); Joan Fontaine (Jean Clemens); Alan Mowbray (Leon Rodowsky); Alan Hale (Detective Flugelman); Billy Gilbert (Krause); Grant Mitchell (District Attorney Ernest Robinson); Erik Rhodes (Spaghetti Nacio); Lee Patrick (Nora Burns); Frank Conroy (Morton Harding); Bradley Page (Rollins); Ada Leonard (The Bride [Miss Goodwin]); Alan Bruce (The Groom [The Director]); Romo Vincent (Truck Driver); Barbara Pepper (Blonde on Bus); Edward H. Robbins (William Goodwin); George Shelley (Barret, a Singer); Jack Carson (Assistant Director); Ralph Lewis, Mary Carr, Ben Hendricks, William Corson (Bits); Ben Hall (Bus Passenger); Jack Mulhall, Larry Steers, Harold Miller, Ralph Brooks (Guests); Grace Hayle (Fat Guest); Mira McKinney (Admirer); George Meeker (Orchestra Leader); Stanley Blystone, Pat O'Malley (Cops); Robert Homans (Desk Sergeant); Milburn Stone (Detective); Harry Tenbrook (Electrician); James Donlan (Suspect with Cold); Russ Powell ("Asleep in the Deep" Singer); Ward Bond (Violet, the Henchman); Sam Hayes (KAFF Announcer); Jac George (Violinist).

A DAMSEL IN DISTRESS   (RKO, 1937) 101 M.

Producer, Pandro S. Berman; director, George Stevens; based on the story by P. G. Wodehouse; screenplay, Wodehouse, S. K. Lauren, Ernest Pagano; music director, Victor Baravalle; orchestral arranger, Robert Russell Bennett; additional arrangements, Ray Noble, George Bassman; songs, George and Ira Gershwin; art director, Van Nest Polglase, Carroll Clark; assistant director, Argyle Nelson; choreography, Hermes Pan; special camera effects, Vernon L. Walker; camera, Joseph H. August; editor, Henry Berman.

Fred Astaire (Jerry Halliday); George Burns (Himself); Gracie Allen (Herself); Joan Fontaine (Lady Alyce Marshmorton); Reginald Gardiner (Keggs); Ray Noble (Reggie); Constance Collier (Lady Caroline Marshmorton); Montagu Love (Lord John Marshmorton); Harry Watson (Albert); Jan Duggan (Miss Ruggles); Pearl Amatore, Betty Rone, Mary Dean, Jac George (Madrigal Singers); Joe Niemeyer (Halliday Impersonator); Bill O'Brien (Chauffeur); Mary Gordon (Cook); Ralph Brooks, Fred Kelsey (Sightseers); Major Sam Harris (Dance Extra).

A MILLION TO ONE   (Puritan, 1937) 68 M.

Producer, Fanchon Royer; director, Lynn Shores; story-adaptation, John T. Neville; production manager, Gaston Glass; camera, James Diamond.

Bruce Bennett (Johnny Kent); Joan Fontaine (Joan Stevens); Monte Blue (John Kent); Suzanne Kaaren (Pat Stanley); Reed Howes (Duke Hale); Kenneth Harlan (William Stevens); Ed Piel (Mac, the Editor); Ben Hall (Joe, a Reporter); Dick Simmons (a Friend).

MAID'S NIGHT OUT (RKO, 1938) 64 M.

Producer, Robert Sisk; director, Ben Holmes; story, Willoughby Speyers; screenplay, Bert Granet; camera, Frank Redman; editor, Ted Cheesman.

Joan Fontaine (Sheila Harrison); Allan Lane (Bill Norman); Billy Gilbert (Popolopolis); Cecil Kellaway (Geoffrey); Hedda Hopper (Mrs. Harrison); William Brisbane (Wally Martin); Vicki Lester (Adele); Hilda Vaughn (Mary); George Irving (Rufus Norman); Frank M. Thomas (Mac); Solly Ward (Mischa); Eddie Gribbon (Hogan).

BLOND CHEAT (RKO, 1938) 62 M.

Producer, William Sistrom; director, Joseph Santley; story, Aladar Lazlo; screenplay, Charles Kaufman, Paul Yawitz, Viola Brothers Shore, Harry Segall; music director, Roy Webb; camera, editor, Jack Hively.

Joan Fontaine (Julie); Derrick de Marney (Michael Ashburn); Cecil Kellaway (Rufus Trent); Cecil Cunningham (Genevieve Trent); Lilian Bond (Roberta Trent); Robert Coote (Gilbert Potts); Olaf Hytten (Paul Douglas); John Sutton (Fred [Percy]); Gerald Hamer (Waiter).

SKY GIANT (RKO, 1938) 81 M.

Producer, Robert Sisk; director, Lew Landers; based on the novel *Ground Crew* by Lionel Houser; screenplay, Houser; camera, Nick Musuraca; editor, Harry Marker.

Richard Dix (Stag); Chester Morris (Ken Stanton); Joan Fontaine (Meg); Harry Carey (Colonel Stockton); Paul Guilfoyle (Fergie); Robert Strange (Weldon); Max Hoffman, Jr. (Brown); Vicki Lester (Edna); William Corson (Claridge); James Bush (Thompson); Edward Marr (Austin); Harry Campbell (Goodwin).

THE DUKE OF WEST POINT (UA, 1938) 112 M.

Producer, Edward Small; director, Alfred E. Green; story-screenplay, George Bruce; camera, Robert Planck; editor, Grant Whytock.

Louis Hayward (Steven Early); Joan Fontaine (Ann Porter); Tom Brown (Sonny Drew); Richard Carlson (Jack West); Alan Curtis (Cadet Strong); Donald Barry (Cadet Grady); Gaylord Pendleton (Cadet Rains); Charles D. Brown (Doc Porter); Jed Prouty (Mr. Drew); Marjorie Gateson (Mrs. Drew); Emma Dunn (Mrs. West); George McKay (Varsity Hockey Coach); James Flavin (Plebe Hockey Coach); Nick Lukats (Plebe Football Coach); William Bakewell (Committee Captain); Kenneth Harlan (Varsity Football Coach); Jonathan Hale (Colonel Early); Art Raymond (Country Boy); Anthony Nace (First Captain of Corps); Mary MacLaren (Nurse); Edward Earle (Surgeon); Alan Connor (Tactical Officer).

GUNGA DIN (RKO, 1939) 117 M.

Executive producer, Pandro S. Berman; producer-director, George Stevens; suggested by the poem by Rudyard Kipling; story, Ben Hecht, Charles MacArthur; screenplay, Joel Sayre, Fred Guiol; art director, Van Nest Polglase, Perry Ferguson; set decorator, Darrell Silvera; gowns, Edward Stevenson; assistant director, Edward Killy, Dewey Starkey; technical advisor, Capt. Clive Morgan, William Briers, Sir Robert Erskine Holland; sound, John E. Tribby, James Stewart; special effects, Vernon L. Walker; camera, Joseph H. August; editor, Henry Berman, John Lockert.

Cary Grant (Cutter); Victor McLaglen (MacChesney); Douglas Fairbanks, Jr. (Ballantine); Sam Jaffe (Gunga Din); Eduardo Ciannelli (Guru); Joan Fontaine (Emmy); Montagu Love (Colonel Weed); Robert Coote (Higginbotham); Abner Biberman (Chota); Lumsden Hare (Major Mitchell); Cecil Kellaway (Mr. Stebbins); Reginald Sheffield (Journalist); Ann Evers, Audrey Manners, Fay McKenzie (Girls at Party); Charles Bennett (Telegraph Operator); Les Sketchley (Corporal); Frank Levya (Merchant); George Ducount, Jamiel Hasson, George Regas (Thug Chieftains); Bryant Fryer (Scotch Sergeant); Lal Chand Mehra (Jadoo); Roland Varno (Lieutenant Markham); Clive Morgan (Lancer Captain).

MAN OF CONQUEST (Rep., 1939) 99 M.

Associate producer, Sol C. Siegel; director, George Nicholls, Jr.; story, Harold Shumate, Wells Root; screenplay, E. E. Paramore, Jr., Root; production manager, Al Wilson; assistant director, Kenneth Holmes; music, Victor Young; Gail Patrick's gowns, Edith Head; art director, John Victor Mackay; costumes, Adele Palmer; sound, Richard Tyler; special effects, Howard Lydecker; camera, Joseph H. August; editor, Edward Mann.

Richard Dix (Sam Houston); Gail Patrick (Margaret Lea); Edward Ellis (Andrew Jackson); Joan Fontaine (Eliza Allen); Victor Jory (William Travis); Robert Barrat (Davey Crockett); George Hayes (Lannie Upchurch); Ralph Morgan (Stephen Austin); Robert Armstrong (Jim Bowie); C. Henry Gordon (Santa Ana); Janet Beecher (Mrs. Lea); Pedro de Cordoba (Oolooteko); Max Terhune ("Deaf" Smith); Ferris Taylor (Jonas Lea); Kathleen Lockhart (Mrs. Allen); Leon Ames (John Hoskins); Charles Stevens (Zavola); Lane Chandler (Bonham); Sarah Padden (Mrs. Houston).

THE WOMEN (MGM, 1939) 132 M.

Producer, Hunt Stromberg; director, George Cukor; based on the play by Clare Boothe; screenplay, Anita Loos, Jane Murfin; art director, Cedric Gibbons, Wade B. Rubottom; set decorator, Edwin B. Willis; gowns-fashion show, Adrian; music, Edward Ward, David Snell; sound, Douglas Shearer; song, Chet Forrest, Bob Wright, and Ed Ward; camera, Oliver T. Marsh, Joseph Ruttenberg; editor, Robert J. Kerns.

(Fashion Show Sequence in Technicolor).

Norma Shearer (Mary Haines); Joan Crawford (Chrystal Allen); Rosalind Russell (Sylvia Fowler); Mary Boland (Countess DeLave); Paulette Goddard (Miriam Aarons); Joan Fontaine (Peggy Day); Lucile Watson (Mrs. Moorehead); Phyllis Povah (Edith Potter); Florence Nash (Nancy Blake); Virginia Weidler (Little Mary); Ruth Hussey (Miss Watts); Muriel Hutchison (Jane); Margaret Dumont (Mrs. Wagstaff); Dennie Moore (Olga); Mary Cecil (Maggie); Marjorie Main (Lucy); Esther Dale (Ingrid); Hedda Hopper (Dolly Dupuyster); Mildred Shay (Helene, the French Maid); Priscilla Lawson, Estelle Etterre (Hairdressers); Ann Morriss (Exercise Instructress); Mary Beth Hughes (Miss Trimmerback); Marjorie Wood (Sadie, Old Maid in Powder Room); Virginia Grey (Pat); Cora Witherspoon (Mrs. Van Adams); Veda Buckland (Woman); Charlotte Treadway (Her Companion); Theresa Harris (Olive); Virginia Howell, Vera Vague (Receptionists); May Beatty (Fat Woman); May Hale (Mud Mask); Ruth Findlay (Pediatrist); Charlotte Wynters (Miss Batchelor); Aileen Pringle (Miss Carter); Florence Shirley (Miss Archer); Judith Allen (Model); Florence O'Brien (Euphie); Hilda Plowright (Miss Fordyce); Mariska Aldrich (Singing Teacher); Leila McIntrye (Woman With Bundles); Dot Farley (Large Woman); Flora Finch (Woman Window Tapper); Dorothy Sebastian, Renie Riano (Saleswomen); Grace Goodall (Head Saleswoman); Lilian Bond (Mrs. Erskine); Winifred Harris (Mrs. North); Gertrude Astor, Nell Craig (Nurses); Grace Hayle, Maude Allen (Cyclists); Natalie Moorhead (Woman in Modiste Salon); Jo Ann Sayers (Debutante); Betty Blythe

(Mrs. South); Dorothy Adams (Miss Atkinson); Barbara Pepper (Tough Girl); Peggy Shannon (Mrs. Jones); Carol Hughes (Salesgirl in Modiste Salon); Virginia Pine (Glamour Girl).

REBECCA (UA, 1940) 130 M.

Producer, David O. Selznick; director, Alfred Hitchcock; based on the novel by Daphne du Maurier; adaptation, Philip MacDonald, Michael Hogan; screenplay, Robert E. Sherwood, Joan Harrison; music, Franz Waxman; art director, Lyle Wheeler; camera, George Barnes; editor, Hal C. Kern.

Laurence Olivier (Maxim de Winter); Joan Fontaine (Mrs. de Winter); George Sanders (Jack Favell); Judith Anderson (Mrs. Danvers); Nigel Bruce (Major Giles Lacey); C. Aubrey Smith (Colonel Julyan); Reginald Denny (Frank Crawley); Gladys Cooper (Beatrice Lacy); Philip Winter (Robert); Edward Fielding (Frith); Florence Bates (Mrs. Van Hopper); Melville Cooper (Coroner); Leo G. Carroll (Dr. Baker); Forrester Harvey (Chalcroft); Lumsden Hare (Tabbs); Leonard Carey (Ben); Alfred Hitchcock (Man outside Phone Booth).

SUSPICION (RKO, 1941) 99 M.

Director, Alfred Hitchcock; based on the novel *Before the Fact* by Francis Iles; screenplay, Samson Raphaelson, Joan Harrison, Alma Reville; art director, Van Nest Polglase; music, Franz Waxman; special effects, Vernon L. Walker; camera, Harry Stradling; editor, William Hamilton.

Cary Grant (Johnnie Aysgarth); Joan Fontaine (Lina); Sir Cedric Hardwicke (General McLaidlaw); Nigel Bruce (Beaky Thwaite); Dame May Whitty (Mrs. McLaidlaw); Isabel Jeans (Mrs. Newsham); Heather Angel (Ethel, the Maid); Auriol Lee (Isobel Sedbusk); Reginald Sheffield (Reggie Wetherby); Leo G. Carroll (Capt. Melbeck); Maureen Roden-Ryan (Winnie, the Maid); Carol Curtis-Brown (Jessie Barham); Constance Worth (Mrs. Fitzpatrick); Violet Shelton (Alice Barham); Pax Walker (Phoebe, the Maid); Leonard Carey (Jenner, the Butler); Gertrude Hoffmann (Mrs. Wetherby); Kenneth Hunter (Sir Gerald); Clyde Cook (Photographer); Faith Brook (Alice Barham); Dorothy Lloyd (Miss Wetherby); Elsie Weller (Miss Wetherby); Aubrey Mather (Mr. Webster); Rex Evans (Mr. Bailey); Edward Fielding (Antique Shop Proprietor); Hilda Plowright (Postmistress); Ben Webster (Registrar); Gavin Gordan (Bertram Sedbusk); Nondas Metcalf (Phyllis Swinghurst); Lumsden Hare (Inspector Hodgson); Clara Reid (Mrs. Craddock); Vernon Downing (Benson); Billy Bevan (Ticket Taker); Alec Craig (Hogarth Club Bit).

THIS ABOVE ALL (20th, 1942) 110 M.

Producer, Darryl F. Zanuck; director, Anatole Litvak; based on the novel by Eric Knight; screenplay, R. C. Sherriff; art director, Thomas Little; camera, Arthur Miller; editor, Walter Thompson.

Tyrone Power (Clive Briggs); Joan Fontaine (Prudence Cathaway); Thomas Mitchell (Monty); Henry Stephenson (General Cathaway); Nigel Bruce (Ramsbottom); Gladys Cooper (Iris); Philip Merivale (Roger); Sara Allgood (Waitress in Tea Room); Alexander Knox (Rector); Queenie Leonard (Violet); Melville Cooper (Wilbur); Jill Esmond (Nurse Emily); Arthur Shields (Chaplain); Dennis Hoey (Parsons); Miles Mander (Major); Rhys Williams (Sergeant); John Abbott (Joe); Carol Curtis-Brown (Maid); Holmes Herbert (Dr. Mathias); Denis Green (Dr. Ferris); Thomas Louden (Vicar); Mary Forbes (Vicar's Wife); Forrester Harvey (Proprietor); Harold de Becker (Conductor); Jessica Newcombs (Matron); Billy Bevan (Farmer); Aubrey Mather, Lumsden Hare (Headwaiters); Heather Thatcher, Jean Prescott (Nurses); Brenda Forbes (Mae, the Singer); Doris Lloyd (Sergeant); Rita Page, Clare Verdera (Corporals); Joyce

Wynn, Valerie Cole, Stephanie Insall, Dorothy Daniels de Becker (WAAF Girls); Alan Edmiston (Porter); Virginia McDowall (Girl); Olaf Hytten (Proprietor); Morton Lowry (Soldier); Wyndham Standing (Doctor); Alec Craig (Conductor); Anita Bolster, May Beatty (Customers); Mary Field (Maid); Cyril Thornton (Station Master); Leonard Carey, Val Stanton (Policemen).

THE CONSTANT NYMPH   (WB, 1943) 112 M.

Producer, Henry Blanke; director, Edmund Goulding; based on the novel by Margaret Kennedy and the play by Kennedy, Basil Dean; screenplay, Kathryn Scola; art director, Carl Jules Weyl; music, Erich Wolfgang Korngold; music director, Leo F. Forbstein; song; Kennedy and Korngold; camera, Tony Gaudio; editor, David Weisbart.

Charles Boyer (Lewis Todd); Joan Fontaine (Tessa Sanger); Brenda Marshall (Toni Sanger); Alexis Smith (Florence Churchill); Charles Coburn (Charles Churchill); Dame May Whitty (Lady Longborough); Peter Lorre (Fritz Bercovi); Jean Muir (Kate Sanger); Joyce Reynolds (Paula Sanger); Eduardo Ciannelli (Roberto); Montagu Love (Albert Sanger); Jeanine Crispin (Marie); Richard Ryen (Trigorin); Doris Lloyd (Hamilton); Joan Blair (Lina); Marcel Dalio (Georges); Andre Charlot (Dr. Renee); Craufurd Kent (Thorpe); Louise Brien (Lady Longborough's Daughter); Geoffrey Steele (Mr. Turtle); George Kirby (Moving Man); Charles Irwin, Donald Stuart (Grooms); Jean Ransome (Maid); Brandon Hurst (Man); Max Rabinowitsh (Caroli); David Clyde (Florist); Mildred Brook (Lady Saunders); Eric Mayne (General Saunders).

JANE EYRE   (20th, 1944) 96 M.

Producer, William Goetz; director, Robert Stevenson; based on the novel by Charlotte Brontë; screenplay, Aldous Huxley, Stevenson, John Houseman; art director, James Basevi, Wiard B. Ihnen; special effects, Fred Sersen; camera, George Barnes; editor, Walter Thompson.

Orson Welles (Edward Rochester); Joan Fontaine (Jane Eyre); Margaret O'Brien (Adele); Peggy Ann Garner (Jane—as a child); John Sutton (Dr. Rivers); Sara Allgood (Bessie); Henry Daniell (Brockelhurst); Agnes Moorehead (Mrs. Reed); Aubrey Mather (Col. Dent); Edith Barrett (Mrs. Fairfax); Barbara Everest (Lady Ingraham); Hillary Brooke (Blanche); Ethel Griffies (Grace Pool); Eily Malyon (Mrs. Sketcher); Ivan Simpson (Mr. Woods); Erskine Sanford (Mr. Braggs); John Abbott (Mason); Elizabeth Taylor (Helen); Mae Marsh (Leah); Mary Forbes (Mrs. Eshton); Thomas Louden (Sir George Lynn); Yorke Sherwood (Beadle); Ronald Harris (John); Charles Irwin (Auctioneer); Gwendolen Logan, Moyna Macgill (Dowagers); Gerald Oliver Smith (Footman at Gateshead); Jean Fenwick, Bud Lawler, John Meredith, Leslie Vincent, Roseanne Murray, Marion Rosamond, Dan Wallace (Guests); Billie Seward, Ruthe Brady, Adele Jergens (Girls at Party); Colin Campbell (Proprietor); Eustace Wyatt (Dr. Carter); Billy Bevan (Bookie); Tempe Pigott (Fortune Teller); Harry Allen, David Clyde, Charles Coleman (Guards); Alec Craig (Footman); Frederick Worlock (Waiter); George Kirby (Old Gentleman); Arthur Gould-Porter (Young Man); Alan Edmiston (Dealer); Barry Macollum, Brandon Hurst (Trustees); Nancy June Robinson (Girl).

FRENCHMAN'S CREEK   (Par.. 1944) C—113 M.

Executive producer, B. G. De Sylva; producer, Mitchell Leisen; associate producer, David Lewis; director, Leisen; based on the novel by Daphne du Maurier; screenplay, Talbot Jennings; music, Victor Young; art director, Hans Dreier, Ernst Fegte; process camera, Farciot Edouart; special effects, Gordon Jennings; camera, George Barnes; editor, Alma Macrorie.

Joan Fontaine (Lady Dona St. Columb); Arturo de Cordova (Jean Benoit Aubery); Basil Rathbone (Lord Rockingham); Nigel Bruce (Lord Godolphin); Cecil Kellaway

(William); Ralph Forbes (Harry St. Columb); Billy Daniels (Pierre Blanc); Moyna Macgill (Lady Godolphin); Patricia Barker (Henrietta); David James (James); Mary Field (Prue); David Clyde (Martin, the Coachman); Charles Coleman (Thomas, the Footman); Paul Oman (Luc); Arthur Gould-Porter (Thomas Eustick); Evan Thomas (Robert Penrose); Leslie Denison (John Nankervis); Denis Green (Philip Rashleigh); George Kirby (Dr. Williams); David Thursby (Ostler); Lauri Beatty (Alice); Ronnie Rondell, George Barton, Victor Romito, Bob Clark, Allen Pinson, Patrick Desmond, Jimmy Dime, Harvey Easton, Henry Escalante, Art Foster, Vincent Gironda, Jacques Karre, John Latito, Rube Schaffer, Sammy Stein, Armand Tanny, Fred Kohler, Jr., John Roy, Neal Clisby, Noble Blake (Pirate Crew); Constance Worth, Phyllis Barry (Women in Gaming House); Edward Cooper (Croupier); Bob Stevenson, Alfred George Ferguson (Jail Guards); Frank Hagney (Cornishman); Keith Hitchcock (Watchman); Leyland Hodgson, Kenneth Hunter, Boyd Irwin, Gordon Richards (Guests).

THE AFFAIRS OF SUSAN   (Par., 1945) 108 M.

Producer, Hal B. Wallis; director, William A. Seiter; story, Thomas Monroe, Laszlo Gorog; screenplay, Monroe, Gorog, Richard Flournoy; art director, Hans Dreier, Franz Bachelin; set decorator, Kenneth Swartz; music, Frederick Hollander; song, E. Y. Harburg and Franz Waxman; assistant director, Dink Templeton; sound, Earl S. Hayman; process camera, Farciot Edouart; camera, David Abel; editor, Eda Warren.

Joan Fontaine (Susan Darell); George Brent (Roger Berton); Dennis O'Keefe (Bill Anthony); Walter Abel (Richard Aiken); Don DeFore (Mike Ward); Rita Johnson (Mona Kent); Mary Field (Nancy); Byron Barr (Chick); Francis Pierlot (Uncle Jemmy); Lewis Russell (Mr. Cusp); Vera Marshe (Brooklyn Girl); Frank Faylen (Brooklyn Boy); James Millican (Major); Robert Sully (Lieutenant); John Whitney, Jerry James (Captains); Crane Whitley (Colonel); Bill Meader, Warren Hymer (Waiters); Ralph Brooks (Messenger Boy); Natalie Draper, Ruth Roman (Girls at *Bright Dollar*); Eddie Laughton (Bartender at *Bright Dollar*); Eddy C. Waller (Grumpy Man at *Bright Dollar*); Alice Fleming (Dowager); Almeda Fowler (Mrs. Oakleaf); Stan Johnson (Reporter); Milton Kibbee (Whortle); Howard Mitchell (Fisherman); Kitty O'Neil (Evie); Gordon Richards (Mr. Giddon); Cyril Ring (Mr. Hughes); Mira McKinney (Actress at First Party); Douglas Carter (Taxi Driver); Jerry James (Elevator Boy); Teala Loring (Girl); Joel Friend (Boy); Renee Dupuis, Grace Gillern (Secretaries); Beverly Thompson, Audrey Westphall, Audrey Young, Wallace Earl, Brooke Evans, June Harris, Lucy Knoch, Mavis Murray, Adelaide Norris, Marjorie Silk, Jane Starr (Chorus Girls).

FROM THIS DAY FORWARD   (RKO, 1946) 95 M.

Executive producer, Jack Gross; producer, William L. Pereira; director, John Berry; based on the novel *All Brides Are Beautiful* by Thomas Bell; adaptation, Garson Kanin; screenplay, Hugo Butler; additional scenes, Edith R. Sommer, Charles Schnee; art director, Albert S. D'Agostino, Alfred H. Herman; set decorator, Darrell Silvera; music, Leigh Harline; music director, C. Bakaleinikoff; songs, Mort Greene and Harline; assistant director, Sam Ruman; sound, Earl Wolcott, Clem Portman; special effects, Vernon L. Walker; camera, George Barnes; editor, Frank Doyle.

Joan Fontaine (Susan); Mark Stevens (Bill Cummings); Rosemary De Camp (Martha Beesley); Henry Morgan (Hank Beesley); Wally Brown (Jake Beesley); Arline Judge (Margie Beesley); Renny McEvoy (Charlie Beesley); Bobby Driscoll (Timmy Beesley); Mary Treen (Alice Beesley); Queenie Smith (Mrs. Beesley); Doreen McCann (Barbara Beesley); Erskine Sanford (Higgler); Polly Bailey (Manageress); Alan Ward (Detective); Sam Lufkin (Husband); Virginia Engels (Woman in Window); Ellen Corby (Mother); George Magrill (Man); Leota Lorraine (Woman); Amelia Romano (Nurse); Jack Gargan (Milkman); Patricia Prest (Girl); Pat Hennigan, Tim Hawkins (Boys);

Bobby Barber (Ice Man); Tom Noonan (Attendant); Moroni Olsen (Tim Bagley); Guy Beach (Magistrate); Ralph Dunn (Bailiff); Joey Ray (District Attorney); Ida Moore (Hairdresser); Alf Haugen (Man in Bar); Nan Leslie (Girl); Charles Wagenheim (Hoffman); Milton Kibbee (Factory Foreman); Manny Harmon (Orchestra Leader); Sally Gordon (Girl on Bridge); Doria Caron (Dispatcher); Theodore Newton (Mr. Brewer).

IVY (Univ., 1947) 99 M.

Producer, William Cameron Menzies; director, Sam Wood; based on the novel *The Story of Ivy* by Marie Belloc Lowndes; screenplay, Charles Bennett; art director, Richard H. Riedel; set decorator, Russell A. Gausman, T. F. Offenbecker; music, Daniele Amfitheatrof; orchestrator, David Tamkin; song, Hoagy Carmichael; assistant director, John F. Sherwood; sound, Charles Felstead, William Hedgcock; camera, Russell Metty; editor, Ralph Dawson.

Joan Fontaine (Ivy Laxton); Patric Knowles (Dr. Roger Gretorex); Herbert Marshall (Miles Rushworth); Richard Ney (Jervis Lexton); Sir Cedric Hardwicke (Inspector Orpington); Lucile Watson (Mrs. Gretorex); Sara Allgood (Martha Huntley); Henry Stephenson (Judge); Rosalind Ivan (Emily); Lilian Fontaine (Lady Flora); Molly Lamont (Bella Crail); Una O'Connor (Mrs. Thrawn); Isobel Elsom (Miss Chattle); Alan Napier (Sir Jonathan Wright); Paul Cavanagh (Dr. Herwick); Sir Charles Mendl (Sir Charles Gage); Gavin Muir (Sergeant); Mary Forbes (Lady Crail); Norma Varden (Joan Rodney); Lumsden Hare (Dr. Lancaster); Matthew Boulton (Tom Lumford); Lydia Bilbrook (Mary Hampton); Alan Edmiston (Jenks); Harry Hays Morgan (Lord Ventner); Holmes Herbert (Mulloy); C. Montague Shaw (Stevens); Claire Du Brey (Shopkeeper); Gerald Hamer (Man from Paris Office); Colin Campbell (Chaplain); Leon Lenoir (Dock Worker); Alan Edmiston (Man in Fortuneteller Scene); David Cavendish, Jean Fenwick, David Ralston, Ella Ethridge, Renee Evans, Judith Woodbury (Guests); Dave Thursby (Groves); Art Foster (Constable); Lois Austin (English Lady); Herbert Clifton (Bates); James Logan (Aviator); Eric Wilton (Steward); Charles Knight (Solicitor); Herbert Evans (Deck Official); Manuel Paris (Cook's Tour Guide); Wyndham Standing (Assistant Chief Justice); Clive Morgan (Assistant King's Council); Elsa Peterson (Yacht Guest); Bess Flowers (Set Rehearsal); James Fairfax (English Newsvendor).

THE EMPEROR WALTZ (Par., 1948) C—106 M.

Producer, Charles Brackett; director, Billy Wilder; screenplay, Brackett, Wilder; assistant director, C. C. Coleman, Jr.; art director, Hans Dreier, Franz Bachelin; set decorator, Sam Comer, Paul Huldschinsky; music, Victor Young; songs, Johnny Burke and James Van Heusen; makeup, Wally Westmore; choreography, Billy Daniels; costumes, Edith Head, Gile Steele; process camera, Farciot Edouart; special effects, Gordon Jennings; sound, Stanley Cooley, John Cope; camera, George Barnes; editor, Doane Harrison.

Bing Crosby (Virgil Smith); Joan Fontaine (Johanna Augusta Franziska); Roland Culver (Baron Holenia); Lucile Watson (Princess Bitotska); Richard Haydn (Emperor Franz Joseph); Harold Vermilyea (Chamberlain); Sig Rumann (Dr. Zwieback); Julia Dean (Archduchess Stephanie); Bert Prival (Chauffeur); Alma Macrorie (Proprietress of the Inn); Roberta Jonay (Chambermaid); John Goldsworthy (Obersthofmeister); James Vincent (Abbe); Harry Allen (Gamekeeper); Eleanor Tennant (Tennis Player); Vesey O'Davoren (Butler); Norbert Schiller (Assistant to Dr. Zwieback); Frank Elliott (Von Usedom); Paul de Corday (Hungarian Officer); Jack Gargan (Master of Ceremonies); Doris Dowling (Tyrolean Girl); Len Hendry (Palace Guard); Cyril Delevanti (Diplomat), Frank Mayo (Parliamentary Politician); Hans Moebus, Albert Petit, Albert Pollet, Count Stefenelli (Elderly Aristocrats); Franco Corsaro (Spanish

Marques); Renee Randall, Jean Marshall, Kathy Young (Tyrolean Girls); Jerry James, William Meader (Kings Guards); Gene Ashley, John "Skins" Miller, Jac Fisher, Leo Lynn (Tyrolean Men); Bob Stephenson, James Logan (Beaters).

KISS THE BLOOD OFF MY HANDS (Univ., 1948) 79 M.

Executive producer, Harold Hecht; producer, Richard Vernon; associate producer, Norman Deming; director, Norman Foster; based on the novel by Gerald Butler; adaptation, Ben Maddow, Walter Bernstein; screenplay, Leonardo Bercovici; art director, Bernard Herzbrun, Nathan Juran; set decorator, Russell A. Gausman, Ruby R. Levitt; music, Miklos Rosza; assistant director, Jack Voglin; makeup, Bud Westmore; special effects, David S. Horsley; sound, Leslie I. Carey, Corson Jowett; camera, Russell Metty; editor, Milton Carruth.

Joan Fontaine (Jane Wharton); Burt Lancaster (Bill Saunders); Robert Newton (Harry Carter); Lewis L. Russell (Tom Widgery); Aminta Dyne (Landlady); Gryelda Hervey (Mrs. Paton); Jay Novello (Sea Captain); Colin Keith-Johnston (Judge); Reginald Sheffield (Superintendent); Campbell Copelin (Publican); Leyland Hodgson (Tipster); Peter Hobbes (Young Father).

LETTER FROM AN UNKNOWN WOMAN (Univ., 1948) 90 M.

Producer, John Houseman; director, Max Opuls; based on the novel *Brief Einer Unbekannten* by Stefan Zweig; screenplay, Howard Koch; art director, Alexander Golitzen; set decorator, Russell A. Gausman, Ruby R. Levitt; technical advisor, Paul Elbogen; music, Daniele Amfitheatrof; orchestrator, David Tamkin; assistant director, John F. Sherwood; makeup, Bud Westmore; costumes, Travis Banton; sound, Leslie I. Carey, Glenn E. Anderson; camera, Franz Planer; editor, Ted J. Kent.

Joan Fontaine (Lisa Berndle); Louis Jourdan (Stefan Brand); Mady Christians (Frau Berndle); Marcel Journet (Johann Stauffer); Art Smith (John); Carol Yorke (Marie); Howard Freeman (Herr Kastner); John Good (Lt. Leopold von Kaltnegger); Leo B. Pessin (Stefan, Jr.); Erskine Sanford (Porter); Otto Waldis (Concierge); Sonja Bryden (Frau Spitzer); Audrey Young (Pretty); William Trenk (Fritzel); Fred Nurney (Officer on Street); Torben Meyer (Carriage Driver); Hermine Sterler (Mother Superior); C. Ramsey Hill (Colonel Steindorf); Will Lee, William Hall (Movers); Lotte Stein (Woman Musician); Ilka Gruning (Woman Ticket Taker for Train Ride); Paul E. Burns (Concierge); Roland Varno (Second); Leo Mostovoy, Shimen Ruskin (Older Men); Celia Lovsky (Flower Vendor); Lester Sharpe (Critic); Michael Mark (Cafe Customer); Lois Austin (Elderly Woman); Lisa Golm (Woman Musician); Rex Lease (Station Attendant); Edmund Cobb (Carriage Driver); Betty Blythe (Frau Kohner); Diane Lee Stewart, Vera Stokes, Doretta Johnson, Lorraine Gale (Girlfriends); Cy Stevens, Doug Carter, Jack Gargan (Men); Arthur Lovejoy (Footman); Guy L. Shaw (Cafe Patron); June Wood (Cashier); Jean Ransome (Maid); Judith Woodbury (Model); Manuel Paris (Baron's Second); John McCallum (Store Helper); Robert W. Brown (First Officer).

YOU GOTTA STAY HAPPY (Univ., 1948) 100 M.

Executive producer, William Dozier; producer, Karl Tunberg; director, H. C. Potter; based on the serialized story by Robert Carson; screenplay, Tunberg; production design, Alexander Golitzen; set decorator, Russell A. Gausman, Ruby R. Levitt; music, Daniele Amfitheatrof; music director, Milton Schwartzwald; assistant director, John F. Sherwood; makeup, Bud Westmore, Lou LaCava, V. Curtis; costumes, Jean Louis; sound, Leslie I. Carey, Joe Lapis; special effects, David S. Horsley; camera, Russell Metty; editor, Paul Weatherwax.

Joan Fontaine (Dee Dee Dillwood); James Stewart (Marvin Payne); Eddie Albert (Bullets Baker); Roland Young (Ralph Tutwiler); Willard Parker (Henry Benson);

Percy Kilbride (Mr. Hacknell); Porter Hall (Mr. Caslon); Marcy McGuire (Georgia Goodrich); Arthur Walsh (Milton Goodrich); William Bakewell (Dick Hebert); Paul Cavanagh (Dr. Blucher); Halliwell Hobbes (Martin); Edith Evanson (Mrs. Racknell); Mary Forbes (Aunt Martha); Peter Roman (Barnabas); Houseley Stevenson (Jud Tavis); Emory Parnell (Bank Watchman); Don Kohler (Ted); Bert Conway (Neil); Hal K. Dawson (Night Clerk); Vera Marshe (Mae); Jimmie Dodd (Curly); Robert Rockwell (Eddie); Joe (Himself); Bill Clauson (Simon); Eddie Ehrhart (Thaddeus); Joe Cook, Jr., Don Garner (Bellhops); Hal Melone, Frank White (Elevator Operators); Beatrice Roberts (Maid); Fritz Feld (Small Man); Arthur Hohl (Cemetery Man); Frank Jenks (Man in Checkered Suit); Frank Darien (Old Man); Edward Gargan (Detective); Don Shelton (Minister); George Carleton (Portly Man); Chief Yowlachie (Indian); Isabell Withers (Maid); Al Murphy (Mechanic); Myron Healey (Day Clerk); Harland Tucker (Mr. Thrush); David Sharpe (Motorcycle Rider); Donald Dewar (Boy); Tiny Jones (Pedestrian); William H. O'Brien (Waiter).

BORN TO BE BAD   (RKO, 1950) 94 M.

Producer, Robert Sparks; director, Nicholas Ray; based on the novel *All Kneeling* by Anne Parrish; adaptation, Charles Schnee; screenplay, Edith Sommer; additional dialog, Robert Soderberg, George Oppenheimer; art director, Albert S. D'Agostino, Jack Okey; music director, C. Bakaleinikoff; camera, Nicholas Musuraca; editor, Frederick Knudtson.

Joan Fontaine (Christabel); Robert Ryan (Nick); Zachary Scott (Curtis); Joan Leslie (Donna); Mel Ferrer (Gobby); Harold Vermilyea (John Caine); Virginia Farmer (Aunt Clara); Kathleen Howard (Mrs. Bolton); Dick Ryan (Arthur); Bees Flowers (Mrs. Worthington); Joy Hallward (Mrs. Porter); Hazel Boyne (Committee Woman); Irving Bacon (Jewelry Salesman); Gordon Oliver (The Lawyer); Sam Lufkin (Taxi Driver); Helen Crozier (Ann); Bobby Johnson (Kenneth); Tim Taylor (Messenger Boy); Peggy Leon (Caine's Secretary); Ray Johnson, John Mitchum, Evelyn Underwood (Guests); Jack Chefe, Barry Brooks, Al Murphy (Men); Homer Dickinson (Art Gallery Attendant); Georgianna Wulff, Ann Burr (Schoolgirls); Frank Arnold (Man at Art Gallery); Don Dillaway (Photographer); Avery Graves (Curtis's Friend).

SEPTEMBER AFFAIR   (Par., 1950) 91 M.

Producer, Hal B. Wallis; director, William Dieterle; based on the story by Fritz Rotter; screenplay, Robert Thoeren; art director, Hans Dreier, Franz Bachelin; music, Victor Young; song, Kurt Weill and Maxwell Anderson; camera, Charles B. Lang, Jr., Victor Milner; editor, Warren Low.

Joan Fontaine (Manina Stuart); Joseph Cotten (David Lawrence); Francoise Rosay (Maria Salvatini); Jessica Tandy (Catherine Lawrence); Robert Arthur (David Lawrence, Jr.); Jimmy Lydon (Johnny Wilson); Fortunio Bonanova (Grazzi); Grazia Narciso (Bianca); Anna Demetrio (Rosita); Lou Steele (Vittorio Portini); Frank Yaconelli (Mr. Peppino); Charles Evans (Charles Morrison); Jimmy Frasco (Francisco); Michael Frasco (Boy); Charles LaTorre (Captain of Plane); Gilda Oliva (Mail Girl); Saverio Lomedico (Italian Man); George Nardelli, Nick Borgani (Italian Workmen); Jeanne Lafayett (French Woman); Dino Bolognese (Flower Vendor); Georgia Clancy (Stewardess); Dick Elliott (Fat Gentleman); Rudy Rama, Franz F. Roehm (Draymen); George Humbert (Waiter); Harry Cheshire (Jim, the Butler); Iphigenie Castiglioni (Maid); Inez Palange (Concierge); Zacharias Yaconelli (Ricardo); Victor Desny (Hotel Clerk); James R. Scott, Stan Johnson, Douglas Grange (Reporters); Larry Arnold (Italian Waiter); Walter Merrill (Taxi Driver).

DARLING, HOW COULD YOU!   (Par., 1951) 96 M.

Producer, Harry Tugend; director, Mitchell Leisen; based on the play *Alice-Sit-By-The-Fire* by Sir James M. Barrie; screenplay, Dodie Smith, Lesser Samuels; art director, Hal Pereira, Roland Anderson; camera, Daniel L. Fapp; editor, Alma Macrorie, Eda Warren.

Joan Fontaine (Alice Grey); John Lund (Dr. Robert Grey); Mona Freeman (Amy); Peter Hanson (Dr. Steve Clark); David Stollery (Cosmo); Virginia Farmer (Fanny); Angela Clarke (Nurse); Lowell Gilmore (Lord Aubrey Quayne); Robert Barrat (Mr. Rossiter); Gertrude Michael (Mrs. Rossiter); Mary Murphy (Sylvia); Frank Elliott (Simms); Billie Bird (Rosie); Willard Waterman (Theatre Manager); Gordon Arnold (Man); John Bryant (Lieutenant); Robin Hughes (Neville); David Eden (Naval Lieutenant); Allan Douglas (Steward); Dave Willock (Usher); Mary Ann Reimer
Maureen Lynn Reimer (Molly); Patsy O'Byrne (Mrs. Jones); Gloria Winters (Girl); Maria J. Tavares (Pretty Nurse); Fred Zendar (Rugged Sailor); William Meader (Ship's Officer); Houseley Stevenson (Old Man); Jimmie Dundee (Girl's Father); Allan Douglas (Customs Officer); Charles Sherlock (Customs Inspector); Mickey Little, Rudy Lee (Boys); Kathryn Towne (Mother); Dolores Hall (Daughter); Percy Helton, Robert E. Burns (Cabbies).

SOMETHING TO LIVE FOR   (Par., 1952) 89 M.

Producer-director, George Stevens; story-screenplay, Dwight Taylor; art director, Hal Pereira, Walter Tyler; music, Victor Young; camera, George Barnes; editor, William Hornbeck.

Ray Milland (Alan Miller); Joan Fontaine (Jenny Carey); Teresa Wright (Edna Miller); Richard Derr (Tony Collins); Douglas Dick (Baker); Herbert Heyes (Crawley); Harry Bellaver (Billy); Paul Valentine (Albert); Frank Orth (Waiter); Bob Cornthwaite (Young Man); Helen Spring (Mrs. Crawley); Rudy Lee (Chris); Patric Mitchell (Johnny); Richard Barron (Headwaiter); Paul Newlan (Bartender); John Indrisano (Party Guest); Jessie Proctor, Lillian Clayes, Genevieve Bell, Patsy O'Byrne, Helen Dickson, Cora Shannon (Old Ladies); Arthur Tovery (Desk Clerk); Joseph J. Greene (Heavy Set Man); Mari Blanchard (Hat Check Girl); James E. Moss, Lee Aaker (Alternate Boys); Douglas Spencer (Joey); Mary Field, Judith Allen (Women); Kerry Vaughn (Cocktail Waitress); Paul Maxey (Hoffstater); Slim Gaut (Derelict); Anne M. Kunde (Cleaning Woman); Raymond Bond (Box-Office Man); Peter Hanson, Laura Elliot, Charles Dayton (Stage Cast); Sherry Jackson, Gerald Courtemarche, Susan Freeman (Little Children); Helen Brown (Miss Purdy); Rolfe Sedan, Marcel De La Brosse, Charles Andre (Frenchmen); Jeanne Lafayette (Frenchwoman); Harold Miller (European); Dulce Daye (Actress); Korla Pandit (Hindu Man); King Donovan (Stage Manager); Al Kunde, George M. Lynn, Don Dillaway (Executives); Gloria Dea, Josette Deegan, Lavonne Battle (Slave Girls); Bob St. Angelo (Slave Boss); Erville Alderson, Maurice Cass (Critics); Eric Alden (Pharaoh); Ida Moore (Woman); Jody Gilbert (Woman in Telephone Booth).

IVANHOE   (MGM, 1952) C—106 M.

Producer, Pandro S. Berman; director, Richard Thorpe; based on the novel by Sir Walter Scott; adaptation, Aeneas MacKenzie; screenplay, Noel Langley; music, Miklos Rozsa; art director, Alfred Junge; sound, A. W. Watkins; costumes, Roger Furse; makeup, Charles Parker; camera effects, Tom Howard; camera, F. A. Young; editor, Frank Clarke.

Robert Taylor (Ivanhoe); Elizabeth Taylor (Rebecca); Joan Fontaine (Rowena); George Sanders (De Bois-Guilbert); Emlyn Williams (Wamba); Robert Douglas (Sir Hugh De Bracy); Finlay Currie (Cedric); Felix Aylmer (Isaac); Francis DeWolff (Font De Boeuf); Guy Rolfe (Prince John); Norman Wooland (King Richard); Basil Sydney (Waldemar Fitzurse); Harold Warrender (Locksley); Patrick Lovell (Philip de Malworsin); Roderick Lovell (Ralph de Vipont); Sebastian Cabot (Clerk of Copmondurst);

John Reedclock (Hundebert); Michael Brennan (Baldwin); Megs Jenkins (Servant to Isaac); Valentine Dysell (Norman Guard); Lionel Harris (Roger of Bermondsley); Earl Jaffe (Austrian Monk).

DECAMERON NIGHTS (RKO, 1953) C—87 M.

Producer, M. J. Frankovich, William A. Szekeley; director, Hugo Fregonese; story, Geza Herczeg; screenplay, George Oppenheimer; music, Anthony Hopkins; camera, Guy Greene; editor, Russell Lloyd.

Main Story: Joan Fontaine (Fiammetta); Louis Jourdan (Boccaccio); Binnie Barnes (Contessa); Joan Collins (Paminea); Mara Lane, Stella Riley, Melissa Stribling (Girls in Villa).

Paganino the Pirate: Joan Fontaine (Bartolomea); Louis Jourdan (Paganino); Binnie Barnes (Countess); Godfrey Tearle (Ricciardo); Elliott Makeham (Governor of Majorca).

Wager Of Virtue: Joan Fontaine (Ginevra); Louis Jourdan (Guilio); Binnie Barnes (Nerina); Godfrey Tearle (Bernabo); Meinhart Maur (Sultan); George and Bert Bernard (Messengers); Ban Boclen (Captain); Gordon Bell (Merchant).

The Doctor's Daughter: Joan Fontaine (Isabella); Louis Jourdan (Bertrando); Joan Collins (Maria); Binnie Barnes (Old Witch); Noel Purcell (Father Francisco); Hugh Morton (King); Marjorie Rhodes (Signora Bucca).

FLIGHT TO TANGIER (Par., 1953) C—90 M.

Producer, Nat Holt; director-screenplay, Charles Marquis Warren; art director, Hal Pereira, John Goodman; music, Paul Sawtell; camera, Ray Rennahan; editor, Frank Bracht.

Joan Fontaine (Susan); Jack Palance (Gil Walker); Corinne Calvet (Nicole); Robert Douglas (Danzar); Marcel Dalio (Goro); Jeff Morrow (Colonel Wier); Richard Shannon (Lieutenant Luzon); Murray Matheson (Franz Kovac); John Doucette (Tirera); John Pickard (Hank Brady); James Anderson (Dullah); Don Dunning, Eric Alden (Moroccans); Bob Templeton (Luzon's Policeman); Peter Coe (Hanrah); Madeleine Holmes (Rosario); John Wengraf (Kalferez); Otto Waldis (Wisil); Jerry Paris (Policeman in Car); Rene Chatenay, Albert D'Arno, Anthony De Mario (Policemen); Karin Vengay (Greek Girl); Pilar Del Rey (Spanish Girl); Josette Deegan (French Girl); Rodric Redwing (Police Orderly); Mark Hanna (Corporal at Airport).

THE BIGAMIST (Filmakers, 1953) 80 M.

Producer, Collier Young; director, Ida Lupino; story, Larry Marcus, Lou Schor; screenplay, Young; music, Leith Stevens; song, Matt Dennis and Dave Gillan; camera, George Diskant; editor, Stanford Tischler.

Joan Fontaine (Eve Graham); Edmond O'Brien (Harry Graham); Ida Lupino (Phyllis Martin); Edmund Gwenn (Mr. Jordan); Jane Darwell (Mrs. Connelley); Kenneth Tobey (Tom Morgan); John Maxwell (Judge); Peggy Maley (Phone Operator); Mack Williams (Prosecuting Attorney); James Todd (Mr. Forbes); James Young (Executive); Lilian Fontaine (Miss Higgins); John Brown (Dr. Wallace); Matt Dennis (Himself); Jerry Hausner (Ray); Kem Dibbs (Tanner Driver); Kenneth Drake (Court Clerk); Mac McKim (Boy on the Street); George Lee (Head Waiter); Collier Young (Barfly).

CASANOVA'S BIG NIGHT (Par., 1954) C—85 M.

Producer, Paul Jones; director, Norman Z. McLeod; story, Aubrey Wisberg; screenplay, Hal Kanter, Edmund Hartmann; music, Lyn Murray, Jay Livingston, and Ray Evans; choreography, Josephine Earl; song, Murray; art director, Hal Pereira, Albert Nozaki; camera, Lionel Lindon; editor, Ellsworth Hoagland.

Bob Hope (Pippo); Joan Fontaine (Francesca); Vincent Price (Casanova); Audrey Dalton (Elena); Basil Rathbone (Lucio); Hugh Marlowe (Stefano Di Gambetta); Arnold Moss (The Doge); John Carradine (Minister Foressi); John Hoyt (Maggiorin); Hope Emerson (Duchess of Castelbello); Robert Hutton (Raphael, Duc of Castelbello); Lon Chaney (Emo); Raymond Burr (Bragadin); Frieda Inescort (Signora Di Gambetta); Primo Carnera (Corfa); Frank Puglia (Carabaccio); Paul Cavanagh (Signor Alberto Di Gambetta); Romo Vincent (Giovanni); Henry Brandon (Captain Rugello); Natalie Schafer (Signora Foressi); Douglas Fowley, Lucien Littlefield (Prisoners); Nestor Paiva (Gnocchi); Kathryn Grant, Marla English (Girls on Bridge); Barbara Freking (Maria); John Doucette (Mounted Guard); Oliver Blake (Amadeo); Torben Meyer (Attendant); Joseph Vitale (Guard on Steps); John Alderson, Richard Karlan (Outside Guards); Joan Shawlee (Beatrice D'Brizzi); Fritz Feld, Walter Kingsford (Ministers); Paul "Tiny" Newlan (Regniatti); Skelton Knaggs (Little Man); Eric Alden (Maggiorin's Ruffian); Keith Richards (Servant); Charley Cooley (Man Servant); Bess Flowers (Marquesa); Dick Sands, Charles Hicks (Assistant Headsmen); Arline Hunter (Girl in Window); Rexene Stevens (Swimmer).

OTHELLO   (UA, 1955) 92 M.

Producer, Orson Welles; associate producer, Giorgio Patti, Julien Derode, Walter Bedone, Patrice Dali, Rocco Facchini; director, Welles; based on the play by William Shakespeare; associate director, Michael Washinsky; costumes, Maria de Matteis; music, Francesco Lavagnino, Alberto Barberis; camera, Anchise Brizzi, Araldo, George Fanto, Obadan Troania, Roberto Fusi; editor, Jean Sacha, Renzo Lucidi, John Shepridge.

Orson Welles (Othello); Michael MacLiammoir (Iago); Suzanne Cloutier (Desdemona); Robert Coote (Roderigo); Milton Edwards (Brabantio); Michael Lawrence (Cassio); Fay Compton (Emilia); Nicholas Bruce (Lodevico); Jean Davis (Montano); Doris Dowling (Bianca); Joan Fontaine (Extra).

SERENADE   (WB, 1956) C—121 M.

Producer, Henry Blanke; director, Anthony Mann; based on the novel by James M. Cain; screenplay, Ivan Goff, Ben Roberts, John Twist; assistant director, Charles Hansen, Dick Moder; costumes, Howard Shoup; songs, Nicholas Brodsky and Sammy Cahn; operatic advisers, Walter Ducloux, Giacomo Spadoni; art director, Edward Carrere; camera, J. Peverell Marley; editor, William Ziegler.

Mario Lanza (Damon Vincenti); Joan Fontaine (Kendall Hale); Sarita Montiel (Juana Montes); Vincent Price (Charles Winthrop); Joseph Calleia (Maestro Marcatello); Harry Bellaver (Monte); Vince Edwards (Marco Roselli); Silvio Minciotti (Lardelli); Frank Puglia (Manuel); Edward Platt (Carter); Frank Yaconelli (Giuseppe); Mario Siletti (Sanroma); Maria Serrango (Rosa); Eduardo Noriega (Felipe); Joseph Vitale (Baritone); Victor Romito (Bass); Norma Zimmer (Mimi in *La Boheme*); Licia Albanese (Desdemona in *Othello*); Francis Barnes (Iago in *Othello*); Lilian Molieri (Tosca in *Tosca*); Laura Mason (Fedora in *Fedora*); Richard Cable (Shepherd Boy in *L'Arlesiana*); Richard Lert (Conductor in *L'Arlesiana*); Jose Govea (Paco); Antonio Triano (Man in The Bull); Leo Mostovoy (Chef); Nick Mora (Luigi, the Waiter); Joe DeAngelo, William Fox, Jack Santora (Busboys); Mickey Golden (Cab Driver); Elizabeth Flournoy (Elevator Operator); Creighton Hale (Assistant Stage Manager); Stephen Bekassy (Hanson); Martin Garralaga (Romero); Don Turner (Bus Driver); Perk Lazelle, April Stride, Diane Gump (Party Guests); Jose Torvay (Mariachi Leader); Martha Acker (American Woman); Vincent Padula (Pagnil).

516

BEYOND A REASONABLE DOUBT   (RKO, 1956) 80 M.

Producer, Bert E. Friedlob; director, Fritz Lang; story-screenplay, Douglas Morrow; song, Herschel Burke Gilbert and Alfred Perry; art director, Carroll Clark; set decorator, Darrell Silvera; music, Gilbert; assistant director, Maxwell Henry; camera, William Snyder; editor, Gene Fowler, Jr.

Dana Andrews (Tom Garrett); Joan Fontaine (Susan Spencer); Sidney Blackmer (Austin Spencer); Philip Bourneuf (District Attorney, Roy Thompson); Shepperd Strudwick (Jonathan Wilson); Arthur Franz (Bob Hale); Edward Binns (Lieutenant Kennedy); Robin Raymond (Terry LaRue); Barbara Nichols (Dolly Moore); William Leicester (Charles Miller); Dan Seymour (Greco); Rusty Lane (Judge); Joyce Taylor (Joan Williams); Carleton Young (Alan Kirk); Trudy Wroe (Hat Check Girl); Joe Kirk (Clerk); Charles Evans (Governor); Dorothy Ford (Blonde); Joey Ray (Eddie); Larry Barton (Customer); Frank Mitchell (Waiter, Burlesque House); Emma Blucher (Patty Gray); Larry Barton (Customer); Billy Reed (M. C.); Carl Sklover (Cab Driver); Phil Barnes (Policeman); Baynes Barron (John Higgins, Fingerprint Man); Jeffrey Sayre (Jury Foreman); Bob Whitney (Bailiff); Hal Taggert (Court Clerk); Dorothy Gordon (Secretary); Bill Boyett, Joel Mondeaux (Staff Members); Eric Wilton (Clergyman); Dave Wiechman (Peters, the Condemned Man); Tony De Mario (Doctor); Harry Strang (Warden); Benny Burt, Myron Cook (Reporters); Ralph Volkie (Photographer); Wendell Niles (Announcer); Franklyn Farnum (Spectator at Electrocution).

ISLAND IN THE SUN   (20th, 1957)   C—119 M.

Producer, Darryl F. Zanuck; director, Robert Rossen; based on the novel by Alec Waugh; screenplay, Alfred Hayes; music, Malcolm Arnold; assistant director, Gerry O'Hara; costumes, David Ffolkes; art director, William C. Andrews; camera, F. A. Young; editor, Reginald Beck.

James Mason (Maxwell Fleury); Joan Fontaine (Mavis); Dorothy Dandridge (Margot Seaton); Joan Collins (Jocelyn); Michael Rennie (Hilary Carson); Harry Belafonte (David Boyeur); Diana Wynyard (Mrs. Fleury); John Williams (Colonel Whittingham); Stephen Boyd (Euan Templeton); Patricia Owens (Sylvia); Basil Sydney (Julian Fleury); John Justin (David Archer); Ronald Squire (Governor); Hartley Power (Bradshaw).

UNTIL THEY SAIL   (MGM, 1957) 95 M.

Producer, Charles Schnee; associate producer, James E. Newcom; director, Robert Wise; based on the story by James A. Michener; screenplay, Robert Anderson; music, David Raksin; song, Raksin and Sammy Cahn; assistant director, Ridgeway Callow; art director, William A. Horning, Paul Groesse; camera, Joseph Ruttenberg; editor, Harold F. Kress.

Jean Simmons (Barbara Leslie Forbes); Joan Fontaine (Anne Leslie); Paul Newman (Capt. Jack Harding); Piper Laurie (Delia Leslie); Charles Drake (Capt. Richard Bates); Sandra Dee (Evelyn Leslie); Wally Cassell ("Shinner" Phil Friskett); Alan Napier (Prosecution); Ralph Votrian (Max Murphy); John Wilder (Tommy); Tige Andrews (Marine); Adam Kennedy (Lt. Andy); Mickey Shaughnessy (Marine); Patrick Macnee (Private Duff); Ben Wright (Defense); Kendrick Huxham (Justice); James Todd (Consul); David Thursby (Trainman); Hilda Plowright (Woman); Nicky Blair, Morgan Jones, Pat Waltz, William Boyett, Jimmy Hayes, Jay Douglas, Pat Colby, Dan Eitner, Tom Mayton, Roger McGee, John Rosser, Jim Cox (Marines); Dean Jones (Marine Lieutenant); Robert Keys (Major Campbell); Ann Wakefield (Mrs. Campbell); Alma Lauton, Dee Humphrey, Dorris Riter, Pamela Light, Phyllis Douglas (New Zealand Girls); Vesey O'Davoren (Minister); Pat O'Hara (Police Inspector); Stanley Fraser (Court Crier).

SOUTH PACIFIC   (Magna, 1958) C—171 M.

Producer, Buddy Adler; director, Joshua Logan; adapted from the play by Oscar Hammerstein II, Richard Rodgers, Joshua Logan, based on the book *Tales of the South Pacific* by James A. Michener; screenplay, Paul Osborn; songs, Rodgers and Hammerstein II; choreography, LeRoy Prinz; costumes, Dorothy Jeakins; assistant director, Ben Kadish; art director, Lyle R. Wheeler, John DeCuir, Walter M. Scott, Paul S. Fox; music director, Alfred Newman; orchestrator, Edward B. Powell, Pete King, Bernard Mayers, Robert Russell Bennett; special camera effects, L. B. Abbott; camera, Leon Shamroy; editor, Robert Simpson.

Rossano Brazzi (Emile De Becque); Mitzi Gaynor (Nellie Forbush); John Kerr (Lieutenant Cable); Ray Walston (Luther Billis); Juanita Hall (Bloody Mary); France Nuyen (Liat); Russ Brown (Capt. Brackett); Jack Mullaney (Professor); Ken Clark (Stewpot); Floyd Simmons (Harbison); Candace Lee (Ngana, Emile's Daughter); Warren Hsieh (Jerome, His Son); Tom Laughlin (Buzz Adams); Beverly Aadland (Dancer); Galvan De Leon (Sub Chief); Ron Ely (Co-Pilot); Archie Savage (Native Chief); Robert Jacobs (Communications Man); Richard Cutting (Admiral Kester); John Gabriel (Radio Man); Darleen Engle, Evelyn Ford (Nurses); Doug McClure, Stephen Ferry (Pilots); Joe Bailey (U. S. Commander); Joan Fontaine (Extra).

A CERTAIN SMILE   (20th, 1958) C—106 M.

Producer, Henry Ephron; director, Jean Negulesco; based on the novel by Francoise Sagan; screenplay, Frances Goodrich, Albert Hackett; music, Alfred Newman; song, Sammy Fain and Paul Francis Webster; costumes, Mary Wills; assistant director, Arthur Lueker; makeup, Ben Nye; sound, Charles Peck, Harry M. Leonard; art director, Lyle R. Wheeler, John Le Cuisir; set decorator, Walter M. Scott, Paul S. Fox; camera, Milton Krasner; editor, Louis R. Loeffler.

Rossano Brazzi (Luc); Joan Fontaine (Francoise Ferrand); Bradford Dillman (Bertrand); Christine Carere (Dominique Vallon); Eduard Franz (M. Vallon); Katherine Locke (Mme. Vallon); Kathryn Givney (Mme. Griot); Steven Geray (Denis); Trude Wyler (Mme. Denis); Sandy Livingston (Catherine); Renate Hoy (Pierre); Carol Van Dyke, Gabrille Del Valle (South Americans); Feridun Colgecan (Hotel Manager); Edit Angold (Cook); David Hoffman (Concierge).

VOYAGE TO THE BOTTOM OF THE SEA   (20th, 1961) C—105 M.

Producer-director, Irwin Allen; story, Allen; screenplay, Allen, Charles Bennett; music, Paul Sawtell, Bert Shefter; song, Russell Faith; assistant director, Ad Schaumer; costumes, Paul Zastupnevich; makeup, Ben Nye; sound, Alfred Bruzlin, Warren B. Delaplain; art director, Jack Martin Smith, Herman A. Blumenthal; set decorator, Walter M. Scott, John Sturtevant; camera, Winton Hoch; editor, George Boemler.

Walter Pidgeon (Admiral Nelson); Joan Fontaine (Dr. Hiller); Barbara Eden (Cathy); Peter Lorre (Emery); Robert Sterling (Captain Crane); Michael Ansara (Alvarez); Frankie Avalon (Chip); Regis Toomey (Dr. Jamieson); John Litel (Admiral Crawford); Howard McNear (Congressman Parker); Henry Daniell (Dr. Zucco); Mark Slade (Smith); Charles Tannen (Gleason); Delbert Monroe (Kowski); Anthony Monaco (Cookie); Robert Easton (Sparks); Jonathan Gilmore (Young); David McLean (Ned Thompson); Larry Gray (Dr. Newmar); George Diestel (Lieutenant Hodges); Robert Buckingham, James Murphy, William Herrin, Richard Adams (Crew Members); Dr. John Giovanni (Italian Delegate); Kendrick Huxham (U. N. Chairman); Art Baker (U. N. Commentator).

TENDER IS THE NIGHT   (20th, 1962) C—142 M.

Producer, Henry T. Weinstein; director, Henry King; based on the novel by F. Scott Fitzgerald; screenplay, Ivan Moffat; music, Bernard Herrmann; song, Sammy Fain and Paul Francis Webster; gowns, Pierre Balmain; costumes, Marjorie Best; assistant director, Eli Dunn; art director, Jack Martin Smith, Malcolm Brown; set decorator, Walter M. Scott, Paul S. Fox; wardrobe, Pierre Balmain, Marjorie Best; special camera effects, L. B. Abbott, Emil Kosa, Jr.; sound, Bernard Freericks, Warren B. Delaplain; camera, Leon Shamroy; editor, William Reynolds.

Jennifer Jones (Nicole Diver); Jason Robards, Jr. (Dick Diver); Joan Fontaine (Baby Warren); Tom Ewell (Abe North); Cesare Danova (Tommy Barban); Jill St. John (Rosemary Hoyt); Paul Lukas (Dr. Dohmler); Bea Benadaret (Mrs. McKisco); Charles Fredericks (Mr. McKisco); Sanford Meisner (Dr. Gregorovious); Albert Carrier (Louis); Mac McWhorter (Colis Clay); Carole Mathews (Mrs. Hoyt); Maurice Dallimore (Sir Charles Golding); Carol Veazie (Mrs. Dumphrey); Arlette Clark (Governess); Leslie Farrell (Topsy Diver); Michael Crisalli (Lanier Diver); Alan Napier (Pardo); John Richardson, Maggi Brown, Linda Hutchins (Bits); Orrin Tucker (Musician); Nora Evans (Singer); Bruno Della Santana (Reception Clerk); Tom Hernandez (Nobleman); Jacques Gallo (Gendarme); Art Salter (Photographer); Eric Feldary (Headwaiter).

THE DEVIL'S OWN (20th, 1967) C—90 M.

Producer, Anthony Nelson Keys; director, Cyril Frankel; based on the novel by Peter Curtis; screenplay, Nigel Kneale; music, Richard Rodney Bennett; Choreography, Denys Palmer; assistant director, David Tringham; music supervisor, Philip Martell; art director, Don Mingaye; production designer, Bernard Robinson; wardrobe, Molly Arbuthnot; camera, Arthur Grant; editor, James Needs, Chris Barnes.

Joan Fontaine (Gwen Mayfield); Kay Walsh (Stephanie Bax); Alec McCowen (Alan Bax); Ann Bell (Sally); Ingrid Brett (Linda); John Collin (Dowsett); Michele Dotrice (Dowsett); Gwen Ffrangcon-Davies (Granny Rigg); Leonard Rossiter (Dr. Wallis); Martin Stephens (Ronnie Dowsett); Carmel McSharry (Mrs. Dowsett); Viola Keats (Mrs. Curd); Shelagh Fraser (Mrs. Creek); Bryan Marshall (Tom).

With Fred Astaire in A DAMSEL IN DISTRESS (RKO '37)

With Allan Lane in MAID'S NIGHT OUT (RKO '38)

With Chester Morris and Richard Dix in SKY GIANT (RKO '38)

With Douglas Fairbanks, Jr., Montagu Love, and Lumsden Hare in GUNGA DIN (RKO '39)

With Joan Crawford, Rosalind Russell, and Norma Shearer in THE WOMEN (MGM '39)

With Cary Grant in SUSPICION (RKO '41)

Along with Pfc. Lambros S. Hajizomenti and Sgt. Carmelo Musumeo, being sworn in as an American citizen in April, 1943

With Brenda Marshall, Charles Boyer, and Joyce Reynolds in THE CONSTANT NYMPH (WB '43)

With Orson Welles and Margaret O'Brien in JANE EYRE (20th '44)

With Cecil Kellaway in
FRENCHMAN'S CREEK (Par '44)

With husband-to-be William
Dozier in May, 1946

With Mark Stevens in FROM
THIS DAY FORWARD (RKO '46)

With Olivia de Havilland and
Lilian Fontaine in 1947

With Louis Jourdan in LETTER
FROM AN UNKNOWN WOMAN
(Univ '48)

With Bing Crosby in THE
EMPEROR WALTZ (Par '48)

With James Stewart in YOU GOTTA STAY HAPPY (Univ '48)

With Robert Ryan, Zachary Scott, Joan Leslie, and Mel Ferrer in BORN TO BE BAD (RKO '50)

With daughter Deborah Leslie in 1950

With Joseph Cotten in
SEPTEMBER AFFAIR (Par '50)

With Finlay Currie in IVANHOE
(MGM '52)

On the set of THE BIGAMIST
(Filmakers '53) with husband
Collier Young and Ida Lupino

In Broadway's TEA AND SYMPATHY (1954) with Tony Perkins

With Harry Belafonte in ISLAND IN THE SUN (20th '57)

With Sandra Dee, Piper Laurie, and Jean Simmons in UNTIL THEY SAIL (MGM '57)

With Rossano Brazzi in A
CERTAIN SMILE (20th '58)

With husband Alfred Wright, Jr.
in 1965

With John Collin in THE
DEVIL'S OWN (20th '67)

Jason Robards, Jr. in TENDER IS THE NIGHT (20th '61)

Becoming a United States citizen in 1939.

5'5"
110 pounds
Reddish-gold hair
Blue-green eyes
Aries

Wendy Barrie

"Include a full-length chapter on Wendy Barrie in a book on cinema history? You've got to be kidding! Why do it?" Granted that Wendy never took her histrionic career seriously and that her acting talents had decided limitations, but for one particular reason this author has always been favorably struck by the Wendy Barrie personality. The spritely spirit that Wendy has displayed in her decades of multimedia work is admirable. Right down the line she has never flinched from being her true self—at whatever cost. On one hand, she indulges her penchant for frivolity and social-butterfly activity, but on the other hand, she almost always laces her dabbler's image with a heavy dose of sharp wit and a piercing ability to center on the truth of a situation or a person.

Most importantly, for the purposes of this book, Wendy represents one distinct brand of stock heroine RKO needed, purchased, and packaged for its slew of 1930s-1940s B-pictures. Because of her British society background, her comely looks, and her fantastic ability to always remain in the news, Wendy could enhance any RKO programmer by her mere presence at an economical salary price RKO could both afford and pay. Her carefree attitude toward her career and her filmmaking was always evident, leading her into several undisciplined screen performances (causing her to be ranked on the movie scene as closer in film type to Peggy Hopkins Joyce than to Olivia de Havilland). But then all Wendy ever asked of her acting work was to enjoy it and to use her salary status to have some good times. All she ever demanded of her fans? "Be a good bunny," of course.

Margaret Wendy Jenkins was born on April 18, 1912, in Hong Kong, of rather impressive ancestry. Her father, Frank C. Jenkins, was one of the outstanding British barristers in the Orient. Her mother, Nell MacDonagh, was a descendant of the Irish king Brian Boru. Wendy's grandfather, General Sir Charles Warren, was the head of Scotland Yard. Her uncle, Sir James Barrie, was a noted English surgeon, and her godfather was the famed writer, Sir James Matthew Barrie,* author of *Peter Pan* and other works. Wendy's sister, Barbara Patricia, was born in 1915.

Wendy had a most peripatetic education, caused as much by her irrepressible high spirits as by her parents' continual desire to have their carefree elder daughter taught at increasingly fancier educational institutions. She first went to the private Peak School in Hong Kong. As soon as she was old enough to make a trip by herself, she was shipped to London to attend the more British-oriented Holy Child and Assumption convent school, and thereafter to a fashionable finishing school in Lausanne, Switzerland. Along the way Wendy matriculated at other institutions of learning, but as she frankly admits, she was expelled from nearly every school she attended because she simply hated to study and relished being instead the perpetual imp. During these school years, it sometimes required a trip halfway around the globe to visit with her parents, for her father constantly changed his professional port of call: from Tokyo, to Singapore, Calcutta, Madras, Rangoon, or the Indian hill country. By the time Wendy was seventeen, she estimated that she had traveled the world's circumference at least seven times.

By 1930 Wendy was settled in London, or so it seemed. She had been given a splashy coming-out party sponsored by Winston Churchill and attended by the proper number of socially elite. Like many another debutante uncertain what to do with her life, Wendy took a flier at several working-girl careers: first as an apprentice beauty-shop operator in Mayfair, than as a secretary; and for a brief spell as an employee in a London department store. But this casual dabbling was scarcely intriguing or satisfying enough for the plucky post-teenager. She next pursued a line of employment time-honored for the lower classes, but still considered unbecoming for a girl of her pedigree—show business.

She landed a chorus part in a West End musical show, *Wonder Bar,* more because of her coquettish good looks than for any song-and-dance talent she may have possessed. Besides, having a chorine of Wendy's social cal-

---

*Hence Wendy's middle name, and the inspiration for her later professional name, Wendy Barrie, which she adopted with her godfather's blessing.

iber in the show was always good for a few extra lines of publicity in the various gossip columns. Then, one day in early 1932, pert, popular, publicity-gathering Wendy was dining with her mother at the swank Savoy Hotel. Seated at a nearby table in the posh restaurant was Hungarian-born film producer-director Alexander Korda. Having made pictures in Hungary, Austria, Berlin, Paris, and Hollywood, Korda had now established his headquarters in London where he had been turning out "quota quickie" features.* Noted for his sharp eye for pretty girls with cinema potential (Maria Corda, Merle Oberon, et al.), Korda immediately spotted Wendy and was quick to introduce himself and suggest she come round to his office to discuss a possible film career. Wendy was flattered by the suggestion and readily consented. Her mother, from whom Wendy had inherited much of her fun-loving spirit, approved of the novel venture, but when word reached Mr. Jenkins of his elder daughter's latest diversion, he was properly horrified. However he was thousands of miles away, and even had he been closer on the scene, it is doubtful whether he could have restrained headstrong Wendy from venturing into the new territory of motion pictures. Wendy met with Korda and quickly acceded to a five-year term contract.

During Wendy's first year with the producer-director, he was in the process of forming London Films with banker Leopold Sutro. Thus, along with others of his contract players, Wendy was loaned out to other cinema producers to keep professionally busy, gain needed screen exposure, and, more importantly, bring a few more pounds into Korda's diminished coffers. Wendy's initial screen roles were as forgettable as the pictures themselves.

She made her cinema debut in *Collision* (July, 1932), a tepid tale of a family man's infatuation for a thieving adventuress (Sunday Wilshin). Wendy was next in *Threads* (September, 1932), also released by the British division of United Artists. The film dealt with a man (John Osborne Wynn) wrongly imprisoned for murder, who is restored to his family's good graces by the ingenuity of his daughter (Wendy). Although the picture's theme was said to be tritely handled "in a flow of dialogue which becomes extremely tedious," Wendy's screen work was praised by the British periodical *Picturegoer*, which noted that she "gives quite a pleasing performance."

Wedding Rehearsal (1932), Wendy's fourth film of the year, finally saw her employed under the direct aegis of Alexander Korda and his new London Films. Roland Young was cast as the Marquis of Buckminster, a Guards officer who has no intention of giving up his eligible-bachelor status. However, his oversolicitous grandmother (Kate Cutler) has different ideas. She prepares a list of eligible young ladies (including Wendy and Joan Gardner) from which Young is prompted to choose a bride. He solves the problem by astutely finding each of the girls a proper mate, including John Loder for Wendy and Maurice Evans for Gardner. But droll Young does not escape the nuptial joys and woes for he falls a victim at last to his

---

*"Quota quickies" were British-made films, produced to fulfill the requirements of a law forcing British exhibitors to show a certain percentage of home product.

grandmother's secretary, Merle Oberon. *Wedding Rehearsal* did not find the public acceptance of Korda's prior *Service for Ladies* (1932, with Leslie Howard and Benita Hume), but it was acknowledged to be a "polished piece of society satire," noteworthy for its inclusion of a scene showing the changing of the Guard. *Wedding Rehearsal* did obtain modest U.S. release, a novelty for such low-budget British productions.

Where Is the Lady (1932) was a very slight musical confection, typical of the helter-skelter entertainment of the time. It boasted music by Franz Lehar but, as the *London Times* observed, the "pity is there are not more good voices to sing it." German actress Marta Eggerth had the lead, Owen Nares was the romantic hero, and third-billed Wendy had a small comedy role.

Thus, Wendy had already made a slight mark as a pretty ingenue in inconsequential features when employer Korda promoted her to the female lead in the featherweight amusement, *Cash* (1933). Robert Donat, who had recently signed with London Films, was seen as the young electrician sent to cut off the lights at the home of Edmund Gwenn, a financial promoter who has had no money since the crash of 1929. Once there, Donat discovers a thief has stuffed a huge sum of money into his work bag. He is quickly persuaded by Gwenn to pose as his new business associate so Gwenn can impress a group of would-be City investors that he is financially solvent. The deal is consummated and Donat demands not only his share of the profits but also the hand in marriage of Gwenn's daughter (Wendy). *Cash* was released in the United States in 1934 under the title *For Love or Money*, after its two young stars had made their reputation in *The Private Life of Henry VIII* (1933). The *New York Times* found Wendy "cool, delectable and charming," although critic Otis Ferguson, then writing in the *New Republic*, pronounced that the film and its cast "carries on each inch of celluloid its trademark, which is the word ham."

In Gainsborough's *It's a Boy* (1933), based on the popular stage comedy, Wendy slipped down to seventh billing. The comedy was directed by American Tim Whelan, who had previously been a gag-man for cinema comedian Harold Lloyd. Whelan had been expressly hired to devise a slapstick flavor for the movie so that the picture might attract more American bookings.* Edward Everett Horton bumbled around in *It's a Boy* as a middle-class Londoner who learns that Albert Burdon is the product of an affair he had in 1914. Wendy, Heather Thatcher, and Helen Haye supplied what was politely termed "diverse charm."

Next came London Films' *The Private Life of Henry VIII*, which gave the floundering British motion picture industry global respectability and commerciality, and, among other honors, won for its star, Charles Laughton, an Oscar. It was also the one memorable opus in Wendy's seventeen-picture

*The picture did receive American release, playing at New York's Westminster Theatre in June, 1934.

British filmmaking career. When the costume drama about a boorish British monarch was in preparation, no one except its originators (Korda and star Laughton) was enthusiastic about its potential. As Laughton later recalled: "During the making of the film we were often apprehensive that while we were saying our lines the sets would collapse and smother us. We finished the picture in five weeks, one of the least expensive big productions ever made. We were fairly satisfied with it but never for a moment did we think it would be the great financial success that it was. We would have sold it to the first bidder. But there were no bidders."

Korda did finally convince a reluctant United Artists to distribute the picture, and even engineered a world premiere for *The Private Life of Henry VIII* at Radio City Music Hall (October 12, 1933), realizing that if New York liked the picture, the later London opening would follow suit. The Gotham press did extol the picture's virtues and liked most every cast member, a critical appraisal repeated by the British reviewers when the movie unreeled at the Leicester Square Theatre on October 24, 1933. *The Private Life of Henry VIII* was a great global commercial success; in 1953 it was still earning 10,000 pounds a year in revivals and made additional profits when released to television in the early 1950s in America and in 1957 in England.

Although bulky Laughton dominated the motion picture with both his physical presence and his hysterical histrionics as the tyrannical, letching ruler, the five actresses portraying Henry's wives (Catherine of Aragon was not depicted) each had appropriate opportunities to make their screen marks. Wendy as Henry's third wife, Jane Seymour, had a smaller and less showy role than those afforded Merle Oberon, Binnie Barnes, and Elsa Lanchester. Wendy is first seen on the day Henry's second wife, Anne Boleyn (Oberon), is to be beheaded. The king is then to wed Wendy. Not a very auspicious start for any bride, but Wendy's Jane Seymour is a fickle and childish dark-haired beauty, unmindful of anyone's fate but her own. She quickly pushes from her mind the gloom surrounding the royal castle, as the ladies-in-waiting sadly observe the preparations being made in the courtyard for Oberon's execution. Wendy's sole concern, however, is to decide which decorated cap she should wear to complete her wedding outfit. Because she cannot decide, she rushes pell-mell into Henry's private court chambers, even though he has an important meeting with his advisors in progress. The annoyed Henry tells his impetuous bride-to-be: "Softly sweetie, we have affairs of state here."

Wendy: "But darling, this is really important. Henry, which one shall I wear?"

The embarrassed Laughton dismisses his grave council, quickly makes a selection among the caps, and, even more quickly, is diverted from his mounting anger by the naive, beautiful twenty-one-year-old whom he will wed and again bed that day. He may call her a "stupid woman" but he is totally beguiled by her physical appeal and childish adoration. Later that day Wendy is momentarily perturbed as the drums announce the demise of Oberon, but it is also the signal for the beginning of her new wedded life, so she traipses off to the ceremony.

It is not long before Wendy's Jane Seymour is pregnant, and one day, while out hunting, Henry is informed that his wife has given birth to a boy child. The overjoyed, cocky Henry is only momentarily disturbed to learn that "poor pretty little Jane" has died in childbirth. "God rest her sweet soul," says Henry, who soon thereafter weds Anne of Cleves (Elsa Lanchester) and then the more worldly Kathreyn Howard (Barnes).

Wendy rightly did not receive much more than passing notice and approval for her participation in *The Private Life of Henry VIII*, but it provided her with a prestigious film credit, one that would stand her in good stead in the many years to come. As with others in the cast, playing in this historical epic proved the threshold event in her career, giving her standing in the industry as a true professional.*

Ironically, *The Private Life of Henry VIII* was the last film Wendy would make for Korda's London Films, as he had already found other ingenues to flesh out the cast lists of his subsequent productions.

Wendy returned to the ranks of seemingly innocuous quota-film leading ladies. In *This Acting Business* (1933) she and Hugh Williams were stage artists who wed in spite of the objections of their parents, veteran Shakespearean troupers. *Kine Weekly*, a trade paper, cited Wendy as "good without being outstanding." In *The House of Trent* (1933) Wendy played the daughter of a newspaper peer, a girl who falls in love with the son (John Trent) of the doctor who died years before while saving her life. The picture was rated a "sincere popular British drama" and Wendy was favorably mentioned for revealing "intelligence" and for being her "attractive" self. She was "sound" as the wife of Henry Kendall in *Without You* (1934), "effective" as the debutante in the farce *The Man I Want* (1934), and "good" in *Freedom of the Seas* (1934) as the daughter of H. F. Maltby. She is attracted to her father's once-timid bank-clerk employee (Clifford Mollison), who later becomes a gallant naval officer in World War I. Equally unmemorable was *There Goes Susie* (1934), set in Brussels, in which Wendy was cast as the carefree daughter of a soap manufacturer (Foaming Hearts Soap Company) who is mistaken for a model by struggling artist Andre Cochet. Lightly draped she poses for a poster by him, which is eventually purchased by her father's firm and turned into a well-distributed advertisement. Compromised by the poster Wendy has no alternative but to wed her jealous suitor, Cochet. British critics found the going heavy-handed, rather than Continental in flavor. *Kine Weekly* described Wendy as "charming and ladylike." *Variety* was even more enthusiastic about Wendy, citing her as a "sweet looking, youthful ingenue lead."

---

*In her fractured way of recalling events, Wendy later said: "I played the part and I got $60 a week for doing it. But I had only one second in the picture. I thought I was sensational, and some people in Hollywood thought I was movie material."

The fragile musical farce, *Give Her a Ring* (1934),* lavishly set on the Continent, found Wendy as a telephone operator who discovers that Clifford Mollison is her boss and that she loves him. Zelma O'Neal, a persistent figure in British pictures of this period, supplied the comedy relief.

Wendy might well have continued for some time as a modestly popular leading lady of undemanding film roles in low-budget pictures. (When her Korda contract expired it is more than likely that some other London producer would have picked up her option to feature her in shoestring pictures.) In August, 1934, she was named an English Baby Star, along with such other girls as Diana Cotton, Peggy Simpson, Grethe Hanson, Jane Cornell, Joyce Kirby, and Gwyneth Lloyd, none of whom achieved anything more than serviceable professional status in the ranks of film players.

But Wendy, like the critics, had never taken her cinema fling seriously. She had much more enthusiastically and imaginatively pursued her major occupation as a leading, romping member of London's social set. Hardly a week went by without a picture in the newspapers of "madcap" Wendy being escorted by some new and very eligible beau to the latest fashionable nightspot. She candidly admitted to the press that her dating experience had long since taught her that American men were the most desirable social companions, particularly because she found herself so much in sympathy with their life-style. Most of all, she expressed a strong preference for Woolworth Donahue, heir to the dime-store millions, and cousin of blueblood butterfly Barbara Hutton. Donahue had squired Wendy about London and had been particularly attentive when they both happened to show up simultaneously at Cannes in mid-1934. When the globe-hopping Donahue had flown over to New York, the London newspapers—at Wendy's prodding no doubt—suggested that Donahue's primary reason for returning to the States was to make arrangements to wed Wendy. However Wendy and the press might have interpreted his sudden westbound departure, Donahue refused to commit himself on the matter. When later contacted by reporters in New York he diplomatically stated re Wendy: "We're good friends, but that doesn't mean we're engaged."

Evidently enterprising Wendy thought differently (or was at least convinced of her persuasive charms), for in September, 1934, she arrived in New York. However, when she docked in Manhattan, she found that Donahue had already departed for Canada, leaving her to confront the formidable society matron Jessie Woolworth Donahue, who made it quite clear that she had no intention of allowing her eldest son to wed an "actress." If twenty-two-year-old Wendy was nonplused by the rapid change of events, she certainly gave no public indication. Following the traditional Horace Greeley advice to "Go West," she soon went to Hollywood to try her luck. Ten days after arriving in the cinema capital, Wendy landed her first Amer-

---

*When this picture reached New York in August, 1935, *Variety* tagged it a "flimsy British musical import" that failed to match up to Hollywood standards of the times, and commented about Wendy and Erik Rhodes—both in Hollywood by then—that "they limp in this one."

ican movie assignment. Not bad for a movie-acting dabbler who had always given more concentration to choosing a new wardrobe than angling for superior movie assignments!

It's a Small World (1935) may have been merely a double-bill-style movie, but it was produced by Fox Pictures and it did have Spencer Tracy as its male lead. This film was Tracy's next-to-last Fox feature, before he moved over to MGM in the spring of 1935, and he certainly was not exerting himself at this time for his outgoing employer, Fox. Wendy followed in the footsteps of such ingenues as Joan Bennett, Claire Trevor, Pat Paterson, Alice Faye, and Ketti Gallian, as performers who shared oncamera scenes with the quietly dynamic Tracy. Within the framework of its satire on small-town life, *It's a Small World* dealt with lawyer Tracy and socialite Wendy, both metropolitan sophisticates from St. Louis who first meet when they are involved in an automobile accident in Hope Center, Louisiana. Taxi-driver-dog-catcher-barber-hotel-owner-sheriff-judge Raymond Walburn arrests the two city slickers, and at the ensuing trial, which is continually interrupted by outrageous distractions from equally bizarre townsfolk, Tracy discovers he is falling in love with Wendy. But it is not until Tracy demonstrates his all-around versatility as a dog-trainer (no less) that the previously irascible Wendy relents and confesses her growing attraction for him. In eight short words *Variety* pinpointed Wendy's impact as a performer in the American cinema: "A looker, but not much of an actress." It was a laser-beam evaluation that would remain accurate throughout the years to come. Unlike others of equal or lesser innate acting talents, Wendy never had pretentions of attaining dramatic peaks in the movies. It was just a glamorous job that had delightful fringe benefits: above-par salary, celebrity status, and, most important of all, entrees into any social circles she wished to enter.

In April, 1935, when *It's a Small World* first went into theatrical release, Wendy was making bigger news in the social columns than on the entertainment page. For she had made a most gallant gesture. As was duly reported in all the society-gossip columns of American and British newspapers, Woolworth Donahue had just called Wendy in Hollywood from Palm Beach, Florida, to inquire whether he might officially break their (alleged) engagement so he could wed Dorothy Fell. Wendy, as she was quick to point out to newsmen, had offered her gracious consent. In actuality, what else could she do?

Even before this news-gathering turn of events, Wendy was considered a marketable personality in cinemaland. Zeppo Marx, her new agent, had little difficulty in engineering a short-term Paramount contract for his British socialite client. In the long run it might well have been wiser if Wendy had held out for better offers, but she was neither then nor later the type of individual to sit around waiting for anything. Impulsive decision-making had always been, and would always be, her guiding rule of living.

Wendy's initial picture at Paramount was a programmer entitled *College*

Scandal (1935), yet another studio entry in the hips-hips-hurrah campus genre. But director Elliott Nugent, let alone his cast, could not decide whether it was to be a musical comedy or a tragedy. What started out as a typical rah-rah coed yarn suddenly switched in mid-picture to a would-be chiller-thriller, triggered by the murders of the campus's newspaper editor and a crooner. Chief of police William Frawley suspects young chemistry professor Kent Taylor, a deduction which amazes Taylor's students, including Arline Judge, Joyce Compton, Wendy (her father is an exchange professor from Paris), not to mention Edward J. Nugent, who almost becomes the third murder victim. No seasoned movie viewer had anything positive to say of the badly garbled *College Scandal*. The *New York American* thought Wendy unsympathetic in her "debut" role,* reasoning that she "deserves a better break." The *Los Angeles Times* reviewer added an interesting postscript about Wendy to his review of *College Scandal*, proving once again that Wendy's proper sphere of reportage belonged on the society-gossip pages and not in the amusement section. Said the reporter: "She arrived here from England last year. A rather new type, she combines beauty and vivacity in the current film and plans to hunt lions while vacationing."

Actually Wendy spent much of early May in 1935 recuperating from a tonsillectomy. She was then assigned to *The Big Broadcast of 1936* (1935), the second of four such Paramount variety-show entries. Director Norman Taurog completed this "goulash of specialty numbers" via a rather unorthodox if practical mode of operation. He would photograph stage acts on the fly, whenever they happened to be passing through California during a given thirteen-month period. As a *modus operandi* to present these unrelated numbers, Taurog borrowed an expedient previously employed in *International House* (Paramount, 1933). Whenever the plot (which has both Jack Oakie and Henry Wadsworth—one the talker, the other the vocalizer, for "Lochinvar," station WHY's on-the-air celebrity and lover—being kidnapped by man-hungry Countess Lyda Roberti and lured to her island retreat) runs amuck, which was often, the storyline makes use of an invention devised by the film's George Burns and Gracie Allen. It is called the radio eye—i.e., television. Thus intermittently throughout the picture Burns and Allen, who are peddling the gadget to WHY, turn on the set and the movie camera then focuses on such acts as Bing Crosby crooning "I Wished on the Moon," Charlie Ruggles and Mary Boland in a domestic comedy sketch, and Ethel Merman singing "The Animal in Me" with a chorus of elephants.†

In *The Big Broadcast of 1936* fifth-billed Wendy was Sue, the well-groomed sidekick of eccentric Roberti, who is paired off romantically with Wadsworth. The spasmodic picture concludes with a madcap chase about the island with none other than the U.S. Marines coming to the rescue. Moviegoers were as baffled as Wendy looked in this tacked-on climax,

*Not many critics had caught or remembered *It's a Small World*.
†This number had been originally filmed for *We're Not Dressing* (Paramount, 1934).

which finds Oakie winning a $250,000 prize in a broadcasting competition for broadcasting a play-by-play account of the zany happenings. Most moviegoers managed to take the picture in stride, as did the *New York Times*, which went a little overboard in its misguided references to Wendy's acting pedigree and to her performance in this production: "Wendy Barrie, whose slim neck fitted her so well for the role of Jane Seymour in *The Private Life of Henry VIII* [she died in childbirth, not at the block, in that film] displays her acid comedy."

Following her chores in *The Big Broadcast of 1936* Wendy was scheduled to make a hasty departure from the United States due to the immigration laws, which required her to return to London and then, after a decent interval, to re-enter the States from Vancouver, British Columbia. Both Wendy and Hollywood's more madcap endorsers were not pleased with this turn of events and an undisclosed compromise was engineered with the federal authorities. Wendy could remain in this country and in Hollywood, in particular. With her alien status solved for the moment, Wendy sent for her mother and sister, inviting them to reside at her new abode, for she had splurged and rented Ramon Novarro's expansive movie-colony home. Meanwhile Wendy had another title to add to her array of Hollywood titles. She was selected by her employers as one of the Paramount Protegees of 1935, along with Grace Bradley, Katherine DeMille, Gertrude Michael, Gail Patrick, and Ann Sheridan. It was a studio-organized self-serving publicity gimmick, but it served its purpose of keeping the girls in the news.

Later in 1935 Wendy and the family received word that her father, Frank C. Jenkins, had been killed in China during a local political revolt. Wendy bore her grief stoically (some cynical Hollywood observers insist she capitalized on it),* put up a brave front for the press, and pushed her schedule of social activities to new heights. Within a short year she had become a more and more prominent figure on the Hollywood nightlife social circuit.

Paramount loaned Wendy to Columbia for *A Feather in Her Hat* (Radio City Music Hall, October 24, 1935). Columbia had intended this class tearjerker to star the queen of the genre, Ruth Chatterton, but she had rejected the project and Pauline Lord was substituted. It was just another hard-boiled drama of mother love, in which Cockney widow Lord runs a small grocery store in London's East End. She has her young son tutored by genteel Basil Rathbone, so that he will be able to rise in the world. As a grown-up the son is played by Louis Hayward. She bravely denies her kinship with him, allowing him to believe he is the son of a once-famous actress (Billie Burke) in whose home he now resides. Hayward has drifted into playwriting and is unaware that it is Lord who has financed his theatrical venture. On opening night she falls gravely ill, but she lives long enough to enjoy a deathbed scene in which she admits to Hayward that she is his true mother. Wendy had only a minor role as Burke's smart-set stepdaughter, who is attracted to

---

*Her "tragedy" brought her and well-heeled Van Renssalear Smith romantically closer for a time.

540

Hayward but almost steps aside because of his past attachment to Cockney Nydia Westman. Although most of the critical attention went to Lord and to Hayward, *Variety* kindly noted Wendy as a "good looking ingenue with plenty of class." This evaluation summed up Wendy's position in Hollywood to a T.

There was little refreshingly novel to recommend *Millions in the Air* (Paramount, 1935), a late arrival in the film genre of let's-kid-the-radio-amateur-talent-shows. In the film "Colonel Edward's Kello Amateur Hour" is offering a top prize of $500 and several would-be contestants are determined to win the loot: Tony the junk peddler (vaudevillian Willie Howard in his belated film debut), John Howard, an ice cream vendor with a stand in front of the Museum of Natural History, and Wendy, who is actually the daughter of soap king George Barbier, the show's sponsor. As single acts. both Howard's saxophone playing and Wendy's vocalizing are busts, but together they produce a winning combination. *Millions in the Air* lacked any big marquee names as a commercial antidote to the stale plot. In fact, one sly reviewer-observer remarked that movies had killed vaudeville and now it was return play. But there were a few redeeming moments in this musical hash: such as Willie Howard's brief singing of selections from *Rigoletto*, Eleanor Whitney's fine dancing, the antics of Billy Gilbert in his recurring characterization of Nikolas Popadopolis, and Joan Davis's comic song, "You Tell Her, I Stutter." In what must have been a burst of patriotic enthusiasm, the British *Daily Renter* graciously accorded that in her nondescript role in *Millions in the Air* Wendy demonstrated that she "improves with her every new appearance."

What had always been clear to Wendy now became evident to Hollywood executives: this was one socialite dilettante who really meant it when she stated she did not give a fig about her movie career. Wendy would devote endless hours to the pursuit of her offcamera activities—nightclub hopping, playing golf and tennis, learning to be an aviatrix—but when it came to playing the career game, she just lost her enthusiasm and drive. Even though she was not in the same league with the aristocratically beautiful Madeleine Carroll or the sharply talented Binnie Barnes, two Britishers who had made their marks in Hollywood, Wendy had untapped potential that might well have carried her above and beyond the rash of stinkers she would soon be permanently gracing with her presence on screen. If only she had cared!

After her Paramount contract ended, Wendy freelanced, starting with RKO's *Love on a Bet* (1936). It was the type of role RKO would soon be handing to contract ingenue Joan Fontaine—the cardboard, skittish socialite who trades an advantageous wedding for marital bliss with a poor but inspiring hero. *Variety* succinctly pegged the audience potential of *Love on a Bet*: "It won't chase 'em out once they're in." In order to win a $15,000 bet, aspiring but impecunious impresario Gene Raymond agrees to a strange wager with his uncle. Raymond is to hitchhike from New York to California in ten days and along the way he must acquire a girl, a pair of trousers, and . . . . one hundred dollars in cash. Thus it is not surprising when one day in the film, Raymond steps out of a cab at . . . . Fifty-ninth Street and Fifth Avenue, clad only in underwear, and without a penny to his name. Moments later he meets Wendy in the process of being proposed to by Addison Randall. This interruption does not endear Raymond to willful rich girl Wendy now, or later when she and her aunt (Helen Broderick) are beginning a cross-country drive and pick up a uniform-clad hitchhiker who turns out to be none other than Raymond. Needless to say, before this trio reaches the West Coast, Wendy and Raymond have fallen in love. If Raymond was overly coy and whimsical in *Love on a Bet,* the acerbic performance of wisecracking Broderick almost counteracted his bland presence. Wendy—well, she was just along for the ride.

Wendy next hopscotched over to MGM for *Speed* (1936), which proved to be the poor man's precursor to Arthur Hailey's novel *Wheels.* The stock triangular love tale was a favorite of programmer producers for it could be readily adapted to "action" tales set on land, at sea, or in the air. This one was concocted to deal with the racetrack. Test driver-mechanic James Stewart of the Emory Automobile Company is certain he can perfect a new high-speed carburetor. Wendy, the niece of the company boss, has obtained a job on her own in the factory's public relations department and is duly impressed with cocksure Stewart. Then there is Weldon Heyburn, a company engineer who is infatuated with Wendy. During a trial run Stewart's improved racer crashes, and it is Heyburn who rescues Stewart, his rival for Wendy's affection. Humbled and discouraged by the accident, Stewart is about to quit the project, but Wendy persuades him to give it another try, and all ends happily. *Speed* owes more to newsreel clips than to its own originality for its padded-out running length. Besides stock footage from the Indianapolis Speedway and other racetracks, there is an extended visual documentary tour of a Detroit automobile factory, none of which was uplifted by the plot's routine sentimentality. Stewart was top-featured in this, his sixth feature film, with Wendy performing "with commendable restraint if little conviction" (*New York Herald-Tribune*). More eye-catching among the distaff cast members were Una Merkel as a plant executive and Patricia "Honeychild" Wilder cavorting about with her deep Georgia drawl.

From high-toned MGM Wendy checked in at poverty-row-plus Republic Studios to co-star with Roger Pryor in *Ticket to Paradise* (1936). Go-getting Chicago businessman Pryor recovers from a taxicab accident, only to discover he is a victim of amnesia. He takes a job as a cabbie, hoping his memory will return. His first passenger is none other than wealthy socialite Wendy (no one had the imagination to cast her as anything else in those days).* She is soon enamored of the unconventional hack driver and be-

*In a rare moment of screen-career concern, Wendy complained: "I always have to be a lady, or a professor's daughter, or something like that. I photograph like a baby, anyway, and my roles always call for sweet smiles and plenty of simpering. I'd like to get hold of a part I could be mean in."

comes a strong factor behind her millionaire father (Claude Gillingwater) offering Pryor a post in his company. Several trials and tribulations later, Pryor is seen recovering in the hospital from a clubside donnybrook. Lo and behold he has regained his memory but now has no recollection of the interim period. Sprightly Wendy walks into his room. He finds her instantly charming but cannot recall anything of their past relationship. Chipper Wendy is undaunted, and she decides to get reacquainted. *Variety* observed with untypical understatement: "[She] appears to be ripe for better things on the screen."

Under Your Spell (20th Century-Fox, 1936) was not one of those "better things." After four MGM pictures of diminishing success in the early 1930s, opera singer Lawrence Tibbett had returned to the Metropolitan Opera in New York, only to be summoned back to filmmaking in 1935 with a two-picture deal at Fox engineered by the studio's new head, Darryl F. Zanuck. The comeback effort, the well-mounted *Metropolitan* (1935), premiered at Radio City Music Hall and collapsed shortly thereafter. Zanuck hastily demanded that Tibbett agree to cancel the scheduled follow-up picture, but Tibbett insisted on his contractual rights. Austrian-born actor-director Otto Preminger was assigned to make his Hollywood film-directing debut with the economy-tinged *Under Your Spell*. The completed product was tossed away with a minor debut at the Palace Theatre (November 6, 1936) as a supporting-bill entry. Once again the obvious was painfully evident: despite an outstanding singing voice, Tibbett was physically and emotionally incongruous as a conventional movie lead. The plot was even more unappealing than his previous entries. Overworked singer Tibbett intends to escape from the atmosphere of work and fame, and his trusty butler Arthur Treacher is just the man to engineer "Project Retreat." But they have not reckoned with blueblood Wendy, who has determined to have celebrity Tibbett perform at her upcoming social bash. Tibbett disappears into the desert on schedule, but with Wendy in hot pursuit. The film has a courtroom finish with Tibbett and Wendy each telling their side of the story to the judge, and Tibbett singing the title tune. Wendy may have won Tibbett in *Under Your Spell*, but she gained few new admirers with this turkey.

The quality of Wendy's film assignments did not increase in 1937 but the quantity did; she was in six releases that year. The upswing in her productivity was not a product of excess career energy but resulted from a far more practical motive. Wendy was broke. In 1936 she had been forced to declare bankruptcy, listing her assets at $94 and her liabilities at $11,000. Work was now a practical necessity for free-spending Wendy.

Breezing Home was the first of seven Universal budget movies in which Wendy would appear. Horse-trainer William Gargan highly regards the nobility of steeds and is none too happy when Alan Baxter and his gangster cronies tamper with racetrack mounts to insure hefty winner's-circle payoffs. Gargan is impressed by the sincerity of horse-owner Binnie Barnes, but he also is diverted by Wendy, who later gains ownership of the horse Galaxy and nurses the injured animal back to health and track victory.

The Rialto Theatre in midtown Manhattan had long been the showcase home for blood-and-bullet action films in the 1930s. Its owner, Arthur Mayer, reasoned he was well qualified to judge his customers' cinema preferences and produced his own entry, *What Price Vengeance?*, filmed on a minimal budget in Canada. In a moment of uncertainty, crackshot policeman Lyle Talbot fails to shoot it out with bank robber Marc Lawrence. The neighborhood denizens are convinced their former hero cop is now yellow, a conclusion in which lunch-counter-owner Wendy concurs. But before the fifty-seven-minute B-picture runs its obvious course, there is plenty of action and gunplay as Talbot redeems his honor and re-establishes his romantic rapport with Wendy. Naturally the film opened at the Rialto Theatre (May 25, 1937) where it received the endorsement of its patrons.

Universal's *Wings over Honolulu* (1937) taxed the viewer's credulity but not his brainpower. The picture opens at a birthday party for nineteen-year-old Virginia belle Wendy, minus any discernible southern accent, at which she is asked by Kent Taylor to marry him. "But you see," Wendy explains, "I don't love you." A few moments later daredevil Navy aviator Ray Milland crash-lands his plane on her plantation field and strolls into her party. Wendy tells the dashing stranger, "I've known you all my life." (Well she should, he was portraying the stock leading-man type of every shoestring feature, and she had worked in enough of them to spot one on sight.) Thereafter Wendy and Milland are wed, but do *not* live happily ever after. When Wendy arrives in Honolulu she is aghast at the small size of their military-supplied quarters and distraught that Navy wives deign to treat her as an outlandish outsider (occasioned by the fact that she won Milland away from Polly Rowles, the admiral's daughter). Wendy is only too eager to relieve her drab existence by an occasional night out on the town, and eagerly accepts Taylor's offer for such an evening. But she does not reckon with the fact that she will become involved in a club brawl, the repercussions of which damage Milland's military career. Wendy leaves Milland, but he comes searching for his estranged spouse and in the process damages his plane. For his unauthorized use of government equipment Milland is court-martialed; spared only when Wendy comes forth at the trial to shoulder the blame. Because the offcamera Wendy was such a well-publicized gadabout individualist, critics such as Howard Barnes of the *New York Herald-Tribune* were always amazed when her real personality did not conflict with her reel-life characterizations: "[She] plays with more credibility and restraint than one might have expected from her."

The high point of Wendy's American film career was being cast in Samuel Goldwyn's filmization of *Dead End* (1937). Not that she had the female lead (Sylvia Sidney portrayed shopgirl Drina, who yearns for respectability and a way to save her brother, Billy Halop, from developing into a slum gangster) or even the flashier supporting woman's role (Claire Trevor was

Francey, the childhood sweetie of punk Humphrey Bogart, who matures into an experienced streetwalker). Instead Wendy was cast as Kay, a kept woman residing in a fashionable East Fifties riverside apartment building near the tenement slums of *Dead End.*

Because of the necessity of adhering to the strict motion picture Production Code of that time, the characters played by Wendy and Claire Trevor remained rather shadowy figures with little explicitly stated about their sordid social status. Wendy's part—and producer Samuel Goldwyn was convinced that because of her well-known real-life British pedigree she could carry it off genteelly—required her to be the temptress who almost lures idealistic architect Joel McCrea away from sloe-eyed proletarian Sidney. In fact, when McCrea is about to collect the police reward for having killed gangster Bogart, he is almost convinced that Wendy is the better girl for him. However, she has already accepted a businessman's offer to take a long cruise on his fancy yacht, leaving dreamy McCrea to reawaken to the virtues of loyal Sidney.

Thus, in her truncated role Wendy had little opportunity to amplify her character or to do more than lend to the production the "beauty and glamour of her personality" (*New York Daily News*). But *Dead End* was considered then, as now, a class film, and it gave Wendy renewed status in a film undustry that was fast forgetting her last prestigious assignment (*The Private Life of Henry VIII*) in the wake of her American programmers.

But then it was back to meat-and-potato pictures. *A Girl with Ideas* (1937) did offer a plot switch on the usual formula newspaper picture. *Morning Dispatch* publisher Walter Pidgeon is the losing defendant in a major slander suit, and he is forced to hand over control of his publication to the young heiress plaintiff (Wendy). Pidgeon may be a gentleman but he wants his revenge, so he attempts to coerce Wendy's new managing editor (Kent Taylor) into running the *Dispatch* into the ground. But all the breaks seem to go Wendy's way. Her ritzy friends take a slumming tour of the newspaper and accidentally let loose such a stream of meaty gossip and hot tips that the *Morning Dispatch* is quickly launched on a successful path. Pidgeon even arranges for the fake kidnapping of Wendy's father (George Barbier) and gives the scoop to a rival newspaper. When that ploy does not bring Wendy to heel, Pidgeon anonymously offers her staff a paid vacation. Obviously, Pidgeon is brought back to his position of authority when Wendy realizes she is not equipped to handle the demanding executive post.

Prescription for Romance (Universal, 1937) was the third of five screen teamings of Wendy and third-string leading man Kent Taylor. S. Sylvan Simon, who had done much better directing *A Girl with Ideas*, helmed this quickie, packaged in three weeks of haste. When Henry Hunter absconds with $500,000, private detective Taylor is hired by the Bankers Protective Association to trail the embezzler and regain the loot. The criminal lands in Budapest with Taylor in fast pursuit, but the local police there mistake the investigator for the culprit and jail him. Wendy, an American doctor (she was at least enjoying variety in her screen characters' professions) stationed in Budapest, bails Taylor out of trouble with the law, believing him to be her old friend Hunter. Taylor has difficulty convincing Wendy that Hunter, auld lang syne or not, is a crook. Eventually circumstances force her to accede to the truth, and she assists Taylor in handing Hunter over to the anxious police. For contrasting feminine appeal there was Hunter's forsaken girlfriend, Dorothea Kent, and for comedy relief there was Frank Jenks, Taylor's bumbling helper. *Prescription for Romance* was a mediocre finish to Wendy's 1937 cinema output.

Every once in a while Wendy's movie career received a little push, seemingly by accident, and never strong enough for others to follow up the casting "break" of which Wendy would only make partial use. *Dead End* had been one, and *I Am the Law* (Columbia, 1938) was another. Granted Wendy did not have a particularly strong part in either production, but both pictures were far from run-of-the-mill ventures, and each was a potential springboard that even a performer far less imaginative or spunky than Wendy could have used to launch a healthy cinema spree. *I Am the Law* was Columbia's contribution to the wave of anticrime films sweeping the cinema. For offbeat casting Edward G. Robinson starred as a law professor appointed as special prosecutor to clean up hometown corruption. Determined Robinson cannot complete the extensive task in the alloted six-month period. Although the district attorney dismisses him from the project, he and his recruited staff operate from his home and utilize most unorthodox methods to eventually corral the town's remaining corrupt elements into a showdown meeting. Via documented motion pictures it is revealed that supposed civic leader Otto Kruger, whose son John Beal is Robinson's top aide, heads the local rackets. And ex-newspaper gal Wendy, who has been so helpful to harassed Robinson, is none other than Kruger's high-class moll and co-conspirator. The unsubtle *I Am the Law* stretched plausibility, but it still emerged as a "slambang, rip-roaring meller" (*Variety*). As the "expressionless gangstress" Wendy provided a distinct contrast to Barbara O'Neil, with the latter far more persuasive as Robinson's understanding, wholesome wife. One of the picture's more savory—and publicized—moments found Wendy and the ex-"Little Caesar" dancing together to "The Big Apple."

On July 23, 1938, at the age of twenty-three, Wendy's sister, "Pat," died in Hollywood of pneumonia. A few months before this unhappy event Wendy admitted that she no longer had the energy or inclination to jump around from Hollywood studio to studio and that perhaps it was time to settle down, at least professionally. Jokingly Wendy referred to herself as Queen of the B-films—and most of Hollywood had come to regard the gallivanting Britisher as just that. So it really was not a situation of choosing among the best offers, but rather a case of accepting among those offered. RKO Radio Pictures, still under the production supervision of Pandro S. Berman, was one of the companies to offer Wendy a contractual studio berth, and she accepted. The terms were not particularly lucrative (her salary was well under $1,000 weekly, with no guaranteed star billing or promises of first-rate assignments), but the contract allowed Wendy ample opportunity to follow her more important life pursuits: society, men, sports. On the structured totem pole of players' status at RKO of 1938-39, Wendy was several pegs down from the top, a lower status than would seem at first since the studio was no longer the elaborate B+ headquarters of Hollywood's swankiest screen sophisticates. Irene Dunne, Katharine Hepburn, and Ginger Rogers were the top-drawing full-time female stars at the Culver City lot, while freelancing Carole Lombard and visiting English luminary Anna Neagle were almost their box-office equals. Lucille Ball, Sally Eilers, Joan Fontaine, and Betty Grable had their strong legions of devotees in the modest programmer division, as did such RKO comediennes as Helen Broderick, Edna May Oliver, studio newcomer Eve Arden, and energetic song-and-dance gal Ann Miller. After a few years in the early 1930s at MGM, fiery Lupe Velez had freelanced until finding a new screen *modus operandi* in an RKO series, *Mexican Spitfire*. And then there was Irish-import Maureen O'Hara, brought over with Charles Laughton's production troupe to co-star in *The Hunchback of Notre Dame*. All of which did not leave too much maneuverability for Wendy to move up the scale in stature with her new contract employer. But this bothered neither Wendy nor RKO, for each was content to milk her celebrity status to the limit in undemanding screen assignments (it was worth several hundred dollars more per week in salary to have Wendy on hand to perform one-dimensional roles in RKO slap-togethers, which could just as well have been acted by contract mini-starlets). Then too, studio supervisor Pandro S. Berman correctly gauged that Wendy's modest screen ambitions would never get the best of her and upset this pre-established balance of interest between studio and player.

While RKO was pegging Wendy to realistic scale, she was conducting her typical erratic interview sessions, which usually bore little correlation to her current range of activities. "I'm a very dull person to interview," Wendy insisted to the press in late 1938, "because I don't collect little snuff bottles or do eccentric things. I'm just plain and healthy. My metabolism is plus one. That's terrific." And it certainly must have been, for Wendy continued to add to the list of celebrities who served as her escorts-of-the-moment. The long list of male acquaintances during Wendy's first Hollywood decade included: William Rhinelander Stewart, A. C. Blumenthal, Frazer Jelke, Randolph Scott, Tyrone Power, Reginald Gardiner, Rudy Vallee, Eddy Duchin, Howard Hughes (ever so briefly), Peter Arno, the Earl of Warwick, Brian Aherne, Macoco, Milton Berle, Gregory Bautzer, Stanley Kahn, Lee Bowman, Jerry Gordon, Arthur Priest, Fritz Lang, Phil Liebman, Horace Luro, Richard Greene, Robert Ritchie, Edmund Anderson, Artie Bulova, Atwater Kent, Jr., Lee Sterling, George Herascu, Joe Gray, and Ralph Morgan.

RKO's *Pacific Liner* opened at the Rialto Theatre on January 17, 1939. It seemed Wendy just could not escape her theatre home away from home.

This modest mixture of he-man action and maritime medicine in a minor *Grand Hotel* style featured doctor Chester Morris and nurse Wendy as hard-pressed medicos attempting to cope with a cholera epidemic which has broken out aboard the S.S. *Arcturus* bound with its cargo of lace and tea from Shanghai to San Francisco. After the first plague victim is dumped into the furnace, the crew's morale noticeably weakens: stoker Barry Fitzgerald philosophizes, Emory Parnell turns to religion, and Paul Guilfoyle commits suicide. In fact, when tyrannical chief engineer Victor McLaglen collapses with fever, Cyrus W. Kendall attempts to instigate a mutiny. By the fade-out order has been restored and Morris now is bent on a new life devoted to combating tropical disease. For Wendy the future promises marriage to Morris and a life of hard work in faraway places (what better fate for the heroine of a low-budget entry?). Since most of the action in *Pacific Liner* occurs among the crew below decks, Wendy had little to do with the plot, but when she was in front of the camera she performed competently and without condescension.

Five days after *Pacific Liner* opened, Universal's earlier product, *Newsboys' Home*, commenced its run at the Central Theatre (January 22, 1939). Universal again featured Wendy as a newspaper owner, this time as the daughter of publisher Samuel S. Hinds, who inherits control not only of his publication but also of its charity offshoot, the Newsboys' Home. Once again it requires much action before Wendy will admit she is a novice and that her boyfriend-editor (Edmund Lowe) is much better equipped for the yellow journalism post—a fact Jackie Cooper and the other newsboys knew from the start of the movie. There was little entertainment value to *Newsboys' Home* and even Wendy, usually a good sport, showed telltale signs of ennui.

Because Wendy was on contract tap at RKO to bolster the "marquee" lure of its programmers, she was frequently assigned to decorate the studio's increasingly large output of series films. Like the budget divisions of other studios, RKO had rediscovered in the late 1930s the public's abiding interest in detective entries, which traditionally focused on a suave amateur sleuth who glibly solves crimes that baffle the police while gallantly flirting with the ladies in the case (heroines and murder suspects alike). RKO had acquired the rights to Leslie Charteris's popular fictional detective, Simon Templar, and cast Louis Hayward in the title role of *The Saint in New York* (1938). The following year suave George Sanders undertook the part for five follow-up entries. Wendy, with her persistent poise and breezy manner, had the dubious distinction of playing the female lead in three of these black-and-white pictures. Although she never essayed the same character twice in these *Saint* pictures, Wendy provided a valid contrast to the brittle, staccato personality of Sanders's lead figure.

Sanders's initial effort, *The Saint Strikes Back* (1939), opens on New Year's Eve at a San Francisco nightclub (decidedly a low-tariff joint, judging from the decor). Suddenly a patron is shot and moments later Sanders and Wendy find themselves out on the street together, anxious to avoid tangling with the fast-approaching law-enforcers. It develops that Wendy's dad, a local police detective wrongly suspected of graft-taking, has committed suicide (before the story opens). Wendy has organized her own gang to seek revenge, with Neil Hamilton, one of her close friends, turning out to be one of her prime targets. Because the Saint has involved himself in the caper, Wendy must not only cope with the cops but also with the self-appointed detective, all of which annoys her immensely. Sanders does beat visiting New York police inspector Jonathan Hale to the criminologist's punch by foiling the culprits and solving the four-murder crime wave. Some of Sanders's crime-solving methods were as laughable as they were exciting, but no matter, the public enjoyed it. Wendy, as a sophisticated denizen of the underworld, was still "extremely easy on the eyes" even if her happy-go-lucky characterization had more than its share of self-contradictions. More ham than humorous relief was provided by Barry Fitzgerald as a comic safecracker who befriends trouble-plagued Sanders.

In a rare moment of career drive Wendy expressed great interest in playing the female role of Britisher Fern in Twentieth Century-Fox's *The Rains Came* (1939).* Darryl F. Zanuck's new discovery, Brenda Joyce, got that assignment, but Fox did utilize Wendy's services for *The Hound of the Baskervilles* (1939). This remake of Arthur Conan Doyle's 1902 Sherlock Holmes tale was the first of two Fox *Sherlock Holmes* pictures to star Basil Rathbone as the Baker Street sleuth and Nigel Bruce as the bumbling Dr. Watson. In dismal Devonshire lies Baskerville Hall, the ancestral home of the famed English family. Strange events lead the occupants to believe that the weird moor legend may be true: that a ghostly hound haunts the family, killing the descendants for a dreadful crime committed centuries ago by their forebears. Holmes and Watson are urged to take up residence at the gloomy Hall to come to grips with the situation, which is driving Richard Greene, the heir to the estate, to near distraction. Using his typically devious deductive methods, Holmes uncovers the diabolical plotters, who are actually using a bloodthirsty hound for their malevolent deeds. Wendy provided the romantic interludes as the supposed daughter of Morton Lowry (really her stepbrother), a naturalist pursuing his studies on the moors. Wendy's Beryl Stapleton is a modern young woman who rides astride with country aristocrat Greene across the moors, and by the end of the thriller she has become engaged to Greene. Wendy was most fetchingly photographed in *The Hound of the Baskervilles*, but her role went no further than being animated set decoration. This was Wendy's last opportunity to rise above her programmer station in Hollywood life, but the chance passed by untapped by night owl Wendy.

RKO contract director John Farrow, who helmed *The Saint Strikes Back*,

---

*Conflict of production schedule, not adversity to the parts, forced Wendy out of Universal's *The Road to Reno* (1938) as a replacement for Irene Dunne—she in turn being replaced by Hope Hampton—and RKO's *Millionaire Playboy* (1940) as a replacement for Lucille Ball, she in turn being replaced by Linda Hayes.

handled that studio's *Five Came Back* (1939). As a Fourth of July holiday gift to action-hungry Rialto Theatre patrons, *Five Came Back* proved to be the programmer sleeper of the year, handling well its "subjective approach to disaster and violence" *(New York Herald-Tribune)*. The clipper plane *Silver Queen* leaves Los Angeles for Panama with a strange and varied set of passengers and crew: tramp Lucille Ball; professor C. Aubrey Smith and his wife, Elisabeth Risdon; wealthy but worthless Patric Knowles, who is eloping with his secretary, Wendy; a gangster's son (Casey Johnson) and his guardian (Allen Jenkins); law-enforcer John Carradine, who has in tow political assassin Joseph Calleia; pilots Chester Morris and Kent Taylor; and steward Dick Hogan. The plane crashes in the Latin American jungle, causing the distraught passengers to reveal their true natures in this desperate situation. Hogan dies in the crash, Carradine and Knowles become parasitic drunkards, Ball demonstrates her basic good instincts, Calleia shows he has inner decency, Wendy awakens to the false glitter of materialistic riches, and glib Morris and Taylor turn out to be good sorts. Smith and Risdon patch up their marital breach, bravely remaining behind to face certain death from the rampaging natives so the chosen five can return to civilization in the patched-up aircraft.

Five Came Back was produced on a shoestring, but was as economical in its expenditure of character emotions as on the outlay for sets.* The end result was a twisted, taut story—unpretentious, well done, and in the best tradition of *Grand Hotel*.† Third-billed Wendy was again short-shrifted onscreen . . . with much more focus given to Ball's wisecracking tart.

Wendy was loaned to Universal for its modestly budgeted *The Witness Vanishes* (1939). It was the fifth and final entry in the studio's first batch of *Crime Club* entries. A man (Barlowe Borland) railroaded into an insane asylum many years before escapes and attempts to kill the four men he feels were responsible for his imprisonment. Borland's daughter (Wendy) had thought her ex-newspaper publisher dad was dead, but now, with the aid of the *London Sun*'s star reporter, Bruce Lester, she sets about to set matters right. Ironically, it is Forrester Harvey, the Glasgow-based reporter for the rival *Tribune*, who solves the caper. Once again, Wendy was able to walk through her cardboard role and still achieve above-par results, which was all that her employers demanded of her oncamera. "[She] presents an ingratiating performance which even surmounts a silly romance with Bruce Lester" *(Variety)*.

Wendy's sixth and final release of the year was Twentieth Century-Fox's *Day-Time Wife*, which debuted at the Roxy Theatre on November 23, 1939. Flavorful eccentric Gregory Ratoff directed this airy comedy, the second

---

*For its main prop, the studio acquired a Capeles C-12 aircraft built in 1928 for a Greek-American syndicate.

†Farrow was evidently very fond of *Five Came Back*, for in 1956 he produced and directed a remake entitled *Back from Eternity* starring Robert Ryan and Anita Ekberg, with Phyllis Kirk in Wendy's role.

feature of star-in-the-making Linda Darnell, and the first of four pictures in which she would co-star with Tyrone Power. In the Art Arthur-Robert Hatari screenplay, dashing young businessman Power still considers himself a newlywed though he is enough of a seasoned spouse to flirt with his comely office employees. On his second wedding anniversary he returns home reeking of Wendy's perfume. Darnell is not about to lose her frivolous husband to any chic secretary, and on the good advice of her much divorced, gossipy pal, Binnie Barnes, she finds employment as secretary to girl-chasing married businessman Warren William. Naturally William makes a play for Darnell, and on one evening about town the two couples (William-Darnell, Wendy-Power) meet at a restaurant and later adjourn to William's apartment, where they spend the night, all in separate rooms. Darnell does make her domestic point and a truculent Power patches up his strained relationship with her in time for a satisfactory ending. *Day-Time Wife* was another of those mindless bits of fluff taken for granted in the 1930s, inconsequential and forgettable, but quite enjoyable. For a second time in Hollywood Wendy was professionally united with Binnie Barnes, her co-player from *The Private Life of Henry VIII*. However, Barnes, firmly established as a seasoned and very versatile second female lead in American movies, was billed above Wendy and had a choicer part, although neither she nor Wendy had sympathetic assignments.

Then it was back again to bread-and-butter pictures at RKO for Wendy. *The Saint Takes Over* (1940), the fifth released in RKO's series, found the ubiquitous detective (George Sanders) returning to New York from a London sojourn. Aboard the transatlantic vessel he is attracted to Ruth (Wendy), ostensibly a member in good standing of the upper-crust set, sporting all the essential prerequisites: charming manner, refined diction, and a sensible wardrobe. As their ship docks Wendy is nearly kidnapped by two thugs. It develops that there is a strong connection between Wendy, the sudden murder of three racetrack fixers, and the attempt to cast suspicion on New York police inspector Jonathan Hale as an underworld accomplice. Sanders as the cool modern Robin Hood plows through the maze of clues and solves the case by gaining a murder confession via a fixed microphone and a shortwave radio broadcast. One of the reasons this was the best *Saint* entry to date was that the film allowed for departures from the standard movie rules, such as having the female lawbreaker (Wendy) taking her medicine and paying for her crimes (she is killed along with wrongdoer Cyrus W. Kendall in a climactic gun battle with the law). With Wendy out of the way at the finale there was no need for the usual forced sequence in which the Saint explains to the heroine that he is not the type to settle down, but must wander about for new adventure and romantic interludes. What was very typical of the *Saint* and other detective series of this vintage, was the increasing amount of footage devoted to dumb comedy-relief characters at the expense of the heroines' oncamera time—herein simple-minded Paul Guilfoyle, once a safecracker and now Sanders's loyal stooge. To say the least, Wendy's character in *The Saint Takes Over* remained mysteriously unfathomable and inconsistent, but, as the *New York Daily Mirror* happily expressed it, "very pleasing to the optics."

Wendy went on loan to Republic for *Women in War* (1940), an old-fashioned melodrama dressed up with mock-contemporary World War II overtones. The economy feature displayed Republic's typical penny-pinching production values all along the line. Headstrong Londoner Wendy is placed on trial for the accidental murder of masher-Army officer Colin Tapley. Two near-strangers are vitally interested in the case: her career officer father (Stanley Logan) and Elsie Janis, her mother, whom her father divorced twenty years before and whom Wendy has not seen since. Without revealing her relationship, Janis arranges for Wendy to join the Overseas Nursing Corps; this weighs heavily in Wendy's favor at the trial, and she is acquitted by the jurors. On the transport ship bound for France reckless Wendy discovers how little she has in common with the other new nurses and it requires a good deal of stern remonstrances before Janis breaks Wendy's freewheeling spirit. Once in France Wendy is attracted to lieutenant Patric Knowles, despite the fact that he is already engaged to nurse Mae Clarke. Wendy eventually comes around to honorably renouncing Knowles, but by then Clarke is so distraught that she determines to kill Wendy and herself. Before Wendy can be rescued from her perilous plight, Clarke has been killed and rescuer Janis badly wounded. At this strategic point Wendy finally learns that Janis is her mom, clearing the air for a salutory finale. "[She] handles the thankless role with persuasion," Howard Barnes of the *New York Herald-Tribune* admitted of Wendy's disillusioned heroine, but it was Janis who gave this lackluster quickie its more than passing value. It proved to be that *Women in War* was the first and last sound feature film of fifty-one-year-old Janis, the former musical-comedy stage star who had become a film scenarist in the 1930s as well as appearing in some Vitaphone talkie shorts.

Recalling the comfortable success of *Love on a Bet* (1936), RKO's prolific budget producer Lee Marcus came up with *Cross-Country Romance* (1940), which was an even closer carbon-copy of the semi-screwball comedy *It Happened One Night*. On the day of her wedding Wendy has a sudden change of heart, much to the chagrin of her high-society-matron mother, Hedda Hopper. Practical-minded Wendy disappears from the ceremonies-to-be and boards the car trailer of doctor Gene Raymond, which (for plot purposes) is conveniently parked on the outskirts of her estate. She tells the westbound medico that her name is Aggie Jones and she is the poor daughter of a drunk. Completing her manufactured tale of woe, she insists she must get to her uncle's home in Pittsburgh. Raymond is a naturally obliging sort and the two set out on their jaunt. They share unusual adventures, fall in love, quarrel and make up, and travel and travel. Even the discovery that Wendy is really the headlined altar-snatched heiress is not a permanent obstacle to the eventual marital bliss of Wendy and the proud, struggling Raymond. (Remember, this is the movies!) Wendy and Raymond (who had recently changed his hair color to a darker shade) performed well together, even in the potentially sticky billing and cooing scenes. The undemanding *New York Daily Mirror* informed its readers: "This story is as old as the hills, but so is love, and both of them are mighty pleasant."

Men against the Sky (1940) suffered from the same basic flaw as many other economy pictures: the action sequences were more exciting—by comparison, that is—than the pallid characters. In this instance even Richard Dix, RKO's longstanding rugged star (now of programmers), could not instill much energy into the routine happenings. Cast as a former flying celebrity, Dix is now a lowly stunt flyer out on the country fair circuit, plagued by periodic drinking bouts. His sober, industrious sister Wendy (they certainly had no physical traits in common) determines to reform him. She joins the staff of West Coast plane manufacturer Edmund Lowe, a "breezy" promoter on the verge of bankruptcy. Wendy persuades Dix to feed her some new engineering concepts over which he has been mulling, and these ideas she passes on to the factory's chief designer (who else but RKO contract player Kent Taylor?). Within seventy-one minutes, Dix is redeemed, Lowe has a new high-speed plane to offer consumers, and Wendy and Taylor have found romance. To his credit, director Les Goodwins did provide the proper atmosphere for vigorous aerial sequences.

Wendy rounded off her 1940 feature film output with *Who Killed Aunt Maggie?*, one of Republic's rare and not very successful excursions into the murder mystery genre. Manhattan advertising executive John Hubbard marries ace radio-writer Wendy, but they fight and separate on their wedding day. Wendy receives word from Aunt Maggie Ambler (Elizabeth Patterson) to come immediately to the family home at Wistaria Hall, for Great Uncle Charles is gravely ill. Meanwhile, doctor Walter Abel, a relative of the Amblers, warns Hubbard that Wendy is headed for grave trouble. Hubbard rushes to the spooky Wistaria Hall, located in an out-of-the-way Georgia town, not only to find that uncle Charles has died but also that his body has disappeared. The will names Wendy as primary beneficiary of Charles's estate, which is to be held in trust until Patterson's death. None of which pleases the other relatives, including Onslow Stevens, Joyce Compton, and Abel's wife, Mona Barrie. Suddenly Patterson is found strangled and Wendy seems the likely suspect, at least in the eyes of bumpkin sheriff Edgar Kennedy. But Wendy, and subsequently Hubbard, are convinced that Patterson's lifelong search for a hidden treasure-room in the mansion is tied into the crime. None other than the cat Yehudi leads Wendy to the mysterious chamber and to the solution of the homicide. *Who Killed Aunt Maggie?* traced its copycat origins back to the genre prototypes, *The Bat* and *The Cat and the Canary*, especially the finely mounted 1939 Paramount film version of the latter. In fact Republic went so far as to utilize Willie Best from Paramount's follow-up Gothic thriller, *The Ghost Catcher* (1940), as an eye-rolling, quaking butler. He was the best thing about *Who Killed Aunt Maggie?*

Meanwhile Wendy, who had taken out her first papers on February 7,

1939, became an American citizen on January 9, 1941, a little more than six and one-half years after she first came to the United States.

By the time of RKO's *The Saint in Palm Springs* (1941), George Sanders's fifth and final impersonation of sleuth Simon Templar, *Variety* was forced to report that "[the series] needs better and fresher story material than provided here, or he will be a forgotten man with film audiences in the secondary houses." The resultant picture was very typical both of the hackneyed product that was foisted on the public and of the performance level required by Wendy in such productions.

No sooner does the Saint arrive in New York aboard the S.S. *Morovia* than inspector Jonathan Hale asks the assistance of the gentleman sleuth. An old friend of the law-enforcer is passing through Manhattan with three Vienna 1856 penny stamps worth over $200,000 which were smuggled out of Europe. The traveler is murdered before Sanders can get in touch with him, and Sanders agrees to "escort" the stamps to their proper recipient: the murdered man's niece (Wendy), who is a tennis instructor at the Twin Palms Hotel in Palm Springs, California. On the transcontinental train trip he just happens to meet Linda Hayes, a junior Ann Sheridan type who later proves to be in the pay of foreign agents. More than one-third of the picture is over before Wendy makes her first appearance, initially seen on the resort's tennis courts giving instruction. Sanders spots the girl, who is wearing a knee-length white sports coat and a white scarf in her hair. "Well, she's charming," says the Saint.

After the Saint tells Wendy of her uncle's death and is nonplused at discovering that he no longer has the three valuable stamps in his possession, she gives him exactly twenty-four hours to return the stamps. She is sufficiently *au courant* to know the Saint's reputation for being a trouble-brewer and a not always happy participant on the side of the law. Later, after police officer Chick Chandler has been murdered at the resort, the Saint realizes he no longer can dawdle and must push his detective resources to the limit to solve the caper. Intermittently Wendy reappears in the story, more as an animate object to request a progress report than as a breathing character. "Did you get them?"—"You really found them"—"Oh" are typical full lines of Wendy's dialog at this point. In the fashion of the typical stage ingenue she wears a pants lounge suit and toys endlessly with the outfit's accompanying scarf.

The one scene in which the repartee between Wendy and Sanders begins to spark occurs late one evening as they are strolling about the resort, engaging in conversation heavily laced with double-entendres.

Sanders: "My forehand isn't what it might be . . . perhaps I move too slowly . . . "

Wendy: "Possibly . . . We've got to have the right partner."

Sanders: "Not doubles. Singles are my game."

All of which is the Saint's roundabout way of establishing that, though he finds Wendy exceedingly attractive and her personality very congenial, he has no intention of settling down professionally or domestically.

Seemingly hard put to pad out the sixty-six-minute programmer, director Jack Hively has several montage sequences of Sanders, Wendy, and the ever-present Linda Hayes (she and Wendy spark antagonism from the start) horseback riding, bicycle riding, tennis playing, and so forth. Sometimes, as in *The Saint in Palm Springs*, Wendy's nonchalant personality did not quite fit the supposed characteristics of her oncamera character. Here she is required to be a rather timorous girl, incapable of mastering the situation when less agile Hayes pulls a gun on her, which seems kind of silly, for Wendy's appearance gave every indication that she was physically able to grab the pistol away from her more decorous adversary. Thus when Wendy kittenishly warns Sanders, "Don't be late. I doubt if my nerves can stand it," the film's believability is stretched a bit thinner than even undemanding audiences should have to accept.

For her final scenes in the picture, costumer Renie provided Wendy with a fetching riding outfit: black pants, white blouse, and a white south-of-the-border-style cowboy hat. At this point Hayes has been murdered, with Wendy and the Saint's trusty but bumbling pal (Paul Guilfoyle) kidnapped by the culprits. Sanders brings the police to the last-minute rescue. With the crooks in hand, the Saint has a moment to parry further with the grateful Wendy. The sleuth asks Wendy not to bother verbalizing her appreciation. "I won't try to, thank you," she lightly says, but the romantic sparkle in her eyes reveals she has in mind a more physical means of showing her thanks. But the Saint is too fast for her, reminding Wendy, "A few more lessons and I'm liable to forget that singles have always been my game."

Then, stealing the closing gimmick from "The Lone Ranger" radio show, the Saint rides off into the desert sunset, with Wendy and Guilfoyle watching the departing figure with admiration and wistfulness.

Even with the typically brief three-week production schedule for a picture like *The Saint in Palm Springs*, it is doubtful that Wendy's role required her presence on the soundstage for more than half that period, for even though she was always second-billed as the female lead in these programmers, her parts were never primary to the plot. As mentioned before, Wendy's strongest assets in portraying these shadowy roles were her healthy good looks (still intact at age twenty-nine); her well-established offscreen pedigree, which helped to bolster the authority of her portrayals; and her persistently radiant good nature, which rarely betrayed any dissatisfaction with the limited scope of her RKO ventures, whether regarding pictures or roles.

There was definitely no fanfare involved with RKO's *Repent at Leisure* (1941).* Department-store general manager Kent Taylor carries on a bus-stop courtship with Wendy, not realizing she is his boss's daughter. They soon wed and as a result of his industry at the office he receives several promotions. But when the proud lad learns of Wendy's parentage he resigns in

*Otis Ferguson in the *New Republic* observed of this wartime picture: "Movie writers are hard put to it these days to concoct something that is (1) national defense (2) no offense to anyone, and so an affair like this gets into a B producer's schedule almost automatically."

a huff and accepts a post with the competition. Meanwhile Wendy and Taylor have adopted an infant who almost dies in a tumble down an elevator shaft. This near tragedy causes the couple to reconcile. Fade-out. By this stage of her film career Wendy could handle such unimaginative, repetitious roles in her sleep; it was a wonder and a blessing that she did not appear to be doing just that.

During 1940 and early 1941 RKO had been experiencing increasing difficulties with Leslie Charteris, author of the original *Saint* stories. Production of the detective series was shifted to England in early 1941 with Hugh Sinclair as the intrepid detective. When contretemps with Charteris still persisted, the studio decided to drop the *Saint* series and to hatch a carbon-copy detective whom the public hopefully would endorse as wholeheartedly as the *Saint*. For a modest sum the rights to Michael Arlen's detective character, the Falcon, were acquired,* and an original screenplay was devised to introduce the new amateur law-enforcer. Produced during June-July, 1941, *The Gay Falcon* debuted in October, 1941. RKO rightly reasoned that there was no better way to establish a "kinship" between the late, lamented Saint and the new Falcon than by having their contract lead George Sanders carry on in the new role, and for good luck to have his frequent co-star Wendy Barrie appear in the new entry. Here the Falcon, now a Wall Street stock-broker, is engaged to Anne Hunter, who wants nothing better than to domesticate her suave beau. But the Falcon still has a very roving eye, and when attractive, single Wendy appears at his apartment begging his assistance, he just cannot resist embarking on a new caper, although his dopey assistant Goldy (Allen Jenkins) insists Wendy should better try Ellery Queen as he is determined to keep his boss far away from "dames and crime."

Sanders makes an appearance at the charity party being given by Wendy's employer (Gladys Cooper). Just as Wendy has predicted there is trouble at the shindig, for Lucille Gleason, after mistakenly slipping Sanders her diamond ring, is shot and killed by an unknown assailant. Naturally police captain Arthur Shields believes Sanders and Jenkins are involved in the homicide, which leads the duo to track down the real murderer. Throughout the proceedings there is a jocular tongue-in-cheek rapport between Sanders and Wendy, the latter used as a means to make Anne Hunter jealous and less possessive. Whether being kissed by Sanders or helping the detective rifle through a suspect's apartment, Wendy was more animated in this picture than previous screenplays had allowed her to be. One of the characteristics of Wendy's Helen Wood in *The Gay Falcon* is that she is forever fainting, both as a result of Sanders's kissing technique and when being unexpectedly confronted by crook Turhan Bey. Wendy just did not look like the type of fragile female who would give in to that kind of emotional ploy. After the caper is solved, Sanders suavely cons Hunter into re-establishing their en-

---

*$5,490 according to facts uncovered by cinema researchers Karl and Sue Thiede in their *Views and Reviews* magazine article, "The Falcon Saga."

gagement, but no sooner does this occur than a very comely girl enters the room imploring the Falcon for his professional help. At the fade-out, good sport Wendy turns to baffled Hunter, once again abandoned by her spouse-to-be, and jauntily asks, "If you're not doing anything tonight, how about a game of gin rummy?" The *Philadelphia Evening Ledger*'s reviewer was among those who voted Wendy the "ideal girl to take along on a man hunt." This "award" documented again the point that people have tended to forget in the intervening decades: throughout her film career, in A-pictures or crummy programmers, Wendy was always regarded as a pert, convivial lass whose lack of dramatic expertise was more than compensated for by her *joie de vivre*, which overcame the shortcomings of her assignments. She may never have been the onscreen darling of upper-class sophisticates, but for action-film audiences, Wendy was a proper dish of tea.

Public Enemies (1941) was Republic's economy version of Twentieth Century-Fox's glossy *Love Is News* (1937), which had starred Tyrone Power and Loretta Young. Police reporter Phillip Terry, hot on the heels of an underworld smuggling ring, becomes involved in the madcap activities of society heiress Wendy. She is so annoyed by Terry's glib interference with her shenanigans that she plants a false story about him, which costs the lad his job. Conscience-stricken by her rash act of revenge, she attempts to assist him in cracking the racketeer syndicate, and finds herself kidnapped by the gang. Along with Edgar Kennedy and William Frawley, who played two humorous ex-cops, Wendy gave the B-picture whatever lift was possible.

A Date with the Falcon, lensed in August-September, 1941, and released in January, 1942, found George Sanders, Wendy, Allen Jenkins, and Eddie Dunn repeating their roles from *The Gay Falcon*. This second entry introduced James Gleason as New York police inspector Mike O'Hara; like his predecessors, he easily assumed that any time Sanders and life intertwined, crime was sure to result. Now that America was involved in World War II there was a legitimate use of espionage and other such topical subjects weaved into the plotline, here involving the kidnapping of the inventor of a new process for making synthetic diamonds, a most valuable wartime industrial commodity. Underworld character Mona Maris invites the Falcon to join her organization. He refuses, but realizes he is hot on the trail of locating the missing inventor. By this episode Wendy was now the Falcon's fiancée, and she is furious that her intended has embarked on a new caper. She reminds the Falcon's dumb Man Friday (Allen Jenkins) that three previous girlfriends of the gentleman sleuth had gotten him to buy engagement rings, but none of them had ever landed the mercurial playboy. While Wendy is busily tracking down her nimble boyfriend, Sanders has allowed himself to be captured by Maris's associates, led by sinister Victor Kilian. Before long Sanders has tricked sultry Maris into disposing of Kilian and has maneuvered the police into capturing the remaining criminal-ring members. At the fade-out, never very cleverly obscured, Wendy and Sanders are finally ready to start off on their delayed trip to meet her parents, with the long-planned-for wedding drawing closer—or is it?

"One of the greatest dangers to any motion picture actress," Wendy warned in an early 1940s press interview, "lies in her becoming so wrapped up in her work that she becomes 100% actress and forgets that she is a woman . . . I am just another girl who hopes someday to be happily married and have a home and children and lead a ordinary, normal, human life; exactly, in fact, what every normal girl hopes and dreams for." But not every or any normal girl was then dating Benjamin "Bugsy" Siegel, head of the Los Angeles branch of Murder, Inc., and the reputed West Coast head of the Mafia. When organized crime infiltrated the motion picture industry in the 1930s, Siegel had changed his base of operations from New York City to Los Angeles, where he soon was traveling in the fastest and flashiest Hollywood social circles. He rented the Holmsby Hill home of Grace Tibbett, the ex-wife of Metropolitan Opera singer Lawrence Tibbett, and soon was ensconced as a popular, if freak, attraction in the movie colony. Siegel's participation in a vast array of gangland activities was always the source of police and public speculation, but not until the brutal slaying of racketeer Big Greenie on November 24, 1939 (on North Vista Del Mar Avenue), did the Los Angeles law-enforcers think they had a solid case to launch against Siegel. He was indicted on a felony charge in November, 1940, which his famed attorney, Jerry Giesler, maneuvered to have dismissed. During these headlined on-again, off-again legal proceedings, Siegel spent some seven weeks in a Los Angeles jail. Not that he allowed this "arrest" to interfere with his hectic social-business life. It was later determined that he had donated over $32,000 to jail officials so that he could be at liberty at will to visit his Beverly Hills dentist, or so he claimed. When pinned down for more concrete facts, Siegel's regular jail guard admitted that on at least one of these eighteen jail leaves (during a given forty-nine-day period) Siegel had lunched with Wendy at Lindy's Restaurant on Wilshire Boulevard. (The guard never did explain where else Siegel had gone during his other "medical leaves" from his jail cell.) Wendy's long-standing romance with Siegel would be capped on March 4, 1943, when she announced her engagement to him. For whatever reason, their relationship thereafter drifted apart and they never did wed.* At any rate, it was right out of *Johnny Eager*, even if Wendy was not Lana Turner, nor Siegel a Robert Taylor.

Meanwhile, Wendy's film career drifted to an end. To wrap up her RKO

---

*Siegel later spread his activities into Las Vegas and was reputed to have roused the ire of the Mafia overlords by subsequently deciding he was the true and sole head of the West Coast operations. On June 13, 1954, he was found shot to death in the home of girlfriend Virginia Hill at 810 Linden Drive, Beverly Hills. His unknown assailants were never traced by the police. Currently, Richard D. Zanuck is planning to produce, for Universal release, a screenplay based on the life and times of Bugsy Siegel, but Wendy's relationship with the gangland czar will not be covered.

contract, she was loaned to Universal for *Eyes of the Underworld* (1942), teamed again with her past RKO co-star Richard Dix. The plot twist involved an aggressive police chief (Dix) determined to halt the rash of crime in his bailiwick. When the law nabs tire and automobile thief Marc Lawrence, the latter recognizes Dix as a former fellow jailmate. Rather than be blackmailed about his unfortunate past, Dix resigns his post. But aided by bodyguard Lon Chaney, Jr. he manages to bring the gang to justice.

Over at RKO, Sir Cedric Hardwicke and the other guiding spirits of the British colony in Hollywood had been preparing *Forever and a Day* (1943). This feature-length paean to the noble British spirit had been in actual production for well over a year, utilizing the services of acting and technical talent as time and facilities permitted. One of the bigger cameo roles in this historical narrative went to Britisher Anna Neagle, who was still in Hollywood making RKO features with her producer-director husband, Herbert Wilcox. The thread holding together this motion picture pageant was the home built by C. Aubrey Smith in 1804, with the picture tracing the various people who occupied the dwelling during the decades right up to World War II. The top-featured stars in *Forever and a Day* included, besides Miss Neagle, Brian Aherne, Ida Lupino, Ray Milland, Robert Cummings, Herbert Marshall, and two of Wendy's *Henry VIII* co-players, Charles Laughton and Merle Oberon. As a matter of fact, Wendy's perpetual B-picture background gave her such little industry standing that she was not even listed among the thirty-six first-billed performers. Wendy was merely seen in passing in the Golden Jubilee sequence as one of Isobel Elsom's two grown-up daughters. Edith (Wendy) and her sister Julia (June Duprez) were shown in their bedroom primping to watch Queen Victoria's historic procession pass by their Pomfret Street home. Clad in her undergarments, and with her braided hair tossed over her right shoulder, Wendy spent most of her brief oncamera moments manicuring her fingernails as she chitchats to Duprez about their unpredictable brother, Wendell Hulett. In fact, most of this scene belonged to Ida Lupino, who as one of the household maids is both in a pickle over her romantic life and busily trying to jump up and peek over the shoulders of the street crowd to witness the goings-on.

Then along came *Follies Girl* (1943), a very minor musical from the poverty-row assembly line of Producers Releasing Corp. In lazy fashion the streamlined production told of a creative dress designer (Wendy) who tangles with her boss's son (Gordon Oliver) and not only wins the soldier's affection but the top professional spot in the firm. Meanwhile, her eccentric boss (J. C. Nugent) has satisfied his ambition to present a burlesque revue on Broadway with Francine La Rue (Doris Nolan) starring in it as the Queen of Showgirls. To give this haphazard movie some timeliness, some of the musical interludes—and there was an overabundance of song-dance-band acts—were situated at a servicemen's canteen. Whatever novelty was possessed by the film's slim premise was dissipated by the company's long delay in releasing the feature, for by October, 1943, filmgoers had witnessed the much more elaborate (and star-laden) *Stage Door Canteen* and Barbara Stanwyck's *Lady of Burlesque*, which employed facets of *Follies Girl*'s plot to far better advantage. In her walk-through role Wendy was criticized for her "pat performance" (*Variety*).

Submarine Alert was produced by Paramount's budget-department specialists, William Pine and William Thomas, during the hectic era of World War II, when situations changed daily. Completed well over fifteen months before the studio tossed it onto the double-bill market in October, 1943, it emerged a badly dated piece of melodrama on the wrong end of a cycle of spy tales. By use of a secret portable shortwave-radio transmitter, Nazi agents were staking out Japanese submarines to sink American tankers in the Pacific. Government agent Richard Arlen is ordered to maneuver himself into the confidence of the spies and destroy the transmitter. Wendy was FBI operative Ann Patterson, who comes to Arlen's rescue in the nick of time in true cliffhanger fashion.

Much before *Submarine Alert* made its belated public appearance, Wendy had called it quits on her decade-old cinema career. She rightly believed she had milked her screen potential to the fullest, and at age thirty-one she did not feel herself physically equipped to compete with the rash of newcomers barraging RKO and the other studios for contract berths. She was definitely a product of pre-World War II living, when being a socialite was sufficient credential for crashing into most any profession with assurance of tacit acceptance by the particular peer group and the public at large. But the 1940s were to see a further fragmenting of the social-class system, and now to a much lesser degree were doors automatically opened or kept from later closing to well-bred young ladies who hankered for excitement beyond their Mayfair-Park Avenue spheres of operation.

Although Wendy was content to abrogate her film career, she was not convinced she should put her show business fling entirely behind her. There was untapped mileage in other mediums to provide income and still-appreciable social entrees. Thus she made the traditional trek from Hollywood to Broadway, where it was assumed her marquee name would not be entirely lost on the theatre-going public. She had already made her American stage debut in the summer of 1941, playing in *Quiet Wedding* at Cambridge, Massachusetts. She was thus hired for a co-lead role in Emlyn Williams's *Morning Star*, which had already had a healthy London run. Unfortunately, in its transatlantic crossing it had lost most of its success quotient. Set in blitzed London, *Morning Star* presented Gregory Peck as the wayward doctor-son of matriarch Gladys Cooper. He is tempted to leave his conventional wife for nitwit blonde Wendy,* but eventually realizes the foolishness of this idea. After unpromising out-of-town tryouts, the drama, staged by Guthrie McClintock, opened at the Morosco Theatre on September 14, 1942—it folded after twenty-four performances. The critics found

*Ambrosine Phillpot had Wendy's role in the London version.

little merit in *Morning Star* as a whole or in Wendy's performance as the shallow, babbling gadabout. "[She] left me cold," claimed Howard Barnes (*New York Herald-Tribune*), while Brooks Atkinson (*New York Times*) was a bit more tactful: "Wendy Barrie is handsomely and expensively impossible."

Morning Star did not provide a new career path for Wendy, but New York living seemed a refreshing change from Hollywood, and Wendy—always adaptable—made Manhattan her new headquarters. Just to keep her finger in the show business pie, she accepted a co-hosting spot on CBS Radio's Wednesday-night quiz show, "Detect and Collect," emceed by rotund Lew Lehr.*

Then, to the surprise of all her new and old acquaintances, Wendy finally married. On June 5, 1945, she wed New York textile manufacturer David L. Meyers, who shared her avid interest in sports—golf in particular. In fact, it was through Meyers that Wendy was launched into her television career. Part of her ritual as the wife of a well-to-do businessman was to participate in country-club golfing. With her athletic prowess, she proved especially talented and was soon shooting eighteen holes in the low eighties and entering amateur tournaments with good results. In May, 1948, golf pro Johnny Farrell invited Wendy to appear on his video sports show, televised over the Dumont Network's flagship, WABD. In those early years of commercial television, self-conscious, stiff-lipped zombies were too often the accepted order of the day, and Wendy's guest-shot appearance proved a refreshing, effervescent change. WABD executives were quick to offer Wendy a hostessing job on the first available program. It happened to be a kiddie show, and that is why she made her full-fledged video debut as the mistress of ceremonies, moderator, and chief entertainer of "Okey Dokey Ranch," a half-hour daily outing. It was for her juvenile audience that Wendy initially coined the expression "Be a good bunny," which for better or worse became her trademark phrase throughout her many television years ahead.

Wendy's chores on this toddler program lasted only six weeks, but the disciplined routine was a tough contrast to her several years of easy living. "It nearly killed me," she candidly confessed, "too much work." Although she was certainly more accustomed to performing for adult audiences, she did admit that the youngsters attending her daily telecasts were live-wires. "At least they'd spit in your face or something."

Dumont did not need to be prodded by Wendy to realize that her forte was helming adult fare, and soon she graduated to hostessing the "Inside Photoplay" program and then was handed her own thirty-minute-a-day afternoon talk-show, soon amassing a steady home-audience following. But Dumont was not satisfied with Wendy just handling this successful berth. They reasoned that since she had been a Hollywood actress, why not feature her in dramatic fare. She was duly cast in a Dumont network dramatic program, portraying a woman killed by her husband because she had a terrible-

---

*Wendy had first appeared on radio in 1938 in several Hollywood-based variety programs.

sounding voice as a result of an adenoid condition. The critics panned Wendy as severely as the inept playlet. Nevertheless, Wendy, the new celebrity of the telewaves, had a marketable name in the new medium, and rival CBS-TV offered her the lead in a projected teleseries based on *Topper*. Wendy refused the lucrative offer, exclaiming, "Why should I try to act when they don't even know I'm acting?"

But Wendy was astute enough to know that Dumont was only a beginning and that she could easily obtain a plusher berth at another network if she waited. She did not have to sit around long, for ABC-TV rose to the occasion and provided her with her own talk-show. She was pleased by the status elevation: "Really, pet. Feel like dear Milton Berle." Her new program debuted on September 12, 1949. Having moved to a more prestigous network, Wendy was duly advised to make her program a more orderly procession. But from the first show onward Wendy was her irrepressible self. ABC-TV had foolishly booked "camp" movie actor Sonny Tufts as her initial guest, which did not please outspoken Wendy one little bit. As prearranged, during the course of the program Tufts was scheduled to play on the drums and cymbals. Wendy, no fan of Tufts, made it very evident to viewers. When he commenced his percussion demonstration, she simply grimaced straight into the camera and then turned full about in her hostess chair and began playing a game of solitaire. Her point was made. Thereafter she chose her own guests, one being actor Marlon Brando, who gave one of his rare interviews on her program.

For those who do not recall madcap Wendy at her television best, Val Adams (*New York Times*) has preserved in writing one of her typical Wednesday-night-at-eight outings from November, 1949: "Wendy Barrie is probably the only television personality who frequently sits on the floor and talks to the viewers. Sometimes she runs the palm of her hand over the rug, patting it gently, and reveals a sudden thought right out loud, 'Gee this would be a great show for a rug sponsor.'" Wendy, a recognized pioneer in the new medium, was not to be toyed with by her network bosses. On one occasion, a bandleader was scheduled as a guest for fifteen long minutes on her show, so ABC could kinescope his segment as an inexpensive pilot to show sponsors. Wendy realized that the guest-to-be was not equipped to entertain viewers for five minutes, let alone fifteen. She offered to buy out the time in order to avoid the wasteland of entertainment she knew would occur, but ABC remained adamant, and the guest went on. Wendy had the final word: she revealed the entire situation to her viewers. On yet another occasion the network decided that Wendy should be shown at her multitalented best. It was felt Wendy's verbal versatility should be matched by musical talent, no matter that she did not play the piano or sing much. Studio executives engineered a video effect that would provide home viewers with the illusion that Wendy was an expert at the ivory keyboards (by blending her image, seated at the piano, with the televised offstage hands of a real pianist). In the midst of this chicanery, Wendy grew bored and resentful. So she plopped her elbows on top of the piano, while offstage the substitute keyboard artist played merrily on.

Wendy continued her ABC-TV stint until late 1950 when her program went off the air. When irate viewers wrote in to the network demanding to know why "their Wendy" was no longer on the air, it was suggested that the show had folded because her sponsor, the Celanese Corporation, makers of aluminum storm windows, had withdrawn its backing (due to the metal shortage occasioned by the Korean War rearmament). Meanwhile Wendy continued to guest on variety programs until March 2, 1951, when ABC provided her with a new Friday night 8:15 P.M. program, again sponsored by the Celanese folks. New York City Mayor Impellitteri and his wife were her first guests.

Although Wendy was at the peak of her video popularity as a forerunner in a field that would soon be crowded with equally vivacious but more persistent souls like Faye Emerson, Virginia Graham, Maggie McNellis, and Lee Graham, her domestic life had long since reached an impasse. She separated from her husband on December 27, 1949, and on April 24, 1950, obtained a Reno divorce. The divorce decree provided that she would receive $400-a-month alimony as long as she did not remarry; but it was not the end of her involvement with Meyers, for in October, 1952, she filed a $250,000 slander suit against her former husband, charging that while he was vacationing at his Florida home he had told the press on three separate occasions that Wendy was openly domiciled with and supporting Cappy Smith, of the race-track set. The headlined case was eventually settled out of court, as was her later suit against a southern hotel, which she visited in 1951 and where she had lost $17,000 worth of jewelry.

At age forty Wendy was still much in demand as a celebrity figure and was often quoted in the press on her views, as when she philosophized: "The only important thing in life is caring for someone who belongs to you." Who that someone might be, she never defined. She confessed that she was very chummy with Joe, the barber at the Waldorf Astoria Hotel, and often went to his Brooklyn home to eat spaghetti and garlic prepared by his family. As the friendly press enjoyed pointing out, Wendy enjoyed chitchatting with her East Side apartment-house doorman as well as hobnobbing with her upper-crust pals.

As the 1950s progressed, Wendy began losing ground in the competition to be television's top video hostess. Her sponsored programs would start and stop, changing time and day frequently, but through it all Wendy remained her nonchalant, effervescent self. By 1954 she was no longer a big New York City video celebrity, but she still had a large following in the hinterland. As part of a $250,000 contract (terms undisclosed) she began in January, 1954, a daily sixty-minute talk-show in Dayton, Ohio, for the Tri-State Network. She was no longer the big banana of the telewaves.

In 1953 Wendy was seen in her last feature film to date. For Columbia, she appeared as a guest performer in Judy Holliday's wacky comedy *It*

Should Happen to You. Wendy was cast along with Ilka Chase, Constance Bennett (another ex-RKO celebrity), and Holliday as television-show panelists—with Melville Cooper as a John Daly-like moderator—interviewing guest Jack Lemmon.*

The following year Wendy was back in New York City with a new video girl-talk show on Channel 5,† and for a time she was a co-host on NBC-TV's "$64,000 Question." One of her Channel 5 showtime guests in July, 1956, was Lawrence Tibbett, her movie co-star of two decades before in *Under Your Spell.* She continued with her format program into 1958, most every segment finding her hugging a bunny, using her tried-and-true formula of helter-skelter questioning of guests (as one reviewer commented: "Garnished with bubbling impertinence and unbelievable naiveté, she manages to elicit a good deal of enlightening information"). There was talk of Wendy doing a new video show to be called "Wendy Barrie Movie Notebook," but it never materialized, nor did "Review," which was to have featured her as a moderator of a panel program discussing all phases of life with assorted experts.

Looking back on her video career, Wendy evaluated: "I was forced into it for money reasons. But I've never really enjoyed the work. It might have been different if I had found a cute one—a cute one that stands about six feet four."

Her last big headline splash occurred in August, 1958, when forty-two-year-old Mickey Lane (a.k.a. Melody Cazes), a former singer, was recommitted to Bellevue Hospital's psychiatric ward. Wendy had brought a co-complaint against Mickey Lane, charging that on a specific date Mickey had phoned her at least nineteen times between 1 and 4 A.M., shouting abuse and fighting over her supposed competitive attention to fifty-year-old captain of waiters Marco Schmoopee Cazes, Mickey Lane's ex-husband. That October there was a court hearing—more humorous than jurisprudential—at which time Mickey Lane screamed at her ex-spouse, "I subpoenaed you to help me and you turn around and try to have me committed." The press tactfully played up the comic elements of the case, ignoring the more lurid implications of the triangular love affair.

Thereafter Wendy only dabbled at work, preferring to venture into the sphere of aviation when a steady diet of party-going proved a bore. She took a flier on a Broadway-bound play in which she starred. It opened and closed in San Juan, Puerto Rico, in 1960. (She had previously done *The Rainmaker* at Atlantic Beach, New Jersey, in 1955.) She was chairman of the women's division of the Committee for Deborah Hospital in 1960, the same year she

---

*In 1970, when Gavin Lambert interviewed the film's director, George Cukor, and the two were discussing *It Should Happen to You*, Cukor recalled the cast of characters on the panel show in the film: In an amused tone of voice he asked Lambert, "And a former actress called Wendy Barrie. Remember her?"

†On Channel 5 Wendy was in competition with such other station talk-show hostesses as Virginia Graham and Maggie McNellis.

began a shortlived midnight talk-show on New York television's Channel 13 (her initial guest was Sandra Dee). Wendy's last acting stint to date was on the *Escape from Kaleandair* episode of ABC-TV's "The Islanders" (January 29, 1961), in which a much-aged Wendy cavorted to diminishing effect.

Wendy has continued to live in Manhattan, most frequently at an East 52nd Street apartment, which is chock-full of trophies from horse shows, golf tournaments, etc. As obeisance to show business, a field she never relished or took very seriously, Wendy returned to radio in the mid-1960s with a syndicated audio show broadcast from the Barbizon Plaza Hotel and distributed to some 365 radio outlets across the country. Like other audio talk-show commentators she played to the hilt the frequently debasing game of hounding the cocktail-party circuit hoping to lure intriguing new guests to appear for minimum-scale fees on her program in a medium relegated to third-best in America. Her last professional video job to date was in the late 1960s, when she turned up in a tacky Manhattan commercial for a West 57th Street thrift fur shop, modeling its second-hand wares. Viewing the amateurish television ad, one could only wonder what had happened to the pert Wendy of only a few years prior.

These days very little is seen of Wendy, save when she walks her dog along Sutton Place or attends an occasional party, at which time she is wont to come on strong with her boisterous, raucous self. As flippant, basic, and candid as ever, she is just as apt to poke a joke at some unsuspecting party guest as herself. Wendy attaches no oversized value to her past social status or to her former celebrity status as a movie or television performer. If stopped on the street by some middle-aged fan who vaguely connects the Wendy that once was, with the now very matronly Wendy of today, she is likely to sign the autograph with the mocking caption, "Look at the old hag now!"

Feature Film Appearances
WENDY BARRIE

COLLISION (UA, 1932) 88 M.

Director, G. B. Samuelson; based on the story by E. C. Pollard.

Sunday Wilshin (Mrs. Oliver); Henrietta Watson (Mrs. Carruthers); L. Tippett (Mr. Carruthers); A. G. Poulton (Mr. Maynard); Irene Rook (Mrs. Maynard); Gerry Rawlinson (Jack Carruthers); Peter Coleman (Brabazon); Wendy Barrie (Joyce).

THREADS (UA, 1932) 77 M.

Director, G. B. Samuelson.

Lawrence Anderson (John Osborne Wynn); Dorothy Fane (Ameila Wynn); Gerald Rawlinson (Arthur); Leslie Cole (James); Wendy Barrie (Olive Wynn); Ben Webster (Lord Grathers); Irene Rooke (Lady Grathers); Aileen Despard (Chloe); Pat Reid (Parsons); Clifford Cobbe (Jefferson Jordan); Walter Piers (Colonel Packinder).

THE CALL BOX MYSTERY (UA, 1932) 72 M.

Director, G. B. Samuelson; story, Joan Morgan; screenplay, Joan Wentworth Wood.

Harold French (Inspector Layton); Warwick Ward (Leo Mount); Harvey Braban (Inspector Brown); Wendy Barrie (Iris Banner); Daphne Mowbray (Rose); Tom Shenton (Pearce); Myno Burnet (Paul Grayle); Gerald Rawlinson (David Ranor).

WEDDING REHEARSAL (Ideal, 1932) 84 M.

Director, Alexander Korda; screenplay, Lajos Biro; dialog, Arthur Wimperis.

Roland Young (Marquis of Buckminister); George Grossmith (Lord Stokeshire); John Loder ("Bimbo"); Maurice Evans ("Tootles"); Wendy Barrie (Lady Mary Rose Stockshire); Joan Gardner (Lady Rosemary Stockshire); Merle Oberon (Miss Hutchinson); Lady Tree (Lady Stokeshire); Kate Cutler (Dowager Marchioness Of Buckminster); Edmund Breon (Lord Fleet); Lawrence Hanray (News Editor); Diana Napier (Mrs. Dryden); Morton Selten (Major Harry Roxbury).

WHERE IS THE LADY? (British Lion, 1932) 77 M.

Director, Lazlo Vajda, W. Victor Hanbury; adaptation, John Stafford; music, Franz Lehar.

Marta Eggert (Steffi Piringer); Owen Nares (Rudi Muller); Wendy Barrie (Lucie Kleiner); George K. Arthur (Gustl Linzer); Gibb McLaughlin (Dr. Schilling); Ellis Jeffreys (Frau Kleiner); Robert Hale (Herr Piringer); O. B. Clarence (Dr. Peffer).

THE BARTON MYSTERY (Par., 1932) 77 M.

Director, Henry Edwards; based on the play by Walter Hackett.

Ion Swinley (Richard Standish, M. P.); Ursula Jeans (Ethel Standish); O. B. Clarence (Sir Everard Marshall); Ellis Jeffreys (Lady Marshall); Lyn Harding (Beverley);

Wendy Barrie (Phyllis Grey); Joyce Bland (Helen Barton); Tom Helmore (Harry Maitland); Franklyn Bellamy (Gerald Barton); Wilfred Noy (Griffiths).

CASH   (Par.-London Films, 1933) 73 M.

Producer, Alexander Korda; director, Zoltan Korda; screenplay, Anthony Gibbs, Dorothy Greenhill, Arthur Wimperis.

Wendy Barrie (Lillian); Robert Donat (Paul Martin); Edmund Gwenn (Gilbert); Lawrence Grossmith (Joseph); Morris Harvey (Meyer); Clifford Heatherley (Hunt); Hugh E. Wright (Jordan); Anthony Holles (Inspector).

IT'S A BOY   (Gainsborough, 1933) 80 M.

Director, Tim Whelan; screenplay, Franz Arnold, Ernest Bach.

Leslie Henson (James Skippett); Albert Burdon (Joe Piper); Edward Everett Horton (Dudley Leake); Heather Thatcher (Anita Gunn); Alfred Drayton (Eustace Bogle); Robertson Hare (Allister); Wendy Barrie (Mary Bogle); Helen Haye (Mrs. Bogle); Joyce Kirby (Lillian); J. H. Roberts (Registrar).

THE PRIVATE LIFE OF HENRY VIII   (UA-London Films, 1933) 95 M.

Producer-director, Alexander Korda; screenplay, Lajos Biro, Arthur Wimperis; art director, Vincent Korda; costumes, John Armstrong; music, Kurt Schroeder; assistant director, Geoffrey Booth; sound, A. W. Watkins; camera, Georges Perinal; editor, Harold Young, Stephen Harrison.

Charles Laughton (Henry VIII); Robert Donat (Thomas Culpeper); Lady Tree (Henry's Old Nurse); Binnie Barnes (Katheryn Howard); Elsa Lanchester (Ann of Cleves); Merle Oberon (Anne Boleyn); Franklin Dyall (Cromwell); Miles Mander (Wriothesley); Wendy Barrie (Jane Seymour); Claude Allister (Cornell); John Loder (Thomas Peynell); Everley Gregg (Katherine Parr); Lawrence Hanray (Cranmer); William Austin (Duke of Cleves); John Turnbull (Holbein); Judy Kelly (Lady Rochford); Frederick Culley (Duke of Norfolk); Gibb McLaughlin (French Executioner); Sam Livesey (English Executioner).

THIS ACTING BUSINESS   (WB, 1933) 54 M.

Director, John Daumery.

Hugh Williams (Hugh); Wendy Barrie (Joyce); Donald Calthrop (Milton Stafford); Violet Fairbrother (Mary Kean); Charles Paton (Ward); Marie Wright (Mrs. Dooley).

THE HOUSE OF TRENT   (Butchers, 1933) 74 M.

Director, Norman Walker; screenplay, Billie Bristow, Charles Bennett.

Anne Grey (Rosemary); John Stuart (John Trent); Wendy Barrie (Angela); Peter Gawthorne (Lord Fairdown); Hope Davey (Joan); Norah Baring (Barbara); Herbert Harben (Editor); Moore Mariott (Ferrier); Jack Raine (Peter); Dora Gregory (Mary); Estelle Winwood (Charlotte); Hay Plumb (Foreman of the Jury); Victor Stanley (Spriggs); Humbertson Wright (Coachman).

MURDER AT THE INN   (WB, 1934) 55 M.

Director, George King; screenplay, Randall Faye.

Wendy Barrie (Angela); Harold French (Tony); Jane Carr (Fifi); Davy Burnaby (Colonel Worthing); Nicholas Hannen (Dedreet); H. Saxon-Snell (Inspector); Minnie Rayner (Aunt).

WITHOUT YOU   (Fox, 1934) 65 M.

Director-screenplay, W. Scott Darling.

Henry Kendall (Tony Bannister); Wendy Barrie (Molly Bannister); Margot Grahame (Margot Gilbey); Fred Duprez (Baron Gustav von Steinmeyer); George Harris (Harrigan); Billy Mayerl (Fink); Joe Hayman (Blodgett).

THE MAN I WANT   (MGM, 1934) 6,162′

Director, Leslie Hiscott.

Henry Kendall (Peter Mason); Wendy Barrie (Marion Round); Betty Astell (Prue Darrell); Davy Burnaby (Sir George Round); Wally Patch, Hal Walters (Crooks).

FREEDOM OF THE SEAS   (Associated British, 1934) 74 M.

Director, Marcel Varnell; based on the play by Walter C. Hackett; screenplay, Roger Bursford; art director, Cedric Dawe; technical advisor, Lieutenant Commander De Burgh, R.N.; sound, A. E. Rudolph; camera, Otto Kanturek; editor, Sidney Cole.

Clifford Mollison (Smith); Wendy Barrie (Phyllis Harcourt); Zelma O'Neal (Jennie); H. F. Maltby (Harcourt); Tyrell Davis (Cavendish); James Carew (Bottom); Cecil Ramage (Berkstrom); Henry Wenman (Wallace); Frederick Peisley (Jackson); Frank Atkinson (O'Hara); Charles Paton (Gamp).

THERE GOES SUSIE   (British International-Pathé, 1934) 70 M.

Producer-director, John Stafford, W. Victor Hanbury; based on the novel by Charlie Roellinghoff, Hans Jacoby; music, Otto Stransky, Niklos Schwalb; music director, Jack Beaver.

Gene Gerrard (Andre Cochet); Wendy Barrie (Madeleine Sarteaux); Zelma O'Neal (Bunny); Gus McNaughton (Brammel); Henry Wenman (Otto Sarteaux); Gibb McLaughlin (Advertising Manager); Bobby Comber (Uncle Oscar); Mark Daly (Sunshine).

GIVE HER A RING   (British International-Pathé, 1934) 79 M.

Producer-director, Arthur Woods; screenplay, Clifford Grey, Marjorie Deans, W. Wilhelm; art director, W. Macdonald Sutherland; music, Harry Acres; songs, Grey and Hans May; camera, Claude Friese-Greene, Ronald Neame; editor, E. B. Jarvis.

Clifford Mollison (Paul Hendrick); Wendy Barrie (Karen); Zelma O'Neal (Trude); Erik Rhodes (Otto Brune); Olive Blakeney (Mrs. Brune); Bertha Belmore (Supervisor); and: Diamond Brothers, Nadine March, Richard Hearne, Jimmy Godden, Stewart Granger.

IT'S A SMALL WORLD   (Fox, 1935) 70 M.

Producer, Edward Butcher; director, Irving Cummings; based on the novel *Highway Robbery* by Albert Treynor; screenplay, Samuel Hellman, Gladys Lehman; music, Arthur Lange; art director, William Darling; sound, S. C. Chapman; camera, Arthur Miller.

Spencer Tracy (Bill Shevlin); Wendy Barrie (Jane Dale); Raymond Walburn (Judge Julius B. Clummerhorn); Virginia Sale (Lizzie); Astrid Allwyn (Nancy Naylor); Irving Bacon (Cal); Charles Seldon (Cyclone); Dick Foran (Motor Cop); Belle Daube (Mrs. Dale); Frank McGlynn, Sr. (Snake Brown, Jr.); Frank McGlynn, Jr. (Snake Brown III); Bill Gillis (Snake Brown, Sr.); Edwin Brady (Buck Bogardus); Harold Minjir (Freddie Thompson); Charles R. Moore (Doorman); Frank Austin, Bob McKinsey, Sam Adams, Lew King, F. M. Watson, W. H. Davis (Bits).

COLLEGE SCANDAL   (Par., 1935) 76 M.

Producer, Albert Lewis; director, Elliott Nugent; story, Beulah Marie Dix, Bertram Milhauser; screenplay, Frank Partos, Charles Brackett, Marguerite Roberts; song, Sam Coslow; camera, Theodore Sparkuhl; editor, William Shea.

Arline Judge (Sally Dunlap); Kent Taylor (Seth Dunlap); Wendy Barrie (Julie Fresnel); William Frawley (Chief of Police Magoun); Benny Baker ("Cuffie" Lewis); William Benedict ("Penny" Parker); Mary Nash (Mrs. Fresnel); Edward J. Nugent (Jake Lansing); William Stack (Dr. Henri Fresnel); Johnny Downs (Paul Gedney); Robert Kent (Dan Courtridge); Joyce Compton (Toby Carpenter); Samuel S. Hinds (Mr. Cummings); Douglas Wood (Dean Traynor); Margaret Armstrong (Dean Elton); Edith Arnold (Posey); Helena Phillips Evans (Melinda); Mary Ellen Brown (Marjorie); Stanley Andrews (Jim, The Fingerprint Man); Samuel T. Godfrey (Doctor); Clarence Geldert (Jury Foreman); Oscar Smith (Generation Jones); Frances Raymond (House Mother); Oscar Rudolph (Olson); Isabelle La Mal (Club Woman); Albert Taylor (Girl's Father); Lillianne Leighton (Fat Lady); Antrim Short (Gas Station Attendant).

THE BIG BROADCAST OF 1936   (Par., 1935) 97 M.

Producer, Benjamin Glazer; director, Norman Taurog; story-adaptation, Walter DeLeon, Francis Martin, Ralph Spence; choreography, LeRoy Prinz; songs, Leo Robin and Richard Whiting; Robin, Whiting, and Rainger; Robin and Rainger; Sam Coslow and Arthur Johnston; Ray Noble; camera, Leo Tover; editor, Ellsworth Hoagland.

Jack Oakie (Speed); George Burns (George); Gracie Allen (Gracie); Lyda Roberti (Countess Ysobel de Naigila); Wendy Barrie (Sue); Henry Wadsworth (Smiley); C. Henry Gordon (Gordonio); Benny Baker (Herman); Bing Crosby, Ethel Merman, Richard Tauber (Themselves); Amos 'n Andy (Grocery Clerks); Mary Boland (Mrs. Sealingsworth); Charles Ruggles (Mr. Sealingsworth); David Holt (Brother); Virginia Weidler (Sister); Sir Guy Standing (Doctor); Gail Patrick (Nurse); Bill Robinson (Dancer); Ray Noble (Band Leader); Ina Ray Hutton (Band Leader); Harold and Fayard Nicholas (Dot And Dash); Vienna Choir Boys (Choir); Akim Tamiroff (Boris); Samuel S. Hinds (Captain); Willy West and McGinty (Builders).

A FEATHER IN HER HAT   (Col., 1935) 73 M.

Director, Alfred Santell; based on the novel by I. A. R. Wylie; screenplay, Lawrence Hazard; assistant director, C. C. Coleman; art director, Stephen Goosson; costumes, Murray Mayer; sound, George Cooper; camera, Joseph Walker; editor, Viola Lawrence.

Pauline Lord (Clarissa Phipps); Basil Rathbone (Captain Courtney); Louis Hayward (Richard Orland); Billie Burke (Julia Trent Anders); Wendy Barrie (Pauline Anders); Nydia Westman (Emily Judson); Victor Varconi (Paul Anders); Thurston Hall (Sir Elroyd Joyce); Nana Bryant (Lady Drake); J. M. Kerrigan (Pobjoy); Lawrence Grant (Dr. Phillips); Doris Lloyd (Liz Vining); David Niven (Leo Cartwright); John Rogers (Henry Vining); E. E. Clive (Higgins, Proprietor Of Pub); Leonard Mudie (Orator); Harry Allen (Alf); Ottola Nesmith (Susan); Tempe Pigott (Katy); Lois Lindsey, Carrie Daumery, Mrs. Wilfrid North, Joyce Colby, Reba Phillips, Eleanor Huntly, Gladys Gale, Dorothy Johnson, Connie Leon, Mildred Hardy, Phyllis Coghlan (Women); Leyland Hodgson (Leading Man); Montague Shaw, Henry Mowbray, Richard Lancaster, Lowden Adams, Phillips Smalley, Major Sam Harris, Lorimer Johnson, Ivan Christy, Frank Ward, Bruce Wyndham, Frank Benson, J. Gunnis Davis (Men); David Dunbar (Truck Driver); Herbert Heywood (Fish Monger); Thomas R. Mills, Robert Cory (Stage Managers); Peggy Wynne (Cockney Woman); Ambrose Barker, John Power, Sonny Roe, D'Arcy Corrigan, George Bunny (Cockney Men); James May

(Butcher); Fred Walton (Heckler); Jimmy Aubrey, Olaf Hytten (Taxi Drivers); William Martin (Richard—as a boy); Alma Chester (Mrs. Wheeler); Elsie Prescott (Mrs. Guernsey); Aggie Steele (Mrs. Probert); Captain John Van Eyck (Hospital Attendant); Gordie Mackay (Messenger Boy); Dan Maxwell (Driver); Doreen Munroe (Mrs. Pobjoy); Kay Deslys (Barmaid); Wilson Benge (Butcher); Robert Hale (Cab Driver); Gil Perkins (Ticket Taker); Larry Dodds (Ticket Seller); Nellie St. Clair, Minnie Steele (Scrub Women); Douglas Gordon (Intern); Vivien Patterson, Corinne Williams (Nurse); John Irwin (Bouncer).

MILLIONS IN THE AIR (Par., 1935) 71 M.

Producer, Harold Hurley; director, Ray McCarey; story-adaption, Sig Herzig, Jane Storm; songs, Leo Robin and Ralph Rainger; Billy Rose and Cliff Friend; camera, Harry Fishbeck; editor, Ellsworth Hoagland.

John Howard (Eddie Warren); Wendy Barrie (Marion Keller); Willie Howard (Tony Pagano); George Barbier (Calvin Keller); Benny Baker (Benny); Eleanore Whitney (Bubbles); Robert Cummings (Jimmy); Catharine Doucet (Mrs. Waldo-Walker); Samuel S. Hinds (Colonel Edwards); Halliwell Hobbes (Theodore); Dave Chasen (Dave); Stephen Chase (Gordon Rogers III); Bennie Bartlett (Kid Pianist); Billy Gilbert (Nikolas Popadopolis); Ralph Malone (Jason); Marion Ladd (Sally); Irving Bacon (Mr. Perkins); Inez Courtney (Miss Waterbury); Harry C. Bradley (Mr. Waldo-Walker); Joan Davis (Singer); Adrienne Marden (Girl); Paul Newlan (Charles Haines, Mechanic); Frances Robinson (Blonde Drunk); Russell Hicks (Davis); Elba Evans (Mary Flynn); Barbara Ray (Gum-chewing Girl); Lillianne Leighton (Fat Lady); Marina Schubert (Blonde); Paddy O'Flynn (Attendant); Harry Tenbrook (Mike); Bess Wade (Tough Girl); Harry Semels (Greek); Florence Dudley (Wise-cracking Dame); Jack Hill, Al Burke (Motor Cops); Sam Ash (Headwaiter); Donald Kerr (Andy); Paul Fix (Hank, The Drunk); Jack Raymond (Kibitzer); Lillian Drew (Woman on Street).

LOVE ON A BET (RKO, 1936) 77 M.

Producer, Lee Marcus; director, Leigh Jason; story, Kenneth Earl; adaptation, P. J. Wolfson, Phil Epstein; camera, Robert de Grasse; editor, Desmond Marquette.

Gene Raymond (Michael); Wendy Barrie (Paula); Helen Broderick (Aunt Charlotte); William Collier, Sr. (Uncle Carlton); Walter Johnson (Stephan); Addison "Jack" Randall (Jackson Wallace); Eddie Gribbon (Donovan); Morgan Wallace (Morton).

SPEED (MGM, 1936) 70 M.

Producer, Lucien Hubbard; director, Edwin L. Marin; story, Milton Krims, Larry Bachman; screenplay, Michael Fessier; camera, Lester White; editor, Harry Poppe.

James Stewart (Terry Martin); Wendy Barrie (Jane Mitchell); Ted Healy (Gadget); Una Merkel (Josephine Sanderson); Weldon Heyburn (Frank Lawson); Patricia Wilder (Fanny Lane); Ralph Morgan (Mr. Dean); Robert Livingston (George Saunders); Charles Trowbridge, William Tannen (Doctors); Walter Kingsford (Uncle); Claudelle Kaye (Nurse); George Chandler (Rustic Bystander); Jack Clifford (Master of Ceremonies); Don Brodie (Track Official).

TICKET TO PARADISE (Rep., 1936) 67 M.

Producer, Nat Levine; director, Aubrey Scotto; story, David Silverstein; screenplay, Jack Natteford, Nathaniel West; additional dialog, Ray Harris; music supervisor, Harry Grey; sound, Terry Kellum; camera, Ernest Miller; editor, Albert C. Clark.

Roger Pryor (Terry Dodd); Wendy Barrie (Jane Forbes); Claude Gillingwater (Mr. Forbes); Andrew Tombes (Nirney); Luis Alberni (Dr. Munson); E. E. Clive (Barkins); John Sheehan (Taxi Driver); Theodore Von Eltz (Small); Russell Hicks (Colton);

Earle Hodgins (Cab Starter); Grayce Hale (Minnie Dawson); Harry Woods (Dawson); Charles Lane (Shyster); Herbert Rawlinson (Townsend); Gavin Gordon (Tony); Harry Harvey (Spotter); Duke York (Milk Man); Harrison Greene (Merry-Go-Round Man); Eric Mayne (Dr. Eckstrom); Bud Jamison (Taxi Driver); Stanley Fields (Kelly); Wallace Gregory (Intern); Fern Emmett, Eleanor Huntley (Nurses).

UNDER YOUR SPELL   (20th, 1936) 60 M.

Producer, John Stone; director, Otto Preminger; screenplay, Frances Hyland, Saul Elkins; music director, Arthur Lange; songs, Howard Dietz and Arthur Schwartz; camera, Sidney Wagner; editor, Fred Allen.

Lawrence Tibbett (Anthony Allen); Wendy Barrie (Cynthia Drexel); Gregory Ratoff (Petroff); Arthur Treacher (Botts); Gregory Gaye (Count Raul Du Rienne); Berton Churchill (Judge); Jed Prouty (Mr. Twerp); Claudia Coleman (Mrs. Twerp); Charles Richman (Uncle Bob); Madge Bellamy (Miss Stafford); Nora Cecil (School Teacher); Bobby Samarzich (Pupil); Joyce Compton, June Gittelson (Secretaries); Clyde Dilson, Boyd Irwin, John Dilson, Lloyd Whitlock, Frank Sheridan, Edward Mortimer, Sam Blum, Jay Eaton, Scott Mattraw, Harry Stafford (Sponsors); Edward Gargan, Frank Fanning (Detectives); Cedric Stevens (Steward); Creighton Hale, Harry Harvey, Charles Sherlock (Photographers); Edward Cooper (Butler); Lee Phelps, Bruce Mitchell (Bailiffs); Pierre Watkin (Allen's Lawyer); Theodor Von Eltz (Cynthia's Lawyer); Sherry Hall, Jack Mulhall (Court Clerks); Dink Trout (Small Man); Kate Murray, Mariska Aldrich (Tall Women); Frank Arthur Swales (Man With Glasses); Troy Brown (Porter); Florence Wix (Dowager); George Magrill (Angry Man); Josef Swickard (Amigo); Ann Gillis (Gwendolyn); Robert Dalton (Announcer); Muriel Evans (Governess); Alan Davis (Pilot).

BREEZING HOME   (Univ., 1937) 64 M.

Associate producer, Edmund Grainger; director, Milton Carruth; story, Finley Peter Dunne, Jr., Philip Dunne; screenplay, Charles Grayson; music director, Charles Previn; songs, Jimmy McHugh and Harold Adamson; camera, Gilbert Warrenton; editor, Otis Garrett.

William Gargan (Steve); Alan Baxter (Joe Montgomery); Wendy Barrie (Gloria); Binnie Barnes (Henrietta); Willie Best (Speed); Raymond Walburn (Clint Evans); Alma Kruger (Mrs. Evans); Elisha Cook, Jr. (Pete Espinosa); Michael Loring (Eddie); Granville Bates (Head Politician); John Hamilton (Chairman); Ivan Miller (Veterinarian); Wade Boteler, James Farley (Detectives); Bob McKenzie (Crony); Lew Kelly (Head Politician Stooge); Pierre Watkin, Selmer Jackson, Bill Gould, Sam Flint (Stewards); Robert E. Homans, George Cleveland, George Ovey (Men); Harry Bowen, Jack Kenney (Touts); Ed Hart (Policeman); Jack Mack, John Morris (Handlers); Forbes Murray (Judge); Eric Wilton, Tony Marlo (Waiters); Al Williams, Jr. (Doran); Tom O'Grady (Bartender); William Cassell, Phyllis Crane, Art Singley (Guests); Bob Quirk (Billy Bender).

WHAT PRICE VENGEANCE?   (Rialto, 1937) 57 M.

Producer, Kenneth J. Bishop; director, Del Lord; screenplay, J. P. McGowan; camera, Harry Forbes, William Beckway; editor, William Austin.

Lyle Talbot (Tom Connors); Wendy Barrie (Polly Moore); Marc Lawrence (Pete Brower); Eddie Acuff (Tex McGirk); Lucille Lund (Babe Foster); Robert Rideout (Slim Ryan); Reginald Hincks (Inspector Blair); Wally Albright (Sandy MacNair); Lois Albright (Mary Connors); Arthur Kerr (Bill MacNair).

WINGS OVER HONOLULU   (Univ., 1937) 78 M.

Executive producer, Charles R. Rogers; associate producer, E. M. Asher; director, H. C. Potter; story, Mildred Cram; screenplay, Isabel Dawn, Boyce De Gaw; camera, Joseph Valentine; editor, Maurice Wright.

Wendy Barrie (Lauralee Curtis); Ray Milland (Lt. Stony Gilchrist); Kent Taylor (Greg Chandler); William Gargan (Lt. Jack Furness); Polly Rowles (Rosalind Furness); Samuel S. Hinds (Admiral Furness); Mary Philips (Mrs. Hatti Penletter); Margaret McWade (Nellie Curtis); Robert Spencer (Wayne); Clara Blandick (Evie Curtis); John Kelly (Gob); Louise Beavers (Mamie); Jonathan Hale (Judge Advocate); Granville Bates (Grocery Clerk); Robert Gleckler (Lt. Commander of Squadron); Joyce Compton (Caroline, Blonde on Telephone); Charles Irwin (Al's Friend, the Drunk); Maude Turner Gordon (Mrs. MacEwen); Maynard Holmes (Tommy); Ivan Miller, Jack Mulhall (Officers); Ruth Robinson (Mrs. MacEwen's Friend); Franklyn Ardell (Al, the Drunk); Milburn Stone (Telephone Operator); George Offerman, Jr., John Bruce, Buddy Messinger (Boys); Rudolph Chavers (Black Boy); Frank Melton (Budge); Mildred Gover (Cook); George H. Reed (Fauntleroy); Max Wagner, Sherry Hall, Frank Marlowe, Jack Egan, Arthur Singley, Marion "Bud" Wolfe (Marines); Virginia Rogan (Hawaiian Dancer); Billy Wayne (Orderly); Capt. P. N. L. Bellinger (Officer on U. S. S. *Ranger*); Phillip "Lucky" Hurlic (Robert Lee); Mabelle Palmer (Woman in Beauty Shop); Louise Latimer (Woman); Isabel La Mal (Woman Shopper); Grace Cunard (Mrs. Strange); Al Kikume (Hawaiian); Martin Turner (Porter); Bernard Kikume (Hawaiian Policeman); Loretta Sayers (Woman with Baby); Hazel Langton (Woman in Beauty Shop); Michael Loring, Robert Anderson (Naval Officers); Ray Turner (Waiter).

DEAD END   (UA, 1937) 93 M.

Producer, Samuel Goldwyn; associate producer, Merritt Hulburd; director, William Wyler; based on the play by Sidney Kingsley; screenplay, Lillian Hellman; art director, Richard Day; music director, Alfred Newman; costumes, Omar Kiam; assistant director, Eddie Bernoudy; set decorator, Julie Heron; sound, Frank Maher; camera, Gregg Toland; editor, Daniel Mandell.

Sylvia Sidney (Drina); Joel McCrea (Dave); Humphrey Bogart (Baby Face Martin); Wendy Barrie (Kay); Claire Trevor (Francie); Allen Jenkins (Hunk); Marjorie Main (Mrs. Martin); Billy Halop (Tommy); Huntz Hall (Dippy); Bobby Jordan (Angel); Leo Gorcey (Spit); Gabriel Dell (T. B.); Bernard Punsley (Milty); Charles Peck (Philip Griswold); Minor Watson (Mr. Griswold); James Burke (Mulligan); Ward Bond (Doorman); Elisabeth Risdon (Mrs. Connell); Esther Dale (Mrs. Fenner, Janitress); George Humbert (Pascagli); Robert E. Homans (Cop); Marcelle Corday (Governess); Charles Halton (Whitey); Bill Dagwell (Drunk); Jerry Cooper (Milty's Brother); Kath Ann Lujan (Milty's Sister); Gertrude Valerie (Old Lady); Tom Ricketts (Old Man); Charlotte Treadway, Maude Lambert (Women with Poodle); Bud Geary (Kay's Chauffeur); Frank Shields, Lucille Brown (Well-Dressed Couple); Micky Martin, Wesley Girard (Tough Boys); Esther Howard (Woman with Coarse Voice); Gilbert Clayton (Man with Weak Voice); Don Barry (Intern); Mona Monet (Nurse); Earl Askam (Griswold's Chauffeur).

A GIRL WITH IDEAS   (Univ., 1937) 70 M.

Producer, Edmund Grainger; director, S. Sylvan Simon; based on an idea by William Rankin; screenplay, Bruce Manning, Robert T. Shannon; music director, Charles Previn; camera, Milton Krasner; editor, Philip Cahn.

Wendy Barrie (Mary Morton); Walter Pidgeon (Mickey McGuire); Kent Taylor (Frank Barnes); Henry Hunter (William Duncan); George Barbier (John Morton);

Dorothea Kent (Isabelle Foster); Samuel S. Hinds (Rodding Carter); Theodore Osborn (Bailey); Horace MacMahon (Al); Edward Gargan (Eddie); George Cleveland (Malladay); Michael Fitzmaurice (Reggie); Robert Dalton (Greg); Frances Robinson (Maggie); Drew Demorest (Hill); Robert Spencer (Charlie); Jimmie Lucas (Tom); William Lundigan (Herman); Billy Bletcher (McKenzie); George Humbert (Toni); Pat Flaherty (Motorcycle Cop); Sam Hayes (Wallie Waldron); Edward McWade (Judge); Norman Willis (Hanson); Fay Helm (Genevieve); Harry Allen (Janitor); Sherry Hall (Jury Foreman); Thomas Braidon (Butler); Fern Emmett, Sidney Bracy (Secretaries); Otto Fries (Policeman); Monte Vandergrift (Truck Driver); James Farley (Private Policeman); George Cleveland (Watchman); Bobby Watson (Vendor); Anthony Warde (Gangster); Mary Jane Shauer (Adele); Art Yeoman, Jack Gardner (Reporters); Matty Roubert (Messenger Boy); Jack Daley (Traffic Officer); Bob McClung (Newsboy); Charles Sullivan (Waiter); Heinie Conklin (Street Sweeper); George Ovey (Bookkeeper); Rebecca Wassem (Girl); Allen Fox (Uniformed Messenger); Kathleen Nelson (Stenographer).

PRESCRIPTION FOR ROMANCE   (Univ., 1937) 70 M.

Producer, Edmund Grainger; director, S. Sylvan Simon; story, John Reinhardt, Robert Neville; screenplay, James Mulhauser, Robert T. Shannon, Albert R. Perkins; music director, Charles Previn; art director, Jack Otterson; camera, Milton Krasner; editor, Paul Landres.

Wendy Barrie (Valerie Wilson); Kent Taylor (Steve Macy); Frank Jenks (Smitty); Mischa Auer (Count Sandor); Gregory Gaye (Dr. Paul Azarny); Dorothea Kent (Lola Carroll); Henry Hunter (Kenneth Barton); Samuel S. Hinds (Major Goddard); Christian Rub (Conductor); William Lundigan (Officer); Constance Moore (Girl); Frank Reicher (Jozsef); Greta Meyer (Marie, the Head Nurse); Torben Meyer (Hotel Desk Clerk); Ralph Sanford (Hungarian Policeman); Theodore Osborn (Corney); Robert C. Fischer (Veterinary); Otto Fries, Bert Roach (Police Sergeants); Elsa Janssen (Elsa); Paul Weigel (Peasant); Joe Cunningham (Farrell); Franco Corsaro (Headwaiter Franz); Jimmie Lucas (Waiter); Alex Palasthy (Hungarian Roue); Dorothy Granger (Cashier); Dick Wessel (Sailor); Michael Mark, George Cleveland, Sid D'Albrook (Cab Drivers); William Gould (Doorman); Hugh Sheridan (Feodor); Fred Gehrmann (Ambulance Driver); Dan Wolheim (Policeman); Paul Newlan (Bearded Hungarian).

I AM THE LAW   (Col., 1938) 80 M.

Producer, Everett Riskin; director, Alexander Hall; based upon the serialized story by Fred Allhoff; screenplay, Jo Swerling; assistant director, William Muller; art director, Stephen Goosson, Lionel Banks; set decorator, Babs Johnstone; sound, Lodge Cunninghams; gowns, Kalloch; music director, Morris Stoloff; camera, Henry Freulich; editor, Viola Lawrence.

Edward G. Robinson (John Lindsay); Barbara O'Neil (Jerry Lindsay); John Beal (Paul Ferguson); Wendy Barrie (Frankie Ballou); Otto Kruger (Eugene Ferguson); Arthur Loft (Tom Ross); Marc Lawrence (Eddie Girard); Douglas Wood (Berry); Robert Middlemass (Moss Kitchell); Ivan Miller (Inspector Gleason); Charles Halton (Leander); Louis Jean Heydt (J. W. Butler); Fay Helm (Mrs. Butler); Emory Parnell (Brophy); Joseph Downing (Cronin); Theodor Von Eltz (Martin); Horace MacMahon (Prisoner); Frederick Burton (Governor); Lucien Littlefield (Roberts); Ed Keane, Robert Cummings, Sr., Harvey Clark, James Flavin, Harry Bradley, Edward J. LeSaint, Billy Arnold, Frank Mayo, Oliver Eckhardt (Witnesses); Kane Richmond, James Bush, Anthony Nace, Robert McWade, Jr., Will Morgan, James Millican (Students); Ed Fetherstone (Austin); Scott Colton, Steve Pendleton, Marshall Ruth, Philip Grant, Alan Bruce, Nick Lukats (Graduate Law Students); Walter Soderling (Professor

Perkins); Bud Jamison (Bartender); Iris Meredith (Girard's Girl); Mary Brodel (Hat Check Girl); Frank Bruno, Chick Collins, Jack Woody (Gangsters); Joseph De Stefani, George Pearce (Cigar Store Proprietors); Eddie Foster, Jeffrey Sayre (Thugs); George Turner, Charles Hamilton, Bud Wiser, Lane Chandler (Policemen); Phil Smalley (University Dean); William Worthington (Committee Man); Lee Shumway (Police Sergeant); Russell Heustis (Man); Ed Thomas (Steward); Walter Anthony Merrill, Lester Dorr (Reporters); Reginald Simpson, Cyril Ring, Allen Fox, Charles Sherlock, Ernie Alexander (Photographers); J. G. MacMahon (Waiter); Bess Flowers (Secretary); Lloyd Whitlock (Headwaiter); Eugene Anderson, Jr. (School Boy).

PACIFIC LINER   (RKO, 1938) 76 M.

Producer, Robert Sisk; production executive, Lee Marcus; director, Lew Landers; story, Anthony Coldeway, Henry Roberts Symonds; screenplay, John Twist; camera, Nicholas Musuraca; editor, Harry Marker.

Victor McLaglen (Crusher McKay); Chester Morris (Dr. Craig); Wendy Barrie (Ann Grayson); Alan Hale (Gallagher); Barry Fitzgerald (Britches); Allan Lane (Bilson); Halliwell Hobbes (Captain Mathews); Cyrus W. Kendall (Deadeyes); Paul Guilfoyle (Wishart); John Wray (Metcalfe); Emory Parnell (Olaf); Adia Kuznetzoff (Silvio); John Bleifer (Kovac).

NEWSBOYS' HOME   (Univ., 1939) 73 M.

Associate producer, Ken Goldsmith; director, Harold Young; story, Gordon Kahn, Charles Grayson; screenplay, Kahn; music director, Charles Previn; art director, Jack Otterson; sound, Bernard B. Brown; camera, Milton Krasner; editor, Philip Cahn.

Jackie Cooper (Rifle Edwards); Edmund Lowe (Perry Warner); Wendy Barrie (Gwen Dutton); Samuel S. Hinds (Howard Price Dutton); Edward Norris (Frankie Barber); Elisha Cook, Jr. (Danny); William Benedict (Trouble); Charles Duncan (Monk); David Gorcey (Yap); Hally Chester (Murphy); Harris Berger (Sailor); Harry Beresford (O'Dowd); Horace MacMahon (Bartsch); George McKay (Hartley); Michael Conroy, Hi Roberts, Bill Cartledge, Billy Graff, Jr., Lee Murray, Lawrence Lathrop (Newsboys); Irving Pichel (Tom Davenport); Joseph Crehan (Sheriff); Edwin Stanley (Bailey); Pat Flaherty (Mulvaney); Peter Lynn (Balke); Matty Fain (Kraft); William Gould (Auctioneer); Edward Earle (FBI Man); Edward Gargan (Policeman); Ralph Dunn (Slugger); Jerry Frank, Howard "Red" Christie (Truck Drivers); Frank Sully (Assistant to Hartley); Jimmy O'Gatty (Mug); Russ Powell, Johnnie Morris (Vendors); Sydney Greylor (Slugger); Kernan Cripps (Pressman); Jack Egan (Daniels); Eric Efron (Man); Francis Sayles (Bill); Frank O'Connor (Rewrite Man); Heinie Conklin (Dominic); Desmond Gallagher (Receptionist); Eric Wilton (Butler); Anthony Warde (Blake).

THE SAINT STRIKES BACK   (RKO, 1939) 64 M.

Producer, Robert Sisk; director, John Farrow; based on the character created by Leslie Charteris; screenplay, John Twist; camera, Frank Redman; editor, Jack Hively.

George Sanders (Simon Templar); Wendy Barrie (Val Travers); Jonathan Hale (Inspector Fernack); Jerome Cowan (Cullis); Neil Hamilton (Allan Breck); Barry Fitzgerald (Zipper Dyson); Robert Elliot (Webster); Russell Hopton (Harry Donnell); Edward Gargan (Pinky Budd); Robert Strange (Commissioner); Gilbert Emery (Martin Eastman); James Burke (Secretary); Nella Walker (Mrs. Fernack).

THE HOUND OF THE BASKERVILLES   (20th, 1939) 80 M.

Producer, Gene Markey; director, Sidney Lanfield; based on the story by Arthur Conan Doyle; screenplay, Ernest Pascal; art director, Thomas Little; music director,

Cyril J. Mockridge; costumes, Gwen Wakeley; sound, W. D. Flech, Roger Heman; camera, Peverell Marley; editor, Robert Simpson.

Richard Greene (Sir Henry); Basil Rathbone (Sherlock Holmes); Wendy Barrie (Beryl Stapleton); Nigel Bruce (Dr. Watson); Lionel Atwill (Dr. Mortimer); John Carradine (Barryman); Barlowe Borland (Frankland); Beryl Mercer (Mrs. Mortimer); Morton Lowry (Stapleton); Ralph Forbes (Sir Hugo); E. E. Clive (Gabby); Eily Malyon (Mrs. Barryman); Nigel De Brulier (Convict); Mary Gordon (Mrs. Hudson); Peter Willes (Roderick); Ian MacLaren (Sir Charles).

FIVE CAME BACK   (RKO, 1939) 75 M.

Producer, Robert Sisk; director, John Farrow; story, Richard Carroll; screenplay, Jerry Cady, Dalton Trumbo, Nathaniel West; art director, Van Nest Polglase; music, Roy Webb; special effects, Vernon L. Walker; camera Nicholas Musuraca; editor, Harry Marker.

Chester Morris (Bill); Lucille Ball (Peggy Nolan); Wendy Barrie (Alice Melbourne); John Carradine (Crimp); Allen Jenkins (Pete); Joseph Calleia (Vasquez); C. Aubrey Smith (Professor Spengler); Kent Taylor (Joe); Patric Knowles (Judson Ellis); Elisabeth Risdon (Martha Spengler); Casey Johnson (Tommy); Dick Hogan (Larry); Frank Faylen (Photographer); Selmer Jackson (Airlines Official); Robert E. Homans (American Official).

THE WITNESS VANISHES   (Univ., 1939) 66 M.

Producer, Irving Starr; director, Otis Garrett; based on the story "You Can't Hang Me" by James Ronald; screenplay, Robertson White; camera, Arthur Martinelli.

Edmund Lowe (Peters); Wendy Barrie (Joan Marplay); Bruce Lester (Lord Noel Stratton); Walter Kingsford (Amos Craven); Forrester Harvey (Allistair McNab); Barlowe Borland (Lucius Marplay); J. M. Kerrigan (Flinters); Vernon Steele (Nigel Partridge); Robert Noble (Inspector Wren); Reginald Barlow (Digby); Leyland Hodgson (Dade); Denis Green (Leets); Boyd Irwin (Ellis).

DAY-TIME WIFE   (20th, 1939) 71 M.

Producer, Darryl F. Zanuck; associate producer, Raymond Griffith; director, Gregory Ratoff; story, Rex Taylor; screenplay, Art Arthur, Robert Harari; art director, Richard Day, Joseph C. Wright; music director, Cyril J. Mockridge; set director, Thomas Little; sound, Arthur von Kirbach, Roger Heman; camera, Peverell Marley; editor, Francis Lyons.

Tyrone Power (Ken Norton); Linda Darnell (Jane); Warren William (Dexter); Binnie Barnes (Blanche); Wendy Barrie (Kitty); Joan Davis (Miss Applegate); Joan Valerie (Mrs. Dexter); Leonid Kinskey (Coco); Mildred Gover (Melbourne); Renie Riano (Mrs. Briggs); Robert Lowery, David Newell (Nits); Frank Coghlan (Office Boy); Alex Pollard (Waiter); Mary Gordon (Scrubwoman); Otto Han (House Boy); Marie Blake (Western Union Girl).

THE SAINT TAKES OVER   (RKO, 1940) 69 M.

Producer, Howard Benedict; director, Jack Hively; based on the character created by Leslie Charteris; screenplay, Lynn Root, Frank Fenton; camera, Fred Redman; editor, Desmond Marquette.

George Sanders (Simon Templar); Wendy Barrie (Ruth); Jonathan Hale (Inspector Fernack); Paul Guilfoyle (Pearly Gates); Morgan Conway (Sam Reese); Robert Emmett Keane (Leo Sloan); Cyrus W. Kendall (Max Bremer); James Burke (Mike); Robert Middlemass (Captain Wade); Roland Drew (Weldon); Nella Walker (Lucy Fernack); Pierre Watkin (Egan).

WOMEN IN WAR (Rep., 1940) 71 M.

Associate producer, Sol C. Siegel; director, John H. Auer; screenplay, F. Hugh Herbert, Doris Anderson; art director, John Victor Mackay; music director, Cy Feuer; wardrobe, Adele Palmer; special effects, Howard Lydecker; camera, Jack Marta; editor, Edward Mann.

Elsie Janis (O'Neil); Wendy Barrie (Pamela Starr); Patric Knowles (Lt. Larry Hall); Mae Clarke (Gail Halliday); Dennie Moore (Ginger); Dorothy Peterson (Frances); Billy Gilbert (Pierre); Colin Tapley (Captain Tedford); Stanley Logan (Colonel Starr); Barbara Pepper (Millie); Pamela Randell (Phyllis); Lawrence Grant (Gordon); Lester Mathews (Sir Humphrey, King's Counsel); Marion Martin (Starr's Date); Holmes Herbert (Chief Justice); Vera Lewis (Pierre's Wife); Charles D. Brown (Freddie); Peter Cushing (Captain Evans).

CROSS-COUNTRY ROMANCE (RKO, 1940) 68 M.

Executive producer, Lee Marcus; producer, Cliff Reid; director, Frank Woodruff; based on the novel *Highway to Romance* by Eleanor Browne; screenplay, Jerry Cady, Bert Granet; music director, Roy Webb; camera, J. Roy Hunt; editor, Harry Marker.

Gene Raymond (Dr. Larry Smith); Wendy Barrie (Diane North); Hedda Hopper (Mrs. North); Billy Gilbert (Orestes); George P. Huntley (Walter Corbett); Berton Churchill (Colonel Conway); Tom Dugan (Pete); Tommy Mack (Stooge); Edgar Dearing (Sweeney, The Motorcycle Cop); Frank Sully (Mike, the Cop); Cliff Clark (Captain G. G. Burke); Dorothea Kent (Millie); Vinton Haworth (Holmby, District Attorney); Maurice Cass (Dr. James J. McGillicuddy); Esther Dale (Mrs. McGillicuddy); George Watts (Sour-Faced Proprietor of Cabins); Lionel Pape (Butler); Yolande Mallot (Jennie, the Maid); Nannette Vallon (Suzette, the Maid); Landers Stevens (Bishop); Edward Dew, Mike Lally, Ronnie Rondell (Reporters); Charles Coleman (Doorman); James Carlyle (Mr. Hildebrant); Joey Ray (Airport Clerk); Louis Mason (Justice of Peace); Earle S. Dewey (Tourist); Dorothy Adams (Tourist's Wife); Joe Bernard (Jake); Herbert Vigran (Reporter from *Star-Herald*); Alan Ladd (Williams, the First Mate); Herbert Rawlinson (Captain Brawley); Kernan Cripps (Tough at Auto Camp); Carl Freemanson (Bit); Ralph Sanford (Henry); Bess Flowers (Secretary); Hank Worden (Wedding Witness).

MEN AGAINST THE SKY (RKO, 1940) 75 M.

Producer, Howard Benedict; director, Les Goodwins; story, John Twist; screenplay, Nathaniel West; music director, Frank Tours; special effects, Vernon L. Walker; camera, Frank Redman; editor, Desmond Marguette.

Richard Dix (Phil); Kent Taylor (Martin); Edmund Lowe (McLean); Wendy Barrie (Kay Mercedes); Granville Bates (Burdett); Grant Withers (Grant); Donald Briggs (Allerton); Charles Quigley (Flynn); Selmer Jackson (Captain Sanders); Lee Bonnell (Capt. Wallen); Jane Woodworth (Miss LeClair); Pamela Blake (Nurse); Chester Tallman, Joe Bordeaux, Ted O'Shea, M. G. McConnell, Jack Gray, Douglas Spencer, Ray Johnson (Mechanics); Lee Phelps (Shop Foreman); Harry Harvey (Reception Clerk); Thornton Edwards (Court Clerk); Roy Gordon (Judge); Paul Everton, Forbes Murray (Bankers); Jan Buckingham (Secretary); Helene Millard (Mrs. McLean); John Sheehan (Bartender); Max Wagner (Electrician); Denis Green (Colonel Kolbec); George Lewis (Lieutenant Norval); Harry Tyler (Passenger); Earle Hodgins (Barker); Eddie Dunn (Cop).

WHO KILLED AUNT MAGGIE? (Rep., 1940) 70 M.

Associate producer, Albert J. Cohen; director, Arthur Lubin; based on the novel by Medora Field; screenplay, Stuart Palmer; additional dialog, Frank Gill, Jr., Hal Fimberg; production manager, Al Wilson; wardrobe, Adele Palmer; art director, John Victor Mackay; music director, Cy Feuer; camera, Reggie Lanning; editor, Edward Mann.

John Hubbard (Kirk Pierce); Wendy Barrie (Sally Ambler); Edgar Kennedy (Sheriff Gregory); Elizabeth Patterson (Aunt Maggie Ambler); Onslow Stevens (Bob Dunbar); Joyce Compton (Cynthia Lou); Walter Abel (Dr. George Benedict); Mona Barrie (Eve Benedict); Willie Best (Andrew); Daisy Lee Mothershed (Bessie); Milton Parson (Mr. Lloyd); Tom Dugan (Trooper Leroy); William Haade (Trooper Curtis); Joel Friedkin (Coroner Dodson).

THE SAINT IN PALM SPRINGS (RKO, 1941) 66 M.

Producer, Howard Benedict; director, Jack Hively; based on the character created by Leslie Charteris; screenplay, Jerry Cady; music, Roy Webb; gowns, Renie; camera, Harry Wild; editor, George Hively.

George Sanders (Simon Templar); Wendy Barrie (Elna Johnson); Paul Guilfoyle (Pearly Gates); Linda Hayes (Margaret Forbes); Jonathan Hale (Inspector Fernack); Ferris Taylor (Mr. Evans); Harry Shannon (Chief Graves); Eddie Dunn (Detective Barker); Gene Rizzi (Bartender); Joey Ray (Hoodlum); Vinton Haworth (Hotel Clerk); Richard Crane (Whitey); Robert Carson (Mystery Man); Chester Tallman; Gayle Mellott (Guests); James Harrison (Bellhop); Frank O'Connor (Brady); Norman Mayes (Club Car Bartender); Edmund Elton (Peter Masson); Charles Quigley (Mr. Fletcher); Lee Bonnell (Tommy); Henry Roquemore (Mr. Flannery); Betty Farrington, Mary MacLaren (Women); Chick Collins (Callahan); Ed Thomas (Waiter); Peter Lynn (Jimmy, the Henchman).

REPENT AT LEISURE (RKO, 1941) 66 M.

Producer, Cliff Reid; director, Frank Woodruff; story, James Gow, Arnaud D'Usseau; screenplay, Jerry Cady; camera, Nicholas Musuraca; editor, H. Marker.

Kent Taylor (Richard Hughes); Wendy Barrie (Emily Baldwin); George Barbier (R. C. Baldwin); Thurston Hall (Buckingham); Charles Lane (Morgan); Nella Walker (Mrs. Baldwin); Rafael Storm (Prince Paul); Ruth Dietrich (Miss Flynn); Cecil Cunningham (Mrs. Morgan); Snowflake Toones (Rufe); George Chandler (Conductor); Charles Coleman (Butler); Hooper Atchley (Floor Walker); Jane Patten (Richard's Secretary); Jack Briggs (Stock Boy); Virginia Vale (Elevator Girl); Michael Dunaway (Baby Richard); Eddie Arden (Messenger); Dorothy Lee (Flip Sales Girl); Wanda Cantlon (Salesgirl); Paul Lepere, Barbara Burke (Clerks); Georgia Backus (Nurse); Norman Mayes (Porter).

THE GAY FALCON (RKO, 1941) 67 M.

Producer, Howard Benedict; director, Irving Reis; based on the character created by Michael Arlen; screenplay, Lynn Root, Frank Fenton; music, Paul Sawtell; art director, Van Nest Polglase; camera, Nicholas Musuraca; editor, George Crone.

George Sanders (Falcon); Wendy Barrie (Helen Reed); Allen Jenkins (Goldy); Anne Hunter (Elinor); Gladys Cooper (Maxine); Edward S. Brophy (Bates); Arthur Shields (Waldeck); Damian O'Flynn (Weber); Turhan Bey (Retana); Eddie Dunn (Grimes); Lucile Gleason (Mrs. Gardiner); Willie Fung (Jerry); Hans Conried (Herman); Jimmy Conlin (Bartender); Walter Soderling (Morgue Attendant); Robert Smith (Cop at Morgue); Lee Bonnell, Virginia Vale (Bits); Bobby Barber (Waiter);

Paul Norby (Cigar Clerk); Mickey Phillips (Newsboy); Frank O'Connor (Cop); Lew Kelly (Jailer); Polly Bailey (Landlady); James Baline (Cop in Hallway); Joey Ray (Orchestra Leader).

PUBLIC ENEMIES   (Rep., 1941) 63 M.

Producer, Robert North; director, Albert S. Rogell; based on a story by Michael Burke; screenplay, Edward T. Lowe, Lawrence Kimble; camera, Ernest Miller; editor, Edward Man.

Phillip Terry (Bill Raymond); Wendy Barrie (Bonnie Parker); Edgar Kennedy (Biff); William Frawley (Bang); Nana Bryant (Emma); Tim Ryan (Trumbull); Paul Fix (Scat); Ken Lundy (Lively); Willie Fung (Lee Hong); Marc Lawrence (Mike); Peter Leeds, Cy Ring, Eddie Fetherston (Reporters); Francis Sayles (Copy Man); Guy Usher (Detective Captain); Lee Phelps (Sergeant Operator); Charles McAvoy (Policeman); Rod Bacon (Tubby, the Reporter); Pat Gleason (Maxie, the Reporter); Dick Paxton (Bellboy); Chuck Morrison, Jack Kenney (Deliverymen); Harry Holman (Fat Reporter); Frank Richards (Shelby); Duke York (Holmes); Sammy Stein (Jake); Francis Pierlot (Priest); Jerry Jerome (Duke); Wally Albright (Tommy, the Newsboy); Sam Bernard (Karmourian); Sammy McKim, Robert Winkler, Douglas Deems, Larry Harris (Newsboys); Russell Hicks (Tregar); Eddy Waller (Olaf); James C. Morton, Dick Rush (Detectives); Arthur Housman (Drunk).

A DATE WITH THE FALCON   (RKO, 1941) 63 M.

Producer, Howard Benedict; director, Irving Reis; based on the character created by Michael Arlen; screenplay, Lynn Root, Frank Fenton; camera, Robert De Grasse; editor, Harry Marker.

George Sanders (Falcon); Wendy Barrie (Helen Reed); James Gleason (Inspector O'Hara); Allen Jenkins (Goldy); Mona Maris (Rita Mara); Victor Kilian (Max); Frank Moran (Dutch); Russ Clark (Needles); Ed Gargan (Bates); Eddie Dunn (Grimes); Alec Craig (Waldo Sampson/H. Sampson); Frank Martinelli (Louie); Jack Carr, Eddie Borden (Taxi Drivers); Roxanne Barkley (Jill); Hans Conried (Hotel Clerk); Eddie Arden (Bellhop); Paul Newlan (Hotel Cop); Earle Ross (Adolph Meyer); Anthony Blair, Mickey Simpson (Cops); Leo Cleary (Brody); Frank O'Connor (Accident Cop); Dick Rush (Desk Sergeant); Selmer Jackson (Wallis); Al Sullivan (Traffic Cop); Youda Hayes (Spectator); William Forrest (Ward); Eddie Hart (Bar Cop); Elizabeth Russell (Girl on Plane); Art Dupuis (Joe, the Bartender); Aline Dixon (Woman); Bud McTaggart, Harry Lee (Mugs); Amarilla Morris (Bit).

EYES OF THE UNDERWORLD   (Univ., 1942) 61 M.

Associate producer, Ben Pivar; director, Roy William Neill; story, Maxwell Shane; screenplay, Michael L. Simmons, Arthur Strawn; art director, George Otterson; music director, H. J. Salter; camera, George Robinson.

Richard Dix (Richard Bryan); Wendy Barrie (Betty Standing); Lon Chaney (Benny); Lloyd Corrigan (J. C. Thomas); Don Porter (Edward Jason); Billy Lee (Mickey Bryan); Marc Lawrence (Gordon Finch); Edward Pawley (Lance Merlin); Joseph Crehan (Kirby); Wade Boteler (Sergeant Clancy); Gaylord Pendleton (Hub Gelsey); Mike Raffetto (District Attorney).

FOREVER AND A DAY   (RKO, 1943) 105 M.

Producer-director, Rene Clair, Edmund Goulding, Cedric Hardwicke, Frank Lloyd, Victor Saville, Robert Stevenson, Herbert Wilcox; screenplay, Charles Bennett, C. S. Forrester, Lawrence Hazard, Michael Hogan, W. O. Lipscomb, Alice Duer Miller, John Van Druten, Alan Campbell, Peter Godfrey, S. M. Herzig, Christopher Isherwood, Gene Lockhart, R. C. Sheriff, Claudine West, Norman Corwin, Jack Hartfield, James Hilton, Emmett Lavery, Frederick Lonsdale, Donald Ogden Stewart, Keith Winters; art director, Albert S. D'Agostino, Lawrence P. Williams, Al Herman; music director, Anthony Collins; special effects, Vernon L. Walker; camera, Robert de Grasse, Lee Garmes, Russell Metty, Nicholas Musuraca; editor, Elmo J. Williams, George Crone.

Anna Neagle (Miriam [Susan]); Ray Milland (Bill Trimble); Claude Rains (Pomfret); C. Aubrey Smith (Admiral Trimble); Dame May Whitty (Mrs. Trimble); Gene Lockhart (Cobblewick); Ray Bolger (Sentry); Edmund Gwenn (Stubbs); Lumsden Hare (Fitts); Stuart Robertson (Lawyer); Claud Allister (Barstow); Ben Webster (Vicar); Alan Edmiston (Tripp); Patric Knowles (Courier); Bernie Sell (Naval Officer); Halliwell Hobbes (Doctor); Helene Pickard (Maid); Doris Lloyd, Lionel Belmore (Bits); Louis Bissinger (Baby); Clifford Severn (Nelson Trimble); Charles Coburn (Sir William); Alec Craig (Butler); Ian Hunter (Dexter); Jessie Matthews (Mildred); Charles Laughton (Bellamny); Montague Love (Sir John Bunn); Reginald Owen (Mr. Simpsen); Sir Cedric Hardwicke (Dabb); Noel Madison (Mr. Dunkinfield); Ernest Cossart (Mr. Blinkinsop); Peter Godfrey (Mr. Pepperdish); Buster Keaton (Dabb's Assistant); Wendy Barrie (Edith); Ida Lupino (Jenny); Brian Aherne (Jim Trimble); Edward Everett Horton (Sir Anthony); Isobel Elsom (Lady Trimble-Pomfret); Wendell Hulet (Augustus); Eric Blore (Selsby); June Duprez (Julia); Mickey Martin (Boy); Queenie Leonard (Housemaid); May Beatty (Cook); Merle Oberon (Marjorie); Una O'Connor (Mrs. Ismay); Nigel Bruce (Major Garrow); Anita Bolster (Mrs. Garrow); Marta Gale (Miss Garrow); Roland Young (Mr. Barringer); Gladys Cooper (Mrs. Barringer); Robert Cummings (Ned Trimble); Herbert Evans (Bobby); Kay Deslys (Woman Drunk); Richard Haydn (Mr. Fulcher); Emily Fitzroy (Mrs. Fulcher); Odette Myrtil (Mrs. Dallas); Elsa Lanchester (Mamie); Sara Allgood (Cook in 1917); Clyde Cook (Taxi Driver); Dorothy Bell (WAAC Girl); Jean Prescott (ATS Girl); Vangie Beilby (Woman Drunk); Robert Coote (Blind Officer); Art Mulliner, Ivan Simpson (Elderly Bachelors); Pax Walker, Lola Vanti (Housemaids in 1917); Bill Cartledge (Telegraph Boy); Charles Hall, Percy Snowden (Men); Donald Crisp (Captain Martin); Ruth Warrick (Leslie); Kent Smith (Gates Pomfret); June Lockhart (Daughter); Lydia Bilbrook (Mother); Billy Bevan (Cabby); Stuart Robertson (Air Raid Warden); Herbert Marshall (Curate); Victor McLaglen (Spavin); Harry Allen (Cockney Watcher); Ethel Griffies (Wife); Gabriel Canzona (Man with Monkey); Joy Harrington (Bus Conductress); Reginald Gardiner (Man); Walter Kingsford (Man); Mary Gordon, Evelyn Beresford, Moyna MacGill, Arthur Treacher, Anna Lee, Cecil Kellaway (Bits); Stuart Hall, Barry Heenan, Barry Norton, Philip Ahlin (Card Players); Daphne Moore (Nurse).

FOLLIES GIRL (Producers' Releasing Corp., 1943) 71 M.

Producer-director, William Rowland; story, Marcy Klauber, Art Jarrett; screenplay, Klauber, Robinson; additional dialog, Pat C. Flick, Lew Hearn; choreography, Larry Ceballos; music director, Ernie Holst; songs, Mary Schaefer; Nick Kenny, Kim Gannon, and Ken Lane; Fred Wise, Buddy Kaye, and Sidney Lippman; Nick and Charles Kenny, Sonny Burke, and John Murphy; Nick and Charles Kenny, and Sonny Burke; Robert Warren; camera, George Webber; editor, Samuel Datlowe.

Wendy Barrie (Anne Merriday); Doris Nolan (Francine La Rue); Gordon Oliver (Private Jerry Hamlin); Anne Barrett (Bunny); Arthur Pierson (Sergeant Bill Perkins); J. C. Nugent (J. B. Hamlin); Cora Witherspoon (Mrs. J. B. Hamlin); William Harrigan (Jimmy Dobson); Jay Brennan (Andre Duval); Lew Hearn (Lew); Cliff Hall (Cliff); Marion McGuire (Trixie); Pat C. Flick (Patsy); Anthony Blair (Somers); Jerri Blanchard (Jerri); Serjei Radamsky (Scarini); G. Swayne Gordon (Doorman); Ray Heatherton and Band, Johnny Long and Band, Bobby Byrne and Band, Ernie Holst and Band, Claire and Arene, Charles Weidman Dancers, Song Spinners, The Heat Waves, Lazare and Castellanos, Fritzi Scheff, Hal Thompson (Specialties).

SUBMARINE ALERT   (Par., 1943) 66 M.

Producer, William Pine, William Thomas; director, Frank McDonald; screenplay, Maxwell Shane; camera, Fred Jackson, Jr.; editor, William Zeigler.

Richard Arlen (Lee Deerhold); Wendy Barrie (Ann Patterson); Nils Asther (Dr. Arthur Huneker); Roger Pryor (G. B. Fleming); Abner Biberman (Commodore Toyo); Marc Lawrence (Vincent Belga); John Miljan (Mr. Bambridge/Captain Haigas Tina); Ralph Sanford (Freddie Grayson); Dwight Frye (Henry Haldine); Edward Earle (Dr. Barclay); William Bakewell (Engineer); Stanley Smith (Clerk).

IT SHOULD HAPPEN TO YOU   (Col., 1954) 81 M.

Producer, Fred Kohlmar; director, George Cukor; story-screenplay, Garson Kanin; art director, John Meehan; music, Frederick Hollander; assistant director, Earl Bellamy; camera, Charles Lang; editor, Charles Nelson.

Judy Holliday (Gladys Glover); Peter Lawford (Evan Adams III); Jack Lemmon (Pete Sheppard); Michael O'Shea (Brod Clinton); Vaughn Taylor (Entrikin); Connie Gilchrist (Mrs. Riker); Walter Klavun (Bert Piazza); Whit Bissell (Robert Grau); Arthur Gilmore (Don Toddman); Rex Evans (Con Cooley); Heywood Hale Broun (Sour Man); Constance Bennett, Ilka Chase, Wendy Barrie, Melville Cooper (TV Show Panelists); Ralph Dumke (Salesman); Mary Young (Old Lady Customer); Cora Witherspoon (Saleslady); James Nusser, Edwin Chandler, Stan Malotte, Robert Berger, Earl Keen, George Becwar, Tom Hennesy, Leo Curley (Board Members); Ted Thorpe, Tom Cound (Assistant Photographers); Sandra Lee, Stephany Hampson (Teenagers); Harold J. Kennedy (Photographer); James Hyland (Bartender); Margaret McWade (Elderly Lady); George Kitchel (Lieutenant); Don Richards (Photographer); Jack Kruschen (Joe); Stanley Orr (Makeup Man); Herbert Lytton (Sound Man); John Saxon (Boy Watching Argument in Park).

With Edmund Gwenn and Robert Donat in CASH (Par-London Films '33)

With Alfred Drayton, Helen Haye, Edward Everett Horton, Albert Bardon, Joyce Kirby, Heather Thatcher, and Leslie Henson in IT'S A BOY (Gainsborough '33)

With Henry Kendall and Fred Duprez in WITHOUT YOU (Fox '34)

With Clifford Mollison and Zelma O'Neal in FREEDOM OF THE SEAS (Associated '34)

With Joyce Compton, Johnny Downs, Arline Judge, and Eddie Nugent in COLLEGE SCANDAL (Par '35)

The PARAMOUNT POTENTIAL OF 1935: *top row*, Gertrude Michael, Gail Patrick, Wendy Barrie, Ann Sheridan; *bottom row*, Grace Bradley, Katherine DeMille

licity pose, c. 1936

WPB-391

With George Shelley and
Maynard Holmes in WINGS
OVER HONOLULU (Univ '37)

With Kent Taylor and Walter
Pidgeon in A GIRL WITH IDEAS
(Univ '37)

With Lloyd Whitlock, Edward G.
Robinson, and J. E. MacMahon
in I AM THE LAW (Col '38)

With Edmund Lowe in
NEWSBOYS' HOME (Univ '39)

With Ed Gargan, George
Sanders, Barry Fitzgerald, and
(on the floor) Russell Hopton in
THE SAINT STRIKES BACK
(RKO '39)

With Kent Taylor, Casey
Johnson, Lucille Ball, and
Chester Morris in FIVE CAME
BACK (RKO '39)

With Mae Clarke, Dennie Moore
(*rear*), and Pamela Randall
(*right*) in WOMEN IN WAR
(Rep '40)

With George Sanders in THE
SAINT IN PALM SPRINGS
(RKO '41)

With Arthur Shields and Allen Jenkins in THE GAY FALCON (RKO '41)

With Nana Bryant in PUBLIC ENEMIES (Rep '41)

With Richard Dix in EYES OF
THE UNDERWORLD (Univ '42)

With Judy Holliday in
IT SHOULD HAPPEN TO YOU
(Col '54)

Wendy Barrie of the mid-1950s

With business executive Norman
B. Orent in a publicity pose in
1966

Lupe Velez in 1940

5'1/2"
112 pounds
Black hair
Brown eyes
Cancer

Lupe
Velez

The greatest merchandising gift Lupe Velez possessed was her inestimable faith in herself and her tremendous zest for life. In her professional days (spanning the years 1927-44) she was a one-woman fireball of energy, utilizing her dynamic life-force and her captivating, accented, south-of-the-border charm to expand what might well have been a very short acting career. For this tiny bundle of shapely beauty had a very limited histrionic range, and by virtue of her features and temperament she was hemmed into a set screen type; as Queen of the Hot-Cha, the Hot Tamale, the Mexican Wildcat, or just simply madcap Velez.

Sloe-eyed Lupe was known as the greatest of fun-lovers, whether on the studio soundstage, at a Hollywood party, or cavorting on a Broadway stage. New York critic John Chapman once penned: "Her temperament is just an excess of enthusiasm; if she is happy she is wildly so; if she is sad she is sad as hell. She is a raucous, tireless horse-player and gagger around a set, buzzing around with the speed and lack of direction of a big horsefly; but once a director calls for action she is instantly quiet, onto her job, and respectful to her boss."

Over the years Lupe has been compared in beauty to Dolores Del Rio, in exotic behavior to Maria Montez, Lily Damita, and Estelita Rodriguez; but in reality there was, and will be, only one Lupe Velez, a tempestuous, vital purveyor of fun, who could blow up a storm of entertainment in even the dreariest of her RKO Mexican Spitfire *series films.*

She was born Maria Guadalupe Villalobos on July 18, 1909, in San Luis de Potosi, a suburb of Mexico City. Her father, Jacob Villalobos, was a colonel in the Mexican regular army; her mother, Josefina, had been an opera singer, performing the lead role of *La Bohème* at the Mexico City Opera House. The Villalobos also had a son named Emigdio and two other daughters, Mercedes and Josefina. As a small child, Lupe was a hellion who thrived on hearty adventures. Years later she vividly recalled riding on military inspection tours with her father* and could recount with precision various political skirmishes she witnessed in which many partisans were slain by the colonel and his troops.

Lupe was barely a teenager when her mother realized that her rambunctious daughter needed more stringent supervision than she could supply, so at the age of thirteen the overly energetic Lupe, who was then insisting she was going to become a champion roller-skater, was packed off to the Our Lady of the Lake convent in San Antonio, Texas. As would be customary throughout her life, Lupe barely paid heed to the uncongenial surroundings of the austere institution, managing to devise her own little dream world of frivolity. As Lupe summed up this facet of her life: "Studied English. Liked to dance. Guess I wasn't much of a success as a student."

Two years later Lupe's father was killed in action during yet another local governmental upheaval in Mexico City. Lupe returned home, intent upon helping her financially strained family make ends meet. She was hired as a salesgirl at the Nacionel Department Store at the modest salary of $4 a week. Although she turned most of her tiny income over to mama, she did retain some pennies in order to take dancing lessons in her spare time. Thirty-seven cents per session was a big expenditure for Lupe, but she wisely reasoned that her already mature figure (37-26½-35) and her zestful personality might earn her a job in the much-higher-paying and more glamorous field of show business. And she was correct in her stage-struck assumption. Later in 1924 Mexican producer Alfeda hired her for a featured dancing role in his new musical revue, *Ra-Ta-Plan*. Lupe, always suffering from an (un)conscious need for exaggeration when dealing with factors in her personal life, later claimed she was quickly elevated to star status in the production and earned a whopping $50 per day (very high pay in the 1920s, particularly in the low-scale Mexican economy). During the run of *Ra-Ta-Plan* Lupe is alleged to have appeared in some film shorts lensed in Mexico City, which, she said, was a factor in her demanding another salary increase from Alfeda. When the $75 per diem was not forthcoming, she hastily withdrew from the show, con-

---

*He was called El Gallo ("The Rooster") by his troops.

templating several professional offers that had come her way—one to go to Cuba, another to star in a Buenos Aires revue—but in the meantime, Mr. and Mrs. Frank A. Woodward, friends of the family, had brought Lupe to the attention of an aging matinee idol of the American stage, Richard Bennett, who was then planning a Los Angeles production of *The Dove.**

So Lupe started for Hollywood, but she got no farther than the Texas border, where the immigration officials refused her admittance into America because she was underage. "All the way back to Mexico City I cried," Lupe recalled, "but I'd show them. I *would* get to Hollywood some way. I appealed to our president, to the ministers, to everybody in Mexico City. After a lot of letter writing between Mexico City and Washington and what you call 'red tape' they said I could cross the border." When determined Lupe finally did arrive in Hollywood she was penniless, for on the train she had met a nice man who held her hand and took her money. To add to her problems, when Bennett finally tested the seventeen-year old girl onstage, he belatedly realized that fiery Lupe was enthusiastic but too inexperienced. More importantly, she looked far too young in contrast to the fifty-three-year-old actor. Dorothy MacKaye was given the part instead.

Two of Lupe's most endearing and fortuitous qualities were her abilities to make friends quickly and to even more quickly find imaginative solutions to any problem at hand. Thus she soon acquired a coterie of Hollywood pals, and while waiting for her big "break" accepted an offer to appear in a Hollywood benefit revue show sponsored by the local traffic policemen. As a result of her onstage cavorting she was signed to a featured dancing spot in Fancon and Marco's *Music Box Revue* (Music Box Theatre, Hollywood, 1926), a variety show starring comedienne Fannie Brice. Lupe quickly garnered her share of the spotlight, more for the vivacity of her personality than for her terpsichorean prowess. Localites were soon comparing her to the already established Mexican actress Dolores Del Rio,† and Florenz Ziegfeld's West Coast agent promptly offered Lupe a sixteen-week contract to perform her eye-catching dances in Ziegfeld's Broadway hit, *Rio Rita*. But Lupe rejected the bid. She was in Hollywood and was determined to make her mark in the cinema.

One day, while still performing in the *Music Box Revue*, she was called for an interview with film producer Hal Roach, then releasing his short-subject comedy product through Pathé Studios. He was convinced the spirited Mexican miss would be a nubile addition to his stable of bathing-beauty talent, which then included Carole Lombard and Jean Harlow, who would be joined shortly thereafter by Paulette Goddard. Roach screentested Lupe and signed her to a three-year contract at minimum salary. Besides posing for the usual Roach cheesecake publicity shots, Lupe appeared in at least two Roach-

---

*Norma Talmadge would star in the 1927 film version released by United Artists, with Dolores Del Rio appearing in a sound adaptation entitled *Girl of the Rio*, released by RKO in 1932.

†The comparison, odious to both parties concerned, would haunt Lupe throughout most of her fledgling Hollywood years.

Pathé comedy shorts. She was little more than an extra in *What Women Did for Me* (August, 1927), directed by and starring Charley Chase, and including such other studio contractees as Eric Mayne, May Wallace, Caryl Lincoln, Viola Richards, and Broderick O'Farrell. The next month Lupe was a striking flapper-style shipboard extra in the Stan Laurel-Oliver Hardy short subject, *Sailors Beware*, directed by Fred Guiol. Anita Garvin, as the con artist in league with midget Tiny Sanford, had the female lead in this two-reeler.

It is sheer speculation how Lupe's career would have progressed had she remained with Roach, who initiated a distribution pact with MGM the following year. Like any actress with loftier ambitions than the custard-in-the-face cinema school (although volatile Lupe was not averse to such antics), Lupe soon departed from the Roach lot, having used her tenure there as a steppingstone to hopefully better projects.

Lupe's natural affinity for the freewheeling, prankster's life made her a logical pal for similarly inclined Douglas Fairbanks, Sr., who was then preparing *The Gaucho* (United Artists, 1928), based on his own story,* adapted for the screen by Lotta Woods. Kingpin Fairbanks was seeking an actress to play a wild mountain girl, definitely of the Spanish variety. Since Dolores Del Rio, who was ideal for the screen role, was too much of a box-office name to accept a featured role, Fairbanks considered her would-be "rival," Lupe. Any doubts Fairbanks and his staff may have had regarding Lupe's histrionic talents were overcome by Lupe's infectious, fun-loving personality. Fairbanks just could not resist signing her for the part, even when Samuel Goldwyn's European import Lily Damita was briefly considered for the picture.

United Artists premiered its $1.50 per ticket silent feature *The Gaucho* at Grauman's Casino Theatre in Hollywood on November 24, 1927. Like the bulk of Fairbanks's 1920s features, this action-packed entry was more noteworthy for verve and panache than for heady performances or solid plotline. Filmgoers who might be tiring of Fairbanks's personable onscreen capering could admire the Technicolor sequences and the on-location south-of-the-border photography. The rambling plot was at least a flimsy excuse for Fairbanks to indulge in 102 minutes of oncamera antics.†

Among the film's visual highlights were Fairbanks's skilled use of the bolas, a T-shaped lasso, and the sequence in which a hundred men on horses pull Fairbanks and Lupe into town. Despite being only the second female lead in *The Gaucho* Lupe made quite an impression on the filmgoing public and the

---

*Written under the pen name of Elton Thomas.

†After a little girl miraculously survives a fall from a mountain ledge into a canyon, the local citizenry label her the "miracle girl." Years later as an adult (Eve Southern) the "girl of the shrine" resides in a specially constructed Miracle City, utilizing her famed healing powers for the benefit of her people. When bandit leader Ruiz (Gustav von Seyffertitz) and his band determine to capture the wealthy city, gaucho Fairbanks leads his band of men to the rescue. All of which makes Lupe, Fairbanks's mountain girlfriend, needlessly jealous, and she turns him over to the local authorities. But he escapes in time to prevent the execution of Southern, save the town, and convince a particularly contrite Lupe to wed him.

critics. "Miss Velez," reported Mordaunt Hall (*New York Times*), "gives a capital characterization as the Mountain Girl, but it does seem strange that she is so suddenly tamed in the end, when she becomes the bride of The Gaucho. Whether in rags or lace, she gives blow for blow when angry." *Variety* was quick to enthusiastically project a rosy future for Lupe: "She scores 100 per cent and is established as a feminine Fairbanks. . . . a beauty and has that freshness that goes with youth. When it comes to acting she does not have to step aside for anyone. They put on a rave about Dolores Del Rio for more than two years out here. Now it's going to go for Lupe. This kid has a great sense of comedy value to go with her athletic prowess."

In her feature film debut Lupe demonstrated the full range of qualities that would make her a continually fascinating, if not always captivating, personality throughout her eighteen-year movie career: striking good looks, energetic behavior (particularly in dancing and cavorting about), a strong sense of comedy timing, and her most marketable screen trait—her ability to enact a prime termagant, a girl quickly fired to anger, who unleashes her pent-up emotions in a barrage of physical assault on her male target. In an age before women's liberation was chic, Lupe's aggressive, volatile screen manner was considered a very engaging trait indeed. It was a "pose" directors would utilize over and over again in her forthcoming film appearances.

Having made a somewhat sensational splash with public and critics alike in *The Gaucho*, the Feature Productions' division of United Artists signed Lupe to a five-year contract. Lupe's enunciated reaction to "overnight" success was phrased in typical Lupe Velez jargon: "Was I happy when *The Gaucho* opened and the public was nice to Lupe? Not happy—delirious!"*

Since silent pictures were still in vogue and it was considered reasonable casting to assign an "exotic" type to play most any nationality, Lupe was loaned to the Cecil B. De Mille division of Pathé Pictures for the Donald Crisp-produced and directed *Stand and Deliver* (1928). In this fifty-seven-minute feature with synchronized sound-effects sequences, Lupe was seen as a Greek peasant girl who is rescued from a burning house by British World War I veteran Rod La Rocque, now posted with the Greek Army. Later La Rocque must kill his superior officer who has attacked Lupe, and the duo escape only to become the captives of mountain bandit Warner Oland and his motley followers. Before the happy finale La Rocque has redeemed himself by thwarting a bandit attack and capturing Oland. Almost needless to say, La Rocque and Lupe discover they have become "that way" about one another. Perhaps the most intriguing aspects of this minor picture were Oland's bravura performance as the greed-crazed brigand and the unique transportation† required to enter-exit the bandit's mountain hideaway. Lupe

---

*Throughout her career, Lupe would maintain, both onscreen and off, her broken English dialect, which she considered a viable gimmick. Reporters furthered her fractured-syntax syndrome by usually rephrasing her remarks into what the public had come to accept as standard Lupeisms.

†A primitive basket-cart-rope-lift.

became overdramatic during the climactic fight between La Rocque and Oland, panting and gesturing in the worst tradition of silent-screen "emoting." Nevertheless she was fetching in her skimpy wardrobe and a properly delightful, spunky little bundle of energy.

In recognition of Lupe's skyrocketing-to-fame work in *The Gaucho*, United Artists named Lupe their WAMPAS Baby Star of 1928, in a year that included such other "newcomers" as: Lina Basquette, Flora Bramley, Sue Carol, Ann Christy, June Collyer, Alice Day, Sally Eilers, Audrey Ferris, Dorothy Gulliver, Gwen Lee, Molly O'Day, and Ruth Taylor. Lupe would soon outdistance all these competitors in the cinema sweepstakes.

Lupe then found herself in a picture being directed by the once-great D. W. Griffith. *Lady of the Pavements* (1929) was the master's third production made under his new Joseph Schenck-United Artists pact, but he had fallen into such strained ways under the modernized production-line filmmaking system of late 1920s Hollywood, that he had been given *Lady of the Pavements* only after Sam Taylor, who wrote the screenplay, proved unavailable to direct it. All of which proved good happenstance for Lupe, because Griffith found it increasingly difficult to cope with the picture's nominal star, Jetta Goudal, and in retaliation deliberately built up Lupe's role to spite the leading lady.

Set in 1868 Paris, the Ruritanian romance finds nobleman William Boyd rejecting countess Goudal as the lady of his life. He tells her that he would rather wed a woman of the streets than her. Goudal does not let this insult pass and determines to make Boyd eat crow. She hires cafe soubrette Lupe to pose as a socially acceptable lady and grooms her, Pygmalion-style, to capture Boyd's fickle heart. When Lupe and Boyd actually fall in love the flabbergasted Goudal speedily informs Boyd of Lupe's true past. Boyd is initially shocked and disgusted—the double standard was in full operation then—but later manages to forgive Lupe her indiscreet pedigree.

Lady of the Pavements (United Artists Theatre, Los Angeles, January 22, 1929) fared poorly with a public anxious for contemporary stories dealing with the spirit of the Roaring Twenties. Nor were moviegoers pleased with maestro Griffith's exasperating experiments with sound in *Lady of the Pavements*.*

As the singer-prostitute of the Smoking Dog Cafe, Lupe made her motion picture singing debut, handling renditions of Irving Berlin's "Where Is That Song of Songs for Me?" as well as "Nena" and "At the Dance." When not vocalizing, she cavorted first as the chanteuse who would rather bite a man's

---

*Griffith historian Iris Barry has noted: "Griffith also had some elaborate ideas about the sound in the film, and tried to increase and decrease the volume of Lupe Velez's singing voice as she approached or retreated from the camera. Unfortunately, this proved to be beyond the abilities of his technicians. There was some question whether the poorly synchronized sound that resulted would be recorded on the film 'as in the Fox method,' but discs won out, and thus the sound for this film is also lost."

hand than caress it, later as the rambunctious pupil of high-toned Goudal, and finally as the burlesque aristocrat whose unique personality and ways win Boyd's snobbish heart. Although it was an honor to work under Griffith's direction, Lupe's personality was quite unsuited to Griffith's old-fashioned ideal of a leading lady, and he fumbled badly with remolding her screen image. As the *New York Sun* saw it: "Mr. Griffith has turned her animalism into cuteness. He has done her hair up into little pompadors, made her pigeon-toed, and rather coy, and when she begins to upset court functions, one is reminded of the gosling days of the [Lillian and Dorothy] Gishes and the [Carol] Dempsters."

Lupe was far more at ease emoting in her own relaxed style, as demonstrated during her personal-appearance tour in connection with the New York opening of *Lady of the Pavements* (Rialto Theatre, March 10, 1929). In the course of her four shows daily at the Rialto, Lupe revealed herself as "a fascinating, vivacious and resourceful little person" (*New York Times*), creating a mild sensation with her songs, and particularly with her zingy imitations of Jetta Goudal, Gloria Swanson, and Dolores Del Rio. Audiences, according to reports of the day, were so intrigued with Lupe's pattern of broken English filled with absurd colloquialisms, that patrons were making return visits to hear the Mexican Spitfire spin through her routine of accented patter.

The United Artists of 1929, which also released Samuel Goldwyn's productions, boasted a roster that included, besides Lupe and its founding stars (Mary Pickford, Douglas Fairbanks, Sr., and Charles Chaplin), John Barrymore, Norma Talmadge, Ronald Colman (of the Goldwyn stable); Camilla Horn, Gilbert Roland, and, soon thereafter, Broadway import Harry Richman. Despite its output of features, United Artists found it more profitable to loan Lupe's professional services to other studios, and so her remaining three 1929 releases were made away from the home lot.

Paramount's *Wolf Song* (1929) was filmed on location in the California Sierras by director Victor Fleming in order to re-create the flavor of the 1840s and outdoors life. Carefree Kentucky trapper Gary Cooper, who usually courts the girls and then leaves them, is so attracted to Lupe, the spirited daughter of a haughty California don, that he carries her off to the mountains and later weds her. Despite strong moments of passion* Cooper yearns for his old free-wheeling ways. Finally heeding the wolf song, he returns to the high mountains and the trapper's way of life. When he is later wounded by marauding Indians, he realizes how much he needs Lupe and crawls back to her abode, where she generously forgives him.

Wolf Song was a commercial success, not only because it had the still novel aspect of being a part-talkie,† but due even more to the blazing offscreen

---

*Prolonged to the point of absurdity in extended close-ups.

†There is a dialog sequence between Lupe and Cooper prior to Lupe's singing her two songs, "Mi Amado" and "Yo Te Amo Means I Love You."

romance between Lupe and her popular, well-established Paramount co-star, Gary Cooper.* Lupe would be "linked" with MGM's John Gilbert in a short-term romance in 1931, but in intensity, scope, and publicity, it was nothing compared to her three-year fling with Cooper, himself cooling from his well-documented affair with the cinema's own It Girl, Miss Clara Bow. Paramount played up the Lupe-Cooper affair to the hilt, which reached a peak when it was learned the lanky 6-foot, 2-inch Cooper and the 5-foot, ½-inch Mexican were sharing a Laurel Canyon retreat. The star duo indulged themselves on a lavish personal-appearance tour for *Wolf Song*, which did much to increase the film's box-office take. Lupe was now at the peak of her cinema popularity, and it little mattered to a captivated public that *Wolf Song* contained one of her lesser performances.†

Cooper eventually deemed it fitting to take Lupe to meet his parents, who were then residing in Los Angeles. Mrs. Cooper took an immediate dislike to Lupe and did all she could to counsel her son against wedding the actress, even encouraging his acquaintanceship with another film performer, Evelyn Brent. In mid-1931 Paramount sent Cooper to Europe on a rest cure, by which time his relationship with Lupe had come to an end. Ever prideful, Lupe informed the press in 1931: "I don't love Gary Cooper. I turned Cooper down because his parents didn't want me to marry him, and because the studio thought it would injure his career. Now it's over, I'm glad I feel so free. I went around New York, did whatever I wanted, had a fine time."‡ As if to finally close the Cooper chapter of her life, Lupe pronounced: "I must be free. I know men too well, they are all the same, no? If you love them, they want to be boss. I will never have a boss."

Lupe and Cooper had one more well-publicized encounter several years later. She arrived at Newark Airport in New Jersey at the same time as Cooper and his wife, Veronica Balfe (whom he wed on December 15, 1933). The couple refused to pose with Lupe, who had traveled East without her husband of two months, Johnny Weissmuller. In a spurt of growing temperament, an embarrassed Lupe explained to the curious press: "I'm happily married and so is he. I wouldn't pose with him." But then her pride got the better of her and Lupe spit forth: "What does Gary Cooper think he is, any-

---

*Following the completion of *Wolf Song* Cooper bestowed a pair of golden eagles on Lupe, a gift sent to him by a Montana fan. The press wanted to know if these love birds symbolized Lupe's unbridled passion for Cooper. "I am not wild." Lupe replied, "I am just Lupe." When asked about the possibility of marriage to Cooper, Lupe answered: "Of course I love him. Marry him? Well, who will know what I do until I do it, eh? Maybe tomorrow, maybe next month, maybe never. But I think maybe."

†"Lupe Velez indulges in a flock of respiratory acrobatics whenever she has a love scene with Gary. Lupe's voice is pleasing enough but she is difficult to understand" (*Motion Picture News*).

‡Despite their public proclamations, both Lupe and Cooper still retained a flame of passion for one another that lasted throughout the mid-1930s. At one point a reporter asked Cooper what was the most exciting thing that had happened to him in the movies. The usually taciturn Cooper unhesitatingly replied, "Lupe Velez!"

way. He's no oil painting! He may be an idol to his mother, but he's nothing to me!"

As a diversion from her torrid Cooper romance, Lupe jaunted to Culver City to participate in MGM's *Where East Is East* (1929), another of the bizarre entries produced and directed by Tod Browning and starring Lon Chaney. The setting may have been Indochina but the atmosphere of the picture reeked of *East Lynne*. Wild-animal trapper Tiger Haynes (Chaney) bears many a scar from his rugged profession. His one constant worldly pleasure is the happiness of his lively half-caste daughter Toyo (Lupe). Lloyd Hughes, the upstanding son of an American circus owner, is enchanted with Lupe and begs Chaney's permission to wed her. Chaney reluctantly agrees, only to have his spiteful ex-wife (Estelle Taylor) return to the jungle outpost and vamp Hughes away from Lupe. Chaney's solution to the intolerable situation is to set loose a killer gorilla who eliminates Taylor but also mortally wounds Chaney. He does live long enough to see Lupe wed to gentle Hughes. In all respects *Where East Is East* was one of the lesser Browning-Chaney collaborations, and box-office grosses went down. Lupe's role in these rambling proceedings was more lackluster than implausible. It was Estelle Taylor, only ten years Lupe's senior, in the flashy assignment of the exotic, slant-eyed Madame de Sylva, who made a strong impression here.

Lupe's first all-talking picture, *Tiger Rose* (1929),* was made at Warner Bros. The story derived from David Belasco's 1917 stage production, which starred Lenore Ulric, who later made a silent version of the Canadian Northwest melodrama in 1923. The new edition of *Tiger Rose* found Lupe second-billed in a role which, by now, had become a stereotyped assignment for her, that of a fiery half-caste. As the tempestuous French-Canadian ward of Tully Marshall, he of the Hudson's Bay Company, she is wooed by Royal Mountie Monte Blue and by Irishman Bull Montana, but it is young railroad engineer Grant Withers whom Lupe loves, much to the annoyance of the ever-present doctor, H. B. Warner. When Withers accidentally kills the deranged Warner in a struggle, he and Lupe flee with the blessing of Blue, who is finally convinced of their sincere love for one another.

Lupe's last United Artists release under her long-term contract was *Hell Harbor* (1930), photographed on location near Tampa, Florida. The prime attraction of this Caribbean-set feature was an excess of gory violence, which was not sufficient to offset the pedestrian melodramatics. Unscrupulous Gibson Gowland, a descendant of Morgan the Pirate, demands that his daughter (Lupe) wed middle-aged pearl trader Jean Hersholt; the latter's price for the bargain is his remaining silent regarding a homicide committed by Gowland. Strong-willed Lupe refuses and turns to American John Holland for succor. In the climactic bout of fisticuffs, Hersholt flings a knife, which finds its target

*The New York premiere, on December 24, 1929, was held at the newly-constructed Beacon Theatre at 74th Street and Broadway; Ben Bernie was the emcee and studio executive Harry Warner was the principal speaker.

in Gowland's hand. (Along with the lensing of well-composed cloud effects, this knife-throwing was the picture's highlight.) Later Gowland kills Hersholt, but Holland insures that he pays for this crime, leaving him and Lupe free to wed. The *New York Times* was rather generous when it cited Lupe's *Hell Harbor* performance as "vivacious and believable."

Lupe's next five pictures were produced at Universal. *The Storm* (1930), directed by William Wyler, was a loose remake of a 1922 Universal feature. This time around, Lupe's Manette Fachard was the lead role,* rather than the fourth-billed part as played by Virginia Valli in the original screen production.† Lupe's role was a stale slice from her prior *Tiger Rose*, as she was again seen as a French-Canadian lass who, along with her smuggler father, is on the lam from the pursuing Northwest Mounted Police. The fugitive duo seek refuge in the Canadian Northwest mountain cabin shared by buddies Paul Cavanagh and William "Stage" Boyd, with the inevitable rivalry arising between the two men for Lupe's fickle affections. The production stagnated under a *déjà vu* approach,‡ leading the *New York Times* to comment: "Miss Velez here possesses a vivacity typical of the roles in which she has previously appeared, but it is somehow curbed by the restraint shown by the other players."

Lupe added another portrait to her growing global gallery of screen half-castes with *East Is West* (1930). As Ming Toy, one of Tetsu Komai's many children, she is rescued from the auction block in China by American Lew Ayres. Later she is placed in the care of E. Alyn Warren and sent to San Francisco to start a new life, but her hoydenish manner and her persistent interest in Occidental ways lead her into difficulties with the waterfront missionary society. To prevent her from being deported back to China, Warren sells her to Edward G. Robinson, the city's egocentric half-caste chop suey king. In the best tradition of trashy pulp fiction, Ayres fortuitously arrives on the scene just in time to rescue her this second time. Ayres would gladly wed Lupe but his aristocratic family is fearfully prejudiced about foreigners; however, everything is righted when it is discovered that Lupe is really an American (minority group lobbyists please note!), the baby of murdered missionaries. *East Is West* had seemed much fresher in 1918 when first presented on the Broadway stage with Fay Bainter, or even in 1922 when made as a silent feature with Constance Talmadge, Edmund Burns, and Warner Oland. If Lupe's portrayal of a child of two cultures was cute but unconvincing, relative screen novice Edward G. Robinson was rather hammy in his interpretation of the semi-Oriental.§

*The part had originally been planned for Laura La Plante.

†A third version of *The Storm* would appear in 1938, starring Charles Bickford and Preston Foster, and with Nan Grey in Lupe's role.

‡There are many plot similarities to Pathé's *High Voltage* (1929), which starred Carole Lombard and William Boyd.

§He would offer an equally theatrical but far more balanced performance as an Oriental in *The Hatchet Man* (1932).

With her bilingual ability to speak Spanish and English, Universal paid Lupe to repeat her *East Is West* role in the studio's restaged Spanish-language version of this feature, entitled *Oriente Es Occidente* (1930). As would remain true throughout the remainder of her screen career, Lupe's wavering popularity in the United States was a half-strength reaction compared to her enduring fan-following in South America, where she was considered far more an artiste than just another gimmicky screen personality.

It was almost inevitable that Lupe should inherit one of Dolores Del Rio's old starring movie vehicles. Universal selected *Resurrection* (1931),* which had been one of Del Rio's biggest commercial successes in the days when she was considered a strong rival to MGM's Greta Garbo. Now Lupe was ranked a bigger motion picture attraction than Del Rio, but the new edition of the Leo Tolstoy fiction—directed by Edwin Carewe, who had helmed the 1927 United Artists original—did nothing to enhance Lupe's box-office standing. The unnecessarily turgid account of 1870s Russia follows the travails of peasant girl Lupe, who is seduced by prince John Boles. She gives birth to his child, but the infant later dies. Disgraced and abandoned, she is forced into a life of prostitution and innocently becomes involved in the death of a merchant. Boles returns in time to proclaim his love for Lupe, but the regenerated miss prefers exile alone in Siberia.

Resurrection suffers greatly from an overdose of amateurish dialog and heavyhanded plotting. Whenever director Carewe was at a creative loss about how to move the plot along, he inserted a heavy dose of pseudo-Russian melodies (hoping to drown out the visuals with the audios), leading more than one disgruntled viewer to assume the mishmash was an abortive operetta. Lupe never came to grips with this, her most challenging role to date, remaining a coquettish poseur whether as the simple, happy peasant girl, or later as the wizened, immoral woman. Obviously the pearl-shaped elocution of Boles in tandem with Lupe's heavily accented speech was a far cry from the tonal qualities of the Russian steppes. Lupe also starred in Universal's Spanish-language version of the feature, which co-starred Gilbert Roland and was entitled *Resurrección* (1931).

MGM was the next studio to bargain for Lupe's services, and United Artists loaned her to Metro's Cecil B. De Mille unit for the director's third rendition of *The Squaw Man* (1931).† This picture, which proved to be the third and final feature for De Mille under his MGM pact, found the veteran megaphoner reaching rather desperately into his grab bag to pull off a success. But the new *The Squaw Man* was a thin rendering of a hoary miscegenation yarn and fared no better than De Mille's prior two Metro efforts. Lupe, with her hair plaited into pigtails, was strikingly photographed as she enacted the

*Yet another remake of the Leo Tolstoy novel was Samuel Goldwyn's elaborate *We Live Again* (United Artists, 1934), which failed to launch European import Anna Sten as an American movie star.

†The 1914 edition starred Dustin Farnum and Red Wing, the 1918 version featured Elliott Dexter and Ann Little.

timeworn account of the Arizona Indian maiden Naturich, who kills braggart Charles Bickford to save the life of British aristocrat Warner Baxter. She later bears Baxter's child (who is played as a grown-up by Dickie Moore) only to find that Baxter, who has wed her, really adores Eleanor Boardman, the widow of his English cousin. Nobility demands that Lupe, still wanted by the law for Bickford's murder, commit suicide. Lupe offered a far more subdued performance than usual, walking and riding through most of the picture with a pinched look of dejection. This new harnessing of her vitality led *Photoplay* to extol: " . . . with scarcely a dozen words of dialogue, [she] holds sympathy every second." One can only wonder how a restrained Lupe might have handled a remake of *Ramona*, another Dolores Del Rio silent success, which was mangled by Loretta Young in a 1936 remake.

After appearing in four screen remakes in a row, Lupe was finally in what is euphemistically termed a screen original. MGM's *Cuban Love Song* (1931), as crudely structured in its way as *The Squaw Man*, was concocted to display the talents of Metropolitan opera star Lawrence Tibbett, who was not destined to become a cinema matinee idol no matter what he did onscreen. Director W. S. Van Dyke used his celebrated ability to grind a property through the motion picture production mill with the minimum of cost, but here he ran afoul of the lumbering screenplay of *Cuban Love Song*, a most unfelicitous amalgam of sentiment and humor.* The film's prime gimmick was the recurrent rendition of the title song, a catchy, perennial favorite of years ago that had recently come into renewed popularity. After a respite of several features Lupe was again cast, according to her determined screen type, as a fiery hot tamale. She reverted to her bag of oncamera tricks, from flashy temper to energetic rhumba dancing, to a barrage of quick-flowing broken English ("You beeg gringo fool, you embecil! Ye de mala madre!"). But her hyperactive Nenita was as out of key with the gawky stodginess of Tibbett's screen manner as the extraneous clubroom comedy of iconoclastic Jimmy Durante. There were several scenes in *Cuban Love Song* in which Lupe came across overly coy, as if determined to steal the limelight away from Tibbett. She did.

By the time Lupe jaunted to Manhattan for the splashy Roxy Theatre opening of *Cuban Love Song* (December 4, 1931), her longtime romance with Gary Cooper had collapsed. But Lupe was never one to want for male company for long, and while on loan-out to MGM she renewed her friendship with another of Hollywood's equally irrepressible personalities, John Gilbert.

---

*On a lark, socialite Tibbett joins the Marines along with two incongruous pals, Ernest Torrence and Jimmy Durante. The trio are shipped to Cuba where they have a high old time, particularly one day when Tibbett slambangs his car into the donkey cart of peanut-vendor Lupe. Tibbett and she feud, fume, and later romance. When the World War I armistice comes, he returns to California to wed his patient blueblood fiancée, Karen Morley. Ten years pass. Suddenly one day Tibbett has a shock of conscience and realizes he must see sweet Lupe again. He returns to Havana to find that she had borne his son (Philip Cooper) and has since died. A remorseful Tibbett returns to America with his child, and is forgiven by his devoted wife.

It was not uncommon to see Lupe and Gilbert cavorting about the cinema capital, indulging each and every one of their impulsive whims, being quite indifferent to conventions or to anything that bridled their desires of the moment. Another familiar sight about Hollywood was Lupe peddling along the main streets on her bicycle, animatedly conversing with her two pet Chihuahua dogs, Mr. Kelly and Mrs. Murphy, who rode in a specially constructed basket.

When Lupe checked into the off-Central Park hotel owned by Marion Davies and thus frequented by MGM luminaries, she was more certain about encountering Johnny Weissmuller there than predicting the public's reaction to *Cuban Love Song*. Weissmuller had recently completed his first starring Metro feature, *Tarzan the Ape Man* ((1932), and was destined to be the studio's most important new star of the year. After the Cooper debacle Lupe had stated about Cooper: "He ees my type of man. I weel only love hees kind," and she was now convinced that the muscular ex-Olympic swimmer fit the bill. According to one account, Lupe spotted Weissmuller in the Manhattan hotel lobby and shortly thereafter called his room: "This is Lupe Velez. I am on the floor below you. Will you come down and have a drink with me?" Weissmuller at first thought it was a practical joke but decided to investigate, and he soon could be seen sipping pink champagne with Lupe in her room. By the time each had concluded a battery of public appearances in New York and was headed back to Hollywood, the couple were a steady nightlife twosome and the constant source of gossip-column items. "Johnnie and I," Lupe told the eager press, "are friends, that ees all!" MGM, which had been instrumental in causing Weissmuller to divorce his first wife, Bobbe Arnst, raised no objection to his building a relationship with Lupe, since they were both then making MGM pictures.

After colorful Lupe appeared in Paramount's *The Broken Wing* (1932), which found Mexican bandit Leo Carrillo courting her but American pilot Melvyn Douglas winning her heart, she decided it was time to reboost her celebrity status by returning to the stage. So she accepted Florenz Ziegfeld's timely offer to co-star in *Hot-Cha!* (Ziegfeld Theatre, March 8, 1932). This was not just one of the typical musical revues then so popular, but a book musical by Lew Brown, Ray Henderson, Mark Hellinger, and Hy Kraft, with songs by Brown and Henderson. The gamey plot revolved around New York club parasite Bert Lahr, who finds himself in Mexico City billed as a fearless matador. Lupe was the Mexican charmer Conchita, with whom philandering was a major industry. Spaced between the antics, Lupe performed three songs: "Conchita," "Say What I Wanna Hear You Say" (sung with Charles "Buddy" Rogers), and "They All Need a Little Hot-Cha." In a season that produced *Of Thee I sing, The Cat and the Fiddle,* and *Face the Music, Hot-Cha!* was mercilessly panned for its archaic book and rather tiresome songs. At least the typical Ziegfeld production values were in evidence, particularly in the fiesta finale. The combination of Bert Lahr and Lupe was sufficient to keep the show going for a modest run of 119 performances.

From the first weeks of rehearsal Lahr realized he had a unique and uncontrollable commodity appearing opposite him in *Hot-Cha!** For when Lupe put her mind to concentrating on some new project she lost whatever sense of perspective and decorum she had gained from her several years of moviemaking. More often than not she would indulge in her habit of stripping down to the buff for a run-through of her scenes (so as not to be encumbered by confining costumes), a situation which amused Lahr but did not please his wife. With undisciplined Lupe, it was not a matter of working into a new role, but simply a case of how she was to adapt her well-defined personality to the part at hand. She was not then nor would she ever be an ensemble player, having no notion of what it meant to work in professional rapport with her fellow performers. She merely did her bits as she saw fit and let the others take their cues from her volatile presence.

Audiences who saw Lupe in *Hot-Cha!* considered her Conchita a rather enticing, frenzied creature. As the tropical adventuress she "deported herself as one consecrated to stimulating, if imprudent, diversion" (*New York Times*). Her enthusiastic dancing in the show was termed "fascinatingly disjointed,"† and her emoting was regarded as a prime example of the best high-powered smoldering taught by the exclusive Copacabana School of Acting.

Meanwhile, filmgoers could see Lupe in Columbia's *Hombres En Mi Vida* (1932), a Spanish-language version of the studio's *Men in Her Life* (1931), starring Lois Moran. Even more intriguing was MGM's *Kongo*, released in December, 1932, after *Hot-Cha!* was long since closed. The violent, atypical Metro feature cast Walter Huston in a repeat of his 1926 stage assignment, which had already been refashioned into Lon Chaney's *West of Zanizibar* (MGM, 1929). Lupe appeared as Huston's Portuguese mistress Tula, an on-the-spot witness to the maniacal revenge of her crippled paramour. Huston lures virginal Virginia Bruce from a Cape Town convent to his African trading-post retreat near Zanzibar, convinced she is the daughter of his long-time enemy, C. Henry Gordon. Only after Bruce has been turned into a prostitute and an alcoholic does Huston learn the white girl is really his own daughter. One of the film's more sadistic moments occurs when Huston punishes impetuous Lupe for her infidelity. While her drugged lover of the moment is immersed to his neck in the reptile-laden swamp, Huston toys with Lupe by twisting her tongue with a loop of wire. Ironically it was neither Huston nor Lupe but fourth-billed Virginia Bruce, a rising MGM contractee and the then latest wife of John Gilbert, who garnered most of the publicity for her sympathetic performance in *Kongo*.

Next volatile Lupe was utilized by RKO to top-cast in *The Half-Naked*

---

*"Working with Lupe was quite an experience," Lahr later recalled. "She couldn't laugh. She cackled—like a duck. I'd say things under my breath to her on the stage and she'd start to cackle. . . . Lupe never washed. When she'd go to the Mayfair or somewhere she'd just put on a dress. Nothing under it—nothing. So when I'd be clowning with her on the stage and I'd notice her dirty hands, I'd say 'You've got your gloves on again.' It would break her up."

†Buried in the chorus of the show was future dancing star Eleanor Powell.

Truth (1932), a picture derived from the anecdotal account of public relations whiz Harry Reichenbach in his book, *Phantom Fame*. David O. Selnick-supervised RKO was the first studio to make use of Lupe as a caricature of her well-known public image, placing the performer into a new facet of her career. No longer was she the apprentice leading lady who, it was forecast, might become as good a dramatic actress as she was exotic, temperamental, and publicity-conscious. Now she was categorized as a celebrity personality whose mercurial behavior could best be channeled into undemanding, one-dimensional, stereotyped screen roles. *The Half-Naked Truth* provided Lupe with a tailor-made part as "Princess Exotica," a publicity-hungry actress posing as an escaped harem beauty, with Eugene Pallette hired as her pseudo-Turkish retainer. To make sure she has not missed any headline-gathering angle, Princess Exotica houses a pet lion in her apartment. Lee Tracy was cast as Lupe's publicity-agent marvel who engineers a starring job for her in producer Frank Morgan's latest Broadway revue (love-struck Morgan has cause to regret his impetuous decision when he actually hears Lupe's heavily accented renditions of American songs). Under Gregory La Cava's direction, Lupe smoothly projected a burlesque version of her typical public self, a pose that would later form the basis for her *Mexican Spitfire* series at RKO.

On a freelance basis Lupe accepted a bid from Fox studio to co-star in *Hot Pepper* (1933), the fourth in the series of screen adventures of Sergeant Harry Quirt (Edmund Lowe) and Top Sergeant Flagg (Victor McLaglen). The first and most famous entry of the continuing series, *What Price Glory?* (1926), had featured Lupe's professional nemesis, Dolores Del Rio, as the fiery French girl Charmaine, while the less plushly mounted *The Cock-Eyed World* (1929) displayed the less effective performance of Lily Damita as the Spanish siren Elenita, and *Women of All Nations* (1931) featured Greta Nissen. Lupe was determined to outshine her three predecessors and supercharged her performance as the South American entertainer, Pepper. Using more than her usual ration of verve Lupe bounded around the sets, but she was still no match for the dominating antics of her two male co-leads. Lowe was again the smug, dapper, smart guy, forever putting one over on his big, gullible comrade, McLaglen. As *Hot Pepper* opens, Lowe and McLaglen have quit the Marine Corps. Three years pass and it is McLaglen, not down-and-out Lowe, who has made his mark as a big league bootlegger with a fancy nightclub of his own. Before long the two rivals are at it again, with Lowe opening his own entertainment spot and stealing away McLaglen's latest performing sensation, who is none other than hotcha south-of-the-border dancer Lupe. From the moment in the picture when stowaway Lupe is discovered aboard one of McLaglen's rum-runners, she provides a nonstop flow of physical energy and spunky dialog* and sings such songs as "Mon Papa." The finale of *Hot Pep-*

---

*Her broken English was a refreshing diversion from the "sez you, sez me" lingo of Lowe and McLaglen.

per found the two hard-boiled gents reinstated in the Marines and on duty in China. Fox planned further adventures of the rugged duo, with or without Lupe as their partner, but the resulting box-office take from the mild *Hot Pepper* did not warrant the investment. At least the *New York Times* endorsed Lupe's performance in this picture, in which she displayed "a good measure of audacity, recklessness and extraordinary vitality."

Lupe and her *Hot-Cha!* sidekick Bert Lahr were among the celebrities of the day corraled to appear in *Mr. Broadway* (1933), a potpourri picture which had been filmed on location at Manhattan nightspots by *New York Daily News* columnist Ed Sullivan. In this filmed travelogue of clubs, Lupe was shown hobnobbing at the Central Park Casino. After a trip to Hollywood to make Fox's *Hot Pepper*, Lupe returned to New York for Lew Brown and Ray Henderson's *Strike Me Pink* (Majestic Theatre, March 4, 1933). She thoroughly enjoyed the refreshing novelty of the Broadway scene, where she was considered a new personality to be courted and indulged. On the more staid East Coast, her spontaneous behavior was considered even more of an attention-grabbing oddity. One thing Lupe thoroughly enjoyed was attention.

Brown and Henderson conceded to the demands of the time and made *Strike Me Pink* a revue-style production. They supplied the songs for the piecemeal production, with Seymour Felix supervising the extensive choreography. However, little jelled properly in *Strike Me Pink*, whether the gagging of Schnozola Jimmy Durante,* the terpsichorean activity of Hal LeRoy, or the contrasting presences of Park Avenue socialite Hope Williams and hot pepper Lupe, "whose duty it was," observed one local critic, "to strut her stuff in the sweet name of Hollywood." Lupe's major contributions to the revue were the song "Love and Rhythm" and the skit "Ultra Modern." She certainly did her best to give live wire Durante a run for his money in the show, causing the *New York Times* to report: "She dances wantonly and some of her seductive gestures might be, if made by a less skillful artiste, a bit abashing." With its $3.30 ticket top, *Strike Me Pink* lasted 122 performances.

By the time *Strike Me Pink* folded, Lupe had negotiated an MGM agreement and was able to return to the West Coast with renewed prestige. Her MGM contract was not magnificent by the standards of such Culver City greats as Norma Shearer, Greta Garbo, Joan Crawford, or even Jean Harlow, but for a quirky personality—and MGM made it clear to Lupe and the public that she was being packaged as a novelty performer, not as an actress—Lupe was doing just fine. Undoubtedly MGM executives were influenced to sign Lupe by her successful Broadway sojourn, and more importantly by her still news-gathering romance with Metro jungle-star Johnny Weissmuller. No matter where pint-sized Lupe and her brawny "Johnnee" went, it seemed, something newsworthy happened. One night they were at the Ciro Club in

---

*With his MGM career floundering, Durante had taken a leave of absence for a Broadway return. It was his first reteaming with Lupe since their oncamera parrying in *Cuban Love Song.*

Hollywood when a patron picked a fight with the screen Tarzan. Weissmuller tried to pass off the incident, but Lupe exploded on the spot and began punching the man. "You beeg ape! You leave my man alone!" The incident was duly given full press coverage, much to the delight of the Metro hierarchy.

After many months of public speculation on their intended domestic status, Lupe and Weissmuller finally did marry, at 4 A.M. on October 8, 1933, in a civil ceremony in Las Vegas conducted by a local justice of the peace. When the couple returned from Las Vegas to Hollywood, they each denied marriage rumors. However on October 28 (perhaps feeling it was time to feed the press some new copy) Lupe announced that she and her man were now wife and husband, explaining her previous denials: "It was my own business. I felt like saying I wasn't married, and now I feel like saying I am married." Who could argue with this logic?

Weissmuller moved into Lupe's two-story Spanish-style mansion at 732 North Rodeo Drive, Beverly Hills. As a wedding gift for his bride he purchased a thirty-four-foot schooner, which he christened the *Santa Guadalupe*. Another addition to Lupe's growing menagerie, which included assorted pets of all species and jungle king Weissmuller, was Joan Del Valle Vallez, the four-year-old daughter of her eldest sister Mercedes. Lupe had "adopted" the girl earlier in the year.

Despite her new marital status, Lupe rushed pell-mell into a busy filming schedule, appearing in four 1934 releases. MGM's investment in Lupe's screen career was relatively minimal, and the studio was primarily interested in garnering as much mileage as possible with the least amount of effort, from Lupe's already existing marquee lure. On paper, *Laughing Boy* (1934) seemed far more promising than it emerged onscreen. It was based on the 1929 Pulitzer Prize-winning novel by Oliver La Farge, which at the time had caused critics to call the fiction a new *Broken Blossoms*. Universal had snapped up the screen rights to *Laughing Boy* in the early 1930s as a vehicle for Zita Johann and Lew Ayres, to be directed by William Wyler. When no satisfactory screen treatment was forthcoming, Universal sold the abortive project to MGM, where it eventually landed on the work assignment sheet for efficient W. S. Van Dyke. It was hoped that he could turn out a passable screen version on a low budget. Although Van Dyke convinced the Metro authorities to allow him to take his cast and crew to the Navajo reservation in northeastern Arizona for on-location filming, the picture still remained pure bunkum. It was no more than a fitful blend of soggy romance and shadowy realism, overly earnest and generally unconvincing. Certainly it was no *Broken Blossoms*. Declining MGM star Ramon Novarro was a less unlikely Indian than Don Ameche would be in *Ramona*, but his Latin-accented speech and high-pitched singing of "The Call of Love" were heavy deficits to overcome. Equally amiss, and everyone knew it from the start, was Lupe's Slim Girl, a Navajo maiden who left the reservation to attend the white man's school and later returned to serve in the home of Caucasian William Davidson. When Novarro, her pious childhood sweetheart, learns of her supposed sin nest, he seeks immediate revenge. In his haste to loose an arrow at Davidson, he fatally wounds Lupe, providing a teary finale at the site of her grave. Although the picturization of *Laughing Boy* met an inglorious box-office death, as recently as 1970 there was legitimate talk of a Hollywood producer resurrecting the archaic story for a proper new filming.

As part of a package deal, Lupe was loaned by MGM to United Artists, along with Jimmy Durante, for a movie version of Ham Fisher's enduring comic strip, *Joe Palooka*. The resulting picture, *Palooka* (Rivoli Theatre, February 27, 1934), was surprisingly chipper, particularly when one considers how the same property would be mishandled later on by Monogram in its movie series. Stuart Erwin played the title role of a yokel who inherits a knack for smacking with his fists from his boxer father (Robert Armstrong),* but it was razzmatazz Durante, taking advantage of the first full-bodied screen role he had had in a long time, who noisily walked away with the picture. Durante's natty and nutty Knobby Walsh became the screen prototype of all conniving boxing managers, but his performance was balanced with a kindhearted warmth and smart wisecracking which added up to top-rate entertainment.

Lupe was not so fortunate in her *Palooka* screen role. She was again a high-spirited *femme fatale*, but here her Nina Madero had few redeeming features. She was an out-and-out "wrecker of champions,"† ego-gratified when bemused Erwin is overcome by her obvious charms and ignores his steadfast hometown sweetheart, Mary Carlisle. Lupe's near-fatal conquest of simplistic Erwin is more than carrying out a favor to Durante (who fears Carlisle will persuade Erwin to abandon the boxing game), it is a self-serving exercise in narcissistic manipulation. Since the entire film was geared to a very unsubtle level, Lupe's turncoat portrayal seemed little different from her past screen efforts. To further detract from possible audience empathy with Lupe in *Palooka* there was Marjorie Rambeau's earthy performance as Erwin's country-town mom. Rambeau gave full dimension to her portrayal of a rough ex-burlesque queen who knows how the fight game can ruin a good man (witness her husband Armstrong having run out on her twenty years prior). So naturally Rambeau sides with Carlisle in steering impressionable Erwin away from Spanish cooch dancer Lupe, and in so doing she devalued Lupe's importance in the picture to a secondary interest.

The audience reaction to *Palooka* taught an uncaring MGM nothing about the proper showcasing of Jimmy Durante or conversely the correct handling of Lupe's screen image, albeit even the new self-mocking guise. The Metro boys blithely tossed the duo into *Hollywood Party* (1934), one of the more noted cinema turkeys of the year. Early in 1933 the project had been bally-

---

*Erwin would earn an Oscar nomination for fulfilling a very similar part in Twentieth Century-Fox's *Pigskin Parade* (1936).

†Early on in *Palooka* it is established that Lupe has already subdued and ruined former boxing champ William Cagney.

hooed as an all-star Culver City film to feature the silver-screen romping of such Metro celebrities as Joan Crawford, Jean Harlow, Marie Dressler, Jean Hersholt, Lee Tracy, and Nils Asther. None of these names graced the final film, which proved to be little more than a dreary series of short subjects and sight-gag skits tacked together within the framework of a watery tale— Durante reads a *Tarzan* novel and dreams he is Schnarzan, the Ape Man, king of Hollywood jungle films. *Hollywood Party* was considered such a turkey, it was released without any directorial credit.

In an opening sequence of *Hollywood Party* Lupe was required to burlesque her real-life relationship to Weissmuller by exchanging blunted barbs with Durante. The comic, dressed in an ill-fitting loin-cloth and an over-the-chest animal-skin ensemble, protests to Lupe: "Beneath this here lion's cloth beats a heart that's seethin' with sentiment." Lupe: "I'll bet you say that to every animal."

Later in the film, which boldly proclaimed there was a laugh for everyone somewhere in the picture, Lupe did have a genuinely hilarious bit of business with comedians Stan Laurel and Oliver Hardy, with whom she had last worked in 1927. After exhausting herself in a club-bar temper tantrum (*de rigueur* for most every Lupe film outing), Lupe tosses off a gold slipper, which wings Laurel and Hardy. Laurel wins the right from his pudgy sidekick to return the shoe to smoldering Lupe. Exasperated Hardy, on the other hand, is ready to crack Lupe on the head with one of his own shoes. But Laurel stops him. Conveniently for the action which then transpires, there is a bowl of eggs on the bar counter. Lupe grabs one, cracks it open, and pours it slowly into Hardy's shoe, leading to a battle of supremacy with the eggs as the chief weapon.*

MGM had no particular plans for either Lupe or Durante at the time so they loaned the performers to RKO for *Strictly Dynamite* (1934). The comedy was offered as the July Fourth holiday treat for the action fans of Broadway's Rialto Theatre, and the *New York Times* quickly passed off the film as strictly "warm weather humor." However, the chipper B-production was an entertaining entry among the several motion pictures dealing with Hollywood's war on the rival radio medium. Durante was appropriately cast as Moxie Slaight, a temperamental radio star with a penchant for multisyllabic words, poetry, luxurious living, and being a pathetically easy prey for adventurous women, fast-talking agents, and authors who could toss long words at him quicker than he could reply. Second-billed Lupe was Vera, Durante's airwaves foil and off-microphone bundle of trouble. Had director Elliott Nugent underplayed the tedious secondary plot (involving idealistic writer Norman Foster and his sweetheart, Marion Nixon), this seventy-one-minute feature would have been all the zestier. As the twentieth-century

---

*This sequence was included in Bob Youngson's compilation feature, *MGM's Big Parade of Comedy* (1964).

Cyrano, Durante mugged all scenes in which he was within fifty feet of the camera. By now Lupe had learned that when teamed with Durante she had better save her outbursts of chili-pepper antics for moments when her co-star was far away offscreen. Before the role of Vera in *Strictly Dynamite* was altered to fit Lupe's personality, RKO had planned the part for rising contract star(let) Ginger Rogers.

Lupe was equally busy offscreen in 1934. On January 24, 1934, she and Weissmuller parted after one of their more serious fights, deriving from their still unresolved relationship. (He was a day person; she a night owl who taught him to smoke and drink, and to socialize on the club circuit. All this went against Weissmuller's grain, not to mention the physical maintenance required to preserve his *Tarzan* physique.) Lupe filed for divorce, but withdrew her suit on July 20 that year. As Lupe related for the edification of the press: "Fight? We all do! Johnee and I may fight, but no more than the rest of Hollywood. They call each other dear and darling een public, and then go home and smack each other een private. When Johnee and I get sore, we get sore, we get sore no matter where we are!" In fact, Lupe insisted, "the way to be happy through marriage ees to fight once a week, maybe more."* When Lupe was on tour that spring and summer, playing the Loew's vaudeville circuit under her MGM contract, Weissmuller joined her in Cleveland. One night while there, the two animal-passion individuals embarked on a wild melee in their hotel room that could not be overlooked by the deafest hotel guest. By morning rumors were spreading that Weissmuller had beaten poor little Lupe black and blue. This attack on "Johnee" so enraged the volatile Lupe that she forgot her anger at Weissmuller and demanded a personal confrontation with a female member of the local press who could then verify that she was unblemished from the noctural argument. "Take a looook," Lupe screamed at the chosen examiner. "See eef you can find one black and blue one. . . . He did not ponch or heet me. . . . Let the world get used to my Johnee and me."

Despite her sizable self-won celebrity status MGM did not choose to renew her option in the fall of 1934. The twenty-five-year-old Mexican personality found the quality and quantity of screen offers anemic, and it required some fast manipulation to restore her sagging career and bank account. Producer William Roland at Columbia offered to star Lupe in the musical *The Girl Friend*, but after initial negotiations Lupe backed out of the project and returned the monetary advance. Two fast-talking French film promoters convinced Lupe to hightail it over to Paris for a loosely described $50,000 motion picture deal. But by Christmas of 1934, Lupe had returned to Hollywood, having learned the hard way that promises and cash on the line are two dif-

---

*Lupe thoroughly enjoyed relating her most intimate home-life scenes to the reporters. She told of waking up one night and staring at Weissmuller, thinking, "He ees so beautiful."

She continued: "Then for no reason I punch him right in the nose. He jumps up and says, 'Mama, you hit me' and I say, 'Darling I am sorree. Heet me back'; and he says, 'Never mind, honey, you couldn't help yourself.' "

ferent matters.* Humiliated but undaunted by her injudicious business *faux pas*, Lupe gifted Weissmuller with a pair of boxing gloves that Christmas, with an attached card reading: "Darling. So you can punch me if I leave you again."

The seven days between Christmas and New Year's of 1934 were more than ample time for Lupe and Weissmuller to force-feed another spat. On January 2, 1935, Lupe again filed for divorce in Los Angeles court, insisting that this time she and "Johnee" were through for good. She would later dismiss this suit, but the marital rift was far more damaging this time, and a sulky Lupe spent the bulk of 1935 and 1936 abroad. Like other Hollywood film celebrities who could not command self-respecting film assignments at home, she found that England offered a pride-saving (and tax dodging) retreat for once stellar marquee names. The British may be many things, but they have a wonderful sense of loyalty to stars of any vintage.

Lupe made her debut in British feature films in *The Morals of Marcus* (English premiere, April, 1935; United States debut, Globe Theatre, January 13, 1936). W. J. Locke's decrepit play was a sorry showcase for Lupe's famous tantrums and other oncamera tricks. The hoary plot called for Lupe to be sold into a Syrian harem. To escape her dire fate she attaches herself to dusty British antique-collector Ian Hunter, stowing away in his stateroom. When they arrive in England her eccentric behavior shocks Hunter's friends (they are so conservative they believe sex is the fundamental blunder of creation). At this trite point she is whisked off to Paris by cad Noel Madison, who has been waiting for a good opportunity to seduce her. But in France he soon abandons Lupe for other, more lively, pursuits, forcing her to eke out a modest living performing in an underworld cafe. Professor Hunter finally comes to Lupe's timely rescue in the last reel. The snails-pace direction by erstwhile actor Miles Mander hampered Lupe's style of tempestuous acting. But in comparison with the phlegmatic performances of Hunter and scheming blueblood Adrianne Allen, Lupe was a glittering star. The *New York Times* aptly observed that the film is tedious when "Lupe Velez is not busy exercising her fiery temper or being unconsciously amusing in her attempts to scale the proverbial dramatic heights."

After making the British *Mad about Money*, which would not find American release until 1938, Lupe returned to America in early 1936 to embark on a vaudeville tour with Weissmuller, the couple earning about $5,500 for the packaged-show unit. Besides singing a medley of songs in the act, Lupe performed her standard imitations of Katharine Hepburn and Gloria Swanson, and winged her way through a skit with Weissmuller that teased his he-man screen image. Lupe then beat a hasty retreat back to England where she starred in another motion picture, *Gypsy Melody* (August, 1936). In this Ruritanian musical comedy she was a gypsy dancer who is finally allowed by the rigid laws of Seeburg to wed her young lover, Alfred Rodo. At most Lupe

*Lupe did collect $25,000 of the sum owed her, plus transportation costs.

was ornamental in this minor picture. The film's primary focus was on Rodo and his *tzigane* (gypsy) orchestra, especially with the group's stylish rendition of Liszt's "Second Hungarian Rhapsody." The archaic book-plot of *Gypsy Melody* even provided a Jewish hatter (Jerry Verno) for standard ethnic-comic relief.

In the fall of 1936, Lupe starred in an Adelphi Theatre revue show in London and then proceeded to make her way back to America, arriving in New York harbor on December 25, 1936, aboard the *Normandie*. When Lupe next turned up in Hollywood after virtually a two-year absence, the professional pickings were very slim. The best deal offered Lupe was the female lead opposite Bert Wheeler and Robert Woolsey in their twentieth and final RKO feature, *High Flyers* (1937). By this point the comedy duo had exhausted the bulk of their box-office worth, which had once been rather high after they made their feature film debut in RKO's *Rio Rita* (1929). Woolsey was suffering from a chronic kidney ailment during the filming of *High Flyers* and a year after its completion would die in October, 1938. RKO production head Pandro S. Berman ordered director Edward Cline to make this entry as cheaply as possible as part of Lee Marcus's RKO economy-production unit. The picture emerged as old-fashioned nonsense and an unsatisfactory diversion even for slapstick devotees. Wheeler and Woolsey were again cast as the perennial nitwits, this time duped by clever criminals into smuggling contraband gems into the country. Only these two scatterbrains could end up on the estate of Paul Harvey and Margaret Dumont, the couple for whom the baubles were originally intended. Lupe seemed befuddled by her role in the worn-out mayhem. Her poolside production number, "Keep Your Head Above Water," was less than memorable. Marjorie Lord, who would much later gain prominence as Danny Thomas's teleseries wife, was the standard ingenue of *High Flyers* and had a lot more in keeping with the picture than Lupe.

Since Lupe and Weissmuller were unable to patch up their emotional differences, she began dating a variety of Hollywood people, sometimes escorted by her business manager, or accompanied by actor Bruce Cabot or producer Eddie Mannix. But capricious Lupe was searching for a substitute for her departed "Johnee" and no one who was available filled the bill. To salve her hurt pride she endorsed an even more extensive nightclubbing program, traipsing about the club circuit with deliberate abandon.

At this juncture Lupe decided it was time to return home to Mexico City, her first visit there in eleven years. She was greeted by a crowd of more than 10,000 fans with a riotous welcome that left her "enchanted but scared to death." The tumultuous reception did much to restore Lupe's deflated self-confidence; more important, she found working conditions in the Mexican film industry particularly salutary and agreed to make a picture for local producers. As a native girl who had made good in Hollywood, she was accorded every cooperation available and treated like the full-fledged star she had always wanted to be. *La Zandunga* (1938), a folk comedy set in the Isthmus of Tehuantepec, told a true tale of love gone astray. The major emphases were

on the romantic relationship between Lupe and sailor Arturo de Cordova*
and on the ample sampling of musical production numbers. When *La Zandunga* played Manhattan's Teatro Hispano Theatre in March, 1938, the *New
York Times* ranked it a "delightful, well proportioned picture" and noted of
Lupe: "In her happier and snappier moods she seems rather calmer than in
her English stage and film work." The critic might have added that with the
restraint imposed by the alien English language gone, Lupe was better able to
effervesce oncamera with more emphasis on vivacity than posturing. Even in
La Zandunga, her standard head scratching, nostril flaring, and teeth flashing
were much in evidence.

Lupe was so pleased by her south-of-the-border filming experience that she
fully planned to return to Mexico in February, 1938, for four additional pictures at a weekly salary of $4,500. However, this event was not to take place
for five more years, as several factors weighed to keep her rooted in Hollywood.

Lupe's relationship to Weissmuller reached the breaking point early in 1938
and she prepared a divorce suit, again claiming cruelty, physical violence, and
mental cruelty, all of which, she explained, upset her so much that she was
emotionally unable to earn her livelihood performing in motion pictures. The
courtroom hearing had its moment of levity when Lupe said that Weissmuller
was so parsimonious he did not even want her to spend the money to go to a
beauty parlor. Judge Charles Burnett interjected: "He probably thought you
didn't need beauty treatment." The divorce would be legally finalized on
August 16, 1939. Under the divorce terms, Weissmuller was to pay Lupe $200
a week for 156 weeks except when she was employed. She was to receive full
possession of their Beverly Hills home and furniture, he to have ownership of
their schooner and speedboat.

Lupe's marital breakup was not the only news-provoking item she excited
in 1938. Sacramento District Attorney Neil McAllister undertook an ambitious
but short-lived campaign to investigate the state of Communism in Hollywood.
He claimed that, among others, James Cagney, Ramon Novarro, Dolores Del
Rio, and Lupe were suspected of left-wing affiliations, linking Lupe with rampant radicalism. For a novel change in recent years, her soon-to-be-ex-spouse
Weissmuller came to Lupe's defense stating, "Why Lupe doesn't even know
what the word Communism means."

Lupe's other English-made picture, *Mad about Money*, finally saw British
release in 1938, and the word-of-mouth about the picture, which crossed the
Atlantic, was unfavorable. The film boasted the presence of four American
movie "names": Lupe, Ben Lyon, Wallace Ford, and Harry Langdon, all of
whom had seen happier professional days in Hollywood. Lupe was cast as
Carla de Huelva, an ambitious actress passing herself off in London as a
wealthy South American cattle queen. Financially pinched film producer Lyon

---

*He would make his brief mark as a Latin Lover type of the American cinema at Paramount
Studios in the early 1940s.

hopes to snag her bankroll for some badly needed front money for his up-coming movie production. And that was the crux of the plot! Obviously money was spent on *Mad about Money*, for the assorted production numbers, none of which really featured Lupe, were far above the usual standards of British filmmaking. But in comparison to the Hollywood product, this Anglo-Saxon entry was flimsy indeed: short on plot, thin on humor, unprofessional in its musical-comedy moments, and saddled with a poorly recorded sound-track to boot. Nothing could be sadder than to see the once legendary Lang-don reduced to wandering through *Mad about Money*, more confused than bemused, in his extraneous, embarrassing role as a tipsy show business angel.

At this new low point in her career Lupe sought another Broadway prop-erty to restore her diminishing professional status. Plans ran afoul for Lupe to star in James Cain's play *7-11*,* but the brothers Shubert recalled Lupe's musical revue work and signed her to co-star with debonair song-and-dance-man Clifton Webb in *You Never Know* (Winter Garden Theatre, September 21, 1938). Before embarking on her latest Broadway venture, Lupe purchased the thirteen-room home in Senseneda, Baja California, that Jack Dempsey had originally had built for his then wife, Estelle Taylor. Ever since the days of *Where East Is East* (MGM, 1929) Lupe and Taylor had been good friends, each bolstering the other's ego in their many times of depression.

During the out-of-town tryouts Lupe was overshadowing her two *You Never Know* confreres, Clifton Webb and class vocalist Libby Holman, both onstage and off. Cole Porter was then in a physical and creative funk, and his transformation of Siegfried Geyer's romantic comedy, *By Candlelight* (1929), was uninspired.† British screenwriter Rowland Leigh continued to rewrite his adaptation and even added a few new lyrics to Porter's songs; librettist Rob-ert Katscher was asked to incorporate one of his tunes into the score; and finally show doctor George Abbott took a stab at revamping the production. While all these internal changes were transpiring, the ragged book being used for the spring tryout favored Lupe's part and she made the most of her mo-ments onstage.‡ During the weeks on the road (New Haven, Boston, Wash-ington, Philadelphia, Pittsburgh, and Indianapolis) Lupe's relationship with Holman deteriorated in direct proportion to the beneficial changes being made in the songstress's role. If Lupe could nonchalantly travel from her hotel to the theatre dressing room each night wearing only a mink coat and slippers, then, reasoned the stage manager, it was just as likely that she meant it when she on several occasions threatened to "keel" Holman. Thus each night Hol-man would be escorted and guarded from her dressing room to the stage en-

---

*Before producer Richard Aldrich shelved the project, Lupe's onetime Hollywood rival, Lily Damita, was announced for the role.

†Despite a cast that included Gertrude Lawrence, Leslie Howard, and Reginald Owen, the show had a very limited run. The 1934 Universal picturization starred Elissa Landi.

‡The well-known plot finds valet Webb posing as his employer to court a lady (Lupe) who is really the maid to the woman (Holman) his employer is pursuing.

trance, for fear Lupe might make good her promise. Dapper Webb attempted to mediate in the growing feud, which he at first thought was pure publicity. But during an after-show supper with Lupe, she showed Webb the ring with which she planned to murder Libby.* Eventually backstage order was restored, but the production was considered to be in such chaotic artistic shape that a summer layoff was ordered, while Porter recuperated in Europe and some new ideas were pushed into the production.

September came and *You Never Know* debuted on Broadway to a tepid response from the critics and public alike. Webb provided the élan, Holman the vocal artistry, while Lupe's performance, according to Brooks Atkinson of the *New York Times*, was "a strange collection of some things that are funny and a great many more that are only perpetual motion." When the action on-stage slowed down, Lupe embellished her performance with imitations of Katharine Hepburn, Shirley Temple, and Vera Zorina. Lupe and Webb dueted "From Alpha to Omega" (a still zingy number) and the title tune, and Lupe held full stage center singing "What Shall I Do?" There was much of Lupe's moviedom antics in her performance as she thumbed her nose at characters and audience alike, gamboling with her traditional hoydenish hokum. But Richard Watts, Jr. of the *New York Herald-Tribune* announced that "my only objection is that she labors a bit too grimly and determinedly at being rowdy and hearty."

During the course of *You Never Know*'s meager seventy-eight-performance run, Lupe did her best to generate some publicity for herself and the show. She (or a public relations man) obligingly selected for the press a list of the ten most interesting men she knew, which included: Johnny Weissmuller,† Franklin Delano Roosevelt, Clark Gable, Lawrence Tibbett, Ed Wynn, Ernest Hemingway, Georges Enesco, John L. Lewis, Jack Dempsey, and George S. Kaufman. For a brief spell Lupe embarked on a new tactic, which was hastily discarded as her chameleonish personality reverted back to old habits. Lupe insisted that it was really the press that gave the public the wrong image of the so-called "Mexican Spitfire" and that she was far less impetuous and temperamental than people had been led to believe. Lupe was probably the only one in captivity who believed this particular train of thought.

After the failure of *You Never Know*, Lupe let it be known that she wanted no further participation in revue shows and would only consider dramatic plays or book musical comedies. There was talk of Lupe headlining Ruth Cumareys's *Ruby Wilson*, but nothing transpired. So Lupe returned to Hollywood and again was rescued from a possible stretch of nonwork by RKO, which paged her for the tailor-written *Girl from Mexico* (Rialto Theatre, June 7, 1939).

---

*Later in the evening, when Lupe had sufficiently calmed down to listen to a modicum of reason, Webb is supposed to have prophetically told her: "Lupe, you must not say such things. One day you'll turn them all against yourself."

†At this juncture Lupe's divorce from "Johnee" was not finalized.

If RKO's *Strictly Dynamite* (1934) and *High Flyers* (1937) had been come-downs in prestige for Lupe, *Girl from Mexico* was the watershed mark. No longer by anyone's imagination could Lupe be termed an ingenue (she was thirty years old). She was now a too-familiar trouper, who, by dint of person-ality and intuitive career maneuvering, had stretched out a see-sawing Holly-wood career for well over a decade. For a long time already American film producers had correctly estimated Lupe's cinematic worth as merely a for-eign novelty who could bolster a mediocre project into commercially accept-able screenfare. With *Girl from Mexico* even Lupe, at least as far as her future Hollywood film career was concerned, tacitly acknowledged that dra-matic stardom was no longer over the proverbial horizon. If producers were willing to pay her for burlesquing her established screen image, why not? Thus Lupe's association with RKO began in earnest in late 1938 when George Schaefer was president of the studio and was restructuring the lot's produc-tion output heavily in favor of programmers that would appeal to rural audi-ences.

RKO economy division producer Robert Sisk had Lionel Houser and play-wright Joseph A. Fields concoct a nonsensical lowbrow comedy vehicle for Lupe, and the resultant *Girl from Mexico*, much to everyone's surprise, not only was financially successful beyond expectation but also paved the way for Lupe's permanent niche in cinema history as the extravagantly headstrong star of the *Mexican Spitfire* series.

Girl from Mexico established all the basic ingredients and cast of char-acters for the eventual series. Manhattan advertising executive Donald Woods is ordered to locate a Mexican girl to sing on a client's radio program. Lupe comes to his attention, and he posts a $10,000 bond guaranteeing her employment and proper moral behavior while in the United States. Naturally the irrepressible Lupe is at odds with north-of-the-border customs; shouts herself hoarse at baseball games and wrestling matches; flirts with Woods, much to the annoyance of his finicky fiancée, Linda Hayes; and, in short, makes a complete nuisance of herself. Only Woods's rubber-legged Uncle Matt (Leon Errol) takes Lupe's side. He eggs her on to be her total natural self, realizing his nephew will eventually choose Lupe as his rightful spouse—and that eventually does happen. *Girl from Mexico* was sneeringly labeled "shrill, spirited, senseless, slapstick comedy" by high-toned critics. But it was mindless entertainment of high satisfaction for audiences of the day. Lupe ex-pended her professional all to be more of a Mexican firecracker than ever, screeching like a parrot, jabbering snatches of unintelligible (to American audiences at least) bits of Spanish colloquialism mishmashed with fractured English, rattling off bits of songs, and performing disjointed sections of Latin American dances. Lupe interplayed her slapstick sequences with Errol to such a high degree of shameless enthusiasm that her old studio boss, Hal Roach, would have stood up and cheered had he been on the set. Interestingly, *Girl from Mexico* contained few close-up shots of now red-headed Lupe. Studio

616

cameraman Jack MacKenzie, who would handle most of Lupe's forthcoming RKO assignments, observed that despite her dark Latin complexion, Lupe's full features were difficult to lense in close proximity without capturing unflattering camera angles.

Studio head George Schaefer was so pleased with the initial exhibitor and audience response to *Girl from Mexico* that he immediately negotiated a picture pact with Lupe.* As a specialty player, distinct from the star roster (which soon would be whittled down to include Lucille Ball, Phyllis Brooks, Maureen O'Hara, Ginger Rogers, and Anne Shirley) Lupe had a limited ceiling to her salary escalations, never rising above $1,500-a-week paychecks. Nevertheless, this sum, bolstered by radio and personal appearance tours, provided a sufficient basis for Lupe to maintain her highstepping California life.

Six months after the debut of *Girl from Mexico*, *Mexican Spitfire* rolled into the Rialto Theatre (December 31, 1939). "Not since Dr. [Mack] Sennett was writing his master's thesis at Keystone College," reported the *New York Times*'s Frank S. Nugent, "has Times Square seen anything like *Mexican Spitfire*. This entry might be better termed a well-pastried bit of buffoonery." For in this picture Lupe marries Donald Woods and soon she and Errol are frolicking through a spree of custard tossing at the wedding reception, outshining each other with their frenzied repartee and double takes. But blueblood Linda Hayes is not about to allow Lupe to emerge the victor in the marriage sweepstakes without paying a penalty. So she later persuades innocent Lupe to pulling some hijinks that embarrass Woods in his business negotiations with stuffy Britisher Lord Epping.† In the course of this slapdash picture Lupe is required to perform her standard Mexican hotblooded bits: fracturing the English of scenarists Joseph A. Fields and Charles E. Roberts, eye-rolling, indulging in obvious double-entendre byplay, and much body movement. But it was Leon Errol who claimed the bulk of audience interest with a routine that would become standard fare in future *Mexican Spitfire* entries. At one point in the inconsequential story, it is imperative that Uncle Matt impersonate Lord Epping in order to smooth over Lupe's latest *faux pas,* which has endangered Woods's future business career. In an overplayed but hilarious exaggeration, Errol rushes pell-mell in one door and out the other with incredibly rubberlegged, breakneck speed, switching from one personality to another. In his alter-ego impersonations Errol has to point up that one gentleman can handle his liquor while the other (Uncle Matt) most certainly cannot. Audiences seemed to have had an abnormally high threshold for this structured vaudeville gambit, and Errol obliged by performing it to the hilt in later installments of the *Mexican Spitfire* series.

---

*Leon Errol, the other ingredient necessary to the series, was already under RKO contract, utilized particularly in a long-running batch of short subjects.

†Whisky magnate Lord Basil Epping bears a striking resemblance to salt-of-the-earth Uncle Matt—and no wonder, since both characters were played with relish by veteran Errol.

With Lupe firmly set as the latest addition to RKO's array of B-picture queens, which now also included Wendy Barrie, the studio contemplated using her in an assortment of other features besides the popular *Mexican Spitfires*. At one point it was decided to reteam Lupe with Victor McLaglen (then at RKO with Edmund Lowe in a further Quirt-Flagg adventure entitled *The Marines Fly High*), but it proved too expensive to obtain the character rights.* Instead Lupe was pushed into *Mexican Spitfire Out West,* her only 1940 release. This entry finds the demanding *tamale* unduly irritated when hubby Woods becomes overly engrossed in closing a business deal with that perennial old duffer, Lord Epping. Not about to be ignored, Lupe packs her bags and rushes off to Nevada to obtain a quick Reno divorce, although she is really more intent on teaching her well-meaning husband a good lesson. This premise allows the cast of regulars to show up in the new western setting, with Lupe's aunt-in-law (Elisabeth Risdon) still angling to wean her malleable nephew Woods away from Lupe and back into the arms of more conventional Linda Hayes. Even more than previously Lupe was relegated to supplying high-powered decoration while the bulk of the comedy burden was placed on Errol's bony shoulders. And he obliged with another rendition of his impersonation-collapsible-legs drunk-Oops, who-am-I-now? routines.

Having established Lupe and Errol as a workable comedy team,† RKO was not averse to loaning the duo out to other studios at a nice profit. Universal provided the necessary coin to borrow the packaged services of Lupe and Errol for its *Six Lessons from Madame La Zonga* (1941), the wacky title deriving from a hit pop tune of the previous year. Lupe was noisier than ever in the role of a loudmouthed Havana club girl hired to transform Manhattanite Helen Parrish into Rosita Alvarez so the latter can return to the States as an in-vogue Latin-rhythm songstress. Errol was on hand in a more subdued manner as a Cuban arrival in search of easy money. Among the "Oklahoma" cowboys involved in the nonsense was actor and polo player Guinn "Big Boy" Williams, who had been Lupe's very steady date for the past year or so. She and Williams had even announced their engagement, but less than a month after the sixty-two-minute *Six Lessons from Madame La Zonga* opened at the Palace Theatre (February 18, 1941), the couple went their very separate paths. Lupe explained: "I am funny in my ways and I like a certain amount of freedom. So does he."

Mexican Spitfire's Baby (1941) was touted by RKO as the "fourth," "final," and "best" entry of the series, but only the first claim proved accurate. Charles "Buddy" Rogers, Lupe's Broadway co-player, was now substituted to play Dennis, Carmelita's harassed advertising-executive husband. Outside of this negligible change, everything was much as before. Using the same plot

*The project was eventually filmed with Chester Morris and Lucille Ball in 1940.
†The chemistry between Lupe and Errol far outshone that provided by her previous teaming with Jimmy Durante.

gimmick as Twentieth Century-Fox's *Sun Valley Serenade* (1941), the picture focused on Lupe and Rogers' interest in adopting a European war orphan. The bundle of happiness who arrives is none other than curvaceous blonde Marion Martin, which triggers a round of complications for all concerned. There was plenty of horseplay throughout, mostly provided by Errol and by flighty ZaSu Pitts, but the cast was obviously straining to dig up laughs at any cost (of energy, not production budget or time). *Mexican Spitfire's Baby* had the historical distinction of being the RKO programmer paired as the co-feature to the studio's controversial *Citizen Kane* when that explosive film played two Manhattan RKO theatres as of September 17, 1941.

Lupe's *Mexican Spitfire* pictures hardly strained her acting resources, but the studio had solid statistics to demonstrate that her name and minimal presence in these pictures was sufficient to produce a tidy box-office profit. Thus in March, 1941, it was decided to extend the *Mexican Spitfire* series for additional entries, and Lupe signed a new three-picture pact with her new home lot. Harry Eddington, RKO production head, acknowledged that since the United States had announced its Latin American good neighbor policy, RKO was sure to benefit from cultural interest in our down-south neighbors by enjoying even wider audience attraction to Lupe and her *Spitfire* pictures. To prove such a point one had only to look at the commercial killing Twentieth Century-Fox was making with its newly pacted Brazilian bombshell, Carmen Miranda.*

Now that Lupe's professional services at RKO were re-extended, it was decided to intermesh her unique personality with the oncamera eccentricities of two other disparate studio contract personalities: bandleader Kay Kyser and aging ex-matinee star John Barrymore. Their ground of operation was to be *Playmates* (1941) and Lupe was to be the catalyst which would make the freak show viable screenfare. The sly premise of *Playmates* made the most of each performer's best-known idiosyncrasies: because a lucrative radio contract depends on it, Barrymore agrees to appear at a Shakespearian festival and to coach publicity-grabbing Kyser into the proper posture to recite the Bard. Lupe was seen as the Mexican bullfighter romance of Barrymore, who again lampooned his once illustrious acting image.† Wiseacre Patsy Kelly brought up the rear as Barrymore's press agent, with bland Peter Lind Hayes cast as Kyser's public relations man. To show where the real emphasis of *Playmates* lay, RKO billed Kay Kyser first and showcased his band vocalist, Ginny Simms, in three mediocre numbers. Lupe, dressed in a revealing gown, had one shimmering conga number, performed while the Kyser ensemble played "Chiquita." For the record, the *Baltimore Evening Sun* reported of this num-

---

*Lupe's long time rival Dolores Del Rio returned to RKO in 1941 to play the female lead in *Journey into Fear* (1942). Since Del Rio was then involved in a highly publicized romance with the star of that thriller, Orson Welles, she enjoyed a prestigious stay at RKO, a fact which caused vituperative Lupe to boil.

† He even recited the *Hamlet* "To Be or Not to Be" soliloquy.

ber: "She makes Miss Carmen Miranda, who also makes such dances a specialty, by comparison seems as retiring as little Elsie Dinsmore, of the nursery books."

Honolulu Lu, made at Columbia in 1941 but not released until early 1942, presented Lupe as Consuelo Cordoba, the sweetheart of the fleet, allowing Lupe to perform a proper sendoff a la Marlene Dietrich's performance in *Seven Sinners* (Universal, 1940), as well as exhibiting her expected mimicry of Katharine Hepburn and Gloria Swanson. Leo Carrillo replaced Leon Errol as Lupe's con-artist uncle, who has latched onto a new gold mine. This gold mine was none other than wealthy Marjorie Gateson, who insists that a refined girl like Carrillo's highly revered niece (Lupe) should win the island's upcoming personality-girl contest. This forces Lupe to do double duty in the film, posing as Carrillo's demure relative when not being her rambunctious self as the sailors' own "Honolulu Lu." In the finale of this scatterbrained musical comedy, Lupe finds herself in heady competition against herself in the contest playoffs. Once again it was Lupe who was energetic and noisy, not the tepid motion picture.

RKO rushed three *Mexican Spitfire* entries into 1942, and the haphazard production values were even more evident. Critics were now acknowledging what had long been obvious to discriminating filmgoers, that Errol was the working mainstay of the series. ("Her frenetic sputterings have as little importance to the drama as can be imagined," *New York Herald-Tribune.*) *Mexican Spitfire at Sea* has Lupe and Charles "Buddy" Rogers on a Honolulu-bound pleasure boat on what she believes is to be a second honeymoon, but is really part of Rogers's scheme to land a big business deal with the social-climbing Baldwins (Harry Holman and Florence Bates). *Mexican Spitfire Sees a Ghost* contains much of Lupe's requisite gnarled phraseology, but had the bolstering novelty of Leon Errol impersonating not two but three characters this time: Uncle Matt, Lord Epping, and Hubbell, the latter's valet extraordinary. The laws of diminishing returns were very much in evidence with the plot of *Mexican Spitfire's Elephant* (1942), but at least Lupe had a slightly larger share of the limelight as she sang snatches of Mexican songs, performed another conga, and abetted Leon Errol in a tall yarn which found diamond-runner Lyle Talbot attempting to smuggle a gem-laden elephant-shaped trinket into the United States via the gullible Lord Epping. To top the proceedings, a pink elephant, of the variety drunks are supposed to envision when inebriated, made a guest appearance in a cafe sequence.

If Lupe thought she would have a different type of role in RKO's *Ladies' Day* (1943) she was badly mistaken. By any other name or outward appearance—here she wore a blonde wig and was Pepita, an ex-burlesque queen—Lupe was still the "Mexican Spitfire." She paraded through her accustomed repertoire of stage antics as the new bride of ace big-league pitcher Eddie Albert, whose teammates (and especially their wives) fear he will forget about baseball because of Lupe's strong diversionary tactics. So Patsy Kelly and the other players' wives kidnap volcanic Lupe and have a hellish time keeping her bound and gagged until after the big game. Detractors of this daffy baseball comedy noted that Albert was short-shrifted in the story and that Lupe "seems to be giving an imitation of Donald Duck in all of her scenes" (*New York Sun*).

Mid-1943 saw the release of *Mexican Spitfire's Blessed Event*, which proved to be the eighth and final series entry, although no one at the time was aware of the fact. The picture's premise was geared to Walter Reed's mistaken belief that Lupe is a mother-to-be.* Actually she has acquired a baby ocelot, but Reed's original assumption proves prophetic for by the end of the programmer Lupe's Carmelita is pregnant. The usual hectic de-livery of the makeshift dialog did not disguise the sparseness of original-ity. For *Redhead from Manhattan* (1943) Lupe transferred her base of operations to Columbia Pictures, but the crosstown trip seemed hardly worth the effort. This film was on the same par as Columbia's rash of Joan Davis and Jinx Falkenburg B-picture entries: harmless, hapless, and hollow. *Redhead from Manhattan,* produced by Wallace MacDonald, who had super-vised *Honolulu Lu,* replayed the gambit of having Lupe enact a dual role. She is first seen as Rita, a stowaway on a transatlantic ship that is torpedoed. She reaches shore safely via a raft and the assistance of saxophonist Michael Duane. Thereafter the script requires her to impersonate both her cousin, musical comedy star Elaine Manners, and Rita, who willingly agrees to sub-stitute for her pregnant relative. Columbia weakly promoted *Redhead from Manhattan* as "Song and Dance . . . Swing and Romance . . . to knock you for a *Lupe.*"

Having survived the spate of B-pictures at RKO and elsewhere, thirty-four-year-old Lupe decided it was high time to return to Mexico City as she had intended to do some five years before. Both Lupe and the new N. Peter Rathvon RKO regime were content to call a halt to further contract-ual negotiations, the studio now busily concentrating on its other series, the *Falcon, Fibber McGee and Molly, Lum and Abner,* and the newly ac-quired *Tarzan* property complete with ex-MGMer Johnny Weissmuller. When Lupe left California in the fall of 1943, she informed the press that she was quitting Hollywood moviemaking "forever"† to restructure her waning movie career in Mexico. After visiting with her mother in Mexico City, Lupe reported to the local Aztec studios, where on October 11, 1943, she began filming a new version of Emile Zola's *Nana.*‡ Before the Christmas holidays she was back in Hollywood, bringing a glowing report of her satis-

---

*Since *Mexican Spitfire's Elephant*, Reed had taken over from Charles "Buddy" Rogers as husband Dennis.

†She always spoke in superlative and emotional finalities.

‡Among the other film versions of *Nana* over the years have been Jean Renoir's 1926 silent with Catherine Hessling, Samuel Goldwyn's 1934 adaptation with Anna Sten, and the Christian-Jaque 1955 color rendition with Martine Carol.

faction with Mexican film production and a firm conviction that once *Nana* was released her new drama-oriented film career was insured.

Since the breakup of her Guinn "Big Boy" Williams romance, Lupe had not been seriously linked with any one man on the Hollywood scene. But then in 1943 she met a twenty-seven-year-old French actor, Harald Ramond. In a burst of romantic bliss Lupe said that her long-ago romance with Cooper had been "kid stuff," that much of her well-documented bickering with Johnny Weissmuller had been engineered strictly for publicity purposes, but that now, at long last, she had found true love. "Harald certainly knows how to handle me . . . " Lupe breathlessly reported. "I've always been used to controlling men, but I try it with Harald and he tells me where to go." Whether Lupe and unemployed Ramond would ever wed was a question left unanswered. Lupe seemingly enjoyed her carefree Hollywood life, with her Beverly Hills home, which she shared with her two sisters and her dogs, and the Laurel Canyon mansion stocked with seventy-five canaries.* At one point in the early 1940s, Lupe told *P.M.* newspaper reporter Mary Morris: "I don't believe in marriage, darling. If there's children, o.k. But to a woman who has a career it means we're here today and gone tomorrow. We travel, and in our work we have a lot of men friends. I'm just being practical when I say husband and career don't mix." Only later, after Lupe's untimely death, would anyone realize how the dilemma of career versus marriage and motherhood haunted the supposedly amoral Lupe, whose Catholic background played a far stronger part in her life than she would ever admit.

The concomitant events shaping Lupe's final year (1944) were only pieced together after the fact. *Nana* premiered in Mexico City at the Palacio Chino Theatre in June, 1944, receiving unenthusiastic reviews. Novice director Celestino Gorostiza was the subject of much critical complaint for failing to make this account of 1870s Paris more than yet another tale of a prostitute with a heart of gold. The critics said that in his staging he fawned too much over the star and her melodramatics, all of which was a detriment to the novel's underlying naturalistic theme. The local reviewers concluded that any comparisons between Norman Foster's Mexican-produced *Santa* and Gorostiza's *Nana* would result in great cruelty to the latter. According to the Mexico City reports, Lupe's Nana had been drastically altered to suit her own Latin Spitfire image, but it was agreed that Lupe gave the best performance of her career.

After evaluating the reviews on *Nana* Lupe decided to wait until the picture opened in the United States before determining the future course of her film career. Meanwhile, it was announced that she and maturing ex-child star Jane Withers would co-star in David Wolper's stage production of *Glad to See You*. Rehearsals were scheduled to commence in October, 1944, and Valerie Bettis was set as choreographer.

*She insisted she knew each bird by name.

Lupe continued her California social life with Harald Ramond now her constant and sole male escort. On November 27, Lupe announced she and Ramond would wed, but a few weeks later (on December 10) the still very changeable Lupe insisted that it was all over between her and Ramond. "I told heem to get out! I like my dogs better!" Only later was it uncovered that Lupe was then four months pregnant and had become frantic over the scandal that would certainly ensue should her child be born illegitimate. But at the same time she was not yet convinced that young Ramond really cared for her, and not for her wealth and position. It was still later revealed that Lupe had even considered the possibility that after her baby's birth, one of her sisters should claim the child as hers. Roman Catholic Lupe never considered the alternative of abortion.

On Wednesday night, December 13, 1944, five days before Lupe was scheduled to go to New York for a radio broadcast and to commence a personal appearance tour, she and her best friend, Estelle Taylor, along with Mrs. Jack Oakie, attended the Hollywood premiere of *Nana*. During the evening Lupe told Estelle: "I am getting to the place where the only thing I am afraid of is life itself . . . I am just weary with the whole world. People think that I like to fight. I have to fight for everything. I'm so tired of it all. Ever since I was a baby I've been fighting. I've never met a man with whom I didn't have to fight to exist."

As the official report determined, Lupe returned to her Beverly Hills home later that night (her family was not in residence at the time), put on her favorite pair of blue silk pajamas, sat down on her eight-foot by eight-foot silk-sheeted bed, and took an overdose of sleeping pills.* The next day, December 14, when her housekeeper could not awaken Lupe, a doctor was summoned, who immediately pronounced her dead. One of the policemen at the scene of the tragedy related: "She looked so small in that out-sized bed that we thought at first she was a doll." Beside the bed were found two notes in Lupe's handwriting. One, addressed to Harald Ramond, stated: "You know the facts for the reason I am taking my life." The other letter was addressed to her companion-housekeeper, Mrs. Beulah Kinder: "My faithful friend, you and only you know the fact for the reason I am taking my life. May God forgive me, and don't think bad of me. I love you many. Take care of your mother, so goodbye and try and forgive me. Say goodbye to all my friends and the

---

*Another published account, filled with inaccuracies but tantalizing in its macabre revelations, claimed that on the day Lupe died, she had ordered a houseload of floral arrangements, had her makeup man and hairdresser prepare her more magnificently than ever before, decked herself out in a lamé dress loaded with jewelry, and then had enjoyed a solitary banquet, with the food heavily spiced as was the Mexican custom. Later she dismissed the servants and went upstairs to her bedroom, where she swallowed a vial of Seconal tablets and lay down on her bed, awaiting her theatrically staged exit. But then the combination of Seconal and the spicy food caused such a tumultuous stomach upset that she raced pell-mell to the bathroom. As she ran toward the toilet bowl, she slipped on the marble tiles, fell head first into the commode, and broke her neck. According to this highly imaginative, unconfirmed report, there she died and was later found, half-submerged in the bowl.

American press that were always so nice to me." A postscript on the other side added: "Take care of Chips and Chops." They were her pet dogs.

Coroner Frank Navie wanted a full investigation made of Lupe's death, stating he was not satisfied by the Beverly Hills police report. However, District Attorney Fred Houser countered that he would not authorize undue expenditures of the taxpayers' money, especially since there was no evidence of foul play beyond Lupe's own evident self-destruction.

Lupe's body lay in state at the Church of the Recessional at Forest Lawn in Glendale before a nondenominational church service was held. More than 4,000 admirers and curiosity-seekers passed by her casket, which was surrounded by her hysterically bereaved mother, sisters, and brother. Among the pallbearers were Johnny Weissmuller, Gilbert Roland, and Arturo de Cordova.

Lupe's will left half her estate to the executrix, Mrs. Kinder, with a trust fund to be established from the remainder to pay a monthly sum to her family.* One of Lupe's sisters (then Mrs. Joseph Anderson of San Antonio, Texas) contested the will, presenting a claim for $45,900.† She informed the judge that she had saved the estate an estimated $21,000 by preventing Lupe's burial in a $12,000 bronze casket and by insisting that neither Lupe's $16,000 diamond ring nor a $15,000 ermine cape should be interred with the body.

June, 1945, saw the finale to Lupe's tangible earthly existence. Her estate was auctioned off to an audience of over five hundred attendees on June 21 and 22. Lupe's Beverly Hills home was sold for $41,750 to Mrs. Virginia Kuppinger, who proudly announced that it would be the postwar abode for her and her Navy officer husband. Among the other items sold at auction was the silver, gold, and ebony headboard of the highly publicized oversized deathbed. This relic went for $45!

A sad ending for Lupe, who not too long before her pointless death had specified the only ambition she had in mind for the rest of her life: "I just want to have a little fun! I know I'm not worth anything. I can't sing well. I can't dance well. I've never done anything like that [well]. . . . [these feelings] come from my heart, or I wouldn't say these things."

---

*Before probate, Lupe's estate was estimated at between $160,000 and $200,000, including $100,000 in diamonds, a $25,000 chinchilla coat, a $20,000 sable coat, and a $15,000 ermine cape.
†The claim was eventually settled for $3,870.

Feature Film Appearances
LUPE VELEZ

THE GAUCHO   (UA, 1928) 102 M.

Producer, Douglas Fairbanks; director, F. Richard Jones; story, Elton Thomas; screenplay, Lotta Woods; art director, Carl Oscar Borg, Harry Oliver, Jack Holden, Francesc Cugat, Edward M. Langley, Marion Larrinaga; assistant director, Lewis R. Foster, William J. Cowen; costumes, Paul Burns; consultants, Wallace Smith, Eugene P. Lyle, Jr.; researcher, Arthur Woods; main titles, Joseph B. Harris; technician, William Davidson; camera, Antonio Gaudio, Abe Scholtz.

Douglas Fairbanks (The Gaucho); Lupe Velez (The Mountain Girl); Geraine Greear (Girl of the Shrine—as a child); Eve Southern (Girl of the Shrine); Gustav von Seyffertitz (Ruiz, the Usurper); Michael Vavitch (Ruiz's First Lieutenant); Charles Stevens (The Gaucho's First Lieutenant); Nigel De Brulier (Padre); Albert MacQuarrie (Victim of the Black Doom); Mary Pickford (Our Lady of the Shrine).

STAND AND DELIVER   (Pathé, 1928) 57 M.

Producer, Donald Crisp; associate producer, Ralph Block; director, Crisp; screenplay, Sada Cowan; titles, John Krafft; assistant director, Emile De Ruelle; art director, Anton Grot; costumes, Adrian; production manager, Richard Donaldson; camera, David Abel.

Rod LaRocque (Roger Norman); Lupe Velez (Jania); Warner Oland (Chika); Louis Natheaux (Captain Dargis); James Dime (Patch Eye); A. Palasthy (Muja); Frank Lanning (Pietro); Bernard Siegel (Blind Operator); Clarence Burton (Commanding Officer); Charles Stevens (Krim); Donald Crisp (London Club Member).

LADY OF THE PAVEMENTS   (UA, 1929) 90 M.

Presenter, Joseph M. Schenck; director, D. W. Griffith; based on the novel *La Paiva* by Karl Gustav Vollmoeller; screenplay, Sam Taylor, Gerrit Lloyd; set design, William Cameron Menzies; song, Irving Berlin; music arranger, Hugo Reisenfeld; costumes, Alice O'Neill; camera, Karl Struss, G. W. Bitzer; editor, James Smith.

Lupe Velez (Nanon del Rayon); William Boyd (Count Karl von Arnim); Jetta Goudal (Countess Diane des Granges); Albert Conti (Baron Finot); George Fawcett (Baron Haussmann); Henry Armetta (Papa Pierre); William Bakewell (Pianist); Franklin Pangborn (M'sieu Dubrey, Dance Master).

WOLF SONG   (Par., 1929) 6,169′

Producer, Victor Fleming; associate producer, B. P. Fineman; director, Fleming; based on the story by Harvey Ferguson; screenplay, John Farrow, Keene Thompson; titles, Julian Johnson; assistant director, Henry Hathaway; music director, Irvin Talbot; songs, Richard Whiting and Al Bryan; supervising music recorder, Max Terr; camera, Allen Siegler; editor, Eda Warren.

Gary Cooper (Sam Lash); Lupe Velez (Lola Salazar); Louis Wolheim (Gullion); Constantine Romanoff (Rube Thatcher); Michael Vavitch (Don Solomon Salazar); Ann Brody (Duenna); Russ Colombo (Ambrosia Guiterrez); Augustina Lopez (Louisa); George Regas (Black Wolf).

WHERE EAST IS EAST   (MGM, 1929) 6,683'

Producer-Director, Tod Browning; story, Browning, Harry Sinclair Drago; adaptation, Waldemar Young; screenplay, Richard Schayer; titles, Joe Farnham; costumes, David Cox; art director, Cedric Gibbons; camera, Henry Sharp; editor, Harry Reynolds.

Lon Chaney (Tiger Haynes); Lupe Velez (Toyo); Estelle Taylor (Madame de Sylva); Lloyd Hughes (Bobby Bailey); Louis Stern (Father Angelo); Mrs. Wong Wing (Ming); Duke Kahanamoku (Wild Animal Trapper); Richard Neill (Rangho the Gorilla).

TIGER ROSE   (WB, 1929) 5,509'

Director, George Fitzmaurice; based on the play by Willard Mack; screenplay, Harvey Thew, Gordon Rigby; titles, De Leon Anthony; song, Ned Washington, Herb Magidson, and Michael Cleary; camera, Tony Gaudio; editor, Thomas Pratt.

Monte Blue (Devlin); Lupe Velez (Rose); H. B. Warner (Dr. Cusick); Tully Marshall (Hector McCollins); Grant Withers (Bruce); Gaston Glass (Pierre); Bull Montana (Joe); Rin-Tin-Tin (Scotty); Slim Summerville (Heine); Louis Mercier (Frenchie); Gordon Magee (Hainey); Heinie Conklin (Gus); Leslie Sketchley (Mounted Police Officer).

HELL HARBOR   (UA, 1930) 90 M.

Director, Henry King; based on the novel *Out of the Night* by Rida Johnson Young; adaptation, Fred De Gresac, N. Brewster Morse; screenplay, Clarke Silvernail; art director, Robert M. Haas; sound, Ernest Rovere; camera, John Fulton, Mack Stengler; editor, Lloyd Nosler.

Lupe Velez (Anita Morgan); Jean Hersholt (Joseph Horngold); John Holland (Bob Wade); Gibson Gowland (Harry Morgan); Al St. John (Bunion); Harry Allen (Peg-Leg); Paul E. Burns (Blinkey); George Book-Asta (Spootty); Rondo Hatton (Dance Hall Proprietor); Habanera Sextette (Orchestra).

THE STORM   (Univ., 1930) 80 M.

Presenter, Carl Laemmle; director, William Wyler; based on the play *Men Without Skirts* by Langdon McCormick; adaptation, Charles A. Logue; screenplay, Wells Root; dialog, Tom Reed; sound, Joseph P. Lapis, C. Roy Hunter; camera, Alvin Wyckoff.

Lupe Velez (Manette Fachard); Paul Cavanagh (Dave Stewart); William "Stage" Boyd (Burr Winton); Alphonse Ethier (Jacques Fachard); Ernest Adams (Johnny); and: Tom London, Nick Thompson, Erin La Bissoniere.

EAST IS WEST   (Univ., 1930) 70 M.

Presenter, Carl Laemmle; associate producer, E. M. Asher; director, Monta Bell; based on the play by Samuel Shipman, John B. Hymer; adaptation, Winifred Eaton; screenplay, Tom Reed; sound, C. Roy Hunter; special effects, Frank H. Booth; camera, Jerry Ash; editor, Harry Marker.

Lupe Velez (Ming Toy); Lew Ayres (Billy Benson); Edward G. Robinson (Charlie Yong); Mary Forbes (Mrs. Benson); E. Alyn Warren (Lo Sang Kee); Henry Kolker (Mr. Benson); Tetsu Komai (Hop Toy); Edgar Norton (Thomas); Charles Middleton (Dr. Fredericks).

ORIENTE ES OCCIDENTE (Univ., 1930)

Director, George Melford; supervisor, Paul Kohner.

Lupe Velez (Ming Toy); Barry Norton (Billy Benson); Tetsu Komai (Hop Toy); and: Manuel Arbó, Daniel F. Rea, José Soriano Viosca, Marcela Nivón, André Cheron, Lucio Villegas, Jim Wong.

(Spanish version of *East Is West* [1930])

RESURRECTION (Univ., 1931) 81 M.

Director, Edwin Carewe; based on the novel by Leo Tolstoy; screenplay, Finis Fox; sound, C. Roy Hunter; music, Dmitri Tiomkin; lyrics, Bernard Grossman; camera. Robert B. Kurrie, Al Green; editor, Edward I. Kahn, Maurice Pivar.

John Boles (Prince Dmitri Nekhludoff); Lupe Velez (Katerina Maslova); Nance O'Neil (Princess Marya); William Keighley (Mayor Schoenbock); Rose Tapley (Princess Sophya); Michael Mark (Simon Kartkinkin); Sylvia Nadina (Eupremia Botchkova); George Irving (Judge); Edward Cecil (Merchant); Mary Foreman (Beautiful Exile); Grace Cunard (Olga); Dorothy Ford (Princess Hasan).

RESURRECCIÓN (Univ., 1931)

Director, David Selman; supervisor, Paul Kohner.

With: Lupe Velez, Gilbert Roland, Amelia Sanisterra, Soledad Jimenez, Faust Rocha, Edwardo Arozamena, Ramon Pereda.

(Spanish version of *Resurrection* [1931])

THE SQUAW MAN (MGM, 1931) 106 M.

Producer-director, Cecil B. De Mille; based on the play by Edwin Milton Royle; screenplay, Lucien Hubbard, Lenore Coffee; dialog, Elsie Janis; sound, Douglas Shearer; art director, Mitchell Leisen; incidental music, Herbert Stothart; camera, Harold Rosson; editor, Anne Bauchens.

Warner Baxter (Captain Jim Wingate); Lupe Velez (Naturich); Eleanor Boardman (Diana Kerhill); Charles Bickford (Cash Hawkins); Roland Young (Sir John Applegate); Paul Cavanagh (Henry, Earl of Kerhill); Raymond Hatton (Shorty); Julia Faye (Mrs. Chichester Jones); DeWitt Jennings (Sheriff Bud Handy); J. Farrell MacDonald (Big Bill); Dickie Moore (Little Hal); Mitchell Lewis (Tabywanna); Victor Potel (Andy); Frank Rice (Grouchy); Eva Dennison (Lady Phoebe Kerhill); Lilian Bond (Babs); Luke Cosgrave (Shanks); Frank Hagney (Clark, Deputy); Lawrence Grant (General Stafford); Harry Northrup (Butler); Ed Brady (McSorley); Chris-Pin Martin (Zeke); Desmond Roberts (Hardwick); Artie Ortego (Naturich's Brother); Herbert Evans (Conductor); Pat Somerset (Officer).

CUBAN LOVE SONG (MGM, 1931) 86 M.

Director, W. S. Van Dyke; story, C. Gardiner Sullivan, Bess Meredyth; screenplay, John Lynch; dialog, Lynch, John Colton, Gilbert Emery, Robert E. Hopkins, Paul Hervey Fox; songs, Dorothy Fields, Herbert Stothart and Jimmy McHugh; camera, Harold Rosson; editor, Margaret Booth.

Lawrence Tibbett (Terry Burke); Lupe Velez (Nenita); Ernest Torrence (Rocket); Jimmy Durante (O. O. Jones); Karen Morley (Crystal); Louise Fazenda (Elvira); Hale Hamilton (John); Mathilde Comont (Aunt Rose); Philip Cooper (Terry, Jr.).

THE BROKEN WING (Par., 1932) 71 M.

Director, Lloyd Corrigan; based on the play by Paul Dickey, Charles Goddard; screenplay, Gordon Jones, William Slavens McNutt; camera, Henry Sharp.

Lupe Velez (Lolita); Leo Carrillo (Captain Innocencio); Melvyn Douglas (Philip Marvin); George Barbier (Luther Farley); Willard Robertson (Sylvester Cross); Claire Dodd (Cecelia Cross); Arthur Stone (Justin Bailey); Soledad Jimenez (Maria); Julian Rivero (Bassilio); Pietro Sosso (Pancho).

HOMBRES EN MI VIDA   (Col., 1932)

Director, William Beaudine.

With: Lupe Velez, Ramón Pereda, Luis Alberni.

(Spanish version of *Men in Her Life* [1931])

KONGO   (MGM, 1932) 86 M.

Director, William Cowen; based on the play by Chester DeVonde, Kilbourn Gordon; screenplay, Leon Gordon; art director, Cedric Gibbons; camera, Harry Rosson; editor, Conrad A. Nervig.

Walter Huston (Flint); Lupe Velez (Tula); Conrad Nagel (Dr. Kingsland); Virginia Bruce (Ann); C. Henry Gordon (Gregg); Mitchell Lewis (Hogan); Forrester Harvey (Cookie); Curtis Nero (Fuzzy).

THE HALF-NAKED TRUTH   (RKO, 1932) 67 M.

Director, Gregory La Cava; titles from the story "Phantom Fame" by Harry Reichenbach; story, Ben Markson, H. N. Swanson; screenplay, Bartlett Cormack, Corey Ford; sound, John Tribby; camera, Bert Glennon; editor, C. K. Kimball.

Lupe Velez (Teresita); Lee Tracy (James Bates); Eugene Pallete (Achilles); Frank Morgan (Farrell); Bob McKenzie (Colonel Willikins); James Donlin (Lou); Shirley Chambers (Gladys); Charles Dow Clark (Sheriff).

HOT PEPPER   (Fox, 1933) 76 M.

Director, John Blystone; based on characters created by Maxwell Anderson, Laurence Stalling; story, Dudley Nichols; screenplay, Barry Conners, Philip Klein; songs, Val Burton and Will Jason; camera, Charles Clarke.

Edmund Lowe (Harry Quirt); Victor McLaglen (Flagg); Lupe Velez (Pepper); El Brendel (Olsen); Boothe Howard (Trigger Thorne); Lilian Bond (Hortense); Gloria Roy (Lily); Russ Clark (Egan).

MR. BROADWAY   (Broadway-Hollywood Productions, 1933) 63 M.

Director, Johnnie Walker; story-screenplay, Ed Sullivan; sound, Harold Walls; camera, Frank Zukor; editor, Marc Arsch.

Ed Sullivan, Jack Dempsey, Ruth Etting, Bert Lahr, Hal LeRoy, Josephine Dunn, Ted Husing, Blossom Seeley, Benny Fields, Lita Grey Chaplin, Joe Frisco, Jack Benny, Mary Livingston, Gus Edwards, Jack Haley, Lupe Velez, Frank H. Gard, Niles T. Granlund, Eddie Duchin & Orchestra, Ernst Lubitsch, Primo Carnera, Maxie Rosenbloom, Johnnie Walker, Tony Canzoneri, Isham Jones & Orchestra, Abe Lyman & Band (Themselves); Dita Parlo (The Girl); William Desmond, Tom Moore (Her Suitors).

LAUGHING BOY   (MGM, 1934) 75 M.

Director, W. S. Van Dyke; based on the novel by Oliver La Farge; adaptation, John Colton, John Lee Mahin; song, Gus Kahn and Herbert Stothart; music, Stothart; camera, Lester White; editor, Blanche Sewell.

Ramon Novarro (Laughing Boy); Lupe Velez (Slim Girl); William Davidson (Hartshorne); Chief Thunderbird (Father); Catalina Rambrila (Mother); Tall Man's Boy (Wounded Face); F. A. Armenta (Yellow Singer); Deer Spring (Squaw's Son); Pellicana (Red Man).

PALOOKA   (UA, 1934) 83 M.

Director, Benjamin Stoloff; based on the comic strip by Ham Fisher; screenplay, Gertrude Purcell, Jack Jevne, Arthur Kober, Ben Ryan, Murray Roth; songs, Harold Adamson and Burton Lane; Ben Ryan and Jimmy Durante; Irving Caesar and Ferde Grofe; Ann Ronell and Joe Burke; camera, Arthur Edeson; editor, Grant Whytock.

Jimmy Durante (Knobby Walsh); Lupe Velez (Nina Madero); Stuart Erwin (Joe Palooka); Marjorie Rambeau (Mayme Palooka); Robert Armstrong (Pete Palooka); Mary Carlisle (Anne); William Cagney (Al McSwatt); Thelma Todd (Trixie); Franklyn Ardell (Doc Wise); Tom Dugan (Whitey); Guinn Williams (Slats); Stanley Fields (Blacky); Louise Beavers (Crystal); Snowflake (Smokey); Al Hill (Dynamite Wilson); Gordon De Main (Photographers' Official); Gus Arnheim and His Orchestra (Themselves).

HOLLYWOOD PARTY   (MGM, 1934) C—68 M.

Director, Roy Rowland; story-screenplay, Howard Deitz, Arthur Kober; songs, Gus Kahn and Walter Donaldson; Dietz and Donaldson; Arthur Freed and Nacio Herb Brown; camera, James Wong Howe; editor, George Boemler.

Jimmy Durante (Jimmy, Schnarzan the Ape Man); Lupe Velez (Lupe); Laurel and Hardy (Themselves); Polly Moran (Henrietta); Jack Pearl (Baron Munchausen); George Givot (Liondora); Eddie Quillan (Bob); June Clyde (Linda); Ben Bard (Sharley); Richard Carle (Knapp); Tom Kennedy (Beavers); Frances Williams, Charles Butterworth, Mickey Mouse, Ted Healy (Specialties); Arthur Jarrett (Singer); Shirley Ross Quartet, Harry Barris, Three Stooges (Themselves); Jed Prouty (Theater Manager); Arthur Treacher (Butler); Robert Young (Himself).

STRICTLY DYNAMITE   (RKO, 1934) 71 M.

Producer, Pandro S. Berman; associate producer, H. N. Swanson; director, Elliott Nugent; based on the play by Robert T. Colwell, Robert A. Simon; screenplay, Maurine Watkins, Ralph Spence, Milton Raison, Jack Harvey; songs, Jimmy Durante; Irving Kahal and Sammy Fain; Harold Adamson and Burton Lane; camera, Edward Cronjager; editor, George Crone.

Jimmy Durante (Moxie Slaight); Lupe Velez (Vera); Norman Foster (Nick Montgomery); William Gargan (Georgie Ross); Marian Nixon (Sylvia Montgomery); Eugene Pallette (Sourwood Sam); Minna Gombell (Miss LeSeur); Sterling Holloway (Fleming); Mills Brothers (Specialty); Stanley Fields, Tom Kennedy (Bodyguards); and: Leila Bennett, Franklin Pangborn, Berton Churchill, Jackie Searl, Irene Franklin, Mary Kornman.

THE MORALS OF MARCUS   (Gaumont-British, 1935) 75 M.

Producer, W. J. Locke; director, Miles Mander; based on the play by Locke; adaptation, Guy Bolton, Mander; dialog, H. Fowler Mear; set decorator, Louis Brooks; art director, James A. Carter; editor, Jack Harris.

Lupe Velez (Carlotta); Ian Hunter (Sir Marcus Ordeyne); Adrienne Allen (Judith); Nocl Madison (Tony Pasquale); and: J. H. Roberts, H. F. Maltby, Arnold Lucy, Frank Atkinson, D. J. Williams, James Raglan, Agnes Imlay, Johnny Nitt.

GYPSY MELODY (Associated British-Pathé, 1936) 73 M.

Director, Edmund T. Greville; supervisor, E. E. Reinert; screenplay, Drury Le Roy, Dan Wellden; songs, Bruce Sievier; camera, Claude Friese-Greene.

Lupe Velez (Mila); Alfred Rode (Capt. Eric Danilo); Jerry Verno (Madame Beatrice); Fred Duprey (Herbert P. Melon); Wyn Weaver (Grand Duke); Margaret Yarde (Grand Duchess); Raymond Lovell (Himself); Monti de Lyle (Marco); Louis Darnley (Hotel Manager); Hector Abbass (Biergarten Manager); G. de Joncourt (Dr. Epstein).

HIGH FLYERS (RKO, 1937) 70 M.

Producer, Lee Marcus; director, Edward Cline; based on the play by Victor Mapes; screenplay, Benny Rubin, Bert Granet; music director, Roy Webb; songs, Herman Ruby and Dave Dreyer; special effects, Vernon L. Walker; camera, Jack Mackenzie; editor, John Lockert.

Bert Wheeler (Jerry Lane); Robert Woolsey (Pierre Potkin); Lupe Velez (Juanita Morales); Marjorie Lord (Arlene Arlington); Margaret Dumont (Martha Arlington); Jack Carson (Dave Hanlon); Paul Harvey (Horace Arlington); Charles Judels (Mr. Fontaine); Lucien Prival (Mr. Panzer); Herbert Evans (Mr. Hartley); Herbert Clifton (Stone); George Irving (Chief of Police); Bud Geary (Sailor); Bruce Mitchell (Police Officer); Frank M. Thomas (Officer Collins); Don Brodie (Accomplice on Boat); Rod Hildebrand (Police Officer); Stanley Blystone (Cop on Pier); Frank M. Thomas (Officer Collins).

LA ZANDUNGA (Films Selectos, 1938) 107 M.

Director, Fernando de Fuentes; story, Rafael M. Saavedra; adaptation, Fernando de Fuentes; dialog, Saavedra, Fernando de Fuentes y Salvador Nova; assistant director, Miguel M. Delgado; music, Max Urban; songs, Urban and Lorenzo Barcelata; choreography, Felipe I. Obregon; sound, B. J. Kroger, Jose B. Carles; camera, Ross Risher; editor, Charles I. Kimball.

Lupe Velez (Lupe); Rafael Falcon (Ramon Miranda); Arturo de Cordova (Juancho, El Jarocho); Joaquin Pardave (Don Cartarino); Carlos Lopez Chaflan (The Secretary); Maria Luisa Zea (Marilu); Manuel Noriega (Don Eulogio); Rafael Icardo (Don Atanasio); Carmen Cortes (Petra); Antonio Mendoz (Pedro); Enrique Carrillo (Juan); Alvaro Gonzales (Jose Antonio); Jesus Melgatejo (El Numero Doce); and: David Silva.

MAD ABOUT MONEY (British Lion, 1938) 75 M.

Producer, William Rowland; director, Melville Brown; story, John E. Harding; screenplay, John Meehan; songs, James Dyrenforth and Kenneth Leslie-Smith; choreography, Larry Ceballos; music, De Wolfe; special effects, Len Lye.

Ben Lyon (Roy Harley); Lupe Velez (Carla de Huelva); Wallace Ford (Peter Jackson); Jean Colin (Diana West); Harry Langdon (Otto Schultz); Mary Cole (Peggy); Cyril Raymond (Jerry Sears); Ronald Ward (Eric Williams); Arthur Finn (J. D. Meyers); Philip Pearman (Prince); Andrea Malandrinos (Ambassador); Olive Sloane (Gloria Dane); Peggy Novak (Secretary); John Stobart (Headwaiter); Ronald Hill (Attorney); Albert Whelan (Judge); Alan Shires (Dance Partner).

THE GIRL FROM MEXICO (RKO, 1939) 69 M.

Producer, Robert Sisk; director, Leslie Goodwins; story, Lionel Houser; screenplay, Houser, Joseph A. Fields; art director, Van Nest Polglase; music director, Roy Webb;

songs, Joaquin Pardave; Romero, Garuse, and De Torre; camera, Jack MacKenzie; editor, Desmond Marquette.

Lupe Velez (Carmelita); Donald Woods (Dennis); Leon Errol (Uncle Matt); Linda Hayes (Elizabeth); Donald MacBride (Renner); Edward Raquello (Romano); Elisabeth Risdon (Aunt Della); Ward Bond (Mexican Pete).

MEXICAN SPITFIRE (RKO, 1939) 67 M.

Producer, Cliff Reid; director, Leslie Goodwins; story, Joseph A. Fields, screenplay, Fields, Charles E. Roberts; art director, Van Nest Polglase; music director, Paul Sawtell; camera, Jack Mackenzie; editor, Desmond Marquette.

Lupe Velez (Carmelita); Leon Errol (Uncle Matt/Lord Epping); Donald Woods (Dennis); Linda Hayes (Elizabeth); Elisabeth Risdon (Aunt Della); Cecil Kellaway (Chumley); Charles Coleman (Butler).

MEXICAN SPITFIRE OUT WEST (RKO, 1940) 76 M.

Producer, Lee Marcus, Cliff Reid; director, Leslie Goodwins; story, Charles E. Roberts; screenplay, Roberts, Jack Townley; art director, Van Nest Polglase; music, Roy Webb; special effects, Vernon L. Walker; camera, Jack Mackenzie; editor, Desmond Marquette.

Lupe Velez (Carmelita); Leon Errol (Uncle Matt/Lord Epping); Donald Woods (Dennis); Grant Withers (Withers); Elisabeth Risdon (Aunt Della); Cecil Kellaway (Chumley); Linda Hayes (Elizabeth); Lydia Bilbrook (Lady Epping); Charles Coleman (Ponsby); Eddie Dunn (Skinner); Charles Quigley (Roberts); Tom Kennedy (Taxi Driver); Gus Schilling (Desk Clerk); Ferris Taylor (Thorne); Dick Hogan (Bellhop); Vinton Haworth (Brown); Charles Hall (Elevator Boy); Youda Hays (Maid); Frank Orth (Window Cleaner); Rafael Storm (Travel Clerk); Rita Owin (Public (Stenographer); Ted Mangean (Page Boy); Lester Dorr (Harry); Warren Jackson (Stranger); Carl Freemanson (Bartender); Sammy Stein (Cowboy); Paul Everton (Dignitary); Herta Margot (Beauty Contest Winner); Jane Woodworth (Bit); John Sheehan (Janitor); Fred Kelsey, Kernan Cripps (Cops).

RECORDAR ES VISIR (Pereda, 1941)

Director, Fernando A. Rivero.

A Compilation feature containing fragments of Mexican sound films starring Lupita Tovar, Fernando Soler, Tito Guizar, José Mojica, Lupe Velez (from *La Zandunga*), Arturo de Córdova, Cantinflas, et al.

SIX LESSONS FROM MADAME LA ZONGA (Univ., 1941) 62 M.

Associate producer, Joseph G. Sanford; director, John Rawlins; story, Ben Chapman, Larry Rhine; screenplay, Stanley Crea Rubin, Marion Orth, Rhine, Chapman; songs, Everett Carter and Milton Rosen; Charles Newman and Jimmy Monaco; camera, John W. Boyle.

Lupe Velez (Madame La Zonga); Leon Errol (Pop Alvarez); Helen Parrish (Rosita Alvarez); Charles Lang (Steve); William Frawley (Beheegan); Eddie Quillan (Skat); Danny Beck (Danny); Guinn "Big Boy" Williams (Alvin); Frank Mitchell (Maxwell); Shemp Howard (Gabby); Lorin Raker (Brady); James Wakely (Pony); John Bond (Tex); Richard Reinhart (Jim); Rosa Turich (Maid); Wade Boteler (Captain); George Humbert (Carriage Driver); Eddie Acuff (Steward); Ken Christy (Employment Manager); Francisco Maran (Officer); Paco Moreno (Jailer); Lee Phelps (Anderson); Jack Clifford (McGuire); Minerva Urecal (Irate Woman); Paul Ellis (Dance Teacher); Jose Tortosa (Banker); James McNamara (Postman); Enrique Acosta (Excited Cuban); Rico de Montez (Bellboy); Demetrius Emanuel (Cuban Policeman).

MEXICAN SPITFIRE'S BABY (RKO, 1941) 69 M.

Producer, Cliff Reid; director, Leslie Goodwins; screenplay, Jerry Cady, Charles E. Roberts, James Casey; camera, Jack Mackenzie; editor, Harry Marker.

Lupe Velez (Carmelita); Leon Errol (Uncle Matt); Charles "Buddy" Rogers (Dennis); ZaSu Pitts (Miss Pepper); Elisabeth Risdon (Aunt Della); Fritz Feld (Pierre); Marion Martin (Suzanne); Lloyd Corrigan (Chumley); Lydia Bilbrook (Lady Epping); Vinton Haworth (Hotel Clerk); Tom Kennedy (Sheriff); Max Wagner (Bartender); Jane Patten (Dennis's Stenographer); Jack Briggs (Orchestra Leader); Jane Woodworth (Cashier); Ted O'Shea (Manager); Dick Rush (Cop); Chester Tallman (Photographer); Jack Grey, Buddy Messinger, Jack Gardner, Jimmy Harrison, Don Kerr (Reporters).

PLAYMATES (RKO, 1941) 96 M.

Producer, Cliff Reid; director, David Butler; story, Butler, James V. Kern, M. M. Musselman; screenplay, Kern; added dialog, Artie Phillips; choreography, Jack Crosby; songs, James Van Heusen and Johnny Burke; camera, Frank Redman; editor, Irene Morra.

Kay Kyser (Himself); John Barrymore (Himself); Lupe Velez (Carmen del Torre); Ginny Simms (Ginny); May Robson (Grandma); Patsy Kelly (Lulu Monahan); Peter Lind Hayes (Peter Lindsey); George Cleveland (Mr. Pennypacker); Alice Fleming (Mrs. Pennypacker); Kay Kyser's Orchestra, featuring Harry Babbitt, Ish Kabibble, Sully Mason (Themselves); Joe Bernard (Thomas); Ray Cooke (Bellhop); Hobart Cavanaugh (Tremble); Jacques Vanaire (Alphonse); Sally Cairns (Manicurist); Fred Trowbridge (Hotel Clerk); Dorothy Babb (Autograph Girl); Leon Belasco (Prince Maharoohu); Grace Lenard (Madeline); Sally Payne (Gloria); Vinton Haworth (Commentator); William Halligan (Mr. Loomis); Jack Carr (Pee Wee); Bill Cartledge (Page Boy); George McKay (Taxi Driver); Billy Chaney (Call Boy); Dave Willock (Cameraman); Marshall Ruth, Wally Walker (Comedy Bull Team); William Emile (Fencing Instructor); Rube Schaffer (Masseur); The Guardsmen (Themselves).

HONOLULU LU (Col., 1941) 72 M.

Producer, Wallace MacDonald; director, Charles Barton; story, Eliot Gibbons; screenplay, Gibbons, Paul Yawitz; added dialog, Ned Dandy; songs, Sammy Cahn and Saul Chaplin; camera, Franz F. Planer.

Lupe Velez (Consuelo Cordoba); Bruce Bennett (Skelly); Leo Carrillo (Don Estaban Cordoba); Marjorie Gateson (Mrs. Van Derholt); Don Beddoe (Bennie Blanchard); Forrest Tucker (Barney); George McKay (Horseface); Nina Campana (Aloha); Roger Clark (Bill Van Derholt); Helen Dickson (Mrs. Smythe); Curtis Railing (Mrs. Frobisher); Romaine Callender (Hotel Manager); John Tyrrell (Duffy); Eileen O'Hearn, Janet Shaw (Debutantes); Joe Bautista (Bellboy); Rudy Robles (Elevator Boy); Lloyd Bridges (Desk Clerk); Ed Mortimer, Elinor Counts, Mary Bovard (Tourists); Harry Bailey (Deaf Man); Charlie Lung (Cab Driver); Dick Jensen, George Barton, Earl Bunn, Charles D. Freeman, Kit Guard, Harry Anderson (Sailors); Ed Mundy (Magician); Hank Mann, Chester Conklin (Comedians); Grace Lenard (Soubrette); Blanche Payson (Mezzo Soprano); Ernie Adams (Pierre); Ray Mala (Native Cop); Sam Appel (Sergeant); Harry Depp (Dentist); Mickey Simpson (Strong Man); Jack Raymond (Mr. Astouras); Kay Hughes (Nurse); Al Hill (Detective); Jamiel Hasson (Police Sergeant); John Harmon (Clerk); Al Bridge (Shooting Gallery Proprietor).

MEXICAN SPITFIRE AT SEA (RKO, 1942) 72 M.

Producer, Cliff Reid; director, Leslie Goodwins; story, Jerry Cady, Charles E. Roberts; screenplay, Roberts; camera, Jack Mackenzie; editor, Theron Warth.

Lupe Velez (Carmelita); Leon Erroll (Uncle Matt/Lord Epping); Charles "Buddy" Rogers (Dennis); ZaSu Pitts (Miss Pepper); Elisabeth Risdon (Aunt Della); Florence Bates (Mrs. Baldwin); Marion Martin (Fifi); Lydia Bilbrook (Lady Epping); Eddie Dunn (Mr. Skinner); Harry Holman (Mr. Baldwin); Marten Lamont (Purser); John Maguire (Ship's Officer); Ferris Taylor (Captain Nelson); Richard Martin, Wayne McCoy (Stewards); Warren Jackson (Shipboard Reporter); Julie Warren (Maid); Lou Davis (Ship's Waiter); Mary Field (Elizabeth's Maid).

MEXICAN SPITFIRE SEES A GHOST   (RKO, 1942) 69 M.

Producer, Cliff Reid; director, Leslie Goodwins; screenplay, Charles Roberts, Monte Brice; art director, Albert S. D'Agostino, Carroll Clark; music director, C. Bakaleinikoff; camera, Russell Metty; editor, Theron Warth.

Lupe Velez (Carmelita); Leon Errol (Uncle Matt/Lord Epping/Hubbell); Charles "Buddy" Rogers (Dennis); Elisabeth Risdon (Aunt Della); Donald MacBride (Percy); Minna Gombell (Edith); Don Barclay (Fingers O'Toole); John Maguire (Luders); Lillian Randolph (Hyacinth); Mantan Moreland (Lightnin'); Harry Tyler (Bascombe); Marten Lamont (Harcourt); Jane Woodworth, Julie Warren (Secretary); Richard Martin (Chauffeur); Linda Rivas, Sally Wadsworth (Bits).

MEXICAN SPITFIRE'S ELEPHANT   (RKO, 1942) 64 M.

Producer, Bert Gilroy; director, Leslie Goodwins; story, Leslie Goodwins, Charles E. Roberts; screenplay, Roberts; assistant director, Ruby Rosenberg; music director, C. Bakaleinikoff; art director, Albert S. D'Agostino, Feild M. Gray; camera, Jack Mackenzie; editor, Harry Marker.

Lupe Velez (Carmelita); Leon Errol (Uncle Matt/Lord Epping); Walter Reed (Dennis); Lyle Talbot (Reddy); Elisabeth Risdon (Aunt Della); Marion Martin (Diana De Corro); Arnold Kent (Jose Alvarez); Luis Alberni (Luigi); Lydia Bilbrook (Lady Epping); Marten Lamont (Arnold); George Cleveland (Chief Inspector); Max Wagner (Headwaiter); Tom Kennedy (Joe, the Bartender); Neely Edwards (Ship's Bartender); Harry Harvey (Ship Steward); Jack Briggs (Lewis); Lloyd Ingraham (Stage Doorman); Vinton Haworth (Parks, the Hotel Manager); Don Barclay (Mr. Smith); Keye Luke (Lao Lee, the Chinese Magician); Ann Summers, Mary Stuart (Maids); Ronnie Rondell (Customs Officer); Ralph Brooks, Bess Flowers (Diners); Eddie Borden (Waiter).

LADIES' DAY   (RKO, 1943) 62 M.

Producer, Bert Gilroy; director, Leslie Goodwins; based on the play by Robert Considine, Edward Clark Lilley, Bertrand Robinson; screenplay, Charles E. Roberts, Dane Lussier; art director, Albert S. D'Agostino, Feild Gray; music, Roy Webb; camera, Jack Mackenzie; editor, Harry Marker.

Lupe Velez (Pepita); Eddie Albert (Wacky Walker); Patsy Kelly (Hazel); Max Baer (Fatso); Jerome Cowan (Updyke); Iris Adrian (Kitty); Cliff Clark (Dan); Joan Barclay (Joan); Carmen Morales (Marianne); Russ Clark (Smokey); Nedrick Young (Tony); George Cleveland (Doc); Eddie Dew (Spike); Jack Briggs (Marty); Richard Martin, Russell Wade, Wayne McCoy, Malcolm McTaggart, Mal Merrihugh, Charles Russell, Jack Shea, Jack Gargan, Cy Malis (Ball Players); Ralph Sanford, Frank Mills, Bud Geary, Kernan Cripps (Umpires); Rube Schaeffer (Runner); Jack Carrington (Announcer on Field); Sally Wadsworth (Cute Blonde); Mary Stuart, Ariel Heath, Mary Halsey, Ann Summers (Wives); Eddie Borden (Man on Field); Don Kerr (Pepita's Assistant); George O'Hanlon (Young Rube); Earle Hodgins (Old-Man Customer); Russell Hoyt (Assistant Director); Henry Hall (Dr. Adams); Wesley Barry (Reporter); Ted O'Shea (Airport Attendant); John Sheehan (Producer); Vinton Haworth (Director); Allen Wood (Locker Boy); Norman Mayes (Pullman Porter); Tom Kennedy (Dugan);

Teddy Mangean (Upstairs Bellhop); Barrie Millman (Baby); Jack O'Connor (Cab Driver); Jack Stewart (Doorman); George Noisom (Airport Mess Boy); Freddie Carpenter (Bellhop).

MEXICAN SPITFIRE'S BLESSED EVENT   (RKO, 1943) 63 M.

Producer, Bert Gilroy; director, Leslie Goodwins; screenplay, Charles E. Roberts, Dane Lussier; art director, Albert S. D'Agostino, Walter E. Keller; music director, C. Bakaleinikoff; camera, Jack Mackenzie; editor, Harry Marker.

Lupe Velez (Carmelita); Leon Errol (Uncle Matt/Lord Epping); Walter Reed (Dennis); Elisabeth Risdon (Aunt Della); Lydia Bilbrook (Lady Epping); Hugh Beaumont (Mr. Sharpe); Aileen Carlyle (Mrs. Pettibone); Alan Carney (Bartender); Marietta Canty (Verbena); Ruth Lee (Mrs. Walters); Wally Brown (Desk Clerk); Joan Barclay, Patti Brill, Margaret Landry, Margie Stewart, Barbara Hale, Rita Corday, Mary Halsey, Ann Summers, Rosemary LaPlanche (Bits); Robert Anderson (Captain Rogers); George Clues (Driver); Eddie Dew (Sheriff Walters); George Rogers, Dorothy Rogers, Don Kramer (Dancers); Billy Edward Reed (Attendant); Charles Coleman (Parker); Eddie Borden (Messenger Boy); June Booth (Nurse); Anne O'Neal (Matron at Orphanage).

REDHEAD FROM MANHATTAN   (Col., 1943) 64 M.

Producer, Wallace MacDonald; director, Lew Landers; story, Rex Taylor; screenplay, Joseph Hoffman; songs, Saul Chaplin and Walter Samuels; art director, Lionel Banks; camera, Philip Tannura; editor, James Sweeney.

Lupe Velez (Rita/Elaine Manners); Michael Duane (Jimmy Randall); Tim Ryan (Mike Glendon); Gerald Mohr (Chick Andrews); Lillian Yarbo (Polly); Arthur Loft (Sig Hammersmith); Lewis Wilson (Paul); Douglas Leavitt (Joe); Clancy Cooper (Policeman); Douglass Drake (Marty Britt); Ben Carter (Boy); Al Herman (Bartender); Alma Carroll, Shirley Patterson (Telephone Operator); Ben Gerien, Peter Dunn (Henchmen); Stanley Brown (Clarinet Player); Jack Gardner (Booker); Lynton Brent (Musician); Donald Kerr (Orchestra Leader); Edythe Elliott (Nurse); Robert Hill (Counter Man); Larry Parks (Man Flirt); Adele Mara (Check Girl); Pat O'Malley (Cop); Dewey Robinson (Truck Driver); Roger Gray, Frank Richards, Richard Talmadge (Fishermen); Jerry Franke, Gertrude Messinger, John Estes, Mickey Rentschler, Frank Sully, Connie Evans, Ezelle Poule (Bits).

NANÁ   (Mexican, 1944) 87 M.

Producer, Albert Santander; associate producer, C. Camacho Corona; director, Celestino Gorostiza, Roberto Gavaldon; based on the novel by Emile Zola; adaptation, Gorostiza, Santander; dialog, Gorostiza; music, Jorge Perez; sound, Consuelo Rodriguez, Fernando Barrera; camera, Alex Phillips; editor, Charles L. Kimball.

Lupe Velez (Nana); Miguel Angel Ferriz (Muffat); Chela Castro (Rosa Mignon); Crox Alvarado (Fontan); Elena D'Orgaz (Satin); Jose Baviera (Van Doeuvres); Sergio Orta (Impresario); Isabelita Blanch (Nana's Aunt); Jorge Reyes (Fauchery); Mimi Derba (Bebe's Mother); Roberto Corell (La Falloise); Virginia Zuri, Pepe del Rio (Bebe); Clifford Carr (Steiner); Luis Alcoriza (de Fauchery); Conchita Gentil Arcos (Zoe); Victorio Blanco (Marques); Rafael Beltran (Felipe); Hernan Vera (Prefect); and: Lupe del Castillo, Jose Elias Moreno, Alfonse Jimenez Kilometro, Emilia Guiu, Lilia Michel.

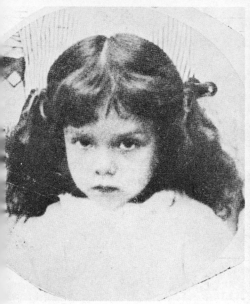

Velez as a child

A publicity pose for Hal Roach
Studios (c. 1927)

AMPAS BABY STARS of
op row, Alice Day,
y Gulliver, Flora Bram-
lly Eilers, Gwen Lee;
row, June Collyer, Sue
Ruth Taylor, Ann
; bottom row, Molly
Audrey Ferris, Lupe
Lina Basquette

With William Bakewell, Albert
Conti, and William Boyd in
LADY OF THE PAVEMENTS
(UA, 1929)

With Gary Cooper in WOLF SONG (Par '29)

With Estelle Taylor in WHERE EAST IS EAST (MGM '29)

With Gaston Glass in TIGER ROSE (WB '29)

With Gary Cooper, c. 1930

With John Holland in HELL HARBOR (UA '30)

With Ernest Torrence, Lawrence Tibbett, and Jimmy Durante in CUBAN LOVE SONG (MGM '31)

With Jimmy Durante on the set
of HOLLYWOOD PARTY
(MGM '34)

With her four-year-old r
Joan Del Valle, in

With Virginia Bruce in KONGO (MGM '32)

Noel Madison in THE
ALS OF MARCUS
nont-British '35)

With Leon Errol in MEXICAN
SPITFIRE OUT WEST
(RKO '40)

elen Parrish and Leon Errol in SIX LESSONS FROM
ME LA ZONGA (Univ '41)

With Marion Martin and Charles "Buddy" Rogers in MEXICAN SPITFIRE'S BABY (RKO '41)

With Nina Campana and Jack Raymond in HONOLULU LU (Col '41)

With Leon Errol, Don Barclay and Luis Alberni in MEXICAN SPITFIRE'S ELEPHANT (RKO '42)

With Eddie Albert and Max Baer in LADIES' DAY (RKO '43)

With Leon Errol and Hugh Beaumont in MEXICAN SPITFIRE'S BLESSED EVENT (RKO '43)

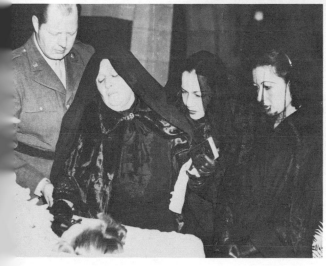

Mrs. Josefina Velez Viuda Villalobos, accompanied by her son-in-law, Pvt. J. Gordon Anderson; her daughter, Mrs. Josefina Anderson; and, *extreme right*, her companion, Delmira Cuniga Lopez; at the funeral of Lupe Velez in December, 1944

In THE HUNCHBACK OF NOTRE DAME (RKO '39)

5'7½"
124 pounds
Titian hair
Hazel eyes
Leo

Maureen O'Hara

For most moviegoers, the name Maureen O'Hara is indelibly associated with sharp images of lush Technicolor swashbucklers starring the fiery, red-headed, Irish-born actress. While a leading lady who excels so nobly at this athletic genre may be tremendously popular (as indeed Maureen O'Hara has been), it is well-nigh impossible for such a screen type to become a super-star.

Because of Maureen's vivid capering as the distaff Douglas Fairbanks, Sr. of the silver screen, her many sensitive performances in subtler movie genres have been too often overlooked. Beyond her sword-and-veil roles, she has provided well-modulated work in screen drama (How Green Was My Valley, Sentimental Journey) *and comedy* (Miracle on 34th Street, Sitting Pretty, McLintok!). *One of her most outstanding talents almost totally ignored by film producers was (and is) her ability to project songs in a charming man-ner, a gift she has exercised to some degree on television, on the stage, and in recordings. All these facts tend to suggest that for too long Maureen's raving beauty has distracted and deterred film executives from providing her with the range of acting opportunities she is fully capable of handling.*

Born Maureen FitzSimons at Millwall, near Dublin, Ireland, on August 17, 1920, she was one of the five children* of Charles FitzSimons, a small-time Dublin clothing merchant and a vice-president of the city's notable soccer team, and Marguerite Rita (Lilburn) FitzSimons, a onetime actress member of the Abbey Theatre.

Maureen had a standard Irish Catholic upbringing, being educated at the nearby Dominican Convent School. She was a rather chubby child, called "Baby Elephant" by her parents and "Fatzer" by her school chums. As a toddler she often made up plays for the enjoyment of the neighborhood kids, and at the age of five she made her stage bow when she was pressed into service to recite a short poem between the acts of a school play. But a theatrical career was not always the child's primary goal. At the age of ten the plucky tomboy fervently wished to become the best truck-driver in Dublin, and she was feisty enough to want to prove that she was physically capable of tackling such an arduous job by engaging any doubters in a fist fight. But soon, under her mother's persuasive prodding, Maureen's ambitions were diverted into more conventional lines, as a possible Shakespearian actress or a ballerina. She was enrolled at Burke's School of Elocution, where she took afternoon classes over the next several years. When she performed on a local radio show and was actually paid a sum, albeit modest, for her participation, it was decided that in the near future she should pursue her mother's occasional profession as an actress. At the age of twelve, she took part in six semiannual sessions in the volunteer ballet corps of the Dublin Operatic Society. Through her mother's professional connections, Maureen was auditioned and enrolled at the Apprentice School of the distinguished Abbey Theatre where she studied drama under Lenox Roberts's tutelage. She soon graduated from spear-carrying parts to small roles in the Theatre's productions. Meanwhile she was exhibiting great mental prowess in her academic pursuits, a facet of her personality often overlooked by associates and reporters in later years. At the early age of fifteen she took her final secondary-education equivalency examinations at Trinity College and was the youngest student to complete the Guildhall School of Music's drama course. Within six months thereafter, Maureen obtained a degree and associateship from the London College of Music, and in an annual scholastic competition she was awarded a medal as the leading honor student for the entire British Isles.

"I never got the chance to do anything worthwhile there," Maureen recalls of her brief Abbey Theatre years, which was a rather modest summation of her short stay there between other academic pursuits. By the age of seventeen she had performed Shakespearian roles with the group and had won the All-Ireland Cup for her portrayal of Portia in *The Merchant of Ven-*

---

*Bridget, one of Maureen's two sisters, would later become a nun, serving with the order of the Sisters of Charity.

ice. Maureen even found time to qualify for her certificate as teacher of education from the Abbey Players.

It was American entertainer-womanizer Harry Richman who brought about Maureen's screen career. After completing a rugged transatlantic flight from New York to Dublin in late 1937, he was the honored guest at a Dublin civic celebration and spotted Maureen among the attendees. He was immediately struck by her peaches-and-cream beauty and took the occasion to briefly speak with her.* When he was in London a few days later preparing for a new motion picture, he mentioned the striking Irish lass to his producers.

Shortly thereafter Maureen was invited to London to screentest for General Film's *Kicking the Moon Around* (1938). Maureen hesitated about making the Irish Sea crossing for she was then being considered for a lead part in one of the Abbey Players' main productions. But she decided to chance it, and, accompanied by her mother, went to London, where she was cast in the Harry Richman film in the tiny role of a secretary. *Kicking the Moon Around* opened in London in April, 1938,† and was rated an above-par quota-quickie picture by *Variety:* "It's the first instance within memory that a British musical enjoyed the advantage of 'going to press' with a suitably prepared script." Evelyn Dall had the Cinderella lead, with Richman singing, dancing, and clowning in his established frenetic style.

While still in London Maureen was hired for the undemanding title role of the modest *My Irish Molly,* made in 1938 but not released in the United States until 1940. The slight tale found Maureen cast as a colleen courted by American reporter Phillip Reed while her true love (Tom Burke) is away in New York attempting to make his fortune. There were several interludes for tenor Burke to perform traditional Irish songs and, for a subplot, there was orphan Binkie Stuart, who is almost bilked out of her inheritance. Teenager Maureen did not photograph well in this helter-skelter production, particularly in the unflattering close-ups, which all too clearly revealed the retention of baby-fat features. A frizzled hairdo crowned her coarse, embryonic screen image. As for the quality of her emoting in this journeyman programmer, *Variety* politely estimated in 1940, "She has improved considerably since."

All along Mr. FitzSimons had been strongly against Maureen's seemingly foolish film foray. After all she was already in the select company of the Abbey Players, and what prouder achievement could a true Irish girl desire? So it was decided by family council that Maureen should return to Dublin, but at the last minute Maureen received an invitation to meet with German

---

*Years later Maureen encountered Richman in Hollywood and stopped him on the street to thank him for setting her movie career into orbit. For the life of him, the singer-playboy could not recall the incident or Maureen.

†*Kicking the Moon Around* was released in the United States as *The Playboy.* Once Maureen had established herself as a Hollywood star the film was reissued in America under the title *Millionaire Merry-Go-Round* (1942).

film producer Erich Pommer. Since the mid-1930s Pommer had been based in London and associated with actor Charles Laughton in Mayflower Productions. Time has blurred the truth about who first saw film clips of Maureen, and decided she would be perfect for the role of the Irish ingenue in Mayflower's projected filmization of Daphne Du Maurier's best-selling *Jamaica Inn*. The honors were subsequently claimed by both Pommer, who a decade earlier had "discovered" Marlene Dietrich during her early German cinema days, and Laughton, who always had a sharp eye for attractive young people, despite his long and apparently happy marriage to actress Elsa Lanchester.

Maureen's meeting with Pommer and Laughton proved so successful that they quickly offered her a contract with Mayflower Productions, a bid which her parents were forced to concede was a little bit of all right. After signing the agreement Maureen was soon put to work on *Jamaica Inn* (1939) in the small but focal assignment of Mary, the late-eighteenth-century Irish orphan colleen who comes to live with her aunt (Marie Ney) and uncle (Leslie Banks) at their inn on the Cornish coast. It develops that the tavern is the headquarters for many strange goings-on, including the harboring of scavengers who wreck ships on the rocky shoreline and then pilfer the booty. A frequent inn visitor is the jowly country squire (Laughton), who adores nice things, including Maureen. At the proper storyline moment, undercover law-enforcer Robert Newton unmasks justice of the peace Laughton as the mastermind of the cutthroats. For the theatrical finale, Laughton, who has attempted to escape with a kidnapped Maureen kicking in tow, jumps from a ship's yardarm to his death.

Because of Laughton's unfortunate dual capacity as both co-producer and star, *Jamaica Inn* emerges as one of the least characteristic productions of film director Alfred Hitchcock. It is a movie dominated not by a hearty plot but by the misguided gusto of its bombastic lead player, who (ogling, lip pursing, nostril-dilating) portrayed the strutting "monster" with great affection. In the presence of such supercharged screen hogging, it was a credit to Maureen's innate cinema abilities that her basically colorless characterization emerged even a little above the one-dimensional.* In her relatively brief screen moments Maureen managed to convey somewhat the contrasting elements of her screen role—soft-voiced but fiery, wide-eyed but self-sufficient, virginal yet brave. She played, wrote the *New York Times*'s Frank S. Nugent, "well this side of ingenue hysteria, with charming naturalness and poise, with even a trace of self-control in her scenes." The *Illustrated London News* was even more perceptive: "Here undoubtedly is a star of the future."

Four months before *Jamaica Inn* opened to popular acclaim at New York's

---

*Had *Jamaica Inn* not required a colleen ingenue, it would have been intriguing to observe how Hitchcock's heroine of *The Lady Vanishes* might have handled the part.

Rivoli Theatre in October, 1939,* Maureen and her mother sailed from England on the *Queen Mary* for New York, in the company of Charles Laughton and Elsa Lanchester. Laughton, who had not been in the States since completing his role in MGM's *Mutiny on the Bounty* (1935), had suddenly concluded a high-priced new contract with RKO, and with the approval of studio president George Schaefer and production head Harry Edington he had selected a rendition of Victor Hugo's *The Hunchback of Notre Dame* for his first new Hollywood-made vehicle. At Laughton's insistence Maureen was to play the gypsy girl Esmeralda in this costume epic. Thus nineteen-year-old Maureen was understandably excited when she arrived in New York harbor on June 18, 1939. There was the matter of the seven-year lease on a Hyde Park house she had signed less than eight weeks before, confident that on the completion of *Jamaica Inn* a London-based film career would be assured. More importantly, when her mentor-employer Laughton advised her they were soon sailing for the United States, Maureen had to make a quick decision regarding her beau, George Brown, a production associate with Mayflower Productions. The couple impetuously solved the dilemma by secretly marrying in London on June 12, 1939, a few hours before Maureen embarked on her transatlantic venture.

The press was naturally on hand to greet camera-hungry Laughton, who in due course suggested the reporters talk with Maureen, whom he jovially tagged "little Miss Menace. She is going far."

Newsmen had dealt with a sufficient number of Irish-born Hollywood imports (Maureen O'Sullivan, Geraldine Fitzgerald, Greer Garson) to instinctively know that Maureen was not going to be the typically scatterbrained wishy-washy ingenue. When one reporter noted she was sipping a Coca-Cola and inquired if that was not a strange drink for a Britisher, Maureen shot back, "We're not so backwards as all that in England."

Maureen candidly discussed Laughton's influence in winning her the coveted role of Esmeralda: "Sure and if he told the studio I could play the part, why wouldn't they believe him? A big man like that. . . . Well I hope I'll not be letting him down."†

It took a woman member of the press contingent, Eileen Creelman of the *New York Sun,* to peg Maureen accurately: "Maureen O'Hara is a spunky piece, and rather the more likeable for it."

Laughton's Hollywood return coincided with the restructuring of RKO, whose management, after a few lean years, was determined to regain its "major studio" status by producing class pictures with class stars. It was a particularly propitious time for Maureen to arrive on the scene, for RKO at this juncture was sorely in need of new female stars. No longer could the lot

---

*Jamaica Inn was part of a film package sold to television early in the game, premiering in the New York City area on March 24, 1950.

†Ballerina Mia Slavenska was the prime contender for the part until Laughton made known his casting preference.

boast of features starring Ann Harding, Constance Bennett, or Katharine Hepburn, all of whom had departed the studio for one reason or another by 1939. Ginger Rogers, teamed with Fred Astaire or solo, was RKO's prime distaff attraction, along with the temporary services of British luminary Anna Neagle, and freelancing Carole Lombard and Irene Dunne. Heading the company's B-unit product were Lucille Ball, Anne Shirley, Joan Fontaine, and Sally Eilers, with a small assortment of minor female contractees in tow, who proved to have little or no cinema future.

Now that Pandro S. Berman had resigned as RKO production chief, George Schaefer was more determined than ever to make *The Hunchback of Notre Dame* a lavish production that in all departments would overshadow the well-remembered Lon Chaney edition (Universal, 1923). The movie was budgeted at close to $2 million, and the studio utilized its eighty-eight-acre ranch at Encino, California, to construct a huge ($250,000) outdoor set, reproducing the square around Notre Dame Cathedral of the 1480s. A record (or so the publicity claimed) 3,500 extras were hired for the extensive crowd scenes. Walter Hampden was lured from Broadway to make his cinema debut. Most publicity was directed to the special makeup being applied daily to Laughton to transform him into the famed misshapened hunchback, Quasimodo. Only profile shots of the "deformed" star were released to the press, geared to insure that his initial onscreen appearance would remain a visual surprise.*

To guarantee a proper send-off for its monumental production, RKO arranged a lavish opening at the Radio City Music Hall on December 31, 1939, which was indeed strange holiday fare. In re-creating Hugo's pictorial drama of fifteenth-century Paris in the reign of King Louis XI, the filmmakers distorted the tale† with too many movieland conventions and much too modern dialog.

For many the sight of the bulbous, mugging Laughton made up as the unspeakably ugly Quasimodo was not horrific but laugh-provoking, especially in the sequence in which the bestial creature undertakes a Tarzan-like rescue of Maureen by swinging from a bell-tower rope to sweep her off the scaffold platform. Once again Maureen was in the predicament of portraying the least colorful character in the proceedings, particularly since the studio and director William Dieterle made her character the major concession in

*A few enterprising photographers sneaked onto the set one day and managed to capture Laughton's grotesqueness from the front.

†Kindhearted gypsy girl Esmeralda (Maureen) comes to Paris to intercede with the King (Harry Davenport) for her people. While there she earns her living as a dancer. Archdeacon Claude (Hampden) is attracted to her and sends the deformed bellringer of Notre Dame Cathedral, Quasimodo (Laughton), to kidnap her. She is rescued by Alan Marshall, a captain of the guard, who is later stabbed by Hampden, with the blame being thrust on Maureen. Under torture she confesses to the crime and is sentenced to be hung, but she is saved by Laughton, who has been her devoted slave since the time she brought him water when he was pilloried and beaten. He leads Maureen to the Sanctuary of the Cathedral. In his misguided attempt to protect Maureen from both the King's men and the surging crowd, Laughton is killed, but Maureen is spared to be later reunited with her poet lover (Edmond O'Brien).

depicting the general filth and beggar-ridden Paris on which the film dearly focuses. It was a carefully garbed and well-cosmetized Maureen who essayed the enchanting Esmeralda, creating a very discordant note in the atmosphere-drenched, freak show-laden drama. "... pretty but a little modern for the Medieval setting and spirit," decided the *New York Sun,* while the *New York Herald-Tribune's* Howard Barnes proclaimed, "[She] did not strike me as the sort of Helen of Troy impersonation." *The Hunchback of Notre Dame* was a commercial success, but not the blockbuster epic for which RKO had hoped, based on the financial success Warner Brothers had been enjoying with its string of Errol Flynn swashbucklers. (Compared to the juvenilia of the Italian-made version of *The Hunchback of Notre Dame* [1957], starring Anthony Quinn and Gina Lollobrigida, the RKO edition was a small masterpiece.)

Despite the rather tepid critical reaction to Maureen's American film debut, RKO was convinced that the lovely newcomer was prime star material and deserved a major buildup. Since 1938 the studio had been planning a remake of *A Bill of Divorcement* to star its own long-term B-picture contractee, Anne Shirley. But now that vibrant, spunky Maureen was suddenly at liberty* it was decided to headline her in the new *Bill of Divorcement,* stoutly forecasting that this production would do as much for Maureen as the 1932 edition had done for launching Katharine Hepburn's screen career.

But RKO term director John Farrow, husband of Maureen O'Sullivan, seemed at a loss how to instill *Bill of Divorcement* (Palace Theatre, July 11, 1940) with the requisite freshness. Granted the decrepit story, set at the Fairfield estate in England, was a huge deficit to overcome, but Farrow allowed the cast to sink in a mire of irrelevant, overblown dramatics. No longer did the viewer find himself applauding the bravery of Sydney Fairfield (Maureen), who reluctantly but firmly relinquished her future happiness with Australian Patric Knowles in order to care for her emotionally jangled father (Adolphe Menjou) after his 20-year stay in a mental institution. Maureen's faltering interpretation led one to the conclusion that here was the practical decision of a rather fanciful young lady who, in a rash of conventionality, does not wish to chance the agony of hereditary insanity striking the children she and Knowles plan to have. "[A] pretty lass," the *New York Sun* reported, "but not yet much of an actress. . . . Her performance still lacks the intensity and desperation it must have; nor does she seem to have a sparkle of humor." Maureen did have one fine dramatic moment in *Bill of Divorcement,* in the scene set at the little railway station where she bids goodbye to Knowles. Had she demonstrated the same poise combined with internal emotional excitement throughout the feature, the new *Bill of Divorcement* really might have been the threshold-to-stardom picture for her.

---

*Plans for Maureen to co-star with Charles Laughton and Elsa Lanchester in a new version of *The Admirable Crichton* were scrubbed when Laughton decided to do *They Knew What They Wanted* (1940) with Carole Lombard.

For a brief spell, David O. Selznick considered Maureen for the female lead in another Daphne Du Maurier story, *Rebecca* (1940), but the part was given to ex-RKO leading lady Joan Fontaine. Instead RKO cast Maureen in Erich Pommer's *Dance, Girl, Dance* (1940), a pleasant but minor Continental-flavored musical helmed by one of Hollywood's few practicing women directors, Dorothy Arzner. Interestingly enough, Maureen, who only a short time before had been described by a *New York Times* reporter as "tallish, with red-brown hair and hazel eyes and more than a touch of Lucille Ball in her makeup," was first-billed in this movie over the studio's contract B-picture star Lucille Ball.* In the movie Maureen plays a ballet-oriented chorine while Ball portrays a predatory showline leg-kicker whose tart quality was a pronoun, not an adjective. Maureen and Ball are both members of a hotcha dance troup, managed by former Russian ballet star Maria Ouspenskaya (who unfortunately is eliminated early in the story). Both girls have a romantic eye on insipid playboy Louis Hayward, who eventually ditches them both to return to his ex-wife, Virginia Field, leaving an open field for ballet producer Ralph Bellamy to pursue Maureen. About the only stock ingredient missing from this backstage story was a sustained sense of comedy. If a display of lofty ideals and frozen emotions is a prerequisite for an aspiring ballerina, then Maureen was more than sufficient for her role. However, she did photograph beautifully and the script wisely kept her display of terpsichorean activity to a noticeable minimum.

By studio standards Maureen had acquitted herself well in the musical-comedy genre, so she was next tossed into *They Met in Argentina* (1941).† By no means was it in the same league with Twentieth Century-Fox's *Down Argentine Way* (1940), which boasted not only Betty Grable, Carmen Miranda, and Charlotte Greenwood, but also gaudy Technicolor. Instead, RKO's black-and-white Latin American salute was structured on a totally anemic plot. Maureen, the forward Argentinian heiress daughter of cattle-owner and horse-breeder Robert Barrat finds her future entwined with James Ellison, a lad sent to South America by his Texas millionaire employer to close an oil-well deal and to purchase Barrat's prize racehorse. For "comedy" relief Ellison's business cohort Buddy Ebsen cavorted antically. North-of-the-border critics declared *They Met In Argentina* "trite and slight" but a passable diversion; however, it was a different story in Argentina. Much to RKO's embarrassment (the studio had ballyhooed the picture as its prime effort in bolstering President Franklin D. Roosevelt's good neighbor policy), Buenos Aires pressure groups demanded that *They Met in Argentina* be withdrawn from its projected release in that country, declaring that on the basis of the North American reviews alone it was obvious that this movie, like Univer-

*The offcamera rivalry between Maureen and Ball on the RKO lot was an obvious stimulant, pushing both gals to give zestier performances than the script required.

†Maureen would later state: 'Now that was a real stinker, but it made lots of money. They all did in those days."

sal's similarly objectionable *Argentine Nights* (1940), was detrimental to the dignity of Argentinians. It was duly pointed out that Alberto Vila, a legitimate South American star imported expressly by RKO to play a major assignment in *They Met in Argentina,* had been reduced to portraying an inferior role as Maureen's gaucho boyfriend (he and Maureen dance the chaco together), whom she quickly jilts for Ellison.

During 1941 RKO was undergoing further financial restructuring, which resulted in the new regime, under president N. Peter Rathvon and production head Joseph Breen, retrenching in all areas of production, including the curtailment of the artistic and financial autonomy afforded Orson Welles's Mercury Theatre production unit. Another money-saving device employed by RKO at this time was to offer other studios joint ownership of some of its players. Thus MGM was allowed to share Charles Laughton's acting services with RKO, and Maureen was parceled off on a joint basis to Twentieth Century-Fox.*

In retrospect it seems almost inevitable that veteran director John Ford would have utilized Gaelic beauty Maureen in one or more of his features. That Maureen's contractual services became available to Twentieth Century-Fox, where Ford was then based and preparing *How Green Was My Valley* (1941) (his last feature film for the duration of World War II), was a lucky happenstance. It solved Ford's ingenue casting problem for the Welsh-set feature and provided Maureen with a legitimate steppingstone to screen stardom.†

Ford worked wonders with Richard Llewellyn's rich novel, originally published in 1940. The film is framed within the narrative of Huw Morgan (Roddy McDowall), now sixty years old and preparing to leave his beloved Welsh valley blighted by decades of indiscriminate coal mining. "I'm packing my belongings in the shawl my mother used to use to go to market . . . ," and soon the viewer is transported back fifty years when Huw, the youngest child of mine superintendent Gwilym Morgan (Donald Crisp), could go walking in the lush green countryside at his father's side. It is at this point that Angharad Morgan (Maureen) makes her first appearance. She is seen standing at the roadside fence in her white-collared dress, neatly attired in apron and shawl, waving to her father and Huw to come home to eat. She is a lovely sight indeed with her hair waving in the breeze. One soon comprehends how vastly she differs in temperament from her hard-working, husband-deferring mother (Sara Allgood) and from Bronwyn (Anna Lee), the devoted girl from the next valley who weds the Morgans' eldest son (Patric Knowles). Although Maureen is well instructed in performing her

---

*Other performers at this time who had unique multistudio pacts were Virginia Gilmore and Dana Andrews, both employed by Twentieth Century-Fox and Sam Goldwyn Productions, the latter then releasing through RKO.

†One shudders to think how any of Fox's contract star(lets) would have handled the assignment, whether Gene Tierney, Ann Baxter, Nancy Kelly, or Linda Darnell.

household chores, from helping with the cooking and dish washing to carrying the buckets of hot water to the backyard for the men's daily post-mining washing ritual, she is a very proud lass with an intrenched spunkiness that defies maidenliness or Welsh tradition. From the moment she spots the new minister, Mr. Gruffydd (Walter Pidgeon), presiding at Knowles's wedding, she is in love with him. With thinly veiled determination she pursues him. For instance, on the night Pidgeon rushes to the Morgan home after Allgood and McDowall have been injured in an accident, she inquires: "Will you be coming to supper soon?" Later on Pidgeon admits: "You'd be queen wherever you are." Unsatisfied by this unprecise expression of praise, Maureen boldly states her matrimonial interest in him: "If the right is mine to give you, you have it." On yet another occasion, when she has not seen him for some days, they encounter and she inquires: "Why am I a stranger now. Have I done anything?" Then one time Pidgeon explains why he has been reticent in their courtship, telling her that he will not allow her to share his poverty-filled existence, insisting she deserves a better lot. Maureen is stunned by this piece of news, but later that night, before they separate, it is she who kisses him. Thereafter when she stands up in church to defend a local girl being castigated for immoral behavior, she and Pidgeon quarrel bitterly over the matter, and a hurt Maureen agrees to wed the mine-owner's snooty son (Marten Lamont).

Then Maureen drifts out of the busy narrative for a time, as the film focuses on Huw and his adventures in the new school in the neighboring valley, and then on the increasing problems at the mines between management and labor. When Huw comes to visit Maureen at her stately new home high on the hill, Mrs. Nicholas (Ethel Griffies), the overbearing housekeeper, does everything possible to make Huw ill at ease, and to keep the newly repressed Maureen toeing the conservative mark. Maureen is a sad sight indeed—anemic, pale, garbed in starched, unbecoming finery, and crowned with a short, curled hairdo. "I look ill. I ought to take care of myself," Maureen informs Huw, and then begs him for news of home and of her beloved clergyman.

Griffies spreads rumors of an unseemly affection between her married mistress, Maureen, and the unconventional minister, Pidgeon. Hints of a pending divorce astonish and shock the staid community. Inhibited further by the malicious gossip, Maureen retreats further into her shell and the incensed Pidgeon resigns his ministry post. But Maureen and Pidgeon have one more meeting, the night of the mine disaster, which claims, among its many victims, her father's life. Maureen and Pidgeon both arrive at the mine-shaftway at about the same time, and spot one another in the anxious crowd. They exchange yearning looks back and forth, capped by mouthed words of love. (This soap-operaish moment, badly handled by both Maureen and Pidgeon, is as jarring to the film's overall mood as the overly cute Welsh-Irish comedy relief of Barry Fitzgerald and Rhys Williams.) Soon the narrative of *How Green Was My Valley* comes to a close, with a final reprise fleetingly showing the main characters in snatches from the film. Maureen is seen waving from the roadside fence, her hair gloriously flowing in the breeze.

How Green Was My Valley was acclaimed "a motion picture of great poetic charm and dignity" *(New York Times)* and won four Academy Awards, including best picture of the year. Although Maureen's spirited performance did not in any way dominate the picture, she cast aside her conventional ingenue guise and established a definite new screen image that would span her succeeding four decades of movie work to date. She personified the fiery Irish lass, as self-sufficient and self-willed as she is beautiful and athletically agile. Maureen, Pidgeon, Crisp, McDowall, and Allgood would recreate their roles from *How Green Was My Valley* on "Lux Radio Theatre" on September 21, 1942.*

Offscreen Maureen had established quite a different impression, as an Irish shamrock miss. Until late 1941 when her mother returned to Ireland to be with her family for the duration of the war, Maureen shared a Hollywood home with her mother and younger brother. (Later she rented a Beverly Hills home with her secretary-companion, Florence O'Neill). Unlike most aspiring Hollywood actresses, Maureen was very reluctant to pose for sexy cheesecake. In fact in her early oncamera lovemaking scenes, she was so overly ladylike that crews tagged her frozen champagne. Because of her marital status Maureen initially eschewed the Hollywood social scene, but as time went on she was frequently seen in the company of Will Price, her dialog coach on *The Hunchback of Notre Dame*. By mid-1941 Maureen had publicly concluded that her hasty marriage to George Brown, who was still in England, had been a youthful mistake. In August-September, 1940, she went to Nevada and established residence for a divorce (an annulment was obtained). On December 29, 1941, Maureen and Price, he on leave from the Marines, went to his hometown of McComb, Mississippi, and were wed at St. Mary of the Pines Convent in nearby Chatawa. After honeymooning in New Orleans, they returned to Hollywood.

Maureen made four more pictures at Twentieth Century-Fox before returning to RKO. *To the Shores of Tripoli* (1942) was a topical, but cliché-ridden, tribute to the United States Marine Corps. The picture relied on Warner Brothers' favorite serviceman-formula plot to push along the manufactured story. Cocky playboy John Payne, a graduate of Culver and whose father had been a leatherneck before him, arrives at the San Diego Marine training station, prepared to mark time until his wealthy fiancée (Nancy Kelly) can maneuver him a soft berth in Washington, D.C. He bridles under the tough discipline of sergeant Randolph Scott, but succumbs to the charms of Maureen, a commissioned Navy nurse. Just as Payne is about to desert the Corps, he learns of the Pearl Harbor attack. With re-

*In the unsuccessful Broadway musical adaptation of the novel-screenplay, entitled *A Time for Singing* (May, 1966, forty-one performances), Shani Wallis inherited Maureen's role as Angharad Morgan.

newed patriotism he returns to his post to do his share in the forthcoming war effort. *To the Shores of Tripoli* may have been an unremarkable service salute, but it provided Maureen with her initial Technicolor feature, allowing filmgoers to finally view in multiple hues the Irish beauty of this performer, famed for her flowing red hair. It was the first of dozens of color features in which Maureen would appear, which soon led the Technicolor Corporation to anoint her the queen of Technicolor. To this day, whenever she starts a new picture, the company sends her a bouquet of red roses.

Continuing in the military-film genre, Maureen took second billing to George Montgomery in *10 Gentlemen from West Point* (1942), a black-and-white semihistorical bit of balderdash dealing with the founding of the austere military academy. Director Henry Hathaway endeavored in vain to make the tribute more than a flag-waving costume drama, as the film traces the adventures of the first class at West Point in the early 1800s. Under the martinet supervision of major Laird Cregar the plebes are soon reduced to ten in number, including buckskin-clad Kentuckian Montgomery and dandy John Sutton. Maureen arrives in the vicinity to visit relatives and soon is romantically dallying with both Montgomery and Sutton, even to the extent of following the men into western Indian territory where they are engaged in routing Tecumseh and his redskin braves. Despite the picture's unsubtle exploitation of patriotism and the tedious blend of fact and fancy, it is reported that back in 1942, after a screening of *10 Gentlemen from West Point,* one Academy officer told his cadets: "It is the least objectionable of the service films." The *New York Times* again complimented Maureen for being "a vision of loveliness."

The Black Swan (Roxy Theatre, December 23, 1942), a handsomely mounted Techinicolor swashbuckler, combined to good results a mixture of piratical Spanish Main hijinks and romantic adventure. The Crown pardons the notorious ex-pirate Henry Morgan (Laird Cregar) and appoints him governor of Jamaica in the place of corrupt George Zucco. None of which endears Cregar or his now law-abiding aide, Tyrone Power, to Zucco's outspoken daughter, Maureen. Power kidnaps Maureen on the eve of her wedding to a prissy gentleman and takes her aboard his ship, *The Revenge.* Before Power succeeds in routing dastardly Captain Leach (red-bearded George Sanders), Maureen's vituperative antagonism for Power has melted into love. Unlike Warner Brothers' Olivia de Havilland, who had effectively graced similar romantic action yarns, usually paired with robust Errol Flynn, Maureen demonstrated she was no milktoast heroine who would be content to remain ladylike on the sidelines. If her love scenes still lacked passionate conviction, her hot-tempered, liberated nature and her beauty were more than sufficient compensation for most viewers and critics. ("Miss O'Hara is no more or no less than her charming self," *New York Herald-Tribune.*)

Maureen was as superfluous to the general effectiveness of *The Immortal Sergeant* (1943) as Carole Lombard had been in Cary Grant-Fredric March's

The Eagle and the Hawk a decade before. Fox's *The Immortal Sergeant* emerged a timely war melodrama and the first American feature to deal with the North African campaign, focusing on a lost patrol in the Libyan desert, of which only four of the original fourteen survive to reach the home base. When title figure Thomas Mitchell is fatally wounded, gentle Canadian Henry Fonda must assume command and in the process must become a decisive, resourceful person. Via disconcerting flashbacks he recalls his tenuous relationship with Maureen, the girl he left behind in London, having been too unsure of himself to ask her to wed him. By the wrap-up he has been awarded the Distinguished Service Cross, received tremendous publicity, and won back Maureen, all of which combines to nearly obscure the original intention of John Brophy's novel (i.e., to detail the inner victory of a once self-effacing individual).

After a two-year absence Maureen returned to RKO, which had undergone a tremendous transformation during the World War II years. The studio now was gearing the bulk of its products to the lowbrow serviceman and rural markets, which meant an overbalance of programmer pictures and low-priced starlets to pepper them. For each major star who had departed RKO, the new regime had added several more small-paid contractees to decorate run-of-the-mill studio products, particularly new installments of such series as *The Falcon, Lum and Abner, Fibber McGee and Molly, Dick Tracy,* the Zane Grey westerns, and Val Lewton's economy line of psychological horror tales. The resultant diminishment in glamour and female-player competition made Maureen much more of a queen bee than ever before on her home lot, second only to Ginger Rogers, who had yet to complete a few remaining studio commitments. There was a wide gap between Maureen and the bulk of the distaff-player stable at RKO, which included such newcomers as Kim Hunter, Nancy Gates, Barbara Hale, Rita Corday, Joan Barclay, and Dorothy Malone.

This Land Is Mine (1943) co-starred Maureen for a third and final time with Charles Laughton. For RKO it was a heavily budgeted feature, a forceful wartorn drama at that. The picture is unspecific in revealing its Continental locale as it depicts a conquered European village's fight for freedom. But it contains a distinctive Gallic flavoring, due no little to the influence of its French director, Jean Renoir. Within the story frame, timid, middle-aged schoolmaster Laughton is securely tied to the apronstrings of his shrewish mother (Una O'Connor), which prevents him not only from telling schoolmarm Maureen of his love for her, but from championing the cause of his country against the Nazi invaders. However, a rapid series of events fortifies jellyfish Laughton with delayed courage. Maureen's brother (Kent Smith), who works for the local underground, is betrayed by O'Connor to save Laughton; the school principal (Philip Merivale) faces the firing squad with dignity; and Laughton is placed on trial for a murder he did not commit. Suddenly blubbering Laughton wakes up emotionally and defies the Nazi authorities, headed by major Walter Slezak. Laughton rises to heroic heights as he delivers an impassioned speech to his class on the meaning of liberty, fully aware that this action will mean his death.

Many of the dramatic incidents in Dudley Nichols's script for *This Land Is Mine* sorely taxed the film's credibility, and anyone expecting the picture to be filled with excitement and suspense was tremendously disappointed, for this feature was pointedly devoted to presenting an inner drama of character. Nevertheless the movie is very rich in theatrical performances,* including Laughton's waddling coward, George Sanders's snide collaborationist, Slezak's menacing Nazi, and O'Connor's termagant mother. As the schoolteacher and zealous patriot who is engaged to Axis-sympathizing railroad superintendent Sanders, Maureen had little to do beyond registering wide-eyed, trembling looks as she voices partisan credos on the necessity for keeping the spirit of freedom alive at any cost. Perhaps it was patriotic compassion which induced the *New Yorker* magazine's reviewer to decide Maureen "seems a peg above her usual self as the girl."

The Fallen Sparrow (Palace Theatre, August 19, 1943) is another one of those murder mysteries which, like *The Big Sleep,* defies rational plot analysis as it gets lost in the convolutions of its storyline twists. There is little zealous hokum in *The Fallen Sparrow,* as it is filled to overflowing with murder, mania, and Nazi cruelty. For a refreshing change, its hero (John Garfield) does not make idealistic speeches or emerge as an improbable supersleuth. Instead, he is a Spanish Civil War veteran who escapes from a Franco prison camp after enduring much torture and later recuperates at an Arizona ranch. When he returns to New York he learns that a boyhood pal has been killed. He properly links the homicide to his knowledge of the whereabouts of a Spanish Civil War battle flag carried by the loyalist Abraham Lincoln Brigade, which destroyed a regiment of Nazi troops. Since the massacred German unit was commanded by a favored officer in the Third Reich, the Nazis are determined to regain this "symbol" of liberty and are quite prepared to go to any lengths to break down Garfield's resistance so he will reveal the flag's whereabouts. Haunted by the dripping sound of water and the shuffling footsteps of his unknown torturer in the Spanish prison, Garfield scurries about Manhattan desperately trying to keep a grip on his sanity and yet remain true to his fallen comrades. There is German refugee Walter Slezak dogging Garfield's steps, and the distracting presence of three women: redheaded milliner Maureen, brunette socialite Patricia Morison, and blonde nightclub singer Martha O'Driscoll. In a bizarre windup Garfield unmasks his adversaries and boards a plane for Lisbon to retrieve the precious flag. In the first of only a few villainous roles in her screen career, Maureen lacked the necessary conviction to be persuasive in her less highly keyed moments, emerging as beautiful as always but far too

---

*One sassy critic insisted there were so many scene-hogging performances in the picture that the movie should have been titled *This Picture Is Mine.*

wooden and ambiguous.* She would recreate her *The Fallen Sparrow* role along with Walter Slezak and substitute male lead Robert Young on "Lux Radio Theatre" on February 14, 1944.

Buffalo Bill (1944) was yet another fanciful re-creation of events in the life of the famed Indian fighter who later brought the Wild West Show to the East. Produced by Harry "Pop" Sherman of *Hopalong Cassidy* fame and directed in overexaggerated style by William A. Wellman, the Twentieth Century-Fox feature failed badly. Blame can be placed either on an overambitious script, which did not focus clearly on individual episodes within its too expansive framework, or on Joel McCrea's stilted performance as Buffalo Bill. Whatever the reason, the resulting Technicolor western lacked zest even in its fierce Indian attack scenes. Maureen was handed a nondescript role as the high-bred eastern girl, the daughter of senator Moroni Olsen, who is rescued by McCrea from an Indian attack. She later weds the great outdoorsman only to witness his sudden championing of the unfairly treated Indians. (The script was geared to create parallels between Buffalo Bill's creed and the high principles enunciated during World War II.) At one point in the film Maureen leaves McCrea, and when their child dies of diphtheria, she loses her will to live. But eventually she is restored to her husband, who has himself found a new productive lease on life performing with his Wild West Show. As one-dimensional as Maureen's role was, it was a far sight more satisfactory than that of Fox star Linda Darnell, who postured as a delicate Indian maiden in love with sturdy McCrea. This time around Bosley Crowther *(New York Times)* termed Maureen a "shimmery vision of loveliness."

For much of the early 1940s Maureen had been a "war widow," since shortly after her marriage to Will Price, he had returned to military duty with the United States Marines and spent a good deal of the war years away from the United States. He was home on leave to attend the 1943 Academy Award ceremonies since one of the short subjects he had made had been nominated for a prize, but he was back overseas by the time Maureen gave birth to her first (and only) child, Bronwyn Bridget,† born on June 30, 1944. Blissfully happy with her new motherhood role, Maureen told the press, "Anyone who would give up a home for a career is crazy."

But Maureen soon had occasion to rescind her dogma, for in March, 1944, she negotiated a new film contract between RKO, Twentieth Century-Fox, and herself. In accordance with her rising box-office appeal she was to be

---

*James Agee writing in the *Nation:* "Good sets and props have done a lot for still another picture this month; excellent lighting, good camera work, and unusually good bit-casting have added so much edge and vitality that *The Fallen Sparrow* passes among many people for the almost-Hitchcock spy melodrama it certainly is not. . . . Someone should tell Maureen O'Hara that if she is pretending to be a granddaughter of a French prince, she should leave off aiding China long enough to avoid calling him 'France Wah.' "

†The child was named Bronwyn after the character in *How Green Was My Valley* and Bridget in honor of Maureen's eldest sister.

featured primarily in Fox films, but was to appear in one RKO picture per year. As soon as she had recuperated from childbirth, RKO paged her for a new film, and Maureen was back in acting harness before she could utter "sweet motherhood" another time.

As her postmaternity vehicle, RKO selected a Hollywood-style pirate yarn, *The Spanish Main* (Palace Theatre, November 6, 1945), rigged out in Technicolor but falling far short of the necessary mark in needed credibility and excitement. Set in the Caribbean, haughty noblewoman Maureen is affianced to the wicked Spanish viceroy (Walter Slezak). However, she is snatched off a passing galleon by an idealistic Dutch merchant captain (Paul Henreid) who weds her in name only—that is, until both Slezak and Maureen have been appropriately tamed. Second-billed Maureen found stiff competition from Binnie Barnes, who provided a hearty performance as Anne Bonney, the roisterous pirate lady very much in love with Continental Henreid.

At the end of World War II Will Price, who had risen from the rank of private to lieutenant in the Marines, was demobilized. Now Maureen could properly voice her domestic plans: "Will and I are hoping to have five more children. It's this family that is our favorite dream of what we want most when he comes home again." Meanwhile having taken out her first papers in November, 1941, Maureen became a United States citizen on January 26, 1946, in Los Angeles federal court. When she was asked to forswear her allegiance to King George VI, she proudly explained that being true-green Irish she never owed it in the first place.

Just as Maureen had been anxious to portray Charlotte Brontë,* a woman of high spirits and restrained behavior, on the screen, so she aspired to win the coveted part of Amber St. Clair in Twentieth Century-Fox's *Forever Amber* (1947). Just in case any of the Fox executives had sparse imaginations, Maureen, on occasion, would sweep into the studio commissary wearing low-cut period gowns and sashay about in the supposed manner of Amber. But Fox's mogul, Darryl F. Zanuck, was not persuaded of Maureen's suitability, and Peggy Cummings was awarded the lead assignment, later to be replaced by Linda Darnell.

However, Fox did heed one of Maureen's more vocal preachments: "Almost every letter I receive," Maureen informed reporters, "asks why Hollywood doesn't take me out of these silly Technicolor pictures and give me dramatic pictures. It's nice to have someone on your side."

Sentimental Journey (Roxy Theatre, March 6, 1946) was the tearjerker supreme of the year, purposefully verging on the lachrymose. But it was so well mounted and so congenially played by its cast that audiences readily accepted its blubbering bathos. The Sutton Place domestic bliss of Broadway star Maureen, wed to stage producer John Payne, would be complete if they only could have a child—and then there is the heart ailment she tries so hard

---

*Warner Bros. gave the role to Olivia de Havilland in *Devotion,* made in 1943 but not released until 1946.

to hide from Payne ("I'll do anything, anything you say doctor, only please don't tell Bill"). During an out-of-town tryout of her latest play, Maureen is sauntering along the seashore when suddenly her fondest wish is answered, as if from heaven. She chances upon little Connie Marshall of the nearby orphanage and is immediately taken with the precocious, lonely child. Naturally Maureen insists that she and Payne adopt Marshall, overriding her husband's objections. The new Broadway play is a smash hit, but Maureen's heart cannot bear the strain of all her professional and domestic joy. She dies. Payne is so overcome by his bereavement that he has neither interest nor time for the little girl. All the weepy child can cling to is Maureen's dying instructions for her never to leave Payne, adding, "But I'll always be around whenever you need me." Little Marshall is eventually drawn back to the seashore spot where she first met her lovely "Lady of the Shiloh." Floating across the water on a breeze Marshall hears Maureen saying: "Everything will be all right now, darling. Now we're really a family. You see, Bill loves you, Hitty." And so he does, for business manager William Bendix has brought Payne back to his muddled senses and the producer hunts for the missing girl, rescuing her just in time from nearly drowning. With dramatic finality Payne informs Marshall: "We're going home, Hitty. We're going home, daughter."

It is true that, as *Time* magazine glibly analyzed, Maureen does "emote heavily in chaste, flowing decorous gowns" in *Sentimental Journey,* being particularly unsubtle in the early sequences, in which she rather clumsily telegraphs portentous events. But in all fairness there were few actresses in Hollywood who could have handled the contrived plot twists with such winning openness and charm.* In addition there were few 1940s female stars, even those much older or less attractive than twenty-six-year-old Maureen, who were willing to play that dreaded of all screen roles: a *mother.*

To demonstrate further to exhibitors, moviegoers, and critics alike that Maureen was indeed highly versatile and capable of handling non-high adventure entries, Twentieth Century-Fox cast her in the Technicolor musical *Do You Love Me?* (1946). Fox was not being entirely altruistic when it made this assignment, for studio blondes Betty Grable and June Haver had already passed up the vehicle. In her first top-billed starring role at Fox, Maureen fought to overcome sizable odds to make herself and the picture a commercial success. She failed. She just was not a seasoned enough performer to carry a very thin musical comedy, nor did she receive much creative support from her two nonactor co-stars, crooner Dick Haymes and trumpeter Harry James. The film's premise presented Maureen as the straightlaced dean of a dignified Philadelphia music academy, en route to New York to arrange for Reginald Gardiner to conduct a symphony-music contest at her institution. On the Manhattan-bound train she strolls into Harry James's private car,

*Just compare Maureen's performance with that of Lauren Bacall in the tattered remake entitled *The Gift of Love* (1958).

where she fails to be impressed by a hot swing session performed by James and his band. He labels her prim miss, but Maureen has the initiative to alter her entire outward appearance, from hairdo to makeup to wardrobe. She is determined to turn the tables on him and to carry out her ploy makes use of Haymes, who, though she does not know it, is a popular vocalist. Thus the rivalry begins, for both James and Haymes are intrigued with the new Maureen, although she protests she is faithfully engaged to colorless Richard Gaines, the business manager of her school. Expectedly all ends well. Maureen, who has lost her post due to what the school board misinterpreted as immodest behavior, is reinstated; Haymes and James prove to the same conservative advisory board that swing has a place in the art of music; and, lo and behold, Maureen and Haymes are reconciled after another lovers' quarrel.

Both Producer George Jessel and Twentieth Century-Fox studio management realized that this musical, originally titled *Kitten on the Keys,* was not in the splashy big league of a Betty Grable outing, and the picture was held back from its planned release for retakes and other tinkering. The restructured film still remained eminently forgettable. While Maureen was again beautifully photographed in color and there were a few catchy minor numbers like "Moonlight Propaganda," what the picture lacked most of all was the presence of one—or all—of Fox's successful triumvirate of RKO's musical comedy stars: Alice Faye, June Haver, and Betty Grable. In fact, during production, even Grable began to think that what the film needed was her presence, particularly when husband James informed her that in the picture's finale he must lose Maureen to Haymes. Due more to this unforgivable *faux pas* than anything else, Grable huddled with executive Zanuck and agreed to appear in an unbilled cameo as the faithful admirer who waits outside the stage door for her favorite trumpeter-bandleader. Even this gratuitous addendum was not enough to goose the entry into more than a "platinum-plated romantic" outing.

RKO alloted a multimillion-dollar budget for Douglas Fairbanks, Jr.'s first post-World War II feature, *Sinbad the Sailor* (1947). The Arabian Nights charade detailed in gaudy hues the seaman's mythical eighth voyage to find the fabled treasure of Alexander on the lost isle of Deryabar. Had the script been written in a more self-kidding vein (as *The Spanish Main* attempted), and had the presentation been less reliant on obvious miniature and special effects, *Sinbad the Sailor* might have become more than just an enjoyable but juvenile film. The studio's advertising campaign for this actioner clearly described Maureen's role: "He stormed a veiled beauty's boudoir . . . and made her love it!" Therefore, before the plotline has greedy, paunchy Walter Slezak done in by his own evilness, Maureen, the slinky adventuress-emissary to emir Anthony Quinn, has fallen prey to Fairbanks's lightning harem-room charms. The two sail off into the studio sunset, having found their own special treasure-trove of love. "[The costumes] worn by Maureen O'Hara are most fetchingly displayed (and most fetchingly display Miss O'Hara) which exhausts the subject of Miss O'Hara" *(New York Times).* But then, with a tongue-in-cheek Fairbanks mouthing such exotic lines as "Ah, Burning Bright . . . O woman of the roses," what more could Maureen do than look bewildered?

From the profitable swashbuckler *Sinbad the Sailor* Maureen turned next to Twentieth Century-Fox's newest horseracing entry, *The Homestretch* (Roxy Theatre, April 23, 1947). The best element of this standard turf drama* was the glorious color photography of equine events at eleven famous racetracks, ranging from Jamaica to England's Grand National. Turning on icy pose number 2-A, Maureen played reserved Bostonian Leslie Hale, who endorses her emotional liberation by ditching her State Department beau (Glenn Langan) to wed raffish Kentucky racing man Cornel Wilde, who in turn had been dallying with bohemian Helen Walker. The expected complications unravel at a snail's pace (which seems all the slower when compared to the horseraces themselves), with everything ending just dandy for all concerned. If only there had been offtrack betting in 1947, all the viewers could have profitably stayed home. But enough moviegoers were appeased by Maureen's shamrock vitality and Wilde's diffuse virility to make the entry an adequate cinema bargain for that season. Maureen and Wilde re-created their *The Homestretch* roles on "Lux Radio Theatre" on May 17, 1948.

From this odoriferous "horse" film Maureen glided into the sweet smell of success with Fox's *Miracle on 34th Street* (Roxy Theatre, June 4, 1947). Questioning the validity of America's traditional belief in Santa Claus, director George Seaton proceeded to present a fantasylike comedy, anchored sufficiently in fact to be disarmingly logical. The advertising manager for the R. H. Macy and Company Department Store, Maureen, blithely hires pixillated Edmund Gwenn to be one of the store's several holiday-time Santa Clauses. When the old gentleman tells customers that if Macy's does not have the Christmas gifts they need, nearby Gimbels surely will, Maureen immediately wants to discharge the disloyal store worker. However, Gwenn's unique helpfulness has caught the press's attention and Macy's receives tremendous free publicity. All of this is fine and dandy, but the neurotic personnel manager, Porter Hall, insists that anyone who believes he is really St. Nick, as Gwenn obviously does, is both a fraud and a mental case and should be treated accordingly. Hall's action on this belief leads to a sanity hearing in which defense attorney John Payne (who along the way succumbs to the charms of widow Maureen and grows to love her cynical young daughter, Natalie Wood) proves to everyone's satisfaction that for all practical purposes Gwenn is Santa Claus.† Although the movie concludes with the viewer still unsure whether Gwenn is or is not St. Nick, the proceedings were

*Twentieth Century-Fox had a penchant for the species: *Maryland* (1940), *Home in Indiana* (1944), etc.

†The logic employed at this strategic point is ridiculous, but, as scenarist Seaton points out in his screenplay, in this insane world reality is downright crazy anyway. The court, nevertheless, buys Payne's argument, which is basically that huge bags of mail addressed simply to "Santa Claus" have been delivered by the Post Office to Gwenn, and since the Post Office is a branch of the government, the government therefore recognizes Gwenn as Santa Claus.

so delightfully concocted that critical endorsement and audience word-of-mouth made this summertime entry a hearty box-office success.

In a very understated manner, which properly kept the focus on Gwenn, Maureen demonstrated her growing adeptness as a light comedienne. She proved that she was one star who did not need to grab the limelight in every scene in which she played. Maureen, along with Payne, Gwenn, and Wood, would re-create her *Miracle on 34th Street* role on "Lux Radio Theatre" on December 22, 1947.*

The Foxes of Harrow was the third of Maureen's three 1947 Twentieth Century-Fox features to play the studio's New York showcase theatre, the Roxy. These showcasings indicated her strong, but still anomalous, position as a Fox performer (i.e., she was a studio star in fact, but technically her screen time was co-owned by RKO, and Fox was not about to push an actress too strongly for another company's possible advantage, even if they were enacting the time-honored silliness of cutting off their nose to spite their face). At some time in the process studio boss Darryl F. Zanuck must have had second thoughts about Wanda Tuchock's screenplay for *The Foxes of Harrow,* for it was decided to lense the costume drama in the more economical black-and-white process. His decision was an astute one, because the movie, directed by John M. Stahl,† emerged as an uneven and overlong (115-minute) picture. Top-billed Rex Harrison, as a bastard Irish philanderer of 1820s New Orleans, proved to be a crashing bore. He is the scamp who earns his first real money via gambling. With his audacity at cards and his gall with people he soon wins himself a plantation and induces haughty, aristocratic Maureen to wed him. Theirs is a strange marriage from the start. On their wedding night they quarrel and thereafter never share the connubial bed until years later when their club-footed son is killed and they are driven together in reconciliation. During the process the rundown plantation nearly falls apart, mostly due to mismanagement and the slaves' preoccupation with voodoo. Nevertheless, spirited Maureen eventually brings Harrison and the workers to their "senses."

Obviously author Frank Yerby had been influenced by *Gone with the Wind* when he wrote the sprawling novel *The Foxes of Harrow,* and Maureen's Odalie was a direct offshoot of Scarlett O'Hara. Maureen performed her role of the comely but arrogant miss as a variation of her *Black Swan* characterization, spunky but sadly diffuse in delineation. Maureen and studio executives realized from *The Foxes of Harrow* that no matter what her dramatic ambitions were, she was no Vivien Leigh. Along with John Hodiak,

---

*The movie was transformed into television specials (including a 1959 version with Ed Wynn, Peter Lind Hayes, and Mary Healy), and thereafter became a nonhit Broadway musical entitled *Here's Love* (1963), with Janis Paige in Maureen's role. A new tv musical of the show appeared on December 14, 1973 on CBS with Jane Alexander, David Hartman, and Sebastian Cabot as Kris Kringle.

†Just as Maureen had lost out on playing *Forever Amber,* so director Stahl had been removed from that production when Peggy Cummings was replaced by Linda Darnell and filming was restarted.

Maureen was heard on the "Lux Radio Theatre" rendition of *The Foxes of Harrow* on December 6, 1948.

Maureen became so identified with her athletic screen-heroine roles in the 1950s that few viewers recall how adroitly she could play a Jane Wyatt-type perfect wife, as in her next picture, the very successful *Sitting Pretty* (Roxy Theatre, March 10, 1948). Created in the same deft light-comedy vein as RKO's *Mr. Blandings Builds His Dream House* (1948), *Sitting Pretty* was a frothy dessert revolving around the timely topic of babysitters.* Businessman Robert Young and his wife (Maureen) reside with their three small sons on Carver Lane in the suburban community of Hummingbird Hill. The rambunctious kids force one maid after another to quit, and when Maureen spots teenaged babysitter Betty Ann Lynn mooning over Young, she promptly advertises for a very mature live-in maid. Prissy Lynn Belvedere answers all of Maureen's standards—except that he is a man (Clifton Webb). But never mind; within a few short days he has her brood so well in tow that she wonders how she ever survived without this versatile eccentric. Now she has spare time to indulge in sculpturing, using Webb for a model, and giving snitty, gossip-snooping neighbor Richard Haydn cause to spread malicious rumors about their innocent relationship. All ends satisfactorily—so well, indeed, for Fox's corporate coffers, that Webb starred in two film follow-ups, *Mr. Belvedere Goes to College* (1949) and *Mr. Belvedere Rings the Bell* (1951), neither of which had Maureen or Young along for reprises. Plans in the mid-1950s to reunite Webb, Maureen, and Young in a further *Belvedere* episode never materialized.

Ten years after *My Irish Molly* Maureen returned to England to star in Twentieth Century-Fox's *The Forbidden Street,* released in May, 1949. It was a dismal failure, making hash of Margery Sharp's novel *Britannia Mews*. As the 1870s London girl from a good family who becomes enraptured with a drunken art teacher (Dana Andrews) who is a resident of the disreputable Mews slums, Maureen projected her character, Adelaide Culver, as a well-groomed automaton. Adelaide, unfortunately, grows no more animated after her husband's timely death, nor even during her eventual remarriage, this time to an unemployed barrister (also played by Andrews). The only apparent spark of human life in the Jean Negulesco production was supplied by Dame Sybil Thorndike as a blackmailing harridan.

Maureen leaped from flop to flop, taking the lead role in *A Woman's Secret* (1949), produced under Dore Schary's late aegis at RKO in early 1948. She was badly miscast as the has-been vocalist who, along with pianist Melvyn Douglas, promotes the songstress career of ex-salesgirl Gloria Grahame, and for her trouble lands in jail on a murder charge. *Time* magazine rightly concluded that the film "might better have been kept under lock and key."

Returning to Fox, Maureen supported Fred MacMurray in *Father Was a*

---

*The post-World War II economy had precluded the feasibility of most upper-middle-class families having domestic servants live in.

Fullback (1949). Despite its title the picture was essentially *not* about sports, but rather a comedy about the generation gap in a campus setting. Unfortunately for this attempt, there was a similar and much better film from the same studio, *Mother Is a Freshman* starring Loretta Young, which was also released in 1949. In *Father Was a Fullback,* MacMurray is harassed on all sides. He is coach of a college football team that cannot win a game, and his two daughters, particularly awkward adolescent Betty Lynn, are giving him constant Excedrin headaches. His cynical maid, Thelma Ritter, who strolls off with the picture's brightest moment, has a simple remedy for Lynn: give her a good sock in the chops. But MacMurray and his patient, radiant wife (Maureen) persist in handling the matter in a more dignified but blundering manner. For the record, *Variety* pointed out that decorative Maureen is "becoming one of the best exponents of helpmeet-mothers on the screen today."

In March, 1949 Maureen participated in a Masquers' Club stage production of *What Price Glory?*, directed by John Ford and Ralph Murphy.

While Howard Hughes, the new boss of RKO, was busily cleaning shop in 1949, and Sid Rogell was supervising what little production was being lensed on the studio soundstages following the sudden departure the year before of Dore Schary, Maureen made what proved to be her final RKO film, *Sons of the Musketeers* (December, 1949). Hughes did not bother releasing the film for three years and made it quite clear that he was not enthused by Maureen's high-priced presence on the lot. As far as he was concerned, any role for which she might be considered "suitable" would certainly be first offered to his protégées, Jane Russell and Faith Domergue. Maureen took the unsubtle hint, packed her belongings, and left the lot.

If RKO in particular and Twentieth Century-Fox to a lesser extent had no pressing need for Maureen's professional services, Universal most certainly did. This latter studio had suffered almost as many financial reverses and executive shakeups in the 1940s as RKO. However, now restructured as Universal-International, it was gearing itself to meet the heavy competition of free television and the wasteland aftermath of the Justice Department's successful antitrust suits, which had forced studios to sell off their movie-house chains. Universal's key to survival was its churned-out Technicolor action programmers, which could be used to saturate the double-bill theatrical market. In order to make these colorful B-pictures Universal needed a variety of attractive players, above and beyond its Rock Hudson, Tony Curtis, Piper Laurie, Julie Adams, Patricia Medina, and Yvonne DeCarlo.

Universal's *Bagdad,* Maureen's fourth and final release of 1949, set the tone for her 1950s film career. In past adventure pictures she had been merely the nervy and decorative distaff lead. Now she moved into the full limelight and claimed the screen title once held by Universal's Maria Montez, and more recently by Yvonne DeCarlo, as queen of the period adventure yarns. More so than Montez or even the more recently successful DeCarlo, Maureen combined her startling screen beauty with an athletic finesse that allowed her to glide through rigorous roles as a gun-toting or rapier-cutting heroine. If Maureen was unable to bring a higher class of talents to the *de rigueur* cardboard damsels of the genre, she certainly exhibited a vigorous enthusiasm in performing her gymnastics. And, more important, Maureen's actioners were relatively inexpensive to mount and almost guaranteed to clean up a tidy box-office profit. Thus at age twenty-nine, Maureen quietly made the final transition from star with dramatic ambition to queen of the B-adventure pictures.

Bagdad contained all the prime ingredients that would typify Maureen's Universal entries: Technicolor lensing; a handsome, if undynamic male co-star; and a weakbrained script which allowed Maureen complete freedom to fight her noble screen causes with her own feminine wiles and many rugged swashbuckling heroics. Midst the formula skulduggery among the sheiks of Bagdad, princess Maureen (who assumes the disguise of a cafe entertainer and sings three songs) learns to her relief that Paul Christian is not the leader of the dastardly Black Riders, a desert gang in cahoots with pasha Vincent Price.

Universal's *Comanche Territory* (1950) found Maureen playing the buck-skin-clad boss of a western town, who seems more at ease in riding breeches, demonstrating her prowess with a black whip and six-shooters, than in an evening gown as the proprietress of the Crooked Tongue Saloon. As she exhorts her placid vis-à-vis, Macdonald Carey, "If you call me a lady once more, I'll fill you full of lead." Less tomboyish than Jean Arthur or cutesy than Doris Day in this Calamity Jane-style role, Maureen inspired the *New York Times*'s Howard Thompson to enthuse: "Framed in Technicolor, Miss O'Hara somehow seems more significant than a setting sun. And she tackles her assignment with so much relish that the rest of the cast, even the Indians, are completely subdued. Maybe the lady was bursting with appreciation for landing out on the prairie after that long siege of rescues from pirates and sultans' harems."

For some time Maureen had wanted to star in a picture directed by her husband, Will Price. Paramount's low-budget producers, William H. Pine and William C. Thomas, gave her just such an opportunity in *Tripoli* (1950), a story Price "uncovered" while attending officers' classes in the Marines. For her male lead Maureen selected her old-time Twentieth Century-Fox co-star, John Payne. In 1805, Marine lieutenant Payne is commanded to head a native army through the Libyan desert to battle Tripolitan pirates. Maureen, the titled daughter of a French diplomat and the ward of a desert despot, disguises herself as a dancing girl so she can trek along with Payne's waste-land scavengers. At best, *Tripoli* abounded with anachronisms (Maureen was labeled "the crowning touch"), but it was a moneymaker, and who but critics ever argue with success?

Maureen still had some buried histrionic desires and jumped at the chance to work with John Ford again. He had in mind a project called *The Quiet Man,* to be shot on location in Ireland. She and John Wayne were to be co-starred. Republic Pictures agreed to finance that seemingly unpromising picture *if* Ford and Wayne first turned out a more likely box-office product, say a hit western. Thus *Rio Grande* (1950), the third member of Ford's cavalry trilogy,* came into being. Maureen brought a fitting maturity to her stereotyped assignment in this film as the estranged, frigid, southern wife of lieutenant colonel Wayne, who has not yet forgiven him for burning her plantation during the recent Civil War. But he was acting under strict orders then as he is now, attempting to maintain a truce calm at his southwestern post, which is besieged by marauding Apaches who continually flee to the safety of Mexico after their raids. Eventually, disobeying orders, Wayne crosses the border with his command (which includes his West Point dropout son, Claude Jarman, Jr.). With the Indians routed and his son having proven his manliness, Wayne reaches a satisfactory rapprochement with Maureen. In the rugged *Rio Grande* Maureen seemed just as much a proper part of the surroundings as Victor McLaglen's hard Irish sergeant or the cavalry sidekicks, Ben Johnson and Harry Carey, Jr.

Self-sufficient Maureen fully intended to join the growing list of Hollywood screen stars participating in independent motion picture production. She was scheduled to film *Paniole* in Hawaii during 1951, but the backers withdrew when there was a threatened injunction over script rights. In mid-1951 she, Will Price, John Payne, and financier L. B. Merman formed Price-Merman Productions, which optimistically announced it would produce seven color features in the next three years, with the on-location *Jamaica* to be the kickoff vehicle. Nothing came of this highly touted corporation. Instead Maureen made the Near East-western *Flame of Araby* (Universal, 1951) as the palpitating princess passionately enamored of hard-riding Jeff Chandler.

Howard Hughes's RKO finally released a retrimmed *Sons of the Musketeers* in April, 1952, under the new title *At Sword's Point*. In this restructured color sequel to *The Three Musketeers,* Maureen, as the titian-haired daughter of Athos, joins the offspring of the other musketeers and the kin (Cornel Wilde) of D'Artagnan in aiding the beleaguered Queen of France (Gladys Cooper) in protecting the throne of King Louis of France (Peter Miles) from nefarious duke Robert Douglas. Sandwiched between the array of thundering hoofs, bobbing plumes, and clashing rapiers, dynamic Maureen and Wilde found ample opportunity for romance. Critical attention focused more on Maureen's proficiency with a sword than on her ability to manage the soggy dialog.

To wind up her Twentieth Century-Fox commitments, Maureen journeyed to Australia to decorate *Kangaroo* (1952), cast as the daughter of cattleman Finlay Currie. In the film she and her dad are almost swindled by adventurers Peter Lawford and Richard Boone before the duo are reformed and assist the landowners with a frantic cattle drive. Maureen seemed very much

---

Fort Apache (1948), *She Wore a Yellow Ribbon* (1949).

out of keeping with the background and action of this programmer, looking and acting more like contemporary Hollywood than the requisite early Twentieth-century Sydney, Australia.

When *The Quiet Man* was released (Capitol Theatre, August 21, 1952), it exceeded everyone's anticipations, garnering two Academy Awards,* several other Oscar nominations, and healthy box-office receipts. At 129 minutes it was a leisurely paced comedy detailing the return of ex-pugilist Wayne to Innisfree, Ireland, where he intends to purchase the cottage in which he was born and thereafter lead a quiet life (since he had not yet gotten over having accidentally killed a man in the ring). But no sooner does Wayne arrive than he spots fiery colleen Maureen with her red hair streaming in the breeze. He woos and weds her easily enough, but he has not reckoned on the ire of her flinty, rich brother, farmer Victor McLaglen, who holds a grudge against Wayne for having bought the very property that separates his spread from that of wealthy widow Mildred Natwick. McLaglen refuses to supply the traditional dowry, and Maureen taunts Wayne for his apparent cowardice in not fighting for what is rightfully theirs. The battle that follows—reputed to be the longest slugfest recorded onscreen for a feature film—has Wayne and McLaglen engaging in the classic donnybrook the townsfolk have long been anticipating with glee. The two men battle through the glens and up and down the hills, and into the village itself, with a breather at the local tavern before they continue, only to eventually collapse exhausted and undefeated. Each now has a healthy respect for the other. Wayne and Maureen are now free to start their married life together.

There are those who object to the "stage Irishisms" rampant in *The Quiet Man,* particularly in the sly performances of matchmaker-bookie-cart driver Barry Fitzgerald and angler-priest Ward Bond. Irish blarney is indeed there in heavy doses, but really as expected a part of the Irish landscape as the country's lush green hedges, meadows, and riverbanks. Maureen was totally in her element in her role as the hot-blooded colleen, whether as the troubled lass trying to explain her problem to salmon-catching Bond, or as the proud beauty whom Wayne dumps at McLaglen's feet ("No dowry, no marriage!").†

What with three of John Wayne's children and Maureen's brother Charles in the cast of *The Quiet Man,* the six weeks of on-location filming in the small town of Cong, County Mayo, Ireland, seemed like a family affair. The film remains one of Maureen's most satisfactory screen experiences.‡

Against All Flags (Universal, 1952), set in 1700 Madagascar, found spunky Spitfire Stevens (Maureen) allied with pirate leader Anthony Quinn, until

---

*Best director, best cinematography.

†In *Donnybrook!,* the short-lived 1961 Broadway musical version of *The Quiet Man,* Joan Fagan inherited Maureen's role.

‡On the *John Ford Salute,* televised on April 2, 1973, Maureen sang selections from the score of *The Quiet Man.*

British naval officer Errol Flynn sweeps her off her feet. For a while it appears that Flynn is more intrigued with kidnapped Indian princess Alice Kelly, whom he duly rescues. But by the fade-out, he and Maureen are passengers on that well-traveled ship to happiness. The combination of an aging Flynn and lackluster direction made this one of Maureen's less pleasing actioners.*

For her next outing, *The Redhead from Wyoming* (1953), Maureen begins on the wrong side of the law. Devious William Bishop, who has gubernatorial aspirations, sets up ex-girlfriend Maureen as a saloon proprietor in Sweetwater, Wyoming, and orders her to purchase maverick cattle rounded up on the open range by settlers. But being an essentially bright lass, Maureen soon catches on to Bishop's overall scheme and organizes a legitimate cattleman's association for the settlers. This good deed pleases staunch sheriff Alex Nicol. Maureen demonstrates all varieties of cowgirl skills in this entry and even did Annie Oakley one better by nonchalantly fighting a range war outfitted in a strapless evening gown!

War Arrow (Universal, 1953), her next film, begins with major Jeff Chandler arriving at Fort Clark, Texas, and finding that commandant John McIntire openly opposes the government-endorsed plan to utilize displaced Seminole Indians to halt the bloody Kiowa raids on soldiers and settlers. In fact, the only person at the fort who is friendly to Chandler is Maureen, the comely widow of captain James Bannon. All the action leads to a tidy finale: Chandler discovers Bannon is very much alive (at least until the end of the picture) and is really the renegade white leader of the Kiowas. In the few allotted action-packed moments in this sluggish entry, the marauding Kiowas are totally subdued. For a rare change Maureen had some stiff competition in the pulchritude department, which was supplied by Suzan Ball as the sultry daughter of the Seminole chief.

While Maureen was busily grinding out these costume pictures and accumulating a tidy bank account, her marriage had deteriorated to the point of an acrimonious divorce. As she testified in court, Will Price moved out of their Bel Air abode on December 29, 1951 (the day of their tenth wedding anniversary!), to "take a Beverly Hills home" without "even an explanation." Maureen filed for divorce in August, 1952, and a year later (August 11, 1953) it was granted. The terms of the divorce provided that she receive $1 in token alimony and $50-a-month child support for Bronwyn (of whom she had custody). Maureen received title to their Bel Air home, various oil leases, and $60,000 in government and municipal-utility bonds. A disgruntled Price let it be known that he did not intend to allow the custody matter to rest.

Meanwhile, two months later on October 6, 1953 (a date that would become very important in a later scandal suit involving Maureen), she left the United States for location-filming on *Fire over Africa* (Columbia, 1954). It

---

*When Universal remade the picture as *King's Pirate* (1967) with Doug McClure, Jill St. John was hired to play Maureen's role.

was the first of her commitments under a five-year Columbia pictures pact, which was later modified to spread the payments over a ten-year period. *Fire over Africa* blithely miscast Maureen as a former OSS girl assigned by her government superiors to track down the unknown leader of a smuggling ring operating out of Tangier's nightlife belt. ("We want a Mata Hari," Maureen's bureau chief informs her.) She does her best. Armed with a pearl-handled revolver strapped to her thigh and a refresher course in judo, she poses as an adventuress and persuades bistro queen Binnie Barnes to let her operate in her busy club. Eventually Maureen and fellow government agent Macdonald Carey (who miraculously survives a deadly barrage of bullets) round up the obvious culprits. While Maureen's onscreen beauty was almost as impressive as the North African scenery, only Binnie Barnes, the real-life wife of the film's producer, M. K. Frankovich, managed to make her stock character jump to life.

Just as it seemed that both the public and Maureen had forgotten that she could act as well as decorate a motion picture, John Ford came to her rescue, casting Maureen in her first grade-A picture in three years. Columbia's *The Long Gray Line* (Capitol Theatre, February 10, 1955) was a rich and rousing tribute in CinemaScope and color to West Point sports instructor Marty Maher (Tyrone Power) and the generations of cadets he had taught and befriended. Ford guided his cast through Maher's fifty years at the Academy, from the time the brash Irish youth steps off the boat in 1898 America in search of a job, until, as an old man, he meets with former student Dwight D. Eisenhower (Harry Carey, Jr.) to plead against being retired. The shamrock-rich tale is employed by Ford to illustrate his point that men like Maher often achieve worthwhile, meaningful lives by pure accident and without ever fully realizing it.

It was a fitting testimonial to Maureen's enduring, fresh beauty that fourteen years after *How Green Was My Valley* she could essay a similar role and still arouse seasoned critics to label her as "[the] perfect colleen to flutter a young bucko's heart" *(New York Herald-Tribune)*. Maureen was seen as the West Point housemaid who catches young Power's eye and heart, and who, as his wife, watches him mature from a fumbling waiter to a bumbling Army enlistee, to an apprentice sports coach under the tutelage of gruff Ward Bond, and then finally to the post of Academy athletic coach. Throughout the chronicle Maureen has her share of touching scenes, as when their baby son dies and she comforts the equally heartbroken Maher ("It's a cruel thing . . . but we have so many boys here"). Along with Donald Crisp, who played Power's dad, brought over from the old country, Maureen, Power, and Bond gave *The Long Gray Line* a solid Irish flavor, which may not have always been true to the ethnic balance of real West Point history, but certainly was consistent with Maine-born Ford's intent. If Maureen fell from her general level of excellence at all in this film, it was in her sequences as an elderly woman shuffling along next to her beloved husband, until, full of years, she peacefully dies.

The Long Gray Line had been one giant step forward in Maureen's film career, but her next entries were definite steps backward. "I did *The Magnificent Matador* [1955]," Maureen says, "because I felt Anthony Quinn and I would be thoroughly convincing lovers on the screen." She was mistaken. Neither their oncamera spooning nor the tedious plotting of this made-in-Mexico Twentieth Century-Fox feature was acceptable. Moreover, the CinemaScope color picture was not in the same league as even the moderately worthwhile *The Brave Bulls* or *The Bullfighter and the Lady,* both 1951 releases. Maureen was obviously ill at ease in *The Magnificent Matador* as she played the rich American cafe-society lady with a yen for bullfighter Quinn. Despite the travelog element (Mexico City, bull-breeding ranches, the arena, etc.), neither the potential excitement of the love story nor the sport itself ever remotely came alive.

Two years after Maureen's divorce from Will Price became final, she was back in court (August, 1955) in a custody hearing regarding Bronwyn. Price claimed in his petition that Maureen had admitted to having allowed Mexican attorney-businessman Enrique Parrahad to move into her home in late 1952. Maureen countered with the argument that Price was $1,700 in arrears on his child-support obligations and that he showed no visible means of paying future installments due. The court promptly decided the case in Maureen's favor.

By the mid-1950s Universal had acquired the performing services of two other former Twentieth Century-Fox stars, Anne Baxter and Jeanne Crain, and decided to shunt Maureen aside into even lesser products than before. At least there was some titillating publicity attached to her portrayal of history's most famous bareback rider, *Lady Godiva* (Universal, 1955). If the repressed public expected a peeping-tom's field day, they were sorely disappointed. The film turned out to be a dully embroidered account of Norman intrigue in eleventh-century England as the foreigners attempt to divide and conquer the Saxon earls, including Maureen's spouse, nobleman George Nader. In the climactic ride through the cardboard town on Universal's backlot, Maureen sat astride a hefty steed, draped with yards and yards of red tresses, which carefully concealed any and all crucial parts of the star's anatomy. And just to be on the safe side, Maureen donned flesh-colored tights for her well-documented saunter.

Maureen did not fare well with her two 1956 releases. Republic's *Lisbon,* produced and directed by co-star Ray Milland, was at best a tepid adventure tale. Its few plus factors were the widescreen (Naturama) and color photography of Portugal and a memorable scene in which the cad, played by Claude Rains, smashes a songbird with his tennis racket as a breakfast treat for his pet cat. As in *The Fallen Sparrow,* Maureen was unconvincing in her villainous role; in this case as the conniving coquette who wants her elderly and rich husband (Percy Marmont) dead so she can collect his fortune. Not only is she unsuccessful in her ploy, but she loses adventurer Milland to Rains's ex-secretary, Yvonne Furneaux.

The double-bill entry *Everything But the Truth* (Universal, 1956) might have been more successful as a television half-hour situation-comedy episode. The film did not attract Maureen's action movie fans and the cloying cuteness of young Tim Hovey was hardly a box-office lure. Maureen was just too attractive and pat as the fourth-grade Fratersville schoolteacher who stands by orphan Hovey when he innocently reveals details of real-estate graft in their small hometown.

Hollywood kingpin and huge moneymaker John Wayne had found Maureen a most agreeable leading lady in *Rio Grande* and *The Quiet Man** and was in full agreement with director John Ford that she should again play his screen spouse in MGM's *The Wings of Eagles* (Radio City Music Hall, 1957), the life story of the late Frank W. "Spig" Wead, Navy aviator hero and later a Hollywood scriptwriter.† *The Wings of Eagles* again boosted Maureen back into a big-league picture, even if she suffered third billing, following Wayne and Dan Dailey, the latter as Wayne's happy-go-lucky sailor pal. Many find the slapstick incidents in the film distractingly unrealistic and undignified for all concerned,‡ but Ford insists that each and every event depicted in the Mack Sennett-like scenes did happen, and that he should know, for he was there.

Maureen was saddled with a very subordinate part in *The Wings of Eagles.* As Wayne's neglected, temperamental wife (she is forever throwing things about the house or morosely drinking herself silly) she finds her dedicated husband constantly spending most of his time and energy on improving the status of Navy aviation. On the night Wayne is appointed skipper of a fighter squadron he breaks his neck in a tumble down the stairs at home. Having packed Maureen off to lead her own life with their children, Wayne is nursed back to health by Dailey and he begins a new civilian career as a respected screenwriter of service films. Just when Wayne and Maureen, she now a successful businesswoman, plan a reconciliation, news is broadcast of the Japanese attack on Pearl Harbor. Maureen is last seen in *The Wings of Eagles* having another bout of Irish temper as she heaves her half-packed suitcase across the room, frustrated that she again has lost Wayne to the Navy. He has induced the brass to send him to the Pacific theatre of war to supervise his revolutionary jeep-aircraft-carrier tactical system.

Not long after *The Wings of Eagles* went into release, Maureen became the subject of a snowballing scandal. It all began when *Confidential,* the spicy gossip magazine, published as the main feature of its March, 1957, issue a news story entitled "It Was The Hottest Show in Town When Maureen O'Hara Cuddled in Row 35." The pointed narrative luridly described the evening of November 9, 1953, when Maureen and an unidentified Latin

---

*Maureen agreed: "When John Wayne and I are teamed something chemically happens which makes both of us more convincing to moviegoers."

†He scripted *Air Mail, Dirigible, They Were Expendable,* etc.

‡E.g., Wayne's plane landing in the swimming pool smack in the middle of the admiral's outdoor tea party; the clubroom fight and cake throwing; the assorted cast members falling into the pool.

American male escort were seated in the balcony of Grauman's Theatre in Hollywood, allegedly conducting their own private love festival despite repeated requests from management to refrain from such undecorous activity. Other stars had been given the same rough going-over by the widely read *Confidential,* but not till Maureen joined in a suit with a few other victims had any celebrity made a firm stand to defend him/herself against the scurrilous accusations.* Maureen demanded $1 million in damages (the amount was later increased to $5 million). In May, 1957, flanked by her two burly brothers, who were then sharing her Bel Air home, Maureen appeared in the Los Angeles court for the jury hearing. Entertainers Liberace and Dorothy Dandridge, who had each been the subject of *Confidential* tell-all stories, agreed to be witnesses in Maureen's suit should it prove necessary. During the course of the protracted hearings, diligently covered by the press for a vastly intrigued public, it was proven via Maureen's stamped passport that she had left the United States for location filming on *Fire over Africa* more than a month before the alleged incident and had not returned to America until January, 1954. Thereafter, Grauman's former assistant manager testified that perhaps he had erred as to the date and that maybe Maureen had been engaged in just a "little affectionate embrace." The jury was taken on a conducted tour of Grauman's theatrical emporium and Los Angeles Superior Court Judge Herbert J. Walker himself visited the then-paralyzed usherette who claimed to have been a witness to the incident. Although stars like Lana Turner, Tab Hunter, Rory Calhoun, and Clark Gable had been subpoenaed by the defense (on the theory that *Confidential* stories on each of them were true and therefore there was a presumption of truthfulness regarding the exposé on Maureen), Judge Walker ruled they could not be forced to testify. Hollywood collectively sighed with relief then and once again in October, 1957, when Maureen's suit was dismissed "with prejudice to *Confidential."* The hung jury just could not decide whom to believe.

Maureen suddenly found herself *Persona non grata* in Hollywood. When the few Hollywood producers who might have considered using her in an adventure film learned she had undergone a slipped-disc operation in May, 1957, and had to wear a neck-to-left-ankle brace for four months thereafter, they refused to take the uninsurable risk of utilizing her in an athletic film assignment.

Maureen herself talked of producing and starring in *Born in Paradise* and *The Morgan Story,* and vaguely considered the possibility of following other out-of-favor American stars to Italy and appearing in features there, such as *The Great Sinner,* in which it was proposed she play Mary Magdalene. But none of these projects came to fruition.

With her sudden, extended liberty, Maureen found more than sufficient time to persuade her parents to come to live in California, and when they agreed she purchased a Brentwood home for them. And after years of al-

*Lizabeth Scott had initiated a huge lawsuit but it was later dropped.

ways planning to do so but never putting her wishes into action, Maureen began taking voice lessons in earnest, hoping that when the rhubarb calmed down she could utilize her potential musical-comedy talent in one medium or another.

By May, 1959, Maureen found herself professionally in demand again. Columbia exercised its option on her services to co-star her with Alec Guinness and Burl Ives in *Our Man in Havana* (1960), a satirical spoof of spy thrillers. Maureen's role as the secretary sent by the British Home Office to aid vacuum cleaner salesman Guinness in his bewildered spying attempt, was decorative at most. But the film served to remind the movie industry and the public that Maureen was still very attractive, albeit now as a more mature leading lady.

Our Man in Havana was just being released when Maureen went into rehearsal for her Broadway debut in the musical comedy *Christine* (46th Street Theatre, April 29, 1960). Back in 1954 she had been considered for the stage musical *Fanny* and had even auditioned for director Joshua Logan and producer David Merrick. In fact, she almost did not get to do *Christine*. Only when negotiations with Margaret Leighton fell through was Maureen handed the lead part. Despite a book by Pearl Buck (based on Hilda Wernhun's novel *My Indian Family*) and songs by Oscar-winners Sammy Fain and Paul Francis Webster, *Christine* proved to be an elaborately mounted ($350,000) but stagnant production about an Irish lady who falls in love with the Hindu doctor-husband of her deceased daughter. Those who had the opportunity to view the show on the road, or during its twelve-performance Broadway run, discovered that Maureen was extremely beautiful in person, possessed an "attractive if small voice" (*Cue* magazine), but was rather wooden in the dramatic interludes.

At about the time Maureen recorded the original cast album to *Christine,** she made a long-playing album for RCA records entitled *Love Letters*. Intent to demonstrate to all that she could put across a song in acceptable fashion, she began accepting guest bookings on various video variety shows ("Dinah Shore," "Perry Como," "Telephone Hour," "Jimmy Dean," "Andy Williams"). On each outing she was charming but, frankly speaking, unexceptional.

Maureen was far more successful with her acting ventures on television. In August, 1958 it was announced she would hostess and star in "Woman in the Case," a half-hour video series for the 1959-60 season to be co-produced by CBS-TV and Tarafilm Productions (owned by Maureen and her brother Charles). That project did not come to be, but beginning with the CBS-TV ninety-minute-special *Mrs. Miniver* (CBS, January, 1960),† Maureen became a popular leading lady of color television specials. Although CBS dropped

*Now a high-priced collector's item.
†Maureen's performance demonstrated that she and Greer Garson, star of the original film version, had more acting traits in common than had been readily apparent.

plans to star her in another Greer Garson movie vehicle, *Valley of Decision,* she did headline a two-segment "Family Classic" rendition of *The Scarlet Pimpernel* (CBS, October, 1960), and continued on in the decade in such productions as *Spellbound* on "Theatre 62" (NBC, February, 1962), with Hugh O'Brian: *A Cry of Angels* on "Hallmark Hall of Fame" (NBC, December, 1963); *High Button Shoes* (CBS, November, 1966) with Carol Lawrence and Garry Moore; and *Who's Afraid of Mother Goose?* (ABC, October, 1967), with Fred Clark.

Walt Disney's *The Parent Trap* (1961), starring teenage box-office magnet Hayley Mills as twin sisters, gave Maureen's sagging movie career a much-needed resuscitation. "Quite unexpectedly," Maureen recalls, "Walt Disney sent for me to play the mother. That started my career out all over again. The picture was tremendously successful [it grossed over $11.3 million] which convinced me my Irish luck was still holding out."

Maureen found working with *Parent Trap* co-star Brian Keith* so congenial that she hired him for *The Deadly Companions* (1961), produced by her brother Charles. It was the initial feature film assignment for the then unknown director Sam Peckinpah, and although *Variety* ranked Maureen's performance as a widowed dancehall woman as "one of her best in some time," few people saw the poorly distributed western, which was set in a ghost town right in the middle of Apache territory.

After a seven-year hiatus Maureen returned to Twentieth Century-Fox for a domestic comedy, more slapstick than her prior *Father Was a Fullback.* In *Mr. Hobbs Takes a Vacation* (1962) Maureen proved to be the most attractive grandmother *onscreen* as she persuades her well-meaning husband (James Stewart) that their entire brood, grandchildren and all, should be reunited for a summer holiday at a freakish old house they have rented on the Pacific coast. The vicissitudes they endure at the hands of their Charles Addams-esque abode are nothing compared to the generation-gap problems created by their assorted offspring. By the conclusion of this slick, if illogical, picture, the spirit had dissipated. Nevertheless, where else in one sitting could one view the drawling charm of Stewart, a still youthful Maureen dancing the twist, the diverse comedy styles of Marie Wilson, Reginald Gardiner, John McGiver, and Minerva Urecal, and the beachside presence of John Saxon and Fabian?

"There is no one in Hollywood quite like me," Maureen told a UPI reporter in October, 1962, shortly after MGM had issued her LP album *Maureen O'Hara Sings Her Favorite Irish Songs.* "The actresses are either youngsters coming up the ladder, or established dramatic stars. I can sing, dance a little, play comedy and dramatic scenes as well.

"No one is in competition for my type of roles. Someone said I fit into the old Myrna Loy category and I think that is about right."

---

*Keith was her estranged husband, with whom she reunites due to the mischievous matchmaking of their twin daughters (Hayley Mills).

But it would be hard to imagine Myrna Loy playing Henry Fonda's wife in Delmer Daves's deluxe rural soap-opera, *Spencer's Mountain* (Radio City Music Hall, May 16, 1963). This was no witty domestic comedy like *Cheaper by the Dozen,* but rather a speciously contrived, sentiment-laden family comedy-drama. Set in Grand Teton, Wyoming, the film's premise revolved around the question of whether the country-bred parents (Maureen, Henry Fonda) of nine spiffily cute children should sacrifice their mountain-top dream home in order to send their eldest child (James MacArthur) to college. The answer was an obvious yes, and the parents do so after 121 minutes of lushly mounted "piety and prurience." Despite its Disney-style ambience, some facet or other of the subject of sex was always rearing its nasty head in *Spencer's Mountain.* It might be Fonda's persistent patting of Maureen's derriere ("Now, Clay; the kids'll see") or MacArthur's torn emotions as to whether to chase after finishing-school belle Mimsy Farmer or court local-grown Kathy Bennett. Despite a resounding critical roasting, *Spencer's Mountain* racked up a lusty $4.75 million revenue in domestic gross rentals.

Much more satisfying filmfare was Maureen's fourth screen teaming with John Wayne in *McLintock!* (United Artists, 1963). It was a deliberate and good-natured gibe at Wayne's own western-format films. Maureen was again a high-toned, proud lass ("Who put that burr under your saddle?" Wayne asks) who had left her husband (Wayne) years ago and gone back East, but she has now returned to his huge cattle ranch to make sure their boarding-school-bred daughter (Stefanie Powers) is not overly influenced by Wayne's drunken, brawling ways. The highlight of the rowdy picture is the fracas between the cattlemen and the homesteaders, all of whom wind up in a mudbath. Wayne and Maureen are vehemently opposed participants in that donnybrook, which ends with Wayne chasing his shrewish spouse back to town. Stripped to her shift, she is dunked in a trough, turned bottom side up, and spanked by Wayne for the whole town to see. Thereafter, a much subdued Maureen takes a running jump to catch a buggy-ride home with her victorious husband. After all, he is a good soul at heart, for he states about his Mesa Verde spread, "I'm gonna leave most of it to the nation for a park."*

It was two years before Maureen made another feature for the still diminishing theatrical-film market. Delmer Daves utilized her services again, this time as the lead figure in *The Battle of the Villa Fiorita* (Warner Bros., 1965), which owed very little to Rumer Godden's novel and was neither the World War II actioner nor the western picture the film's title would seem to indicate. The sluggish soap opera opens with stiff-lipped Englishman Richard

---

*It was sad to note how frazzled Yvonne DeCarlo looked in *McLintock!* Although she was a contemporary of Maureen, she had grown plump and lined, and as the cook-housekeeper for the Wayne household was as unconvincing in her performance as she had been in her Universal heyday some two decades before.

Todd returning home to Maureen and their two children after a two-month business trip. "Something binding, inescapable, unforgettable has happened to me," Maureen bravely confesses to her husband. The tumultuous event turns out to be rather mundane. She has fallen madly in love with Italian composer Rossano Brazzi and intends to follow him to his home on Lake Garda in northern Italy. This she does, but her two determined young children follow after her and, in league with Brazzi's equally precocious daughter, make their elders so guilt-stricken that there is no option but to give up the passionate romance. Most agreed that Maureen "remains one of the most beautiful women on the screen" *(New York Morning Telegram),* but she was no competition for the sumptuous natural scenery, nor could she rise above the creeking mechanisms of this vulgarized tearjerker.

Andrew V. McLaglen, who had helmed *McLintock!,* directed Universal's *The Rare Breed* (1966), which reunited Maureen with both James Stewart and Brian Keith. It was a strange B+ western dealing with English widow Maureen and her daughter (Juliet Mills), who venture to America in 1884, determined to sell their prize white-faced Hereford bull, Vindicator, for breeding new cattle stock. Halfway through the picture Stewart, who had earlier tried to swindle Maureen, repents for his past actions and tries to befriend her. Meanwhile she is being wooed first by slick beef-buyer David Brian and then by Scotsman-widower Keith, the latter most unsparing in his hammy antics. The picture was not well distributed and was all too quickly forgotten.

Since the early 1950s, Maureen had been dating Enrique Parrahad, now one of Mexico's richest men. He had been separated from his wife for the past decade and owned a ranch spread in Stone Canyon, California, as well as a home in Mexico City. As Maureen informed the press: "I told Rich's family I am quite prepared to sign a paper that, in the event of our marriage, he can leave me completely out of his will. . . . All I can say about him is that he is the best man I have ever met." For very personal reasons, the couple never did wed, but on March 11, 1968, in Charlotte Amalie, Virgin Islands, Maureen married Charles F. Blair, whom she had met several years before in Ireland.* He sold his Connecticut real estate and she her California home, and they moved to a two-towered round house on St. Croix in the Virgin Islands. Besides this residence they also maintained a sixty-five-foot yacht and a Manhattan apartment on Sutton Place South. Later they purchased a twenty-eight-acre site in Glengarriff, County Cork, Ireland, and built a four-bedroom home there.

---

*Born in Buffalo in 1920, Blair had been a Pan American World Airlines pilot for twenty-nine years. He was the first man to fly solo over the North Pole in a single-engine plane, for which he won the Harmon Trophy in 1952, and in late 1967 he set a New York to London speed record in a Mustang fighter plane. He was also the author of *Red Ball in the Sky.* More recently, as a retired Air Force brigadier general, he had established the Antilles Air Boats Company, which flies scheduled flights in and out of the Caribbean. Blair has two children, Suzanne (born 1935) and Christopher (born 1950), by his first wife, Janice, whom he divorced shortly before wedding Maureen.

Maureen, now a grandmother,* was perfectly content to ignore her career—the offers coming in were not very attractive to begin with—until Jackie Gleason paged her to co-star with him in Cinerama's *How Do I Love Thee* (1970). Maureen was attracted to the role of playing the extremely devout wife of beefy Gleason, whom she has taken to Lourdes, hoping for a miracle since the specialists cannot diagnose his seemingly fatal ailment. Actually he is suffering only from a guilt complex, mistakenly believing God heard and granted his hasty wish that the head of Drinkwater College's philosophy department would die so his instructor son (Rick Lenz) would inherit the post. The amateurish color comedy was advertised with the line, "They *do* make movies like this anymore." Perhaps that is why former moviegoers with good memories stayed away in droves from this flop.

After the misfire of *How Do I Love Thee,* Maureen was quite ready for another cinema outing with John Wayne in George Sherman's *Big Jake* (National General, 1971). Originally the producers had insisted Maureen should wear a white wig in the picture, but she says, "I refused, Absolutely refused!" In the picture, when Richard Boone and his scurvy gang kidnap her grandson from her ranch, Maureen summons her two sons (Patrick Wayne, Chris Mitchum) to organize a rescue party to pay Boone the demanded $1 million ransom and retrieve Little Jake (Ethan Wayne). But thinking the situation over, Maureen concludes "It will require an extremely harsh and unpleasant kind of man to deal with it." Naturally this description fits her long-departed roustabout husband, Wayne,† who handles the task with dispatch and success. Maureen did not have a very substantial role in *Big Jake,* but she provided a splendid introduction to the action story at hand and as always worked extremely well in her scenes of love-hate-admiration-disgust with Wayne. *Big Jake* went on to gross $7.5 million, which by Hollywood rules made the fifty-one-year-old Maureen a viable film commodity once again.

Maureen's next professional appearance was on the 1971-filmed nostalgia salute. *The Fabulous Fordies,* finally televised on February 29, 1972 by NBC-TV. Ineptly hosted by Ernie Ford, and largely concerned with the sentimental reunion of Betty Grable and Dick Haymes, Maureen provided a refreshing touch to the hour telecast by looking great and warbling more than adequately "It's a Grand Night for Singing" and "I Don't Care."

In August, 1972, Maureen returned to the cameras again, this time for a *Bell Telephone Family Special* (NBC-TV, March 18, 1973), a color rendition of John Steinbeck's *The Red Pony.* Maureen inherited the role played by Myrna Loy in the 1949 feature film version: the rancher wife whose husband

---

*Bronwyn, who legally changed her name to Bronwyn FitzSimons in 1963, a year after her father, Will Price, died, made her acting debut in a video episode of "Surfside 6" (1962) and in *Spencer's Mountain* had a four-line role. Subsequently she wed Foster Vincent Yoakum and gave birth to a son, Foster Vincent Yoakum III.

†A standing joke throughout *Big Jake* has everyone, upon meeting Wayne, exclaiming: "But I thought you were dead."

(Henry Fonda) is just as much at a loss as she in coping with the fanatic devotion of their son (Clint Howard) to a newly acquired pony. The two-hour Universal telefeature—which producers Frederick Brogger and James Franciscus are marketing in the rest of the world as a theatrical film—contained a few surprises, particularly with the "unexpected amount of harsh and vivid violence included in its footage" (*Variety*). Most of the camera time was devoted to Fonda's overbearing attempt to make his son self-reliant before his time, leading to myriads of conflicts between the two before the ultimate happy resolution. Maureen, looking radiant as always (there were references to her hair being the same color as that of the pony), had little opportunity to emote, being relegated to the sidelines as the patient wife and mother, hoping that her menfolk would eventually resolve their relationship problems on their own.

Not too long ago, Maureen analyzed herself: "I talk too much, and I lose my temper and socially I'm always late. But never professionally or in business. . . . When I have a project I attack it like a tiger." Seemingly she does not miss her once strenuous Hollywood production schedule, preferring now her rather plush private life. However, she does have a hankering to someday direct a western film: "I have a facility for telling other people what to do, even if I can't do it myself.

"I couldn't care less about the passage of time. If you're just a glamour girl it could be very hard on you. But I'm an actress who enjoys her work, so there's no problem. I can't wait to grow old. I'm going to be the nastiest old lady you ever saw.

"My one real tragedy," Maureen admits, "is not the parts I missed, but the children I didn't have."

Feature Film Appearances
MAUREEN O'HARA

KICKING THE MOON AROUND*   (General Film, 1938) 78 M.

Director, Walter Forde; story, Tom Geraghty; screenplay, Michael Hogan, Angus MacPhail, Roland Pertwee, H. Fowler-Mears; songs, Michael Carr and Jimmy Kennedy; camera, Francis Carver.

Ambrose and His Orchestra (Themselves); Evelyn Ball (Pepper Martin); Harry Richman (Himself); Florence Desmond (Flo Hadley); Hal Thompson (Bobbie Hawkee); Denier Warren (Mark Browd); Julian Vedey (Herbert Stoker); Max Bacon (Gus); Les Carew (Streamline); Dave Burnaby (Magistrate); George Carney (P. C. Truscott); Maureen O'Hara (Secretary).

*U.S. title: THE PLAYBOY (1942); reissue title: MILLIONAIRE MERRY-GO-ROUND.

JAMAICA INN   (Par., 1939) 99 M.

Producer, Erich Pommer, Charles Laughton; director, Alfred Hitchcock; based on the novel by Daphne du Maurier; adaptation, Alma Reville; screenplay, Sidney Gilliat, Joan Harrison; dialog, Gilliat, J. B. Priestley; special effects, Harry Watts; sets, Tom N. Moraham; costumes, Molly McArthur; music, Eric Fenby; music director, Frederic Lewis; sound, Jack Rogerson; camera, Harry Stradling, Bernard Knowles; editor, Robert Hamer.

Charles Laughton (Sir Humphrey Pengalian); Horace Hodges (Butler); Hay Petrie (Groom); Frederick Piper (Agent); Leslie Banks (Joss Merlyn); Marie Ney (Patience); Maureen O'Hara (Mary); Emlyn Williams (Harry the Peddler); Wylie Watson (Salvation Watkins); Robert Newton (Jem Trehearne); Stephen Haggard (Boy); William Devlin (Tenant); Basil Radford, Jeanne de Casalis (Friends); and: George Curzon, Morland Graham, Edwin Greenwood, Mervyn Johns, Herbert Lomas, Clare Greet, A. Bromley Davenport.

THE HUNCHBACK OF NOTRE DAME   (RKO, 1939) 117 M.

Producer, Pandro Berman; director, William Dieterle; based on the novel by Victor Hugo; adaptation, Bruno Frank; screenplay, Sonya Levien; assistant director, Argyle Nelson, Edward Killy; costumes, Walter Plunkett; choreography, Ernst Matray; technical advisor, Louis Van der Ecker; makeup, Perc Westmore; dialog director, Will Price; special effects, Vernon L. Walker; music, Alfred Newman; camera, Joseph August; editor, William Hamilton, Robert Wise.

Charles Laughton (Quasimodo, the Hunchback); Sir Cedric Hardwicke (Frollo); Thomas Mitchell (Clopin); Maureen O'Hara (Esmeralda); Edmond O'Brien (Gringoire); Alan Marshal (Phoebus); Walter Hampden (Claude); Harry Davenport (Louis XI); Katharine Alexander (Madame De Lys); George Zucco (Procurator); Fritz Leiber (Nobleman); Etienne Giradot (King's Physician); Helene Whitney (Fleur); Minna Gombell (Queen of Beggars); Arthur Hohl (Olivier); Rod La Rocque (Phillippe); Spencer Charters (Court Clerk).

MY IRISH MOLLY   (Alliance, 1940) 66 M.

Producer, John Argyle; director, Alex Bryce; story, J. F. Argyle; screenplay, Ian Walker, Alex Bryce; camera, Ernest Palmer; editor, F. H. Beckerton.

Maureen O'Hara (Eileen O'Shea); Binkie Stuart (Molly Martin); Tom Burke (Danny Gallagher); Phillip Reed (Bob); Maire O'Neil (Mrs. O'Shea); C. Denier Warren (Chuck); Maureen Moore (Hannah Delaney); Franklyn Kelsey (Liam Delaney); Leo McCabe (Corney); Paddy (Herself).

BILL OF DIVORCEMENT   (RKO, 1940) 70 M.

Producer, Lee Marcus; director, John Farrow; based on the play by Clemence Dane; screenplay, Dalton Trumbo; assistant director, Argyle Nelson; camera, Nicholas Musuraca; editor, Harry Marker.

Maureen O'Hara (Sydney Fairfield); Adolphe Menjou (Hilary Fairfield); Fay Bainter (Margaret Fairfield); Herbert Marshall (Gray Meredith); Dame May Whitty (Hester Fairfield); Patric Knowles (John Storm); C. Aubrey Smith (Dr. Alliot); Ernest Cossart (Rev. Dr. Pumphrey); Kathryn Collier (Basset); Lauri Beatty (Susan).

DANCE, GIRL, DANCE   (RKO, 1940) 88 M.

Producer, Erich Pommer; director, Dorothy Arzner; story, Vicki Baum; screenplay, Tess Slesinger, Frank Davis; songs, Edward Ward, Chester Forrest, and Robert Wright; choreography, Ernst Matray; camera, Russell Metty; editor, Robert Wise.

Maureen O'Hara (Judy); Louis Hayward (Jimmy Harris); Lucille Ball (Bubbles); Virginia Field (Elinor Harris); Ralph Bellamy (Steve Adams); Maria Ouspenskaya (Madame Basilova); Mary Carlisle (Sally); Katharine Alexander (Miss Olmstead); Edward Brophy (Dwarfie); Walter Abel (Judge); Harold Huber (Hoboken Gent); Ernest Truex, Chester Clute (Baileys); Lorraine Krueger (Dolly); Lola Jensen (Daisy); Emma Dunn (Mrs. Simpson); Sidney Blackmer (Puss in Boots); Vivian Fay (Ballerina); Ludwig Stossel (Caesar); Edno Verebes (Fitch); Ruth Seeley (Dimples); Thelma Woodruff (Mary); Marjorie Woodworth (Jane); Lasses White (Stage Manager); Philip Morris, Wade Boteler, Lee Shumway (Cops); Robert Emmett O'Connor, Lee Phelps (Plainclothesmen); Paul Rensy (Headwaiter); Tony Martelli, Gino Corrado (Waiters); Milton Kibbee, Lew Harvey, Paul Burns, Paul Phillips (Reporters); Clyde Cook (Claude); Leo Cleary (Clerk); Kernan Cripps (Bailiff); Ray Cooke, Don Kerr (Photographer); Bob McKenzie (Fat Man); Harry Tyler (Barker); Jean La Fayette (Nanette); Paul Fung (Chinese Waiter).

THEY MET IN ARGENTINA   (RKO, 1941) 76 M.

Producer, Lou Brock; director, Leslie Goodwins, Jack Hively; story, Roy Hunt, Harold Daniels; screenplay, Jerry Cady; choreography, Frank Veloz; songs, Richard Rodgers and Lorenz Hart; music director, Lud Gluskin; special effects, Vernon L. Walker; camera, J. Roy Hunt; editor, Desmond Marquette.

Maureen O'Hara (Lolita); James Ellison (Tim Kelly); Alberto Vila (Alberto Delmonte); Buddy Ebsen (Duke Ferrel); Robert Barrat (Don Enrique); Joseph Buloff (Santiago); Diosa Costello (Panchita); Victoria Cordova (Nina Maria); Antonio Moreno (Don Carlos); Robert Middlemass (George Hastings); Chester Clute (His Secretary); Carlos Barbe (Nicanor); Francisco Maran (Don Ramon); Fortunio Bonanova (Pedro); Luis Alberni (Don Frutos).

HOW GREEN WAS MY VALLEY   (20th, 1941) 120 M.

Producer, Darryl F. Zanuck; director, John Ford; based on the novel by Richard Llewellyn; screenplay, Philip Dunne; art director, Richard Day, Nathan Juran; set decorator, Thomas Little; costumes, Gwen Wakeling; music, Alfred Newman; camera, Arthur Miller; editor, James B. Clark.

Walter Pidgeon (Mr. Gruffydd); Maureen O'Hara (Angharad Morgan); Donald Crisp (Mr. Morgan); Anna Lee (Bronwyn Morgan); Roddy McDowall (Huw Morgan); John Loder (Ianto Morgan); Sara Allgood (Mrs. Beth Morgan); Barry Fitzgerald (Cyfartha); Patric Knowles (Ivor Morgan); Welsh Singers (Themselves); Morton Lowry (Mr. Jonas); Arthur Shields (Mr. Parry); Anne Todd (Genwen); Frederick Worlock (Dr. Richards); Richard Fraser (Davy Morgan); Evan S. Evans (Gwinlyn); James Monks (Owen Morgan); Rhys Williams (Dai Bando); Lionel Pape (Old Evans); Ethel Griffies (Mrs. Nicholas); Marten Lamont (Iestyn Evans); Mae Marsh (Miner's Wife); Louis Jean Heydt (Miner); Denis Hoey (Motschell); Tudor Williams (Singer); Eve March (Meillyn Lewis); Clifford Severn (Mervyn); Mary Gordon (Woman); Mary Field (Eve); Herbert Evans (Postman); Tudor Williams (Ensemble Singer); Irving Pichel (Narrator).

TO THE SHORES OF TRIPOLI   (20th, 1942) C—82 M.

Producer, Darryl F. Zanuck; associate producer, Milton Sperling; director, Bruce Humberstone; story, Steve Fisher; screenplay, Lamar Trotti; music, Alfred Newman; camera, Edward Cronjager, William Skall, Harry Jackson; editor, Allen McNeil.

John Payne (Chris Winters); Maureen O'Hara (Mary Carter); Randolph Scott (Sergeant Dixie Smith); Nancy Kelly (Helene Hunt); William Tracy (Johnny Dent); Maxie Rosenbloom (Okay Jones); Henry Morgan (Mouthy); Edmund MacDonald (Butch); Russell Hicks (Major Wilson); Minor Watson (Captain Winters); Michael "Ted" North (Bill); Basil Walker (Joe Sutton); Charles Tannen (Swifty); Alan Hale, Jr. (Tom Hall); Margaret Early (Susie); Frank Orth (Barber); Iris Adrian (Blonde); Joseph Crehan (Uncle Bob); John Hamilton (General Gordon); Stanley Andrews (Doctor); Richard Lane (Lieutenant); Gordon Jones, Steve Gaylord Pendleton, Anthony Nace (Corporals); Robert Conway (Ensign); James C. Morton (Bartender); Hillary Brooke, Patricia Farr (Girls); James Flavin (Warden); Knox Manning (Newscaster); Harry Strong (Chief Petty Officer); Pat McVey (Radio Operator); Hugh Beaumont (Orderly).

10 GENTLEMEN FROM WEST POINT   (20th, 1942) 104 M.

Producer, William Perlberg; director, Henry Hathaway; based on a story by Malvin Wald; screenplay, Richard Maibaum; additional dialog, George Seaton; camera, Leon Shamroy; editor, James B. Clark.

George Montgomery (Dawson); Maureen O'Hara (Carolyn Bainbridge); John Sutton (Howard Shelton); Laird Cregar (Major Sam Carter); Shepperd Strudwick (Henry Clay); Victor Francen (Florimond Massey); Harry Davenport (Bane); Ward Bond (Scully); Douglass Dumbrille (Gen. William H. Harrison); Ralph Byrd (Maloney); Joe Brown, Jr. (Benny Havens); David Bacon (Shippen); Esther Dale (Mrs. Thompson); Louis Jean Heydt (Jared Danforth); Stanley Andrews (Captain Sloane); James Flavin (Captain Luddy); Edna Mae Jones (Letty); Charles Trowbridge (Senate President); Tully Marshall (Grandpa); Edwin Maxwell (John Randolph); Uno (Old Put); Edward Fielding (William Eustis); Morris Ankrum (Wood); Selmer Jackson (Sersen); Noble Johnson (Tecumseh); Edward Dunn (O'Toole); Frank Ferguson (Alden Brown).

THE BLACK SWAN   (20th, 1942) C—85 M.

Producer, Robert Bassler; director, Henry King; based on the novel by Rafael Sabatini; screenplay, Ben Hecht, Seton I. Miller; music, Alfred Newman; art director, Richard Day, James Basevi; camera, Leon Shamroy; editor, Barbara McLean.

Tyrone Power (James Waring); Maureen O'Hara (Margaret Denby); Laird Cregar (Henry Morgan); Thomas Mitchell (Blue); George Sanders (Leech); Anthony Quinn

(Wogan); George Zucco (Lord Denby); Edward Ashley (Ingraham); Fortunio Bonanova (Don Miguel); Stuart Robertson (Captain Graham); Charles McNaughton (Fenner); Frederick Worlock (Speaker); Willie Fung (Chinese Cook); Charles Francis (Captain Higgs); Arthur Shields (Bishop); Keith Hitchcock (Major-Domo); John Burton (Captain Blaine); Cyril McLaglen (Captain Jones); Clarence Muse (Daniel); Olaf Hytten (Clerk); David Thursby, Charles Irwin, Frank Leigh (Sea Captains); Arthur Gould-Porter, C. Montague Shaw, Boyd Irwin, George Kirby (Assemblymen); Rita Christiani (Dancer); Bryn Davis, Jody Gilbert (Women); Billy Edmunds (Town Crier).

THE IMMORTAL SERGEANT   (20th, 1943) 90 M.

Producer, Lamar Trotti; director, John Stahl; based on the novel by John Brophy; screenplay, Trotti; camera, Arthur Miller; editor, James B. Clark.

Henry Fonda (Corporal Colin Spence); Maureen O'Hara (Valentine); Thomas Mitchell (Sergeant Kelly); Allyn Joslyn (Cassidy); Reginald Gardiner (Benedict); Melville Cooper (Pilcher); Bramwell Fletcher (Symes); Morton Lowry (Cottrell); Bob Mascagno, Italia De Nubila (Specialty Dancers); Jean Prescott (Nurse); Peter Lawford, Gordon Clark, John Whitney, John Meredith, Robert Herrick, Hans von Morhart, Henry Guttman (Soldiers); John Banner (Officer); Anthony Marsh (Assistant Post Corporal); Leslie Vincent (Runner); Donald Stuart (Post Corporal); Bud Geary (Driver); Guy Kingsford (Lorry Driver); Sam Waagenaar (German); David Thursby (Bren Carrier Driver).

THIS LAND IS MINE   (RKO, 1943) 103 M.

Producer, Jean Renoir, Dudley Nichols; director, Renoir; screenplay, Nichols; music, Lothar Perl; music director, C. Bakaleinikoff; dialog director, Leo Bulgakov; camera, Frank Redman; editor, Frederick Knudtson.

Charles Laughton (Albert Lory); Maureen O'Hara (Louise Martin); George Sanders (George Lambert); Walter Slezak (Major Von Keller); Kent Smith (Paul Martin); Una O'Connor (Mrs. Emma Lory); Philip Merivale (Prof. Sorel); Thurston Hall (Mayor); George Coulouris (Prosecutor); Nancy Gates (Julie Grant); Ivan Simpson (Judge); John Donat (Edmund Lorraine); Frank Alten (Lieutenant Schwartz); Leo Bulgakov (Little Man); Wheaton Chambers (Mr. Lorraine); Cecil Weston (Mrs. Lorraine); Louis Donath (German Captain); Lillian O'Malley (Woman in Street); Philip Ahlm (German Lieutenant); Terrellyne Johnson (Girl); Hallene Hall (Woman at Window); Lester Sharpe, Russell Hoyt, Sven Borg, Nick Vehr, Bill Yetter, Albert d'Arno (German Soldiers); Ferdinand Schumann-Heink (Karl); Gus Taillon (Newsman); Mary Stuart (Photo Double); Casey Johnson (Boy); Joan Barclay (Young Woman); Mildred Hardy, Margaret Fealy (Old Women); Linda Ann Bieber (Emily); George Carleton (Jury Foreman); John Dilson (Mayor's Secretary); Ernest Grooney (Priest); Otto Hoffman (Printer); Hans von Morhart (Soldier Who Is Slapped); Henry Roquemore (Butcher); Hal Malone (Bit in Courtroom); Lloyd Ingraham (Paper Business on Street).

THE FALLEN SPARROW   (RKO, 1943) 91 M.

Producer, Robert Fellows; director, Richard Wallace; based on the novel by Dorothy B. Hughes; screenplay, Warren Duff; assistant director, Sam Ruman; special effects, Vernon L. Walker; camera, Nicholas Musuraca; editor, Robert Wise.

John Garfield (Kit); Maureen O'Hara (Toni Donne); Walter Slezak (Dr. Skaas); Patricia Morison (Barby Taviton); Martha O'Driscoll (Whitney Hamilton); Bruce Edwards (Ab Parker); John Banner (Anton); John Miljan (Inspector Tobin); Hugh Beaumont (Otto Skaas); George Lloyd (Sergeant Moors); Russ Powell (Priest); Lee Phelps (Cop); Stanley Price (Caterer); Charles Lung (Carlo); Rosina Galli (Mama);

Marty Faust (Chef—Carlo's Cafe); Lillian West (Receptionist); Miles Mander (Dr. Gudmundson); Edith Evanson (Nurse); Bud Geary (Cab Caller); William Edmunds (Papa); Nestor Paiva (Jake); Jack Carr (Danny); Andre Charlot (Peter); Eric Wilton (Butler); Erford Gage (Roman); Rita Gould (Dot); Joe King (Desk Sergeant); Al Rhein (Man); Babe Green, George Sherwood (G-Men); Billy Mitchell (Porter); Sam Goldenberg (Prince deNamur); Margaret Landry, Mary Halsey (Bits); Russell Wade (Flower Clerk).

BUFFALO BILL   (20th, 1944) C—90 M.

Producer, Harry Sherman; director, William A. Wellman; based on the story by Frank Winch; screenplay, Aeneas MacKenzie, Clements Ripley, Cecile Kramer; music, David Buttolph; art director, James Basevi, Lewis Creber; special effects, Fred Sersen; camera, Leon Shamroy; editor, James B. Clark.

Joel McCrea (Buffalo Bill); Maureen O'Hara (Louise Cody); Linda Darnell (Dawn Starlight); Thomas Mitchell (Ned Buntline); Edgar Buchanan (Sergeant Chips); Anthony Quinn (Yellow Hand); Moroni Olsen (Senator Frederici); Frank Fenton (Murdo Carvell); Matt Briggs (General Blazier); George Lessey (Mr. Vandevere); Frank Orth (Sherman); George Chandler (Trooper Clancy); Chief Many Treaties (Tall Bull); Chief Thundercloud (Crazy Horse); Sidney Blackmer (President Theodore Roosevelt); Evelyn Beresford (Queen Victoria); Cecil Weston (Maid); Vincent Graeff (Crippled Boy); Fred Graham (Editor); Harry Tyler, Arthur Loft, Syd Saylor (Barkers); Robert Homans (Muldoon, the Policeman); Cordell Hickman, Gerald Mackey, Eddie Nichols, Fred Chapman, George Nokes (Boys); John Reese (Tough Guy); John Dilson (President Hayes); Edwin Stanley (Doctor); Tatzumbia Dupea (Old Indian Woman); Margaret Martin (Indian Servant); George Bronson (Strong Man).

THE SPANISH MAIN   (RKO, 1945) C—110 M.

Producer, Robert Fellows; director, Frank Borzage; associate producer, Stephen Ames; story, Aeneas MacKenzie; screenplay, George Worthing Yates, Herman J. Mankiewicz; music, Hanns Eisler; technical director, Capt. Fred Ellis; art director, Albert S. D'Agostino, Carroll Clark; set decorator, Darrell Silvera, Claude Carpenter; sound, John E. Tribby; music director, C. Bakaleinikoff; second unit director, B. Reeves Eason; special effects, Vernon L. Walker; assistant director, Lew Borzage; camera, George Barnes; editor, Ralph Dawson.

Paul Henreid (Laurent Van Horn); Maureen O'Hara (Francisca); Walter Slezak (Don Alvarado); Binnie Barnes (Anne Bonney); John Emery (Da Bilar); Barton MacLane (Captain Black); J. M. Kerrigan (Pillory); Fritz Leiber (Bishop); Nancy Gates (Lupita); Jack LaRue (Lieutenant Escobar); Mike Mazurki (Swaine); Ian Keith (Captain Lussan); Victor Kilian (*Santa Nadre* Captain); Curt Bois (Paree); Antonio Moreno (Commandante); Alfredo Sabato (Sailing Master); Brandon Hurst (Captain Salter); Bob O'Connor (Master at Arms); Tom Kennedy (Captain McLeon); Marcelle Corday (Senora Perez); Norma Drury (Senora Montalvo); Abe Dinovich (Singer); Max Wagner, Ray Spiker (Bullies); Juan De La Cruz (Major-Domo); Leo White (Hairdresser); Cosmo Sardo, Leo Schlessinger (Spanish Guards); Jack Wise (Manicurist); Dan Seymour (Jailer); Ray Cooper, Jamiel Hasson, Alf Haugan, Al Haskell, George Bruggerman, Chuck Hamilton, Jean Valjean, Demetrius Alexis, Carl Deloro (Officers); Don Avalier (Pirate).

SENTIMENTAL JOURNEY   (20th, 1946) 94 M.

Producer, Walter Morosco; director, Walter Lang; story, Nelia Gardner White; screenplay, Samuel Hoffenstein, Elizabeth Reinhardt; art director, Lyle Wheeler, Albert Hogsett; set decorator, Thomas Little, R. Murray Waite; costumes, Kay Nelson; sound, Bernard Freericks, Roger Heman; makeup, Ben Nye; song, Bud Green,

683

Les Brown and Ben Homer; special camera effects, Fred Sersen; camera, Norbert Brodine; editor, J. Watson Webb.

John Payne (Bill); Maureen O'Hara (Julie); William Bendix (Donnelly); Sir Cedric Hardwicke (Dr. Miller); Glenn Langan (Judson); Mischa Auer (Laurence Ayres); Connie Marshall (Hatty); Kurt Kreuger (Wilson); Trudy Marshall (Ruth); Ruth Nelson (Mrs. McMasters); Dorothy Adams (Martha); Mary Gordon (Agnes); Lillian Bronson (Miss Benson); Olive Blakeney (Mrs. Deane); James Flavin (Detective); William Haade (Bus Driver); Mary Field (Chaperon); Byron Foulger (Clerk in Toy Store); George E. Stone (Toy Hawker); John Davidson (Floorwalker); Carol Ann Beekly, Shirley Barton, Mary Anne Bricker, Peggy Miller, Carol Coombs, Donna Cooke (Girls); Bert Hicks (Actor).

DO YOU LOVE ME? (20th, 1946) C—91 M.

Producer, George Jessel; director, Gregory Ratoff; story, Bert Granet; adaptation, Robert Ellis, Helen Logan; additional dialog, Dorothy Bennett; music director, Emil Newman, Charles Henderson; choreography, Seymour Felix; songs, Harold Adamson and Jimmy McHugh; Charles Henderson, Lionel Newman, and Harry James; Harry Ruby, Herb Magidson, and Matt Malneck; art director, Lyle Wheeler, Joseph C. Wright; special effects, Fred Sersen; camera, Edward Cronjager; editor, Robert Simpson.

Maureen O'Hara (Katherine Hilliard); Dick Haymes (Jimmy Hale); Harry James (Barry Clayton); Reginald Gardiner (Herbert Benham); Richard Gaines (Ralph Wainwright); Stanley Prager (Dilly); Harry James Music Makers (Themselves); B. S. Pully (Taxi Driver); Chick Chandler (Earl Williams); Alma Kruger (Mrs. Crackleton); Almira Sessions (Miss Wayburn); Douglas Wood (Mr. Dunfee); Harlan Briggs (Mr. Higbee); Julia Dean (Mrs. Allen); Harry Hays Morgan (Professor Allen); Eugene Borden (Headwaiter); Lex Barker (Guest); Harry Seymour (Headwaiter); Sam McDaniel (Bartender); William Frambes (Usher); Betty Grable (Clayton's Admirer); Jesse Graves (Bartender); Evelyn Mulhall (Woman); Esther Brodelet, Jack Barnett, Lillian Porter, Marjorie Jackson (Dancers); Les Clark, Jimmy Cross (Bellhops); Marla Shelton (Miss Fairchild); Kay Connors (Secretary); Philip Morris, Fred Graham (Doormen).

SINBAD THE SAILOR (RKO, 1947) C—116 M.

Producer, Stephen Ames; director, Richard Wallace; story, John Twist, George Worthington Yates; screenplay, Twist; assistant director, Lloyd Richards; marine technical director, Capt. Fred F. Ellis; art director, Albert S. D'Agostino, Carroll Clark; set decorator, Darrell Silvera, Claude Carpenter; music, Roy Webb; sound, John E. Tribby, Clem Portman; special effects, Vernon L. Walker, Harold Wellman; camera, George Barnes; editor, Sherman Todd, Frank Doyle.

Douglas Fairbanks, Jr. (Sinbad); Maureen O'Hara (Shireen); Walter Slezak (Melik); Anthony Quinn (Emir); George Tobias (Abbu); Jane Greer (Pirouze); Mike Mazurki (Yusuf); Sheldon Leonard (Auctioneer); Alan Napier (Aga); John Miljan (Moga); Barry Mitchell (Maullin).

THE HOMESTRETCH (20th, 1947) C—99 M.

Producer, Robert Bassler; director, Bruce Humberstone; screenplay, Wanda Tuchock; assistant director, Henry Weinberger; art director, James Basevi, Leland Fuller; set decorator, Thomas Little, Walter M. Scott; music score, David Raksin; music director, Alfred Newman; sound, E. Clayton Ward, Harry M. Leonard; special camera effects, Fred Sersen; camera, Arthur Arling; editor, Robert Simpson.

684

Cornel Wilde (Jock Wallace); Maureen O'Hara (Leslie Hale); Glenn Langan (Bill Van Dyke); Helen Walker (Kitty Brant); James Gleason (Doc Kilborne); Henry Stephenson (Don Humberto Balcares); Ethel Griffies (Aunt Martha); Tommy Cook (Pablo); Margaret Bannerman (Ellamae Scott); Nancy Evans (Sarah); John Vosper (Cliff); Michael Dyne (Julian Scott); Edward Earle (Mac); Charles Stevens, Nina Campana (Mexican Parents); Fernando Alvarado, Jose Alvarado, Miguel Tapia, Robert Espinoza (Mexican Boys); Anne O'Neal (Maid); George Economides, Michael Economides (Gypsy Boys); Inez Palange (Gypsy Woman); David Cavendish, Arthur Little, Jr., Rebel Randall, Shirley Chambers (Guests); Juan Torena (Hernandez); Ed Cobb (Mac's Helper); Buddy Roosevelt (Brakeman).

MIRACLE ON 34th STREET   (20th, 1947) 95 M.

Producer, William Perlberg; director, George Seaton; story, Valentine Davies; screenplay, Seaton; assistant director, Arthur Jacobson; art director, Richard Day, Richard Irvine; set decorator, Thomas Little, Ernest Lansing; music, Cyril Mockridge; sound, Arthur L. Kirbach, Roger Heman; special effects, Fred Sersen; camera, Charles Clarke, Lloyd Ahern; editor, Robert Simpson.

Maureen O'Hara (Doris Walker); John Payne (Fred Gailey); Edmund Gwenn (Kris Kringle); Gene Lockhart (Judge Henry X. Harper); Natalie Wood (Susan Walker); Porter Hall (Mr. Sawyer); William Frawley (Charles Halloran); Jerome Cowan (Thomas Mara); Philip Tonge (Mr. Shellhammer); James Seay (Dr. Pierce); Harry Antrim (Mr. Macy); Thelma Ritter, Mary Field (Mothers); Theresa Harris (Cleo); Alvin Greenman (Albert); Anne Staunton (Mrs. Mara); Robert Hyatt (Thomas Mara, Jr.); Richard Irving, Jeff Corey (Reporters); Anne O'Neal (Secretary); Lela Bliss (Mrs. Shellhammer); Anthony Sydes (Peter); William Forrest (Dr. Rogers); Alvin Hammer (Mara's Assistant); Joseph McInerney (Bailiff); Ida McGuire (Drum Majorette); Percy Helton (Santa Claus); Jane Green (Mrs. Harper); Marlene Lyden (Dutch Girl); Jack Albertson, Guy Thomajan (Post Office Employees); Robert Lynn (Macy's Salesman); Jean O'Donnell (Secretary); Snub Pollard (Mail-Bearing Court Officer); Robert Karnes, Basil Walker (Interns); Herbert Heyes (Mr. Gimbel).

THE FOXES OF HARROW   (20th, 1947) 115 M.

Producer, William A. Bacher; director, John M. Stahl; based on the novel by Frank Yerby; screenplay, Wanda Tuchock; art director, Lyle Wheeler, Maurice Ransford; set decorator, Thomas Little, Paul S. Fox; music, David Buttolph; music director, Alfred Newman; assistant director, Joseph Behm; sound, George Leverett, Roger Heman; camera, Joseph LaShelle; editor, James B. Clark.

Rex Harrison (Stephen Fox); Maureen O'Hara (Odalie); Richard Haydn (Andre); Victor McLaglen (Mike Farrel); Vanessa Brown (Aurore); Patricia Medina (Desiree); Gene Lockhart (The Vicomte); Charles Irwin (Sean Fox); Hugo Haas (Otto Ludenbach); Dennis Hoey (Master of Harrow); Roy Roberts (Tom Warren); Marcel Journet (St. Ange); Kenneth Washington (Achille); Helen Crozier (Zerline); Sam McDaniel (Josh); Libby Taylor (Angelina); Renee Beard (Little Inch); A. C. Bilbrew (Tante Caleen); Suzette Harbin (Belle); William Ward (Etienne Fox); Clear Nelson, Jr. (Little Inch—age 3); Henri Letondal (Maspero); James Lagano (Etienne—age 3); Dorothy Adams (Mrs. Fox); Andre Charlot (Dr. Terrebone); Georges Renavent (Priest); Jasper Weldon (Jode); Celia Lovsky (Minna Ludenbach); Eugene Borden (French Auctioneer); Joseph Crehan (Captain); Randy Stuart (Stephen Fox's Mother).

SITTING PRETTY   (20th, 1948) 84 M.

Producer, Samuel G. Engel; director, Walter Lang; based on the novel *Belvedere* by Gwen Davenport; screenplay, F. Hugh Herbert; assistant director, Gaston Glass;

art director, Lyle Wheeler, Leland Fuller; set decorator, Thomas Little, Ernest Lansing; music, Alfred Newman; makeup, Ben Nye; costumes, Kay Nelson; sound, George Leverett, Roger Heman; special effects, Fred Sersen; camera, Norbert Brodine; editor, Harmond Jones.

Robert Young (Harry); Maureen O'Hara (Tacey); Clifton Webb (Lynn Belvedere); Richard Haydn (Mr. Appleton); Louise Allbritton (Peggy); Randy Stuart (Peggy); Ed Begley (Hammond); Larry Olsen (Larry Kirg); John Russell (Bill Philby); Betty Ann Lynn (Ginger); Willard Robertson (Mr. Ashcroft); Anthony Sydes (Roddy); Grayce Hampton (Mrs. Appleton); Cara Williams, Marion Marshall (Secretaries); Charles Arnt (Mr. Taylor); Ken Christy (Mr. McPherson); Ann Shoemaker (Mrs. Ashcroft); Minerva Urecal (Mrs. Maypole); Mira McKinney (Mrs. Phillips); Sid Saylor (Cab Driver); Ruth Warren (Matron); Isabel Randolph (Mrs. Frisbee); Ellen Lowe (Effie); Dave Morris (Mailman); Anne O'Neal (Mrs. Gibbs); Albin Robeling (Maitre D'); Josephine Whittell (Mrs. Hammond); Mary Field (Librarian); Billy Wayne (Newsreel Man); Charles Owens, Iris James, Robert Tidwell, Barbara Blaine (Jitterbugs); Gertrude Astor (Woman); Jane Nigh (Mabel); J. Farrell MacDonald (Cop); Charles Tannen (Director); Dorothy Adams (Mrs. Goul).

THE FORBIDDEN STREET   (20th, 1949) 91 M.

Producer, William Perlberg; director, Jean Negulesco; based on the novel *Britannia Mews* by Margery Sharp; screenplay, Ring Lardner, Jr.; assistant director, Guy Hamilton; art director, Andre Andrejew; music, Malcolm Arnold; music director, Muir Mathieson; sound, Buster Ambier; sound editor, Ben Hipkins; camera, George Perinal; editor, Richard Best.

Maureen O'Hara (Adelaide Culver); Dana Andrews (Gilbert Lauderdale/Henry Lambert); Dame Sybil Thorndike (Mrs. Mounsey); June Allen (Adelaide—As a Child); Anthony Tancred (Treff Culver); Anthony Lamb (Treff—As a Child); Wilfred Hyde-White (Mr. Culver); Fay Compton (Mrs. Culver); Anne Butchart (Alice Hambro); Suzanne Gibbs (Alice—as a Child); Diane Hart (The Blazer); Heather Latham (Blazer —as a child); Herbert Walton (The Old 'Un); A. E. Matthews (Mr. Bly); Mary Martlew (Milly Lauderdale); Gwen Whitby (Miss Bryant); Scott Harold (Benson); Neil North (Jimmy Hambro).

A WOMAN'S SECRET   (RKO, 1949) 84 M.

Executive producer, Dore Schary; producer, Herman J. Mankiewicz; director, Nicholas Ray; based on the novel *Mortgage on Life* by Vicki Baum; screenplay, Mankiewicz; assistant director, Dorian Cox; art director, Albert S. D'Agostino, Carroll Clark; set decorator, Darrell Silvera, Harley Miller; music, Frederick Hollander; music director, C. Bakaleinikoff; makeup, Gordon Bau, James Barker, Jack Barron; costumes, Edward Stevenson; sound, Frank Sarver, Clem Portman; special effects, Russell A. Cully; camera, George Diskant; editor, Sherman Todd.

Maureen O'Hara (Marian Washburn); Melvyn Douglas (Luke Jordan); Gloria Grahame (Susan Caldwell); Bill Williams (Lee); Victor Jory (Brook Matthews); Mary Philips (Mrs. Fowler); Jay C. Flippen (Fowler); Robert Warwick (Roberts); Curt Conway (Doctor); Ann Shoemaker (Mrs. Matthews); Virginia Farmer (Mollie); Ellen Corby (Nurse); Emory Parnell (Desk Sergeant); Dan Foster (Stage Manager); Alphonse Martel (Waiter); Charles Wagenheim (Piano Player); Marcelle De La Brosse (Baker); Lynne Whitney (Actress); Rory Mallinson (Benson); George Douglas, Lee Phelps, Mickey Simpson, Tom Coleman, Guy Beach (Cops); John Laing (Radio Announcer); Bert Davidson (Radio Director); Alvin Hammer (Fred); Frank Marlowe (Whitey); John Parrish (Professor Camelli); Oliver Blake (Mr. Pierson).

FATHER WAS A FULLBACK   (20th, 1949) 84 M.

Producer, Fred Kohlmar; director, John M. Stahl; based on a play by Clifford Gold-smith; screenplay, Aleen Leslie, Casey Robinson, Mary Loos, Richard Sale; art direc-tor, Lyle Wheeler, Chester Gore; set decorator, Thomas Little, Stuart Reiss; assistant director, Arthur Jacobson; costumes, Kay Nelson; makeup, Ben Nye, James Barker, Ernie Parker; sound, Arthur Charles Hall; special effects, Fred Sersen; camera, Lloyd Ahern; editor, J. Watson Webb, Jr.

Fred MacMurray (George Cooper); Maureen O'Hara (Elizabeth Cooper); Betty Lynn (Connie Cooper); Rudy Vallee (Mr. Jessop); Thelma Ritter (Geraldine); Natalie Wood (Ellen Cooper); Jim Backus (Professor Sullivan); Richard Tyler (Joe Burch); Buddy Martin (Cheerleader); Mickey McCardle (Jones); John McKee (Cy); Charles J. Flynn (Policeman); William Self (Willie); Joe Haworth (Reporter); Gwen Fields (Daphne); Gilbert Barnett (Stinky Parker); Tommy Bernard (Delivery Boy); Mike Mahoney (Sailor); Tom Hanlon (Radio Announcer); Pat Kane (Bellhop); Forbes Murray (College President); Lee MacGregor (Cheerleader); Don Hicks (Bill); Wilson Wood, Rodney Bell, Don Barclay (Grandstand Coach); Bill Radovich (Football Player); Harry Carter, Bob Adler (Grandstand Bits); Bob Patten (Manager); Bess Flowers (Woman).

BAGDAD   (Univ., 1949) C—82 M.

Producer, Robert Arthur; assistant producer, Morgan Cox; director, Charles Lamont; story, Tamara Hovey; screenplay, Robert Hardy Andrews; art director, Bernard Herz-brun, Alexander Golitzen; set decorator, Russell A. Gausman; songs, Jack Brooks and Frank Skinner; assistant director, Jesse Hibbs; makeup, Bud Westmore, Emil LeVigne; choreography, Lester Horton, Bella Lewitsky; costumes, Yvonne Wood; sound, Leslie I. Carey, Glenn E. Anderson; camera, Russell Metty; editor, Russell Schoengarth.

Maureen O'Hara (Princess Marjan); Paul Christian (Pasha Ali Nadim); Vincent Price (Hassan); John Sutton (Raizul); Jeff Corey (Mohammed Jad); Frank Puglia (Saleel); David Wolfe (Mahmud); Fritz Leiber (Emir); Otto Waldis (Marengo); Leon Belasco (Beggar); Ann Pearce (Tirza).

COMANCHE TERRITORY   (Univ., 1950) C—76 M.

Producer, Leonard Goldstein; director, George Sherman; story, Lewis Meltzer; screenplay, Oscar Brodney, Meltzer; special effects, David S. Horsley; camera, Maury Gertsman; editor, Frank Gross.

Maureen O'Hara (Katie); Macdonald Carey (James Bowie); Will Geer (Daniel Seeger); Charles Drake (Stacey Howard); Pedro De Cordoba (Quisima); Ian Mac-Donald (Walsh); Rick Vallin (Pakanah); Parley Baer (Boozer); James Best (Sam); Edmund Cobb (Ed); Glenn Strange (Big Joe).

TRIPOLI   (Par., 1950) C—95 M.

Producer, William H. Pine, William C. Thomas; director, Will Price; story, Price, Winston Miller; screenplay, Miller; art director, Lewis H. Creber; music, David Chud-now; camera, James Wong Howe; editor, Howard Smith.

Maureen O'Hara (Countess D'Arneau); John Payne (Lieutenant O'Bannon); How-ard Da Silva (Captain Demetrios); Philip Reed (Hamet Karamanly); Grant Withers (Sergeant Derek); Lowell Gilmore (Lieutenant Tripp); Connie Gilchrist (Henriette); Alan Napier (Khalil); Herbert Heyes (General Eaton); Alberto Morin (Il Taiib); Gran-don Rhodes (Commodore Barron); Frank Fenton (Captain Adams); Rosa Turich (Seewauk); Ray Hyke (Crawford); Walter Reed (Wade); Paul Livermore (Evans); Gregg Barton (Huggins); Don Summers (Langley); Jack Pennick (Busch).

RIO GRANDE (Rep., 1950) 105 M.

Producer, John Ford, Merian C. Cooper; director, Ford; based on the story "Mission With No Record" by James Warner Bellah; screenplay, James Kevin McGuinness; art director, Frank Hotaling; set decorator, John McCarthy, Jr., Charles Thompson; music, Victor Young; songs, Stan Jones; Dale Evans; Tex Owens; second unit director, Cliff Lyons; camera, Bert Glennon; second unit camera, Archie Stout; editor, Jack Murray; assistant editor, Barbara Ford.

John Wayne (Lt. Col. Kirby Yorke); Maureen O'Hara (Kathleen Yorke); Ben Johnson (Trooper Tyree); Claude Jarman, Jr. (Trooper Jeff Yorke); Harry Carey, Jr. (Trooper Sandy Boone); Chill Wills (Dr. Wilkins); J. Carroll Naish (Gen. Philip Sheridan); Victor McLaglen (Sgt. Maj. Tim Quincannon); Grant Withers (Deputy Marshal); Peter Ortiz (Captain St Jacques); Steve Pendleton (Captain Prescott); Karolyn Grimes (Margaret Mary); Alberto Morin (Lieutenant); Stan Jones (Sergeant); Fred Kennedy (Heinz); The Sons of The Pioneers (Regimental Singers); Chuck Roberson (Indian); Pat Wayne (Boy); Cliff Lyons (Soldier); Jack Pennick (Sergeant); and: Tommy Doss.

FLAME OF ARABY (Univ., 1951) C—77 M.

Producer, Leonard Goldstein; director, Charles Lamont; story-screenplay, Gerald Drayson Adams; art director, Bernard Herzbrun, Hilyard Brown; music director, Joseph Gershenson; camera, Russell Metty.

Maureen O'Hara (Princess Tanya); Jeff Chandler (Tamerlane); Lon Chaney (Borka Barbarossa); Buddy Baer (Hakim Barbarossa); Maxwell Reed (Prince Medina); Richard Egan (Captain Fezil); Dewey Martin (Yak); Royal Dano (Basra); Susan Cabot (Clio); Judith Braun (Calu); Henry Brandon (Mallik); Neville Brand (Kral); Tony Barr (Malat); Frederic Berest (Ibid); Cindy Garner (Elaine); Norene Michaels (Zara); Richard Hale (King Chanda); Virginia Brissac (Alhena); Dorothy Ford (Naja); William Tannen (Captain of the Guards); Andre Charlot, Joe Kamaryt (Physicians); Lillian Ten Eyck (Elaine's Mother); Leon Charles (Huntsman); Chuck Hamilton (Ayub); Barry Brooks (Guard).

AT SWORD'S POINT (RKO, 1952) C—81 M.

Executive producer, Sid Rogell; director, Lewis Allen; based on the novel *Twenty Years After* by Alexandre Dumas; adaptation, Aubrey Wisberg, Jack Pollexfen; screenplay, Wallace Ferris, Joseph Hoffman; art director, Jack Okey, Albert D'Agostino; music director, C. Bakaleinikoff; music, Roy Webb; set decorator, Darrell Silvera; William Stevens; sound, John Cass, Clem Portman; makeup, Mel Burns; gowns, Edward Stevenson; camera, Ray Rennahan; editor, Samuel E. Beetley, Robert Golden.

Cornel Wilde (D'Artagnan); Maureen O'Hara (Claire); Robert Douglas (Duc de Lavalle); Gladys Cooper (Queen); June Clayworth (Claudine); Dan O'Herlihy (Aramis); Alan Hale, Jr. (Porthos); Blanche Yurka (Madame Michom); Nancy Gates (Princess Henriette); Edmond Breon (Queen's Chamberlain); Peter Miles (Louis); George Petrie (Chalais); Moroni Olsen (Old Porthos); Boyd Davis (Dr. Fernand); Holmes Herbert (Mallard); Lucien Littlefield (Corporal Gautler); Claude Dunkin (Pierre); Joseph Hall (Father Luvoir); Pat O'Moore (Monk); Al Cavens (Ledoux); Mickey McCardle (Queen's Messenger); John McKee, Ned Davenport, Tristram Coffin, Gregg Barton, Fred Kohler, George Holmes, Don Turner (Regent Guards); Eric Alden, Allen Matthews, Glen Gallagher, Keith McConnell (Captain of Regent Guards); Art Dupuis (Servant); Philip Van Zandt (Jacques); Serena McKinney (Maid); Gregory Marshall (Henrique); Ed Hinton (Sergeant of Guard); Georgia Clancy (Florette).

KANGAROO   (20th, 1952) C—84 M.

Producer, Robert Bassler; associate producer, Robert Snody; director, Lewis Milestone; story, Martin Berkeley; screenplay, Harry Kleiner; music, Sol Kaplan; music director, Alfred Newman; art director, Lyle Wheeler, Jack-Lee Kirk; camera, Charles G. Clarke; editor, Nick De Maggio.

Maureen O'Hara (Dell McGuire); Peter Lawford (Richard Connor); Finlay Currie (Michael McGuire); Richard Boone (Gamble); Chips Rafferty (Trooper Leonard); Letty Craydon (Kathleen); Charles Tingwell (Matt); Ron Whelan (Fenner); John Fegan (Burke); Guy Doleman (Pleader); Reg Collins (Ship's Officer); Clyde Combo (Aborigine Stockman); Henry Murdock (Black Tracker); Sid Chambers, Joe Tomal, Archie Hull, James Doogue, Bill Bray, Ossie Wenban, Alex Cann, Kleber Claux (Sailors); Larry Crowhurst (Cockatoo at Door); Dennis Glenny (Well-Dressed Cockatoo); Stan Tolhurst (Policeman); John Clark (Ferret Face); Frank Catchlove (Publican); Eve Abdullah (Woman Servant); Frank Ransome (Burton—Station Foreman); Douglas Ramsey (Kelly—Station Foreman); Alan Bardsley (Cook on Cattle Drive).

THE QUIET MAN   (Rep., 1952) C—129 M.

Producers, John Ford, Merian C. Cooper; director, Ford; based on the story by Maurice Walsh; screenplay, Frank S. Nugent; art director, Frank Hotaling; set decorator, John McCarthy, Jr., Charles Thompson; music, Victor Young; songs, Dr. Arthur Colahan and Michael Donovan; Thomas Moore; second unit directors, John Wayne, Patrick Ford; assistant director, Andrew McLaglen; camera, Winton C. Hoch; second unit camera, Archie Stout; editor, Jack Murray; assistant editor, Barbara Ford.

John Wayne (Sean Thornton); Maureen O'Hara (Mary Kate Danaher); Barry Fitzgerald (Michaeleen Flynn); Ward Bond (Father Peter Lonergan); Mildred Natwick (Mrs. Sarah Tillane); Francis Ford (Dan Tobin); Eileen Crowe (Mrs. Elizabeth Playfair); May Craig (Woman at Railroad Station); Arthur Shields (Rev. Cyril Playfair); Charles FitzSimons (Forbes); Sean McClory (Owen Glynn); James Lilburn (Father Paul); Jack McGowran (Feeney); Ken Curtis (Dermot Fahy); Mae Marsh (Father Paul's Mother); Major Sam Harris (General); Harry Tenbrook (Policeman); Joseph O'Drea (Guard); Eric Gorman (Railroad Conductor); Kevin Lawless (Fireman); Paddy O'Donnell (Porter); Webb Overlander (Railroad Station Chief); Hank Worden (Trainer in Flashback); Patrick Wayne, Antonia Wayne, Melinda Wayne (Children); Elizabeth Jones (Tiny Woman); Douglas Evans (Ring Physician).

AGAINST ALL FLAGS   (Univ., 1952) C—83 M.

Producer, Howard Christie; director, George Sherman; story, Aeneas MacKenzie; screenplay, MacKenzie, Joseph Hoffman; music, Hans J. Salter; assistant director, John Sherwood, Phil Bowles, James Welch; art director, Bernard Herzbrun, Alexander Golitzen; set decorator, Russell A. Gausman, Oliver Emert; sound, Leslie I. Carey, Joe Lapis; camera, Russell Metty; editor, Frank Gross.

Errol Flynn (Brian Hawke); Maureen O'Hara (Spitfire Stevens); Anthony Quinn (Roc Brasiliano); Alice Kelley (Princess Patma); Mildred Natwick (Molvina MacGregor); Robert Warwick (Captain Kidd); Harry Cording (Cow); John Alderson (Harris); Phil Tully (Jones); Lester Mathews (Sir Cloudsley); Tudor Owen (William); Maurice Marsac (Captain Moisson); James Craven (Captain Hornsby); James Fairfax (Barber); Lewis Russell (Oxford); Arthur Gould-Porter (Lord Portland); Olaf Hytten (King William); Renee Beard (Archimedes); Maralou Gray (Harem Girl); Carl Saxe, Chuck Hamilton (Pirates).

689

THE REDHEAD FROM WYOMING   (Univ., 1952) C—81 M.

Producer, Leonard Goldstein; director, Lee Sholem; story, Polly James; screenplay, James, Herb Meadow; art director, Bernard Herzbrun, Hilyard Brown; set decorator, Russell A. Gausman, Joseph Kish; sound, Leslie I. Carey, Corson Jowett; music director, Joseph Gershenson; camera, Winton Hoch; editor, Milton Carruth.

Maureen O'Hara (Kate Maxwell); Alex Nicol (Stan Blaine); Robert Strauss ("Knuckles" Hogan); William Bishop (Jim Averell); Alexander Scourby (Reece Duncan); Gregg Palmer (Hal Jessup); Jack Kelly (Sandy); Jeanne Cooper (Myra); Stacy Harris (Chet Jones); Dennis Weaver (Matt Jessup); Edmund Cobb (Sprague); Philo McCullough (Aldrich); Keith Kerrigan (Girl in Katie's Place); Betty Allen (French Heels); Bob Merrick (Professor); Ray Bennett (Wade Burrows); Syd Saylor (Drunken Settler); George Taylor (Doctor); Harold Goodwin (Henchman); Buddy Roosevelt (Man); David Alpert (Wally Beggs); Jack Hyde (Chuck); Rush Williams (Ned); Joe Bailey (Jack).

WAR ARROW   (Univ., 1953) C—78 M.

Producer, John W. Rogers; director, George Sherman; screenplay, John Michael Hayes; assistant director, Frank Shaw, Terry Nelson; art director, Bernard Herzbrun, Alexander Golitzen; dialog director, Irvin Beck; sound, Leslie I. Carey, Richard De Weese; music director, Joseph Gershenson; assistant director, Frank Shaw; costumes, Edward Stevenson; set decorator, Russell A. Gausman, Joseph Kish; camera, William Daniels; editor, Frank Gross.

Maureen O'Hara (Elaine Corwin); Jeff Chandler (Maj. Howell Brady); John McIntire (Col. Jackson Meade); Suzan Ball (Avis); Noah Beery (Sgt. Augustus Wilks); Charles Drake (Sgt. Luke Schermerhorn); Henry Brandon (Maygro); Dennis Weaver (Pino); Jay Silverheels (Santanta); James Bannon (Capt. Roger Corwin); Steve Wyman (Captain Neil); Brad Jackson (Lieutenant); Lance Fuller, Bill Ward (Troopers); Dee Carroll (Hysterical Woman); Roy Whaley (Lieutenant); Darla Ridgeway (Crying Child).

FIRE OVER AFRICA   (Col., 1954) C—84 M.

Producer, M. J. Frankovich; director, Richard Sale; screenplay, Robert Westerby; music, Benjamin Frankel; art director, Vincent Korda, Wilfred Shingleton; camera, Christopher Challis, A. Ibbetson; editor, A. S. Bates.

Maureen O'Hara (Joanna Dane); Macdonald Carey (Van Logan); Binnie Barnes (Frisco); Guy Middleton (Soames Howard); Hugh McDermott (Richard Farrell); James Liburn (Danny Boy); Harry Lane (Augie); Leonard Sachs (Paul Dupont); Ferdy Mayne (Mustapha); Eric Corrie (Pebbles); Bruce Beeby (Potts); Gerard Tichy (Cronkhite); Mike Brendell (Rodrigo); Derek Sydney (Signor Amato); Jacques Cey (Monsieur Ducloir).

THE LONG GRAY LINE   (Col., 1955) C—138 M.

Producer, Robert Arthur; director, John Ford; based on the book *Bringing up the Brass* by Marty Maher with Nardi Reeder Campion; screenplay, Edward Hope; art director, Robert Peterson; set decorator, Frank Tuttle; assistant director, Wingate Smith, Jack Corrick; technical consultant, Francis Cugat; music, Morris Stoloff; sound, John Livadary, George Cooper; makeup, Clay Campbell; gowns, Jean Louis; camera, Charles Lawton, Jr.; editor, William Lyon.

Tyrone Power (Martin Maher); Maureen O'Hara (Mary O'Donnell); Robert Francis (James Sundstrom, Jr.); Donald Crisp (Old Martin); Ward Bond (Capt. Herman

J. Koehler); Betsy Palmer (Kitty Carter); Phil Carey (Charles Dotson); William Leslie (Red Sundstrom); Harry Carey, Jr. (Dwight D. Eisenhower); Patrick Wayne (Cherub Overton); Sean McClory (Dinny Maher): Peter Graves (Capt. Rudolph Heinz); Milburn Stone (Capt. John Pershing); Erin O'Brien-Moore (Mrs. Koehler); Walter D. Ehlers (Mike Shannon); Don Barclay (Major Thomas); Martin Milner (Jim O'Carberry); Chuck Courtney (Whitey Larson); Willis Bouchey (Doctor); Jack Pennick (Sergeant); Norma La Roche, Pat Harding, Jean Moorhead, Dorothy Seese (Ad-Lib Girls); Pat O'Malley, Harry Denny (Priests); Jack Pennick (Recruiting Sergeant).

THE MAGNIFICENT MATADOR   (20th, 1955) C—94 M.

Producer, Edward L. Alperson; associate producer, Carroll Case; director, Budd Boetticher; story, Boetticher; screenplay, Charles Lang; music director, Raoul Kraushaar; song, Alperson and Paul Herrick; sound, Manuel Topete; technical advisor, Carlos Arriya; camera, Lucien Ballart; editor, Richard Cahoon.

Maureen O'Hara (Karen Harrison); Anthony Quinn (Luis Santos); Manuel Rojas (Rafael Reyes); Thomas Gomez (Don David); Richard Denning (Mark Russell); Lola Albright (Mona Wilton); William Brooks Ching (Jody Wilton); Eduardo Noriega (Miguel); Lorraine Chanel (Sarita Sebastian); Anthony Caruse (Emiliano); and: Jesus Solarzano, Joaquin Rodriguez, Rafael Rodriguez, Antonio Velasquez, Jorge Aguilar, Felix Briones, Nacho Tevino (Themselves).

LADY GODIVA   (Univ., 1955) C—89 M.

Producer, Robert Arthur; director, Arthur Lubin; story, Oscar Brodney; screenplay, Brodney, Harry Ruskin; art director, Alexander Golitzen, Robert Boyle; music director, Joseph Gershenson; camera, Carl Guthrie; editor, Paul Weatherwax.

Maureen O'Hara (Lady Godiva); George Nader (Lord Leofric); Eduard Franz (King Edward); Leslie Bradley (Count Eustace); Victor McLaglen (Grimald); Torin Thatcher (Lord Godwin); Rex Reason (Harold); Arthur Gould-Porter (Thorold); Robert Warwick (Humbert); Grant Withers (Pendar); Sim Iness (Oswin); Alec Harford (Tom the Tailor); Arthur Shields (Innkeeper); Anthony Eustrel (Prior); Kathryn Givney (Abbess); Thayer Roberts (William); Clint Eastwood (First Saxon); Rhodes Reason (Sweyn); Olive Sturgess (Girl); Tom Cound, Judith Brian (Listeners); Maya Van Horn (Frenchwoman); Jack Grinnage (Blacksmith's Son); Philo McCullogh (Captain).

LISBON   (Rep., 1956) C—90 M.

Producer-director, Ray Milland; story, Martin Rackin; screenplay, John Humberto Madeira; music, Nelson Riddle; camera, Jack Marta; editor, Richard L. Van Enger.

Ray Milland (Capt. Robert John Evans); Maureen O'Hara (Sylvia Merrill); Claude Rains (Aristides Mavros); Yvonne Furneaux (Maria Maddalena Masanet); Francis Lederer (Serafim); Percy Marmont (Lloyd Merrill); Jay Novello (Joao Casimiro Fonseca); Edward Chapman (Edgar Selwyn); Harold Jamieson (Phillip Norworth); Humberto Madeira (Tio Rabio).

EVERYTHING BUT THE TRUTH   (Univ., 1956) C—83 M.

Producer, Howard Christie; director, Jerry Hopper; screenplay, Herb Meadow; music director, Milton Rosen; art director, Alexander Golitzen, Bill Newberry; camera, Maury Gertsman; editor, Sherman Todd.

Maureen O'Hara (Joan Madison); John Forsythe (Ernie Miller); Tim Hovey (Willie Taylor); Frank Faylen (Mac); Les Tremayne (Lawrence Everett); Philip Bourneuf (Mayor Parker); Paul Birch (Senator Winter); Addison Richards (Roger Connolly); Barry Atwater (Arthur Taylor); Jeanette Nolan (Miss Adelaide Dabney); Roxanne Arlen (Blonde); Ray Walker (Doctor); Howard Negley (Chairman of School Board);

Bill Walker (Waiter); Elizabeth Flourney (Salesgirl); Don Dillaway (Official); Ken Osmond (Orrin Cunningham); Bill Anders (Passenger); Dorothy Abbott (Hostess); Arnold Ishii (Japanese Reporter); Gertrude Astor (Bit).

THE WINGS OF EAGLES   (MGM, 1957) C—109 M.

Producer, Charles Schnee; associate producer, James E. Newcom; director, John Ford; based on the life and writings of Comdr. Frank W. Wead, U.S.N.; screenplay, Frank Fenton, William Wister Haines; art director, William A. Horning, Malcolm Brown; set decorator, Edwin B. Willis, Keogh Gleason; costumes, Walter Plunkett; music, Jeff Alexander; assistant director, Wingate Smith; aerial stunts, Paul Mantz; music, Jeff Alexander; camera, Paul C. Vogel; editor, Gene Ruggiero.

John Wayne (Frank W. "Spig" Wead); Maureen O'Hara (Minnie Wead); Dan Dailey (Carson); Ward Bond (John Dodge); Ken Curtis (John Dale Price); Edmund Lowe (Admiral Moffett); Kenneth Tobey (Herbert Allen Hazard); James Todd (Jack Travis); Barry Kelley (Capt. Jock Clark); Sig Ruman (Manager); Henry O'Neill (Captain Spear); Willis Bouchey (Barton); Dorothy Jordan (Rose Brentmann); Peter Ortiz (Lt. Charles Dexter); Louis Jean Heydt (Dr. John Keye); Tige Andrews ("Arizona" Pincus); Dan Borzage (Pete); William Tracy (Air Force Officer); Harlan Warde (Executive Officer); Jack Pennick (Joe); Bill Henry (Naval Aide); Alberto Morin (Second Manager); Mimi Gibson (Lila Wead); Evelyn Rudie (Doris Wead); Charles Trowbridge (Admiral Crown); Mae Marsh (Nurse Crumley); Fred Graham (Officer in Brawl); Stuart Holmes (Producer); Olive Carey (Bridy O'Faolain); Major Sam Harris (Patient); May McEvoy, Janet Lake (Nurses); William Paul Lowery (Wead's Baby "Commodore"); Chuck Roberson (Officer); and: Cliff Lyons, Veda Ann Borg, Christopher James.

OUR MAN IN HAVANA   (Col., 1960) 107 M.

Producer, Carol Reed; associate producer, Raymond Anzarut; director, Reed; based on the novel by Graham Greene; screenplay, Greene; assistant director, Gerry O'Hara; art director, John Box; camera, Oswald Morris; editor, Bert Bates.

Alec Guinness (James Wormold); Burl Ives (Dr. Hasselbacher); Maureen O'Hara (Beatrice Severn); Ernie Kovacs (Captain Segura); Noel Coward (Hawthorne); Ralph Richardson ("C"); Jo Morrow (Milly Wormold); Gregoire Aslan (Cifuentes); Paul Rogers (Hubert Carter); Maxine Audley (Teresa); Timothy Bateson (Rudy); Jose Prieto (Lopez); Raymond Huntley (Army Representative); Maurice Denham (Navy Representative); Hugh Manning (Air Force Representative).

THE PARENT TRAP   (Buena Vista, 1961) C—129 M.

Producer, Walt Disney; associate producer, George Golitzin; director, David Swift; based on the novel *Das Doppelte Lottchen* by Erich Kastner; screenplay, Swift; music, Paul Smith; songs, Richard M. and Robert B. Sherman; assistant director, Ivan Volkman; costumes, Bill Thomas; art director, Carroll Clark, Robert Clatworthy; sound, Dean Thomas; camera, Lucien Ballard; editor, Philip W. Anderson.

Hayley Mills (Sharon McKendrick/Susan Evers); Maureen O'Hara (Margaret); Brian Keith (Mitch); Joanna Barnes (Victoria Robinson); Charles Ruggles (Charles McKendrick); Una Merkel (Verbena); Leo G. Carroll (Rev. Dr. Mosby); Cathleen Nesbitt (Louise McKendrick); Ruth McDevitt (Miss Inch); Crahan Denton (Hecky); Linda Watkins (Edna Robinson); Nancy Kulp (Miss Grunecker); Frank DeVol (Mr. Eaglewood).

THE DEADLY COMPANIONS   (Pathé-America, 1961) C—90 M.

Producer, Charles B. FitzSimons; director, Sam Peckinpah; based on the novel by A. S. Fleischman; screenplay, Fleischman; music, Marlin Skiles; sound, Robert J.

Callen; song, FitzSimons and Skiles; camera, William H. Clothier; editor, Stanley E. Rabjon.

Maureen O'Hara (Kit Tildon); Brian Keith (Yellowleg); Steve Cochran (Billy); Chill Wills (Turk); Strother Martin (Parson); Will Wright (Doctor Caxton); Jim O'Hara (Cal); Peter O'Crotty (Mayor); Billy Vaughan (Mead Tildon); Robert Sheldon, John Hamilton (Gamblers); Hank Gobble (Bartender); Buck Sharpe (Indian); Riley Hill (Gambler); Chuck Hayward (Card Sharp).

MR. HOBBS TAKES A VACATION   (20th, 1962) C—115 M.

Producer, Jerry Wald; associate producer, Marvin A. Gluck; director, Henry Koster; based on the novel by Edward Streeter; screenplay, Nunnally Johnson; music, Henry Mancini; assistant director, Joseph E. Rickards; song, Johnny Mercer and Mancini; costumes, Don Feld; sound, Alfred Bruzlin, Warren Dlaplain; orchestrator, Jack Hayes, Leo Shuken; special camera effects, L. B. Abbott; makeup, Ben Nye; camera, William C. Mellor; editor, Marjorie Fowler.

James Stewart (Mr. Hobbs); Maureen O'Hara (Peggy Hobbs); Fabian (Joe); John Saxon (Byron); Marie Wilson (Mrs. Turner); Reginald Gardiner (Reggie McHugh); Lauri Peters (Katey); Lili Gentle (Janie); Valerie Varda (Marika); John McGiver (Mr. Turner); Josh Perne (Stan); Natalie Trundy (Susan); Minerva Urecal (Brenda); Michael Burns (Danny Hobbs); Richard Collier (Mr. Kagle); Peter Oliphant (Peter Carver); Thomas Lowell (Freddie); Stephen Mines (Carl); Dennis Whitcomb (Dick); Michael Sean (Phil); Barbara Mansell (Receptionist); Maida Severn (Secretary); Ernie Gutierrez (Pizza Maker); Darryl Duke (Boy); Doris Packer (Hostess); Sherry Alberoni, True Ellison (Girls in Dormitory).

SPENCER'S MOUNTAIN   (WB, 1963) C—121 M.

Producer-director, Delmer Daves; based on the novel by Earl Hamner, Jr.; screenplay, Daves; art director, Carl Anderson; set decorator, Raiph S. Hurst; music, Max Steiner; sound, M. A. Merrick; assistant director, Gil Kissel; second unit director, Robert Totten; camera, Charles Lawton; editor, David Wages.

Henry Fonda (Clay Spencer); Maureen O'Hara (Olivia Spencer); James MacArthur (Clayboy); Donald Crisp (Grandpa Zebelon); Wally Cox (Preacher Goodson); Mimsey Farmer (Claris); Virginia Gregg (Miss Parker); Lillian Bronson (Grandma); Whit Bissell (Dr. Campbell); Hayden Rorke (Col. Coleman); Kathy Bennett (Minnie-Cora); Dub Taylor (Percy Cook); Ken Mayer (Mr. John); Hope Summers (Mother Ida); Med Flory, Michael Greene, Mike Henry, Lawrence Mann, Buzz Henry, James O'Hara, Victor French, Raymond Savage (Zebelon's Other Children); Bronwyn FitzSimons (Secretary to Dean).

McLINTOCK!   (UA, 1963) C—127 M.

Producer, Michael Wayne; director, Andrew V. McLaglen; screenplay, James Edward Grant; music, Frank De Vol; assistant director, Frank Parmenter; costumes, Frank C. Beetson; song, DeVol; technical advisor, Cliff Lyons; sound, Jack Solomon; camera, William H. Clothier; editor, Otho Lovering.

John Wayne (McLintock); Maureen O'Hara (Katherine McLintock); Yvonne DeCarlo (Louise Warren); Patrick Wayne (Devlin Warren); Stefanie Powers (Becky McLintock); Jack Kruschen (Birnbaum); Chill Wills (Drago); Jerry Van Dyke (Matt Douglas, Jr.); Edgar Buchanan (Bunny Dull); Bruce Cabot (Ben Sage); Perry Lopez (Davey Elk); Michael Pate (Puma); Strother Martin (Agard); Gordon Jones (Matt Douglas); Robert Lowery (Governor); Ed Faulkner (Young Ben Sage); Pedro Gonzales, Jr. (Carlos); Hal Needham (Carter); Chuck Roberson (Sheriff Lord); Aissa Wayne (Alice Warren); H. W. Gim (Ching); Leo Gordon (Hones); Hank Worden (Jeth); Mary Patterson (Beth); John Hamilton (Fauntleroy); Ralph Volkie, Dan

693

Borzage (Loafers); John Stanley (Running Buffalo); Kari Noven (Millie); Mari Blanchard (Camille); Frank Hagney (Bartender); Bob Steele (Engineer).

THE BATTLE OF THE VILLA FIORITA (WB, 1965) C—111 M.

Producer-director, Delmer Daves; based on the novel by Rumer Godden; screenplay, Daves; art director, Carmen Dillon; sound, Les Hammond, Len Shilton; wardrobe, Emilio Pucci; music, M. Spoliansky; camera, Oswald Morris; editor, Bert Bates.

Maureen O'Hara (Moira); Rossano Brazzi (Lorenzo); Richard Todd (Darrell); Phyllis Calvert (Margot); Martin Stephens (Michael); Elizabeth Dear (Debby); Olivia Hussey (Donna); Maxine Audley (Charmian); Ursula Jeans (Lady Anthea); Ettore Manni (Father Rossi); Richard Wattis (Travel Agent); Clelia Matania (Celestina); Finlay Currie (Emcee); Rosi Di Pietro (Guiletta).

THE RARE BREED (Univ., 1966) C—97 M.

Producer, William Alland; director, Andrew V. McLaglen; screenplay, Ric Hardman; art director, Al Ybarra; assistant director, Terry Morse, Jr., Tom Schmidt; camera, William H. Clothier; editor, Russell F. Schoengarth.

James Stewart (Burnett); Maureen O'Hara (Martha Price); Brian Keith (Bowen); Juliet Mills (Hilary); Don Galloway (Jamie); David Brian (Ellsworth); Jack Elam (Simons); Ben Johnson (Harter); Harry Carey, Jr. (Mabry); Perry Lopez (Juan); Larry Domasin (Alberto); Alan Caillou (Taylor).

HOW DO I LOVE THEE (Cinerama, 1970) C—109 M.

Producer, Everett Freeman, Robert Enders; director, Michael Gordon; based on the novel *Let Me Count the Ways* by Peter DeVries; screenplay, Freeman, Karl Tunberg; assistant director, Ted Swanson; art director, Walter M. Simonds; set decorator, Ned Parsons; music, Randy Sparks; music director, Jim Helms; song, Sparks and Freeman; camera, Russell Metty; editor, Ronald Sinclair.

Jackie Gleason (Stanley Waltz); Maureen O'Hara (Elsie Waltz); Shelley Winters (Lena Mervin); Rosemary Forsyth (Marion Waltz); Rick Lenz (Tom Waltz); Maurice Marsac (Bishop); Don Beddoe (Dr. Littlefield); Jack Nagle (Dean Bagley); J. Edward McKinley (Hugo Wellington).

BIG JAKE (National General, 1971) C—110 M.

Producer, Michael A. Wayne; director, George Sherman; screenplay, Harry Julian Fink, R. M. Fink; assistant director, Newton Arnold; costumes, Luster Bayless; makeup, David Grayson; art director, Carl Anderson; set decorator, Raymond Moyer; music, Elmer Bernstein; sound, John Ferguson; special effects, Howard Jensen; camera, William Clothier; editor, Harry Gerstad.

John Wayne (Jacob McCandles); Richard Boone (John Fain); Maureen O'Hara (Martha McCandles); Patrick Wayne (James McCandles); Chris Mitchum (Michael McCandles); Bobby Vinton (Jeff McCandles); Bruce Cabot (Sam Sharpnose); Glenn Corbett (O'Brien); Harry Carey, Jr. (Pop Dawson); John Doucette (Buck Dugan); Jim Davis (Head of Lynching Party); John Agar (Bert Ryan); Gregg Palmer (John Goodfellow); Robert Warner (Will Fain); Jim Burk (Trooper); Dean Smith (Kid Duffy); John Ethan Wayne (Little Jake McCandles); Virginia Capers (Delilah); William Walker (Moses Brown); Jerry Gatlin (Stubby); Tom Hennesy (Saloon Brawler); Don Epperson (Saloon Bully); Everett Creach (Walt Devries); Jeff Wingfield (Billy Devries); Hank Worden (Hank); Chuck Roberson (Texas Ranger); Roy Jenson (Tracker); John McLiam (Officer); Bernard Fox (Scotch Sheepman).

Maureen O'Hara in 1939

In THEY MET IN ARGENTINA
(RKO '41)

With Charles Laughton in JAMAICA INN (Par '39)

With Sara Allgood and Donald Crisp in HOW GREEN WAS MY VALLEY (20th '41)

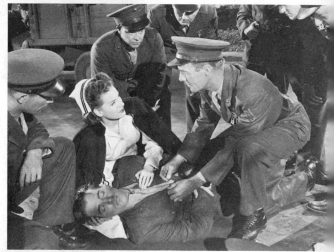

With John Payne and Randolph Scott in TO THE SHORES OF TRIPOLI (20th '42)

With Charles Laughton in THIS LAND IS MINE (RKO '43)

With John Banner, Sam Goldenberg, John Garfield, and Walter Slezak in THE FALLEN SPARROW (RKO '43)

With John Payne in
SENTIMENTAL JOURNEY
(20th '46)

With Paul Harvey, *right,* in
DO YOU LOVE ME? (20th '46)

With Douglas Fairbanks, Jr. in
SINBAD THE SAILOR (RKO '47)

With Hugo Haas, Rex
Harrison, and Richard Haydn
in THE FOXES OF HARROW
(20th '47)

With husband Will Price in 1948

With Robert Young and
Clifton Webb in SITTING
PRETTY (20th '48)

In THE FORBIDDEN STREET
(20th '49)

With Ian MacDonald,
Macdonald Carey, and Parley
Baer in COMANCHE
TERRITORY (Univ '50)

With Barry Fitzgerald in
THE QUIET MAN
(Republic '52)

With Tyrone Power in
THE LONG GRAY LINE
(Col '55)

With Kathryn Givney in
LADY GODIVA (Univ '55)

With brothers Charles and James FitzSimons in September, 1957

With Paul Roebling, Juliet Mills, and Leo Genn in MRS. MINIVER (CBS-TV, January 7, 1959)

With Alec Guinness in OUR MAN IN HAVANA (Col '60)

With James Stewart in MR.
HOBBS TAKES A VACATION
(20th '62)

With John Wayr
MC LINTOCK! (UA

With Rossano Brazzi in THE
BATTLE OF THE VILLA
FIORITA (WB '65)

With husband Charles
in March.

Tennessee Ernie Ford and Betty Grable on *Fabulous Fordies* (NBC-TV,
uary 29, 1972)

A pinup pose, c. 1943

5'7"
132 pounds
Brown hair
Brown eyes
Gemini

Jane
Russell

For most people the chief allure of Jane Russell has always been her amazingly buxom figure, in particular her thirty-eight-inch bustline. In case any potential filmgoer doubted the value of spending coin at the box office to ogle the natural wonders of Jane onscreen, RKO producer-director-owner Howard Hughes spent hundreds of thousands of dollars promulgating the uniqueness of Jane's breast size, making Jane the first movie star to ride onto a crest of popularity strictly through her mammary assets.

With this tremendous publicity concentration on Jane's anatomy, there was little opportunity for the public or the film industry to correctly determine what other professional assets Jane might have to carry along her film career. She was frequently branded by the critics as a sneering stoneface of as tawdry a character as her films, and a person with a one-dimensional acting quotient. As a distinct credit to Jane, she herself remained unperturbed by the shower of international attention on her cheesecake qualifications, preferring to treat her natural endowments as a fortuitous gift of the Lord, and her film career as just a well-paying job.

As the decades passed and other well-stacked cinema beauties replaced Jane in movie popularity, she hoped that she might have the opportunity to express and experiment with her seasoned range of acting abilities. But the chances onscreen and onstage were few and far between. More frequently than not, the post-fifty-year-old Jane of today will snap about her show business career: "The whole thing was really an accident. . . . I've never had any of that [star] aggressiveness. I do things because I like to do them. . . . I'm impulsive but pliable."

The reasons for Ernestine Jane* Geraldine Russell's birth occurring in Bemidji, Minnesota, at 6 A.M. on June 21, 1921, are rather dramatic in origin. Jane's maternal forebears traced their arrival in North America back to Otto Reinhold Jacobi, a painter to the Prussian court who settled in Canada. Jane's mother, Geraldine Jacobi, was reared in Grand Forks, North Dakota, where she met her future husband, Roy William Russell, in high school. But several years would intervene before they married, because she had won two declamation medals in high school and persuaded her parents to send her to Emerson College of Drama and Oratory in Boston.† Upon graduation she found employment with two Boston stock companies where she remained until she was hired to play a lady-in-waiting in George Arliss' *Disraeli,* which was booked into Boston's Plymouth Theatre. Later Geraldine toured with Arliss in *Daddy Long Legs,* playing the role of Julia Pendleton. During the show's tour, Arliss's group offered a performance at an Army camp where First Lieutenant Roy Russell was then stationed. Although he and Geraldine had not seen each other in six years, they had corresponded regularly. Russell proposed marriage, and three days later (on March 22, 1918) they were wed in Kalamazoo, Michigan. Because Russell was to be sent overseas, the twenty-seven-year-old Geraldine rejoined the Arliss tour. But she had to quit the show in Toronto when she learned she was pregnant. She returned to her parents' home in Grand Forks. When Russell was demobilized in November of 1918 the couple moved to Edmonton, Canada, where he had obtained a post with a stockbrokerage firm. There their first-born child, a son, took ill and died at the age of fifteen months. Disconsolate Geraldine planned to resume her theatre career as a diversion, but found that she was again pregnant, and so, instead, she returned to her parents' care; they were then summering at Bemidji, Minnesota.

When Mrs. Russell and little Jane returned to Edmonton, Mr. Russell had already begun a builders'-supply business. When it failed, the Russells decided to move to California, where Mrs. Russell's sister and brother-in-law were engaged in the real-estate business in Glendale. On April 7, 1922, the Russells arrived in San Francisco by ship from Vancouver, but it was several months before Mr. Russell could obtain adequate employment. He eventually was

*The Jane part of her name was in honor of actress Jane Cowl.

†Cinema writer Ray Hagen unearthed the fact that while at Emerson, Geraldine posed for a painting by her art teacher, Mary B. Titcimb. *Portrait of Geraldine J* has an interesting history: after being exhibited at the 1915 Panama-Pacific Exposition in San Francisco, it was hung in the White House, and later Woodrow Wilson's widow rehung it over the fireplace in her home in Washington, D.C.

hired by the Andrew Jergens Company to replace an office manager in their Los Angeles office. They purchased a home in Burbank and had four additional children: Tommy (1924), Kenny (1925), Jamie (1927), and Wally (1929). Meanwhile in 1924, Mrs. Russell organized classes in elocution and drama for the neighborhood youth, convinced that some phase of theatre should always be part of her life.

By 1932 Mr. Russell had risen to general manager of Jergens's West Coast factory, and the family moved to Van Nuys, where, on an eight-acre plot near Foothill Boulevard, they built a Mexican-type ranch house. With her own rambunctious personality and four energetic younger brothers, it was no wonder that gangly Jane would spend most of her childhood as a dominating tomboy, her favorite game being to play Dead-by-the-roadside (much to the annoyance of gullible passers-by). Not that Mrs. Russell allowed Jane to ignore the cultural aspects of life. Jane learned to play the piano as part of the Russell family orchestra, while on occasion she performed at neighborhood functions. In her Van Nuys High School class play, Jane played the lead in *Shirt Sleeves*.

By the time Jane graduated from high school she had already decided upon a career. "The subjects at school in which I was any good were art, drama and music," Jane clearly recalls. "Well my mother was an actress, so to rebel from the start, I decided on being a designer." But Jane's father died in 1937 after a gallstone operation, and it was necessary for her to help support the family. She took a $10-a-week job as a chiropodist's receptionist. To supplement this salary, the now physically mature Jane* began modeling outergarments for photographer Tom Kelly (who later lensed the famed calendar shots of Marilyn Monroe).

Jane candidly admits that "the whole show business thing was really an accident." By 1940 she had saved up enough money to at long last begin a design course. "The school I went to on a Friday with my tuition check told me to come back Monday. During the weekend I went to see a friend who was studying drama, decided I'd do that instead and gave them the money on Monday." Egged on by her mother, Jane enrolled at Max Reinhardt's Theatrical Workshop, but after one term switched to Maria Ouspenskaya's school, where she studied for six months.† Through Mme Ouspenskaya's industry connections, Jane was given screen tests at both Warner Bros. and Twentieth Century-Fox, but nothing materialized.

Then two Howards (Hawks and Hughes) entered Jane's life and nothing was ever the same again. When iconoclastic billionaire Hughes decided to return to filmmaking in 1939 after a seven-year absence, he hit upon the triangular love story of outlaws Billy the Kid, Doc Holliday, and the half-breed

---

*Her dimensions were 38-24-36.

†Jane's recollections of dramatic classes with the great teacher are rather sketchy. She does remember: "One day Ouspenskaya told all of us to imagine we were egg beaters. We felt awfully silly at first. She says if you can do things like that you can do almost anything in the presence of others and not be embarrassed."

girl Rio. Hughes signed Hawks, who had directed his prior production, *Scarface* (1932), to handle the new production. Both Hughes and Hawks favored utilizing newcomers for the leads, and merrily initiated a talent hunt. At one point, Leatrice Joy Gilbert, the daughter of film celebrities John Gilbert and Leatrice Joy, was set for the Rio role, then Jane Russell burst onto the scene. It has never been conclusively determined whether it was Hawks or Hughes who actually discovered Jane. Hawks has repeatedly stated that one day he was visiting a doctor's office in Van Nuys and spotted receptionist Jane wasting away behind the secretarial desk. Other sources suggest that agent Levis Green, knowing of Hughes's girlhunt, showed some of photographer Tom Kelly's camera work of Jane to Hughes's talent staff, and that eventually Hughes was made aware of the photographs and the girl.* Whatever the real facts may be, Hughes did sign Jane to a seven-year contract, which started at $50 weekly and provided for annual escalations and revisions.

But publicity-conscious Hughes, who had hired public relations genius Russell Birdwell to helm the campaign for his new western, did not immediately announce that Jane was to be the female star of the forthcoming picture. It was too much fun "discovering" new luscious dolls to be methodically considered for the role.† Finally in the fall of 1940 it was officially disclosed that newcomers Jane and Buetel were to star in a new Howard Hughes film entitled (eventually) *The Outlaw* and that they would be supported by veterans Walter Huston (Doc Holliday) and Thomas Mitchell (Sheriff Pat Garrett). Hawks took his cast and crew to Moencopi, Arizona, near Yuma, and production finally got underway.‡

Early in the actual shooting of *The Outlaw,* Birdwell began his hard-sell ballyhooing of Jane to the public, proclaiming her to be the new Jean Harlow. "Before I even went on location for the picture," Jane remembers, "they started giving me the buildup. I christened boats, I judged baby contests, I reclined in haystacks, I sprawled on beaches—always in a low-cut blouse." It was not long before Jane became a leading contender in the cheesecake sweepstakes, climaxed for some admirers when the Anthropology Club of Harvard College named her Miss Anatomy of the first half of the twentieth century. Once the film company was actually on location for the highly touted

*According to Noah Dietrich, Hughes's business aide, it was at this point that Hughes said, "Today I saw the most beautiful pair of knockers I've ever seen in my life."

†Cinematographer Lucien Ballard told Leonard Maltin, as quoted in *Behind the Camera* (1971): "We filmed those tests on 16mm in Hughes' basement. . . . Hughes had already picked the two he wanted, but we went ahead anyway. So after a while I told Howard I wanted to do some tests of my own, and I took Jane Russell, because she'd been hanging around me for a while, always asking why I did that and why I did this—she was just a kid at the time. So Howard said OK, and asked me to use Jack Buetel, who he liked quite a bit for the role. Anyway I made these tests in the haystack, used cross-lights so her tits show big, and Hughes went wild for it. I didn't know it then, but he had a thing for tits; he had the scene made into a loop, and he'd run it over and over again. So anyway, he cancelled the two people he'd signed for the leads, and decided to use Jane Russell and Jack Buetel.

‡By this point Hughes had almost given up trying to beat MGM, which had a similarly storied western, to the finish line. Metro's *Billy the Kid,* with Robert Taylor, Brian Donlevy, and Mary Howard, debuted at the Capitol Theatre on June 19, 1941.

The Outlaw, the publicity campaign took on even greater dimensions. Jane found herself constantly posing on and off the set for cameramen, usually with the cameras' lenses aimed down her cleavage. One time the crafty photographers had the naive, nineteen-year-old, blouse-clad Jane bend over to pick up two pails of water, then snap went the cameras. "Or else," Jane recalls, "they would tell me to jump up and down in bed in the nightgown while they shot from above and below. I didn't realize what they were doing. I was green as grass." Jane soon caught on to the reporters' ploys and in tears ran to Hawks, who advised her: "You're a big girl. You have to learn to say no to those photographers."

The Outlaw was in production for just over a week when Hughes suddenly arrived on the set and began taking greater and greater interest in the directorial aspects. Hawks grew exasperated, particularly when Hughes issued an edict that the film must be a much more elaborate picture in all departments. Hawks threw in the towel and gave his notice, and, as expected, Hughes gleefully took over as director. Filming would continue for several more months, with takes and retakes of the indoor scenes usually being lensed between the hours of 3 P.M. and midnight to comply with Hughes's predilections. All told, *The Outlaw,* originally budgeted at $440,000, snowballed into a $3.4 million production before it was finally completed in November, 1941.

Even before actual shooting began on *The Outlaw,* Hughes was engulfed with the Motion Picture Producers and Distributors of America (a.k.a. the Hays Office) in difficulties over his script, which the Hays Office insisted must be altered if it were to be approved. Hughes listened to their solemn advice and then proceeded to lens the proscribed sequences. In May, 1941, he submitted the completed master copy of *The Outlaw* to the Hays Office and was promptly told to snip a scene here and there. He refused, appealed, and then, when the matter had seemingly been milked dry of publicity value, he relented and made the change. Code approval was bestowed, but then Hughes had a better idea. Why not withhold distribution of *The Outlaw* for an indefinite period, simultaneously feeding the public with titillating tidbits of items about the alleged morally controversial nature of the sagebrush tale? In his heart of hearts Hughes knew *The Outlaw* was not a cinematic masterpiece nor strong enough on its own as a word-of-mouth audience-grabber. This deceptively coy campaign was put into execution with a brilliance that warranted Russell Birdwell receiving his own special Oscar. Finally Hughes announced the world premiere of *The Outlaw* for February 5, 1943, at the Geary Theatre in San Francisco.

To tout the long-awaited opening, a huge billboard sign was erected outside the theatre, depicting newcomer Jane in an exceedingly languorous pose, capped by a caption which read "Sex has not been rationed" and a qualifying phrase that *The Outlaw* was "the picture that couldn't be stopped." (These advertisements had deliberately not been submitted to the Hays Office.) On opening night an obviously nervous Jane and Jack Buetel made personal appearances on the Geary's stage, greeted the audience, and then walked into the wings, as the house lights darkened and the movie unreeled on screen.

By today's standards *The Outlaw* is an exceedingly tame story, even with its overabundance of puerile sexual overtones.* But the World War II-weary audiences of 1943 had not been subjected to an oversatiation of cheap pornography, and the promise of deviations from standard Hollywood filmfare was sufficient to drag in over 300,000 paying customers during the seven weeks *The Outlaw* played in San Francisco.† The feature might have played in San Francisco indefinitely, but after the first day's showing, the local chief of police hit the scene, prompted by outraged protests from the San Francisco branch of the Legion of Decency, whose national office had condemned the film. Despite a police ban on the film, the movie continued to be shown while Hughes's attorneys won a court order permitting the film to be publicly screened. It was at Hughes's order that *The Outlaw* was withdrawn from distribution at the end of its self-shortened San Francisco engagement. He had whetted the public's appetite and wished to build further audience anticipation before saturating the film in national release.

Self-appointed critics took the cue from the rhubarb in San Francisco, and soon everyone was getting into the act by supporting or decrying the morality of *The Outlaw*. Most of the ruckus stemmed from the deliberately alluring photographing of Jane's breastwork, with the cameras continually dollying in on her billowing bosom (which led one critic to advise, "They forgot to milk her!").‡ The censors were particularly upset by the ranch-bedroom sequence

---

*The plot of *The Outlaw* is as follows: Outlaw William Bonny (Jack Buetel), known as Billy the Kid, was not killed as legend has it, but continued on. In Lincoln, New Mexico, the Kid claims ownership of a strawberry roan, which Doc Holliday (Walter Huston), a cardsharp, gunman, and deputy sheriff, insists is his. The two men argue. Later the Kid is at the livery stable, where he is shot at by the half-breed Rio (Jane), who wants revenge for the Kid having killed her brother in a gunfight. Her shot misses its target. The next day sheriff Pat Garrett (Thomas Mitchell) attempts to arrest the Kid and in the gunplay the outlaw is wounded. Holliday comes to his rescue and rides him to the ranch where Holliday is staying with Rio and her Aunt Guadalupe (Mimi Aguglia). Rio nurses the wounded lawbreaker, and soon they fall tempestuously in love and secretly wed. Holliday senses what is going on and, disgusted with the display of non-loyalty by the Kid, denounces him, but again helps him to escape into the desert from the sheriff's pursuing posse. There the Kid and Holliday discover that Rio has filled both their canteens with sand, demonstrating her contempt for each of her men. Later Garrett captures Holliday, and at a further point in the tale he is forced to shoot his old friend during an escape attempt. Meantime the Kid has corraled Rio, planning his own physical revenge, but thinking better of it, frees her. After tricking Garrett, who is left handcuffed to the porch pillar of Rio's ranch, the Kid and Rio ride off into the sunset. (A twenty-minute epilog was excised before this initial public engagement.)

†Three weeks at the Geary and an additional four at the Tivoli Theatre, with a gross of over $158,000.

‡Jane has always insisted that the elaborately "leaked" story of Hughes having developed a special brassiere for her to wear in *The Outlaw* and thereafter was and is sheer nonsense. Which leads one to question Murray Schumach's statements in *The Face on the Cutting Room Floor* (1964): "The camera explored Miss Russell's cleavage during the rape, and even more in the bed-warming scene. He [Hughes] even put generous shares of her bosom on display when she was riding a horse, moving around a fire or bound for whipping." At one point in the production of *The Outlaw,* Schumach insists Hughes said: "We're not getting enough production out of Jane's breasts." Then adds Schumach: "The designer of planes repaired to his drawing board. He designed a special bra for Miss Russell that would make the breasts more revealing than ever, but keep them from bobbing about too much and spoiling their contours."

in which Jane, clad in an ill-fitting blouse, bends over Buetel's bed and leans forward looking into a mirror. Accentuating the mammary-oriented nature of *The Outlaw* were the special advertisements prepared for the movie, one famous pose having scanty-white-blouse-clad Jane standing in front of a haystack with gams planted firmly apart and a pistol in each clenched fist. The ad copy for this layout read: "Mean, Moody and Magnificent."*

During all this scrimmaging over *The Outlaw,* a picture more talked about than seen during World War II, Jane, along with such established cinema personalities as Betty Grable, Lana Turner, Dorothy Lamour, and Paulette Goddard, had become one of the most popular pinup beauties of armed-services troops everywhere.† An extraordinary feat for Jane, considering that the general public had yet to see her in even one film.

Poor Jane, who was anxious to prove herself to the public as something more than an abstract sex symbol, found herself relegated to the cinematic sidelines for the duration. Hughes had decided that he did not want his valuable "property" to lose her potential publicity value by making her national screen "debut" in any other film before *The Outlaw* was put into full release. Thus he refused Darryl F. Zanuck's offer to pay him $35,000 a week for Jane to appear as Dona Sol in Twentieth Century-Fox's bullfighting epic, *Blood and Sand* (1941). Rita Hayworth was substituted instead. Other offers poured in, but Hughes pointedly refused each and every one of them for an assortment of well-heralded reasons. Boss Hughes did have the good sense to send his histrionically untutored employee for dramatic lessons with Florence Enright and other coaches. It helped pass the time for Jane, as she struggled week after week to gain the desired sense of screen poise and personality. Another incentive to develop talents beyond those supplied by Mother Nature was Jane's awareness that at any time the mercurial Hughes might whimsically substitute one of his constant stream of movie "discoveries" in her spot on the future film-star totem pole, and at that time she would need other assets to display if she wished to remain a viable item in the movie game.

In sharp contrast to Jane's well-promoted hyper-sex-symbol status was her apple-pie romance with her high school sweetheart, Bob Waterfield, who had become the star quarterback for the Cleveland Rams football team. She had met him when she was fourteen, began steadily dating him when she was seventeen, and now at twenty she eloped with Waterfield to Las Vegas (on April 24, 1943) to be wed. At this time he was certainly a far more proven commodity in his field than Jane was in hers. Three weeks after their marriage, Waterfield, inducted into the Army, was off to Officer Candidate School at Fort Benning, Georgia. A week later Jane followed him to nearby Columbus, where she filled her idle days by working in a beauty parlor and participating in local war-bond drives. Although Hughes had no movie assignments

---

*As Jane later evaluated this merchandising campaign: "They sold me like a can of tomatoes."

†Said a most demure Jane at the time: "A pin-up reputation is a very flattering thing, and I am happy if some of my stills have helped brighten life for the boys. But that isn't a career. I want to act." A decade later a more outspoken, conservative Jane spoke forth about 1950s pinups: "They're going too far—and too vulgar."

on the immediate agenda for Jane, he promptly put her on suspension, with-holding her $75 weekly paycheck.

In 1945 Waterfield received a medical discharge from the Army and the couple returned to California. Jane re-established her professional relationship with Hughes, who had not been idle in the film field (having dabbled momen-tarily with the careers of Jane Greer and Terry Moore, while focusing a good deal of attention on promoting the cinema potential of Faith Domergue). Hughes weakened in his insistence on keeping Jane professionally under wraps—the national release of *The Outlaw* was now in the offing—and acceded to the importuning of producer Hunt Stromberg to loan out Jane for the title role in *Young Widow* (United Artists, 1946). Hughes majestically announced that *Young Widow* was "the best woman's part in ten years" and proceeded to finance part of the picture's production costs, along with Ida Lupino, whose ex-husband, Louis Hayward, was to co-star in the tearjerker. Jane, who had returned to acting classes with Florence Enright, confided to columnist Hedda Hopper: "Hedda, I feel this chance I'm getting in *Young Widow* is a debut instead of a comeback because the public never saw me, only a few people in San Francisco. They saw an awkward, bewildered girl. I really didn't know what it was all about. As I look back at it now it's just a haze of vague recol-lections, like trying to recapture the essence of a dream. I feel I've matured a lot since then."

Just before the much-discussed *Young Widow* was scheduled for public viewing, Hughes relaunched *The Outlaw*. Hughes arranged a public appear-ance tour for Jane and had his business associate, producer-director-scenarist Preston Sturges, pen special material to bridge Jane's pointed singing of "It Had to Be You," "Bye Bye Blues," and "Talk of the Town." United Artists, which was releasing *Young Widow,* was given the distribution rights to *The Outlaw* and at Hughes's urging, a fresh publicity campaign was ground out for the western, again featuring breast-oriented poses of Jane, but with a new caption: "What are the TWO great reasons for Russell's success?" Civic protest to this promotional tactic arose across America. The Code seal, which Hughes had finagled in 1941, was suddenly revoked (much to Hughes's glee), and he was "forced" to take his civil liberties case to court in each state where the film was summarily banned. Judge Twain Michelsen told the San Fran-cisco jury that acquitted *The Outlaw* of an indecency charge: "We have seen Jane Russell. She is an attractive specimen of American womanhood. God made her what she is." But it was a different legal story in Baltimore, where the judge upheld a state ban on the picture, remarking that Jane's breasts "hung over the picture like a thunderstorm spread out over a landscape." The majority of the court decisions went against *The Outlaw*, forcing Hughes to withdraw the picture once again.

During this renewed contretemps over *The Outlaw, Young Widow* pre-miered at the pedestrian Globe Theatre. Almost until the time of its public bow *Young Widow* was ballyhooed in the same lofty terms as *Gone with the Wind,* suggesting that viewers were in for a rare cinematic treat. But as July

28, 1946, the date of *Young Widow*'s unveiling, came closer, the advertising campaign was suddenly switched, and it became all too clear that the new picture, like *The Outlaw,* would be little more than a physical showcase for Jane. The advertisements were now reading: "The World's Most Exciting Brunette . . . She can't help what she does to men. Nature made her that way." And producer Hunt Stromberg, who had used as many as three different directors on the project, now went on public record as saying he had had Jane's anatomy "psychoanalyzed" for the film project. The publicity releases went on to say that special custom-made suits from an undisclosed Oregon knitting mill had been ordered to properly encase Jane's monumental figure and that, yes, by popular demand, she did wear a sheer black nightie in one sequence, and a tight-fitting bathing suit in another scene.

There was very little to recommend *Young Widow* beyond Jane's physically dynamic presence. The plot was stale,* the direction boorish, and the acting childish. First-billed Jane fared very poorly with the critics. Wanda Hale, in her two-star *New York Daily News* review, observed that the role of Joan Kenwood "should have been handed to a more experienced actress. Or to one, who has at least a couple of changes of facial expression." The *New York Times* confirmed: "Miss Russell's expressions and her written lines add little to this neophyte's trite and flat role." A disgusted Boston film journalist later snapped: "If the young widow had [only] died when the husband did, the picture need never have been made."

After the all-around letdown of *Young Widow* Jane found herself faced with another long filmmaking hiatus. Hughes was again firm that she would make no more pictures until *The Outlaw* had seen the light of movie screens everywhere. Jane became so bored and restless with her overflow of free time that she took up interior decorating and started her own business. She also was tired of public appearance tours on which "they always gave me some corny speech to make. I felt ridiculous." She absolutely refused to hit the road

---

*The flat plot is as follows: When Jane's pilot husband is killed in a mission over Berlin during World War II, she returns to the United States from England, where he had been based. Kent Taylor, managing editor of the newspaper on which she and her husband had worked, greets her in New York and offers her the old job back any time she wants to work. But Jane rejects this option, insisting that she must return to the Virginia farm where she and her late spouse had shared some happy moments. Haunting memories soon force Jane to leave the farm, and on the train back to Manhattan she meets Louis Hayward. Much as she likes him, she is fearful of a new romance drowning out the memories of her past love. Jane settles into the New York City apartment of Marie Wilson and Penny Singleton and agrees to take up her old newspaper post. Just when life is falling into a comfortable rut she runs into Hayward again, and they begin dating. She even changes her mind about having a steady affair with him, as demonstrated by her telling her pal, Faith Domergue, not to break her own engagement to a serviceman for fear of becoming a war widow. Later Hayward proposes to Jane in a Southampton Beach scene. She is about to accept, when suddenly she hears the strains of the tune that she and her husband had called "their song." A dejected Hayward is ordered overseas. Jane arrives at the airport too late to see him off. Her good friend Kent Taylor expresses his opinion that this is a rotten break, but Jane disagrees, saying, "It was meant to be that way," and that besides she is not yet ready for another marriage. If and when she is ready, she knows in her heart, Hayward will return.

again unless she could perform as a full-fledged songstress.* Hughes relented, and Jane prepared a new vocalizing act, which she tried out for a week at the Latin Quarter Club in Miami Beach at a $15,000 salary. Thereafter she made a guest appearance on "Kay Kyser's Kollege of Fun and Knowledge" radio show (ABC, January, 1947) and was so well received that the bandleader signed her to a twelve-week stint on his program. At this time she recorded "Boin-n-ng" and "If My Heart Had a Window" as a single disc for Columbia Records, followed by an album of eight torch-style ballads for the same label.†

To the general public Jane was known as a very erotic sex object, a sex goddess with no illusory veil of romance to soften her image. But offcamera, to her small circle of friends and acquaintances, she was best associated with her mother's Chapel in the Valley, in which the self-ordained Mrs. Russell conducted religious services for friends and local folk. Two of the most constant attendees were Chili Williams, the erstwhile "Polkadot Girl," and Gail Russell, actress and divorced wife of Guy Madison. Both girls claimed that Mrs. Russell's ministerial work helped them to overcome their severe drinking problems.

At the time the press did not choose to emphasize Jane's sincere religious interest, but was willing to quote her frequently on the subject of matrimony, reasoning that the acknowledged sex bomb might have some worthwhile pointers for less-endowed distaff readers. Jane, always unimpressed by the extraordinary news coverage given her anatomy, was content to answer the press questions to the best of her simple knowledge. She theorized that her domestic bliss must be due to the fact that she and Waterfield were contrasting types: "He's a boy, I'm a girl. He's conservative—that's the English in him. I'm not—maybe that's the Polish in me. He likes sports, except the ones I like—swimming and riding. Football I can take so much of and no more. He loves golf. I loathe it. . . . Robert doesn't know or want to know from art, music and drama. We have huge arguments about it, and that's all, no nagging, no picking."

At this critical point in Jane's meandering film career,‡ she had the good fortune of coming to the professional attention of Bob Hope, a past master at employing beautiful leading ladies to good advantage in his screen comedies. Hughes wisely agreed to loan Jane to Paramount for the Technicolor comedy *The Paleface,* which would open as the holiday attraction at the Paramount Theatre on December 15, 1948. In this western spoof Jane was second-billed as outlaw Calamity Jane who, in the 1870s, is paroled by law-enforcers in order to accomplish a special mission out west. She is to track down a gang of smugglers who are selling rifles to the rampaging Indians. When Jane stumbles across a bumbling correspondence-school dentist, one Painless

---

*A popular quip of the time was, "You can't take your eyes off her voice."

†The LP, *Let's Put Out the Lights,* contained: "Body and Soul," "I Must Have That Man!," "Let's Put Out the Lights," "Do It Again," "Love For Sale," "Two Sleepy People," "A Hundred Years from Today," and "Until the Real Thing Comes Along."

‡In 1971 Jane would state: "*The Outlaw* typed me and set a pattern that I could never break. I never had a chance to do really good movies. I never had any choice in my pictures. When you are under contract, you must do the movies they order you to do."

Peter Potter (Hope), she hastily weds him in order to give herself a cover-up identity. Throughout the course of this sight-gag comedy, it is dead-shot Jane (she packs her pistols in petticoat holsters) who fends off the Indians and the desperadoes, allowing buffoon Hope to take the credit and garner the admiration of the townsfolk. By the finale she realizes Hope is a man of courage —of sorts—and her former contempt turns to true love.

One of the best assets of *The Paleface* is the fun poked at Jane's sex image. This approach provided Jane with a far more human, realistic frame of reference within which to work. For example, on first meeting Jane, Hope quips: "Now I know what Horace Greeley meant!" One of the standing gags of the film is that everytime Hope and Jane embrace, Ski Nose literally passes out, for she accompanies each kiss with a crack on the back of his head with her gun-butt (so she can attend to her government business unhampered by clumsy Hope). The typical Hope-ian sexual innuendoes aimed at Jane's shapely presence seemed to buoy her performance, inducing her to give a far more lively, flippant accounting than she would ever again exert oncamera.* Jane sometimes fumbled her comic lines, and occasionally resorted to being a tall, dark, and sullenly expressionless mannequin, but as master comedian Hope phrased it: "Don't let her fool you. Tangle with her and she'll shingle your attic." *The Paleface* did just dandy at the box office, grossing over $4.5 million in domestic net rentals.

Jane was not so lucky with her two other 1948 films. *Montana Belle* was made on loan to Fidelity Pictures and filmed by director Allan Dwan at Republic Studios in Truecolor. When Hughes saw the completed results, he purchased the picture for some $600,000 and shelved its release indefinitely. Having taken over control of RKO, Hughes utilized the facilities to team Jane with Frank Sinatra and Groucho Marx in *It's Only Money,* but the finished product seemed so tepid—and both Sinatra and Marx were undergoing bad spells in their careers—that it too was shelved.

But no one could shelve the real-life Jane, and at the Academy Award ceremonies in 1949 she was a resounding success, singing the tune "Buttons and Bows," which had been performed by Bob Hope in *The Paleface* and would win an Oscar as the best song of the movie year. That September, when Hughes unleashed *The Outlaw* for a third go-round, Jane made a personal appearance on the stage of the Broadway Theatre where it was being showcased. Nearly nine years after its completion Jane's celebrated appearance in *The Outlaw* was finally being officially reviewed by the full estate of New York critics.‡ The *New York Times* said Jane "is undeniably decorative

*Howard Barnes (*New York Herald-Tribune*) was able to report: "Miss Russell does not exactly act in the part of Calamity Jane, but she is extremely effective in underlying the ludicrous quality of the show."

†Universal would remake *The Paleface* as *The Shakiest Gun in the West* (1968), starring Don Knotts.

‡Screen historians William K. Everson and George N. Fenin in *The Western* (1962): "One of the better film biographies of Billy the Kid (no more accurate than the others, but less sentimentalized), it would in fact have been a *very* good Western but for the obtrusive eroticism. . . . Many looked upon the film as a deliberate insult to womanhood, specifically pointing out the scene in which Billy and Doc Holliday gamble and cannot decide whether the winner should take Rio or a horse."

in low-cut blouses, [but she] is hopelessly inept as an actress," while the *New York Herald-Tribune* remarked: "She is far from persuasive and none too attractive. Her sultry advances to the young desperado are more amusing than licentious." But still the public was curious to see what the "celluloid turkey" was all about, and *The Outlaw* grossed over $3 million in its 6,153 domestic engagements, and an additional $1.5 million in foreign distribution. Later Hughes, as he had done with *Scarface,* would withdraw the picture from theatrical release. *The Outlaw* has yet to be made available for television showings.

With *The Outlaw* finally in her past, Jane journeyed to London in October, 1949, to present her stage act at the Princess Theatre, singing an assortment of pop standards, including such provocatively titled tunes as "Look What They've Done to Me." When she returned to the United States, Jane joined with Bob Hope in a March, 1950, engagement at the Paramount Theatre. In their relaxed, bantering act, she clowned with the quipster, and sang "Great Day" and "The Lady Is a Tramp." Jane was not entirely absent from the screen in 1950. She was to be briefly seen in Columbia's 9½-minute short subject *Hollywood Rodeo,* along with such other oncamera western stars as John Wayne and Gene Autry.

By 1950 Howard Hughes had weeded so much so-called chaff from RKO that the studio threatened to die of staff malnutrition, let alone of deficits in the financial end. Of the thirty-two features released that year, two were from Samuel Goldwyn's stable (*Our Very Own, Edge of Doom*), two from Walt Disney (*Cinderella, Treasure Island*), two were European-made imports (*Stromboli, The Tattooed Stranger*), four were low-budget westerns, and the rest comprised an assortment of mild product ranging from John Ford's *Wagonmaster* to anemic efforts by three former cinema queens (Claudette Colbert in *Secret Fury,* Irene Dunne in *Never a Dull Moment,* and Joan Fontaine in *Born to Be Bad*). Included in this bundle of semi-junk were two pictures starring Jane's chief competitor on the RKO lot. *Where Danger Lives* and the much-revised *Vendetta* both were geared to spotlight Hughes's enduring protégée, Faith Domergue, but they demonstrated instead that Hughes's forte was obviously airlines and not would-be screen luminaries. No matter what he may have wished and no matter how much of the RKO money he cavalierly spent (especially on the ill-fated *Vendetta*), the public remained persistently indifferent to the uncrystalized screen charms offered by Miss Domergue. (Nor did Hughes fare much better with another infatuation, Miss Janet Leigh, whom he borrowed from MGM to star in *Holiday Affair* [1949], the tattered, anachronistic musical *Two Tickets to Broadway* [1951], and the Josef von Sternberg-directed fiasco *Jet Pilot,* not released until 1957, seven years after its making on the RKO lot.)

Notwithstanding these poor showings by her rivals on the RKO payroll, Jane was in none too strong a professional position in 1950. In five times at the cinematic bat she had struck out with *Young Widow,* been walked twice with two shelved pictures, received a no-play decision for her nonacting appearance in *The Outlaw,* and only on loan-out to Paramount had made a hit with *The Paleface* (and the umpires insisted that was only due to the co-starring presence of Bob Hope). Therefore when Jane appeared on the RKO soundstages in the spring of 1950 to start *His Kind of Woman,** her future was very much in the air. If the picture did not click at the box office—even modestly, for it was not an expensive production—Jane could well have been washed up in Hollywood and allowed to pasturize by chameleon Hughes. Given these circumstances, she was indeed fortunate to have experienced director John Farrow to helm her new project and, more importantly, to have the boosting presence of RKO's hottest marquee attraction, Robert Mitchum, as her screen partner.†

His Kind of Woman is perhaps the most typical of all Jane's RKO vehicles, displaying every facet of her screen persona showcased against the full backdrop of RKO production values, cut-rate 1950s style. As was its frequent penchant, the studio opted for a south-of-the-border setting of a dude ranch somewhere beyond Nogales, Mexico, although nearly all the sets—outdoor and indoor—were constructed on the studio soundstages. Professional gambler Mitchum is on his way to the resort to collect a $50,000 fee in exchange for carrying out an unspecified job. On a stopover at a small airport he saunters into a nearby cafe, where he chances upon Jane. She is a sight to behold in her Michael Woulfe outfit: a revealing ensemble complete with a white-collar top, a spray of flowers at her cleavage, and ankle-strap shoes. Sleepy-eyed Mitchum takes a good gander at Jane, missing no detail of her expansive geography, but she initially pays no heed for she is nonchalantly singing "Five Little Miles from San Perdoo" (performed in a very relaxed, professional style). Obviously director Farrow was not intimidated by Jane's renowned immobile face for he pans in on her for several close-ups during the catchy number. A few minutes later Jane, now modeling a pointed coolie hat, and trenchcoat-clad Mitchum find themselves the sole passengers on the same small plane heading for the resort.

In the course of the flight Jane informs Mitchum, "I'm what you call a spoiled child and rich." (Obviously no one ever told or showed her how to dress properly.) In a later bit of plane-side chitchat Mitchum tosses out a gem of spoken ambiguity that can be interpreted a myriad of ways, even to scriptwriter Frank Fenton poking unsubtle fun at Hughes's protégée. Mitchum drawls in his lackadaisical style, "I've heard better [referring to her informal jam session], but you sing like you do it for a living." A justly nonplused Jane allows this remark to slip by.

Once at the isolated resort ‡—and now the actual plot finally gets underway—Mitchum learns to his chagrin that he is to be the patsy for Raymond Burr, a

---

*Working title, *The Smiler with a Gun*; it completed production in May, 1950, and premiered at the Paramount Theatre on August 23, 1951.

†He received top, above-the-title, billing.

‡Furnished in accustomed barren, economical RKO style and filled with equally chintzy, stereotyped dress-extras and crackpot character-types.

Lucky Luciano-type gangster who had been deported from the United States and is now attempting a re-entry by assuming another person's identity via plastic surgery and doctored passports. And Jane, God love her, is not really a blueblood playgirl, despite her persistent "I spend most of my time on the Continent—Europe." Her grandfather was not a member of the Four Hundred social set but a barber of forty years, and she is really not Lenore Brent, but fortune-hunting Liz Brady, who had gone to Europe on a USO tour and one thing led to another and . . . RKO contract co-star Vincent Price was ideally cast as a hammy Hollywood matinee idol, fond of pretentious speech and vicarious high adventure, but less pleased that his dowdy estranged wife (Marjorie Reynolds) has seen fit to pursue him to the out-of-the-way ranch.

Before the black-and-white features completes its 120-minute course, Jane has sung "You'll Know," and reprised "Five Little Miles" in a beachside scene with Mitchum. In that awkwardly plotted sand bit, Jane modeled a strategically taut black bathing suit for the benefit of male filmgoers. (Not to ignore the distaff viewers, *His Kind of Woman* contains a sadistic sequence in which Mitchum, stripped to the waist, is mauled by Burr's henchmen.) For the climax of the picture Price leads a Wild West-style rescue squad of Mexican police to Burr's boat, by which the gangster and his men are disposed of and Mitchum rescued. The fade-out has Price, who had first met Jane at St. Moritz, decide to stick with Reynolds. Jane thereafter saunters into Mitchum's hotel room, where she finds him ironing a shirt (he always irons things when nervous or bored). As she relieves him of the iron and they kiss, she absent-mindedly allows the hot iron to scorch his shirt—get the rampant symbolism?—and then fade-out, "The End."

The advertising copy for *His Kind of Woman* carried an endorsement by Louella Parsons:* "The hottest combination that ever hit the screen." It was not exactly dynamite screen magic between Jane and Mitchum, but their joint presence was the one redeeming aspect of what the *New York Herald-Tribune* aptly defined as a "nonsensical melodramatic hodgepodge."† Mitchum provided his expected virile nonchalance coupled with histrionic understatement, which allowed Jane too full range to exercise her bag of cinematic guises: tough babe with a heart of gold, a liberated female who still craves to be dominated by a right guy, a former small-town innocent who has drifted into the morally ambiguous world of show business and now has the scars to prove her apprenticeship. What distinguished Jane's screen presence was her marvelously unpretentious attitude. She is totally un-self-conscious about her too-well-proportioned torso, equally unimpressed by her thrush abilities (modest as they are), and plainly aware that she may not be the most intellectual broad around town, and she is totally well intentioned. Whatever variations of these essential characteristics a script imposed on Jane's stated

---

*Daughter Harriet Parsons was then an RKO producer.

†A far cry from the conservative RKO of old, which would never have endorsed such a hogwild mixture of hokum and violence. But in the 1950s, with moviemaking Hollywood desperate for survival, anything went.

movie presence, they were at best fripperies that no one could take seriously for a moment.

"Treat yourself to a double exposure of fun and foolishness!" suggested the publicity for *Double Dynamite,* her next film, which debuted—three years after its completion—at the Paramount Theatre on Christmas Day, 1951. It was not a very generous holiday gift from RKO to the public. Meek bank-teller Frank Sinatra rescues a bookie (Nestor Paiva) about to be beaten up by hoods, and out of gratitude Paiva places a sure bet on a nag in Sinatra's name. The filly wins, and the suddenly $60,000 richer Sinatra can now afford a new car for himself and a mink coat for his bank co-worker and sweetheart, Mildred "Mibs" Goodhue (Jane). But it just so happens that back at the bank there has been a $75,000 shortage. Sinatra is concerned lest he be thought the culprit because of his sudden, unexplainable windfall, but it is Jane who is suspected because the shortage has registered on her adding machine. Eventually all does end happily, with Sinatra and Jane marrying. Bridging the lumbering plotline is Groucho Marx, appearing as Emile J. Keck, waiter at the local Italian bistro. His threadbare wisecracks and not-so-mobile raised eyebrows were the highlights of the picture. Sinatra sings "It's Only Money" as he and Groucho skip along to the bank one day, while Sinatra and Jane duet "Kisses and Tears."* They were not TNT tunes! Because Sinatra was then undergoing a prolonged period of professional unpopularity, he was played down in the promotion of *Double Dynamite* and Jane was top-billed. But she was not artistically equipped to carry the comedy burden. As the *New York Herald-Tribune* quipped, "Jane Russell tries so hard to act that it's touching, but farce is not her pianissimo." It certainly did not help visual matters—a strong factor in Jane Russell films—that Jane's wardrobe was several years out of style.

Midst the vicissitudes of her career, Jane was solving her domestic ambitions with much more success. She and her husband had wanted children for a long time, and finally in 1951 they decided to adopt one.† The adoption of their first child, a newly born girl named Tracy, was completed on February 15, 1952. Later in the year Jane made a well-publicized trip to England to find a new baby as a companion for Tracy. During her London stay, Jane was presented to the Royal Family. One day she was visited at her Savoy Hotel suite by Mrs. Michael Kavanaugh, the wife of an impoverished carpenter foreman who had read of Jane's baby search and suggested that Jane adopt her third child, fifteen-month-old Tommy, so he could "get a good home and a fine education." Jane was agreeable, but the case came to the attention of the English courts because of the British Child Adoption Act, which then forbade the adoption of any British subject by non-citizens who are not blood

---

*Later recorded for Columbia Records

†One of the ironies closely associated with the established sex symbols of the mid-twentieth century (Jane, Marilyn Monroe, Sophia Loren, Brigitte Bardot) is that they could (would?) not fulfill their natural functions as women by giving birth to children, or if they did, as in Loren's case, it was after several miscarriages.

relations. The Court, sternly announcing that its decision was not to be regarded as a precedent, allowed Jane to bring Tommy to America "as a visitor" and did not press charges against the Kavanaughs. In December, 1952, the Waterfields legally adopted Tommy.* At the time Waterfield, who was making a $20,000 annual salary as a gridiron star of the Los Angeles Rams, was about to retire from the playing field to become one of the team's head coaches.

Jane's busiest year onscreen was 1952 with five pictures in release. *The Las Vegas Story* (Paramount Theatre, January 30, 1952) unhappily teamed Jane with muscular but stolid Victor Mature in a corny romantic-triangle crime yarn, unfortified by the Nevada gambling capital backdrop. The reluctant story told of former cafe singer Jane, who has wed New York investment broker Vincent Price. She is disinclined to stop at Las Vegas, where, unknown to Price, she has a past. (Years before, when she had been a singer at the downtown Last Chance Club, she fell in love with Mature of the U.S. Air Force. When he went overseas without asking her to wed him, she married Price on the rebound.) It is not long before Price has amassed a huge gambling debt, and he is later accused of stealing his wife's $50,000 diamond necklace to pawn and get the eventual insurance recoupment. None other than local police officer Mature comes to Price's timely rescue. He makes it obvious that he still loves Jane. When she is kidnapped by Bradford Dexter, the actual culprit, Mature becomes frenzied with anger and charges across the desert after Dexter via a helicopter. The sleazy picture ends with Price turning out to be wanted back in New York on embezzlement and grand theft charges, which leaves Jane free to remain in Las Vegas, resume her old singing job, divorce Price, and renew her abortive relationship with Mature. In the course of the picture Jane offered renditions of "I Get Along without You Very Well" and "My Resistance Is Low." Much more effective as musical-interlude relief from the tedious plot was Hoagy Carmichael's rendition of his own novelty number, "The Monkey Song."

Nothing then—or even now in the rosy glow of nostalgia—glittered in *The Las Vegas Story,* certainly neither the innuendo-spiked dialog, the stiff leading man, nor Jane in a severely tailored wardrobe ("looking as though she had been first carved out and then lacquered," said the *New York Herald-Tribune*). Director Robert Stevenson brought out all the minus-values in Jane, permitting her to render a most unrelaxed performance.† Her scenes with Mature seemed more appropriate to something out of *Zombies on Parade.*

*Jane's experiences in adopting her child led to her organizing the Women's Adoption International Fund (WAIF), dedicated to assisting American couples in adopting foreign-born babies (because of the shortage of American children available for adoption). Co-founders of WAIF were Irene Dunne, Loretta Young, and June Allyson. WAIF later merged with the International Social Service, and the combined WAIF-ISS has been responsible for bringing to the United States, and providing homes for, over 19,000 orphans from all corners of the globe.

†"Miss Russell's figure, which is the sole prop of her acting career, seems to be the one consistent point of reference to which director Robert Stevenson turns throughout the film," reported the *New York Times*'s Bosley Crowther, who did not cotton to Jane's "petulant pout and twangy whine."

Howard Hughes mistakenly assumed that Josef von Sternberg had the proper directorial acumen and personal chemistry to work great improvements in Jane's screen image, and therefore assigned him to direct her in *Macao* (lensed between August and October, 1950, but not released until April 30, 1952, at the Paramount Theatre). Von Sternberg was twenty years away from structuring the box-office wonder of Marlene Dietrich in *Morocco* (1930). Not only was the veteran filmmaker having great difficulty adjusting to the changed social mores of post-World War II moviegoers, but he was in no way equipped to deal with the new-style production-line filmmaking in Hollywood, especially not under the dictatorial setup of Hughes, who displayed such minor regard for directors.*

The *Macao* that emerged onscreen was at best a routine exercise in melodrama. Certainly the ambience created by the blend of newsreel footage and soundstage sets did not at all suggest that Macao was an exotic, sinful, teeming Portuguese colony off the China coast. The unrealized plot opens with the arrival of a steamer in the port of Macao. Aboard are Robert Mitchum,† a former lieutenant in the Signal Corps who is still on the run because of a minor scrape he had back in New York and who has just lost his passport; Jane, a cabaret singer; and William Bendix, ostensibly a happy-go-lucky salesman. Soporific Mitchum expends a bit of unexpected energy just before the boat docks, for he is involved in a tangle with rambunctious Jane. After they each calm down he queries her about her past.

Jane: "Got any small questions? I don't warm up to questions when I don't know the answers myself."

Eventually she reveals that she had formerly been a cigarette girl and photographer at a Miami Beach club, then was a fortuneteller, and now is coasting along as a songstress. Once again Jane's character is self-indulgently introspective but refreshingly candid: "I was never considered a brain." "I'm a creature of moods." Her philosophy is: "Everybody's lonely, worried, and sorry. Everybody's looking for something. I don't know whether it's a person or a place. But I'll keep on looking." If Mitchum is impressed by her personality probe, his laconic expression gives no indication of such an interest.

Upon landing Jane is quickly hired by criminal Brad Dexter to chirp at his Club Quick Reward, much to the annoyance of his girlfriend and gaming-joint croupier, Gloria Grahame. Jane is soon at work, singing to the gambling crowd a version of "You Kill Me." Her sole facial expression for this number consists of rolling her eyes about in perpetual searching, as if to say, "Aw gee, what the heck. Here goes nothing." Meantime Dexter and his corrupt police crony, lieutenant Thomas Gomez, have been alerted that one of the three

---

* According to von Sternberg scholar Herman G. Weinberg, nearly all of *Macao* was reshot by Nicholas Ray, with little of von Sternberg's original intent left intact.

† Mitchum, again top-billed, had a good rapport with Jane, and quite enjoyed making pictures with her. He jokingly called her "Hard John" because of her total candor and her Runyonesque speech (her vocabulary included: *guys* for *men*, *dames* for *girls*, *malarky* for *flattery*, *just stuff* for *fame*, and "Old Stone Face" or "The Old Man" when referring to her husband.

newcomers is an undercover police officer sent to bring Dexter back to justice by tricking him into coming outside the three-mile limit of Macao (which has no extradition treaties). The criminal twosome assume that Mitchum is the law-enforcer when in reality it is burly Bendix. The latter is killed by error when Dexter's henchmen knife him instead of Mitchum. Good-sport Mitchum insists upon following through on Bendix's assignment. With the aid of Jane he does entice Dexter into open territory and eventual police capture.

Jane's highlight, if it can be called that, in *Macao* was her offering of the song "One for the Road," for which she was enshrined in a twenty-six-pound gold-silver-mesh lamé dress,* capped by gaudy, dangling rhinestone earrings, and a wide-smeared lipstick streak, which accentuated her jutting square chin (and overall her broad, square shoulders). The sexual allure of the outfit to one side, being fitted in precious metal supplied by Dexter symbolically stressed Jane's initial rejection of Mitchum's offer to give up their wandering and to instead settle down on the proverbial desert island. But as the turgid drama pushes toward its expected resolution, Jane and Mitchum fall into harmony. One good but brief bit has him charging after her in her dressing room with a fan, she holding up a pillow in mock protection, and the room soon becoming filled with billowing feathers. Later Jane becomes even more com-

---

*In a memo addressed to RKO studio manager C. J. Tevlin, Hughes, ever sexually infantile in his concepts, enunciated: "This dress is absolutely terrific and should be used, by all means.

"However, the fit of the dress around her breasts is not good and gives the impression, God forbid, that her breasts are padded or artificial. They just don't appear to be in natural contour. It looks as if she is wearing a brassiere of some very stiff material which does not take the contour of her breasts. . . .

"I am not recommending that she go without a brassiere, as I know this is a very necessary piece of equipment for Russell. But I thought, if we could find a half-brassiere which will support her breasts upward and still not be noticeable under the dress, or alternatively, a very thin brassiere made of very thin material so that the natural contour of her breasts will show through the dress, it will be a great deal more effective. . . .

"Now, it would be extremely valuable if the brassiere, or the dress, incorporated some kind of a point at the nipple because I know this does not ever occur naturally in the case of Jane Russell. Her breasts always appear to be round, or flat, at that point so something artificial here would be extremely desirable if it could be incorporated without destroying the contour of the rest of her breasts. . . .

"You understand that all the comment immediately above is with respect to the dress made of metallic cloth.

"However, the comment is equally applicable to any other dress she wears, and I would like these instructions followed with respect to all of her wardrobe.

"Regarding the dresses themselves, the one made of metallic cloth is OK, although it is a high-necked dress, because it is so startling.

"However, I want the rest of her wardrobe, wherever possible, to be low-necked (and by that I mean as low as the law allows) so that the customers can get a look at the part of Russell which they pay to see and not covered by cloth, metallic or otherwise." Hughes then went on to add in this historic letter:

"In the test, both Jane Russell and Joyce MacKenzie [then being considered for the role assumed by Gloria Grahame] were played chewing gum. If this was inadvertent and Russell merely did so because she considered it a wardrobe test, I suppose that is of no consequence.

"But if Von Sternberg intends to play these girls in the picture chewing gum, I strongly object as I do not see how any woman can be exciting while in the process. Incidentally, even in a wardrobe or make-up test, I can certainly tell better what the girl looks like without this indulgence. . . ."

placent. She informs Mitchum, "You'd better start getting used to me fresh out of the shower." And by the wrap-up sultry Jane (forever being photographed chest-level leaning toward the camera's lens) and frequently barechested Mitchum are sympatico. They have decided to give up their eternal drifting and establish domestic roots.

While no one at this time, least of all Jane, pretended that she was a seasoned screen performer, the recurring gaucheries of her accepted acting manner were a source of embarrassment that could not be disguised by von Sternberg, the costumes, or Mitchum's manly presence. For example, when Jane hails a rickshaw in front of the Quick Reward Club she accidentally simulates a ludicrous image of a tired New Yorker hailing a Yellow Cab in midtown Manhattan. Her efforts to capture a sense of hard-boiled ennui often caused her to render her dialog flatter than written. (E.g., caught in a dangerous situation in *Macao*, Mitchum calmly suggests they may soon be killed. Hopefully brittle Jane feebly snaps back: "From what I hear. Once is once too much.")

While *Macao* was playing the theatrical circuit, Hughes finally dragged the four-year-old *Montana Belle* out of the vaults. The fermentation period did not miraculously create good vintage film. Jane was cast as the West's most celebrated female outlaw.* Director Allan Dwan could not whip any interest into the ridiculous storyline or the determinedly pedestrian cast. In addition, the garishly hued early Truecolor process was no asset to the proceedings. Belle Starr (Jane), an outlaw's widow and a crack markswoman, has a misunderstanding with Scott Brady and the three other outlaw Dalton Brothers. She joins with Forrest Tucker and Jack Lambert in a holdup rampage, gaining an even more unsavory reputation. Later she returns to her old stamping grounds of Guthrie disguised sufficiently so that no one recognizes her. Because gambler-saloonkeeper George Brent has $50,000 in funds that Jane is itching to acquire, she persuades him to make her an associate at his saloon. As the new presiding mistress of the establishment she finds time to vocalize "The Gilded Lily"† and to reason that Brent is basically a good guy after all (even though he is hellbent on bringing the Daltons and Belle Starr to justice). Of her modest performance *Variety* acknowledged, "It's safe to say that her more recent efforts are much better."

In upbeat contrast to these RKO dismals, Jane reteamed with Bob Hope in *Son of Paleface* (1952), a film which provided her with an even more advantageous screen role than the original. It must be noted that a great deal of Jane's success with both *Paleface* ventures was directly due to the highcaliber mounting provided by Paramount, a quality uniformly missing from Jane's RKO ventures. It was not simply a case of Jane seeming to be better than she really was because of slick technical production values and a more

*A role previously played onscreen by Gene Tierney in *Belle Starr* (1941) and by Isabel Jewell in *Badman's Territory* (1946).
† Subsequently recorded as a single on the Mills Music label.

high-powered cast. She actually rose to the occasion in Grade-A surroundings. Her frequently vulgar screen image * lost much of its hard-boiled crude overtones when in classier company, and she was transfigured frequently into a more brittle character exhibiting confidence, ease, and experience.

Son of Paleface presents second-billed Jane as the flashy proprietress of the Dirty Shame Saloon in Sawbuck Pass of 1895. On the sly, she is the Torch, the leader of a notorious bandit gang that has been robbing the local citizenry with great success. Jane's equilibrium is disturbed by the arrival of medicine-showman Roy Rogers, for whom she takes a strong fancy. But he is a secret service agent out to capture the Torch. He cares for nothing beyond the accomplishment of his mission and the care of his trusty horse, Trigger. There is another newcomer in town, Hope, the son of the late Painless Peter Potter, who, despite being a Harvard graduate, is a chip off the old block. Like his old man, Hope is a supercilious, cowardly braggart. If Hope is disappointed to discover that the only legacy his dad left him was a rash of bad debts, he is soon overwhelmed by plucky Jane. When he swaggers into her saloon, he is apprised that Jane "was tops in California." To which Hope adds his own instant appraisal: "She ain't so bad in North and South Dakota." Dressed in tights and net hosiery (showing off her very shapely gams) and garnished with opera-length white gloves, she is a knockout. At times Jane's authoritarian role is submerged into that of straight woman for Hope's gaggery:

Hope to Jane: "Wouldn't you like to take a stroll around the rock quarry? In college I majored in geology, anthropology, and running out of gas on Bunker Hill."
Or later:
Jane: "I think you're the handsomest person in the world." (She is out to con him for one of her devious plans.)
Hope: "I wouldn't say that, but I appreciate your honesty." Before they actually reach the kissing stage, Hope advises the statuesque gal: "Before you know where you are, you'll be kissing me full on my rich red ruby lips. . . . How I envy her."
When they eventually do kiss, Hope's feet leave the ground and his oversized spurs start spinning.

Jane is at her best in the saloon sequence in which she reprises the Oscar-winning song "Buttons and Bows" with a fresh set of lyrics, later belting out "Wing Ding Tonight" and dueting with Hope in "Am I In Love."† In the movie tradition of Jean Harlow *(Red Dust)* and Claudette Colbert *(The Sign of the Cross),* Jane has her own alluring bubble-bath scene, using—according to the publicists, anyway—the same tub Paulette Goddard had graced on-camera in her 1940s moviemaking days.

Son of Paleface has its moral but twisted happy ending. By the time Jane

---
*A recurring characteristic more due to Hughes's structuring of her screen presentation than to Jane's own personality.
†Later re-recorded for Capitol Records.

and her gang are caught, she and Hope have fallen fully in love. They wed and she troops off to jail to serve her sentence. Upon her release, Hope is at the prison gate to greet her. Smirkingly he tells the movie viewer, "Let's see television top this," as a squad of little Painless Potters pop into sight, trailing behind Jane. This wild and woolly spoof of the Old West did quite well at the box-office, restoring some of Jane's marquee lure.

Rounding out her five 1952 releases, Jane made a brief guest appearance in Paramount's sixth *Road* picture, *Road to Bali.* To spruce up the laugh travelog, *Road to Bali* interpolated into its zany plot a clip of Humphrey Bogart pulling *The African Queen,* and cameos by Dean Martin, Jerry Lewis, and Bob Crosby, with Jane reserved for the finale. Scantily clad Jane is conjured up from a basket by Hope, who is playing on his magic horn. She promptly joins Dorothy Lamour in linking arms with romantic victor Bing Crosby, and the trio walk off into the sunset, leaving the ill-fated Hope nonplused.

Before, during, and after the fact, it was inspired casting on the part of Twentieth Century-Fox producer Sol C. Siegel to borrow Jane from Hughes-RKO to co-star (with top billing!) opposite homelot sex queen Marilyn Monroe in *Gentlemen Prefer Blondes* (1953).* The comparatively sophisticated musical movie found Jane as the best friend and stage partner of Lorelei Lee (Monroe). The duo are heading for Paris on the *Ile de France,* financially bolstered by a letter of credit from Monroe's fiancé, Tommy Noonan. Sex-hungry Jane immediately becomes involved with shipmate Elliott Reid, not knowing he is a detective hired by Noonan's father to spy on gold-digging Monroe. (Unfortunately Jane's exchanges of repartee with Reid are her weakest moments in the movie.) Monroe is aghast that Jane can so promptly forsake money for sex and love, and hastily tries to match her pal with a more bank-account-worthy candidate. Her choice is Henry Spofford III, who, it turns out, is deep-voiced child George "Foghorn" Winslow. While Jane is spending her time with Reid or cavorting in the men's gymnasium, Monroe is toying with elderly merchant Charles Coburn, who gives her his wife's diamond tiara, allowing the wide-eyed blonde to show Jane that diamonds are really a girl's best friend. The saucy gals reach Paris, accept a nightclub job when Noonan temporarily abandons them, and later in court prove that it was Coburn who gave—and not Monroe who unlawfully took—his wife's costly head adornment. The wrap-up of one of the classic musicals of 1950s Hollywood has Jane wedding Reid and Monroe marrying Noonan in a double ceremony.

Gentlemen Prefer Blondes demonstrated Jane's innate flair for musical

---

*Fox paid $150,000 for the film rights to the 1949 Broadway smash hit (740 performances), based on the 1926 stage comedy and 1928 silent film. The resultant 1953 Technicolor movie, directed by Howard Hawks, grossed in excess of $5.1 million. At one point before Fox acquired the screen rights, Columbia had planned to use *Gentlemen Prefer Blondes* as a vehicle for Judy Holliday, Paramount as a showcase for Betty Hutton, and Hal Wallis as a property for the Broadway original, Carol Channing. Fox originally tagged the project back in 1951 for Betty Grable.

comedy, a forte neglected by Hughes and RKO. "She has the knack of snapping out gags with deadpan sarcasm" *(New York Herald-Tribune)*. Jane and Monroe—the haystack brunette versus the blowtorch blonde—worked very well indeed together. Snapped one quipster: "Marilyn looks best walking away while Jane takes first place in passing." Vocally the girls were in harmony as they dueted "Two Little Girls from Little Rock" and "When Love Goes Wrong." Each had her stanzas of "Bye Bye Love." Jane was snappy performing an ode to romance, "Ain't There Anyone Here for Love" (sung to a gym full of squirming athletes). But she came dramatically alive in the French courtroom scene in which she pretends to be Monroe. Garbed in blonde wig and full-length coat she parodies her buddy for the sake of the gullible judge, then to prove she is really her friend, she launches into a rendition of "Diamonds Are a Girl's Best Friend." As she tears into the number, she yanks off her coat, revealing a wow of a white-sequined tights outfit. Jane's run-through of the song also includes the unforgettable lines, "Pear shape or square shaped, these rocks don't lose their shape," underlining the lyrics by cupping her breasts. This was the Jane Russell that Hughes had always hoped for but never knew how to create.

If anyone expected a battle royal to occur between the two contemporary sex goddesses—both Geminis, by the way—he was sorely disappointed. Thirty-two-year-old Jane, on foreign soil at the Fox Studios, was on her best behavior, and twenty-seven-year-old Monroe, gliding into her peak stardom years, was at her friendliest, warm, if vague, self. "We got along nicely," Monroe later confirmed. "Jane called me the 'Round One.' I don't know what she means by that, but I assume she means it to be friendly." Jane even got her co-star to attend nondenominational services at her mother's Chapel in the Valley. Monroe admired the dedication of the Episcopalian Mrs. Russell and her energetic sermons. "Wonderful," said Monroe. "They didn't happen to turn me into a deeply religious person, but if anybody could do that, Jane could. That girl can do anything she puts her mind to—anything!"

With Monroe taking the lead, the reporters now expressed some interest in Jane's religious fervor. As she explained to columnist Mike Connolly: "Look it's really very simple. God gave me certain physical attributes that made it possible for me to become a star. But that didn't change the kind of person I am—deep down. The church and showbusiness are all the same to me—part of my life."

On another occasion Jane rationalized it all more colloquially: "God is a living doll. If you love your neighbor, you'll automatically keep all the commandments."

Hughes, who was never interested either personally or professionally (as a publicity angle) in dealing with Jane's religious or domestic status, was very intrigued with the possibility of carrying on the momentum created by *Gentlemen Prefer Blondes*. He reasoned that another cinematic ocean voyage should be equally welcome at the box-office, particularly if it were concocted by another Loos (Mary, niece of writer Anita). But what Hughes did not reckon on, was that all the vital ingredients that had combined to make the Fox water-trek so entertaining would be missing in RKO's transatlantic journey: in particular, taste, satire, pacing, and plush production values.

The French Line (1953) opens on the eve of Jane's wedding to Craig Stevens. When she learns that he has jilted her because he is fearful of marrying a Texan wealthy enough to be a diversified corporation, she follows the advice of her folksy guardian (Arthur Hunnicutt) and takes a trip incognito. Which brings Jane to New York to see her childhood friend Mary McCarty, who now owns a swank dress salon and is about to shepherd a flock of models to Paris on the S. S. *Liberte* for an upcoming international fashion show. Presto: Jane switches identities with model Joyce MacKenzie, who just happens to be secretly married. Meantime Hunnicut hires impecunious playboy Gilbert Roland to serve as Jane's secret protector during the hazardous trip, leading to a clichéd mistaken-identity crisis. Of course Jane and Roland unscramble the mess and affirm their love by the time they land in France.

Hughes counted on two company-made promotional gimmicks to hardsell *The French Line.* The musical had been lensed in the new three-dimensional film process (with fuzzy color) so the advertisements heartily proclaimed: "Jane Russell in 3-D . . . it'll knock *both* your eyes out!" More important to the well-being of the new picture, Hughes engineered another censorship controversy in the tradition of *The Outlaw.* On its own, Jane's lusty bubble-bath scene in *The French Line* was salacious enough, but it was the finale fashion-show production number that caused the well-perpetuated rhubarb. For this sequence Jane was outfitted in a skimpy one-piece black-satin tights outfit. To make matters worse (or better?) three huge leaf-shaped pieces had been scissored from the midriff area and a sprinkling of spangles used to cover the navel. Clad thusly, Jane performed a vulgar bump-and-grind shimmy dance while belting out the song "Lookin' for Trouble."

This one sequence was sufficient to cause the Breen Office to refuse the picture a film industry Production Code seal of approval.* A responsible RKO immediately jumped into action, promulgating editorial copy about *The French Line* being one of the first films to be nationally released without a Production Code seal. The Breen Office fined RKO $25,000 for its audacity, which did not stop the studio from proceeding with plans to debut *The French Line* in St. Louis in late 1953. The archbishop of the Archdiocese of St. Louis immediately banned the film, and *The French Line* was withdrawn, slightly re-edited, and released with much hoopla in mid-1954. It would not be until late 1955

*A Breen Office spokesman stated, "Some glaring breast shots of Jane Russell and a dance sequence by that lady during her rendition of 'I Want a Man,' . . . will certainly bring the cops to any theater where it is shown."

Although RKO's promotional material for *The French Line* proclaimed that "Miss Russell personally supervised the creation of the gorgeous and daring costumes," Jane later told her own version: "I fought and beefed and argued over scenes in the picture. Some of the camera angles are in horrible taste. I had an awful time with some of the dance costumes they wanted me to wear. They were really bad—hardly anything at all. I don't like the accent on sex and never have." Jane's final words on the film were: "I hope and pray the studio will see the light and make the cuts required."

that RKO and Code administrators would reach a compromise agreement on the picture, resulting in *The French Line* finally achieving Code-approved status. The never-paid fine was lifted. (As late as 1958 *The French Line* was still engendering morality controversies. A San Antonio television station had to cancel a planned showing of the film, stating that the famed dance sequence was too immodest for home-viewer consumption and too lengthy to be cut without being missed.)

The censors may have been prompted to debate the morality merits of *The French Line,* but the critics were of one accord about the film's artistic qualifications. "The picture has Miss Russell. She is female. That angle is worked hard" *(Newsweek).* "It's a cheap exhibitionist thing in which even the elaboration of the feminine figure eventually becomes grotesque" *(New York Times).* Of the highly promoted bubble-bath interlude, one disgruntled viewer wrote, "She wades into the assignment like a substitute—coming off the bench in the fourth quarter, in a clear case of misplaced enthusiasm." Perhaps *Time* magazine best summed up the values exhibited in *The French Line:* "long on notoriety and short on entertainment."

Particularly when viewing *The French Line* today, one wonders if Hughes's creative teams at RKO were out to sabotage Jane's career permanently. She emerges from this stinker of a picture not as a rich Texan tomboy but as a dime-store cheapie in personality. The first view of Jane is at her Texas ranch as she changes outfits, allowing for an extended, unsubtle, but tame strip-tease, as she flings off layer upon layer of garments behind a screen. She tells her guardian (Hunnicutt) that she is as excited as "a bull mink in moltin' season." (An analogy which well defines the state of the scriptwriters' intellect.) Casting Mary McCarty as Jane's oncamera pal was another bad breach of judgment for the often unrefined Miss McCarty only emphasized the crudity of Jane's character in this picture. Jane's wardrobe was intended to emphasize her anatomy for the 3-D cameras, but it was also in the height of non-fashion, making the big-boned gal appear anything but femininely vulnerable as the script would suggest. At one point Jane arrives oncamera in one of her celebrated abbreviated outfits and is promptly told: "You look like something unlawful." Tawdry would be closer to the mark. Capping the overall lack of refinement of Jane's Mary Carson was the actress's undefined southern drawl, which was all the more unappealing when heard together with the strange Parisian lingo of Gilbert Roland.*

Much more emotionally rewarding to Jane was her show business venture with Beryl Davis, Connie Haines, and Della Russell (the latter, no relation to Jane, was replaced later by Rhonda Fleming). The performers were all members of Jane's Hollywood Christian group and as a lark had decided to professionally record "Do Lord" for Coral Records in 1954, billing themselves as "The Four Girls." Their rendition of the old religious spiritual proved quite popular and the quartet was persuaded to record three additional songs ("He's

*For the record, Billy Daniel's choreography of Jane's musical interludes ("What Is That That I Feel?," "Well I'll Be Switched," "I Want a Man," and her duet with McCarty, "Any Gal from Texas") presented Jane at her awkward worst, totally graceless and very amateurish.

Got Time," "Unto the Lord," and "Make a Joyful Noise") and then an LP *(Make a Joyful Noise)* on the Coral label before switching to the Capitol Company where they recorded the LP *The Magic of Believing* and some singles. The group made several nightclub bookings at a $15,000 weekly salary and were, for several seasons, a popular television attraction. The girls donated all the profits from the venture to WAIF-ISS and to other church charities.

Jane's next film, *Underwater!,* filmed in late 1953, but not released until 1955, was her last commitment under her current Howard Hughes-RKO contract. Aside from the novelty use of SuperScope, RKO's shortlived wide-screen process, *Underwater!* was essentially a routine treasure-hunt yarn with Jane, as a girl named Theresa (her Spanish accent was atrocious), involved with both Gilbert Roland and Richard Egan above and below the water as they dive for a fabled treasure hidden in the wreck of a Spanish galleon in the Caribbean. In the course of ninety-nine minutes, the cast spouts a plethora of clichés—which made Jane's underwater scenes, in which she just blew bubbles, a blessing—before Jane and Roland, Egan and Lori Nelson pair off satisfactorily. What of the treasure, the crux of the film? Bandit Joseph Calleia grabbed most of that, while priest Robert Keith acquires a big gold cross.

Underwater was touted as costing $3 million and requiring three years to film. Part of the expense occurred when director John Sturges finally had to abandon underwater location shooting off Kona, Hawaii, and restage many scenes on soundstage-built sets at RKO. The ads for *Underwater!* read: "With Jane Russell as you've never seen her before"—referring, of course, to her specialized wardrobe for this picture. It included one-piece and two-piece bathing suits, high-cut shorts, low-cut dresses, a nightgown and pajamas, and, just for a little variety, an aqualung and skin diving equipment. The one memorable vision from the entire picture is of Jane swimming directly toward the camera's eye, garbed in a clinging red bathing suit, looking intent yet bewildered. As Bosley Crowther *(New York Times)* framed it in his review: "This presentation of Miss Russell is like one of those fountain pens that is guaranteed to write underwater. It is novel, but impractical."

To wrap up the *Underwater!* venture, RKO decided to stage the premiere of its latest Jane Russell offering in Silver Springs, Florida (January 10, 1955) at a specially built theatre twenty feet underwater. Jane was present, adorned, like the adventurous audience, in swim suit, aqualung and flippers, preparatory to viewing the subaqueous unspooling of the feature. Ironically it was another Jane, Jayne Mansfield, who attracted most press attention by arriving at the special premiere in a most revealing bikini. It was the start of her motion picture ascent. To herald the New York opening of *Underwater!* at the Mayfair Theatre (February 9, 1955), RKO invested $50,000 in an eighty-five-foot sign stretched across the theatre's marquee. Despite the critical roasting, *Underwater!* had the distinction of racking up more theatrical bookings than any RKO picture in the preceding decade.

After completing *Underwater!* Jane awaited the termination of her

Hughes-RKO pact in February, 1954, to see what move her long-standing boss would make. At this point Hughes had long ago relinquished all claims on Faith Domergue, who had married, had a baby, and had temporarily deserted the cinema. She had been followed by Gina Lollobrigida, whose broken English was not the only obstacle to her becoming the queen of RKO, and she, in turn, was followed by Britisher Jean Simmons, whose husband, Stewart Granger, successfully helped her break an oral contract with Hughes and RKO. Mitzi Gaynor of Twentieth Century-Fox claimed she had won Hughes's heart, but it was only temporary, as was Hughes's liaison with actress Terry Moore. But another Fox star(let), Jean Peters, proved to be a different story, for she and Hughes were wed in Washington, D.C., on May 29, 1954. Not that there had ever been the least suggestion of a romance between Hughes and Jane, but still the thirty-three-year-old personality had good cause to wonder what her cinema future would be if the boss's wife should dampen his continued enthusiasm for promoting the amply proportioned Jane. Then, too, there were already rumors that Hughes was fast losing interest in the declining motion picture industry and might already be negotiating to sell out his interest in RKO, a studio he never set foot on in seven years of "ownership." So to play it safe, Jane formed Russ-Field Productions with her husband, Bob Waterfield, as executive producer. But Hughes evidently had further plans for Jane, for in early 1955 he negotiated a new movie contract with her, which committed her to make five pictures for Hughes (RKO). Her salary was to be $1,000 a week for twenty years. In explaining his rationale for this well-publicized contract to his associate, Noah Dietrich, Hughes said: "I'm paying her a million dollars for five pictures—two hundred thousand per picture for a star of her status is not bad at all. But by paying her over a twenty-year period, I'm using the theory you taught me about 'present worth.' I'm really paying her only half a million, because I can invest the money and get back a half-million in interest."

With high-priced Jane now under contract again, Hughes opted to loan her out to other studios, taking full advantage of her still-viable box-office name. Universal's *Foxfire* (1955) teamed Jane with Jeff Chandler in a contemporary Arizona-set soap opera. Wealthy New Yorker Jane, vacationing out west, encounters boozy doctor Dan Duryea and his pal, half-breed Apache Chandler. Soon predatory Jane (wearing a most unattractive, close-cropped hairdo) and brooding Chandler are taking moonlight strolls. He mumbles to her: "You're a spoiled society type and I'm just a poor mining engineer. What's a guy like me walking around with a gal like you for?"

Jane: "Would you like to stand still and find out." They quickly embark on a mutual ego-boosting trip.

Chandler: "You are so beautiful."

Jane: "So are you." The rugged western scenery and the glimpses of Apache ceremonies were undeniably the best features of *Foxfire*.

Much more of a box-office worthy was Twentieth Century-Fox's expensive western *The Tall Men* (1955), which paired Jane with Clark Gable. Ex-bushwacker Gable first meets Jane in a Rocky Mountain cabin during a blizzard. There she advises Gable: "I want a man with great big dreams, who's goin' places—and has room for a passenger." Gable, who "dreams small," has one immediate reaction to her platform speech. He snarls: "Help me pull off this boot." (Jane is forever bending over for the advantage of the CinemaScope color cameras in *The Tall Men,* assisting the menfolk in removing their clodhoppers, which usually requires each male to balance a foot on her derriere. At least it provided a new variation on the standard Jane Russell screen pose.) Jane and the mature Gable* developed a good screen rapport, making it believable that the self-sufficient gal could be tamed by a free and easy man who is hard on his women but thoughtful to his wrangler pals. In the film she sang "I Want a Tall Man" and even garnered some decent reviews for her efforts ("With each film [she] seems to grow in power and surly confidence").

Jane's fourth 1955 release, *Gentlemen Marry Brunettes,†* opened October 30 at the Mayfair Theatre. Although decked out in CinemaScope and color with a production tab of $2 million, this entry was no fitting successor to *Gentlemen Prefer Blondes.* The weary plot cast Jane and Jeanne Crain as a singing "sister" act; Crain is the practical one, while Jane is just a girl who can't say no. More earnest than intelligent, Jane has promised herself in marriage to six different beaus, with the ceremonies all scheduled for the same night. Reluctantly she agrees, "I guess I just don't have all my marbles." Crain accedes to this generous estimation, suggesting they make a fresh start in Paris, where their agent, Scott Brady, has maneuvered a Folies Club engagement for them. Once in Gay Paree they chance upon aging boulevardier Rudy Vallee, who fondly recalls his 1920s escapades with their mothers, the famed flappers who made such a hit as the singing Jones Sisters. (This allows for extended flashbacks in which the two co-stars portray their gold-digging moms.) Jane is eventually paired off with Brady, and Crain succumbs to the charms of wealthy Alan Young. Jane and Jeanne Crain sang a wide selection of standard nostalgic tunes,‡ but the whole affair had a tacky *déjà vu* air that nothing could dispel.

Before Jane and the four-years-younger Crain went to Paris for on-location filming for *Gentlemen Marry Brunettes,* no one would have taken odds that Crain would overshadow Jane in the publicity sweepstakes. But Crain, recently released from a long-term Twentieth Century-Fox contract, was eager to change her girl-next-door image by revealing that her 36½-24-36 figure entitled her to other screen considerations. Once in France it was Crain who monopolized the press (and later the film's reviews) as the sexier gal.

*Then age fifty-four.
†The first actual motion-picture venture of Russ-Field Productions.
‡Jeanne Crain's singing was dubbed by Anita Ellis.

Columbia's *Hot Blood* (Palace Theatre, March 23, 1956) was a mistake from all points considered, being a puerile Hollywood rendition of life and love among the gypsies.* Had scriptwriter Jesse Lasky, Jr. and/or director Nicholas Ray had any intriguing premises to offer, the presentation might have been bearable. But there were few who could become engrossed with the problems of conniving gypsy Joseph Calleia, who supports his family by betrothing daughter Jane to any willing clansman, then pocketing the money and scrambling out of town.† One of Calleia's more persistent customers is Luther Adler, head of the Los Angeles gypsies, who purchases Jane as the bride for his younger brother (Cornel Wilde), a foolish lad who would rather dance than be a husband.

In *Hot Blood* Jane provided bit roles for her brothers Jamie and Wally. In real life during 1956 she added to her own family when she and Waterfield adopted a third child, nine-month-old Robert John.

Because Twentieth Century-Fox was unable to hoodwink Marilyn Monroe into starring in *The Revolt of Mamie Stover* (1956), producer Buddy Adler hired Jane to play the whore with a heart of gold. (Evidently Fox "star" Jayne Mansfield was not considered up to the demands of the dramatic role.) Raoul Walsh, who had already directed Jane in *The Tall Men,* stated succinctly why he considered Jane of value to his new CinemaScope color production: "The most important ingredient in most pictures is still going to be sex. You can't get away from it. That's why Jane Russell is worth $200,000 a picture, and Lassie is on television."

That *The Revolt of Mamie Stover* emerged as bland filmfare was quite a trick, considering the fact that William Bradford Huie's novel about an enterprising whore who put her work on an assembly-line basis was popular smut from cover to cover. In fact, a less perceptive viewer of *The Revolt of Mamie Stover* might easily conclude that Jane's Mamie was just a hard-luck broad from the wrong side of the tracks, and *nothing more.* The distilled screenplay, set in 1941, has Jane being escorted by the San Francisco police to the entrance galley of a ship leaving town. She is advised not to return—ever! Aboard the Hawaii-bound vessel she chances upon clean-cut science fiction writer Richard Egan. He proves to be the first man in her versatile lifetime who respects her as a person. Naturally she is duly impressed. Once they dock, she lands a job at the Bungalow Club, presided over by domineering madam Agnes Moorehead. According to the movie, servicemen were lining up for blocks just for the opportunity to dance and talk (but definitely nothing more) with Moorehead's "hostesses," particularly the ever popular Jane. Poor Jane is shunned by the better element in town, who do not appreciate her patriotic contribution. Her conscience forces her to tell Egan: "No, Jimmy, I can't let you ruin

*Broadway failed with the same subject matter with the flop musical *Bajour* (1964).
†A variation on this con gambit was used in *Skin Game* (1971).

your life. You can't lick the whole island—I've got a number on my back and they all know it." Egan is positive that some compromise can be worked out, but in the meantime he goes off to war. While he is away Jane is determined to make all the social abuse worth enduring and becomes the queen of Moorehead's house. When Egan returns on leave to Honolulu he is dismayed to find that Jane is the star attraction of the Bungalow Club. The shock of it all pushes him back into the refined arms of his society fiancée, Joan Leslie, who has that nice home high on the hill. And Jane? She has made a killing in post-Pearl Harbor real estate, but, now being a regenerated girl, she gives away her fortune and leaves Hawaii. She braves the scorn of the San Francisco police as she passes through town, bound home for Mississippi, her sordid past all behind her.

Jane wore a bright red wig as the brash, eye-catching lass of *The Revolt of Mamie Stover,* but she was definitely no screen descendant of Moll Flanders or Sadie Thompson, as had been intended. Midst the bathos of the laundered plot Jane sang "Keep Your Eyes on the Hands" and "If You Wanna See Mamie Tonight" (the latter tune reminiscent of Rita Hayworth's "Put the Blame on Mame" from *Gilda*). The critics soundly panned *The Revolt of Mamie Stover,* and the public preferred watching television in the comfort of their homes to venturing to the theatres to see this *Pollyanna*-style film.

Jane and Waterfield via Russ-Field had linked together with Clark Gable to form Gabco-Russ-field (with Gable as president) and to produce the western *Last Man in Wagon Mound* for United Artists in 1956, with Gable and Jane reteamed. By the time production started under Raoul Walsh's direction, Jane was busy elsewhere, and the picture, released under the title *The King and Four Queens,* had Eleanor Parker as the co-star. (The picture did only modest business and it was the quiet end for the Gabco-Russ-Field joint cinema ventures.) Meanwhile, Jane agreed to star in *The Fuzzy Pink Nightgown* (1957). It was her first black-and-white screen venture since *Macao* and her biggest box-office lemon of the decade. The film's premise situated Jane as movie star Laurel Stevens, who has just completed *The Kidnapped Bride.* Her agent, who must have seen Lucille Ball's *The Affairs of Annabel* (1938) years before, decides it would be a good publicity gimmick to have Jane "kidnapped" by ransom-demanding gangsters. Naturally, Damon Runyonesque hoods Keenan Wynn and Ralph Meeker really do abscond with Jane, and the reluctant victim becomes enamored of muscular Meeker. United Artists was not impressed by the completed product and dumped it onto the showcase distribution market (October 30, 1957) where it promptly died. Less than four years later it was filler in the late-night-television movie slot.

With the resounding failure of *The Fuzzy Pink Nightgown,* film distributors were leery of co-financing any future pictures with Jane's production company, nor were other producers anxious for her screen services. Howard Hughes had already ditched the bulk of his RKO investments, and that studio had all but disbanded its theatrical-film production activities. Thirty-six-year-old Jane now found it difficult to sniff out suitable movie roles, for there was a very limited number of parts being written for young-matron sexpots.

However, there was always television. Other performers of higher caliber than Jane were drifting into the rival medium for series work, grabbing quick money while their names still had some drawing power. Jane had already made occasional video appearances, usually as a guest performer on variety shows (with or without her nightclub group act). In 1957 there was talk of Jane starring in "Guestward Ho," a CBS-TV series based on the Patrick Dennis book. At a later point she actually made a teleseries pilot entitled "MacCreedy's Woman," dealing with a female nightclub operator in San Francisco. Although the pilot was aired on the "Colgate Theatre" (NBC, September 23, 1958), a series never developed. Jane claims: "I decided against it when I found out how much work was involved." Jane did make a guest appearance on "Desilu Playhouse" in the western episode entitled *Ballad for a Bad Man* (CBS, January 26, 1959) but thereafter confined her video showcasing to variety programs.

Having been ruled out of movies, and having ruled out television, Jane returned to the nightclub circuit, debuting with a solo act, which opened at the Sands Hotel in Las Vegas in October, 1957. Carried onstage on an ornate couch, the strikingly garbed Jane sang such songs as "Be Happy with the Yacht You've Got." For a time her brother Wally was a featured part of the act. The following October she played New York's Latin Quarter in a restaged routine devised by Jack Cole. The critics found her delivery of the blues numbers far more appealing than her singing of pop tunes like "Volare." Later Jane fulfilled engagements in Mexico, South America, Europe, Canada, and back in the United States (Chicago, Houston, and Palm Springs) with successful, if not outstanding, results.

When still no film offers came her way, Jane tackled summer stock, debuting in a tour of *Janus* in New England in the summer of 1961, which was followed by a run of *Skylark* at the Drury Lane Theatre in Chicago that fall. A year later she was seen in an edition of *Bells Are Ringing,* which inaugurated its run at the Westchester Town House, Yonkers, New York, (November, 1962).

Meanwhile Jane continued with her WAIF-ISS volunteer work. "My image is a plus instead of a minus in charity work," Jane stated. "Many people are curious to see me. Then they get hooked on the work of the organization." Endorsing each and every one of Jane's various charity and professional activities was her husband. As far as the public knew, the Waterfields had a model marriage, made complete by their three adopted children. Religion was still a vital part of Jane's way of life. "If I've learned anything in life," she said, "it's that you can't buck the Lord. He's your best friend, and from the female angle, the only one more important than your husband."

Throughout the early 1960s there were recurrent rumors that forty-year-old Jane would make her screen comeback in this or that vehicle. Jane was signed to play a role in the Capri-filmed *Never Enough* for MGM in 1963, but the project fell through, as did Richard Condon's *A Talent for Loving,* which was to have been lensed in England. But Jane claimed she did not mind the screen inactivity. "I never got a charge about seeing myself up there on the screen. That build-up of me as a sex-goddess—what a joke! What a tribute to the power of publicity and a 40-inch bust! I never took any of it seriously. . . . Who wants to work in films when you've got a loving husband and family at home? Who needs it?"

Then suddenly Jane showed up in Twentieth Century-Fox's *Fate Is the Hunter* (1964), fifth-billed in a cameo role as herself entertaining troops at a remote outpost during World War II. She sang "No Love, No Nothing, Not Until My Baby Comes Home." Two more years passed before Jane was onscreen again, this time second-billed in two A. C. Lyles low-budget color westerns churned out for Paramount Pictures and the double-bill markets. *Johnny Reno* (1966) cast her as a saloon owner and the former fiancée of marshal Dana Andrews, while *Waco* (1966) featured the one-time movie star as the wife of corrupt preacher Wendell Corey. Neither project did anything but confirm that Jane's screen stardom days were well behind her. It was a sad sight indeed for more than one viewer to view a middle-aged Jane hampered beyond her years by unattractive hairdos and careless lighting.

But then Jane's dying screen career picked up a bit later in 1966 when she was signed for *The Honorable Frauds,* to film on location in New York. Jerry Shaw was to direct a cast that would include Peter Savage and Betty Bruce. Jane was assigned the part of a wealthy woman who loses all her financial holdings and is among those waiting for a rich relative to pass away. As suddenly as publicity about this feature appeared in print, so news of its progress disappeared from media sources. Not until January 27, 1967, did further word of this $500,000 project, financed by real-estate man Forest Bedell and actor-director Savage, find its way into print. A small item in the New York newspapers announced that the master print of *The Honorable Frauds* had been screened at Movielab on New York's West 54th Street and sold at auction for $1,000 by the Franklin National Bank, which had a lien on the picture.

Those still-loyal fans of Jane who thought the onetime cinema name could sink no deeper into the career doldrums were sadly mistaken. For along came *Born Losers,* pushed onto the market by American International Pictures on August 18, 1967. Like the same studio's *The Wild Angels* (1966) and its carbon-copy successors, *Born Losers* was a cheaply engineered exploitation entry. But it had two distinguishing differences, it reeked with morality about the evil and sadism of motorcycle gangs, and it boasted the presence of Jane Russell as the third-billed Mrs. Shorn, a trailer-camp-living waitress residing on the outskirts of a California town. Frazzled Jane portrayed the mother of teenager Janice Miller. Jane's daughter is among a group of adventurous teeny-boppers who participate in a cyclist sex orgy, and then, thinking better of their lark, claim they were raped by the wandering gang on wheels. Jane refuses to allow her girl to testify to the authorities, fearful of gang reprisals. In her few oncamera scenes, Jane photographed badly, her features very thickened and her portrayal too jerky and overdramatic. Industry observers insisted that very little of the solid box-office returns of *Born Losers* could be attributed to the curiosity value of Jane's presence.

Jane had often stated: "If there's one thing about the Russell family that stands out more than others, it is the fact that when we get married we're determined to *stay* married. Among hundreds of cousins and uncles and aunts, there hasn't been a single divorce. That's the truth. The record proves it. You can see that for yourself." Thus it came as rather a surprise when on February 2, 1967, Jane filed for divorce in the courts of Los Angeles. She charged Waterfield with "physical abuse," and her suit concluded that "the basis of marriage has been destroyed." In her divorce petition Jane asked for $4,950-a-month temporary support for her three children.* In his cross-complaint, Waterfield charged that Jane was guilty of drunkenness and cruelty and that despite his efforts to curb her drinking habits, she continually concealed large supplies of liquor at home. A year later, in July of 1968, Jane received her final divorce papers and obtained custody of her two older children, while Waterfield acquired custody of their twelve-year-old son, Robert.

Less than a month after her divorce, Jane wed actor Roger Barrett, who was the same age as Jane (forty-seven). They had met while doing stock in Niles, Michigan. They were married August 25, 1968, at the Community Presbyterian Church in Beverly Hills by Dr. Bernard MacDougall Looner, professor of philosophy and religion at the Berkeley Baptist Divinity School. Jane and Barrett purchased a new Hollywood home. But their marital bliss was short-lived, for on November 17, 1968, he died of a heart attack. Jane took the tragedy very hard. As she phrased it: "I went into one of those darling depressions and couldn't care less about anything. Nothing mattered. Nothing at all. . . . I went to a psychiatrist and also prayed more than I ever have in my life. Many people thought I was suffering because of the way my career was going. That had nothing to do with it. My husband's death almost destroyed me."

Gradually Jane emerged from her depression and began searching for creative projects to fill her empty days. She designed a new bedding kit, aimed at eliminating the drudgery of making up bunk beds. Jane even be-

---

*Jane was then earning about $102,000 a year (mostly from her Howard Hughes contract). Her estate at the time was valued at several million dollars.

gan searching anew for film roles that would be appropriate to her age status. She gamely parceled out her postmenopause thoughts to the public. "I think I can act, given the opportunity. I'm begging to be a character actress, to play parts with some depth to them. I'm willing to try anything! I'm ready to be my age and look like hell, if necessary. That's how much I want to get out of this sex rut."

Then Shelley Winters, an established pro at turning character parts into starring, scene-stealing assignments, told novice Jane: "It will happen, honey. Look for the good directors, then find out if there's a splashy role in whatever movie they're doing, and go ask for it.

"The role doesn't need to be big. It just has to have guts. Then, if you get the job, you do the rest."

Jane evidently thought she had followed Miss Winters' sterling advice to a T, for she soon signed to play in *Darker than Amber* (1970), the first of a projected series of the adventures of John D. MacDonald's literary character, Travis McGee (Rod Taylor). Jane enthused about her comeback assignment. "I'm a noisy, good-hearted drink-'em-up dame known as The Alabama Tiger [*sic*] who lives on a boat and is a flamboyant hostess at a party that never loses steam, because there's always more guests arriving."

When *Darker than Amber* snuck into showcase release in August, 1970, Jane, along with British actor James Booth, was listed in the credits as a guest star. Booth had a fairly sizable scene as Taylor's eccentric friend who is murdered, but Jane was not so fortunate. She appeared in only two very brief scenes, which did not last more than a minute and a half in total. The viewer first spots Jane as Taylor's boat churns past her yacht, which is overcrowded with raucous partygoers. Taylor tells his boatmates that the party has been going full steam for over a year and that her husband had died only a few months before. Taylor waves to Jane, who is dressed in a hostess gown and is leaning over the yacht rail with a drink clutched in her hand. She yells to Taylor: "Charley wants me to lend him $30 million to buy a movie studio."

Taylor: "That's the only way you'll get to be a movie star." Taylor smiles with his fleshy Irish grin. End of scene. (The embarrassing ramifications of this snatch of dialog remain to haunt any staunch Jane Russell devotee.) Near the movie's finale Taylor's craft chugs back to dock again, and again passes Jane's yacht. The camera pans across her party still in progress, and Jane can be spotted with difficulty in a long shot. So much for her role in *Darker than Amber,* and so much for Jane's film career to date.

In the spring of 1971 Jane was playing in a stock version of *Catch Me If You Can* at the Meadowbrook Dinner Theatre in New Jersey. She was still newsworthy enough to grab a few inches of column space, telling one reporter that she preferred stage work to, say, television, where "you have to work too hard." As Jane explained it, "I enjoy the actual performance but it's the time between that is so empty."

On one of her days off from the New Jersey show, Jane came into Manhattan to see the Tony-winning musical *Company*. Producer-director Hal Prince talked with Jane that day and asked her if she would consider replacing Elaine Stritch, who was about to leave the show. Although *Company* was largely an ensemble production, the role of Barbara, the thrice-married sophisticate, was the outstanding female part. Jane readily agreed to the assignment. "When I was married and the children were growing up, I always felt the worst thing that could happen would be to get into a long-running show. Now it doesn't matter where I live."

Jane almost did not make her Broadway debut as Barbara, the moderately dipso-nymphomaniac, for shortly before she was to step into Stritch's stage shoes, she panicked and hid out in Chicago. "Well, you dumb ass," Jane recalls telling herself, "the Lord opened the door—He'll give you strength to go through it." So on May 10, 1971, Jane became a working member of Broadway's *Company*. She appeared onstage wearing a simple, black-paneled evening gown. "She's still a knockout looker," *Variety* reported, "whose first entrance is met by silent whistles from the men and envious sighs from the women in the audience." Jane's big moment in the show occurred when she sang the hit number "Ladies Who Lunch." She may not have possessed the tart punch of Stritch's delivery, but Jane's interpretation had a validity all its own. She remained with the show through October of 1971, when she was replaced by another former, but lesser, film personality, Vivian Blaine.

During her months with *Company,* Jane found plenty of time to talk with the press, who were now eager for publishable quotes from the 1940s sexpot. "I'm very glad I'm not starting out in pictures today. I simply wouldn't play.

"In the days when I was a pinup girl I always wanted to look like Marjorie Main. Marjorie never had to worry how she looked. And now that I'm older, I'd like to play more mature parts.

"I didn't enjoy it [stardom] at all. For me, it was a way to earn money to do the other things in life I enjoyed more, like interior decorating.

"I've just finished nine [*sic*] months on Broadway in *Company* and I played a character I could identify with because she was my age and I was no longer Jane Russell, sex idol."

Particularly because of the Clifford Irving-Howard Hughes biography hoax, Jane was asked one set of questions repeatedly. "Everybody wants to pick my brains about Hughes. I refuse to talk about him. If he doesn't want any publicity, why should I go around blabbing about his private life. I'm not going to be any information center about the man." On another occasion she added: "I don't like to see all this adverse publicity about him. As far as I'm concerned, he is a great man who has been kind and generous and a very, very close friend for many years . . .

"We were once very close and I've always felt that I should honor that close relationship by not giving interviews concerning him. My feeling is that if he doesn't want publicity about himself, then it's my place to keep quiet."*

After *Company,* Jane returned to California, but time still hung heavy on her. Son Thomas was in the National Guard, Tracy was a college student, and Robert still lived with Waterfield. Jane did the best she could to make sense out of her all-too-free days. She did the rough sketches for Taco West in the San Fernando Valley, an eighty-unit luxury apartment complex, structured as a replica of the nation's oldest apartment building, the adobe system used by the Pueblo Indians for over a thousand years. A design student was hired to complete Jane's sketches, and Jane's contractor brother, Tom, handled the actual construction. In early 1972 Jane moved into one of the apartments. "I'm getting sick of moving. I never want to leave this place. I'm looking forward to designing another apartment complex."

Jane was next in the news when she turned up at the "Fabulous Forties" party at Manhattan's Roseland Dance Hall in June, 1972, a charity event held for the benefit of Odyssey House. Jane led the conga line. More recently Jane was to be seen in a new Playtex eighteen-hour living bra television commercial promoting the product designed for "full-figured women."†
Seated in the living-room set of the ad, Jane made a particularly lovely spokeswoman—women's liberation to one side—being photographed in a most flattering light, and displaying a softness of approach never present before in her professional delivery.

Just when it seemed that Jane, once the most desired girl in America, was wilting on the romantic vine, she upped and married forty-nine year old John Calvin Peoples, a real estate man. The couple were wed in a tiny gold chapel in the gardens of the Santa Barbara, California home of the Right Reverend Michel d'Obrenovic on January 31, 1974. Said Jane of her third husband, "John is the sweetest, dearest man in the world! . . . I've known John for several years, ever since he started dating my close friend Merilyn Garcin [who was Jane's attendant at the Russell-Peoples wedding]. Then on night, a long time after he broke up with her, he asked me to dinner . . . and then our ro-

*Jane maintained this dignified silence in print and person (even in the face of some determined late-night-television-show interviewers who persisted in pushing a closed subject with Jane. On each occasion she would politely decline to answer the question about Hughes or would kiddingly say, "You probably know more on the subject than I do." Which made it strange when one national weekly newspaper of dubious journalistic standards printed a story alleged to be based on a new interview with Jane, who suddenly was giving out loose talk of her Hughes years. These statements she later flatly disclaimed having ever made: "After World War II, when he was making more films, he'd have the director shoot two separate movies of the same script—one that was shown in public theatres and the other where everyone in the picture was nude.

"But he only showed those reels to the cast.

"I never participated in this, although I was naked from the waist up in some scenes in *The Outlaw.* But they were re-shot with me wearing a top.

"He did throw some wild parties though, really wild. I can't go into detail about this."

†She had previously done a cat food video commercial.

mance just sort of happened. . . . John likes all the things I do, like golf, bike riding and boating. You know, it's funny. I've had a big boat for many years and never really enjoyed it. Now all of a sudden I love it—because of John." Said the beaming groom, "I must be the envy of millions of American men. She is my woman. Every time I meet her, it's like finding home plate in a baseball game."

On the 1970s professional front, thanks largely to persistent interest in the enigmatic billionaire Howard Hughes, Jane is not an entirely unknown commodity to the new generations who never saw or even heard about *The Outlaw*. However, the prospects for Jane's professional future are shaky at best. In the permissive new age, even Jane's legitimate screen successors are finding it difficult to obtain satisfactory roles in any medium. With the proliferation of the hard-core skin flicks and the live massage palaces, it is hard to find customers for restrained screen and television entertainment starring aging busty gals.

But Jane is not asking for the show business moon again in her bid for more work. "It's not an egocentric thing. It's not that I want to be fawned over, but more that I don't relish being ignored."

Feature Film Appearances
JANE RUSSELL

THE OUTLAW (RKO, 1943) 126 M.*

Producer, Howard Hughes; supervising film director, Otho Lovering; directors, Howard Hawks, Hughes; screenplay, Jules Furthman; music director, Victor Young; assistant director, Sam Nelson; art director, Perry Ferguson; special effects, Roy Davidson; second unit camera, Lucien Ballard; camera, Gregg Toland; editor, Walter Grissell.

Jack Buetel (Billy the Kid); Jane Russell (Rio); Thomas Mitchell (Pat Garrett); Walter Huston (Doc Holliday); Mimi Aguglia (Guadalupe); Joe Sawyer (Charley); Gene Rizzi (Stranger); Frank Darien (Shorty); Pat West (Bartender); Carl Stockdale (Minister); Nena Quartaro (Chita); Dickie Jones, Frank Ward, Bobby Callahan (Boys); Ethan Laidlaw, Ed Brady, William Steele (Deputies); Wally Reid, Jr. (Bystander); Ed Peil, Sr. (Swanson); Lee "Lasses" White (Coach Driver); Ted Mapes (Guard); William Newell (Drunk Cowboy); Cecil Kellogg (Officer); Lee Shumway (Dealer); Emory Parnell (Dolan); Martin Garralaga (Waiter); Julian Rivero (Pablo); Arthur Loft, Dick Elliott, John Sheehan (Salesmen).

*Post-1943 showing, 117 minutes.

YOUNG WIDOW (UA, 1946) 100 M.

Producer, Hunt Stromberg; director, Edwin L. Marin; based on the novel by Clarissa Fairchild Cushman; screenplay, Richard Macaulay, Margaret Buell Wilder; additional dialog, Ruth Nordli; music, Carmen Dragon; production design-art director, Nikolai Remisoff; assistant director, Harold Godsoe; sound, William H. Lynch; camera, Lee Garmes; editor, James Newcom.

Jane Russell (Joan Kenwood); Louis Hayward (Jim Cameron); Faith Domergue (Gerry Taylor); Marie Wilson (Mac); Kent Taylor (Peter Waring); Penny Singleton (Peg Martin); Connie Gilchrist (Aunt Cissie); Cora Witherspoon (Aunt Emeline); Steve Brodie (Willie); Norman Lloyd (Sammy); Richard Bailey (Bill Martin); Robert Holton (Bob Johnson); Peter Garey (Navy Lieutenant); Bill Moss (Marine Lieutenant); Bill "Red" Murphy (Army Lieutenant); Gerald Mohr (Charlie); James Burke (Motorcycle Cop); Jimmie Dodd (Officer Friend); Harry Barris (Officers' Club Pianist); William Newell (Charlie); Dick Wessel (Cabby); George Meader (Photographer); George Lloyd (Man on Platform); James Flavin (Conductor); Walter Baldwin (Miller).

THE PALEFACE (Par., 1948) C—91 M.

Producer, Robert L. Welch; director, Norman Z. McLeod; screenplay, Edmund Hartman, Frank Tashlin; additional dialog, Jack Rose; art director, Hans Dreier, Earl Hedrick; set decorator, Sam Comer, Bertram Granger; music, Victor Young;

songs, Joseph J. Lilley; Jay Livingston and Ray Evans; choreography, Billy Daniel; costumes, Mary Kay Dodson; sound, Gene Merritt, John Cope; assistant director, Alvin Ganzer; special effects, Gordon Jennings; process camera, Farciot Edouart; camera, Ray Rennahan; editor, Ellsworth Hoagland.

Bob Hope ("Painless" Peter Potter); Jane Russell (Calamity Jane); Robert Armstrong (Terris); Iris Adrian (Pepper); Robert Watson (Toby Preston); Jack Searl (Jasper Martin); Joseph Vitale (Indian Scout); Charles Trowbridge (Governor Johnson); Clem Bevans (Hank Billings); Jeff York (Joe); Stanley Andrews (Commissioner Emerson); Wade Crosby (Web); Chief Yowlachie (Chief Yellow Feather); Iron Eyes Cody (Chief Iron Eyes); John Maxwell (Village Gossip); Tom Kennedy (Bartender); Henry Brandon (Wapato, the Medicine Man); Francis J. McDonald (Lance); Frank Hagney (Greg); Skelton Knaggs (Pete); Olin Howlin (Undertaker); George Chandler, Nestor Paiva (Patients); Earl Hodgins (Clem); Arthur Space (Zach); Trevor Bardette, Alan Bridge (Horsemen); Edgar Dearing (Sheriff); Dorothy Grainger (Bath House Attendant); Charles Cooley (Mr "X"); Eric Alden (Bob); Babe London (Woman on Wagon Train); Loyal Underwood (Bearded Character); Billy Engle, Houseley Stevenson, Al M. Hill (Pioneers); Margaret Field, Laura Corbay (Guests); Duke York, Ethan Laidlaw (Henchmen); John "Skins" Miller (Bellhop); Wally Boyle (Hotel Clerk); Stanley Blystone, Bob Kortman (Onlookers); Lane Chandler (Tough-Looking Galoot); Oliver Blake (Westerner); Carl Andre, Ted Mapes, Kermit Maynard (Horsemen); Dick Elliott (Mayor); Betty Hannon, Charmienne Harker, Dee La Nore, Marie J. Tavares, Marilyn Gladstone, June Glory (B-Girls); Harry Harvey, Paul Burns (Justices of the Peace).

HIS KIND OF WOMAN   (RKO, 1951) 120 M.

Producer, Howard Hughes, Robert Sparks; director, John Farrow; story, Frank Fenton, Jack Leonard; screenplay, Fenton; art director, Albert S. D'Agostino; music director, C. Bakaleinikoff; songs, Sam Coslow; Harold Adamson and Jimmy McHugh; camera, Harry J. Wild; editor, Eda Warren.

Robert Mitchum (Dan Milner); Jane Russell (Lenore Brent); Vincent Price (Mark Cardigan); Tim Holt (Bill Lusk); Charles McGraw (Thompson); Marjorie Reynolds (Helen Cardigan); Raymond Burr (Nick Ferraro); Leslye Banning (Jennie Stone); Jim Backus (Myron Winton); Philip Van Zandt (Jose Morro); John Mylong (Martin Krafft); Carleton G. Young (Hobson); Erno Verebes (Estaban); Dan White (Tex Kearns); Richard Berggren (Milton Stone); Stacy Harris (Harry); Robert Cornthwaite (Hernandez); Jim Burke (Barkeep); Paul Frees (Corle); Joe Granby (Arnold); Daniel De Laurentis (Mexican Boy); John Sheehan (Husband); Sally Yarnell (Wife); Anthony Caruso (Tony); Robert Rose (Corle's Servant); Tol Avery (The Fat One); Paul Fierro, Mickey Simpson (Hoodlums); Ed Rand, Jerry James (Cops); Joel Fluellen (Sam); Len Hendry (Customer); Joey Ray, Barry Brooks (Card Players); Gwen Caldwell, Don House (Guests); Barbara Freking, Mamie Van Doren, Joy Windsor, Jerri Jordan, Mary Brewer (Girls); Maria Sen Young (Chinese Waitress); Bud Wolfe (Seaman); Bill Nelson (Captain Salazarr); William Justine (Gyppo); Ralph Gomez (Mexican Foreman); Peter Brocco (Short and Thin); Mike Lally (Henchman); Gerry Ganzer (Countess); Saul Gorss (Viscount); Mariette Elliott (Redhead).

DOUBLE DYNAMITE   (RKO, 1951) 80 M.

Producer-director, Irving Cummings; based on characters created by Mannie Manheim; story, Leo Rosten; screenplay, Melville Shavelson; additional dialog, Harry Crane; art director, Albert S. D'Agostino, Feild Gray; set decorator, Darrell Silvera, Harley Miller; assistant director, James Lane; music, Leigh Harline; songs,

Sammy Cahn and Jule Styne; makeup, Gordon Bau; sound, Phil Brigandi, Clem Portman; camera, Robert De Grasse; editor, Harry Marker.

Frank Sinatra (Johnny Dalton); Jane Russell (Mildred Goodhue); Groucho Marx (Emil J. Keck); Don McGuire (Bob Pulsifer); Howard Freeman (R. B. Pulsifer, Sr.); Nestor Paiva (Man with Sunglasses); Frank Orth (Mr. Kofer); Harry Hayden (McKissack); William Edmunds (Baganucci); Russ Thorson (Tailman); Joe Devlin (Frankie Boy); Lou Nova (Max); Benny Burt (Waiter); Bill Snyder (Wire-Service Man); Bill Erwin, Charles Regan, Dick Gordon, Mike Lally, Jack Jahries, Gil Perkins, Jack Gargan (Men); Claire Du Brey (Hatchet-faced Lady); Charles Coleman (Santa Claus); Ida Moore (Little Old Lady); Harry Kingston, Kermit Kegley (Goons); Jean De Briac (Maitre D'); George Chandler (Messenger); Hal Dawson (Mr. Hartman); Virgil Johnansen (Santa Claus); William Bailey (Bank Guard); Jack Chefe (Chef); Al Murphy (Waiter); Jim Nolan, Lee Phelps (Detectives); Lillian West (Hotel Maid); Dickie Derrel (Boy); Charles Sullivan (Sergeant); Harold Goodwin (Lieutenant).

THE LAS VEGAS STORY   (RKO, 1952) 88 M.

Executive producer, Samuel Bischoff; producer, Robert Sparks; director, Robert Stevenson; screenplay, Earl Felton, Harry Essex; art director, Albert S. D'Agostino, Feild Gray; set decorator, Darrell Silvera, John Sturdevant; music director, C. Bakaleinikoff; songs, Hoagy Carmichael; Carmichael and Harold Adamson; gowns, Howard Greer; makeup, Mel Burns; special effects, Harold Wellman; camera, Harry J. Wild; editor, George Shrader.

Jane Russell (Linda Rollins); Victor Mature (Dave Andrews); Vincent Price (Lloyd Rollins); Hoagy Carmichael (Happy); Brad Dexter (Tom Hubler); Colleen Miller (Mary); Chet Marshall (Bill); Gordon Oliver (Drucker); Jay C. Flippen (Harris); Bill Welsh (Martin); Will Wright (Mike Fogarty); Ray Montgomery (Desk Clerk); Syd Saylor (Cab Driver); Clarence Muse (Pullman Porter).

MACAO   (RKO, 1952) 80 M.

Executive producer, Samuel Bischoff; producer, Alex Gottlieb; director, Josef von Sternberg;* story, Bob Williams; screenplay, Bernard C. Schoenfeld, Stanley Rubin; (uncredited additional scenes shot by director Nicholas Ray scripted by Walter Newman); songs, Johnny Mercer and Harold Arlen, Jule Styne and Leo Robin; music, Anthony Collins; art director, Albert S. D'Agostino, Harley Miller; costumes, Michael Woulfe; set decorator, Darrell Silvera, Harley Miller; makeup, Mel Berns; camera, Harry J. Wild; editor, Samuel E. Beetley.

Robert Mitchum (Nick Cochran); Jane Russell (Julie Benson); William Bendix (Lawrence Trumble); Thomas Gomez (Lieutenant Sebastian); Gloria Grahame (Margie); Brad Dexter (Halloran); Edward Ashley (Martin Stewart); Philip Ahn (Itzumi); Vladimir Sokoloff (Kwan Sum Tang); Don Zelaya (Gimpy); Emory Parnell (Ship Captain); Nacho Galindo (Bus Driver); Philip Van Zandt (Customs Official); George Chan (Chinese Photographer); Sheldon Jett (Dutch Tourist); Genevieve Bell (Woman Passenger); Tommy Lee (Coolie Knifed in Water); Alex Montoya (Coolie Bartender); James B. Leong (Knifer); Alfredo Santos, Marc Krah (Hoodlums); Marc Krah (Desk Clerk); May Taksugi (Barber); Lee Tung Foo (Chinese Merchant); Maria Sen Young, Iris Wong (Croupiers); Manuel Paris (Bartender); Art Dupuis (Portuguese Pilot); William Yip (Rickshaw Driver); Michael Visaroff (Russian Doorman); W. T. Chang (Old Fisherman); Weaver Levy (Chang); Trevor Bardette (Bus Driver); Rico Alaniz (Alvaris); Walter Ng (Fisherman).

*Much of the film was redirected by Nicholas Ray.

MONTANA BELLE (RKO, 1952) C—81 M.

Producer, Howard Welsch; associate producer, Robert Peters; director, Allan Dwan; story, M. Coates Webster, Welsch; screenplay, Horace McCoy, Norman S. Hall; art director, Frank Arrigo; set decorator, John McCarthy, Jr., George Milo; costumes, Adele Palmer; music, Nathan Scott; song, Portia Nelson and Margaret Martinez; special effects, Howard and Theodore Lydecker; camera, Jack Marta; editor, Arthur Roberts.

Jane Russell (Belle Starr); George Brent (Tom Bradfield); Scott Brady (Bob Dalton); Forrest Tucker (Mac); Andy Devine (Pete Bivins); Jack Lambert (Ringo); John Litel (Matt Towner); Ray Teal (Emmett Dalton); Rory Mallinson (Grat Dalton); Roy Barcroft (Jim Clark); Holly Bane (Ben Dalton); Eugene Roth (Marshal Ripple); Gregg Barton (Deputy Stewart); Glenn Strange, Pierce Lyden, George Chesebro (Deputies); Ned Davenport (Bank Clerk); Dennis Moore (Messenger); Stanley Andrews (Marshal Combs); Dick Elliott (Banker Jeptha Rideout); Kenneth MacDonald (Sheriff Irving); Rodney Bell (Hotel Clerk); Iron Eyes Cody (Cherokee); Rex Lease (Barfly); Charles Soldani (Indian); Hank Bell (Bartender); Franklyn Farnum (Man in Audience); Frank Ellis (Kibitzer); Paul Stader (Double for Scott Brady); Terry Wilson (Double for Forrest Tucker); Dave Sharpe (Rider for Iron Eyes Cody); Tom Steele (Rider for Stanley Andrews); Joe Yrigoyen (Double for Jack Lambert).

SON OF PALEFACE (Par., 1952) C—95 M.

Producer, Robert L. Welch; director, Frank Tashlin; screenplay, Tashlin, Welch, Joseph Quillan; choreography, Josephine Earl; songs, Jay Livingston and Ray Evans; Jack Brooks, Jack Hope and Lyle Moraine; art director, Hal Pereira, Roland Anderson; music, Lyn Murray; special camera, Gordon Jennings, Paul Lerpae; process camera, Farciot Edouart; camera, Harry J. Wild; editor, Eda Warren.

Bob Hope (Junior); Jane Russell (Mike); Roy Rogers (Himself); Bill Williams (Kirk); Lloyd Corrigan (Doc Lovejoy); Paul E. Burns (Ebeneezer Hawkins); Douglass Dumbrille (Sheriff McIntyre); Harry Von Zell (Stoner); Iron Eyes Cody (Indian Chief); Wee Willie Davis (Blacksmith); Charley Cooley (Charley); Robert L. Welch, Cecil B. DeMille, Bing Crosby (Guest Spots); Charles Morton (Ned); Don Dunning (Wally); Leo J. McMahon (Crag); Felice Richmond (Genevieve); Charmienne Harker (Bessie); Isabel Cushin (Isabel); Jane Easton (Clara); Homer Dickinson (Townsman); Lyle Moraine (Bank Clerk Weaverly); Hank Mann (Bartender); Michael A. Cirillo (Micky, the Bartender); Isabel Cushin (Becky, the B-Girl); Chester Conklin (Townsman); Flo Stanton (Flo); John George (Johnny); Joseph Epper, George Russell, Lewis H. Morphy, Danny H. Sands, James Van Horn, Charles Quirk (Posse); Frank Cordell (Dade); Willard Willingham (Jeb); Warren Fiske (Trav); Carl Andre (Pedra); Anne Dore (She-Devil); Gordon Carveth (Indian); Freddie Zendar (Ollie); Al Ferguson (Man); Rudy Lee (Boy); Hazel Boyne (Old Lady); Wally Boyle (Perkins); Rus Conklin (Indian); Oliver Blake (Telegrapher); Bob St. Angelo (Lem); Howard Joslin (Sam); Rose Plummer (Townswoman); Art Cameron (Art); Geraldine Farnum (Cigarette Girl); Louise Lane, Joanne Arnold, Marie Shaw, Blanche Renze (Dance-Hall Cuties); Sue Carlton, Valerie Vernon (Girls in Bedroom Scene); Marie Shaw (Matron); Jonathan Hale (Governor); Jean Willes (Penelope); Jack Pepper (Customer in Restaurant).

ROAD TO BALI (Par., 1952) C—91 M.

Producer, Harry Tugend; director, Hal Walker; story, Frank Butler, Tugend; screenplay, Butler, Hal Kanter, William Morrow; art director, Hal Pereira, Joseph McMillan Johnson; set decorator, Sam Comer, Russ Dowd; sound, Gene Merritt,

John Cope; music director, Joseph J. Lilley; choreography, Charles O'Curran; orchestral arranger, Van Cleave; songs, Johnny Burke and James Van Heusen; camera, George Barnes; editor, Archie Marshek.

Bob Hope (Harold Gridley); Bing Crosby (George Cochran); Dorothy Lamour (Lalah); Murvyn Vye (Ken Arok); Peter Coe (Gung); Ralph Moody (Bhoma Da); Leon Askin (Ramayana); Jane Russell, Dean Martin, Jerry Lewis, Bob Crosby, (Themselves); Jack Claus (Specialty Dancer); Bernie Gozier (Bo Kassar); Herman Cantor (Priest); Shela Fritz, Ethel K. Reiman, Irene K. Silva (Chief's Wives); Charles Mauu, Al Kikume, Satini Puailoa (Warriors); Mylee Haulani (Beautiful Girl in Basket); Kukhie Kuhns (Fat Woman in Basket); Michael Ansara (Guard); Larry Chance (Attendant); Bunny Lewbel (Lalah at 7); Pat Dane, Sue Casey, Patti McKaye, Judith Landon, Leslie Charles, Jean Corbett, Betty Onge (Handmaidens); Roy Gordon (Eunice's Father); Harry Cording (Verna's Father); Carolyn Jones (Eunice); Jan Kayne (Verna); Allan Nixon (Eunice's Brother); Douglas Yorke (Verna's Brother); Mary Kanae (Old Crone); Raymond Lee, Luukia Luana (Boys); Bismark Auelua, Bhogwan Singh, Chanan Singh Sohi, Jerry Groves (Lesser Priests).

GENTLEMEN PREFER BLONDES   (20th, 1953) C—91 M.

Producer, Sol C. Siegel; director, Howard Hawks; based on the play by Anita Loos, Joseph Fields; screenplay, Charles Lederer; art director, Lyle Wheeler, Joseph C. Wright; songs, Hoagy Carmichael and Harold Adamson; Jule Styne and Leo Robin; music director, Lionel Newman; choreography, Jack Cole; camera, Harry J. Wild; editor, Hugh S. Fowler.

Jane Russell (Dorothy); Marilyn Monroe (Lorelei Lee); Charles Coburn (Sir Francis Beekman); Elliott Reid (Malone); Tommy Noonan (Gus Esmond); George "Foghorn" Winslow (Henry Spofford III); Marcel Dalio (Magistrate); Taylor Holmes (Esmond, Sr.); Norma Varden (Lady Beekman); Howard Wendell (Watson); Henri Letondal (Grotier); Steven Geray (Hotel Manager); Alex Frazer (Pritchard); Robert Fuller (Man); George Chakiris (Dancer); Leo Mostovoy (Phillipe); George Davis (Cab Driver); Alphonse Martell (Headwaiter); Jimmie Moultrie, Freddie Moultrie (Boy Dancers); Jean De Briac, Peter Camlin, George Dee (Gendarmes); Harry Carey, Jr. (Winslow); Jean Del Val (Ship's Captain); Ray Montgomery (Peters); Alvy Moore (Anderson); Robert Nichols (Evans); Charles Tannen (Ed); Jimmy Young (Stevens); Charles De Ravanne (Purser); John Close (Coach); William Cabanne (Sims); Philip Sylvestre (Steward); Jack Chefe (Proprietor); John Hedloe (Athlete); Max Willenz (Court Clerk); Rolfe Sedan (Waiter); Robert Foulk, Ralph Peters (Passport Officials); Harris Brown, A. Cameron Grant (Men); Harry Seymour (Captain of Waiters); Donald Moray (Airport Porter); Deena Dikkers (Hotel Clerk); Richard La Marr (Man); Fred Stevens (Stagehand).

THE FRENCH LINE   (RKO, 1953) C—102 M.

Producer, Edmund Grainger; director, Lloyd Bacon; story, Matty Kemp, Isabel Dawn; screenplay, Mary Loos, Richard Sale; art director, Albert S. D'Agostino, Carroll Clark; songs, Josef Myrow, Ralph Blane and Robert Wells; music, Walter Scharf; choreography, Billy Daniel; gowns, Michael Woulfe, Howard Greer; camera, Harry J. Wild; editor, Robert Ford.

Jane Russell (Mary Carson); Gilbert Roland (Pierre Du Quesne); Arthur Hunnicutt (Waco Mosby); Mary McCarty (Annie Farrell); Joyce MacKenzie (Myrtle Brown); Paula Corday (Celeste); Scott Elliott (Bill Harris); Craig Stevens (Phil Barton); Laura Elliot (Katherine Hodges); Steven Geray (Francois); John Wengraf (First Mate); Michael St. Angel (George Hodges); Barbara Darrow (Donna Adams); Barbara Dobbins (Kitty Lee); Jean Moorehead, Mary Rodman, Kim

Novak, Jarma Lewis, Jane Easton, Suzanne Alexander, Doreen Woodbury, Ellye Marshall, Pat Sheehan, Maureen Stephenson (Models); Bess Flowers (Saleslady); Ramona Magrill (Seamstress); George Wallace (Cowboy); William Forrest (Sam Baker); Jack Chefe (Wine Steward); Allen Ray, Jeffrey Sayre, Robert Dayo, Renald Dupont (Reporters); Wayne Taylor (French Bellhop); Toni Carroll (Toni); Mary Jane Carey (American Nurse); Dede Moore, Gloria Pall, Helen Chapman, Sue Casey, Mary Ellen Gleason, Joi Lansing (Showgirls); Shirley Patterson (Elsie); Fritz Feld (French Cabbie); Bert Le Baron (Doorman).

UNDERWATER! (RKO, 1955) C—99 M.

Producer, Harry Tatelman; director, John Sturges; story, Hugh King, Robert B. Bailey; screenplay, Walter Newman; music, Roy Webb; costumes, Michael Woulfe; assistant director, William Dorfman; underseas camera, Lamar Boren; camera, Harry J. Wild; editor, Stuart Gilmore.

Jane Russell (Theresa); Gilbert Roland (Dominic); Richard Egan (Johnny); Lori Nelson (Gloria); Robert Keith (Father Cannon); Joseph Calleia (Rico); Eugene Iglesias (Miguel); Ric Roman (Jesus); Robert Polo (Deck Hand); Max Wagner, Dan Bernaducci (Waiters); Jamie Russell (Cab Driver).

FOXFIRE (Univ., 1955) C—91½ M.

Producer, Aaron Rosenberg; director, Joseph Pevney; based on a novel by Anya Seton; screenplay, Ketti Frings; art director, Alexander Golitzen, Robert Clatworthy; music, Frank Skinner; music supervisor, Joseph Gershenson; song, Jeff Chandler and Henry Mancini; assistant director, Ronnie Rondell, Phil Bowles; camera, William Daniels; editor, Ted J. Kent.

Jane Russell (Amanda Lawrence); Jeff Chandler (Jonathan Dartland); Dan Duryea (Hugh Slater); Mara Corday (Maria); Frieda Inescort (Mrs. Lawrence); Barton MacLane (Mr. Mablett); Robert F. Simon (Ernest Tyson); Eddy C. Waller (Old Larky); Celia Lovsky (Saba); Charlotte Wynters (Mrs. Mablett); Lillian Bronson (Mrs. Potter); Arthur Space (Foley); Phil Chambers (Mr. Riley); Robert Bice (Walt Whitman); Guy Wilkerson (Mr. Barton); Mary Carroll (Mrs. Riley); Vici Raaf (Cleo); Grace Lenard (Rose); Lisabeth Fielding (Mrs. Foley); Dabbs Greer (Bus Driver); Hal K. Dawson (Man Tourist); Charmienne Harker (Rowena); Grace Hayle (Woman Tourist); Beulah Archuletta (Indian Woman); Billy Wilkerson (Apache Chief); Chebon Jadi (Bellhop); Leon Charles, Jimmy Casino, Charles Soldani, Martin Cichy (Miners); Manley Suathojame (Indian Husband); R. H. Baldwin (Hoist Operator).

THE TALL MEN (20th, 1955) C—122 M.

Producer, William A. Bacher, William B. Hawks; director, Raoul Walsh; based on the novel by Clay Fisher; screenplay, Sydney Boehm, Frank Nugent; music, Victor Young; songs, Ken Darby and Jose Lopez Alaves; costumes, Travilla; assistant director, Stanley Hough; art director, Lyle R. Wheeler, Mark-Lee Kirk; camera, Leo Tover; editor, Louis Loeffler.

Clark Gable (Ben Allison); Jane Russell (Nella Turner); Robert Ryan (Nathan Stark); Cameron Mitchell (Clint Allison); Juan Garcia (Luis); Harry Shannon (Sam); Emile Meyer (Chickasaw); Steven Darrell (Colonel); Will Wright (Gus, the Bartender); Robert Adler (Wrangler); Russell Simpson (Emigrant Man); Tom Wilson (Miner); Tom Fadden (Stable Owner); Dan White (Hotel Clerk); Argentina Brunetti (Maria); Doris Kemper (Mrs. Robbins); Carl Harbaugh (Salesman); Post Park (Stagecoach Driver); Gabrile Del Valle (Man); Meyito Pulito, Gilda Fontana (Spanish Girls); Frank Leyva (Waiter); Jack Mather (Cavalry Lieutenant).

GENTLEMEN MARRY BRUNETTES   (UA, 1955) C—97 M.

Executive producer, Robert Bassler; producer, Richard Sale, Robert Waterfield; associate producer, Mary Loos; director, Sale; based on the story "But Gentlemen Marry Brunettes" by Anita Loos; screenplay, Mary Loos, Sale; assistant director, Basil Keys, Robert Genore; music, Robert Farnon; choreography, Jack Cole; songs, Walter Donaldson; Richard Rodgers and Lorenz Hart; Fats Waller and Andy Razof; Sidney Clare and Lew Pollack; Bob Troup; Bert Kalmar, Herbert Stothart, and Harry Ruby; costumes, Travilla; gowns, Christian Dior; camera, Desmond Dickinson; editor, G. Turney-Smith.

Jane Russell (Bonnie and Mimi Jones); Jeanne Crain (Connie and Mitzie Jones); Alan Young (Charlie Biddle, Mrs. Biddle, Mr. Biddle, Sr.); Scott Brady (David Action); Rudy Vallee (Himself); Guy Middleton (Earl of Wickenware); Eric Pohlmann (Monsieur Ballard); Ferdy Mayne (Monsieur Dufond); Leonard Sachs (Monsieur Dufy); Guido Lorraine (Monsieur Marcel); Derek Sydney (Stage Manager); Body Caheen (Philot); Robert Favart (Hotel Manager); Duncan Elliot (Couturier); Edward Tracy (Chauffeur); Michael Balfour (Stage Doorman); Penny Dane (Wardrobe Woman).

HOT BLOOD   (Col., 1956) C—85 M.

Producer, Howard Welsch, Harry Tatelman; director, Nicholas Ray; story, Jean Evans; screenplay, Jesse Lasky, Jr.; music, Les Baxter; choreography, Matt Mattox, Sylvia Lewis; assistant director, Milton Feldman; art director, Robert Peterson; songs, Baxter and Ross Bagdasarian; camera, Ray June; editor, Otto Ludwig.

Jane Russell (Annie Caldash); Cornel Wilde (Stephan Torino); Luther Adler (Marco Torino); Joseph Calleia (Papa Theodore); Mikhail Rasumny (Old Johnny); Nina Koshetz (Nita Johnny); Helen Westcott (Velma); Jamie Russell (Xano); Wally Russell (Bimbo); Nick Dennis (Korka); Richard Deacon (Mr. Swift); Robert Foulk (Sergeant McGrossin); John Raven (Joe Randy).

THE REVOLT OF MAMIE STOVER   (20th, 1956) C—92 M.

Producer, Buddy Adler; director, Raoul Walsh; based on the novel by William Bradford Huie; screenplay, Sydney Boehm; art director, Lyle R. Wheeler, Mark-Lee Kirk; music director, Lionel Newman; music, Hugo Friedhofer; songs, Tony Todaro and Mary Johnston, Paul Francis Webster and Sammy Fain; costumes, Travilla; assistant director, Joseph E. Richards; special camera, Ray Kellogg; camera, Leo Tover; editor, Louis Loeffler.

Jane Russell (Mamie Stover); Richard Egan (Jim); Joan Leslie (Annalea); Agnes Moorehead (Bertha Parchman); Jorja Cutright (Jackie); Michael Pate (Harry Adkins); Richard Coogan (Eldon Sumac); Alan Reed (Gorecki); Eddie Firestone (Tarzan); Jean Willes (Gladys); Leon Lontoc (Aki); Kathy Marlowe (Zelda); Margia Dean (Peaches); Jack Mather (Bartender); John Halloran (Henry); Boyd Red Morgan (Hackett); Naida Lani, Anita Dano (Hula Dancers); Dorothy Gordon, Irene Bolton, Merry Townsend, Claire James, Sally Jo Todd, Margarita Camacho (Dance-Hall Girls); Richard Collier (Photographer); Max Reed (Hawaiian Cop); Janan Hart (Hostess); Johnny Caler (Soldier); Sherwood Price (Sailor); Frank Griffin (M.P.); Charles Keane (Detective); Jay Jostyn (Doctor); Arthur Grady (Young Soldier); Kayoka Wakita (Japanese Girl).

THE FUZZY PINK NIGHTGOWN   (UA, 1957) 87 M.

Producer, Robert Waterfield; director, Norman Taurog; based on the novel by Sylvia Tate; screenplay, Richard Alan Simmons; music, Billy May; assistant director, Stanley H. Goldsmith; costumes, Travilla; art director, Serge Krizman; camera, Joseph LaShelle; editor, Archie Marshek.

Jane Russell (Laurel Stevens); Keenan Wynn (Dandy); Ralph Meeker (Mike Valla); Fred Clark (Sergeant McBride); Una Merkel (Bertha); Adolphe Menjou (Arthur Martin); Benay Venuta (Daisy Parker); Robert H. Harris (Barney Baylies); Bob Kelley (TV Announcer); Dick Haynes (Disc Jockey); John Truax (Flack); Milton Frome (Lieutenant Dempsey).

FATE IS THE HUNTER (20th, 1964) 106 M.

Producer, Aaron Rosenberg; director, Ralph Nelson; based on the novel by Ernest K. Gann; screenplay, Harold Medford; music, Jerry Goldsmith; assistant director, Ad Schaumer; costumes, Moss Mabry; sound, Carl Falkner; art director, Hildyard Brown; camera, Milton Krasner; editor, Robert Simpson.

Glenn Ford (Sam McBane); Nancy Kwan (Sally Fraser); Rod Taylor (Capt. Jack Savage); Suzanne Pleshette (Martha Webster); Jane Russell (Herself); Wally Cox (Bundy); Dorothy Malone (Lisa Bond); Nehemiah Persoff (Ben Sawyer); Mark Stevens (Mickey Doolan); Max Showalter (Crawford); Howard St. John (Hutchins); Robert Wilke (Stillman); Bert Freed (Dillon); Dort Clark (Wilson); Mary Wickes (Mrs. Llewelyn); Robert F. Simons (Proctor); Peter Ford (Attendant); Harold Goodwin (Art Baldwin); Marianna Case (D'Arcy); Pauline Myers (Mother); John Hubbard (Robbins); Joseph Hoover (Newsman); Richard Walsh (Radio Newscaster); John Lawrence (Priest); Hal Taggart (Doctor); Tony Barr (Coordinator); Kort Falkenburg, Joe Scott (Controllers); Rusty Lane (Supervisor); Morgan Len Justin (TV Camera Crewman); George Dockstader (Policeman); James Secrest (Orderly); Marshall Reed, Paul Lukather, Ralph Thomas, Rusty Burrell, Robert Duggan, John Stevens (Reporters); Kem Dibbs, Robert Adler (FBI Men); Evadne Baker (Secretary); Angela Dawson (Child); Stanley Adams (Bartender); Francois Andre, David BeDell (Technician); Iris Adrian (Ad-Libber).

JOHNNY RENO (Par., 1966) C—83 M.

Producer, A. C. Lyles; director, R. G. Springsteen; story, Steve Fisher, Lyles; screenplay, Fisher; music, Jimmie Haskell; art director, Hal Pereira, Malcolm Brown; set decorator, Jerry Welch; assistant director, Jim Rosenberger, Bob Jones; makeup, Wally Westmore, Lou Haszillo; sound, Harold Lewis; camera, Hal Stiner; editor, Bernard Mates.

Dana Andrews (Johnny Reno); Jane Russell (Nona Williams); Lon Chaney (Sheriff Hodges); John Agar (Ed Tomkins); Lyle Bettger (Jess Yates); Tom Drake (Joe Connors); Richard Arlen (Reed); Tracy Olsen (Maria Yates); Paul Daniel (Chief Little Bear); Dale Van Sickle (Ab Connors); Robert Lowery (Jake Reed); Reg Parton (Bartender); Rodd Redwing (Indian); Charles Horvath (Wooster); Chuck Hicks (Bellows); Edmund Cobb (Townsman).

WACO (Par., 1966) C—85 M.

Producer, A. C. Lyles; director, R. G. Springstein; based on the novel by Harry Sanford, Max Lamb; screenplay, Steve Fisher; art director, Hal Pereira, Al Roelofs; set decorator, Robert Benton, Charles Pierce; music Jimmie Haskell; song, Haskell; sound, Terry Kellum, John Wilkenson; assistant director, James Rosenberger; camera, Robert Pittack; editor, Bernard Mates.

Howard Keel (Waco); Jane Russell (Jill Stone); Brian Donlevy (Ace Ross); Wendell Corey (Preacher Sam Stone); Terry Moore (Dolly); John Smith (Joe Gore); John Agar (George Gates); Gene Evans (Deputy Sheriff O'Neill); Richard Arlen (Sheriff Billy Kelly); Ben Cooper (Scotty Moore); Tracy Olsen (Patricia West);

DeForest Kelly (Bill Rile); Anne Seymour (Ma Jenner); Robert Lowery (Mayor Ned West); Willard Parker (Peter Jenner); Jeff Richards (Ike Jenners); Reg Parton (Kallen); Fuzzy Knight (Telegraph Operator).

BORN LOSERS   (American International Pictures, 1967) 112 M.

Executive producer, Delores Taylor; producer-director-screenplay, Tom Laughlin; music producers, Mike Curb, Al Simms; art director, Rick Beck-Meyer; sound, Leroy Robbins; assistant director, Paul Lewis; makeup, Louis Lane; camera, Gregory Sandor; editor, John Winfield.

Tom Laughlin (Billy Jack); Elizabeth James (Vicky Barrington); Jane Russell (Mrs. Shorn); Jeremy Slate (Danny Carmody); William Wellman, Jr. (Child); Robert Tessier (Cue Ball); Jeff Cooper (Gangrene); Edwin Cook (Crabs); Tex (Tex); Paul Prokop (Speechless); Julie Cahn (Lu Ann Crawford); Susan Foster (Linda Prang); Janice Miller (Jodell Shorn); Stuart Lancaster (Sheriff); Jack Starrett (Deputy); Paul Bruce (District Attorney); Robert Cleaves (Mr. Crawford); Ann Bellamy (Mrs. Prang); Gordon Hobar (Jerry Carmody).

DARKER THAN AMBER   (National General, 1970) C—97 M.

Producer, Walter Seltzer, Jack Reeves; director, Robert Clouse; based on the novel by John D. MacDonald; screenplay, Ed Waters; music, John Parker; art director, Jack Collis; assistant director, Ted Swanson; makeup, Guy Del Russo, Marie Del Russo; set decorator, Don Ivey; camera, Frank Phillips; editor, Fred Chulack.

Rod Taylor (Travis McGee); Suzy Kendall (Vangic/Merrimay); Theodore Bikel (Meyer); Jane Russell (Alabama Tigress); James Booth (Burk); Janet MacLachlan (Noreen); William Smith (Terry); Ahna Capri (Del); Robert Phillips (Griff); Chris Robinson (Roy); Jack Nagle (Farnsworth); Sherry Faber (Nina); James H. Frysinger (Dewey Powell); Oswaldo Calvo (Manuel); Jeff Gillen (Morgue Attendant); Judy Wallace (Ginny); Harry Wood (Ginny); Michael De Beausset (Dr. Fairbanks); Marcy Knight (Landlady); Warren Bauer, Wayne Bauer (Roy's Companions); Don Schoff (Steward).

With Thomas Mitchell, Walter Huston, and Jack Buetel in THE OUTLAW (RKO '43)

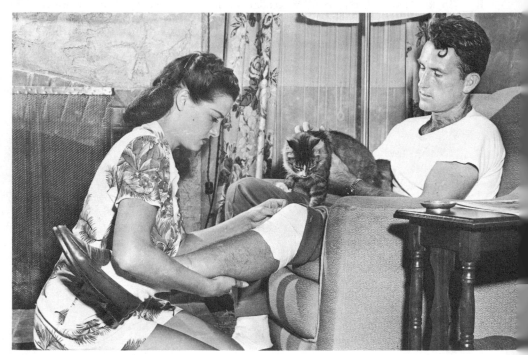

With husband Robert Waterfield in October, 1944

With Louis Hayward on the set of YOUNG WIDOW (UA '46)

Jane Russell, c. 1948

With Bob Hope in THE PALEFACE (Par '48)

With Robert Mitchum and
Vincent Price in HIS KIND
OF WOMAN (RKO '51)

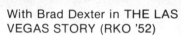

With Brad Dexter in THE LAS
VEGAS STORY (RKO '52)

With Frank Sinatra in
DOUBLE DYNAMITE (RKO '51)

In MACAO (RKO '52)

In THE FRENCH LINE
(RKO '53)

With George Brent in
MONTANA BELLE (RKO '52)

In GENTLEMEN PREFER
BLONDES (20th '53)

With Beryl Davis, Connie Haines
and Della Russell at the
recording session for
"Do Lord" in 1954

With Scott Brady, Alan Young, Derek Sydney, and Jeanne Crain in GENTLEMEN MARRY BRUNETTES (UA '55)

With Cornel Wilde in HOT BLOOD (Col. '56)

With Richard Egan in THE REVOLT OF MAMIE STOVER (20th '56)

With Keenan Wynn in THE
FUZZY PINK NIGHTGOWN
(UA '57)

Appearing on the nightclub
circuit in Italy in 1960

With Rod Taylor in FATE IS
THE HUNTER (20th '64)

VACO (Par '66)

With husband Roger Barrett in August, 1968, after their wedding

ARKER THAN AMBER
(National General '70)

Leading the conga line at the "Fabulous Forties" night (June 5, 1972) at Roseland Dance City, New York City

In FIRST YANK INTO TOKYO (RKO '45)

5'5½"
115 pounds
Brown hair
Hazel eyes
Aries

Barbara Hale

Today Barbara Hale is still best known to the general public as stalwart secretary Della Street, a role she played for nine video seasons (1957-66) on the Raymond Burr "Perry Mason" show. Her present chores as television spokeswoman for a home oven product have done nothing to alter this firm image.

Scanning Barbara's four-decade film career, it is easy to write her off as just one more run-of-the-mill 1940s leading lady of the once-proud RKO studios. She glided through a seven-year hitch at that film factory, where, during the 1940s, the major policy thrust was to churn out programmers, make a buck, and forget 'em, along with the starlets who populated the productions. Moreover, her enunciated career plans were never that lofty. She was a small-town midwestern gal with modest professional goals, tastes, and desires. She enjoyed acting and the above-average pay scale it provided, but she was far more earnest about wanting the complete life of a housewife-mother.

Obviously some perspective on the subject is necessary. On one hand she matched neither Anne Baxter in acting range nor Gene Tierney in looks, but on the other she cannot be passed off with a snap of the fingers as a movie player whose middle-class ambience and husky-toned voice *add up to nothing more than a glorified Rosemary DeCamp type. The mere fact that Barbara so far outdistanced the bulk of her studio and industry contemporaries of the World War II years proves her ability to arouse the interest of moviegoers, who found satisfaction in her sincere performances in a rash of mediocre pictures.*

Barbara was born in DeKalb, Illinois, on April 18, 1921, the second child* of Luther Ezra Hale, a landscape gardener, and Willa (Calvin) Hale. The Hales were of Scotch-Irish descent, and their forebears had resided in the Kentucky-Virginia area for generations. When Barbara was little more than two years old, the Hales moved to Rockford, Illinois, then a city of 100,000 population. Barbara grew up in a bungalow-styled house on elm-tree-lined North Central Avenue. From the age of twelve, she studied tap dancing and ballet, was considered a fairly talented painter, and participated in the city's little-theatre productions. During her high school years she held part-time jobs as a department store clerk, and, later, as a soda fountain waitress. She thought she might like to become a nurse or even a news reporter. In short, Barbara's daily life was as typically American as anything Ann Rutherford's Polly Benedict experienced in the *Andy Hardy* series. But whereas most girls of Barbie's upbringing would have been content to remain in their hometowns, to marry, have children (like her sister, Juanita, who was now a housewife with two children, Jimmy and Diana), and to grow old contentedly in the Middle American tradition, Barbara had an unsolidified creative urge that persuaded her to leave Rockford upon graduation from high school.

With her parents' blessing and financial support she moved to Chicago and enrolled at the Chicago Academy of Fine Arts, where she pursued a commercial art course. But Barbara's fellow students at the Academy were a far more talented conglomerate than those she had competed against in Rockford, and after two years she decided she did not have the makings for real success in the field. The clincher occurred one day when she returned to the classroom after a painting session in the nearby park. "I'll never forget," Barbara recalls, describing her nervous tension when the instructor inspected her latest effort, "as she held up the painting in front of the class, she looked at it upside down, then from one side and then the other, but never right side up. Finally she commented: 'Let me tell you one thing. When you go the the park to paint, try capturing one tree. Don't paint the whole park.'"

Barbara was not about to return to Rockford as an unproven "talent." She remembered that one day some months before, while she had been crossing a busy Chicago thoroughfare, a car had pulled up to the intersection of Michigan Avenue and Oak Street and a man stuck his head out the window. He called her over and handed her a business card, telling her

*The Hales' elder daughter, Juanita, had been born in 1913.

that if she ever wanted to model, to look him up. So Barbara, who had been the May Queen during her senior year at Rockford High School, and who had posed for the cartoon strip "Ramblin' Bill" during her art school days, went to the offices of the Chicago Model Bureau and was signed on by its proprietors, Corrine and Al Seaman. As soon as she grasped the basic techniques of her new profession, Barbara found herself much in demand as a model. Her salary rose to $100 weekly, permitting her to move out of the YWCA and into a small apartment, which she shared with a girlfriend. In the course of her work assignments she did photo modeling for Stanley Johnson, posed for Gil Elvgren for an Orange Crush drink layout, and, because of her quick popularity in modeling one particular product, was tagged the "Long Woolies Girl."

Barbara's employer, Al Seaman, was so enthusiastic about her rapid advance in the field that he was convinced his prize employee should be in the movies. Recalling that a classmate of his, Perry Lieber, was now a minor executive at RKO Studios (in the publicity field), Seaman sent him a photograph of Barbara. A short time later, when Arthur Willi, head of the RKO talent department, was returning to the Coast from New York, he stopped off in Chicago. Barbara was summoned to his suite at the Sherman Hotel. He was satisfied with her film potential and passed in a favorable report to Charles W. Koerner, then general manager of the studio. When Koerner was next in Chicago he met with Barbara and signed her to a stock contract.

If Barbara's life to this point seemed more glamorous and exciting than that of her hometown contemporaries, her values remained level-headed, modest, and undemanding. It was not the magnetic glitter of Hollywood and a chance to become a screen celebrity that decided her to accept the movie offer, but a more romantic reason. She was dating a soldier who had just been transferred to the West Coast and realized this would be a good way of joining him. Barbara packed her belongings, and, with a studio-supplied ticket on the Super Chief train, embarked one day in October, 1942, for California. She remembers spending most of the two-day trip in a state of tears, wondering to what dubious future she had committed herself.

No sooner had Barbara arrived in Hollywood and registered at the Studio Club for a $15-a-week room, than she was advised to check in at the studio. Within a day twenty-one-year-old Barbara was at work on the first of eight RKO pictures in which she would appear in 1943. In her first several films Barbara was only entrusted with bit parts, really mere walk-ons. RKO had passed its halcyon days as the creator of smart women's pictures with such stars as Ann Harding and Irene Dunne, and as the supplier of tasteful Fred Astaire-Ginger Rogers musicals. Commandeering Orson Welles and his Mercury Players had already proved a costly failure. So now the financially shaken corporation was embarked on a programmers-for-the masses output, geared to make up in quantity what the individual pictures lacked in quality. It was a realistic, if unimaginative, way of capitalizing on the lucrative World

War II theatre market. Because of RKO's recommitment to a heavy B-picture policy, it made sense to keep a constant turnover of low-priced contractees who could handle a stream of undemanding bit assignments. If any neophyte proved to have acting potential and, more importantly, box-office appeal, so much the better. These chosen few would be elevated to featured screen roles and given the "big" buildup—that is, until they became too costly in their salary demands and were allowed to try their luck at other, higher-paying, lots. Under this hit-or-miss method governed by a strenuous watch-the-budget dictate, some budding new players flowed right in and out of the studio. There had been a young girl in the late 1930s named Constance Keane who by the early 1940s had gained international prominence as Veronica Lake. Later there was another fledgling, Dorothy Malone, who went on to prominence at Warner Brothers and an academy award at Universal.

Barbara's initial seven RKO pictures reveal very little about her potential screen abilities, but the films themselves tell a good deal about the studio itself. Of all the Hollywood film factories RKO was the most enthusiastic about utilizing radio-series personalities in feature versions of their audio successes.* The obvious rationale was that a built-in audience existed that could be tapped with a minimum of publicity expense on the studio's part. So, in the late 1930s, Edgar Bergen and Charlie McCarthy became RKO studio fixtures along with Marion and Bill Jordan of "Fibber McGee and Molly" fame, Kay Kyser of the "Kollege of Musical Knowledge," Chester Lauck and Norris Goff of "Lum and Abner," and Harold Peary, who as Throckmorton P. Gildersleeve, water commissioner of Summerville, was known to seventeen million radio fans as The Great Gildersleeve. *Gildersleeve's Bad Day,* released in mid-1943, was Peary's second starring vehicle in the four-entry series.† Directed in a *laissez-faire* style by Gordon Douglas, this sixty-two-minute programmer found Gildersleeve the sole hold-out on a hung jury, which does not endear him to his fellow townsfolk. Later on, becoming involved with a gang of safecrackers is more of an exertion than rotund, odd-noise Gildy had expected. "The resultant slapstick situations are not as bad as they might be, but that's no reason for you to go out of your way to see if you can take it." To which, if Gildy had read this Archer Winsten *(New York Post)* critique, he might well have replied with his pet expression: "Ain't it the truth." In this film Barbara, along with such newcomers as Patti Brill, Margie Stewart, Ann Summers,‡ and Betty Wells, was merely set dressing. Joan Barclay had a slightly bigger part as Grant Withers's daughter, while Nancy Gates, who had not yet been at the studio a year, was featured as Margie Forrester, Gildersleeve's sweet niece.

*The fact that RKO's parent corporation, Radio Corporation of America, was heavily involved in the radio-network field and tied in with the major talent agencies in block-booking for the stage acts utilized on the Keith-Orpheum vaudeville circuit spurred on this policy.
†As The Great Gildersleeve, Peary had appeared as a subordinate figure in RKO's *Look Who's Laughing* (1941) and *Seven Days' Leave* (1942).
‡She made a small name for herself on Broadway in the late 1940s and early 1950s.

Mexican Spitfire's Blessed Event (1943) was the eighth and final entry in a slapdash series that starred fiery Lupe Velez and rubber-legged Leon Errol. Because of America's hasty, backslapping rapport with its Latin American neighbors, RKO and the other Hollywood studios had been grinding out pseudo-south-of-the-border-flavored concoctions for some time. Had not Lupe Velez committed suicide in 1944, it is likely the series, which had begun in 1939, would have continued until at least the end of the war. In *Mexican Spitfire's Blessed Event* Barbara was briefly utilized, along with the RKO stock female crew (Joan Barclay, Patti Brill, Rita Corday, Mary Halsey, Rosemary LaPlanche, Margie Stewart, Ann Summers), to flesh out the feeble storyline: Velez's oncamera husband (Walter Reed) believes he will soon be a father, only to learn that his temperamental wife has latched onto a baby ocelot, not impending motherhood.

The Seventh Victim (1943), scripted by DeWitt Bodeen and Charles O'Neal,* was another entry in producer Val Lewton's special B-unit at RKO, which spewed out economy thrillers geared to raise chills through inexpensive-to-mount, psychologically taut scenes rather than costly special effects. RKO announced loftily that Lewton's features, especially contrived as a patriotic gesture, were aimed at enabling audiences to escape the daily pressures of wartime life through super-horror entertainment. *The Seventh Victim* studied contemporary devil worship in New York City, focusing on "The Order of Palla." Kim Hunter quits her fashionable boarding school to locate her affluent sister (Jean Brooks), who has mysteriously disappeared. Twice Hunter almost catches up with Brooks only to lose her trail again. It develops that Brooks had been talked into breaking her cult pledge by visiting psychiatrist Tom Conway.† In one plotline montage, Barbara was spotted as a young Manhattanite lover with her boyfriend. With its brooding Greenwich Village locales and the plethora of offbeat characters, ranging from the one-armed devil worshipper (Evelyn Brent) to shrieking, frightened beautician Isabel Jewell, *The Seventh Victim* rightfully holds its own minor niche in the annals of the cinema psychological thriller.

Barbara was next handed a minor part in what was for RKO of the 1940s an A-picture. *The Iron Major* (1943), the story of the late football coach Frank Cavanaugh, was partially inspired by the recent box-office success of such other sports biopictures as *The Pride of the Yankees* (1942)‡ and, in particular, *Knute Rockne—All American* (Warner Bros., 1940), since that film's star, Pat O'Brien, was now an RKO contract lead. The storyline of *The Iron Major* opens in 1942 as Cavanaugh's seven children (including Barbara as Sarah) enlist in various branches of the armed services. Cavanaugh's widow (Ruth

---

*Bodeen scripted the well-received *The Cat People* (1942), and with O'Neal would prepare the screenplay for *The Curse of the Cat People* (1944). O'Neal is the father of actor Ryan O'Neal.
†In a repeat of his *The Cat People* characterization, even though he had been killed off in that 1942 entry.
‡Produced by Samuel Goldwyn and released by RKO.

763

Warrick) and her close friend, Father Tim Donovan (Robert Ryan), reminisce about the deceased sports coach. The viewer is then treated (or subjected to, depending on your tolerance level for synthesized Americana) to a flashback covering forty years of the Irish-American's constructive life, from the time in Worcester, Massachusetts, when schoolboy O'Brien becomes an attorney, turns to football coaching, and weds Warrick, up to the peak of his success as the Holy Cross football coach at the age of forty, when he enlists in the Army during World War I. While stationed in France he is promoted to the rank of major and is wounded in action, thus earning the sobriquet "Iron Major." Once demobilized he returns to coaching, this time at Boston College, where he learns he has at most only five years left before his eyesight will fail. He hurriedly accepts a lucrative offer from Fordham University to whip their losing gridiron squad into championship shape, which he does, before he dies in 1933. The point is pounded home in an extremely lachrymose style that Cavanaugh loved God, his country, and his family, all of which makes for an exemplary man but hardly provides a remarkable or moving cinema drama.

The "seasoned" Barbara was then assigned as a stocking clerk in *Gildersleeve on Broadway* (1943), in which Gildy (Harold Peary) hops to New York with pharmacist Peavy (Richard LeGrand) for a druggists' convention. It is not long before Gildy, engaged to hometown girl Ann Doran, is mixed up with wealthy widow Billie Burke and blonde siren Claire Carleton. After extricating himself from a series of ludicrous escapades he returns to Summerville and Doran, hopefully a wiser man. True to RKO monetary strictures, most of the picture's Gotham activity transpired within the confines of a hotel, which saved the expense of even rear-projection photography.

For one of its really prime ventures of the year, *Government Girl* (1943), RKO borrowed Olivia de Havilland from Warner Bros. and Sonny Tufts from Paramount, and paired them in a slapstick comedy about hectic working and living conditions in the nation's very overcrowded capital. Despite the combined scripting efforts of Adela Rogers St. John, Budd Schulberg, and Dudley Nichols, the film suspiciously resembled a "sugar-coated pill." With de Havilland straining to play a half-witted office employee at the War Construction Board who becomes enamored of lumbering production engineer Tufts, the genuine laughs were too few and far apart. This derivative movie was climaxed by a madcap motorcycle chase, which owed more to the efforts of stunt riders and rear projection than to the comic artistry of the two co-stars. RKO stalwart Anne Shirley was merely featured as de Havilland's ever-hungry roommate, determined that she and her new spouse (James Dunn) shall have the hotel suite promised to them in order to consummate their marriage. Barbara and the other RKO junior starlets filled in the background space as secretarial types.

As "the old professor," popular Kay Kyser had made a radio hit with his *"Kollege of Musical Knowledge"* and was imported to Hollywood to make a series of five RKO films. *Around the World* (1943), his final RKO entry, was the weakest of the lot, for it was not one of his usual spoofs, such as his amusing mock-horror fillip, *You'll Find Out* (1940), but was rather a bland hodgepodge of musical interludes in which Kyser and his aardvark band (including Ish Kabibble, Harry Babbitt, and Sally Mason) embark on a hectic globetrotting tour of military installations. Occasionally the script found a small bit of a plot as the musical gang became involved with Axis agents, but most of the Allan Dwan-produced-directed quickie focused on the song-and-dance segments, with comedy relief thankfully supplied by Joan Davis, and, to a lesser extent, by contractee cutups Wally Brown and Alan Carney. All the members of the RKO female stock company were drawn into the proceedings as USO hostess-helpers, and they were allowed to use their own given names in the casual proceedings. Thus, Barbara was "Barbara" for the first time onscreen.

Barbara's unexpected rise from the regular studio ranks was largely due to RKO producer-director Tim Whelan choosing her to play opposite the lot's singing sensation, Frank Sinatra, in *Higher and Higher* (1944). Not that Barbara or even hot crooner Sinatra had the actual leads in the black-and-white picture. On the contrary, vaudevillian Jack Haley, who had headlined the Broadway version of the story years earlier, was cast in the central role. As valet to Leon Errol, he devises a scheme to pass off the kitchen maid (Michele Morgan) as Errol's debutante daughter, hoping that she can attract a wealthy husband in the very near future. Haley cannot make up his mind whether the playboy next door (Sinatra) or titled foreigner Victor Borge would be the better catch. It develops that Borge is a bogus nobleman, and Sinatra actually prefers authentic socialite Barbara. Of course, Haley and Morgan are then free to pair off, with Errol set to transform his mansion into a swank club. By the time *Higher and Higher* opened at the Palace Theatre on January 21, 1944,* Sinatra was firmly entrenched as the bobby-soxers' newest delight, and the movie was promoted as his "real" screen debut.† Bosley Crowther *(New York Times)* complained that the movie was a "slapdash setting for the incredibly unctuous renderings of 'the voice'." Other critics noted that it was tough to judge the screen performances because of the continually distracting waves of squeals from the overexcitable younger members of the audience. Ninth-billed Barbara, playing the polite, sweet daughter of overbearing society matron Elizabeth Risdon, was conventionally dressed in standard evening and day garb but less effectively coiffed (her hair had an unflattering fuzzy styling). Certainly she was no match for the more sophisticated and very striking Michele Morgan. Barbara did have the distinction in this film of presenting Sinatra with his first screen kiss, but she spent most of her brief scenes standing demurely on the sidelines while Sinatra and Marcy McGuire (as the housemaid) handled the movie's five tunes.

*The previous New Year's Eve, fifty theatres on the RKO circuit in the metropolitan New York area previewed the film at a $1.10 admission tag.
†He had had guest band-vocalist parts in three previous pictures.

Viewing *Higher and Higher* today one would hardly guess that Barbara was considered a likely candidate for leading-lady grooming even at second-rate RKO, for her oncamera personality was as undefined as her approach to on-screen emoting. Nevertheless she possessed just the qualities RKO demanded during its 1940s programmer regime.* She was a "girl-next-door" type who fulfilled lower-middle-class dream-girl standards, and at the same time could be professionally serviceable as the stereotyped self-sufficient cinema variety who peppered the studio's detective series. Barbara was not as pretty or as cloyingly sweet as Warner Brothers' Joan Leslie or Joyce Reynolds, nor as professionally naive and trusting as Samuel Goldwyn's Teresa Wright or MGM's Marsha Hunt. None of these ladies, by the way, would have fit in with RKO's concepts at the time, but Barbara possessed two very serviceable oncamera characteristics: a husky voice and a straightforward manner of eyeing her onscreen vis-à-vis.

Now slated for more important roles, Barbara was next cast in the eighth of RKO's thirteen *Falcon* pictures, *The Falcon out West* (Rialto Theatre, March 17, 1944). Shot in less than three weeks at a cost of $146,000, this entry had the distinction of moving away from the usual metropolitan back-drops, even if most of the smaller outdoor sets for *The Falcon out West* were stock units assembled on an RKO soundstage. Playboy Tom Lawrence (Tom Conway), better known to police and underworld alike as the Falcon, is dining at the packed Flamingo Club in New York City when wealthy Texas rancher Lyle Talbot suddenly collapses and dies on the dance floor. The ever-present Inspector Donovan (Cliff Clark) and his equally dumb assistant (Ed Gargan) are convinced the Falcon is tied into the crime. Therefore, the model amateur sleuth must follow up the clues to prove his innocence. Like Carole Gallagher, Talbot's fiancée, Conway pinches a train ticket from dead Talbot's wallet and jaunts out to the late millionaire's Texas spread. There he must cope with Gallagher, the ex-Mrs. Talbot (Joan Barclay), Talbot's Lawyer (Don Douglas), Talbot's partner (Minor Watson), the latter's independent daughter (Barbara), and the omnipresent Clark and Gargan. Barbara is first seen when Conway and company depart the train to take a stage to Talbot's ranch. Suddenly there is a volley of shots (to welcome the new dude guests to the area) and Conway finds himself rumbling along on a runaway coach. Barbara, in a basic cowgirl outfit with a short, curly hairdo, rides her horse at high speed and succeeds in bringing the stage horses under control. Wry Conway then observes: "Horses, weather and women! You can never be sure of them."

As *The Falcon out West* proceeds with its unfulfilled but intriguing mixture of two genres, Barbara is displayed in an assortment of outfits and hairstyles,

---

*According to one fan magazine writer, describing the Barbara of early 1944, "Miss Hale looks like a Petty Girl gone wholesome. She has Those Legs and That Figure—but her nails are not red, her pretty face is almost minus make-up, and instead of wearing gossamer transparencies, she traipses around in tailored suits of red. Her short curly hair is brown . . . and her eyebrows are arched like an elf's."

a most unusual showcase for RKO to give any of its minor players. At the barbecue she wears her hair down and sports dangling earrings that complement her spangle-clad skirt and white blouse. On another occasion her hair is in an upsweep, revealing how much she resembled a young Janis Paige or Ruth Roman. Barbara offered an appealing contrast to the film's other two female leads. Gallagher, a willowy blond whose dull personality matched her vapid role, offered no competition; whereas Joan Barclay, as the right-thinking divorcee, demonstrated an affirmatively pleasing personality, which indicated she might well have given Barbara a good professional run for her money had the script been so inclined. It was typical of such detective quickies that Barbara had an essentially ambiguous role. She vaguely flirts with Conway, once having gotten over the fact that he had suspected her and/or her dad of the murder of Talbot and the later poisoning of Douglas. It is vampish Gallagher, however, who occupies most of Conway's romantic interest—that is, until she is proven a co-agent in the crimes along with her ranch-foreman boyfriend (Lee Trent). True to form, the Falcon remains romantically uncommitted at the end of this entry, bidding everyone a fond farewell, and hopping on a train in pursuit of a Spanish gal in distress. Barbara is thus left at the fade-out to kiss Ed Gargan—a most unrewarding finish for her.

After the *Falcon* Barbara continued to move from one B-picture to another, next in line being *Heavenly Days* (1944). Jim Jordan and his wife, Marion, had been entertaining the listening public with the spats and adventures of Fibber McGee and Molly of 79 Wistful Vista since 1936. The title for this RKO feature was derived from one of Molly McGee's pet expressions. At the request of their Washington bigwig cousin, Charles Trowbridge, the McGees hike off to the nation's capital to participate in a proposed postwar planning program. On the way Fibber decides to find the "average man" and extract his viewpoint on current events. Fibber enlists the aid of Dr. Gallup and his polling organization. Once in Washington Fibber is given a pass to the Senate gallery, where, egged on by reporters, he begins addressing the august body on what the man in the street really wants. The Senators are duly shocked. The McGees later return home only to find that the Senate fracas has caused so much publicity that Fibber is now a national celebrity and Dr. Gallup has chosen him the winner of the "average man" contest. All of which annoys proud Fibber, the great individualist, until he realizes he cannot vote in the pending national elections because he forgot to register. Thus he realizes that he is very human and average after all. Sixth-billed Barbara functioned as newspaper gal Angie, who is in love with a reporter on a rival paper, Gordon Oliver. It is Oliver who encourages Fibber to speak his piece to the governmental representatives.

One would hardly think that this harmless yarn could have caused a federal rumpus, but it did. When government observers viewed the picture they decided that Fibber's unobtrusive moral blandishments to the South were too political. So under the Soldiers' Vote Law, the War Department declared

Heavenly Days, along with Twentieth Century-Fox's biographical epic *Wilson* as unfit for showing at Army camps. All of which led the *New York Sun's* reviewer to quip about the film, "it is about as political as the funnies!"*

Goin' to Town (1944) was the fifth of seven Chester Lauck-Norris Goff comedy features made for RKO. The two comedians carried over into this film their long-standing radio characterizations of Lum and Abner, whose crackerbarrel activities were centered on their Jot 'Em Down General Store in Pine Ridge, Arkansas. In this screen outing, the duo and the townsfolk are the victims of a practical joke perpetrated by an oil promoter visiting the rural hamlet. This leads the local folk to invest in what proves to be a worthless oil scheme. Lum and Abner decide to teach the city slicker a well-deserved lesson by going to Chicago to unload their useless stock back on the joker (Dick Elliott). Third-billed Barbara was Sally, Elliott's secretary, who takes a kindly attitude to the suckers and directs them to the Ski Hi Club, where Elliott can be found (allowing for the interpolation of chorus-girl sequences featuring Nils T. Granlund and some of his show dolls). In a very conventional assignment, Barbara had little opportunity to contribute much to the picture beyond her increasingly comely looks and direct manner.

The Falcon in Hollywood (1944) next claimed Barbara's oncamera presence. The dapper detective (Tom Conway) is enjoying an afternoon at the Santa Anita racetrack when he encounters two cinema "celebrities," Peggy Calahan (Barbara) a former club dancer and now a musical film star, and Lillo D'Allio (Rita Corday), a foreign movie import. Conway learns the latter is the ex-sweetheart of gangster Sheldon Leonard. The sleuth becomes intrigued with Barbara when she accidentally takes Corday's bag with her upon leaving the racetrack. He follows them back to the Sunset Studios (the RKO lot). There, on a soundstage, the Falcon discovers the body of the actor-husband of studio dress-designer Jean Brooks. With the *corpus delicti* at hand and inspector Emory Parnell and assistant Frank Jenks breathing hot and heavy down his neck, Conway is motivated into solving the caper. There is a full range of suspects: (1) Brooks, who had been unfaithful to her spouse and is in love with insulting director Konstantin Shayne; (2) Corday, who also has a yen for Shayne; (3) Shayne, who is spotted hiding the murder weapon in a plaster vase; (4) Shakespeare-spouting producer John Abbott, who owned the homicide weapon; (5) jealous ex-convict Sheldon Leonard, who is later killed; and (6) Barbara, who already has a bad track record with the Falcon—she had seriously wounded Shayne on one occasion with a prop gun that turned out to be very real. Director Gordon Douglas wrapped up *The Falcon in Hollywood* in eighteen days (July 12-29, 1944) at a cost of $131,000. Although the picture was branded a "run-of-the-RKO mill murder mystery" by the *New York Daily News* and failed to reach its potential, it is this author's favorite entry in the

---

*Because of the political turmoil created by *Heavenly Days* and *Wilson,* a special Taft anti-political amendment was thereafter added to the Soldiers' Vote Law.

series. *The Falcon in Hollywood* may not have provided much insight into the behind-the-cameras workings of a studio, but the variety of movie colony stereotypes has an offbeat appeal. In particular there is the garrulous taxi driver played to the hilt by Veda Ann Borg, who insists upon helping the Falcon solve the crime. The Barbara of *The Falcon in Hollywood* did not exactly physically fit into the Betty Grable or even Ann Miller mold of cinema dancing star, but this casting discrepancy was politely ignored by everyone concerned. Maybe the film's scriptwriter, Gerald Geraghty, reasoned that an Americanized carbon-copy of Vera Hruba Ralston would do just fine.

Barbara only decorated two 1945 releases. Several factors contributed to this slowdown in her screen work. World War II was fast coming to a close, bringing about already foreseeable signs of cutback in Hollywood production-line feature-filmmaking. RKO had undergone yet another corporate shakeup and William Dozier was now in charge of studio production. He was attempting to limit the lot's inflated program schedule. Also, Barbara was now at the point in her film career where, by RKO standards, she was a recognizable name and not to be so quickly pushed into just any available part. Not that anyone, least of all Barbara, considered her a strong dramatic actress or a refined screen beauty. Barbara was still thought to be most serviceable as a pleasant leading-lady type who could knowledgeably dress up the scenery of modestly budgeted features. After all, RKO asked no more of its low-paid starlets.

In later 1944 RKO tested Barbara opposite Rory Calhoun for a projected picture, *The Prodigal Woman*,* but the venture was never filmed. Instead she made another western, *West of the Pecos* (1945). (In the mid-1940s RKO was remaking several Zane Grey sagebrush yarns that had starred Richard Dix a decade before.) Robert Mitchum played a sleepy-eyed cowboy who cares little for common justice until his own lackadaisical life-style is interrupted and he is forced to take an interest. Barbara was cast as "Bill," the well-bred niece of Chicago meatpacker Thurston Hall. When Hall is ordered to take a health vacation on his Texas ranch, Barbara, accompanied by her French maid (Rita Corday), joins irascible Hall on the trip. On the way to Hall's spread their stagecoach is held up. Barbara disguises herself as a boy to save being imposed upon by the outlaws and in this guise encounters devil-may-care cow-puncher Mitchum. He proceeds to treat "Bill" like any other annoying young kid, which leads to predictable embarrassing situations. Eventually Mitchum and his sidekick, Richard Martin, rout the outlaws; by this time he has discovered that Barbara is a most attractive woman. She ditches her lawyer fiance to wed the quick-shooting hero. Not a very unusual B-western, but for Barbara the picture had its own special rewards. Cast in a supporting role in

---

*DeWitt Bodeen, who scripted *The Prodigal Woman,* recalls that Barbara offered a very even-keeled, fitting performance in the screentest.

West of the Pecos was studio contractee Bill Williams.* She and Williams quickly developed a strong mutual romantic interest, although Barbara jokingly admits: "It took me two years to talk him into marrying me."

Meanwhile, *First Yank into Tokyo* splashed into the Palace Theatre on October 24, 1945. This picture had the distinction of being the first American-made feature to deal with the Allied atomic bombing attacks on Hiroshima (August 6, 1945) and Nagasaki (August 9, 1945). This topical coup was not the result of RKO's foresightedness—rather just the opposite. *First Yank into Tokyo* had been sitting in the can for some weeks (having gone into production on February 1, 1945, under the title *First Man into Tokyo*), prepared as merely another entry in the vein of the studio's rather successful *Behind the Rising Sun* (1943). All of a sudden V-E Day (May 8, 1945) occurred and was followed by the Japanese surrender on August 14, 1945, with the subsequent V-J Day (September 2, 1945). In order to contemporize what had become an outdated story, the studio tacked on clips of the A-bomb attack via Pathé Newsreel with an accompanying new finale narration for the picture.

First Yank into Tokyo suffered from a rather outrageous plotline prepared by the film's producer, J. Robert Bren, in collaboration with Gladys Atwater. Compounding the picture's credibility gap was the usual RKO malady: blatantly obvious soundstage sets executed in stringently economical fashion. This latter factor prompted one reviewer to retag the movie *First Spy into Studio's Japan*. The plot asked the viewer to believe the following contrived tale: U.S. Air Force major Tom Neal, who was raised in Japan and fully comprehends the Nipponese customs and language, is requested by his superiors to handle a dangerous mission. He has to undergo plastic surgery to remold his facial features from Occidental to Oriental† and then is smuggled into a Japanese prisoner-of-war camp to contact Army ordnance expert Marc Cramer, who had been working on an atomic bomb project before his capture. The plan is put into operation and everything goes smoothly until Neal arrives at the prison camp. There he encounters his fiancee, Barbara, who he thought had died on Bataan. She is a captured Army nurse now in charge of the Allied prisoners' hospital. Naturally she does not recognize the slant-eyed version of her beloved, a situation which Neal suffers stoically. (An idyllic flashback sequence recalls their beachside rendezvous in the simpler days of old.) Who

---

*Born William Katt on May 21, 1926, in Brooklyn, the 6-foot, 190-pound, blond-haired, brown-eyed New Yorker was educated at Brooklyn Technical High School and then attended Pratt Institute, preparing for a career in construction engineering. In 1934 and 1935 he was junior scholastic champion in the 220-440-meter swim meet. Thereafter, he devoted his time to exhibition diving, when out of the blue he was offered an opportunity to earn higher pay in St. Louis as an adagio dancer. Later in 1935 he joined the Municipal Opera Company in St. Louis in a minor dancing capacity, but shortly thereafter he left to form his own adagio act, touring Europe and playing the London Palladium. During World War II he enlisted in the U.S. Army for the air service branch, but was later demobilized on medical grounds. He gravitated to Hollywood, where he made his screen debut in Universal's *Murder in the Blue Room* in 1944 and that same year joined RKO as a stock player.

†One of the peculiar plot twists is the doctors' repeated statement that subsequent plastic surgery cannot erase his new face.

else is at the compound? None other than colonel Richard Loo, the militant Japanese officer who had been Neal's college roommate. Despite the action-filled years since they last met, Loo distinctly remembers—in fact he has news-reel footage of Neal on the gridiron to prove it—that whenever his old roomie becomes overly tense, he is subject to involuntary nervous mannerisms. This suspected Japanese, of course, has those same telltale twitches. Neal's fate is sealed, but not before he distracts the bestial Japs so that Cramer, Barbara, and captain Michael St. Angel can escape. As the pasted-on newsreel-clip finale points out, Neal's patriotic sacrifice paved the way for the "necessary" nuclear attacks on Hiroshima and Nagasaki.

Perhaps of all Barbara's RKO screen work to date, *First Yank into Tokyo* was most representative. It was her fourth and final professional association with studio contract director Gordon Douglas. The film was mounted by the full complement of standard studio department-heads: art designs by Albert S. D'Agostino, music by Leigh Harline, and the camera work by Harry J. Wild. All were slickly serviceable, but highly unimaginative. *Variety* cited Barbara's performance here as "effective," a rather euphemistic way of stating she was competent in her one-dimensional characterization as Neal's subordinate vis-à-vis. If anything, it was the combination of Barbara's wholesome looks (increasingly more like Ruth Roman than June Haver), her deep-toned pro-jection, and her essential quality of unobtrusively backstopping her co-players, that allowed the midwestern miss to become an RKO leading lady. While most of her onetime RKO contract contemporaries, such as Rita Corday, Myrna Dell, Jane Randolph, and Rosemary LaPlanche, had fallen by the pro-fessional wayside into early retirement or moved over to Producers Releasing Corp. or Monogram on poverty row, Barbara had survived. Nonetheless, she was hardly in the same league with RKO-Twentieth Century-Fox personality Maureen O'Hara, or as classy as RKO newcomer Jane Greer, or even as filled with eye-catching appeal as the Darryl F. Zanuck reject, Simone Simon, who had come to RKO in the early 1940s. In fact, had Barbara been a member of the actress stable at Warner Brothers, MGM, Paramount, or Twentieth Cen-tury-Fox, it is more than likely that by this time her option would have been dropped.

Barbara's middle-of-the-road career pattern at RKO was accurately reflected by the public's only vague awareness of her. Habitués of first-run metro-politan theatres showing strictly Grade-A features probably were totally unac-quainted with Barbara's cinema existence. Only the high-powered bigtime studios could demand and afford that all their players, of whatever caliber, be given comprehensive coverage in the media. Actor members of lesser film factories had to be satisfied with a far less effective publicity buildup. For example, in contrast to every splashy newspaper or magazine interview pro-moting Paramount's latest Broadway import, Joan Caulfield, there might be at most a one-liner announcing Barbara's latest film assignment. It was rare indeed that Barbara or her counterparts at other smaller studios had the oppor-tunity to be showcased on the prestigious radio anthology series like "Lux Radio Theatre" or "Screen Guild of the Air." Flipping through national magazines of the time, there would rarely be an interview or photo layout of the nonstartling players from middle-league studios; that is, unless the newcomer latched onto some gimmick—as did Universal term performer Diana Barrymore, heiress to generations of famous actors, or RKO's newly arrived Jane Greer, the ex-wife of Rudy Vallee.* More frequently than not, the chief magazine exposure for players of the caliber of Barbara, Cheryl Walker, Peggy Stewart, et al., was in photographic advertisements endorsing new consumer products.

Barbara's exception to the above general publicity embargo occurred when she and Bill Williams were wed. Granted their legalized union did not smack of the romanticized fascination surrounding the decade-later union of Debbie Reynolds and Eddie Fisher, but still it was considered an apple-pie marriage. Taking full advantage of the post-World War II back-to-normalcy drive, RKO had the ceremony covered in depth by as many high-level magazines as possible. For a change the studio's publicity chief, Perry Lieber, had salable copy in Barbara, which *Life* magazine, among others, bought. The wedding took place on June 22, 1946, in Rockford, Illinois, with the Reverend B. E. Allen officiating. All of Barbara's family and hometown friends were present for the traditional affair. Williams's old vaudeville stage partner, Stuart Morgan, was the best man. As a special "treat" for the local citizenry, RKO premiered Williams's latest movie, *Deadline at Dawn*. Barbara, ever the happy bride, admitted she did not mind Bill making love to *Deadline at Dawn* co-star Susan Hayward—on the screen, that is. The couple then honeymooned at—where else?—Niagara Falls, before returning to Hollywood.

Barbara's sole 1946 release, *Lady Luck,* played the Palace Theatre as of October 30. Teamed with easygoing ex-MGM demistar Robert Young, the light comedy presented second-billed Barbara as the prim owner of a Beverly Hills bookshop. Because she is descended from a long line of ill-fated gamblers—her grandfather, Frank Morgan, being a prime example—she has a strong aversion to the species. But Barbara's Mary, female and human, succumbs to the charms of Young, who is an out-and-out gambler. To rationalize her attraction to Young, Barbara insists she can reform this professional dice thrower. She foolishly leaves Morgan in charge of her shop while she and Young venture to Las Vegas, of all places, for their honeymoon. Once there she is quickly convinced he has returned to his gambling ways, and in a huff she leaves him. Young promptly calls upon his Damon Runyonesque pals to infect Barbara with the gambling fever, which is not tough to accomplish, since in her absence Morgan has turned her bookshop into a gamblers' haven. Soon Barbara opens her own green-felt club and becomes as die hard a gambler as Young ever was. However, within the alloted screen time, domestic bliss is restored through the intervention of kindhearted Morgan.

*For a period in 1943-44, Louise Albritton and Margaret Landry were Barbara's roommates at the Hollywood Studio Club—or so the publicity handouts claimed.

Because *Lady Luck* had a ludicrously transparent storyline in which the adeptness of both Barbara and Young at handling the give-and-take of romantic scenes was wasted, no one really bothered to take time out to appreciate the quality of the co-stars' efforts. Perhaps if this potentially diverting study of gambling had not been sidetracked into a conventional account of newlyweds, things might have been different.

Before *Lady Luck* went into release, RKO was made aware that *Look* magazine had voted Barbara "the most promising newcomer of 1945," citing "her natural American beauty, wholesome charm and honest talent [which] makes her top-star material." With this accolade in mind, RKO altered its promotional campaign on Barbara. A year before the studio had tagged her a "delectable lovely"; now, in keeping with her *Look* award and her marital status, she was billed as "RKO's bright and Promising Young Attraction."

Meanwhile Barbara had a few thoughts of her own to convey to the press, telling reporters about her dual occupation as both film actress and wife: "It's like walking a tightrope, this business of career and marriage. I've never walked a tightrope before, but I guess I'll have to learn how."

A Likely Story (1947) reunited Barbara and her real-life husband onscreen in a very thin fling at pixillated comedy. It was very weakly directed by H. C. Potter. On the train to New York, midwestern artist Barbara, accompanied by her ten-year-old brother (Lanny Rees), meets ex-GI Williams. During the trip Williams is accidentally banged on the head and later wakes up in a Manhattan hospital, where he mistakes another patient's diagnosis as his own. Assuming he has only a short time to live, he romantically decides that it would be a marvelous gesture to make Barbara his beneficiary and give this struggling young artist a financial uplift. Williams convinces ex-mobster Nestor Paiva to purchase a flush life-insurance policy on him, and meanwhile to advance him a stated sum, which he hands over to his lady love. When both he and Paiva discover that his supposed fatal disease is non-existent, Paiva decides to have Williams killed—to little avail, of course. To promote *A Likely Story,* Barbara and Williams went on a personal appearance tour in the spring of 1947. Three months after the release of the picture, Barbara gave birth to her first child, Barbara Willa Johanna Williams, born July 24, 1947.

RKO's *The Boy with Green Hair* (1948) had a peculiar production history. Begun in 1947 when Dore Schary, executive vice-president in charge of RKO production under president N. Peter Rathvon, was riding the crest of his topical success, *Crossfire,* this new color feature was an overt paean of antiwar sentiment, budgeted at a plush $876,325 with a thirty-five-day production schedule. It was the first feature assignment for director Joseph Losey, who would later be blacklisted from Hollywood during the McCarthy Communist witchhunt.* By the time the picture had completed its postproduction gestation

*Adrian Scott, husband of former RKO star Anne Shirley and the original producer of *The Boy with Green Hair,* was removed from the picture when he was named one of the Hollywood Ten at the House Un-American Activities Committee hearings.

in June, 1948, Howard Hughes had purchased the RKO Pictures plant and Dore Schary was only a few weeks away from "resignation." Hughes, a violent anti-Communist, required only one quick viewing of *The Boy with Green Hair* to appreciate its pacifist-oriented (Red-inspired?) message. Immediately he yanked the film from its scheduled Thanksgiving release date and ordered it entirely restructured; anything to remove its message-laden, leftist taint.* Several months of monkeying with the finished product ensued, including the shooting of new sequences, but nothing could be done to alter the picture's basic content. Finally, in disgust and with his typical hot-then-cold attitude on policy decisions, Hughes pushed *The Boy with Green Hair* out onto the market.†

There was nothing subtle about the picture, which *Time* magazine berated: "It labors so clumsily to cram its idea into the mold of entertainment; it was an out-and-out pacifist parable, told within the framework of a flashback."‡ RKO's publicity department was ordered to palm the picture off on the public with a twisted advertising campaign ("Please don't tell why his hair turned green!"), but no one was fooled. Considering the artistic soundness of two other post-World War II studies of the effects of the ravaging war on youth, *Shoeshine Boy* and *The Search,* the *New York Times* was generous when it judged *The Boy with Green Hair* "a bright notion gone wrong." Barbara's role in this misfire was inconsequential, her screen time minimal. At this point in her life she was not the freethinking individual she later became, and diplomatically she remained quiet about her reactions to the bizarre situation which failed to launder *The Boy with Green Hair.*

Following the July, 1948, personnel cutback at RKO, Hughes pushed a few

*In July, 1948, Hughes for all practical purposes suspended operations at RKO, obstensibly to ferret out any possible Reds on the personnel roster. The closedown paved the way for a new economy wave, which reduced the lot's working force by considerably more than one-half.

†A similar releasing fate was suffered by another, less expensive, RKO effort, the Robert Stevenson-directed *I Married a Communist* (1949), a.k.a. *Woman on Pier 13.*

‡War orphan Dean Stockwell relates to police psychiatrist Robert Ryan that his parents went to England years before, and he has been shunted from relative to relative ever since, until he came to live with Gramps (Pat O'Brien), an ex-circus performer, now a singing waiter. The boy is happy and secure with Gramps, until one day, while taking part in a school drive for clothing war orphans, he learns that he too is a war orphan, that his parents were killed in a London bombing raid. The next morning he awakens to discover his hair has turned green. Everyone is disturbed by the phenomenon, including Stockwell. His schoolteacher (Barbara) tries to reassure him: "How many boys have brown hair? How many have red hair? And how many have green hair?" but the little boy is not calmed. Ostracized by his playmates he runs into the woods, where suddenly the war orphans in his school poster appear before him and explain that they have turned his hair green to attract attention, and that when questioned he is to reply that war is bad and it must cease. The deeply impressed child returns to town. No one will listen to his message, and the townspeople insist he have his hair shaved off. He complies but later, feeling he has betrayed the war orphans, runs away. As he finishes telling Ryan the story, O'Brien, Hale, and doctor Samuel Hinds arrive. Stockwell goes home with Gramps. There the boy is read a letter from his father, written just before he died, in which he reminds his son that his parents died in the struggle against war and that the living must be reminded continually why they died. Stockwell then tells Gramps that he will crusade against war and that when his hair grows in again he hopes it will be green.

quickies into production that fall to take advantage of talent and technical staff still under contract. *The Clay Pigeon* (March, 1949), one of these programmers, was turned out in sixteen days at the end of September, 1948. Although it was tossed away in release it had a better than expected flavor, not so surprising when one considers the people involved in the project: director Richard Fleischer (he later helmed *Compulsion, Fantastic Voyage, The Boston Strangler*), screenwriter Carl Foreman (who subsequently scripted *Champion, Home of the Brave, The Men,* scripted-produced *The Guns of Navarone,* produced *Born Free* and *Young Winston*), and cameraman Robert de Grasse, RKO lenser since 1935. The premise of this sixty-three-minute thriller finds Bill Williams a war-dazed sailor forced to clear himself of treason charges, which allege he sold out to the Japanese during World War II. Escaping from the naval hospital, he contacts his old prison-camp buddy (Richard Quine), who immediately promises to assist his good pal in tracking down Richard Loo, the prisoner-of-war-camp guard tied into the treason-counterfeiting racket. It did not take a supersleuth to figure that overly solicitous Quine was the villain,* but the programmer moved at a rapid enough clip to make this production error forgivable. One brief but very effective scene in *The Clay Pigeon* occurred near the wrap-up as the cops close in on the culprits and the villains attempt to shove pesky Williams under a passing railway train. Second-billed Barbara had a typical subordinate role in this outing, being Williams's pleasant romantic interest.

An entirely different matter was *The Window* (1949). This film had gotten underway in early November, 1947, when Dore Schary approved the forty-four-day production schedule, which called for the movie to be filmed largely on location in New York City. Neither Schary (who would be settled in at MGM as executive vice-president in charge of production by the time the film was released) nor anyone else involved in the low-budget project had any inkling that this film adaptation of Cornell Woolrich's story, "The Boy Who Cried Wolf," would prove to be a major sleeper picture of 1949. Director Ted Tetzlaff† shepherded his small cast to Manhattan to lens much of the seventy-three-minute black-and-white suspense yarn against the backdrop of a condemned tenement block on East 105th Street. The well-known tale had twelve-year-old Bobby Driscoll‡ as the overly imaginative Tommy Woodry, whose fanciful mind has whipped up so many tall tales that no one, least of all his hard-working, unsophisticated parents (Barbara and Arthur Kennedy), can believe his latest whopper: that he really did see their neighbors (Paul Stewart, Ruth Roman) murder a seaman. In fact Barbara is so out of sorts

*Turning to directing, Quine would function more effectively, if not more artistically, behind the camera. Among the films he has directed are *The Solid Gold Cadillac, Operation Mad Ball, Sex and the Single Girl,* and *Synanon.*

†A longtime cameraman at Paramount, Columbia, and RKO, Tetzlaff had directed John Barrymore's *World Premiere* (1941) and then a trio of Pat O'Brien RKO entries in the late 1940s.

‡On special loan-out from Walt Disney Productions, which was then still distributing its product through RKO.

775

with her young son that she insists he apologize to the homicidal couple, all of which leads to a tense game of hide-and-seek played out against the cluttered city backlot.

The Window debuted on August 7, 1947, at the Victoria Theatre, and *Cue* magazine delivered the majority opinion: "[It] begins on a trembling note of foreboding, and concludes on a shrieking tremolo of breathtaking melodrama, guaranteed to leave you limp with exhaustion." Most of the picture's attention was focused on the cat-and-mouse exercise of wide-eyed Driscoll versus sinister Stewart and his sloppy wife Roman, but housedress-clad Barbara was in enough evidence as the painstakingly patient wife and mother for *Variety* to describe her performance as "unusually sympathetic, without being sticky."* Any viewer who as a child had experienced injustice at the hands of "all-knowing" parents certainly gave a silent cheer of approval at the film's climax, when the contrite Barbara and Kennedy accompany their hero son to the police station. *The Window* created such a favorable impression with the public that years later its story would be rehashed three more times (*The Boy Who Cried Murder* [1966], *Sudden Terror* [1971] and *The Boy Who Cried Werewolf* [1973]) to far less satisfactory results.

The ripples from the success of *The Window* did nothing to advance Barbara's RKO career, for by the time of its long-delayed release, Barbara and Bill Williams had long since departed from Hughes's RKO, which chose to retain the services only of such protégées as Jane Russell and Faith Domergue, hot box-office attraction Robert Mitchum, and such useful holdovers as Jane Greer. Some ex-RKO contractees, like Williams, floated into freelance and others, like newcomer Martha Hyer, went on to term contracts at Universal.

But Barbara, who had amazed more than one astute Hollywood observer by surviving three changeovers in the RKO regime, engineered her own relatively spectacular coup. Realizing that the September, 1948, shooting of *The Clay Pigeon* was the end of the road at RKO, she quietly shopped around for a new studio berth, not such an easy task for a demure performer with no sensational screen credits to her name. She brought herself to the attention of Columbia Pictures' veteran producer Sidney Buchman, who was then seeking a wholesome screen type to play opposite Larry Parks in *Jolson Sings Again* (1949), the projected sequel to the studio's $8 million musical money-maker, *The Jolson Story* (1946). Bypassing such Columbia term or picture contractees as Joyce Reynolds, Lola Albright, Jeff Donnell, and even Lucille Ball, who might have been equally acceptable in the role of Al Jolson's bright "second" wife, Buchman cast Barbara as Ellen Clark. The deal was announced in the trade papers on October 27, 1948, which stated that Barbara had signed a Columbia term pact and would co-star in *Jolson Sings Again*. Three days later the film went into production on the Gower Street soundstages.

The ninety-six-minute Technicolor *Jolson Sings Again,* in production forty-

*Barbara's presence in this film, both in appearance and projection, was akin to the standard tenement mother played so effectively by Warner Brothers' contractee Rosemary DeCamp, who had similarly emoted in RKO's *From This Day Forward* (1946).

seven days, picks up its storyline where its predecessor ended, with Jolson (Larry Parks) having separated from his actress wife (Evelyn Keyes) in 1939 and returned to the New York stage to forget his marital woes. Director Henry Levin traces the great showman's professional decline into near-oblivion in the face of the new-breed entertainer, and shows how Jolson embarked on an extensive USO tour from the Aleutians to the Caribbean during World War II. More than a third of the way into the biopicture, Jolson contracts a serious fever in North Africa, is hospitalized, and is nursed back to health by Ellen Clark (Barbara).* As the technician from Little Rock, Arkansas, Barbara photographed prettily in color. Her cute finishing-school drawl with Judy Canova-esque overtones was an effective contrast to the pulsating cadence of Parks's Jolson delivery. While courting the love-stricken Barbara, Parks "sings" "Baby Face," and, when they must part for a time, he then croons to her "After You're Gone." After they wed Barbara coaxes the veteran star, who has lost a lung, to resume his career. The last portion of *Jolson Sings Again* deals with the making of *The Jolson Story,* allowing for the strange onscreen sight of actor Parks appearing as the aging Jolson watching Parks the screen performer emote in front of the camera in the movie-within-the-movie.

Jolson Sings Again premiered at Loew's State Theatre on August 17, 1949. As is typical with most movie sequels, neither the critics nor the public were as enthused by the padded-out but sincere follow-up. Nevertheless it did chalk up a hefty $5 million gross in United States and Canadian release. There was little new for the critics to state about Parks's tidy aping of Jolson (with the longtime singer supplying his own offcamera vocalizing) or about Ludwig Donath, Tamara Shayne, William Demarest, or Bill Goodwin, who repeated their prior characterizations. The surprise of the movie was Barbara! Thomas Pryor, writing in the *New York Times,* declared: "Miss Hale emerges in the picture a new and captivating personality with a peaches and cream complexion that is strikingly beautiful in Technicolor, after something like six years of competent but undistinguished work in Westerns and run-of-the-mill pictures. . . . She finally has got hold of a part which permits her to blossom like a fresh personality." Barbara, Al Jolson, Demarest, Donath, et al., would recreate their *Jolson Sings Again* roles for "Lux Radio Theatre" on the May 22, 1950, broadcast.

Barbara, who had never clicked with the public while at RKO, was suddenly news. Her freshness and charm were ballyhooed in the best Hollywood publicity tradition, and when she went to New York to promote *Jolson Sings Again* she was mobbed by fans.

Upon signing her seven-year Columbia contract, Barbara unpretentiously informed the press: "I probably am being trite, but I'm being honest when I

*Barbara was a close physical lookalike to the real-life Erle Chennault Galbraith, a relative of General Claire Chennault, who married Jolson in 1945, becoming his fourth wife. Columbia's two-picture Jolson biography chose to ignore the performer's first two wives, Henriette Keller, whom he wed in 1906 and divorced in 1919, and Ethel Delmar, his spouse from 1922 to 1926.

say that I would like to do parts that I believe in. Otherwise how can I do my best work? I might add that I have done both kinds."

Barbara was next reteamed with Robert Young—he received top billing—in Columbia's *And Baby Makes Three* (Palace Theatre, December 22, 1949), directed by Henry Levin, who had guided her so successfully in *Jolson Sings Again*. When Barbara catches Young in a compromising situation, she hastily applies for a Reno divorce and is about to wed stuffed-shirt Robert Hutton on the rebound. Just as the new wedding ceremony is about to take place, Barbara faints, not from nuptial fright, but, so the diagnosis goes, because she is pregnant. When Young refuses to give up custody of the baby-to-be, Hutton and his flibbertigibbety socialite mother (Billie Burke) are frightened off. Eventually Barbara and Young reunite, even though it is determined that she is not pregnant after all. "It has practically everything but a story that hangs together" (*New York Herald-Tribune*).

Her next picture, *Emergency Wedding* (1950), wilted on the vine before it was released. It was a pedestrian updating of *You Belong to Me,* which even back in 1941 had seemed anemic, but was saved by the expertise of stars Barbara Stanwyck and Henry Fonda. To compound the errors of the remake, Barbara and co-lead Larry Parks, who had such fine oncamera rapport in *Jolson Sings Again,* were operating on different levels in *Emergency Wedding,* he being listless and overly coy, and she appearing very uncomfortable in her characterization. The would-be farce presented comely physician Barbara wedding wealthy playboy Parks. She soon becomes disenchanted with his vapid existence and allows eager attorney Willard Parker to court her. Jealous Parks hastens to reform. He comes upon the bright notion of utilizing his surplus funds to establish a hospital where foreign medics can interne properly, thus earning himself Barbara's everlasting respect. Director Eddie Buzzell continually relied on sight gags and cliches as substitutes for satire and full-bodied characters. These faults become all the more transparent when the film suddenly switches genre and goes dramatic near the climax. *Emergency Wedding* was the last screen teaming of Barbara and Parks, the latter soon to be *persona non grata* in the film industry due to his past Communist affiliations.

Barbara frankly admitted that her blossoming screen career, as such, had its adverse effects on maintaining a steady marital relationship, particularly in the late 1940s when Williams suffered a back injury, was hospitalized, and then found movie freelancing even tougher than before. "When Bill and I were both under contract to RKO," Barbara recalls, "they wanted to build both of us. But, when I went to Columbia and Bill started freelancing, my studio—naturally—wanted to build me. They didn't care about Bill. He wasn't the investment. They were only concerned in grooming the lamb for the shearing.

"What happens when you do husband-and-wife stories and layouts when the studio wants YOU to steal the limelight? Your husband winds up with the back of his head [showing]. The magazine comes out, and it's all about you. The damage has been done. You can't undo it. Your husband has been put in second place."

Careerwise, Barbara fared much better on loan-out. One day after the strictly support feature *Emergency Wedding* opened at the Palace Theatre, a much superior film, *The Jackpot,* debuted at the Roxy Theatre (November 23, 1950). The Twentieth Century-Fox release had Barbara playing opposite James Stewart in a zany but wholesome comedy that took potshots at the current craze of radio giveaway shows. *Jackpot* was based on the real-life incident of Jim Caffrey of Wakefield, Rhode Island, who correctly named Louis B. Mayer as the "mystery voice" on the "Sing It Again" show and won $24,000 in prizes, which turned out to cost him more than they were worth. In the film Stewart portrayed a small-town Indiana department-store executive with a nice wife (Barbara) and two normal kids (Natalie Wood, Tommy Rettig). With the aid of a newspaper pal (James Gleason) he correctly guesses on the telephone the correct answer to the prize question on the "Name the Mystery Husband Contest." Thereafter his home is deluged with thousands of dollars worth of merchandise, including 7,500 cans of Campbell's soup, a portable swimming pool, $4,000 worth of shrubbery, and assorted other goodies, all of which he must pay income tax on for having received. To compound his growing problems, the other prizes include a visit by a chic artist (Patricia Medina) who is to paint his portrait—which makes Barbara jealous—and free consultations by a bizarre interior decorator (Alan Mowbray) who has his own distinct notions of how to remodel Stewart's living room. Everything ends happily, of course, but not before Stewart has nearly been fired by his boss (Fred Clark), has tangled with the police, and has become enmeshed with a bookie to whom he tries to sell some of his loot. Stewart was at his folksy usual in *The Jackpot.* As his exasperated but loving wife Barbara was winning, but she was easily outshone by Medina, who sparkled in her brief role as the crafty interloper.

Producer Edward Small, who had a profitable penchant for churning out low-costing versions of adventure classics,* rather grandly announced in early 1950 that he would refilm the Richard D. Blackmore romantic drama *Lorna Doone* on location in England. The novel had been twice produced on screen by the British (1913, 1935), and an American rendition had been brought out by Associated First National in 1922 with Madge Bellamy and John Bowers in the lead roles. By the time actual production began on this new version in the early summer of 1950, Small and Columbia had compromised on a less expensive mounting, utilizing the Yosemite National Park for colorful background. Barbara was assigned the title role, completing her principal photography long before it became obvious that she was pregnant. She gave birth to her second child, William, on February 16, 1951. *Lorna Doone* was released in June of that year.

Set in the reign of Charles II in seventeenth-century England, *Lorna Doone*

The Last of the Mohicans, The Count of Monte Cristo, etc.

traces the return of Britisher Richard Greene to his home valley to find the area controlled by Carl Benton Reid and the tyrannical Doone family. Adventurous Greene organizes the oppressed farmers to attack the Doone stronghold, but before he does so, he encounters Barbara, who has escaped from the fortress, fearful that her cousin (William Bishop), the heir to the Doone largess, will force her to wed him. After several skirmishes in which the seesaw of power sways each way, Bishop is disposed of, and the path is clear for Barbara and Greene to wed. But wait, it is then discovered that Barbara is not a Doone after all, but of noble parentage, which requires her to journey to the royal court. There her true love, Greene, befriends Charles II, is knighted, and he and Barbara finally do wed. The *New York Times* may have pouted that the film was "stale meat and flat drink," but director Phil Karlson geared his Technicolor feature directly to the demands of the intended action and kiddie markets, and viewers had cause to be well satisfied. Greene, once a serious contender to Tyrone Power as Twentieth Century-Fox's most popular young leading man, was properly agile and gallant as the swashbuckling John Ridd. Barbara did all that her cardboard heroine's role required of her, mouthing her lines convincingly, flirting amorously, and maintaining a fetching look throughout the action.

Next in line for her, Columbia whipped together *The First Time* (1952) for the double-bill theatrical market, although this very slight domestic farce was far more suitable for a half-hour television-comedy-show format. The assembly-line story dealt with the trials and tribulations of a young married couple (Robert Cummings and Barbara) with their first baby. To make the picture even more cutesy, the episodic account is bridged by the baby's own narration. Having vicariously endured the trials and tribulations of parenthood, the audience is expected to howl (chuckle, moan) with anticipation of future mishaps when, at the climax, Barbara has a renewed spasm of desire for banana sandwiches, the food craving that signaled her initial pregnancy.

Barbara's busiest screen year since her early RKO days was 1953 with four releases, although it is unlikely she spent more than a combined four months in front of the cameras. Andre DeToth had little material with which to work in the programmer western *Last of the Comanches* (trade screened in December, 1952; released in February, 1953). Six cavalrymen, led by burly Broderick Crawford, survive a devastating Indian raid on a plains town. After a hundred-mile desert trek, they are joined by an assortment of stranded stagecoach passengers, a vagrant group of diverse types in the true John Ford-derivative tradition, ranging from heroine Barbara to a murder suspect and an Indian lad (Johnny Stewart). Almost needless to say, the reserve cavalry arrive in the nick of time to save laconic Crawford and his contingent from a redskin massacre. Barbara appeared properly harried yet brave, but she had little business to perform in this conventional B-film, boosted a little by color photography, but spoiled by trite anachronistic dialog.

On loan to Universal Barbara was cast opposite Rock Hudson in *Seminole*

(1953). The Technicolor western was directed by Budd Boetticher, who would gain eminence by helming Randolph Scott westerns later in the decade. *Seminole* is set at Fort King in the Florida territory of 1835, where Army lieutenant Hudson is charged with the murder of a sentry. At the court-martial he recounts his story: the wary co-existence between the settlers and the Indians was threatened by the martinet commander (Richard Carlson) of the Army fort. Hudson's childhood sweetheart, Barbara, agreed to meet with Osceola (Anthony Quinn), a mutual friend from their youth who had given up his own Army career to become head of the Seminole tribe. Through her influence and Quinn's respect for Hudson, the redskin leader eventually came to the stockade under a truce flag. But Indian-hating Carlson imprisoned Quinn in a pit, the latter died, and the situation deteriorated from bad to worse until the Indians rescued Hudson, who had been jailed by Carlson for killing a soldier while trying to restore peace. Once again Barbara's major asset in the film was her physical presence, providing a tone of sincerity.

Also for producer Howard Christie's programmer unit at Universal, Barbara appeared in the George Sherman-directed *Lone Hand* (1953). Filmed in color, *Lone Hand* was a wholesome family-style western outfitted with a respectable plot twist. A principled, gentle widower, Joel McCrea, and his son arrive in Timberlake, a western town of the 1870s. The settlement is overrun with a pack of killer bandits. Instead of joining the vigilantes as might be expected, McCrea offers his allegiance to the outlaws and participates in a stagecoach robbery—so, he says, he can wed widow Barbara. None of this pleases the law-abiding townsfolk or McCrea's newly enlarged family unit, who despise his crookedness. Because the finale reveals that McCrea is actually a Pinkerton undercover detective, he has the dual benefit in this film of being both a glamorous desperado and a nobler, more virtuous law-enforcer. *Variety* described Barbara as "properly sweet." Despite her colorless role, Barbara did have one good screen moment when McCrea confesses his real identity to her. She berates his eleventh-hour revelation as a "dirty trick."

Her only major film appearance of the year was in Warner Bros.' *A Lion Is in the Streets* (1953), produced by William Cagney and starring his brother James. The Cagneys had purchased the film rights to the sizzling political novel in 1945 for $250,000. Unfortunately for this film, four years before it was made and released, Columbia distributed the Academy Award-winning *All the King's Men,* an even more biting rendition of the same theme: the rise and fall of a Huey Long-like demagogue. In *A Lion Is in the Streets,* Cagney is seen peddling his wares in the back-hills country of a cotton-growing southern state. He falls for comely Barbara, a sympathetic grade-school teacher from up North. They wed and honeymoon in a cottage supplied by aristocratic Warner Anderson. But soon Cagney awakens to the possibilities of a grab-all political career in which he could easily become the kingpin of the state. Paralleling his unsavory career rise is Cagney's increased interest in a tramp, Flamingo (Anne Francis), a predatory tart who in a fit of jealousy nearly does away with her competitor (Barbara) in a premeditated swamp accident. Barbara leaves the cooling home fires to recuperate up North. Francis moves in, and that takes care of the schoolmarm. Just before grasping Cagney reaches the political bigtime in the gubernatorial elections he is shot down by Jeanne Cagney, the widow of sharecropper John McIntire. Once again second-billed Barbara was sweet, charming, and understanding, but she has the least showy role in a film full to the bursting point with well-delineated colorful characters flavorfully performed by a very seasoned cast.

By the time *A Lion Is in the Streets* was released, Barbara had given birth to a third child, Laura Lee, born on December 22, 1953. Thereafter Barbara was off the screen for over a year. The domestic-minded actress admitted: "All I want is to pay off the mortgage [on their new Bel Air home] and to have Daddy succeed with his own show."* On another occasion she explained: "It's very easy for me to fall into a domestic routine. I love to stay home. I love the children and Bill. I don't like to be away at the studio. But Bill is old-time vaudevillian. He likes to get out—see the town, do things. He would be bored with a girl who was just a little housewife. I keep just enough career going to keep Bill interested in what I'm doing."

With the above in mind, it is little wonder that Barbara calmly allowed her film assignments to deteriorate, paving the way for her being permanently relegated oncamera to cheap, cardboard leading-lady roles in increasingly inconsequential pictures.

Unchained (Victoria Theatre, January 27, 1955) would have been a quickly forgotten minor prison melodrama but for several plus factors: despite a contrived storyline, the Warner Bros. drama was based on fact and earnestly endeavored to reflect reality; its theme song was Oscar-nominated and has become a standard pop tune; it offers the sincere if amateurish performance of ex-football player Elroy "Crazylegs" Hirsh, contrasted with a hard-pressing enactment by Chester Morris as the founder-warden of an experimental penal institution. When rancher Hirsh assaults and nearly kills an employee he suspects of stealing, he is imprisoned and then transferred to Chino. At first he is an uncooperative prisoner. Along with inmate Jerry Paris he plans a break to freedom from the unbarred institution. Later, having become a member of Chino's respected men's council, he recognizes his own emotional shortcomings and decides to serve out his sentence, a redeemed citizen.

Since the bulk of *Unchained* dealt with the inmates' day-to-day existence, there was little opportunity to weave female characters into the account. As Hirsh's wife, Barbara is first seen arriving on visiting day to share a picnic

---

*Williams, who had been having poor luck in the feature film field, had come to the attention of director Lew Landers, who used him on a radio western series and then starred him as television's *Kit Carson* (1952-56, 104 episodes), tied in with a seven-year Coca-Cola sponsorship contract.

lunch with her distraught husband. Dressed in a white-collared, short-sleeved cotton dress, looking very much like Ruth Hussey, she once again personified the model lower-middle-class housewife—pert, loyal, and hardworking. Conversing with Hirsh in her deep-voiced tones, she offered as sympathetic as possible a performance within the script's limitations. But producer-director-scenarist Hall Bartlett focused much of this visiting day sequence on the interaction between Jerry Paris and his doll-moll (Peggy Knudsen), who professes her abiding love for Paris—after all, did she not make peanut-butter-and-jelly sandwiches for the occasion?—while pressuring him for details of his alleged hidden loot. Her Marilyn Monroe-like facial mannerisms riveted the viewer's attention, and Barbara was temporarily lost in the shuffle. Barbara's second sequence, another Sunday picnic scene, reflected her concern at Hirsh's failure to adjust to his new surroundings, but more importantly the medium shots of Barbara revealed very noticeable wrinkles in her forehead. Thirty-four-year-old Barbara was no longer an ingenue! Her third scene—yet another weekend mealtime outing—found her clad in a frilly white blouse and plain skirt, with a white sweater thrown over her shoulders, very reminiscent of the Barbara Hale of the earlier RKO programmers. But the bulk of this segment was devoted to Hirsh's timorous interplay with his confused youngster (Tim Considine), who finds it difficult to accept that his father is a convict.*

Unchained did not fare well on the release market. Not only did it lack kinetic zing to give it box-office impetus on even a modest scale, but too many well-publicized and ugly prison riots were occurring in the United States at the time for the sweetness-and-light Chino prison farm to seem real to filmgoing America. Along with Oscar-winning Columbia contract star Donna Reed, Barbara next found herself shunted over to Paramount's budget-production unit for *The Far Horizons* (1955). The inexpensively produced feature boasted Technicolor and widescreen VistaVision, but bore the burden of a monosyllabic script and Rudolph Mate's distinctly routine direction. Above all, Fred MacMurray and Charlton Heston seemed to have written off this chore from the start of shooting. As the two explorers assigned by President Thomas Jefferson to explore the Louisiana land purchase in 1803, they growled and scowled at one another (MacMurray had caught Heston kissing MacMurray's fiancée, Barbara, behind a White House portico), and later competed for the affection of their Shoshone Indian guide, Sacajawea (Reed), even though squaw Reed has told savior Heston: "You fought for me. Now I belong to you. It is the custom of my people." Because of the overemphasis on the romantic turmoil, the all-important historical exploration trip seemed inconsequential at best. Barbara attempted to instill winning sincerity into her two brief scenes, but it was a losing cause.

Three years and five pictures after *Last of the Comanches,* Barbara finally

*At least Barbara did not suffer the fate of ex-MGM player Rita Johnson, whose scenes as Chester Morris's wife were deleted altogether from the final-release print of *Unchained.*

returned to her home lot on Gower Street to co-star with Gene Barry in *The Houston Story* (1956), produced by the king of inexpensive movie-making, Sam Katzman. It was yet another entry in the extended cycle of exposé pictures then peppering theatres (e.g., *Las Vegas Shakedown, Phoenix City Story, New Orleans Uncensored, Miami Expose, New York Confidential, Chicago Confidential,* etc.). The British *Monthly Film Bulletin* rightly pegged *The Houston Story* as "a machine made racketeer picture which lacks distinction in all departments." The picture did have one difference, Barbara was blonde this time, but her role consisted mostly of reaction shots as the tale unfolded. The storyline has oil worker Barry perfect a plan to steal "black gold" directly from the Houston wells. He gains admission to a crime syndicate, which puts the scheme into operation. Soon Barry maneuvers himself to the top of the heap, but the enemies he incurs along the way engineer his downfall. Rather than be murdered, he surrenders to the police.

For her next outing Barbara joined the growing company of actresses who were given the opportunity to provide feminine adornment for Randolph Scott's string of efficient Technicolor westerns.* *Seventh Cavalry* (1956) offered a twist on the story of General Custer's last stand. After the massacre of Army troops at Little Big Horn, captain Randolph Scott is branded a coward for having been away from the post and thus not in action at the time of the slaughter. Scott later heads a suicide patrol into the Indian-infested Black Hills to attempt the recovery of the dead officers' bodies. This time it is not the cavalry that rides to the beleaguered soldiers' rescue—rather, the presence of Custer's riderless battle mount convinces the aroused Indians to allow the patrol to leave the area unharmed. Barbara's token assignment required her to prance about as the daughter of post commander Russell Hicks.

Now a very seasoned hand at underplaying western leading ladies, Barbara was again cast opposite Joel McCrea in *The Oklahoman* (1957), shot in De-Luxe color and CinemaScope by Academy Award-winning editor-turned-director Francis D. Lyon. "No matter what people think," says widower-physician McCrea, who has settled in Cherokee Wells, a midwestern prairie town of the 1870s, he will not allow the greedy ranchers to pin a dubious murder charge on Indian Michael Pate (a rich flow of oil on Pate's land has stirred the white men's avarice). This situation sets the stage for the inevitable duel of power between justice-fighter McCrea and the grasping locals, led by skunk Brad Dexter. To complicate matters, McCrea has Pate's young daughter (Gloria Talbott) employed as a housekeeper on his spread, which arouses the jealousy of widow Barbara, who has already set her sights on eligible McCrea. Howard Thompson (*New York Times*), who decided the "corn is well arranged on the cob" in this oater, also called attention to the performance of the "always excellent" Barbara. But it was really Talbott as the spunky Indian who livened up the cloying domestic interludes. *The Oklahoman* was crammed full

*Dolores Dorn, Joan Weldon, Dorothy Malone, Angela Lansbury, Jocelyn Brando.

of screen veterans, including Gertrude Astor, Esther Dale, Kermit Maynard, Scotty Beckett, and Verna Felton, the latter best known as the co-star of the "December Bride" video series.

Both Barbara and Bill Williams appeared briefly as guest performers in Universal's western spoof *Slim Carter* (1957), playing a very middle-aged Hollywood husband-and-wife acting team. Then came the Twentieth Century-Fox programmer *Desert Hell* (1958), which proved to be Barbara's last feature film for a decade. This black-and-white entry, filmed in Regalscope, had a French Foreign Legion (studio) backdrop, with Brian Keith and Richard Denning, the sole survivors of an Arab ambush, uncovering a plot to start a new Arab-French war in Africa. They embark on a dangerous field mission to substantiate their evidence, combating not only the Tuareg natives but each other, since Keith has caught Denning kissing his wife (Barbara). In the dying programmer theatrical market, *Desert Hell* had little to offer with its fake desert, plot, and characters. The triangular love tale was reminiscent of *The Far Horizons,* but the plot itself bore a remarkable resemblance to the far superior *The Last Outpost* (1935), starring Claude Rains and Cary Grant. Although Barbara was second-billed in *Desert Hell,* she was scarcely in evidence during the picture's sluggish eighty-two-minute running time.

By 1956, with her Columbia contract nearly completed, Barbara turned to television work, accepting assignments more for the fun of it and the ready cash than from any aggressive career plan. She had debuted on the medium in *The Divided Heart* on "Ford Theatre" (NBC, November 27, 1952) opposite Stephen McNally, followed by sporadic appearances on such anthology series as "Schlitz Playhouse of Stars," "Climax," "Screen Directors Playhouse," "Science Fiction Theatre" (with Bill Williams), "Loretta Young Theatre," and "Playhouse 90."

But the highlight of Barbara's television career, and the event that ultimately made her name well known to Americans, was being selected to portray secretary Della Street on the "Perry Mason" series, the first sixty-minute weekly segment of which debuted on CBS-TV on September 21, 1957, with the episode *The Case of the Restless Redhead.* Barbara had been the personal choice of the producer of the series, former actress Gail Patrick Jackson, who no doubt agreed with one leading television critic of the time that "no leading lady blushes quite as prettily as Barbara Hale." And no one was perhaps more qualified than Barbara to assume a major yet subordinate assignment, which would require her to be alert and pert, but never overshadowing, in her portrayal of the self-sufficient but not hard-boiled secretary to master lawyer-sleuth Perry Mason (Raymond Burr).

The *Perry Mason* property already had a long and lucrative history before reaching the small screen. California lawyer Erle Stanley Gardner wrote the first of his fifty-two *Perry Mason* novels in 1933: *The Case of the Velvet Claws* and *The Case of the Sulky Girls.* To date the *Perry Mason* capers have sold over 140 million copies in the United States alone. The book series had never adapted well to the screen,* and it was not until the property was transformed into a radio show in 1943 on CBS that its multimedia potential began to be realized.†

From the start of the long-running teleseries (271 episodes) the format remained almost rigidly the same: a much-troubled client asks the assistance of criminal attorney Perry Mason (Burr). With the aid of private investigator Paul Drake (William Hopper), Mason and secretary Della Street (Barbara) marshal together all the facts in the case, despite the continual interference of detective-lieutenant Arthur Tragg (Ray Collins). In the standard courtroom finale Mason proves, much to the chagrin of crusading district attorney Hamilton Burger (William Talman), that the defendant suspect is innocent. If a courtroom witness on the stand does not break down under pressure at the crucial moment to reveal the expected denouement, an epilogue section has Della and Drake querying Mason on just how he figured out the crime and persuaded the culprit to reveal his guilt.

In the initial *Perry Mason* novels Della Street had been described as a pert girl of twenty-two, while Barbara was thirty-six years old when the "Perry Mason" teleseries commenced and forty-five when the show faded in the spring of 1966. But in all other aspects it was felt that Barbara was admirably cast as lawyer Mason's ever-loyal secretary. In some episodes, Barbara would have no more than six lines of dialog, but each line might occur in a different day setting within the storyline, requiring six changes of outfits and demanding her presence on the set each day at CBS's Hollywood studio. Although her role was consistently small on the show, it was an essential facet of the program's successful makeup, and all concerned, from producer Jackson to star Burr, agreed that Barbara's participation was a key to the show's spectacular popularity with the public. As Burr described it: "Barbara, without being ostentatious about it, is a remarkably intuitive actress. She has an instinct for doing exactly the right thing when it is needed." Barbara would half-jokingly admit: "I could hardly drag myself to the parking lot to drive home each day. I was so exhausted from standing around."

Before the first season was over, the show had established itself as a solid hit with home viewers,‡ and it remained a very popular entry for eight ad-

---

*There were seven low-budget entries produced between 1934 and 1937: *The Case of the Howling Dog* (1934) with Warren William as Perry Mason and Helen Trenholme as Della Street; *The Case of the Curious Bride* (1935) with Warren William and Claire Dodd; *The Case of the Lucky Legs* (1935) with Warren William and Genevieve Tobin; *The Case of the Black Cat* (1936) with Ricardo Cortez and June Travis; *The Case of the Velvet Claws* (1936) with Warren William and Claire Dodd; *Special Investigator* (1936); and *The Case of the Stuttering Bishop* (1936) with Donald Woods and Ann Dvorak.

†During its radio run the series successively starred Bartlett Robinson, Santos Ortega, Donald Briggs, and John Larkin as Perry Mason; Gertrude Warner and Jan Miner as Della Street. On the short-lived 1973-1974 CBS "New Perry Mason" series, Monte Markham was Mason, with Sharon Acker as Della Street, Harry Guardino as Hamilton Burger, Albert Stratton as Paul Drake, and Dane Clark as Lieutenant Tragg.

‡One publicity handout stated that when Barbara learned the series would be renewed for a second season she invested in a silver belt buckle, initialed with the letters D.S. (Della Street).

ditional video seasons. In the course of its long run, Burr won two Emmy awards, with Barbara earning her Emmy from the Academy of Television Arts and Sciences in 1959 for best supporting actress in a video series, and receiving another nomination in 1961. Had the Academy not frequently fluctuated its award categories so drastically, it is likely Barbara would have won additional Emmys.

With a rich yearly salary from "Perry Mason" Barbara felt no need to expand her professional activities beyond the time-consuming video show, although she guested on television in "Custer" (ABC) on November 22, 1961. But with the end of "Perry Mason" in 1966 (but not of residuals, since "Perry Mason" is still in continual domestic and foreign syndication), Barbara agreed to appear in A. C. Lyles's programmer western *Buckskin* (1968). The fact that Lyles agreed to cast Bill Williams as her husband in this economy feature insured her acceptance.* In standard Lyles style, *Buckskin* boasted a bevy of movie-television veterans, headed by 1940s cinema star Joan Caulfield, playing a saloon tart. This color programmer was set in Gloryhole, Montana, where Wendell Corey is bilking the miners in his gambling establishment and harassing landowners to leave their homesteads so he can take possession of their potentially rich lands. To prompt their removal from the valley, Corey has had a dam constructed to deprive the homesteaders of needed water supply. But territorial marshal Barry Sullivan rides fearlessly into town and soon sets matters straight. He removes crooked sheriff Lon Chaney from office. When he fights off Corey's henchmen so he can dynamite the dam, his young ally, Michael Larrain, the son of Barbara and Williams, is killed. In the final showdown, Sullivan emerges victorious and wins no less a prize than Miss Caufield. Barbara's screen moments in *Buckskin* were few but telling. *Variety* appraised: "Barbara Hale rises above her material in the chilling moment when she sees the dead body of her son. Death, so cavalierly treated so often in Westerns, is here responded to freely."

The following year Barbara was among the assortment of established names who graced Ross Hunter's glossy production, *Airport* (1970), based on Arthur Hailey's best-selling novel. The movie was slick and more vapid than the computer-plotted book original, but it possessed a vital major ingredient: smooth, suspenseful entertainment—so much so, that *Airport* to date has made more than $44.5 million in domestic gross receipts. In the eleventh-billed role of Sarah Bakersfeld Demerest, Barbara was cast as the sister of Burt Lancaster, the general manager of Lincoln International Airport. She is married to senior jet-passenger-plane pilot Dean Martin, knowing full well that he has a reputation for fraternizing with the stewardesses. As she tells Lancaster, she sticks with Martin because she loves him and knows he will always come back

---

*Williams had not been doing very well on the video scene after his "Kit Carson" series. He starred with Betty White in an abortive comedy series, "A Date with the Angels" (1957), and in 1960 was co-lead of a thirty-nine-episode loser titled "Assignment: Underwater." He occasionally guested on drama and western series.

787

home to her eventually. But she has not counted on his steamy romance with hostess Jacqueline Bisset, who announces to childless Martin before their fateful flight to Rome that she is pregnant. Before the 707 jet airliner has passed over the Appalachian Mountains, passenger Van Heflin has set off his briefcase bomb and the crippled aircraft must limp back to Lincoln International Airport. Barbara did not have much showcasing in *Airport* compared to the scene-stealing performances of Helen Hayes or Maureen Stapleton, but two of her brief scenes stick in the viewer's mind. One in which she drives Martin to the airport in her full-length fur coat and bids him goodbye. The worried smile on her face fully conveys her realization that some third party is jarring their domestic relationship once again. In the final-resolution sequence, a much-concerned Barbara waits at the terminal entrance to learn whether Martin has survived the bombing ordeal intact. Although the camera quickly passes over to focus on the "stars," Barbara, with experienced pantomime, manages to suggest a sequence of relief, then despair, and finally resignation, as she witnesses Martin accompanying the stretcher-carried Bisset from the rampway onto the main concourse.

Barbara's most recent feature is *Soul Soldier* (1971),* geared to exploit the rising tide of Hollywood-style black-power features. *Soul Soldier* starred former Olympic decathlon champion Rafer Johnson as a member of a black cavalry unit posted at Fort Davis, Texas, following the Civil War. Essentially a standard western, it was given a black twist, as the cavalrymen complain about the rigors of Army life and ponder the morality of fighting another minority group, the redskins. Barbara very much looked her age, portraying the wife of post commander Cesar Romero. She had five scenes in the film, usually seen talking to Romero on the porch of their fort home, or shopping at the post store. One sequence called for her to wear her hair down and utilize a fall, accentuating the aging process, which had broadened her features. On another occasion she used a pair of silver-rimmed spectacles, once again looking very much like a Rosemary DeCamp type. Her bits of dialog were merely contrivances to explain the uncertain plot action, or even worse, aimless chatter with her oncamera spouse (e.g., "I've heard you say some nasty things to officers").

Soul Soldier was conceived too early in the black-power cycle to boast flagrant racism and fast-paced violence as did the later *The Legend of Nigger Charley* (1972), but even the superficial *Soul Soldier* found its own relatively profitable market. When the film was finally reviewed by the *New York Times*, the write-up noted that Barbara and Cesar Romero "bring up the rear with some dignity."

Barbara and Bill Williams guested on the September 29, 1971, episode of the "Adam 12" (NBC) series, she playing the mother of Katy Garver. In November of that year Barbara was professionally reunited with Raymond Burr

*First released in 1970 under the title *The Red, White, and Black*.

788

for the first time since the spring of 1966, when she guest-starred as a playwright on the *Murder Impromptu* segment of the police-detective series "Ironside" (NBC, November 2, 1971). That fall she began her chores as a television spokeswoman for the Amana Company, promoting their oven appliances, a post she still holds.

Now, as several decades ago, Barbara is still most comfortable as a housewife and mother, and being a performer is a very decidedly second in her order of priorities. She obviously has never forgotten the time in the late 1940s when she and Williams, according to rumor, had marital problems, stemming from her career upswing and his professional stagnation. If pressed for an interview, she will usually decline unless the requester agrees to talk with Williams too, a factor that has made Barbara a rarely covered subject in the press today.* Much of the Williams's yearly income is derived from Chatsworth and from desert real estate which they have acquired over the years. Their son William made his motion picture debut in 1971 in the independently produced Anne Baxter feature *The Late Liz,* in which he went by the professional name of William Kaat.

*Williams, whose last feature film to date was a small assignment in Buena Vista's *Scandalous John* (1971), has always had career attitudes that put off the press and the public. For example, c. 1958 he stated: "I have always tried to avoid the star bit. Too many headaches, too much backbiting. People will never go to a picture just to see me, but on the other hand producers will always use me because they know my name is comfortably familiar and that I'll always do a good competent job for them. These multi-million dollar deals with your production company simply leave me cold." Reviewing Williams's career to date, this theory sounds more sour grapes than abject modesty.

Feature Film Appearances
BARBARA HALE

GILDERSLEEVE'S BAD DAY   (RKO, 1943) 62 M.

Producer, Herman Schlom; director, Gordon Douglas; screenplay, Jack Townley; music director, C. Bakaleinikoff; art director, Albert S. D'Agostino, Carroll Clark; camera, Jack Mackenzie; editor, Les Milbrook.

Harold Peary (Gildersleeve); Jane Darwell (Aunt Emma); Nancy Gates (Margie); Charles Arnt (Judge Hooker); Freddie Mercer (Leroy); Russell Wade (Jimmy); Lillian Randolph (Birdie); Frank Jenks (Al); Douglas Fowley (Louie); Alan Carney (Toad); Grant Withers (Henry Potter); Richard Legrand (Peavy); Dink Trout (Otis); Harold Landon (George Peabody); Charles Cane (Police Chief); Ken Christy (Bailiff); Ann Summers, Patti Brill, Betty Wells, Margie Stewart, Barbara Hale (Bits); Joey Ray (Tom); Joan Barclay (Julie Potter); James Clemons, Jr. (Boy); W. J. O'Brien, Morgan Brown, Ralph Robertson, Broderick O'Farrell, Lou Davis, Herbert Berman, Richard Bartell, Eddie Borden, Larry Wheat (Jurors); Warren Jackson (Joe, the Cop); Earle Hodgins (Mason, the Cop); Fern Emmett (Mrs. Marvin); Lee Phelps (Ryan); Danny Jackson (Messenger Boy); Fred Trowbridge (Defense Attorney); Arthur Loft (Lucas); Jack Rice (Hotel Clerk); Edgar Sherrod (Minister).

MEXICAN SPITFIRE'S BLESSED EVENT   (RKO, 1943) 63 M.

Producer, Bert Gilroy; director, Leslie Goodwins; screenplay, Charles E. Roberts, Dane Lussier; art director, Albert S. D'Agostino, Walter E. Keller; music director, C. Bakaleinikoff; camera, Jack MacKenzie; editor, Harry Marker.

Lupe Velez (Carmelita); Leon Errol (Lord Epping/Uncle Matt); Walter Reed (Dennis); Elizabeth Risdon (Aunt Della); Lydia Bilbrook (Lady Epping); Hugh Beaumont (Mr. Sharpe); Aileen Carlyle (Mrs. Pettibone); Alan Carney (Bartender); Marietta Canty (Verbena); Ruth Lee (Mrs. Walters); Wally Brown (Desk Clerk); Joan Barclay, Patti Brill, Margaret Landry, Margie Stewart, Barbara Hale, Rita Corday, Mary Halsey, Ann Summers, Rosemary LaPlanche (Bits); Robert Anderson (Captain Rogers); George Plues (Driver); Eddie Dew (Sheriff Walters); George Rogers, Dorothy Rogers, Don Kramer (Dancers); Billy Edward Reed (Attendant); Charles Coleman (Parker); Eddie Borden (Messenger Boy); June Booth (Nurse); Anne O'Neal (Matron at Orphanage).

THE SEVENTH VICTIM   (RKO, 1943) 71 M.

Producer, Val Lewton; director, Mark Robson; screenplay, Charles O'Neal, DeWitt Bodeen; music, Roy Webb; music director, C. Bakaleinikoff; art director, Albert S. D'Agostino, Walter E. Keller; camera, Nicholas Musuraca; editor, John Lockert.

Tom Conway (Dr. Louis Judd); Kim Hunter (Mary Gibson); Jean Brooks (Jacqueline Gibson); Hugh Beaumont (Gregory Ward); Erford Gage (Jason Hoag); Isabel Jewell (Frances); Chef Milani (Mr. Romari); Marguerite Sylva (Mrs. Romari); Evelyn

Brent (Natalie Cortez); Mary Newton (Mrs. Redi); Jamesson Shade (Swenson, the Cop); Eve March (Mrs. Gilchrist); Tola Nesmith (Mrs. Lowood); Edythe Elliott (Mrs. Swift); Milton Kibbee (Joseph, a Devil Worshipper); Marianne Mosner (Miss Rowan); Elizabeth Russell (Mimi); Joan Barclay (Gladys); Barbara Hale (Young Lover); Mary Halsey (Bit); William Halligan (Radeaux); Wheaton Chambers, Ed Thomas (Men); Edith Conrad (Woman); Lou Lubin (Irving August); Bud Geary, Charles Phillips, Howard Mitchell (Cops); Lloyd Ingraham (Watchman); Dewey Robinson (Conductor); Ann Summers (Miss Summers); Tiny Jones (News Vendor); Adia Kuznetzoff (Ballet Dancer); Sarah Selby (Miss Gottschalk); Betty Roadman (Mrs. Wheeler); Eileen O'Malley, Lorna Dunn (Mothers).

THE IRON MAJOR (RKO, 1943) 85 M.

Producer, Robert Fellows; director, Ray Enright; story, Florence M. Cavanaugh; screenplay, Aben Kandel, Warren Duff; technical football advisor, William "Hiker" Joy; assistant director, Edward Killy; music, Roy Webb; music director, C. Bakaleinikoff; art director, Albert S. D'Agostino, Carroll Clark; camera, Robert De Grasse; editor, Robert Wise.

Pat O'Brien (Frank Cavanaugh); Ruth Warrick (Florence "Mike" Ayres Cavanaugh); Robert Ryan (Father Tim Donovan); Leon Ames (Robert Stewart); Russell Wade (Private Manning), Bruce Edwards (Lieutenant Jones); Richard Martin (Davis Cavanaugh); Robert Bice (Coach); Virginia Brissac (Mrs. Ayres); Robert Anderson, Mike Lally, Lee Phelps, Craig Flanagan, Michael Road (Bits); Arnold Stanford, Bob Thom (Soldiers); Lew Harvey (Lieutenant); Bud Geary (Sergeant); Walter Brooke (Lieutenant Stone); Louis Jean Heydt (Recruiting Sergeant); Frank Puglia (Nurse); Pierre Watkin (Colonel White); Walter Fenner (Doctor); Louis Borell (French Officer); Billy Roy (Bob—as a boy); Robert Winkler (Frank—as a boy); Henry Roquemore (Evans); Barbara Hale (Sarah Cavanaugh); Joel Davis (Davie—as a boy); Cy Ring (Ross); Wheaton Chambers (Army Doctor); Dean Benton (William Cavanaugh); Myron Healey (Paul Cavanaugh); Kirk Alyn (John Cavanaugh); James Jordan (Philip Cavanaugh); Victor Kilian (Francis Cavanaugh); Margaret Landry (Sis Cavanaugh); Ian Wolfe (Professor Runnymead); Harry Tyler, Eddie Woods (Friends); Pat O'Malley (Charlie); Gloria Duran, Ramon Ros (Dancers); Bonnie Braunger (Baby); Sada Simmons, Mary Currier (Nurses); Joe Crehan (Judge); Joe King (Defense Attorney); Eddie Hart (Bailiff); Milton Kibbee (Watkins); Paul LePere (Court Clerk); Joe O'Connor (Second Defense Attorney); Harold Landon, James Courtney, Buddy Yarus, Mel Schubert, Greg McClure (Boston College Players); Charles D. Brown, William Forrest (Officials); Sam McDaniel (Pete); John Miljan (Oregon Coach); Larry Lund, Robert Benton, Steve Barclay (Football Players); Walt Robbins, Sid Jordan (Drivers Of 2-Up); James Flavin, Russ Clark (Umpires); Brooks Benedict, Brandon Beach (Alumni); John B. Williams (Pullman Porter); Florence Hansen (Bob's Girlfriend); Fred Kohler (Boston College Captain); John Dilson (Doctor); James Magill, Steve Winston, Gordon Clark (Students); Dorothy Vaughan (Ma Cavanaugh); Frank Shannon (Pa Cavanaugh); Paul McVey (Athletic Coach); Chuck Hamilton (Fordham Player); Richard Davies (Chuck, a Player); Roland Dupree, Michael Miller, Bobby Larson, Richard Dillon (Boys).

GILDERSLEEVE ON BROADWAY (RKO, 1943) 65 M.

Producer, Herman Schlom; director, Gordon Douglas; story-screenplay, Robert E. Kent; music director, C. Bakaleinikoff; art director, Albert S. D'Agostino, William Stevens; camera, Jack Mackenzie; editor, Les Milbrook.

Harold Peary (Gildersleeve); Billie Burke (Mrs. Chandler); Claire Carleton (Francine Gray); Richard LeGrand (Peavy); Freddie Mercer (LeRoy); Hobart Cavanaugh (Homer); Margaret Landry (Margie); Leonid Kinsky (Window Washer); Ann Doran

(Matilda); Lillian Randolph (Birdie); Michael Road (Jimmy); Rita Corday, Elaine Riley, Shirley O'Hara, Daun Kennedy, Rosemary LaPlanche (Models); Harry Clay (Bellboy); Tom Burton, Steve Winston, Barbara Coleman, Dorothy Malone (Bits); Lee Phelps (Clancy); Larry Wheat (Man); Sylvia Andrew (Spinster); Teddy Infuhr (Stanley); Phyllis Dare (Little Girl); Forrest Lewis (Carson); Robert Anderson (Hotel Clerk); Frank Dawson (Minister); George Carleton (Hawkins); Eugene Borden (Headwaiter); Lawrence Tierney (Cab Driver); Barbara Hale (Stocking Clerk); Fred Essler (LeMaire); Ken Christy (Delaney); Jack Norton (Mr. Dobrey); Walter Tetley (Bellboy); Herbert Evans (Butler); Charles Miller (Judge).

GOVERNMENT GIRL   (RKO, 1943) 94 M.

Producer, Dudley Nichols; associate producer, Edward Donahue; director, Nichols; story, Adela Rogers St. John; adaptation, Budd Schulberg; screenplay, Nichols; music, Leigh Harline; music director, C. Bakaleinikoff; special effects, Vernon L. Walker; camera, Frank Redman; editor, Roland Gross.

Olivia de Havilland (Smokey); Sonny Tufts (Browne); Anne Shirley (May); Jess Barker (Dana); James Dunn (Sergeant Joe); Paul Stewart (Branch); Agnes Moorehead (Mrs. Wright); Harry Davenport (Senator MacVickers); Una O'Connor (Mrs. Harris); Sig Rumann (Ambassador); Jane Darwell (Miss Trask); George Givot (Count Bodinsky); Paul Stanton (Mr. Harvester); Art Smith (Marqueenie); Joan Valerie (Miss MacVickers); Harry Shannon (Mr. Gibson); Emory Parnell (The Chief); Ray Walker (Tom Holliday); J. O. Fowler (Man); Russell Huestes, Larry Steers, James Carlisle, Bert Moorhouse, Fred Norton, Demetrius Alexis, Larry Williams, Chester Carlisle, Harry Denny, Tom Costello, Ronnie Rondell, Charles Meaken (Business Men); Norman Mayes, Karl Miller (Janitors); Clive Morgan (Officer); Harold Miller (Naval Officer); Major Sam Harris (American General); Rita Corday, Patti Brill, Margaret Landry, Mary Halsey, Barbara Coleman, Barbara Hale, Marion Murray (Bits); Lawrence Tierney, Bruce Edwards, Ralph Dunn, Al Hill, David Newell, George Ford, Alex Melesh (FBI Men); Fred Fox, Babe Green, Frank McClure, Harry Bailey, Donald Hall, Louis Payne, Wally Dean, James Kirkwood (Senators); Ralph Linn, Josh Milton, Tom Burton, Harry Clay, Steve Winston (Reporters); June Booth (Secretary); Ivan Simpson (Judge Leonard); Charles Halton (Clerk); Ian Wolfe (Hotel Clerk); David Hughes (Guest); J. Louis Johnson (Mr. Wright's Father); Chef Milani (Hotel Waiter); Frank Norman (Tough Sergeant); John Hamilton, Edward Keane, George Melford (Irate Men); Joe Bernard (Workman); George Riley (Cop).

AROUND THE WORLD   (RKO, 1943) 81 M.

Producer-director, Allan Dwan; story-screenplay, Ralph Spence; special material, Carl Herzinger; art director, Albert S. D'Agostino, Hal Herman; music, George Duning; songs, Jimmy McHugh and Harold Adamson; camera, Russell Metty; editor, Theron Warth.

Kay Kyser (Kay); Mischa Auer (Mischa); Joan Davis (Joan); Marcy McGuire (Marcy); Wally Brown (Clipper Pilot); Alan Carney (Joe Gimpus); Georgia Carroll (Georgia); Harry Babbitt (Harry); Ish Kabibble (Ish); Sully Mason (Sully); Julie Conway (Julie); Diane Pendleton (Diane); Kay Kyser's Band (Themselves); Jack and Max, Lucienne and Ashour, Little Fred's Football Dogs, Jadine Wong and Li Sun, Al Norman (Specialty Acts); Robert Armstrong (General); Buford Turner (Turner); Mary Halsey (Mary Jane); Joan Barclay (Barclay); Margie Stewart (Marjorie); Barbara Hale (Barbara); Barbara Coleman (Coleman); Rosemary LaPlanche (Rosemary); Shirley O'Hara (Shirley); Daun Kennedy (Daun); Sherry Hall (Clipper Steward); Renny McEvoy (Band Man); Colin Kenny (Dock Worker); Josh Milton, Drake Thorton, Jack Alfred, George Hoagland, John Albright (Officers); Bill Manning (Handsome Sergeant); Charles Straight (Orderly); Peter Chong (Mr. Wong); Joan Valerie (Countess Olga); Frank Puglia (Native Dealer); Duncan Renaldo (Dragoman); William Vaughn, Arno Frey, Walter Bonn (Germans); Norman Mayes (Black Orderly); Ivan Lebedeff (Menlo); Henry Guttman (Balso); Chester Conklin (Waiter); Claire Carleton (WAAC Lieutenant Spencer); Selmer Jackson (Consul); Clarence Peterson, Carl Saxe, Bernie Sell, Gene Stone, Bud Townsend, Hansel Werner, James Waters, Billy Wilkerson, Mike Kilian, Ed Astran, Richard Clarke, James Courtney, Ken Cutler, George Ford, George Golden, Charles Heard, Don Kemp, Harold Knight, Nils Althin, Don Bryan, John Jenkins, Joe Roach (Soldiers); James Westerfield (Bashful Marine); Allen Jung (Ring); Philip Ahn (Foo); Fred Cavens (Instructor); Arnold Stanford (Orderly); Ralph Littlefield (B. H. Colonel); Faith Kruger (Singer); Roland Got (Rickshaw Driver); Paul Kay (Army Captain).

HIGHER AND HIGHER   (RKO, 1943) 90 M.

Producer, Tim Whelan; associate producer, George Arthur; director, Whelan; based on the play by Gladys Hurlbut, Joshua Logan, Richard Rodgers, Lorenz Hart; screenplay, Jay Dratler, Ralph Spence; additional dialog, William Bowers, Howard Harris; music director, Constantin Bakaleinikoff; orchestrator, Gene Rose; music, Roy Webb; vocal arranger, Ken Darby; choreography, Ernst Matray; art director, Albert S. D'Agostino, Jack Okey; set decorator, Darrell Silvera, Claude Carpenter; gowns, Edward Stevenson; assistant director, Clem Beauchamp; songs, Jimmy McHugh and Harold Adamson; sound, Jean L. Speak, James G. Stewart; camera, Robert De Grasse; editor, Gene Milford.

Michele Morgan (Millie); Jack Haley (Mike); Frank Sinatra (Frank); Leon Errol (Drake); Marcy McGuire (Mickey); Victor Borge (Fitzroy Wilson); Mary Wickes (Sandy); Elisabeth Risdon (Mrs. Keating); Barbara Hale (Catherine); Mel Torme (Marty); Paul Hartman (Byngham); Grace Hartman (Hilda); Dooley Wilson (Oscar); Ivy Scott (Miss Whiffin); Rex Evans (Mr. Green); Stanley Logan (Hotel Manager); Ola Lorraine (Sarah, the Maid); King Kennedy (Mr. Duval); Robert Anderson (Announcer); Rita Gould (Woman Assistant); Harry Holman (Banker); Warren Jackson (Contractor); Anne Goldthwaite (Debutante); Shirley O'Hara, Elaine Riley, Dorothy Malone, Daun Kennedy (Bridesmaids); Drake Thorton (Bellboy); Edward Fielding (Minister); Buddy Gorman (Page Boy).

THE FALCON OUT WEST   (RKO, 1944) 64 M.

Producer, Maurice Geraghty; director, William Clemmons; based on the character created by Michael Arlen; story-screenplay, Billy Jones, Morton Grant; art director, Albert S. D'Agostino, Alfred Herman; music director, C. Bakaleinikoff; music, Roy Webb; dialog director, Donald Dillaway; assistant director, James Carey; costumes, Renie; camera, Harry Wilk; editor, Gene Milford.

Tom Conway (Falcon); Carole Gallagher (Vanessa); Barbara Hale (Marion); Joan Barclay (Mrs. Irwin); Cliff Clark (Inspector Donovan); Minor Watson (Caldwell); Ed Gargan (Bates); Don Douglas (Hayden); Lyle Talbot (Tex); Lee Trent (Dusty); Perc Launders (Red); Wheaton Chambers (Sheriff); Chief Thundercloud (Eagle Feather); Tom Burton (Photographer); Steve Winston (Caldwell Cowboy); Harry Clay (Hall); Robert Anderson (Wally Waldron); Edmund Glover (Frank Daley); Mary Halsey (Cissy); Daun Kennedy (Gloria); Rosemary La Planche (Mary); Chef Milani (Manager); Elaine Riley (Cigarette Girl); Shirley O'Hara, Patti Brill (Hat Check Girls); Michael St. Angel (Bit); Eddie Clark (Coroner); Joe Cody (Toni); Bert Roach (Charlie, the Drunk); Norman Willis (Callahan); Kernan Cripps (Murphy); Slim Whitaker (Cowboy); William Nestell (Chef); Zedra Conde (Carlita); Norman Mayes (Pullman Porter).

HEAVENLY DAYS (RKO, 1944) 72 M.

Producer, Robert Fellows; director-story, Howard Estabrook; screenplay, Estabrook, Don Quinn; art director, Albert S. D'Agostino, Ralph Berger; set decorator, Darrell Silvera; William Stevens; makeup, Mel Burns; music, Leigh Harline; music director, C. Bakaleinikoff; special effects, Vernon L. Walker; camera, Roy Hunt; editor, Robert Swink.

Jim Jordan (Fibber McGee); Marian Jordan (Molly McGee); Eugene Pallette (Senator Bigbee); Gordon Oliver (Dick); Raymond Walburn (Mr. Popham); Barbara Hale (Angie); Don Douglas (Dr. Gallup); Frieda Inescourt (Mrs. Clark); Irving Bacon (Butler); The King's Men (Themselves); Emory Parnell (Detective); Charles Trowbridge (Mr. Clark); Chester Carlisle, Bert Moorhouse (Sergeants-at-Arms); J. M. Sullivan (Detective); Henry Hall, Ed Peil, James Farley, Lloyd Ingraham, Fred Fox, Brandon Beach, James Carlisle, J. O. Fowler, Lou Payne, Henry Herbert, Ed Mortimer, Wilbur Mack, Joseph Girard, Dick Rush, John Ince (Senators); Ed Stanley (Vice President Wallace); Harry Humphrey (Southern Senator); George Reed (Servant); Norman Mayes (Waiter); Helena Benda (Czech Lady); Bertha Feducah (French Lady); William Yip (Chinese Man); Esther Zeitlan (Russian Lady); John Duncan (Boy); Clinton Rosemond (Black Servant); Eva McKenzie (Clerk); Teddy Infuhr (Czech Boy); Oleg Balaeff (Russian Boy); Pat Prest (Dutch Girl); Maurice Tauzin (French Boy); Dena Penn (Belgian Girl); Walter Soo Hoo (Chinese Boy); Yvette Duguay (Greek Girl); Joel Davis (English Boy); Eddie Clark (Scout); Larry Wheat (Butler); Bryant Washburn (Airport Official); Lane Chandler (Minute Man); Gil Perkins (Confederate Soldier); Ken Ferrel (Union Soldier); Selmer Jackson (Sunday Editor); Rosemary La Planche, Margie Stewart (Bits); Sheldon Jett (Big Fat Man); Richard Thorne (World War I Soldier); Erville Alderson (Farmer); Glen Stephens, John Benson (Military Police); Ronald Gaye, Erwin Kaiser (Drum Boys); John Elliot, Charles Griffin, Elmer Jerome (Men); Virginia Sale, Elaine Riley (Secretaries); Molio Sheron (Russian).

GOIN' TO TOWN (RKO, 1944) 68 M.

Executive producer, Frank Melford; producer, Jack William Votion; director, Leslie Goodwins; screenplay, Charles E. Roberts, Charles R. Marion; music director, Lud Gluskin; choreography, Paul Oscard; art director, Alfred C. Ybarra; assistant director, John E. Burch; sound, Percy Towsend; camera, Robert Pittack; editor, Hanson T. Fritch.

Chester Lauck (Lum); Norris Goff (Abner); Barbara Hale (Sally); Florence Lake (Abigail); Dick Elliott (Squire); Grady Sutton (Cedric); Dick Baldwin (Jimmy Benton); Herbert Rawlinson (Wentworth); Ernie Adams (Zeke); Jack Rice (Clarke); Sam Flint (DeCrane); Andrew Tombes (Parker); George Chandler (Jameson); Ruth Lee (Mrs. Wentworth); Danny Duncan (Grandpappy Spears); Marietta Canty (Camellia); Nils T. Granlund (N.T.G.).

THE FALCON IN HOLLYWOOD (RKO, 1944) 67 M.

Producer, Maurice Geraghty; director, Gordon Douglas; based on a character created by Michael Arlen; screenplay, Gerald Geraghty; art director, Albert S. D'Agostino, L. O. Croxton; music director, C. Bakaleinikoff; choreography, Theodore Rand; camera, Nicholas Musuraca; editor, Gene Milford.

Tom Conway (Falcon); Barbara Hale (Peggy Calahan); Veda Ann Borg (Billie Atkins); John Abbott (Martin S. Dwyer); Sheldon Leonard (Louis Buchanan); Konstantin Shayne (Alex Hoffman); Emory Parnell (Inspector McBride); Frank Jenks (Higgins); Jean Brooks (Roxana Miles); Rita Corday (Lilli D'Allio); Walter Soderling (Ed Johnson); Usaf Ali (Nagari); Robert Clarke (Perc Saunders); Carl Kent (Art

Director); Gwen Crawford, Patti Brill (Secretaries); Bryant Washburn, Sammy Blum (Actors' Agents); Nancy Marlow (Mail Clerk); Chris Drake (Assistant Cameraman); George De Normand (Truck Driver); Jimmy Jordan (Operator); Perc Launders (Zoller); Jacques Lory (Musician); Wheaton Chambers, Bert Moorhouse (Bits); Chester Clute (Hotel Manager); Chili Williams (Beautiful Blonde); Margie Stewart, Greta Christensen (Girls).

WEST OF THE PECOS (RKO, 1945) 66 M.

Executive producer, Sid Rogell; producer, Herman Schlom; director, Edward Killy; based on the novel by Zane Grey; screenplay, Norman Houston; art director, Albert S. D'Agostino, Lucius Croxton; set decorator, Darrell Silvera, William Stevens; music, Paul Sawtell; music director, C. Bakaleinikoff; sound, John E. Tribby, Terry Kellum; assistant director, Harry Mancke; camera, Harry J. Wild; editor, Roland Gross.

Robert Mitchum (Pecos); Barbara Hale (Rill); Richard Martin (Chito Rafferty); Thurston Hall (Colonel Lambeth); Rita Corday (Suzanne); Russell Hopton (Jeff Stinger); Bill Williams (Tex Evans); Bruce Edwards (Clyde Morgan); Harry Woods (Brad Sawtelle); Perc Launders (Sam Sawtelle); Bryant Washburn (Dr. Howard); Philip Morris (Marshal); Martin Garralaga (Don Manuel); Sammy Blum, Robert Anderson (Gamblers); Italia De Nubila (Dancer); Carmen Graneda (Spanish Girl); Ariel Sherry, Virginia Wave (Mexican Girls); Ethan Laidlaw (Lookout); Jack Gargan (Croupier); Allan Lee (Four-Up Driver); Larry Wheat (Butler).

FIRST YANK INTO TOKYO (RKO, 1945) 82 M.

Producer, J. Robert Bren; director, Gordon Douglas; story, Bren, Gladys Atwater; screenplay, Bren; assistant director, Sam Ruman; music, Leigh Harline; music director, C. Bakaleinikoff; art director, Albert S. D'Agostino, Walter Keller; set decorator, Darrell Silvera, Charles Nields; technical advisor, R. Andrew Smith; sound, John L. Cass; camera, Harry J. Wild; editor, Philip Martin.

Tom Neal (Major Ross); Barbara Hale (Abby Drake); Marc Cramer (Jardine); Richard Loo (Colonel Okanura); Keye Luke (Haan-Soo); Leonard Strong (Major Nogira); Benson Fong (Captain Ianabe); Clarence Lung (Major Ichibo); Keye Chang (Captain Sato); Michael St. Angel (Captain Andrew Kent); Edmund Glover, Robert Clarke, Johnny Strong, Eden Nicholas, Jimmy Jordan (Prisoners); Bruce Edwards (Captain Harris); Artarne Wong, Larry Wong (Koreans); Albert Law (Jap Pilot); Gerald Pierce (Waist Gunner); Selmer Jackson (Colonel Blaine); Ralph Stein (Bellhop); Harry Anderson (Submarine Commander); Dorothy Curtis, Gwen Crawford, Betty Gillette, Frances Haldorn, Ione Reed, Aline Goodwins, Bobby La Salle, Noreen Lee (Nurses); Weaver Levy, George Chung, Spencer Chan, James Leong, Thomas Quon Woo (Bits); Joseph Kim (Sergeant Osami); Beal Wong (Lieutenant Kono); Paul Fung (Captain Yamanashi); Bob Chinn, Chet Vorovan (Jap Soldiers); Tommy Lee, Richard Wang (Jap Sentries); Bo Ching (Dancer); George Lee (Chinese Captain); Peter Chong (Dr. Kai Koen); Eddie Luke (Ling Wan); Wallace Clark (Dr. Langley); John Hamilton (Dr. Stacey); Russell Hicks (General Stanton); Ken McDonald (Colonel Thompson).

LADY LUCK (RKO, 1946) 97 M.

Executive producer, Robert Fellows; producer, Warren Duff; director, Edwin L. Marin; story, Herbert Clyde Lewis; screenplay, Lynn Root, Frank Fenton; music, Leigh Harline; music director, C. Bakaleinikoff; art director, Albert S. D'Agostino, Feild Gray; set decorator, Darrell Silvera, James Altwies; sound, Clem Portman, John L. Cass; gowns, Edward; assistant director, James Anderson; camera, Lucien Andriot; editor, Ralph Dawson.

Robert Young (Scott); Barbara Hale (Mary); Frank Morgan (William Audrey); James Gleason (Sacramento Sam); Don Rice (Eddie); Harry Davenport (Judge Martin); Lloyd Corrigan (Little Joe); Teddy Hart (Little Guy); Joseph Vitale (Happy Johnson); Douglas Morrow (Dan Morgan); Robert Clarke (Southern Officer); Larry Wheat (Calm Card Player); Alf Haugan (Sign Maker); Alvin Hammer (Man in Book Store); Betty Gillette (Stewardess); Russell Simpson (Daniel Boone); Harry Depp (Elderly Gent); Grace Hampton (Woman in Book Shop); Pat Prest (Girl); Eric Mayne, Major Sam Harris, Henry Herbert, J. W. Johnson, Carl Faulkner, Forbes Murray, Billie Snyder, Sayre Deering, Clyde McAtee, Jack Ford, Jack Arkin, Sam Lufkin, Paul Lacy, Brick Sullivan, Sammy Shack (Gamblers); Bert Moorhouse, Jack Stoney (Billiard Players); Mary Field (Tall, Thin Woman); Forrest Taylor (General Sherman); Dick Elliott (Fat Man); Joe Whitehead, Jack Norton (Bartenders); Al Rhein (Croupier); Myrna Dell (Mabel); Harry Harvey (Desk Clerk); Eddie Dunn (Police Lieutenant); Nancy Saunders (Manicurist); Frank Dae (Man in Hallway); Lorin Raker (Process Server); Cosmo Sardo (Barber).

A LIKELY STORY (RKO, 1947) 88 M.

Executive producer, Jack Gross; producer, Richard H. Berger; director, H. C. Potter; suggested by a story by Alexander Kenedi; screenplay, Bess Taffel; art director, Albert S. D'Agostino, Feild Gray; set decorator, Darrell Silvera, James Altwies; music, Leigh Harline; music director, C. Bakaleinikoff; assistant director, Harry Mancke; sound, Richard Van Nessen, Terry Kellum; special effects, Russell A. Cully; camera, Roy Hunt; editor, Harry Marker.

Barbara Hale (Vickie North); Bill Williams (Bill Baker); Lanny Rees (Jamie); Sam Levene (Louie); Dan Tobin (Phil Bright); Nestor Paiva (Tiny); Max Willenz (Mr. Slepoff); Henry Kulky (Tremendo); Robin Raymond (Ticket Girl); Mary Young (Little Old Lady); Nancy Saunders (Blonde on Train); Bill Shannon (Major); Charles Pawley, Drew Miller, Carl Hanson, Larry Randall (Reporters); Sam Flint, Emmett Vogan (Doctors); Isabel Withers, Mary Treen, Dorothy Curtis (Nurses); Paul Newlan (Truck Driver); Joe Green (Senator); Jack Rice (Secretary to Senator); Cy Schindell (Criminal); Jack Arkin, Mike Lally, Hal Craig (Photographers); Clarence Muse (Porter); Dick Rush (Detective); Tom Noonan, Sam Lufkin, Jack Gargan (Taxi Drivers); George Magrill (Express Man); Chester Clute (Dr. Brown); Pat McKee (Smoky); Hal K. Dawson (Dr. Fraser); Jason Robards (Cop); Eddie Parks (Drunk); Bill Wallace (Limousine Driver); Lee Phelps (Cop at Intersection); Jessie Arnold (Landlady); Semion J. Grenvold, Katherine Lytle, Ethelreda Leopold (Artists); Al Murphy, Charles Sullivan, Joseph Palma, Philip Freidman, Cy Malis (Poker Players); Patsy O'Bryne (Flower Woman); Kid Chissell (Gym Attendant); William Gould (Doorman); Phil Warren (Intern); Dick Elliott (Conductor); Alan Wood (Elevator Operator); William Self, Phil Warren (Interns).

THE BOY WITH GREEN HAIR (RKO, 1948) C—82 M.

Executive producer, Dore Schary; producer, Stephen Ames;* director, Joseph Losey; based on a story by Betsy Beaton; screenplay, Ben Barzman, Alfred Lewis Levitt; art director, Albert S. D'Agostino, Ralph Berger; set decorator, Darrell Silvera, William Stevens; music, Leigh Harline; orchestrator, Gil Grau; music director, C. Bakaleinikoff; song, Eden Ahbez; assistant director, James Lane; costumes, Adele Balkan; makeup, Gordon Blau; sound, Earl Wolcott, Clem Portman; camera, George Barnes; editor, Frank Doyle.

Pat O'Brien (Gramp); Robert Ryan (Dr. Evans); Barbara Hale (Miss Brand); Dean Stockwell (Peter); Richard Lyon (Michael); Walter Catlett ("The King"); Samuel S.

*Adrian Scott, the film's original producer, was removed from the project during production.

Hinds (Dr. Knudson); Regis Toomey (Mr. Davis); Charles Meredith (Mr. Piper); David Clarke (Barber); Billy Sheffield (Red); John Calkins (Danny); Teddy Infuhr (Timmy); Dwayne Hickman (Joey); Eilen Janssen (Peggy); Curtis Jackson (Classmate); Charles Arnt (Mr. Hammond); Don Pietro (Newsboy); Patricia Byrnes, Carl Coombs, Cynthia Robichaux, Georgette Crooks, Donna Jo Gribble (Girls); Diane Graeff (Tiny Girl); Wendy Oser (Frail Girl); Billy White, Russ Tamblyn, Baron White, Spear Martin, Michael Losey (Boys); Roger Perry (Small Boy); Peter Brocco (Mr. Hammond #1); Max Rose (Man); Anna Q. Nilsson, Lynn Whitney (Townswomen); Carl Saxe (Plainclothesman); Kenneth Patterson, Dale Robertson (Cops); Sharon McManus (Girl Who Cries); Ann Carter (Eva); Howard Brody (Eva's Brother); Ray Burkett, Warren Shannon (Little Old Man); Eula Guy (Mrs. Fisher).

THE CLAY PIGEON   (RKO, 1949) 63 M.

Producer, Herman Schlom; director, Richard O. Fleischer; screenplay, Carl Foreman; art director, Albert S. D'Agostino, Walter E. Keller; set decorator, Darrell Silvera, Harley Miller; music, Paul Sawtell; music director, C. Bakaleinikoff; assistant director, Jimmy Casey, Maxwell Henry; sound, Phil Brigandi, Clem Portman; makeup, Bill Phillips; special effects, Clifford Stine; camera, Robert de Grasse; editor, Samuel E. Beetley.

Bill Williams (Jim Fletcher); Barbara Hale (Martha Gregory); Richard Quine (Ted Niles); Richard Loo (Tokoyama); Frank Fenton (Lieutenant Commander Prentice); Frank Wilcox (Hospital Doctor); Marya Marco (Helen Minoto); Robert Bray (Blake); Martha Hyer (Receptionist); Harold Landon (Blind Veteran); James Craven (John Wheeler); Grandon Rhodes (Clark); Kenneth Terrell (Davis); Dan Foster (Bellboy); Ann Doran (Nurse); Eddie Lee (Cashier); Harry Cheshire (Doctor); Jim Nolan (Faber); Howard Negley (Sergeant); Joel Friedkin (Motorist); G. Pat Collins (Abbott); Joe Bernard (Hotel Manager); Kernan Cripps (Chief Jones).

THE WINDOW   (RKO, 1949) 73 M.

Producer, Frederic Ullman, Jr.; director, Ted Tetzlaff; based on the story "The Boy Who Cried Wolf" by Cornell Woolrich; screenplay, Mel Dinelli; art director, Albert S. D'Agostino, William E. Keller, Sam Corso; set decorator, Darrell Silvera; assistant director, Fred Fleck, Earl Harper; music, Roy Webb; music director, C. Bakaleinikoff; makeup, Gene Romer; sound, Earl Wolcott; production manager, Walter Daniels; camera, William Steiner; editor, Frederic Knudtson.

Barbara Hale (Mrs. Woodry); Bobby Driscoll (Tommy Woodry); Arthur Kennedy (Mr. Woodry); Paul Stewart (Mr. Kellerton); Ruth Roman (Mrs. Kellerton); Anthony Ross (Ross); Richard Benedict (Seaman Being Murdered); Jim Nolan (Stranger on Street); Ken Terrell (Man); Lee Phelps, Eric Mack, Charles Flynn, Budd Fine, Carl Faulkner, Lloyd Dawson, Carl Saxe (Police Officers); Lee Kass (Reporter); Tex Swan (Milkman).

JOLSON SINGS AGAIN   (Col., 1949) C—96 M.

Producer, Sidney Buchman; director, Henry Levin; screenplay, Buchman; art director, Walter Holscher; set decorator, William Kiernan; music, George Duning; music advisor, Saul Chaplin; orchestrator, Larry Russell; music director, Morris Stoloff; song stager, Audrene Brier; songs, Al Dubin and Harry Warren; Noble Sissle and Eubie Blake; Edgar Smith and John Stromberg; B. G. De Sylva and Louis Silvers; Irving Caesar and George Gershwin; Mort Dixon and Harry M. Woods; De Sylva, Al Jolson, and Joseph Meyer; Joe Young, Sam Lewis, and Jean Schwartz; Gus Kahn and Walter Donaldson; Kahn, Tony Jackson, and Egbert Van Alstyne; Benny Davis and Harry Akst; assistant director, Milton Feldman; makeup, Clay Campbell; costumes, Jean

Louis; sound, George Cooper, Philip Faulkner; production manager, Jack Fier; camera, William Snyder; editor, William Lyon.

Larry Parks (Al Jolson); Barbara Hale (Ellen Clark); William Demarest (Steve Martin); Ludwig Donath (Cantor Yoelson); Bill Goodwin (Tom Baron); Myron McCormick (Ralph Bryant); Tamara Shayne (Mama Yoelson); Eric Wilton (Henry); Robert Emmett Keane (Charlie); Larry Parks (Himself); Frank McLure, Jock Mahoney (Men); Betty Hill (Woman); Charles Regan, Charles Perry, Richard Gordon, David Newell, Joe Gilbert, David Horsley, Wanda Perry, Louise Illington, Gertrude Astor, Steve Benton, Eleanor Marvak (Bits); Margie Stapp (Nurse); Nelson Leigh (Theatre Manager); Virginia Mullen (Mrs. Bryant); Philip Faulkner, Jr. (Sound Mixer); Morris Stoloff (Orchestra Leader); Helen Mowery (Script Girl); Michael Cisney, Ben Erway (Writers); Martin Garralaga (Mr. Estrada); Dick Cogan (Soldier); Peter Brocco (Captain of Waiters).

AND BABY MAKES THREE   (Col., 1950) 83 M.

Producer, Robert Lord; associate producer, Henry S. Kesler; director, Henry Levin; screenplay, Lou Breslow, Joseph Hoffman; art director, Robert Peterson; set decorator, Louis Diage; music, George Dunning; music director, Morris Stoloff; assistant director, Earl Bellamy; makeup, Clay Campbell; costumes, Jean Louis; sound, Russell Malmgren; camera, Burnett Guffey; editor, Viola Lawrence.

Robert Young (Vernon Walsh); Barbara Hale (Jacqueline Walsh); Robert Hutton (Herbert Fletcher); Janis Carter (Wanda York); Billie Burke (Mrs. Fletcher); Nicholas Joy (Mr. Fletcher); Lloyd Corrigan (Dr. William Parnell); Howland Chamberlin (Otto Stacy); Melville Cooper (Gibson); Louise Currie (Miss Quigley); Grandon Rhodes (Phelps Burbridge); Katharine Warren (Miss Ellis); Wilton Graff (Root); Michael Cisney (Martin); Joe Sawyer, James Cardwell (Police Officers); Everett Glass (Minister); Lulumae Bohrman, Mary Benoit (Bits); Claire Meade, Wanda Perry, Doris Stone (Women); Paul Marion (Phillips, the Chauffeur); Robert Strong (Man); Mary Treen (Mrs. Bennett); Teddy Infuhr (Danny); Joe Recht (Elevator Operator); Gilbert Barnett (Bobby); Vernon Dent (Umpire); Lela Bliss (Laura Payton); Mary Bear (Clerk); Herbert Vigran (Mr. Woodley); Theresa Harris (Maid); Barbara Wooddell (Mrs. Carter); Dick Cogan, Garry Wilkin, Al Eben (Cops); Alvin Hammer (Mr. Pruitt); Virginia Chapman, John Doucette (Married Couple); John Mantell (Newsboy); Victor Sen Young (Lem Kee); Elizabeth Flournoy (Stock Clerk); Marjorie Stapp (Peggy); Torben Meyer (Waiter); John Hubbard (York); Mary Emory (Secretary).

EMERGENCY WEDDING   (Col., 1950) 78 M.

Producer, Nat Perrin; director, Eddie Buzzell; story, Dalton Trumbo; screenplay, Nat Perrin, Claude Binyon; art director, Carl Anderson; music director, Morris Stoloff; camera, Burnett Guffey; editor, Al Clark.

Larry Parks (Peter Kirk); Barbara Hale (Helen Hunt); Willard Parker (Vandemer); Una Merkel (Emma); Alan Reed (Tony); Eduard Franz (Dr. Heimer); Irving Bacon (Filbert); Don Beddoe (Forbish); Jim Backus (Ed Hamley); Teru Shimada (Ito); Myron Welton (Freddie); Ian Wolfe (Dr. White); Helen Spring (Miss Toomey); Greg McClure (Richard Andrews); Queenie Smith (Rose); Jerry Mickelsen (Newsboy); George Meader (Motel Manager); Dorothy Vaughn (Woman Patient); Boyd Davis, Sydney Mason, Pierre Watkin (Doctors); Lucille Shamburger, Arthur Howard, Virginia Cruzon, Grace Burns, Elsa Peterson (Bits); Cosmo Sardo (Headwaiter); Joe Palma, Frank Arnold (Waiters); Wilson Benge (Frederick, the Butler); Myron Healey, Mike Lally, Warren Mace, Shirley Ballard, Jean Willes, Mary Emory (Guests); Thomas F. Martin (Bartender); Stephen Chase (Kirk); Thomas Patrick McCormick (Baby); Billy Nelson (Cab Driver); James O'Gatty (Pedestrian); Ted Jordan (Orderly); William E. Green

(Chairman); James Conaty, James Carlisle (Committee Men); Bobby Johnson (Sammy); Vivian Mason (Kitty); Kathleen O'Malley (Mabel); Louise Kane (Switchboard Girl); Harry Harvey (Dr. Wilson); William Forrest (Personnel Director); Frank Cady (Mr. Hoff); Ann Tyrrell (Miss Nielson); Simon "Stuffy" Singer (Little Boy); Paul Bradley, John Kascier, Richard LaMarr (Barbers); Elizabeth Flournoy (Saleswoman); Mary Newton (Governess); Ruth Warren (Shopper); Virginia Cruzon (Dignified Woman); Muriel Maddox (Mrs. Crain); Marjorie Stapp (Mrs. Young); Beverly Crane (Mrs. Hayes); Ted Stanhope, Henry Sylvester (Clerks).

THE JACKPOT   (20th, 1950) 85 M.

Producer, Samuel G. Engel; director, Walter Land; based on a story by John McNulty; screenplay, Phoebe Ephron, Henry Ephron; art director, Lyle Wheeler, Joseph C. Wright; orchestrator, Earle Hagen; camera, Joseph La Shelle; editor, J. Watson Webb, Jr.

James Stewart (Bill Lawrence); Barbara Hale (Amy Lawrence); James Gleason (Harry Summers); Fred Clark (Mr. Woodruff); Alan Mowbray (Leslie); Patricia Medina (Hilda Jones); Natalie Wood (Phyllis Lawrence); Tommy Rettig (Tommy Lawrence); Robert Gist (Pete Spooner); Lyle Talbot (Fred Burns); Charles Tannen (Al Vogel); Bigelow Sayre (Captain Sullivan); Dick Cogan (Mr. Brown); Jewel Rose (Mrs. Brown); Eddie Firestone (Mr. McDougall); Estelle Etterre (Mrs. McDougall); Claud Stroud (Herman Wertheim); Caryl Lincoln (Susan Wertheim); Valerie Mark (Mary Vogel); Joan Miller (Mabel Spooner); Walter Baldwin (Watch Buyer); Syd Saylor (Ernie, the Mailman); John Qualen (Mr. Ferguson); Fritz Feld (Long-Haired Pianist); Kathryn Sheldon (Mrs. Simpkins); Robert Dudley (Mr. Simpkins); Minerva Urecal (Strange Woman); Milton Parsons (Piano Player); Kim Spaulding (Mr. Dexter); Dulce Daye (Mrs. Dexter); Andrew Tombes (Pritchett); Marjorie Holliday (Telephone Operator); Harry Carter, Colin Ward, Ken Christy (Men); Peggy O'Connor (Salesgirl); Jack Roper, Dick Curtis, Guy Way (Moving Men); June Evans (Washerwoman); Elizabeth Flournoy (Woman); Harry Hines (Elevator Man); Carol Savage (Switchboard Operator); Franklin "Pinky" Parker (Poker Player); Robert Bice, Tudor Owen, John Roy (Policemen); John Bleifer (Bald Man); Bill Nelson (Truck Driver); Phil Van Zandt (Flick Morgan); Jack Mather, Jay Barney (Detectives); Ann Doran (Miss Bowen); Jerry Hausner (Al Stern); Frances Budd (Saleslady); George Conrad, Sam Edwards (Parking Lot Attendants).

LORNA DOONE   (Col., 1951) C—88 M.

Producer, Edward Small; director, Phil Karlson; based on the novel by Richard D. Blackmore; adaptation, George Bruce; screenplay, Jesse L. Lasky, Jr., Richard Schayer; art director, Harold MacArthur; music director, Morris Stoloff; music, George Duning; camera, Charles Van Enger; editor, Al Clark.

Barbara Hale (Lorna Doone); Richard Greene (John Ridd); Carl Benton Reid (Sir Ensor Doone); William Bishop (Carver Doone); Ron Randell (Tom Faggus); Sean McClory (Charleworth Doone); Onslow Stevens (Counsellor Doone); Lester Mathews (King Charles II); John Dehner (Baron de Wichehalse); Gloria Petroff (Lorna Doone —as a child); Orley Lindgren (John Ridd—as a child); Dick Crutis (Carth); Anne Howard (Annie Ridd); Katharine Warren (Sarah Ridd); Malcolm Keen (Lord Lorne); Queenie Leonard (Gwenny); Trevor Bardette (Jan Fry); Myron Healey (Todd Darcy); Harry Lauter (Calvin Oates, Jr.); Norman Rainey (Parson Bowden); Trevor Ward (Farmer Dyke); Betty Fairfax (Mrs. Lacy); Allen Pinson (Jonas); Ted Jordan (Gurney); Glenn Thompson (Billy); Bruce Lester (Walt Snowe); Leonard Mudie (Cal Oates, Sr.); Ray Teal (Farmer Ridd); Fred Graham (Outrider); Paul Collins (Charleworth—as a child); Jerry Mickelsen (Carver Doone—as a child); Sherry Jackson (Annie Ridd—as a child);

James Logan (Farmer); Pat Aherne (Judge Jeffries); Wheaton Chambers (Priest); Eric Wilton, Gerald Hamer (Doctors); House Peters, Jr., Bill Hale (Patrol Leaders).

THE FIRST TIME   (Col., 1952) 89 M.

Producer, Harold Hecht; director, Frank Tashlin; story, Jean Rouverol, Hugo Butler; screenplay, Rouverol, Butler, Tashlin; Dane Lussier; art director, Ross Bellah; music director, Morris Stoloff; music, Frederick Hollander; camera, Ernest Laszlo; editor, Viola Lawrence.

Robert Cummings (Joe Bennet); Barbara Hale (Betsey Bennet); Bill Goodwin (Mel Gilbert); Jeff Donnell (Donna Gilbert); Carl Benton Reid (Andrew Bennet); Mona Barrie (Cassie Mayhew); Kathleen Comegys (Florence Bennet); Paul Harvey (Leeming); Cora Witherspoon (Miss Salisbury); Bea Benaderet (Mrs. Potter); Joy Windsor (Rita); Ida Moore (Old Lady); Norma Jean Nilsson (Violet); Jean Willes (Fawn); Sandra Gould (Telephone Operator); Arthur Tovey, Lyle Moraine, Bill Wilkerson, Charles J. Stewart (Salesmen); Dennis Ross (Boy); Patti Ann McKenzie (Girl); Shimen Ruskin (Tidy Didy Man); Evelyn Russell (Cashier); Paul Bradley (Nigel #2); Shirley Whitney, Virginia Christine (Nurses); Larry Dobkin (Doctor); Harry Stanton (Boyfriend); Diana Dawson (Woman).

LAST OF THE COMANCHES   (Col., 1953) C—85 M.

Producer, Buddy Adler; director, Andre DeToth; screenplay, Kenneth Gamet; art director, Ross Bellah; set decorator, Frank Tuttle; sound, George Cooper; music, George Duning; music director, Morris Stoloff; camera, Charles Lawton, Jr.; editor, Al Clark.

Broderick Crawford (Sgt. Matt Trainor); Barbara Hale (Julia Lanning); Johnny Stewart (Little Knife); Lloyd Bridges (Jim Starbuck); Mickey Shaughnessy (Rusty Potter); George Mathews (Romany O'Rattigan); Hugh Sanders (Denver Kinnaird); Ric Roman (Martinez); Chubby Johnson (Henry Ruppert); Martin Milner (Billy Creel); Milton Parsons (Prophet Satterlee); Jack Woody (Corporal Floyd); John War Eagle (Black Cloud); William Andrews (Lieutenant Floyd); Carleton Young (Major Lanning); Jay Silverheels, Rod Redwing (Indians); Harry Harvey (Civilian); Bud Osborne (Wagon Driver); George Chesebro (Pete).

SEMINOLE   (Univ., 1953) C—86 M.

Producer, Howard Christie; director, Budd Boetticher; story-screenplay, Charles K. Peck, Jr.; art director, Alexander Golitzen, Emrich Nicholson; set decorator, Russell A. Gausman, Joseph Kish; technical advisor, Col. Paul R. Davison; dialog director, Jack Daniels; sound, Leslie I. Carey, Glen Anderson; costumes, Rosemary Odell; makeup, Bud Westmore; assistant director, Tom Shaw, Gordon McLean; music, Joseph Gershenson; camera, Russell Metty; editor, Virgil Vogel.

Rock Hudson (Lt. Lance Caldwell); Barbara Hale (Revere Muldoon); Anthony Quinn (Osceola/John Powell); Richard Carlson (Maj. Harlan Degan); Hugh O'Brian (Kajeck); Russell Johnson (Lieutenant Hamilton); Lee Marvin (Sergeant Magruder); Ralph Moody (Kulak); James Best (Corporal Gerard); Dan Poore (Trooper Scott); Frank Chase, Earl Spainard, Scott Lee (Troopers); Fay Roope (Zachary Taylor); Don Gibson (Captain Streller); John Day (Scott); Howard Erskine (Corporal Smiley); Duane Thorsen (Hendricks); Walter Reed (Farmer); Robert Karnes (Corporal); Robert Dane (Trader Taft); John Phillips (Major Lawrence); Soledad Jimenez (Mattie Sue Thomas); Don Garrett (Officer); Bob Bray (Captain Sibley); Peter Cranwell (Sentry); Alex Sharp (Officer); Jack Finlay, Jody Hutchinson (Guards); William Janssen (Bit).

LONE HAND (Univ., 1953) C—79½ M.

Producer, Howard Christie; director, George Sherman; story, Irving Ravetch; screenplay, Joseph Hoffman; art director, Alexander Golitzen, Eric Orsom; camera, Maury Gertsman; editor, Paul Weatherwax.

Joel McCrea (Zachary Hallock); Barbara Hale (Sarah Jane Skaggs); Alex Nicol (Jonah Varden); Charles Drake (George Hadley); Jimmy Hunt (Joshua); Jim Arness (Gus Varden); Roy Roberts (Mr. Skaggs); Frank Ferguson (Mr. Dunn); Wesley Morgan (Daniel Skaggs).

A LION IS IN THE STREETS (WB, 1953) C—88 M.

Producer, William Cagney; director, Raoul Walsh; based on the novel by Adria Locke Langley; screenplay, Luther Davis; music, Franz Waxman; assistant director, Willima Kissel; makeup, Otis Malcolm; sound, John Kean; special effects, Roscoe Cline; camera, Harry Stradling; editor, George Amy.

James Cagney (Hank Martin); Barbara Hale (Verity Wade); Anne Francis (Flamingo); Warner Anderson (Jules Bolduc); John McIntire (Jeb Brown); Jeanne Cagney (Jennie Brown); Lon Chaney (Spurge); Frank McHugh (Rector); Larry Keating (Robert Castleberry); Onslow Stevens (Guy Polli); James Millican (Mr. Beach); Mickey Simpson (Tim Peck); Sara Haden (Lulu May); Ellen Corby (Singing Woman); Roland Winters (Prosecutor); Burt Mustin (Swith); Irene Tedrow (Sophy).

UNCHAINED (WB, 1955) 75 M.

Producer-director, Hall Bartlett; based on the book *Prisoners Are People* by Kenyon J. Scudder; screenplay, Bartlett; music, Alex North; assistant director, Bob Farfan; orchestrator, Maurice de Packh; sound, Hal Bumbaugh; camera, Virgil E. Miller; editor, Cotton Warburton.

Elroy Hirsh (Steve Davitt); Barbara Hale (Mary Davitt); Chester Morris (Kenyon J. Scudder); Todd Duncan (Bill Howard); Johnny Johnston (Eddie Garrity); Peggy Knudsen (Elaine); Jerry Paris (Joe Ravens); Bill Kennedy (Leonard Haskins); Henry Nakamura (Jerry Hakara); Kathryn Grant (Sally Haskins); Bob Patten (Swanson); Don Kennedy (Gladstone); Mack Williams (Mr. Johnson); Tim Considine (Win Davitt); Saul Gorss (Police Captain).

THE FAR HORIZONS (Par., 1955) C—108 M.

Producer, William H. Pine, William C. Thomas; director, Rudolph Mate; based on the novel *Sacajawea of the Shoshones* by Della Gould Emmons; screenplay, Winston Miller, Edmund H. North; costumes, Edith Head; music, Hans Salter; assistant director, William McGarry; art director, Hal Pereira, Earl Hedrick; camera, Daniel L. Fapp; editor, Frank Bracht.

Fred MacMurray (Meriwether Lewis); Charlton Heston (Bill Clark); Donna Reed (Sacajawea); Barbara Hale (Julia Hancock); William Demarest (Sergeant Gass); Alan Reed (Charboneau); Eduardo Noriega (Cameahwait); Larry Pennell (Wild Eagle); Argentina Brunetti (Old Crone); Julia Montoya (Crow Woman); Ralph Moody (Le Borgne); Herbert Heyes (President Jefferson); Lester Mathews (Mr. Hancock); Helen Wallace (Mrs. Hancock); Walter Reed (Cruzatte); and: Bill Phipps, Tom Monroe, LeRoy Johnson, Joe Canutt, Bob Herron, Herman Scharff, Al Wyatt, Voltaire Perkins, Vernon Rich, Bill Walker, Margarita Martin, Frank Fowler, Frank Bennett.

THE HOUSTON STORY (Col., 1956) 79 M.

Producer, Sam Katzman; director, William Castle; story-screenplay, James B. Gordon; art director, Paul Palmentola; assistant director, Gene Anderson, Jr.; camera, Henry Freulich; editor, Edwin Bryant.

Gene Barry (Frank Duncan); Barbara Hale (Zoe Crane); Edward Arnold (Paul Atlas); Paul Richards (Gordie Shay); Jeanne Cooper (Madge); Frank Jenks (Louie).

SEVENTH CAVALRY   (Col., 1956) C—75 M.

Producer, Harry Joe Brown; associate producer, Randolph Scott; director, Joseph H. Lewis; story, Glendon F. Swarthout; screenplay, Peter Packer; assistant director, Abner E. Singer; art director, George Brooks; music director, Mischa Bakaleinikoff; camera, Ray Rennahan; editor, Gene Havlick.

Randolph Scott (Capt. Tom Benson); Barbara Hale (Martha Kellogg); Jay C. Flippen (Sergeant Bates); Jeanette Nolan (Mrs. Reynolds); Frank Faylen (Kruger); Leo Gordon (Vogel); Denver Pyle (Dixon); Harry Carey, Jr. (Corporal Morrison); Michael Pate (Captain Benteen); Donald Curtis (Lt. Bob Fitch); Frank Wilcox (Major Reno); Pat Hogan (Young Hawk); Russell Hicks (Colonel Kellogg); Peter Ortiz (Pollock).

THE OKLAHOMAN   (AA, 1957) C—78 M.

Producer, Walter Mirisch; associate producer, Richard Heermance; director, Francis D. Lyon; screenplay, Daniel B. Ullman; assistant director, Austen Jewell; music, Hans Salter; art director, Dave Milton; sound, Charles Schelling; camera, Carl Guthrie; editor, George White.

Joel McCrea (Dr. John Brighton); Barbara Hale (Anne Barnes); Brad Dexter (Cass Dobie); Gloria Talbott (Maria Smith); Michael Pate (Charlie Smith); Anthony Caruso (Jim Hawk); Douglas Dick (Mel Dobie); Verna Felton (Mrs. Waynebrook); Peter Votrian (Small Charlie); Adam Williams (Bob Randell); Diane Brewster (Eliza); John Pickard (Marshall Bill); Sheb Wooley (Cowboy-Henchman); Ray Teal (Jason, the Stableman); Harry Lauter (Grant); I. Stanford Jolley (Storekeeper); Mimi Gibson (Louise Brighton); Esther Dale (Mrs. Fitzgerald); Robert Hinkle (Ken, the Driver); Doris Kemper, Dorothy Neumann, Gertrude Astor (Women); Wheaton Chambers (Lounger); Earle Hodgins (Sam, the Bartender); Watson Downs, Tod Farrell (Farmers); Rankin Mansfield (Doctor); Don Marlowe (Rider); Laurie Mitchell, Jenny Lea (Girls); Scotty Beckett (Messenger at Ranch); Tod Farrell (Tommy); Lennie Geer (Bushwacker); Al Kramer (Wild Line); Kermit Maynard (Townsman); Bill Foster (Dobie Henchman).

SLIM CARTER   (Univ., 1957) C—82 M.

Producer, Howie Horwitz; director, Richard Bartlett; story, David Bramson, Mary C. McCall, Jr.; screenplay, Montgomery Pittman; art director, Alexander Golitzen, Eric Orbom; music director, Joseph Gershenson; music, Herman Stein; songs, Ralph Freed and Beasley Smith; assistant director, William Holland; gowns, Bill Thomas; sound, Leslie I. Carey, Corson Jowett; special camera, Clifford Stine; camera, Ellis W. Carter; editor, Fred McDowell.

Jock Mahoney (Slim Carter [Hughie Nash]); Julie Adams (Clover Doyle); Tim Hovey (Leo Gallagher); William Hopper (Joe Brewster); Ben Johnson (Montana Burriss); Joanne Moore (Charlene Carroll); Walter Reed (Richard L. Howard); Bill Williams (Frank Hannemann); Barbara Hale (Allie Williams).

DESERT HELL   (20th, 1958) 82 M.

Executive producer, Charles Marquis Warren; producer, Robert Stabler; director-story, Warren; screenplay, Endre Boehm; art director, James W. Sullivan; set decorator, Raymond Boltz, Jr.; music, Raoul Kraushann; sound, Jack Goodrich; assistant director, Hathan R. Barragar; wardrobe, Byron Munson; special camera effects, Jack Rbain, Louis DeWitt; camera, John M. Nicholaus, Jr.; editor, Fred W. Berger.

Brian Keith (Captain Edwards); Barbara Hale (Celia Edwards); Richard Denning Sergeant Benet); Johnny Desmond (Lieutenant Forbes); Philip Pine (Captain Parini); Richard Shannon (Private Hoffstetter); Duane Grey (Private Arussa); Charles Gray (Private Bandurski); Lud Veigel (Private Knapp); Richard Gilden (Private Kebrissyan); Ronald Foster (Private Bergstrom); Patrick O'Moore (Private Corbo); John Verros (Knifra); Bill Hamet (Private Brocklin); Roger Etienne (Private Sirmay); Felix Locher (Maisays); Ben Wright (Bob Remy); Albert Carrier (Sergeant St. Clair); Bhogwan Singh (Holy Marabout); and: Fred Dale, Bill Hickman, Bert Rumsey.

BUCKSKIN (Par., 1968) C—97 M.

Producer, A. C. Lyles; director, Michael Moore; screenplay, Michael Fisher; assistant director, Joseph Kenny; art director, Al Roelofs; music, Jimmie Haskell; sound John R. Carter; camera, W. Wallace Kelley; editor, Jack Wheeler.

Barry Sullivan (Chaddock); Wendell Corey (Rep Marlowe); Joan Caulfield (Nora Johnson); Lon Chaney (Sheriff Tangley); John Russell (Patch); Barbara Hale (Sarah Cody); Bill Williams (Frank Cody); Gerald Michenaud (Akii); Barton MacLane (Doc Raymond); Aki Aleong (Sung Li); Michael Larrain (Jimmy Cody); Leo Gordon (Travis); George Chandler (Storekeeper Perkins); Richard Arlen (Townsman); Craig Littler (Browdie); James X. Mitchell (Baker); Emile Meyer (Corbin); Robert Riordan (Telegrapher); LeRoy Johnson (Bartender); Manuela Thiess (Moni).

AIRPORT (Univ., 1970) C—137 M.

Producer, Ross Hunter; associated producer, Jacques Mapes; director, George Seaton; based on the novel by Arthur Hailey; screenplay, Seaton; art director, Alexander Golitzen, E. Preston Ames; set decorator, Jack D. Moore, Mickey S. Michaels; music, Alfred Newman; costumes, Edith Head; assistant director, Donald Roberts; technical advisors, John N. Denend, Capt. Lee Danielson; makeup, Bud Westmore; sound, Waldon O. Watson, David H. Moriarty, Ronald Pierce; special camera effects, Don W. Weed, James B. Gordon; camera, Ernest Laszlo; editor, Stuart Gilmore.

Burt Lancaster (Mel Bakersfeld); Dean Martin (Vernon Demerest); Jean Seberg (Tanya Livingston); Jacqueline Bisset (Gwen Meighen); George Kennedy (Patroni); Helen Hayes (Ada Quonsett); Van Heflin (D. O. Guerrero); Maureen Stapleton (Inez Guerrero); Barry Nelson (Lt. Anson Harris); Dana Wynter (Cindy Bakersfeld); Barbara Hale (Sarah Bakersfeld Demerest); John Findlater (Peter Coakley); Gary Collins (Cy Jordan); Jessie Royce Landis (Mrs. Harriet DuBarry Mossman); Larry Gates (Commissioner Ackerman); Peter Turgeon (Marcus Rathbone); Whit Bissell (Mr. Davidson); Virginia Grey (Mrs. Schultz); Eileen Wesson (Judy); Paul Picerni (Dr. Compagno); Robert Patten (Captain Benson); Clark Howat (Bert Weatherby); Ilana Dowding (Roberta Bakersfeld); Lew Brown (Reynolds); Lisa Garritson (Libby Bakersfeld); Patty Poulsen (Joan); Ena Hartman (Ruth); Malila Saint Duval (Maria); Sharon Harvey (Sally); Albert Reed (Lieutenant Ordway); Jodean Russo (Marie Patroni); Nancy Ann Nelson (Bunnie); Walter Woolf King (Cindy's Father); Dick Winslow (Mr. Schultz); Lou Wagner (Schuyler Schultz); Janis Hansen (Sister Katherine Grace); Mary Jackson (Sister Felice); Shelly Novack (Rollings); Chuck Daniel (Parks); Charles Brewer (Diller); Damian London (Father Seen Praying).

SOUL SOLDIER* (Fanfare, 1971) C—84 M.

Producer, James M. Northern, Stuart Z. Hirschman; director, John Cardos; screenplay, Marlene Weed; music, Tom McIntosh; art director, Phedon Papamichael; camera, Stu Phillips; editor, Lewis J. Gunn, Mort Tubos.

*Formerly titled: THE RED, WHITE, AND BLACK.

Rafer Johnson (Private Armstrong); Robert DoQui (Trooper Eli Brown); Lincoln Kilpatrick (Sergeant Hatch); Isaac Fields (First Sergeant Robertson); Janee Michell (Julie); Cesar Romero (Colonel Grierson); Barbara Hale (Alice Grierson); Robert Dix (Walking Horse); and: Steve Drexel, Russ Nannarello, Jr., Otis Taylor, Bill Collins, John Fox, Byrd Holland.

Barbara Hale as Victory
Garden Queen of California
in June, 1943

With Claire Carleton and
Harold Peary in
GILDERSLEEVE ON
BROADWAY (RKO '43)

With Michele Morgan and
Frank Sinatra in HIGHER AND
HIGHER (RKO '43)

RKO publicity pose, 1944

Publicity pose for A LIKE
STORY (RKO

With Ed Gargan, Cliff Clark, Joan Barclay, and Tom Conway in THE FALCON
OUT WEST (RKO '44)

With Bobby Driscoll and Arthur Kennedy in THE WINDOW (RKO '49)

With Larry Parks, Ludwig Donath, and William Demarest in JOLSON SINGS AGAIN (Col '49)

With Robert Young and Robert Hutton in AND BABY MAKES THREE (Col '50)

With husband, Bill Williams
and children, Barbara Willa
and William Theodore (Ma
1951)

With Richard Greene, Malcolm Keen, Lester Mathews in LORNA DOONE
(Col '51)

With Robert Cummings in
THE FIRST TIME (Col '52)

With Broderick Crawford in
LAST OF THE COMANCHES
(Col '53)

With Sara Haden, Anne Francis,
James Cagney, and Lon
Chaney, Jr. in A LION IS IN
THE STREETS (WB '53)

With Tim Considine and Elroy Hirsch in UNCHAINED (WB '55

With Gene Barry in THE HOUSTON STORY (Col '56)

With Jock Mahoney, Tim Hovey *(foreground),* William Hopper, Bill Williams, Ben Johnson, and Julie Adams in SLIM CARTER (Univ '57)

Television Emmy winners of 1959: Bob Hope, Jack Benny, Barbara Hale, and Raymond Burr

With Dean Martin in AIRPORT (Univ '70)

BARBARA HALE FOR AMANA:
'Make the greatest cooking discovery since fire."

Commercial spokeswoman, 1970s style

RKO publicity pose, *c.* 1944

5'5"
115 pounds
Dark brown hair
Brown eyes
Virgo

Jane Greer

Among the wide variety of ambitious starlets popping onto movie screens in the 1940s, few had more promising potential than RKO's Jane Greer. Her well-chiseled features and deep-timbred voice were encased in a calm, un-ruffled screen reserve, further enhanced by what critics called her "Mona Lisa" look (actually caused by a childhood ailment that had temporarily para-lyzed part of her face).

Beyond the fact that Jane never diligently pursued her screen career—too content being a wife and a mother—it was a difficult task for any of the tough-broad types at post-World War II RKO to make an enduring impression on the public (witness the fate of Gloria Grahame and Lizabeth Scott in their RKO tenure days). The public might, and did, cotton to this trio of screen dames, but would only accept them in a limited number of assignments before turning its interest back to more conventional leading-lady types. By the time Jane left RKO to try her luck at MGM and then finally at freelancing, the Hollywood studio system had been so eroded, and she had become so much more interested in activities outside the film profession, that there was no guiding force to push her into the cinema popularity she so rightly deserved.

Bettejane Greer and her twin brother, Donne,* were born in Washington, D.C., on September 9, 1924, the only children of Charles and Bettejane Greer. Mr. Greer was a small-time salesman jumping from one consumer product to another (oil burners, fire extinguishers, etc., changing companies about every four months as he became bored). He preferred to devote most of his energies to inventions, in particular an onion peeler. His business vagaries led the family into one minor financial crisis after another, particularly after the Depression saturated America. There were times in the Greer household when food was in such short supply that Mrs. Greer would dole out precious pennies to her children to purchase lemon-flavored hard candies, an old-fashioned remedy to stave off hunger.

Jane's mother had always nurtured career ambitions for herself, but her family had disapproved. The closest she came to pursuing any path in the arts was her poetry writing (several of her poems being published in anthologies). In addition, in 1932-34, she ran the "Aunt Bettie's" column for a Sarasota, Florida newspaper. Her frustrated vocational goals led her to hope that her children would consider the arts as their destined future. Jane, in particular, became the career her mother never had. There were talent contests, beauty pageants, and such, to occupy Jane's childhood, with professional modeling added at the age of twelve. Jane never won any of the contests, but she told the author: "Mother was undaunted. . . . She was never guilty of pushing me. I rather enjoyed all the attention at that age. However, no doubt my twin brother suffered."

Bettejane was attending Western High School in Washington, where she was a member (and later president) of the dramatics club, when the first big crisis of her life occurred. How she handled the potentially devastating problem provides a clear insight into the internal fortitude of the girl. As Jane recalls the event she was just a typical fifteen-year-old schoolgirl at the time:

"I'll never forget that night. It was a big evening. My crush, a seventeen-year-old high school boy who delivered our daily newspaper, had deigned to attend the party. He liked my dress. It was black—my first black dress, and almost off the shoulder. Suddenly for no apparent reason at all, he looked at me so strangely.

" 'What's the matter?' I asked him.

"He replied: 'Why are you making such a funny face?'

" 'Oh, I always look this way,' I quipped. What was the matter with him! Was my lipstick smudged or something? I walked to a mirror. And screamed!

"My left eye was bloodshot and watering. My mouth, slack jawed, gaped open. The left side of my face was distorted in a Frankenstein grin.

"I cried myself to sleep that night, sleep which only came when my hand

*He considered becoming an actor ("He was talented," Jane says), but World War II intervened. Through his talents as an artist, he entered the field of motion picture prop designing and set decorating after the war, which eventually led to his becoming a producer-director of low-budget motion pictures in Hollywood. His latest feature is a children's film shot in Malaysia. He is married to a model and has four children.

pushed down the left eye to close it. I woke up the next morning with one side of my face completely paralyzed."

The doctors diagnosed Jane's neurological disturbance as Bell's palsy, a disease from which very few people ever completely recover. But she was determined.

"I rented a heat lamp, had it on and off a few minutes at a time for a month. I held a hot water bottle to my face all day and night long. I tried to feel, to see. One side of my face felt numb, but I kept moving it. It took me months, just trying to make it go up to match the other side. Then one day it went up an eighth of an inch—just a flicker, but the doctor knew that the muscle wasn't completely dead. And I knew I could do it.

"For hours at a time I'd say 'ah' and study my jaws. They had to be exactly even. And finally they were. Then I went to work on my left eye. I had to open and close it with my finger tips."

Encouraged by her mother, Jane rationalized that her arduous physical therapy sessions had a dual purpose. "I'd always wanted to be an actress, and suddenly I knew that learning to control my facial muscles was one of the best assets I could have as a performer. Emotions often must be portrayed from an inner feeling, of course, but I had a double advantage because I was learning to direct my as-yet expressionless feelings, as well as gaining an ability to express emotion by a very conscious manipulation of my muscles."

After two months away from school, Jane was persuaded to return to the classroom. At the time she was terribly self-defensive and aloof, fearful that her classmates would shun her because of the disfiguring infirmity. At the time it was still necessary for her, before she went out each day, to lift the left corner of her mouth into a smile. (One unforeseen "benefit" from this grueling experience was that the ailment gave Jane a strange trademark, her "Mona Lisa" smile. "It made me different, and people remembered me.")

Jane did not graduate from high school, for money was still in short supply in the Greer household. She quit her education in her senior year, to take a job with Ralph Hawkins's band at the seemingly tremendous salary of $100 weekly.* Thereafter she auditioned for Enric Madriguera's orchestra, which had just been hired to play at Washington's Club Del Rio. Madriguera's group was noted for its handling of good society-type music and well-orchestrated Latin American melodies. Jane vocalized the Spanish songs in her deep rich voice, but admits she did not understand the phonetically learned foreign words. ("Later I discovered some of the words were not as written. His band was putting me on.") Jane remained with Madriguera for about eight months, also participating in his nightly radio program.

By this time America was involved in World War II and Mrs. Greer had

---

*"Of course," Jane recalls with typical joviality regarding her career events, "I fell asleep at the side of the piano every night and would be jostled awake by the piano player just before my numbers. The name of the nightclub was the Crossroads and my father would drive over an hour delivering me at 8 P.M. and picking me up at 2 A.M. This did not last for long as I contracted measles from fatigue (most unglamorous)."

been hired for a minor War Department job. When she learned that the newly created Women's Army Auxiliary Corps* was seeking applicants to model its newly styled uniforms, she suggested her daughter for the assignment. It proved to be a steppingstone to Jane's long-desired acting career. She was soon featured in a recruiting poster advertisement and then in a photo layout of women at war for *Life* magazine (issue of June 8, 1942). She repeated her WAC-outfit modeling for a spot in a Paramount newsreel. "The reason I was given the close-up of the WA(A)C cap was that it was raining. I pinned up my limp hair into a bun at the neck. An officer found a regulation stipulating the hair should be one inch off the collar, so they chose me for the close-ups. The other two models had permanents which were unperturbed by the weather."

Paramount's talent department viewed the newsreel and had Jane screen-test for a possible studio contest. She thought her audition "awful," but they signed her to a contract which she misunderstood. (It was not a firm commitment but an option which they could drop within thirty days.) Bettejane and her mother understandably thought they were on their way to Hollywood and had many going-away parties to celebrate the occasion. As she and her mother awaited the arrival of the plane tickets, a letter came from the studio informing her, "Sorry, we have so many of your type." † A much-embarrassed Jane remained in Washington ("Immediate seclusion was my goal"). However, her family talked her into facing defeat, and she fibbed to her friends that her attorney had decided she must not sign the Paramount deal.

In the interim Jane's *Life* magazine and newsreel exposure did not go unnoticed by the public in general or by Rudy Vallee in particular. The forty-one-year-old crooner, known for his enthusiastic womanizing, had spotted the WAC-outfitted Jane and through associates acquired data about the seventeen year old. He obtained her telephone number and called her at the Greer's Washington apartment. He explained that he thought she had cinema potential and suggested that if she came to Hollywood he would endeavor to guide her into a film career. Vallee also made it clear that he was personally interested in the young lady. Jane's social life was then still being strictly supervised by her ever-present mother, and, although Jane and (especially) Mrs. Greer were flattered by Vallee's attention, it was decided that because she was legally underage, it would be best to reject his offer of sponsorship.

Several months after Jane's unsatisfactory Paramount test, David O. Selznick had Jane tested in New York. This time it was a good one,‡ photographed by Stanley Cortez. When the screentest was shipped to California, Freddie Schuessler, who was then casting director for both Selznick and Howard Hughes, learned that Selznick was not too thrilled with the test. Schuessler showed it to billionaire Hughes, who had one of his talent scouts

* The original designation for the Women's Army Corps (WAC), created on May 14, 1942.
† In particular the frizzled-haired Jane of 1941-1942 bore a striking resemblance to Paramount contractee Diana Lynn (and the slightly later Mimi Chandler).
‡ Ella Raines and Willard Parker were tested the same day.

in New York come to Washington to take photographs of Jane ("*No* make-up—unretouched"). Hughes signed Jane to a contract with options expiring every thirty days. (The final contract was signed about six months after she arrived in California.)

Jane and her mother arrived in Hollywood in early, 1943,* and was duly impressed into the company of Hughes's other publicized protégées, Jane Russell and Faith Domergue. Following the usual procedure Jane began a battery of coaching sessions to prepare her for the cinema: drama (Florence Enright), coordination, and poise. From the start Jane found Hughes a most congenial employer. "He charmed all of us and performed many kind acts." What intrigued Jane even more than Hughes's headlined mentorship of Russell and Domergue "was the other secret twenty girls also under [personal] contract [to Howard Hughes]. The drama coach [Florence Enright] whom Hughes used would have us leave on the half hour so we would avoid meeting each other. You can imagine how curious we were. Finally I couldn't stand it and hid behind a bush across from the bus stop and managed to glimpse a dark haired beauty entering her home."

In due course Jane was asked to audition for the chief himself. Hughes always had the new girls read scenes from the script of *The Awful Truth.* Jane memorized the scenario and when ushered into Hughes's imposing office, began her dramatic recitation at top voice, knowing that Hughes was hard of hearing. For a multitude of reasons Hughes was impressed with her and renegotiated her option into a firm contract. Now that her future was "secure," Mr. Greer, Donne, and the family dog, Ripley, joined her and Mrs. Greer in Hollywood, where they had rented a house.†

If Hughes was then still preoccupied with manipulating the screen future of *The Outlaw,* Jane's would-be protector, Rudy Vallee, was not so remiss. He recalls: "Hughes forbade her to go out in public, but she remembered the phone call and was soon singing at some of my Coast Guard band appearances. A more charming, talented, and gracious person I shall never know."

A romance of sorts developed between Jane and Vallee, and on December 2, 1943, they were wed at the Hollywood-Westwood Community Chapel. There were full military trappings for the "high-ho everybody" man, with the couple passing through an arch of crossed sabers uplifted by a contingent of Coast Guard men.‡

---

* A few years later Jane was reported as saying that Hughes had sent her two drawing room tickets for the cross-country trek. "I wasn't rolling in dough, so I switched the drawing room tickets for two berths, upper and lower, saved $200 and bought some clothes. The Pullman was due in California two hours before the drawing room so we'd have plenty of time to jump on the drawing room train and walk off as if we belonged on it." Unfortunately, the Pullman section was sidetracked for five hours, and an increasingly worried Jane sent telegram after telegram to Hughes. Meanwhile Hughes had checked at the train station and the drawing room train was on time. He waited and waited for his new contractee. When Jane finally arrived at the station and disembarked from the train, she said weakly, "Are we late? So sorry."

† Mr. Greer would die in August, 1963; Mrs. Greer passed away in July, 1964.

‡ Looking at photographs of the occasion, the Jane of today quipped: "Can you imagine wearing gold lame to your first wedding. It matched the braid on Rudy's uniform, that's why."

Although Jane outwardly seemed to be the compleat wife, she must have had reservations about both domesticizing Vallee and manipulating her own career. He graciously introduced her to the plush life of residing in a twenty-room San Fernando Valley home (once owned by Ann Harding), and gallantly designed chic black-on-black and ultra-pink satin suits for her. In March, 1944, Jane and Vallee separated for the second time* with the would-be starlet explaining that they were happier living apart than together. In June of that year they parted for keeps. The ex-bride claimed, "There's something about the possessiveness of marriage that won't work for us." But physically separating from and forgetting the charming Vallee were two different things. In September, 1944, three months after their divorce, Jane told the press: "Rudy is the only one for me. Our marriage will last forever now. Our divorce has brought us closer together than ever." Her youthful optimism proved inaccurate for they again stopped dating, and he went his own merry way, marrying for a fourth time in 1949 to Eleanor Kathleen Norris.†

Jane was under contract to Howard Hughes from January, 1943, to mid-1944.‡ But she soon saw that she might wait in the wings for years for even a bit screen role to develop from this pact, leading her to buy out Hughes's agreement for the sum of $7,572. As the story is popularly told, money-conscious Jane had paid the wealthy eccentric two weekly installments of $25 each when she suddenly decided that since he was so much richer than she, there was no point in bothering to continue the gesture. Later Hughes admitted to Jane that he had not expected any refund whatsoever.

Jane went on to occupy a berth at RKO Pictures. At the time it was said that she was enabled to sign on there through one of Rudy Vallee's many industry connections. Discussing this today, however, she says, "I really can't remember." Middle-class RKO was then enjoying the full flush of the lush World War II filmmaking years and was choked with a bevy of contract players, mostly lower-echelon screen types used economically to fill out the array of programmers being churned out by the studio. Although Jane was not immediately cast into any feature work—there were drama coaching from Lillian Albertson and singing lessons with Robert Keith—Vallee still was pitching for the girl who was soon to be his ex-spouse. He suggested to Walter Wanger that she be borrowed for his upcoming Universal release, *Salome, Where She Danced* (1945). ("But with those legs . . ." Jane now says, laughing off this "absurd" casting notion, Wanger declined Vallee's initial suggestion. He later cast another Vallee protégée in the part, and Yvonne De Carlo went on to stardom.)

Eventually Jane went in front of the RKO cameras in early August, 1944,

---

*They had gone their separate ways for a twenty-four-hour period that February.

†His first two marriages were to Fay Webb and Leonia Cauchers.

‡In between reconciliations with Vallee, Jane dated Howard Hughes. "He loved going to amusement parks," Jane recalls, "throwing baseballs at lead milk bottles. I had quite a collection of kewpie dolls and stuffed animals he had won. He has a charming little boy quality about him that was very endearing to women."

for her screen debut in *Two O'Clock Courage,* which crept into the Rialto Theatre on March 13, 1945. It was a double-bill item about which one reviewer snapped, it "has less guts than its title." The drab murder mystery had Tom Conway as an amnesia victim suspected of killing a Broadway producer and therefore forced to locate the real murderer to establish his own innocence. He is aided in this uninspired chore by taxi driver Ann Rutherford and comical newsman Richard Lane. Seventh-billed Jane was rung into the act as the spirited girlfriend of Lester Matthews, he being a play-stealing skunk. Her minor role made no impression on the critics or the public. Jane's reaction to seeing herself onscreen for the first time was distinctly negative: "My mouth was much too large, my eyes turned out and my legs were toothpicks. Aside from that, I was numb."

Her next picture, *Pan-Americana,* which completed shooting on September 8, 1944, debuted at Loew's State Theatre on March 22, 1945. It was yet another of RKO's frugally constructed musicals, a lackluster combination of preprogrammed storyline and unspectacular musical numbers.* Its one gimmick was to utilize authentic Latin American talent within its plot framework: staff members of a "chic" American pictorial magazine take a picture-postcard tour (courtesy of stock-footage photography) of South America to select local talent for an upcoming musical revue the magazine is promoting. Several of the newer RKO apprentice-contractees were utilized as Pan American girls (Virginia Beaumont, Patti Brill, Greta Christensen, Rita Corday, Rosemary La Planche, Susan Walsh) while Jane had a so-called featured role as Miss Downing. She appears very briefly in one of the south-of-the-border production numbers, has a tiny splattering of dialog ("Yes sir. I mean, Yes, ma'am!"), and, in a dressing room sequence, casts snide looks at her fellow hoofers. Not much of a beginning for a $100-a-week contract player.

The third of her four pictures that year was *George White's Scandals* (1945), a dirt-cheap musical that pretty much wasted Joan Davis and Jack Haley, except for their satirical number, "Who Killed Vaudeville?" Nor did the musical interludes of Ethel Smith at the organ or Gene Krupa and Orchestra upgrade the feature to a worthwhile level. Jane was cast as Billie Randall, a clumsy dancer who has her thoughtless heart set on show director Phillip Terry, although she is well aware that he is busily courting Martha Holliday (a British socialite who has slipped into the cast of the *Scandals*—the show-within-the-movie—to prove her worth as a ballet dancer). Jane's cinematic comeuppance here is in keeping with the low tenor of the picture's aspira-

---

*James Agee (in the *Nation*) had words to write on this John H. Auer-produced and directed feature: " . . . another of those buckets of good-swill that make me wish some Latin American movie people would come north, for a change, and take fair vengeance on the United States; a job at which I would be only too happy to help out. In some other respects, however, I rather liked the picture. There is a general air of casual lousiness about it—the aching dreariness of the climactic stage tableaux for instance which seems very friendly and fresh compared with the high-finished pink granite gravestones which are normally released as musical comedies. The song-and-dance numbers are mainly poor, but with the fierce unembalmed poorness of the real things; as you see it in night clubs."

tions, for her misplaced ardor is cooled off with a bucket of paint dumped over her head.

Jane's entree into RKO economy-series picture-making was *Dick Tracy* (1945), the first of four features on Chester Gould's famed cartoon detective that RKO would produce.* *Variety* complimented this entry for being a "nifty action melodrama" whose "pace is fast and production mounting good. Cast is excellent and brings the Gould characters alive without the grotesqueness of the newspaper strip features." The plot revolved around the machinations of the hideously disfigured criminal, Splitface (Mike Mazurki), who vows revenge on those who sent him to jail years before. He eliminates three victims and almost brings about the demise of Tess Trueheart (Anne Jeffreys) and Junior (Mickey Kuhn) before indomitable Dick Tracy (Morgan Conway) makes his timely rescue. For the first time on the screen Jane was billed as "Jane Greer" as she played the daughter of intended victim Morgan Wallace.† Compared to the picture's leading lady (Jeffreys), Jane did not have much screen time, but she had the good sense to give her characterization a little bite and dimension.

Besides emoting oncamera, Jane, now earning $200 a week at RKO, was kept busy posing for the studio's publicity department. One photo layout pictured Jane as a typical Hollywood starlet who shared a comfortably modest apartment with two other RKO stock contractees, Vonne Lester and Myrna Dell. (Not true, she was still living with her family). A more uncharacteristic stunt imposed upon Jane occurred when the publicity people used her for an Easter Egg gimmick. In a series of continuity photos Jane is shown popping out of an oversized egg shell. Needless to say, this juvenilia was so alien to her fun-loving, but sensible, nature that the montage photos revealed a telltale look of discomfort on Jane's face.

Since she had functioned more than adequately as a junior bad girl in several programmers, RKO executive producer Sid Rogell agreed to assign Jane to several bigger but similar roles in 1946. Jane was tested for a George Raft vehicle, *Nocturne* (1946), but the screen tough guy wanted a "name" in the part and would not even look at her test, so it went to Lynn Bari. But Jane was in *The Falcon's Alibi* (1946), RKO's twelfth entry in the popular detective series. Critics of the day were excessively blasé about this B-picture ("We can do nothing this morning but give the Rialto's latest offering the bird"). Actually *The Falcon's Alibi*, shot on the usual $140,000-plus budget on a shooting schedule of under three weeks, had the merit of a good, gimmicky plotline, which substantially enhanced the whodunit. Tom Lawrence (Tom Conway) and his intrepid stooge-helper Goldie (Vince Barnett) are called upon by heroine Rita Corday to prevent her being accused of stealing her employer's jewelry, which is insured for $100,000. Needless to say the gems are stolen, there are three murders, Inspector Blake (Al Bridge) is convinced the

*Republic had already produced several serials on the subject.

†Jane was happy enough to chop her surname down to marquee size, for she hated the moniker "Bettejane."

Falcon is implicated in the crimes, and the tricky murderer is caught within the allotted sixty-two minutes.

Corday functioned smoothly as Esther Howard's feckless private secretary, but her performance was as unmemorable here as in most of her RKO work. On the other hand, Jane displayed a quality of showmanship that would individualize her screen work over the years. She was cast innocuously enough, as the band vocalist at the Barbary Towers Hotel, singing two songs during the course of the picture.* Her first, "How Do You Fall in Love?", was sung from her platform stance at the Barbary Bowl Club. Beret in hand, Jane performed with more animation and conviction than had been her custom in previous studio outings. Her facial expressiveness riveted the viewer's attention, despite the busy action going on around her in the scene. By the time she goes into her paces for her second number, "Come Out—Wherever You Are," the audience knows that Jane is secretly married to weasel disc jockey Elisha Cook, Jr., who performs his nightly radio show from a penthouse apartment at the hotel. But even more to the point, she is carrying on an affair with bandleader Paul Brooks, playing him for the proverbial sucker. For when he insists that she leave Cook and the club, she reveals her true colors: "I can't leave now I'm just getting somewhere. . . . I have a career to think about." She has more than that to think about, for her neurotic hubby is none other than a jewelry-stealing crook (where else is he going to get the money to keep materialistic Jane content?), who has added murder to his dossier of crimes. "I don't want any part of this . . . " stammers a frightened Jane as she realizes that nebbishy, seemingly affable Cook is a determined lawbreaker, "You can't involve me." Now there is a nervous twitch to Jane's mouth, accentuating the breakdown of the previously tough broad into a cowardly babe. Not long thereafter Cook catches Jane trying to scram from the scene, and he does what any self-respecting killer would do—adds another homicide to his record. (Cook then meets his own cinematic just reward. He is killed trying to get away down the fire escape.)

Variety had good words for Jane's performance as Lola Carpenter in *The Falcon's Alibi*: "Femme honors go to Jane Greer, nitery canary and one of the victims. Miss Greer wraps up two pop songs in fine style and registers strongly on acting and in dramatic scenes with Elisha Cook, Jr." Granted Jane had yet to refine her physical appearance to its apogee,† but she was no run-of-the-mill 1940s movie toughie, as was clearly demonstrated when she paraded about in her sequinned two-piece floor-length black gown, tearing into her song, the dialog, and her co-players.

The Bamboo Blonde (1946)‡ was songstress Frances Langford's first film

---

*She recorded her own song numbers.

† In some of her eight scenes there were still traces of her fast-disappearing baby-fat figure, and her hair style was not yet the sleek coiffure she would display in the late 1940s.

‡ Filmed before *The Falcon's Alibi*. In the detective picture, Elisha Cook, Jr. spins a recording of Frances Langford singing "Dreaming Out Loud" from *The Bamboo Blonde*, a none-too-sly bit of self-serving studio promotion.

after returning from entertaining the troops during World War II. It was not much of a tribute to her (she photographed badly as well), nor hardly an indication of the screen work director Anthony Mann would later turn out in Hollywood. The plot had Langford as a third-rate club star whom promoter Ralph Edwards launches into stardom when B-29 pilot Russell Wade has her likeness painted on the side of his bomber and his plane makes victory headlines in the Pacific theatre of war. Thereafter Edwards has Langford publicized as the in-person "Bamboo Blonde." Jane had the rather thankless task of playing Eileen Sawyer, the catty ex-fiancée of blueblood Wade. Most of the picture's few diversions were offered by wisecracking Iris Adrian, here cast as Edwards's tough-talking gal.

Sunset Pass (1946)* was the third filming of Zane Grey's tale of an express-company detective (James Warren) who falls in love with Nan Leslie, the demure sister of rancher John Laurenz. The latter is responsible for a series of mysterious train and bank robberies, which forces Warren into the stale situation of doing his duty at the possible expense of losing his girl. If one wondered why Jane, who had already graduated to better roles, was seen only briefly as Helen, a dance hall girl in the Lone Pine Saloon, there is a ready explanation. "*Sunset Pass* was done in 1945," Jane recalls, "just after *Two O'Clock Courage*. I was literally hysterical in the part. Not realizing I had the flu, 102° temperature. I ruined more takes laughing at myself. They took me off the picture."

Despite the policy shakeup at RKO in 1946 when Charles Koerner died and Dore Schary replaced him as executive vice-president in charge of production, Jane's studio position continued to escalate along with her salary ($500 a week in 1946, $750 in 1947). But one would hardly have known that Jane's career was on the upswing from her role in *Sinbad the Sailor* (1947). This quasi-major feature starred Douglas Fairbanks, Jr., in his first post-World War II film, and Maureen O'Hara, who was continuing her joint RKO-Twentieth Century-Fox acting pact. The color swashbuckler was reputed to have cost as much as $3-4 million, but the feature boasted telltale expense-saving devices, ranging from a tongue-in-cheek script, which relied more on narration than action, to an overabundance of miniature effects for the "spectacular" sequences. As Pirouze, O'Hara's faithful slave handmaiden, Jane was decked out in Near East-by-way-of-Hollywood costuming, a pantaloon-bra affair with bare midriff. It was not the script's original intention that Jane should be quite so indistinguishable from the backdrops in this, her first color film. But obviously cinema star Miss O'Hara had second thoughts about distracting competition from the onscreen presence of veil-clad Jane. "The veil worn by me in *Sinbad* became thicker every day. Finally you could see only eyes." With characteristic raconteur charm Jane added to this remembrance

---

*It would be one of a package of six RKO features reissued in 1951 on the double-bill, action-theatre circuit. Thereafter the rights to *Sunset Pass* reverted back to the Zane Grey estate and the feature is currently unavailable for television showings.

of studio politicking: "I begged the makeup man to make me up only to the nose since no one would see the lower half of my face."

For most performers there is usually *the* role in *the* film which provides the watershed for their career, either pushing them onward to fame or proving, at least in retrospect, that glory was never to be theirs. Jane's opportunity to step out of the starlet's vestibule into the main chapel of cinema prominence occurred with *They Won't Believe Me* ((1947). In Jane's previous eight RKO pictures she had been typecast as a baddie, but in this Irving Pichel-directed melodrama she had a more sympathetic, full-bodied role. Jane succinctly accounts for this important transition: "'Baddie' roles I attribute to my dark hair. When I lightened it, my face softened and *They Won't Believe Me* came along, thanks to Joan Harrison, producer."

The story of *They Won't Believe Me* is unreeled from the witness stand where Robert Young is on trial for homicide. He has been a conscienceless playboy wed to wealthy Rita Johnson. When she pulls the purse strings, he drops his merry fling with magazine writer Jane Greer, and he moves from Manhattan to Los Angeles where an interest in a brokerage house has been purchased for him. Young rapidly forgets ditched Jane after becoming infatuated with money-hungry secretary Susan Hayward. He and Hayward run away together to Reno, Nevada, but on the way she is killed in an automobile crash. The authorities think the victim is Johnson. This leads to desperate complications when Young returns home and finds his wife has committed suicide. He disposes of the body, only to have the cops assume that the second body is that of Hayward. Although the ironic finale was essentially a cop-out to skirt the Breen Office Production Code, the film received overall critical plaudits.* Young may have been miscast as the louse, but the trio of female players were a fine lot of performers, providing the needed contrasting characterizations. Both Rita Johnson and Susan Hayward had been on the movie scene too long to garner where-has-she-been type reviews, but not so Jane. "A comely beginner," said James Agee in the *Nation.* "A young hopeful with plenty to back up any hopes," was *Photoplay*'s evaluation. Evidently the RKO hierarchy agreed, for Jane was elevated to star billing, being listed third above the film's title. After five years in Hollywood she was definitely on her way.

As a result of the favorable response to her work in *They Won't Believe Me*, Jane not only had her RKO-lot dressing room moved from the top floor to the first ("with private shower. What luxury!"), but she was assigned to the leading role opposite Robert Mitchum in *Out of the Past* (1947). It was a prestigious bit of casting for Jane as sleepy-eyed Mitchum was fast becoming one of Hollywood's major attractions in the post-World War II setup. Thanks to the tempered direction of Jacques Tourneur† and the imaginative camera

---

*Over the years *They Won't Believe Me* has gained a reputation as a fitting genre follow-up to *Double Indemnity.*

†Jane recalls: "Jacques Tourneur's direction was very simple to understand. 'Impassive' was his favorite word of direction. It worked."

work of Nicholas Musuraca, *Out of the Past* was not just another hard-boiled private eye picture abounding with sleazy characters. Maybe it was not quite the "honey of a thriller" the *New York Daily Mirror* insisted, but as Wanda Hale analyzed in her three-star *New York Daily News* review, "Morbid curiosity in the fate of these intriguing people is the film's holding power."

Framed within a flashback, *Out of the Past* has Bridgeport, California, gas station owner Mitchum explain to his wide-eyed girl (Virginia Huston) who he really is, and just why a hoodlum has ordered him to report to Kirk Douglas's Lake Tahoe retreat the next morning. It evolves that Mitchum was formerly a Manhattan private detective, hired by mobster Douglas to track down Jane. She not only had taken potshots at Douglas but had grabbed $40,000 of his funds and taken off for parts unknown. As lion Mitchum sizes up panther Douglas (and vice versa), Douglas assures his would-be employee that he has no intention of harming Jane. He merely wants her back, along with his money. That seems fair enough to the junior Sam Spade and he accepts Douglas's deal. Fade-out. Fade-in on Mexico City,* where trenchcoat-clad Mitchum is lazing in Pablo's cafe, convinced his prey will eventually turn up for a nightcap. Presto, in slithers Jane, adorned in a wide-brim white hat that dramatically sets off her ambiguous presence against the tawdry surroundings. Soon she and Mitchum are engaged in some seminifty non sequitur conversation, with the detective slyly admitting: "You're going to make any man you meet curious."

Very soon Jane convinces Mitchum that she has much more to offer him than client Douglas, and they tacitly agree to become a steady twosome. After dodging an overanxious Douglas, who just happens to be in the vicinity of Mexico City, Jane and Mitchum head for San Francisco and the proverbial new life ahead. Their plans are quickly short-circuited by mushy Steve Brodie, Mitchum's agency partner, who has trailed Mitchum to the West Coast so Douglas's case can be completed and the fee paid into the kitty. Brodie and Jane quickly evaluate one another. He calls her a "cheap piece of baggage." Jane's response is more to the point, as she asks Mitchum, "Why don't you break his head?" When Mitchum remains too genteel in the matter Jane nonchalantly shoots Brodie. This leads to a split with Mitchum. The flashback then blends into the present where Mitchum is nonplussed to find Jane housekeeping at Douglas's Lake Tahoe spread. Closed-mouth Jane explains: "I had to come back. What else could I do?" Evidently Mitchum thinks plenty.

But feline Jane is a past master at getting her way and before long has her claws out to play Mitchum for a sucker again. This time there is one difference. He outmaneuvers her. Finally, even Douglas, in big tax trouble with the U.S. government, awakens to Jane's primeval nature. "You dirty little phoney. I should have kicked your teeth in." Before he finishes snarling Jane calmly plugs him. Thereafter she "convinces" Mitchum that he has no alternative but to beat a quick retreat with her. Her logic is simple: "You're no good and

*Still a favorite locale for RKO films.

824

neither am I. We deserve each other." When Jane senses that basically honest Mitchum is perhaps stringing her along, she shoots him too. But justice prevails. Ensnaring law-enforcers soon riddle her car and body with well-placed bullets.

At one point in *Out of the Past*, Virginia Huston optimistically says of Jane to Mitchum: "She can't be all bad. No one is."

Taciturn Mitchum replies: "She comes the closest." The critics responded very favorably to Jane's low-keyed performance. *Variety* found her most admirable as a "sleek and charming baby-faced killer" and James Agee (*Time* magazine) zeroed in with: ". . . can best be described, in an ancient idiom, as a hot number." On its more modest scale, *Out of the Past* was for Jane what *Double Indemnity* had been for Barbara Stanwyck, and what *Too Late for Tears* (United Artists, 1949) would be for Lizabeth Scott, *Tension* (MGM, 1949) for Audrey Totter, and *Human Desire* (Columbia, 1954) for Gloria Grahame. Dore Schary was enthusiastic enough about Jane's work in this RKO offering that he agreed to renegotiate her contract from $750-a-week to $1,000-a-week. Had both Barbara Bel Geddes and Gloria Grahame not been grabbing the assignments in the RKO pictures that more-versatile-than-was-apparent Jane could have easily handled, her impact at the studio and on the public would have been far greater and more enduring in the long run of her career.*

But at this strategic point in Jane's galloping career she chose to end her bachelor days, and on August 21 she wed wealthy attorney-producer Edward Lasker,† then an associate of Walter Wanger. She had first met him in New York in 1945.

Despite Jane's growing repute in the cinema field, she was not director Sidney Lanfield's first choice to play the saloon queen in *Station West* (RKO, 1948). He had wanted Marlene Dietrich for the role of Charlie, who doubles as gaming-house hostess and secret head of a gang robbing gold from the big shippers of this 1880s western mining town. Lanfield made Jane constantly aware that he considered her a poor second to Dietrich. The situation on the set became very strained. "Since I was twenty-two [*sic*] at that time, I was

---

*Twenty-five years after the fact, Jane looks back on this film with fondness and a refreshing degree of frankness about her performance:

"Bob [Mitchum] used to ask 'What are the lyrics?' of the script boy before rehearsing a scene. This lulled me into thinking I too could learn the dialogue under the dryer in make-up.

"I soon found out he was letter-perfect while I was fumbling around for the words. This put an end to my 'winging it.'"

Jane has contrasting opinions of her two co-stars. Of Mitchum: "He is a marvelous actor and was so considerate of me. I am very fond of him."

Of Kirk Douglas: "Kirk is a more physical actor. He bruised my arms grabbing me, and my face was roundly slapped. How he did *Champion* without maiming his partner is a miracle."

†Lasker was born in Chicago in 1912. A former bigtime advertising executive, he had been in charge of the radio division of the powerful Lord and Thomas Agency in the late 1930s. Thereafter he was associated with Howard Hawks and Wanger in filmmaking. At age forty Lasker went to UCLA Law School, graduated with honors, and is now practicing law in Los Angeles. He had been previously married for eleven years to New Yorker Carol Gimble.

quite defenseless," Jane recalls. "Dore [Schary] came to my rescue and threatened to remove Mr. Lanfield if such insults continued. Dore became a good friend of mine socially."

The storyline of *Station West*, which found Army undercover man Dick Powell posing as a disagreeable gent, became predictably obvious if one read the movie's advertising slogan: "Sometimes a man *Has* to double-cross the woman he loves." But there was good background flavor with Agnes Moorehead as a harassed mine owner, Burl Ives as the laconic hotel-keeper, Guinn Williams as Jane's powerful but dumb henchman, and Regis Toomey as Powell's earnest co-worker. One of the film's best points was its snappy repartee, which proved that Jane was no fledgling when it came to matching Powell in seemingly off-the-cuff banter.

Jane: "Have you ever made love to a woman?"

Powell: "Only from the doorway."

Jane: "You haven't made love to me."

Powell: "Let's go over to the doorway."

The screenplay for *Station West*, based on Luke Short's novel, allowed Jane to perform a pretty Mort Greene-Leigh Harline tune, "Sometime Remind Me to Tell You," which she handled in a suitable torchy fashion. Jane's portrayal of the conscienceless heavy who meets a timely end aroused *Time* magazine to report: "Miss Greer wears an extensive and luscious assortment of jig-sawed gowns [designed by Renie], and uses her eyes, mouth and bosom so effectively that it soon becomes clear that she was born too late. Back in the disreputable old days of silent movies when sex was sex, she would have become a major star very fast. Today, she seems so anachronistic as a Virginia loyalist. But it is a pleasure to watch her." The *Hollywood Reporter* was more direct in its appraisal of Jane, terming her a "luscious looking lady heavy." Jane, Dick Powell, and Agnes Moorehead trudged to Chicago for the world premiere of *Station West* (RKO Palace Theatre, October 19, 1948), appearing in a local parade there and endorsing the film in a special session on Mutual Network televised from that city.

Long before *Station West* went into national release, Jane had given birth to her first child, Albert, born June 23, 1948, and RKO had undergone yet another change of management. Howard Hughes had acquired the studio, leading to Dore Schary's resignation in July, 1948, and the substitution of Sid Rogell in his place as executive vice-president in charge of production. Rogell was favorably inclined to Jane, but it was decided that it might be better box office to borrow Lizabeth Scott from Hal B. Wallis-Paramount to team with Robert Mitchum in *The Big Steal*, a film to start production under Don Siegel's direction in October, 1948. Then, on August 31, 1948, Mitchum, Hollywood's rebel, was arrested on a charge of possession of marijuana cigarettes. Hughes-RKO may have been conventionally intolerant of any potential Communists on the lot,* but Hughes (and David O. Selznick, who shared

---

*During the 1947-52 Red fear in Hollywood, RKO's Dore Schary and Howard Hughes were both notably disinclined to back any studio member tainted by the House Un-American Activities Committee hearings.

826

Mitchum's $250,000-a-year contract) was not about to ditch his valuable male lead in his time of need. As soon as the actor was released on bail from the drug charge, he was hustled right over to the RKO soundstages to begin shooting of *The Big Steal*. But by this time Lizabeth Scott had bowed out of the film, and Jane had been substituted a week later.* During filming Mitchum was sentenced to sixty days at a Los Angeles County honor farm, and production on the cops-and-robbers thriller was suspended until his release at the end of March, 1949. Meantime Jane had learned she was pregnant again, so the movie had to be rushed to a hasty completion.

"Mitchum's newest picture" and he's reteamed with "gorgeous Jane Greer," read the ads for *The Big Steal* (Mayfair Theatre, July 10, 1949), which described the cast of Mitchum, Jane, and William Bendix as "A Man of Ice, A Woman of Fire, A Guy with a Gun." The plot of this flick most closely resembled target practice at a gang of characters on a carnival shooting-gallery treadmill. In the story, a steamer docks at Vera Cruz, where Bendix informs Mitchum he's under arrest for implication in the theft of a $300,000 Army payroll (really stolen by Patric Knowles). Mitchum's response is to knock Bendix out cold and take his papers. He and fellow passenger Jane go ashore, where she encounters Knowles and demands $2,000 he borrowed from her. Ungentlemanly Knowles takes off for Thehuacan, with Jane, Mitchum, and Bendix in pursuit, and law-enforcer Ramon Novarro standing in readiness as he calmly observes this conga-line manhunt. If one ignores the confused plotline (which has Knowles in the pay of international crook John Qualen, and Bendix one of his devious aides), there is some saucy dialog and a credible rapport between Mitchum and Jane (they have a two-day romance during which time she delights in his murdering of the Spanish language). And as has always been typical of director Don Siegel's *oeuvre*, there are plenty of shootings and a big climactic chase. Bosley Crowther (*New York Times*) thought Jane's role was "prettily played," and Howard Barnes (*New York Herald-Tribune*) graciously acknowledged that "she plays with a cool detachment that is perfectly in key with a bang-bang South-of-the-border melodrama."

On October 7, 1949, Jane gave birth to her second child, Lawrence. That year she found time to head the GI Gift Lift for the Los Angeles Junior Chamber of Commerce (which supplied Christmas presents for United Nations soldiers in Korea). More importantly she went to battle with Sid Rogell at RKO, demanding that she be given a better break in the studio's decreased lineup of pictures. She was tired of portraying the stereotyped sinister screen roles. Jane had far-reaching ambitions, which she revealed in a press statement. She was itching to garner an Oscar! "I know it means hard work and a great deal of trying and trying again, but I'm sticking to my guns. If I don't win as a leading lady, I'll keep plugging and win it for a character portrayal. In any case I want one of those Oscars to show my children!" RKO tempo-

---

*"Bob was much more hurt and humbled by this episode than the public was led to believe," Jane recalls "I was eager to work with him again, but was not mad about the script."

rarily appeased Jane by talking of starring her in a comedy, *The Richest Girl in Jail* by Michael Fessier, in which she would essay a zany heiress who commits one minor offense after another. That project did not transpire, and Jane found herself playing second fiddle to Lizabeth Scott in *The Company She Keeps*, which was made in early 1950 but did not see release until its opening at Loew's Criterion Theatre on January 28, 1951.*

The one novelty of the soggy *The Company She Keeps* was that it gave Miss Scott an opportunity to play against type. She plays the halo-adorned, trenchcoated Los Angeles parole officer of Jane, the latter released after two years of a five-year sentence for check forgery. Scott exudes a cloying (and very unconvincing) abundance of saintly patience as wisecracking Jane aggressively sways back and forth on the hackneyed road to redemption. A mere drop of one of Jane's hairpins, and Scott is on the scene allaying any fears her charge may have about its moral repercussions. The tale was basically filled with clichéd romantic melodrama, but its dialog had occasional sparks of foreshadowed women's lib, as when Jane discusses her prison job as nurse's aide.

Jane: "Working for women—waiting on women—being bossed by women. You don't know how I hate women!"

Scott: "There are men patients, too."

Jane: "I like my men on their feet."

And so she does. For Jane, always hankering for a good time and stimulating male companionship, sets her sights on newspaper reporter Dennis O'Keefe, who just happens to be Scott's boyfriend. Later on Scott has an opportunity to prove herself humanly frail by sending Jane back to prison for violating the parole regulations. But guardian angel Scott is too dedicated to do thusly, so she stretches her authority, and sacrificially sends Jane off to live (happily?— who knows?) ever after with besmitten O'Keefe. Even genteel Bosley Crowther (*New York Times*) champed at the bit over this plot maneuvering. "Things might have been a little better if Miss Scott had sent Miss Greer back to jail," he wrote. So they would have, despite director John Cromwell's tasteful try with the picture.

By 1950 the production output at RKO had reached a new low, and Howard Hughes was anxious to recoup overhead costs by loaning out players and technical talents to other companies. Jane was loaned to Twentieth Century-Fox for two films. *You're in the Navy Now* (1951) is one of those stillborn comedies that appears so much better on the scripting boards than in actuality. The combination of box-office magnet Gary Cooper and slick, commercial director Henry Hathaway seemed surefire. Under the title *U.S.S. Teakettle* the picture premiered at the Roxy Theatre in February, 1951. Bosley Crowther (*New York Times*) enthused in a backhanded manner: " . . . most explosively funny service picture that has come along since the nickelodeon

---

*"The part in *Company* was written by Ketti Frings with me in mind. I loved the part." Regarding Miss Scott on the set, Jane recalls: "Friendly, but she kept to herself quite a bit."

versions of the sinking of the battleship Maine." But the public was seemingly not amused by the fragile account of ninety-day-wonder officer Cooper, who during World War II is put in charge of a patrol craft (PC 1168) powered by steam turbine. The film's only suspense relies on everyone's anticipation of the eventual explosion of the craft's newfangled motor. Jane was oncamera ever so briefly as Cooper's patient WAVE wife. The picture engendered so little box-office response that it was hastily withdrawn, retitled *You're in the Navy Now*, and pushed back out on the release market with mild results.

After making the weak Twentieth Century-Fox musical *Down among the Sheltering Palms*, which was shelved for two years before being dropped onto the distribution circuit in 1953, Jane found herself at a crossroads. She had had enough of the RKO treadmill. It might have been a friendly, secure home base, but in the early 1950s studio head Howard Hughes was too busy promoting Jane Russell, Faith Domergue, and unsung other protégées to have any concrete interest in redefining Jane's screen career. "I didn't want my sons to have to grow up and when someone asked what their mother did, to have to reply, 'Oh Mom's a gunmoll.'" So Jane's husband, Edward Lasker, negotiated a settlement to her RKO career, buying her out of her pact there with Hughes.

With the blessing of her longtime friend Dore Schary, now heading production at MGM, Jane signed a short-term agreement with Metro. But MGM of the 1950s, having long since bid farewell to its golden age, was fumbling in the face of television competition, and dubious management by Mr. Schary. Like such other shaded semi-luminaries at MGM as Jean Hagen, Jane floundered in the massive studio setup. She was not given any career direction by company executives and was not a big enough celebrity-personality to engineer her own professional future with any degree of success.

You for Me (Globe Theatre, September 24, 1952) was a pleasant little screwball comedy from MGM's economy unit, and that was just the trouble. It was too modest in concept and execution to stand on its own. So it was foisted off as an undistinguished double-bill item, geared for the so-called youth audience, when in actuality its premise was quite adult. Playboy Peter Lawford (billed in oversized type below the title, but before Jane's billing) gets birdshot in the backside and hastens to the local hospital. Since he is a heavy financial contributor ($100,000 a year) to the institution, he expects a great deal of VIP treatment. To the contrary he receives no sympathy at all, particularly from outspokenly flip nurse Jane. When he announces that he is withdrawing his annual monetary support from the hospital, abrasive doctor Gig Young urges Jane to patch up the rhubarb by making a pass at Lawford. She does, but finds herself in the dilemma of having to decide between wealthy Lawford (her wacky family naturally votes for him) and struggling physician Young. MGM's ads for *You for Me* proclaimed: "She's a little bit of Eve, a little bit of Delilah . . . and a gal who just can't say 'no'!" But she does, and chooses Young. Despite Jane's intentionally callous characterization, which led the *New York Times* to state that she "acts angry about the whole thing which is understandable," Paul V. Beckley (*New York Herald-Tribune*) was of a different opinion: "As the nurse with the ironic tongue, Jane Greer gives this role an amusing and sympathetic run for its money." Unfortunately, not enough of the discriminating public saw this programmer to make Jane's performance count with studio executives.

Jane enjoyed making *You for Me* and would have liked to do more comedy, but it was not to be, for she was next shunted to the Technicolor-mounted Ruritanian swashbuckler *The Prisoner of Zenda* (1952), playing the fifth-billed Antoinette de Maubam. As the jealous love of Robert Douglas, the sinister half-brother of king Stewart Granger, Jane was "appropriately hot-headed as the familiar femme fatale" (*New York Times*). She never looked lovelier onscreen than as "the Beautiful Conspirator Who Lures Men to Doom," but there was an indefinably derivative quality to her performance that constantly made one harken back to the splendid rendition of the same role by Mary Astor in the 1937 filmization of *The Prisoner of Zenda*.* Thus the popular new edition of Anthony Hope's enduring novel did nothing to joggle Jane's stagnating cinema career.

When actress Betsy Drake rejected a co-starring role in MGM's economy feature *Desperate Search* (1952), Jane was unceremoniously substituted, which gives a good indication of how little influence either Jane or her agent, Famous Artists Agency, had with the studio bosses.† Jane portrayed the warm second wife of Canadian charter pilot Howard Keel.‡ It is her love and devotion that rescue him from the depths of alcoholism induced by his first marriage to famed, but selfish, aviatrix Patricia Medina. When Keel's two children are lost in the northern wilds after their plane crashes, Jane must fight Medina, who is still trying to emasculate Keel by having him grounded during the search crisis. The film was little more than a trim but very slim suspense saga that more closely resembled one of today's telefeatures than a full-blown theatrical movie. But given the nature of the picture, Jane helped immeasurably in giving *Desperate Search* whatever class it attained. As the worried wife and stepmother she displayed sensibility with understated playing, but she also could show fire as when she angrily tells Medina to "get off your rump" and arrange for Keel to fly again.

Jane was making more of a splash offscreen in 1952, particularly in her forthright, flip views. She told columnist Earl Wilson (and remember these opinions were stated long before they became clichés of the movie set):

"Hollywood's biggest mistake is trying to make everybody believe the stars are like the girl next door.

*Only years later did this author learn from Jane: "The director [Richard Thorpe] had me run a movieola of Mary Astor in the part every day on the set. That is why I was so bad in the movie. I took him literally when he asked me to repeat her performance. Little did I know the remainder of the cast were playing tongue-in-cheek."

†Jane had been eager for the role of silent screen vamp Lina Lamont in *Singin' in the Rain* (MGM, 1952), but the studio did not even test her for the part, giving it to Jean Hagen instead.

‡Few cared that singing star Keel was making his dramatic film debut after already having appeared in several musicals.

"Now that's silly. If they were like the girl next door, nobody'd ever go to the movies. They'd go next door to see the girl next door."

Or:

"I wouldn't go near the kitchen. If I did, the cook would laugh herself sick. The way to a man's heart is through a good cook. . . . "

That same year Jane had a bylined King Features' newspaper article entitled: "How to Get Rid of a Man." Among her novel suggestions was one rather drastic alternative: "Dropping dead!"

Jane's final MGM venture was Red Skelton's *The Clown* (1953), an anemic remake of Wallace Beery and Jackie Cooper's *The Champ* (1931).* This ragged feature barely skirted pathos as it told of ex-Ziegfeld star Skelton, now a broken-down amusement park clown and a drunk, who has difficulty caring for his son (Tim Considine). After Skelton is arrested in a stag show raid, his ex-wife Jane (now wed to Philip Ober) begs him to give her custody of their son, so he can be raised in a proper atmosphere. The finale finds Skelton, just on the brink of television-comeback success and a long-awaited reunion with his loyal son. But at the crucial moment Skelton collapses and dies of a heart attack. *Variety* kindly cited Jane as "exceptionally good . . . giving the role a warmth that makes it believable." If anything the role in *The Clown* foreshadowed her passive screen assignments in the years to come.

Down among the Sheltering Palms was finally released at the Palace Theatre on June 12, 1953. Everyone in the industry was aware of the problems that had dogged the picture from its inception. When Fox musical-comedy star June Haver rejected the property because of the script's morality values, Jane was substituted in her place. Director Edmund Goulding, then feuding with studio head Darryl F. Zanuck, made a mess of *Down among the Sheltering Palms* as a way of getting even.† The film's flimsy premise had William Lundigan, an Army captain in charge of a troop command sent to occupy the remote South Pacific island of Midi at the end of World War II. Because of the Army's rigid rule against fraternization with the natives, he attempts to set a good example by stifling his romance with Jane, the comely niece of local missionary Gene Lockhart. Then sexy newsreporter Gloria De Haven arrives on the island. When Lundigan has the audacity to spurn her ardent advances, she reveals to the public that the isle's king (Billy Gilbert) has cheerfully offered his daughter (Mitzi Gaynor) for Lundigan's pleasure. The harmless tale nosedives to a feeble end with everyone suitably matched and contented—all save the audience. Jane authoritatively sang her two allotted tunes, "Who Will It Be When the Time Comes?" and "When You're in Love," in her mezzo-soprano voice. Her comedy highlight, if it can be adjudged that, occurs after Lundigan informs Jane she is causing just too much

---

*Skelton's motion picture popularity was decidedly on the wane by the time of *The Clown,* and the spotty production values and release pattern of the picture attest to this.

†Jane recalls: "Everyone under contract to 20th in *Palms* was dropped from contract. Mitzi, Bill Lundigan, etc. Zanuck was very small and unreasonable.

"Since I was not under contract, this did not affect my career, except for the film itself."

attention among the women-hungry GIs. Obligingly, she dons baggy Army fatigues, horn-rimmed glasses, a sensible hairdo, and no makeup. Big deal! To television-diverted America, *Down among the Sheltering Palms* was no more impressive than Paramount's equally silly and very similar effort, *Girls of Pleasure Island*, released earlier that year.

Jane was very dissatisfied with her year-long stay at MGM, where she was offered (and rejected) more mediocre assignments than she cares to remember. Very quietly she negotiated her release from Metro and was thereafter off the screen for three years, during which time she gave birth to a third son, Steven, born on Mother's Day (May 9), 1954, at Cedars of Lebanon Hospital.

When she did return to moviemaking, it was as a freelance player in United Artists' *Run for the Sun* (1956), produced by Jane Russell's husband, Robert Waterfield. When asked what prompted her cinema "comeback," Jane casually replied: "I like the role of being a mother and a wife very much. But it got to be sort of monotonous. But more importantly, I began thinking of myself as a typical drab housewife. I decided to do something about it and here I am."

As the third-billed Katy Connors in *Run for the Sun*, Jane offered one of her most satisfying screen characterizations to date. She portrayed the intelligent magazine writer sent to Mexico to ferret out why adventurer-writer Richard Widmark has suddenly stopped his output of writing. She tracks the author down in his out-of-the-way retreat and learns the blunt truth. When he lost his wife, he substituted blue jeans and drink for ambition and allowed his literary prowess to vegetate. Insisting he is a lost cause, he has enough gentlemanly qualities left to offer to fly Jane back to Mexico City in his small aircraft. On the way a magnetized notebook in her pocketbook throws the plane's compass off center and the craft crashes into the jungle. They find themselves at the warped mercy of Nazi war criminal Peter Van Eyck and his sadistic henchmen, who regard the unwanted intruders as suitable material for a refreshing manhunt. Sound familiar? Richard Connell's story "The Most Dangerous Game" had been filmed at least twice before (in 1932 with Joel McCrea and in 1946 as *Game of Death* with John Loder). Dudley Nichols's generally taut screenplay occasionally went banal, as when Widmark and Jane are facing doom at an abandoned church.

Widmark: "Our luck's run out. I'm sorry."

Jane: "I don't care, as long as it happens to both of us."

Variety's reviewer performed a bit of justified proselytizing when he editorialized: "It should be noted that Miss Greer should do more films; she has the needed looks and ability."

The following year Jane was cast in the most prestigious film of her entire career. *Man of a Thousand Faces* (Universal, 1957) starred James Cagney in a loosely constructed rendering of Lon Chaney's life story, filmed in black and white. Cagney himself requested Jane for the role of the second Mrs. Chaney, a former showgirl who is a paragon of virtue and understanding, filled with all the standard cinema devotion and sentiment. Jane's blandly conceived part

832

gave her little material with which to work, leading the *New Yorker* magazine to decide that she was "pretty enough but about as appetizing as a cake of soap." It was Dorothy Malone, still riding the crest of her Oscar win for *Written on the Wind* (1956), who had the juicy assignment of portraying the first Mrs. Chaney, a neurotic miss who sacrifices Chaney and their son to resume her freewheeling stage career only to later perversely swallow a vial of acid to destroy her voice. Since *Man of a Thousand Faces* was labeled Universal's Fiftieth Anniversary Salute Picture, a big hoopla was accorded the biopic when it debuted at the Palace Theatre on August 13, 1957, with Cagney, Jane, and Robert Evans (who portrayed Irving Thalberg in the picture) on hand to trumpet the merits of this screen biography.

Despite her essentially tough, resilient screen image, there were phases of show business that frightened Jane. She was terrified at the thought of performing in front of live audiences, and never once considered the possibility of participating in stage plays. As for radio, she had one horrendous experience. While at RKO she was assigned to co-star on "Lux Radio Theatre" with Tyrone Power and David Niven in *The Bishop's Wife* (CBS, December 19, 1949). Jane can still vividly recall the petrifying experience. "My pages shook so, they pasted each page of my script to cardboard. The script was then about three feet high on the stage beside me. . . . I would grab a hunk of pages from the pile. Very funny sight to the audience." But television was a different story since it was prepared much the same as motion pictures, only with less fuss. Jane made her small-screen debut on "Ford Theatre" in the episode *Look for Tomorrow* (NBC, May 15, 1953) in which she played a young singer in love with her voice coach (William Ching). With her debut behind her, Jane returned to the medium that fall in "Mirror Theatre" in an episode entitled *Summer Dance* (CBS, November 21, 1953), a simply constructed but effective yarn of a young woman (Jane) who learns that her sister (Barbara Bates) loves the same man she had romanced years before. One of her more effective performances was on an anthology show episode called "One Man Missing" (NBC, June 9, 1955) in which she, Audrey Totter, Ellen Drew, and Helen Wallace were four wives assembled in a mountain lodge to await news of their husbands, who had been involved in a plane crash.*

More often than not, Jane was wasted in western series episodes,† providing sturdy performances that led her now sporadic career nowhere. Occasionally there would be an offbeat job such as in *Portrait without a Face* on "Thriller" (NBC, December 25, 1961). The program itself was of low caliber and as preposterous as a poverty row melodrama of the 1940s. Nevertheless, Jane was dignified and lovely as the widow of a murdered painter (John Newland, also the director). Her last video performance to date was a brief cameo on the detective series "Burke's Law" (ABC, April 17, 1964).‡

*Very similar in plot to *Three Secrets* (Warner Bros., 1950).
†E.g., "Zane Grey Theatre," "The Westerner," "Bonanza," and "Stagecoach West."
‡Jane made one television commercial in the early 1960s, for Clairol. ("That was a favor to a friend. However, the money wasn't bad.")

If any year can be called an off-year for Jane, it was 1963. She and Edward Lasker divorced on November 6 in Juarez, Mexico, not too long after she underwent a heart operation.* To get her back into the professional swing of things, Frank London, casting director for Edward Dmytryk, suggested her for a role in Dmytryk's *Where Love Has Gone* (Paramount, 1964). "Although I was terribly weak and underweight, the experience was good for me," says Jane, "and I am grateful for the chance."

As most everyone knows, *Where Love Has Gone* derives from Harold Robbin's exploitative novel, a not even thinly veiled rendering of the sordid details involved in the Lana Turner-Cheryl Crane-Johnny Stompanato love-homicide triangle. Despite the onscreen presence of vituperative Bette Davis (as the domineering matriarch) and explosive Susan Hayward (her self-destructive, sculptress daughter), the garish color feature was bogged down by John Michael Hayes's script, which "manages to make every dramatic line . . . sound like a caption to a *New Yorker* cartoon" (*Saturday Review*). Judith Crist of the *New York Herald-Tribune* was in a quandary, unable to "decide whether to laugh or throw up." A listless Jane was fifth-billed as Marian Spicer, the understanding juvenile-division probation officer of Joey Heatherton (Hayward's sexually precocious teenager). Jane's few scenes and snatches of dialog went generally unnoticed by the public. *Variety*, kind as always, reported Jane to be "beautiful and excellent" in the film.

When producer-actor Peter Lawford fashioned a moderately successful Broadway domestic comedy, *Time Out for Ginger,* into *Billie* (United Artists, 1965), a musical-feature vehicle for Patty Duke, Jane was signed to portray the wife of Jim Backus and the mother of tomboyish Duke. Most of the film's inconsequential goings-on were devoted to Duke's adeptness as a high school track-and-field star (she feels the rhythm of sprinting) who consistently outdistances her male competitors on the track but not in the social arena. More than one level-headed film critic thought Duke's character was more in need of a psychiatrist than track coaching. Jane was relegated to the screen sidelines, occasionally used to bolster her husband's courage in his mayoral campaign against Billy De Wolfe, or counseling her elder daughter (Susan Seaforth), who has secretly married Ted Bessell and is now embarrassingly pregnant. Jane's presence was an asset to the color picture, as the critics agreed ("bears up very nicely under the burden" [*New York Morning Telegraph*]; "comes off best" [*New York Herald-Tribune*]).

Since then Jane has been content to remain professionally inactive, satisfied to be just a mother.† She makes recordings for the blind, participates in charity work (Share, Inc., in particular), and enjoys painting. She has no great interest in reviving her career, reasoning: "It was great fun and satisfaction

---

* In March, 1963, the pericardium (the sac around the heart) was removed. It took over a year for Jane to fully recuperate.

† Her children are well on the way to professional maturity. Albert is a graduate of the UCLA film school and is planning on a career in film directing; Lawrence has completed Yale College, where he was a journalism major; and Steven entered UCLA in the fall of 1972.

in my youth. I have no ambitions now. No regrets." On the other hand, Jane still attends film screenings at the Academy of Motion Picture Arts and Sciences in Hollywood. She admits that she maintains more than a general filmgoer's interest in the medium: "It is a very exciting time for films. Much more can be shown of reality than in former years."

Up until March, 1973, Jane had been categorized by the film industry as semiretired; then out of the blue she accepted a role in MGM's *The Outfit*, produced by Carter De Haven, Jr., and starring Robert Duvall, Karen Black, and Joe Don Baker. The film deals with a professional bankrobber who declares war on organized crime to avenge the murder of his brother. Still maintaining a solid perspective on her career, life, and the world, Jane nonchalantly announced to the press that this latest role was not a comeback, but just a return to professional chores. From a note the actress sent this author re her recent screen casting, the private, chipper Jane Greer is actually quite delighted to be back in front of the cameras, doing what she knows best— entertaining the public with her well-modulated talents.

Feature Film Appearances
JANE GREER

As Bettejane Greer:

TWO O'CLOCK COURAGE   (RKO, 1945) 66 M.

Producer, Ben Stoloff; director, Anthony Mann; story, Gelett Burgess; screenplay, Robert E. Kent; art director, Albert S. D'Agostino, L. O. Croxton; music, Roy Webb; special effects, Vernon L. Walker; camera, Jack Mackenzie; editor, Philip Martin, Jr.

Tom Conway (The Man); Ann Rutherford (Patty); Richard Lane (Haley); Lester Mathews (Mark Evans); Roland Drew (Maitland); Emory Parnell (Brenner); Bettejane Greer (Helen); Jean Brooks (Barbara); Edmund Glover (O'Brien); Bryant Washburn (Dilling); Philip Morris (McCord); Nancy Marlow (Hat-Check Girl); Elaine Riley (Cigarette Girl); Jack Norton (Drunk); Guy Zanett (Headwaiter); Harold de Becker (Judson); Bob Alden (Newsboy); Chester Clute (Mr. Daniels); Almira Sessions (Mrs. Daniels); Eddie Dunn, Bob Robinson (Cops); Charles Wilson (Brant); Sarah Edwards (Mrs. Tuttle); Maxine Seamon (Maid); Chris Drake (Assistant Editor); Carl Kent (Dave Rennick).

PAN-AMERICANA   (RKO, 1945) 84 M.

Executive producer, Sid Rogell; producer-director, John H. Auer; story, Frederic Kohner, Auer; screenplay, Lawrence Kimble; music director, C. Bakaleinikoff; choreography, Charles O'Curran; songs, Mort Greene and Gabriel Ruiz; Bob Russell and Marguerita Lecuona; special effects, Vernon L. Walker; camera, Frank Redman; editor, Harry Marker.

Philip Terry (Dan); Audrey Long (Jo Anne); Robert Benchley (Charlie/Narrator); Eve Arden (Hoppy); Ernest Truex (Uncle Rudy); Marc Cramer (Jerry); Isabelita (Lupita); Rosario and Antonio, Miguelito Valdes, Harold and Lola, Louise Burnett, Chinita Marin, Chuy Castillion, Padilla Sisters, Chuy Reyes and His Orchestra, Nestor Amaral and His Samba Band (Themselves); Bill Garvin (Sancho); Frank Marasco (Miguel); Armando Gonzales (Carlos); Joan Beckstead (Miss Peru); Valerie Hall (Miss El Salvador); Luz Vasquez (Miss Mexico); Betty Joy Curtis (Miss Bolivia); Goya Del Valle (Miss Panama); Carmen Lopez (Miss Paraguay); Aldonna Gauvin (Miss Uruguay); Velera Burton (Miss Dutch Guiana); Ruth Lorran (Miss Honduras); Alma Beltran (Miss Guatemala); Nina Bara (Miss Argentina); Rita Corday, Patti Brill, Rosemary La Planche, Susan Walsh, Greta Christensen, Virginia Belmont (Pan American Girls); Shirley Karnes (Miss Dominican Republic); George Mendoza (Waiter); Bettejane Greer (Miss Downing); Mary Halsey (Switchboard Operator); Nancy Marlowe (Pretty Office Girl); Elaine Riley (Girl); Francis Revel, David Cota (Waiters); Hugh Hendrikson (Juan); Fernando Ramos (Jose); Leif Argo (Pedro); Albano Valerio (Mexican Ambassador); Tom Costello (Brazilian Ambassador); Douglas Madore, Boots Le Baron (Boys); Evita Lopez (Mexican Flower Girl); Julian Rivero (Pablo); Jesus Castillion (Specialty).

GEORGE WHITE'S SCANDALS (RKO, 1945) 95 M.

Producer, Jack J. Gross, Nat Holt, George White; director, Felix E. Feist; story, Hugh Wedlock, Howard Snyder; screenplay, Wedlock, Snyder, Parke Levy, Howard Green; choreography, Ernest Matray; music director, C. Bakaleinikoff; songs, Jack Yellen and Sammy Fain; B. G. De Sylva; Lew Brown and Ray Henderson; Tommy Peterson and Gene Krupa; art director, Albert S. D'Agostino, Ralph Berger; special effects, Vernon L. Walker; camera, Robert de Grasse; editor, Joseph Noriega.

Joan Davis (Joan Mason); Jack Haley (Jack Williams); Phillip Terry (Tom McGrath); Martha Holliday (Jill Martin); Ethel Smith (Swing Organist); Margaret Hamilton (Clarabelle); Glenn Tryon (George White); Bettejane Greer (Billie Randall); Audrey Young (Maxine Manners); Rose Murphy (Hilda); Fritz Feld (Montescu); Beverly Wills (Joan—as a child); Gene Krupa and His Band (Themselves); Rufe Davis (Impersonations); Wesley Brent, Grace Young, Lorraine Clark, Diana Mumby, Linda Claire, Susanne Rosser, Marilyn Buford, Marie McCardle, Vivian Mason, Vivian McCoy, Virginia Belmont, Rusty Farrell, Nan Leslie, Chili Williams, June Frazer, Virginia Cruzon, Annelle Hayes, Joy Barlow, Barbara Thorson, Ruth Hall, Ethelreda Leopold, Alice Eyland, Linda Ennis, Lucy Cochrane, Zas Varka (Showgirls); Frank Mitchell, Lyle Latell (Ladder Gag); Effie Laird, Hope Landin (Scrubwomen); Shelby Bacon, Edwin Davis, Edwin Johnson, John Stanley, Allen Cooke, Eric Freeman, Vonn Hamilton, Walter Stone (Dancers); Carmel Myers (Leslie); Ed O'Neil (John the Baptist); Neely Edwards (Lord Quimby); Dorothy Christy (Lady Asbury); Holmes Herbert (Lord Asbury); Harry Monty, Buster Brodie (Box Gag); Betty Farrington (Buxom Woman); Harold Minjur (Hotel Clerk); Rosalie Ray (Chorus Dame); Tom Noonan (Joe); Edmund Glover (Production Man); Nino Tempo (Drummer); Sammy Blum (Cafe Proprietor); Larry Wheat (Pop).

As Jane Greer:

DICK TRACY (RKO, 1945) 61 M.

Executive producer, Sid Rogell; producer, Herman Schlom; director, William Berke; based on the cartoon strip by Chester Gould; screenplay, Eric Taylor; music director, C. Bakaleinikoff; music, Roy Webb; art director, Albert S. D'Agostino, Ralph Berger; set decorator, Darrell Silvera, Jean L. Speak; assistant director, Clem Beauchamp; sound, Jean L. Speak, Terry Kellum; camera, Frank Redman; editor, Ernie Leadley.

Morgan Conway (Dick Tracy); Anne Jeffreys (Tess Trueheart); Mike Mazurki (Splitface); Jane Greer (Judith Owens); Lyle Latell (Pat Patton); Joseph Crehan (Chief Brandon); Mickey Kuhn (Tracy, Jr.); Trevor Bardette (Professor Lynwood P. Starling); Morgan Wallace (Steven Owens); Milton Parsons (Deathridge); William Halligan (Mayor); Edythe Elliott (Mrs. Caraway); Mary Currier (Dorothy Stafford); Ralph Dunn (Detective Manning); Edmund Glover (Radio Announcer); Bruce Edwards (Sergeant); Tanis Chandler (Miss Stanley); Jimmy Jordan, Carl Hanson (Pedestrians); Franklyn Farnum (Bystander at Murder); Jack Gargan, Sam Ash, Carl Faulkner, Frank Meredith, Bob Reeves (Cops); Tom Noonan (Johnny Moko); Harry Strang, George Magrill (Detectives); Robert Douglass (Busboy); Alphonse Martell (Jules, the Waiter); Gertrude Astor (Woman); Jack Chefe (Headwaiter); Florence Pepper (Girl); Wilbur Mack, Jason Robards, Sr. (Motorists).

THE FALCON'S ALIBI (RKO, 1946) 62 M.

Executive producer, Sid Rogell; producer, William Berke; director, Ray McCarey; based on the character created by Michael Arlen; story, Dane Lussier, Manny Seff; screenplay, Paul Yawitz; assistant director, James Anderson; dialog director, Madeleine Dmytryk; art director, Albert S. D'Agostino, Lucius Croxton; set decorator,

Darrell Silvera; sound, Francis M. Sarver, Terry Kellum; music director, C. Bakaleinikoff; camera, Frank Redman; editor, Philip Martin, Jr.

Tom Conway (The Falcon); Rita Corday (Joan Meredith); Vince Barnett (Goldie Locke); Jane Greer (Lola Carpenter); Elisha Cook, Jr. (Nick); Emory Parnell (Metcalf); Al Bridge (Inspector Blake); Esther Howard (Gloria Peabody); Jean Brooks (Baroness Lena); Paul Brinkman (Alex Olmstead); Jason Robards, Sr. (Harvey Beaumont); Morgan Wallace (Bender); Lucien Prival (Baron); Edmund Cobb (Detective Williams); Betty Gillette (Elevator Operator); Forbes Murray (Mr. Thompson); Alphonse Martel (Louie); Edward Clark (Coroner); Bonnie Blair (Telephone Operator); Myrna Dell (Girl with Falcon); Nan Leslie (Girl); Bob Alden (Bellhop); Joe La Barba, Eddie Borden (Men); Mike Lally, Jack Stoney (Thugs); George Holmes (Man); Harry Harvey (Race Fan); Alf Haugen (Doorman).

THE BAMBOO BLONDE   (RKO, 1946) 67 M.

Executive producer, Sid Rogell; producer, Herman Schlom; director, Anthony Mann; based upon the story "Chicago Lulu" by Wayne Whittaker; screenplay, Olive Cooper, Lawrence Kimble; art director, Albert S. D'Agostino, Lucius Croxton; set decorator, Darrell Silvera; sound, Jean L. Speak, Earl B. Mounce; assistant director, James Casey; choreography, Charles O'Curran; songs, Mort Greene and Lew Pollack; music director, C. Bakaleinikoff; vocal arranger, Robert Keithe; special effects, Vernon L. Walker; camera, Frank Redman; editor, Les Milbrook.

Frances Langford (Louise Anderson); Ralph Edwards (Eddie Clark); Russell Wade (Patrick Ransom, Jr.); Iris Adrian (Montana); Richard Martin (Jim Wilson); Jane Greer (Eileen Sawyer); Glenn Vernon (Shorty Parker); Paul Harvey (Patrick Ransom, Sr.); Regina Wallace (Mrs. Ransom); Jean Brooks (Marsha); Tom Noonan (Art Department); Dorothy Vaughan (Mom); Larry Wheat (Pop); Eddie Acuff, Steve Barclay (MP's); Jason Robards, Sr. (Colonel Graham); Jimmy Jordan (Larry); Robert Manning (Ollie); Robert Clarke (Jonesy); Al Martini, Don Evers (Crew Members); James Leahy (Top Gunner); Bruce Edwards (Lieutenant); Paul Brinkman (Jackie); Betty Gillette (Maid); Harry Harvey (Airport Clerk); Mary Worth (Mrs. Sawyer); Don Davis (Boy); Jean Andren (Woman); Frances Ring (Girl); Alexander Pollard (Butler); Nan Leslie (Bit in Train); Bob Randall (Soldier); Lou Short (Baldheaded Man); Eric Mayne (Bearded Man); Herbert Evans (Sour-faced Man); Walter Reed (Montgomery); Vonne Lester (Secretary); Carl Hanson, Jack Arkin (Photographers); Lee Elson, Dennis Waters, Bonnie Blair (Bits).

SUNSET PASS   (RKO, 1946) 58 M.

Executive producer, Sid Rogell; producer, Herman Schlom; director, William Berke; based on the novel by Zane Grey; screenplay, Norman Houston; art director, Albert S. D'Agostino, Lucius Croxton; set decorator, Darrell Silvera, William Stevens; sound, Jean L. Speak, Roy Granville; assistant director, Doran Cox; music, Paul Sawtell; music director, C. Bakaleinikoff; camera, Frank Redman; editor, Samuel E. Beetley.

James Warren (Rocky); Nan Leslie (Jane); John Laurenz (Chito); Jane Greer (Helen); Robert Barrat (Curtis); Harry Woods (Cinnabar); Robert Clarke (Ash); Steve Brodie (Slagle); Harry Harvey (Doab); Slim Balch, Roy Bucko, Steve Stevens, George Plues, Clem Fuller, Bob Dyer, Artie Ortego, Buck Bucko (Posse Men); Slim Hightower, Boyd Stockman, Glen McCarthy (Robbers); Carl Faulkner (Passenger); Frank O'Connor (Station Agent); Florence Pepper, Vonne Lester (Dancers); Robert Bray, Dennis Waters (Bank Clerks); Maria Dodd, Dorothy Curtiss (Women at Station).

SINBAD THE SAILOR   (RKO, 1947) C—116 M.

Producer, Stephen Ames; director, Richard Wallace; story, John Twist, George Worthington Yates; screenplay, Twist; assistant director, Lloyd Richards; Marine technical director, Capt. Fred F. Ellis; art director, Albert S. D'Agostino, Carroll Clark; set decorator, Darrell Silvera, Claude Carpenter; music, Roy Webb; sound, John E. Tribby, Clem Portman; special effects, Vernon L. Walker, Harold Wellman; camera, George Barnes; editor, Sherman Todd, Frank Toyle.

Douglas Fairbanks, Jr. (Sinbad); Maureen O'Hara (Shireen); Walter Slezak (Melik); Anthony Quinn (Emir); George Tobias (Abbu); Jane Greer (Pirouze); Mike Mazurki (Yusuf); Sheldon Leonard (Auctioneer); Alan Napier (Aga); John Miljan (Moga); Barry Mitchell (Maullin).

THEY WON'T BELIEVE ME   (RKO, 1947) 95 M.

Executive producer, Jack J. Gross; producer, Joan Harrison; director, Irving Pichel; story, Gordon McDonnell; screenplay, Jonathan Latimer; art director, Albert S. D'Agostino, Robert Boyle; set decorator, Darrell Silvera, William Maginetti; music, Roy Webb; music director, C. Bakaleinikoff; sound, John Tribby, Clem Portman; assistant director, Harry D'Arcy; special effects, Russell A. Cully; camera, Harry J. Wild; editor, Elmo Williams.

Robert Young (Larry); Susan Hayward (Verna); Jane Greer (Janice); Rita Johnson (Gretta); Tom Powers (Trenton); George Tyne (Lieutenant Carr); Don Beddoe (Thomason); Frank Ferguson (Cahill); Harry Harvey (Judge Fletcher); Wilton Graff (Patrick Gold); Janet Shaw (Susan Haines); Glen Knight (Parking Lot Attendant); Anthony Caruso (Tough Patient); George Sherwood (Highway Cop); Perc Launders (Police Stenographer); Byron Foulger (Mortician); Hector Sarno (Nick); Carl Kent (Chauffeur); Lee Frederick (Detective); Jean Andren (Maid); Paul Maxey (Mr. Bowman); Herbert Heywood (Sheriff); Elena Warren (Mrs. Bowman); Lillian Bronson (Mrs. Hines); Martin Wilkins (Sailor); Dot Farley (Emma); Milton Parsons (Court Clerk); Lee Phelps (Bailiff); Frank Pharr (Patrick Collins); Ellen Corby (Screaming Woman); Matthew McHugh (Tiny Old Man); Bob Pepper (Officer Guarding Larry); Ira Buck Woods (Waiter); Irene Tedrow (Woman); Berta Ledbetter (Untidy Woman); Lida Durova (Girl at Newsstand); Bob Thom (Hotel Clerk); Ivan Browning, Jack Gargan (Bartenders); Madam Borget (Mrs. Roberts); Harry Strang (Rancher); Bud Wolfe (Driver); Sol Gorss (Gus); Lovyss Bradley (Miss Jorday); Harry D'Arcy (Fisherman); Jack Rice (Tour Conductor); Netta Packer (Spinster).

OUT OF THE PAST   (RKO, 1947) 97 M.

Executive producer, Robert Sparks; producer, Warren Duff; director, Jacques Tourneur; based on the novel *Build My Gallows High* by Geoffrey Homes; screenplay, Homes; music, Roy Webb; music director, C. Bakaleinikoff; assistant director, Harry Mancke; sound, Francis M. Sarver, Clem Portman; art director, Albert D'Agostino, Jack Okey; set decorator, Darrell Silvera; special effects, Russell A. Cully; camera, Nicholas Musuraca; editor, Samuel E. Beetley.

Robert Mitchum (Jeff Bailey); Jane Greer (Kathie Moffett); Kirk Douglas (Whit); Rhonda Fleming (Meta Carson); Richard Webb (Jim); Steve Brodie (Fisher); Virginia Huston (Ann); Paul Valentine (Joe); Dickie Moore (The Kid); Ken Niles (Eels); Lee Elson (Cop); Frank Wilcox (Sheriff Douglas); Jose Portugal, Euminio Blanco, Vic Romito (Mexican Waiters); Jess Escobar (Mexican Doorman); Primo Lopez (Mexican Bellhop); Tony Roux (Joe Rodriguez); Sam Warren (Waiter—Harlem Club); Mildred Boy, Ted Collins (People at Harlem Club); Caleb Peterson (Man with Eunice); Theresa Harris (Eunice); James Bush (Doorman); John Kellogg (Baylord); Oliver Blake (Tillotson); Wallace Scott (Petey); Michael Branden (Rafferty); William Van Vleck (Cigar-Store Clerk); Phillip Morris (Porter); Charles Regan (Mystery Man); Harry Hayden (Canby Miller); Adda Gleason (Mrs. Miller); Manuel Paris (Croupier).

STATION WEST (RKO, 1948) 91 M.

Executive producer, Dore Schary; producer, Robert Sparks; director, Sidney Lanfield; based on the novel by Luke Short; screenplay, Frank Fenton, Winston Miller; art director, Albert S. D'Agostino, Feild Gray; set decorator, Darrell Silvera, James Altwies; music, Heinz Roemheld; music director, C. Bakaleinikoff; songs, Mort Greene and Leigh Harline; sound, Frank Sarver, Terry Kellum; assistant director, Max Henry; makeup, Gordon Bau; costumes, Renie; special effects, Russell A. Cully; camera, Harry J. Wild; editor, Frederic Knudtson.

Dick Powell (Haven); Jane Greer (Charlie); Agnes Moorehead (Mrs. Caslon); Burl Ives (Hotel Clerk); Tom Powers (Captain Iles); Gordon Oliver (Prince); Steve Brodie (Stallman); Guinn "Big Boy" Williams (Mick); Raymond Burr (Mark Bristow); Regis Toomey (Goddard); Olin Howlin (Cook); John Berkes (Pianist); Michael Steele (Whitey); Dan White (Pete); John Kellogg (Ben); John Doucette (Bartender); Charles Middleton (Sheriff); Suzi Crandall (Girl); Al Hill (Croupier); Jack Stoney, Stanley Blystone (Bouncers); Joey Ray (Stickman); Marie Thomas (Dance-Hall Girl); Robert Gates (Sam); Robert Jefferson (Boy); Leo McMahon (Rider); William Phipps (Sergeant); Bud Osborne, Ethan Laidlaw, Monte Montague, Lomax Study (Men).

THE BIG STEAL (RKO, 1949) 71 M.

Executive producer, Sid Rogell; producer, Jack L. Gross; director, Don Siegel; based on the story "The Road to Carmichael's" by Richard Wormser; screenplay, Geoffrey Homes, Gerald Drayson Adams; music, Leigh Harline; music director, C. Bakaleinikoff; art director, Albert D'Agostino, Ralph Berger; set decorator, Darrell Silvera, Harley Miller; costumes, Edward Stevenson; makeup, Gordon Bau, Robert Cowan; assistant director, Sam Ruman; camera, Harry J. Wild; editor, Samuel E. Beetley.

Robert Mitchum (Duke); Jane Greer (Joan); William Bendix (Blake); Patric Knowles (Fiske); Ramon Novarro (Colonel Ortega); Don Alvarado (Lieutenant Ruiz); John Qualen (Seton); Pasqual Garcia Pena (Manuel); Henry Carr, Jose Logan, Primo Lopez (Bellhops); Alfonso Dubois (Police Sergeant); Frank Hagney (Madden); Ted Jacques (Cole); Virginia Farmer, Carmen Morales, Lillian O'Malley (Women); Edward Colebrook (Mexican Tourist); Paul Castellanos, Dimas Sotello, Frank Leyva, Elios Gamboa, Juan Duval (Vendors); Rodolfo Hoyos (Custom Inspector); Salvador Baguez (Morales); Arturo Soto Rangel (Pedro); Beatriz Ramos (Carmencita); Tony Roux (Parrot Vendor); Felipe Turich (Guitar Vendor); Nacho Galindo (Pastry Vendor); Carl Sklover, Bing Conley (Dockhands); Gregorio Acosta (Chaney); Alfred Soto (Gonzales); Paul Guerrero (Pepe); Juan Varro (Gonzales); Carlos Reyes (Taxi Driver); Alphonse Sanchez Tello (Basquez).

THE COMPANY SHE KEEPS (RKO, 1951) 81 M.

Producer, John Houseman; director, John Cromwell; story-screenplay, Ketti Frings; art director, Albert S. D'Agostino, Alfred Herman; music director, C. Bakaleinikoff; camera, Nicholas Musuraca; editor, William Swink.

Lizabeth Scott (Joan); Jane Greer (Diane); Dennis O'Keefe (Larry); Fay Baker (Tilly); John Hoyt (Judge Kendall); James Bell (Mr. Neeley); Don Beddoe (Jamieson); Bert Freed (Smith); Irene Tedrow (Mrs. Seeley); Marjorie Wood (Mrs. Haley); Marjorie Crossland (Mrs. Griggs); Virginia Farmer (Mrs. Harris); Parley Baer (Steve); Dick Ryan (Waiter); Harry Cheshire (Cliff Martin); Jasper Weldon (Redcap); Jack Gargan (Hospital Attendant); Kathleen Freeman (Jessie); Geraldine Carr (Rita); Helen Brown (Helen Johnson); Eileene Stevens (Bess Kreiger); Charles Wagenheim (Pete); Frances Driver (Rosabelle); Jane Crowley (May); Royce Milne (Girl); Jerry Mullins (Boy); Gail Bonney (Nurse); Sally Corner (Patient); Don Greer (Fred); Kenneth Tobey (Rex); David Clarke (Barkley); Paul Lees (Kendall's Secretary); Gerald Pierce (Office Boy); Claudia Constant (Peggy); Torben Meyer (Waiter in Restaurant); Charles McAvoy (Counterman); Kate Lawson (Mrs. Spencer); Dewey Robinson (Sergeant); William Ruhl (Joe); Barry Rooks (Cop Outside); Victoria Horne (Marcia); Maria Costi (Laura); Theresa Harris (Lilly); Adrienne Marden (Amy); Virginia Vincent (Annabelle); Hilda Plowright, Don Dillaway (Victims); June Benbow (Myrtle); Forrest Dickson, Alyn Lockwood (Policewomen); Eric Alden (Sergeant of Detectives); Larry Barton (Store Detective); George Volk, Peter Michaels (Detectives); Edith Evanson (Miss Holman); Jeff Bridges (Baby at Station); Beau Bridges (Boy at Station); Lela Bliss, Virginia Mullen (Women Shoppers); Frances Morris (Mrs. McLean); Elizabeth Flournoy (Mrs. May); Gertrude Hoffman (Miss Kaufman); Erskine Sanford (Professor); Fred Hoose (Ticket Agent).

YOU'RE IN THE NAVY NOW   (20th, 1951) 93 M.

Producer, Fred Kohlmar; director, Henry Hathaway; based on article by John W. Hazard; screenplay, Richard Murphy; art director, Lyle Wheeler, J. Russell Spencer; set decorator, Thomas Little, Fred J. Rode; costumes, Charles Le Maire; music director, Lionel Newman; technical advisor, Joseph Warren Lomax, U.S.N.; makeup, Ben Nye; music, Cyril Mockridge; special camera effects, Fred Sersen, Ray Kellogg; sound, W. D. Flick, Roger Heman; camera, Joe MacDonald; editor, James B. Clark.

Gary Cooper (Lt. John Harkness); Jane Greer (Ellie); Millard Mitchell (Larrabee); Eddie Albert (Lt. Bill Barron); John McIntire (Commander Reynolds); Ray Collins (Admiral Tennant); Harry Von Zell (Captain Eliot); Jack Webb (Ens. Anthony Barbo); Richard Erdman (Ens. Chuck Dorrance); Harvey Lembeck (Norelli); Henry Slate (Ryan—Chief Engineer); Ed Begley (Commander); Fay Roope (Battleship Admiral); Charles Tannen (Houlihan); Charles Bronson (Wascylewski); Jack Warden (Morse); Ken Harvey, Lee Marvin, Jerry Hausner, Charles Smith (Crew Members); James Cornell (New Sailor); Glen Gordon, Laurence Hugo (Shore Patrolmen); Damian O'Flynn (Doctor); Biff McGuire (Sailor Messenger); Norman McKay (Admiral's Aide); John McGuire (Naval Commander); Elsa Peterson (Admiral's Wife); Herman Cantor (Naval Captain); Joel Fluellen (Mess Boy); William Lester (C.P.O.); Ted Stanhope (Naval Officer); Rory Mallinson (Lieutenant Commander).

YOU FOR ME   (MGM, 1952) 70 M.

Producer, Henry Berman; director, Don Weis; story-screenplay, William Roberts; art director, Cedric Gibbons, Eddie Imazu; set decorator, Edwin B. Willis, Alfred A. Spencer; music supervisor, Alberto Colombo; camera, Paul C. Vogel; editor, Newell P. Kimlin.

Peter Lawford (Tony Brown); Jane Greer (Katie McDermad); Gig Young (Dr. Jeff Chadwick); Paula Corday (Lucille Brown); Howard Wendell (Oliver Wherry); Otto Hulett (Hugo McDermad); Barbara Brown (Edna McDermad); Barbara Ruick (Ann Elcott); Kathryn Card (Nurse Vogel); Tommy Farrell (Rollie Cobb); Paul Smith (Frank Elcott); Helen Winston (Flora Adams); Elaine Stewart (Girl in Club Car); Perry Sheehan (Nurse); Stephen Chase (Bretherton); Ned Glass (Harlow Douglas); Nikki Justin (Maid); Martha Wentworth (Lucille's Mother); Jerry Hausner (Patient); John Rosser (Brill); John Close, Robert Smiley (Cops); Ivan Browning (Pullman Porter); Hal Smith (Malcolm); Alvy Moore (Friend); Ralph Grosh (Photographer); Joann Arnold, Diann James, Marjorie Jackson, Kathy Qualen (Nurses); Tommy Walker (Elevator Operator); Alan Harris (Court Clerk); Julia Dean (Aunt Clara).

THE PRISONER OF ZENDA   (MGM, 1952) C—101 M.

Producer, Pandro S. Berman; director, Richard Thorpe; based on the novel by Anthony Hope and the dramatization by Edward Rose; adaptation, Wells Root;

screenplay, John Balderstone, Noel Langley; music, Alfred Newman; art director, Cedric Gibbons, Hans Peter; sound, Douglas Shearer; set decorator, Edwin B. Willis, Richard Pefferie; assistant director, Sid Sidman; makeup, William Tuttle; costumes, Walter Plunkett; special effects, Warren Newcombe; camera, Joseph Ruttenberg; editor, George Boemler.

Stewart Granger (Rudolf Rassendyll/King Rudolf V); Deborah Kerr (Princess Flavia); Louis Calhern (Colonel Zapt); Jane Greer (Antoinette de Mauban); Lewis Stone (Cardinal); Robert Douglas (Michael, Duke of Strelsau); Robert Coote (Fritz von Tarlenheim); Peter Brocco (Johann); Francis Pierlot (Josef); James Mason (Rupert of Hentzau); Tom Brown (Henry Detchard); Eric Alden (Krafstein); Stephen Roberts (Lauengram); Bud Wolfe (Bersonin); Peter Mamakos (DeGautet); Joe Mell (R. R. Guard); Peter Votrian (Newsboy); Elizabeth Slifer (Woman); Alex Pope (Husband); Mary Carroll (German Wife); Jay Adler (Passport Official); Michael Vallen (Assistant Passport Official); George Slocum (Sandwich Vendor); Charles Watts (Porter); Kathleen Freeman (Gertrude); Bruce Payne (Court Chamberlain); Alphonse Martell, Manuel Paris (Noblemen); Forbes Murray (Nobleman with Cardinal); John Goldworthy (Archbishop); Guy Bellis (Lord Chamberlain); Frank Elliott, Gordon Richards (Dignitaries); Stanley Logan (British Ambassador); Doris Lloyd (Ambassador's Wife); Emilie Cabanne (Lady with Cardinal); Hugh Prosser, George Lewis (Uhlan Guards); Paul Marion (Guard); William Hazel, Victor Romito (Aides).

DESPERATE SEARCH   (MGM, 1952) 73 M.

Producer, Mathew Rapf; director, Joseph Lewis; based on the novel by Arthur Mayse; screenplay, Walter Doniger; assistant director, Joel Freeman; art director, Cedric Gibbons, Eddie Imazu; music director, Rudolph G. Kopp; sound, Douglas Shearer; set decorator, Edwin B. Willis, Ralph Hurst; special effects, A. Arnold Gillespie, Warren Newcombe; camera, Harold Lipstein; editor, Joseph Dervin.

Howard Keel (Vince Heldon); Jane Greer (Julie Heldon); Patricia Medina (Nora Stead); Keenan Wynn (Brandy); Robert Benton (Wayne Langmuir); Lee Aaker (Don); Linda Lowell (Janet); Michael Dugan (Lou); Elaine Steward (Stewardess); Jonathan Cott (Detective); Jeff Richards (Ed); Dick Simmons (Communicator).

THE CLOWN   (MGM, 1953) 92 M.

Producer, William H. Wright; director, Robert Z. Leonard; story, Frances Marion; adaptation, Leonard Praskins; screenplay, Martin Rackin; art director, Cedric Gibbons, Wade B. Rubottom; music, David Rose; camera, Paul Vogel; editor, Gene Ruggeiro.

Red Skelton (Dodo Delwyn); Jane Greer (Paula Henderson); Tim Considine (Dink Delwyn); Loring Smith (Goldie); Philip Ober (Ralph Z. Henderson); Lou Lubin (Little Julie); Fay Roope (Dr. Strauss); Walter Reed (Joe Hoagley); Edward Marr (Television Director); Jonathan Cott (Floor Director); Don Beddoe (Gallagher); Steve Forrest (Young Man); Ned Glass (Danny Dayler); Steve Carruthers (Maitre D'Hotel); Billy Barty (Midget); Lucille Knoch (Girl); David Saber (Silvio); Sandra Gould (Bunny); Gil Perkins (Dundee); Danny Richards, Jr. (Herman); Mickey Little (Lefty); Charles Calvert (Jackson); Karen Steele (Blonde); Jack Heasley, Bob Heasley (Twins); Helene Millard (Miss Battson); Forrest Lewis (Pawnbroker); Charles Bronson (Eddie); Robert Ford (Al Zerney); John McKee (Counterman); Jan Kayne, Vici Raaf (Women); Jesse Kirkpatrick (Sergeant); Martha Wentworth (Neighbor); Inge Jolles (Secretary); Harry Staton (Hogarth); Linda Bennett (Judy); Wilson Wood (Wardrobe Man); Frank Nelson (Charlie); Thomas Dillon (Clancy); Paul Raymond (Young Man); James Horan, Al Freeman (Men); Tom Urray (Vendor); Mary Foran (Heavy Girl); Sharon Saunders (Girl); David Blair (TV Page Boy); Brick Sullivan (Stagehand); Cy Stevens (Makeup Man); G. Pat Collins (Mr. Christenson); Shirley Mitchell (Mrs. Blotto); Robert R. Stephenson (Counterman); Jimmie Thompson, Allen O'Locklin, Tony Merrill (Ad-Libbers); Al Hill, Jerry Schumacher, Barry Regan (Dice Players); Lennie Bremen (George); Lee Phelps (Sergeant); Joe Evans, Walter Ridge, George Boyce, Donald Kerr, Mickey Golden (Attendants); Roger Moore (Man with Hogarth); Jules Brock, Eve Martell, Neva Martell (Dancers).

DOWN AMONG THE SHELTERING PALMS   (20th, 1953) C—86 M.

Producer, Fred Kohlmar; director, Edmund Goulding; based on the story "Paradise with Serpent" by Edward Hope; screenplay, Claude Binyon, Albert Lewis, Burt Styler; art director, Lyle Wheeler, Leland Fuller; songs, Harold Arlen and Ralph Blaine; music, Leigh Harline; choreography, Seymour Felix; makeup, Ben Nye; special camera effects, Fred Sersen; camera, Leon Shamroy; editor, Louis Loeffler.

William Lundigan (Capt. Bill Willoby); Jane Greer (Diana Forrester); Mitzi Gaynor (Rozouila); David Wayne (Lt. Carl G. Schmidt); Gloria DeHaven (Angela Toland); Gene Lockhart (Reverend Edgett); Jack Paar (Lt. Mike Sloan); Alvin Greenman (Corporal Kolta); Billy Gilbert (King Jilouili); Henry Kulky (First Lieutenant); Lyle Talbot (Major Curwin); Ray Montgomery (Lieutenant Everly); George Nader (Lt. Homer Briggs); Charles Tannen (Radio Operator); Claud Allister (Woolawei); Edith Evanson (Mrs Edgett); Fay Roope (Colonel Parker); David Ahdar (Witch Doctor); Sailofi Jerry Talo (Taomi); Clinton Bagwell (Aide to Colonel); Steve Wayne, Richard Grayson, John Baer (Officers); Jean Charney (Native Girl); Barncy Phillips (Murphy); Lee Marvin (Snively); Henry Slate (Thompson); Joe Turkel (Harris); David Wolfson, James Ogg, Ray Hyke, Roger McGee, Richard Monohan (GI's).

RUN FOR THE SUN   (UA, 1956) C—98 M.

Executive producer, Robert Waterfield; producer, Harry Tatelman; director, Roy Boulting; based on the story "The Most Dangerous Game" by Richard Connell; screenplay, Dudley Nichols, Boulting; art director, Al Y'Barra; music director, Frederick Steiner; songs, Steiner and Nestor Amaral; assistant director, Ed Killy, Bob Stillman; camera, Joseph LaShelle; editor, Fred Knudtson.

Richard Widmark (Mike Latimer); Trevor Howard (Browne); Jane Greer (Katy Connors); Peter Van Eyck (Van Anders); Carlos Henning (Jan); Juan Garcia (Fernandez); Margarito Luna (Hotel Proprietor); Jose Chavez Trowe (Pedro); Guillermo Talles (Paco); Enedina Diaz de Leon (Paco's Wife); Guilermo Bravo Sosa (Waiter).

MAN OF A THOUSAND FACES   (Univ., 1957) 122 M.

Producer, Robert Arthur; director, Joseph Pevney; story, Ralph Wheelwright; screenplay, Ivan Goff, R. Wright Campbell, Ben Roberts; art director, Alexander Golitzen, Eric Orbom; music, Frank Skinner; music director, Joseph Gershenson; assistant director, Phil Bowles; special effects, Clifford Stine; camera, Russell Metty; editor, Ted Kent.

James Cagney (Lon Chaney); Dorothy Malone (Cleva Creighton Chaney); Jane Greer (Hazel Bennct); Marjorie Rambeau (Gert); Jim Backus (Clarence Logan); Robert J. Evans (Irving Thalberg); Celia Lovsky (Mrs. Chaney); Jeanne Cagney (Carrie Chaney); Jack Albertson (Dr. J. Wilson Shields); Roger Smith (Creighton Chaney—at age 21); Robert Lyden (Creighton Chaney—at age 13); Rickie Sorensen (Creighton Chaney—at age 8); Dennis Rush (Creighton Chaney—at age 4); Nolan Leary (Pa Chaney); Simon Scott (Carl Hastings); Clarence Kolb (Himself); Danny Beck (Max Dill); Phil Van Zandt (George Loane Tucker); Hank Mann, Snub Pollard (Comedy Waiters).

WHERE LOVE HAS GONE   (Par., 1964) C—111 M.

Producer, Joseph E. Levine; director, Edward Dmytryk; based on the novel by Harold Robbins; screenplay, John Michael Hayes; assistant director, Michael Moore;

art director, Hal Pereira, Walter Tyler; set decorator, Sam Comer, Arthur Kram; music, Walter Scharf; song, Sammy Cahn and James Van Heusen; costumes, Edith Head; sound, John Carter, Charles Grenzbach; special effects, Paul L. Lerpae; process camera, Farciot Edouart; camera, Joseph MacDonald; editor, Frank Bracht.

Susan Hayward (Valerie Hayden); Bette Davis (Mrs. Gerald Hayden); Michael Connors (Luke Miller); Joey Heatherton (Dani); Jane Greer (Marian Spicer); DeForest Kelley (Sam Corwin); George Macready (Gordon Harris); Anne Seymour (Dr. Sally Jennings); Willis Bouchey (Judge Murphy); Walter Reed (George Babson); Ann Doran (Mrs. Geraghty); Bartlett Robinson (Mr. Coleman); Whit Bissell (Professor Bell); Anthony Caruso (Rafael).

BILLIE   (UA, 1965) C—86 M.

Executive producer, Peter Lawford; producer-director, Don Weis; based on the play *Time Out for Ginger* by Ronald Alexander; screenplay, Alexander; art director, Arthur Lonergan; music, Dominic Frontiere; choreography, David Winters; assistant director, Dick Moder, Dale Coleman; songs, D. Lampart, Z. Crane, Jack Gold, and B. Ross; camera; John Russell; editor, Adrienne Fazan.

Patty Duke (Billie Carol); Jim Backus (Howard Carol); Jane Greer (Agnes Carol); Warren Berlinger (Mike Benson); Billy De Wolfe (Mayor Davis); Charles Lane (Coach Jones); Dick Sargent (Matt Bullitt); Susan Seaforth (Jean Matthews); Ted Bessell (Bob Matthews); Richard Deacon (Principal Wilson); Bobby Diamond (Eddie Davis); Michael Fox (Ray Case); Clive Clerk (Ted Chekas); Harlan Warde (Dr. Hall); Jean MacRae (Nurse Webb); Allan Grant (Himself); Georgia Simmons (Mrs. Hosenwacker); Arline Anderson (Mrs. Clifton); Layte Bowden (Miss Channing); Mathew M. Jordan (Reporter); Shirley J. Shawn (Mrs. Harper); Maria Lennard (Adele Colin); Breena Howard (Mary Jensen); Craig W. Chudy (Starter).

THE OUTFIT   (MGM, 1973) C—102 M.

Producer, Carter De Haven; director, John Flynn; based on the novel by Richard Stark; screenplay, Flynn; music, Jerry Fielding; art director, Tambi Larsen; set decorator, James I. Berkey; assistant director, William McGarry; sound, Richard Raguse, Jall Watkins; camera, Bruce Surtees; editor, Ralph E. Winters.

Robert Duvall (Macklin); Karen Black (Bett Harrow); Joe Don Baker (Cody); Robert Ryan (Mailer); Timothy Carey (Menner); Richard Jaeckel (Chemey); Sheree North (Buck's Wife); Felice Orlandi (Frank Orlandi); Marie Windsor (Madge Coyle) Jane Greer (Alma); Henry Jones (Doctor); Joanna Cassidy (Rita); Tom Reese (Man); Elisha Cook (Carl); Bill McKinney (Buck); Ania O'Day (Herself); Archie Moore (Packard) Tony Young (Accountant); Roland LaStarza (Hit Man); Roy Roberts (Bob Caswell); Edward Ness (Ed Macklin); Tony Andersen (Parking Attendant); Emile Meyer (Amos); Roy Jenson (Al); Philip Kenneally (Bartender); Bern Hoffman (Jim Sinclair); John Steadman (Gas Station Attendant); Paul Genge (Pay-Off Man); Francis De Sales (Jim); James Bacon (Bookie); Army Archerd (Butler); Tony Trabert (Himself).

e Greer as a child

With Gloria Pechett and Inga Rurdvold, posing for the WAAC uniform (1942)

With husband-to-be Rudy Vallee in December, 1943

With Martha Holliday, Audrey Young, Lorraine Clark, Suzanne Rosser, Tanis Chandler, Virgini Belmont, and, *seated,* Vivian Mason, Marie McCardle in GEORGE WHITE'S SCANDALS (RKO '45)

With Mickey Kuhn and Anne Jeffreys in DICK TRACY (RKO '45)

With Rita Corday in THE FALCON'S ALIBI (RKO '46)

An RKO publicity pose, *c.* 1945

In SUNSET PASS (RKO '46)

With Douglas Fairbanks, Jr
SINBAD THE SAILOR (RKO

With George Tyne and Don Beddoe in THEY WON'T BELIEVE ME (RKO '47)

OUT OF THE PAST

With husband Edward Lasker in
Los Angeles in August, 1947

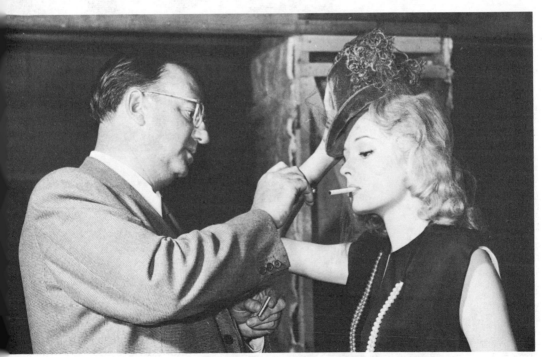

n the set of OUT OF THE PAST (RKO '47) with director Jacques Tourneur

With Gordon Oliver and Dick Powell in STATION WEST (RKO '48)

In THE BIG STEAL (RKO '49)

With Otto Hulett, Paul Smith, Peter Lawford, Barbara Ruick, and Barbara Brown in YOU FOR ME (MGM '52)

th Jack Albertson and Robert Evans in MAN OF A THOUSAND FACES (Univ '57)

In BILLIE (UA '65)

APPENDIX A
A CAPSULE HISTORY OF RKO RADIO PICTURES

1883: More than a decade before the first fledgling motion pictures were shown to the public, the nucleus of the Keith-Albee vaudeville circuit was established with the opening of a variety theatre in South Boston.

1920: The British firm of Robertson-Cole, which distributed the Roamer automobile and exported Hollywood film product from its American branch to the Continent and England, opened its own Hollywood studio, with *Mistress of Shenstone* (1921) its first self-produced film at the new facility.

1922: Robertson-Cole was reorganized; the corporate name of the film division was changed to FBO (Film Booking Office of America), with P. A. Powers, formerly of Universal Pictures, as the new president.

1923: The English banking firm of Graham's of London acquired control of the studio, with Major H. C. S. Thomson brought in to supervise the reorganization and succeed Powers as president.

1926: J. G. Hawks, who had succeeded B. P. Fineman as production chief for FBO, was replaced by Edwin King, who was appointed vice-president in charge of production. Later in the year, Hayden, Stone and Company bought FBO from the British interests, with King remaining in charge of production under the new company president, Joseph P. Kennedy.

1928: William LeBaron replaced Edwin King, who resigned.

1929: Radio Corporation of America purchased control of FBO and merged the studio with the Keith-Albee-Orpheum vaudeville circuit enterprise. Joseph I. Schnitzer was named president of the new corporate studio outgrowth (RKO), with William LeBaron as vice-president in charge of production, and B. B. Kahane as secretary-treasurer. First all-talking picture shot on the lot was *Street Girl,* directed by Wesley Ruggles.

1930: On November 28, RKO purchased Pathé Exchanges and Studio (an organization that traced its United States origins back to 1904, when it was formed as a continuation of a business organized in France in 1898).

1931: E. B. Derr resigned as president of Pathé, with Lee Marcus appointed president of RKO Pathé. In February, Charles R. Rogers was named production head of RKO Pathé, which was technically stated to be a separate producing company from RKO Radio Pictures. On October 21, RKO Radio Studios and RKO Pathé became a corporate unity, with Hiram Brown named president of RKO Corporation, David O. Selznick, head of RKO Studio productions (replacing William LeBaron).

1932: On February 24, Joseph I. Schnitzer resigned as president of RKO Studios with Hiram Brown as temporary replacement. On April 13, M. H. Aylesworth was selcted as the new president of RKO, succeeding Brown, and Benjamin B. Kahane was elected president of RKO Studios when the company went into Chapter 77-B bankruptcy receivership. Harold B. Franklin became general manager of RKO Theatres, slated to succeed Joseph Plunkett as president.

1933: On February 2, David O. Selznick resigned as production head of the combined RKO Studios, with Merian C. Cooper named as his replacement.

1934: Pathé Exchange, Inc., formed under a five-year agreement with RKO Studios, was reorganized into Pathé Film Corporation under control-ownership of RKO Studios.

1935: Floyd B. Odlum of Atlas Corporation, an investment trust with various film holdings, including an important stake in Paramount, gained domination of RKO by acquiring, in association with Lehman Brothers, RCA's controlling stock in the company. As of October 22, Leo Spitz was named RKO president, with Merlin H. Aylesworth as chairman of the board (succeeding David Sarnoff), J. R. McDonough as executive vice-president and Sam Briskin as vice-president in charge of production at the studio.

1936: On March 8, Pandro S. Berman was chosen production head of RKO, replacing Sam Briskin. Benjamin B. Kahane resigned on August 9 as vice-president of RKO Studios, becoming vice-president of the corporation.

1937: On May 1, RKO Studios became RKO Radio Pictures, Inc.

1938: George Schaefer, formerly United Artists vice-president in charge of distribution, became president of RKO Radio Pictures (Leo Spitz had resigned). Ned Depinet became RKO Radio Pictures vice-president and J. J. Nolan was placed in charge of production. J. R. McDonough was vice-president in charge of finances, and Harry Edington was executive producer.

1939: On May 27, Pandro S. Berman resigned as production head of RKO, effective October 1.

1940: On January 8, Harry Edington, new production head of RKO Radio Pictures, was joined by J. J. Nolan as executive assistant to the president.

1941: On April 28, producer Samuel Goldwyn signed a distribution pact with RKO. Joseph Breen resigned from his post as president of the Production Code Administration of the Motion Picture Association to succeed Harry Edington as production head of RKO Radio Pictures, but later in the year he resigned from his RKO berth to return to the PCA, being replaced at RKO by Charles Koerner, the new general manager of RKO Radio Pictures' studios.

1942: In June, N. Peter Rathvon was appointed chairman of the board of RKO Corporation, with Ned Depinet elected president of the studio.

1943: Floyd B. Odlum of the Atlas Corporation was elected chairman of the board of RKO Corporation.

1944: Keith Albee Corporation, formed in 1928 through the merger of the Keith and Orpheum vaudeville circuits, was dissolved, with the stock passing to B. F. Keith Corporation, 99.9 percent of which was owned by the RKO Corporation.

1946: Following the death of Charles Koerner (February 2), N. Peter Rathvon became president of RKO Pictures.

1947: As of February 5, Dore Schary was executive vice-president in charge of production at RKO. On August 13, Harry Michaelson was named president of RKO Pathé, replacing Fred Ullman, Jr., who resigned to become producer at RKO Radio.

1948: Howard Hughes on May 11 took over control of RKO Radio Studios and RKO Theatres from Floyd B. Odlum's Atlas Corporation. On July 1, Dore Schary resigned as production head of RKO, with Sid Rogell as his temporary replacement. On September 3, Floyd B. Odlum resigned as chairman of board of RKO Corporation, along with N. Peter Rathvon, who left his post as corporate president. As of September 8, Ned Depinet was named president of RKO Corporation.

1949: At the July 11, 1949, meeting of the board of directors of RKO Corporation, Howard Hughes assumed the post of managing director-producer, assuming "general supervision of that portion of our business which relates to the production of motion pictures and the operation of our studio." Earlier in the year (March 2), RKO (and Paramount) agreed to the separation of theatrical film exhibition and distribution under the government consent decree.

1950: On May 18, Sid Rogell, who earlier in the year had been named executive production head at RKO, resigned, with Howard Hughes temporarily appointing Sam Bischoff as his successor. On August 14, Jerry Wald-Norman Krasna Productions signed an extensive five-year production-management pact with RKO covering $50 million and sixty films. On December 13, C. J. Trevlin was named vice-president in charge of studio operations.

1951: October 9 saw Howard Hughes winning the United States Supreme Court hearing to air a lower court decision that he dispose of 929,000 shares of the new RKO Theatres Corporation by February 20, 1955. As of October 26, Sam Bischoff left RKO to return to Warner Brothers.

1952: On September 23, Howard Hughes sold his 1,013,420 shares of common stock in RKO, carrying control of RKO to a group composed of Ralph Stolkin, Abraham L. Koolish, Ray Ryan, Edward Burke, Jr., and Sherrill C. Corwin, at a $7,093,940 price tag, with the terms to be completed by January 1, 1955. On October 2, the Stolkin group took control of RKO, with Ned E. Depinet retained as consultant, and Arnold M. Grant as board chairman of the reconstituted directorate. Arnold M. Picker, of United Artists, was named as the company's new executive vice-president. As of October 22, the Stolkin group was out of RKO, with Grant also resigning thereafter, and Charles Boasberg, William Zimmerman, and Ross Hastings later being placed on the RKO Radio Pictures board of directors. On December 12, Howard Hughes announced he would resume management control, with the subsequent return of C. J. Trevlin as vice-president in charge of studio operations.

1953: As of November 6, Howard Hughes sold his 929,020 shares of RKO Theatres stock to Albert A. List, New England industrialist, the latter having acquired 200,000 shares of RKO Pictures stock some eighteen months prior. Meanwhile, Hughes gained 246,500 shares of RKO common stock, bringing his holdings up to 1,262,120 shares. James R. Grainger, former executive vice-president and distribution chief at Republic, signed a three-year RKO executive pact. Walt Disney Productions formed Buena Vista Distributing Company to release certain pictures apart from its RKO commitments.

1954: In late March, Howard Hughes purchased, for $23,489,478, all the assets of RKO Pictures, including RKO Radio Pictures.

1955: On July 18, Howard Hughes sold the company in toto to General Tire and Rubber Company, through the latter's subsidiary, General Teleradio, for $25 million. On December 23, RKO Radio Pictures perpetually leased its entire film inventory (740 features, some 1,100 short subjects) to C and C Super Corporation, stock-controlled by Matthew Fox and headed by Walter S. Mack, for $15,200,000. The purchaser acquired not only worldwide television and 16mm rights, but the theatrical rights outside the United States and Canada. Daniel

T. O'Shea became president of RKO Radio Pictures, a division of RKO Teleradio Pictures. Hughes personally acquired back from the purchaser two self-produced features, *The Conqueror* and *Jet Pilot* (at a $12 million tag).

1956: In May, the corporate shell, RKO Pictures, merged into Atlas Corporation, and RKO Theatres emerged as List Industries via merger. As of December, RKO Teleradio decided to close the RKO Pathé New York studios and consolidate the latter's production activities in the Culver City plant. William M. Dozier was in charge of production during this transformation year.

1957: On February 1, RKO announced its discontinuation of domestic film distribution, turning over its current pictures and eleven other unreleased films to Universal Pictures. Late in the year, RKO Teleradio sold both RKO Radio studios to Desilu, Inc., for $6 million, but did not wholly withdraw from production, joining in a co-deal with Warner Brothers to film *The Naked and the Dead* in Panama. RKO Radio's interest in the Churubusco Studios in Mexico was sold to the studio company for $800,000.

1958: On March 25, RKO Teleradio Pictures signed a long-term agreement with the British-based J. Arthur Rank Organization to handle overseas processing for RKO. On March 27, Daniel P. O'Shea resigned the RKO Radio Pictures presidency, with John B. Poor named as general manager of the RKO Radio Pictures division of RKO Teleradio. On July 20, William O'Neil, president of General Tire and Rubber Company, confirmed that RKO Teleradio would quit the theatrical motion picture field. Later RKO Radio turned over its Mexican film distribution to the Gold Chain.

APPENDIX B

PANDRO S. BERMAN was born in Pittsburgh, Pennsylvania, on March 28, 1905. The son of Harry M. Berman, who was general manager of Universal and FBO, he was educated at DeWitt Clinton High School in New York City, thereafter becoming an assistant director at FBO (for five years) and then a film editor for FBO, a film and title editor at Columbia Studios, and chief film editor of RKO Productions.

Berman moved into an executive assistant post, serving under William LeBaron and David O. Selznick. In 1931 he was made an RKO producer, responsible for such pictures as *Symphony of Six Million, The Silver Cord, Morning Glory, The Life of Vergie Winters, The Gay Divorcee, Of Human Bondage, Roberta, Alice Adams,* and *Top Hat.* As of March 8, 1936, Berman was chosen as production head of RKO Radio, replacing the departing Sam Briskin. Berman held the post until October, 1939. He remained at the studio until 1941 (as an executive producer) turning out such films as *The Story of Vernon and Irene Castle* and *In Name Only.*

In January, 1941, Berman joined MGM as a producer, responsible for such products as *Rio Rita, Somewhere I'll Find You, National Velvet, The Seventh Cross, Dragon Seed, Sea of Grass, Father of the Bride, Knights of the Round Table, The Long, Long Trailer, Butterfield 8,* and *The Sweet Bird of Youth.* Most recently he produced *A Patch of Blue* (MGM, 1966) and *Justine* (Twentieth Century-Fox, 1969).

He is married to Viola V. Newman, who is not involved in the film profession.

MERIAN C(OLDWELL) COOPER was born in Jacksonville, Florida, on October 24, 1894. His father was a lawyer who became chairman of the Federal Reserve Board in Florida. After attending a local elementary school Cooper journeyed to the Lawrenceville School, near Princeton, New Jersey, and in 1911 received an appointment to Annapolis. He resigned from the Naval Academy in his senior year, finding life too exciting for the restraints imposed by military service.

After an abortive attempt to ship out on the transatlantic run as an able seaman, he accepted a post as a reporter on the *Minneapolis Daily News,* later moving on to the *Des Moines Register-Leader* and then to the *St. Louis Post-Dispatch.* In 1916 he joined the Georgia National Guard in order to participate in the roundup of Pancho Villa in Mexico; the following year he joined the Army's aviation service and was sent to France for active duty. After recuperating from being shot down in action, he joined the Polish Army in 1919.

When Cooper returned to New York in 1921, he found work as a feature writer-reporter on the *New York Times,* but soon thereafter he was off to Singapore to join Capt. Edward A. Salisbury on a global tour, as a result of which he and Salisbury wrote the book *The Sea Gypsy* (1924). (Cooper also wrote the autobiographical *Things Men Must Do,* published in 1927.)

One of Cooper's cohorts on the Salisbury trek had been Ernest B. Schoedsack, a former combat photographer. Cooper and Schoedsack later filmed life among the Bakhtiari nomad tribe of Western Iran, editing their material into the feature-length *Grass* (1925). Paramount successfully distributed that picture and financed Cooper's next one, *Chang* (1927), filmed in the jungles of Siam. Next came *Four Feathers* (1929), with much of the local color actually filmed on location in Africa.

Through mutual friends Cooper was introduced to David O. Selznick, then production chief at RKO. The latter asked Cooper to assist him in putting RKO back on an even financial keel, and Cooper was made Selznick's executive assistant. During this period he pushed his pet project into realization, the making of *King Kong* (1933). When Selznick left RKO to establish himself at MGM, Cooper (in February, 1933) was appointed in his stead. Among the properties turned out during Cooper's regime were: *Morning Glory, Professional Sweetheart, Little Women, Flying Down to Rio,* and *The Lost Patrol.*

Cooper had joined with Jack Whitney in the formation of Pioneer Pictures in May, 1933, for the purpose of promoting the new three-color Technicolor process, and after Cooper returned from his year-long honeymoon trip with actress Dorothy Jordan, he relinquished his supervisory control at RKO, agreeing to personally produce *She* and *The Last Days of Pompeii,* both 1935 releases.

As executive producer for Pioneer Pictures, Cooper negotiated the merger of Pioneer Pictures with Selznick-International in 1936, becoming a vice-president of the new company. In late 1938 Cooper left Selznick to form Argosy Pictures with director John Ford, the two turning out *Stagecoach* and *The Long Voyage Home.* In the late 1930s, Cooper was also associated with MGM in the capacity of producer, taking time out from his functions at that studio to work on the pre-production of Alexander Korda's *Jungle Book* and Universal's *Eagle Squadron.*

In 1941 he offered his services to the U.S. Air Force and became an assistant executive and intelligence officer in the Pacific, later serving with the Fifth Air Force. After World War II, Cooper and John Ford re-established Argosy Pictures and turned out such films as *The Fugitive, Fort Apache, Rio Grande,* and *Wagonmaster.* Meantime, Cooper embarked on another *King Kong*-like project, which evolved as *Mighty Joe Young* (1949). The last two ventures of Argosy Pictures were *The Quiet Man* and *The Sun Shines Bright.*

By this point, Cooper had become intrigued with the Cinerama widescreen process, and he was induced by Lowell Thomas and Mike Todd to assume supervision of the Cinerama Company's first feature-length venture, *This Is*

Cinerama (1952). The same year Cooper was given a special Oscar for his many innovations and contributions to the art of the cinema. Cooper remained at Cinerama for two years, then formed C. V. Whitney Productions, which produced, among others, *The Searchers* (1956), directed by John Ford. It was not until 1963 that Cooper produced another picture, the compilation project, *The Best of Cinerama.*

Cooper died on April 21, 1973, of cancer. He was survived by his widow; a son, Maj. Richard M. Cooper; and two daughters, Mrs. B. G. Henderson and Mary Caroline.

NED E. DEPINET was born in Erie, Pennsylvania, on September 9, 1890. After high school he entered the employ of the Imported Film and Supply Company in New Orleans, serving as booker and film salesman. In 1911 he joined Universal Pictures as southern division manager; in 1924 he was appointed one of three sales directors of the Universal home office in New York. Two years later he became member of the sales cabinet and manager of the southern territory of First National Pictures; later he was named general sales manager.

When Pathe and RKO merged, Depinet joined that company, and was elected in 1932 to the board of directors of RKO Radio and RKO Pathé. He was elected president of RKO Distributing Corporation in 1934, and in 1937 he was named vice-president of RKO Radio and president of Pathé News, Inc. Later he was named vice-president and director of Radio-Keith-Orpheum Corporation; in June, 1942, he was elected president of RKO Radio. Four years later he was named vice-chairman of the board and executive vice-president of the Radio-Keith-Orpheum Corporation. By 1948 he was president and board chairman of RKO Theatres, Inc., and in 1950 he was named president of RKO Pictures Corporation. He resigned his RKO posts in October, 1952.

Depinet has served as president of COMPO (1951), president of the Motion Picture Pioneers (1957-60), and president of Will Rogers Memorial Hospital (1962 and thereafter).

WILLIAM M. DOZIER was born in Omaha, Nebraska, on February 13, 1908. After receiving his B.A. degree from Creighton University and then completing two years of law school, he migrated to Hollywood, where he was soon in charge of the story and writer department of the Phil Berg-Bert Allenberg, Inc. talent agency. In 1941 he joined Paramount as head of the scenario and story department.

Dozier joined RKO in 1944 as general production aide to Charles Koerner's supervisory regime. In 1946 he moved over to Universal-International as vice-president and associate head of production; this studio for a time released the product of Rampart Productions, a joint venture he conducted with his actress wife, Joan Fontaine. He canceled his Universal contract in 1949, going over to Columbia, where he produced *Harriet Craig* and *Two of a Kind,* and then in 1951 became story editor-assistant to Samuel Goldwyn. Later that year he was hired in a similar capacity by CBS-TV, where he remained in an executive position until 1956, when he returned to RKO Radio Pictures to be in charge of production.

In 1957, Dozier returned to CBS-TV as general program executive, later becoming vice-president in charge of West Coast operations for Screen Gems and in the 1960s forming Greenway Productions, which was berthed at Twentieth Century-Fox and turned out series like *Batman* and *The Green Hornet*. In 1969 he was a producer at Warner Brothers-Seven Arts, responsible for *The Big Bounce*.

HOWARD HUGHES was born in Houston, Texas, on December 24, 1901, the son of Alena Gano and Howard R. Hughes (the latter, who died in 1924, was a brother of writer Rupert Hughes; he founded the Hughes Tool Company and was one of the outstanding men identified with the Texas oil industry). Hughes was educated at the Fessenden School in West Newton, Mass.; the Thatcher School in Ojal, California; the California Institute of Technology in Pasadena; and Rice Institute in Houston. At the age of twenty he took over the management of his father's business.

By 1927 he was in Hollywood, where he established Caddo Company to produce motion pictures. His first venture, *Two Arabian Knights* (United Artists, 1927), won recognition for both its character star (Louis Wolheim) and its director (Lewis Milestone). Thereafter, Hughes's company, which signed distribution agreements with both Paramount and United Artists, handled *The Racket* (1928), *The Mating Call* (1928), *Hell's Angels* (1930), *The Front Page* (1931), *The Sky Devils* (1932), and *Scarface* (1932).

In the mid-1930s Hughes established several solo airplane records (1935, 1936, 1937) and was the recipient of the Harmon Trophy as the world's outstanding flier (1938) after a record round-the-world flight, with a crew of four.

Hughes returned to film production (and direction) with *The Outlaw* (1941-43), initially released by RKO. In 1944 he formed, with producer-director Preston Sturges, Hughes-Sturges Productions. As of May 11, 1948, Hughes assumed control of RKO Radio Studios and RKO Theatres, personally supervising a series of that studio's releases starring Jane Russell, Faith Domergue, and other protegées, while assuming more financial and management control of the studio, until July, 1955, when he sold the company to General Tire and Rubber Company, through the latter's subsidiary, General Teleradio.

Hughes was married in 1925 to Ella Rice, a Houston debutante—a marriage that ended in divorce after four and one-half years. Throughout the 1930s, 1940s, and early 1950s, he dated a succession of movie personalities, ranging from Ginger Rogers to Katharine Hepburn to Gina Lollobrigida, and in 1957 he wed Twentieth Century-Fox star(let) Jean Peters. They were divorced in 1970.

Hughes once owned a brewery in Texas, but was more famous for his 75 percent interest in Trans-World Airlines, which he sold for $500 million.

In recent years Hughes has remained based in near total seclusion, whether in Las Vegas, Paradise Island in the Bahamas, Nicaragua, or Canada. The 1971 Clifford Irving biography hoax (an allegedly confidential account of Hughes's life written for publication by McGraw-Hill), brought the very eccentric billionaire once again into the public limelight and spurred the issuance of several unauthorized biographies, as well as a myriad of anecdotal statements by a host of celebrities in far-reaching fields.

CHARLES W. KOERNER was born in New Orleans on September 10, 1896. As a youth he worked at odd jobs in motion picture theatres after school. He attended Shattuck Military Academy in Montana, and prior to World War I he operated a movie theatre in Havre, Montana. After the war he served with the Jensen and Von Herberg theatre chain in the Pacific Northwest, becoming their branch manager, followed by a similar post with First National Pictures in their offices in Portland, Oregon, and Butte, Montana. In 1925, he became part-owner and general manager of the George Mann circuit of northern California theatres. When this circuit was sold to the Hughes-Franklin organization in 1931, Koerner became the personal representative of Harold B. Franklin.

After Franklin became president of RKO, Koerner was put in charge of operating the RKO theatres in the Southwest division. Thereafter Koerner became chief of the Upstate New York and New England divisions of RKO theatres under pool with Chris Buckley. After being transferred from Albany to Boston, he found himself in charge of RKO New England Theatres. By 1939 he had become division manager for the RKO West Coast Theatres; in 1941 he was elevated to general manager of the company's national theatre circuit. The following year saw Koerner made general manager of the RKO studios, at which time he set out to reorganize the production lineup on a more commercial and less experimental basis, dropping some $500,000 worth of studio committed projects. When Koerner took over RKO the company was in debt to the tune of $1.6 million; two years later the corporation had turned a profit of $4 million. (Actor Pat O'Brien, in his memoirs, *The Wind at My Back* [1964], insists of studio boss Koerner: "He was endowed with more warmth, charm and generosity that anyone who had ever headed a studio during my time. . . . When he died, so did RKO.")

Koerner was appointed head of production of RKO in 1943, a post he retained until his death in Hollywood on February 2, 1946, of leukemia. He was survived by his wife, Vivian.

WILLIAM LEBARON was born February 16, 1883, in Elgin, Illinois. He attended the University of Chicago and later New York University. By 1918 he was managing editor of *Collier's* magazine and had written such plays as *Apple Blossoms, Her Regiment, The Love Letter, Moonlight,* and *The Very Idea.*

LeBaron's first entry into motion pictures was in 1919 when he was hired as a scripter for Cosmopolitan Productions in New York. He remained there for five years, eventually directing some of the company's films. In 1924 he joined Famous Players' Long Island Studios as an associate producer, continuing in this post through 1927, when he left to join Film Booking Office (FBO) as vice-president. In 1928 LeBaron became production chief for FBO, and the following year he was made vice-president in charge of production for the company's successor, RKO Radio Pictures. In this new capacity he personally produced such features as *Street Girl, Rio Rita, Cimarron,* and *Beau Geste.*

He returned to Paramount in 1932 as an associate producer, supervising such films as *Terror Abroad, College Humor, Rumba, Here Comes Cookie,* Mae West's *She Done Him Wrong, I'm No Angel, Goin' to Town,* and *Belle of the Nineties,* and W. C. Fields's *The Old Fashioned Way* and *The Man on the Flying Trapeze.* After Ernst Lubitsch's short reign as Paramount's chief in 1935, LeBaron succeeded him as "studio czar," a post he retained through 1941. During this time he co-scripted *Baby Face Harrigan* (MGM, 1935) and produced the Bing Crosby musical *Rhythm on the River* (Paramount, 1940).

In 1941 he moved over to Twentieth Century-Fox as an independent producer and supervised such musical features as *Kiss the Boys Goodbye, Weekend in Havana, Song of the Islands, Iceland, Springtime in the Rockies,* and *Pin-Up Girl,* and the low-budget comedy *Don Juan Quilligan.* After leaving Fox, he produced United Artists' *Carnegie Hall* (1947).

In the 1950s LeBaron was announced as co-producer on several pending television-series projects, one for Mae West, but none of them ever materialized. He died on February 9, 1958, at the age of seventy-five.

KENNETH MACGOWAN was born in Winthrop, Massachusetts, on November 30, 1888, growing up in St. Louis, where his father founded a cordage manufacturing company. He attended Harvard University, and after graduation in 1911 he became the assistant of *Boston Transcript* theatre reviewer H. T. Parker. Thereafter he became the amusement editor of the *Philadelphia Evening Ledger* and in 1917 moved on to New York where he became involved in theatrical productions as a publicity manager. Later there were posts as publicity director for Goldwyn Pictures Corporation, feature writer on the *New York Tribune,* and a stretch as drama critic of the *New York Globe.*

By 1922 Macgowan had become involved with the struggling Provincetown Playhouse, serving as its managing director until 1926, when he transferred his activities to becoming a lecturer, writer, and independent producer. Between 1929 and 1932, in partnership with Joseph Verner Reed, Macgowan produced seven Broadway plays.

It was at the suggestion of Macgowan's actor friend, Irving Pichel, that David O. Selznick hired Macgowan as story editor at RKO in early 1932. Later in the year, Macgowan was made an associate producer at RKO, his first film being *The Penguin Pool Murder.* Later he was responsible for such studio projects as *Topaze, Little Women,* and *Rafter Romance.*

In 1933 the new production head of RKO, Merian C. Cooper, assigned

Macgowan to produce, for John Hay Whitney, the Technicolor short subject *La Cucaracha,* followed more than a year later by his producing *Becky Sharp,* the feature-length three-color Technicolor version of *Vanity Fair.*

Macgowan left RKO in 1935 to join Darryl F. Zanuck's newly formed Twentieth Century-Fox studios, where Macgowan produced *King of Burlesque, Lloyds of London, In Old Chicago, Kidnapped, The Story of Alexander Graham Bell, Young Mr. Lincoln, The Return of Frank James, Brigham Young,* and *Man Hunt.* In 1941, Macgowan took a leave of absence from Fox to serve as Director of Production in the Motion Picture Division of the Office for Coordination of Commercial and Cultural Relations between the American Republics under the Council of National Defense. He returned to Fox the following year, working on *Jane Eyre* and then on *Happy Land* and *Lifeboat,* before moving over to Paramount in 1944 for *Easy Come, Easy Go.*

When he was offered an opportunity to organize a theatre arts department at the University of California in Los Angeles in 1944, he accepted; the following year he commenced there a scholarly publication devoted to the motion pictures, entitled the *Hollywood Quarterly.*

On April 27, 1963, he died in Los Angeles of cancer. Shortly before his death, he had completed a book on the cinema, *Behind the Screen: the History and Techniques of the Motion Picture.*

NATHANIEL PETER RATHVON was born in Denver, Colorado, on April 26, 1891. A graduate of Culver Military Academy, the University of Colorado, and the University of Colorado Law School, he later went to China as counsel for New York mining interests. From 1918 to 1922 he represented various mining interests in Europe and Asia. When he returned to the United States in 1922, he was counsel and officer of Newmont Mining Corporation, and thereafter a partner in Munds, Winslow & Potter, a New York Stock Exchange member.

In 1933 Rathvon helped to form the Atlas Corporation, a mutual trust fund operation, becoming its vice-president, and president of Pacific Eastern Corporation, its subsidiary. In those capacities, he reorganized RKO Pictures out of bankruptcy. In 1939 he was elected chairman of the executive committee and director of RKO. In June, 1942, he was named president of RKO. In this new capacity, he was responsible for the construction of Churubusco Studios in Mexico City, in association with Mexican interests. Rathvon was instrumental in aligning independent producers (Samuel Goldwyn, Walt Disney, John Ford) with the RKO facilities. He resigned from RKO in 1943; in 1944 he formed the Motion Picture Capital Corporation, engaged in motion picture production and financing. Still later he produced theatrical films in Europe and various film subjects for USIA.

Rathvon held the French Legion of Honor and was a longtime member of the Academy of Motion Pictures Arts and Sciences. He also served on numerous boards as a director, including the Madison Square Garden Corporation. He retired to Mexico City in 1957.

Rathvon died suddenly on May 26, 1972, while visiting friends in New York. He was survived by three children (his wife Helen Hall, whom he wed in 1917, died in 1964) and eleven grandchildren.

SID ROGELL was born on January 16, 1900, in St. Joseph, Missouri. He attended North Central High School in Spokane, Washington. He entered the motion picture field in an administrative capacity, soon becoming associated with producer Harry Joe Brown, with whom he worked for four years, handling business matters on the series of Ken Maynard-First National westerns. (Many of these Maynard oaters were directed by Rogell's younger brother, Albert.) When Maynard signed with Universal in 1933-34 for his own production unit, he had Rogell hired as his financial-business advisor. Rogell then became a Columbia producer during 1935.

From 1936 to 1941 he served as studio manager for RKO. He returned to the studio in June, 1942, and was appointed an executive producer in 1943, supervising the production of such films as *The Falcon in Mexico, Here Comes the Bride,* and *Murder My Sweet.* In 1947, with his feature-length production *Design for Death,* he received an Academy Award for distinctive achievement in the documentary field.

In January, 1950, the Howard Hughes regime named Rogell chief studio executive, a post he resigned in May of that year. Subsequently he became an executive production manager for Twentieth Century-Fox in the early 1950s.

Rogell married actress June Clayworth on February 7, 1938, and they had a son Anthony.

Rogell died at his West Los Angeles home on January 17, 1974, at the age of seventy-four.

CHARLES R. ROGERS was born in New York City on July 15, 1892. He completed his high school training in the Boston public schools. Later he entered the theatre business with his Star Theatre in Buffalo, followed by his opening of an exchange in that city. Thereafter he was appointed general sales manager for Select Pictures; still later he became an independent producer, also becoming a partner in the company of Asher, Small, and Rogers, which produced Corinne Griffith pictures for First National and a series of Ken Maynard westerns.

In February, 1931, Rogers was named production head of RKO Pathé, a post he held for over a year before producing pictures independently for Paramount release, including *Song of the Eagle, I Love That Man, Sitting Pretty, Eight Girls in a Boat,* and *Hold 'Em Yale.* March, 1936, saw Rogers becoming executive vice-president in charge of production at Universal; for this studio he functioned as executive producer of such features as *My Man Godfrey, The Magnificent Brute, Flying Hostess, Three Smart Girls,* and *A Letter of Introduction.* He resigned from Universal in 1938, but continued on their board of directors.

Throughout the 1940s, Rogers served as an independent producer, turning out such pictures as *She Knew All the Answers* (Columbia, 1941), *Adventure in Washington* (Columbia, 1941), *The Powers Girl* (United Artists, 1942), *Song of the Open Road* (United Artists, 1944), *Delightfully Dangerous* (United Artists, 1945), *Angel on My Shoulder* (United Artists, 1946), and *The Fabulous Dorseys* (United Artists, 1947).

Rogers was married to Helen Weiss and they had one son, John W., who became a film producer. Rogers died in Hollywood on March 29, 1957, from injuries suffered on February 18 of that year in an automobile crash. He was survived by his wife, his son, and three brothers and sisters.

GEORGE J. SCHAEFER was born in Brooklyn, New York, on November 5, 1888. Educated at the Heffley Institute, he entered business with an automobile manufacturing concern, remaining there until 1914, when he became secretary to L. J. Selznick and his New York-based production company. Two years later Schaefer was appointed assistant sales manager of World Film Company. He was promoted to district manager for that company the following year. In 1920 he joined Paramount as booker at the New York exchange and one year later was promoted to district manager of the New England territory. He was appointed sales manager for district number one in 1926, rising to become general sales manager and then general manager of the Paramount division, and in 1935 he was named president of Famous Theatres, Inc., and vice-president of the reorganized Paramount. That same year he resigned from Paramount, and in 1936 he became vice-president and general manager in charge of domestic and Canadian sales for United Artists.

In 1938 Schaefer resigned from United Artists to become president and director of Radio-Keith-Orpheum Corporation, chairman of the board thereafter, and president and a director of RKO Radio Pictures, Inc., Pathé News, Inc. and Keith-Albee-Orpheum Corporation. In 1941 he was named general manager of RKO Theatres. In June, 1942, he resigned his RKO posts.

During the World War II years he was national chairman of the War Activities Committee of the Motion Picture Industry. In 1945 he entered independent production and distribution, becoming associated with Stanley Kramer Distributing Corporation. From 1957 to 1959 he was president of the Todd-AO Corporation, and presently he is president of Selected Pictures Corporation.

DORE SCHARY was born August 31, 1905, in Newark, New Jersey, and was educated at that city's Central High School. He developed his hobby of little-theatre directing-acting into a professional career, while also branching out into the newspaper field, first as editor for the state "Y" papers, then as a columnist for the *Newark Sunday Call* and *Charm* magazine. He turned to playwriting *(One Every Minute, Gentlemen of Distinction, Man of Ideas, Violence),* but by 1932 had moved into the film scripting field with *He Couldn't Take It* (Monogram), *Fog* and *Fury of the Jungle* (both Columbia), and *Comin' Round the Mountain* (MGM). By the mid-1930s he was a full-fledged scripter, preparing scenarios for many of the major studios. For his original story of *Boys Town* (MGM, 1938) he received an Oscar. In 1942 he was appointed executive producer at MGM, where he supervised such features as *Journey for Margaret, The War against Mrs. Hadley, Lassie Come Home,* and *Joe Smith, American.*

Schary resigned from MGM in 1943 to join David O. Selznick's Vanguard Company as producer, the new company releasing its product through RKO. In February of 1947 he was appointed executive vice-president in charge of production of RKO, where he remained for sixteen months before resigning due to conflict with the new studio head, Howard Hughes. Schary immediately accepted a similar berth at MGM, where he became vice-president in charge of production (1948-56).

In 1957 Schary authored *Sunrise at Campobello* and produced it in conjunction with the Theatre Guild. Since that time he has authored several unsuccessful Broadway ventures *(Banderol, Something about a Soldier, The Highest Tree),* while writing-producing-directing the film version of *Act One* (Warner Bros., 1963).

Schary married Miriam Svet in 1932.

DAVID O. SELZNICK was born on May 10, 1902, in Pittsburgh, Pennsylvania, the son of pioneer motion picture promoter-distributor Lewis J. Selznick. (David's five-years-older brother, Myron, would become a noted Hollywood talent agent.) From 1920 to 1925, Selznick served as publicity man-story editor for his father's Select Pictures; the following year he was hired as assistant story editor by MGM, but was fired by Irving Thalberg in 1927. In 1928 he was appointed producer at Paramount, rising to become assistant general manager of the studio.

On March 29, 1930, Selznick wed Louis B. Mayer's daughter, Irene; they had two sons: Lewis Jeffrey (1932) and Daniel Mayer (1936). In the fall of 1931, Selznick was appointed head of the combined RKO Radio and RKO Pathē studios, a post he held until February, 1933, when he resigned to take up the reins of his own production unit at MGM (where he prepared, among other films, *Dinner at Eight, Dancing Lady, Viva Villa!, David Copperfield,* and *Anna Karenina).* Selznick left MGM in 1935 to go into independent production with his Selznick-International Pictures, which produced *Little Lord Fauntleroy, A Star Is Born, Tom Sawyer, Gone with the Wind,* and *Rebecca* (he won best production Oscars for the latter two films).

In 1940 Selznick dissolved Selznick-International Pictures and founded David O. Selznick Productions, later merging it into Vanguard Films, which turned out *Since You Went Away* and *I'll Be Seeing You.* In 1949 he was appointed president of Selznick Releasing Organization and continued to turn out features, including *The Paradine Case, Portrait of Jennie,* and, in co-production with London Films, *The Third Man* and *The Wild Heart.* Selznick's last film venture was the remake of *A Farewell to Arms* (Twentieth Century-Fox, 1957), which starred his actress wife, Jennifer Jones. (Selznick had divorced Irene in 1949, marrying Jennifer Jones on July 13, 1949; by her he had a daughter, Mary Jennifer, who was born on August 12, 1954.)

Selznick died on June 22, 1965.

APPENDIX C

JAMES ROBERT PARISH, New York-based freelance writer, was born near Boston on April 21, 1944. He attended the University of Pennsylvania and graduated as a Phi Beta Kappa with a degree in English. A graduate of the University of Pennsylvania Law School, he is a member of the New York Bar. As president of Entertainment Copyright Research Co., Inc. he headed a major researching facility for the film and television industries. Later he was a film reviewer-interviewer for *Motion Picture Daily* and *Variety*. He is a member of the *Kate Smith U.S.A. Friends Club*. He is the author of such volumes as *The Great Movie Series, The Fox Girls, The Paramount Pretties,* and *Actors Television Credits.* He is the co-author of *The Cinema of Edward G. Robinson* and *The MGM Stock Company: The Golden Era.*

T. ALLAN TAYLOR, the godson of the late Margaret Mitchell, was born in Greenwich Village, attended Wesleyan University, and is currently the production manager at Engineering Index, Inc. He was manuscript editor on *The Fox Girls, The Paramount Pretties, Good Dames, The Great Spy Pictures,* and many other cinema history volumes. Mr. Taylor, a noted archivist of classical recordings, is also a commentator on classical music for various record journals.

Since the age of five, thirty-four year old-Brooklynite JOHN ROBERT COCCHI has been viewing and collating data on motion pictures and is now regarded as one of the most energetic film researchers in the United States. He is the New York editor of *Boxoffice* magazine and the co-founder of a leading Manhattan film society. He was research associate on *The American Movies Reference Book, The Slapstick Queens,* and many other volumes, and has written extensive cinema history articles for such journals as *Film Fan Monthly* and *Screen Facts.*

New York-born FLORENCE SOLOMON attended Hunter College and then joined Ligon Johnson's copyright research office. Later she was appointed director for research at Entertainment Copyright Research Co., Inc. and she is currently a reference supervisor at ASCAP's Index division. Miss Solomon has collaborated on such works as *The American Movies Reference Book, TV Movies, The Great Movie Series,* and *Film Directors' Guide: The U.S.A.* She is the niece of the noted sculptor, the late Sir Jacob Epstein.

Index

877